P9-CPW-407

Almost All Aliens

Immigration, Race, and Colonialism in American History and Identity

Paul Spickard

Routledge
Taylor & Francis Group
New York   London

Routledge
Taylor & Francis Group
270 Madison Avenue
New York, NY 10016

Routledge
Taylor & Francis Group
2 Park Square
Milton Park, Abingdon
Oxon OX14 4RN

© 2007 by Taylor & Francis Group, LLC
Routledge is an imprint of Taylor & Francis Group, an Informa business

Printed in the United States of America on acid-free paper
10 9 8 7 6 5 4 3 2

International Standard Book Number-10: 0-415-93593-8 (Softcover) 0-415-93592-X (Hardcover)
International Standard Book Number-13: 978-0-415-93593-7 (Softcover) 978-0-415-93592-0 (Hardcover)

No part of this book may be reprinted, reproduced, transmitted, or utilized in any form by any electronic, mechanical, or other means, now known or hereafter invented, including photocopying, microfilming, and recording, or in any information storage or retrieval system, without written permission from the publishers.

Trademark Notice: Product or corporate names may be trademarks or registered trademarks, and are used only for identification and explanation without intent to infringe.

Library of Congress Cataloging-in-Publication Data

Spickard, Paul R., 1950-
    Almost all aliens : immigration, race, and colonialism in American history and identity / Paul Spickard.
        p. cm.
    Includes bibliographical references.
    ISBN 0-415-93592-X (hardback : alk. paper) -- ISBN 0-415-93593-8 (pbk. : alk. paper)
    1. United States--Emigration and immigration--History. 2. United States--Emigration and immigration--Government policy. 3. Discrimination--United States. I. Title.

JV6450.S75 2007
304.8'73--dc22   2006031874

Visit the Taylor & Francis Web site at
http://www.taylorandfrancis.com

and the Routledge Web site at
http://www.routledge.com

Almost All Aliens

To my students

Racism is the elephant in the living room in this country. And we pretend it does not exist. Until we acknowledge it, until we acknowledge the past, we are not moving forward.

Rita Bender, widow of Michael Schwerner, a White civil rights worker slain in Mississippi in 1964. Quoted in Josh Gitlin and Elizabeth Mehren, "Still a Long Ways from Justice," (*Los Angeles Times,* January 8, 2005).

Contents

CONTENTS

Acknowledgments

This book is dedicated to my students. I worked out many of its ideas before several thousand of them over 30 years at Harvard, Berkeley, Solano Community College, San Francisco State, Bethel College, Nankai University, Capital University, Brigham Young University-Hawai'i, the University of Hawai'i, and University of California, Santa Barbara (UCSB). They listened to and critiqued my ideas, contributed their own insights, wrote papers that informed me or set me thinking, and suggested books I should read. They are too numerous to credit individually, but I am very aware of my debt to them and acknowledge it with gratitude.

Several colleagues have contributed over the course of many years to the idea structure that lies beneath this book. Most prominent among them is Patrick Miller, who has been a faithful friend and collaborator on more adventures than I can count. He read every word of this book, suggested sources, critiqued ideas, and deflated pomposities. If the book is not as good as it might be, it is not because he did not try to get me to make it better. Steve Cornell and Al Raboteau have supported this project and many others with steadfast friendship and unfailing good humor. Some other people who have had particular influence on these ideas include Hank Allen, Elaine Aoki, Larry Cloud Morgan, Reg Daniel, Roger Daniels, Kip Fulbeck, Debbie Hippolite Wright, Jane Iwamura, Winthrop Jordan, Harry Kitano, Larry Levine, Davianna McGregor, Laurie Mengel, Jim Morishima, Michael Omi, Lori Pierce, Sally Sumida, Haunani-Kay Trask, Bill Wallace, Diane Wong, and David Yoo.

I would not have been able to envision the perspectives taken in this book had I not been formed by my associations with the people surrounding Garfield High School in Seattle; San Francisco's Chinatown; and the Kanaka Maoli and islander communities of O'ahu's North Shore. I began to think about writing the book in response to conversations with David Stannard and Peter Coveney about other books I might have written and did not; I owe them thanks for their early encouragement. I worked out the structure for the book during many hours spent with Don Spickard, watching 007 videos and sometimes talking. I am grateful for his company and mourn his passing.

ACKNOWLEDGMENTS

Several friends offered suggestions for the shape of the book: Marc Coronado, Rudy Guevarra, Matt Kester, Jeff Moniz, José Moreno, Chidinma Offoh-Robert, Travis Smith, David Torres-Rouff, Joan Ullman, Neha Vora, and Isaiah Walker. Oscar Fierros, Tom Guglielmo, Kimberly Hoang, Elena Olivera, Ingrid Page, Zaragosa Vargas, and Ben Zulueta read chapters and offered valuable insights. Others offered specific ideas and leads, or shared their work with me: Lilynda Agvateesiri, Richard Alba, Luis Alvarez, Evelyn Alsultany, Brahim Aoude, Ralph Armbruster-Sandoval, Jennifer Baker, Elliott Barkan, Edwina Barvosa-Carter, Moustafa Bayoumi, Jim Bergquist, Randy Bergstrom, Shana Bernstein, Mehdi Bozorgmehr, Mark Braude, Jeff Burroughs, Max Burroughs, Trish Casey, Josef Castañeda-Liles, Cassie Chavez, Sarah Cline, Eli Contreras, Angela Cottrell, Kevin Cragg, Claus Daufenbach, John Decker, Taoufik Djebali, Gabe Dudley, Richard Dunn, Grace Ebron, Mark Elliott, Ed Escobar, Flora Furlong, Sonia Gaha, Nancy Gallagher, Martín Garcia, Hank Gemery, Anita Guerinni, David Gutiérrez, Carl Gutiérrez-Jones, Yvonne Haddad, Lisa Hajjar, Barbara Hanrahan, Ambi Harsha, Toshi Hasegawa, Maria Herrera-Sobek, Fred Hoxie, Joe Illick, Camille Jacinto, Kevin Johnson, Violet Johnson, Walter Kamphoefner, Bryan Kim, Rasmia Kirmani, Paul Kramer, Patsy Kurokawa, Marla Kurtz, Ed Lara, John Lee, Sam Lee, Mark Leo, Crystal Lewis-Coleman, Nelson Lichtenstein, Rebecca Loman, Dan Lombardo, Elena Lopez-Guzman, Roseanne Macias, Patrick McCray, Sears McGee, Pyong-Gap Min, Kathie Moore, Olga Moore, Nadine Naber, Sharleen Nakamoto, Norman Newkirk, Alice O'Connor, Mike Osborne, Bernt Ostendorf, Jessica Paredes, John Park, Paul Parvanian, Chelsea Pearson, Marina Petronoti, Liam Riordan, Alicia Rivera, Joanne Rondilla, Curtiss Rooks, Joaquin Ross, Jane Rudolph, Vicki Ruiz, Alicia Saldaña, Monica Sanchez, Mark Shanks, Jaideep Singh, Jim Spickard, Steve Striffler, Christine Su, Diane Taniguchi, Kim Tellez, Russ Thornton, Julie Vongkhamchanh, FlorenceMae Waldron, Angie Wei, Lily Welty, Elana Wenocur, Richard White, Susanna Whitmore, Henry Yu, and Naomi Zack. I'm pretty sure I have left out a lot of people who should be included in this list; I apologize for the oversight and hope that if they read this book they may take some satisfaction in seeing their ideas reflected.

My intellectual debt to many other scholars will be found in the footnotes. I want to stress my gratitude to them and my admiration for their work. Even when I have disagreed with some of them, I have not once failed to be impressed by their minds and their erudition. Scholarly research and writing are hard, lonely work. Trying to figure things out and put them together in a way that has meaning is never an accomplishment to be taken lightly. So even as I have sometimes been critical, I have never meant to be disrespectful.

I am grateful to UCSB for providing a stimulating intellectual environment and a steady paycheck, as well as for time off to do some of the writing. I am conscious that such time to reflect and write is a luxury that colleagues at many institutions are not afforded. The UCSB Interdisciplinary Humanities Center supported this project in its early stages, as it has generously supported other projects in the past. I owe a debt as well to the generous and efficient staffs of two fine libraries: Valley Library at Oregon State University (OSU) and Davidson Library at UCSB. I am especially grateful to the OSU students for leaving the books on the shelves so I could use them. Matt Kester helped me immensely with research assistance, as he did on several previous projects before going off to his own teaching post. I also benefited from research assistance by Theresa Christensen, Rania Azzam, Chrissy Lau, and Kathy

Patterson. I depended on technical assistance by Jimmy Grablev, Scott Wilson, Alex Nyers, Dan Haskell, and a slew of generous UCSB history colleagues and graduate students when I was being a technological nincompoop. Randy Lamb, Hunter Howatt-Nab and their colleagues at UCSB photographic services helped prepare the illustrations.

Several of the chapters were drafted during a year in residence at the Oregon State University Center for the Humanities. In that extraordinary intellectual environment, overseen by David Robinson and Wendy Madar and assisted by the incredible Sara Ash and Quynh Le, I benefited not only from the generosity of the University and the Center, but also from stimulating conversations with colleagues and friends, including Neil Davison, Elizabeth Abel, Mary Braun, Nick Cline, Tracy Daugherty, Aaron David, Paul Farber, Gary Ferngren, Erlinda Gonzalez-Berry, Charlotte Headrick, Maureen Healy, Anita Helle, Bill Husband, Alana Jeydel, Barbara Loeb, Andrea Marks, Dunya Nuaimi, Bob Nye, Mary Jo Nye, Mike Oriard, Kurt Peters, Bill Robbins, Lani Roberts, Patti Sakurai, Robert Thompson, and Jun Xing.

A second season of writing was sponsored by the Rockefeller Foundation, through their study center in Bellagio, Italy—a place justly celebrated for its unique blend of beauty, solitude, and good company. Among the extraordinary intellectuals I met there were several who contributed directly to the ideas in this book: Roshni Chowdhury, Henri Cole, John Decker, Istvan Kecskes, Bob Jaffe, Parekawhia Mclean, Charles Royal, Paul Sniderman, and Mary Ellen Strom. I also owe thanks to center director Gianna Celli, Pilar Palacia, Susan Garfield, and their kind and wonderfully helpful colleagues, among them Elena Ongamia, Vittorio Gicardoni, and Nadia Gicardoni.

Karen Wolny, my first editor at Routledge, was an enthusiastic supporter and excellent critic from the beginning. Her successors, Bill Germano and Kimberly Guinta, have been equally supportive of this and other projects. At the press I am also grateful for the help I have received from Sarah DeVos, Jaclyn Bergeron, Gilad Foss, Brendan O'Neill, Linda Leggio, and Daniel Webb. Special thanks are due to John Coltrane, Aaron Sorkin, and Joe Williams, for helping me make it through the night.

I have spent much of my life preparing to write this book. For the last quarter-century of it I have been daily in the emotional and often the physical company of two remarkable moral intellectuals, Naomi Spickard and Daniel Spickard. They have challenged and supported me in ways and to a degree that I have never experienced from any other source in this life. Other books have been dedicated to them, but I hope they will accept this one as well. During the period I was writing this book I fell under the spell of Anna Martinez, and am grateful for her rock-solid companionship and constant intellectual engagement. She also contributed in most of the ways I have attributed to others above.

Despite my gratitude to all those named here, I alone am responsible for any deficiencies that may remain.

Preface

The purpose of this book is to tell the story of American immigration. But that story will be told here from rather a different point of view than that which most readers have experienced before. *Almost All Aliens* proposes a paradigm shift. A paradigm is an orientation, a lens, a way of seeing and interpreting an object. From time to time in intellectual affairs, an old paradigm that once seemed fresh and full of insights becomes tired and worn out. Thomas Kuhn famously describes the paradigm shift that took place in late medieval Europe: from an Aristotelian, deductive, Christian-church-centered view of the cosmos to an inductive, modern, scientific way of seeing. Gradually over a few generations, the observations and musings of people like Tycho Brahe, Copernicus, Kepler, and Galileo chipped away at the old way of seeing things and a new vision emerged. It wasn't that the earth-centered, God-driven view that had lasted for centuries was not useful in describing the motions of stars and planets in the sky. But as people began to be able to make observations and measurements that were ever more precise, another paradigm, another angle of vision, proved more helpful in seeing and explaining more things more accurately. Thus was born first the notion of a heliocentric universe, and then of one without a center, held together by forces like gravity. Thus was born modern science.[i]

So, on a less cosmic scale, it has been with the study of the American West. For nearly a century, the ideas of Frederick Jackson Turner and his disciples dominated the intellectual landscape. His notion of a moving frontier line, with Europeans and civilization pressing on one side and Native peoples and savagery retreating on the other, reflected Americans' sense of themselves as virtuous settlers of virgin territory. The frontier paradigm drew from and reinforced Americans' sense of themselves as cowboys and settlers of the plains, as rough-and-ready democrats, as manifestly destined to overwhelm the landscape. It led to uncountable studies of pioneer life, each important and even revelatory in its own way, but each operating within the same Turnerian frame of reference.[ii] Although much of my work has been about peoples who came to live in the American West, when I was a graduate student I did not go into Western history precisely because the paradigm seemed dead to me. There was little left to talk about within the frontier interpretation. Fortunately, Richard White, Patricia Nelson Limerick, and others did go into Western history and, in one of the most important advances in American historical studies in the last half-century, they overturned Turner's paradigm. Their work describes, not a frontier line separating civilized Americans from savage Native people, but a wide zone of interaction among multiple peoples, a region constantly in flux, not a barrier between one people and another, but rather a zone of connection.[iii]

After 30 years of studying the peoples who have migrated to the United States, I'm convinced that the reigning paradigm in immigration history is just about worn out. *Almost All Aliens* sketches the outlines of a new, and I think better, one. If I have a wish for this book, it is that it might begin to overturn the immigrant assimilation paradigm that has dominated studies of U.S. immigration for many generations. So, much of the material in this book, many of the characters and subplots, will be familiar to readers of immigration history (some will not). But the paradigm, the angle of vision, the mode of interpretation, will be different. It is my hope that, on completing this book, the reader will look at immigration and American identity differently than he or she did before picking it up.

Almost All Aliens builds on the work of two generations of scholars—both immigration historians and, more particularly, scholars of ethnic studies. Nearly all immigration historians (and, indeed, sociologists, demographers, and students of policy) work from some version of the Ellis Island paradigm of immigrant assimilation. Since the 1960s, immigration historians have been stretching the assimilation model in several new directions. Scholars like Roger Daniels, Donna Gabaccia, and Elliott Barkan (they have had many co-workers in this endeavor) have provoked insights that have made us begin to rethink how immigration has occurred and what it has meant.[iv] For all that these are brilliant historians doing pathbreaking work, their work does not amount to a paradigm shift. They have been chipping away at the existing immigrant assimilation model, stretching it to see new subjects and address new issues, not proposing a new way to see the overall nature and meaning of immigration.

The ground for the new approach I propose in *Almost All Aliens* has been laid even more significantly by scholars in ethnic studies. For them, race, not culture change, is the main issue, and they do not assume normative Whiteness. They insist, as do I, that race matters. The experiences of White immigrants have certain areas of similarity to—and very large territories of difference from—the experiences of African, Asian, Latin American, and Middle Eastern migrants. Immigrants of color, now as throughout American history, are not variations on a theme set by European immigrants; they are different in fundamental ways. European immigration, contra the Ellis Island model, had consequences, not just for the immigrants, but for the Native peoples who inhabited the land before them. I will have much more to say about such matters in the chapters to come.[v]

Almost All Aliens attempts, then, to build on the work of immigration historians and ethnic studies scholars, complete the paradigm shift, and break free from the strictures of the assimilation model—not because that model is wrong but because it is only partial, and because it obscures as much as it illuminates. The chapters to follow should make clear how this is so.

One part of the shift will be immediately apparent to the reader. Throughout *Almost All Aliens*, the geographical limits of the America that the book addresses are constant. That is, it refers to the territory that came to be the fifty states by the middle of the twentieth century. Some may regard this as anachronistic, but it is done for a reason. Most histories of U.S. immigration (and, indeed, of the United States) have an initial frame of reference confined to a few spots on the eastern seaboard. This they gradually expand to include all the thirteen colonies and then states; then leap to the Mississippi; then add the Louisiana Purchase, then Texas, then the Southwest, the Northwest, and finally Alaska and Hawai'i. That approach emphasizes the building of the American nation. However, it tends to obscure the effects of European immigrants on the Native peoples in lands they did not control at first but would later take over. It tends to exaggerate the centrality of the stories of a tiny number of Europeans, and also to mask the devastating effect of European Americans on the continent as a whole. I have taken pains to calculate the impact on the whole.

The writing of immigrant history is very often an act of filial piety. So, for example, the first words of Jon Gjerde's excellent monograph, *From Peasants to Farmers: The Migration from Balestrand, Norway, to the Upper Middle West*, are: "This study, like all historical inquiry, is, in part, a personal search. Deep in my family's folklore are observations about the causes of emigration from Norway." Perhaps all serious writing must respond to some inner pulse on the part of the writer. But it seems Gjerde is asserting something more specific than that, perhaps even that one's topic and one's angle of interpretation come necessarily from one's life experience. In his own case, the book may be seen as one about his family's past, writ larger onto the Norwegian immigrant experience, and larger still onto the migrant experience generally.

Gjerde's assertion may not apply to all writers of history, but he seems to be on to something when it comes to writers of immigration history. Listen to the list of contributing authors to a respected collection of essays on *Swedish-American Life in Chicago*: Anderson, Blanck, Beijbom, Olsson, Olson, Lovoll, Runblom, Lintelman, Barton, Wendelius, Wright, Furuland, Swanson, Erickson, Carlsson, Nordstrom, Nordahl, Westerberg, Williams, Jarvi, Johannesson, Lund, Olsson, Johnson; almost all are Swedes. Immigrant history, for most of its practitioners, is family history. This is not to suggest that such personal motivation, nor the writing it produces, is misguided. Some of the very best writing on immigrants springs from a mood of remembering family, and in so doing, to write out from one's life and illuminate the experiences of a broader range of Americans—one thinks of Richard White's *Remembering Ahanagran* or Ronald Takaki's *Strangers from a Different Shore*. One nonetheless must caution against the tendency to imagine that the story one remembers of one's own ancestors is somehow the main story of immigration around which all other stories revolve, and against which they must be measured.[vi]

Close to the filial piety trap is the illusion that a particular place—New York City—sets the pattern for all of American immigration. For example, a prominent conference of immigration scholars was held in New York City in 2003.[vii] It was billed as an assessment of "the state of the field" that would bring together many of the top sociologists, historians, economists, political scientists, and anthropologists working on immigration issues. It was indeed a very distinguished group of scholars, all of them brilliant and enormously accomplished. The conference was well funded and could afford to bring in people (the present author included) from other parts the country. Yet only five of the participants were from the West, five from Southern universities, seven from the Midwest—and thirty-three from the Northeast. Over and over again throughout the conference, much was made of the fact that even most of those people present who worked at universities outside the Northeast originally hailed from New York. And speaker after speaker insisted that the story of immigration to New York *is* the story of immigration.[viii] It isn't true. New York has for much of American history been one very important port of entry for immigrants, and many immigrants and their descendants have lived long in that city, but the story of New York's immigrants is only one part of the immigrant story. It is part of the whole; it does not stand for the whole.

One of the things that this book may do is make steps toward deflating some of the self-congratulatory stories about immigration that we Americans have told ourselves for generations. It may help us see a clearer picture of the shape and meaning of immigration in U.S. history. Some readers may make the mistake of thinking that there is a political agenda behind the writing of this book. That is not true. There is no agenda here regarding current or future immigration policy. It is not a book about what we *should do*. It is about what we *have done*. Our past is our past; there is no point in hiding from it or making up a different past in order to make us feel better about ourselves. I have no particular feelings about the history of immigration in America, although I do have some observations and a critique. Some few readers may even go so far in error as to question my patriotism, for not everything I have to say in this book reflects well on the attitudes and actions of the American people and our government at various times in our history. We live in an age when patriotism is everyone's plumage and it is easy and fashionable to question the patriotism of others. That is socially unfortunate, but such is our era. Let it be said clearly: I am a patriot. I love America and America's peoples. I regard the writing of this book as a patriotic act. Americans at our best are a people who can see ourselves and the world clearly, who can act fairly and with generosity of spirit. Among the hopes that I have for this book in the present and future is that it may call Americans to be our best selves.

Chapter 1

Immigration, Race, Ethnicity, Colonialism

Buffalo, New York, December 2004. Thirty-four American citizens are detained for up to six hours at the U.S. border on their return from a religious conference in Toronto, entitled "Reviving the Islamic Spirit." They are forced by U.S. Customs and Border Protection agents to surrender their fingerprints. Newspapers the same day report that the United States has failed in its efforts to compile a national fingerprint data bank. They also report that the border has been reopened, after a mad cow disease scare, for cattle from the United States and Canada to move freely back and forth without restrictions or security checks. None, it may be assumed, are crossing the border to attend conferences on "Reviving the Bovine Spirit."[1]

Queens, New York, June 6, 1993. The *Golden Venture*, a rusting freighter of Indonesian registry, runs aground a few hundred feet off Rockaway Beach. After four months in the dank hold, 286 Chinese aspiring immigrants run onto the deck and plunge into the ocean, flailing toward shore. Ten drown and the others are arrested. Only about 10 are granted asylum; 100 are deported to Central America; and another one-third are sent back to China. Later, after nearly four years in jail, the final 53 are paroled by the Clinton administration and become immigrants of a sort. On that same day, a shining 747 disgorges several hundred Irish tourists at JFK airport. Dozens, perhaps scores of them overstay their visas and melt into the White American population. They become students, bartenders, actors, and accountants. No one hunts them down as illegal aliens. A decade later, some return to Ireland as its economic upturn begins to reverse the Irish exodus. Meanwhile, the Chinese would-be migrants await deportation.[2]

Los Angeles, April 29, 1992. A multiethnic riot erupts after a racially charged trial that results in the acquittal of four police officers who beat motorist Rodney King. The news media portray the riot as largely a Black-against-Korean confrontation. They show African American rioters targeting Korean American businesses and attacking random White passersby, while Korean shopkeepers defend their property with guns. The Koreans are portrayed as the good minorities—owners of property, hard-working small business people, and law abiding—while the Blacks are lawless, violent, and bad minorities. Subsequent information and arrest records show that more Latinos than African Americans were arrested for looting, that Whites also took part in the looting, and that Black-owned businesses were also burned. Enduring issues such as police violence against Latinos and African Americans, the lack of jobs in the central city, and business flight from minority neighborhoods take a backseat to racial sensationalism.[3]

Pasadena, 1945. H. S. Tsien, Goddard Professor of Aeronautics at Cal Tech, is awarded a top security clearance, goes to Europe, interrogates Nazi scientists, brings their rocketry research back to the United States, and jump-starts the U.S. missile program. Five years later, the Federal Bureau of Investigation (FBI) accuses him of spying for China, the land of his birth, and revokes his security clearance. After another five years filled with McCarthy-era harassment, humiliation, and virtual house arrest, Tsien gives in to Immigration and Naturalization Service (INS) attempts to deport him and moves to China. There he is chosen to head up the Chinese missile program and designs the Silkworm missile that is later sold to Iran and Iraq.[4]

The Southwest, 1930s. Under pressure from the federal government and local leaders, as many as one million Mexican Americans leave the United States. Some go voluntarily, some are coerced. In rural Texas, Los Angeles, the mines of Arizona, the fields of the San Joaquin Valley, and Henry Ford's Detroit, the INS sweeps up hundreds of U.S. citizens along with noncitizens, deposits them in northern Mexico, and denies them re-entry to the land of their birth. Two thousand Filipinos are similarly repatriated.[5]

Washington, D.C., 1924. Congress passes the Johnson–Reed Act. It bans immigration from Asia, including the foreign-born wives and children of U.S. citizens of Asian ancestry, and severely limits migration from Southern and Eastern Europe. Meanwhile, it leaves wide the gates for Northwest Europeans. President Calvin Coolidge and the bill's author Albert Johnson tie it explicitly to a theory of Nordic supremacy and their desire to keep America's people from being "diluted by a stream of alien blood." Many Asian and South and East European immigrants return home, discouraged. Others stay and try to find ways to bring their families together in America.[6]

Arizona Territory, September 1886. Goyathlay (Geronimo) and the Chiricahua Apaches surrender to the U.S. Army. Geronimo and his followers are taken from their homeland to a prison compound in Florida, then to Alabama. They are never allowed to return home. One-quarter century later Geronimo dies in captivity at Fort Sill, Oklahoma. The Chiricahua Apache surrender follows on the heels of warfare and death or incarceration for other Native peoples of the American West: Captain Jack and the Modocs in 1872; Crazy Horse and the Oglala Sioux in 1877; Chief Joseph and the Nez Percé in the latter year; and many other Native groups. Thus ends the era of Indian armed resistance to European immigration.[7]

Russia, 1881. The murder of Tsar Alexander II leads to a wave of *pogroms*, officially encouraged riots targeted at Jewish communities. Thousands are rendered homeless. Coming after decades of punitive laws and followed by decades more of violence, the *pogroms* send into exile two million Jews—one-third of the East European Jewish population. Many make their way to America, through Castle Garden to the Lower East Side of Manhattan or to other destinations, there to build new Jewish communities and a new Judaism.[8]

Promontory Point, Utah Territory, May 10, 1869. Leland Stanford, president of the Central Pacific Railroad, drives the Golden Spike, completing the Transcontinental Railroad. Engineers shake hands. Euro-American train operators, dignitaries, and laborers (many of them immigrants) look on. Missing from the picture are the thousands of Chinese immigrant workers who also built the railroad, constructing the more difficult and dangerous western half of the route. Missing, too, are the tens of thousands of Native Americans who will be forced to leave their homes to make way for land-hungry Euro-American immigrants brought by the train.[9]

Northern Mexico, May 30, 1848. The United States concludes its war of aggression against Mexico by seizing the Mexican northlands. That territory later forms the greater part of seven southwestern U.S. states. By the Treaty of Guadalupe Hidalgo, some of the 100,000 Mexican citizens who live in the transferred territory become American citizens. They are granted elements of formal, legal Whiteness, though ever after they are relegated to second-class social Brownness. Others become foreigners in their native land. Land titles are voided, occupations are blocked, lynching is common. The United States seeks to Americanize its new empire from Texas to California, imposing the English language, American laws and courts, American food and dress, and American racial hierarchy on the inhabitants.[10]

Ireland, 1846. A particularly vicious fungus attacks potatoes across Ireland for the second year in a row, turning 80 percent of the main food crop into rotting, gooey, black blobs in the ground. Faced with starvation and a hostile English master class, hundreds of thousands of Irish peasants leave their lands. Many go to work in factories in Liverpool and the British Midlands, others to Australia and New Zealand. The largest number join the stream to America that will total four million Irish migrants by the founding of the Irish Republic in 1921–1922. Most are near penniless when they arrive. They land in eastern cities where they form the shock troops of the U.S. Industrial Revolution. Ireland never regains its lost population—eventually nine times as many Irish descendants live in the United States as in the Old Sod.[11]

Cherokee Nation, 1838. Under orders from Congress and President Andrew Jackson, General Winfield Scott and U.S. troops round up substantially the entire population of the independent, sovereign Cherokee Nation and place them in stockades. Over the ensuing months, several detachments—some guarded by U.S. soldiers, some under tribal leaders like John and Lewis Ross—make the 800-mile trek to a new "Indian Territory" west of the Mississippi River. At least one-quarter of the Cherokee population, and perhaps as many as 8000, die in the stockades or along the way. This Trail of Tears is the final removal of Native peoples from the Southeastern

United States, preceded by the removal of the Chickasaw, Creek, Choctaw, and Seminole peoples, to make way for Euro-American migration into their homelands.[12]

East Coast, December 1773 to March 1776. Eight thousand migrants from England come to the thirteen colonies in eastern North America. Hailing from London and the Thames Valley, from Yorkshire, and from points all over the island, the largest numbers land in ports such as New York, Philadelphia, and Baltimore. Leaving unemployment and landlord tyranny, or seeking to become landowners themselves, they quickly spread across the landscape from New England to the Carolinas. Others like them go to Nova Scotia and the West Indies.[13]

Taos, New Mexico, August 10, 1680. The Pueblo Indians revolt against their Spanish overlords. After eighty years of mostly peaceful Spanish occupation and agricultural cooperation, Native peoples from most Pueblos in New Mexico rise in revolt. They kill or drive out the Spanish friars, farmers, and ranchers from the countryside and lay siege to Santa Fe. On September 21 they allow a remnant of Spanish soldiers and citizens to evacuate the smoldering town. The Spanish do not reclaim the territory until a dozen years later.[14]

Chesapeake Colonies, 1640–1700. Slavery and race become entwined. African immigrants and their descendants are gradually pushed from a semi-free condition as indentured servants into slavery. The labor force on tobacco plantations is transformed from mostly White to mostly Black, from mostly indentured to mostly enslaved. In 1640 John Punch, a Black indentured servant, runs away with two White comrades. When they are caught, the Whites are sentenced to extra years as servants, and Punch to slavery for life. In 1676 Nathaniel Bacon leads a revolt of White servants and African slaves against the colony's leaders in a dispute over Indian policy. The revolt fizzles, but the White elite is convinced that they need a stronger hold on the working population and makes a rapid transition to African American slavery as the labor system of choice.[15]

Plymouth, December 21, 1620. A boatload of illegal immigrants from England sneaks ashore. Chartered to make their homes in Virginia, the Pilgrims, led by Governor John Carver and soldier of fortune Miles Standish, wander off course—either accidentally or intentionally, we cannot be sure. They suffer terribly that first winter: half of them die from cold, scurvy, and malnutrition. They survive only because Squanto and the Wampanoag Indians give them food and show them how to prosper in this new place, in return for their pledge to help the Wampanoags fight against the neighboring Narragansetts. Squanto does not ask for their green cards.[16]

All of these are parts of the story of immigration in U.S. history.

Beyond Ellis Island—How Not to Think about Immigration History[17]

"America is a nation of immigrants." Who has not heard this phrase? It is a sentiment close to the core of America's vision of itself. The statement is formally true—more than 99 percent of the current U.S. population can at least theoretically trace its ancestry back to people who came here from somewhere else. In this sense,

American history is inevitably the history of immigration. Yet this perspective also obscures a great deal about the nature of the peoples who have made up America and the relationships among them.

The rhetorical vision of the United States as a nation of immigrants has a marvelous quality of national self-celebration about it. It proclaims proudly that we are a people made up of all the world's peoples. Here, all the varieties of humankind are fused into one American identity. J. Hector St. John Crèvecoeur, himself an immigrant from France to late-colonial America, put the matter perhaps first and most memorably in his *Letters from an American Farmer* in 1782:

> What then is the American, this new man? He is either an European, or the descendant of an European, hence that strange mixture of blood, which you will find in no other country. I could point out to you a family whose grandfather was an Englishman, whose wife was Dutch, whose son married a French woman, and whose present four sons have now four wives of different nations. *He* is an American, who, leaving behind him all his ancient prejudices and manners, receives new ones from the new mode of life he has embraced, the new government he obeys, and the new rank he holds. He becomes an American by being received in the broad lap of our great *Alma Mater*. Here individuals of all nations are melted into a new race of men, whose labours and posterity will one day cause great changes in the world. Americans are the western pilgrims, who are carrying along with them the great mass of arts, sciences, vigour, and industry which began long since in the east; they will finish the great circle. The Americans were once scattered all over Europe; here they are incorporated into one of the finest systems of population which has ever appeared, and which will hereafter become distinct by the power of the different climates they inhabit. The American ought therefore to love this country much better than that wherein either he or his forefathers were born.[18]

Soaringly poetic though it be, this vision masks the profound power dynamics that have existed among America's peoples. Carl Wittke wrote the first large, comprehensive, and widely read history of American immigration, which he titled *We Who Built America: The Saga of the Immigrant*. Wittke rhapsodized about the glorious mix of peoples who made up the United States. But for Wittke as for Crèvecoeur, that meant Northwest European peoples. Four-fifths of Wittke's 500-plus pages described immigrants from Holland, France, Wales, Ireland, Germany, Scandinavia, and so on. Less than one-fifth of the pages were devoted to South and East European migrants; they were numerous, but presumably they were not as central to the American project as the others. Wittke had only fourteen pages for Asians, three for Mexicans, and none at all for Africans or Native Americans—apparently they did not contribute to the building of America.[19]

This understanding of immigration is built on an interlocking set of unexamined assumptions about how various racial and ethnic groups have in fact functioned in relationship to each other in American history. For example, while the nation-of-immigrants ideology perfunctorily recognizes that the people who came to North America from England were immigrants, it does not treat them that way. On the contrary, it posits the English as by definition native to the American landscape, and measures others with respect to English Americans. Milton Gordon identified this assumption a couple of generations ago as "Anglo-conformity": all other people in the United States would be expected to change their behavior to approximate that of Americans of English descent.[20] There is something more insidious, however, than mere Anglo-conformity going on here. "Conformity" implies a certain volition on the part of the conforming person, a willingness to give up her or his preferred behavior patterns in return for a measure of acceptance. But in the case of Anglo-Americans, the assumption is unspoken but insistent that English people are natural Americans and every other sort of people are less so. One might call this "Anglo-normativity."

We can see Anglo-normativity at work in the writing of Peter Brimelow. Here a recent immigrant from England talks savagely and disparagingly about how inappropriate are immigrants from other places, as if his very Englishness made him a natural American: "The problem is not necessarily immigration in principle—it's immigration in practice. Specifically, it's the workings of the 1965 Immigration Act and its subsequent amendments. ... [Before the 1965 act], immigrants came overwhelmingly from Europe ... ; now, immigrants are overwhelmingly visible minorities from the Third World. ... The mass immigration so thoughtlessly triggered in 1965 risks making America an *alien nation* ... America will become a freak among the world's nations because of the unprecedented demographic mutation it is inflicting on itself" by taking in non-White, non-English immigrants. "[C]urrent immigration policy is Adolf Hitler's posthumous revenge on America."[21]

Oscar Handlin was for many years regarded as the premier historian of U.S. immigration. His book *The Uprooted*, a monument to historical empathy, begins with the words: "Once I thought to write a history of the immigrants in America. Then I discovered that the immigrants *were* American history." Yet all of Handlin's immigrants are Europeans, and none of them are English. The same is true for Handlin's book *Immigration as a Factor in American History*. He goes on at length about "old world background, the economic adjustment, immigrant organization," and other issues. But he only talks about Asians in a few pages on "color prejudice" near the end of the book, and does not talk about English Americans, nor about other peoples of color at all; apparently they are not part of the immigrant experience. In a more recent generation, John Bodnar contested many of Handlin's conclusions in *The Transplanted*. But still, for Bodnar as for Handlin, immigration meant primarily non-English Europeans. Like so many others who think about U.S. immigration, for these authors English people were not immigrants but natural Americans, and non-White peoples were not in the picture at all.[22]

The story of American immigration has thus almost always been portrayed as a series of one-way migrations by successive waves of European but non-English peoples, from an Old Country (which was for one reason or another a bad place to live) to the New Country (which was by self-definition good). They left the Old Country—uprooted in Handlin's telling, transplanted in Bodnar's—and came to America on a one-way ship. Crèvecoeur assumed that anyone who left Europe for America had been poor and miserable in Europe, and that one came to America to become prosperous and happy. That is the understanding that Emma Lazarus celebrated when she wrote the words that appear at the base of the Statue of Liberty: "Give me your tired, your poor, Your huddled masses yearning to breathe free, The wretched refuse of your teeming shore. Send these, the nameless, tempest-tost to me, I lift my lamp beside the golden door!"[23]

We may call this the Ellis Island paradigm[24] or the immigrant assimilation model. According to the model, the task of these peoples was to become Americanized, that is, to become facsimiles of English-descended Americans. Secretary of

State John Quincy Adams put the issue clearly, in an 1819 letter to German Baron von Furstenwäther responding to a question about the prospects for German migrants in the United States: "To one thing they must make up their minds, or, they will be disappointed in every expectation of happiness as Americans. They must cast off the European skin, never to resume it. They must look forward to their posterity rather than backward to their ancestors"—they must, in short, assimilate to Anglo-American norms.[25]

Thus the story of immigration has been presented as the same story over and over again. Wittke enunciated the paradigm, but its outlines had been agreed upon for many decades before he wrote, and they remain barely challenged today. First there was "The Old Immigration" of the middle of the nineteenth century: people from Ireland, Germany, and Scandinavia came to America and became like Anglo-Americans. Then there was "The New Immigration" of the period 1880 to 1924: people came from Italy, Poland, Greece, and other parts of Southern and Eastern Europe and did their best to become like Anglo-Americans.[26] Each of these "waves" of immigration is treated analytically as more or less the same.[27] In the twentieth century, writers have referred to "The Third Wave" and even "The Fourth Wave," all following more or less the same pattern, though with populations that diverged more and more from the assumed Anglo-American central group, and so were less able to make the prescribed cultural transformation.[28]

According to the immigrant assimilation model, culture change is the story. In the migrant generation the people in question were foreign to the mainstream American identity. They spoke a "foreign" language (so regarded because the natural language of the United States is presumed to be English); they wore foreign clothes, ate foreign foods, thought in ways that were foreign to Anglo-America. By choice or by compulsion, they associated mainly with people from their ancestral homeland. In succeeding generations they peeled off the cultural markers of their difference—they learned unaccented American English, changed their clothes and manners, adopted new associates—and gradually they became Americans. Richard Alba and Victor Nee put the matter succinctly:

> The mainstream of American life has demonstrated since the colonial period a remarkable capacity to draw into its swift currents the descendants of successive waves of immigrants. Individuals and families descended from the mass immigrations of the late nineteenth and early twentieth centuries have joined the mainstream. ... The descendants may choose to celebrate their ethnic identity and cultural roots, but their ethnicity has greatly diminished as an ascriptive trait that decisively shapes life chances. The processes that brought about this outcome are the motor of American assimilation.[29]

Thus relationships between groups had nothing to do with power, economic station, race, slavery, oppression, discrimination, or displacement of Native peoples. They had only to do with how well immigrants adapted culturally to the Anglo-American norm. There is no power, there is only culture.[30]

It is as if America were a giant metaphoric escalator. Every new group starts at the bottom and makes its way inexorably up to the top over the course of three or four generations. It is mechanical, inevitable; it just happens that way. Along the way, in order to stay, each group must jettison the things that distinguish it from other

Americans: language, religion, ways of thinking. At the top, people are all the same and cease to have ethnicity. They are simply Americans, and American democracy is triumphant.[31]

Part of the embrace of a self-celebratory paradigm may have to do with people's filiopietistic motivations for studying immigration history. I have written elsewhere that those who write the history of Christianity almost always place their own denominational roots at the center of the story. Their religious grandparents, if you will, are for them the pivot point around which the whole of Christian history revolves, the seed crystal that gives form to the entire edifice. A Roman Catholic, a Baptist, and a Russian Orthodox history of Christianity resemble each other only in the vaguest of outlines.[32] So it is with the history of immigration. As Diane Johnson reminds us, "Just as civilizations have foundation myths, Americans have arrival myths, the whole collective notion of the huddled masses yearning to breathe free mixed with the particular memories of a grandparent arrived at Ellis Island. ... Underlying the arrival story in each region of America [and for each ethnic group]— and all are different—was the same explicit promise of freedom and opportunity, usually meaning freedom from persecution and freedom to become rich."[33]

So for most historians of immigration, their own forebears or some other group with whom they identify become the template for all immigration experiences. And just as almost all historians of immigration are European Americans, nearly all the templates are European American templates. The stories of their European immigrant ancestors, coming through Castle Garden or Ellis Island in New York and settling in the northeastern part of the United States, become *the* story of immigration. Everything that does not fit that story is epiphenomenal. European American experiences are the really real. If some peoples of color have different experiences, those are just exceptions.

The story of European immigration through places like Ellis Island is *part* of the story of immigration in American history, but it is only a part, and it has never been more than that. *Almost All Aliens* tells that story, but it tells the other stories too, and it relates them one to another.

The Ellis Island version of immigration history leaves out a mountain of essential material and vital perspectives. As noted above, it treats English Americans as the quintessential natives, not as immigrants. It ignores the fact that tens of thousands of English people kept coming to the United States each year throughout the supposed periods of the Old and New Immigration and after. It may surprise some readers to learn that more than twice as many migrants came to the United States from Britain in the single decade of the 1880s than came from all of Europe during the entire colonial era. It may surprise them further to learn that as many British immigrants came to the United States during the 1990s as during the seventeenth and eighteenth centuries combined.[34]

Whether those English people migrated in the 1690s or the 1960s, they entered a multicultural America. The European-centered assimilation model also ignores the fact that America has always been a profoundly multicultural place, a nation of peoples far more diverse than that model has room for. Yet the most knowledgeable people in such matters refuse to let us see the South in the colonial era as simply Black and White, and insist that it was always a zone of complex interactions between various peoples whom it is probably unfair to simplify into merely Red, White, and Black. Likewise, California, Texas, Kansas, the Pacific Northwest, and other parts of the country were zones characterized for a very long time by complex, evolving sets of relationships between multiple peoples: Native Americans of various groups, different sorts of Europeans, Mexicans, African-descended peoples, several kinds of Asians.[35]

The Ellis Island interpretation further refuses to treat Africans as part of the history of migration to North America at all. Because they do not fit the escalator model, they are epiphenomenal. Will Herberg, much-revered pioneer scholar of immigrant religion, had only a footnote for Blacks and Latinos:

> Two major groups stand measurably outside this division of American society into three "melting pots" [Protestant, Catholic, and Jewish]—the Negroes and the recent Latin-American immigrants (Mexicans in the southwest, Puerto Ricans in New York and other eastern centers). Ethnic amalgamation within the religious community does not yet include them to any appreciable extent; their primary context of self-identification and social location remains their ethnic or "racial" group. … The future of the Negroes in the United States constitutes a much more difficult problem, about which very little may be said with any assurance today.[36]

African-descended people had been on the continent for 350 years, but still very little could be said about them, because they did not fit the model; they were exceptions to be ignored.

Some immigration writers have actually tried to fit African Americans into an escalator model, arguing that they did not get on the escalator until the early decades of the twentieth century, when large numbers migrated from the rural South to the urban North. Hence, if they are a people apart still in America, it is only because of their very late entry. It has nothing to do with racial division and oppression. No one is to blame.[37]

Africans were in fact migrants, though compelled, and I argue in the chapters to come that they have undergone processes that are in some ways very similar to those of other immigrant groups—and in some ways they are profoundly different. It is essential to see both the similarities (many of which have to do with cultural processes) and also the differences (which have to do with race and power).[38] The relevant comparison for African American migrants is to compare the descendants of slaves and servants who came starting in the 1620s with the descendants of English people who came starting in the 1620s, not to compare Black Americans who migrated from the South to the North and West beginning at the dawn of the twentieth century with European immigrants to eastern seaports about the same time. Most U.S. historians would be surprised to learn that, in the generation before the American Revolution, between 1720 and 1760, more African migrants came to the thirteen colonies than European migrants: 159,000 Africans compared to 105,000 Europeans. African American migration dominated the demography of that era to an even greater extent than did European migration dominate the last decades of the nineteenth century and the first decades of the twentieth century.[39]

Likewise, the immigrant assimilation model has no way to deal with Native Americans. In fact, like much of American mythic history, it tends to treat Native peoples like parts of the natural landscape—like antelopes and cougars, if you will, sometimes threatening and sometimes benign, but subject to removal and extermination without thinking.[40] It is this very naturalizing that leads a lot of White Americans to claim some Native American ancestry (always several generations back and usually an Indian woman, preferably Cherokee).[41] As historian Philip Deloria put it, "Americans wanted to feel a natural affinity with the continent, and it was Indians who could teach them such aboriginal closeness. Yet, in order to control the landscape they had to destroy the original inhabitants." White Americans have played at being Indians, from the Boston Tea Party to the Boy Scouts to the New Age, in order to establish a national identity on the North American continent and to identify with that continent—in Deloria's words, "to encounter the authentic amidst the anxiety of urban industrial and postindustrial life. ... Over the past thirty years, the counterculture, the New Age, the men's movement, and a host of other Indian performance options have given meaning to Americans lost in a (post)modern freefall. ... Playing Indian is a persistent tradition."[42] Kevin Costner can dance with wolves and claim some Native American ancestry, in part because it costs him nothing and it makes him more American to do so. To be Native American, unlike to be Black, is to be naturally, primordially part of America. What this construction ignores is the manifestly larger and more important historical issue: White people killing Indians, spreading across the landscape, and taking it. All that is about race, power, and colonialism. These are central issues in the story of American immigration.

Nor does the Ellis Island model deal well with Mexican Americans. It insists on treating Mexicans as recent immigrants (*pace* Herberg above), when many are not immigrants at all, but rather the descendants of people who lived in lands that the United States conquered and took. In effect, the border crossed them. Others came later but still have lived in the United States for several generations—many for a century or more—yet the Ellis Island model treats them as recently arrived aliens.[43] The immigrant assimilation model posits a long distance between the country of origin and the United States, and with that distance little ongoing contact. The Old Country is left and the New Country is embraced. Many Mexican and other Western Hemisphere immigrants, by contrast, have maintained ongoing connections with their ancestral homelands, even as they have been full Americans.[44]

The immigrant assimilation model likewise cannot deal with such non-European immigrants as Chinese and Japanese. If Asians are included in the traditional interpretation at all, they are regarded as part of the New Immigration: more foreign culturally, more difficult to assimilate than Old Immigrants (so, by implication, if they have a hard time in America, it is their own fault for being culturally incompatible). How is it, then, that 230,000 Chinese came to the United States during the period of the Old Immigration, and only half that number during the period of the New? The Ellis Island paradigm has no answer. But Roger Daniels does: "The old typology between old and new simply assumed that immigrants were Europeans. Chinese, who came in the era of the old, and Japanese, who came in the period of the new, were treated as exotic exceptions when they were not written off as sojourners and thus not immigrants at all."[45]

The immigrant assimilation model also has no explanation for the stubborn fact that today American-born U.S. citizens of Asian and Mexican descent are regarded as foreigners in their native land by Whites, even those whose ancestry in the United States may be of substantially shorter duration. As Lisa Lowe puts it, "[T]he Asian is always seen as an immigrant, as the 'foreigner-within,' even when born in the United States and the descendant of generations born here before."[46] During the 1996 campaign of Washington State Governor Gary Locke, an American-born lawyer of Chinese descent, a third-generation American, he received the endorsement of the *Seattle Times*, the state's most prominent newspaper. Nonetheless, the *Times* felt constrained to have an investigative reporter go through the list of contributors to Locke's campaign, highlight all the Chinese surnames, and check to see if they were U.S. citizens, hence eligible to contribute. They did not go through his opponents' lists of contributors looking for English or Scandinavian names and check to see if those people were citizens. Asians are treated as perpetual foreigners indeed.[47]

Moreover, the immigrant assimilation model is relentlessly unanalytical about key issues. For example, it never asks: What is a White person? What is a Black person, or an Italian for that matter? It merely assumes categories.[48]

Not Assimilation But Race Making

Race is a central, not a marginal, issue in U.S. immigration history. *Almost All Aliens* offers a new paradigm for interpreting the whole history of American immigration and identity, placing race at the center of the analysis, rather than on the margins as with the previous paradigm. This new view of U.S. immigration history will hold in tension three ways of thinking about their subject: the immigrant assimilation paradigm, the transnational diasporic model, and the theory of panethnic formation.

The Immigrant Assimilation Model

The Ellis Island paradigm, which I have been discussing for much of this chapter, tells part of the story. It is good at detailing the changes that take place in the behavior and cultural skills of migrants as they leave one place and enter another. Its emphasis on culture change over generations is particularly helpful when considering the dynamics within specific immigrant communities over extended periods of time.

The main rhetorical mode of the immigrant assimilation paradigm is the Melting Pot. Everyone since Crèvecoeur has heard that America is a great melting pot. The melting pot myth is an extremely powerful rhetorical tool. The idea is that people will come to the United States from all over the world. Each group will contribute a portion of its culture—food, language, religion, physical appearance. Out of the melting pot will come a proportional blend of all the peoples who make up America. It is a hopeful vision indeed. It promises respect for every individual and group. It promises that everyone who comes to America will change, and all will change together.

Ralph Waldo Emerson struck the note boldly: "[A]s in the old burning of the Temple at Corinth, by the melting and intermixture of silver and gold and other metals a new compound more precious than any, called Corinthian brass, was formed; so in this continent,—asylum of all nations,—the energy of Irish, Germans, Swedes, Poles, and Cossacks, and all the European tribes,—of the Africans, and of the Polynesians,—will construct a new race, a new religion, a new state, a new literature."[49] Israel Zangwill's 1908 play, *The Melting Pot*, echoed Emerson's theme. There, a Russian Jewish immigrant named David Quixano, in love with a native Gentile woman, nearly sings his joy in America: "America is God's crucible, the great Melting Pot where all the races of Europe are melting and re-forming! Here you stand, good folk, think I, when I see them at Ellis Island, here you stand in your fifty groups, with your fifty languages and histories, and your fifty blood hatreds and rivalries. But you won't be long like that, brothers, for these are the fires of God you've come to—these are the fires of God. A fig for your feuds and vendettas! Germans and Frenchmen, Irishmen and Englishmen, Jews and Russians—into the Crucible with you all! God is making an American."[50]

The melting pot rhapsody underlay a 1993 special issue of *Time* magazine, on "How immigrants are shaping the world's first multicultural society." Never mind that there have been lots of multicultural societies before, from Byzantium to the Swahili Coast to Tang China to the Philippines. A little self-celebration sells magazines. On the cover was a picture of an impossibly beautiful woman, "The New Face of America." She was not an actual human being, but a computer creation, morphed from photos of dozens of actual people—purporting to represent the mathematical average of all the physical types present in the American population, in precise proportion to the size of the various groups half a century hence: 15 percent Anglo-Saxon, 17.5 percent Middle Eastern, 17.5 percent African, 7.5 percent Asian, 35 percent Southern European, and 7.5 percent Latino (Figure 1.1).[51]

All this is pleasant, positive, hopeful. The promise of the melting pot is that America will become a happy place where everyone blends together and turns out somewhere in the physical and cultural middle. But there is another—a hegemonic—side to the melting pot idea.

As Milton Gordon noted so trenchantly four decades ago, when someone invokes the melting pot, that person really means Anglo-conformity. That person is acting rhetorically, attempting to establish Anglo-American hegemony over other peoples in the United States.[52] As Will Herberg admitted, "Our cultural assimilation has taken place not in a 'melting pot,' but rather in a 'transmuting pot' in which all ingredients have been transformed and assimilated to an idealized 'Anglo-Saxon' model."[53] Whenever people invoke the melting pot, they are really pushing Anglo-conformity.[54] Gordon offers us another useful insight: a distinction between assimilation and acculturation. That is, "assimilation" he describes as the incorporation of an immigrant or racial minority group into the dominant Anglo-American group structurally, in terms of participation in dominant-group institutions, intermarriage, and common identification as one people. "Acculturation"—adoption of the cultural skills of the dominant Anglo-American group—Gordon argues, can take place without significant structural assimilation. Immigrants can learn English and eat American dishes without abandoning their connections with others from their immigrant group. Yet here, too, Gordon assumes that the change will be a one-way thing: the immigrant will acculturate to Anglo-American norms (speak English, become a Christian, and so forth). "Acculturation" is as laden with Anglo-conformity as is "assimilation."[55]

Eileen Tamura shows us a more fruitful way to think about acculturation. She makes a distinction between acculturation and Americanization. She analyzes the behavior of Nisei (that is, second-generation Japanese Americans) in Hawai'i in the decades surrounding World War II. Haoles (that is, Whites) controlled the social and political processes of the islands and used the public schools to Americanize the Nisei. They forced Nisei to learn national standard English, Anglo-American table manners, handwriting by the Palmer method, and the like. The Whites' goal was to create an educated Nisei servant class. The generation of Daniel Inouye and Patsy Mink, however, took those cultural tools and turned them against their would-be betters. They used their education and Anglo-American cultural skills, not to become servants to White people, but to seize control of the islands politically (and, to a lesser extent, socially).[56]

Figure 1.1 "The New Face of America," according to *Time*.

The question remains unresolved, however: must acculturation always be a one-way thing, non-Anglo Americans changing to conform to Anglo-American norms? Or can acculturation ever be a genuinely multiple-sided process, with all the peoples who make up America changing to meet with all the others? Can the promise of the melting pot become reality? It seems unlikely.

Even if there can be no melting pot, and there must be only Anglo-conformity, there are nonetheless issues and patterns that are common to the experience of many immigrant groups: the rigors of the journey, the shock of the new, alienation of the second generation from their parents, and a host of other processes. Yet I want to be wary of the unspoken assumption of the Ellis Island model: that every group in U.S. history is going through more or less the same process of assimilation and incorporation into a nonethnic American mass. The assumption of assimilation scholarship is that all American ethnic and racial groups are marching along the same pathway; perhaps they are at different points on that pathway, but they are all marching relentlessly, in Richard Alba's memorable phrase, "into the twilight of ethnicity" when they will be just undifferentiated Americans.[57] A couple of early twenty-first-century books even predict that, by 2050, Latinos and Asians will be White.[58] Can one imagine a person who used to be Chinese and now is White? It is a nonsensical assertion.

The contention of the assimilationists that all ethnic groups are traveling the same pathway is not accurate for the United States today, nor has it ever been accurate. Whatever similarities we may find between various groups, there is a fundamental difference between the experiences of peoples of color and those of White immigrants. Matthew Jacobson makes the case that there have been from time to time different shades or degrees of Whiteness.[59] Yet there is also a fundamental divide, historically and currently, between the experiences of the pigment poor and those of the pigment rich.[60] The assimilation model does not work for people of color. No amount of wishing will make it so.

The Ellis Island Museum in New York Harbor presents Ellis Island as "America's Gate." Well, it is one of America's gates. The story of Ellis Island and the Lower East Side is one of the stories of American immigration. European immigrant uplift over generations into fairly undifferentiated Whiteness is part of American immigration history, but there are other parts. The story of American immigration is also the story of Angel Island and East Los Angeles, and of the Rio Grande Valley, and of Miami, and the Canadian border. Many points of entry, many vectors of immigrant experience. Not just in the present but for all of America's past, the story of American immigration and identity has been a more complex one than the immigrant assimilation model can fully comprehend.

The Transnational Diasporic Model

Two interpretive paradigms, the transnational diasporic model and the panethnic or racial formation model, are useful as partners with the immigrant assimilation model.[61]

Much has been made in recent years about the diasporic nature of human migrations. People who have come to America typically have not, contrary to the assimilation model, cut off their ties to the places from which they came. That was as true for George Washington and Benjamin Franklin as for 1990s dot-com wizards from Madras. Washington, for example, was indeed America's first great general, national hero, and president. But he also was heir to a country house in the north of England where he might instead have chosen to live out his days as a gentleman. Franklin spent a third of his adult life in England and France, and he very nearly might have chosen to remain in Britain at the start of the American Revolution. Instead of a roll-the-dice, once-and-for-all abandoning of the ancestral homeland and siding with the United States, for almost every American immigrant group, there has been a going and a coming, a continuing connectedness with the homeland, and also with other places to which migrants from one's homeland have gone. Many Greek and Italian villages by the 1930s and 1940s had aging residents who had spent their young adult years in the United States. And the Italians did not just come to the United States: many went to North Africa, Argentina, Brazil, and other places, just as the eighteenth- and nineteenth-century English went not only to the United States and Canada, but also to Australia, India, East and South Africa, Aotearoa, Fiji, South America, and other places as well.[62]

Roger Rouse writes on the linked Mexican communities of Aguililla (Michoacán) and Redwood City (California):

> It has become inadequate to see Aguilillan migration as a movement between distinct communities, understood as the loci of distinct sets of social relationships. Today, Aguilillans find that their most important kin and friends are as likely to be living hundreds or thousands of miles away as immediately around them. More significantly, they are often able to maintain these spatially extended relationships as actively and effectively as the ties that link them to their neighbors. In this growing access to the telephone has been particularly significant, allowing people not just to keep in touch periodically, but to contribute to decision-making and participate in familial events from a considerable distance.[63]

The Internet and the World Wide Web have tied them closer together still. That is a new view of Mexicans that the immigrant assimilation model could not accommodate.

The diasporic process is not new. People in migration have always been linked and have moved back and forth. What is new is that we have a conceptual orientation, the transnational model, that allows us to see that pattern. People were moving around what is now the U.S. Southwest and the Mexican North long before there was a United States or a Mexico. In the trans-Pacific Chinese family, adolescent boys for several generations left South China and went out to work in the United States, Hawai'i, Southeast Asia, and elsewhere. Women and children stayed home. The men would make a trip or two back to China, marry, sire children, and return overseas. The family went on for decades, even generations, existing simultaneously on both sides of the Pacific or in two regions of Asia. After World War II, the War Brides Acts were designed to allow American soldiers to bring home, outside racially motivated immigration quotas, women they had married abroad during wartime; several thousand Chinese American soldiers used them to bring over their wives of many years.[64]

If the diasporic or transnational model has perspectival and explanatory strength, it is not without its detractors among ethnic studies scholars.[65] They argue against the diasporic concept on essentially political grounds, citing the centrality of service to communities of color in the mission of ethnic studies. If ethnic studies scholarship is to be useful for much, it ought to empower the powerless, and they feel that the diasporic perspective detracts from that purpose. On the one hand, it concentrates on the migrating generation—on first-generation Chinese or Samoans, for example, around the globe. In doing so it turns its attention away from the issues of succeeding generations in any given location. Asian Americans and Asians are not the same people, despite the tendency of non-Asians to confuse them. Similarly, one may say that Italians and Italian Americans, Poles and Polish Americans, are not quite the same people, either, though surely they are linked.

Second, the critics are troubled by what they see as an upper-class bias in diasporic studies. Sau-ling Wong wonders "to what extent a class bias is coded into the privileging of travel and transnational mobility in … articulations of denationalization" and diasporas. People can go and come because they have the money to do so and jobs and comfortable homes to return to. The diasporic model, says Wong, "is, at least in part, extrapolated from the wide range of options available to a particular socioeconomic class, yet the class element is typically rendered invisible."[66]

It might also be argued that the emphasis of the transnational model on the immigrant generation and connections with ancestral homelands may jeopardize the well-being of immigrants in racialized states. In the United States, it is true that there are woeful limitations on the life chances of immigrants, especially people of color. But there is at least the countervailing influence of the immigrant assimilation model, which asserts that anyone born in America is an American and belongs to America. Contrast that to the situation in places like Germany, Austria, France, and Denmark, where entrenched nativist parties insist that even second- and third-generation Turks, Algerians, and Hungarians do not belong.[67]

One particularly interesting take on transnational relationships that may drive migration comes from work on international labor migration by Edna Bonacich and Lucie Cheng. They argue that, at least under the conditions of a mature international capitalist economy such as has existed in much of the world since the mid-nineteenth century, economic forces link the sending places and the receiving places. Some other, simpler models talk about "push factors" such as war, disease, and rural impoverishment driving people out of their ancestral homelands. They talk about separate "pull factors" such as cheap land, good public education, and abundant job opportunities that pull people to a place like the United States.[68] Cheng and Bonacich say that such factors may be linked, and the mechanism that links them is the global market economy. Figure 1.2 shows their conceptual diagram explaining their theory.[69]

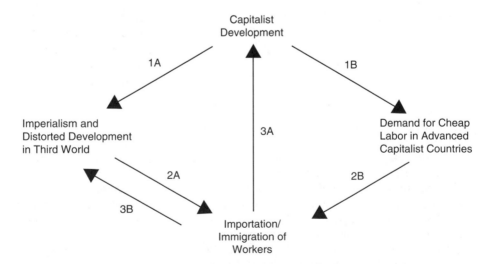

Figure 1.2 Bonacich and Cheng's conceptual diagram of international labor migration.

One can see how such dynamics might have linked China with Britain and the United States in the mid-nineteenth century. Capitalist development in Britain in the age of the Industrial Revolution sent British merchant fleets abroad seeking markets (vector 1A). The British East India Company provoked two Opium Wars in China, which resulted in imperial encroachment on Chinese sovereignty, not only by England, but also by the United States and several other industrializing powers. As the Chinese central government lost control of its southeastern provinces, rebellion and warlordism drove peasants off the land. Some of them took ship for Southeast Asia and America (2A). In the United States, Chinese laborers on railroads and in mines built essential parts of the infrastructure of industrial capitalism (3A). But their leaving left parts of rural China underpopulated and unstable (3B). In a simpler and more obvious set of connections, industrial capitalist development in Europe and the United States, as well as imperialist development by the United States and Europe abroad (1B) led to a demand for cheap labor, both in those countries and in overseas colonies such as Singapore and Indochina. Hence (2B) workers were imported, and this contributed further (3A) to the development of capitalist power in Europe and the United States.

Not only, then, was there a back-and-forth quality to the migrations of peoples, some of whom ended up in the United States. Those peoples in motion were part of vast international webs by which people moved from Europe, Africa, Asia, Latin America, and the Pacific to North America. They also moved within each of those regions; and from Europe to Africa and Africa to Europe; from Asia to Africa, Latin America, and the Pacific and back; and so on and on. The pathways of migration were also the pathways of trade and of colonial economic and political connection. It was a complicated set of interlocking patterns, far more complex than can be comprehended by the assimilation model alone.

The Panethnic Formation Model

The other necessary supplement to the Ellis Island paradigm is the panethnic or racial formation model. Richard Alba and Victor Nee write that, by about the third generation in any immigrant group, "their ethnicity has greatly diminished as an ascriptive trait that decisively shapes life chances."[70] Nonsense! It may well be that, for instance, the lives of the great-grandchildren of Irish American immigrants are not shaped in any meaningful way by their Irishness. I am one of those. I am Irish on March 17 and whenever anyone offers Guinness, but Irish identity does not in any meaningful way shape my life chances. What does shape my life chances is the fact that I am White. *That* is my ethnicity, and it is powerful. My ethnicity has not diminished. It is not less than the ethnicity of my purely Irish great-grandmother. It has changed. She was Irish; I am White.

What Alba and Nee fail to see is *the major fact* of ethnic identity in American history: panethnic formation. Yen Le Espiritu coined the term "panethnicity" to describe a process that has been going on in the world for a very long time: the lumping together of formerly separate ethnic groups, frequently in a new geographical or political setting. People came to this country as members of ethnic groups that were frequently defined by place of origin. In the United States, they became members of larger panethnic groups, which we sometimes call races. Igbo, Hausa, Fon, Fulani, Asante, Yoruba, and dozens of other groups became Negroes by late in the eighteenth century or early in the nineteenth, and then, in the fullness of time, they came to be called Blacks, and then African Americans. Sicilianos and Milanos became Italians; Litvaks and Galitsianers became East European Jews; and then those Italians and Jews, and English descendants and Swedes and Poles and Irish, became White people. Osage, Choctaw, and Potawatomi became Indians. Beginning in the 1950s and 1960s, Chinese, Japanese, Koreans and others began to become Asian Americans. In the last third of the twentieth century and the first part of the twenty-first, Dominicans, Cubans, Puerto Ricans, Mexicans, and others may be becoming Latinos. Everyone has ethnicity. No one's ethnicity has been diminished. Rather, it has been transformed. People whose ancestors were members of smaller, nationally defined ethnic groups have become in America members of races. They are not less ethnic; they are differently ethnic.[71]

What is happening, then, is not simple assimilation, but panethnic or racial formation. The panethnicity model, like the immigrant assimilation model, empha-sizes the experiences of people in the place to which they migrate—in the present case, the United States. It is similar to the immigrant model in that it tends to focus on the experiences of succeeding generations in the new place, and de-emphasizes connections to places of origin. It is different from the immigrant model in that it does not presume the ultimate absorption of the immigrant people into some amor-phous American mass. Rather, it highlights the formation of larger, enduring ethnic collectivities through which people may act together. Together these three ways of conceiving ethnic processes—the immigrant assimilation theory, the transnational diasporic paradigm, and the panethnic formation model—help us see clearly what has gone on in the history of American immigration.

Race vs. Ethnicity: The Difference, and the Difference It Makes

Ethnicity and race, then, are among the central concerns of this book. But what exactly are they, and how do they relate to each other?[72] At the broadest level, I see at least two ways that people tend to think about these matters. One way comes to us from the eighteenth- and nineteenth-century pseudoscience of Blumenbach, Gobineau, Cuvier, and their intellectual descendants (right down to Charles Murray and Richard Herrnstein, J. Philippe Rushton, and Jon Entine as the twentieth cen-tury turns to the twenty-first).[73] Their vision is the one that most lay people assume to be the way things are.

According to the pseudoscientists, there are four or five big races and smaller subsidiary ethnic groups. In this view, race is about biology, genes, phenotype, the body. It is physical, inherited, and immutable. The races are discrete from each other, each marked not only by specific distinguishing bodily features—skin color, hair texture, nose shape, and so forth—but also by specific character qualities that cannot be erased. These character qualities are heritable, immutable, hard-wired into people's genes. They may be suppressed, but eventually they will out.

In this same mode of thinking, ethnicity is based on smaller human sub-divisions of race. The various ethnic groups within a race look very much, if not completely, alike. Their differences are based on cultural or national divisions, such as language, citizenship, religion, child-rearing practices, food habits, clothing, and so forth. Ethnic differences, in this way of thinking, are mutable. Ethnicity derives from an ancestral group, but it can be changed by changing behavior.

(racist)
In this view,
race = stagnant
ethnicity = date

18

An alternative view emphasizes the plasticity and constructedness of groups, whether we call them "races" or "ethnic groups."[74] It notes that groups that are often called races have cultures, and that there are average physical differences that can be observed among the peoples who are called ethnic groups, so the race/ethnic group dichotomy tends to break down pretty quickly. It emphasizes that race is not a thing or a condition but a *process*. This alternative view notes further that the understanding of the pseudoscientists was created in a particular time and place (Europe and the United States in the late eighteenth to early twentieth centuries). It was created among a set of people who were trying to explain the varieties of peoples that Europeans and Euro-Americans were encountering as they made colonies around the globe. Some would say that they were trying to naturalize colonialism, to lay it onto the genes of people.[75]

History and logic argue for the use of "ethnicity" rather than "race" as a generic term for kinds of groups that operate on more or less the same bases.[76] Both are social and political constructs based on real or fictive common ancestry, which were generated in particular contexts and which have gone through particular histories. If one is focusing on internal group processes, they are much the same kinds of groups, whether one calls them "races," "ethnic groups," "ethno-racial groups," or some other common term (more about those processes in the next section of this essay). To distinguish between "race" and "ethnicity" is to give in to the pseudoscientific racists by adopting their terminology. It is to conjure up visions of large, physical, immutable races and smaller, cultural subgroups that are ethnic groups.

In the United States, it is true, the markers of the largest social groups do in fact more or less correspond to Blumenbach's pseudoscientific racial categories: Native, Asian, African, Latin, and White Americans. Those are the meaningful racial formations in American society.[77] But elsewhere, it is other markers that make the big divisions. In Britain, at least for a time in the 1970s and 1980s, people whom Americans would call Asians and Africans, many Britons joined together under the single term "Black."[78] Taoufik Djebali argues that, in North Africa throughout much of its history, it was religion that constituted the big divider. There, religion is, in power terms, a "racial" divider, in that people on either side of the religious divide see each other as fundamentally, immutably different from themselves. So, too, Han Chinese and Tibetans, Japanese and Koreans have something like "racial" differences between them.[79]

The Racial Moment. Despite such evident similarities between "racial" and "ethnic" groups, there *is* nonetheless a critical juncture in relationships between peoples when they come to see each other, and are seen by outsiders, as fundamentally, essentially, immutably different from one another. At such a juncture, the differences they perceive are often laid on the body and the essential character. That is what I would call *the racial moment*. At such times, that racializing move is accompanied by at least an attempt by one group to exert power over the other, or to highlight its own disempowerment. It is worth noting that "race" is a term that seems static and essential, while "racialize" emphasizes agency and process: ongoing action taken to make hierarchy, to position oneself and to create an Other.

At its point of origin and in its ongoing formations, race is a story about power, and it is written on the body. That is, dividing into peoples has usually been done for reasons of asserting power vis-à-vis one another. Those with more power have frequently dictated the shape of the division: who would be in each group, what would be the criteria for group membership, what would be the relationships between the

19

groups, and what members of each group would have to do henceforth. Subordinate groups may do some reflexive policing of their own, but the impetus comes from the powerful. This racialization process tends to create the impression of permanence. A sociopolitical process of dividing and dominating comes to be viewed as an essential, biological difference between peoples. The purpose of writing racial division onto the body is to naturalize it, to make it inevitable, and thus no one's fault.[80]

In the United States, for instance, much of race relations has depended on the one-drop rule: race relations have been defined as being between Black and White, and any person with any known African ancestry has been regarded as Black.[81] That was in order to keep the part-White sons and daughters of slave owners and slave women as slaves and to keep them from asserting any measure of Whiteness. Then subordinate status was written onto the Black body itself. Whites (and others) assumed that the people whom they defined as Black possessed particular character qualities and life chances, and that the people they defined as White naturally, by virtue of their supposed biological inheritance, were blessed with more positive character qualities and better life chances.

Yet for other groups in the United States, the one-drop rule does not apply, at least not in the same way and with the same pervasiveness. People who are part-Indian and part-White are sometimes reckoned Native American and sometimes White, depending on the degree of their connectedness to Native peoples, cultures, and institutions. People who are part-Indian and part-Black are generally reckoned Black. People who are part-Asian and part-something else have much more complex sets of ethnic possibilities and constraints. We shall see how these differences have come to be.[82]

Ethnic Formation Processes

It is worth thinking about what kinds of things hold ethnic groups together and what allows them to come apart.[83] Ethnic groups are not primordial units of human relationship. They are social groupings that form, and change their shape and the glue that holds them together, and sometimes they are subsumed into larger ethnicities.

In the twentieth century, most systematic thinking about ethnicity has been done by social scientists. Beyond the common-sense understanding of ethnicity as shared ancestry—as kinship writ large—a survey of social-scientific writing identifies three forces that shape the creation, sustenance, dissolution, and re-formation of ethnic groups.[84] These are shared interests, shared institutions, and shared culture. All three are important. No one of them is more fundamental than the others to the nature of an ethnic group. Each has a role to play in shaping group consciousness and action at various times in the history of the ethnic group. Many theorists have been inclined to see one of the three as fundamental and the others as superstructural. It is not true.

Shared Interests, political or economic, are usually the things that pull an ethnic group together in the first place. That is, if a set of people perceive themselves to share a common heritage and also have concrete economic or political reasons for affiliating with each other, they may begin to form an ethnic group.[85]

One example of this type of group formation is occurring among Latinos in the United States today. Latinos, or "Hispanics," as some call them, are not a single group. The three largest groups—Mexicans, Puerto Ricans, and Cubans—have very little in common. Mexican Americans live throughout the country but are concentrated in the Southwest, exhibit an ancestral mixture of mainly Spanish and Indian, are concentrated in the lower and middle classes, and vote heavily for the Democratic Party. Some have been in what is now the United States since before the American Revolution, while others arrived yesterday. Puerto Rican Americans are concentrated mainly in the industrial cities of the Northeast, mix Black ancestry along with Spanish and Indian, are heavily working class, and generally vote Democratic. Cuban Americans are concentrated in Florida, are visibly lighter of skin on the average than the other two groups, have many more members of the upper middle class, are often attuned to anti-Communist politics in their ancestral homeland, and usually vote for the Republican Party. Each of these groups came to the United States at a different time—Mexicans throughout U.S. history—and for very different reasons. They spoke different varieties of Spanish and pursued subtly different varieties of Catholic Christianity.[86]

All share certain cultural similarities, but there is no strong cultural uniformity. What all three groups have most in common is an *interest*. Independently, none of the groups is large enough to attract much attention from the U.S. government or the public at large outside the locale of its highest concentration. But together they can muster millions of voters. Thus, Mexican, Cuban, and Puerto Rican Americans have a political *interest* in banding together as Latinos. In time, we may see Latinos forming shared institutions and creating shared culture that will sustain them as a group.

While interests may bring a group together initially, interests change easily—they are external to the group and largely determined by others. Latinos are becoming a single ethnic group in America, not because of any substantial natural commonality among them, but because there is a major tangible advantage to be gained by acting as a single group, and because Anglos have a hard time telling them apart. Yet interests are only a short-term basis for group cohesion. If an ethnic group endures, it is usually because it forms shared institutions and builds up shared culture.

Shared Institutions are the ways people within the ethnic group organize themselves to achieve their interests, practice their culture, and maintain their group identity.[87] There are any number of examples of ethnic institutions. The United Farm Workers is a mainly Mexican American ethnic institution that expresses and protects the interests of laboring Chicanos. Cumberland Presbyterian Church in San Francisco is an ethnic institution where Chinese Americans come together to worship and to socialize. Hadassah is an ethnic institution where Jewish women gather to connect with each other, reinforce their Jewishness, and serve their ethnic community. The Daughters of the American Revolution is an Anglo-American ethnic institution that seeks to celebrate and maintain the elite position of the dominant group in American society. The National Association for the Advancement of Colored People (NAACP) is an ethnic institution that acts to create and defend the rights of African Americans.

Ethnic institutions are the places where members of a group come together to pursue group interests—the United Negro College Fund is an example, as is the Anti-Defamation League of B'nai B'rith. But ethnic institutions are also places where **Shared Culture** is created and maintained. It is in Chinese churches, Chinese families, and Chinese neighborhoods that Chinese language—an item of culture—is spoken and the ability to speak is passed on. The culture is not just what people do in institutions, however. It is, on its own, an important binding agent that keeps group identity alive. Ethnicity-as-culture is an old view of these things, associated with people like Robert Ezra Park and E. Franklin Frazier.[88] But it has a lot to recommend it. What do an Israeli farmer, a New York journalist, and a London businessman have in common? Nothing at all, in terms of interests or institutions. Yet once a year they all say the same words at a Passover *seder*, and that ritual act—that piece of culture—binds them tightly together. Because they share culture, they all see themselves as Jews and as fundamentally related, indeed as essential to each other. They have a strong bond of identity and emotion.[89]

Shared culture may be outward and apparent to the noninvolved observer. Italian food, Polish language, and Vietnamese Buddhism are examples. Or shared culture may be inward and more or less invisible. It can have to do with shared values, orientations, ways of framing issues, or seeing the world. A trivial example will illustrate. Most Americans flip a switch and say they "turned on the light." But most Chinese Americans, down to the third generation, including those who speak no Chinese at all, on performing the same act, say they "opened the light." Most American-born Chinese do not even realize that their expression derives from the Chinese-language term, which connotes opening a gate to allow a current to flow. This is inward shared culture, albeit of a relatively inconsequential sort. Aspects of inward shared culture include patterns of childrearing, facial affect, talking with one's hands, and a host of other items.

To summarize, the forces of shared interests, institutions, and culture interact in a dynamic way to provide the glue that holds together ethnic consciousness. Most ethnic groups form, in the beginning, on the basis of some tangible shared interest, as Latinos seem to be doing in the late twentieth century and the early twenty-first. They create ethnic institutions by which they organize themselves to pursue their common interests. As people come together in those institutions, they interact and create shared culture—rituals, habitual turns of phrase, behaviors, and understandings that bind them together. Institutions and especially culture are much longer lived than are interests. They enable ethnic groups to survive changing circumstances. After an initially shared interest changes or disappears, culture and institutions may even hold the group together long enough for a new set of interests to emerge.

One can imagine a number of situations in which ethnic groups might find themselves with regard to these three factors: interests, institutions, and culture. It is possible to represent these factors in ethnic group development schematically as three continua (Table 1.1).[90]

At any given point in the history of an ethnic group, one ought to be able to locate that group with respect to each factor in ethnic group saliency. Some ethnic groups—African Americans today, for example—are high on all three indices. Although there is tremendous regional and class variety, there is also a good quantum of shared culture among Black Americans, from dialect to food to affective

Table 1.1 Factors in Ethnic Group Development

Interests	low	medium	high
Culture	low	medium	high
Institutions	low	medium	high

behavior. There are shared interests, insofar as Blacks as a group still suffer systematic social and economic disabilities, and insofar as they may also all potentially benefit from, for example, affirmative action. And there is a web of shared institutions, from the NAACP to First A.M.E. Zion Church. African American ethnicity seems to be quite high.

There are also groups that are high on only one or two of the three indices. Latinos today, for example, are a group that may be high in certain sorts of interests and elements of shared culture, but quite low in institutions. Yet they are even now creating and expanding shared institutions such as the various Hispanic or Latino caucuses in government and professional circles. In time, they may build up a good deal more shared culture—language and religion are similar enough to provide a basis for some of that. Much will depend on whether or not they function historically as a group in the future.

There are other groups that are high on culture yet low on institutions and interests. There is a tremendous amount of shared religious, intellectual, and emotional culture among American Jews—at the same time that Jews are arrayed across the class spectrum and perhaps a third of the Jewish population has not been inside a synagogue or community meeting in over a year. Interests are fairly low, institutional connectedness is not much higher, but certain aspects of culture (not necessarily including formal religious observance) are fairly high. Ethnicity remains.

One must be wary about this schema, as with all social scientific models, not to allow the model to rcify one's perceptions of ethnic processes that are fluid and dynamic. Such models may be aids to insight, but they are not realities in their own right. Family and community relationships, identity claiming, ethnic relationships, perceived common social interests, and so on are the things that bind people together in a group.

Colonialism and Race Making

The reinterpretation of American immigration offered in this book highlights the role of colonialism. It will not surprise knowledgeable readers that many important American ideas about racial and ethnic hierarchy were shaped by colonial encounters between light-skinned Americans and darker-skinned peoples in places like the Philippines and Hawai'i. European American expansion across the North American continent also had a colonial quality to it—it was the homeland of other peoples, and the United States took it by force and made subjects of the former owners—and racial hierarchy was made in that enterprise. The argument here highlights the ways that, when Europeans made racial hierarchy in their interactions with Africans and Native Americans, they did so in a colonial context. It explores the ways immigration (by Europeans, Asians, and Latin Americans) to the newly colonized territories was partly a colonial story as well as a migrant story. Immigration and ethnic identity in U.S. history have been intimately tied to race and slavery, on the one hand, and to colonial expansion across the continent, on the other.

Race making is done in the context of colony making. In the eighteenth and nineteenth centuries, pseudoscientific ideas about race were created by English, German, and French colonizers who went to Africa and Asia, and by those who stayed behind and enjoyed the fruits of empire. Those racial ideas were means to explain the peoples that Europeans found in such places, and to rationalize Europeans' violent domination of those peoples. English people went to South and East Africa, to India, to Fiji, and a host of other places. In each of those locations they developed an ideology of the natural superiority of Europeans in general and English people in particular, of the fitness of such people to lead the darker masses, and of the appropriateness of colonial rule. Rudyard Kipling expressed English racial, colonial condescension in "The White Man's Burden," as he encouraged his American cousins to seize the Philippines:

> Take up the White Man's burden—
> Send forth the best ye breed—
> Go bind your sons to exile
> To serve your captives' need;
> To wait in heavy harness,
> On fluttered folk and wild—
> Your new-caught, sullen peoples,
> Half-devil and half-child.[91]

Lest one think that such imperial, racial condescension is a uniquely British trait, Elisabeth Schäfer-Wünsche instructs us that German pseudoscientific racial ideas were born in the conquest and near-annihilation of the Hereros in Southwest Africa, long before they were applied to Jews in Europe. Taoufik Djebali and Richard Fogarty find the French making similar racial-colonial distinctions in their dealings with North Africans. The making of racial distinctions and laying them on the body occurred in other colonial encounters that did not involve Europeans at all. Miyuki Yonezawa finds them in Japanese imperial expansion against the Ainu and Ryukyuans. And Han Chinese have long laid a discourse of innate primitivity and racial inferiority on Tibetans, Uygurs, and other colonized peoples.[92]

United States racial ideas owe profoundly to three encounters between Euro-Americans and other peoples: Africans whom Euro-Americans encountered in the act of enslaving them; Native peoples whom Euro-Americans encountered in the acts of displacing and destroying them; and later, in such overseas places as the Philippines, dark-skinned peoples whom Euro-Americans encountered in the process of making formal empire.[93] I would contend that these are all colonial encounters. In its classic form, colonialism involves several acts of domination: military intervention; political transfer of sovereignty; economic domination; and ultimately cultural domination. Those were all true in the cases of slavery, of Native American removal and genocide, and of the overseas adventures of the late nineteenth century. In some instances, the cultural domination was so complete as to amount to what Antonio Gramsci termed "hegemony": that domination so complete that the one dominated knows not he is being dominated, but thinks it the natural order of things.[94]

The consistent pattern of relationships between the races since the seventeenth century has been this: Non-White persons have possessed lesser rights than have White persons. People of color have not possessed full, individual identities in the eyes of Whites or before the law. They could be (and frequently were) treated as an undifferentiated mass. They could be (and frequently were) moved out to make room for others (of European descent) who were seen as individuals with rights.

Albert Memmi, in *The Colonizer and the Colonized*, points out with excruciating precision how it is just such relationships that constitute the core of colonized—and, we may add, of racialized—relationships.[95]

It has become fashionable in recent years to talk about European immigrants to the United States as if they once suffered the same disabilities as have peoples of color.[96] It isn't true. There is no question that many eighteenth- and nineteenth-century European immigrants to the United States had a tougher time than native Whites of their era, or than those immigrants' own descendants, and that they were subjected to humiliations and poverty. But the Native peoples were killed or pushed out of New England. Five large tribes were ousted from the Southeast in forced marches in the 1830s. In 1885 and 1886, the entire Chinese populations of Seattle and Tacoma, Washington and Rock Springs, Wyoming, were shipped out of those towns, and many were murdered. In the 1930s, a million Mexican Americans—many of them U.S. citizens—were forced to leave the country. During World War II, 120,000 Japanese Americans—two-thirds of them U.S. citizens—were jailed on account of their race. And let us not forget the master case of all this: Black racial slavery. No group of White Americans was ever subjected to anything like these sorts of racial domination and abuse.

These are all racial dominations that occur in the ongoing context of Euro-American colonial relationships with peoples of color in the United States. One cannot say that "since the colonial period" such-and-such has happened in U.S. history. The colonial period of American history continues. The first fact of the history of American immigration is genocide: the displacement and destruction of the Native peoples of North America. That is part of the story of *immigration*; it is not some other, parallel history. The two—immigration and genocide—are two interlocking parts of the same story. This is an inescapable fact that we must keep always before us.

It is not that the Ellis Island model is incorrect, but rather that it is only partial. The Ellis Island pattern of immigrant assimilation and uplift over generations is accurate, more or less, for explaining the experiences of White immigrants to the United States. But it has never accurately represented the experiences of peoples of color. What *Almost All Aliens* attempts to do is to retell the story of American immigration, taking race off the margins and putting it in the middle of the analysis. We shall find as we go along that processes of assimilation and acculturation have indeed happened in U.S. history for every migrant people. But they have been by no means uniform in the ease and speed with which they have occurred. Moreover, peoples have assimilated not to some abstract and ethnicity-free "American" identity, but rather into one of five large panethnic groups—White Americans, African Americans, Native Americans, Asian Americans, or Latinos—through complex processes of racial formation and identity negotiation.

Words Matter

Words are not neutral objects. They do not simply denote meanings taken directly from dictionary definitions. Frequently, they are laden with extra meanings that are consequential. Here are some words about which I want to be careful in writing this book and about which I hope the reader will be careful when she or he reads this book and others.

Some Terms the Reader May Want to Think about Differently

American. Sometimes the term is used simply to refer to people who live in the United States or who are U.S. citizens. With apologies to my friends from Canada and Latin America, who might prefer a term like "USian," I have no quarrel, at least for the purposes of the present volume, with using "American" to refer to the people of the United States of America. There is, of course, also the related problem of what to call this place that became the United States of America before that nation had declared its existence. One can hardly call it the United States before 1776. Perhaps it is unavoidable that there should be some unsatisfying slippage among such terms, ideas, and usages.

My main concern in this book about the term "American" is that I want to be careful not to use it as a synonym for "Euro-American." That is very often the way the word is used, by Euro-Americans and also by others, when describing relationships between Euro-Americans and other peoples such as Asian Americans and Latinos. I know more than one Asian American who refers to "the Sansei [third-generation Japanese American] girl who is dating an American boy," when that person really means "the Sansei girl who is dating the White boy."

Settler. Throughout the literature of American history, one finds the term "settler" used to refer to Europeans who came to North America to displace the local Native Americans. In other historical contexts, one finds it used for British people who went to Aotearoa (New Zealand) to displace the local Maori; for Dutch people who went to South Africa to displace the local Xhosa; for Russians who went to Central Asia to displace the local Turkmen; and for Jewish Israelis who went to the West Bank to displace the local Palestinians. The term implies that there was no one there before the "settlers" came, or that the people who were there were heathen barbarians—that it was a wild land in need of settling by civilized people like the Europeans, British, Dutch, Russians, and Israelis. Hence the Puritan "errand into the wilderness" populated only by animals and "savages" was a mission to settle and "civilize" a wasteland.[97] I will try not to use the word "settler."[98]

Tribe is a word that also takes on connotations of barbarism. At its base meaning, tribe is a lineage-based system of social organization. But it takes on other connotations as well. Indians come in tribes—primitive, animal-like—and so we are not bound to respect them. They are not like Europeans who come in families and communities, modes of social organization that we are committed to support. Sometimes it is almost impossible to avoid using the word "tribe" in referring to groups of Native Americans, but I shall try.

Alien. This is a formal, legal term for one who is living outside the place of his or her citizenship. I have no quarrel with that formal definition. Yet the reader must be aware of the other connotation that comes with "alien." An alien is a foreigner, an outsider, one who does not belong. Aliens come not just from other countries but from other planets. Aliens are invaders from outer space. They are irreducibly Other. If I refer to a migrant as an "alien," then I am creating in the reader's mind a prejudice; I am dehumanizing that person and defining his or her presence in the United States as illegitimate.

There is self-conscious irony in my choice of a title for this book. "Almost All Aliens" is intended to draw the reader's attention to this problem with the use of the word "alien," and to highlight the fact that nearly all Americans are guests on the North American continent. It is the thing we have most in common.

Caucasian. From time to time, I have a student who complains about being called "White." On such occasions, the person in question says that being labeled White sounds like an accusation. Usually, she or he expresses a preference for being called "Caucasian." We shall see in Chapter 6 that the term "Caucasian" echoes the pseudoscientific racism of the latter nineteenth and early twentieth centuries, which worked to rationalize hierarchy and domination. I will use "White" rather than "Caucasian." It is not an accusation; it is a description.

Immigration. There is a human experience and there are policy issues. In the latter case, the talk is of "immigration" and it is usually described as a "problem" to be solved or managed.[99] This book will lean heavily toward the former. This is a book more about immigrants than about immigration. The reader should note that *Almost All Aliens* is not a book about U.S. immigration policy, either in the present or in the past. Of course, policy, like demography, shapes immigrant experiences. But this book is primarily about those human experiences. It emphatically does not advocate any particular policy for immigration in America's future. Some readers may change their views on policy issues based partly on what they read here, but that is not my goal. I simply want to write an account that is true to the human experiences of the past.

I hope to use "migrant" and "migration" as frequently as "immigrant" and "immigration." The latter pair focuses on the place to which migrants come—in our case, the United States—and suggests that the important thing about their experience is their coming to the United States. "Migration" and "migrant" are, it seems to me, more neutral terms, that express an openness to the possibility that the persons in question are moving from one place to another, but do not demand special privilege for the place to which they move.

An Idea That May Be New

This book employs some concepts that may not be familiar to all readers. One of these is **Normative Whiteness.** This is a way to describe the very common assumption that, unless we are informed to the contrary, the people under discussion are White. Normal people are, by definition and without remark, White people. If one is White, then one is a person, but if one is not White, then one's not-Whiteness needs to be explained. When we read the pages of most daily newspapers, we find race marked only for people of color. There are people, and then there are Black people. There are people and there are Native Americans. People (that is, White people) have names and personalities; non-White people have races. We only mark those who diverge from the norm we presume, which is normative Whiteness. (It is worth noting that most publications also assume a normative maleness and a normative heterosexuality).[100]

We mark our privilege by what we do not want to talk about. A colleague who teaches racial issues at an Ivy League university reports that, on the first day of class, she always asks each student to identify him- or herself. There are no further instructions, although the students are aware that it is a course on racial this and that. Student A says she is a Black single mother, and the class knows pretty much who she is. Student B says she is a woman, and one doesn't need to look—one can be sure that she is White. Student C presents him- or herself as a citizen, an American, or a human being, and one can be sure without looking that this is a White male. And none of the students in question is highlighting the fact that they are all students at an Ivy League college that tends to attract the hyper-privileged and to confer substantial privilege upon even those students who did not previously possess it. We mark our privilege by what we do not want to talk about.

Normative Whiteness reared its head very publicly in 1995, in the hubbub surrounding the murder trial of athlete and celebrity O. J. Simpson. Since the trial was televised, Judge Lance Ito became a familiar figure to audiences across the country. Ito is a third-generation Japanese American, the grandson of immigrants. U.S. Senator Alfonse D'Amato of New York made an appearance on Don Imus's radio talk show. D'Amato is a third-generation Italian American, the grandson of immigrants. On the radio, D'Amato criticized the slow pace of the trial, and then launched into what he imagined to be a thick Japanese accent. Anyone who had seen the trial on TV (that is, any American) knew that Ito speaks with sharp consonants, round vowels, and not a trace of an accent, whereas D'Amato has a pronounced New York accent. Nonetheless, it seems that D'Amato saw himself as an American on the basis of his Whiteness, whereas Ito, he apparently assumed, must be reckoned a foreigner on account of his Asian ancestry. Both were middle-class, politically successful grandchildren of immigrants. Yet D'Amato saw his Whiteness as natural, but felt called to remark disparagingly upon Ito's Asianness.[101]

One key example of normative Whiteness is the attempt to present the story of European immigration as if it were the story of immigration. White immigrants are simply immigrants; their Whiteness is not named. So if another group has a different experience than that of Ellis Island White immigrants, their differences are just the exceptions to the rule. The privilege granted to White experiences is not named.

Immigrant assimilation, transnationalism, panethnic formation, colonialism. Shared interests, institutions, and culture. New terms like normative Whiteness and old ones about which we may wish to be careful. Let us keep all these thoughts in mind as we go forward to explore the story of immigration in American history. But let us remember that it is a story. It tells of the lives of people, not just of the relationships between peoples—far less of abstract theories. Let us always keep before us that this is a human story. And so we begin.

Chapter 2

Colliding Peoples in Eastern North America, 1600–1780

Thanksgiving

giving thanks
should be a very personal thing
like the legendary settlers in New England learned
when they arrived as illegal immigrants
and the natives
though wary of their guns and swords
taught them to plant
corn together with fish
and shared their harvest with them
late in the year
. . .
giving thanks is a very human thing
it shows that we are aware
of the fragility of our life
of how it always depends
on the kindness of strangers
who help us to survive
in their world

Walter Hölbling[1]

In the Beginning There Were Indians

Variety

The history of American immigration begins with Indians, because what is now the United States was not empty before Europeans came. The first concept to grasp is diversity. North America was not a unitary place, and it was not inhabited by only one sort of people prior to the European invasion. Take language. More different languages were spoken in what is now California alone than in all of Europe in 1500. Perhaps as many as 143 language *families*—as different from each other as the Sino-Tibetan language family is from the Indo-European—coexisted in America north of Mexico. Some families of related languages like the Algonquian family (including languages spoken by the Pequot, Abnaki, Menominee, Chippewa, and many more Native groups) were spoken over wide territories by relatively large numbers of people. Others like the languages in the Ritwan family were employed in only very limited locales by small numbers of closely related peoples. Scholars figure there were about 1000 different Native American languages in all (Figure 2.1).[2]

Figure 2.1   Tribal groups.

Figure 2.2 Kicks Iron.

Take physical features. Here are pictures of three Indian men from different parts of western North America: Kicks Iron of the Dakota Sioux (Figure 2.2); Tswawadi, a Kwakiutl (Figure 2.3); and Mishongnovi, a Hopi (Figure 2.4).[3] It's not just the clothes. These guys do not look alike. Native Americans were not just one sort of people.

Take social organization. There was enormous variety in the density and complexity of different Native groups. In the thirteenth century, the city of Cahokia sprawled along the Mississippi River not far from the present-day location of St. Louis. With a population of 20,000 to 30,000, it was smaller than Texcoco, the Chichimec city, or Tenochtitlan, the later seat of the Aztec empire. But Cahokia's population was on the same order of magnitude as London's or Rome's.[4] Cahokia was the epitome of what the archeologists call Mississippian culture. Cahokians made fine jewelry and sophisticated pottery. They worked in metal and stone, herded deer, and planted corn, pumpkins, squash, beans, and tobacco. The city was arranged around a central plaza with a huge rectangular earthen mound. The central pyramid, with a wooden temple at its top, covered fifteen acres and stood as high as a

Figure 2.3 Tswawadi.

modern ten-story building. Smaller mounds dotted the surrounding territory. There was a rigid class system and a ritual life focused on issues of mortality. Cahokia drew tribute from surrounding towns and farming communities. It was the center of a vast regional trade network. Mississippian mound-building culture and commerce stretched from Florida to Wisconsin, from Ohio to Oklahoma.[5]

The Native peoples of the Northwest Coast, Salish and others, built networks of towns rather than central cities, but they approached similar levels to the mound builders in terms of prosperity, population density, social complexity, and regional trade in the centuries before Europeans came to the continent. The Southeastern flood plains and the forests and rivers of the Northwest were rich physical environments that supported large settled populations. Some other peoples, such as the Shoshone and Bannock who lived in the Great Basin of Nevada and Utah, found the desert a less salubrious climate. Their population was sparse and on the move, small bands with no permanent dwellings, gathering seeds and roots and hunting small game. Other Native peoples assorted themselves between these two extremes of nomadism versus settlement, hunting and gathering versus agriculture and urban life.[6]

Figure 2.4 Mishongnovi.

North America, then, was inhabited by a great variety of peoples. They had no common consciousness of themselves as "Indians." Robert Berkhofer reminds us that, "[s]ince the original inhabitants of the Western Hemisphere neither called themselves by a single term nor understood themselves as a collectivity," it was only in the minds of White people that they were "Indians."[7]

North America was also inhabited by a lot of people. The best estimates of the total population of North and South America before Columbus left the Canary Islands range from 54 million to 75 million: about 15 percent of the total world population at the time, as many as lived in Europe.[8] Most of those people lived in fairly dense agricultural and urban settings in Mexico and in Central and South America. But a substantial number also lived north of the Rio Grande. Scholars' estimates of the total have grown over the past century, as they have become more sophisticated in their understanding of the archeological record and of how European diseases probably spread among Native peoples even before they came into actual physical contact with Europeans. William Denevan estimates that 3.8 million people lived north of Mexico in 1492. Russell Thornton puts the number at more than seven million: a

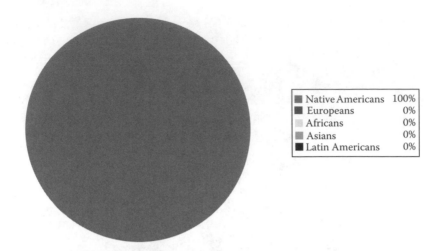

■ Native Americans	100%
■ Europeans	0%
□ Africans	0%
■ Asians	0%
■ Latin Americans	0%

Figure 2.5 Population of North America, North of Mexico in 1500.

bit over five million in what is now the contiguous United States and something over two million in Canada, Alaska, and Greenland. Thus five million people lived in the continental United States. Add the nearly one million who lived in Hawai'i, and the total number of Native people in the territory that later became the United States probably adds up to about six million. (Compare that to the total number of European- and African-descended people counted within the United States by the first census of 1790: 3.9 million.) The lands to which Europeans migrated at the dawn of the modern era were far from empty.[9]

Figure 2.5 represents the racial makeup of the lands that would eventually become the United States, at the time of the beginning of European migration into the Americas. I recognize that the racial designations—Native American, European, etc.—are anachronistic. They do not stand for people groups as anyone recognized them in 1500. Even such concepts as "English" and "Spanish" were tenuous then. I have no wish to arrogate to myself the right to specify what were the relevant groups at any other time in history. But I do want the reader to get a sense of how broadscale racial demography has changed over the centuries; hence I have chosen to introduce these very modern racial categories. I will place similar figures at appropriate points throughout this volume—roughly one every half-century starting with 1600. They allow us to think comparatively with a wide lens about broad trends in population dynamics. In the beginning, there were Indians.

Origins

How did all these people come to be in North America? The dominant theory—and it is just that, for there are no historical records and only fragments of archeology to prove it—is that they came from Asia via a land bridge sometime before 12,000 years ago. During each of several ice ages between 90,000 and 10,000 years ago, the annual temperature of the earth dropped several degrees below current levels. Much of the Northern Hemisphere was covered with thick sheets of ice. Since the earth is a bounded system, the water to make that ice had to come from somewhere.

The level of the world's oceans dropped between 100 and 300 feet, depending on which period one is talking about. The Bering Sea is less than 200 feet deep. All this meant that, during the coldest centuries, what is now sea floor was then land. Asia and North America were not connected by a narrow "land bridge"; they were a single continent, joined by a section several hundred miles wide. It was all cold territory and much of it covered with ice, but some parts had little snowfall and amounted to polar desert pathways. Large game animals—horses, mammoths, camels, caribou, and bison—migrated across the territory and made their first appearance in the Western Hemisphere. The theory is that Asian hunters followed them and—many generations later when temperatures moderated, the ice melted, and the oceans rose again—found themselves on the eastern side of the divide. They migrated east and south through the two continents, multiplied and filled the landscape, and reached the southern tip of South America around 12,000 years ago.

Some archeologists speculate that the first humans may have entered North America as much as 40,000 years ago or even earlier; others put that date at less than 15,000 years ago. Some think that they came not on foot across the icy wastes, but in small boats along the coast warmed by the Japan current and feeding off fish and marine mammals. Others point out that migration was also possible (indeed likely) from northern Norway across Arctic ice to Greenland and Baffin Island. DNA and blood group studies suggest a close link between Native Americans and Asians, but also some remote European ancestry. Linguistic studies suggest three major migrations, one involving the ancestors of most Native peoples of the new world, a second the ancestors of Northwest Coast Indians, and the third and most recent involving Inuits and Aleuts.[10]

That is the theory that is traditionally most common among anthropologists. The theory that is traditionally most common among Native Americans is that they originated here. Each Native people has its own story recounting how humans were first created, how some of them came to live in their particular part of North America, and various matters pertaining to social order, ethics, and spiritual life. Some of these stories tell of travel across land or water, but more tell a story of creation in this place or of emergence from an underworld. For example, the Hopi origin stories regard this as the fourth world, into which people came to escape evil. After climbing up from the third world through a reed or bamboo, they scattered across the earth. Groups who were to become the Hopi clans wandered across the Southwest and came to Black Mesa and the surrounding lands where Hopi have dwelt in modern times. These too are theories.[11]

Of course, it is possible that some people came to the Americas from some other place in much more recent centuries, after the time of the Ice Age yet before Columbus. There is something strangely Eurocentric about the land bridge theory. It posits that Native Americans must be descended from people who came here very, very long ago and by primitive means—hence they are part of the natural landscape, not modern human beings. And of course, because only Europeans can build big ships and sail long distances, anyone else who was here must have walked. Even if one does not subscribe to the theories of Ivan Van Sertima and others, who insist that there was considerable ancient communication and trade between Africa and South America, one can recognize the probability of other, middle-era contacts. Polynesian seafarers traveled successfully back and forth across many thousands of miles of open ocean throughout the first millennium CE. If they could reach Hawai'i, Aotearoa, and Rapa Nui—which they did—then surely they might have reached

Chile and Peru. China's huge Ming Dynasty fleets plied the Indian Ocean, traded on the coast of Africa, and may have reached Australia. There is some speculation that Chinese ships, then or much earlier, might have reached Mexico as well. One is on more solid evidentiary ground noting that in winter Inuit from Alaska have traded and married with Siberians across the frozen Bering Straits for as long as outsiders have observed them, using centuries-old travel technology—so ongoing connection in the pre-Columbian era is likely. And Norse sailors like Eirik Thorvaldsson, Bjarni Herjulfsson, and Leiv Eiriksson explored the northeast coast of North America and planted some colonies at the dawn of the second millennium. Still, even though there may have been some such small-scale contacts, the major infusions that formed the population of Native Americans clearly came much earlier, in the very remote past.[12]

Except for Native American origin stories, all these theories posit Indians as the first immigrants to America. They may indeed have come from Asia or some other place, but in this book I will speak of them as Native peoples, for however and whenever they came to be in this land, they began here a very long time ago. I will treat them as the original inhabitants.[13]

There Goes the Neighborhood: European Incursion and "Settlement"

Spanish, French, and Dutch Encounter Native Peoples

Several generations passed between Columbus's discovery of the Americas and the first European migration into what would later become the United States. The Spanish were the most active in the early period. Hundreds and then thousands of soldiers and civilians came to the islands of the Caribbean from the 1490s, and after 1519 they came to Mexico as well. They seized control of lands by force and by treachery. Their arms and especially their diseases—plague, smallpox, influenza, measles, cholera, typhus, and others to which Native Americans had no natural immunity—decimated the local population. On Hispaniola, nearly eight million people died in Columbus's generation. Disease marched ahead of the invaders along Native routes of trade and communication (Figure 2.6). A very partial list of early epidemics, each of which killed thousands of people, would include:

1516	Yucatan	Smallpox
1520	Southern Mexico	Smallpox
1615–1622	Chesapeake	Smallpox
1616–1620	New England	Smallpox
1633–1635	New England	Smallpox
1659	Florida	Measles
1660	New England	Smallpox
1746	Nova Scotia	Typhoid
1780–1800	Texas	Smallpox and measles
1782–1783	Columbia River Valley	Smallpox
1784	Western Great Lakes	Smallpox
1790	Northwest Canada	Tuberculosis

1797	Central Mexico	Smallpox
1830	Columbia River Valley	Influenza
1831–1838	Lower Mississippi River	Cholera
1837	Upper Missouri River	Smallpox
1838	Western Great Lakes	Smallpox
1847	Pacific Northwest	Measles
1849–1860	Colorado	Cholera
1869–1870	Upper Missouri River	Smallpox
1891–1901	Southwest Canada	Tuberculosis[14]

By the time the killing had stopped, 95 percent of the Native American population had been wiped out.[15]

Spanish soldiers wandered around Florida and the Southwest, finding their way among the local inhabitants. In 1565 Pedro Menéndez de Avilés founded St. Augustine, Florida, the first permanent European town in the territory that would later become the United States. In 1598 Juan de Oñate led an expedition of Spanish to plant a colony among Native peoples in New Mexico. On the same trip he destroyed the ancient mountaintop Pueblo at Ácoma. A dozen years later, Spanish immigrants founded the city of Santa Fe. These most northerly of the Spanish immigrant outposts were not very profitable for Spain, but their dominion over the rich and populous central Mexican plateau brought millions of tons of gold into Spanish coffers.[16]

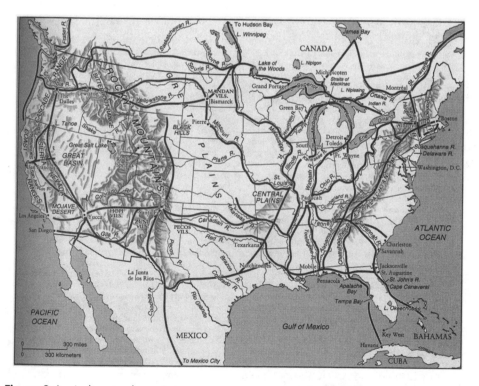

Figure 2.6   Indian trade routes.

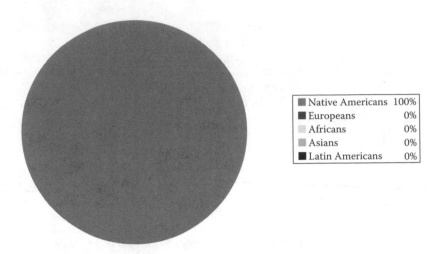

■ Native Americans	100%
■ Europeans	0%
▢ Africans	0%
▢ Asians	0%
■ Latin Americans	0%

Figure 2.7 Population in 1600 of the territory that would become the United States.

If the Spanish came to the southern part of North America as conquerors and extractors of wealth, the French came to the northern region as traders. Early on, two small groups of Huguenots—Protestant refugees from the Catholic reaction against the Reformation—tried and failed to establish colonies in what are now South Carolina and Florida in 1562 and 1564. Other French people had better luck far to the north, where the St. Lawrence River gave them access to the Great Lakes and they could trade with Native peoples for furs to be sold in European markets. French people founded towns at Port Royal in Nova Scotia in 1604 and Quebec in 1608. The French were a tiny number of people compared to their Native American hosts. The Dutch, too, came in small numbers to trade with the Native peoples, planting trading posts near Albany in 1614 and at New Amsterdam (later New York) in 1621 (Figure 2.7).[17]

A Micmac leader gave a sense of the relative power of immigrants and Natives in these words spoken circa 1677 to Chrestien LeClerq, a Recollet missionary:

> Thou sayest of us also that we are the most miserable and most unhappy of all men, living without religion, without manners, without honour, without social order, and, in a word, without any rules, like the beasts in our woods. ... Well, my brother, if thou dost not yet know the real feelings which our Indians have towards thy country and towards all thy nation, it is proper that I inform thee at once. I beg thee now to believe that, all miserable as we seem in thine eyes, we consider ourselves nevertheless much happier than thou. ... [T]hou deceivest thyself greatly if thou thinkest to persuade us that thy country is better than ours. For if France, as thou sayest, is a little terrestrial paradise, art thou sensible to leave it? And why abandon wives, children, relatives, and friends? Why risk thy life and thy property every year ... in order to come to [our] country ...? ... We believe, further, that you are incomparably poorer than we. ... As to us, we find all our riches and all our conveniences among ourselves, without trouble and without exposing our lives to the dangers in which you find yourselves constantly through your long voyages. ... [T]here is no Indian who

does not consider himself infinitely more happy and more powerful than the French.[18]

Neither Spanish, nor French, nor Dutch, nor English people were inclined to respect their Native American hosts. European ideas about Native North Americans were unevenly split. The minor chord was a romantic image of the New World as a paradise on earth, with Indians cast as nature's noble and gentle dwellers of the forest. Robert Berkhofer describes the enduring image of "the good Indian":

> [T]he good Indian appears friendly, courteous, and hospitable to the initial invaders of his lands and to all Whites so long as the latter honored the obligations presumed to be mutually entered into with the tribe. Along with handsomeness of physique and physiognomy went great stamina and endurance. Modest in attitude if not always in dress, the noble Indian exhibited great calm and dignity in bearing, conversation, and even under torture. Brave in combat, he was tender in love for family and children. Pride in himself and independence of other persons combined with a plain existence and wholesome enjoyment of nature's gifts. According to this version, the Indian, in short, lived a life of liberty, simplicity, and innocence.[19]

But that image always took second place to the dominant portrayal of Native peoples as savages; as bloodthirsty, primitive barbarians; and perhaps worst, as heathen worshippers of non-Christian gods. David Stannard sums up European thinking about Indians:

> [O]ne of the preconditions for the Spanish and Anglo-American genocides against the native peoples of the Americas was a public definition of the natives as inherently and permanently—that is, as racially—inferior beings. To the conquering Spanish, the Indians more specifically were defined as natural slaves, as subhuman beasts of burden, because that fit the use to which the Spanish wished to put them. ... Since the colonizing British, and subsequently the Americans, had little use for Indian servitude, ... the Indians were Satan's helpers, they were lascivious and murderous wild men of the forest, they were bears, they were wolves, they were vermin. Allegedly having shown themselves to be beyond conversion to Christian or to civil life—and with little British or American need for them as slaves—in this case, straightforward mass killing of the Indians was deemed the only thing to do.[20]

In European eyes, Europeans were individuals who had names, stories, and discernible personalities. Indians did not have names, individual identities, personalities, or stories. They were interchangeable, faceless, menacing, and to be destroyed.[21]

For their part, Native peoples returned a considerable measure of disrespect. Cornelius Jaenen reminds us that it was Europeans' egotism and folly, not their actual experiences with Native peoples, that led them to assume "that the native tribesmen viewed [European] culture with awe and admiration, that they often attempted to imitate the Europeans, and usually aspired to elevate themselves to the superior level of the white man." To the contrary, although in some cases Native peoples feared European metal weaponry, and surely they must have been demoralized by the bewildering toll taken by European diseases, on balance they thought the Europeans' religion to be sorcery and their manners to be inferior. They thought it barbaric that, as they had heard from those who came from Europe, in places like England and France there was an abundance of food, yet some people were poor and forced to beg in the streets. Among Native North Americans, such hard-heartedness would never have been tolerated.[22]

While a sense of superiority infected the French and Dutch people who came to live in America, the balance of power made them less likely than the Spanish to act aggressively against local people. The number of French and Dutch immigrants was so small, and they depended so heavily on the goodwill of their Algonquian and Iroquois hosts to maintain their trade relationships, that for a long time they stayed, for the most part, on good terms with their Native neighbors.

English Immigrants Encounter Native Peoples

Add to this mix the English people who migrated into the middle region of eastern North America late in the sixteenth century and early in the seventeenth. They, too—small in number and weak at first—began on a more or less positive footing with the Native peoples whose lands they entered. But quickly relationships turned sour.[23]

A word must be said about terms. The *Harvard Encyclopedia of American Ethnic Groups* sets forth the standard scholarly view on each of its hundreds of subjects. The otherwise fine essay on English Americans makes the silly, self-absorbed, and unfortunately all-too-common distinction between "17th-Century Settlement" and "18th-Century Immigration." I will not use the term "settlement" because that implies North America was a howling, empty wilderness in need of "settling," and this it surely was not. It was a place full of many different peoples, and the English who came here were immigrants. The encyclopedia also makes the strange assertion that "By the time of independence these English people and their descendants constituted about half the population." Half of what? Half of the White population? Probably. Half of the combined White and Black population of the thirteen new states? Less likely. Half the total population of the portion of North America that would later become the United States? Certainly not. The English part of *that* population was about one-sixth. It is essential that we not lose sight of the larger picture of peoples and their interactions. If we focus only on the White population of the easternmost part of the continent, as almost all histories of the period do, then we begin to go down a slippery slope toward excusing genocide and slavery as natural, inevitable, and therefore no one's fault.[24]

trans-national

The first attempt at English immigration took place at Roanoke Island in Pamlico Sound, in what is now North Carolina. Sir Walter Raleigh was an adventurer and an intimate of Queen Elizabeth I (the Virgin Queen whose reputed sexual status gave its name to the first American colony). Raleigh sent an exploratory mission to the southeast coast in 1584, looking for a place to begin the kind of rich conquest that Spanish adventurers had been making for most of the century. His soldiers were received warmly by a Roanoke chief named Wingina, who thought he might be able to use the English as allies in his efforts to establish power over some neighboring chiefs. Two Roanoke Indians went back to England with the visitors. They returned a year later with a militarized expedition of English people. One of the Indian emissaries, Manteo, thought the English would make good allies. The other, Wanchese, perceived inequality and suffering in English society and warned against trusting English intentions. The immigrants demanded that Wingina and his people provide them with food and made known their intention to enslave their hosts. The local people got fed up, but before they could act the English attacked their village and killed Wingina and most of the Native leaders. Unable to establish the colony, the adventurers returned to England.[25]

In 1587 Raleigh sent out a civilian party, including women and children, led by John White, with the intention that they would co-exist peacefully with local Indians, not try to kill or enslave them. They were supposed to go to another location, further north, on Chesapeake Bay, but the ship captain who delivered them dropped them off at Roanoke Island instead. By this time, Wanchese had assumed leadership of the Roanoke Native community, whose members were still angry about the earlier encounter. The English and Native communities exchanged attacks, then White sailed back to England looking for reinforcements. But a war between Spain and England intervened and he did not make it back for three years. When he finally was able to return in 1590, the English colony had disappeared. Roanoke's fate was treated as a mystery for many years, but recent research suggests that at least some of the Roanoke English ended up taking refuge fifty miles away on Croatoan Island. There, among friendly Indians related to the optimistic emissary Manteo, they appear to have maintained a separate English community for a while. In the end they seem to have taken up the ways of their hosts and blended into the Native population by the early 1600s. So the first act of immigrant assimilation in what was to become the United States was English people becoming Indians.[26]

In this period when English people were first trying to migrate into the southeastern part of North America, the main focus of their attention was the lands around Chesapeake Bay. Bankrolled by English investors, the migrants' hope was to start a colony where they could make a return on that investment. But no one was quite sure how to make the colony pay for itself. Some hoped to discover gold, others to trade with the Native inhabitants, and still others to sell forest products to the English navy. A long-term goal was to find a sea passage to the Pacific and thence to Asia. In May 1607 three small ships, commanded by Captain Christopher Newport and bearing 120 migrants, dropped anchor at a place they named Jamestown after their new king, sixty miles from the mouth of Chesapeake Bay. The newcomers and their provisions were put ashore and the ships returned to England. When Newport returned with more immigrants and supplies the following January, only thirty-eight of the men he had left ashore remained alive.

They had not found gold or silver. They had not found a rich, populous Native civilization they could conquer and enslave, nor with whom they could trade. They had fallen to bickering and scheming among themselves, and they had proved unable to feed themselves. Reinforced by several shiploads of immigrants and supplies over the next few years, Jamestown limped along for a time, able to survive only because of the calculated generosity of Powhatan, a local Native chief. The people of the Chesapeake region were divided into perhaps as many as fifty different tribes, each of them made up of several towns, and each tribe with its own chief. Powhatan was paramount ruler over perhaps two dozen of those tribes. He saw in the English another tribe of people whom he might use in alliance to maintain and strengthen his paramount position in the region (after all they had guns, hatchets, and other metal implements, and they seemed to like fighting). Powhatan had his people trade with the English and supply them with food. Powhatan's people captured the English leader, an adventurer named John Smith, in December 1607. When Smith was brought before Powhatan, the chief and his preteen daughter Pocahontas enacted a richly choreographed ceremony by which Powhatan symbolically adopted Smith and invested him as an honorary, but lesser, chieftain or *werowance*, beholden to Powhatan. Smith thought he was about to be killed and that Pocahontas had saved his life—that was the story passed down on the English side.[27]

Despite Powhatan's friendship, the English behaved brutally and relationships soon deteriorated. In 1609, Powhatan complained to John Smith:

> Captaine Smith, you may understand that I having seene the death of all my people thrice, and not any one living of these three generations but my selfe [Powhatan probably refers to three epidemics that had swept through the area before the English arrived]; I know the difference of Peace and Warre better than any in my Country. ... that you are come to destroy my Country, so much affrighteth all my people as they dare not visit you. What will it availe you to take that by force you may quickly have by love, or to destroy them that provide you food. What can you get by warre, when we can hide our provisions and fly to the woods? Whereby you must famish by wronging us your friends. ... Thinke you I am so simple, not to know it is better to eate good meate, lye well, and sleepe quietly with my women and children, laugh and be merry with you, have copper, hatchets, or what I want being your friend: then be forced to flie from all, to lie cold in the woods, feede upon Acornes, rootes, and such trash, and be so hunted by you, that I can neither rest, eate, nor sleepe; but my tyred men must watch, and if a twig but breake, every one cryeth there commeth Captaine Smith: then must I fly I know not whether: and thus with miserable feare, end my miserable life, leaving my pleasures to such youths as you, which through your rash unadvisednesse may quickly as miserably end, for want of that, you never knew where to find. Let this therefore assure you of our loves, and every yeare our friendly trade shall furnish you with Corne; and now also, if you would come in friendly manner to see us, and not thus with your guns and swords as to invade your foes.[28]

Warfare followed, with atrocities on both sides. Powhatan stopped trading with the English, determined to starve them out. In the winter of 1609 to 1610, the English population of nearly 500 dwindled to 60, but in spring the Virginia Company sent more immigrants. In 1613 a party of English seized Pocahontas as she was visiting friends along the Potomac River. Kept as a hostage at Jamestown, she converted to Anglicanism and became engaged to the widower John Rolfe. Their marriage the following year was not just a personal union, but a diplomatic way to end five years of warfare. She gave birth to a son, Thomas Rolfe, and then in 1616 was taken to London and feted as *"la belle sauvage."* She met King James I and partied with high society, but she contracted pneumonia, died at age twenty-two, and was buried far from home. Her son, Thomas Rolfe, went back to Virginia in 1640 as a planter. His workers grew tobacco on lands that had once belonged to his mother's tribe, but he himself had assimilated into British society.

Meanwhile, 600 miles to the north, a different sort of English immigrants were interacting with a different set of Native peoples. For a couple of generations, English fishing boats had plied the waters from Newfoundland to Cape Cod, and adventurers like John Smith had brought ships to trade. An unintended accompaniment to such contacts was the passing of European microbes. For instance, in the plague of 1616 to 1619, probably 90 percent of the Massachusett Indians who inhabited the coastal area were wiped out. When a boatload of religiously motivated Puritans arrived in 1620, the Massachusetts were reeling. Neighboring Indian groups such as the Wampanoags and Narragansetts were pressing upon them. These Puritans had received a charter to go to the Chesapeake, but they went off course, either accidentally or because they wanted to found their own colony outside the control of the Virginia Company (we cannot be sure which). Arriving just before Christmas, with few preparations for a harsh New England winter, the Pilgrims suffered terribly, and half of them died by spring from cold, scurvy, and malnutrition.[29]

Enter Squanto and Massasoit. Squanto had already had a remarkable life. He had been kidnapped from his Patuxet village by an English trader in 1614 and taken to Spain to be sold as a slave. It is unclear how he escaped, but by 1617 he had made his way to England. After a trip with English sailors to Newfoundland, he returned home to find that the Patuxet and most other Wampanoag groups had been wiped out by disease. In the spring of 1621, because he spoke English and the local language, he was able to insert himself between the Pilgrims and their Wampanoag neighbors. He taught the newcomers how to plant corn using fish fertilizer, and so enabled them to feed themselves in their new world. Massasoit was sachem, or hereditary leader, of the Wampanoags who surrounded the Plymouth colony. He saw in these English people a potential ally against his Narragansett rivals and so made a mutual defense treaty with them in 1621. Without the friendship of Squanto, Massasoit, and the other Wampanoags, the English people likely would not have survived.[30]

So, despite negative European presumptions about Native Americans, the Europeans who came to places like Plymouth and the Chesapeake got along fairly well with their Native neighbors at first. Still, before long conflict came to dominate their relationships whenever they encountered one another. The first problem was disease. European diseases to which they lacked immunity, combined with wars and changes in ways of living, contributed to a sharp decline among the Indians of Virginia: from 25,000 when Jamestown was founded in 1607 down to 2,000 in 1700 (meanwhile the non-Indian population of Virginia had grown from zero to about 100,000). Disease frequently ran ahead of substantial person-to-person contact between Europeans and Native peoples. In 1670, the Native population of Illinois was more than 10,500; by 1736 it had dropped to 2,500, and by 1800 to 500. Over the whole area that would become the continental United States, the Native population dropped from more than 5 million in 1600 to just 600,000 in 1800. The dynamics were similar in other places that came to be part of the United States, although somewhat later in time. In Hawai'i when Captain Cook arrived in 1778 the population numbered between 800,000 and 1 million. Disease ravaged the Hawaiians, who could count only 80,000 people in 1849, and 45,000 in 1876. The pattern throughout the Americas was that Europeans' diseases and European aggression killed, on the average, between 90 and 95 percent of each group of Native people.[31]

Soon, land became the issue. In places like New England and the Chesapeake, Europeans inserted themselves amid declining Native populations. Eager to obtain land and build farms and villages after the style of rural England, sometimes they arranged to buy land from local people and sometimes they just took it. To the English, North America was an empty continent (and, indeed, their diseases had made it less populous than it had been previously). The Natives were, in English eyes, as beasts of the forest, not as people who lived on the land. America was an empty wilderness in need of civilizing by Europeans. The English attitude toward Native land claims is summed up in these 1629 words of John Winthrop, who was to go on to serve many years as Governor of Massachusetts Bay Colony: "As for the Natives in New England, they inclose noe Land, neither have any settled habytation, nor any tame Cattle to improve the Land by, and soe have noe other but a Naturall Right to those Countries, soe as if we leave them sufficient for their use, we may lawfully take the rest, there being more than enough for them and us." In such an interpretation, to live on the land, to "settle" it, was to build a farm with a fence around it, a barn, and put cows in the field. By such an interpretation, since Native peoples farmed but not after the European style, because they were in that interpretation not fully humans, the land was empty and available for the taking.[32]

Resistance, Conflict, Genocide

Of course, the land was not empty and the Indians who lived on it were often quite unhappy about being asked or forced to vacate. Powhatan's people fought three wars against the Chesapeake English in 1610 to 1614, 1622 to 1632, and 1644 to 1646. By the end of the third war, European diseases and superior firepower had just about wiped out the Powhatan Indians. Some of the remnant moved west, others were sold into slavery in the Caribbean, and a few adopted White ways and lived among Europeans (Figure 2.8). The Virginians who fought the 1622 to 1632 war established a policy of open-season warfare against all Indians. Thereby, English people were able to expand their area of habitation into lands that had formerly been Indian homes.[33]

In 1636 a nasty English trader named John Oldham who had been thrown out of towns up and down the coast was killed at Block Island, off the eastern tip of Long Island, apparently by some Pequot Indians with whom he had been trading. The Pequots had been expanding their power over other tribes in southern New England

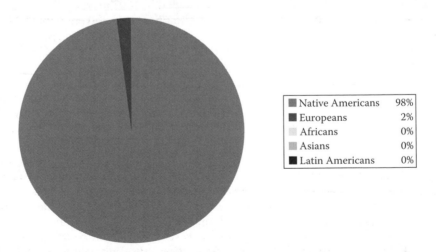

Native Americans	98%
Europeans	2%
Africans	0%
Asians	0%
Latin Americans	0%

Figure 2.8   Population in 1650 of the territory that would become the United States.

since before the English began to immigrate, and they were now the most powerful Native group in the region. But the English possessed armor, muskets, and cannon. An expedition from the Bay Colony attacked the Pequots and burned their homes to the ground, killing hundreds of women and children along with adult men. As John Mason interpreted the end of the Pequot War, "Thus was God pleased to smite our enemies and to give us their land for an inheritance." The Pequot War reduced the most powerful Indian people in the region to a tiny remnant, as the English sold many Pequots into slavery and attached others to neighboring tribes such as the Narragansetts who were friendly to the English. The war also opened up the fertile Connecticut River valley for another colony of Puritans.[34]

Three decades later, half the remaining Native population of New England rose up against the English. They were led by a Wampanoag sachem, Metacom, whom the English called King Philip, and who was Massasoit's son. Several tribes were involved. The conflict stemmed from the continued expansion of English people from Plymouth, Massachusetts Bay, and most recently Connecticut into lands occupied by Native peoples. With the decline of the beaver population along the coast, several coastal tribes had nothing to trade with the English any longer. Their populations were declining and they were demoralized. Metacom gave them an inspiration to resist the colonizers, and young men from several tribes such as the Nipmunks and Narragansetts responded. Metacom's War has been called the bloodiest war in the history of North America, which would be quite a distinction. Initially, in 1675, Metacom's warriors succeeded brilliantly. Hundreds of English immigrants fled outlying farms and villages for the safety of Boston and other larger towns. But English firepower prevailed in the end, allied with some large, powerful tribes to the west like the Mohawks, who still had furs to trade with the English. In the end, Metacom's wife, his son, and hundreds of other Indians were captured and sold into slavery. Metacom was killed and beheaded; his head remained on display in the fort at Plymouth for twenty-five years.[35]

Thus ended Native resistance to English domination in the Northeast. And thus was introduced genocidal warfare. Native peoples of the lands that would one day become the United States did not traditionally fight wars against whole civil populations. In the main, war was confined to limited retaliation, as in raiding a village, taking a life for a life. Frequently captives were seized and adopted into tribes to replace those who had been killed. With the coming of Europeans, all that began to change. As Francis Jennings trenchantly observes: "Civilized war is the kind *we* fight against *them* (in this case, Indians), whereas savage war is the atrocious kind that they fight against us." English people after Metacom's War feared Indians as bloodthirsty barbarians because they refused to make way for English expansion into their homelands and they resisted militarily. David Stannard adds: "The European habit of indiscriminately killing women and children when engaged in hostilities with the natives of the Americas was more than an atrocity. It was flatly and intentionally genocidal. For no population can survive if its women and children are destroyed." The English who fought the Pequot War and Metacom's War were making genocide against their neighbors, as surely as were Serbs making genocide against their Muslim and Croatian neighbors in Bosnia-Herzegovina late in the twentieth century.[36]

Whatever our high school textbooks may have told us, America in the seventeenth century was not limited to the lands claimed and increasingly populated by English people along the eastern seaboard. There were Europeans migrating in that same era into other territory far to the west. Since the time when Juan de Oñate and a troop of soldiers stumbled into what is now New Mexico in 1598 looking for gold, Franciscan friars had been trying to convert local Indians to Christianity and other Spanish ways. In and around the valley of the Rio Grande lived thousands of Native people whom the Spanish named Pueblo because they lived in permanent towns (apartment houses, even) built of adobe. They farmed and wore what the Spaniards could recognize as clothing. In the manner of their residence, occupation, and dress, then, the Spanish saw them as civilizable (that is, convertible into facsimiles of Europeans) and so they sought to make Christians of them. After Oñate's butchery at the Ácoma Pueblo in 1599—the Spanish killed 800 people outright and enslaved the other 600, cutting one foot off each of the 80 men whom they allowed to live—other Indians in the area submitted to the Spanish for more than three generations. The Spanish forced them to convert to Christianity, to pay tribute, and to labor to support the immigrants. They punished anyone who still practiced their ancestral religion. But economic hard times followed a six-year drought, and neither the Spanish nor their god was able to protect the Pueblo Indians from slave-taking raids by Apaches and Navajo. The Spanish squashed a Native spiritual revitalization movement in 1675 by hanging its leaders and flogging several dozen followers.

Five years later, in a carefully timed plot led by a religiously motivated Pueblo named Popé, 17,000 Indians from 25 pueblos, half the population of the territory, rose in bloody revolt. They killed more than 400 Spanish residents, burned Santa Fe, and forced the remaining 2000 Spanish to flee New Mexico. The Pueblo Revolt was the most successful of what Jack Forbes has called an "epidemic" of Indian rebellions across northern New Spain in the 1680s. A loose coalition of Pueblos kept the Spanish out of New Mexico until 1692; thereafter the Spanish allowed the Native peoples more freedom of culture and religion than under the previous regime. During the Spanish absence, Navajos and Apaches made off with herds of Spanish sheep and horses. The Navajos changed their lifestyle to sedentary herding, while the Apaches raised horses and traded them with other Indian peoples to the north. The arrival of horses on the Great Plains ushered in the birth of horse-riding, buffalo-hunting Plains Indian culture. Now Native peoples were able to hunt buffalo efficiently. The Great Plains were able to support a much larger population, and tribes from the east and west crowded into what had been a sparsely populated region.[37]

Not all Indian-European relationships were so thoroughly conflict ridden. In some instances, Native peoples managed to coexist with European immigrants with fairly long periods of peace, in a regime of mutual accommodation and trade. Key items in maintaining such harmony were an economic nexus framing relationships, a physical distance between concentrations of Europeans and Natives, and military power in the hands of well-organized Indian confederacies. The prototypical confederacy was the Iroquois. The Pequots, Wampanoags, Powhatans, and other coastal tribes were small in size, militarily weak after the first generation or two of Europeans had arrived, and not centrally organized. The League of the Iroquois was the opposite. Many thousands strong, the confederacy had been in place for at least a century before Europeans showed up in North America. It comprised five large tribes: the Mohawks, Oneidas, Onandogas, Senecas, and Cayugas (the Tuscaroras were added in 1722). They met in annual councils with complex rules for regulated decision making. They made war on their neighbors effectively and negotiated treaties as a sovereign nation. The Iroquois controlled a huge territory, from the Adirondacks to the Great Lakes, in what later became New York and Pennsylvania. Since they controlled the eastern Great Lakes, they could monopolize the fur trade with pelt-hungry Europeans. By skillful diplomacy, they played first the Dutch and then their New York successors the English off against the French. It was only after the French lost the Seven Years War in 1763 and were forced out of Canada that Iroquois power began to decline. No other Native people was as strong as the Iroquois, but a few large southern tribes like the Creeks and Cherokee maintained autonomy and peace on similar terms.[38]

Several assumptions that Europeans made about their relationships with Native peoples turned out not to have been well founded. For one thing, European immigrants, particularly the English and Spanish, seem to have convinced themselves that Native Americans would readily change to become like Europeans. Proselytizing for Christianity was one of the supposed motivations for European involvement in North America. To be sure, some Native people did adopt new styles of clothing within a couple of generations of meeting European immigrants. Some became Christians, and many learned English, Spanish, or French. Yet, as James Axtell and Theda Perdue have conclusively shown, it was just as likely that Europeans would acculturate to Native ways. Axtell tells of hundreds of English immigrants who either lived near Indian groups or were captured by them, who then became "White Indians"—and who when offered rescue by other Whites chose to remain as Indians. Axtell speaks of "the extraordinary drawing power of Indian culture." Eighteen-year-old James Smith was captured and baptized into the tribe of his captors with these words:

> My son, you are now flesh of our flesh and bone of our bone. By the ceremony that was performed this day, every drop of white blood was washed out of your veins. You are taken into the Caughnewaga nation and initiated into a warlike tribe. You are adopted into a great family and now received with great seriousness and solemnity in the room and place of a great man. After what has passed this day you are now one of us by an old strong law and custom. My son, you have now nothing to fear. We are now under the same obligations to love, support, and defend you that we are to love and to defend one another. Therefore you are to consider yourself as one of our people.

Smith was skeptical at first, but came to conclude, "They treated me ... in every way as one of themselves."[39] Perdue writes of the mixed families of European-derived men and Native women in the Southeast. The men were traders and Indian agents, their wives often prominent women among the Creeks or another tribe. Contrary to the men's expectations, it was they who were the newcomers and dependents. They seem to have imagined that their children would be raised as English Americans, but they found out that Native matrilineal norms swept the children into the Native orbit.[40]

The point of this section is to remind us that European people in the beginning were immigrants, guests in Native America. Sometimes they came with power, as did the Spanish in central Mexico. Other times they came in a posture of weakness, as did the Pilgrims in Plymouth and the early English immigrants to the Chesapeake. Seldom were the Europeans socially polished. Their predisposition to believe that Native peoples were savages led them to disregard the Indians' perspectives and to run roughshod over them when they were able. The Europeans killed most of the Native population, through sharing diseases and by force of arms. Assimilation was a two-way street: some Europeans became Indians, and many Indians took on the ways of Europeans. But from the beginning in North America, English people were immigrants. They went through processes of change and adjustment to life in their newly adopted land, as we shall see in the next section. And they kept coming.

A Mixed Multitude: European Migrants

English Immigrants

The largest single group of immigrants who came to the colonies of British North America during the seventeenth and eighteenth centuries were themselves British.[41] But "British" meant a lot of different things. David Hackett Fischer argues that one can most fruitfully conceive of these British people as migrating to America in four distinct waves, from different regions and strata of society in the land they left, forming four distinct societies (and cultures) in British North America.[42]

For English working people, migration itself was not a new thing, in that for many generations people had been moving around England and indeed around Europe. Young men went out of their villages to work; they maintained ties to their ancestral homes and often returned after a period away. Others made more permanent moves to the towns and cities that were growing at the dawn of the modern era. As the sixteenth century turned to the seventeenth, the number of such migrants increased. Some were driven by the pressure that an expanding rural population laid on the land. Others were cast off by the enclosure movement. British landlords began turning farmland into pasture for sheep and cattle. Herding paid good profits and it required fewer hands. The landholding class increased its wealth, and farmers who had formerly been attached to the land were cast adrift. They went to towns and cities looking for work. As Bernard Bailyn described it, "in its earliest phase, the [English] peopling of North America was a spillover—an outgrowth, an extension—of these established patterns of mobility in England." London was a mecca for migrants: between 1650 and 1750, half the natural increase of the English countryside was absorbed by that growing city. But London and other cities were also charnel houses, rife with poverty and disease. Against such a grim backdrop, emigration to North America must have seemed a reasonable alternative. And so the move to the city extended across the Atlantic: between 1640 and 1700, 69 percent of the countryside's natural increase went to North America (Figure 2.9).[43]

This pattern repeats itself over and over in the history of American immigration. Japanese peasants late in the nineteenth century, and Italians, Poles, and many others first went out to work and came back. Then they, or their children or grandchildren, moved from village to town and from town to city. Only then, by and large, did they make the leap across the ocean. To be sure, there were important exceptions to this pattern, such as the abrupt, forced removal of Africans from their homes into slavery in the seventeenth and eighteenth centuries, and the equally abrupt forcing of East European Jews out of the *shtetl* and out of Russia by *pogroms* in the nineteenth century. In both those cases, the migrants were forced to leave behind family, friends, and nearly everything they held dear. But a much more widespread pattern was a generations-long process of going and coming, of connectedness between the places from which one came and the places to which one was moving.

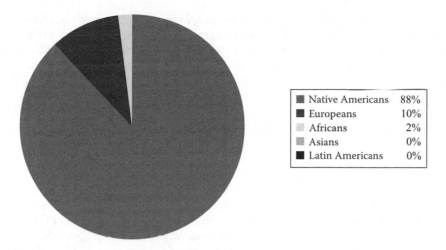

■ Native Americans	88%
■ Europeans	10%
■ Africans	2%
■ Asians	0%
■ Latin Americans	0%

Figure 2.9 Population in 1700 of the territory that would become the United States.

Another theme in the English migration to North America is a certain intentionality. The Virginia Company recruited volunteers to go to America and told them big whopping lies about how easy it would be to make a living there. The company's investors needed colonists in Virginia, growing crops for the British market, if they were to earn a return on their investment. In 1991 a famous historical journal printed Walter Woodward's parody, "Jamestown Estates," which caught the flavor of the Company's effort:

JAMESTOWN ESTATES

For As Little As £10 12s. 6d., You, Too, Can Own a Share of Paradise.

From the moment the gentle, southern breezes waft your pinnace to the verdant, gardenlike shore, you'll know this is where you belong. Jamestown Estates, where only a few are living a life those in England can hardly imagine. … Jamestown Estates offers one of the most active labor markets in the New World. Whatever you do, you can do it better here. Our employment office has many people anxious to welcome you to our growing work force. … Consider … some of these exceptionally valuable Jamestown Pluses:

- 24-hour security, palisaded grounds.
- Hunting, fishing right on premises. Native guides teach you to hunt like a lord.
- The Sotweed Garden Center—learn how to plant like a pro. No experience necessary …

Virginia … A WHOLE NEW WORLD[44]

William Penn had a few more scruples about telling the truth, but he was no less active in sending out advertisements and agents, not only within England but to Germany and other parts of Europe as well, to recruit immigrants for Pennsylvania.

The Puritans and their companions—the first large wave of English migrants to what would become the United States—also migrated with intent. The bulk of the

Puritan migration came from the flatlands of eastern England to Massachusetts in the period between 1628 and 1640. They certainly were intentional, organized, and energetic in their move abroad. In those years 80,000 English people—2 percent of the total population—left England. Of those, 58,000 went across the Atlantic to the Caribbean and North America. Most of the several thousand who went to New England (Plymouth, Massachusetts Bay, Connecticut, and Rhode Island) went with a religious purpose. They were Puritans, members of one radical fringe of the Protestant Reformation who had been uncomfortable in an England dominated in turns by the Catholic Church and the Church of England.

Modern-day Fundamentalists would recognize kindred in the Puritans. They were serious folk, Bible readers and believers, people who had been born again spiritually by a powerful conversion experience. They believed God had a special role for them to fulfill in the destiny of humankind. Despairing of the sorry state of religion and society in England, they went to America by the tens of thousands to establish "A City On a Hill": a godly commonwealth where biblical Christianity was practiced, a model that those they left behind in Europe might one day learn to emulate.[45]

Unlike other early immigrants to British North America, the Puritans came in families and created replicas of English villages. They scattered a hundred towns from New Hampshire to Connecticut, pushing back the Native people as they did so. The Puritans were probably the best educated of any large group of immigrants in American history, except for late-nineteenth- and early-twentieth-century Japanese and late-twentieth-century Filipinos, Koreans, South Asians, and Arabs. They built schools and colleges that set the standard for one of America's now nearly abandoned sources of strength and unity: the public school system. They organized themselves into towns and congregations, and even though they included less fervent believers in their midst, Puritan religion held sway. Pastors and male lay leaders stood at the head of society. Those who challenged their leadership were likely to be whipped, hanged, or thrown out of the community, whether they be proselytizing Quakers or orthodox but outspoken Puritan women like Anne Hutchinson.

The Puritans weathered three crises in the seventeenth century that fundamentally reshaped the New England regime. The first was Puritan success in old England. From 1642 to 1649 Puritan politicians and armies fought for control of the English government. In the latter year they overthrew King Charles I, executed him, and placed Oliver Cromwell at the head of a nominally republican government. For the next 15 years, no one was looking to the City On a Hill—they had a larger Puritan experiment to attend to in England. Many New Englanders went back to England to take part in the great adventure. Others who stayed turned away from England and began to form an American identity.

As a second generation of Puritan migrants came of age in America, a crisis of faith hit New England. Members of the first generation had been marked by the intervention of the Holy Spirit in their lives; each knew that she or he had been converted by God's personal caress. In mid-century a second generation grew up with a different experience from that of their parents. Nearly all of them believed with their minds and hearts all that their parents had believed. But few among them had felt God's touch in a personal conversion experience; therefore, they were not admissible to church membership, hence they could not be full citizens. A new generation of leaders solved the impasse by instituting what later generations called the Halfway Covenant—such believers could have partial church membership and so their children in turn could be baptized. It was an attempt to preserve Puritan culture by taking a realistic view of what was possible to demand in the new environment. This constituted a classic second-generation move, as we shall see with other immigrant groups in American history.[46]

As New England grew into a stable, prosperous province, more and more people crowded in. Most were English, but few of the latecomers were Puritans. Then, at the end of the century, a series of witchcraft outbreaks—the most famous at Salem, Massachusetts, in 1692—tested the fabric of New England society. All the new diversity brought out gender, class, theological, and interpersonal conflicts. Some people accused others of consorting with dark forces. It may have been in part real warfare of the spirit world. People were tried, found guilty, and executed. When the wave of hysteria subsided, New Englanders went back to building a prosperous, middle-class society out of increasingly diverse elements. With each passing decade they became less and less unanimous spiritually, and more and more American (as opposed to English) in outlook.

Most English people, indeed most Europeans, were believing Christians of one sort or another at the dawn of the modern era. But that does not necessarily mean that religion played a part in their coming to America. The Puritans' motivation was genuinely religious; in this they were highly unusual. The second big wave of British immigrants comprised a royalist elite and a mass of indentured servants who came to America from south England between 1640 and 1675. As we saw earlier in this chapter, a fragile colony was planted at Jamestown despite great loss of life and morale, and it held on for a third of a century. In the 1640s, however, things began to look up, at the same time and for the same reason that things were looking down for migration into New England. The gathering Puritan revolution in Old England destabilized not only the Stuart dynasty, but the lives and fortunes of a large cohort of nobles and would-be aristocrats.

Sir William Berkeley, a supporter of the King, came in 1641 and served as Governor of Virginia for more than thirty years. According to David Hackett Fischer's description, "His appearance was that of a nobleman—short cloak, deep bands, great boots, belted sword, and long hair cascading in ringlets around his patrician face. His manners were those of a courtier, polished by years in the presence of the King. His speech was that of a scholar, knighted on the field of honor by Charles I."[47] Such descriptions lent themselves over the years to the creation of the Cavalier Myth, that Southern Whites are descended from English nobility. Berkeley consciously recruited royalist aristocrats (many of them younger sons who would not inherit family lands in England) to come to Virginia. They came mainly from royalist strongholds in the south and west of England. He awarded them large lots of land and important civil positions. About the same time, for reasons that are not clear, the Virginia population ceased to die off at the horrific rate it had suffered in the first several decades. During Berkeley's tenure as governor, the English population of Virginia exploded from 8,000 to 40,000. The economy expanded, too, with tobacco being the main crop, grown for consumption in Europe.

These privileged landowners imported workers, also mainly from the south and west of England, to plant, tend, and harvest their tobacco fields. In return for the planters paying their passage, the workers served indentures that usually lasted four to seven years. The planters were awarded a headright: fifty acres of land for each person they brought into the colony. Those workers who survived to the end of their indenture were then turned out to find their own means of support.[48] They went looking for land on which to farm. With most of the land in the tidewater region—the flat, fertile territory along the rivers near Chesapeake Bay—taken, these former servants and some late-coming people of higher class found themselves squatting on backcountry land that was inhabited by Indians. It was a situation destined for conflict. Governor Berkeley tried to keep the English and the Indians separate by decree, but the land-hungry English would have none of it.

Conflict came to a head in 1675 to 1676. A dispute over some hogs between a group of Doeg Indians and some English immigrants resulted in English killing Doegs, then Doegs killing English, then English killing not just Doegs but Susquehannocks, who had been English allies for two generations. Some Indian groups raided outlying English farmsteads, and the English in the Chesapeake began to fear a war like the one Metacom was just then fighting with another set of English people in New England. Led by a disgruntled aristocrat and former friend of the governor named Nathaniel Bacon, English farmers attacked the Indians they found most convenient to hand: Appomattoxes, Pamunkeys, Occaneechees, and others who were friendly and who lived within the area of White residence. They killed hundreds. Bacon excused this slaughter disingenuously, saying that the peaceful Indians "have been soe cunningly mixt among the severall Nations or families of Indians that it hath been very difficult for us, to distinguish how, or from which of those said Nations, the said wrongs did proceed"—so he would just kill them all. Indians are all alike, and the only good ones are dead. Governor Berkeley attempted to impose order by marching against both Indians and Bacon's militia. Bacon and his followers chased Berkeley across Chesapeake Bay and burned Jamestown to the ground. But then Bacon contracted dysentery and died, and the rebellion collapsed. From that time forward, the White planter class began to turn away from importing White servants under indenture, and began to bring in ever-larger numbers of African slaves to do their work.[49]

The third large wave of English migrants came from the northern Midlands and Wales to the Delaware Valley between 1675 and 1725. William Penn was granted a charter to build a colony as a refuge for his fellow members of the Society of Friends, or Quakers. Even more radical than the Puritans, the Quakers believed that God spoke directly to each individual human heart, and so they had no place for ecclesiastical authorities. In the early years of their religion, which coincided with the founding of New England, Quakers were physically abused in both Old and New England. By the end of the century their main disability was social ostracism from Anglicans and Puritans alike. Pennsylvania was to be a place of refuge for Friends, but quickly it became home to a mixed multitude of people from many parts of English life as well as from other parts of Europe, and Philadelphia, its port and capital, became a hub of commerce.[50]

Immigration Policy under the British

During the generations when the British Crown ruled, the government's consistent policy was one of encouraging immigration by Europeans.[51] In 1616 the Virginia Company began to grant the headright. If an employer brought in indentured servants or slaves, then he got to keep the headrights for them.[52] In 1740, Parliament passed the Plantation Act, "An Act for naturalizing such foreign Protestants, and others herein mentioned, as are settled or shall settle, in any of his Majesty's Colonies in America." Its goal was both to encourage immigration and to make an orderly process for turning migrants into English subjects:

> Whereas the Increase of People is a Means of advancing the Wealth and Strength of any Nation or Country; And whereas many Foreigners and Strangers from the Lenity of our Government, the Purity of our Religion, the benefits of our Laws, the Advantages of our Trade, and the Security of our Property, might be induced to come and settle in some of His Majesty's Colonies in America, if they were made Partakers of the Advantages and Privileges which the natural born Subjects of this Realm do enjoy.

The act went on to specify that, except only for Quakers and Jews, any applicant for naturalization must take communion in a Protestant church.[53]

Later, when the British government did not promote immigration to their satisfaction, the English-descended people in America rebelled. The *Declaration of Independence* is partly a high-minded document full of noble abstractions about unalienable rights and the pursuit of happiness, but it is mainly a bitter catalogue of English Americans' complaints about their faraway king. One of the complaints that British North Americans voiced most often in the period after 1763 was that George III had failed to encourage immigration. The *Declaration* reads in part:

> When in the course of human events it becomes necessary for *one people* to dissolve the political bands which have connected them with *another* ... a decent respect to the opinions of mankind requires that they should declare the causes which impel them to the separation. ... The history of the present King of Great Britain is a history of repeated injuries and usurpations, all having, in direct object, the establishment of an absolute tyranny over these States. ... He has endeavored to prevent the population of these States, for that purpose, obstructing the laws for naturalization of foreigners, refusing to pass others to encourage their migration hither.

Note the words in italics. By the 1770s, enough generations had passed that the grandchildren and great-grandchildren of English immigrants now thought of themselves as not English people but Americans. They were peeved at the English king for failing, in their estimation, his duty to bring more migrants to this country they increasingly saw as not his but their own. There is a grim paradox in the fact that they would then go on to impose their own hegemony over newcomers henceforth.

Other Europeans

The growth of the middle colonies in the eighteenth century gave rise to a fourth wave of British migration, and along with it a large influx of peoples from other parts of Europe. First, the peoples from other parts. A small troop of Dutch immigrants founded New Amsterdam in 1624. They left their names on towns, streets, neighborhoods, and public buildings far out of proportion to their actual population, which was tiny. Holland maintained a small post for fur trading with Native peoples, but it was not until the British took over in 1664 and renamed the town New York that the place began to grow.[54]

Among the many European peoples who later streamed into New York, Philadelphia, and other eastern ports were various sorts of Germans. It is essential to remember that Germany was not yet a nation but a collection of principalities stretching from the mouth of the Rhine in Holland up to the Alps in Switzerland, and from Alsace in the west far into Central Europe. Large parts of that territory would coalesce into the modern state of Germany in the latter nineteenth century, while others would remain outside the German polity yet within the German cultural sphere. All of the peoples of those various places spoke varieties of the German language, although those varieties were not all mutually intelligible. So the line between Dutch and German, between German and Swiss, or between German and Czech was not always as clear as it might seem today. A term like "Pennsylvania Dutch" thus has an elliptical quality to it. On the one hand it was a corruption of *Deutsch* ("German") which once referred to all those different peoples. On the other hand, the actual Dutch—that is, people from Holland—were among the several Germanic peoples who came to the middle colonies. The vast majority, however, came from other German places.[55]

Some of the Pennsylvania Dutch were members of radical Protestant sects, such as the thirteen Quaker and Mennonite families who founded Germantown, Pennsylvania, in 1683. But most were either Lutherans or Reformed, members of established state churches in their ancestral principalities. Large-scale German migration began in 1709, when 13,000 people left the Palatinate, a wine-growing principality along the Rhine. They had suffered overpopulation, border wars against the French, and recent harsh winters. They went first to England, then nearly 3000 of them were sent on by the British government to New York's Hudson River Valley. Some soon moved north and west up the Hudson and the Mohawk, while others made their way southwest to Pennsylvania, where land was more readily available. They wrote back to those at home about the land to be had in America and a stream of migration was begun, not just from the Palatinate but from other German-speaking lands all up and down the Rhine, and indeed from all over Central Europe. By mid-century, German migrants were pushing west into central Pennsylvania and coming into conflict with Native populations there. Others made their way south and west, through Maryland and into Virginia up the Shenandoah Valley. By the time of the American Revolution, German farms and villages were planted all along the Allegheny foothills and into the Carolina backcountry.[56]

The largest German impact came in Pennsylvania. Many German immigrants served indentures in their early years in America, but most became independent farmers before long. By the time of the Revolution they numbered more than one-third of the colony's White population. They did not gather into cities, but became the largest group in parts of the countryside. Concentrated in half a dozen southeast Pennsylvania counties stretching between Philadelphia and York, the Germans were the most segregated of the colony's ethnic groups; for example, in 1790 they made up 72 percent of the population of Lancaster County and 73 percent of Berks. One could live in such areas, not speak a word of English, and get along quite nicely. Ethnic Germans were a force with which to reckon in Pennsylvania society and politics. They took to English citizenship more freely than any other non-English group— they constituted 94 percent of the people naturalized into English citizenship within the thirteen colonies during the eighteenth century. They formed an ethnic swing vote in colonial politics between the Quaker party and that of the colony's proprietor, Thomas Penn. When the Revolution came in 1776, Germans formed the largest ethnic minority bloc in the new state assembly (Table 2.1).[57]

Table 2.1 German Immigration to British North America by Decades, 1700–1775

Decade	Number
Before 1700	153
1700–1709	41
1710–1719	2,981
1720–1729	4,801
1730–1739	16,728
1740–1749	10,361
1750–1759	48,081
1760–1769	9,341
1770–1775	5,011
Total	111,211

Source: Marianne S. Wokeck, *Trade in Strangers: The Beginnings of Mass Migration to North America* (University Park: Pennsylvania State University Press, 1999), 45–46.

Thousands of British people came to America in the middle of the eighteenth century, during the main era of German immigration between 1710 and 1775. Many of them were English, as before, but there were new populations: Scots, Irish, and Scotch-Irish. They constituted the fourth wave in David Hackett Fischer's typology of British migrants: coming from the north of England, Scotland, Northern Ireland, and Ireland proper, many thousands of them ended up in the same backcountry zone as the Germans, stretching from Pennsylvania to Georgia. Like the migrations to the Delaware Valley and New England (and unlike the Chesapeake migration), these immigrants typically came in families. The largest part of this group was from Ulster, the northeastern part of Ireland where the British government had planted colonies of Scots in an attempt to subdue the native Irish. As Maldwyn Jones described their situation as servants of English colonizers in Ireland, these displaced Scots were "surrounded by a hostile people whom they despised, yet themselves regarded as inferior by the ruling English." In the 1730s and 1740s their numbers began to swell until, on the eve of the Revolution, they constituted the largest group of migrants except Africans.[58]

These people, who would have called themselves Ulstermen, have been variously denominated by others as Ulster Scots, Scotch-Irish, and Anglo-Irish. Most were Presbyterians, and so they had much in common with the people who came direct from Scotland in these same decades. Like those Scots and also the northern English with whom they did not share a common religious commitment, the Scotch-Irish were pushed by rising rents and pulled by the desire to own farmland of their own. Like those others, the Scotch-Irish had long existed in an unstable border zone where violence between clans and between the English and their neighbors was endemic. On the average, these various Scots, Scotch-Irish, and northern English brought less education and less wealth with them than the more middle-class New Englanders, or the British and German populations of Pennsylvania and the Delaware Valley. They entered America through Philadelphia and other middle coast ports. Quickly they fanned out into the backcountry and, like the Germans, moved south and west, some as far as the Carolinas.

Driven though they were by difficult circumstances, the Scotch-Irish and others who made up this last pre-Revolutionary wave of migrants from the northern parts of the British isles nonetheless came to have a positive view of the migration experience. Samuel Johnson reported from the Isle of Skye in 1773 that local people had America very much on their minds, and that they saw themselves as having a future there.

> Whether the mischiefs of emigration were immediately perceived, may be justly questioned. They who went first, were probably such as could best be spared; but the accounts sent by the earliest adventurers, whether true or false, inclined many to follow them; and whole neighborhoods formed parties for removal; so that departure from their native country is no longer exile. He that goes thus accompanied, carries with him all that makes life pleasant. He sits down in a better climate, surrounded by his kindred and his friends: they carry with them their language, their opinions, their popular songs, and hereditary merriment: they change nothing but the place of their abode.[59]

Johnson and his friend James Boswell attended a party to celebrate those who had migrated and those who would:

> [W]e performed with much activity a dance which I suppose the emigration from Skye has occasioned. They call it "America." A brisk reel is played. The first couple begin, and each sets to one—then each to another—then as they set to the next couple, the second and third couples are setting; and so it goes on till all are set a-going, setting and wheeling round each other, while each is making the tour of all in the dance. *It shows how emigration catches till all are set afloat.* Mrs. Mackinnon told me that last year when the ship sailed from Portree for America, the people on shore were almost distracted when they saw their relations go off; they lay down on the ground and tumbled, and tore the grass with their teeth. This year there was not a tear shed. The people on shore seemed to think that they would soon follow.[60]

This completes the four waves of British migration to North America. Those British immigrants and their descendants were certainly not the only peoples in what would become the United States. They were not the only Europeans. But together the various British immigrants and their descendants made up the larger part of the White population of the colonies on the eve of nationhood. They formed four distinct culture zones in eastern North America. The Puritan migration brought religiously motivated, well-educated, strong nuclear families from the south of England to New England in the middle third of the seventeenth century. Then aristocrats, would-be aristocrats, and their servants created a very different society in the tidewater—less well educated, less socially integrated, and more hierarchical. Then a mixed multitude led by a moderate and tolerant Quaker government inhabited the Delaware Valley and surrounding country. Finally, families from Ireland, Scotland, and the north of England came through Pennsylvania and spread out over the southern backcountry. Each wave of migrants had its distinctive origins, its typical family characteristics. Each created a distinctive society in America, with its own dialect and patterns of social organization.

Aaron Fogleman estimated the numbers of migrants of various ethnic origins to the thirteen British colonies between the beginning of the eighteenth century and the start of the Revolution (Table 2.2). His estimates vary a bit from those for Germans in Table 2.1 or for Africans in Tables 2.3 and 2.4, but they give a rough estimate of the relative sizes of the different migrant flows in this period.

All this meant that, by the time of the American Revolution, the European American population was a mixed multitude. Figure 2.10 shows the percentages of people from various European national origins who were recorded by the first U.S. Census of 1790. Note that the large size of the English population is due not to a large number of recent immigrants so much as to a large amount of natural increase from immigrants who had come generations before.

Indenture

Most European migrants came as indentured servants. Someone—a broker in the old country, a ship captain, or, on rare occasions, an employer in America—paid their passage. When they arrived they were obliged to work off their debt for four, five, or even seven years. In 1750, Gottlieb Mittelberger was a passenger on a ship with 400 redemptioners, as they were also called. It took him from May to October to make the trip from his native Württemberg to Pennsylvania: seven weeks down the Rhine to Rotterdam and then fifteen weeks on board ship before reaching Philadelphia. He described the voyage:

> During the journey the ship is full of pitiful signs of distress—smells, fumes, horrors, vomiting, various kinds of sea sickness, fever, dysentery, headaches, heat, constipation, boils, scurvy, cancer, mouth-rot, and similar afflictions, all of them caused by the age and the highly-salted state of the food, especially of the meat, as well as by the very bad and filthy water, which brings about the miserable destruction and death of many. Add to all that shortage of food, hunger, thirst, frost, heat, dampness, fear, misery, vexation, and lamentation as well as other troubles. Thus, for example, there are so many lice, especially on the sick people, that they have to be scraped off the bodies. All this misery reaches the climax when in addition to everything else one must also suffer through two to three days and nights of storm, with everyone convinced that the ship with all aboard is bound to sink. In such misery all the people on board pray and cry pitifully together.[61]

When they arrived in America the redemptioners were sold. Mittelberger described the scene at the docks in Philadelphia:

> This is how the commerce in human beings on board ship takes place. Every day Englishmen, Dutchmen, and High Germans come from Philadelphia and other places, some of them very far away, sometimes twenty or thirty or forty hours' journey, and go on board the newly arrived vessel that has brought people from Europe and offers them for sale. From among the healthy they

Table 2.2 Immigration by Ethnic Group into the Thirteen Colonies, by Decade, 1770–1775

Decade	Africans	Germans*	Scotch Irish	Irish	Scots	English	Welsh	Other	Total
1700–09	9,000	(100)	(600)	(800)	(200)	[400]	[300]	[100]	(11,500)
1710–19	10,800	(3,700)	(1,200)	(1,700)	(500)	[1,300]	[900]	[200]	(20,300)
1720–29	9,900	(2,300)	(2,100)	(3,000)	(800)	[2,200]	[1,500]	[200]	(22,000)
1730–39	40,500	13,000	4,400	7,400	(2,000)	[4,900]	[3,200]	[800]	(76,200)
1740–49	58,500	16,600	9,200	9,100	(3,100)	[7,500]	[4,900]	[1,100]	(110,000)
1750–59	49,600	29,100	14,200	8,100	(3,700)	[8,800]	[5,800]	[1,200]	(120,500)
1760–69	82,300	14,500	21,200	8,500	10,000	[11,900]	[7,800]	[1,600]	157,800
1770–75	17,800	5,200	13,200	3,900	15,000	7,100	[4,600]	[700]	67,500
Total	278,400	84,500	66,100	42,500	35,300	[44,100]	[29,000]	[5,900]	(585,800)

Figures are rounded to nearest 100 immigrants. The estimates are divided into three categories: most dependable for accuracy (no demarcation), less dependable ( ), and least dependable [ ].

Aaron Spencer Fogleman, *Hopeful Journeys: German Immigration, Settlement, and Political Culture in Colonial America, 1717–1775* (Philadelphia: University of Pennsylvania Press, 1996), 2; see also Fogleman, "Migrations to the thirteen British North American Colonies, 1700–1775: New Estimates," *Journal of Interdisciplinary History*, 22 (1992): 691–709.

* Includes all German-speaking peoples, including Swiss and Alsatians.

Table 2.3 African Migrants through the Slave Trade, Exported, and Imported by Region of Destination

	1450–1600	1601–1700	1701–1810	1811–1870	Total
Exported from Africa	367,000	1,868,000	6,133,000	3,330,000	11,698,000
Total arrived at market	274,900	1,341,100	6,051,700	1,898,400	9,566,100
British North America			348,000	51,000	399,000
Spanish America	75,000	292,500	578,600	606,000	1,552,100
British Caribbean		263,700	1,401,300		1,665,000
French Caribbean		155,800	1,348,400	96,000	1,600,200
Dutch Caribbean		40,000	460,000		500,000
Danish Caribbean		4,000	24,000		28,000
Brazil	50,000	560,000	1,891,400	1,145,400	3,646,800
Old World	149,900	25,100			175,000

Sources: Philip D. Curtin, *The African Slave Trade: A Census* (Madison: University of Wisconsin Press, 1969), 268; Paul E. Lovejoy, "The Volume of the Atlantic Slave Trade: A Synthesis," *Journal of African History,* 23 (1982), 473–500. See also David Northrup, ed., *The Atlantic Slave Trade* (Lexington, MA: Heath, 1994); Herbert S. Klein, *The Atlantic Slave Trade* (Cambridge: Cambridge University Press, 1999). James A. Rawley raised Curtin's estimates of imports about 16 percent, thus:

Region or Country	Curtin est.	Rawley est.
British North America	399,000	523,000
Spanish America	1,552,100	1,687,000
British Caribbean	1,665,000	2,443,000
French Caribbean	1,500,200	1,655,000
Dutch Caribbean	500,000	500,000
Danish Caribbean	28,000	50,000
Brazil	3,646,800	4,190,000
Old World	175,000	297,000
Total	9,566,100	11,345,000

James A. Rawley, *The Transatlantic Slave Trade* (New York: Norton, 1981), 428.

Table 2.4 Estimated Immigration to British North America by Race, 1620–1780

Years	European Migrants	African Migrants	Total Migrants
1620–1660	7,000		7,000
1660–1680	60,000	5,000	65,000
1680–1700	35,000	15,000	50,000
Total 1620–1700	102,000	20,000	122,000
1700-1720	32,000	37,000	69,000
1720-1740	70,000	72,000	142,000
1740-1760	35,000	100,000	135,000
1760-1780	67,000	86,000	153,000
Total 1700-1780	204,000	295,000	499,000
Grand Total	306,000	315,000	621,000

Sources: These numbers were taken mainly from the exhibit, "The Peopling of America," at the Ellis Island Immigration Museum, New York Harbor (viewed October 28, 2003); listed consultants: Russell R. Menard and Henry A. Gemery. The numbers here are based on my estimates of the numbers displayed in three-dimensional bar graph form. Gemery and Menard's estimates for Africans are lower than several other demographers'. Accordingly, I have supplemented them with information from Philip D. Curtin, *The Atlantic Slave Trade: A Census* (Madison: University of Wisconsin Press, 1969), 140. See also Henry A. Gemery, "Emigration from the British Isles to the New World, 1630–1700: Inferences from Colonial Populations," *Research in Economic History*, 5 (1980), 179–231; Gemery, "European Emigration to North America, 1700–1820: Numbers and Quasi-Numbers," *Perspectives in American History*, New Series, 1 (1984), 283–343; Gemery, "The White Population of the Colonial United States, 1607–1790," in *A Population History of North America*, Michael R. Haines and Richard H. Steckel, Eds., (Cambridge: Cambridge University Press, 2000), 143–190; Philip D. Curtin, *The Atlantic Slave Trade: A Census* (Madison: University of Wisconsin Press, 1969), 140; Paul E. Lovejoy, "The Volume of the Atlantic Slave Trade: A Synthesis," *Journal of African History*, 23 (1982), 473–501; Joseph Inikori and Stanley L. Engerman, Eds., *The Atlantic Slave Trade* (Durham, NC: Duke University Press, 1992); James A. Rawley, *The Transatlantic Slave Trade* (New York: Norton, 1981), 167; Michael A. Gomez, *Exchanging Our Country Marks: The Transformation of African Identities in the Colonial and Antebellum South* (Chapel Hill: University of North Carolina Press, 1998), 20.

pick out those suitable for the purposes for which they require them. Then they negotiate with them as to the length of the period for which they will go into service in order to pay off their passage, the whole amount of which they generally still owe. When an agreement has been reached, adult persons by written contract bind themselves to serve for three, four, five, or six years, according to their health and age. The very young, between the ages of ten and fifteen, have to serve until they are twenty-one, however.

Many parents in order to pay their fares in this way and get off the ship must barter and sell their children as if they were cattle. Since the fathers and mothers often do not know where or to what masters their children are to be sent, it frequently happens that after leaving the vessel, parents and children do not see each other for years on end, or even for the rest of their lives.

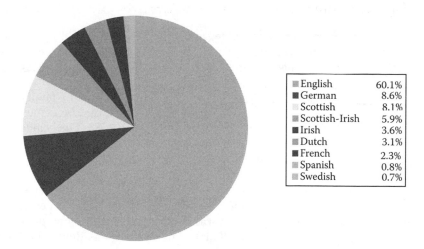

■ English	60.1%
■ German	8.6%
Scottish	8.1%
■ Scottish-Irish	5.9%
■ Irish	3.6%
■ Dutch	3.1%
■ French	2.3%
■ Spanish	0.8%
■ Swedish	0.7%

Figure 2.10 Varieties of White people in the 1790 census.

People … who have children under the age of five, cannot settle their debts by selling them. They must give away these children for nothing to be brought up by strangers; and in return these children must stay in service until they are twenty-one years old.

… When either the husband or the wife has died at sea, having come more than halfway, then the surviving spouse must pay not only his or her fare, but must also pay for or serve out the fare of the deceased.[62]

Indentured servants were put to every sort of work imaginable: clearing forests, planting and tending crops, working the docks as longshoremen, and body servants to the wealthy. A minority learned skills such as smithy or cooperage, but most just labored with their bodies. The conditions of work were arduous. By the time they had worked off their indenture, many servants were broken wrecks, barely able to work any longer. There was no incentive for masters to treat servants with care or respect, and every incentive for them to work their charges nearly to death. Some colonies passed laws restricting masters from physically abusing indentured servants, but abuses—ranging from overwork to beatings to rape— were common nonetheless. If a servant ran away, extra time was added to his or her term of indenture; in South Carolina, a 1691 law authorized adding a week for every day a servant went missing, and a year for every week absent (in the northern colonies the ratio was usually two to one). Yet White servants did possess some rights; they were not slaves. They could sue and testify in court, though they could not vote. They could not engage in trade, but they could own property. And their children did not inherit their servitude.[63] Even so, Mittelberger concluded that his fellow Germans ought not make the immigrant bargain: "So let people stay in their own country and earn their keep honestly for themselves and their families. … [T]hose people who may let themselves be talked into something and seduced into the voyage by the thieves of human beings are the biggest fools. … How sad and miserable is the fate of so many."[64]

From English to American

One of the striking features of seventeenth-century English social life in North America was a gradual but marked transition of identity. English people in America at the dawn of that century had children, and those children had children. Over the course of those three generations, their identity changed: they came to see themselves as, and to call themselves, "Americans." One can see this in the family of that archetypal American, Benjamin Franklin. Josiah and Anne Franklin came to Boston with three small children, Benjamin's older siblings, in 1683. They came partly for economic reasons and partly out of a religious motive: Charles II had reclaimed the throne and the Puritan republic had collapsed. Though the Franklins' migrant motives may have been mixed, their Puritan commitment was not. Among the core Puritan beliefs was the idea that each person had a "calling." Each had been selected by God for a particular vocation, and it was each person's duty to pursue that vocation with zeal. Anne and Josiah had several children, and after Anne died Josiah had several more with his second wife Abiah. The last boy was Benjamin, born in 1706, almost a generation younger than his oldest siblings. By the time the young Franklin had lived out his long life and finished his distinguished career, he had helped create not only an American identity through his writings and his publishing, but a separate American nation. Franklin was a typical second-generation child of immigrants. When he ran away from his family at age seventeen and took off for Philadelphia, he began a rebellion against the immigrant generation and a transformation of identity and culture. Where his parents saw themselves as English people in America, Benjamin came to see himself as an American with English origins and ties. And where they believed deeply in the doctrine of the calling—following God with all one's heart in pursuing one's vocation—in Benjamin that idea degenerated to a secular ideology of working hard for work's own sake, and for the pecuniary rewards that would result. Identity was changing, culture was changing, generation by generation. It was not just Franklin, it was people throughout the colonies. As Richard Bushman put it, "Sometime between 1690 and 1765 Connecticut Puritans became Yankees."[65]

For all that the grandchildren of English immigrants began to call themselves "Americans," we must remember that they were not the only Americans. There were German Americans, Ulstermen, other European Americans, African Americans, and Native Americans of many tribes (Figure 2.11). Yet there was already in eighteenth-century America an Anglo-American core identity to the Euro-American racial formation that would later emerge.

Out of Africa

David Brion Davis, eminent historian of slavery both in the United States and throughout the world, wrote that "racial slavery and its consequences [are] the basic reality, the grim and irrepressible theme governing the settlement of the Western hemisphere and the emergence of a government and society in the United States that white people have called 'free.'"[66] Perhaps Davis erred in ignoring that other grim and irrepressible reality, genocide against Native peoples, but he is not wholly off the mark. These two facts—enslavement of Africans and destruction of the Native

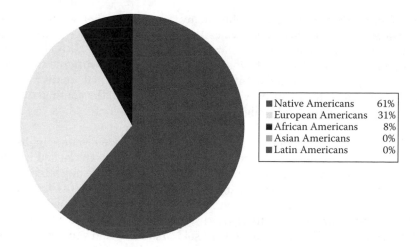

■ Native Americans	61%
European Americans	31%
■ African Americans	8%
Asian Americans	0%
■ Latin Americans	0%

Figure 2.11 Population in 1750 of the territory that would become the United States 3 million people.

peoples of the United States—are the two founding facts of American history and culture. They are surely both central facts in the story of American immigration.

African slaves were immigrants. They came under brutal compulsion. But, as we shall see, they went through many of the same cultural processes of adaptation, accommodation, culture change, and identity transformation as did migrants who were not compelled. Only they were not transformed from English people into Americans; rather, they lost their various African ethnic identities and became Negroes. This was the first fully realized panethnic formation in American history.[67]

To Become a Slave

Picture yourself a child in a West African village, in the rich, populous savannah region known as the Sudan (not to be confused with the modern nation that has since taken that name). This territory of farms and city-states stretched across what is now Burkina Faso, the northern parts of Guinea, Ivory Coast, Ghana, Togo, Benin, and Nigeria, and sections of Mali and Niger. Your family is literate and owns a farm. Your parents are working and you are playing on the edge of the village. Someone grabs you, ties a bag over your head, and whisks you away. You never see your family or home again.

Venture Smith was one such child, taken from his home about 1734 at the age of five. Some strangers came to his town and demanded money and slaves from his father, who was a local hereditary political leader. His father fought them while his wives and children hid.

> They then came to us in the reeds, and the very first salute I had from them was a violent blow on the back part of the head with the fore part of a gun, and at the same time a grasp round the neck. Then I had a rope put about my neck, as had all the women in the thicket with me, and was immediately led to my father, who was likewise pinioned and haltered for leading. In this condition we were all led to the camp. The women and myself being pretty submissive,

had tolerable treatment from the enemy, while my father was closely inter-rogated respecting his money which they knew he must have. But as he gave them no account of it, he was instantly cut and pounded on his body with great inhumanity, that he might be induced by the torture he suffered to make the discovery. All this availed not in the least to make him give up his money, but he despised all the tortures which they inflicted, until the continued exercise and increase of torment, obliged him to sink and expire.[68]

You are chained together in a line with others seized from your neighborhood. Children are tied by ropes at the neck (Figure 2.12). Adults are locked into large wooden collars with spikes protruding a foot or more to impede any attempt to run away. You walk for days, sleeping out in the open. Your captors are Africans, but not people whose language or manners you recognize. You come to a town where they sell you to other slavers. The others from your village are sold to one broker and led away north toward the Sahara. You are sold to another and you keep marching, chained together with other slaves you have not seen before. After several weeks of walking through strange forests you arrive at the largest lake you have ever seen, blue water stretching to the horizon. There your captors throw you into a big cage with dozens of other people. You know no one, but you can understand and talk with a few people. The others are utterly foreign. All are scared.

Olaudah Equiano was another little boy in that situation, seized in 1756, who was traded from hand to hand and walked for months until he reached the Bight of Benin:

Figure 2.12 Slave coffle.

All the nations and people I had hitherto passed through, resembled our own in their manners, customs, and language; but I came at length to a country, the inhabitants of which differed from us in all those particulars. ...

The first object which saluted my eyes when I arrived on the coast was the sea, and a slave ship, which was then riding at anchor, and waiting for its cargo. These filled me with astonishment, which was soon converted into terror, when I was carried on board I was immediate handled, and tossed up, to see if I were sound, by some of the crew; and I was now persuaded that I had got into a world of bad spirits, and that they were going to kill me. Their complexions, too, differing so much from ours, their long hair, and the language they spoke (which was very different from any I had ever heard), united to confirm me in this belief. ... When I looked round the ship too, and saw a large furnace of copper boiling, and a multitude of black people of every description chained together, every one of their countenances expressing dejection and sorrow, I no longer doubted of my fate; and quite overpowered with horror and anguish, I fell motionless on the deck and fainted. When I recovered a little, I found some black people about me, who I believed were some of those who had brought me on board, and had been receiving their pay; they talked to me in order to cheer me, but all in vain. I asked them if we were not to be eaten by those white men with horrible looks, red faces, and long hair. They told me I was not. ...

I was soon put down under the decks, and there I received such a salutation in my nostrils as I had never experienced in my life: so that, with the loathsomeness of the stench, and crying together, I became so sick and low that I was not able to eat, nor had I the least desire to taste anything. I now wished for the last friend, death, to relieve me; but soon, to my grief, two of the white men offered me eatables; and, on my refusing to eat, one of them held me fast by the hands, and laid me across, I think the windlass, and tied my feet, while the other flogged me severely. I had never experienced anything of this kind before, and, although not being used to the water, I naturally feared that element the first time I saw it, yet, nevertheless, could I have got over the nettings, I would have jumped over the side, but I could not; and besides, the crew used to watch us very closely who were not chained down to the decks, lest we should leap into the water; and I have seen some of these poor African prisoners most severely cut, for attempting to do so, and hourly whipped for not eating.[69]

Thus you begin your journey across the Middle Passage. A strange, translucent creature with long, straight hair comes to the place you are caged, pokes your flesh, and examines your gums. You are stripped naked and your body parts are examined. Money changes hands, you are branded with a hot iron and led away in chains along with most of the others who were in the cage. Placed in a small boat with half a dozen others, you are rowed out to a ship at anchor. You fear that these pale people are going to eat you.

You are taken into the hold and chained in place. You are made to lie on one of three layers of wooden platforms, with other slaves above, below, and alongside

(Figure 2.13). There is only a small clearance between the platforms, so you cannot sit up. You are chained to the people on either side of you, so if you want to turn over, they must turn, too. The ship weighs anchor. You are seasick and vomit and soil yourself. When the weather is good, you are let out on deck twice a day in small, chained groups and carefully guarded while you eat. Then you are returned to the hold. Light barely filters down from the hatch in good weather. If it is stormy, you are in blackness for days on end amid the smells and groans of your fellow captives. Food is passed to you in a bucket, and you defecate the same way. The person on your left dies of dysentery. You are chained to a corpse for several days before the crew takes the body away.

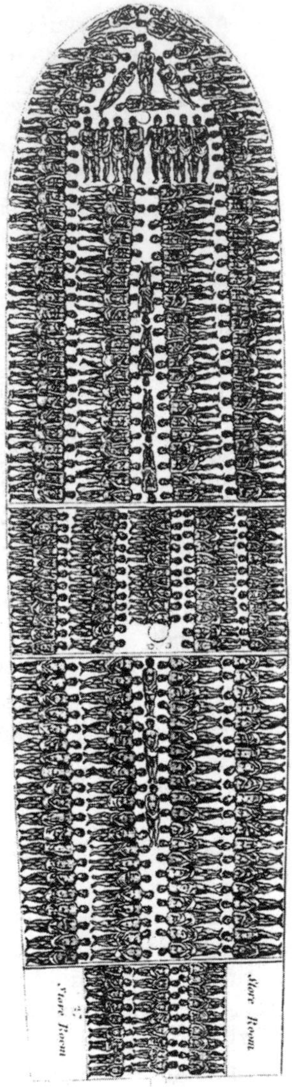

Slave traders were of two minds as to how best to accommodate their human cargo. Advocates of loose packing preferred to bring smaller numbers of slaves on each vessel, feed them better and exercise them, on the theory that more would survive the journey and they would be in better shape on arrival in the Americas, hence they would each command a higher price and the lot would mean a solid profit for the slaver. Tight packers argued it was more efficient to cram as many people as possible into the hold of the ship and throw overboard those who died along the way. Records indicate that 15 to 20 percent of those who boarded ship did not make it to market in the Americas. That was just an average: the mortality rate was higher in the fifteenth and sixteenth centuries and then declined over the later centuries as slavers got better at their job.

After weeks at sea, they let you out on deck, chained together in a small group. Exercise and better food make you stronger and, you will learn, more marketable. The ship takes you first to Barbados, an island in the Caribbean. There you are stripped, exhibited, poked, measured, fondled, sold, and transshipped.

Equiano reported:

Figure 2.13 Slave ship.

At last we came in sight of the island of Barbados ... we plainly saw the harbor, and other ships of different kinds and sizes, and we soon anchored amongst them, off Bridgetown. Many merchants and planters now came on board. ... They put us in separate parcels, and examined us attentively. ... We thought by this, we should be eaten by these ugly men, as they appeared to us; and, when soon after we were all put down under the deck again, there was much dread and trembling among us, and nothing but bitter cries to be heard all the night from these apprehensions, insomuch, that at last the white people got some old slaves from the land to pacify us. They told us we were not to be eaten, but to work, and were soon to go on land, where we should see many of our country people. This report eased us much. And sure enough, soon after we were landed, there came to us Africans of all languages. ...

On a signal given (as the beat of a drum), the buyers rush at once into the yard where the slaves are confined, and make choice of that parcel they like best. The noise and clamor with which this is attended, and the eagerness visible in the countenances of the buyers, serve not a little to increase the apprehension of terrified Africans. ... In this manner, without scruple, are relations and friends separated, most of them never to see each other again.[70]

Barbados, Jamaica, and other transshipment points in the Caribbean marked a sharp division of life fortunes for enslaved Africans. By far the majority of male slaves were sent to work in Brazil and the Caribbean. The largest component of a slave's price was the cost of transporting her or him. Because of closer proximity to Africa, it was more efficient in Latin America and the Caribbean to import mainly male workers, work them hard, wear them out, and then bring some more over from Africa. Thus the slave trade brought over more people to Brazil and the Caribbean than to North America. Smaller numbers of slaves were shipped to North America, and a higher percentage of them were women. They were brought, if not to form families, then at least to breed more slaves. This does not mean that the slave regime was gentler in North America nor more humane, just that the economics worked out differently.

Equiano failed to attract a buyer in Barbados and so was shipped on to Virginia:

We were landed up a river a good way from the sea, about Virginia county, where we saw few or none of our native Africans, and not one who could talk to me. I was a few weeks weeding grass and gathering stones in a plantation; and at last all my companions were distributed different ways, and only myself was left. I was now exceedingly miserable, and thought myself worse off than any of the rest of my companions, for they could talk to each other, but I had no person to speak to that I could understand. I was constantly grieving and pining, and wishing for death rather than anything else.[71]

Dimensions and Effects

The European slave trade out of Africa was one of the largest people movements in world history.[72] The best estimates suggest that at least 11.7 million people were shipped out of Africa in the European-conducted slave trade between 1450 and 1870, and that perhaps 9.6 million of them survived to market.

It is worth pointing out that, in terms of absolute numbers, more Africans than Europeans crossed the Atlantic to the Americas until some time in the third decade of the nineteenth century. Table 2.5 shows informed estimates for just those who came to British North America.

Note that, whereas the slave trade to Latin America and the Caribbean was enormous very early, it did not emerge in what would later become the United States

Table 2.5 African Americans as a Percentage of the Combined Black and White Population of the British Colonies, 1660–1780

Year	New England	Middle Colonies	Upper South	Lower South	West Indies
1660	1.7	11.5	3.6	2.0	42.0
1700	1.8	6.8	13.1	17.6	77.7
1740	2.9	7.5	28.3	46.5	88.0
1780	2.0	5.9	38.6	41.2	91.1

Source: John J. McCusker and Russell R. Menard, *The Economy of British America, 1607–1789* (Chapel Hill: University of North Carolina Press, 1985), 222. I list these as percentages of the "combined Black and White population" because those regions also included Indians, but their numbers were not recorded.

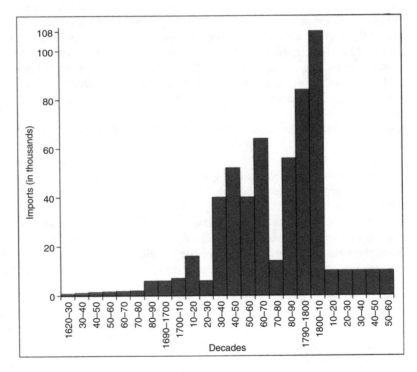

Figure 2.14 U.S. Imports of slaves per decade, 1620–1860.

until the eighteenth century. But note, too, that far more African migrants than Europeans entered the thirteen colonies between the start of that century and the time of the American Revolution (Figure 2.14).

All these numbers are for those who made it across to the Americas, or who were recorded as having been shipped out of Africa. We have no figures, of course, for those who were smuggled or whose captors kept no records. Likewise, we do not know how many died between their initial capture and taking ship, nor how many died, were maimed, or rendered homeless by the wars fought to take slaves. Certainly, those numbers must have been enormous. They would probably add many millions to the totals, but we cannot know for sure just how many.

Nor can we measure with any precision the other effects all this had on Africa. As David Northrup put it: "The effects of the slave trade varied widely in Africa. They depended on how long and how much a society was involved, on whether its people were the slave traders or the slaves traded, and on how well a society managed the strains introduced by the trade." Walter Rodney argued that, by the forcible transshipment of millions of human beings and the introduction of an attendant level of violence and civil chaos, "Europe underdeveloped Africa" during the centuries of the slave trade. He contended that, at the start of the slave trade, Europe and Africa were on similar plateaus in terms of population size, infrastructure development, education, health, and other indices of economic and social development. During the period of the slave trade, Europe grew rapidly in all these areas, while Africa stagnated or declined. Rodney attributed Africa's decline to the impact of the slave trade, and credited slave labor with providing much of the capital that later fueled Europe's industrial revolution.[73]

Rodney may have overestimated the degree to which it was slave labor that formed the capital crucial to fund the European industrial revolution—there was considerable capital formation within Europe as well. But there is no doubt that the European slave trade destabilized numerous societies in West and Central Africa. Settled and prosperous states of the interior fell prey to marauding armies and went into eclipse. They lost a huge portion of their population to death and enslavement. Was it twenty million? Thirty million? We cannot tell. Commerce was interrupted. Kingdoms fell. Small, previously poor states along the coast grew into powerful but unstable, militarized states whose main goal seems to have been to make war on their neighbors, enslave those neighbors, enrich themselves, and avoid being made slaves themselves.

Some may object to calling this the European slave trade. They may say that slavery had long existed in Africa before Europeans arrived on the scene, that the slave catchers and internal slave traders were Africans, that they benefited from the trade, and that European slavers were just latecoming exporters serving an already established African slave system. Yes, there was slavery in Africa, although it looked a good deal more like the personal, family-and-community-connected slavery practiced by Native Americans than it did like gang labor on plantations. Some Africans did indeed prosper as a result of the trade in human lives. But overall, Africa suffered terribly from the European slave trade, and it has not yet recovered. Thus Africa was ushered into a worldwide, capitalist economic system that was beginning to form. It entered on terms of inequality, it became much poorer and less populous relative to Europe, and millions of its people were forced to migrate to the Americas. As the Cheng and Bonacich model described in Chapter 1 suggests, these are linked phenomena.[74]

How "Black" and "Slave" Came to Mean the Same Thing

We have become accustomed to the idea that African-descended people were all slaves, and that slaves were necessarily Black. Yet there is nothing about slavery as a labor system that requires a racial or physical demarcation between slaves and free people. Extensive slave systems existed in ancient China, the Roman Empire, Mesoamerica, and the Middle East without slavery becoming associated with a particular group marked by ethnicity or physical features. But in North America, by about 1700, it was widely assumed that all slaves would be African in origin, and that Black people normally would be slaves.[75]

In the early decades of British involvement in North America, free English wage earners worked alongside European indentured servants, Native people who were paid or coerced, and slaves who were brought from Africa. The people who funded colonies searched for ways to make their investments pay; in the Chesapeake and Carolina they eventually hit upon staple crops (tobacco, rice, and indigo) that they could grow in large quantities for sale in Europe. These crops required gangs of relatively unskilled workers throughout most of the year, so a large, dependable workforce was essential.

Gradually over the second half of the seventeenth century, as the tobacco economy expanded, slavery became the labor system of choice, and Africans became the slaves of choice. This was not a systematic policy decision, but rather the result of countless individual decisions made by employers at the local level. The demand for labor was so great as the economy expanded rapidly, that free wage laborers could demand a premium and could not be counted on to stay in one place. European indentured servants were not much better. They found it easy to run away from their masters and sell their labor with no questions asked, or to squat on land in the borderlands between European territory and Indian territory. And especially after Bacon's Rebellion, free Whites spelled trouble in the minds of Virginia's leaders. So an element of compulsion came to seem essential. The economic success of slavery throughout Latin America and the Caribbean offered employers an attractive alternate model.

Some Europeans had scruples about enslaving other Christians; enslavement of Turks and other non-Christians captured in war had long been viewed as acceptable in Europe, although it was not practiced on a large scale. The British tried enslaving Native Americans, and for a time there was a brisk trade in Indian slaves, with some tribes like the Creeks and Yamasee growing strong by attacking and selling their neighbors. But Native peoples were at home in North America and could run away easily enough. Moreover, close contact with Europeans caused Indian slaves to die off from European diseases at rates that some employers found unaffordable. Finally, British colonists feared Indian tribes would retaliate with raids against European towns and farms. Tens of thousands of Indians were enslaved, but most of them were transshipped to British colonies in the Caribbean where they had fewer deficiencies as slaves. Deportation was a means of genocide, as those Indians quickly were worked to death in the islands.[76]

In all these regards, Africans made better slaves for the British colonies in North America. Except for a very few from European-colonized areas like Angola, they were "heathen"—that is, non-Christians. As natives of the Old World, they had some immunities to European diseases such as smallpox and cholera that killed Indians in large numbers. As natives of the tropics, they could bear the climate of the Carolina Low Country better than Europeans, and some West Africans had experience with gang labor. They looked very different from Europeans, so they could not run away and easily blend into the European-descended population. If they ran to the frontier, then they would stand out among the Native population. They could not call on Native tribes to make war on their behalf.

These were all parts of the calculus, but what tipped the balance decisively in favor of African slavery was the fact that English people felt less guilty enslaving

Africans than they did enslaving other peoples. They were not Christian brothers and sisters. Long before English people first met Africans, the former group associated the color black with evil, ugliness, sin, and duplicity, just as they associated the color white with beauty, righteousness, purity, honesty, and godliness. Many English people believed that God in the Old Testament had placed a curse on Ham, one of the sons of Noah. People from south of the Sahara had been identified as Hamitic peoples, and in this era many Whites came to believe that slavery was the natural result of God's ancient curse. Finally, English people associated Africans with the animal world. They were frankly amazed by the animals that they found in Africa, especially the great apes. They seem not to have been able to distinguish completely between African apes and African people, and they entertained themselves with lurid descriptions of supposed physical and temperamental similarities between the two, even with tales of interspecies mating. So where English people saw Indians as savage human beings, they saw Africans as beasts.

Of course, not every African in America was a slave. In the early decades, quite a number seem to have achieved freedom after a period of bondage, not unlike White indentured servants. There were always some free people of African descent, and there was a larger amount of social mixing between Black and White free workers on terms of rough social equality in the colonial era than at any time until the last third of the twentieth century.[77]

Virginia laws began to recognize permanent, inherited slave status for African immigrant workers by the 1660s. The decision was a racial one, not mitigated by religion or any other factor. Laws explicitly indicated that conversion to Christianity was not sufficient to alter slave status. By 1705, the identification of Africanity and slavery was complete. Robert Beverley visited Virginia that year and described the situation:

> Their Servants they distinguish by the Names of Slaves for Life, and Servants for a time.
>
> Slaves are the Negroes, and their Posterity, following the Condition of the Mother, according to the Maxim, *partus sequitur ventrem*. They are call'd Slaves, in Respect of the Time of their Servitude, because it is for Life. Servants, are those which serve only for a few Years. ... The Male-Servants, and Slaves of both Sexes, are imployed together in tilling and manuring the Ground, in sowing and planting Tobacco. ... Sufficient Distinction is also made between the Female-Servants, and Slaves; for a white Woman is rarely or never put to work in the Ground ... Whereas on the other hand, it is a common thing to work a Woman Slave out of Doors.[78]

By the dawn of the eighteenth century, then, the idea was firmly in place that Africans were slaves, slaves were Africans, and European-descended people were something other than either.

Variations on a Theme

The situation for African slaves was not the same everywhere in British North America. African-descended people lived in all the colonies, but their numbers were very small in the northern colonies. In 1770, 14,892 slaves lived in New England, between New Hampshire and Connecticut. Never more than 2 or 3 percent of the total population of that region, African Americans were mainly sailors, longshoremen, and household servants. More African Americans were free than slave in New England. There were larger numbers of Blacks in the middle colonies. In 1770, New York, New Jersey, and Pennsylvania were home to 32,843 slaves. African Americans, slave and free, lived particularly around the cities of New York and Philadelphia, where they worked the docks and as industrial laborers. There was a higher percentage of slaves in those places than there was further north: for example, in Philadelphia in 1775, only 14 percent of the Black population was free and the rest were slaves. Thus, slavery was primarily an urban phenomenon in the northern colonies, African Americans lived mainly in cities there, and the numbers of Black people, slave and free, were relatively small.[79]

The southern colonies had urban Africans, too, but far more of them lived in rural areas. Their numbers were vastly larger in those colonies, and an even higher percentage of them were slaves than in the north. In 1770, 322,854 slaves lived in the Chesapeake, and less than 5 percent of African-descended people in that region were free. African-derived slaves amounted to more than 40 percent of the population of Virginia, and two-fifths of the total slave population of the colonies lived in Virginia. The dominant crop in Virginia was tobacco. A tobacco plantation was usually not the huge affair one imagines from movies, but rather consisted of several parts, or quarters, scattered amid other people's farms. Slaves typically lived in small work groups and worked from dawn to dusk. They were bought in small lots from slave ships that traveled the region's navigable rivers deep into the interior, stopping at each plantation to sell a few souls. So in Virginia the various African ethnicities were mixed together quite early. Slavery dominated the Virginia economy, politics, and social life thoroughly.[80]

Contrast that pattern to the one found in the South Carolina low country. South Carolina got started on slavery later than the Chesapeake, but quickly caught up in percentage terms. By 1770, 92,178 slaves lived in South Carolina and Georgia. Rice was the staple crop, and the low country along the coast was covered with large plantations, each with many slaves. The low country, in fact, had a Black majority. There was more urban slavery in South Carolina because there was more urb: Charleston was the sole port, and slave trading went through that city. Slaves in South Carolina tended to be sold in larger lots, which meant that people from a particular African language or cultural group had a greater chance of living together and maintaining culture and identity from the Old World.

Despite such variations in the numbers of Africans in the population in various places, the percentages who were slaves, and the pattern of slavery, it is important to remember that all Americans were complicit in slavery. Slavery was legally established in all the colonies. The ship captains of Boston, Salem, and Providence made their fortunes in the slave trade. The docks and industries of New York and Philadelphia depended on slave labor, as much as did the plantations of Virginia and South Carolina. It is likewise important to remember that Indians as well as Africans were slaves.

From Igbo and Bambara to Negro

A remarkable transformation took place in America before the end of the eighteenth century. Migrants who had come to the colonies as members of a variety of West and

Table 2.6 Origins of African Migrants to North America, by Region in America 1700–1800 and Percent

African Region of Origin	Chesapeake	South Carolina	Louisiana
Mozambique	4	0	2
West Central Africa (Congo, Angola)	16	40	25
Bight of Biafra	38	7	8
Bight of Benin	0	3	25
Gold Coast	16	9	2
Upper Guinea	11	18	6
Senegambia	15	23	32

Source: Helen Hornbeck Tanner, *The Settling of North America* (New York: Macmillan, 1995), 50.

West Central African ethnic groups found themselves treated, not as Igbo or Hausa or Fon, but as Black and slave. By the time their grandchildren came of age, they had largely ceased to identify in terms of various African ethnicities, and they had become simply Negroes.[81]

The sources of African migration to North America began in the Senegambia region (surrounding Cape Verde), and as time went on, extended down the coast through Upper Guinea, Sierra Leone, the Gold Coast, the Bight of Benin, the Bight of Biafra, and on to Congo, Angola, and eventually Madagascar. People in West and West Central Africa usually reckoned their identities according to family and lineage, village and town. Some seem to have had senses of themselves as belonging to larger ethnic identities, and certainly they marked one another with broader ethnic labels, which were often associated with linguistic differences. The list of all such groups would be very long; among them would be Fon, Asante, Mandinka, Oyo, Fula, Ewe, Yoruba, Ife, Mande, Kong, Nok, Ukwu, Akan, Fante, Bambara, Igbo, Hausa, Ibibio, Ngwa, Efik, Twi, Baule, Ga, Kissi, Kono, Wolof, Coromanti, Temne, Aja, and many more. Precise percentages for these various ethnic groups are not available, but we do know approximately how many African migrants to North America came from which parts of Africa (Table 2.6).

People from the Senegambia region contributed significant percentages of the African population of all three major slave zones in what would become the United States. They, and people from Upper Guinea, were preferred by South Carolina slavers because they brought knowledge of rice cultivation. West Central Africa contributed a large percentage of Carolina and Louisiana slaves. Igbo and other peoples imported from the Bight of Biafra dominated Virginia's slave population.

The transformation from an African ethnic identity to an American Negro identity began even before the slaves took ship. People began their journey into slavery along with others captured in their own home areas. If they came from near the coast, then they might remain with ethnic compatriots and be shipped together. But peoples like the Bambara and Mandinka, who came from the upper reaches of the Niger River, and the Hausa, who hailed from what is now northern Nigeria, were forced to walk hundreds of miles to the sea. On the way they were mixed with people from other ethnic groups. Upon arrival at the shore, they entered the barracoon stage, when they were placed in forts or cages awaiting sale and shipment. There, they were part of a mixed multitude whose only common characteristic was that they were Black Africans. They were placed in ships, guarded and abused by White people. Michael Gomez wrote about this process:

> Africans of varying ethnicities, who had never considered their blackness a source of reflection let alone a principle of unity, became cognizant of this feature perhaps for the first time in their lives. ... A second factor also encouraged a sense of community among those remaining at journey's end: their very survival. They had survived the death angel's Passover only to enter a whiteman-made Hades on Earth. They had witnessed starvation and suicide. They had endured the dizzying days and the sickening nights and somehow remained. They were those who fought and scratched and clawed their way through, yet comforting one another in their collective despair. They had shared what little they had with those who were on the verge. They had made the necessary sacrifices and had extended themselves in so many charitable acts, large and small, none of which has been preserved for posterity. But that they occurred is beyond doubt, for how else could they have emerged from the belly of the great fish?[82]

The cross-ethnic bonds that united shipmates formed the beginnings of a panethnic African identity that would grow in America.

In South Carolina, ships' cargoes were unloaded wholesale and plantations were large, so some ethnic contingents remained intact. But in Virginia, shipmates were distributed across the countryside. New slaves in both places were seasoned—that is, trained in the ways of being a slave—by those who had undergone the transformation earlier. Among the things they had to do was learn to communicate. Some Africans clung stubbornly to their native languages, but that was possible only if there were others around with whom they could speak and be understood. Quickly slaves developed pidgin languages to communicate among themselves. Whites heard these as merely English poorly performed, but in fact they seem to have been independent inventions, with grammar and syntax drawn from various West African tongues, but using substantial numbers of words borrowed from English. Using this common language—to respond to the master class, to be sure, but mainly among enslaved Africans of various ethnic backgrounds—hastened the identification between all peoples of African ancestry.[83]

Religion played a critical role in bringing peoples together in the migrant generation and after. Some groups, such as the Bambara who came through the Senegambia and the Hausa who came via the Bight of Biafra, were mostly Muslims. Islam is a universalist religion that recognizes brother- and sisterhood among all adherents. It was easy for Muslim slaves to see themselves as having a common identity with other Muslims who came from different ethnicities and regions. Later, during the first Great Awakening of the mid-1700s, and especially during the Second Great Awakening that swept America from the 1790s through the 1830s, Christianity became a common denominator that bound African-born and African-descended slaves of many ethnic origins in a sense of community and identity. It is significant that by the time of the Second Great Awakening (which affected Whites as well as Blacks) most European-descended Americans had accepted the idea that they could share their religion with slaves without sharing full social brother- and sisterhood with them. So active acceptance of Christianity did help create common identity among various sorts of African Americans, even while it did not bridge the racial gap.[84]

Africans took spouses and had children in America. Some could find partners who shared their ancestral ethnicity, but many could not. Groups who came from near the African coast were imported in nearly equal numbers of men and women, but for inland groups like the Bambara, slavers imported only half as many women as men.[85] That meant mixing and culture change at the point of making families. The advent of children carried the process further. They surely knew their ancestry, heard stories of Africa, and saw more African newcomers around them as they grew up. But like the second generation of any immigrant group, they came to have as much identification with the place where they grew up as with the places from which their parents had come. Some spoke African languages and others spoke mainly the pidgin patois of the quarters. Some worshipped in African ways—this seems to have been the longest-lasting feature of African culture in Black America. But gradually, over the course of the first two centuries of African history in America, and over the first two or three generations in any family, identity shifted.

These people were not becoming undifferentiated Americans. The assimilation theorists are just wrong in casting the issues that way. These migrants did not cease to be foreigners and become raceless Americans. Instead, they entered into a panethnic African or Black racial formation. They were no longer Fon or Fula or Ife; they were Negroes. The varieties among the Black populations of different parts of the country—differences in their ethnic and linguistic backgrounds as well as differences in demography, degrees of freedom, and patterns of slavery—made for very different groups of African Americans early on, as different as the different varieties of Europeans or Native Americans by the time of the American Revolution.[86] But what is striking about the experience of Africans is the degree to which they had, by that point in their history, accepted the common identity that had been thrust upon them.

African American identity was bolstered in the slavery centuries primarily by a common interest. That is how most ethnic groups begin to form. In this case, the common interest was to survive slavery, humiliation, degradation, and desperation, and to carve out for themselves a place in America. Culture was a mixed bag. Some people continued to speak African languages, at least on their own, when they were out of hearing of the master class. Such languages bolstered their individual ethnicities, but did not foster a common African identity as effectively. But most also spoke a pidgin amalgam of several African languages and English. The same was true of religion. Islam and various localized West African religious practices continued. But some of these were transmuted into hybrid, West-African-derived practices such as hoodoo. Meanwhile other slaves adopted Christianity and adapted it to African cosmologies. In these senses—language and religion—a common African American culture had begun to form. As to institutions, again the analysis is mixed. Slavery was a powerful institution that almost all African Americans shared in common at the beginning of the American Revolution, and that affected those who were nominally free, too. But the slave regime had kept other institutions, even the family, from being fully formed and stable enhancements of community and identity.

Merging Peoples, Blending Cultures

The End of an Age

Ethnic dynamics began to change drastically in the British colonies in North America after the middle of the eighteenth century. The in-migration of thousands of African slaves every year continued. There was a brief, dramatic increase of European migrants as well, both English people and a host of others.[87] But the situation for Native peoples changed abruptly when the French lost the Seven Years' War in 1763. Suddenly the French were removed from the continent and the British claimed everything east of the Mississippi. That left Native peoples, especially the Iroquois Confederation, unable any longer to play off one European power against the other. Iroquois power declined rapidly, Europeans flooded onto Indian lands, and some Native peoples began to look to move westward, away from the encroaching British. The English government tried to avoid conflict between its subjects and Native peoples by declaring the Appalachian crest a line of demarcation between European and Indian, but Europeans swarmed westward in defiance of the prohibition.[88]

At the end of that war, British soldiers may have engaged in germ warfare against Native people. The Ottawa leader Pontiac led resistance to the British after the French had surrendered. Lord Jeffrey Amherst, after whom the Massachusetts city is named, commanded the army that was tasked with putting Pontiac down. Lord Amherst wrote his subordinate, Col. Henry Bouquet, approving a plan to put smallpox-infected blankets where the Ottawa were likely to find them, for the purpose of introducing the disease into their population. Amherst wrote, "Could it not be contrived to send the Small Pox among those disaffected tribes of Indians? We must on this occassion use every stratagem in our power to reduce them. ... [We must] try Every other method that can serve to Extirpate this Execrable Race." It is unclear whether Bouquet's men did in fact pass out infected blankets, although an epidemic devastated the Ottawas a couple of months thereafter.[89]

The era of the Revolution saw the last large surge of slave immigration. One hundred thousand Africans migrated under compulsion to British North America in the period 1740 to 1760; 86,000 between 1760 and 1780; and 92,000 more between 1780 and 1810. Then the trade declined to an estimated 10,000 per decade through the 1850s. That number has to be estimated because no one kept records—because the importation of slaves was formally outlawed in 1808, though enforcement was lax. The U.S. Constitution enshrined slavery as part of the fundamental law of the republic (see Chapter 3). Among its provisions was Article II, Section 9, Paragraph 1, which read: "The migration or importation of such persons as any of the States now existing shall think proper to admit, shall not be prohibited by the Congress prior to the year one thousand eight hundred and eight, but a tax or duty may be imposed on such importation, not exceeding ten dollars for each person." But sentiment built against the slave trade, based in England and in those parts of the United States that had few slaves. In 1807, Congress passed a measure banning importing slaves into the country; the ban took effect on January 1, 1808. Smugglers continued to bring in African slaves in smaller numbers from that time on until the Civil War, but the era of massive African migration to the United States had ended.[90]

Identity: Black, White, and Red

By the era of the Revolution, America's first racial formation was complete. Scores, if not hundreds, of separate African peoples had blended into one panethnic group. Those who were new to the colonies (later states) may have carried the name Mandinka or Yoruba or Fulani in their own minds, but in the eyes of others—Blacks as well as Whites and Indians—they were just Africans or Negroes. The children and grandchildren of earlier generations of slave migrants no longer identified with the individual peoples of their ancestors, but instead saw themselves and were seen by others simply as Negroes.

The various European peoples had also begun the move toward becoming one panethnic people, the White race. Winthrop Jordan and Theodore Allen, working with very different materials and under very different assumptions, find that English, Scots, Irish, Germans, and others came together and began calling themselves White people in the Chesapeake region by the 1660s, largely in response to their construction of various African peoples as Black. Allen, at least, believes that the transformation was complete by the early eighteenth century.[91] Jon Butler puts the transformation somewhat later, and shifts the point of contrast that drove self-definition from Africans to Europeans. He describes a long process lasting from 1680 to 1760, during which many varieties of European immigrants and their descendants came, in their own minds and in the minds of others, to be Americans. Even as he draws that distinction, however, he is clear that he is talking about White Americans, and that Blacks and Indians were excluded.[92] David Roediger and Noel Ignatiev would place the decisive period in the formation of the White race later, in the period 1820 to 1850, when the United States was undergoing an industrial revolution and the White working class was affirming its White racial status (and eliding its class consciousness) by setting itself off from the Black working class, slave and free.[93] Jordan, Butler, and Allen would seem closer to the truth. It is worth noting (and we will take this matter up in detail in Chapter 3) that the 1790 Naturalization Act specified that only "free, White persons" could become U.S. citizens through naturalization—and from that date forward, all the peoples who are now thought of as White were accorded that privilege, even as Asians, Africans, and Native Americans were denied it.

By the time of the Revolution if not well before, most White Americans had lost any sense of the differences among Rappahanock, Creek, and Narragansett; they were all just Indians in the White mind. It took several generations longer, however, for Native peoples to begin to think of themselves and to act as one, so strong were tribal identities. White people like Lord Amherst may have seen them as all one "Execrable Race," but Indians saw themselves as myriad distinct peoples for years to come.

Assimilation

Last, we come to the issue of assimilation. The assimilation of peoples, one into another, is one of the main themes of this first period of American immigration history. From the beginning of intercontinental contact in America, English people were assimilating and became Indians—think of the Roanoke colony and of many individual "White Indians." At the same time Indians like Thomas Rolfe, Pocahontas's son, assimilated to become English people in the seventeenth century, and White people in the eighteenth. The other major development on this theme was the legion of other, non-English European Americans who, together with English immigrants and their descendants, by the mid-eighteenth century were assimilating to become White people.

English people were immigrants. They underwent the same processes of culture and identity change over generations as did immigrants from other places. They ceased to be English folk or Yorkshiremen and became, in their own minds, Americans (and White people). Africans, too, were immigrants, for all that they were compelled to come. They, too, underwent immigrant-style culture and identity change. They, however, became not Americans but Negroes. Native Americans were not immigrants, at least not in the period under discussion here. But they are irrevocably part of the immigrant story, if only because they were forced out so that White immigrants could take their places. In the heat of contact, Indians, too, underwent culture and identity change, though of a quite different sort than that experienced by immigrant peoples.

Chapter 3

An Anglo-American Republic? Racial Citizenship, 1760–1860

This government of ours is founded on the white basis. It was made by the white man, for the benefit of the white man, to be administered by white men. … a negro, an Indian, or any other man of inferior race [should be permitted only those] rights, privileges and immunities which he is capable of exercising consistent with the safety of society … the signers of the Declaration … had no reference either to the negro, the savage Indians, the Fejee, the Malay, or any other inferior and degraded race, when they spoke of the equality of men.

Stephen Douglas[1]

A contest took place between the middle of the eighteenth century and the middle of the nineteenth over who would be recognized as an American. The decision was largely racial in nature. Political power—hence the authority to determine citizenship—rested squarely in the hands of adult, White, free, male owners of property. White Americans fought their revolution claiming freedom for themselves from British tyranny. During the era of that war and the founding of the republic, some thought to extend liberty to African-descended people and full citizenship to White women. This era saw the loosening of the slave regime in parts of the new United States during that time, the creation of a small but significant class of Blacks who were not legal slaves, and the gradual end to African slave immigration. And it witnessed the hardening of the line between Whites and others via the invention of the one drop rule and the racial character of the first immigrant naturalization act in 1790.

European immigration declined from prewar levels during the first decades of this fragile new country. But by the beginning of the middle third of the nineteenth century, many thousands of European migrants were arriving each year. They gathered together to form the second great American panethnicity: the White race. That race was made up of all the varieties of European-descended people who lived in the United States, although not all of them equally. The White race was defined, not only against African-descended Americans, but also against Asians and Indians. In a sad twist of race-making, the White Americans chose to anchor their new common identity partly by appropriating the symbols and ersatz versions of identities of the Native peoples they were removing and killing. In another twist, they invented the language of the melting pot to characterize ethnic social processes in America, even as they were insisting, in practical fact, on Anglo-conformity.

This chapter overlaps in time somewhat with the ones that precede and follow it, but here the angle of analysis is different. Previously we attended to the beginnings of the European colonial enterprise in North America. Now we turn to focus on the membership question—the Europeans who came, the relations among them, and how they defined who would be an American. Chapter 4 returns to the subject of European American colonialism and carries it farther in time and space, as White Americans marched across the continent and kept making racial hierarchy in the very act of colonizing.

As a caution against thinking that the story of European-descended people is the whole story of America in this period, consider Figure 3.1. It represents the population in 1800 of the territory that would before long be encompassed by the United States. Note, by comparison with earlier, similar charts, that European-instigated warfare and disease had by this time taken their toll: Native peoples had been reduced to one-fifth of the population and Europeans now—for the first time—constituted a solid majority.

Slavery and Antislavery in the Era of the American Revolution

Thinking about Freedom, and Not

In the era of the American Revolution, many European-descended Americans saw themselves as engaged in a political project to free themselves from tyranny at the hands of the British crown and government. Some even spoke of themselves as slaves to the British. It did not escape their notice that, even while they cast their movement for political independence in such extreme rhetorical terms, many among them were holding their fellow human beings in a slavery that was far more tangible. The revolutionary era constituted a brief period of time when the idea of liberty became modestly contagious.[2]

Slavery meant moral agony for some. Thomas Jefferson, for example, genuinely abhorred slavery, though perhaps more for what he regarded as the moral degradation it thrust on the slave owner than for the suffering it thrust on the slave. Even so he could not bring himself to emancipate more than a few of his own slaves (and those probably his own kin). He did feel guilty for enslaving hundreds of his fellow humans. He envisioned and wrote about, though he did not work to implement, gradual schemes by which he and other slave owners might be relieved of

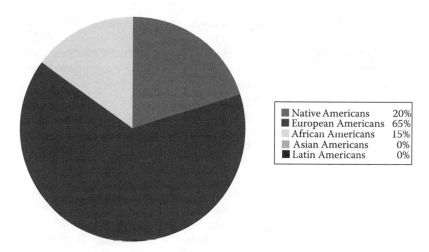

■ Native Americans	20%
■ European Americans	65%
African Americans	15%
■ Asian Americans	0%
■ Latin Americans	0%

Figure 3.1 Population by race in 1800 of the territory that would become the United States—6.7 million people.

the moral burden of slave owning without having to sacrifice their wealth or social position and without being troubled by the company of large numbers of free Black fellow citizens. But in the end he retreated from emancipation via the comforting twin rationalizations that the country was not ready for free Black people and that African-descended slaves were not yet ready—might never be ready—to be free members of American society.

Patrick Henry, like Jefferson a Virginian, an American patriot, and the owner of many slaves, was in Jefferson's words "The idol of the country beyond any man who ever lived." He was the oratorical firebrand of the Revolution, most famous for his passionate pro-war speech to the Second Virginia Convention in Richmond on March 23, 1775. That speech included these words: "Is life so dear, or peace so sweet, as to be purchased at the price of chains and slavery? ... I know not what other course others may take. But as for me—give me liberty, or give me death!" Yet two years earlier, Henry had written to his Quaker friend Robert Pleasants, thanking Pleasants for a book by Anthony Benezet that called for an end to the slave trade. Henry called slavery "totally repugnant" and spent several paragraphs blaming slavery's existence on encouragement from "the professors of Christianity." And then he weaseled:

> Would anyone believe I am a master of slaves of my own purchase! I am drawn along by the general *inconvenience* of living here without them. I will not, I cannot justify it. ... I believe a time will come when an opportunity will be offered to abolish this lamentable evil. Everything we can do is to improve it, if it happens in our day. If not, let us transmit to our descendants, together with our slaves, a pity for their unhappy lot and an abhorrence of slavery.

Patrick Henry would fight British tyranny to the death, but domestic tyranny was too convenient for him to forego.[3]

Some Whites were more willing to act. In the 1770s, led by Quakers like Benezet and John Woolman, some White Americans began to agitate for an end to the slave trade, for private manumissions by individual slaveholders, and for the abolition of slavery itself. They launched an intensive campaign of pamphleteering, personal persuasion, and political pressure. Their efforts paid off rather well in the next two decades. The Continental Congress temporarily suspended slave imports in 1774. Many masters North and South—and notably in Virginia, the largest slave state—were persuaded to free their human property during the Revolution and after. Former President George Washington was one, by his will of 1799. The Vermont constitution in 1777 outlawed slavery in that new state. In 1780 the Pennsylvania legislature enacted a gradual abolition law that freed all children born to slaves after its passage, although it left their parents in bondage for life. The following year a Massachusetts court declared that slavery was inconsistent with the rights granted to all humans in that Commonwealth's 1780 constitution. For official purposes, slavery immediately ceased to exist in the Bay State. Three years later Connecticut also enacted gradual emancipation. By contrast, New York did not come to begin gradual emancipation until 1799, and New Jersey took five years more to reach the same conclusion. And states south of Mason's and Dixon's Line, where nine-tenths of all African American people lived, did not end slavery at all.

The crucial difference was the degree to which each locality was economically dependent on slavery—Henry's inconvenience factor. There were only 5000 African Americans in Massachusetts, less than 2 percent of the population; abolishing slavery there was a moral choice, but one without much economic impact. In New York, 20,000 slaves constituted 8 percent of the population and a vital element in the harbor workforce; there, gradual manumission was a more convenient public policy choice than sudden emancipation. Farther south, in Virginia and South Carolina, slaves made up more than 40 percent of the population, they numbered in the hundreds of thousands, and the economic stakes were much higher.[4] Virginia did make it easier for a time for individual masters to manumit their slaves and for slaves to buy their freedom. But then after Gabriel's Rebellion in 1800 they cracked down hard on the liberties of so-called "free Blacks"—they were not formally slaves, but they were forbidden to own firearms or testify in court—and no more free people of color would be allowed to enter the state. In South Carolina, the master class was so traumatized by news of the bloody slave revolt in Haiti in 1793, which overturned the French slave regime there, that they kept the lid nailed down tight. Calling antislavery treason and complaining that free Black people made unfair competition for White working people, they expelled the small number of legally free African Americans who lived in the state and squelched all dissent against the slave regime.

Whites, however, were not the only actors. Gordon Wood reminds us that "By the time of the battle of Yorktown, a quarter of Washington's Continental Army was made up of blacks."[5] Most had begun the war as slaves and were slaves still in the eyes of the law. But many had a sense they were fighting for their own personal freedom as well as that of their country. One named Saul petitioned for his freedom after the war:

To the Honorable, the Speaker, and Members of the General Assembly.

The petition of Saul, a black slave, the property of Geo. Kelly, Esqr. Humbly sheweth.—In the beginning of the late War, that gave America Independence, Your Petitioner Shouldered his Musket and repaired to the American Standard. Regardless of the Invitation, trumpeted forth by British Proclamations, for slaves to Emancipate themselves, by becoming the Assassins of their owners, Your Petitioner avoided the rock, that too many of his colour were Shipwrecked on. [a large number of slaves did achieve freedom by running away to serve in the British army]—He was taught to know that War was levied upon America, not for the Emancipation of Blacks, but for the Subjugation of Whites, and he thought the number of Bond-men ought not to be augmented; Under those impressions, your Petitioner did actually Campaign in both Armies,—in the American Army, as a Soldier,—In the British Army as a Spy.... In this double Profession, Your Petitioner flatters himself that he rendered essential service to his Country, and should have rendered much more had he not, in the Campaign, of 1781, been betrayed by a Negro whom the British had employed upon the same business. ... Your Petitioner was at the time, In Portsmouth, a British Garrison, collecting Information for Colonel Josiah Parker, and his heels saved his neck. ...

Your Petitioner. ... [is] Hoping the Legislatures of a Republick will take his case in consideration and not suffer him any longer to remain a transferable property.

The Virginia General Assembly was persuaded, and on November 13, 1792, Saul was granted his freedom, with the state paying his master for the loss of his property.[6]

The framers of the Declaration of Independence considered calling for an end to slave immigration in that document. Most of us know the noble words about unalienable human rights that begin the Declaration, but the larger part of the document is a list of grievances against British King George III. In an early draft, one clause read:

He has waged cruel war against human nature itself, violating its most sacred rights of life and liberty in the person of a distant people who never offended him; captivating and carrying them into slavery in another hemisphere, or to incur miserable death in their transportation thither. This piratical warfare, the opprobrium of infidel powers, is the warfare of the Christian king of Great Britain. Determined to keep open a market where men should be bought and sold, he has prostituted his negative for suppressing every legislative attempt to prohibit or restrain this execrable commerce.[7]

That clause was excised, apparently on the theory that it would not do to alienate the slave-owning class, many of whose members were leaders of the rebellion—indeed, one of whose members was the Declaration's main author. The matter came up again at the 1787 Constitutional Convention. There, the question was put off for two more decades, to 1808. In that year, the international trade in slaves finally became illegal, the numbers of African immigrants who were imported as slaves each year fell dramatically, and the remaining trade went underground.

Three-Fifths of a Person

The U.S. Constitution does not contain the word "slave" or "slavery," yet it enshrined African American slavery at the core of American government and self-identity.

Article 1, Section 2, Paragraph 3 reads: "Representatives and direct taxes shall be apportioned among the several States which may be included within this Union, according to their respective numbers, which shall be determined by adding to the whole number of free persons, including those bound to service for a term of years, and excluding Indians not taxed, three fifths of all other persons." Those "other persons" were African American slaves. Indians were outside the matter entirely—not taxed, not citizens, not able to vote, not represented, not people at all in the eyes of the founding document of the United States.

Black slaves, though not named, were on the agenda in the Constitution. The northern states wanted the new government to count slaves for purposes of possible future federal taxation, but not for purposes of representation. If their view had prevailed, then Virginia, South Carolina, and other states with large numbers of slaves would have had fewer representatives in Congress and the Electoral College, and they would have paid more for the government if Congress ever decided on a per capita tax levied directly on the population (it did not ever do so).[8] The White slave owners who controlled Southern politics wanted the opposite: they did not want slaves counted for tax purposes, but did want them counted for purposes of representation, even though the slaves would not themselves have any say in government.

James Madison of Virginia, himself the lifelong owner of many slaves, was one of the politicians who brokered a compromise: each slave would be counted as three-fifths of a person for purposes of both representation and taxation (remember, the taxation never came to pass). So Southern Whites gained representation in Congress and the Electoral College out of proportion to their numbers; three-fifths of the number of slaves were added to their population for those purposes. It was thus no accident that four of the first five presidents hailed from Virginia. The compromise embodied ambivalent, some would say self-serving, thinking on the part of European Americans about the African-descended people among them who were their fellow countrymen but not their fellow citizens. Madison explained that thinking in *The Federalist Papers*, propaganda sheets designed to drum up support for the Constitution:

> We subscribe to the doctrine ... that representation relates more immediately to persons, and taxation more immediately to property, and we join in the application of this distinction to the case of our slaves. But we must deny the fact that slaves are considered merely as property, and in no respect whatever as persons. The true state of the case is that they partake of both these qualities: being considered by our laws, in some respects, as persons, and in other respects as property. In being compelled to labor, not for himself, but for a master; in being vendible by one master to another master; and in being subject at all times to be restrained in his liberty and chastised in his body, by the capricious will of another—the slave may appear to be degraded from the human rank, and classed with those irrational animals which fall under the legal denomination of property. In being protected [sic], on the other hand, in his life and in his limbs, against the violence of all others, even the master of his labor and his liberty; and in being punishable himself for all violence committed against others—the slave is no less evidently regarded by the law as a member of the society, not as a part of the irrational creation; as a moral person, not as a mere article of property. The federal Constitution, therefore, ... views them in the mixed character of persons and of property.[9]

It is worth noting that Madison regarded himself as an opponent of slavery through-out his adult life, although he never manumitted his own slaves.[10]

Table 3.1 shows the effects of the three-fifths clause on representation in Congress and the Electoral College. Even in the northern states, formal and informal strictures kept voting mainly in the hands of Whites.[11] The three-fifths clause gave extra representation in Congress and in presidential elections to Southern Whites. For example, Virginia had a White population of 442,000, Pennsylvania had 424,000, and New York had 414,000—all of a similar order of magnitude. But with three-fifths of the slave population added in, that White Virginia population had an effective representation of 671,000, vastly more than the 433,000 for Pennsylvania and 432,000 for New York. Virginians had, effectively, one and a half times as much representation per White capita as citizens of the northern states.

Partly-Free People of Color and One Drop of Blood

This is not a book about slavery or race per se, but rather mainly about immigration, so from this point forward I will address the situation of African Americans and other peoples already resident in the United States for several generations only when there is a major shift in the status of a significant group among them. Such was the case in the early decades of the nineteenth century for those African-descended people who had achieved legal freedom. I say "legal freedom" following the logic of Stephen Small: "It is misleading to call people of color who were not enslaved 'free,' as if they had the same civil and social rights as White people. Their rights were legally and socially curtailed at all times. I use the term 'legally free' in preference to 'free' to mark their difference in legal status from those who were enslaved and their difference in social status from Whites, who enjoyed all the rights and privileges of freedom."[12]

Ira Berlin refers to such legally free African Americans as "slaves without masters." Certainly that was an accurate description for the slave states of the South. In that region, those African Americans who were legally not slaves nonetheless had few of the rights of European Americans. In most states they could not vote, serve on juries, testify in court against White people, or keep firearms. They were subject to warrantless searches, assaults, and detentions by White law officers and often by any Whites who felt like harassing them. The 1819 Virginia Black code declared that every legally free Black person had to register with the county authorities each year, much like sex offenders at the dawn of the twenty-first century. Legally free Blacks were forbidden to meet with slaves at night. Legally free Blacks were forbidden to administer medicine on pain of death (apparently Whites feared poisoning at Black hands). Legally free African Americans had to pay a special tax each year. If a legally free person of African descent were convicted of a crime, after being punished he or she was liable for deportation. And so on and on.[13] All such strictures were intended to bind those Blacks who were legally free into something not far different from slavery, so that the White population could control them.

Things were not a great deal better in the North and West. Legal freedom did not mean social equality there either. Whites in the North, as much as in the South, believed African-descended people to be inferior and unassimilable into an American society defined and controlled by European-descended people. At various times between the Revolution and the Civil War, New Jersey, Connecticut, Rhode Island,

Table 3.1 Impact of the Three-Fifths Clause on Congressional Representation 1790 Census

States with over 200,000 Population	Whites	Free Blacks	Total Free Persons	Slaves	Total Actual Population	Effective Total for Representation	Ratio Effective Total to Whites
New Hampshire	141,097	630	141,727	157	141,884	141,821	1.01
Massachusetts	373,324	5,463	378,787	0	378,787	378,787	1.01
Connecticut	232,374	2,271	234,645	2,648	237,293	236,234	1.02
New York	414,142	4,682	418,824	21,193	440,017	431,540	1.06
Pennsylvania	424,099	6,531	430,630	3,707	434,337	432,854	1.02
Maryland	208,649	8,043	216,692	103,036	319,728	278,514	1.33
Virginia	442,117	12,866	494,983	292,627	747,610	670,559	1.52
North Carolina	288,204	5,041	293,245	100,783	394,028	353,715	1.23
South Carolina	140,178	1,801	141,979	107,094	249,073	206,235	1.47

Source: US Bureau of the Census, *Negro Population in the United States, 1790–1915* (Washington, DC: Government Printing Office, 1918), 45, 57.

and Pennsylvania disenfranchised Black voters. Ohio passed its own Black code in 1804, which required each African American who entered the state to provide evidence he or she was legally free and to post a bond of $500, although the latter provision was not always enforced. It also forbade Black people to serve on juries, to testify against Whites, or to join the militia. In 1829, the White citizens of Cincinnati used such laws to expel between 1100 and 2200 of their Black neighbors from the city. Several other northern or western states and territories considered, and some enacted, bars against African-descended people entering their jurisdictions. Many municipalities created segregated schools and other public facilities. All but a few states outlawed marriages between Blacks and Whites. And the Dred Scott decision and the Fugitive Slave Law meant that even legally free people of African descent might be captured by slave hunters and taken south into formal slavery.[14]

Despite such limitations, legally free Black people outside the South gradually created communities, built institutions, and secured economic places for themselves. Richard Allen became a Christian, preached to his fellow slaves, converted his master, and bought his freedom. When he and other African-descended Philadelphians were turned away by St. George Episcopal Church in 1787, he walked out and began to form his own congregation. By 1816 it was a denomination, the African Methodist Episcopal Church, and Allen was its bishop. Black churches, schools, literary societies, and businesses anchored the largely urban, often economically marginal population of legally free Black people and provided a small but growing middle class that would one day give leadership to post-slavery Black America.[15]

The story of the many stigmas borne by free people of color was inevitably bound up with definitions of who was Black. By the middle of the nineteenth century, the free population of African origins was visibly lighter, on average, than the slave population. In the seventeenth century, interracial social and sexual mixing took place primarily between Black slaves and White indentured servants, out of sight of the master class.[16] By the first third of the nineteenth century, a tighter regime that made race and not class the primary mode for creating and enforcing hierarchy had reduced social mixing among the lower orders. In its place, however, men of the master race had developed the habit of visiting themselves sexually upon slave women. The numbers of people who carried mixed African and European ancestry expanded much more rapidly than either monoracial population. White men of the master class did not only exploit slave women; sometimes they made families with them. In the antebellum period and even after, it was not unusual for a rich White man to keep a White family in a large house on the front of his property while he also maintained an interracial household in a more discreet location. Most people of mixed ancestry remained in slavery, but some slave owners saw fit to emancipate their offspring. Thus most of those African Americans whose families were legally free during the slave era can trace at least some of their ancestry to European Americans. The proportions are quite striking. A free African-descended population that numbered 60,000 in 1790 grew to 488,000 by 1860. In the latter year, only 10 percent of the slave population had mixed ancestry, but 41 percent of the free African Americans who lived in the southern states recognized some White ancestry.[17]

The existence of a substantial group of people with mixed ancestry called into question the racial line that had been drawn between slave and free. The solution was the one drop rule. By the middle of the nineteenth century, the consensus outside a few pockets such as New Orleans and Charleston was that "one drop of Black blood"—one known African-descended ancestor—made one Black. This was an unusual way to handle the issue of multiraciality. Other multiracial societies that had experienced extensive commingling arranged themselves differently. In South Africa there emerged a Coloured caste, partway between Black and White. In Brazil and Jamaica, there was an elaborate hierarchy based on class, color, and ancestry. In all three of those places, as in the United States, Whites who believed they were unmixed stood at the top of the social system. But only in the United States did Whites draw so radical a line as that created by the one drop rule. In the United States, the one drop rule was the key tool for creating not just the Black race but also the White race. It was the essential means by which Whites could draw a sharp line between themselves and slaves. They might mate with African-descended people, but thanks to the one-drop rule, when they did so their multiracial offspring would be Black, and those offspring would most often remain in slavery.[18]

Africans and Indians

The making of mulattoes by European- and African-descended Americans was a mixing of two immigrant stocks. Other mixing also took place, between Europeans and Native peoples, and between Africans and Indians. From Pocahontas on, Native women and men married and mated with European immigrants and their descendants. Her son became an Englishman, as did many other people of mixed ancestry. Just as many became Indians. By the 1830s, about a quarter of the members of the Cherokee and Chickasaw tribes were recognized as having some European ancestry. Osceola, the great Seminole war chief and leader of the resistance against White America, was the son of William Powell, a British trader who lived among the Upper Muskogee Creeks, and Polly Copinger, who was herself of mixed Creek and British ancestry. There was no one drop rule where relationships between Indians and Europeans were concerned. Depending on one's circumstances, one might live one's life on the White side of the line, on the Native side, or perhaps both, and many members of both groups were recognized as mixed. Native ancestry did not disqualify one from membership in the White race, and White ancestry did not prevent one from being an Indian. Indeed, most southeast Indians reckoned lineage through the maternal line, so those like Osceola whose fathers were Europeans were more likely to live as Indians.[19]

Just as Osceola was a Seminole of part-White ancestry, so too there were Indians of part-Black ancestry. In the last quarter of the eighteenth century, the Seminole nation came together out of Creeks, Yamasees, and other Indians who broke off from their tribes and migrated into the northern part of Spanish Florida. Some runaway slaves joined the new Indian nation; some among them formed separate African Seminole communities, and other individuals were integrated directly into the nation. Early on, as Theda Perdue describes it: "The Creeks accepted Africans into their society because traditionally Creeks had no concept of race. Kinship, not physical features, distinguished one Creek individual from another, and the Africans whom Indians incorporated had matrilineal ties to Creek clans through birth or adoption." A White man named Samuel Bend killed a woman of the Cherokee Deer clan in the 1770s. As a replacement he gave the clan an African American slave named Molly. The clan adopted Molly, she took the name Chickaw, married a Cherokee man, and had two sons who enjoyed full, free Cherokee citizenship. In time, White influence led many Indians to take up racial slavery and European ideas about racial hierarchy. The Creek and Cherokee adopted Black codes and kept large African-descended slave populations. Yet these tribes were themselves already mixed multitudes, with ancestry that was Native, European, and also African.[20]

Free White Persons: Defining Membership

One's race determined one's eligibility for citizenship in the United States right from the start. The 1740 British Naturalization Act endorsed the value of immigrants and encouraged their importation, although its authors seem to have contemplated only European immigrants and it limited naturalization to baptized Christians and Jews. The individual colonies, and then the states, made their own citizenship laws, but in general these followed the outlines of the 1740 act. The tenor of America's self-image on immigration and naturalization was enunciated in 1783 by General George Washington in a letter to his fellow soldiers: "The bosom of America is open to receive not only the Opulent and respected Stranger, but the oppressed and persecuted of all Nations and Religions; whom we shall welcome to a participation of all our rights and privileges, if by decency and propriety of conduct they appear to merit the enjoyment." Washington, too, seems to have been thinking only of European immigrants.[21]

One of the first acts of the new government of the United States was to pass "An Act to Establish a Uniform Rule of Naturalization" in 1790:

> Be it enacted by the Senate and the House of Representatives of the United States of America in Congress assembled, That any alien, *being a free white person*, who shall have resided within the limits and under the jurisdiction of the United States for the term of two years, may be admitted to become a citizen thereof, on application to any common court of record, in any one of the states wherein he shall have resided for the term of one year at least, and making proof to the satisfaction of such court, that he is a person of good character, and taking the oath of affirmation prescribed by law, to support the constitution of the United States, which oath or affirmation such court shall administer; and the clerk of such court shall record such application, and the proceedings thereon; and thereupon such person shall be considered as a citizen of the United States. And the children of such persons so naturalized, dwelling within the United States, being under the age of twenty-one years at the time of such naturalization, shall also be considered as citizens of the United States. And the children of citizens of the United States, shall be considered as natural born citizens; Provided, That the right of citizenship shall not descend to persons whose fathers have never been resident in the United States; Provided also, That no person heretofore proscribed by any state, shall be admitted a citizen as aforesaid, except by an act of the legislature in the state in which such person was proscribed.[22]

This act set up several themes that have guided U.S. naturalization law ever since. After a period of residence (later laws specified different durations) a noncitizen could apply to become naturalized. State and local governments would set any more detailed procedures, for a person would become a citizen of a state and of the United

States at the same time. State and local courts would handle the investiture. Minor children of the applicant would become U.S. citizens automatically upon a parent's naturalization. An oath of allegiance to the U.S. constitution would be required. Children of U.S. citizens would be considered natural born citizens and would not have to be naturalized. And naturalization would be restricted to "free white person[s]."[23]

African-descended slaves, as we have seen, were not citizens but property. Legally free Blacks had a kind of attenuated citizenship status. Born in the United States, they might have been treated as citizens, but they nonetheless had their citizenship rights sharply limited by state legislatures and local governments. No African-descended person could become naturalized, because such a person, even if free, was not White. White persons, even if they were serving indentures and thus were not fully free, nonetheless were eligible for naturalization. The line drawn was a racial one. Chancellor James Kent of the New York Court of Errors (that is, appeals) pronounced the noncitizen status of Native Americans in an 1823 ruling: "Though born within our territorial limits, the *Indians* are considered as born under the jurisdiction of their tribes. They are not our subjects, born within the purview of the law, because they are not born in obedience to us. They belong, by birth, to their own tribes, and these tribes are placed under our protection and dependent upon us, but we still recognize them as national communities." That same year the federal courts agreed: Indians were "of that class who are said by jurists not to be citizens, but perpetual inhabitants, with diminutive rights. ... [an] inferior race of people, without the privileges of citizens, and under the perpetual protection and pupilage of the government."[24]

Native Americans were not citizens, but members of "domestic, dependent nations." They were not quite foreign, for their lands and lives could be trampled by the government with relative impunity, but they did not possess the rights guaranteed to U.S. citizens by the Constitution. A few Native individuals—perhaps 3000 before the Civil War—did become U.S. citizens, but not by going through naturalization. In some cases European-American pressures forced tribes to disband. In others, individuals who had mixed Native and White ancestry left their tribes and melted into the mass of White people. In such cases, the courts and public opinion ruled that they had become Whites and, by virtue of their nativity on U.S.-claimed soil, were U.S. citizens. Asians—and there were a few in early America—were defined as aliens ineligible to citizenship on racial grounds. Later in this chapter we shall have occasion to consider whether there were differences among Europeans with respect to what was meant by "White persons." But certainly that category did not include people of Native, African, or Asian descent, right from the beginning.[25]

It is worth noting that the granting and taking on of American citizenship had a ceremonial quality to it from the beginning. A candidate for naturalization had not only to meet the qualifications and make application. The candidate had to appear before a judge, swear an oath of allegiance to the United States, forswear allegiance to any other governments, declare his or her devotion to the principles of the Constitution, and present credible witnesses to his or her good character. This public performance of fealty was inherited from British customs of the feudal era, passed down through colonial practices. A group of Lutherans from Salzburg settled in Georgia in 1733 and went through such a ceremony. Their pastor's diary entry read:

> On December 21st, on which day our Saltzburgers were bound by oath and had to promise with hand and mouth to be subject to the English government,

their present authority, and, as subjects, to show obedience in their enjoyment of the rights and freedoms of the land. On this occasion the following ceremony took place: There appeared before us Captain [Thomas] Coram, deputy for the trustees, and also the captain of our ship [Tobias Fry] and an English merchant [William Sale]. In their presence Commissioner [Philip Georg Friedrich] von Reck [who led this group of immigrants] gave a brief address in which he praised the good deeds done for the Saltzburgers and urged upon them gratitude to God and to their benefactors. After they had promised obedience with a loud *yes*, a proclamation, *written in German*, was read to them in the name of the Trustees, which told them about the freedom and privileges they were to enjoy in this land and also about their duties. Hereafter the names of the Saltzburgers were written on the bottom of the proclamation. The Saltzburgers had to touch the paper and were asked whether they meant to honor all of this. They confirmed it with a yes and then shook the deputy's hand.

Subsequent ceremonies varied, but there was always a ceremony, performed before a judge, whereby individuals—usually in a group—formally took on the mantle of American citizenship. In Britain, such ceremonies declined. Eventually, all one had to do was fill out a form, swear an oath in a lawyer's office, pay a fee, and wait for one's citizenship papers in the mail. But in the United States, citizenship was bound up right from the start with a performance of fealty and celebration of America as a place with special rights, liberties, and duties for its citizens. Note also that it seemed appropriate in the early republic to hold such rituals, not only in English, but largely in the native language of the immigrants.[26]

Playing Indian: White Appropriations of Native American Symbols and Identities

About the time that Europeans began to succeed in genocide on a grand scale, in the generations around the American Revolution when the Native population declined rapidly, White Americans started to appropriate Indian identity for their own. Whether it be Boston Tea Partiers donning feathers and paint, Boy Scouts singing *faux* Indian songs and joining the Order of the Arrow, or Kevin Costner dancing with wolves, White Americans seem to feel they have a natural right to style themselves as if they were Indians.[27]

The logic goes something like this: Native peoples are not full human beings to be interacted with, and do not have rights, opinions, and power that must be respected. Indians are part of the natural landscape, like deer and foxes, perhaps even like rocks and trees. As such, they are fit candidates for being moved or disposed of. In fact, they have been disposed of. Indians *are* not, they *were*. That is, White people view Indians as having died out—hence the overwhelmingly strong narrative of the inevitable disappearance of their race throughout the late eighteenth, nineteenth, and early twentieth centuries. As Robert Berkhofer reflected on this discourse, "civilization was destined to triumph over savagery, and so the Indian was to disappear." Novelists like James Fenimore Cooper and anthropologists like Arthur Kroeber proclaimed the vanishing Indian in mournful tones; others chose triumphal ones. D. H. Lawrence, in writing about Cooper's novels, critiqued this theme: "Benjamin Franklin had a specious little equation in providential mathematics: Rum [he might have said genocide] + Savage = 0. Awfully nice! … Rum plus Savage may equal a dead savage. But is a dead savage nought? Can you make a land virgin by killing off its aborigines?"[28]

Native Americans, in this view, are nature's noble people. They are part of a common past that is available to anyone, perhaps particularly to those people who extinguished them. Sacajawea the domesticated Indian is our symbolic foremother and her image is on the dollar coin. European Americans or others can feel themselves becoming more American, more rooted in the landscape, in the very earth, by adopting the trappings of what they believe to be an Indian identity. Thus, a White, suburban, 50-something woman feels perfectly comfortable making a New Age statement about what a natural person she is by donning buckskin, beads, and moccasins as she drives to Kroger's in her Jeep Grand Cherokee. Thus, RJR Tobacco markets Natural American Spirit, an additive-free, "natural" cigarette, with a stylized emblem of a thunderbird at the top of the box and a logo of a Plains Indian chief in a feathered headdress, smoking a peace pipe, all in earth tones (Figure 3.2). White people make themselves feel more natural, and more elementally American, when they pretend to Indianness.[29]

Meanwhile, White Americans were not treating Native peoples very well. The Northwest Ordinance, which organized the lands between the Appalachian Mountains, the Ohio River, and the Mississippi River in 1787, promised "The utmost good faith shall always be observed toward the Indians; their lands and property shall never be taken from them without their consent; and, in their property, rights, and liberty, they never shall be invaded or disturbed, unless in just and lawful wars authorized by Congress; but laws founded in justice and humanity shall, from time to time, be made, for preventing wrongs being done to them and for preserving peace and friendship with them." Such noble sentiments masked a more acquisitive set of motives on the part of the Euro-American population. President Thomas Jefferson wrote to Benjamin Hawkins, the U.S. government's agent to the Creeks, in 1803:

> I consider the business of hunting as already become insufficient to furnish clothing and subsistence to the Indians. The promotion of agriculture, therefore, and household manufacture, are essential in their preservation, and I am disposed to aid and encourage it. This will enable them to live on much smaller portions of land … while they are learning to do better on less land, our increasing numbers will be calling for more land, and thus a coincidence of interests between those who have such necessaries to spare, and [those who] want lands. … Surely it will be better for them to be identified with us, and preserve the occupation of their lands, than be exposed to the many casualties that may endanger them while a separate people.[30]

Few Indians—for that matter few White people—perceived such a benevolent-sounding "coincidence of interests." White people wanted Indian land, and they wanted Indians off it. The Iroquois Confederacy had been overwhelmed by White Americans in the eastern Great Lakes region after the French left North America in 1763. The Iroquois went into a long, swooping decline that was punctuated only briefly by a religious resurgence late in the century in which a prophet, Handsome Lake, counseled accommodation with the Europeans. Many Native groups who nurtured a more resistive mentality bet on the losing side in the war for White American independence from Britain. Alexander McGillivray led his mother's people, the

Figure 3.2 Natural American Spirit ad.

Creeks, skillfully, but not successfully, through a series of international negotiations from the 1770s until his death in 1793. He attempted to keep White Georgians from seizing Creek lands: first by siding with the British in the war, then by talking with Midwest tribes about a pan-Indian alliance, later by allying with the Spanish in Florida, then by attempting to build a centralized Creek state, and finally by extracting a treaty from President George Washington that promised Creek autonomy and control over their ancestral lands. Before long, however, Creek territory was overrun by White Georgia farmers.[31]

The War of 1812 gave some Indians another shot at resistance to the encroachment by Euro-American migrants. Again, they bet on the side that gave up and went back to England. The Shawnee war chief Tecumseh and his brother, the prophet Tenskwatawa, attempted to rally Indians from many tribes in the Ohio Valley and southern Great Lakes, to form a grand, pan-Indian confederation to defend their lands and their way of life against the invaders. Tecumseh spoke eloquently of the need for pan-Indian unity in resistance:

> It is true I am a Shawnee. My forefathers were warriors. Their son is a warrior. From them I only take my existence; from my tribe I take nothing. I am the maker of my own fortune; and oh! that I could make that of my red people, and of my country, as great as the conceptions of my mind, when I think of the Spirit that rules the universe. I would not then come to Governor Harrison, to ask him to tear the treaty, and to obliterate the landmark; but I would say to him, Sir, you have liberty to return to your own country. The being within, community with the past ages, tells me, that once, nor until lately, there was no white man on this continent. That it then all belonged to red men, children of the same parents, placed on it by the Great Spirit that made them, to keep it, to traverse it, to enjoy its production, and to fill it with the same race. Once a happy race. Since made miserable by the white people, who are never contented, but always encroaching. The way, and the only way to check and stop this evil, is, for all the red men to unite in claiming a common and equal right in the land, as it was at first, and should be yet; for it never was divided, but belongs to all, for the use of each. That no part has a right to sell, even to each other, much less to strangers; those who want all, and will not do with less. The white people have no right to take the land from the Indians, because they had it first; it is theirs. They may sell, but all must join. Any sale not made by all is not valid. … It requires all to make a bargain for all. All red men have equal rights to the unoccupied land.[32]

The attempt to forge a pan-Indian alliance did not succeed, Tecumseh was killed in battle, and Indian resistance deflated. In the years after the war, a young U.S. Army colonel named Andrew Jackson made a national reputation for himself, hunting Indians—any Indians—and independent African-descended communities in Florida and the parts of the Southeast not yet occupied by Whites, torching villages, and slaughtering women and children.[33]

European Immigrants

In the preceding pages I have outlined the racial background to the story of European immigration between the time of the American Revolution and the Civil War. Beginning with the revolutionary generation, European Americans declared that the United States would be a White republic. In the eyes of some, it would be an Anglo-Saxon republic.[34]

Beginnings of U.S. Immigration Policy

In the United States in the twenty-first century, it is frequently uttered as if its truth were self-evident, that no nation can prosper and grow if it does not first control its borders.[35] That has not been true in America's own historical experience. For the first two-and-a-half centuries of European residence in North America, and for the first century of the existence of the United States as an independent nation, no government made a noticeable attempt to control U.S. borders, and in that time the American people and nation prospered famously and grew enormously. During much of that period, the locations of the borders between the United States and its northern, southern, and western neighbors were not known in full nor with precision. On several occasions they were in dispute, and they kept changing (see Chapter 4). Even after the United States had extended its claim all the way across the continent, and after theoretical borders had been legally established, there was only light regulation on a tiny part of the vast length of the U.S. borders with Canada and Mexico. No one kept records of the comings and goings of people along the U.S. borders with Mexico and Canada until well into the twentieth century (and for that reason, if for no other, government figures for immigration from and emigration to those places were grossly understated). Individuals came and went, and groups migrated back and forth across the borders with impunity and without apparent *transnational* negative effect.[36]

Insofar as the U.S. government addressed immigration at all before the Civil War, it was mainly to encourage it. The 1790 naturalization law was intended to facilitate White foreigners becoming American citizens. True, the Alien and Sedition Acts of 1798 gave the president the power to deport "dangerous" foreigners, but these laws constituted an attempt by the John Adams administration to keep out would-be supporters of his rival Thomas Jefferson, not to limit immigration, which was seen as a good thing. Congress did formally outlaw the bringing of one class of immigrants—slaves—in 1808, but a scaled-down international slave trade continued in violation of the law. In 1819 the U.S. government began for the first time to count immigrants who entered the country. And in 1847 the City of New York began to require the captains of incoming ships to hand in passenger lists. These slight measures were attempts to count, not to control or limit. The various levels of government in the United States kept the door wide open to immigrants until after the Civil War.[37]

Immigration, But Not "Old" or "New"

The stream was small at first. It arrived uncounted before 1820, and the numbers in those years were probably very small. Only 151,824 immigrants came in the 11 years 1820 to 1830—a bit under 14,000 per year. But the numbers jumped and jumped again: to 599,125 in 1831 to 1840 (that is, nearly 60,000 per year); 1,713,251 in 1841 to 1850; and 2,598,214 in 1851 to 1860—19 times the yearly rate of the 1820s. By the eve of the Civil War, more than 13 percent of the U.S. population was foreign born. Nearly all of these people came from Europe, but the stories of their comings (and goings) are several different stories.[38]

Once upon a time, a book of this sort would have devoted this entire chapter to "The Old Immigration": Irish, Germans, and Scandinavians, so went the story; people from the northwestern part of Europe who were perceived to be similar in language, religion, and physical appearance to "American stock"—that is, to English Americans. Carl Wittke made the classic statement of this mode of interpretation:

> In the nineteenth century, and with increasing volume after 1830, the tide of emigration set in again from Europe. Wave after wave rolled over the cities and prairies of the New America. The Irish, the Germans, and the Scandinavians, in more or less sharply defined but overlapping streams, poured into the United States; these major groups, together with several minor ones, constitute the "old emigration" from western and northern Europe, in contradistinction to the newer groups that came in the last quarter of the century from the south and east.[39]

Wittke contrasted this Old Immigration to the "New Immigration"—people from southern and eastern Europe and from Asia whom he regarded as very different from old stock Americans in language, religion, and physiognomy. Such people, in the popular view, posed a much bigger problem for America because they were "unassimilable." Unlike the Old Immigrants, they could not, in this view, morph into facsimiles of Anglo-Americans. Wittke again:

> [I]t is only since 1880 that the "new" immigrant tide reached the proportions of a great inundation. That there were significant and striking differences between the new arrivals and the older German, Irish, Scandinavian, and Anglo-Saxon stock is apparent to even the most casual observer. The newcomers from southern and eastern Europe represented peoples who were strikingly different in language, customs, political experiences and ideologies, and personal standards of living. … The newer immigrants arrived in great masculine hordes. A large proportion were merely "birds of passage," a new phenomenon in the history of American immigration; for they came, not to stay and to acquire citizenship, but to save enough money to return as speedily as possible to the fatherland. As a result, they were less concerned with the American standard of living than earlier immigrants, who looked upon the United States as their permanent home.[40]

Wittke liked immigrants, the new ones not much less than the old ones, but he unselfconsciously gave away his alarm by using phrases like "horde of immigrants" and "alarming fecundity" to describe this second batch of newcomers. The Old Immigrants came in waves, but they washed benignly across the landscape; the New Immigrants caused "a great inundation." They were not, in this view, permanent immigrants, but sojourners who came to make a buck and take it back home. Most ominous, they were different, not just in outward appearance and speech, but in "ideologies, and personal standards."[41]

Lest the reader think that Wittke's is an antiquated and therefore irrelevant paradigm, a recent survey of U.S. history textbooks revealed that eleven out of fourteen reproduced some version of his Old versus New Immigration schema.[42] Even more troubling, the best textbooks on immigration history, written beautifully by knowledgeable specialists, fall very close to Wittke's general interpretation, even as they are so strong on many aspects of immigration history's details.[43]

Table 3.2 British Immigration, 1820–2000

Decade	British Immigration	Percent of Total Immigration
1820–1830	27,489	18.1
1831–1840	75,810	12.7
1841–1850	267,044	15.6
1851–1860	423,974	16.3
1861–1870	606,896	26.2
Total 1820–1870	1,401,213	
1871–1880	548,043	19.5
1881–1890	807,357	15.3
1891–1900	271,538	7.4
1901–1910	525,950	6.0
1911–1920	341,408	6.0
1921–1930	339,570	9.7
Total 1871–1930	2,833,866	
1931–1940	31,572	6.0
1941–1950	139,306	13.5
1951–1960	202,824	8.1
1961–1970	213,822	6.4
1971–1980	137,374	3.1
1981–1990	159,173	2.2
1991–2000	151,866	1.7
Total 1931–2000	1,033,937	
Total All Years	5,271,016	8.0

Source: Appendix B, Table 9.

The problem with Wittke, of course, was that he had a lot of his information wrong, blinded as he was by the simple elegance of his paradigm. Consider the evidence of numbers. Wittke and the other authors cited in the footnotes to the paragraph above wrote a lot about immigrants, but English people were never the immigrants under discussion. It was assumed that the English in America all came during the early part of the colonial era and set the pattern for American culture and citizenship thereafter. The issues for English people were never immigrant issues. There weren't significant numbers of English immigrants at any time after the seventeenth century. These were the assumptions of Wittke and those who followed his lead. Yet consider Table 3.2. British immigrants came in large numbers in every decade of U.S. history except the 1820s and during the Great Depression. Great Britain was the third largest source of migrants (after Ireland and Germany) over the course of the nineteenth century. And the reader may choose any decade from the 1840s through the 1920s—more British people migrated to the United States during that decade *alone* than during the *entire* colonial period. The narratives created by historians have naturalized English people as if they were nonimmigrant Americans already on arrival, when in fact they were one of the largest groups of immigrants who continued to come, right through U.S. history.[44]

The Old vs. New Immigrants paradigm misplaces Scandinavians and Chinese. Wittke's paradigm placed Scandinavians in the Old Immigration because he perceived their Germanic languages, Protestantism, and light-colored skins and eyes to be similar to those of Anglo-Americans; therefore, he thought them susceptible to assimilation without incident. Yet only 411,077 Scandinavians came to the United States during the period of the alleged Old Immigration (1820 to 1880), whereas 1,934,992—nearly five times as many—came during the period of the New (1880–1930). Conversely, Wittke and others following his lead posited Chinese migrants as members of the New Immigration: they came from a land far distant, were speakers of a tongue strange to English lips, heathens, and physically very unlike Anglo-Americans. Yet the only period when Chinese constituted a significant portion of the immigrant stream was before 1882.[45]

So we will have no talk of Old and New Immigration in this book, nor any remnants of that kind of analysis in some other disguise. Instead, we will speak of European migrants to the eastern parts of the United States in the first generations of the republic: British, Germans, Irish, and Jews. Chinese immigrants, who came mainly to the western United States, appear in Chapter 4, not because of chronology, but because that chapter is about America's colonial adventure across the continent, the migration of European Americans into lands recently owned by Mexicans and Indians, and the immigration of others—from Europe, China, and other points of the globe—close on their heels.[46] Scandinavians appear in Chapter 5, which discusses the very large flow of immigrants from southern, eastern, northern, and western Europe between 1880 and 1930.[47] Now, to some of the patterns of European migration in the early decades of the republic.

British

Though the migrants were many, sources of information about British immigration into nineteenth-century America are few; almost no historians have bothered to pay attention to the phenomenon. One who has, Charlotte Erickson, refers to them as "invisible immigrants."[48]

In fact, hundreds of thousands of migrants left the British Isles for the United States in the decades after 1840, as the United States went through an industrial revolution that created millions of jobs and as the portion of the continent available to White farmers expanded rapidly. The total number of British immigrants recorded for just the four decades 1820 to 1860 was nearly 800,000; it was more than five million by the end of the twentieth century. Those were the figures recorded by U.S. immigration officials at East Coast ports of entry, but the actual number of immigrants was far higher. Many British immigrants who came to the United States landed first in Canada and then came across the border uncounted. William E. Van Vugt, the leading scholar of British immigration, believes that U.S. immigration officials regularly recorded many British migrants as being Irish instead. The reader should note that the United States was not the only destination for British emigrants. It is true that in the period 1846 to 1854, for instance, 72.6 percent of recorded British emigrants (442,049 people) came to the United States. But at least 86,000 went to

British North America in those same years, and nearly 72,000 to Australia and New Zealand, with smaller numbers going to other points in the empire.[49]

The motor for the migration from Britain to the United States was the linkage between the two nations' economies. As Van Vugt, put it, "Britain and the United States were from 1820 to 1860 the two most interconnected countries [in the world] in terms of culture and economic growth."[50] There was no single economic pattern that drove the migration, but rather a number of situations pushing people out of the isles and another bunch attracting them to the United States. The migrants were English, Scottish, and Welsh. They were farmers and city people, miners and industrial workers. A popular ditty went like this:

> From Liverpool as I before had stated
> We sail'd a motley set we surely were
> With coals and iron was our vessel freighted
> Scotch Irish Welsh and English were there
> Going out to see if emigration was a recipe against starvation
> There were ploughboys weavers blacksmiths tailors
> Irish peasants and Welsh mountaineers
> Together with a family of nailors
> Scotch from the lowlands and some highland seers
> Butchers bakers carpenters and joiners
> There were also a lot of Cornish miners[51]

The 1840s were lean times for farmers and other workers in England, and even more so for Scots and Irish people as the potato famine hit those areas. But in fact emigration from Britain was modest in the most depressed years and picked up just as good times began to return in the late 1840s and early 1850s. By 1850 only one-fifth of the British population was engaged in agriculture and more than half the people lived in towns and cities. By comparison, four-fifths of the U.S. labor force still worked the land. But industry was beginning to build, especially in the Northeast, where more than one-third of the labor force worked in textile mills or other industrial enterprises. The United States suffered, as it always has, from a surplus of resources and an inadequate labor supply. Thus wages in Pennsylvania coal mines, Michigan iron mines, and a host of other industries were two or three times what they were in England.

The other big attraction was land, plentiful and cheap. The U.S. government passed a number of acts in the 1840s and 1850s that drove prices down below a dollar per acre on lands the government had recently wrested from Native peoples. Some migrants added religious motives to economic ones. Throughout the mid-century decades, the two nations were in the throes of a transatlantic revival that brought various religious enthusiasms from the United States to Britain and back again, and people followed their congregations. Notable among these were Primitive Methodists, who began in the American Second Great Awakening and secured a burgeoning audience in England, many of whom migrated then to the founding country of their faith. English Mormons, several tens of thousands of them, also made the transatlantic journey.

British immigrants went everywhere in America. They worked in New England textile mills and mid-Atlantic buggy factories, in mines in Pennsylvania and throughout the Midwest. Most of the people who came with farming ambitions and cash—and this was largely a migration not of impoverished people but of individuals looking to move up—made their homes in the Midwest. Several thousand ventured as far as California to mine or to farm.

Van Vugt argues that "British immigrants ... could assimilate more readily than other immigrant groups thanks to the language and essential cultural traits and traditions they held in common with most native-born white Americans."[52] These observations are not incorrect, but they are incomplete. Such analysis misses the essential point of perceived racial sameness. Christmas tree decorating and Halloween costuming are pretty easy for any immigrant to learn to perform. Anyone who has been to a restaurant in small-town America that advertises "Chinese and American food" knows that folkways like food production are easy for non-Europeans to pick up. And the children of the Chinese family that runs such a restaurant speak unaccented American slang. Non-White immigrants might perform Americanness perfectly, but they were still not assimilated as easily as English immigrants because they were perceived by the dominant White American group to be racially foreign. English immigrants, by contrast, disappeared effortlessly into the White American population—indeed, their very status as immigrants was usually ignored—because they were thought of as being already the same people as native, American Whites on the day they arrived, or at most, very shortly thereafter.

That does not mean that individual British immigrants did not have issues relating to cultural adjustment and identity revision. British versions of the English language were different from American Englishes; one could communicate on arrival, but it took time to learn to sound like a native. Immigrants missed the friends, homes, and communities they left behind. It took time to find a job, establish a home, and make new friends. These are processes common to all migrants. But British immigrants were treated as Americans right from the start. One indication of the native status that British immigrants acquired immediately on landing is the fact that, alone among immigrant groups, they voted Whig and Republican—parties with anti-immigrant platforms. All the other immigrant groups of the era except the Chinese (who were forbidden to become citizens and could not vote) supported the Democratic Party.

Mary Wrightson was born in the north English coalfield hamlet of Middlestone, thirty miles southwest of Newcastle, to an English miner and his Irish wife. When she was six, her father and brothers took the family to Pennsylvania, where they worked in the mines near Scranton for the rest of their lives. Mary's older sisters married coal miners of British and German descent, her brothers the daughters of mining families—some immigrant, some native, but all White. Mary went to grammar and high school, worked for the YWCA, and eventually married Russell Adkins, a medical doctor and Mayflower descendant. She lived the rest of her adult life among the country club set in Chicago, Indianapolis, Los Angeles, and Seattle. Although she was an immigrant and the child of immigrants, she said that, in the ninety-eight years of her life, never once did anyone question her instantaneous, authentic, and unproblematic Americanness.[53]

In some respects, the British immigrants who came to the United States in the middle of the nineteenth century were very much like the Japanese who came at the end of that century. These British and those Japanese were the two best-educated immigrant groups to enter the United States before the last quarter of the twentieth century. Nearly all were literate (nearly all the Japanese had, in fact, six years of primary education—more than the native White U.S. population). Both these immigrant populations mixed city people with farmers, and both came to dwell in urban as well as rural areas. The British, like the Japanese, came in families or formed them quickly in the United States, and they both had smaller households with fewer children than was common among many other migrant groups. Some British immigrants, like some Japanese, returned whence they came, and others hoped to but never managed to make it back to their respective homelands. The big difference between British immigrants and Japanese immigrants had to do with the reception they received in the United States. Because of racial sameness, a roughly common language, and a sense of shared history, British immigrants were accepted as natural Americans. They amalgamated with the native White population easily. Native Whites did not see English people, even those who were fresh off the boat, as foreigners. They saw them as natural Americans. Citizenship, intermarriage with the local population, acceptance into the society of native born Americans—these all were easily available to British immigrants, where they were not available to Japanese immigrants. The difference was race.[54]

Germans

Germany contributed the largest number of immigrants to the United States over the course of U.S. history. Germany was either the largest or the second-largest sending country of migrants to the United States in the following decades: the 1830s, 1840s, 1850s, 1860s, 1870s, 1880s, 1930s, 1940s, and 1950s. In the middle decades of the nineteenth century, the proportion of the immigrant stream that came from Germany ranged as high as 37 percent. More than a million and a half Germans came to the United States between 1820 and the start of the Civil War. Over the whole of the history of the republic, Germany was the source of nearly 11 percent of immigrants to the United States: a total of more than seven million people (see Table 3.3).[55]

It is essential to remember that, strictly speaking, there was no Germany in the first two-thirds of the nineteenth century. Speakers of Germanic languages lived across a huge territory from Austria to Schleswig-Holstein and from the Rhine Valley to East Prussia—indeed, there was a longstanding colony of German speakers far to the east on the Volga. But Germany as a single people inhabiting a united nation was only an idea then, although it was an idea being pursued in central Europe both by republicans and by would-be makers of a pan-Germanic empire. The dream did not become reality until Bismarck's forces won the Franco-Prussian War of 1870 to 1871. So the "Germans" who came to America in the first two-thirds of the nineteenth century were in their own minds Saxons or Prussians, Bavarians or Bohemians, and so on. They were diverse in other ways, as well. About a third were Catholics, more were Lutherans, and others were freethinkers or Jews (German Jewish immigration will be treated in a separate section below). Fewer were Pietists than had been the case in the eighteenth century. The immigrants ranged across the spectra of age and class. They were farmers and townspeople, cottage weavers and industrial workers.

Germans who left their homeland did so, often, because of a complex of economic circumstances that rendered their situation there tenuous. Partly it had to do with customary rules of inheritance. Most parts of Germany practiced primogeniture, with a family farm passing from father to oldest son (German women were not allowed to inherit land in this period). This kept the landholding together so it could

Table 3.3 German and Irish Immigration, 1820–2000

Decade	German Immigration	Percent of Total Immigration	Irish Immigration	Percent of Total Immigration
1820–1830	7,729	5.1	54,338	35.8
1831–1840	152,454	25.5	207,381	34.6
1841–1850	434,626	25.4	780,719	45.6
1851–1860	951,667	36.6	914,119	35.2
Total 1820–1860	1,546,476		1,956,557	
1861–1870	787,468	34.0	435,778	18.8
1871–1880	718,182	25.5	436,871	15.5
1881–1890	1,452,970	27.7	655,482	12.5
1891–1900	505,152	13.7	388,416	10.5
1901–1910	341,498	3.9	339,065	3.9
1911–1920	143,945	2.5	146,181	2.5
1921–1930	412,202	10.0	211,234	5.1
Total 1861–1930	4,631,417		2,613,027	
1931–1940	114,058	21.6	10,973	2.1
1941–1950	226,578	21.9	19,789	1.9
1951–1960	477,765	19.0	48,362	1.9
1961–1970	190,796	5.7	32,966	1.0
1971–1980	74,414	1.7	11,490	0.2
1981–1990	91,961	1.3	31,969	0.4
1991–2000	92,606	1.0	56,950	0.6
Total 1931–2000	1,268,278		212,499	
Total 1820–2000	7,176,971	10.9	4,782,083	7.2

Source: Appendix B, Tables 10 and 11. Irish figure includes Northern Ireland through 1925.

sustain that son's family, but in an age of expanding population it cast younger sons adrift. They were ripe for the lure of opportunity abroad. In some other parts of Germany like Hesse and the Rhineland, farmers bequeathed their land by *Realteilung*, that is, in equal shares to all their sons. In such cases, holdings got smaller and smaller. Farm families took up ancillary trades such as linen weaving and other cottage industries to make ends meet. In the middle of the nineteenth century, textile factories began to replace cottage weaving. In some regions, former farmer-weavers made the transition to industrial labor. In others, no factories were built and the former weavers simply lost that source of income; this forced many to look for opportunities elsewhere. There was one other force pushing Germans to migrate: political strife. German intellectuals supported a series of attempts in various principalities to overthrow monarchies. Some people fled the unrest, which reached its zenith in 1848. More left because they were on the losing—that is, the republican—side.[56]

It is worth noting that most German emigrants, like most British migrants, were not "poor, huddled masses yearning to breathe free." They were people of middling economic circumstances who had at least family memories of owning farms, who may have fallen temporarily on harder times, but who still could manage to pay for passage to America and on into the hinterlands, and who could reasonably hope to be able to afford to buy land in America, if not at once, then in the course of their lives. Very few of them came because of religious or political persecution, although after 1848 politics was a minor theme in the German emigrant saga.

Migrants were drawn to America by the same things that attracted English, Irish, and others in the same period: jobs at better wages than in Europe, and the possibility of owning land. The pattern of their settling in the United States reflects the sinews of the transportation system. Going by ship, significant numbers of Germans ended up in port cities like New York, Philadelphia, Baltimore, and New Orleans. In the latter half of the century, in fact, New York was the third most populous German city, after Berlin and Vienna. Many immigrants went on to regional transportation hubs: Cincinnati, Chicago, Milwaukee, Cleveland, or St. Louis. One might even say that immigrants built a town like Milwaukee. In 1835 the outpost had only 125 inhabitants. By 1848 they numbered 16,521—58 percent of those were immigrants, 35 percent Germans. A dozen years later the town had grown to 45,246 inhabitants and 49 percent were native born. But many of those surely were the American-born children of immigrants, and Germans of the immigrant generation still accounted for 35 percent of the total; one must conclude that at least half the city's people were members of German immigrant families.[57]

They clustered together with other Germans at first—friends, relatives, at least people who spoke a language the immigrants could understand, ate familiar food, and brewed good beer.[58] They founded places called Germantown in several states—in New York, Maryland, Pennsylvania, and Wisconsin, plus two each in Tennessee, Ohio, and Illinois—and countless other towns and neighborhoods echoing German names, from New Leipzig in North Dakota to New Braunfels in Texas. James Bergquist wrote in 1984:

> A century ago nearly every major American city had its "German district," a visible and tangible reminder of the presence of the country's largest foreign-speaking element, and an image which hovered in the minds of most native-born Americans when the question of immigration was discussed. Typically, the German area began not far from the central business district, and extended outward to more newly-settled neighborhoods, including some small acreages on the edge of the city. Within it a visitor could walk for blocks, perhaps for miles, hearing little else but strange Teutonic sounds. The pervasive "foreignness" [read: non-Englishness] of the district was reinforced by the sight of shops bearing signs in German, restaurants and public housing advertising their German fare, German bookshops and newspaper offices, German physicians, grocers and banking houses—all the elements of a rather complete and self-contained community. To many native Americans, of course, such a place seemed to be almost defiantly proclaiming German separateness and resistance to American standards.[59]

Old-country divisions persisted in the new land. In cities like Chicago and New York the migrants from each of the German principalities tended to form their own separate newspapers, schools, mutual aid societies, literary circles, theaters, singing societies, and the like. A town with a large German population might have several varieties of German Lutheran church depending on the derivation of the majority of the congregation. They also would have at least one Catholic parish where Germans numbered prominently among the faithful. In general, the Catholic church adhered to the parish principle: one church building and congregation per locality. The church hierarchy did grant German Catholics the right to form separate ethnic parishes, something the church made difficult for later French Canadian immigrants and denied to twentieth-century Mexican Americans. But even in the German case, the ethnic parishes proved difficult to maintain in multiethnic cities, as the numbers of Irish people in the same neighborhoods were high and they came to church, too. There were not many German American priests, and some German Catholics chafed under the leadership of French or Irish American priests.[60]

The same was true in rural areas, which contained more than half of the German American population. Few of the German migrants were rich, but a lot came with sufficient money to purchase a ticket to the Midwest, and some even had enough to buy a plot of land and begin farming. Some did this as individuals, but more often they came in groups to plant German farm communities in American soil. Early in the century, some of these were pietist communal societies like Harmony, Pennsylvania, in 1805; Economy, Pennsylvania, in 1825; and Amana, Iowa, in 1843. As the century wore on and German migration expanded and became more secular, aristocrats and real estate speculators led bands of immigrants whom they had gathered both in Germany and in the German neighborhoods of U.S. cities to plant agricultural colonies in places like Berlin, Wisconsin, in 1846; New Ulm, Minnesota, in 1854; and New Braunfels, Texas, a year later.[61]

We can see several ethnic processes at work on German Americans in the middle decades of the nineteenth century. One of these is panethnic formation. Germany was just coming together as a unified nation in those decades, and so were German Americans. But by the latter decades of the century, they were seeing themselves and referring to themselves, as they were referred to by others, as Germans, not Westfalians or Rhinelanders any longer. Those subethnic Lutheran churches became simply German Lutheran churches by the end of the century. As we shall see later in Chapter 5, similar processes of panethnic fusion took place for Japanese and Italian immigrants between the 1880s and the 1920s.

As the second generation grew up, in areas of high German population concentration, they grew into German America, more than into the wider Anglo-American-defined White community. Consider the concentrated German population in southeast Pennsylvania. That was the first state where Germans congregated, during the eighteenth century, and one of its notable features was its longstanding commitment to maintaining bilingualism. In the late 1900s, it became fashionable to believe that English had always been the near-official U.S. language and that a bilingual citizenry could not hold together. To the contrary, Pennsylvania managed a thriving bilingual existence for more than a century and a half, as did German American communities in other states to lesser degrees. German was the language of the German community in southeast Pennsylvania, not just in the colonial period, and not just among those who were immigrants themselves (an ever-renewing set of people), but also among those born and raised in the state, and through the second half of the nineteenth century. It began early in the eighteenth century, with public officials disregarding Benjamin Franklin's warnings and publishing official documents—including the Declaration of Independence and the Constitution—in both languages.[62]

In that same early era, from the 1710s, German-language schools thrived in towns and rural areas that had large German populations. The Pennsylvania Germans saw this as a matter more of religious fealty than of language autonomy. They were deeply dedicated to the Lutheran, Reformed, and Mennonite churches that nourished their souls and gave them community. Communal spiritual life included raising up each young generation in family and in faith. The historian of Pennsylvania German schools, Clyde Stine, put it this way:

> The Pennsylvania German farmer, when the public school system was introduced in the nineteenth century, could not understand why the state wanted to educate his children. For him real education took place on the farm, where children were already at nine years of age integral parts of the farm community. The school, he thought, was to teach his children how to read, write, and calculate enough for the purposes of the rural economic and social world in which they lived. *His* was the responsibility for their turning out to be worthwhile members of the community.
>
> The only interference he would brook in this system of education was from the church, which undertook to teach his children what he regarded as the eternal truths. And since both he and the pastor were agreed that one of the aims of learning to read and write was to read with understanding the Scriptures, he took it for granted that the church would supervise directly or indirectly the school where his children were to learn reading, writing and arithmetic.
>
> Of course, the instruction in the schools was to be in German, since that was not only his own language, but that of the Luther Bible, the book of books for the early Pennsylvania Germans. English might be taught sufficiently to let the children get enough for the occasions when business or exercise of voting privileges brought them in contact with that language, but it had no real place in the well-knit farm community.[63]

The state attempted to get into the education business as early as 1802, but it had no impact on the German-language schools. German Pennsylvanians and other Pennsylvanians simply went to separate schools for many decades. By the 1830s the Reformed Church supported 160 schools, the Lutherans nearly 250, and there were also German-language neighborhood schools that proceeded without church affiliation. English-speaking public officials made several attempts to curb German-language education, but with very little effect. It was only after an 1873 revision of the state constitution that English-advocating state authorities began to make inroads, starving the German-language schools of money and trained teachers. The last German-language schools closed by about 1890, but many other schools continued to teach on a bilingual basis. German continued to be the language of the people, even as formal schooling in German declined. It was not until 1911 that the English-speaking-dominated legislature dared to declare that English would be the sole language of instruction henceforth.[64]

German American communities were a century younger in most other places and so less well entrenched, yet similar conflicts occurred in St. Louis, New York, and Chicago over German American desires to maintain institutional and language autonomy. At the same time, there were always German Americans who were leaking into the generic White population, speaking English, forgetting most of their German, moving out of German towns and neighborhoods, marrying non-German-descended

White people, and perhaps anglicizing their names. German American separatism was mainly a self-asserted thing, not an imposition from the majority group. As I will explain below, British-descended Americans did mount an anti-Catholic nativist movement in the 1840s and 1850s, but that was only a temporary impediment to the absorption of the German American population into an almost undifferentiated White America. Even in the places with the largest German concentrations, by the third generation most German Americans were just White people with some vestigial family memory of German this or that—village festivals, perhaps, or favorite beers— what Herbert Gans later called "symbolic ethnicity." The fact of their assimilation was masked to the view of outsiders because more Germans kept coming to renew the immigrant membership and folk culture of German American neighborhoods and institutions. As James Bergquist put it, "[T]he German-American community was a way-station rather than a permanent home." Throughout the nineteenth century and ever since, in most places, Germans slipped into White America almost as smoothly as did their contemporaries who were immigrants from Britain.[65]

Peasants into City People: The Famine Irish

The presence of Irish people in the United States is related to the long, troubled, colonial history between England and Ireland. Prior to the era of emigration, Ireland was fairly sparsely inhabited by peoples of mainly Celtic and Anglo-Norman ancestry, the latter themselves immigrants from England in the fifteenth and sixteenth centuries. British monarchs from Henry VII to James I used military and political means to create a subject state in Ireland. They gave control over Irish lands and peasants to their loyal, ethnic English supporters. As England embraced a version of the Protestant Reformation, the Irish common people remained almost all Catholics. England imported Protestant Scots into Ulster by the tens of thousands and Protestant English to rule the other provinces. The English overlords discriminated against Irish Catholics: James I closed Catholic schools and forced Catholic children to attend Protestant schools. Another law forbade any Catholic to buy land from a Protestant. Oliver Cromwell confiscated Catholic landholdings. In 1801 England annexed Ireland outright. By the end of the seventeenth century, Catholics in Ireland were confined to a social position not unlike the one occupied by free Blacks in America: legally not enslaved, but not entitled to full citizenship, either. The salient differences were that Catholics in Ireland constituted a large majority of the population, not a tiny minority, and they were the bottom rung of society. American free Blacks were a middle set of people, between the majority free White population and the large and severely oppressed Black slave class.[66]

The Irish who came to America in the colonial period were almost all Protestants—either Ulster Scots who had been planted in Ireland a generation or two earlier, or Protestant Anglo-Irish from the southern provinces. The bulk of Irish migrants to the United States continued to be Protestants up through the 1830s. Overall U.S. immigration numbers were just beginning to pick up in those years, and Ireland contributed more than one-third of the total: 54,000 in the 1820s, 107,000 in the 1830s. Then disaster struck Ireland, and emigration exploded.[67]

Ireland's agricultural economy was relatively prosperous until the peace of 1815 ended the Napoleonic Wars and prices for Irish grain began to drop. Thereafter, landlords (mainly Protestants but some Catholics, many English but also many

Irish) found it efficacious to remove the peasants who lived on their lands. Some began to use labor-saving farm machinery, which left cottagers unemployed. Others shifted from cultivation to animal husbandry. They enclosed their fields, planted grass, and ran herds of sheep, which, like mechanized farming, required fewer hands and threw people out of work. Meanwhile, agricultural disaster was brewing. The potato had been brought from the Americas to Europe in the 1570s. Hardy, nutritious, and requiring only small plots of land to support a large population, after 1780 the potato became the staple crop of the Irish peasantry—nutritious and cheap enough to set off a population boom.

So the Irish peasant population was expanding, just as landlords were pushing peasants off the land. And then the potato crop failed. There had been partial crop failures in several earlier years, due to poor weather or disease. But in 1845 a hitherto unknown fungus attacked the potato plants. Leaves blackened and crumbled at the touch, tubers turned into black, gooey, stinking, inedible globs. Thirty to forty percent of the country's crop was destroyed that year, and people began to starve. In 1846 the blight returned, and destroyed all but 20 percent of the crop. People were reduced to eating their seed potatoes. In 1847, although the fungus was gone, only one-fifth as many acres were planted as had been planted two years before.

Thus came the Great Hunger. Between 1845 and 1851, at least a million and perhaps as many as a million and a half people died of starvation and disease. A visitor to the northern midlands reported in 1846 that he "saw sights that will never wholly leave the eyes that beheld them, cowering wretches almost naked in the savage weather, prowling in turnip fields, and endeavoring to grub up roots ... little children ... their limbs fleshless, ... their faces bloated yet wrinkled and of a pale greenish hue, ... who would never, it was too plain, grow up to be men and women." Historian Kerby Miller describes the scene: "[O]thers fed on grass, seaweed and shellfish, rotten potatoes, dead animals, even human corpses. Weakened by malnutrition, thousands fell victim to typhus or 'black fever,' scurvy, 'famine dropsy,' cholera, relapsing fever, and dysentery or the 'bloody flux.' Many simply barricaded themselves in their hovels and waited for death; others wandered about searching for food, spreading disease throughout the island."[68] The British government did nothing. They blamed the suffering on congenital Irish indolence.

Another two million Irish, perhaps, went abroad. The very poorest, even if they avoided starvation, could not manage the £2 to £5 fare to North America, nor the cost of food for that trip. Several hundred thousand made their way by boat or barge to British ports like Liverpool, Glasgow, and London, where they filled up slum districts and where some of them found jobs in factories, construction, or domestic service. Those with a few more resources scraped together the fare and took ship for America (smaller numbers went to Australia and New Zealand) (Figure 3.3). The voyage was not easy: in their weakened condition, as many as one-third of the migrants from British ports to Canada in 1847 died at sea or shortly after arrival.

The nature of Irish emigration had changed. Before the famine, the emigrants were mainly Protestants from Ulster and people of a middling sort—farmers, artisans, and shopkeepers who were hoping to move up. Famine emigrants came from all four regions of Ireland. They were overwhelmingly poor, rural, and Catholic. A significant number spoke Gaelic rather than English.

We should not imagine that all the Irish who migrated to America came as a result of the potato famine. Those who fled the famine were not the first Irish to emigrate in large numbers, nor were they the last. The population of Ireland continued

Figure 3.3   Leaving Queenstown.

to drop until the end of the nineteenth century, and Irish migration to the United
States did not falter until the 1910s. Yet that cataclysmic event seized the imagination of generations of Irish people in both Ireland and America, and it is their self-
defining collective diasporic memory, much as slavery is for African Americans,
wartime imprisonment is for Japanese Americans, or the Great Trek is for Boers.
Ask an Irish American when his or her ancestors came to the United States, and
like as not you will hear they came fleeing the famine—even if that particular person's ancestors, in fact, came earlier or later or under different circumstances. The
symbol of the famine meant Irish immigrants to America were not, in their minds,
voluntary migrants trying to better their lot, but rather desperate individuals fleeing a holocaust. Historian Florence Gibson characterized them as homesick exiles:
"Many Irish-Americans had moved to the United States physically, but spiritually

and emotionally they were back home in Ireland." Kerby Miller may overstate the case, but his comments help us understand the continuing hold that Ireland and the famine have had on the imaginations of Irish Americans:

> First, both collectively and individually the Irish—particularly Irish Catholics—often regarded emigration as involuntary exile, although they expressed that attitude with varying degrees of consistency, intensity, and sincerity. Second, this outlook reflected a distinctive Irish worldview—the impact of a series of interactions among culture, class, and historical circumstance upon Irish character. Finally, both the exile motif and its underlying causes led Irish emigrants to interpret experience and adapt to American life in ways which were often alienating and sometimes dysfunctional, albeit traditional, expedient, and conducive to the survival of Irish-American nationalism.[69]

In the decades immediately following upon the famine, Irish nationalism and resentment of the British blossomed. Nationalism flourished as much in Irish America as in the old soil. Elizabeth Gurley Flynn was born near the end of the century in New Hampshire, and the politics to which she refers are of a later era, but her description of the hold of Ireland on the Irish diaspora is compelling: "The awareness of being Irish came to us as small children, through plaintive song and heroic story. ... As children, we drew in a burning hatred of British rule with our mother's milk. Until my father died, at over eighty, he never said 'England' without adding, 'God damn her!'"[70] The rise of an Irish nationalist movement fed the sense of exile, and together those fed a twin consciousness among Irish Americans: Over the generations they became relentlessly American, members of the White race, and very few went back compared to other immigrant groups like the Germans or English. But they maintained a psychic connection with Ireland that led to ongoing involvements, the sending of remittances to even distant relatives, and support for the Irish national cause from the mid-nineteenth century, across the twentieth, and into the twenty-first century.

More than any other immigrant group until the end of the nineteenth century, famine Irish migrants made their new homes in U.S. cities. Four out of five of the Irish-born U.S. population lived in the urbanized states of the industrializing Northeast. Nearly one-third lived in just ten cities (see Table 3.4).

At the time of the famine, the United States was still an agricultural country: 85 percent of the people lived in rural districts. The countryside was where the most attractive opportunities lay. Other groups of immigrants—English, Germans, Ulster Scots—had made a beeline for the hinterlands and taken up land for farming. Not so the famine Irish. Though they came from rural areas in Ireland and had themselves tilled the land, finances trapped them in East Coast cities. Once they hit Boston or Philadelphia or New York, their feet sought out a cheap place to live and a job at whatever wage was available. Thus there grew up vibrant, densely populated Irish neighborhoods in places like Five Points, Manhattan, and Boston's wharf district. Many—women as well as men—found work in New England and Middle Atlantic factories. Others, particularly women, worked as domestic servants in middle-class Anglo-American households. Some men found jobs digging sewers and canals, or laying railroad track. A few made it out to California in the boom years of that new state. Later, Irish immigrants would figure prominently in the building of the first transcontinental railroad in the 1860s and other pick and shovel work throughout

Table 3.4 Irish-Born in Select U.S. Cities, by Number and Percent of Total City Population, 1860

City	Number	Percent of City Population
New York (incl. Brooklyn)	260,450	24
Philadelphia	95,548	16
Boston	45,991	26
St. Louis	29,926	19
Chicago	19,889	18
Providence	9,534	19
San Francisco	9,363	16
Pittsburgh	9,297	19
Jersey City	7,380	25
Cleveland	5,479	13
Total	492,857	
Total Irish-Born in the U.S.	1,611,304	

Source: Kathleen Neils Conzen, "Irish," in *Harvard Encyclopedia of American Ethnic Groups* (Cambridge, MA: Harvard University Press, 1980), 531.

the West. But by far the majority languished in the cities of the East. There, peasants became city people (Figure 3.4). Historian Donald B. Cole described the Irish who came to Lawrence, Massachusetts:

> Massed on the decks, the survivors [of the crossing] looked hopefully on the new world as the ship entered Quebec or Boston. Those landing at Quebec found new horrors as unemployment drove them to the long foot journey down through Canada to New England. After months of agony Irish men, women, and children trickled into the mill cities of the Merrimack Valley, one of them Lawrence. The Boston arrivals found the walk or train ride to Lawrence relatively simple. ... Once in the city the Irish flocked to Wards Two and Three, which were soon the most densely populated areas. South of the Common they lived in the mill boarding houses and to the north they settled on the "plains." Many also inhabited a shanty village along the river near the dam. ... The wooden huts above the dam were responsible for the label "shanty" Irish. These were shacks of slabs and unfinished lumber with over-lapping boards for the roofs. Above each roof rose a stovepipe chimney and piled high around the walls was sod for insulation.[71]

In such dismal conditions, immigrants from Ireland became the shock troops of the American industrial revolution. In Lawrence and dozens of other cities they found work in textile, shoe, and other factories, laboring seven days a week, ten to twelve hours a day, for pennies per day.[72]

Figure 3.4 Irish squatters in Central Park.

Sephardim and German Jews

As many as a quarter million Jews migrated from Germany to the United States in the late colonial and early national eras. It would be possible to treat those people as merely a religious subset of the German migration to the United States in those years.[73] Certainly, their numbers did not put Jews among the largest groups of people migrating into the United States in this period. Yet it is important to highlight the ties between this German Jewish migration and the other Jewish migrations that occurred before and after it. Some secularized Jewish radicals who fled the failure of the 1848 revolutions probably saw themselves as simply German immigrants, or as proletarian members of a worldwide working class, or even perhaps as humanists, citizens of the world. But many more people had a strong sense of themselves as Jews. Certainly they were treated that way in Europe, and they continued to be a people somewhat apart from other Whites, and indeed from other German immigrants, once they arrived in America.[74]

The first Jews to come to North America were Sephardim: Spanish and Portuguese Jews fleeing persecution in Europe for the relative safety of America. Coming as early as 1654, they formed outposts of Judaism in places like Rhode Island and New Amsterdam (later New York). These were Orthodox Jews, but possessors of a culture far removed from the life of the Orthodox East European Jews who would come more than a century later. Most Sephardi Jews entered the world of commerce and finance in America. Several, like Haym Solomon and Aaron Lopez, were prominent financiers of the American Revolution. Others fought in that war. At the time of America's first national census in 1790, Jews numbered only 1500 out of 3.9 million Americans. By the early years of the nineteenth century, Sephardi immigration had all but stopped, and Sephardim were fast losing their distinct identity, blending either into the Gentile population or into the mass of Jewish newcomers.[75]

After about 1825, the Sephardim were rapidly overtaken by a wave of Ashkenazi immigrants—members of that other great arm of Judaism in Central and Eastern Europe. In 1840, the American Jewish population stood at about 15,000—a tenfold increase in five decades. In 1848, the population was 50,000; in 1860, over 150,000; and in 1880, over 230,000.[76] By that time, almost all American Jews were of Germanic origin; even those who came from Hungary, Austria, Bohemia, and western Poland spoke German rather than Ladino, Yiddish, or Hebrew and were influenced by German Jewish culture. The best estimate is that about one-quarter of Germany's 600-odd thousand Jews made their way abroad in the course of the nineteenth century. Some went to England, France, and elsewhere in Europe. But the majority went to the United States. They kept coming from the 1820s through the end of the century, although in the last couple of decades their numbers were dwarfed by rising numbers of Jewish immigrants from farther to the east (see Chapter 5).

These were years of emigration for many sorts of Germans besides Jews—Protestant sectarians, Catholics, Lutherans, political dissidents, and Germans who merely sought a chance at raising their standard of living. Many German Jews were caught up in the latter two movements. Most came to America seeking economic opportunity. Unlike the relatively well-to-do Sephardim, whose family connections stretched to merchant houses all over the Americas, the German Jewish immigrants of the mid-nineteenth century were mainly people of the middle and lower social classes. They came particularly from Bavaria, Baden, Württemberg, and the Palatinate. Many were merchants, peddlers, money lenders, or dealers in cattle or grain. As the agricultural economy declined, their fortunes did, too. Some left the countryside for German cities. This was common for non-Jewish Germans in the same period, but those Gentiles who migrated generally were young, single men going to work in mines and factories, whereas Jews who migrated within Germany did so mainly as whole families and went to work in trade and finance. Other Jews left Germany entirely. In this case, most often a young man would go to seek his fortune, working his way across Germany to Bremen or Hamburg, and then taking ship to the United States. If he prospered, he would then send back to Germany for parents, brothers, and sisters.

Some Jews left Germany for specifically Jewish reasons, fleeing the humiliations and economic restrictions that were the lot of their people in Europe. The rise of German nationalism brought new difficulties for Jews all across Central Europe. Laws in various localities restricted Jews' rights to marry and to reside in the places of their birth. Between 1819 and 1848, riots targeted Jewish neighborhoods in Baden, Frankfurt, Munich, and other cities, burning homes and looting shops. In 1840, the *Israelitische Annalen* wrote from Swabia (in modern Baden-Württemberg): "The emigration fever has steadily increased among Israelites of our district and seems about to reach its high point. In nearly every community there are numerous individuals who are preparing to leave the Fatherland early next year and seek their fortune on the other side of the ocean."[77]

New York was the largest port of entry, but there were others: New Orleans, Philadelphia, Baltimore, and Boston. Peddling was an employment niche that German Jewish immigrant men quickly took over. Avraham Barkai described the scene:

> [T]he Jews had indeed succeeded to "transplant Bavaria to America." Settling all over the land, preferably in regions of strong German settlement, they almost immediately went back to "carry a pack" and peddle their wares among the newly upgrowing farms like their fathers in the old homeland. Even learned artisans who initially started work in their skilled trade found it more profitable to return to peddling. Not, of course, as a permanent station, but as a favorable transitional way to earn a living and gain some capital during the early period of economic adjustment.[78]

It was a simple mode of self-employment and kept them from being beholden to Gentile employers. It did not require much capital to start, and one need not speak English if one traded mainly with other Germans at first. As one picked up capital and knowledge of the new country, one could branch out. The Jewish peddler became a stereotype immortalized in doggerel and popular fiction. Jewish men hawked their wares not just in the seaboard cities but also throughout the South and West, and established small Jewish communities wherever they went.[79] They invented installment sales. They went first to inland cities where Germans congregated, like Cincinnati, St. Louis, and Milwaukee. But soon they were selling all over the South and West. Solomon Spiegelberg drove a team of oxen over the Santa Fe Trail in 1846, got a contract to provision the U.S. Army in its war on Mexico, and later with his brothers founded what became the territory's largest retail establishment. Adam Gimbel came from Bavaria to New Orleans in 1835 and sold this and that up and down the Mississippi. Then he opened a dry goods store in Vincennes, Indiana. In time, he and his sons owned a chain of stores in Milwaukee, Philadelphia, and New York. Bloomingdale's also had peddler origins. Other Jews with names like Kuhn, Loeb, and Seligmann became the core of New York's German Jewish financial aristocracy by the latter decades of the nineteenth century. Most immigrants did not achieve such spectacular success, but by the time the second generation turned to the third, most German Jews had entered the ranks of the middle class in urban America.

German Jews brought with them a jumble of theological persuasions, from strict Orthodoxy to radical free thought. One of these was Reform Judaism, the cutting edge of Jewish intellectual liberalism in Germany. Anxious to be accepted into American (as into German) Gentile society, the Reformers tried to modernize Judaism, to deemphasize the ritual aspects and Mosaic imperatives that set their religion apart from Christians. They discounted the age-old notion that the Jews were a people somehow different from other peoples and presented Reform Judaism as just another denomination, like Presbyterianism.[80] Their rationale was that Judaism had always changed its face to accommodate the tastes and state of knowledge of the time. They also stressed that Jews had a special mission to reach all people, not just to recreate the historic nation of Israel, and so they must be flexible in their appeal. Orthodox leaders in America and especially in Europe looked upon the Reformers with horror. They felt that Reform struck at the very heart of proper Judaism: ritual adherence to Mosaic law. But in America, unlike Europe, the Reformers had a relatively free hand to change Judaism as they pleased, for there were no official ecclesiastical structures and few long-established Orthodox bodies to stand in their way. Reform Jews took over the Charleston synagogue in the 1820s, and others led by Rabbi Leo Merzbacher founded Temple Emanu-El in New York City in 1845. It is probably true that most American Jews remained more or less Orthodox, but by the time of the Civil War, most of the elite were adherents of Reform.[81]

Reform Judaism began as an adaptation to the intellectual imperatives of German Enlightenment culture, but it also became an expression of American Jewish independence from Europe. Isaac Meyer Wise, the great leader of American Reform, called for a separate American synod (note the word borrowed from Christianity) in 1855, a call that resulted in an independent body of Reform leaders and congregations that diverged further and further from Orthodoxy. Two decades later, a Reform gathering in Pittsburgh set out these very modernist religious principles:

> *The God-Idea.* We recognize in every religion an attempt to grasp the Infinite One, and in every mode, source or book of revelation held sacred in any religious system the consciousness of the Indwelling of God in man. … *The Jewish People.* We recognize in Judaism a progressive religion ever striving to be in accord with the postulates of reason. We are convinced of the utmost necessity of preserving the historical identity with our great past. Christianity and Islam being daughter religions of Judaism, we appreciate their mission to aid in the spreading of monotheistic and moral truth. We acknowledge that the spirit of broad humanity of our age is our ally in the fulfillment of our mission, and therefore we extend the hand of fellowship to all who cooperate with us in the establishment of truth and righteousness among men. *Tora.* We recognize in the Mosaic legislation a system of training the Jewish people of its mission during its national life in Palestine, and today we accept as binding only the moral laws and maintain only such ceremonies as elevate and sanctify our lives, but reject all such as are not adapted to the views and habits of modern civilization.

They sound a bit like Unitarians. Judaism was changing to fit the social ambitions of its assimilating adherents in their American environment.[82]

Not only was the trend toward Reform. It was also toward upward social and economic mobility. The German Jewish population was not made up entirely of economic successes, but the second generation was making a place for itself in the

White American middle class by the 1880s, just when a new wave of very different Jews began showing up—but that is a story for Chapter 5.

Issues in European Migration

How are we to interpret all this? Are there big patterns and larger meanings to these movements of Europeans into the United States in the decades between the founding of the republic and the Civil War? Historians of immigration have raised a number of interpretive issues that are worth contemplating.

Individual Choice or Embedded in a Web of Industrial Capital?

Many Americans cherish a story (sometimes more than one) about the coming of their own family to America once upon a time. Usually it is a story with a heroic quality to it, such as a great, great grandfather choosing to leave his ancestral home for reasons noble, adventuresome, or pious. Or perhaps he was fleeing persecution, or avoiding the sheriff. But in any case, it is usually an individual story, even an adventure. A person or a family left the country of their birth and chose to come to the United States because things were bad for them where they were and because they envisioned America as a land of freedom or opportunity. And surely, many immigrants made individual decisions in more or less that way.

Historians, however, like to search for patterns in such individual actions. And patterns there were aplenty in the case of international migration. The most common way historians treat migration is to speak of "push factors"—those elements of the social situation in the sending country that make individuals want to leave—and "pull factors"—those features that draw them to a particular destination.[83] Perhaps understandably, the July Fourth rhetoric of American political triumphalism has tended to emphasize pull factors. People chose to come here because the United States is wonderful. Its economic bounty or promise of liberty compelled them to come. In the case of each of the European immigrant groups dealt with in this chapter, it is easy to see push factors. Irish emigrants fled famine. German Jews left under the sting of social discrimination. Gentile Germans and English folk were in less dire circumstances in the old country. For them, the push factors may have existed—a migrant might not have stood to inherit the family farm, for instance—but it is unlikely that, for the bulk of British and German migrants in this period, push factors were decisive. Rather, the pulls of high wages and cheap farmland were what drew these more middle-class migrants to the United States.

That makes sense, but was it really that simple? Or is it possible that there may have been something connecting the sending places and the receiving place? If that be true, then perhaps the push factors and the pull factors did not operate independently of each other, but were part of a larger, transnational web of causation. Dirk Hörder and other scholars have described three such transnational webs operating in the nineteenth century (Figure 3.5). The Russo-Siberian System, between 1815 and 1915, drew 10 million people from European Russia (and other parts of Central and Eastern Europe) across the Eurasian land mass to inhabit the lands Catherine the Great had claimed in the latter eighteenth century. The Asia and Pacific System sent 14.5 million people, mainly contract laborers in plantation agriculture, back and

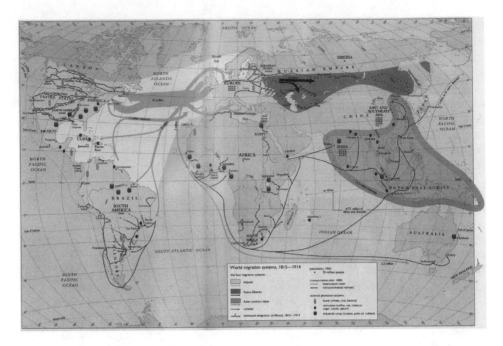

Figure 3.5 World migration systems.

forth across that part of the world. South Chinese went to Malaysia, the Philippines, and elsewhere. Filipinos went to Hong Kong. Indians went to Malaysia, the Dutch East Indies, and Fiji. Japanese went to Korea. And another million Asians spun off into North and South America. There they connected with the System of the Atlantic Economies. In that system, thirty-five million people migrated from Europe to North America, eight million to South America. Seven million went back. Another half million went along the pathways of European colonialism to Africa and Asia, and 2.5 million migrated to Australia.[84]

The common thread operating in all three of these systems was colonialism, but the three systems presented different varieties of colonial connection. In the Russo-Siberian system, the colonialism was straightforward: Russians going across the continent, making it their own, and incorporating it into the Russian state, much like European Americans taking the North American continent in the nineteenth century (see Chapter 4). In the Asia–Pacific system, there were several European and American colonial powers (operating formally as in India and less formally as in China). The relationships between European colonizer and would-be colonizer countries, on one side, and Asian colonized countries on the other, provided the pathways for migration by Asians and islanders as well as Europeans. In the Atlantic system, there were elements of formal and less formal colonialism: Americans across the continent; British in Central America.

In Chapter 1, I described the international labor migration model proposed by Lucie Cheng and Edna Bonacich. It would seem to be an appropriate device for attempting to understand the dynamics within each of these three systems of economic connection and movement of peoples. Cheng and Bonacich's model posits a core, industrializing country—say, Britain—and one or more places that are tied to it in a subordinate way. They have agricultural economies that supply crops, raw materials, and migrants as the industrial core has need of them. At its simplest, this model would have predicted American workers would have left home to migrate to England and take work in booming British textile mills in the nineteenth century. The people were moving the other way, so something seems amiss. As we shall see in Chapters 4 and 5, the Cheng and Bonacich model works fairly well for some groups such as Chinese and Japanese moving from Asia to the United States in the latter nineteenth and early twentieth centuries, and quite well for Mexicans, Filipinos, and Central Americans moving to the United States in the late twentieth and early twenty-first centuries. But it seems less well suited to explain European migration streams to the United States in the first two-thirds of the nineteenth century.

Instead, let us follow historian William Van Vugt and recognize that the British and American economies were indeed intimately connected, but in more complex ways than the Cheng and Bonacich model allows. Imagine a single North Atlantic economy headed by the industrializing regions of the English Midlands, with secondary centers in the Ruhr Valley and New England. As Britain's industrial transformation changed its own landscape and Ireland's, and cut loose large numbers of farm people (some of the middling sort, some desperately poor), industrialization was also turning loose significant numbers of people in Germany. This economic system then reallocated those laborers to factories in England, Germany, and the American Northeast, as well as to farms across the United States. John Bodnar, preeminent American historian of U.S. industrial labor immigration, described it this way:

> The movement to America of millions of immigrants in the century after the 1820s was not simply a flight of impoverished peasants abandoning underdeveloped, backward regions for the riches and unlimited opportunities offered by the American economy. This tremendous population shift depended not only on the growth of American industrial capitalism but on transformations occurring in immigrant homelands as well. People did not move randomly to America but emanated from very specific regions at specific times. ... Economic changes in the immigrant homeland rather than American industrial growth accounted for the cycle of each immigrant stream. ... The immigrant did not encounter capitalism for the first time in American cities; he had already encountered some of its manifestations prior to departing. ... [C]apitalism intruded. ... as transportation networks expanded from industrial cities, cheaper manufactured goods flooded rural markets undercutting the economic base of independent artisans and household producers. ... [T]he rise of industrial cities created a huge new market for agricultural produce. Agriculture conducted on a large scale ... moved from a subsistence base to ... cash crops.[85]

Many of the people thus cast off the land became the working class of Europe's cities. Millions more ended up going to the United States.

Recruitment and Chain Migration

Migrants did not just choose to go to America. In addition to being propelled along the sinews of an interlocking international economic system, they were actively recruited and conducted. There was money to be made in international labor migration. Sailing and steamship companies, land speculators, employers in the United States, and a host of others had an interest in expanding the migration stream, as it would bring them customers, buyers, and workers. They advertised in newspapers throughout Britain, Ireland, and Germany in this period—and later in other parts of Europe as well. Some large employers and transportation companies sent agents to Europe to recruit migrants. A hot market sprang up in guide books for would-be emigrants. Some were aimed at the general population, others at specific groups with particular destinations in mind. One of the most popular, *Wiley & Putnam's Emigrant's Guide*, promised reliable instruction for everything from the initial decision to emigrate to securing a job and a place to stay in America. The opening chapter's contents read:

> Who should emigrate. The choice of a ship. Dishonest runners. Extract from the circular of the New York Emigrant Society. How to know whether a passenger-agent is respectable or otherwise. The difference in ships. Good and bad points about a ship so plainly stated that an emigrant can choose a ship for himself. A ship should be of good height between decks—should have good conveniences for cooking—good water-closets. When a ship is properly loaded. The character of the captains and officers important. Facts illustrative of the difference between a bad captain and a good captain. Emigrants should speak well of a good ship and good treatment.

The guide listed what food to take, names of shipping agents in various cities, how to handle conflict with other passengers, and a host of other necessaries.[86] Similar guides were written in German for both Jewish and Gentile readerships. Specialized guidebooks instructed Mormons how to make their way by covered wagon to the valley of the Great Salt Lake and told Europeans how to reach the California goldfields.

Once recruited, migrants entered migration chains. These have been a near-constant feature of large voluntary movements of people in modern world history. A few people from a particular place—a town, a village, a rural district, an urban neighborhood—in a particular sending country or region would go abroad and have a good experience. They would write to relatives and friends back home, tell of their success, and suggest that those people come, too, perhaps offering to help pay passage. Some of those people would then join them in the new place, have success, and write back to others. And soon a link was established between the old place and the new.

We see chain migration at work in the period under discussion in this chapter among German, English, Irish and other immigrants. Anna Maria Schano wrote from New York, back to her family in Germany in 1850:

> I've saved up to now in the time we've been married some 40 dollars in case, not counting my clothes. Dear parents and brothers and sisters, I certainly don't want to tell you what to do, do what you want, for some like it here and some don't, but the only ones who don't like it here had it good in Germany, but I also think you would like it here since you never had anything good in Germany. I'm certainly glad not to be over there, and only those who don't want to work don't like it here, since in America you have to work if you want to amount

to anything, you mustn't feel ashamed, that's just how you amount to something, and so I want to tell you again to do what you want, since it can seem too trying on the journey and in America as well, and then you heap the most bitter reproaches on those who talked you into coming, since it all depends on whether you have good luck, just like in Germany. Dear parents, you wrote me that Daniel wants to come to America and doesn't have any money, that is certainly a problem. Now I want to give you my opinion, I've often thought about what could be done. I thought 1st if he could borrow the money over there, then when he has saved enough over here then he could send it back over, like a lot of people do, and secondly, I thought we would like to pay for him to come over, but right now we can't since it costs 28 dollars a person and I also want to tell you since my husband wrote to you, the money we want to send you, whether you want to use it to have one or two come over here or if you want to spend it on yourselves, you just have to let us know so that we have an idea how much you still need, and you'll have to see to it that you have some more money, too, since we can't pay it all. ... Dear parents and brothers and sisters, if one of you comes over here and comes to stay with us we will certainly take care of you, since we are now well known, and you needn't be so afraid of America, when you come to America, just imagine you were moving to Stuttgart, that's how many Germans you can see here.[87]

The same pattern held for other migrant groups. For that reason, some localities and some extended families, over a period of years or perhaps decades, essentially moved en masse to America. Others nearby, in similar circumstances but without an American connection, remained where they were or migrated to European cities instead.[88]

One feature of the migration chain is return migration. Links to the homeland brought people over, but they also kept one connected to the place one left. The triumphal narrative of American immigration posits that people who migrate to the United States do so with the intention to stay forever. They cast off the chains or poverty of the old country and put on the freedom and prosperity of the new. They embrace cultural change so that they become new people in the American mold. Surely, sentiments something like these must have characterized some immigrants in every age. But for many more, surely there was ambivalence about the venture. Many migrants—in every age and from almost every group—came to America with the initial intent to return to their original homes, perhaps a bit richer than when they left. A prime goal of many was to assemble the wherewithal to buy some land back home. Others who hoped to live permanently in the United States found it did not work out as well as they had dreamed. Oftentimes they had more difficulty with language and strange American customs than they had anticipated. Frequently they encountered opposition from other European Americans whose ancestors had come a generation or two earlier. Sometimes they just decided they liked their former home better.[89]

Over the course of the nineteenth century, one out of five immigrants to the United States from Europe returned whence they came. William Van Vugt tells of Eli Beckley making ten trips back to England to import horses after his initial migration to Illinois in 1854. "The mid-century immigrants would make return visits for almost any imaginable reason: to preach a funeral sermon, for health reasons (which surely included homesickness), to find suitable brides, to see family, or to fight in the

Is that a lot?

Crimean War." He estimates that, between 1870 and World War I, 40 percent of English and Scottish immigrants returned home permanently. Charles Dickens wrote about a trip of his own back to England following a book tour in the United States in 1842: "We carried in the steerage nearly a hundred passengers: a little world of poverty. … Some of them had been in America but three days, some but three months, and some had gone out in the last voyage of that very ship in which they were now returning home. Others had sold their clothes to raise the passage-money, and had hardly rags to cover them; others had no food, and lived upon the charity of the rest. They were coming back, even poorer than they went."[90]

From Puritan exiles in Massachusetts to twenty-first-century Korean entrepreneurs riding jumbo jets, going and coming have ever been part of the immigrant story, although they have not been acknowledged in the dominant paradigm of immigrant assimilation. Of the groups we have witnessed in this chapter, only the Irish and Jews failed to go back to their former homeland in significant numbers. In the Irish case, the old country's economy just would not support them. Instead of an actual return, Irish Americans substituted a psychic one—ongoing involvement in the Irish national cause and a plaintive song of exile. In later chapters we will see other immigrant groups following both these patterns. We shall see Chinese, Italian, Greek, and other migrants maintaining strong ties to the homes and families they left behind, sending remittances to support the people back home, and significant numbers of them eventually going back themselves. From time to time we will see others such as Hmong maintaining the mood of exile, even though the rate of actual return is slight.

Changes in Transportation Technology and Travel Conditions

One of the things that made return migration practical was improvements in transportation technology. The trip from Liverpool to New York took about five weeks by sailing ship. If the weather was bad, it could take as much as fourteen weeks. Conditions had not improved much since Gottlieb Mittelberger's crossing (see Chapter 2). By mid-century most ships had two or three classes, but the better cabins were beyond the means of most immigrants, who ended up in steerage. Their accommodations were cramped: "besides two tiers of berths on the sides, the vessel was filled with a row of berths down the centre, between which and the side berths there was only a passage of about three feet. The passengers were thus obliged to eat in their berths. In one were a man, his wife, his sister, and five children; in another were six full-grown young women, whilst that above them contained five men, and the next one eight men."[91]

Most travelers probably had good passages, despite certain hardships. There were times of excited anticipation, especially at the beginning of the journey: "The morning was fine, and the ebbing tide in a few hours carried us out of the river. During the day the wind, though light, continued favorable, and we had, literally speaking, a pleasure sail. Every heart was light and every face wore a smile." But before long it became pretty grungy: "It was scarcely possible to induce the passengers to sweep the decks after their meals or to be decent in respect to the common wants of nature; in many cases, in bad weather, they would not go on deck; their health suffered so much that their strength was gone, and they had not the power to help themselves. Hence the between-decks were like a loathsome dungeon. When the hatchways were opened under which the people were stowed, the steam rose and the stench was like that from a pen of pigs. The few beds they had were in a dreadful state, for the straw, once wet with sea water, soon rotted, besides which they used the between-decks for all sorts of filthy purposes." The water was foul. The food was rotten, or at best monotonous. Cholera and "ship fever" ran through the steerage cabin. For some, it was worse. Harriot Veness wrote: "We were very sick for three weeks [on account of a storm] coming over. We had the misfortune to lose both our little boys. We were very much hurt to have them buried in a watery grave."[92]

Steamships began to make transatlantic passages in the 1840s. The conditions in their steerage were no better, but the crossing took a fraction of the time: about twelve days. As late as the latter 1850s, 95 percent of migrants still traveled under sail. Gradually over the next three decades the migrant traffic shifted from sail to steam, so that by the time of another large surge in immigration late in the century most people had to endure only much shorter voyages. Significantly improved conditions on shipboard would not come until the twentieth century.[93]

Nativism

One of the responses to all this immigration, from White Americans who were born in this country, was a nativist movement. Protestant, English-descended people saw themselves as the truest sort of Americans from early in the colonial period. Some had a long-standing suspicion of non-English Whites—for example, Ben Franklin's fulminations against Pennsylvania Germans. As immigration grew in the 1830s to 1850s, nativism grew with it. It reached a high point—one of several in American history—with the launching of the American or Know Nothing Party in the 1850s on an explicitly anti-immigrant platform.[94] John Higham summarized "the ideological core of nativism. ... Whether the nativist was a workingman or a Protestant evangelist, a southern conservative or a northern reformer, he stood for a certain kind of nationalism. He believed—whether he was trembling at a Catholic menace to American liberty, fearing an invasion of pauper labor, or simply rioting against the great English actor William Macready—that some influence originating abroad threatened the very life of the nation from within. Nativism [was] intense opposition to an internal minority on the ground of its foreign (i.e., 'un-American') connections."[95]

The upsurge of Irish, German (and, unacknowledged by the nativists, British) immigration came at the same time much of the United States was in the throes of the Second Great Awakening, a generation-long revival of Protestant religious excitement and intimacy with God. It was perhaps natural that in an era of enthusiasm about Protestantism, some people should express hostility to the great rival of their church.

Among the charges against the Roman Catholic Church was that its members would never be free citizens of the United States but slaves to the pope. Samuel F. B. Morse, the telegraph inventor, published in 1835 *Imminent Dangers to the Free Institutions of the United States through Foreign Immigration*, which was mainly a diatribe against the supposed evils of the Catholic Church. Thomas Whitney contrasted "Romanism" with "American Republicanism" (not to be confused with the Republican Party, which was born in this era and did not oppose immigration) in 1856:

American Republicanism cultivates intelligence among the people. Romanism suppresses intelligence.

American Republicanism recognizes and secures to all men the right of trial by jury. Romanism adjudicates in the somber dungeon of the inquisition. ...

American Republicanism ensures the freedom of the press, and the right of free speech. Romanism silences, or else muzzles the press and forbids discussion. ...

American Republicanism secures the full liberty of conscience to all its people, and to the stranger within its gates. Romanism pronounces liberty of conscience to be a wicked theory.

American Republicanism permits every human creature to read and study the Word of God. Romanism forbids it. In a word, American Republicanism is FREEDOM; Romanism is *slavery*.[96]

Beyond the fantasy of sinister foreign control over American citizens, anti-Catholics had lurid tales to tell about deeds done in darkness in Catholic precincts. They alleged that German and especially Irish Catholics brought crime and disease to U.S. cities, and that they stole the jobs of native-born people. In 1836, some anti-Catholic activists helped a woman named Maria Monk write *Awful Disclosures of the Hotel Dieu Nunnery of Montreal*, where she told tales of priests tunneling into nuns' cloisters and forcing themselves on the women, of the resultant babies being strangled by church authorities, and of her own supposed escape with a priest's child in her womb. It all turned out to be fabricated, but it sold a lot of copies, prompted a sequel, and whipped up a frenzy against Catholic immigrants.[97] Similar tales formed the backdrop for violence against Catholics. On the night of August 11, 1834, egged on by Lyman Beecher, the most famous Protestant preacher in America at the time, a Boston mob burst into the Ursuline convent in nearby Charlestown and burned it to the ground. At least a dozen other church buildings were torched in the next two decades, and an anti-Catholic riot in Philadelphia in 1844 killed thirty people and injured hundreds.

By the mid-1850s, the anti-Catholic crowd had gathered themselves into what they called the American Party, with which they hoped to replace the fading Whigs. They operated like a secret society and it was said they would not talk for the record, hence others called them "Know Nothings" derisively. Their central issue was to enact federal restrictions on immigration and naturalization. Specific provisions varied, but generally they included a twenty-one-year wait for naturalization and a bar on serving in any but the lowest government offices. Other proposals included banning immigrants who were paupers, insane, feeble-minded, or had criminal backgrounds or certain diseases.

The Know Nothings flashed boldly across the American political landscape in the 1850s. They elected governors in six states and took control of nine state legislatures. Yet it is important to remember that the nativists did not prevail. The Know Nothings flamed out; in 1856 Millard Fillmore ran for president on both the Know Nothing ticket and the Whig, and both parties died in the process. Out of their ashes came a Republican Party that was committed to "Free Soil, Free Labor, Free Men":

immigration would go unrestricted, the government would provide public lands to would-be farmers cheap or free, and slavery would be overturned.[98]

The nativist movement of the mid-nineteenth century has always been portrayed as an anti-Catholic and especially, as we shall see in the next section, an anti-Irish movement. That is true, in the sense that anti-Catholicism was the focus of the Know Nothing party and people like Morse and Whitney. But those same years saw the beginnings of a not wholly unrelated movement against Jews. European Christians had long harbored some pretty appalling prejudices against Jews. As European Jews were emancipated and began to ascend the social and financial ladders over the course of the nineteenth century, they came in for increasing anti-Semitic abuse. The European prejudices had their echoes on the North American continent. But the American expressions of anti-Semitism were muted by comparison. Three states required voters to swear on the Christian Bible, which effectively eliminated Jews from voting. Yet two of those states (Rhode Island and New Hampshire) overturned the ban in 1842—at the height of anti-Catholicism—and the other (North Carolina) joined them in 1868. In that same era, David Yulee of Florida (1846) and Judah P. Benjamin of Louisiana (1852) were elected to the U.S. Senate. And rabbis gave the opening prayers to the Virginia House of Delegates and constitutional convention. So Jews seem to have been accorded places of civic legitimacy in American society, and despite personal prejudices and some social discrimination, they were not made a specific target of anti-immigrant hostility in this period. That would wait until after the Civil War.[99]

The issue in all this was: Who was fit to become a full member of American society? Since the Naturalization Act of 1790, one had to be White. Now, it seemed, there was increasing sentiment that one must be Protestant as well. There was also an undercurrent of offense taken by Anglo-Americans at the insistence by some Germans on separate German-language schools. Some Irish and German Catholics established Catholic parochial schools, and in some cases they suggested that the public help fund those schools on the same basis that it funded schools with Protestant leanings. This offended a lot of Anglo-Protestants. Jews continued to inhabit a kind of second-class status. Yet these were all discussions—even disagreements and attacks—within the community of White people. Catholics and Jews were marginal to America's Anglo-Protestant self-definition, but they were within the realm of Whiteness. Blacks, Indians, Mexicans, Chinese were all entirely outside.[100]

Despite the failure of the Know Nothings and their platform, nativist ideas were not spent. Nativism—not with its own party but as a minority strain within both major parties—reached full flower after the Civil War. In 1882, when immigration patterns were still much as they had been in the 1850s (a new burst of immigration from new places was just beginning), *Atlantic Monthly* editor Thomas Bailey Aldrich published the poem "Unguarded Gates," which read in part:

> Wide open and unguarded stand our gates,
> And through them presses a wild motley throng—
> Men from the Volga and Tartar steppes,
> Featureless figures of the Hoang-Ho,
> Malayan, Scythian, Teuton, Kelt, and Slav,
> Flying the Old World's poverty and scorn;
> These bringing with them unknown gods and rites,
> Those, tiger passions, here to stretch their claws.

In street and alley what strange tongues are loud,
Accents of menace alien to our air,
Voices that once the Tower of Babel knew!
O Liberty, white Goddess! is it well
To leave the gates unguarded? On thy breast
Fold Sorrow's children, soothe the hurts of fate,
Lift the down-trodden, but with hand of steel
Stay those who to thy sacred portals come
To waste the gifts of freedom. ...[101]

Such racist, xenophobic ideas have proved hard to put away, no matter that they have never had any basis except in fear and unreason. There is a direct line from Samuel F. B. Morse and Thomas Whitney in the mid-nineteenth century, through Thomas Bailey Aldrich to Madison Grant and Lothrop Stoddard in the early twentieth century (see Chapter 6), and on to Pat Buchanan and Richard Lamm in the early twenty-first century (Chapter 9).

Were the Irish Ever Not White?

If full citizenship was to be limited to White people, and if some American citizens, so defined, wanted to keep out Irish or German Catholics, did that mean that the Irish and German Catholics were not White? So it has been alleged, more or less. There is a large, rapidly growing literature on Whiteness, and much of it springs from a consideration of the place of Irish immigrants in the first two-thirds of the nineteenth century.[102] The term "White," used as both an adjective and a noun to refer to people of European descent and to distinguish them from Africans and Native North Americans, goes back in English usage as far as 1604. By the end of that century, White was the common appellation for European-descended people in North America. Winthrop Jordan wrote: "[T]here seems to have been something of a shift during the seventeenth century in the terminology which Englishmen in the colonies applied to themselves. From the initially most common term *Christian*, at mid-century there was a marked shift toward the terms *English* and *free*. After about 1680, taking the colonies as a whole, a new term of self-identification appeared—*white*."[103]

As we have seen, English-descended people regarded themselves as central to the American identity. But right from the start they had room for other European-descended people as citizens of the thirteen colonies and of the new nation. Some scholars have stood up in recent years to assert that Irish people were not White in the first three-quarters of a century of the American republic. They point to real disabilities suffered by Irish people—some discrimination, even mob violence—and contend that popular culture portrayed Irish in the same way it portrayed Blacks. Yes, there is one famous cartoon from 1876 where an Irish man with simianized features is set on a scale in balance with a Black man (Figure 3.6).

But in that case, Thomas Nast was not saying that Irish people were Black. Rather, he was saying that Irish American support for the Democratic Party in the North balanced out the votes of newly freed African Americans in the South, and he was implying that he didn't think much of either group. Nast did draw the Irish figure with ape-like features, and neither it nor the portrait of the Black man opposite is a sympathetic portrait.[104] But this is one of only a very few such portrayals

THE IGNORANT VOTE—HONORS ARE EASY.

Figure 3.6 A cartoon by Thomas Nast, *Harper's Weekly*, 1837.

in America of Irish as physically distinguishable from other Whites. There were many such bestial images in British depictions of Irish people, but few in America. A legitimate argument can be made that the colonial relationship between Britain and Ireland resulted in the creation in British minds of the idea of an Irish Other that had racial qualities to it. But it is not, in my judgment, possible to do the same in the American context.[105]

The test is not how a person or group is caricatured by cartoonists who oppose that person or group. Democratic-leaning cartoonists in the first decade of the twenty-first century made the American president look like Alfred E. Newman. The test is how a person or group is portrayed by those who are sympathetic. Did such people draw Irish Americans as not looking White? Artists who sympathized with the situations of Native Americans, African Americans, and Chinese Americans in the latter nineteenth century nonetheless portrayed them as racially other, as physically different from Whites, in fact as looking unlike any living Indian, Black, or Chinese (Figure 3.7). By contrast, artists who sympathized with Irish people showed them as looking just like other Whites (Figure 3.8). There were a great many cartoons that looked like this in American publications in the nineteenth century, and very few that looked like Nast's caricature.

The actual record of discrimination against Irish Americans exists, but it is much thinner than for any people of color. Irish were White in America.

125

Figure 3.7 Distorted Indian, Chinese, and Black caricatures, *Harper's Weekly*, 1879.

Making a White Race

What we see happening in the first decades of the republic is the culmination of a process that began in the 1600s, when Europeans began to define themselves as White—first against Native peoples and then against Africans. By the middle of the nineteenth century at the very latest, consensus had been reached that to be of European descent made one White, and that one must be White if one aspired to full U.S. citizenship.

Jon Gjerde tells this story in his brilliant work of historical ethnography and imagination, *The Minds of the West*:

> My mother is a daughter of the middle border. Born in 1908, she was reared by a Danish father and a Yankee mother on a farm in southwestern Minnesota. She cherishes still the memories of her Danish grandmother who lived with the family and remembers well being schooled in Methodist ways by her mother. When she came of age, she chose to marry the son of a Norwegian

Figure 3.8 Irish American prizefighter.

Lutheran pastor who had been raised in deeply rural Norwegian communities of the American Northwest. It probably came as little surprise to her when her son some years later wed a German American Roman Catholic. In sum, she lived in a region where ethnic and religious identities were clearly defined but where interaction between people ... was relatively common and boundaries were often breached. Her narrative is emblematic of the rural Middle West.[106]

So it is indeed. Gjerde does not acknowledge it here, but this is a story about the formation of the White race. His mother and the others whose lives he portrays in the book show the ease with which people of various European ancestries blended together socially and familially. There are no African Americans in Gjerde's mother's Middle West, no Indians or Asians or Mexicans. There are just White people, but they are not labeled White. Instead, they are labeled Swedes, Danes, Dutch, Norwegians, Germans, and lots of other things. Their Whiteness is masked by the discussion of their ethnic particularities. And their ethnic particularities (including religious identities from Mennonite to Catholic to Presbyterian) matter to them as badges of identity. Gjerde's people mark those identities all the time in discourse casual and purposeful. Except that those identities don't ultimately count for much. Nearly everyone in this story is, like Gjerde's mother, in fact ethnically mixed. Their friends come from lots of different kinds of White people and include no people who are not White. The people in *Minds of the West* have other ethnic labels, and they have lots of knowledge about the places with which those labels are associated, but they are just White people.

From very early on, the American imagination celebrated the myth of the melting pot. America would be a land where all the world's peoples were welcome to come and where they all merged into a new people. J. Hector St. John de Crèvecoeur, himself a French immigrant, made the classic melting pot statement in 1782 (see page 5). It is a powerful vision of blending and creating a new identity based on interaction among peoples and response to republican political institutions. But it is a vision limited to White people.

Even among such White people, practically speaking, differences were drawn. Crèvecoeur's rhapsody did not admit what was happening on the ground. In practical fact, not all Whites were blending together equally. From the very beginning, as we have seen, Anglo-Americans assumed primacy. What was happening was not the melting pot but, as sociologist Milton Gordon explained, "Anglo-conformity." From the beginning there was "a central assumption [of] the desirability of maintaining English institutions (as modified by the American Revolution), the English language, and English-oriented cultural patterns as dominant and standard in American life"[107] (Figure 3.9).

Compare Figure 3.2 to Figure 3.1 at the beginning of this chapter. What happened in the first half of the nineteenth century, demographically speaking? The overall U.S. population exploded, from less than 7 million to nearly 24 million. Perhaps 3 million of those people were immigrants of European origin. The rest came from natural increase. The number and proportion of Native peoples declined sharply, and African American numbers rose modestly. The United States was indeed becoming a White man's country—in terms of who made up the largest part of the population as well as who set the cultural agenda for society—just as the nation was marching across the continent and ingesting it. The latter is the story of Chapter 4.

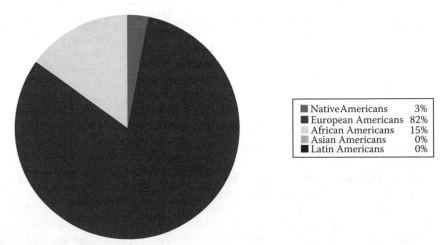

■ Native Americans	3%
■ European Americans	82%
▢ African Americans	15%
▨ Asian Americans	0%
■ Latin Americans	0%

Figure 3.9 Population in 1850 of the territory that would become the United States (23.9 million people).

Chapter 4

The Border Crossed Us: Euro-Americans Take the Continent, 1830–1900

"Of all conquerors, we were perhaps the most excusable, the most reasonable, the most beneficent. The Mexicans had come far short of their duty to the world. Being what they were, they had forfeited a large share of their national rights."

Justin Smith
The War with Mexico[1]

Almost All Aliens is not organized according to strict chronology. The general movement of the book is from past to present, but this chapter, for example, overlaps the one that precedes it considerably with respect to the time periods to which they attend. Chapter 3 addresses the period 1760 to 1860, while Chapter 4 runs from 1830 to 1900. Rather than just chronology, each chapter highlights a particular theme or issue. Chapter 3 was about a connection between immigration and race, one of the topics promised in the book's subtitle. That is, at its core it described the formation of the White race out of various immigrant peoples from Europe, with English-descended people holding the place at the unexamined center. Chapter 4 is mainly about the other connection in the book's subtitle: between immigration and colonialism.

The nineteenth century was one of Euro-American colonial enterprise. Embracing the ideology of Manifest Destiny and westward expansion, White Americans marched across the North American continent and took it. They made war on many Native peoples and tried to exterminate some. Others they removed from their ancestral lands and sent to places far away, where they were restricted to ever smaller and more remote reservations. In two great gulps in the 1830s and 1840s, Euro-Americans seized the Mexican northlands and incorporated Mexico's conquered people with a measure of Whiteness: legal citizenship, but social

Brownness. In the wake of all this colonial expansion, several different patterns of race-making emerged between Euro-Americans on the one hand and Mexicans, Indians, Asians, and Blacks on the other, in various parts of the borderlands that became the American West and Southwest.

This chapter also explores the nature of Chinese immigration and compares the anti-immigrant movement against the Irish with the movement against the Chinese. It examines the tension between different vectors of the international recruitment of labor for industrializing America—recruiting future citizens from Europe and recruiting noncitizen guest workers from Asia and Latin America. It assesses the conflict over slavery and the making of a new racial order in the South after the Civil War: the remaking of the meaning of personhood and a measure of citizenship for African-descended people. Finally, it explores the ways that disparate groups of Indians were forced together on reservations and began to build a common Native American panethnicity.

U.S. Colonial Expansion across North America

Late in the twentieth century and early in the twenty-first century, we are in the habit of talking about immigration as having consequences for the people who are already here now. We weigh the expected value to the American economy and social structure of immigrant workers, investors, and families against the supposed costs to American citizens in terms of jobs, wages, health care, education, and so forth. Such policy inquiries are reasonable, even important considerations to undertake. But it is also true that, as we contemplate the past, we need to talk about past immigration's consequences for the people who were already here before. What did it cost the Native peoples of North America for previous generations of immigrants to come to their country? It cost a lot.

Making Empire, Making Race: Manifest Destiny and Westward Expansion

From very early in the history of the republic, Euro-Americans asked themselves, "What shall be the geographical limits of our nation?" but their underlying meaning was, "Where shall we go and what shall we take?" Thirteen little colonies fought a war against their British relatives, France intervened at a key moment, and England gave up. In 1783 the United States formally acquired England's claim to all the lands between the Appalachian crest and the Mississippi River. They didn't own it or occupy it, of course. There were Native peoples living there, but the White Americans pressed in upon them for the next three generations until they had pushed nearly all of them out. In the revolutionary generation, some argued grandly that the United States should spread from Atlantic to Pacific and from the Arctic to Tierra del Fuego. Such, they said, were the natural limits of the American empire. By comparison, the eventual American empire, stretching from ocean to ocean but only from the Gulf of Mexico to the 49th Parallel, seems a more modest land grab. The great prize was the Louisiana Purchase in 1803, by which some kind of paper title to another large chunk of Native American lands was transferred from France to the United States. In 1819 the United States acquired Florida and the Gulf Coast

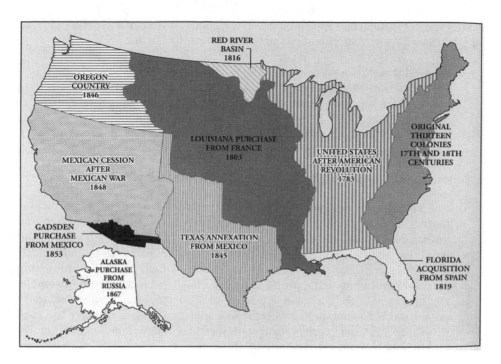

Figure 4.1 Growth of U.S. land claims.

from Spain. The 1840s saw the territory Texas claimed, the Oregon Country, and Mexico's extreme northwest all fall into America's lap (Figure 4.1).

Of course, there were people living on those lands. Under relentless military and economic pressures, one group of Native Americans, and then another, and then another was forced to cede their lands to the United States.

In the first half of the nineteenth century, Euro-Americans freely called this the making of an empire (later they repented of the term, but not of the deed). They constructed for themselves an ideology—Manifest Destiny—that explained why this empire was a good thing.[2] The phrase was coined famously in 1845 by New York newspaper editor John O'Sullivan, but the sentiment had been building at least since the war of 1812: "The American claim is by the right of our manifest destiny to overspread and to possess the whole of the continent which Providence has given us for the development of the great experiment of liberty and federative self-government entrusted to us. It is a right such as that of the tree to the space of air and earth suitable for the full expansion of its principle and destiny of growth."[3] That is, America's vaguely theologized experiment with democracy for White men was so noble that it justified seizing the lands of darker peoples.

Manifest Destiny's historian, Albert Weinberg, wrote that " 'Manifest Destiny,' the once honored expansionist slogan, expressed a dogma of supreme self-assurance and ambition—that America's incorporation of all adjacent lands was inevitable fulfillment of a moral mission delegated to the nation by Providence itself."[4] Manifest Destiny's poet, Walt Whitman, extolled the romantic vision of American virtue o'erspreading the continent when, in "Pioneers! O Pioneers!" he called young Euro-Americans from every corner of the land to course westward, rushing, pulsing, saving the very landscape by bringing White American energy and democracy. In "A Broadway Pageant" he extended the vision across the Pacific:

> I chant the world on my Western sea,
> I chant copious the islands beyond, thick as stars in the sky,
> I chant the new empire grander than any before, as in a vision it
>   comes to me,
> I chant America the mistress, I chant a greater supremacy,
> I chant projected a thousand blooming cities yet in time ... .[5]

Manifest Destiny's propagandist, William Gilpin, wrote that

> The *untransacted* destiny of the American people is to subdue the continent—to rush over this vast field to the Pacific Ocean—to animate the many hundred millions of its people, and to cheer them upward ... —to establish a new order in human affairs ... —to teach old nations a new civilization—to confirm the destiny of the human race—to carry the career of mankind to its culminating point—to cause a stagnant people to be reborn—to perfect science—to emblazon history with the conquest of peace—to shed a new and resplendent glory upon mankind—to unite the world in one social family—to dissolve the spell of tyranny and exalt charity—to absolve the curse that weighs down humanity, and to shed blessings round the world!

All this could be accomplished, in Gilpin's view, by making war on Mexico, seizing a path to the Pacific, and building a transcontinental railroad. The rest of these glories would naturally follow.[6]

Empire making is race making. George Will, conservative nationalist pundit of the late twentieth century and early twenty-first century, understood this. He was writing about U.S. atrocities in Iraq in 2004, but he might have been writing about the U.S. war on Mexico in the 1840s, the war against the Chiricahua Apaches in the 1880s, or the war against the Philippines after 1898: "[E]mpire is always about domination. Domination for self-defense, perhaps. Domination for the good of the dominated, arguably. But domination." Such domination requires the dominator mentally to dehumanize the people he or she dominates, to make them something less than fully human.[7] Something of the ways that dominators used race to mark those they dominated, and then congratulated themselves for being racially superior, comes through in these words by a White planter in Hawai'i (what would eventually become America's Farthest West) in the mid-nineteenth century:

> The word in the beginning seems to have been spoken to the white man, when he was commanded to 'subdue the earth and have dominion over it.' Europe was given to the white man, America to the red man, Asia to the yellow man and Africa to the black man. And with slight exceptions the white man is the only one that has ventured beyond the 'bounds of his habitations.' He has run over Europe, and crossing the Atlantic westward has taken possession of America, and is 'monarch of all he surveys' from Cape Horn to Behring's Strait. He has stepped across the Pacific Ocean, leaving the imprint of his enterprising foot upon the various islands of the sea; he has taken possession of Australia and India, with their countless thousands; he has gone to Africa. ... The coming

of the white man ... means government, enterprise, agriculture, commerce, churches, schools, law and order. It will be better for the colored man to have the white man rule.[8]

Reginald Horsman, historian of the connection between race and Manifest Destiny, summarized the matter this way:

By 1850 American expansion was viewed in the United States less as a victory for the principles of free democratic republicanism than as evidence of the innate superiority of the American Anglo-Saxon branch of the Caucasian race ... in the era of the Mexican war ... the Anglo-Saxons [conceived of themselves] as a separate, innately superior people who were destined to bring good government, commercial prosperity, and Christianity to the American continents and to the world. This was a superior race, and inferior races were doomed to subordinate status or extinction.[9]

Indian Deportation to the West

The first candidates for subordinate status or extinction were Native Americans. European in-migration and Indian out-migration were intimately intertwined. As European immigrants and native-born Euro-Americans moved out of the eastern seaboard and into what some would one day call the nation's heartland, they killed or moved out the Native people who lived in those places. In the first decades of the nineteenth century, Whites built (or had their slaves build) a network of roads leading from eastern cities into the interior, ultimately connecting all the territory east of the Mississippi River. These roads conveyed tens of thousands of European-descended people across the Midwest and the South (Figure 4.2).

Especially in the South, Whites clamored for the government to move out the Indian inhabitants, and the government responded. These were not the first big Native American migrations. Anthropologists believe the Navajo made the long walk from northern Canada into what is now New Mexico some time before the fifteenth century. The eastern Sioux are believed by some to have moved from what is now the Carolinas to Minnesota before that.[10] But despite the scale and the distances covered, those almost certainly were gradual migrations, giving people time to adjust to the new landscape. By contrast, the forced removals of the nineteenth century wrenched people out of their homes and livelihoods, killed many thousands, and left the rest in political, economic, and cultural disarray.[11]

The so-called Five Civilized Tribes—the Cherokee, Chickasaw, Choctaw, Creek, and Seminole—lived in the Southeast on lands coveted by the rapidly expanding White population. At least the first four had responded positively to the assimilation policy enunciated by President Thomas Jefferson. They all practiced settled agriculture, fenced their fields, kept herds of cows and horses, bought and sold slaves. In 1827 the Cherokee nation passed a constitution, and all these tribes had written law codes. In 1828, the Cherokees began publishing a newspaper. Many Indian children went to White-run missionary schools. But all that did not satisfy President Andrew Jackson or his constituents. They did not care that Indians were becoming like White people. They wanted the Indians out. Jackson publicly refused to honor treaty obligations to protect these tribes from trespass and attacks by Whites. In 1830, Congress passed and Jackson signed the Indian Removal Act. It

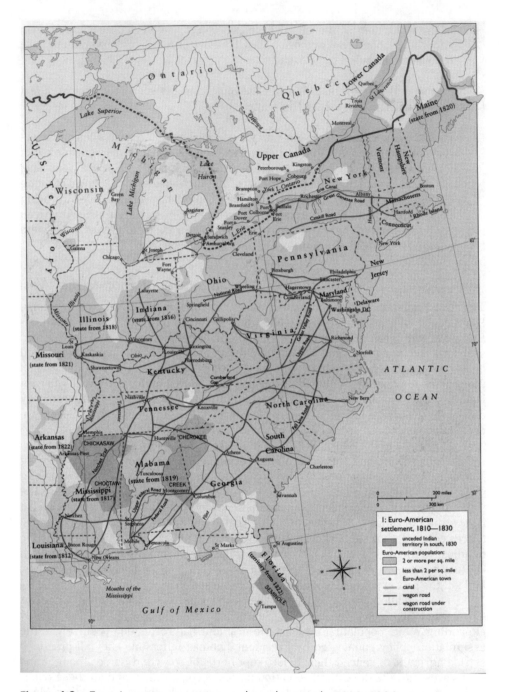

Figure 4.2 Euro-American incursion and road network, 1810–1830.

empowered the president to take Indian lands in the vicinity of White populations and give those tribes land in exchange on the west side of the Mississippi, which "the United States will *forever* secure and guaranty to them, and their heirs"—well, for a while.[12]

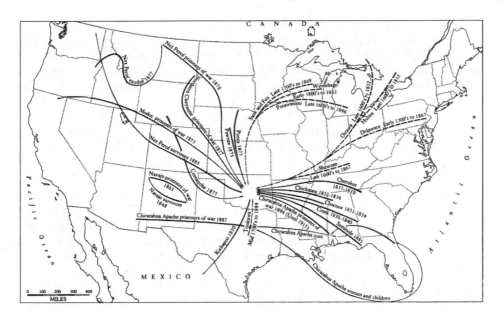

Figure 4.3 Migrations into Indian Territory.

It would seem the law was on the Indians' side, but insofar as that was true, it did little good. The U.S. Supreme Court under Chief Justice John Marshall ruled in 1831 and 1832 that Georgia law did not apply on Cherokee lands, because the Cherokee and other tribes were "domestic dependent nations," which had given up certain rights in treaties they signed with the United States, but which retained their sovereignty in all other matters. Yet the White population kept pressing in. For years, small bands of Indians had given up their homes and made their way west to Indian Territory—what is now Oklahoma and parts of Kansas, Nebraska, and Iowa. There they joined Indians such as the Huron, Ottawa, Potawatomi, and Winnebago who had been migrating out of the Great Lakes region under White pressure since the 1700s (see Figure 4.3).

White pressure on the southeastern tribes became irresistible after the Indian Removal Act. The Choctaw were the first to go en masse, in the winter of 1831. They were gathered into stockades by federal troops and marched northwest out of Mississippi and Alabama, only to encounter a blizzard and subzero temperatures on the way. More than 13,000 reached the Red River district. Seven thousand more stayed behind in Mississippi; over time, most of those who stayed and had money blended into the surrounding White population, the others into the Black. The main body of Creeks started leaving Alabama and Georgia in 1836. An overloaded steamboat sank on the way, taking 311 lives; nearly half the Creek population perished either en route or in the first few years west of the Mississippi. The following year, four thousand Chickasaws made a better-financed expedition and arrived in Indian Territory with their numbers more or less intact.

Cherokee removal from Georgia and parts of neighboring states commenced in 1838. The Cherokees were the largest and most powerful tribe to go through forced removal. They had on their side several court decisions affirming their sovereignty, and they were trying to accommodate Whites—indeed, they had already applied to become a separate state of the Union. They had a strong leader and skilled negotiator in John Ross, and they were determined to remain in their ancestral homes. But federal troops launched surprise raids on Cherokee villages and farmsteads and herded 16,000 people into stockades. A White missionary named Evan Jones stayed with his flock when they were taken away and sent these words to the *Baptist Missionary Magazine*:

> The Cherokees are nearly all prisoners. They have been dragged from their houses, and encamped at the forts and military posts, all over the nation. In Georgia, especially, multitudes were allowed no time to take any thing with them, except the clothes they had on. Well-furnished houses were left a prey to plunderers, who, like hungry wolves, follow in the train of the captors. These wretches rifle the houses, and strip the helpless, unoffending owners of all they have on earth. Females, who have been habituated to comforts and comparative affluence, are driven on foot before the bayonets of brutal men. ... The poor captive in a state of distressing agitation, his weeping wife almost frantic with terror, surrounded by a group of crying, terrified children, without a friend to speak a consoling word, is in a poor condition to make a good disposition of his property and is in most cases stripped of the whole, at one blow.[13]

One-quarter of the Cherokee nation died of hunger and cold on the walk to the west that winter. About 1000 escaped into the North Carolina mountains. The rest were dumped unceremoniously in Indian territory.

The Seminoles were the last to go, 3000 of them in 1843, with another several hundred holding out in the Florida Everglades in a long, inconclusive war of resistance. Altogether, perhaps 30,000 Native Americans died on these southeastern Indians' Trails of Tears. Many thousands more were to die as the story was repeated over and over. The expanding Euro-American population, fueled by immigration and a high birthrate, entered one region and then another seeking land. From Minnesota to Arizona to Oregon, whole peoples were packed off and their lands given to White migrants.

The southeastern Indians who walked west were a mixed multitude. They owned some 8000 African-descended slaves. Most of the slaves had some Indian ancestry, and many of the Indian members of such tribes as the Cherokee, Creek, and Seminole had some African ancestry. Slavery was maintained in Indian Territory until after the Civil War. Thereafter, these tribes maintained a strange (given the manifest mixed ancestry of both "Indian" and "Freedman") system of segregation along fictive racial lines.[14]

Resistance and Genocide

As we saw in earlier chapters, White incursion onto Native lands brought conflict with and resistance from Native peoples, from the time of the Roanoke Island colony to the age of Tecumseh. Such resistance continued through the era of formal, federally coordinated Indian removals. Cherokees who refused to go to the West ran off into the Appalachians and fought on sporadically into the 1850s. Osceola led a mixed band of Seminoles and Creeks against U.S. troops in Florida during the Seminole wars of the 1810s, and kept on fighting until he was captured in 1837. Some

Seminoles, Cherokees, and others fought on, but most eventually made their peace with the move into the West.

From the 1850s, and with increasing energy after the Civil War, White Americans turned their attention to the lands beyond the Mississippi. Government policy changed from removal to extermination. The U.S. Army turned its energies to clearing out the Indians, both those like the Sioux who had lived long on the plains, and also those other tribes who had only recently—within a generation—been banished there. The Indian story of heroic resistance and death has been told many times.[15] It is part of the elemental lore of Americana. From Mari Sandoz's classic book *Cheyenne Autumn* to the movie *Little Big Man*, the destruction of the Indians of the western plains by the U.S. cavalry is one of the great, tragic themes of American history and literature. Historians such as Richard White rightly object to the mythic quality of much of this writing, and point to strategic and political counter-narratives, such as the long-term expansion of the power of the western Sioux through the first half of the nineteenth century. The Sioux and their allies expanded at the expense of other plains Indian tribes, and used their acquired strength to hold off the power of Euro-America for quite a long time. But in the end they too were subdued, many were killed, and the remainder sequestered on much smaller pieces of land called reservations.[16]

Here, two stories may suffice to stand for many, with acknowledgement of the wide variety of circumstances in different Indian-White encounters. The Modoc Indians lived for many centuries along the shores of Tule Lake and the Lost River, in the high valleys where the borders of California, Nevada, and Oregon now meet. They quarreled occasionally with their neighbors, the Paiutes and Klamaths. But for the most part they lived quietly off the land's bounty of fish, marshland plants, and waterfowl. From the 1820s on, White trappers, then prospectors, then ranchers and farmers came to the valley. They polluted the rivers, depleted the salmon runs, scared away the game, and took hunting grounds for farms. The Modocs retaliated by attacking wagon trains and rustling cattle. In 1852 a White rancher named Ben Wright led the slaughter of forty-one Modocs; later he was himself killed by a Modoc woman whom he had stripped naked and whipped in public. The incidents back and forth continued until the government got Modoc leaders to sign a peace treaty in 1864. The Modocs would not be allowed to stay on their lands. Instead, they were shuffled off to the Klamath Indian reservation in Oregon, where they became a minority in close quarters with their old enemies, the Klamaths and Paiutes.

After a few years, some among the Modocs could take confinement no more. Led by Kintpuash, whom the Whites called Captain Jack, 150 Modocs left the reservation and returned home, where they took up residence alongside White farmers. The Whites objected, and called on the U.S. government to take the Modocs away again. In November 1872, several hundred federal troops arrived to round up the Indians. A fight broke out that killed three Modocs, including a woman and child, as well as one soldier. The troops burned the Modoc village to the ground. The Modocs fled into the barren moonscape that is now Lava Beds National Monument, where they holed up in caves and lava tubes for four months. Their natural fortifications kept the Army at bay.

President Ulysses S. Grant sent Brig. Gen. Edward Canby to make a peace treaty. Kintpuash asked for a meeting with Grant in Washington, DC, and a guarantee of 2000 acres near the Lost River. Canby refused; Kintpuash killed Canby; in the ensuing firefight, the Modocs escaped. After several weeks of running, Kintpuash and a few remaining warriors were captured. Several were put in prison. Kintpuash and three others were hanged. Their heads were cut off and shipped in alcohol to the Army Medical Museum. The remaining 150 Modocs were banished to the Quapaw Indian Agency in Oklahoma, forbidden ever to use their language or practice their religion again. More than thirty years later, a few remaining Modocs were allowed to return to the Klamath reservation.[17]

The most famous statement of Native American capitulation to government pressure on behalf of White immigrants came from Chief Joseph. He spent much of his youth on the Nez Percé reservation in the Wallowa country of northeast Oregon, but Whites discovered gold there and prospectors flooded in. The government seized six million acres of reservation land and ordered the Nez Percé to a reservation in Idaho one-tenth the size in 1877. Chief Joseph was one of the leaders who engineered a daring flight by 200 Nez Percé warriors and their families, pursued by two thousand U.S. troops and Indian auxiliaries, nearly 1400 miles over more than three months, east and north toward Canada. After several pitched battles and only twenty-five miles from freedom, but with war chiefs dead and warriors scattered, Joseph surrendered, saying:

> I am tired of fighting. Our chiefs are killed. Looking Glass is dead. Toohool-hoolzote is dead. The old men are all dead. It is the young men who say, "Yes" or "No." He who led the young men is dead. It is cold, and we have no blankets. The little children are freezing to death. My people, some of them, have run away to the hills, and have no blankets, no food. No one knows where they are—perhaps freezing to death. I want to have time to look for my children, and see how many of them I can find. Maybe I shall find them among the dead. Hear me, my chiefs! I am tired. My heart is sick and sad. From where the sun now stands I will fight no more forever.[18]

The troops slaughtered most of the Nez Percé's Appaloosa horses—their means of livelihood—and took the rest as booty. The remaining Nez Percé were imprisoned at Fort Leavenworth, Kansas, then taken to a reservation in Oklahoma. There many died of malaria. In 1885, some were allowed to go to the Idaho reservation with other Nez Percé, but Joseph and half his remaining followers lived out their days on a reservation in northeast Washington, far from either their home or the rest of their tribe.[19]

The Remnant: Reservation Indians

Native peoples who lived in what was becoming the eastern United States had been pushed out of their homelands and into the West. Then Europeans and Euro-Americans poured into the lands to which they had so recently banished the same Indians. There, White Americans made war on Indians, killed them, and took their lands. The Native population of the lands that would become the United States numbered 6 million before Europeans came to the continent, 1.3 million in 1800. By the end of that century, only 250,000 remained (Figure 4.4).[20] By that time, most of the remnant had been restricted on tiny reservations.

Historian Frederick Hoxie describes the Crow Indians' move from freedom to the reservation as "immigration in reverse":

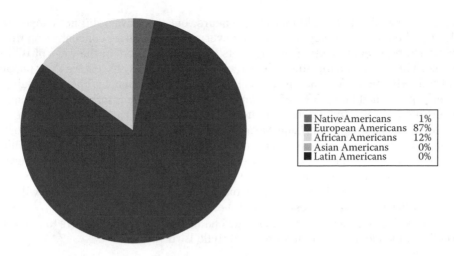

■ Native Americans	1%
■ European Americans	87%
African Americans	12%
■ Asian Americans	0%
■ Latin Americans	0%

Figure 4.4 Population in 1900 of the territory that would become the United States.

In early April 1884, 130 families began a journey ... down from the foothills of the Beartooth range to the flatlands of the Bighorn and Little Bighorn valleys. Over 900 people, accompanied by wagons and guarded by federal agents, began their passage. ... Like countless others who had passed across the barrier of the mountains, they came to the flatland with the expectation that their new homeland, while demanding new skills, would open a door to a new way of life. ... Prior to that event, the Crows were relatively free from the daily intrusions of white settlers and cattlemen; afterwards they lived amidst rail traffic, cattle drives and enterprising farmers. Before the relocation, missionaries and government schoolmasters were infrequent visitors; afterwards, missions and boarding schools became fixtures within the community. And before the agency moved to the prairies south of the Yellowstone, the tribe had been free to range across a large area in search of game and enemy raiders; afterwards the entire population was expected to locate permanently on a gradually shrinking reservation. ... Like their fellow [White] pioneers in Washington, Idaho, the Dakotas, and Colorado, these 900 [Indian] Montanans appeared to be moving from an area of marginal subsistence to a place that promised abundant crops and new prosperity. ... [but] their experience mirrored, rather than paralleled, the westward migrations of other nineteenth-century Americans.[21]

Reservation life varied enormously. After the U.S. Army conquered the Navajo people in 1864, the soldiers took the defeated Indians to live with Mescalero Apache in a reservation at Bosque Redondo in southeastern New Mexico. Traveling 400 miles under guard, the captives arrived starving, impoverished, and demoralized. "Shortages of food and fuel were continual, and the alkaline water caused dysentery. Other illnesses at the reservation included malaria, pneumonia, rheumatic fever, measles, and venereal disease. The Indians report that sometimes military personnel beat them and that Navajo women were raped. Further, the Navajo were raided by other Indian tribes." The government had in mind making the Navajo into centrally organized agricultural entrepreneurs, but the Navajo did not cooperate. They worked hard, but they resisted the government's plans for concentrating their living arrangements as well as its attempts at schooling them in the ways of White people. They called on the Squaw Dance and the Coyote Way to restore their people and smite their enemies, and these held them together as a people. They complained bitterly, petitioned for their freedom, and many ran off to their former lands despite government threats to hunt and kill them. Finally, the government in 1868 gave up and let the remaining reservation Navajo go back to their ancestral lands. It is worth noting that this unusual Indian achievement of relative autonomy, in the face of White attempts to restrict them, took place in territory that had garnered far less interest from Euro-American farmers and land speculators than the lands of the Sioux, the Crow, or the Nez Percé. Perhaps that accounts for the government's ultimate willingness to allow the Navajo to resume control of their homelands.[22]

Most Indians who endured the huge change from traditional ways to reservation life could identify with the words of Buffalo Bird Woman:

> I am an old woman now. The buffaloes and black-tail deer are gone, and our Indian ways are almost gone. Sometimes I find it hard to believe that I ever lived them.
>
> My little son grew up in the white man's school. He can read books, and he owns cattle and has a farm. He is a leader among our Hidatsa people, helping teach them to follow the white man's road.
>
> He is kind to me. We no longer live in an earth lodge, but in a house with chimneys; and my son's wife cooks by a stove.
>
> But for me, I cannot forget our old ways.
>
> Often in summer I rise at daybreak and steal out to the cornfields; and as I hoe the corn I sing to it, as we did with I was young. No one cares for our corn songs now.
>
> Sometimes at evening I sit, looking out on the big Missouri. The sun sets, and dusk steals over the water. In the shadows I seem again to see our Indian village, with smoke curling upward from the earth lodges; and in the river's roar I hear the yells of the warriors, the laughter of little children as of old. It is but an old woman's dream. Again I see but shadows and hear only the roar of the river; and tears come into my eyes. Our Indian life, I know, is gone forever.[23]

Disappearing Peoples

If Buffalo Bird Woman lamented that the ways of Indians were gone forever, a lot of White Americans were eager to have Indians themselves gone forever. Removal, the extermination campaigns of the wars for the West, and reservation life had killed off a lot of people. Whites were eager to conclude that this was part of the inevitable extinction of American Indian peoples. Because doom was inevitable, it was sad, perhaps, but it was nobody's fault. Scholarly books and popular theater from the 1820s through the 1990s are filled with references to "the vanishing American" and "a superseded race." Charles Sprague, a Boston banker and poet, in 1825 expressed this enduring trope of White American popular culture:

As a race they have withered from the land. Their arrows are broken, their springs are dried up, their cabins are in the dust. Their council-fire has long since gone out on the shore, and their war-cry is fast dying away to the untrodden west. Slowly and sadly they climb the distant mountains, and read their doom in the setting sun. They are shrinking before the mighty tide which is pressing them away; they must soon hear the roar of the last wave, which will settle over them forever.

Ishi, a Yahi Indian discovered by Berkeley anthropologist Alfred Kroeber in 1911 and made into a living museum exhibit and enduring cultural icon, was celebrated as "the last wild Indian in North America." I am not questioning the genuineness of the sympathies of people like Kroeber or Sprague for the difficult circumstances faced by the remaining Indians. But it is hard not to sense an undercurrent of celebration beneath such laments. Native peoples' extinction, for many Whites if not for these, was an affirmation of White superiority, and it paved the way for Whites to appropriate Indian identities and symbols for their own, and thereby to naturalize themselves in the American landscape.[24]

Whites tried to speed the process by taking away even the reservations. In 1887 the Congress passed the General Allotment or Dawes Act. The idea was to turn Indians into citizens by breaking up the reservations into individual holdings for farming or ranching. In the process, it was hoped, Indians would assimilate to White ways, for it was thought that land ownership had the power to "civilize." Not incidentally, a lot of land would become, as the government put it, "surplus"—it would be freed up for Whites to occupy. The Board of Indian Commissioners began to survey reservation lands, divide them into parcels, and award them to individual Native Americans. Naturally, they started with the reservations on the Great Plains that White farmers coveted the most; more barren and remote lands like the Navajo reservation were saved for last, and so they remain largely intact today. Indian agents encouraged those who received allotments not to work the land themselves, but rent it to White farmers and ranchers. Soon tens of thousands were rendered landless, and total Indian landholdings were reduced over four decades from 138 million to 48 million acres. In 1898, Rep. Charles Curtis, himself a Kaw Indian, sponsored a bill in Congress that hastened the project of dismantling the tribes, by abolishing tribal courts and providing legislative machinery for the dissolution of the so-called Five Civilized Tribes.[25]

Another tactic was to try to obliterate Indian identity by sending children away from their families to boarding schools. All Native peoples had, of course, educated their young. And some such as the Choctaw and Cherokee had created their own schools that taught Euro-American style curriculum, as a supplement to raising children in the ways of their ancestors. But beginning with the Carlisle Indian Industrial School in Pennsylvania, missionaries and bureaucrats built boarding academies. They usually located the schools quite far from the homes of their charges—often hundreds of miles distant. Richard Henry Pratt, Carlisle's founder, coined the phrase that became that school's motto: "Kill the Indian and save the man" (Figure 4.5). There and at other Indian boarding schools, children taken from their parents often as young as toddlers lived away from their families and communities for years on end. They suffered loneliness, deracination, and sometimes abuse. They were raised to think and act as White people, at the same time they were prepared with skills for industrial labor.[26]

Figure 4.5   Before-and-after photos of Tom Torleno, Navajo, at Carlisle Indian Industrial School, c. 1880s.

In 1883 Sun Elk left the Taos pueblo in northern New Mexico to attend Carlisle. He told his story:

> When I was about thirteen years old I went down to St. Michael's Catholic School. Other boys were joining the societies and spending their time in the kivas and being purified and learning the secrets. But I wanted to learn the white man's secrets. I thought he had better magic than the Indian. ... So I drifted a little away from pueblo life. My father was sad but he was not angry. He wanted me to be a good Indian like all the other boys, but he was willing for me to go to school. ...
>
> Then at the first snow one winter ... a white man—what you call an Indian Agent—came and took all of us who were in that school far off on a train to a new kind of village called Carlisle Indian School, and I stayed there seven years. ...
>
> They told us that Indian ways were bad. They said we must get civilized. I remember that word too. It means "be like the white man." I am willing to be like the white man, but I did not believe Indian ways were wrong. But they kept teaching us for seven years. And the books told how bad the Indians had been to the white man—burning their towns and killing their women and children. But I had seen white men do that to Indians. We all wore white man's clothes and ate white man's food and went to white man's churches and spoke white man's talk. And so after a while we also began to say Indians were bad. We laughed at our own people and their blankets and cooking pots and sacred societies and dances.

After seven years at Carlisle, Sun Elk returned to Taos, unable to speak his first language any longer. His father was told by tribal elders: "'He cannot even speak our language and he has a strange smell. He is not one of us.' The chiefs got up and walked out. My father was very sad. I wanted him to be angry." Stunned and hurt, Sun Elk went to White people's towns and drifted from job to job as a printer, blacksmith, and farm hand. He said, "All this time I was a white man." Many years later he returned to the pueblo. The land had been divided, and his father gave him some to farm. Sun Elk married and "became an Indian again. I let my hair grow, I put on blankets, and I cut the seat out of my pants."[27]

Native American Panethnic Formation

As Stephen Cornell writes, "In the pattern of their subjugation lies the shape of their resistance."[28] From Columbus's geographical mistake onward, Europeans and Euro-Americans piled all Native peoples of the Americas into one conceptual basket more often than they comprehended the manifold differences among them. From the late eighteenth century through the end of the nineteenth century, Native Americans—irrespective of their tribe and region, their culture, behavior, or material condition—came in for shared restriction, removal, annihilation, and racial replacement at the hands of Whites.

In this same period we can discern the beginning elements of a shared pan-Indian consciousness, born of gathered resistance to common oppression. Often, it took the form of pantribal cultural or religious revivals that began in particular tribes, spread across wide regions, and provided an element of cultural glue to support armed resistance. The teaching of the Delaware Prophet, Neolin, that Native peoples must put off the corruption of White ways, underlay a widespread uprising against British forts by Ottawas, Hurons, Chippewas, Potawatomis, and other Great Lakes and Ohio Valley tribes in 1763. The Washani Creed revealed to the prophet Smohalla served as ideological support for passive resistance against White incursions and treaty impositions by thousands of Indians across the Northwest from the 1850s to the 1870s. The Ghost Dance, revealed in 1889 to a western Nevada Paiute named Wovoka, spread quickly across the Great Basin and Plains. Lakota Ghost Dance followers were wearing sacred shirts they believed would protect them from U.S. Army bullets when they were massacred at Wounded Knee in 1890.

Such revelations came to individuals in particular tribes, but they were received by many kinds of Indians across wide territories. These were the beginnings of a common consciousness among members of a third panethnic or racial formation—Indians or Native Americans—to stand alongside Blacks and Whites. The panethnic bond for Native peoples was weaker. As with Blacks, there was the strong common interest that attended the assault by Euro-Americans. Indians had every reason to band together to protect themselves. But they had substantial impediments that kept them from doing so fully. The primary barrier was tribal divisions. Tribal allegiances were still very strong, and these militated against making common cause against the Whites. Outsiders perceived a wide variety of Native peoples to practice similar cultures and lifestyles. But in fact, very different modes of sustenance, mutually unintelligible languages, and very different customary traditions kept them apart.

This Native American story is part of the story of American immigration, because immigration has consequences, and not just for the immigrants. Native peoples were killed and moved out of their homes by the U.S. government and groups of White people—over and over again, many hundreds of times, many thousands of people, many millions of acres of land—so that European immigrants and their descendants could move in.

Taking the Mexican Northlands

The United States' mid-nineteenth-century adventure into what is now called the American Southwest is an immigration story, too. Like the spreading onto Indian lands in the Great Plains and Northwest, it is not the story of foreigners migrating into the United States, but rather the story of the United States migrating onto other peoples: in this case Mexicans as well as Indians.

Mexicans have long had an ambivalent relationship to Native peoples and racial identity. On one hand, Mexico inherited a European racial identity from the Spanish who slaughtered the Aztecs and built a rich colony in the central highlands on the backs of Native laborers, beginning in the sixteenth century. On the other, from very early on Mexico's people acknowledged they were a mixed multitude: Spanish- and Indian- and (some finally admitted) African-descended people. Not everyone had mixed racial ancestry, but lots of people did and their numbers kept getting larger, due to generations of Spanish men mating with Native, African, and Mestizo women, and then their progeny mating with one another. In time, a distinct Mestizo population emerged and became the numerically dominant group. There was a pretty clear racial hierarchy, with people who possessed light skin and lots of European ancestry toward the top and others arrayed in ever-darker layers below.[29]

Such racialized social hierarchy and ambivalence about racial identity played themselves out in the Mexican northlands during the decades before the Anglo-American invasion. Societies with distinctive features evolved in Texas, New Mexico, and California, but all had three broad racial tiers: a Mexican elite that had some Iberian ancestry and frequently pretended to racial purity; a growing Mestizo Mexican population; and Indians—often non-Spanish-speaking—who remained in separate congeries of groups and whose numbers were declining. We must be clear that the Spanish dominion in Mexico was as much a European colonial project as was the English dominion in eastern North America up to the respective moments of national independence for the two countries, although the two colonial systems were differently organized. By the same token, the actions taken toward Native peoples in the northern provinces by the Mexican government after independence in 1821—a government dominated by European-descended people—were colonial acts just as were those taken by European-descended people in the American West. Spanish policies, however, sought to harness Native labor and harvest Native souls, and they included a substantial element of social mixing, especially in the northlands. By contrast, the main Anglo-American tactics were to separate themselves from Indians and try to exterminate them, and then to segregate the remnant on nineteenth-century equivalents of later South African Bantustans.

Most of the Mexican northern land claims were in fact territory controlled by Native peoples, not Mexicans, just as most of the western territory claimed by the United States was, in fact, occupied by Native peoples, not Euro-Americans. The three main centers of Mexican residence and development were in the southern parts of California, the Rio Grande valley in New Mexico, and the vicinity of San Antonio in south Texas. Under Spanish rule, residents of all three territories were forbidden to trade with non-Spanish outsiders. Spain granted large tracts of land to favored sub-jects who came to ranch and to rule. The Catholic Church gathered Indians around its missions as converts and bond laborers in California and Texas, whereas it made use of existing pueblos in New Mexico to organize and control the local people. Small, not very prosperous farming and ranching outposts grew slowly. The hinterlands remained under the control of various Native peoples, but not for long.[30]

Forget the Alamo: Taking Texas for Slavery

Mexico threw off the yoke of the Spanish empire in 1821. The new government was quite amenable to contacts with non-Spanish outsiders. International trade sprang up immediately along a wagon road between Missouri and Santa Fe. Into this sparsely populated borderland came Anglo-Americans[31]: traders, trappers, and increasingly immigrants. In 1824, the Mexican National Congress passed a law to welcome new immigrants. Tejano representative José Erasmo Seguín led the advocates of this new policy, urged on by his American friend Stephen F. Austin. Texas was the region that felt the most impact. The law (together with legislation in the state of Coahuila-Texas) gave huge grants of land to *empresarios*, or developers, provided they brought immigrants to work the land, became Mexican citizens and Roman Catholics, and obeyed the law. The idea in the capital was to introduce a stable, European-derived population to the frontier region that would tie it to Mexico and provide a buffer against Indians farther north and west.[32]

Stephen Austin received the first such *empresario* grant. The Austin land grant covered 200,000 acres, stretching along the Gulf Coast from Galveston Bay to Tres Palacios Bay, and north to the San Antonio-Nacogdoches road. Austin was respon-sible for bringing in migrants, surveying the land, setting up a government, and building roads, schools, and granaries. Soon, immigrants were flowing freely into Texas and taking up residence without regard to the niceties of citizenship, conver-sion, or lawful behavior. Thousands of White Southerners flooded across the border from the United States into East Texas. Many of them brought slaves, in defiance of an 1824 constitutional provision that had outlawed slavery in Mexico. This was a continuation of the gradual spread of racialized slavery from the Chesapeake and the Carolinas across the American South to Alabama, Mississippi, and Louisiana. Now, accompanying the expansion of the cotton economy, it crossed the Sabine into Mexico.

Texas soon was dominated numerically by White Americans. In 1836 the region held 30,000 White Americans, 5,000 African Americans (nearly all slaves), 3,470 Mexicans, and 14,200 Indians.[33] But Texas was only one part of the state of Coahuila-Texas, which was ten times its size. Thus, the only Anglo-dominated part of Mexico found its distinctive voice drowned out in national politics. Motivated by intertwined desires for home rule and for slavery, White Texans began to agitate for independence from Mexico and annexation by the United States. Some Mexican Texans, or Tejanos, including José Seguín's son Juan, joined their cause. Nervous, the central government closed Texas to further U.S. immigration in 1830, although the law could not be enforced effectively.

The central government, attempting to establish its authority, tried to stop Anglo-American smugglers and collect customs duties in the coastal town of Anáhuac in 1835. Instead of meekly complying, the smugglers gathered weapons and captured a garrison. The new president of Mexico, Antonio López de Santa Anna, sent an army to bring the region to heel. He chose to go first to San Antonio de Béxar, which had the largest concentration of Mexicans and could be expected to provide support. But most of the San Antonio Tejanos evacuated the town, leaving an outmanned garrison of mainly Anglo-Americans (a few Mexicans stayed) to defend the Alamo. They all died on March 6, 1836, in a battle that passed quickly into myth. Santa Anna's army executed another 400 Anglo-Texans in Goliad. The Alamo's defenders had not heard the news, but days before, a gathering of Anglo-Texan leaders (and three Tejanos) had declared independence. Inflamed by the brutality of Santa Anna's victories, the Anglo-Texans turned with fury that took an increasingly racialized tone. The war's climactic battle took place on April 21, 1836, at San Jacinto, where the Anglo-Texans, along with a Tejano regiment (commanded by the younger Seguín), thumped the Mexican army. They captured Santa Anna and forced him to sign documents that soon led to Texan independence.

The new Texas Republic applied immediately for admission to the United States as a state, but Northern antislavery politicians blocked the deal for nearly a decade.[34] The Alamo has been remembered in American lore as a moment of heroic virtue and sacrifice: the Anglo-Texans' lives were lost, but soon democracy triumphed over tyranny.[35] Lost in this rhetoric of narcissistic nationalism is the fact that one of the core issues in this war was a desperate yearning on the part of White American expatriates to keep racialized slavery, contrary to the Mexican constitution to which those Anglo-Texan immigrants had sworn fealty. On a visit to the Alamo shrine and museum today, one sees room after room of artifacts with abundant curatorial commentary. Nowhere do the exhibits hint that this was a war fought to keep slavery. That untidy fact has been erased.

In the next few years, the place of Mexicans in Texas began to be erased as well. White Southerners and their slaves continued to pour in. The leaders of the new nation sent recruiters to Europe. They came back with thousands of German colonists who settled along the Indian frontier north of the San Antonio-Nacogdoches road. Texas, a formerly Indian place that had become a partly Mexican place, was now awash in White Americans and Europeans. Prior to the war, Americans and Tejanos had gotten along amicably, perhaps because they lived mainly in separate parts of the territory. The Texas Revolution, as the Anglo-Americans called it, was more a war for independence and slavery than a race war by Whites against Mexicans.

Yet the Americans held flagrant anti-Mexican prejudices. Those prejudices grew upon a foundation laid by centuries of English and Anglo-American anti-Catholicism, abetted by the Black Legend of Spanish treachery. Historian David Weber comments:

> American visitors to the Mexican frontier were nearly unanimous in commenting on the dark skin of Mexican mestizos who, it was generally agreed, had inherited the worst qualities of Spaniards and Indians to produce a "race" still more despicable than that of either parent. ... North Americans, then, combining their inherited belief in the Black Legend with racism and their exposure to frontier Mexican culture, came to the conclusion that Mexican people were inferior. They were contemptuous of Mexican government and of Catholicism, and they viewed Mexicans as indolent, ignorant, bigoted, cheating, dirty, bloodthirsty, cowardly half-breeds.[36]

Expanding Aggression

The stage was set for the next war to become a race war. The fate of Juan Seguín is instructive as to the course race relations were taking. A Texan hero of the Battle of San Jacinto, Seguín was elected mayor of his native town, San Antonio, still an almost all-Tejano place. But a Mexican expeditionary force seized San Antonio in 1842 in an attempt to retake Texas. The crafty Mexican commander pronounced Seguín a loyal Mexican despite his role on the Texan side of the 1836 war. Seguín said he was a Texan, not a Mexican, and led the forces that chased the army back across the Nueces River, Texas's traditional southern border. But an Anglo-Texan volunteer army moved into San Antonio, labeled Seguín an enemy, and forced him into hiding. Leaderless and threatened by an army of lawless thugs, many San Antonio Tejanos went south into Mexico, despite their loyalty to the Lone Star Republic. Seguín was among them.[37]

The American war against Mexico began simply enough. Anglo-Texans sent an army to "liberate" New Mexico in 1841 and attacked merchants on the Santa Fe Trail. The next year a Texan expedition invaded Mexico, crossing not only the Nueces River, but also the Rio Grande farther south. Both efforts failed, but as a precaution the Mexican government closed the Santa Fe Trail in 1843. Since the Texas Revolution, Mexico had warned it would view a U.S. annexation of Texas as an act of war. The United States did just that in 1845, and President James K. Polk then set his sights on California. In 1846 the U.S. Army under General Zachary Taylor set up a post at the mouth of the Rio Grande and blockaded the river, an act of war under international diplomatic standards. A skirmish later that year, on disputed territory north of the river, was Polk's pretext for declaring war with unbridled hypocrisy: "Mexico has passed the boundary of the United States, has invaded our territory and shed American blood upon American soil. ... War exists, not withstanding all our efforts to avoid it."[38]

The war was brief but brutal. Colonel Stephen W. Kearny led the Army of the West and volunteers into New Mexico in August 1846 and claimed the province for the United States in what at first appeared to be a peaceful transfer of power. Four months later, Indians at the Taos Pueblo and local Mexicans revolted against the Americans; the Taos rebels were crushed and hundreds died. An American expedition into California met resistance from an army organized belatedly by Californios. The Californios held most of Southern California for a while, but by 1847 they, too, had been conquered.

The U.S. Army and a horde of volunteers, including a gang of thugs calling themselves the Texas Rangers, invaded central Mexico under General Taylor.[39] The American atrocities were extreme. George Gordon Meade, later a Civil War general, was one of the soldiers, and he wrote this report:

> [July 9, 1846] They [the volunteers] have killed five or six innocent people walking in the street, for no other object than their own amusement. ... They rob and steal the cattle and corn of the poor farmers, and in fact act more like a body of hostile Indians than civilized Whites. Their officers have no command or control over them. ... [December 2, 1846] They plunder the poor inhabitants of everything they can lay their hands on, and shoot them when they remonstrate; and if one of their number happens to get into a drunken brawl and is killed, they run over the country, killing all the poor innocent people they find in their way to avenge, as they say, the murder of their brother.[40]

Taylor and General Winfield Scott could not control the volunteers' butchery. A young soldier named Samuel Chamberlain wrote this account of what he found on following Yell's Cavalry up a ravine:

> On reaching the place we found a "greaser" shot and *scalped*, but still breathing; the poor fellow held in his hands a Rosary and a medal of the "Virgin of Guadalupe," only his feeble motions kept the fierce harpies from falling on him while yet alive. A Sabre thrust was given him in mercy, and on we went at a run. Soon shouts and curses, cries of women and children reached our ears, coming apparently from a cave at the end of the ravine. Climbing over the rocks we reached the entrance, and as soon as we could see in the comparative darkness a horrid sight was before us. The cave was full of our volunteers yelling like fiends, while on the rocky floor lay over twenty Mexicans, dead and dying in pools of blood. Women and children were clinging to the knees of the murderers shrieking for mercy. ... Most of the butchered Mexicans had been scalped; only three men were found unharmed. A rough crucifix was fastened to a rock, and some irreverent wretch had crowned the image with a bloody scalp. A sickening smell filled the place. The surviving women and children sent up loud screams on seeing us, thinking we had returned to finish the work! ... No one was punished for this outrage.[41]

By the time the war was over, Mexico had lost half of its land area to its aggressive neighbor to the north. The Americans added the last piece of their contiguous empire in 1853 when they acquired, through the Gadsden Purchase, a transcontinental railroad route and copper deposits in what is now southern Arizona.[42]

Incorporating Mexico's People, and Not

The war ended with the signing of the Treaty of Guadalupe Hidalgo on February 2, 1848. Some, like Sam Houston, a U.S. Senator from Texas, argued for taking all of Mexico: "The Mexicans are no better than Indians, and I see no reason why we should not go on in the same course now and take their land."[43] Others demurred, on no less racially charged grounds. John C. Calhoun of South Carolina ranted on the floor of the Senate:

> It is without example or precedent, either to hold Mexico as a province, or to incorporate her into our Union. No example of such a line of policy can be found. We have conquered many of the neighboring tribes of Indians, but we never thought of holding them in subjection—never of incorporating them into our Union. They have either been left as an independent people amongst us, or have been driven into the forests. I know further, sir, that we have never dreamt of incorporating into our Union any but the Caucasian race—the free white race. To incorporate Mexico, would be the very first instance of the kind of incorporating an Indian race; for more than half of the Mexicans are Indians, and the other is composed chiefly of mixed tribes. I protest against such a union as that! Ours, sir, is the Government of a white race. ... Are they fit to be connected with us? Are they fit for self-government and for governing

you? Are you, any of you, willing that your States should be governed by these twenty-odd Mexican States, with a population of about only one million of your blood, and two or three millions of mixed blood, ... all the rest pure Indians, a mixed blood equally ignorant and unfit for liberty, impure races, not as good as the Cherokees or Choctaws?[44]

The government of Mexico lay prostrate before the Americans and was forced to give up its remaining northern lands—California, nearly all of the territory that now makes up the states of New Mexico, Arizona, Nevada, Utah, and Colorado, plus parts of surrounding states as well. They could do very little for the Mexican citizens they were abandoning to these White Americans who regarded them as a racially inferior people, unfit for American citizenship. The Mexican government did succeed, however, by the Treaty of Guadalupe Hidalgo, in conferring American citizenship on those Mexicans who wanted it. Some Mexicans feared that they would be pushed into a position like that of African American slaves (or into a position nearly as bad—the not-quite-citizen status occupied by legally free Blacks). Citing the precedent of the French and Spanish citizens who became American citizens with the acquisition of Louisiana and the Floridas, the Mexican government pushed for the same arrangement for the Mexican citizens it was being forced to abandon.[45] Articles VIII and IX read in part:

> Mexicans now established in territories previously belonging to Mexico, and which remain for the future within the limits of the United States, as defined by the present treaty, shall be free to continue where they now reside, or to remove at any time to the Mexican Republic, retaining the property which they possess in the said territories, or disposing thereof, and removing the proceeds wherever they please; without their being subject, on this account, to any contribution, tax or charge whatever.
>
> Those who shall prefer to remain ... may either retain the title and rights of Mexican citizens, or acquire those of citizens of the United States. But they shall be under the obligation to make their election within one year from the date of the exchange of ratifications of this treaty: and those who shall remain ... after the expiration of that year, without having declared their intention to retain the character of Mexicans, shall be considered to have elected to become citizens of the United States.
>
> ... [P]roperty of every kind, now belonging to Mexicans, not established there, shall be inviolably respected. The present owners, the heirs of these, and all Mexicans who may hereafter acquire said property by contract, shall enjoy with respect to it, guaranties equally ample as if the same belonged to citizens of the United States. ...
>
> The Mexicans who ... shall not preserve the character of citizens of the Mexican Republic ... shall be incorporated into ... the United States according to the principles of the Constitution; and in the mean time shall be maintained and protected in the free enjoyment of their liberty and property, and secured in the free exercise of their religion without restriction.[46]

The treaty as originally signed included an Article X, which guaranteed to Mexicans title to the land they had held under grants from the Mexican government. The U.S.

Senate struck Article X, fearing that land that Anglo-Texans and other Whites had seized from Mexicans would have to be given back. In fact, in all the conquered territories, White Americans over the next few decades took most of the land that had been granted by the Mexican government away from its Mexican owners, just as they and the Mexicans had been taking away land that Indians inhabited.

By Articles VIII and IX, if a person who had been a Mexican citizen wanted to retain Mexican citizenship, he or she had to file notice within one year of the treaty. If he or she did nothing, that person was supposed to be made a U.S. citizen. In practical fact, however, many if not most of the 80,000 to 100,000 people who were entitled to American citizenship by this provision never received it. Whites assumed them to be noncitizens, as Whites have treated people of Mexican descent as foreigners ever since, whatever their parentage and wherever their birth. Thus, the border crossed them: America moved onto the lands and lives of Mexicans in the Southwest, and they became foreigners in the land of their birth.

So arose a strange anomaly in the American racial system. A set of people, Mexicans, was in practical fact marked off socially as a distinct race.[47] But because of the treaty's guarantees, and because of aspirations to a fictive Whiteness on the part of some upper-class Californios and Hispanos, Mexicans retained elements of formal, legal Whiteness. Mexicans were admitted to citizenship, and citizenship was limited to "free White persons," so on one level they must have been considered sort of White. But in their social relationships they were manifestly treated as Brown, not White. In the twentieth century, this contradiction would lead to a strange fiction perpetuated by the U.S. census. Throughout U.S. history the census has asked some kind of "race" question. Terminology has changed several times, but there have long been places for White or Caucasian or European Americans; Black or Negro or African Americans; American Indians or Native Americans; and Asian Americans under various definitions. Despite the practical existence of Mexican Americans (later Latinos or Hispanics as the numbers of people with origins in other Latin American countries increased) as a distinct racial group, there was no race category in the census for them to reflect that fact. In the twentieth century, the census came to include a separate, so-called "ethnicity" question. It asked variations on the question, Is the respondent Mexican or not, Hispanic or not, Spanish-surnamed or not, Spanish-speaking or not? This has meant an enormous amount of confusion, and made it impossible to know accurately the numbers of Mexican Americans or other Latinos.[48]

The situations in the three main areas of Mexican-derived population—New Mexico, Texas, and California—were different, and each evolved more or less independently of the others over the next half-century. But in each case a complex, somewhat fluid racial system emerged, with Whites on top, Blacks and Indians in separate social spheres at the bottom, and Mexicans a separate racial group (despite the Treaty) somewhere in between. Historian Neil Foley calls their status that of "partly colored people." He posits a bipolar racial system, with Whites on top and Blacks on the bottom, and Mexican Americans negotiating a degree of Whiteness while Whites sought to push them toward Blackness. But we have seen a tripolar system at work in the eastern United States from the beginning: White, Black, and Red. In Texas and New Mexico in the nineteenth century, the racial system grew a fourth pole and so was White, Red, Black, and Brown. California added a fifth pole: Yellow.[49]

Making Race in California

Between 1769 and 1823, Franciscan friars planted a string of twenty-one missions up and down California, from San Diego to Sonoma. They brought some local Indians into their orbit as agricultural laborers and Christian converts; others remained free and in control of most of the region. The pertinent racial distinction in Spanish California was between Indians and Spaniards. The Spaniards were almost all themselves of mixed Iberian, Native American, and African ancestry, although their descendants told a tale of Whiter ancestry than that. Some of the nonmission Indians continued to pursue their precontact ways of life, while others took to raising cattle and horses and trading with the Mexicans. The Indian population of Alta California had dropped by the early 1840s to fewer than 100,000. Mexican citizens numbered about 12,000. Perhaps another 2500 were White immigrants from the United States.[50]

After the mission lands were secularized in 1834, the church receded and the strongest authorities left in California society were the Californio elite. Some were the descendants of members of early Spanish expeditions into the region who had been given large grants of land by the Spanish crown. When the missions closed and the Indians were dispossessed, those lands were given away by the Mexican government, and the ranks of Californios swelled. The larger part of the Mexican population lived in what is today Southern California; the northern half of the modern state was only lightly populated by Mexicans and mainly in Indian hands. Thus the racial-social groups in Mexican California were: (1) a Californio elite with pretensions to pure European ancestry; (2) a growing number of mestizo Mexican working people; (3) a dwindling number of mission Indians; and (4) a large number of nonmission Indians.

American traders began to come to California in the 1840s. American troops came with the U.S.-Mexican War. The floodgates opened in 1848, when gold was discovered in the Sierra foothills in north-central California, on a land grant owned by Johann Augustus Sutter, a Swiss immigrant and Mexican citizen. Tens and then hundreds of thousands of foreigners poured in. Eighty percent of them came from the United States; another 10 percent or so from Mexico. Others came from Europe, Peru, Chile, China, the Pacific Islands—indeed, from all points of the globe. California was remade overnight. The balance of population shifted to the north. San Francisco boomed as the entrepôt for the goldfields. A rough, transient, and near-lawless society ruled the mining camps.

The period between the 1840s and the end of the century witnessed the formation of a new racial order in Southern California. The coming of the U.S. regime led to a period of "Americanization." That term would take on quite a different meaning across the country a half-century later, when it would come to stand for the transformation of immigrant individuals into people who were able to perform American language and culture. In California in the 1850s–1870s, "Americanization" meant the immigrants were transforming the local culture and making it American. Not only did the dominant language shift gradually from Spanish to English, laws changed from an Iberian model to an Anglo-American style. Californio politicians, judges, and other leaders became less and less common, and Anglo-Americans took over.

At first an uneasy alliance of American immigrants and upper-class Californios stood together at the top of society, cooperating to keep control over the Mexican masses, and beneath them, the Indians. But over that time period, three processes added to the numbers of Mexicans. Many former mission Indians took Spanish names and gradually merged into the Mexican working class. Some nonmission Indians wandered in from the cold and joined them. Some migrants came north from Mexico, though it is not clear how many they were. Not only was no one keeping accurate statistics, but in an atmosphere that was increasingly defining status in racial terms, the dominant Whites saw anyone Mexican as an immigrant, whether that person was born in California or not. At the same time, as White Americans solidified their hold on local power in places like Santa Barbara and Los Angeles, they gradually pushed the upper-class Californios into the Brown Mexican category as well.[51]

The dynamics were rougher in the goldfields. Despite the polyglot population, the mining country quickly came to be viewed by White Americans, now the largest group, as their national and racial property. In 1848, an estimated 1300 Californios rushed to work in the gold mines. Soon they were joined by thousands more Mexicans (some from Mexico, some probably from other parts of California) and other Latin Americans. Anglo miners took offense at Brown people taking gold out of the ground. A host of lynchings, shootings, beatings, robberies, and claim-jumping went unpunished. In the fall of 1849, Luis de la Rosa, the Mexican ambassador to Washington, lodged a formal protest, which the U.S. government ignored. In 1850 the California Assembly passed the Foreign Miners' Tax: all non-U.S. citizens would be charged twenty dollars a month for the privilege of prospecting. The tax was enforced against anyone Mexican (U.S. citizen or not), against other Latin Americans, Pacific Islanders, and Chinese. It was not enforced against Whites, even if they were not U.S. citizens. Many Mexicans left the goldfields by the mid-1850s because of such abuses. Things got so bad that in 1857, Don Manuel Domínguez, a Californio politician who had been a signer of the California Constitution of 1849, was denied the right to testify in court because he had some Indian ancestry.[52]

Mexican Californians did not take all this lying down. Some fought in court to keep their land and citizenship. Some continued to participate in politics in places like Los Angeles and Santa Barbara until they were finally pushed out late in the century. None of the resisters against the new racial order, in California or elsewhere in America's newly conquered provinces, was more celebrated than bandit hero Joaquín Murrieta. Murrieta may have been a single person or a legendary amalgam of several men who were bandits in the eyes of Anglo-Californians and heroes in the eyes of the Mexican Californian masses. Certainly, people named Murrieta and others from what became the Mexican states of Sonora, Sinaloa, and Michoacán had been migrating back and forth to California for many generations by the time the Americans took claim to California. It seems one Joaquín Murrieta and perhaps a dozen family members made their way back into California around the time gold was discovered. They seem to have been working in the mines and capturing mustangs and trading them from roughly 1849 to 1851.

Then some Anglos got in a dispute with Joaquín's half-brother Jesús Carrillo Murrieta. They lynched Jesús, horsewhipped Joaquín, and raped Joaquín's wife, Rosa Felíz de Murrieta. For the next two years Joaquín and a band of other Sonorans went on a rampage. Whites said they were killing and looting indiscriminately. Mexicans said they were hunting down the men who had assaulted them, one by one, and dragging them to death behind Joaquín's horse. In 1853 the Assembly paid for a Los Angeles deputy sheriff, Harry Love, to raise a squad of California Rangers who were to hunt Murrieta down and arrest him. They hunted Murrieta down, and instead of bringing him to justice, killed him and several of his compatriots, bottled two of their heads, and put them on public display. Joaquín Murrieta was an outlaw in the eyes of White Americans, but he was a hero in the eyes of many Mexican Americans, just as were a host of others who resisted White domination in California, Texas, Arizona, and New Mexico. José Canales, biographer of Juan Cortina, reminds us: "Whether a man is called a 'bandit' or a 'hero' often depends just upon one word—SUCCESS; for very often a successful bandit turns out to be a real hero and true patriot, such as … [George] Washington." Such men as Juan Cortina, Gregorio Cortez, Elfego Baca, Tiburcio Vásquez, and Joaquín Murrieta were the subjects of song and legend from that generation to this, celebrating their resistance to Anglo domination. They resisted, they were crushed, and the Whites triumphed in the end.[53]

As in Texas, so also in California, on a different time schedule and with different details. White Americans came into a country that was inhabited mainly by Indians and claimed by Mexico. They took the land by force and remade the local class hierarchy and racial system, placing themselves at the top and pressing the lower orders together. Some of the local people collaborated with the conquerors, some resisted, but in the end their day had passed. The immigrants—White Americans—did not assimilate into their new land. They remade their new land as their own racial possession.

Racial Replacement

The process we have witnessed in this chapter so far is not simple immigration, but something more sinister: *racial replacement.* The White people of the United States took the western two-thirds of the U.S. continental swath away from Red and Brown peoples (after taking away the eastern third in earlier generations). They killed as many of the Indians as they could and took away most of the land where the remainder had lived. They took land and citizenship rights away from Mexicans, too. At the same time, White Americans were recruiting Europeans to emigrate to America, to fill in those same lands. Western railroad companies, which had been given grants of former Indian land along their planned routes, raised money to build the tracks by selling land to immigrants from the eastern states and from Europe. They hired agents and sent them to Europe with handbills like the one in Figure 4.6 to entice people to come.[54]

Frederick B. Goddard published *Where to Emigrate and Why* in 1869. It was aimed at European readers (Goddard took time to explain American democratic institutions) and contained descriptions of each state and territory in the West and South, including Alaska, the claim to which had been purchased from Russia two years before. He wrote in part:

> During the last two years more than six hundred thousand sturdy [European] immigrants have landed upon our shores, and there is no ebb to the flowing tide. Our land is ringing with the din of her internal improvements; cottages are springing up far away to the west upon sunny acres where, but yesterday, roamed the Indian and the buffalo. Grand lines of railroad are stretching out across the continent. … And all we have, and are, or may be, as a nation, we offer to share with the struggling millions of the earth."[55]

THE FINEST FARMING LANDS

WHEAT — CORN — COTTON — FRUITS & VEGETABLES

EQUAL TO ANY IN THE WORLD!!!
MAY BE PROCURED

At FROM $8 to $12 PER ACRE.
Near Markets, Schools, Railroads, Churches, and all the blessings of Civilization.
1,200,000 Acres, in Farms of 40, 80, 120, 160 Acres and upwards, in
ILLINOIS, the Garden State of America.

12

13

Figure 4.6 Land advertisements such as this lured Europeans to the United States to replace Native Americans, *Harper's Weekly*, 1863.

Presumably, he did not include recently dispossessed Indians or Mexicans among those struggling millions to be welcomed.

Goddard loved the Homestead Act of 1862. He called it "one of the most beneficent enactments of any age, or country, and one which has done more than any other to honor the American name, and make it loved throughout the earth."[56] As with Goddard, so with most historians of the Homestead Act and White "settlement" of the West. The previous inhabitants are glossed over, naturalized, and romanticized as that now-disappeared and therefore fondly remembered pair of fauna: "the Indian and the buffalo." In the words of historian Frederick Hoxie, the literature on the Homestead Act is "incurious about the impact of the act and the newcomers' presence on the peoples who inhabited those lands previously."[57]

Several historians have written eloquent accounts of the peopling of the Great Plains, Southwest, and Far West by European immigrants. There, are, for example, stirring histories of immigrant Germans colonizing Texas, Old Order Amish on the Great Plains, Swedes in the Dakotas, and so on and on.[58] In *The Minds of the West*, Jon Gjerde has written as good a book as a historian can write. It is a vividly imagined, painstakingly researched, and movingly written book about the coming together of many varieties of European immigrants in farm, family, and community in the rural Middle West in the nineteenth century. But nowhere does *Minds of the West* project any sense that these White people were pursuing their lives, building their farms, making their families, blending their ethnicities, learning new languages and foods, and changing their identities on land that had been taken from Native Americans just a few years before. In fact, Indians appear in only one sentence out of the book's

426 pages: "Herbert Quick … remembered that 'Old Ebenezer McAllister used to say that among the Injuns the women did all the work, among the Hoosiers it was equally divided, and among the Yankees the men did it all.'" We mark our privilege by what we fail to talk about.[59]

Few historians are willing to make the connection between homesteading and genocide that Mari Sandoz did, as she recalled the stories of old-timers from her childhood in northwest Nebraska: "At that time [1854] the white men in the region were only a few little islands in a great sea of Indians and buffaloes. Twenty-three years later, in 1877, the buffaloes were about gone and the last of the Indians driven to the reservations—only a few little islands of Indians in a great sea of whites. This exploit of modern man is unrivaled in history: the destruction of a whole way of life and the expropriation of a race from a region of 350,000,000 acres in so short a time." Sandoz knew whereof she wrote: she was herself the daughter of Swiss immigrant homesteaders. But unlike some other writers of similar background, she was attuned to the situations of the Native peoples around her. It is significant that it is historians of Native America, not historians of immigration or the westward movement of White people, who are willing to make this connection.[60]

The Homestead Act of 1862 was a key tool for bringing Europeans into the American West. For decades the government had been selling off former Indian lands to would-be farmers and, more frequently, to speculators who then resold them to farmers. As vast tracts of land in the West came under government control after 1850, political pressure increased, calling on them to open up lands for free. This had much to do with the Jeffersonian myth of the yeoman farmer, which held that virtue and democracy resided in a nation consisting of small freeholders. From Washington Irving to Hamlin Garland to Walt Disney to Garrison Keillor, this theme runs deep in American literature and popular culture.[61] The most virtuous—indeed, the most *American*—people are White family farmers living on the land and in small communities. Selling land cheaply to such people was a good thing; giving it to them would be even better. So the Homestead Act proposed to fill the West with virtuous Euro-American citizens who would bring social stability and civic engagement, and it would not cost anyone anything—well, except those pesky Indians.[62]

Part of the rationale for the Homestead Act was specifically to bring in Europeans, to make them democracy-loving Americans, and so to increase America's standing in the world's eyes. Rep. Dunham of Indiana said in support of the homestead bill on the floor of Congress, "By this bill, which places within the reach of all the power of becoming owners of the soil, you demonstrate the beneficent spirit of our institutions, you add to their reputation and give a new impulse to the cause of liberty throughout the world." Rep. Willard Hall added: "[I]f by a system of legislation at once just and beneficial to our citizens generally, we can induce the foreign immigrant to make his home in the West we secure his attachment and fidelity to our institutions. As soon as he finds himself in possession of a home of his own and occupying a position that makes him a freeman free from the control, direction and oppression of a superior, he will and must feel proud of American citizenship."[63]

The Homestead Act offered up to 160 acres of land to any person who was at least age twenty-one or a head of household. He or she must be a U.S. citizen, or else must declare the intention to become a U.S. citizen. That provision encouraged European immigrants to come and take advantage of the U.S. government's generosity, at the same time it made nearly all Blacks, Indians, and Asians ineligible for homesteading, because they could not become citizens (the situation of African

Figure 4.7 Cherokee land run.

Americans changed with the Fourteenth Amendment, and there were some Black homesteaders after the Civil War). The claimant had to occupy the land, build a house, live on it for five years, and grow crops. At the end of five years, with the payment of an eighteen dollar fee and filing some papers, the land would belong to the farmer. The Homestead Act gave farms to 400,000 White Americans by the time it was repealed in 1976 (Alaskan homesteading continued until 1986). Hundreds of thousands more Whites bought former Indian lands at bargain prices from the government or from land agents.[64]

Together, European immigrants and Euro-Americans flooded onto the lands that had only recently been inhabited by Mexicans and Indians. They even took much of Oklahoma, which had been designated as Indian Territory in perpetuity, but which had been shrinking as first one then another piece was given away. In a series of "land runs"—races for the best farmland—beginning in 1889 and continuing through the 1890s, land from which the Cherokee and several other tribes had just recently been removed went over to White ownership (Figure 4.7).[65]

The impact of land sales and land runs on Native Americans was enormous. Craig Miner and William Unrau studied "the end of Indian Kansas." Between 1854 and 1871, a Native American population of more than ten thousand was reduced to only a few dozen Indians. Kansas was originally supposed to be the permanent home of several tribes that had been removed from the eastern states, as well as the tribes that had lived in the region before the first great removal; they included Sacs and Foxes, Potawatomis, Kickapoos, Comanches, Kiowas, Pawnees, Cheyennes, and Arapahos. But as the Civil War approached, White people cast longing eyes on those supposedly perpetual Indian lands. In the eastern part of the state, the government pushed Indians to accept individual tenure to land parcels, which vastly reduced the total size of Indian holdings, and then they sold off the rest to Whites. They forced some tribes to disband, and sold the land to Whites. In the west, the U.S. Army attacked Native peoples, killed their buffalo supply, and drove them onto reservations in Oklahoma. "Leaving Kansas required of the tribes a terribly difficult psychological adjustment, since many of them were being torn from established homes for the second time in thirty years. Ottawa chief John Wilson repeated over and over as he walked south to Indian Territory that he did not want to go. He died on the road of a chill contracted while trying to catch some of his horses in a rainstorm. … 'I feel,' said one Indian, 'as if I were standing on the end of a log, and a very light one too, which is floating on water one hundred feet deep, and that the log is liable at any moment to turn over with me and drown me.'"[66]

A few Native Americans found jobs in Wild West shows, playing Indians attacking stagecoaches and wagon trains. Far more Indians who lost tribal lands and identities took up farming or ranching. In places like Oklahoma, with very large Native populations, they most often retained their Indian identities, but in many places they did not, and over generations blended into the rural White working class. A campaign by government officials, missionaries, and educators over the period from the 1880s through World War I managed to assimilate large numbers of Native people into the White population.[67]

The point is this: there was an intimate tie between exterminating Indians and dispossessing Mexicans, on one hand, and bringing in Europeans on the other. Both were purposeful actions taken by the White American public and the U.S. government acting on their behalf. Dispossession of two peoples and importation of a third were parts of the same process, twined together. They amounted to racial replacement, and that was one of the dominant themes of nineteenth-century U.S. history.

East from Asia

Chinese Immigrants

Among the several million immigrants into the American West in the nineteenth century were a quarter of a million Chinese.[68] They came on quite different terms than did the European and Euro-American migrants. Alone among the significant groups of nineteenth-century immigrants, Chinese were Asian, and therefore ineligible to become naturalized U.S. citizens. Alone among immigrant groups, they were soon banned, in a national fit of racist hysteria.[69]

The Bonacich and Cheng integrated model of international labor migration described in Chapter 1 seems to align itself fairly well with the pattern for Chinese migration into the United States: industrial development in Europe and North America leading to trade with, military intervention in, and destabilization of a pre-industrial region, which is in turn accompanied by the movement of people from the pre-industrial to the industrial region. In such a model, international trade is a kind of colonial relationship, and one of the things the colonial relationship creates is migration.

The United States was a junior partner to the United Kingdom in the British attempt to open China to Western trade. The Chinese government was reluctant to allow much foreign trade of any sort, and the product the British wanted to sell was opium, so they were unwelcome but persistent salespeople. In two opium wars in 1839 to 1842 and 1856 to 1858, Britain, France, the United States, and several European nations pried China open to international trade and missionary activity. The first center of foreign influence was the southeast coastal province of Guangdong. The Portuguese maintained a colony in nearby Macau, and after 1842 the British held Hong Kong. They sold opium up the Pearl River and along the coast under the protection of British gunboats, and thereby drained vast amounts of money from the Chinese economy. The combined impact of military intrusion and economic drain was destabilization of the Chinese government and an element of lawlessness in Guangdong. Peasants were impoverished. Bandits roamed the countryside. The Taiping Rebellion and the Red Turban Revolt began in Guangdong, lasted from 1851 to 1864, and killed more than twenty million people.

One way out of all this chaos was to leave China. Several million Chinese did that over the course of the nineteenth century. Pooling family savings to pay for passage or signing away their freedom for a contractual period, young men in their teens and twenties went abroad to work. The plan was to send some money home and return one day as rich men. Chinese laborers went out from Guangdong and neighboring Fujian province mainly to Southeast Asia—to Malaya and Siam, where international migration networks were already established before the beginning of the nineteenth century, as well as to the Philippines and the new British colony of Singapore. They also went to Hawai'i, Peru, Louisiana, Cuba, and Jamaica.

The United States was just one destination among many. Lee Chew told of learning about America:

> I worked on my father's farm till I was about sixteen years of age, when a man of our [clan] came back from America and took ground as large as four city blocks and made a paradise of it. He put a large stone wall around and led some streams through and built a palace and summer house and about twenty other structures, with beautiful bridges over the streams and walks and roads. Trees and flowers, singing birds, water fowl and curious animals were within the walls.
>
> The man had gone away from our village a poor boy. Now he returned with unlimited wealth, which he had obtained in the country of the American wizards. After many amazing adventures he had become a merchant in a city called Mott Street, so it was said. ...
>
> Having made his wealth among the barbarians this man had faithfully returned to pour it out among his [clansmen], and he is living in our village now very happy, and a pillar of strength to the poor.[70]

Lee Chew followed the path blazed by his kinsman to the United States. The first Chinese people to come to the United States in significant numbers arrived in California in 1849 with the intention of mining for gold. Many did. They persisted in the goldfields after most of the Mexicans had been run off, and even after the mines began to wear out and most Whites left, too. By 1870, one-quarter of California's 36,000 miners were Chinese. Other Chinese men entered building trades or found service work, running laundries and restaurants from San Francisco to the gold country. Cooking and washing were traditionally female tasks in Euro-America. Since Gold Rush California was nearly all male, this was an economic niche that any enterprising set of people could fill. The Chinese chose to fill this niche. Thus began the feminization of Asian men in the minds of Euro-Americans, despite the manifest masculinity of Chinese males (Figure 4.8).[71]

Figure 4.8   "This guy carried laundry, but he was a hunk."

Some Chinese went back with their bags filled with gold. For more, the pot remained unseized at the end of the rainbow, and they stayed on. Others came to join them. Thousands worked on building the nation's first transcontinental railroad. Irish immigrants, other White workers, and some African Americans provided the labor for the long, flat eastern portion. A nearly all-Chinese work force built the much tougher and more dangerous western section. They built trestles over gorges and blasted tunnels through mountains. No one kept track of how many died. When the two work teams met in the middle, former California governor Leland Stanford and a band of dignitaries nailed the Golden Spike near Promontory Point, Utah (Figure 4.9). Chinese, Black, and Irish workers witnessed the ceremony, but the commemorative drawings erased the Chinese and Blacks.

Other Chinese immigrants worked in agriculture. Seventy-five percent of California's farm laborers in the 1880s were Chinese. They raised fruits and vegetables and planted vineyards and citrus orchards. As farming and railroad work expanded into the Northwest and the mountain states, Chinese workers went to those places, too. They cut and milled lumber in Washington and Oregon, mined silver in Colorado and Nevada, and canned salmon on the British Columbia coast. Tough, energetic, enterprising young men, they went wherever there was work and labored long hours for low wages. Some ventured as far away as North Adams, in western Massachusetts, where they worked in a shoe factory.

In some of these places, Chinese worked alongside Whites, in others alongside Blacks or Indians or, in the Northwest forests, alongside Hawaiians and Native

COMPLETION OF THE PACIFIC RAILROAD—MEETING OF LOCOMOTIVES OF THE UNION AND CENTRAL PACIFIC LINES; THE ENGINEERS SHAKE HANDS.

Figure 4.9   Driving the Golden Spike. Granger Collection, New York.

Americans. But for the most part they maintained separate work gangs organized by immigrants from the early years who had mastered some English and served as labor contractors. The role of the ethnic labor contractor—who often ran a store or flophouse in a West Coast port city—was crucial in developing a market for Chinese workers, arranging passage and housing for new recruits, helping them get their bearings in the new country, having letters written and sent home, arranging for the bones of a Chinese who died in the United States to be sent back to the village in China, and mediating between the Chinese immigrant community and the wider society.[72]

The immigrant Chinese economized every way they could, They would sleep several men to a room, go without luxuries, and send their pay back to their families in China. Some politicians at the time, and some scholars since, have made much of the fact that most Chinese immigrants did not form families in the United States, that they hoped to go back to China one day, that while they viewed America as a land of economic opportunity, it was not their first choice for a permanent home. Such people have contrasted this pattern to what they presume to be the American norm: immigrants leave the old country behind and embrace the new. Immigrants come in families, women and children as well as men. Soon, their ties to the old place wither, they change their language, clothing, and mannerisms, and they assimilate into the White American mainstream. But as we have seen, most other immigrant streams were preponderantly male in the beginning. Quite a high percentage of English and German immigrants returned to their homelands, and others went back and forth several times before making the move permanent. Had they been allowed to assimilate in America, it is quite possible the Chinese, too, would have blended in and given up their dreams of home. But that was not possible, for they were marked off by race for special discrimination.[73]

Another way to interpret the sojourner quality of Chinese immigration is to note that Euro-Americans were very active in recruiting European immigrants, while the Chinese came to the United States largely on their own initiative. In going after European immigrants, White America was recruiting people they hoped would become future citizens. Insofar as they accepted Chinese, Mexicans, Hawaiians, and other immigrants of color, White Americans saw themselves as allowing the entry of foreign guest workers who, the Whites hoped, would one day go back where they came from. No White people, not even those who protested against the violence of the anti-Chinese movement, argued that the Chinese would make good American citizens. They were not given that chance.

The Anti-Chinese Movement

The first generation of Chinese residents in the United States suffered an unremitting series of atrocities at the hands of Whites, accompanied by a crescendo of demagoguery and legislative attempts to harass them, drive them out, and bar them from the country. In 1850 the California Assembly passed the Foreign Miner's Tax, which was supposed to levy twenty dollars a month on any noncitizen miner. In practice, the tax was collected only from Latin Americans and Chinese, and after the first couple of years, only from the Chinese. European noncitizens did not have to pay.[74]

In October 1853 three White men went on trial in Nevada County for the murder of Ling Sing. One White and three Chinese testified against George W. Hall and his codefendants, and the jury returned a guilty verdict. On appeal, the California Supreme Court overturned the verdict. They ruled that, since the state's criminal proceedings act said, "No black or mulatto person, or Indian, shall be permitted to give evidence in favor of, or against, any white person," Chinese were also barred from testifying. Speaking for the court, Chief Justice Hugh C. Murray ruled that Chinese were effectively either Blacks or Indians. He went on to say that, if Chinese were allowed to testify in court, White Americans would "soon see them at the polls, in the jury box, upon the bench, and in our legislative halls." That prospect horrified him, since he regarded the Chinese as a race "whose mendacity is proverbial; a race … nature has marked as inferior, and … incapable of progress or intellectual development beyond a certain point."[75]

Some early Chinese immigrants probably came to the United States under pre-existing labor contracts (something like indentures), but most came as free laborers. In either case, they violated the law of China, which forbade emigration. That changed in 1868 with the Burlingame Treaty, a trade pact that said in Article V: "The United States of America and the Emperor of China cordially recognize the inherent and inalienable right of man to change his home and allegiance, and also the mutual advantage of the free migration and emigration of their citizens and subjects respectively from one country to the other for the purpose of curiosity, of trade, or as permanent residents."[76]

The American welcome mat did not stay out for long. The completion of the Transcontinental Railroad threw several thousand men out of work in 1869. Some, both White and Chinese, made their way to western cities and towns in search of jobs. Unemployed White workers began to grumble about the Chinese who, they said with increasing frequency and bitterness, were driving down wages and taking away jobs that ought to belong to White people. Chinese people were harassed in many locations, among them Los Angeles. On October 24, 1871, a White police officer walking near Chinatown heard shots down a narrow alley. He called together whatever armed White men he could find, and they entered the alley. There they found a dispute between two groups of Chinese men over which owned a young Chinese woman. One man lay dead on the ground. The White posse went wild, shooting Chinese people at random, looting buildings, and burning them. Boys as young as ten or twelve were hacked to pieces, as was a wealthy Chinese doctor who pleaded for his life. In all, at least twenty-one Chinese immigrants died that day, fifteen of them hanged on gallows erected impromptu on the spot.

San Francisco was hardly better. In 1873 the board of supervisors passed three laws aimed to pressure Chinese immigrants into leaving. As one board member said, "The General Government has so tied our hands by the treaty with China, that we must depend entirely upon local legislation to discourage the immigration of Chinese."[77] First on the docket was the laundry ordinance. Chinese laundrymen had come to dominate the clothes-washing business in San Francisco and elsewhere in the state. They organized themselves into a powerful craft union, the Tung Hing Tong, which set prices and regulated who among the Chinese could enter the business. For the 1300 Chinese laundry workers in San Francisco, theirs was a labor-intensive trade. They washed clothes by hand and delivered them on foot, while the few White launderers used horse carts. The laundry ordinance charged eight dollars a year to any laundry that made its deliveries using a single horse-drawn cart, sixteen dollars if it used two carts, and sixty dollars a year if it didn't have a cart at all.

The cubic air ordinance, ostensibly a health measure, played on the fact that several Chinese men would share sleeping quarters in order to save money, often sleeping in shifts. The ordinance required that any living quarters provide 500 cubic feet of air for each inhabitant. Hundreds of Chinese immigrants were rousted out of bed and jailed for violating this law, which was not enforced against the White population. They were packed in jail to the point where they had scarcely 100 cubic feet of air apiece. And there they encountered the queue ordinance. The jailers tried to shave their heads, also ostensibly a health measure. But it was far more than that to the Chinese, and the leaders of White San Francisco knew it. China was governed by a foreign dynasty, the Qing, who were ethnic Manchus. To distinguish themselves from the Han Chinese majority, they decreed that all ethnic Chinese men had to wear a distinctive hairstyle, with the front half of the head shaved and the hair grown long and braided in a queue at the back. Any Han Chinese who did not wear his hair this way was assumed to be a rebel by government authorities and executed on the spot. So any Chinese immigrant in America who did not keep his queue could not go back to China on pain of death.

Other laws forbade anyone to disinter the bones of a Chinese person who died in the United States and ship those bones back to the family in China; imposed a $1000 penalty on anyone bringing in a Chinese or Japanese immigrant; denied "aliens ineligible to citizenship"—Chinese and Japanese—from owning land; denied those same groups business licenses; excluded Chinese granite from San Francisco public works; and so on and on. Such laws were petty but not insignificant attempts to harass California's Chinese residents and encourage them to go away. In many cases such laws worked, as men went back to China in triumph or in defeat. But those who stayed fought back, with the help of White religious leaders like the Reverend Otis Gibson, a Methodist minister, and some of the state's best lawyers. In time, most of the local anti-Chinese ordinances were overturned in the California courts.

The most outspoken leader of the anti-Chinese movement was Denis Kearney, himself an immigrant who had come from Ireland in 1868. By 1872 he was running a cartage business in San Francisco and agitating under the slogan, "The Chinese Must Go!" Kearney became the demagogue-in-chief at the head of the California Workingmen's Party. Kearney fulminated in an 1877 speech:

> We intend to try and vote the Chinaman out, to frighten him out, and if this won't do, to kill him out, and when the blow comes, we won't leave a fragment for the thieves to pick up. We are going to arm ourselves to the teeth, and if these land-grabbers and thieves go outside the Constitution, we will go outside the Constitution, too, and woe be to them. You must be prepared. The heathen slaves must leave this coast, if it cost 10,000 lives. We want to frighten capital and thereby starve the white men so that they will be exasperated and do their duty. This is the last chance the white slaves will ever have to gain their liberty. … We have the numbers to win at the ballot box, but you will be cheated out of the result, and all history shows that oppressed labor has always to get its right at the point of the sword. If the Republican robber and the Democratic thief cheat you at the election, as I know they will, shoot them down like rats. You must be ready with your bullets. We will go to Sacramento and compel them to enact such laws as we wish.[78]

The Workingmen's Party—and a whole lot of other White citizens and noncitizens— took part in an orgy of anti-Chinese violence that began in July 1877 and carried on to the end of the decade. Mary Roberts Coolidge reported:

> In the first riot alone twenty-five wash houses were burned at a loss of twenty-thousand dollars and the laundrymen fled into hiding in Chinatown. Then followed an orgy of outrage; for months afterward no Chinaman was safe from personal outrage even on the main thoroughfares and the perpetrators of the abuses were almost never interfered with so long as they did not molest white men's property. The epidemic of arson, robbery and personal abuse spread to the surrounding country. In town after town Chinese laundries and quarters were set on fire by incendiaries; and when the inmates tried to escape they were often robbed and shot and sometimes left to die in burning buildings. … The Chinese could no longer safely attend the Mission night schools in the towns and fled to the mountains and the remote country districts for work. Many … went back to China, never to return. The culmination of this insane resentment was reached in a riot at Truckee in November, 1878, when the town was in a state of anarchy and the Chinese population of about 1000 persons was driven out. … The white men were seldom American citizens; it was, in fact, an uprising of European foreigners, generally led by Irishmen, against Oriental foreigners.[79]

The violence culminated in the Denver anti-Chinese riot of November 1880. A White man got in a poolhall fight with two Chinese men. Soon word spread—

Figure 4.10   Anti-Chinese cartoon, "The Coming Man."

inaccurately—that a Chinese man had killed a White. A mob of several hundred Whites roared through the streets assaulting any Chinese person they saw, burning laundries and restaurants, and looting. One Chinese man was killed, scores were wounded, and property damage totaled more than $50,000. That same year the California Assembly in 1880 passed an anti-miscegenation law that stipulated that no White person would be allowed to marry "a negro, mulatto, or Mongolian."[80]

Soon the anti-Chinese movement became a national political issue. In 1875 Congress passed the Page Law, which barred immigration by women who were being brought into the country "for lewd and immoral purposes." The law specifically gave the U.S. consuls in "China, Japan, or any Oriental country"—but not in any European country—the responsibility of ascertaining whether women were in fact coming as prostitutes. Selective enforcement and heavy interrogation meant that the numbers of Chinese immigrant women, already small, dropped almost to nothing.[81]

An essential part of the anti-Chinese campaign was a rhetoric that portrayed Chinese people as deformed subhumans. The men were monsters and the women their monstrous slaves (Figure 4.10).

In 1878 a Congressional committee report alleged that Chinese people were unfit for entry because "[t]hey bring with them neither wives nor families, nor do they intermarry with the resident population. … Mentally, morally, physically, socially and politically they have remained a distinct and antagonistic race." Here in crystalline form was the argument against Chinese immigrants: they were supposed to be permanently, biologically, and characterologically different from White people, inferior to White people, and incapable of change for the better.[82]

Then came the *pièce de résistance*: the Chinese Exclusion Act. In 1879 Congress passed an act to stop any further Chinese immigration. President Rutherford B. Hayes vetoed it on the ground that it violated the 1868 Burlingame Treaty, which guaranteed the right of immigration and permanent residence to Chinese people. In 1881 Congress ratified an amended treaty, and in 1882 passed a new exclusion act over the veto of President Chester A. Arthur. Slated to last ten years, it barred "any Chinese laborer" from entering the United States. Merchants, students, and travelers could continue to come, but people who worked with their bodies could not. A year later, Emma Lazarus wrote "Give me your tired, your poor"—presumably Chinese migrants were not part of the huddled masses she envisioned. The exclusion act was renewed in 1892 and 1902, and made permanent in 1904. Other legislation made it first difficult and then illegal for Chinese U.S. residents to go back to China for a visit and then return to the United States.[83]

The anti-Chinese movement did not end there. In 1885 Congress passed a law banning contract labor: that is, paying someone's passage in return for that person working a term in the United States, as had been the case for White indentured servants in the colonial era, and for some Chinese in the Gilded Age. That same year, a mob led by Tacoma's most prominent White citizens attacked that Washington town's several hundred Chinese residents, herded them together, and put them on a boat for San Francisco. The next year a Seattle mob very nearly succeeded in doing the same thing. Also in 1885, miners and other White residents of Rock Springs, Wyoming, set upon the 300-plus Chinese who lived there and worked in mines run by the Union Pacific Railroad. They set buildings afire and shot men as they ran from the flames. Twenty-eight Chinese men were killed and fifteen wounded. It took federal troops to put down the massacre (Figure 4.11).

At the height of their greatest numbers, Chinese people never constituted so much as one-twentieth of the total U.S. immigrant stream. But they were the first nationality group against whom specific ethnic restrictions were directed. The example set by this decision to exclude Chinese immigrants on racial grounds echoed through American history as other groups—Japanese, South Asians, Mexicans, Koreans, and Filipinos—all would suffer similar treatment.[84]

The aftermath of the anti-Chinese movement was dismal for Chinese Americans. A population that had spread across the western landscape now drew back. Abandoning work on railroad and farm, in mine and forest, Chinese people retreated into slum neighborhoods in towns and cities. They left holes in the labor market that other immigrants would soon be called to fill. It was in the 1880s and 1890s that every western city came to have its Chinatown, a neighborhood into which outsiders did not trespass and out of which few Chinese dared go. Chinese people built their own social institutions, a kind of internal community government, that dealt with outsiders and kept them away. This was mainly a bachelor society. As time went on, with no new immigrants coming, the population aged. Their homeland became an ever more distant memory. Meanwhile, the anti-Chinese movement morphed into the anti-Asian movement and went on to other targets. The anti-Asian movement has continued through the twentieth century and into the twenty-first.[85]

How different this early anti-Chinese movement was—how much more severe the attacks, how much more racial in tone, how much more tragic the human cost—than the comparatively insignificant movement against Irish immigration a generation earlier!

Figure 4.11 Massacre of Chinese miners at Rock Springs, *Harper's Weekly*, 1885.

Slave and Citizen

It is not the place of this book or this chapter to attempt a comprehensive description and assessment of slave life and culture, the economics and demography of slavery, slave resistance, or the movement to end the slave institution. Such matters are the province of a very large literature.[86] I am interested here in African Americans *as an immigrant group*—who were brought under brutal compulsion, but who nonetheless went through many of the same processes of culture and identity change as other, more voluntary migrants. It is worth asking the question, how did African Americans in the second two-thirds of the nineteenth century compare with other immigrant peoples of their time?

As we saw in Chapter 2, many disparate African peoples had formed a common pan-African American ethnic identity by the era of the American Revolution. It did not mean that they retained no memory of African culture, nor of ethnic distinctions that had been meaningful in Africa. It meant only that by the third generation or so in America they had become Americans in many ways, including language, dress, political values, and in many respects religion. Old world differences faded into unimportance compared to the huge gulf that separated Blacks from Whites in the United States. When Asante, Mandinka, and other African peoples came to America, they assimilated into the Black racial category. When Germans, Scots, and other European peoples came, they assimilated into the White. White people—yes, even Irish, Italians, and Jews, and even fairly recent immigrants—possessed Whiteness, freedom, and full citizenship. Black people, no matter how many generations they had lived in the United States, possessed none of these.

The 1850s saw a steep rise in the activity and urgency of the people, Black and White, who agitated to end slavery. The Dred Scott decision, the Fugitive Slave

Act, and the experiences of thousands of quasi-free Blacks who found themselves enslaved or in jeopardy signaled aggressive resistance by pro-slavery people to any attack on their prerogatives. An 1850 Congressional compromise between pro- and antislavery forces over the possible extension of slavery into lands wrested from Mexico and the fate of the large slave market in Washington, D.C., resulted in the Fugitive Slave Act, which read in part:

> [W]hen a person held to service or labor in any State or Territory, ... shall ... escape into another State or Territory ... the person or persons to whom such service or labor may be due, or his, her, or their agent or attorney ... may pursue and reclaim such fugitive person, either by procuring a warrant ... or by seizing and arresting such fugitive ... without process. ... In no trial or hearings under this act shall the testimony of such alleged fugitive be admitted in evidence. ... [A]ll good citizens are hereby commanded to aid and assist in the prompt and efficient execution of this law.

The act overrode laws in nine northern states that had protected runaway slaves. It empowered, in effect, any White person to claim ownership of any Black person and to enslave that person without any proof other than their claim of ownership. Many hundreds of Blacks, some of whom had been born free, were captured and hauled off in chains. Twenty thousand northern Blacks left for Canada.[87]

Dred Scott was born a slave around 1800. He moved with his master Peter Blow from Virginia to Alabama and then Missouri. When Blow died, Scott was bought by John Emerson, an army surgeon. Scott lived with Emerson in Missouri, which recognized slavery, and then in the free state of Illinois and the free territory of Wisconsin. When Emerson was transferred back south, Scott and his wife Harriet traveled unaccompanied more than 1000 miles to Louisiana to rejoin him. When Emerson died in 1843, his widow hired Scott out to another master. Scott first tried to buy freedom for himself and his wife. When Mrs. Emerson refused to sell, Scott sued for his freedom.

Scott's lawyers argued in 1850 that he had become free by virtue of living in a free state and territory. As the case wound its way through a succession of Missouri and federal courts, judges ruled in turn both for and against him. Finally, in 1857, the U.S. Supreme Court ruled against Dred Scott, on the ground that, because he was Black, he was not a citizen and therefore had no right to sue for anything. Chief Justice Roger B. Taney wrote the majority opinion, which read in part:

> The question is simply this: Can a negro ... become a member of the political community formed and brought into existence by the Constitution of the United States, and as such become entitled to all the rights, and privileges, and immunities, guaranteed by that instrument to the citizen? One of which rights is the privilege of suing in a court. ...
>
> The question before us is, whether ... [people of African descent] compose a portion of this people, and are constituent members of this sovereignty? We think they are not, and that they are not included, and were not intended to be included, under the word "citizens" in the Constitution, and can therefore claim none of the rights and privileges which that instrument provides for and secures to citizens of the United States.

On the contrary, they were at that time considered as a subordinate and inferior class of beings, who had been subjugated by the dominant race, and, whether emancipated or not, yet remained subject to their authority, and had no rights or privileges but such as those who held the power and the government might choose to grant them.

Dred and Harriet Scott subsequently went free despite the ruling, for they were bought and manumitted by the sons of Peter Blow, Dred Scott's first master. But the status of African-descended Americans was clear: they could not be U.S. citizens, even if they were free.[88]

The Fugitive Slave Act and the Dred Scott decision added fuel to the flames of the antislavery movement, as they also mobilized proslavery people to defend their cherished institution. In the next decade, the nation fought a devastating war—not its largest nor the longest, but certainly the most traumatic and the one that had the greatest impact on American identity. That war had many causes and consequences, but among them was bringing an end to slavery.

After an initial period of euphoria, the lives of many Black Americans did not improve enormously in material terms after slavery's end.[89] Yet the Civil War did bring one crucial change: formal citizenship and recognition of legal personhood for African Americans. The critical documents were the hard-won Thirteenth, Fourteenth, and Fifteenth Amendments to the United States Constitution. Section 1 of the Thirteenth Amendment, passed at war's end in 1865, read: "Neither slavery nor involuntary servitude, except as punishment for crime whereof the party shall have been duly convicted, shall exist within the United States, or any place subject to their jurisdiction." At a stroke, slavery—the White South's labor system of choice and a long-honored American institution—was legally ended. Of course, it took quite a long time to readjust actual social and economic relationships. And within a generation Black peasants were again tied as sharecroppers to the land that their parents had once worked as slaves. But African Americans were accorded at least a measure of freedom.

The Fourteenth Amendment, not passed until 1868, was just as important. It read in part:

> All persons born or naturalized in the United States and subject to the jurisdiction thereof, are citizens of the United States and of the State wherein they reside. No State shall make or enforce any law which shall abridge the privileges and immunities of citizens of the United States; nor shall any State deprive any person within its jurisdiction the equal protection of the laws. ... Representatives shall be apportioned among the several States according to their respective numbers, counting the whole number of persons in each State, excluding Indians not taxed.

This completed the formal incorporation of African-descended former slaves as supposedly full citizens. It erased the three-fifths clause of the original Constitution. For a brief period of time, Blacks indeed voted and ran for office in many southern states. Some were governors and senators, mayors and legislators. Soon enough, however, a White backlash set in, and Blacks were prevented from enjoying the full benefits of citizenship (more about this in Chapter 6). Note that Indians were specifically excluded from citizenship and enumeration. Blacks born in other countries were now eligible to become naturalized U.S. citizens, but Asians and Native Americans were still excluded.

Despite legal freedom and citizenship status, African Americans were still denied many of the rights to which they were formally entitled. Reasoning that the most basic right of U.S. citizenship is the right to vote, the Reconstruction-era Congress passed the Fifteenth Amendment in 1870: "The right of citizens of the United States to vote shall not be denied or abridged by the United States or by any State on account of race, color, or previous condition of servitude. ... The Congress shall have power to enforce this article by appropriate legislation." Progress was made in fits and starts, but nearly a century and a half further on, the promise of the Fifteenth Amendment has yet to be fulfilled. African Americans thus emerged from the end of formal slavery with only partial citizenship. Race limited the access that they had to full membership in an American society that was defined by Whites.

Colonialism and Race Making

In this chapter we have seen the intimate connection between the U.S. imperial project and the making of race in North America. Race in America has never been about Black and White alone. From the beginning, there have always been at least three poles in the U.S. racial system: Red, White, and Black. But as White Europeans launched themselves across the continent in the nineteenth century, they encountered peoples more various than they had known hitherto. These they began to group conceptually into Red, White, Black, Yellow, and Brown. The first three racial formations were complete in White minds well before 1900. It took somewhat longer for Native peoples to grasp a common identity in their own minds, but the seeds of pan-Indianness were well sown by Whites' campaigns of restriction and wars of extermination. Common Latino and Asian identities would not form in the minds of those peoples for another half century or more. But colonial conquest and racialized oppression of Mexicans and Chinese in the nineteenth century laid the groundwork for the Asian and Latino panethnicities that later would form.

Lest the reader think this was all a simple, linear process, neatly conceived and achieved, I conclude the chapter with a story that may seem to complicate these emerging racial categories: the tale of Solomon Bibo, the Jewish chief of the Acoma Pueblo. Bibo was born in Prussia in 1853, the sixth of eleven children. His older brothers migrated to America and ended up working for the Spiegelberg family, pioneer merchants in Santa Fe. The brothers moved to Ceboletta, a tiny village, where they set up a trading post among Navajo Indians. In 1869 the sixteen-year-old Solomon took ship for the United States. He worked with his brothers serving several southwest tribes at a series of trading posts. They bought Indian produce and sold it to the U.S. Army to supply forts in the region. In 1882 Solomon Bibo set up a trading post at the Acoma Pueblo west of Albuquerque.[90]

Soon Bibo was asked by some Acoma Indians to help represent them in disputes over land ownership. A large portion of the Acoma Pueblo's traditional lands had been given by the Spanish crown in land grants to Mexican soldiers, some of whose descendants continued to hold them. Bibo helped the pueblo get some of its lands back, despite the opposition of Pedro Sanchez, the U.S. Indian agent in Santa Fe. In 1885, Bibo married Juana Valle, granddaughter of the governor of the Acoma Pueblo. Three years later he was chosen to succeed his wife's grandfather.

He served a five-year term and stayed on in Acoma for five years more. Wiped out financially in the depression of the 1890s, he and Juana took their children to San Francisco, where they raised them in a Jewish community and gave them a Jewish education. Solomon Bibo ultimately rebounded and opened an upscale grocery. He died in San Francisco in 1934; Juana followed seven years later. They are both buried in the Jewish cemetery in nearby Colma.

Solomon Bibo was always White and remained Jewish to his dying day. Yet like racial boundary crosser John Ross, the mixed-blood Cherokee leader, and countless White traders who lived among Native peoples and worked their way into the communities in which they lived, Bibo integrated himself to an unusual degree into Acoma life. He and Juana lived to some extent on both sides of the White-Indian racial divide. His children grew up in San Francisco, ultimately on the White side of the line, but for a time at least, the Acoma Pueblo had a Jewish governor. Later in life, the San Francisco Jewish community had Native American members.

Chapter 5

The Great Wave, 1870–1930

Takao Ozawa addressed the court.

> In name, General Benedict Arnold was an American, but at heart he was a traitor. In name, I am not an American, but at heart I am a true American. I set forth the following facts which will sufficiently prove this. (1) I did not report my name, my marriage, or the names of my children to the Japanese Consulate in Honolulu; notwithstanding all Japanese subjects are requested to do so. These matters were reported to the American government. (2) I do not have any connection with any Japanese churches or schools, or any Japanese organizations here or elsewhere. (3) I am sending my children to an American church and American school in place of a Japanese one. (4) Most of the time I use the American (English) language at home, so that my children cannot speak the Japanese language. (5) I educated myself in American schools for nearly eleven years by supporting myself. (6) I have lived continuously within the United States for over twenty-eight years. (7) I chose as my wife one educated in American schools … instead of one educated in Japan. (8) I have steadily prepared to return the kindness which our Uncle Sam has extended me … so it is my honest hope to do something good to the United States before I bid a farewell to this world.[1]

Ozawa was a resident of the Territory of Hawai'i, a graduate of the University of California, a Christian, and an American patriot. He was born in Japan, then came to the United States as a teenager. He applied for U.S. citizenship in 1914 and was denied on racial grounds—citizenship, by an 1870 law, was limited to Whites and people of African descent. Ozawa sued the U.S. government for the right to have his American identity confirmed. He argued that he was a model candidate for citizenship in every way, and further, that his skin was in fact whiter than the skin of a lot of Europeans. "My skin is white, I am a white person. I've lived in this country more than twenty-eight years. I deserve citizenship." (Figure 5.1). He cited authorities legal, theological, and anthropological.

Figure 5.1 Takao Ozawa.

The U.S. Supreme Court said no. They said in their 1922 decision that they thought Ozawa a fine fellow, and did not disagree with the assertions of experts that the Japanese were an "enlightened" people. But they said he was racially inappropriate for admission to American citizenship. Ozawa, said the court, "is clearly of a race which is not Caucasian and therefore belongs entirely outside the zone" of White people. As to the question of skin color, "Manifestly the test afforded by the mere color of the skin of each individual is impracticable, as that differs greatly among persons of the same race, even among Anglo-Saxons. ... Hence to adopt the color test alone would result in a confused overlapping of races and a gradual merging of one into the other." Takao Ozawa died a Japanese citizen.[2]

Takao Ozawa migrated to the United States during a time of unprecedented economic growth. The U.S. economy exploded in the period between Reconstruction and the end of World War I. From 1870 to 1920, the fraction of the American labor force that worked in industry and transportation doubled from a quarter to a half. The number of manufacturing workers more than tripled, from just over 2 million to 6.5 million workers. Bituminous coal production jumped twenty-sevenfold, from 20,471 tons to 568,667 tons. Raw steel production expanded 600-fold, from 77 tons to 46,183 tons. The Gross National Product was multiplied by twelve times. The per capita income of Americans more than doubled, and the U.S. share of world manufacturing jumped from 23 percent to 42 percent. The wages of farm laborers more than doubled. The amount of land devoted to farming also more than doubled, from 4.1 to 9.6 million acres.[3]

One of the keys to all this growth was the ability of the U.S. economy to call on a deep and flexible pool of new workers. At the dawn of the industrial age in the mid-nineteenth century, the United States was blessed with an extraordinary list of advantages: enormous natural resources of land and minerals; free security, sheltered by wide oceans and bordered by weak and quiet neighbors; the world's second best education system after Japan (which meant a skilled labor force could easily be trained); abundant sources of capital, both domestic and foreign; and key developments in technology, from water power to steam to railroads to machine processes. None of America's advantages stood out more consistently than these two features: the United States, throughout its history, has had, thanks to conquest, abundant territory and too few people, at least by comparison with the other industrializing nations of the world. This meant that, as the country and the economy grew, it was easy to attract a flexible labor supply out of other nations' surpluses. Wages were high relative to Europe and Asia because American enterprises had to pay wages that high in order to attract labor.

A great wave of immigrants swept over the United States in the last third of the nineteenth century and the first third of the twentieth century. Their presence in industrial America created a complex dynamic between the migrants and those Americans who were already here. This chapter and the one that follows it are, on one hand, about the provenance of the labor supply for mature American industrialism in the formative years between the end of the Civil War and the dawn of the modern age. On the other, they are also about the racial dilemma faced by Takao Ozawa.

From New Sources and Old, to America and Back

The period addressed by this chapter, 1870 to 1930, is the era in which the Ellis Island immigration station was built and flourished. More importantly, it is the only era in American history during which much of the immigration to the United States actually resembled the Ellis Island model. Millions of Europeans came to the United States, many of them through New York Harbor and other eastern ports. They continued to come in very large numbers from Germany, Britain, and Ireland, as they had in the preceding decades. To their number were added millions more who came from Southern, Eastern, and Northeastern Europe. In the western part of the United States, hundreds of thousands of Asians and Mexicans entered as well. Their experiences were very different from those of the various Europeans who came to the East.

Although it has become axiomatic that the largest flow of so-called "new" immigrants came from Southern and Eastern Europe, and prominent textbooks have asserted that "Italians were the most numerous" and "[t]wo million Jews comprised the second largest body of immigrants arriving in the late nineteenth and early twentieth centuries,"[4] the actual numbers are more revealing. Table 5.1 shows the comparative numbers for the countries that sent the most people to the United States in those decades.

Italy did indeed send the largest number of people from any single nation in this period: 4.6 million. Yet the Italian numbers were about the same order of magnitude as those from several other places: 4.1 million from the Austro-Hungarian Empire, 3.6 million from Germany, 3.3 million from Russia, 2.8 million from Britain, 2.6 million from Canada, and 2.2 million each from Scandinavia and Ireland. And, as we shall see below, while Jews were very important, it is not because their number—about 2 million—was so large. Even granted that some portion of the national numbers attributed to Austria-Hungary, Russia, and Germany in Table 5.1 represented Jewish migrants (others were Poles in addition to Hungarians, Germans, Russians, Czechs, Slovaks, and others), the roughly 2 million Jews who migrated to the United States in the period under discussion were fewer than the migrants from half a dozen other groups. Jews have had a very large impact on how Americans have perceived European immigration, but it is not because of numbers alone.

Several issues stand out as one looks at Table 5.1. First, the total number of migrants to the United States grew substantially in the last decades of the nineteenth century and continued to ascend into the twentieth century, then dropped off as World War I created a barrier for many who might otherwise have left Europe. Second, immigration from new places—Italy, Austria-Hungary, Russia, and Scandinavia—grew very rapidly, starting in the 1880s and continuing through the 1910s. Third, immigration from the Western Hemisphere, specifically Canada and Mexico, increased sharply in the 1910s and again in the 1920s. Fourth, the immigration numbers for long-established sources of the American population—Germany, Britain, and Ireland—remained high throughout. Finally, the immigrant groups—Asians—about which there was the most controversy and opposition, and over whom a substantial amount of immigration law was being made, never constituted more than a small fraction of the incoming population.

It is important to remember that migration was almost never just a one-way, one-step process. In all periods, for migrants of almost all derivations, there was a degree of back and forth. Theodore Saloutos, a pioneer immigration historian, put the matter bluntly:

> Americans by reputation are a smug, self-satisfied people who find it difficult to believe that anyone, native or foreign-born, who has lived in their midst over a period of years would forsake their country for residence abroad. For years they gloried in their achievements as a nation, their spiritual and economic values, their bountiful resources, and their limitless opportunities. As proof they cited the millions of Europeans who settled in the United States during the nineteenth and twentieth centuries. But in the process these same self-centered Americans overlooked the millions ... who left the United States to return to their native land.[5]

In this time when tens of millions of people were crossing the Atlantic east to west, millions were crossing west to east.

Table 5.1 Immigration by Origin, Leading Sending Countries and Regions, 1871–1930

Decade	Italy	Austria–Hungary	Germany	Russia*	Britain	Canada	Scandinavia	Ireland	Asia	Mexico
1871–1880	55,759	72,969	718,182	39,284	548,043	383,640	243,016	436,871	124,160	5,162
1881–1890	307,309	353,719	1,452,970	213,282	807,357	393,304	656,494	655,482	69,942	1,913
1891–1900	651,893	592,707	505,152	505,290	271,538	3,311	371,512	388,416	74,862	971
1901–1910	2,045,877	2,145,266	341,498	1,597,306	525,950	179,226	505,324	339,065	323,543	49,642
1911–1920	1,109,524	896,342	143,945	921,201	341,408	742,185	203,452	146,181	247,236	219,004
1921–1930	455,315	63,548	412,202	61,742	339,570	924,515	198,210	211,234	112,059	459,287
Total 1871–1930	4,625,677	4,124,551	3,573,949	3,338,105	2,833,866	2,626,181	2,178,008	2,177,249	951,802	735,979

Sources: See Appendix B, Tables 5, 8, 10, 11, 12, 13, 14, 15, 22, 23.
* Soviet Union after 1917.

Moreover, it was not a one-step process from point of origin to the United States. Migration across the Atlantic was an extension of the long-standing practice of laborers going out from their home districts in search of work for a season or for a few years. Between 1850 and 1930, several hundred thousand Swedes went to the United States, but 300,000 traveled to work in other parts of Europe (40,000 to Germany alone) and most of those people eventually returned to their homeland. Mark Wyman described the European component of the Italian diaspora: "A study of four Italian villages found that from 16 to 37 percent of the twenty-year-old men were 'away from Home' at any time in the years from 1820 to 1900. Italy's Commissariato dell'Emigrazione reported in 1912 that 900,562 Italians were then in the rest of Europe, led by the 400,000 in France, the 180,000 in Germany, and the 135,000 in Switzerland."[6] Other Italians went to South America, South Africa, and even Australia. Poles went to Germany, Denmark, and Austria. People migrated from region to region, and from countryside to city, within every European country, just as they had been doing for generations. In this pattern the migrants of the late nineteenth century and the early twentieth century were no different from the English, Scots, Irish, and Germans who had migrated from town to city, to other countries within Europe, and across the Atlantic to the United States between a half-century and two centuries earlier.[7]

Still Coming from Northwest Europe

Although many histories of immigration describe this period from the 1870s to the 1920s as one when the sources of migrants shifted from Northwest Europe to Southern and Eastern Europe—the "Old Immigration" versus the "New Immigration," Northwest Europeans continued to come and stay in very large numbers. Table 5.2 shows the numbers of foreign-born Europeans in the U.S. population recorded in census years between 1850 and 1990, divided between Northwest Europe, Eastern Europe, and Southern Europe. Note that the number of foreign-born Americans from Northwest Europe continued to climb through 1890, and then only declined gradually. In every census year, foreign-born people from Northwest Europe ranked ahead of Eastern and Southern Europeans.

The summary numbers offered in census publications in the late nineteenth century (and through most of the twentieth century)—and the historical writing that used those numbers—tended to obscure the fact that the largest group of foreign-born Americans was still Northwest Europeans. The census people did this by placing Germans in a "Central and Eastern Europe" category along with Poles, Russians, and so forth. That was not in fact their social positioning in the United States. Socially, they were much closer to Scandinavians and English people than to Poles and Romanians—they were middle class, many were Protestants, and they had a centuries-long history in the United States—and so they should have appeared in the Northwest European group (as they have in the most recent censuses). The number of German foreign-born residents was so large throughout the first half of the twentieth century as to tip the perceptual scales dramatically toward Eastern Europe. The numbers recorded by the census tended to support the misperception that this was a period of "New Immigration," when immigrants were coming mainly from Eastern and Southern Europe.[8] In fact, large numbers of English, Irish, Germans, and other Northwest Europeans continued to come to the United States every year.[9]

Table 5.2 Foreign-Born European Americans
by Region of Birth, 1850–1990

Year	Northwest Europe[a]	Eastern Europe[b]	Southern Europe[c]
1850	2,021,249	2,360	8,258
1860	3,748,286	35,519	20,493
1870	4,815,171	93,664	26,155
1880	5,461,226	219,829	59,470
1890	7,165,646	633,896	208,487
1900	6,866,101	1,471,389	540,110
1910	6,550,304	3,670,561	1,558,105
1920	5,516,202	4,443,453	1,916,497
1930	5,336,864	4,286,728	2,108,552
1940[d]			
1950	3,261,131	3,186,177	1,653,878
1960	2,962,840	2,728,092	1,528,473
1970	2,369,687	1,973,129	1,343,510
1980	2,036,540	1,440,914	1,336,805
1990	2,355,085	1,253,685	1,054,141

Sources: See Appendix B, Table 32.

[a] Belgium, Denmark, France, Germany, Iceland, Ireland, Luxembourg, Netherlands, Norway, Sweden, Switzerland, United Kingdom.

[b] Albania, Austria, Bulgaria, Czechoslovakia, Estonia, Finland, Hungary, Latvia, Lithuania, Poland, Romania, Russia/U.S.S.R. (from 1990 its successor republics), Yugoslavia (from 1990 its successor republics).

[c] Greece, Italy, Spain, Portugal.

[d] There are no data for this subject in the 1940 census.

British

Nearly 3 million British people migrated to the United States between 1870 and 1930. The high watermark, in fact, for the entire history of British immigration was the decade of the 1880s, when 807,357 people arrived on American shores from the United Kingdom (Table 5.1). The fact is that we just don't know very much about the English, Scots, and Welsh who came to America in this period, for few scholars have addressed the issue. Did these migrants come from the same kinds of backgrounds and for the same kinds of reasons as earlier cohorts of English migrants? Were their experiences on their entry to American society similar? We do not know.

John Wrightson; his wife Isabella; her two adult sons by a previous marriage, William and David Kennedy; John and Isabella's young son Arthur; and their four daughters Sarah, Margaret Jane, Isabella, and Mary Ellen all lived in a stone cottage in the tiny hamlet of Middlestone in Durham County. The Wrightson men did body work in the Leasingthorne colliery, a coal mine that went down under the ground from a spot a half-hour's walk downhill from Middlestone across a smoking moonscape of slag heaps and discarded metal. In 1886 the entire Wrightson family left Middlestone. They took a train to Liverpool and then a ship across the Atlantic. A few weeks later they found themselves in Scranton, Pennsylvania, where John and the boys took jobs in another coal mine. Before long they had worked their way up to become middle managers in the employ of a mining company. The girls graduated from an American high school and married middle-class men. Did the Wrightsons leave northern England because they knew they would find a greater opportunity for economic advancement in the United States? Did their nonconforming faith—they were Primitive Methodists—draw them to a place where they thought they could more comfortably practice their version of Christianity? Did other British migrants in this period have similar economic or religious motives? Were the ambitions of those other migrants realized, as they seem to have been for the Wrightsons? We just do not know.[10]

We have some scraps of information. We know, for instance, that the British emigration to the United States, large though it was, still was just one part of a massive migration by Britons to several English-speaking territories overseas. Canada received nearly as many Britons as the United States in this period, and Australia was not far behind. We know that 40 percent of the English migrants to the United States were listed as laborers on their entry documents in the 1880s, and that that number declined to 12 percent by 1910. The small percentage of farmers was declining too. So we may assume that an increasing percentage of British immigrants to the United States in this period were urban members of the middle class before they left the United Kingdom.[11]

Some things about the social and cultural experiences of British migrants in America seem clear. Americans tended to blend together in their thinking people from different parts of the island—Welsh and Scots, Yorkshiremen and Merseysiders—and regard them all as "English." They did not see English people as very foreign, even on first arrival. Britons who entered America found the new country's class system more fluid than the one they had known, and many reveled in that improvement, as they did in the economic opportunities American presented. The language was comprehensible, as were many social customs, from the way Americans celebrated Christmas to the way they cooked their breakfast and made their bed. But where many American customs were vaguely familiar, they were not necessarily comforting, for they seemed at best pale imitations of British customs. Some British American migrants adopted a position of haughty superiority. As Rowland Berthoff put it, "In … all things but money and quick promotion, British-Americans thought the United States a debased copy of their homeland. Many seemingly familiar customs and institutions had lost their British essence. 'The Land of Slipshod,' one immigrant in 1885 called the country, its language not English but 'a silly idiotic jargon—a mere jumble of German idioms and popular solecisms, savored by a few Irish blunders,' the enforcement of its basically English legal code 'totally farcical,' and its children half-educated, spoiled, and unruly."[12]

Further, not all British migrants stayed in the United States; quite a number went back to Britain. American and British records differ substantially on this subject, because they asked different questions, and it is not clear how many of the persons recorded as sailing east were going home for a visit versus remigrating for

Figure 5.2 It was easier for those who were middle class.

good. Berthoff reports that "According to the British figures between 1895 and 1918, 55 percent as many Englishmen and Welshmen, taken as one group, came back as left for the United States; among the Scots the proportion was 46 percent, and among the Irish, 42 percent." Some came to the United States for a season to work, with no intention ever of staying. Berthoff notes that "American [stonecutter's] unions objected to the Scots ... because their sudden mass appearance each spring during the 1880's and 1890's dashed hopes of labor shortage and high wages. American winters shut down quarries and the open cutting sheds for three or four months a year; in Great Britain a man could work in any season, though for lower wages. The steamship gave the answer. In March and April crowds of Scotsmen landed at Boston and New York, worked through the season, and sailed back about Christmas 'with a good bag o' siller for their mothers and sweethearts.'"[13]

The middle-class position of British American migrants aided remigration (Figure 5.2). As Wilbur Shepperson described it, "fewer Britons, in fact, than members of any other national group [were forced] to enter American life at the lowest level. The British seldom left the United States because of congestion, trouble with the law, labor-organization difficulties, nativist discrimination, or resentment of their religion, speech, color, or culture. They were not one of the submerged minorities."[14] Ships' manifests suggest that, at least after 1900, more British emigrants returned to the United Kingdom from the United States than from Canada, although the westward migrations from Britain to those two countries were approximately equal in size by that time.[15]

The study of English Americans as immigrants has been slighted for earlier time periods. For the half-century after the Civil War, the subject has been almost wholly ignored. It is as if these Britons are assumed to have become undifferentiated Americans from the moment their feet hit the dock. British immigrants *qua* immigrants are erased from the historical narrative almost entirely, even though their numbers were large and, one may assume, their impact not insignificant. A systematic history of British migrants to the United States in this period still awaits its chronicler.[16]

Germans

Between 1870 and 1930, 3.5 million Germans migrated to the United States. The high point was reached in the 1880s, when 1.5 million Germans entered the United States, but the numbers continued strong throughout the period, and indeed as late as the 1950s (Appendix B, Table B.10).[17] German Americans throughout this period continued their gradual blending into the White panethnic formation that had gone on in the previous half-century. There was a brief upsurge in German-language public schools after the Civil War, but gradually German ethnic separateness and language use declined to the point where segregated German-language schools were no longer supportable, and by the end of the century they had all disappeared.[18]

Cities like Cincinnati and Milwaukee that had been homes to very large, distinct German American communities began to expand, industrialize further, and attract immigrants from a host of other countries. Although Germans continued to immigrate, they ceased to maintain the vibrant ethnic communities, nor the political clout, that they had manifested in early decades. In short, German Americans were still a recognizable ethnic group, but gradually they were becoming simply White people—not very different from, nor socially separate from, English Americans or Swedish Americans or any other Whites. German individuals and families kept coming to the United States, and individuals and families continued to go through immigrant processes—language learning, culture change, identify shift, attenuated connection to once-familiar places, people, and ways of being. But the German American community itself had become assimilated into White America. So when individual Germans assimilated, they were not assimilating into German Americanness any longer, but simply into Whiteness.

Germans did stand out from other Americans politically for a time, in that, as an ethnic community, they tended to oppose both prohibition and U.S. imperial adventures abroad in places like Cuba and the Philippines. Beer was a food not an alcoholic beverage in Germany and among German Americans, and some were active in defending their sumptuary habits against the religious zealots of the Prohibition Party. But otherwise Germans blended into mainstream White America.

In 1901 a number of German American business and community leaders, as well as representatives of the German-language press, schools, and various local clubs, came together to form the National German-American Alliance, or *Deutsch-Amerikanische Nazionalbund*. The plan was to foster the preservation of German culture in the United States, and also to advocate for immigrants and for community issues. The organization ultimately planted chapters in 44 states and claimed 2.5 million members. It was effective in gathering community members around local focal points, in helping brewers hold off prohibition for a time, and in encouraging German immigrants to learn English and take out U.S. citizenship papers. But ultimately the Alliance foundered during World War I when it tried to advocate for American nonintervention in the European war.[19]

Most other Whites seemed inclined to accept German Americans as simply American White people up until the middle of World War I. During the war's first years, Americans debated whether to join the struggle or to stay out. There was some sentiment in favor of Britain and little in favor of Germany, but most people seemed inclined at first not to choose sides. Gradually the U.S. government turned toward the British and in 1917 the United States entered the war. Swiftly and savagely, other White Americans turned on their German-descended fellow countrymen, in a smaller-scale preview of the tragedies that would later be thrust on Japanese Americans in the 1940s and Arab Americans in the 2000s. Prominent German-American intellectuals, artists, businesspeople, and community leaders who had not acquired U.S. citizenship were interned. Twenty-six states passed laws prohibiting the use of the German language, and many stopped teaching the language in public schools. Novels and movies offered lurid tales of German spies in America's midst.

German Americans were assaulted on the streets of many cities and towns. The extreme in anti-German hysteria was reached on April 4, 1918, when a German American coal miner, Robert Prager, was seized by a mob in Collinsville, Illinois. He was rescued by police, but then the good citizens came to the jail and demanded him. The police then escorted the mob and Prager outside the city limits so that the lynching would not take place within their jurisdiction. The mob's leaders were acquitted after a trial that even the local newspaper described as "a farcical patriotic orgy."[20]

As a result of all this pressure and harassment, the assimilation process of Germans into White America that had been well along before the war increased its pace. To take just one example, in 1894 there were 800 German-language newspapers in the United States; in 1910 there were 554; by 1920 there were only 278. The National German-American Alliance closed shop. By the end of the 1920s, German Americans had become simply White people.[21]

Irish

Irish immigration had not stopped, either. More than 2 million Irish people came to America between 1870 and 1930 (Table 5.1).[22] But unlike an earlier generation, these Irish were not fleeing famine. The pre-eminent historian of Irish migration, Kerby Miller, assesses the motivations of late-nineteenth-century Irish emigrants like this: "[T]he vast majority of Irish Catholic migrants left home for essentially mundane reasons similar or identical to those that produced mass migration from other European countries: crop failures, falling agricultural prices, and, most important, the increasing redundancy of petty farmers, farmers' children, and agricultural laborers that had been brought about by the dynamics of agrarian and industrial capitalism ... by the decline in cottage industries and by the shift from subsistence to commercial agriculture."[23]

In fact, by the late nineteenth century Irish Americans were poor no more, whether they were immigrants or born in America. They were mainly middle-class people with property. As a group, Irish Americans had risen to a position of influence in the Catholic church, the ranks of labor, and the Democratic Party.[24]

In one of the great American success stories, Irish Americans had become intimately connected to the political system. During the decades after Reconstruction, Irish-dominated machines of political patronage ran the Democratic Party, and, indeed, the cities of New York, Boston, and other eastern metropolises. John Breen's machine ran Lawrence, Massachusetts, with their main power base the votes of Irish immigrants and their children. A piece of Breen's campaign propaganda asked and answered:

Q. Whose is the ready ear and helping hand to the poor and suffering?

A. Breen's ... .

Q. Whose efforts any laboring man cannot honestly say were ever idle in securing him employment when at all possible?

A. Breen's.

Breen's machine found jobs for hundreds of immigrants in the health and public works departments. They provided protection to illegal drinking, gambling, and vice establishments. They mediated between management and labor to prevent strikes or mitigate their effects.[25]

In New York, Tammany Hall machine politician George Washington Plunkitt distinguished between "honest graft" and "dishonest graft." In politics, he said,

honesty doesn't matter; efficiency doesn't matter; progressive vision doesn't matter. What matters is the chance of a better job, a better price for wheat, better business conditions. ... There's an honest graft, and I'm an example of how it works. I might sum up the whole thing by sayin': "I seen my opportunities and I took 'em."

Just let me explain by examples. My party's in power in the city, and it's goin' to undertake a lot of public improvements. Well, I'm tipped off, say, that they're going to lay out a new park at a certain place. I see my opportunity and I take it. I go to that place and I buy up all the land I can in the neighborhood. Then the board of this or that makes its plan public, and there is a rush to get my land, which nobody cared particular for before. Ain't it perfectly honest to charge a good price and make a profit on my investment and foresight? Of course, it is. Well, that's honest graft. ...

When the voters elect a man leader, they make a sort of a contract with him. They say, although it ain't written out: "We've put you here to look out for our interests. You want to see that this district gets all the jobs that's comin' to it. Be faithful to us, and we'll be faithful to you." ... no Tammany man goes hungry in my district.[26]

The Irish machine dominated Boston politics until after the middle of the twentieth century. In the fullness of time, other European immigrant groups—Italians in New York, Poles in Chicago—took out citizenship papers, began to vote, and entered the political arena. In each city, the Irish machines made places for ethnic captains from these other groups.[27]

Just as Irish-dominated political machines took over Democratic politics in this period, so Irish priests were taking over the American Catholic hierarchy. Irish Americans made up about half of the American Catholic church in 1900, but they were nearly two-thirds of the priests, bishops, and teachers in parochial schools. Irish Americans set the agenda for the American Catholic church and the communities that gathered around its parishes. Other Catholic immigrant groups resented this Irish dominance, of course, to the point where Polish American Catholics and others mounted unsuccessful challenges to Irish American church hegemony. Irish dominance of the church went so far that, in the words of church historian Jay Dolan, "people began describing the church in the United States as One, Holy, Irish, and Apostolic."[28]

Even though on arrival Irish migrants found places firmly within White America and many soon entered the middle class or achieved positions of political or ecclesiastical power, Irish Americans' memory was one of having struggled up from terrible poverty and disempowerment. All were, in their own imagining, famine Irish, who continued to suffer deprivation in the United States. This led them, Kerby Miller demonstrates, to hold in tension two opposing visions of America: "as a land of incredible and easily attainable wealth—as 'sort of a halfway stage to heaven'—or else as an awful, forbidding place where many, if not most, Irish emigrants pined and starved their way to early graves." From this tension sprang the theme of exile and yearning to return to Ireland and overthrow "'British misgovernment,' 'Protestant Ascendancy,' [and] 'landlord tyranny.'"[29]

Thus Irish Americans for several generations remained involved with the homeland they had left but not quite left behind. Some of it had to do with the perception they were discriminated against in America. Michael Davitt spoke at Cooper Union in 1880: "[A]id us in Ireland to remove the stain of degradation from your birth and the Irish race here in America will get the respect you deserve."[30] More of it was expressed as a yearning for freedom and prosperity for those left behind. As the poet Joseph O'Halloran wrote in 1898,

> Think of the myriads who gave
> the crimson current of their veins,
> Our darling motherland to save
> from the Oppressor's cruel chains!
> While still one rusty fetter clanks,
> Close up the ranks! Close up the ranks!

Such appeals brought money into the coffers of the Fenians and other Irish nationalist organizations, and when the final conflict came in the 1910s, some Irish Americans enlisted in the fight for independent Ireland. Even the majority who remained in the diaspora had their eyes on the Old Sod. As Robert Ellis Thompson wrote, "[T]he larger Ireland, which English misgovernment and deportation has created, sends its confirmation back to the old Ireland of its love and its hate. From every quarter of the inhabited world the Irish race watch and wait for the hour of deliverance."[31]

That came with independence in 1921, although there was no wholesale rush of Irish Americans back to Ireland. They were White Americans now, whatever their affections for their ancestral homeland. But they were not yet completely undifferentiated White people. As Timothy Meagher has persuasively argued, in the final decades of the nineteenth century and the first decades of the twentieth century, the second generation of Irish Americans, born in the United States, moved decisively into the middle class and took on White American Catholicism—something broader than Irish but not so broad as the entire White race—as their primary identity. It would be only late in the twentieth century that Irish-descended people became simply, unproblematically White Americans.

The Northwest European migrants who came to the United States in the last third of the nineteenth century and the first third of the twentieth century constitute a subject that has been understudied by scholars up to this point. We do not know much, and we ought to know more, for contrary to historical stereotype,

Northwestern Europe continued to be the largest single regional source of U.S. immigrants well into the twentieth century.

New Sources of Workers in Southern Europe

Nonetheless, the Old-versus-New-Immigration model has one element of truth to it. There were indeed some new sources of very large numbers of migrants late in the nineteenth century and early in the twentieth century: Italy, Greece, Poland, Russia, the Austro-Hungarian Empire, and Scandinavia.

Italians

More than 4.5 million Italians emigrated to the United States in the period 1870 to 1930 (Table 5.1).[32] They were just one part of a much larger Italian migration web that began in Italy itself and spanned much of the globe. Italy was just barely a nation in 1870. "Italy" had been a descriptive term used to lump together conceptually a hodgepodge of only marginally related kingdoms and principalities. The *risorgimento*, a movement of cultural nationalism that gradually turned to political and military means, gathered strength over the first two-thirds of the nineteenth century. In 1861, after years of warfare among shifting participants, a Kingdom of Italy was proclaimed, but the new nation did not include Rome, Italy's most important city, until 1870. The peoples of the Italian peninsula remained divided by language, culture, and identity well into the twentieth century—indeed, many northern Italians see themselves as fundamentally different from southerners even today. The north entered the world of industrial capitalism early and established itself as the heart of Italian industry. Northern agriculture became mechanized and much more productive than farming in the south. The southernmost provinces were devoted to peasant agriculture using premodern practices and they were dominated by feudal social relationships until very late. The new national government's taxation policies favored the industrial north and traumatized the southern economy. Cheap consumer goods flowed in from other industrialized countries and put southern artisans out of work. Competition from industrialized agriculture in the north and abroad reduced southern farmers' ability to subsist. The south was poor, overpopulated, and ripe for emigration.[33]

People went out, not just from the south but from all parts of Italy, both before and after the achievement of national unity. There was a long-established pattern of seasonal migration between Italian regions, and between Italy and such industrializing countries as France, Belgium, and Germany. The numbers of migrants, especially from the south, jumped dramatically after 1880: 30 million people left Italy for other countries between that year and 1930. Two-thirds of the northerners migrated to other parts of Europe; nine-tenths of the southerners went to the Americas. More than 4 million went to the United States alone; nearly 3.5 million went to Mexico, Argentina, and Brazil.[34] The people who went abroad in the late nineteenth and early twentieth centuries did not see themselves as Italians so much as Siciliani, Calabresi, Milani, and so on. Chains of migration connected particular parts of Italy with particular new places. Thus, most of the people carrying Italian documents who ended up in San Francisco Bay's fishing industry hailed from the north: Liguria, Piedmont, and Lombardy. The same was true of the

Italians who came to St. Louis. New York's Italians, and Boston's and Baltimore's, came mainly from the extreme south, from Sicily and the mainland provinces of the Mezzogiorno.[35]

The Italian migration to the United States involved mainly young men in the beginning, either single or married men who left their families at home in Italy. Micaela di Leonardo describes an "Italy-based [economic strategy]: migrants arrived with little capital (that was left with relatives in Italy) and worked as proletarians in occupations requiring little investment. They sent the bulk of their savings back to Italy and periodically returned home themselves. They did not attempt to acquire American badges of status: proficiency in English, literacy, property, a high-status occupation."[36]

A key figure in recruiting Italian workers and directing them to jobs was the *padrone*—literally "patron," but usually translated "boss." A young man who thought to go abroad seldom knew how to get to America, much less where to find work or a place to live once he got here. *Padroni*, men who had gone out before and made return visits to their home regions, who knew the steamship lines and spoke a little English, who had established relationships with employers in the United States, set up networks to recruit workers in Italy and bring them to America. They might advance a young man money to pay his ticket across the Atlantic and then set him up with housing and a job in the United States. *Padroni*, like labor contractors who worked with Greek, Italian, Japanese, and Chinese immigrants, lent money, ran flophouses, and wrote letters back home for illiterate clients. They organized gangs of workers and delivered them to employers on contract. Typically they took a cut of each man's paycheck, and also charged him for food, housing, and other services rendered. *Padroni* were the first Italian American community leaders.[37]

Most Italian immigrants started out as body laborers with little idea of staying on in the United States. In any case, they did not have the capital to buy land in America—that was a privilege left to middle-class migrants like Germans, Britons, and Scandinavians. The whole point of migrating for Italians was to amass such capital, and then to use it back home. Their intention was to make some money and send it back to their families in Italy, in hopes they could buy land or start a business and move up in Italian society. So these Italian peasants became industrial workers for a time. Saverio Rizzo spoke later of his coming to America:

> I was born in the town of Cimigliano, in the province of Catanzaro, Italy, which I left at the age of sixteen in 1903. I was preceded to America by two of my brothers, one of whom was killed in a mining accident in New Jersey.
>
> Most of the men who had emigrated from my town had intended to return, expecting to remain in America for perhaps five or six years simply to earn money. Cimigliano, however, had no industries and there was a scarcity of work and a certain amount of poverty. Yet, after a short time, some did return.
>
> One of those who returned was a neighbor of ours who arrived from America with a few hundred dollars, which in those days was considered a great sum, and asked me if I wanted to emigrate with him on his return trip. I answered that I would be glad to come but that he would have to ask my parents' permission. He did and, since he was a good man, they did not object. He promised that we would look after me like a father, and since I was a minor and had to have a guardian, he would take that responsibility.

Rizzo and his guardian walked eight miles to a town with a railroad station, then took a third-class train to Naples. There followed a nineteen-day voyage across the Atlantic, a medical examination and paper stamping at Ellis Island, a train ride from Grand Central to Albany, then another train and a cart ride to a talcum mine in upstate New York.

> "To the mine"? I asked myself, it must be the village name. The carriage came to a stop between two shanties and we descended. ... The town I had imagined to be a beautiful place caused my heart to shrink with disappointment. My home was a dirty shanty in the camp ... I was soon introduced to the man who ran the store and who wished to be called "Uncle Gabriel." Before long I concluded that this man was not sincere in his dealings with the miners. ... the men had all been recruited by Uncle Gabriel, and he seemed to have some kind of control over them. He had obtained the concession for a store on company property where the miners were required to buy all their commodities as a recompense to him for having found work for them. No one was permitted to trade in the village stores where the prices were lower and the merchandise of better quality. Any transgression would have cost the transgressor the loss of his job. ...
>
> [I began as a blacksmith's helper.] To me $3 a week seemed a fortune. Converted to Italian money, I was going to earn triple the amount my father was earning at home. What I did not know was that there was also triple the cost of living.[38]

Many did go back to Italy eventually. Precise proportions are difficult to calculate, but the best estimate is that at least 1.5 million Italian migrants to the United States—perhaps one-third of the total—returned to Italy between 1900 and 1914. This was not happenstance, nor a reflection of a failure to make it in the United States, but rather the success of the plans they had made when first they went abroad. That is, they were migrating with the limited objective of making some money in America and returning richer to their homes in the old country, like first-generation English people who went to colonial Virginia or mid-nineteenth-century Chinese who went to California. When Italian authorities began in 1901 to require emigrants to state whether they intended to return, only one-quarter said they were leaving Italy for good.[39]

Life in America was hard, but it could be endured if one were making money and succeeding in one's plan to return to Italy. Some of the men who went abroad found themselves staying on longer than they had originally planned. They began to make a foothold for themselves in America. Many of this group then brought over their families, and some of those families stayed on in America. Joseph Baccardo's father came before him in the 1890s.

> He suffered over here and we suffered over there, because he wasn't able to send us very much. ... Finally my father came back to bring us to this country [in 1902]. He brought a little money with him, and we all came back the cheapest way—steerage. By then I was about nine or ten years old. Of course, we'd never been out of our own town. We went to Palermo and there we got a ship and came to New York. ... and then out here to Pennsylvania, where a friend of my dad's was working. Dad had been boarding with him while he was here.

We rented two rooms in an old house and bought some furniture from a young couple who were moving out. They sold us a little stove and four chairs and a table and a few pots and pans and a bed for my mother and dad. First my brother and I slept on the floor, and then they bought a couple of little folding cots for us. We slept in the kitchen and mother and father in the other room. That's all we had for about ten years.

Pop was doing manual work, you know; that's all he knew. He was working with a gang building the county road out to Chester. It was a gravel road then. He used to get up at 2:00 in the morning on Monday and walk to the job. That was about ten miles. That first summer I got a job there, too, as a waterboy. I carried water to the men working on the road. We stayed in a shanty during the week, and then Saturday night we walked back home. I was getting 40 cents a day for ten hours, and dad was getting $1.10 a day. We tried to live off my 40 cents, so that we could bring $6.00 back home. ...

I hear people talk about the good old days. Well, look how many people suffered. All those bridges, all those roads, all those railroads—they were built by people who worked hard to build them.[40]

As time went on, some of the emigrants—both the men who went out to work and the families they brought behind them—took up more permanent residences and formed distinct Italian communities in American towns and cities, some in rural districts. The family was the cornerstone of community life. Much of family life was carried over from Italy, although there was a fictive quality to some Italian Americans' visions of what life had been like in the old country. Humbert Nelli observed: "Immigrants and their descendants firmly believed that the Southern-Italian family was recreated in the Little Italys of America. Actually the Old World family and community they remembered fondly was largely a myth. Thus one second-generation Italian-American leader in Chicago during the 1920s described his neighborhood as having 'the same kind of warmth, friendliness, and intimacy in our community life that was to be found in the small towns of Sicily from whence our parents came.' Family 'unity and strength' in Southern Italy and Sicily was, in actuality, more an ideal than an accomplished fact."[41] Paul Campisi showed a gradual shift in the characteristics of the Italian family as it moved from Sicily to the United States (see Table 5.3).

Certainly, the realities of living in crowded American cities must have created new social dynamics, not just for Italians but for other immigrants to industrial cities like New York and Philadelphia. Consider the crowding of human beings evident in the picture of Hester Street on New York's Lower East Side in Figure 5.3.

People lived jammed into tenement houses, "boxes arranged like drawers in a bureau."[42] Figure 5.4 is a schematic, top-down diagram of a dumbbell tenement, which was actually an improvement over earlier building styles, because every room now had at least a small window on an airshaft. Large families would be crowded into tiny apartments, four to a floor, in walk-up buildings five and six stories tall. They would typically have the use of a living room, a kitchen, and one or two bedrooms, with toilets and wash facilities either in the hall, downstairs on the ground floor, or out in the backyard.

Nearly every major industrial city had at least one concentration of Italian immigrants by the time of the First World War: Boston's North End, San Francisco's North Beach, New York's Little Italy, and so on. New York led the way with 145,433 Italian residents in 1900, 340,765 a decade later. In 1900, more than two-thirds of

Table 5.3 Differences between the Southern Italian Peasant Family in Italy and the First- and Second-Generation Italian American Family

Southern Italian Peasant Family in Italy	First-Generation Italian American Family	Second-Generation Italian American Family
Patriarchal	Fictitiously patriarchal	Tends to be democratic
Active community life	Inactive in the general American community but somewhat active in the Italian American community	Inactive in the Italian neighborhood, but increasingly active in the general American community
Emphasis on the sacred	Emphasis on the sacred is weakened	Emphasis on the secular
Children live for the parents	Children live for themselves	Parents live for the children
Many family celebrations of special feasts, holidays, etc.	Few family celebrations of feasts and holidays	Christmas the only family affair, with Thanksgiving being variable
Large-family system	Believe in a large-family system but cannot achieve it because of migration	Small-family system
Father has highest status	Father loses high status, or it is fictitiously maintained	Father shares high status with mother and children; slight patriarchal survival
Mother center of domestic life only and must not work for wages	Mother center of domestic life but may work for wages and belong to some clubs	Mother acknowledges domestic duties but reserves time for much social life and may work for wages
Son is expected to work hard and contribute to family income	Son is expected to work hard and contribute to family income, but this is a seldom-realized goal	Son is expected to do well in school and need not contribute to family income
Marriage in early teens	Marriage in late teens or early twenties	Marriage in early or middle twenties
Selection of mate by parents	Selection of mate by individual with parental consent	Selection of mate by individual regardless of parental consent
Must marry someone from the same village	Same-village marriage is the ideal, but marriage with someone from the same province is tolerated; very reluctant permission granted to marry outside nationality; no permission for marriage outside religion	Increasing number of marriages outside nationality and outside religion
No birth control	Some birth control	Birth control is the rule
No divorce allowed	No divorce allowed, but some do divorce	Religion forbids divorce, but it is practiced

Source: Abridged from Paul Campisi, "Ethnic Family Patterns: The Italian Family in the United States," *American Journal of Sociology*, 53 (May 1948), 444–446.

Figure 5.3 Hester Street scene, 1900.

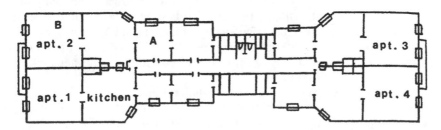

Figure 5.4 Dumbbell tenement.

Table 5.4 Immigration from Greece and Turkey, 1881–1930

Decade	Greece	Turkey
1881–1890	2,308	3,782
1891–1900	15,979	30,425
1901–1910	167,519	157,369
1911–1920	184,201	134,066
1921–1930	51,201	33,824
Total, 1881–1930	421,208	359,466

Source: Theodore Saloutos, "Greeks," in *Harvard Encyclopedia of American Ethnic Groups*, Thernstrom, Ed., 432.

those Italian Americans were crowded into the Lower East Side of Manhattan. Philadelphia was next with 45,308 Italians in 1910, followed by Chicago with 45,169, Boston with 31,380, and San Francisco with 16,918.[43]

It was in Italian neighborhoods that labor contractors ran their businesses. In Italian neighborhoods, Italian restaurants catered to both an Italian clientele and the wider public. Bocce courts were temples of male camaraderie. Catholic churches held services in Latin and parish meetings in Italian, sometimes with English translation. Newspapers published in Italian brought news from back home and interpreted America to the immigrants. Italian American bankers handled people's savings and dispensed loans. Mutual aid societies based on old-country regional distinctions provided insurance and social functions. Yans-McLaughlin points to the role that Italian communities played in the migration process itself: "Providing a stable reference point after the shock of immigration, it helped immigrant families to make the transition from rural peasants to urban workers. It was 'urban villages,' not the entire society, that absorbed the Italians and other national groups. While substantially different from the villages abroad, they still supplied a familiar orientation. Most important, they embraced those networks of kin relationships and friendships which were so necessary for the preservation of family traditions."[44]

Greeks

The story for Greek migrants was much like that for Italians: an impoverished peasantry in a region unblessed by the industrial revolution, driven abroad in search of means to improve their economic situation at home, extending seasonal migration patterns that already existed farther afield into the Americas, and many of them returning in the end to the villages they had left behind.[45] Other ethnic Greeks fled their homes in Turkey, when they, along with Armenians and Assyrians, were forced to flee persecution by the Ottoman government.[46] Table 5.4 gives the numbers of migrants from Greece and Turkey into the United States, by decades during the height of immigration, 1881 to 1930.

These figures suggest that at least one-half million Greeks, and perhaps more, migrated to the United States during those decades. Like other European migrants, most Greeks headed to the mills and tenements of eastern cities. Perhaps as many as 50,000 went west to work in mines and smelters in Colorado and Utah, lured there by the same kind of *padrone* system as that subscribed to by Italian workers.

Like the Italian migration of the same years, like the Chinese migration a generation earlier (and, indeed, like the first English migration), the Greek migrant stream was overwhelmingly male. In the years 1890 to 1898, 9996 men arrived in the United States from Greece, as against 420 women; that is, nearly 24 men to every Greek woman.[47] These guys intended to go back from the start. Probably about half of the Greeks who came to the United States in the early decades of the century did in fact eventually return to their homeland. Their stories were as varied as their motivations for coming in the first place. Some, like Mr. S., interviewed by Theodore Saloutos, had succeeded in making a lot of money and took it back home to invest.

> Mr. S. heads the largest dairy farm in Greece. Like other repatriates, he founded his business with dollars and experience earned in America. ... A Peloponnesian from Arcadia, he came to the United States in 1905 and lived in Chicago. In 1912 he and his brothers formed an ice-cream company as a family concern. That same year he left the United States to fight in the Balkan Wars and returned in 1916. In 1928 he made another of his many trips to Greece, this time to marry a native girl, and again returned to the United States. He repatriated himself in 1934. ... The theory of pasteurization had been known in Greece before Mr. S. formed his company, but the capital and the managerial and technical skills needed to put it to practical use were lacking. ... Mr. S. ... introduced pasteurized milk in 1935 with equipment imported from the United States. A technician from the family firm in Chicago was brought to teach the process to Greek workers. The people most receptive to the idea of pasteurized milk proved to be returned Greek-Americans. ... The local milk dealers, however, fought the innovation. ... At first Mr. S.'s company was looked upon as a foreign firm.

Before long, however, Mr. S. became one of the largest milk producers in Greece. Mr. M. D.'s story was more humble.

> Mr. M. D. is a small sidewalk merchant in Salonika. He sells baskets. He was born in 1889 in a small village in East Thrace and left for the United States in 1913, right after the First Balkan War, to escape serving in the Turkish army. ... He sailed from Constantinople for Piraeus on a Russian ship, from Piraeus for Patras on a Greek ship, and from Patras for New York on an American one. He worked for a brick company in Joliet, Illinois, from 1913 to 1919. Mr. M. D. would have remained in the United States had it not been for his parents who were refugees in Salonika and whom he wanted to bring to America. ... [When he got there] the city was in ruins. ... Salonika appeared like a village. Worse still ... his parents did not care to go to the United States. Instead, they wanted him to remain in Greece. When pressures of the most inconceivable types were exerted to prevent his departure, Mr. M. D. decided to remain in Greece. He had had $3,500 when he reached Greece, the result of six years of labor and saving in the United States. After a few months' vacation, he left for a village in East Thrace where he invested his money in a general store. He managed this until he was compelled to serve in the Greek army, and then his brother took over the management. When the Turks invaded the region and drove out the Greeks, he lost his investment.[48]

From Eastern Europe, Too

Another new source of large numbers of immigrants in this period was Eastern Europe.[49]

Polonia

We do not have good numbers for Polish immigration because U.S. officials kept records by nationality, not ethnicity, and Poland did not enjoy national sovereignty during the main period of migration to America.[50] Rather, what had once been and later would be Poland was carved up between Russia, the Austro-Hungarian Empire, and Prussia (later Germany). For example, 4.3 million ethnic Poles were recorded by the Austrian census of 1910 as living within that empire; they constituted about 15 percent of the national total.[51]

Despite the absence of precise numbers, we can say a few things about the shape of the Polish migrant population. According to government estimates, ethnic Polish immigrants to the United States numbered 820,696 in the years 1899 to 1909. Of those, 377,134 (46 percent) came from Austria-Hungarian-controlled Poland, 33,708 (4 percent) came from Prussian Poland, and 407,743 (50 percent) came from Russian Poland. The peak year of Polish immigration was 1907, when 138,033 Poles arrived on American shores. The total number of ethnic Polish immigrants between 1899 and 1932 has been estimated at between 1.1 and 2 million, out of perhaps 3 million Poles who went abroad altogether.[52] The best estimates suggest that between 2.2 and 4 million Poles, immigrant and native born, lived in the United States by 1908: perhaps half a million in Pennsylvania, mainly in Philadelphia, Pittsburgh, and the coal mining country of the southeastern part of the state; between 350,000 and 500,000 in New York; 390,000 to 450,000 in Illinois; 200,000 to 250,000 in Wisconsin; 160,000 to 250,000 in Michigan; 130,000 to 300,000 in Massachusetts; and lesser numbers in other urban, industrial states.[53] The Poles were one of the largest East European immigrant groups, more numerous by far than Russians and about the same in number as East European Jews.

The factors drawing Poles away from their homeland were various and interlocking. Before 1860, a few thousand Polish emigrants were political refugees who had been on the losing side of one of several nationalist uprisings against foreign rule. They were as likely to go to Paris, London, or Geneva as to New York or Chicago. Mass labor emigration began after 1870. In assessing motivations for migration in this period, one must distinguish between the situations in the three Polands: German-, Austrian-, and Russian-controlled territories. All three found themselves locked increasingly into an international web of capitalist agriculture that pushed peasants off the land and left them in an impoverished state. John Bukowczyk's characterization of the whole is apt: "Polish rural society became a cauldron of social and economic change in which a population increase, the expansion of commercial agriculture, and the growth of transportation, industry, and urban markets would forever disrupt the manorial world. The dissolution of the ties that bound the rural populace to the land and the creation of a large pool of surplus labor would later impel the mass migration of the late nineteenth and the early twentieth century."[54] Despite similar overall effects, the shapes of the economies and the courses of government policies in the three Polands were quite different.

The first large migrant stream came from Pomerania and Poznan, regions under Prussian control. The overwhelming majority of Poles were peasant farmers, tied to the land by longstanding law and custom, working small plots for subsistence and perhaps producing a small surplus for market. In the 1820s, the Prussian government emancipated the Polish peasantry, setting them free from feudal dues and also denying them feudal rights of residence and cultivation. As the century went on, German- and Polish-owned estates claimed a larger and larger proportion of agricultural land. A high birthrate sent the population soaring. Less than 2 percent of the landowners owned 60 percent of the farmland, while two-thirds of the peasants were relegated to only 3 percent of the farmland.[55] At the same time, the new government that unified Germany in the 1870s attacked the Polish Catholic church in a campaign of *Kulturkampf,* or "struggle for culture." The government made a policy of giving Polish lands to German colonizers and trying to Germanicize Poles. Such changes pushed Polish peasants off the land in search of work at the same time they devalued Polish culture and autonomy. Some found work in the agribusiness estates, others in German cities, but many took the more radical step across the Atlantic.

In Galicia, the Austrian province of Poland, the Austrian government ended serfdom in 1848 yet left the peasants on the land. But it insisted on partible inheritance rather than primogeniture. This meant that, as the generations went on, individual peasant landholdings got so small that they no longer would support subsistence. Meanwhile, most of the land remained in the hands of Galician nobles. Heavy taxes on the peasantry, a potato blight to rival the one suffered in Ireland, and epidemics of cholera and typhus all combined to make peasants miserable and eager to find a way out.

Tsarist policy in Russian Poland promoted commercial agriculture in its sector of Poland. It removed peasants from the land but did not give them land of their own, at the same time it required them to continue to perform compulsory labor on the new commercial farms as they had for the nobles under feudalism. This resulted in the creation of a landless rural proletariat, desperately in search of work at any wage. British protectionist laws and competition from American grains caused the collapse of the Russian-Polish agricultural economy. In Russian Poland, however, there was also a growing industrial sector that for a time drew workers off the land and into cities like Warsaw and Lodz. Then, class strife within the Russian empire after the turn of the century, a disastrous war lost to Japan in 1904 to 1905, an unsuccessful revolution in 1905 to 1906, and new Tsarist policies that moved industry out of Poland and into Russia proper, all contributed to the decline of Polish industry and joblessness among the Polish working class.

In whichever part of Poland, the results were much the same: hundreds of thousands of peasants, formerly tied to the land in subsistence agriculture, found themselves cast adrift in search of a way to make a living. Many went abroad within Europe along paths that had been worn by seasonal migrations in years past. In 1907, the leaders of the Roman Catholic diocese in Kraków surveyed migration out of Galicia and found their parishioners distributed thus:

Jordanów: to Prussia, Saxony—400; to Budapest—10; to America—400
Letownia: to Saxony, Silesia, Denmark—1500; to Budapest—50; to America—20
Maków: to Saxony—220; to Prussia—483; to Budapest—140; to America—290
Osielic: to Prussia—300; to America—70

Raba Wyznia: to Prussia—50; to Budapest—25; to America—50
Rabka: to Prussia—60; to Saxony—20; to America—110
Sidzina: to Prussia—60; to America—130
Spytkowice: to Prussia—30; to Saxony—20; to America—450
Zawoja: to Prussia, Silesia, Wroclaw—500; to Saxony—1500; to America—200.[56]

Whether to Denmark, to Hungary, to one of the German states, or across the sea to America, it was all part of the same migrant outflow.

Polish migrants had long seen America as a land of extraordinary wealth and opportunity, based partly on the fanciful tales of labor recruiters, partly on letters sent by those Poles who had gone before and been successful, partly on the fantasies of poets and playwrights. Here is a sampling of letters from some early migrants who went to rural parts of America: "The land is big and there is plenty of space, with settlers few and far between; for example, the distance between Indijonol and Victoria [in Texas] is 50 miles. … and only ten people live there; they are all prosperous and wealthy as some raise 2000 cattle, pigs and innumerable other animals." "Cows and oxen are bigger in size. … There are plenty of trees on the farm … both for building and burning." "The climate is always healthy; although there are heat waves in summer, cool, refreshing winds blow continuously."[57]

Amateur theater troupes enticed people with descriptions like these: "To America. … There you'll be given land for which you'll be paying for 20 years, as well as cattle and timber for building a house; … I have just heard from my brother-in-law who's in America that all our peasants who emigrated became very rich." "There are no taxes there. … No man will be drafted. … There is no king and there are no noblemen, as all people are equal. … And if someone has little money or no money at all, but wants to go there, I'll give him everything for free, in return for signing a contract, where he'll declare that he will work on a farm for two years." "I know a country where gold is dug out like clay here and where all potters become goldsmiths. People live there as in paradise. … Gold is not deep underground, on the surface golden wheat grows, its grains are as big as noodles, it's pot-ready, it only needs boiling, buttering and can be eaten—real paradise." Polish migrants hoped for a chance to find such a paradise—if not to make a permanent new home for themselves, then at least a place to make some money and return home wealthy.[58]

Some of the earliest German-Polish immigrants in the 1850s came at a time when land prices were low, and they often came with enough cash to buy small farms in places as various as Texas, Minnesota, Ohio, and Wisconsin, all of which had rural Polish communities.[59] But the vast bulk of Polish immigrants came after 1880, they came with very little, and in any case, like Greeks and Italians, they came with the intention to earn some money as fast as they could and return to Poland and buy land there. They were not the poorest of the poor; such people did not have the money to pay for the journey. That typically began with a day's walk from one's home village to a railhead, followed by a bone-crushing third-class train ride across Poland and Germany to the port of Hamburg or Bremen (Galician Poles usually sailed out of Trieste). Then a wait of a week or two in huge barracks near the wharf, then two weeks deep in the dark, smelly hold of a steamship, eating salt meat and throwing up much of the time.

Most of the Polish migrants arrived with their funds exhausted, as had their Irish predecessors, and in far worse financial shape than most German, British, or Scandinavian migrants. Some Poles managed the price of a ticket to Chicago,

Figure 5.5 Some Polish American children worked in coal mines.

Milwaukee, Pittsburgh, or Detroit, but many did not make it much past the port of entry, Boston or New York or Philadelphia. Very few of them became farmers after about 1870. A 1911 survey found that only 10 percent of Polish immigrants worked in agriculture, either as owners or as farm laborers, compared to 14 percent of Irish, 27 percent of Germans, 30 percent of Swedes, 32 percent of Czechs, and 50 percent of Norwegians.[60]

Captains of American industry in the late nineteenth century subscribed to racialized ideas about the supposed characters and capabilities of various ethnic groups. Poles, they thought, were not suited to work that demanded complex thought, but they were very good at dangerous jobs that required muscles and obedience to authority. Poles, for their part, were primarily interested in making money they could then use back in Poland, so they went for the quick dollars, rather than trying to build careers in the United States. Poles worked the docks and warehouses in New York. They went down into the ground to dig coal out of mines in eastern Pennsylvania (Figure 5.5). They worked in the stockyards of Chicago, the steel mills of Pittsburgh, the new automobile assembly plants in Detroit, and other dirty, dangerous industrial venues.[61]

For all that most Polish migrants came with the initial intention to make some money and return home, there is little evidence of a large re-emigration like that of Italians or Greeks. Quite quickly, Polish women came to join their men and form families. As with many migrants of the era, Polish immigrant women lived mainly within the household and raised the five to ten children that were typically their responsibility, cooking and cleaning and teaching and supervising from long before dawn until long after everyone else was asleep. Men's sphere was outside the household, in the world of work and the life of the street. Men, accordingly, were more

Figure 5.6 Polish, Irish, and Turkish kids in the yard outside their mill town dwelling.

likely to learn English than were their wives. But the network of mothers became the glue that held together the Polish American community.

Poles formed communities around ethnic parishes of the Roman Catholic Church and around saloons where men congregated after work. They were less likely than Italians to live in mono-ethnic neighborhoods; they simply lived near their work, in multiethnic, working-class, industrial neighborhoods (Figure 5.6). They did build an array of Polish American institutions: mutual benefit societies that provided insurance and loans, as well as a place to hang out; Polish-language newspapers (often several in a given city); parochial schools. Unions were not specifically ethnic institutions, but almost all the Poles in the Chicago packing houses, for example, were union members, and there were some ethnic Polish chapters within multiethnic unions. It was symbolic of the central place of these two institutions that giant St. Joseph's Roman Catholic Church was built in 1914 at the corner of 48th and Hermitage, in Chicago's Back of the Yards neighborhood—right across the street from the offices of Amalgamated Meat Cutters Polish Local 554.[62]

No institution was more important to American Polonia than the Roman Catholic Church. It was, as William Galush wrote, "the one institution that transcended the partitions" in Polish society, and so it was a powerful force for Polish nationalism. Polish nationalism, in fact, grew in Polish America, especially in the church, because here Poles from all three colonized regions came together and nurtured a common ethnic identity. Sometimes that Polish nationalism leaked into church politics. In Poland, nobles had controlled the local parishes and appointed the priests. In America, the parishioners thought a more democratic principle should be followed, that they should hold title to parish property and should run parish affairs. The Irish-dominated Roman Catholic hierarchy in the United States thought otherwise, and insisted that property and decision-making should be in the hands of the clergy. Matters came to a head in many parishes, none more pointedly than St. Stanislaus Kostka parish in Chicago in the 1870s. The parish had been founded by a Polish mutual aid society, but soon those with democratic (and Polish nationalistic) convictions tired of Irish priestly authority, split off, and formed their own new church, Holy Trinity, only three blocks away from St. Stanislaus. Historian Jay Dolan describes the scene: "The [Irish American] priests at St. Stanislaus tried to take over Holy Trinity parish, but the people would not allow it. For the next twenty years the two groups fought. One priest walked the neighborhood armed with a pistol; people rioted in the streets and demonstrated in church, throwing hymnals, yelling, and stamping their feet; several times, the parish was closed by the bishop, and finally the people appealed their case to Rome." Much to everyone's surprise, the Vatican backed the Holy Trinity parishioners, a new priest (Polish this time) was called, and peace was restored. This was a fight for democratic parish control, but it was also a fight by Polish Catholics against Irish priests by whom they did not wish to be dominated.[63]

East European Jews

The other very large group of East European migrants to the United States were Jews from Russia, Poland, the Ukraine, Hungary, and elsewhere in Eastern Europe.[64] These were a different sort of Jews than the Sephardim and German Jews who preceded them to America (see Chapter 3), and this was the beginning of a new era for American Jewry. Altogether, between 1881 and the restriction of East European immigration in 1924, 2.3 million East European Jews came to America.[65] In 1880, the American Jewish population stood at roughly one-quarter of a million. By 1900 it had quadrupled, and it quadrupled again to reach 4 million by the 1920s (see Appendix, Table 33). Table 5.5 shows the number of Jews who came to the United States as immigrants each year from 1899 to 1924, as well as the percentage of the total immigration stream in those years who were Jews.

Almost all of these Jewish immigrants came from Eastern Europe: 68 percent from Russia and Poland, 14 percent from Austria-Hungary, and 6 percent from Romania. Less than 1 percent came from Germany.[66]

Not only did this folk invasion dwarf the existing, mainly German-derived Jewish community in America, these were a different kind of Jews. They were very orthodox, having lived for centuries in a segregated, intensely Jewish environment. Jews in the Russian Empire were confined mainly to the Pale of Settlement, a wide swath of territory stretching from the Baltic states through Poland and western Russia to the Ukraine and the Black Sea (see Figure 5.7).

In American Jewish communal memory, they lived in the *shtetl*, Yiddish for "small town." But it was a particular kind of small town: a totally Jewish environment. Chaim Waxman described it this way: "The person from the *shtetl*, living in a traditional monoreligious culture, would probably not have even understood the Western distinction between religious group and ethnic group. To him or her, there were only *Yidn*, Jews, and *Yiddishkeit*, Jewishness, the Jewish way of life."[67] The language of the *shtetl* was Yiddish, a medieval amalgam of German and Hebrew, written in the Hebrew script, morphed over time into a family of mutually more-or-less intelligible local dialects. God spoke and scholars wrote in Hebrew. In Irving Howe's words,

Table 5.5 Jewish Immigration, 1899–1924

Fiscal Year	Jewish Immigrants (in thousands)	Jews as Percent of Total U.S. Immigration
1899	37	12.0
1900	61	13.5
1901	58	11.9
1902	58	8.9
1903	76	8.9
1904	106	13.1
1905	130	12.7
1906	154	14.0
1907	149	11.6
1908	103	13.2
1909	58	7.7
1910	84	8.1
1911	91	10.4
1912	81	9.6
1913	101	8.5
1914	138	11.3
1915	26	8.1
1916	15	5.1
1917	17	5.9
1918	4	3.3
1919	3	2.2
1920	14	3.3
1921	119	14.8
1922	54	14.3
1923	50	9.5
1924	50	7.1
1899–1924	1,838	10.4

Source: Hersch, "International Migration of the Jews," 474.

God was a living force, a presence, more than a name or a desire. He did not rule from on High; He was not a God of magnificence; nor was he an aesthetic God. The Jews had no beautiful churches, they had wooden synagogues. Beauty was a quality, not a form; a content, not an arrangement. The Jews would have been deeply puzzled by the idea that the aesthetic and the moral are distinct realms. One spoke not of a beautiful thing but a beautiful deed. ... Yiddish culture was a culture of speech, and its God a God who spoke. He was a plebian God, perhaps immanent but hardly transcendent. Toward Him the Jews could feel a peculiar sense of intimacy: had they not suffered enough on His behalf? In prayer His name could not be spoken, yet in or out of prayer He could always be spoken to.[68]

Figure 5.7 The Pale of Jewish Settlement.

Life in the *shtetl* was built around family, tight-knit community, and religious devotion. A premium was put on knowledge of the Hebrew Bible and of centuries of commentaries by learned men. The highest status people were not those who had the most, but those who were most devoted to understanding God.

The *shtetl* was out in the countryside, but it was not remote from its non-Jewish neighbors. Jews, mainly merchants or skilled tradespeople, served their neighbors as much as they did other Jews. As serfdom was abolished, and commercial agriculture and industry drew people to cities, the economy of the *shtetl* declined, and many thousands of Jews—even whole communities—were rendered destitute. Some went off to cities. By the 1870s, many East European Jews lived in towns and cities, driven there by the decline of the *shtetl* economy and drawn by the rise of industry. There, many came in contact with a host of new idea-systems, from Zionism to socialism to secular Yiddishism. Many East European Jews had had little contact with the Enlightenment ideas that their German predecessors had imbibed. The minority among them who had experienced a broader intellectual world had learned not Goethe but Marx. They were free-thinkers and Zionists and laborites and socialists, not seekers after Protestant refinement. Even in cities they lived a segregated existence in almost-all-Jewish neighborhoods and schools. The majority of those who came to America either came directly from the *shtetl* themselves or were but a generation removed from it.[69]

Those Jews—religious and secularist—who left Russian-controlled lands did so for very different reasons than other Poles and Russians who went abroad. The main Jewish reason was persecution. In 1881, Tsar Alexander II was assassinated by terrorists who wanted to overthrow the monarchy. Alexander had for twenty-five years pursued a relatively benign policy toward the country's Jewish minority. His son and successor, Alexander III, was not so inclined. Agents of the Russian government encouraged Gentile Russians to attack their Jewish neighbors. Mary Antin recalled learning as a child about *pogroms*—government-sponsored anti-Jewish riots—from victims who fled the countryside and took refuge in her town of Polotzk: "[T]he Gentiles made the Passover a time of horror for the Jews. Somebody would start up that lie about murdering Christian children, and the stupid peasants would get mad about it, and fill themselves with vodka, and set out to kill the Jews. They attacked them with knives and clubs and scythes and axes, killed them or tortured them, and burned their houses. ... little babies [were] torn limb from limb before their mothers' eyes."[70] The Russian government also acted against its Jewish citizens. In 1882 Jews were banished from many villages and their trade in cities was restricted. In 1891 Moscow expelled 20,000 Jews, and St. Petersburg and Kharkov soon did likewise. There were new waves of *pogroms* in 1903 and 1905.[71]

As a result of all this persecution, one third of the East European Jewish population fled the region between 1881 and 1914. Because the conditions driving Jews out of Eastern Europe were so unrelenting, this was one group of immigrants who did not come with the intention to return. Only 5 percent of Jewish migrants turned around and went back, compared to 10 percent for Irish immigrants, 16 percent for Germans, 19 percent for English, 40 percent for Poles, 47 percent for Greeks, and more than half of the Russian, Italian, and Balkan migrants (see Appendix B, Table B.29).

Just because the Russian government had looked the other way while Russians and Poles killed and burned and looted, that did not mean that they would give Jews permission to emigrate. The Tsar's government refused passports and exit visas, yet it tolerated clandestine border crossings. Many Jews went on foot, carrying their few belongings and sneaking across the border into Austria-Hungary or Germany. From there they made their way by train to ports in Germany and the Low Countries: Hamburg, Bremen, Rotterdam, Amsterdam, and Antwerp (Figure 5.8).

They did not know where they were going. Mary Antin described the ignorance and sense of anticipation among those about to leave Russia in 1891: "America was in everybody's mouth. Businessmen talked of it over their accounts; the market women made up their quarrels that they might discuss it from stall to stall; people who had relatives in the famous land went around reading their letters for the enlightenment of less fortunate folk ... children played at emigrating; old folks shook their sage heads over the evening fire, and prophesied no good for those who braved the terrors of the sea and the foreign goal beyond it; all talked of it, but scarcely anyone knew one true fact about this magic land."[72]

The earlier wave of German Jewish immigrants had spread out across the American landscape, working as peddlers and in other mobile pursuits, before they settled into the country's cities and established careers and businesses small and large. Not so this new addition to American Jewry. They were city people from the start. Most had exhausted their resources by the time they reached America, so like

Figure 5.8 Romanian Jewish *fusgeyer.*

the Irish before them they were stuck in ports of entry. They took up residence in eastern cities that already had concentrations of Jews and synagogues where they could worship. Mary Antin and her family ended up in an impoverished immigrant neighborhood in Boston's South End. Others went to Philadelphia. Only a few in this wave made it on to cities in the interior. The largest group by far—more than 60 per-cent of all Jewish immigrants in this period—went to New York.[73] And most of those began their American lives on the Lower East Side.

This was a family society from the start. More than a third of the Jewish immi-grants were children under the age of sixteen, and nearly 42 percent of the adults were women.[74] They filled up the tenements on the Lower East Side. Irving Howe describes tenement conditions:

> Just north of Canal Street and extending from Mott to Elizabeth stood the "Big Flat," an enormous tenement occupying six city lots [and occupied by Jews and some Italians]. Water was supplied to tenants from one tap on each floor, set over a sink outside the north wall. These sinks, serving as the only receptacles for refuse, were loathsome, especially in the winter, when the traps beneath them would freeze. Each apartment had three rooms and drew its light from a single window in the "living room." The two inner rooms were always dark and without ventilation, since the space allotted each resident averaged out to 428 cubic feet [about 7 x 7.5 feet of floor space] per head. ... The annual death rate ... came to 42.40, as compared to 25.72 for the city as a whole; nearly 62 per-cent of the deaths in the "Big Flat" were of children under five years of age.[75]

Three-quarters of the East Side residents slept three, four, five, or more to a room.

The Jewish immigrant population came impoverished, but they brought more in the way of social capital than most other immigrant groups: many were skilled craftspeople, and the men had an 83 percent literacy rate (compared to 74 percent

Figure 5.9 This sewing factory was cleaner, better lighted, and more spacious than most.

for all other immigrants combined).[76] Despite a certain level of skill and knowledge, however, by far the majority found themselves working in dismal conditions, as peddlers and rag-pickers or in factories and sweatshops, for extremely low wages. Many Jews worked in the garment industry. Immigrants made that choice of employment partly because many of the owners of clothing manufacturing businesses were German Jews, partly because many of them already had some skill with needle and thread, and partly because the industry expanded rapidly in just the years of East European Jewish migration (Figure 5.9).[77]

In Jewish New York, women worked outside the home for wages nearly as often as did the men. Women and men brought strength to the labor movement and worked tirelessly to improve their wages and working conditions. Nineteen-ten was a year of countless strikes in New York's Jewish industries. Then in the spring of 1911, a fire broke out in the Triangle Shirtwaist Company, one of the largest garment factories on the East Side. Flammable materials were everywhere, doors were locked from the outside. One hundred forty-six workers—mainly Jewish and Italian young women and girls—burned, were asphyxiated, or jumped to their deaths. A reporter described what he saw:

> [A] young man helped a girl to the window sill on the ninth floor. Then he held her out deliberately, away from the building, and let her drop. He held out a second girl the same way and let her drop. He held out a third girl who did not resist. They were all as unresisting as if he were helping them into a street car instead of into eternity. He saw that a terrible death awaited them in the flames and his was only a terrible chivalry. He brought around another girl to the window. I saw her put her arms around him and kiss him. Then he held her into space—and dropped her. Quick as a flash, he was on the window sill himself. His coat fluttered upward—the air filled his trouser legs as he came down. I could see he wore tan shoes.[78]

Figure 5.10 Triangle fire victims.

All of working-class New York was in mourning for weeks (Figure 5.10). Rose Schneiderman, a leader of the Women's Trade Union League, spoke at a memorial meeting: "This is not the first time girls have been burned alive in this city. Every week I must learn of the untimely death of one of my sister workers. Every year thousands of us are maimed. The life of men and women is so cheap and property is so sacred!"[79]

From tragedies like the Triangle Shirtwaist Fire, and the poor wages and terrible working conditions that Jews and other workers, mainly immigrants, had to endure, came a strong Jewish labor movement in New York. Jewish unions, like Polish unions in Chicago, were important community organizations. And in fact, thousands of Jews populated hundreds of labor unions, workers' leagues, socialist study groups, and other activist organizations running across a wide political spectrum.[80] Other organizations bustled about the Lower East Side. None were more important than the *landsmanshaftn*, mutual aid societies based on region of origin in Eastern Europe.[81]

The Lower East Side was home to a vast cacophony of Jewish voices: dozens of newspapers, most in Yiddish, some in English, and a few in Hebrew; scholars, both Hebraists and secular thinkers, writers, and speakers; poets, novelists, and playwrights in Yiddish and English; Zionists; anarchists; socialists; and free-thinkers. For all the poverty and suffering, New York's Jewish community in the first decades of the twentieth century was a bubbling pot of people and ideas.[82]

The contrast was so great between the East Europeans and the now middle- and upper-class German Jews who had preceded them that most Germans did not at first want to be associated with the new immigrants. The existing Jewish community dutifully, and gingerly, extended a helping hand to these new Jews, but did not welcome them as brothers and sisters. In the words of the historian Moses Rischin, "Nothing in the newcomers seemed worthy of approval. Yiddish, or Judeo-German, 'a language only understood by Polish and Russian Jews,' though intelligible to non-Jewish Germans, was denounced as 'piggish jargon.' Immigrant dress, ceremonials, and rabinical divorces were anathema. Yiddish theaters were barbarous, Yiddish newspapers, collectively stigmatized as 'socialistic,' even worse. Furthermore, 'dangerous principles' were 'innate in the Russian Jew.'" A German Jewish writer complained: "Our newspapers have daily records of misdemeanors, marital misery, and petty quarrels that may largely be attributed to the same source. The efforts of intelligent brethren to raise the standards of Judaism have been frustrated." It was a class division and an ethnic one, between well-established German Jews who lived uptown and Russian and Polish Jews, new to the country, who lived downtown.[83]

Nor, as we shall see in Chapter 6, did the American Gentile community welcome East European Jews. They were White people, and so from the start were legally entitled to a place in American society. They could become citizens and take part in public life, but in social terms they were White people of a distinctly different color even than Irish, Greeks, Italians, and Poles.

Northeast Europeans

Scandinavian immigrants have usually been treated in the same category with the British, Germans, and Irish, as part of the Old Immigration, because of their light coloring and the Protestant religion that characterized their communities. Late-nineteenth-century scholars and policy advocates saw them as compatible with Anglo-Americans and wanted to draw a distinction between them—as acceptable immigrants—and South and East European peoples, whom they portrayed as more foreign and therefore inappropriate for inclusion in American society. That is to say, rarely did Scandinavian customs or stereotypes show up in nativist screeds.

In fact, Swedes, Norwegians, and other Scandinavian migrants came in large numbers not before the Civil War but after. During the period 1840 to 1860, the so-called Old Immigration years, Scandinavians never constituted so much as 1 percent of the immigrant population. That jumped to 5.5 percent in the 1860s, 8.6 percent in the 1870s, 12.5 percent in the 1880s, and 10.1 percent in the 1890s, and then it tapered off. So the era of the so-called New Immigration was actually the high point of Scandinavian immigration, and Scandinavians had not come before that time in significant numbers. Their placement by earlier scholars as part of a light-skinned, Protestant Old Immigration is simply an error, caused by racial and cultural categorizing, not demographic reality (see Table 5.1 and Appendix B, Table 14).[84]

Swedes

Swedes, like the Germans, Britons, Japanese, Jews, and other Scandinavians, were a middle-class immigrant group.[85] They almost all arrived in the United States with enough cash on hand to buy a ticket to the Midwest, and often with enough to set themselves up on a farm. Many of those who lacked the cash on arrival to satisfy their land hunger were able to work hard and soon acquire it, or to take advantage of the homestead acts that were racially slanted in their favor. Others made their way into city occupations; most moved quickly into middle-class positions.

Nonetheless, a few Anglo-Americans found even Scandinavians distasteful. One story stands out for its pungency, but also because it was so anomalous. Horace Glenn wrote back to his family in New York from Smith's logging camp in Marcy, Minnesota, in the winter of 1901, telling a fond tale of Anglo-American racial, economic, and pugilistic superiority:

> 9/10th of the men are Roundheads [immigrants] & the most disgusting, dirty, lousy reprobates that I ever saw. I want to hit them every time I look at them. I licked one last week & kicked him bad & I get so mad sometimes I could whip a dozen if I had to. There are probably 15 *white* men here to 60 Swedes & those 15 keep them so they don't dare to say their soul is their own. Every time a Swede gets gay he is promptly squelched & it is done so quick & decisively that he don't try it again. It is getting worse every year & soon there will be nothing else up here. The idea is that the poorest wages & board in this country are so far above anything the Swede ever dreamed of that he is contented with anything here & therefor makes a first class scab. In any labor requiring a degree of skill he cannot be used, however. In all the camps I have been in I have never seen a Swede cant hook man & only one Swede teamster & he got fired & they are none too good at anything else. When I get out of here I never want to see a Swede again. … If I had my way with them I would have them carroled & made to take a bath & instructed in the use of a handkerchief at the point of a bayonet.[86]

But Glenn's was decidedly a minority opinion. Discrimination against Swedish immigrants and their children was miniscule. Other Americans recognized them as a distinct ethnic group and respected their right to form their own community, but otherwise viewed Swedes simply as White people.

Sweden lost about one-quarter of its population to the United States in two great gulps, in 1868 to 1873 (103,000) and 1880 to 1893 (475,000). That did not end the migration: 219,000 Swedes came to the United States in the first decade of the twentieth century, another 92,000 in the 1920s. The majority of Swedish immigrants came from rural backgrounds. Some were junior members of families that owned some land, but not enough for all the children to become farmers in their own right. Others were landless agricultural laborers. Both classes of people went to America in search of a homestead. They went primarily to the Midwest, in very large numbers to Minnesota and Illinois in particular. Some Swedes from industrial and mining regions in Sweden chose industrial New England instead; others from lumbering and fishing backgrounds sought similar employment in the Pacific Northwest. But the majority of Swedish immigrants came to cities like Chicago and Minneapolis and then fanned out over the countryside and set up farms.

Walter Lindstrom grew up on an island just off the coast of central Sweden near the industrial port city of Sundsvall. Eldest son of a farming family that worked marginal lands—hard work and not much return—Lindstrom acquired the wanderlust at school. He and his mates were connected, by education and the growing web of industrial capitalism, with the outside world.

> The library at our public school was a treasure house, full of books from the whole world. It had *Robinson Crusoe, Gulliver's Travels, Uncle Tom's Cabin, Huckleberry Finn*, Jack London, *Tom Sawyer, Around the World in Eighty Days*. There was no end to what we could choose from. Nor was this all. The boys in the neighborhood and I ganged up and bought paperbound books every week from a bookstore in the city on the mainland; books the school library didn't have—Sherlock Holmes, Nick Carter, Buffalo Bill. ... What a man! And what a country. America! Huckleberry Finn, Tom Sawyer, running away from conformity on a raft in the river to freedom, where they didn't have to comb their hair or take orders from the widow. You could probably say that it was because of those books that I finally came to America.

When Lindstrom turned fourteen and school ended, he had to go to work.

> Work, work, all the time. No end. No compensation. Only an existence. I kept on pressing my father that I wanted to go. Somewhere, someplace. Anyplace. Maybe on a ship. Maybe to America. I always remembered the alluring tales of the Wild West—Indians, buffaloes, everything. And what tales the immigrants had to tell when they returned form America, the promised land! Nuggets of gold hanging on Christmas trees, diamonds on the waysides, sparkling pearls in crystal water begging to be held by human hands. And how good those homecomers looked—fur coats, cuffs on well-creased trousers, and money!

In 1913, at age seventeen, Lindstrom decided to go to Minnesota, where he worked as a farmhand. Then there were stints on a riverboat on the Mississippi, as a hospital orderly, a long career as a fireman on the Baltimore and Ohio Railroad, and another running a small construction business in Chicago until he retired in his seventies.[87] The lure of America was so strong for people like Lindstrom that, even in the U.S. depression decade of the 1890s, the immigrant flow from Sweden continued undiminished.

As was the case for many immigrant groups, churches were the central sources of Swedish American community. As in Sweden, most Swedish Americans attended Lutheran churches tied to the established church back home, although Baptists and Covenant church people also formed their own Swedish denominations in the United States. Swedes and Norwegians banded together for a time to form the interethnic Augustana Synod, but soon the Norwegians branched off and formed their own Lutheran denomination.

Swedish Americans were a key element in the Democratic-Progressive-Farmer-Labor coalition that animated politics in the Upper Midwest from the 1890s through the 1980s. Bill Carlson, a St. Paul Democratic Party leader in the 1980s and 1990s, recalled fondly how conservative religion and liberal politics went together for his Swedish immigrant grandfather. "When you went to Grandpa's house, there were only three things you could read, and they were all there on his coffee table. You could read the Bible. You could read the Baptist General Conference newsletter. Or you could read the union paper."[88]

Norwegians

Norwegians preceded Swedes to the United States, although they were not so plentiful, nor did they ever achieve as much public prominence.[89] Still, emigrant Norwegians represented an even larger proportion of the old country population than did emigrant Swedes. More than 850,000 Norwegians migrated to North America between 1820 and 1975—nearly as large a number as the entire population of Norway in 1820. Three big waves defined the flow: nearly 98,000 in the 1860s, another 186,000 in the 1880s, and 190,000 more in the first decade of the twentieth century.

Like Swedes, Norwegians were drawn to the United States by a vision of a country where land was cheap and people were free to do as they pleased. The legacy of primogeniture and quasifeudal obligations, together with a population expansion for much of the nineteenth century, turned thousands of formerly secure peasants into landless workers. Unlike Denmark, where farmers made a successful transition from grain production to livestock raising (partly because their population did not increase so much), in Norway farmers saw themselves as desperate. Those who went to the United States settled primarily in the Upper Midwest—Minnesota, Wisconsin, and the Dakotas—and along the waters of Puget Sound.

Ole Beheim was one of these. He was a younger son, and so would have spent his life as a laborer on the farm that his older brother was due to inherit. His mother encouraged him to try America and gave him money to pay his passage. Not speaking a word of English, he went by ship and train to Minneapolis. In a few years' time he was running a general store in a small town in Iowa. He taught himself English, simplified his name to Beim, and stopped speaking Norwegian. He married an American woman of English descent, buried her a few years later, and started a second family with another Anglo-American woman. Then gold was discovered in the Klondike in 1897 and he was off. He abandoned his family for nearly two years, went to Alaska by boat from San Francisco, and made a small fortune in the downstream gold diggings before returning to storekeeping in South Dakota. Ole Beim lived out his later days as an insurance salesman, traveling up and down the Pacific Coast and selling small policies to immigrants and other working people. He died in the 1930s in a business hotel in San Francisco. By that time his children had achieved education—some through college and one the holder of two master's degrees—grown to adulthood, and acquired middle-class status, professional jobs, and large houses.[90]

By the 1920s, the Scandinavian immigrant stream had declined to a trickle. Both Swedish and Norwegian American communities were coming to be dominated not by immigrants but by the American born. Even when they had grown up in Scandinavian enclaves, by the time they reached adulthood, these people acted and were treated as simply White Americans.

Making a Multiethnic Working Class in the West

Just as Poles and Irish, Italians and Serbs, and other White immigrants and their children formed a common class of workers in the industrial cities of the East and Middle West, so too Chinese, Japanese, Filipinos, Mexicans, and others—including Whites—formed a multiracial working class in the factories that were the fields, mines, and forests of the West. They worked together building railroads, digging for

Figure 5.11 *Alamo City Employment Agency.*

minerals, canning fish, harvesting crops, and felling trees. Sometimes they worked in racially segregated work teams, but often they were hired and worked together. Figure 5.11 shows a crowd of Mexican, White, and Black Americans gathered outside San Antonio's Alamo City Employment Agency in 1924.

Frequently the Whites lived separately from Blacks, Mexicans, and Asians, but sometimes the latter groups intermingled in work camps and urban neighborhoods. Whites—both American-born and immigrants—struggled to maintain a position of racial superiority over the various peoples of color. The dynamics of race and class relationships were different in each part of the region—Hawai'i, California, the Pacific Northwest, the mountain states, the desert Southwest, and Texas—and in each place, those racial hierarchies changed over time. But in all of them, the racial systems were not just Black and White, nor Red and White, but Black and Red and White and Yellow and Brown from the beginning.[91]

Chinese

Chinese Americans were one part of that Western working class.[92] In 1880 they formed the largest ethnic contingent in the pool of California agricultural workers. Twenty years later, they had all but left agriculture. After further immigration by Chinese workers was banned in 1882, the Chinese population—which had formerly spread out across the landscape in field and forest, mine and mill—turned in upon itself. Every town and city in the West came to have a largely self-segregated Chinese neighborhood—a "Chinatown"—by the end of the century. There, Chinese people built an enclave economy. Some took jobs outside, whether they worked in cigar factories in San Francisco or in fish canneries in Seattle. But many lived and worked within Chinatown's confines, in shops and restaurants and groceries and noodle factories. Chinese American merchants and professional people served Chinese Americans almost exclusively. There was the Chinatown lawyer, the Chinatown doctor, the Chinatown dentist and optometrist and druggist.

Chinatown was largely a self-governing community. The merchants and leaders of family and regional associations banded together in the *chung-wah kung-so*, or Chinese Consolidated Benevolent Association (the version in San Francisco, the largest Chinatown, was called the Six Companies). Chung Wah took care of maintaining order in the Chinese community. They spoke for the community to the mayor and police, and in fact did a lot of the policing of Chinatown themselves, using the services of tongs—secret societies with links to politics and the underground economy back in China. The sealed-off quality to Chinatown society, as well as the presence of these mysterious secret societies (whose partners in China were in fact the only organs of political opposition to be found there), lent themselves to the creation of Orientalist mythology surrounding Chinatown.[93] In fact, Chinatown was just a dense, segregated, monoracial slum. It was a bachelor society, where aging Chinese working men, too poor and too proud to go back to China, forbidden to bring over wives and make families, lived out their days in toil and quiet desperation, as Madeline Hsu put it, "dreaming of gold, dreaming of home."[94]

The tong connection, and the ongoing interest of the Chinese American population in the country they had not quite left behind, helped make the career of Dr. Sun Yatsen. Sun was an exile from South China who learned his medical trade in Hawai'i and spent most of his adult life among the Chinese diaspora in the United States, Hawai'i, Southeast Asia, and Europe. He was involved with various secret societies in lobbying for political change as the Qing Dynasty gradually collapsed through the 1890s and 1900s. When armed rebellion broke out in 1911, Sun was raising money and agitating for revolution among Chinese people in Denver. He hurried to join the revolutionaries back home, just in time to lead them to victory over a hapless and exhausted imperial dynasty, and be named the first president of the Republic of China.[95]

A small number of Chinese immigrants did manage to save enough money to start modest businesses, often in partnership with several others. That transformed them from laborers to merchants in the eyes of the U.S. government, and it qualified them to bring over wives from China. Others were able to achieve family and other life goals by virtue of a historical accident. In 1906, a massive earthquake and fire leveled San Francisco, including its Chinatown. Government records were destroyed in the fire. Within days, hundreds and then thousands of Chinese immigrant men descended on the emergency government offices that were set up, asking in broken English for copies of their birth certificates in San Francisco County. Of course, none such existed, but then neither did any other birth certificates. The men swore they were native born, and they brought friends and relatives to attest to that fact. What could the government do? Thus several thousand Chinese immigrant men became American citizens despite the law against naturalization (these were smart guys). Some of them lived out their days in America. Others went back to China permanently or for visits, secure in the knowledge that their American papers would allow them re-entry. Often they would report having a child (usually a son) when they visited their wives. Then, years later, those sons, or other young men who bought their papers, came over to join their fathers in the United States. These "paper sons," as they came to be called (and some paper daughters) were the means by which the Chinese American population renewed itself and kept refreshing contact with China over the next several decades.[96]

Japanese

The Chinese left Western agriculture during the 1880s, but the economy was expanding rapidly and work still needed to be done.[97] Quickly labor recruiters turned elsewhere in Asia.

Japan had opened its shores to foreigners only a generation earlier, after more than two centuries sequestered from the outside world. For more than half a century after the 1868 Meiji revolution, the Japanese people suffered through wave after wave of disorienting struggle with the forces of modernity as the government wrenched the country from agrarian isolation to industrial engagement with the world as a major economic and military power. Japan took colonies abroad in Asia and the Pacific. At home, Asia's largest industrial economy was built in a single generation on the backs of the peasants. They were taxed to the point of losing their land—one-seventh of the country's rice lands underwent foreclosure in 1884 to 1886 alone. Kanagawa farmer-leader Sunaga Renzo petitioned the government in 1884:

> The 200,000 people of this prefecture are unable to repay their debts because of declining prices and the depressed state of the silkworm business and textile industry in general. They are plagued day and night with worries, sorrow, frustration, and hardship. People are being crushed underfoot by the usurers as if they were ants. The demonstration by the members of the Debtors' party in this prefecture in mid-1884 proved to be fruitless; all we got was a lecture from the authorities. No lenience or generosity was forthcoming.[98]

Hundreds of thousands of jobless peasants went out to work temporarily in Japanese cities. Finding wages there low and working conditions dreadful, some extended their working sojourn across the Pacific. Like Chinese, Italians, and most other migrants who came to America, the initial goal of most was to work hard, make some money, return home, and buy land or otherwise enable their families to live better than they had been doing. American wages varied between five and twenty-five times as high as those in Japan. The migrants were mainly young men in the beginning, from a handful of rural prefectures in southwestern Japan where Hawaiian and American labor recruiters went first. They were the best-educated immigrant group in American history to that point: nearly all had the government-mandated six years of primary education, 60 percent had completed middle school, and 21 percent were high school graduates. That meant they were better educated than the native U.S. White population at the time. The Japanese government was mindful of its international reputation and wary of giving Europeans or Americans any reason to impose colonialism. It took care that sick people, criminals, and the indigent were not allowed to go abroad, and it required that every emigrant have two or three propertied Japanese citizens to act as guarantors lest the migrant become a public charge.

Japanese movement abroad began in earnest in the 1880s and increased rapidly. The first outward thrust was to Hawai'i, where *imin*, or emigrants, signed contracts to cut cane and harvest pineapples. At the end of their three-to-five-year contracts, some went back to Japan. More headed to towns in Hawai'i or shipped on to the continental United States, which did not seize formal control of the islands until 1898 but was already much involved in Hawaiian affairs. Meanwhile, other Japanese went abroad to places like Peru and Brazil, and later others went to islands in the southwest Pacific and to mainland East Asia.

Growing in number throughout the 1890s and well into the first decade of the twentieth century, Japanese men and some women came to the western United States and worked—some 150,000 in all. Like Italians and Chinese, they worked in monoethnic gangs organized by labor contractors who were immigrants themselves; some doubled as hotel keepers or store owners in Western towns. Inota Tawa's experiences were typical:

It was 1893 when I entered Idaho as a member of Tadashichi Tanaka's group of workers. … We dressed like American railroad workers in shirts and dungarees and American shoes. … We worked ten hours a day and made $1.15, out of which 10 cents was withheld as employment commission. White workers got $1.45 per day. Two or three months every winter we were out of a job. … One or two hundred workers waited in Nampa camp until the snow melted in spring. Room and board there cost approximately $7 or $8 per month, and the system was that we would pay it back when we started working again in spring. …

The section life at that time was very crude. Between six and ten people were living together per section. The foremen were all whites, and they lived by twos in separate buildings. They were high-salaried men making $60 to $70 per month. Since it was a camp in the mountains, there was no recreation available. … The only pleasure was pay day once a month. Receiving our checks, we went off into town, bought bourbon at $1 or $2 a bottle, canned salmon and— secretly—rice. We cooked the rice, put vinegar over the salmon and piled that on top of the rice. We called it "sushi" and enjoyed it gleefully. Getting drunk on the cheap whiskey, we sang the songs of our homeland and talked about the memories of home. …

For three years and a half I worked this way and sent the money—nearly three thousand yen—to my father in Okayama. He bought about a five-acre field [a very large farm by Japanese standards] and suddenly became a rich man in the village. As I had realized the first goal of coming to the states, I decided to work for myself after that, and went down south to San Francisco.[99]

The *imin* worked all over the West: as farm laborers on the West Coast, and also in Arizona, as far east as Texas, and down into Mexico; as miners in Colorado; as ranch hands in Montana and Alberta; and as orchardists from northern California through eastern Oregon and Washington and up into British Columbia—the borders didn't matter much in those days. They built rail lines, roads, and bridges. They fished off the coast from San Diego to Vancouver. They cut down forests and milled lumber. They worked the canneries of the Northwest coast as far as Alaska. They began doing city work—as domestic servants and in hotels and restaurants.

By the second decade of the twentieth century, some had made the money they hoped for and so they went back to Japan. A lot of non-Japanese Americans encouraged them to leave. Two hundred thousand stayed on, however, and gradually became committed to making more-or-less permanent homes in the United States. Some of them amassed enough capital to go into business for themselves. In agriculture, for most that meant tenant farming at first, then buying a small piece of land of their own. Japanese Americans owned about one-third of the orchards in Placer County, California, by the 1920s. City Japanese Americans opened barber shops, grocery stores, restaurants, and hotels catering to the transient interracial working class. More than a few went to school. T. Takayoshi ran the only store, a tiny laundry/grocery, in Port Blakely, Washington, but his passion was his photography business, which he operated out of a horse-drawn cart.

Business ventures often were financed by *tanomoshi*, rotating credit clubs in which groups of immigrants pooled their resources so that one person could start a business. As he repaid his loan and others continued contributing, another business could be started, then another, and another. They formed farm organizations and business leagues, and *kenjinkai*, clubs based on their province of origin in Japan. The Japanese Association of America was formed by business leaders with the blessing of the Japanese government. It often acted as an intermediary between the Japanese community and Americans, including local government. Japanese Americans planted Buddhist temples and erected Shinto shrines. They responded to the entreaties of American home missionaries and became Christians in surprising numbers, segregated into ethnic Japanese congregations. They gave all the appearances of settling down in America for the long haul.

This included marrying and forming families. While the early immigrant flow from Japan was 80 percent male, after 1908 the proportion nearly reversed, as few men came over and many sent for wives or went back to Japan and brought them over. The popular image is of the picture bride: A man, lonely in America, writes back to his relatives, asking them to find him a mate. They scout around and find someone willing to go to America. There is a proxy ceremony and she is bundled onto a ship. Weeks later she stands at the rail, armed with a picture of a much younger and handsomer man than the fat old guy she sees down there on the dock waving at her. That is all very cinematic, but it seems to have happened much less frequently than is usually assumed.[100] There were in fact Japanese American picture brides, as there were picture brides in European immigrant communities, and as there are weddings today of couples who met first on the Internet. But more Japanese men were already married before they left Japan than is widely assumed. They were sending for or fetching wives from whom they had endured some years apart, not sending for strangers to become their wives. Others did come single and later went back themselves to look for Japanese wives. And more than a few Japanese women came on their own, without males attached.

Mexicans

Over the latter two-thirds of the nineteenth century, Anglo intrusion into what had once been northern Mexico dramatically altered the calculus of political power and racial definition in the territory that was becoming the American Southwest.[101] Elite Mexicans such as the Tejanos in south Texas, Hispanos in New Mexico, and Californios on the coast lost their positions of local dominance to Anglo invaders. Gradually they were pushed down by the Anglo intruders into a broad class of Mexicans, and those Native peoples who remained outside reservations were pulled up into that same class. A few Californios, Tejanos, and Hispanos maintained the fiction of pure Castillian aristocratic heritage and claims to the status of White people—thus was born the myth of Zorro—but by far the majority became simply Mexicans, foreigners in their native land.[102]

The U.S. Southwest had all been part of Mexico, and its most populous group of inhabitants in the middle of the nineteenth century were still Mexican-descended people. Rapidly over the next half-century many thousands of Whites, along with lesser numbers of Asians, poured into this region. The Native population was dec-imated, absorbed into the Mexican group, or restricted onto reservations. At the end of the nineteenth century and into the twentieth century, the White popula-tion finally outstripped the darker peoples throughout the region. As Rodolfo Acuña observed: "In 1900, New Mexico, Arizona, and Oklahoma had not been admitted into the Union. New Mexico and Arizona had too many Mexicans; Oklahoma had too many Indians. Rapid population change [to a White majority] made statehood possible."[103]

As agriculture, mining, and other rural industries expanded rapidly in the twentieth century, and as Asian supplies of labor were excluded one by one, demand for workers exceeded even the flood of Whites. A new wave of migrants came across the border from Mexico to join them. This was not a group of people wholly new in the region—many had relatives or friends in the Southwest United States, and some who lived in the Mexican north were descended from people who had formerly lived in what had more recently become American territory. We do not have anything like good figures for this migration, for *la frontera*, the border, was a broad region of coming and going, not a well-defined line that one crossed. Neither the U.S. nor the Mexican government was good at keeping track of who came and went. Most scholars think that somewhere between 1 million and 1.5 million Mexican nation-als—about one-tenth of the country's population—entered the United States more or less permanently between 1890 and 1930.[104]

Beginning in the 1880s, thousands of peasants began to flow out of the Mexican countryside and into cities, fleeing the oppressive land policies of the government led by dictator Porfirio Diaz. The government encouraged the breakup of communal land holdings devoted to subsistence farming by *campesinos*, and helped create in their places so-called "modern" mega-farms and ranches devoted to export agri-culture. In the process, many thousands of peasants were thrown off the land and became wanderers. Some went to cities like Guadalajara and Mexico City to work; others were drawn to mines in Mexico's north. Before long, many of them started to travel north along an expanding rail network into what was now the American South-west (Figure 5.12). The revolt against Diaz in 1910 brought chaos to the countryside and swelled the northward flood. The nation was engulfed in civil war throughout the decade, with armies of rebels—some representing the legitimate grievances of Indians and peasants—fighting various pretenders to national leadership, and some-times one another. Some supporters of the Diaz regime went into political exile, but the majority of the emigrants were simply people caught in the crossfire. Half a mil-lion people died in the revolution; many others fled.

They were drawn first north within Mexico, and then across the border, by the American Southwest's rapidly expanding economy. That expansion was the prod-uct of several large-scale changes that came in the last quarter of the nineteenth century: a vast network of rail lines constructed by workers for such carriers as the Union Pacific and Southern Pacific; the introduction of refrigerated railway cars that allowed producers to carry vegetables long distances to market; and new irrigation projects that brought huge tracts of land into cultivation. All these meant jobs by the tens of thousands. The American rail infrastructure connected with new rail lines on the Mexican side of the border that also facilitated people movement.

The largest group of Mexican immigrants in this period became migratory field laborers at first, establishing a pattern that would last for generations. They moved from planting to planting and harvest to harvest, in year-long cycles. Some

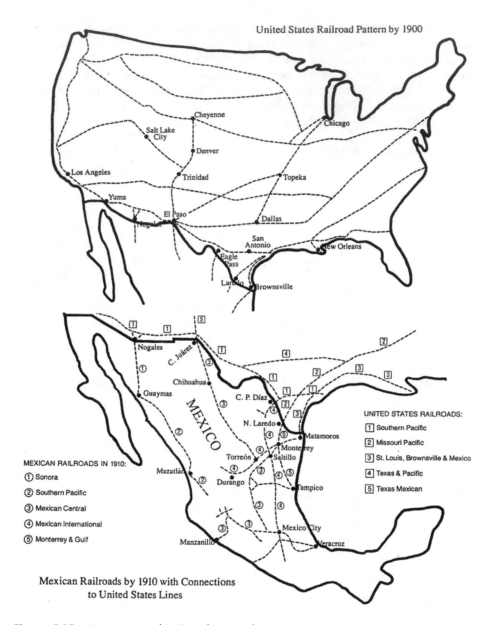

United States Railroad Pattern by 1900

Mexican Railroads by 1910 with Connections
to United States Lines

Figure 5.12 Mexican and U.S. rail networks.

would go, for instance, from the cotton fields of the Imperial Valley in California's extreme south; north through the nuts and vegetables in the San Joaquin and Salinas Valleys; as far north as the Yakima Valley and Columbia Basin orchards; and back again. Some made shorter cycles within particular regions. Living conditions in migrant labor camps were appalling: shacks and tents, no plumbing or running water. Mexicans did the lowest-paid and most backbreaking labor. Whole families, including very small children, worked in the fields and orchards. The children of migrating families had to catch education where they could, and often ended up with little.

Carlos Ibáñez told sociologist Manuel Gamio in 1926 or 1927:

> I came to this country more than twenty-five years ago. My object, like that of all those who come here, was to seek a fortune; I wanted to work hard in order to see if I could get something together for old age. ... In Zacatecas, at the time when I left there, I worked as a peon in San Francisco and scarcely earned my food and a few cents daily. ... I came to California. After living here for a while I went to work in the beet fields, in the railroad tracks, and at other jobs from one place to another until finally I came back to this city [Los Angeles]. ... At times I have had work and at other times I haven't. When I have had work I have saved a little of my wages. ... I haven't wanted to get married because the truth is I don't like the system of the women here. They are very unrestrained. They are the ones who control their husband and I nor any other Mexican won't stand for that. ... I have learned a little English especially at my work. I do anything and work hard when there is work. It is certain that I live better here than in Mexico, but I wouldn't change my citizenship on that account for anything in the world.[105]

Gradually, over time, people who followed the crops and other employment up and down the West Coast, or along a similar corridor that stretched north from Texas, found ways to settle down in particular locations. In Texas, many families found themselves working as tenants on land owned or leased by Anglos. They paid a portion of their crop, usually a larger portion than was demanded of White tenant farmers. Anastacio Torres told Gamio about his experiences as wage worker, share-cropper, and tenant:

> I was about seventeen years old, in 1911, when I came to the United States with my brother-in-law. ... We crossed the border at Ciudad Juarez and when we got to El Paso, Texas, we signed ourselves up for work in Kansas. We first went to work on the railroad and they paid us there $1.35 for nine hours of work a day. As that work was very hard I got a job in a packing house where I began by earning $1.25 a day for eight hours work but I got to earning as much as $2.00. ... I was married to a girl from La Piedad, Michoacan, in Kansas City. She died there after we had been married about a year, leaving our little son. While working in the packing plant I broke my leg. ... About the end of 1918 I went to Ciudad Juarez for my sister and her children. My father also came with her. Then we went to Calipatria and the whole family of us engaged in cotton picking. ... They paid us $2.00 or $1.75 for every 100 pounds of cotton which we picked and as all of the family picked we managed to make a good amount every day. When the cotton crop of 1919 was finished we went to Los Angeles and then I got a job as a laborer with a paper manufacturing company. They paid me $3.40 a day for eight hours work. I was at that work for some time and then returned to the Imperial Valley for lemon picking. ... In 1921 a Japanese friend for whom I was working as a laborer told me to keep the farm, for he was going to go [back to Japan] soon. The owner of the land who was an American furnished the land, the water and the seeds, and we went halves on the other

expenses. Half of the crop was his and half mine. ... Afterwards, encouraged by the first good crop that I got, I rented forty acres at $30 a year for each acre. I had to furnish the water and the seed and this time things went bad for me. The crop wasn't any good, the seed was lost and I had to go and look for work elsewhere.[106]

While the majority of Mexican Americans in this period engaged in farm work, the growing number of city people also merits attention. By the 1920s 40 percent of Mexican Americans were living in urban areas. The population of Los Angeles County grew from 101,000 in 1900 to 2.2 million three decades later. As late as the 1950s, towns like Gardena and San Fernando were zoned for mixed farming and residential housing. In such locations, Mexican Americans and other workers could be close to farm jobs, and they or family members could also work in construction or factory labor. All these jobs paid minimal wages and entailed long hours of back-breaking, often dangerous work. But in the city one could live in a house, however tiny and rundown. One could send one's children to school, even if it was segregated and substandard. Immigrants and native Mexican Americans made their way to Los Angeles, El Paso, San Antonio, and other Southwestern towns, as well as to Midwestern cities like Chicago, St. Paul, and Detroit where they could find industrial work.

For the most part, unions ignored Mexican American workers, as they ignored Black workers in this period, even as they recruited Hungarians and Poles: unions were for White people. Not only because of unions' racially motivated unwillingness to attend to Mexican Americans, but also because many of the latter were not U.S. citizens, many did not speak much English, and they were frequently on the move, it was difficult for labor unions to organize Mexican American farm workers, even had they been inclined to do so. Miners were the one part of the Mexican American working population that did experience the benefits of membership in organized labor. The Western Federation of Miners and the Industrial Workers of the World, both active in the mines of the West, were exceptions to the racial policy of ignoring Mexican workers. U.S. mining companies had recruited laborers in Mexico as early as the 1870s. Mexican American copper and coal miners in Arizona and elsewhere became union members and struck for higher wages and better working and living conditions several times from the 1910s on.

Mexican Americans and Whiteness

For all that the Treaty of Guadalupe Hidalgo had supposedly conferred on Mexican Americans the full citizenship of White people, and for all that Mexican workers were essential to industry and agriculture in the West, Anglos insisted on seeing them as un-American and not White—legally, socially, and culturally.[107] Sarah Deutsch describes the cultural end of this equation: White people's "arbitrary depiction of Hispanic values. These 'values' include blind loyalty to and dependence on ethnic leaders (or 'patrons'), a dislike of competition and personal initiative ... and a resistance to social change. Hispanics were supposed to be isolated, static, inflexible, paternalistic, and passive. Nearly all these traits were perceived as threats to democracy, capitalism, and progress. Hispanic culture, thus defined, was conveniently the antithesis of all that was meant by 'American.' ... Hispanics were generally seen as victims, but of their own heritage."[108] Mexicans were outside the circle of what it meant to be American. Such sentiments were foundational to the dehumanization of Mexican American workers that took place throughout the twentieth century, as well as to particularly sordid episodes such as the forced expatriation of Mexican Americans during the Depression and the anti-Mexican riots of the 1940s (see Chapter 7).

For their part, Mexican Americans expressed a variety of orientations toward their racial placement in the United States. The population of Mexico from which they came was profoundly mixed: Spanish and other Europeans, Indians of many tribes and nations, Africans brought as slaves, Filipinos, and Chinese. *Mestizaje*, the modern Mexican myth of racial identity, embraced the Iberian and the Indian, but pushed the others out of the national memory.[109] That first treaty had promised Mexican citizens in the newly conquered territories that they would enjoy the full benefits of U.S. citizenship on the same basis as White Americans. That promise was fulfilled episodically in a formal legal sense, but very seldom in social life at large. Mexicans remained at best second-class U.S. citizens, and frequently had a story of foreignness written on them by Anglos.

There were a number of ways by which Mexican-descended Americans tried to resist racial subjugation. One was denial. In New Mexico especially, people who had been long in the land took the term "Spanish" for themselves and pretended to pure Castillian ancestry, in order to distinguish themselves from more recent (and in their view more Indian) immigrants from Mexico. Californios and their descendants made a similar pretense for similar reasons in the Golden State. As Charles Montgomery put it: "In New Mexico, 'Mexicans' became 'Spanish-Americans' by staying put. They came to be known by the new label only because they continued to occupy the picturesque villages founded by their ancestors. ... When twentieth-century New Mexicans spoke of 'Spanish-Americans,' they recalled the longstanding distinction, reaching back to colonial times, between *español* and *indio*, the Christian Spanish colonist and the non-Christian Indian. That division was always more formal than real."[110] In several instances, Mexican Americans tried to convince the courts that they were indeed European descendants—in order, for instance, to claim places in schools that were racially segregated. Sometimes, people who were themselves immigrants from earlier decades or the children of such immigrants spoke disparagingly of "those Mexicans" as if they were a people racially apart from themselves.[111]

Such attempts by Mexican Americans already resident in the United States to disassociate themselves from more recent immigrants seldom convinced non-Mexican Americans that they were indeed White people. As Neil Foley has noted, "the word 'Mexican' denoted a race as well as a nationality. A fifth-generation Mexican American was still a 'Mexican' rather than an American in the eyes of most Anglos."[112] When, in 1904, a group of New York nuns brought forty Irish American orphans to a lonely mining town in Arizona, in order to place them with Mexican Catholic families, the local Anglos became apoplectic. A mob very nearly lynched the nuns and a priest, kidnapped the children, and placed them with White families. The Catholic Church sued to get the children back, but the courts sided with those who believed in racial solidarity over religious fealty.[113]

Another mode of resistance to racial degradation was to form solidarity with other people of Mexican descent. Then a claim could be made for full U.S. citizenship, on the basis, not of White racial placement, but rather of American birth. These contrary impulses—some wanting to identify with and claim full citizenship in White America, others wanting to mark themselves off as Brown and of Indian descent, or at least to proclaim solidarity with immigrants of Indian ancestry—bedevil Mexican American communities to this day.

Filipinos and Other Asians

The agricultural and industrial expansion of the 1910s and 1920s that called tens of thousands of Mexicans to what had recently become the American West also called Filipinos.[114] The Philippines endured Spanish rule for more than three centuries, and so felt the imprint of colonialism more thoroughly than any other Asian or Pacific nation. In 1898, Filipinos had nearly succeeded in driving out the Spanish, only to have their country seized by the United States. By 1902, perhaps one-third of a million Filipinos had died in the unsuccessful war for national liberation. Late Spanish economic changes continued under the Americans, chief among them the consolidation of land into large holdings dedicated to crops such as sugar, coffee, and tobacco. Subsistence farming in rice and other food crops gave way to export agriculture. Farmers were impoverished and many were thrown off the land. The Americans transformed Philippine society, planting American institutions, requiring the use of English, building an American-style education system, and spreading among educated Filipinos the idea that the United States was a wonderful country.

The first migrants from the Philippines were *pensionados*, elite students, mainly Tagalog speakers from around Manila, who were sponsored by the colonial government and came to attend American schools and colleges. With U.S. entry into World War I, some Filipinos joined the U.S. Navy, serving mainly as stewards in a segregated force. From that time forward, Filipino stewards were a fixture in U.S. naval culture. Julio Ereneta joined the U.S. Navy in the Philippines in 1919 when he was seventeen. He served first as a cabin boy on the *Eider*, one of the minesweepers that cleared the North Sea after the armistice. He made the Navy his career, fought in World War II as an airplane radio operator and gunner, and rose to the rank of chief warrant officer. After the war he worked as an electronics technician in the aerospace industry.[115]

Another narrative relates, yet again, to manual labor and factories in the fields. Filipino emigrants were recruited by the Hawaiian Sugar Planters Association (HSPA). Between 1909 and 1934, the HSPA brought in 118,556 workers from the Philippines. Soon they were going to the continental United States as well. By the 1920s there was a huge demand for workers in West Coast agriculture. Along with Mexicans and Whites, Filipinos filled the bill. They came in the tens of thousands, mainly from the Ilocano provinces of Luzon Island, northwest of Manila. Bruno Lasker told this story of three young men:

> Narciso, José and Manuel did not share the good fortune of the earlier student group. ... Narciso is the oldest of the trio. He has left a wife and two children at home, in a village of Southern Ilocos. This is not his first trip abroad, for he has worked for three years on a sugar plantation in Hawaii. In fact, his children were born there; and he has taken his family back to his home town to buy a piece of land adjoining his father's farm. Now the savings are all invested or spent. Narciso is ambitious for his children. He has seen that in Hawaii the children of laborers go to high school, and that it is easy to become an *illustrado*, a member of the upper class, even when you have no money to start with.

He does not want his children to slave all their lives; but he does not want to go back to Hawaii either, for there "a man has no freedom," and he is still young and wants to see something of the world. After all, California is not so much farther, and he has heard that one can earn $4 a day there—enough to support the family and to have something over, in two or three years, to send the children to high school and, maybe, to buy a larger farm.

José is his younger brother and is brought along to help in this purpose. But José, at the age of fifteen, has ideas of his own. It took no urging to make him come along; but his mind is on the pictures he has seen of the great cities of America and on the stories he has read of the country where all men are free and equal, where a poor peasant may be President, and where one can learn to fly. He has thought it out many a time: What his country needs most is an airplane service from island to island, to make it truly one nation. To José his dreams are more real than the sordid reality of the long steerage passage; and as his eye sweeps over the sky-line of San Francisco, his heart leaps with joy.

Manuel has a cousin in Stockton. He has had many letters calling him across the ocean to that center of Filipino life in America. At first his family would not hear of it. But the decision of their neighbor Narciso to try the great experiment was the clinching argument. The cousin in Stockton had sent $50 toward the passage money, to be paid back out of Manuel's wages. But it was not money nor the advantage of older neighbor's protection during the trip that had fired Manuel's ambition. Rather it was the letters and photographs passed around among the young fellows at home that had long persuaded him—letters telling of automobiles bought on the installment plan, photographs of girls. The work of cutting asparagus was hard, it appeared; but it brought more money in a week than at home one could earn in two months.[116]

They all ended up working in the fields.

Precise figures are difficult to calculate, for the U.S. government regarded their Filipino colonial subjects as U.S. "nationals"—an ambiguous status that meant they could come and go to the United States freely but did not enjoy other benefits of citizenship. Table 5.6 shows the U.S. Census numbers of Filipinos in the United States and Hawai'i.

In Hawai'i, Filipinos worked on sugar and pineapple plantations, in ethnically separated gangs alongside groups of Chinese, Japanese, and other imported

Table 5.6 Filipino American Population, 1910–1940

Year	Continental United States Total	California	Hawai'i
1910	406	5	2,361
1920	5,603	2,674	21,031
1930	45,208	30,470	63,052
1940	45,876	31,408	52,569

Sources: Harry H. L. Kitano and Roger Daniels, *Asian Americans* (Englewood Cliffs, NJ: Prentice Hall, 1988), 80; Posadas, *Filipino Americans*, 15.

workers. On the continent, Filipino workers traveled the migrant cycles that had been set by Chinese, Japanese, and Mexican laborers before them. They worked the fields, forests, and fisheries from California's Imperial Valley up into British Columbia (Figure 5.13).

Wherever there were Mexicans on the West Coast, there were Filipinos, too. Ultimately, by the 1930s and 1940s, the two groups formed interlocking communities from San Diego and East Los Angeles, to Porterville and Stockton, to Salinas and San Francisco.[117]

This Filipino migrant population was young and male—more than four-fifths were under thirty, more than 90 percent were men. Some, like Narciso, had wives back home. But many did not, and they sought the companionship of local women. When those women were Mexican Americans, Indians, or other people of color as was frequently the case, it seldom caused a public stir. But if they were White women, White men responded with fury. In San Francisco in January 1930, two young Filipino men were walking home with their White dates (one was the man's wife). A gang of White youths set upon them, taunted the women for dating Filipino men, and started to beat the men up. When the police arrived the attackers scattered. The police arrested the Filipinos for disturbing the peace. Margaret and Virgil Duyungan frequently lost housing due to neighbors' complaints. As she said, "One year alone we moved thirteen times. And if we get into a house and the landlord likes us then the neighbors would kick, and the next thing I knew we were asked to move."[118]

California banned marriages between Whites and "Mongolians," and the courts usually ruled that for the purpose of this law Filipinos were Mongolians (in Oregon, they were ruled to be "Kanakas"). Despite harassment and the intermarriage ban, many Filipino men did date and marry local women. In fact, both Mexican and White women like Margaret Duyungan played a major role in making community among Filipino Americans.[119]

Other Asians came to the United States in the first decades of the twentieth century in very small numbers. Perhaps six or seven thousand Koreans came to Hawai'i and some went on to the continental United States. Their immigration was cut off after, first, Japan seized Korea in 1905, and then in 1907 to 1908 made the Gentlemen's Agreement.[120] A similarly small number of South Asians immigrated in the same era. Most were from the Punjab and were either Sikhs or Muslims, although non-South Asian Americans insisted on calling them all Hindus. Entering first from Canada as part of the scattering of Indians throughout British-connected domains, the South Asian immigrants worked first in eastern Washington State. Driven from there, they moved to California and entered agricultural labor alongside Mexicans. Some made the transition to petty middle-class status in the Imperial and San Joaquin valleys. Like Filipinos and Chinese, these early South Asians were almost all men, though some had families back in the Punjab. Some married local women, usually Mexican immigrants on account of the California ban on Asian marriages with Whites. Thus there grew up in those valleys little Indian American communities maintained largely by Mexican American women and their racially mixed children.[121]

Expunging Native Peoples

Except for genocidal warfare, all the processes discussed in Chapter 4, by which the government and White people of the United States tried to restrict and eliminate

Figure 5.13 Filipinos and Mexicans worked side by side in the fields.

Native peoples, continued into the new century.[122] The U.S. government continued the process of dismantling tribes begun under the Dawes Act, consolidating them on ever-smaller reservations, doing its best to convert Indians from members of tribes into individual, compliant, ethnically not-very-distinct citizens. Wherever possible, the Bureau of Indian Affairs (BIA) tried to push ahead with allotment. Tribe by tribe, reservation by reservation, government officials put out the word that individuals could renounce their tribal affiliation in return for 160 acres of farm or grazing land. The BIA said that the idea was "to make all Indians self-supporting, self-respecting, and useful citizens of the United States."[123] Not incidentally, in the process, ever more non-Indians came into possession of Indian land, including very large proportions of most reservations. Between 1887 and 1934, tribal land holdings were reduced from 138 million acres to 48 million acres. By 1920, 50 percent more land on Indian irrigation projects was being cultivated by Whites than by Indians.[124] Theodore Roosevelt gave the justification in *The Winning of the West* in 1910. He wrote, "It was wholly impossible to avoid conflicts with *the weaker race*," and went on:

> It cannot be too often insisted that they did not own the land; or, at least, that their ownership was merely such as that claimed often by our own white hunters. If the Indians really owned Kentucky in 1775, then in 1776 it was the property of Boone and his associates; and to dispossess one party was as great a wrong as to dispossess the other. To recognize the Indian ownership of the limitless prairies and forests of this continent—that is, to consider the dozen *squalid savages* who hunted at long intervals over a territory of 1,000 square miles as owning it outright—necessarily implies a similar recognition of the claims of every white hunter, squatter, horse thief, or wandering cattleman. ...
>
> Nowadays we undoubtedly ought to break up the great Indian reservations, disregard the tribal governments, allot the land in severalty (with, however, only a limited power of alienation), and treat the Indians as we do other citizens, with certain exceptions, for their sakes as well as ours. ...
>
> As a nation, our Indian policy is to be blamed because of the weakness it displayed, because of its shortsightedness and its occasional leaning to the policy of the sentimental humanitarians. ... our government almost always tries to act fairly by the tribes; the governmental agents ... are far more apt to be unjust to the whites than to the reds. ... The tribes were warlike and bloodthirsty.

Those who disagreed with his analysis, said TR, were "maudlin fanatics." In his heart of darkness, Roosevelt was an exterminationist.[125]

The government continued to take children away from their families and communities and place them in boarding schools. There they received, in David Adams's apt phrase, "education for extinction"—not necessarily their individual physical demise, but the death of their Indian identity and their tribal group. Indian schools run by missionary teachers at the behest of the BIA left an ambiguous legacy. Without question, they were designed to destroy Native cultures and replace them with White American habits and values. And surely they broke up families, caused terrible heartache, destroyed Native languages, and undermined community. Yet they taught some useful things despite the tragedy, and many students gradually turned their captivity into an opportunity to make places for themselves in a changing world, some even a means to resist. Many looked back on their school years with a mixture of pain and regret, on one hand, and fondness for their classmates and gratitude for what they had learned, on the other. Things got just a little bit better when, after the turn of the century, the government began to allow students to attend boarding schools on their own reservations. Rather than being shipped across the country, many students were able to have at least some contact with their families.

Boarding school graduates used the things they learned—the English language, how to read and write, and job skills—to make their way in the world of White people, and also to serve their Indian communities. It is no accident that the so-called "Red Progressives" who founded the Society of American Indians, the first pan-Indian organization, in 1911, were educated, many of them at boarding schools. One of their leaders, Arapaho Episcopal priest Sherman Coolidge, wrote that the Society was "managed solely for and by the Indians. ... the hour has struck when the best educated and most cultured of the race should come together to voice the common demands, to interpret correctly the Indians' heart, and to contribute in a more united way their influence and exertion with the rest of the citizens of the United States in all lines of progress and reform, for the welfare of the Indian race in particular, and all humanity in general." This was assimilationist leadership to be sure, but it was a generation of leaders that was created in part by the boarding schools.[126]

The net result of the reservation, allotment, and boarding school policies was that the total number of Indians continued to decline. By 1900 it had reached its nadir: 250,000 people or less.[127] It was mainly because millions of Native Americans had died, victims of war and disease, casualties of the immigration of Europeans into their land. But the Native American numerical decline was also partly because many people, who in another social climate might have been reckoned as Indians, in this social climate chose or were assigned to be White or Black or Mexican. Census takers in those years did not ask what one's ethnicity might be; they eyeballed a person and made a choice. Many people with substantial Native ancestry thus were assigned to be Black or Mexican, even on and near reservations.[128] The government complicated matters early in the twentieth century by inserting the idea of blood quantum into Indian affairs. Drawing on the laws of southern states regarding membership in the Black race, and inverting the one-drop rule, they calculated one's Native ancestry in sixteenths and established rules for each tribe that specified an individual must have a certain blood quantum—a certain percentage of tribal ancestry—in order to be certified a member of the tribe. If one did not have the proper documentation or had the wrong mix of ancestors, one was forced out of the tribe and could not claim tribal benefits, such as the right to live on the reservation or to receive a land allotment. Blood quantum was not a Native American way of determining membership; it was a Euro-American imposition designed to reduce the number of Indians and their claims to land rights.[129]

Throughout the nineteenth century and into the twentieth century, in parallel with the actual decline in the numbers of people who were counted as Indians, there grew a widespread public assumption that the world was witnessing the inevitable extinction of American Indians. This assumption was a long, sentimental tale, one of the most resilient tropes of American popular culture. It had tragic heroes, real and fictional, from Hiawatha to Crazy Horse. It became a fundament of American identity. It has been used to excuse much that is loathsome in American history. If Indians were destined to die out anyway—if they were "the weaker race," in Theodore

Roosevelt's phrase—then it was no one's fault that they were killed or dispossessed. It was just the natural way of things. And if others—Whites—benefited, well, that was no one's fault, either.[130]

Meanwhile, a lot of people (again, mainly Whites) were engaged in a reciprocal move: they were appropriating Indianness for themselves, to make themselves feel more elementally part of America.[131] Early in the twentieth century the nation was awash in local "Indian" pageants made up by White people to celebrate their connection with the race that had lived anciently in North America, that had now died, and so was ripe for appropriation. The same impulse was apparent in the early development of the Boy Scouts of America, founded in 1910. Scouting not only put White boys in the woods—the supposed natural environment of Indians—it created ersatz "Indian" rituals such as the Order of the Arrow in tandem with a militaristic celebration of U.S. patriotism. Americans celebrated a vogue of naming collegiate sports teams after Indian mascots. According to cultural historian Patrick Miller:

> It was principally during the 1920s that various nicknames, mascots, and half-time ceremonies began to associate college sporting teams with Native Americans. … North Dakota State became the "Fighting Sioux," Central Michigan adopted "Chippewas," and Southeastern Oklahoma State competed nominally as "Savages" … . upholding the notion that painted-faced, buckskin-clad, spear-wielding, war-whooping white guys who danced at halftime honestly spoke to pride in the native American "traditions" of their regions. … it wasn't the *presence* of first nations in the American landscape that was being honored, but ironically, and ethnically cleansed *past*. … In effect, "playing Indian" occurred only after a vast majority of Native Americans had been killed off or compelled to live on reservations while their distinctive cultures were forcibly eradicated or left to languish.[132]

Some of the move to appropriate Indianness was energized by late-nineteenth-century anthropologists who were fascinated by the Indians' decline and eager to make laboratory objects out of those who remained. This was part scientific curiosity, part mass entertainment. Buffalo Bill's Wild West Show, which toured the United States and abroad from the 1880s through the 1910s, put Indians on display. They wore ceremonial dress and engaged in mock battles with White people. The Chicago World's Fair of 1893 celebrated the fourth centenary of Columbus's stumbling upon the Americas by bringing live exhibits of so-called "primitive" or "pre-modern" people into the view of White Americans. Among the peoples on exhibit were North American Indians. Some Indians participated in the exhibitions; Sitting Bull, erstwhile chief of the Lakota federation, took part in Cody's Wild West Show in 1885, despite the decades he had led the fight against European American encroachment. Others resisted. Simon Pokagon must have surprised some listeners with "The Red Man's Greeting" on the opening day of the Chicago fair:

> In behalf of my people, the American Indians, I hereby declare to you, the pale-faced race that has usurped our lands and homes, that we have no spirit to celebrate with you the great Columbian Fair now being held in this Chicago city, the wonder of the world.

No; sooner would we hold the high joy day over the graves of our departed than to celebrate our own funeral, the discovery of America. And while you who are strangers, and you who live here, bring the offerings of the handiwork of your own lands and your hearts in admiration rejoice over the beauty and grandeur of this young republic and you say, "Behold the wonders wrought by our children in this foreign land," do not forget that this success has been at the sacrifice of *our* homes and a once happy race.

Pokagon thus expressed the resentment of many American Natives against the European immigrants who had come and taken.[133]

By 1920, two-thirds of the people who were identified as American Indians possessed U.S. citizenship. Many of these lived off reservations and were beginning to integrate into the Western working class. They worked in the Puget Sound fishing fleet and St. Paul's construction industry, in Colorado mines and California orchards. Most had names that bore little trace of native derivation. The line between Native American and European American had begun to blur, not only in the sense that many possessed mixed ancestry. Many also now saw themselves as American citizens of Indian descent rather than as Indians whose lands had been occupied by foreigners.

World War I was a critical moment for those who espoused Indian participation as citizens. Some 16,000 Indians fought in American uniforms. When the war ended, Carlos Montezuma, a Yavapai, exhorted Native soldiers to act as citizens: "[Y]ou have demonstrated to the world by taking up arms for your country and standing shoulder to shoulder with your pale face comrades that the Indian race is not helpless and incompetent for freedom and citizenship. ... Now, what is your duty? Carry on the fight ... for the freedom and citizenship of your race. ... You have been loyal to your country. Your country is indebted to you. ... Your mission, at this hour, is to preach the gospel of truth that your race is ready for freedom and citizenship."[134] Not all Indians shared Montezuma's view—the Iroquois Confederacy declared war against Germany separately, on the ground that they were a sovereign nation allied to the United States, not domestic American citizens. But White Americans' desire to abolish a separate Indian identity went so far that in 1924, the government declared that the remaining one-third of the Native population would henceforward be U.S. citizens.

Interlocking Discriminations

In the era of the largest flow of immigrants, 1870 to 1930, the working class of the Western United States was made up somewhat differently than that of the East, South, or Middle West.[135] The various colored peoples who inhabited the lower rungs of the social ladder and who did the body work in the American West constituted one vast multiethnic underclass, tied together by a web of interlocking discriminations based on race. Asians, Mexicans, off-reservation Indians, and the region's few Blacks all did harder and more dangerous work, on the average, than did White laborers, including White immigrants—whether they worked in the mines, the forests, railroad building, or factories in the fields. They worked with their bodies for lower pay, at more marginal occupations, with less job security, at more danger to themselves. Even in semi-independent agriculture, Mexican tenant farmers in Texas were forced to accept smaller shares of the crops they produced than did White sharecroppers.

The Western colored working class was forced to submit to residential segregation, whether they were Native Americans on reservations or residents of all-Mexican villages in New Mexico, segregated barrios in Southwest cities, Chinatowns, or Little Manilas. Beginning in the 1870s and with increasing frequency and thoroughness as the nineteenth century passed into the twentieth century, the education systems in several Western states were segregated, with Black, Chinese, and Mexican children separated from Whites. The various peoples of color did come together occasionally—as in the 1920 interethnic O'ahu sugar strike of Japanese, Filipino, Chinese, and some Hawaiian workers.[136] But for the most part, the coming together of various peoples of color was something caused by common White discrimination. California, Arizona, and several other Western states prohibited marriages between Whites and most of the populations of color; Mexicans were supposed to be White for the purposes of most such laws, but in fact they were usually interpreted to be Indians, and so marriage to Whites was outlawed.

Finally, Whites withheld full citizenship from the working peoples of color in the West. Chinese and Japanese immigrants were denied the right to naturalize. Filipinos were called "nationals" but were not full citizens. Some Mexicans were citizens formally, but many were treated as immigrants even when their families had lived for generations in the United States. Indians were denied formal citizenship until 1924.

For much of American history and in the eastern part of the country, the interests of immigrants and the interests of Natives necessarily ran counter to one another. There, immigrants came mainly from Europe and Africa, and they displaced Native people. But in the West, late in the nineteenth century and early in the twentieth century, among working-class people of color, the immigrant project and the Native project finally came together in some measure. They were tied together by a common system of racial discrimination that was directed, in its various manifestations, against everyone who was not White.

Chapter 6

Cementing Hierarchy: Issues and Interpretations, 1870–1930

How They Lived and Worked

Much of the literature on immigrant history has made two characteristic mistakes with regard to the class positions of migrants in this period. First, it has tended to assume that all new immigrants were members of the unskilled working class who were relegated to working with their bodies under miserable conditions and for low pay. These things were true for many immigrants, but not all, and not for all groups equally. Second, the literature on immigration has treated men as immigrants and women as incidental baggage. As a result of the first mistake, some immigration historians have tended to focus on the history of the union movement as if it were the central part of the history of immigrants.[1] It is true that the majority of immigrants in this period became industrial workers in the United States, even when they came from rural backgrounds in Europe, Asia, or Latin America. For them, and for native-born industrial workers, the union movement was a godsend, a much needed way to fight the degradation of their lives thrust on them by industrial capitalism. But many immigrants, including a majority of some ethnic groups such as English, Jews, Scandinavians, and Japanese, brought with them considerable social capital that made their entry into the U.S. economy considerably easier. Even when they began their lives in America doing body work, quite quickly they were able to enter the ranks of the petty middle class.

Contradicts next page

The Immigrant Working Class

Most of those who streamed into the United States, East or West, in the decades surrounding 1900 were indeed very poor people who labored with their bodies. Ewa Morawska recorded the voices of East European peasants who found themselves trapped in the maw of the American industrial machine. A Pennsylvania steel worker wrote home to his brother:

> If you want to, you can come to the same city where I live. Here you will find work right away as long as you are willing to work. But I tell you … that here work is not the same as in the old country. In the old country, you can work the way you like and every Sunday and holiday, you can rest. But here in America, it is not like that, because here, as soon as you start a job, you have to work day and night and holidays and non-holidays. … you have to work straight through just like the horses or oxen back home.

Another wrote: "Here work never stops. The furnaces are going day and night, seven days a week, all the year round. I work, eat, sleep, work, eat, sleep until there are times when I couldn't tell my own name." Another wrote home: "Because I was very ill, I lost my job. … Those beautiful dollars of gold and silver, which I earned with hardship and with my blood, disappeared all too soon because my illness was serious and unfortunate. … And now I have plenty of debts to pay off." In the mining towns of Pennsylvania, Magyar immigrants sang:

> Coal-dust soaks up our tears,
> Our laughter is drowned in smoke,
> We yearn to return to our little village,
> Where every blade [of grass] understood Hungarian.[2]

The sweatshop was a way of organizing manufacturing that did not involve large capital outlays for plant and equipment, and that tended to inflict horrific conditions on workers. John DeWitt Warner, head of a Congressional investigating committee, described New York sweatshops in 1895, in terms that would not have been unfamiliar to clothing workers a century later:

> The "ready-made" business has developed new economies, especially in divisions of labor and the method of its employment. Middle-men have been given a place between the "manufacturer" and the actual operative, processes have been cheapened, and labor degraded.
>
> The materials are cut and "bunched" for each garment by the manufacturer. They are then distributed in large lots to special jobbers, known as "contractors," each a specialist in his line. For example, one makes coats, another cloaks, another pantaloons, while some make special grades or sizes. With this distribution the wholesaler washes his hands of the business, his ignorance of how and where his goods are actually made up being as ideal as intentional.
>
> Not far from one-half of the goods thus distributed are made up in the contractors' factories. As to the other half, the first contractor sublets the work to a "sweater," whose shop is generally one of the two larger rooms of a tenement

flat, accommodating from six to fifteen or twenty "sweating" employés—men, women, and children. In the other large room of the flat are his living, sleeping, and cooking arrangements, overflowing into the workroom. Employés whom he boards, who eat at their work, and who sleep on the goods, frequently complete the intimate connection of home and shop. ...

Single families, inhabiting one or more rooms, generally having a family as subtenants, or a number of lodgers or boarders, subcontract work from the tenement "sweaters." ... The homes of these home-workers include many of the most wretched in which human beings exist among us. The conditions of squalor and filth are frequently such as to make even inspection impossible, except by one hardened to the work, while the quarters in which this work is centered are those into which tend the most helpless of our population.

From the wholesale manufacturer, handling each year a product of millions, through the contractor to the "Sweater," and on to the "home-worker," the steps are steadily downward—of decreasing responsibility, comfort, and compensation. The profit of each (except the wretch at the bottom) is "sweated" from the next below him. ...

The lot ... of ... "sweat-shop" workers is luxury compared to that of those engaged in tenement home work. The home-worker is generally a foreigner just arrived, and frequently a woman whose husband is dead, sick, or worthless, and whose children keep her at home. Of these tenement home workers there are more women than men, and children are as numerous as both. The work is carried on in the one, two, or three rooms occupied by the family, with its subtenants or boarders. No pretence is made of separating shop work from household affairs. The hours observed are those which endurance alone limits. Children are worked to death beside their parents. Contagious diseases are especially prevalent among these people; but even death disturbs from their occupation only the one or two necessary to dispose of the body.[3]

Not All Were Working Class

Some immigrant groups, by contrast, comprised mainly members of the middle class from the start.[4] Scandinavians and British were two such groups. Other immigrants began in body work, but soon made their way into the middle class.[5] Usually, it was because they brought with them substantial social capital in the form of skills and education.

Japanese migrants began in body labor in western fields and forests, but by the 1920s many had made the transition to the small-scale entrepreneurial class. They were tenant farmers, or owners of their own small plots, shopkeepers, restaurant owners, or hotel operators. Likewise, although many Jews arrived without much money, most came with some social capital. Most could read and many were skilled tradespeople such as tailors. Demographer Liebmann Hersch observed:

Skilled laborers are much more common among immigrants from northwestern Europe than among those from southern and eastern Europe. For no other people, however, is the percentage of skilled laborers as high as that found among the Jews. ... The proportion of skilled laborers among Jewish

Table 6.1 Percentage of Immigrants over Age 14 Who Were Literate, 1900

Group	Percent Literate	Group	Percent Literate
Scandinavian	99.2	Slovak	72.0
English	98.0	Russian	71.2
Scotch	97.9	Polish	68.4
Irish	96.8	Croatian/Slovenian	62.6
German	94.2	Mexican	61.7
Japanese	91.1	Filipino	50.0
Northern Italian	88.2	Southern Italian	45.5
Magyar	83.1	Portuguese	40.0
Greek	82.5	Turkish	21.3

Source: Emily Greene Balch, *Our Slavic Fellow Citizens* (New York: Arno, 1969; orig. 1910), 479.

immigrants … was greater by two-fifths than that among the English; it was more than double that among the French or Germans, more than three times that among the Scandinavians and five times that among the Irish.[6]

Table 6.1 gives the percentage of adults who possessed literacy among various immigrant groups in 1900. Such wide disparities in social capital made for very different experiences and possibilities for immigrants in the United States.

Limits on Mobility

The contrast between the social capital that middle-class immigrants like the Japanese, Scandinavians, and Jews brought with them, and the relative lack of such capital brought by working-class immigrants, can be seen in a study made by W. Lloyd Warner and his graduate students between 1930 and 1935. They examined Newburyport, Massachusetts, in painstaking detail, collecting data on every inhabitant of this industrial town. They surveyed the entire population of 17,000 people and catalogued the occupational and social class status of various ethnic groups as it rose over their generations of residence in the United States. The changing social class and occupational status of Jews, Irish, Armenians, Greeks, French Canadians, Italians, Russians, and Poles are plotted in Figure 6.1, with a numerical value assigned to each group's status.[7]

Three things stand out as one contemplates this graph. The first is mobility. Every immigrant group showed real occupational mobility between the first generation and the second, and the group who had been in Newburyport into the third and fourth generations (Irish) continued to ascend. On the other hand, not all the immigrants started out in the same place on the occupational scale: Jews, for example, came with considerable social capital in the form of literacy and work skills, whereas Poles brought less social capital with them and began lower on the ladder. Finally, the rate of increase—the slope of the lines on the graph—went up much more steeply for those groups like Jews and Irish who came with more social capital. If the rates were to continue, Poles and Italians would never catch up to the other groups (and so it has proved to be).[8]

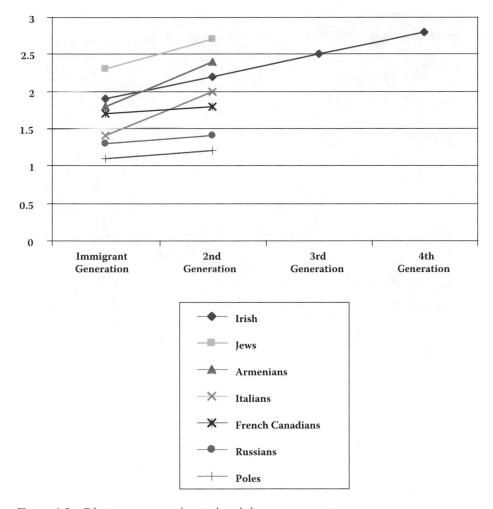

Figure 6.1 Ethnic groups and social mobility.

Leading the Poor

The working-class immigrant poor who entered the United States, especially the Eastern and Midwestern cities, were the target clients of four sets of would-be social leaders: religious leaders, political bosses, union organizers, and middle-class social reformers. Religious figures were perhaps the most natural community leaders from the beginning.[9] Whether they were Irish American Catholic priests, Jewish American rabbis, or Japanese American Buddhist priests, they were sent by their religious orders into emigrant communities to minister to those far from home. Like Jewish rabbis and Irish, Polish, and other Catholic priests, religious leaders also played a vital role in Japanese American communities right from the start. Bishop Yemyo Imamura was a sixteenth-generation Buddhist priest and the premier leader of the Honolulu Japanese community from 1901 until his death in 1931. He mediated a

Figure 6.2 Striking Polish miners armed with sticks and rocks lost the fight to goons armed with guns, Shenandoah, Pennsylvania, 1888.

potentially violent strike by Waipahu sugar cane workers against White plantation owners and overseers, and the Buddhist church under his leadership provided the sites for subsequent labor organizing.[10] On the American side, missionaries were intent on winning the hearts of immigrant communities. Baptists and Methodists were especially active in home missions. For their part, many immigrants who did not particularly share the belief structure of American Protestantism nonetheless appreciated the attentions of missionaries and the classes they offered in the English language, citizenship procedures, American table manners, and other matters intended to ease their adjustment to life in the United States.

Political bosses like George Washington Plunkitt served in those communities where immigrants were allowed to become American citizens and participate in the political process. Many thousands of European migrants became citizens, and their political leaders were important in local politics in every industrial city, especially in the Democratic Party. Likewise, labor unions sought to organize immigrant workers. Many labor organizers, like Samuel Gompers who helped found and nurture the American Federation of Labor, were immigrants themselves (Figure 6.2).[11]

No one was more interested in leading immigrants to a better life than the social reformers of the progressive era.[12] From Boston to Honolulu, liberal Anglo-Americans and like-minded people of other ethnicities built settlement houses in immigrant neighborhoods in the 1890s and 1900s. They tutored people in the English language and American manners. They helped people find jobs. Some of them helped expose the suffering of industrial workers and the residents of poor urban slums, and so motivated slum clearances and laws regulating wages, hours, and working conditions. The settlement house movement, abetted by similar activities on the part of home missionaries, helped tens of thousands of poor immigrants and laid the foundation for the social work profession. Some observers have criticized progressive reformers for being condescending toward immigrants, making them docile before the forces of capitalism, and seeking to control their behavior; such criticisms are not without merit. But many immigrants would have echoed the sentiments of an Italian woman named Rosa concerning her settlement house experience:

> Mrs. Reuter ... and Miss Gray. ... used to tell us that it's not nice to drink the beer, and we must not let the baby do this and this. ... Pretty soon they started the classes to teach us poor people to talk and write in English. The talk of the people in the settlement house was different entirely than what I used to hear. I used to love the American people, and I was listening and listening how they talked. That's how I learned to talk such good English. Oh, I was glad when I learned enough English to go by the priest in the Irish church and confess myself and make the priest understand what was the sin! But I never learned to do the writing in English. I all the time used to come to that class so tired and so sleepy after scrubbing and washing the whole day—I went to sleep when thcy starting thc writing. ... I have to tell about another good thing the settlement house did for me. That winter my [baby] Leo died we were still living in that little wooden house in the alley. All my walls were thick with frosting from the cold, and I got bronchitis on the lungs, with blood coming up. So one of those good ladies from the Commons, she arranged and sent me to a kind of home in the country where people go to get well. They had the nice nurses in that place and they cured me up good. I had a good time there, too.[13]

Gender and Migration

The most common immigrant story we are used to hearing runs something like this[14]: A young man went out from his home in a country far away. He left his family behind and made his way to a port city, then boarded a ship for America. In the United States he found a job and sent letters and money back home, telling his wife or fiancée of the wonderful new land. The woman came to join her man. They established a home in America, they raised children, changed their speech and clothes and habits, and gradually they became Americans together.

Consider this rather different story: Margaret Duyungan Mislang married her first husband, Virgil Duyungan, in Washington State in 1924. He was a Filipino labor contractor and union activist. They moved frequently in search of work, and often because they were evicted on account of race. After Virgil was murdered in 1936, Margaret took their seven children, ages four months to eleven years, to the Philippines in the hope that his family would help them make ends meet. A few years later the U.S. government demanded that Margaret return to the United States to testify about union activities, so she and two children returned (the government would let her, legally a Filipina, bring only those two and required that the others remain in the Philippines). Later she married Virgil's union colleague Joe Mislang, in accordance with her late husband's wish. Margaret Duyungan Mislang—widow, resident of the Philippines and of the U.S. West Coast, head of a Filipino American family, wife of two Filipino labor organizers—was a White woman, born in Seattle to Scottish immigrant parents. The story of women in immigration is a complex one, not easily reducible to roles and stereotypes.[15]

The story of American immigration has usually been told as a man's story. In this story, men were immigrants. Women who migrated were the wives of immigrants or the children of immigrants; they were not immigrants themselves. Intention, destination, life trajectory, and decision making were all in men's hands. Change happened to men; women followed behind. Women's identity (including their racial identity) was often subsumed under their husbands' and fathers'. Historians wrote phrases such as "the immigrants and their wives," assuming that men made the family decisions, that women had no will of their own, and that—however important they were to their families and communities, however great the hardships they may have endured—they were just along for the ride, kind of like luggage. In the last few decades such language has begun to disappear. A generation of historians has explored the complex ways that women's experiences of migration differed from those of men, and also the ways that women migrants from different points of origin differed one from another.

I have tried to highlight gender differences and commonalities throughout this volume, but it is worthwhile to attend to a few issues in a separate analytical section here. In the nineteenth and twentieth centuries, immigrants—women and men—were drawn away from home mainly by the intrusion of international capitalism into their homelands. As Donna Gabaccia, an Ellis Island historian but a revisionist on gender and transnationalism, has written, "As conquest, capitalist investment, and ties of commerce disrupted subsistence production around the world, they generated first regional and then global markets for settlers and workers from developing nations. … But while capitalism and centralizing governments introduced fairly uniform changes in the hinterlands of the world, people's responses varied considerably with culture and gender."[16] As the world market economy penetrated rural Japan, Italy, Hungary, and many other places, family and gender roles began to change. Some people, mainly young women and men, who once would have stayed at home and worked in the fields, went out for a time to work for wages in towns and cities within their region, sending money back to their families. Then some made the longer leap across the ocean to America. More men than women made that leap. As one can see from Table 6.2, before the depression decade of the 1930s, women made up only about 40 percent of the immigrants who came to the United States. Thereafter, responding to changes in U.S. immigration policy, women became the majority.

Most peasant women who migrated to the United States in the late nineteenth and early twentieth centuries came from patriarchal societies, whether in Europe, Asia, or elsewhere. They were expected to keep the home, to nurture the children, sometimes to work in the fields, and to perform other domestic labor that was not monetarily compensated. Decision making was supposed to be mainly in the hands of husbands and fathers. While that is all more or less true, it is important to recall that the market economy had begun to penetrate the places that sent migrants abroad. Migrating women almost all had had some prior experience with work for pay outside their homes before they left for America.

Table 6.2 Percentage of Females among Immigrants to the United States, 1820–2000

Decade	Percent Female	Total Immigration
1820–1829	32.0	128,502
1830–1839	37.6	508,381
1840–1849	44.5	1,497,277
1850–1859	41.2	2,670,513
1860–1869	39.8	2,123,219
1870–1879	39.0	2,742,137
1880–1889	38.8	5,248,568
1890–1899	38.4	3,694,294
1900–1909	30.4	8,202,388
1910–1919	34.9	6,347,380
1920–1929	43.9	4,295,510
1930–1939	55.3	699,375
1940–1949	61.2	856,608
1950–1959	53.7	2,499,268
1960–1969	55.6	3,213,749
1970–1979	53.0	4,336,001
1980–1989		
1990–1999		

Source: Donna Gabaccia, *From the Other Side: Women, Gender, and Immigrant Life in the U.S., 1820–1990* (Bloomington: Indiana University Press, 1994), 28.

Insofar as it attends to women, the story of immigrant assimilation in the Ellis Island model suggests that migration was for women a liberatory experience. As women came to America, so goes the story, they put off the old-country patriarchal roles and learned allegedly more enlightened American mores. They imbibed middle-class American soft-core feminist ideas, received education, and took jobs that brought them out of the home and into broader society. And so it was for some. But for others, life in America just meant more work. With their menfolk away long hours at the shop or factory, many women had to shoulder the entire burden of domestic responsibilities, at the same time they worked long hours outside the home themselves. Kathie Friedman-Kasaba studied the experiences of Jewish and Italian women migrants and found that young, single women who came on their own indeed did find "a degree of emancipation from old world hierarchies and greater self-determination." But women who came as wives and mothers did not experience so much liberation. For them, she found "migration ... to intensify existing subordination, as well as to subject women to new forms of control and domination," both by immigrant men and by American society at large. Domesticity meant something different for immigrant women than for American natives (Figure 6.3). According to Gabaccia:

Figure 6.3 "This Hungarian immigrant mother had plenty to do, caring for her children and managing her home."

Although both found themselves listed in censuses as housewives, immigrant women with families labored under conditions that can scarcely be compared to those of their middle-class white counterparts in the nineteenth century. Most earned money. Few could employ a servant to help with household work. Even the daughters, sisters, and nieces who might have helped them out served instead as maids and cooks in middle-class households. The tasks that defined middle-class domesticity—particularly the moral and spiritual supervision of a small group of children—fell near the bottom of an immigrant housewife's long list of chores.[17]

John Bukowczyk paints a vivid picture of the workload of an immigrant woman and its implications:

While her husband ... worked over twelve hours a day in mine or factory, Maria Kowalska's toil would literally never have been done. For a woman, the workday began well before dawn. She would have lighted a fire in the wood stove, after emptying out the ashes from the previous day, and cooked breakfast before she roused her husband and the male lodgers. ... After the men left for work, Maria would have turned her attention to the daily and weekly round of household chores. If her house or apartment did not have indoor plumbing yet, hauling water for cooking and washing. ... trying to keep her home clean in a neighborhood that ... had dirt sidewalks and streets. ... Once a week, this immigrant wife scrubbed laundry by hand in a steaming tub set on a chair in the kitchen and ironed next to the crackling stove. She ... made a weekly trip to the farmers' market and the corner store—where she had to negotiate credit—for goods she could neither make nor grow. More regularly, she would have tended the family's vegetable garden—canning produce in the summer—and looked after the ducks and chickens ... in a shed behind the house. ... [Soon it was] time for her to serve the evening's pot of soup ... and wait on the men as they returned at dusk, dirty and tired from a day in the mines or mills.

An immigrant wife like Maria Kowalska would have worked long and hard, the strain on her body increased by frequent pregnancies. Polish women who obeyed the Church resolutely foreswore birth control. ... Maria Kowalska could have expected to bear five to ten children during her fertile years. ... [C]aring for a succession of offspring multiplied the already heavy workload. With men at work most of the waking day, women reared their children virtually single-handedly. ...

In addition to domestic chores and child-rearing, immigrant women like Maria Kowalska made more direct economic contributions. ... [working] outside the home at domestic service or light manufacturing until she bore her first child. ... Since Polish wives kept the household accounts, Maria Kowalska would have "made" money for the family by saving it [and by taking care of] boarders and lodgers. ...

The economic role of women like Maria Kowalska in America seems greater than what it had been in rural Poland; her authority within the home seems to have grown accordingly. ... As kinship ties and friendship networks increasingly followed female lines, Polish immigrant families took on the matrifocal form common to other migrant, working-class groups.[18]

The classic immigrant tale has a man going abroad, making a place, and then calling over his woman. But women often migrated for their own reasons, more or less independent of men. One of the most celebrated variants of the women-as-luggage story is the myth of the picture bride, which I described with reference to Japanese migrants in Chapter 5. Picture brides are said to have been common among Japanese, Chinese, Armenians, Jews, Germans, and many other immigrant groups. Cinematic as this story may be (and in fact there have been movies made on the theme), picture brides seem not to have been so common a phenomenon as has often been supposed. Far more frequently, a man was married before he left for America and sent for his wife and perhaps his children later on. Or if he were single, most often he would travel back home to meet and marry a woman, who then came to America as his wife. Many of these were indeed arranged marriages, but very few were picture brides.[19]

The picture bride narrative rests on the assumption that women who went abroad to join mates were migrating in order to marry. That is, their primary life goal was to find themselves a husband; in order to land a man, they had to take the extraordinary step of going abroad. Laurie Mengel's careful study of Japanese immigrant women in turn-of-the-century Hawai'i suggests that something else was going on for a lot of women. Many of the women she studied were marrying in order to migrate. That is, they saw the men they were going to join as a means of getting to America. They often had some education, were somewhat more liberated than other Japanese women, and were intent on emigrating. Picking a mate in the United States was an easy way to free themselves from family responsibilities and to leap bureaucratic hurdles. Women traded husbands at dockside, ran away, sought divorces, and by many other means took charge of their lives in the country to which they had decided to emigrate. Many women surely went abroad to make families, but lots of women migrated under their own power and for their own purposes.[20]

The special role of women as enforcers of racial rules can be seen in Linda Gordon's account of *The Great Arizona Orphan Abduction*. When nuns from New York brought Irish American orphans west to Arizona mining camps and placed them with Mexican American Catholic families, it was Anglo men who kidnapped the children and attacked church officials. But the animus against Mexican families, and the impetus to take the racist steps, came from Anglo women, who saw themselves as keepers of racial morality and who valued racial purity over religious homogeneity.[21]

There is even a gendered aspect to anti-immigrant movements. In the 1880s, one of the common assertions of the anti-Chinese crowd was that Chinese women were all prostitutes. Because of the supposedly debased sexual nature of Chinese women, hence of Chinese society, Chinese people (women and men) must be kept out. This argument—based on very little evidence—was the basis first of the Page Law (1875), which meant that almost all Chinese women were barred from the country, and not long after (1882) of Chinese exclusion itself. Moreover, Chinese men were even cast as something like female in this interpretation. According to Karen Leong, "Depictions of Chinese prostitutes and the illicit sexuality associated with Chinese laborers implicated the Chinese male as immoral, uncivilized, and fundamentally unfit for American citizenship. The architects of the anti-Chinese movement and subsequent exclusion laws expanded this theme into a broad-ranging, gendered argument against the Chinese as a race. ... Chinese men did not meet the ideal of Anglo-American masculinity and thus could not be virtuous republican citizens." Chinese men were not real men.[22]

Angles of Entry

America's understanding of its immigrant past has been dominated by the image of Ellis Island. Built on a rock in New York Harbor, the Ellis Island Immigration Station opened in 1892. It was the place of entry for more than 12 million immigrants between that year and its closing in 1954, more than any other immigration station. But Ellis Island was just one angle of entry, its story just one part of the story. The story has many parts; the crucial difference among them is race.

Typically, a ship arriving from Europe would land its first-class passengers at a pier on the Hudson River. They underwent a cursory check of their papers by immigration officials and moved smoothly into the New York City streets. The occupants of steerage were treated with greater scrutiny. They were ferried back out into the harbor and disgorged onto Ellis Island. There they entered the cavernous Great Hall and waited for several hours, crowding onto benches or sitting on their bundles on the floor. Each immigrant went through a careful check of his or her papers and a medical exam before being released to board another ferry and enter the United States (Figures 6.4 and 6.5).[23]

Some of the people who applied for entry through Ellis Island were denied by the first round of immigration inspectors. They were held and examined again by a board of immigration officials; if their appeal was turned down, the ships that

Figure 6.4 An Ellis Island interrogator is flanked by an interpreter and a man aspiring to enter.

Figure 6.5 Immigrants were subjected to a medical exam.

Table 6.3 Classes of Immigrants Restricted from Entry

Year	Restricted Class
1875	Some Asian women
1882	Chinese laborers; lunatics; people likely to become public charges; convicts
1885	Contract laborers
1891	Persons suffering from a loathsome or dangerous contagious disease; felons; polygamists; persons guilty of moral turpitude
1901	Anarchists
1903	Epileptics
1907	Children unaccompanied by a parent; tuberculosis patients; people with mental or physical defects likely to affect their ability to make a living
1910	Women imported for immoral purposes
1917	People who cannot read in some language; Asians except Japanese and Filipinos
1924	Asians except Filipinos
1950	Members of Communist party; people who might engage in activities which would be prejudicial to the public interest or would endanger the welfare or safety of the United States
1978	Nazi war criminals

Source: Appendix A: Chronology of Immigration and Naturalization Laws and Decisions

brought them to America had to take them back to Europe. It was a heartbreaking situation. Families were broken up, hopes were dashed, and lives ruined. One man recalled, "I decided if they ever have to send me back, I jump in the water. I never go back to Russia." He was admitted.[24] Table 6.3 shows the laws that Congress passed and the immigration service enforced, in an ever-stricter attempt to control who would be allowed to enter the United States. The largest numbers of people denied entry at Ellis Island were mental or physical "defectives"—often people with symptoms of tuberculosis, trachoma, or mental illness—and people whom the inspectors thought were "likely to become public charges." In the period 1892 to 1930, 284,508 people were sent back from various immigration stations under these categories of rejection (see Appendix B, Table 3). Much smaller numbers of political radicals, criminals, and people who lacked literacy skills were also denied. Altogether, at Ellis Island, about 2 percent of those who tried to enter were refused. The others passed on into New York City after a sometimes frightening and humiliating period of a couple of hours or perhaps an overnight stay on the island.

As important as it was to the image of immigrant America, Ellis Island was only part of the story. Many hundreds of thousands more came earlier through Castle Garden, which was the New York immigration station from 1855 to 1890 (in fact, a lot of people whom their descendants believe came through Ellis Island in fact entered through Castle Garden). And they came through several other portals.

The most famous immigration station on the West Coast was Angel Island in San Francisco Bay. Opened in 1910 to perform functions on the West Coast analogous to those of Ellis Island on the East Coast, Angel Island turned out to be a detention and interrogation center that processed far fewer immigrants and held them for

Figure 6.6 Chinese boy being interrogated at Angel Island.

much longer. The posture of the immigration service in the West was more severe. On the East Coast, in places like Ellis Island, immigration officials tried mainly to manage and document the flow of European immigrants and make sure that a few people who were sick or criminal were kept out. In the West, their task was racial. To be sure, White immigrants entered through San Francisco. But Angel Island existed specifically to intercept, interrogate, and send back Chinese immigrants. In time, Japanese and some other Asians were added to their number.[25]

Where European immigrants at Ellis Island might have to wait a couple of hours or even overnight before they were allowed to enter, Chinese immigrants at Angel Island had to wait weeks, months, or even years. Where 2 percent of the Europeans who applied for entry were sent back, Asians were sent back at more than ten times that rate. Z. B. Jackson, an Angel Island immigration inspector, recalled: "[O]ur job was to go over every minute detail of the history of an arriving child— where he lived, where he went to school—and compare what he said with what his father said." They were looking to flush out paper sons and daughters (Figure 6.6). While they were interrogating, the prisoners languished. Lee Puey You recalled that "Everyone was feeling low. We all suffered, emotionally. No one had any energy. We slept all day. So much mental anguish, you know, we cried more than anything else. It was hard. And time went by so slowly." Mock Ging Sing remembered that during his imprisonment, "Every night at ten they turned out the lights. There would be a guard posted to watch over us in case we ran away or somehow escaped from the

UNITED STATES IMMIGRATION ISLAND, ELLIS ISLAND, NEW YORK HARBOR.

Figure 6.7 Ellis Island was a grand processing center, a symbolic port of entry.

island." The Ellis Island station was a grand public building with towers and turrets and huge windows (Figure 6.7). Angel Island and the other stations where authorities examined Chinese immigrants were cramped jails with bars on the windows (Figure 6.8). Ellis Island was a processing center; Angel Island was a prison—the difference was race.[26]

To visit what remains of the Angel Island jail is to revisit the suffering of so many despondent immigrants. There, on the walls of their cells, they carved their emotions:

Sadly, I listen to the sounds of insects and angry surf.
The harsh laws pile layer upon layer; how can I dissipate my hatred?
Drifting in as a traveler, I met with this calamity.
It is more miserable than owning only a flute in the marketplace of Wu.

* * *

Living on Island away from home elicits a hundred feelings.
My chest is filled with a sadness and anger I cannot bear to explain.
Night and day, I sit passively and listlessly.

* * *

Barred from landing, I really am to be pitied.
My heart trembles at being deported back to China.
I cannot face the elders east of the river.
I came to seek wealth but instead reaped poverty.

* * *

I thoroughly hate the barbarians because they do not respect justice.
They continually promulgate harsh laws to show off their prowess.
They oppress the overseas Chinese and also violate treaties.
They examine for hookworms and practice hundreds of despotic acts.[27]

In the 1970s I knew an old Chinese American woman, a fervent Christian whose son had gone from Chinatown to the University of California and become a

CHINESE EXAMINATION STATION, MALONE, N. Y.

Figure 6.8 The Chinese examination station at Malone, New York, was a barn made into a jail.

suburban dentist. She always showed a warm, sunny disposition and generous spirit. We spent scores of hours together. Only once did I ever hear her express a negative emotion. When I asked her about Angel Island, she spat with bitterness and called it "the time they put me in jail."

Ellis Island and Angel Island were cinematic places, but they were only part of the story. Immigrants came to America through several other angles of entry. Boston, Philadelphia, Baltimore, Miami, New Orleans, Los Angeles, Seattle, and Honolulu were all major ports of entry for immigrants in this period. And the United States also possessed vast border regions, north and south, which had few border controls and across which people wandered unrecorded and unimpeded. Sui Sin Far's turn-of-the-century short story, "The Smuggling of Tie Co," described the career and strange love affair of Jack Fabian, a Canadian who smuggled scores of young Chinese men and a woman through the woods into upstate New York. Then, as now, America's northern border was very open, and people came and went without heed.[28] The first attempt at border control was directed at that northern border. During the 1920s, bootleggers brought in millions of gallons of alcohol in defiance of Prohibition. In 1924, Congress established the U.S. Border Patrol to interdict the trade. Only much later did it direct its attentions to people crossing the border with Mexico.[29]

Making Jim Crow in the South

On June 7, 1892, a shoemaker named Homer Plessy boarded a train on the East Louisiana Railway. On the side of the car was a sign that said "White." Plessy looked White, and indeed seven of his eight great-grandparents were White. But by

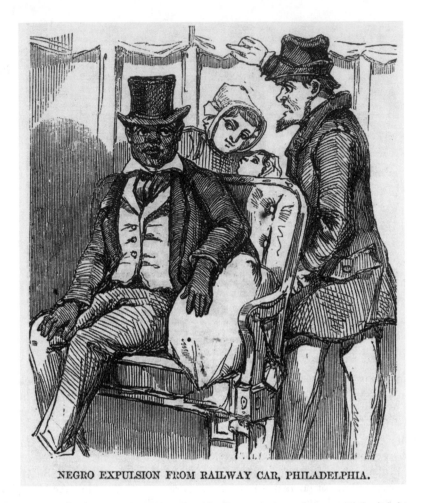

NEGRO EXPULSION FROM RAILWAY CAR, PHILADELPHIA.

Figure 6.9 A Black passenger is ordered off a segregated car in Philadelphia.

Louisiana law, following the one-drop rule, that one Black great-grandparent made him Black. In 1890 the Louisiana legislature had mandated that Blacks and Whites must travel in separate cars. Plessy and a group of other Louisiana Creoles—people of mixed ancestry whose families had long lived an in-between racial existence— decided to challenge the law. First Daniel Desdunes rode on a segregated interstate train. Desdunes won his case against so-called separate-but-equal public facilities, on the ground that only the U.S. government had the power to regulate interstate commerce, so Louisiana's law could not be applied to a train that crossed the state line. Then Plessy and his supporters challenged the law on a train that ran only within the state. Based on his phenotype, Plessy probably could have traveled in the White car undetected. So the challengers arranged with a conductor and a private detective for Plessy to be detained. He was arrested and tried. The same judge who had ruled for Desdunes ruled against Plessy (Figure 6.9). The case ultimately made its way to the U.S. Supreme Court, which ruled 7 to 1 that Louisiana's law was valid. The majority opinion said in part that a "distinction which is founded in the color of the two races, and which must always exist so long as white men are distinguished from the other race by color—has no tendency to destroy the legal equality of the two races." That is, segregated facilities for Blacks and Whites were justified. Lost for six decades was the minority opinion of Justice John Harlan in the Plessy case: "Our Constitution is color-blind, and neither knows nor tolerates classes among citizens."[30]

The *Plessy* case was the turning point in a long campaign by White southerners to build a new system of racial domination after slavery was ended by the Civil War.[31] An end to slavery did not mean full freedom for African Americans. The initial euphoria at being emancipated was followed for many by fearful uncertainty about what lay ahead. How would one earn a living? How could people who had for generations been slaves suddenly take their places as full citizens? Would Whites, who retained the vast bulk of economic resources, let them be free? For a brief period in the late 1860s and 1870s called Reconstruction, it appeared possible that a new, fairly equal racial regime might be created. Union troops took control of southern states. New state governments worked under new constitutions. There were Black officeholders in legislatures, statehouses, and the U.S. Congress. The federal government made promises of land and education to newly freed people.

Before very long, a White backlash set in. The Ku Klux Klan, a shadowy organization of supremacist thugs whose membership ran across the southern White population from working class to elite, terrorized Blacks and their would-be White supporters. Economic promises to former slaves were abandoned one by one. The U.S. federal government turned its attention away from the South and let the sons of the former slaveholding class make a new racial order, White over Black just as surely as before, but this time without formal slavery. Most Black southerners never were allowed to advance very far out of agrarian peonage. They were held by White landholders in semiserfdom via the mechanism of sharecropping. A landowner would rent portions of farmland to his family's former slaves or other Blacks (and some poor Whites) in return for a share of the crop. He would advance money for seeds and food to get the farmer through until harvest. At that time the landlord or another of his class would sell the crop and divide the proceeds between farmer and landowner. Seldom indeed could a sharecropper produce enough to advance out of debt. And so long as there was debt, laws and sheriffs prevented the debtor from leaving the land to look for a fresh start. During the same time that Black former slaves were being reduced to a new kind of near bondage, the electoral rights they had briefly enjoyed were taken away by a number of subterfuges—including literacy tests and poll taxes—as well as outright intimidation by White terrorists.

A key element in cementing White hegemony was the gradual descent into segregation in the urban South.[32] There was formal residential segregation—the White side of town and the Black side of town. There were hotels for Whites in one neighborhood and smaller, less comfortable ones for Blacks in another. There were separate schools; separate hospitals; separate sections in parks and playgrounds (pools were often off-limits to Blacks entirely); separate sections on streetcars; separate washrooms and drinking fountains; and separate sections in theaters. The fiction enunciated by the justices in the *Plessy* decision was that such facilities, though separate, were equal. In fact, the White facilities were vastly superior to the Black facilities in every case. Along with segregation was an etiquette of racial subjugation. White people demanded that Black people be obedient, even subservient. No Black person dared look a White person in the eye. A Black man was not supposed to even look at a White woman; under no circumstances was he to touch her. Black people were to come to the back doors of White homes, not the front. They were not supposed to raise their voices to Whites or question their racial superiors.

In this period, the one-drop rule was enforced more sharply than ever before. Black people who had been free under the slave regime at first made up a kind of intermediary class between White and Black. But as the nineteenth century drew to a close, they were pushed down into the Black race, and any social distinctions between those who had some White ancestry and those who had little, between those who had been born free and those who had been slaves, disappeared.[33]

One means of enforcing Black subjugation was racially sanctioned lynching.[34] Blacks were not the only people killed by vigilante force; depending on the period and method of counting between 12 and 30 percent of lynching victims nationwide were White, Mexican, Indian, or Asian. But the vast majority of lynchings took place in the South, and the vast majority of victims were Black people. Lynching—the seizure and killing of people without recourse to law—became a common tool in the Southern White fight to put Blacks back in a position where Whites could control them (Figure 6.10). An act of terror, lynch gangs were as likely to be made up of White employers and their goons seeking to terrorize Black field laborers into accepting lower wages as they were to be KKK night riders with a more overtly political agenda. Early in its history, lynching was a deed done in darkness. But when segregation came to flood tide after 1890, lynching also became a public spectacle. Grace Hale described the phenomenon: "[P]eople who went to church some days watched or participated in the torture of their neighbors on others. ... Lynchers drove cars, spectators used cameras, out-of-town visitors arrived on specially chartered excursion trains, and the towns and counties in which these horrifying events happened had newspapers, telegraph offices, and even radio stations that announced times and locations of these upcoming violent spectacles." White people sent postcards of lynchings to their friends and families. A national campaign against lynching led by Black leaders Ida Tarbell and Walter White resulted in the gradual diminution of the practice, though segregation and Black subjugation continued.

Lynching was only the most horrific variety of violence perpetrated by Whites against Blacks in this period. As common as lynchings were (about two a week occurred somewhere in the South for four decades), far more common were beatings and rapes—what W. J. Cash called "private violence."[35] Black southerners lived in a climate of restriction and unremitting fear. Not every African American knew someone who had been lynched, but every Black southerner surely knew someone who had been beaten or raped in order to keep that person in subjection.

Making Racial and Ethnic Hierarchy in the North

Whiteness of Several Colors

Between 1870 and 1930, a national debate took place over membership in American society, and an ethnic and racial hierarchy was built among different kinds of White people. Some were deemed more natural candidates for membership in American society than were others. People who were never thought of as immigrants at all, even if they had just stepped off the boat (that is, English Americans) stood at the top of the ladder. Members of the supposed Old Immigration came next, first Protestants and Catholics. They were followed by New Immigrant Catholic groups like

Figure 6.10 The lynching of Lige Daniels, August 3, 1920, Center, Texas.

Italians and Poles. And at the nether edge of Whiteness stood East European Jews.[36] This hierarchy forms a part of an unspoken, hierarchical understanding of just who belongs in America that was reflected in the drastic change in immigration law that was passed in 1924 (see below).

That understanding of ethnic differences in membership in American society persists to this day. In 1978, as a young teacher at UC Berkeley, I made up an exercise to help my students understand the 1924 Immigration Act. I listed ten U.S. ethnic groups on the board, stressed that they were all *American* ethnic groups, not foreign peoples, and asked them to "Rank these groups according to how closely they approximate the core of what if means to be an American." I have repeated this exercise well over one hundred times, with groups of students and audiences at lectures from Honolulu to Boston and Texas to Minnesota. Indeed, I have presented it to audiences who were knowledgeable about American affairs in Germany, France, England, and China. Every single time, if the audience numbered more than twenty-five, their average responses came out like this:

English Americans
Swedish Americans or Irish Americans
Polish Americans
Jewish Americans
Black Americans or American Indians
Mexican Americans
Japanese Americans
Arab Americans[37]

There is, indeed, by common consent in American society, hierarchy among White people—Whiteness of different colors, in Matthew Frye Jacobson's phrase. In the late nineteenth century especially, some Whites were more central to the American project than others. Some—Poles, Greeks, Italians, Jews—were lower on the hierarchy than were English, Irish, Germans, or Scandinavians. They were darker Whites, by Jacobson's way of thinking. But like the Irish we examined in Chapters 3 and 4, these people were never something other than White. There was always a sharp line between Whites of various sorts and peoples of color, and people who were rich in pigment were always poorer in social status and life's goods. The difference between Whites as a group and people of color is apparent even when Jacobson asserts that European immigrant workers were not White:

Reconstruction collapsed in the south, raising new questions about the relations among whites and blacks in an era of black Emancipation and the reintegration of the South into national political life. In the aftermath of Custer's demise ... the Great Sioux Wars ended with the defeat of the Minneconjou Sioux; Sitting Bull escaped to Canada, and Crazy Horse surrendered to federal troops. A vocal and often violent anti-Chinese movement coalesced in the West, particularly in California, where white workers decried the labor competition of "Mongolians" and were wracked by labor unrest which *raised questions in some quarters* about the white immigrant working class itself.[38]

"Raised questions" versus killed, enslaved, imprisoned on reservations, lynched, raped, and excluded from the country. Yes, there were groups of Whites who were set off from the dominant group, and they had less privilege, but that does not mean that they were racially separate from dominant-group Whites, nor that their disadvantage came close to that experienced by peoples of color. They could enter the country, they could vote, they were eligible for naturalization, and no one was killing them on account of their ethnicity.

I have heard some people assert that Italians did not begin their time in the United States as White people, but rather found themselves in a social position much like that of Blacks when they arrived in America. Then over the course of a couple of generations, according to this line of thinking, Italians gradually became White people, in their own eyes and the eyes of others, by virtue of class mobility, intermarriage, and strategic display of anti-Black racism. That is part of the argument of David A. J. Richards's book *Italian Americans: The Racializing of an Ethnic Identity*. It is similar to the arguments found in other books on other White groups, such as *How the Irish Became White*, *How Jews Became White Folks*, and *How America's Immigrants Became White*. It is not accurate.[39]

Certainly there was a lot of race talk directed against Italian Americans late in the nineteenth century and early in the twentieth. Italians were described physically as all resembling an imagined Sicilian prototype—swarthy, muscular, built low to the ground. They were spoken of as inferior intellectually and morally to Nordic peoples, as related to the peoples of Africa. Violence, guile, criminality, and lustfulness were attributed to their character, to their essence, to their very genes.[40] There was indeed discrimination against Italians, even violence. Some native Whites in the Mississippi Delta tried to segregate Italian schoolchildren into the local Black school—and they failed. Other Whites in Louisiana tried to deny Italian immigrants the vote in 1898—and they failed.[41]

One key piece of evidence often adduced to demonstrate the initial non-Whiteness of Italian Americans is the lynching of eleven men, at least three of them Sicilian immigrants, in New Orleans in 1891. A jury had acquitted them of murdering Police Chief David Hennessy and some townspeople disagreed with the verdict.[42] The assumption seems to be that lynching was always and only a racial act, something reserved for African Americans and a terrorist buttress to White supremacy. Indeed, there were a lot of racial lynchings: 353 lynchings of Blacks by White mobs in Louisiana alone in the period 1878 to 1946. But there were also thirty-five lynchings of Whites by White mobs in those years. Those percentages seem to carry across the South as a whole. Between 1882 and 1930, the best records indicate there were 2805 lynchings, 2462 with Black victims, 284 (something over 10 percent) with White victims, and 55 (2 percent) with victims of another or unrecorded racial identity.[43]

The White-on-White lynchings seem not to have been acts taken to enforce racial hierarchy. Rather, they seem to have resulted from an overzealous desire for retribution against assumed miscreants, fueled by doubts about the capacity of the system to deliver justice. Into which category, then, did the Italians fall? Were they lynched as Whites or as people of color? And what are we to make of the fact that there were many hundreds of lynchings in the Southwest, West Coast, and Midwest, and almost none of the victims in those places were Black; instead almost all were White, Chinese, Mexican, or Indian? The simple equation of lynching and non-Whiteness would not seem to carry the easy validity its advocates assume.[44]

Nineteen scholars led by Jennifer Guglielmo and Salvatore Salerno undertook to evaluate the claim of Richards and others that Italians were once not White, in a book with the provocative title, *Are Italians White?*[45] They explored Italian American experiences, particularly early in the twentieth century, in various locales and social situations. Their conclusions were not uniform in all their details, but generally they saw Italians placed socially toward the bottom of the White category—not as people of color, nor in a position intermediate between Blackness and Whiteness.

Even in Louisiana, where violence against Italian victims reached its peak, according to Vincenza Scarpaci, "their black coworkers on the plantations … appear to have considered Sicilians to be white." These experts' views were summed ably by Thomas Guglielmo:

> [I]n the late nineteenth century and continuing well into the twentieth century, … discrimination and prejudice aimed at Italians, southern Italians, Latins, Mediterraneans, and "new" immigrants were fierce, powerful, and pervasive. And some of this anti-Italian sentiment and behavior questioned Italians' whiteness on occasion. In the end, however, Italians' many perceived … inadequacies aside, they were still largely accepted as whites by the widest variety of people and institutions—the U.S. census, race science, newspapers, unions, employers, neighbors, real estate agents, settlement houses, politicians, political parties, and countless federal and state laws regarding naturalization, segregation, voting rights, and "miscegenation." … In so many of these situations, one color line existed separating "whites" from the "colored races"—groups such as "Negroes," "Orientals," and "Mexicans." And from the moment they arrived in the United States—and forever after—Italians were consistently and unambiguously on the side of the former. If the Italians were … undesirable in the eyes of many [white] Americans, they were white just the same.

They were, as Gugliemo put it, "White on arrival."[46]

The extent to which the merging of various European-derived identities into a single White racial identity, often disguised by the term "American," was complete is apparent in this fragment from John Bukowczyz's dedication of his definitive study of Polish immigrants: "to my second cousins … Greek/Irish/Polish-Americans, or just plain Americans?"[47] I would suggest they were White Americans.

Beginnings of Black Migration

Chapter 5 had much to say about the making of an interracial working class in the West out of local people (Indians and Mexicans) and recent immigrants (Asians, Whites, Blacks, and other Mexicans). It also described the migration of many thousands of European working people into the industrial cities of the Northeast and Midwest. The second half of this period, from the dawn of the century through 1930, saw a similar interracial working class begin to form in Northeastern and Midwestern cities. The element left to describe in that class formation was Black workers who migrated from the South.[48] Between 1910 and 1940, 1.75 million southern Blacks moved into northern and western cities. Their reasons for going were many. On the negative side, more than a few fled the atmosphere of violence and repression, and the daily humiliations of the Jim Crow South. In the 1910s boll weevil infestations destroyed cotton crops across the South. In later decades, mechanization threw thousands out of work. On the positive side, Black migrants hoped to find jobs that paid better, homes that were sturdier and prettier, better schools for their children, and a measure of social equality.

Like many European migrants, when African Americans left the land they went first to cities in their region—such as Savannah, Birmingham, Shreveport, and Houston—and then on to places like New York, Pittsburgh, and Chicago. They swelled to a steady stream after about 1900. World War I caused a major expansion of Black

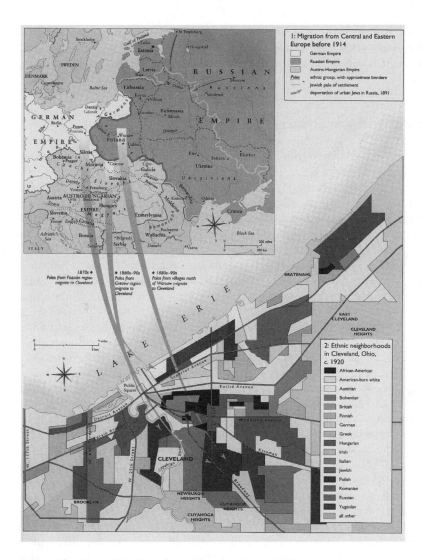

Figure 6.11 Ethnic neighborhoods in Cleveland, c. 1920.

migration by interrupting immigration from Europe. New York's Black population jumped by two-thirds between 1910 and 1920, from 91,709 to 152,467. Chicago's was multiplied by one and a half times; Cleveland's by three times; Detroit's by six.[49]

Together two great groups of peasants, Black migrants from the American South and White migrants from Europe, became fodder for the American industrial behemoth. Industrial jobs were often segregated by race, with White workers on the assembly line and Blacks sweeping the shop floor, Whites in the union and Blacks left out. White and Black workers lived in inner city neighborhoods within walking or streetcar distance from factories (Figure 6.11). Some neighborhoods were largely segregated. But places like the Strip District and Polish Hill in Pittsburgh housed Polish, Italian, and African Americans in almost equal numbers. That kind of mixing was even more common for those Blacks who ventured farther, to cities in the

West. In Seattle's Central District, the Western Addition in San Francisco, and Boyle Heights in Los Angeles, Blacks, White immigrants, Chinese, Japanese (and in Los Angeles, Mexicans) all lived near one another by the 1920s.[50]

Empire and Race Making

Americans do not like to think of ourselves as imperialists. Of course, that does not mean that we have not been. This book has already described European Americans marching across the North American continent, taking land, and ejecting, destroying, or domesticating peoples—that is the story told in Chapter 4. For reasons deriving from the persistent fantasy of American exceptionalism, many Americans (scholars included) have engaged in what Sarah Deutsch calls "imperialism's saltwater fallacy—that is, if salt water is not crossed, aggression and domination are not imperialistic." Take, for instance, these perhaps not fully considered words from an otherwise eminent American historian, Arthur Schlesinger, Jr.: "Americans, unlike the Romans, the British, and the French, are not colonizers of remote and exotic places. We never developed a colonial outlook." Nonsense. Of course we did, but neither Schlesinger nor most White Americans are comfortable with admitting it.[51]

At the very end of the nineteenth century, the Congress and the public engaged in a surreal debate over whether or not the United States should become an imperial power, when manifestly it had been an imperial power for more than a century. Strangely conceived though that debate may have been, it did reflect the fact that several of the nations of Europe—Britain, France, Belgium, Germany, and Portugal—and one Asian nation, Japan, had been expanding and consolidating overseas empires in the last decades of the nineteenth century. The debate was over whether the United States should join in a parallel overseas imperial venture of its own, but the debate masked the fact that the United States had already been engaged in empire for a very long time.[52]

For Americans, in fact as opposed to fantasy, there was a clear connection between the continental and overseas empires, and some prominent White Americans admitted it. Recall how Walt Whitman connected these two zones of empire, as he dreamed of an American imperium stretching across the continent and encompassing the western sea. After the turn of the century, America's favorite historian, Frederick Jackson Turner, echoed Whitman's celebratory tone: "[T]hese energies of expansion ... and the demands for a vigorous foreign policy, for an interoceanic canal, for a revival of our power upon the seas, and for the extension of American influence to outlying islands and adjoining countries, are indications that the movement [to acquire lands and peoples] will continue."[53]

Making War on Our Little Brown Brothers

The United States did in fact become not just a continental but an oceanic imperial power in 1898 when it seized the Philippines, Puerto Rico, Guam, and Hawai'i. White Americans, like their British cousins, justified these colonial adventures as self-sacrificial attempts on their part to bring Christian civilization to hopeless brown heathen. Rudyard Kipling summed his sentiments in favor of the American action in the Philippines in the poem, "The White Man's Burden," which is quoted in part in Chapter 1. The poem continues:

> Take up the White man's burden—
>   The savage wars of peace—
> Fill full the mouth of Famine
>   And bid the sickness cease;
> And when your goal is nearest
>   The end for others sought,
> Watch Sloth and Heathen Folly
>   Bring all your hope to nought.
>   * * *
> Take up the White Man's burden—
>   Ye dare not stoop to less—
> Nor call too loud on Freedom
>   To cloak your weariness;
> By all ye cry or whisper,
>   By all ye leave or do,
> The silent, sullen peoples
>   Shall weigh your Gods and you.[54]

Kipling's poem was widely read and approved in the United States. The U.S. president at the time, William McKinley, told a visiting delegation of clergy how he came to the decision to annex the Philippines. His words show a similar self-ennobling condescension:

> I walked the floor of the White House night after night until midnight, and I am not ashamed to tell you, gentlemen, that I went down on my knees and prayed Almighty God for light and guidance more than one night. And one night late it came to me this way—I don't know how it was, but it came: (1) That we could not give them back to Spain—that would be cowardly and dishonorable; (2) that we could not turn them over to France or Germany—our commercial rivals in the Orient—that would be bad business and discreditable; (3) that we could not leave them to themselves—that they were unfit for self-government—and they would soon have anarchy and misrule over there worse than Spain's was; and (4) that there was nothing left for us to do but to take them all, and to educate the Filipinos, and uplift and civilize and Christianize them, and by God's grace do the very best we could by them, as our fellowmen for whom Christ also died. And then I went to bed, and to sleep, and slept soundly.[55]

The United States took the Philippines after a war that both reflected and helped shape American racial ideas.[56] Spanish colonial power was on the decline around its global dominions as the nineteenth century neared its close. Some local people, in Cuba and the Philippines especially, clamored for self-government and an end to Spanish rule. A Filipino nationalist movement called Katipunan started an armed rebellion in 1896, just about the same time that Cuban guerillas began operations half a world away. The United States got involved when an American battleship blew up mysteriously in Havana harbor in 1898. The Americans, intent on attacking the Spanish in the Philippines as well, transported exiled rebel leader Emilio

Aguinaldo back from Hong Kong to the Philippines to help organize the guerillas against the Spanish. Filipino forces, some led by Aguinaldo, defeated the Spanish on land and the U.S. Navy destroyed the Spanish fleet at sea. The Filipinos had taken possession of nearly the entire archipelago except the capital city, Manila, when the Spanish surrendered, and they declared a republic. The Americans had other plans: the Philippines would be the first piece of their overseas empire and their gateway to the China market. The United States turned on its erstwhile ally, and war raged from 1899 to 1902. American troops slaughtered whole villages and put towns and crops to the torch. Between two and three hundred thousand Filipinos died before the United States could claim some semblance of victory; underground conflict rumbled for several years.

Even before hostilities were complete, an army of American administrators, investors, and missionaries began to pour into the Philippines. They made a new government and school system on American models. They took over the Philippines economy. There were two themes in the language of White American leaders as they gazed upon their new colonial domain in the Philippines. The first was naked White racism. McKinley and other Americans viewed Filipinos as half-naked savages incapable of acquiring the manners of White civilization. That racism was masked, however, by the second theme, a language of mission and uplift. William Howard Taft, appointed U.S. governor over the Philippines in 1901, referred to the people of the Philippines with imperial condescension as "our little brown brothers."

McKinley, the American president, called the U.S. policy in the Philippines "benevolent assimilation." By that phrase, he drew a link between the White American encounter with colonized brown people abroad and the European American encounter with non-White immigrants at home. In both cases, the putative task of the racialized underclass was to "assimilate," to become like White Americans: in the United States, to become absorbed into Anglo-America; in the Philippines, to become a facsimile of Americans (Figure 6.12). And of course, in both cases, McKinley and other U.S. policy- and opinion-makers were certain that the underclass would fail at its assigned task.[57]

Perhaps the most flagrant expression of the perceptions and motivations, racial and mercantile, behind the American adventure in the Philippines came in the words of Albert Beveridge on the floor of the U.S. Senate in 1900:

> Mr. President, the times call for candor. The Philippines are ours forever, "territory belonging to the United States," as the Constitution calls them. And just beyond the Philippines are China's illimitable markets. We will not retreat from either. We will not repudiate our duty in the archipelago. We will not abandon our opportunity in the Orient. We will not renounce our part in the mission of our race, trustee under God, of the civilization of the world. ... The Pacific is our ocean. ... China's trade is the mightiest commercial fact in our future. ... [Filipinos] are a barbarous race, modified by three centuries of contact with a decadent race [the Spanish]. ... there are not 100 men among them who comprehend what Anglo-Saxon self-government even means. ... They are not capable of self-government. How could they be? They are not of a self-governing race. They are Orientals, Malays. ... The Declaration [of Independence] applies only to people capable of self-government.[58]

THE METAMORPHOSIS

Figure 6.12 These two photos of a Bontoc Igorot boy, taken in 1904 and 1913, recall the representations of cultural transformation prescribed for Native Americans like Tom Torleno.

Armed with naked pecuniary ambitions, White Americans nonetheless positioned themselves as racially superior to Filipinos, and as benevolent leaders of that benighted race (Figure 6.13).[59]

Queen Lili'uokalani Loses Her Country

The final piece in taking the American West away from brown peoples was the U.S. seizure of the Hawaiian islands in several steps that culminated in 1898.[60] American Congregational missionaries came to Hawai'i in the 1820s, not long after Kamehameha I had unified the islands and proclaimed them a kingdom. Those missionaries, American businessmen, and their descendants married into Hawaiian noble families and began to infiltrate the government. Foreign diseases reduced the Native Hawaiian population by 95 percent within a generation. In 1848, missionary-descended foreigners convinced the Hawaiian government to allow the sale of island land to outsiders for the first time; within two decades most of the agricultural land lay in the hands of non-Hawaiians. Like European Americans in the western part of the continent, Americans in the islands looked on the local inhabitants with a mixture of disgust and sentimentality. They predicted the inevitable extinction of the noble, brown Hawaiian race, even as they took steps to subordinate Hawaiians and supplant them by bringing in tens of thousands of Asian laborers to work foreign-owned sugar plantations.

In 1887, soldiers led by White Americans forced on King Kalakaua what came to be called the Bayonet Constitution, by which the king was made to cede most of his authority to a legislature dominated by American expatriates. Six years later,

Figure 6.13 White America's racialized view of the very good and self-sacrificial thing it was doing by bringing civilization to the primitive Filipinos.

the foreigners, backed by American troops and a warship in the harbor, overthrew the Hawaiian monarchy, and imprisoned Kalakaua's successor, Queen Lili'uokalani. They proclaimed a "republic" on July 4, 1893; the date was no coincidence. As in Texas, the rebels applied immediately to be incorporated into the United States. As in Texas, the United States dragged its heels before complying—this time in 1898. Two years later, with the Organic Act, U.S. law became the law of Hawai'i; this meant, among other things, that both contract labor and Chinese immigration were now forbidden. All the while, Americans in the islands were remaking the social structure along racial lines, with themselves at the top, various Asian peoples in between, and Hawaiians at the bottom. To cover over this racial hierarchy and promote tourism, they created what Lori Pierce calls "the discourse of aloha"—a myth of Hawai'i as a racial paradise—and marketed it abroad.[61]

In both the Philippines and Hawai'i, there was an intimate connection between building empire and making race. The point is not just that colonial links to the Philippines, Hawai'i, and other places spurred the growth of migration between those places and the United States. Surely they did that. Tens of thousands of Filipinos came to the United States from the 1910s to the 1930s, and many Japanese and others came to the continental United States through Hawai'i. In later generations, thousands more migrants came from Puerto Rico and Guam. Colonial connections provided the channels of migration.[62] It is essential to understand that, in the colonial encounter between White Americans and darker peoples abroad, racial ideas that had been born in slavery and genocide on the North American continent were extended and elaborated, and those ideas reverberated back home with new force. Making colonies was making race, both in the colonies and in the United States.[63]

This perspective was well understood by the Black American soldiers who went over to the Filipino side in the turn-of-the-century war of conquest and resistance. David Fagen was an American corporal with a good service record who went AWOL in 1899, joined the Filipino army, fought against his erstwhile comrades in northern Luzon, rose to the rank of captain, and married a Filipina. He acquired a certain legendary presence as the leader of a mixed group of Filipinos and African American former U.S. soldiers. The Americans chased him all over Luzon until he was finally snagged by a bounty hunter and his head was delivered to the U.S. Army in December 1901. About the time Fagen deserted, a group claiming to represent "the colored community of Boston" published this letter in Black newspapers across the country: "To the colored people of the U.S.: We, the undersigned, address you at one of the most important points in your history. If there ever was a war of races in this world, the war now going on in the Philippine Islands is precisely that." Many Black Americans, including soldiers like David Fagen, understood that what White Americans were doing in the Philippines—building racial hierarchy violently and to the detriment of Filipinos—was intimately involved with the project of racial hierarchy building to the detriment of African Americans that was going on at home in those same years.[64]

Law, Race, and Immigration

Race and Gender before the Law

One of the key tools that has been used in crafting both immigration patterns from abroad and racial hierarchy in the United States is the law.[65] Several acts of the U.S. government defined the rules for entry and citizenship in ways that were framed by race, gender, and class. In 1875, Congress passed the Page Law. It declared "That the importation into the United States of women for the purposes of prostitution is hereby forbidden." On the face of it, that seems not an unreasonable requirement—designed, perhaps, to protect women from being brought to the United States against their will and forced into sex work. But the law further provided "That in determining whether the immigration of any subject of China, Japan, or any Oriental country, in the United States, is free and voluntary, ... it shall be the duty of the consul-general or consul of the United States ... to ascertain whether such immigrant has entered into a contract or agreement for a term of service within the United States, for lewd and immoral purposes."[66] There was no such instruction to U.S. consuls in other countries. The law pointed directly at a persistent theme in the paranoid fantasies of the anti-Chinese movement: the contention that all Chinese women (and indeed all Asian women) were by nature prostitutes who degraded all who came in contact with them. In 1872, U.S. Senator Cornelius Cole, a California Republican, said while campaigning for re-election: "I have no fear of the Chinese overrunning this continent, and yet when I look upon a certain class of Chinese who come to this land—I mean the females—who are the most undesirable of population, who spread disease and moral death among our white population, I ask myself the question, whether or not there is a limit to this class of immigrants? There is, and Congress will so legislate."[67] The "moral death" Cole cited was, presumably, the punishment to be meted out by God or nature on White men for hiring Chinese women to have sex with them. The disease that Cole, newspaper reporters, and professional race-baiters attributed to Chinese women was syphilis. Dr. J. Marion Sims, president of the American Medical Association, asserted in 1876 that the "Chinese slave … breeds moral and physical pestilence" in California, where "even boys eight or ten years old have been syphilized by these degraded wretches." Note that the emphasis in such ravings was the supposedly degraded character of Chinese women, not of White men who purchased their services. The problem was Chinese women who "syphilized" White men; they were the actors. White men were the victims; they were not responsible.[68]

Surely, some Chinese women were in fact brought to the United States to be prostitutes. Chinese men were barred from marrying White women in several states, so they could not form families with local women as they did in Hawai'i and Thailand. Many had wives and families back in China. Like Whites and others, married and not, Chinese men hired prostitutes. And some non-Chinese prostitutes refused to serve Chinese men. So, whatever one may be tempted to think about the morality of sex for hire, Chinese women who came (many under compulsion but some perhaps not) as prostitutes were filling a recognizable social and economic niche. Yet, just as surely as there were prostitutes among the Chinese, so too there were prostitutes among the women from all the other immigrant groups, and many more prostitutes among native women as well. But the Page Law was aimed only at Chinese immigrant women, and it fell equally on the majority of Chinese women migrants who were not prostitutes and came as wives and daughters of Chinese men already here. George Anthony Peffer, the historian of early Chinese women's migration, notes that "Chinatown's prostitution industry so dominated the popular imagination as to render other classes of female immigrants all but invisible." Indeed, a generation of White missionary social workers—like "Chinatown's avenging angel," Donaldina Cameron of San Francisco—made their careers out of "rescuing" Chinese women.[69] Chinese Exclusion followed the Page Law in 1882 as a matter of political continuity (see Chapter 4), and was renewed twice before Congress made it permanent in 1904.

Gender drove the Expatriation Act of 1907 as well. It provided that "any American woman who marries a foreigner shall take the nationality of her husband." That is, she was deemed to be, not an independent agent, but rather an extension of her husband's identity. This was a boon to some European women who could become naturalized citizens derivatively despite lacking literacy themselves. But it also meant that American women (even those born in the United States) who married Asian men became aliens ineligible for citizenship. Fifteen years later, following a campaign by women's groups, the Cable Act severed White women's citizenship status from that of their husbands. But Asian American women who married Asian men continued to lose their U.S. citizenship on account of their marriages.[70]

Legal Whiteness

A series of legal decisions between the 1870s and the 1920s turned on the critical question of who was reckoned White. As we have seen, Whiteness was the critical requirement for access to full citizenship. And so, members of first one ethnic group, then another, and another tried to prove their claim to Whiteness. The first case was *In re Ah Yup*, decided in federal circuit court in San Francisco by Judge Lorenzo Sawyer in 1878. Ah Yup was an immigrant from China who sought naturalization into U.S. citizenship. Judge Sawyer ruled that, based on both common usage and the scientific theories of Blumenbach and Cuvier (see following section), Chinese were not White or Black but rather Mongolians, and so they were not eligible to be naturalized.[71]

If Chinese people could not be naturalized, did that mean they were racially barred from citizenship entirely? The U.S. legal custom had long been that anyone born anywhere to American-citizen parents was entitled to U.S. citizenship under the doctrine of *jus sanguinis*. In addition, anyone of whatever parentage born on U.S. soil was also entitled to U.S. citizenship under the doctrine of *jus soli*. Wong Kim Ark was born in San Francisco in 1873 to Chinese parents who were barred from being naturalized themselves. In 1890 he made a visit to relatives in China and returned. Although Chinese immigration had been banned, the customs collector allowed him to enter on the ground that he was a U.S. citizen by virtue of his American birth. Four years later he went again to China and he returned in 1895. This time he was denied entry, on the ground that he was not a citizen. He sued for the right to enter the United States and to have his U.S. citizenship recognized. Ultimately, the case ended up before the United States Supreme Court, which decided that birth superseded race in deciding U.S. citizenship based on birthplace. Justice Horace Gray, writing for the court, cited "the broad and clear words of the Constitution [in the first clause of the Fourteenth Amendment], 'All persons born in the United States, and subject to the jurisdiction thereof, are citizens of the United States.'" Race mattered, and Wong was not White, but he was born in the United States and so was a citizen.[72]

In subsequent decades, two groups, Arabs and Armenians, were measured for Whiteness and found the cloak fit. Perhaps as many as 100,000 Armenians fled mass persecutions in their Turkish- and Russian-controlled homeland in the first quarter of the twentieth century. Armenian Americans became mainly an urban people, concentrated in northeastern cities like New York, Boston, and Providence. Their one rural concentration was in and around Fresno, California, where they constituted something of a separate ethnic group in the first decades of the twentieth century. In California, unlike eastern cities where they mixed among the European immigrant masses, Armenians were distinctly lower in social status than were either native-born White Americans or other White immigrants. White Californians used restrictive covenants on real estate to segregate Chinese, Japanese, Mexicans, Blacks, and in Fresno, Armenians. So their place among White Americans was in question, at least in Fresno. Initially, U.S. immigration officials classified Armenian migrants as Asians, since they came from Asia Minor. But their commitment to Christianity going back to the first centuries after Christ, along with perceived physical similarity to Europeans, meant that soon Armenians were classed as Whites. In 1909 a federal circuit court ruled that Armenians were indeed White and entitled to naturalization.[73]

Several tens of thousands of Arabs, mainly from the semiautonomous Syrian province of Mt. Lebanon, came to the United States in the last decades of the nineteenth century and first decades of the twentieth century. Like Armenians, they were initially classified as Asians, because they came from Turkish domains, and the Turks were supposed to be related to the Mongols. In several different cases, federal courts ruled that Arabs could not be naturalized because they were Asians and therefore not White. The crucial case was *Dow v. United States*, decided in 1915. George Dow was a Syrian immigrant who applied for naturalization as a U.S. citizen. Federal courts in South Carolina initially turned him down, but on appeal he was judged to be White—partly because of his lawyer's argument that Syrians were "the purest type of the Semitic race" who had a "better claim upon the White Race than that of the modern nation of Europe." The decisive factor in Dow's favor, however, was that he and other Syrian immigrants were Christians. The court presumed that, because of their Christianity, they had been acculturated to European ways of thinking and being.[74]

From that era until the 1970s, Arab Americans were White people, more or less. But their hold on White status was more fragile than that of any other people, including Armenians and Jews. In 1942 a Muslim Arab was denied U.S. citizenship on the ground that he was not White, only two years after another federal court found another Muslim Arab to be White and therefore entitled to citizenship.[75] Arab Americans' tenuously White racial status began to decline in the waning decades of the twentieth century. As Arab nationalism and oil-derived power made themselves felt in the world, White Americans began to recalculate the racial position they assigned to Arab Americans, and to move them decisively from White to Brown (see Chapter 9).

So Armenians and Arabs, after some confusion, landed in the White column. By contrast, Japanese immigrants, Filipinos, South Asians, and Mexicans found themselves shut out of the domain of White people, hence of full membership in American society. Chapter 5 opened with the declaration of Takao Ozawa before the United States Supreme Court. The justices did not disagree with Ozawa's contention that he, as an individual, was a model of the qualities that they would like to see in an American citizen—educated, devoutly Christian, polite, hard-working, patriotic, devoted to family and community. But because he was Japanese, and therefore "clearly of a race which is not Caucasian and therefore belongs entirely outside the zone" of White people, he could not be a citizen. Historian Yuji Ichioka commented on the significance of this decision for Japanese immigrants' position in America:

> Without the right of naturalization, Japanese immigrants stood outside the American body politic. … Japanese immigrants shared much in common with their European counterparts. Yet every European immigrant group, regardless of national origin, had the right of naturalization. And precisely because they possessed it, no matter how beleaguered they were, they were able to enter the political arena to fight for their rights. … Japanese immigrants never had the option of entering the political arena to defend themselves. … Excluded from the political process, Japanese immigrants were political pariahs who had no power of their own to exercise. This state of powerlessness is a central theme in Japanese immigrant history.[76]

The same was true for other Asians. Federal courts ruled consistently that Filipinos were not White and not entitled to become citizens, although for a time they had some of the benefits of citizenship under the ambiguous heading of "nationals."[77] For South Asians, the reasoning was even more convoluted, and the result was the same. Bhagat Singh Thind was an immigrant student who worked summers cutting lumber in Oregon to pay his way through the University of California. He volunteered for service in World War I in 1918. Based on his military service and the fact that several dozen other South Asians had already been granted U.S. citizenship, Thind applied for naturalization in 1920. A Portland judge awarded him citizenship, but the federal government appealed, and the case ended up before the U.S. Supreme Court in 1923. Thind's lawyers argued that, according to anthropologists, South Asians were Caucasians, indeed they were Aryans, like Germans and Scandinavians. Their brief read in part: "Being a high caste Indian and having no intermixture of Dravidian, or other alien blood, and coming from the Punjab, one of the most northwestern provinces of India, the original home of the Aryan conquerors, unless all the historical, ethnological and philological authorities cited in this brief are disregarded it must be held that Bhagat Singh Thind belongs to the Caucasian or white race." The same court that had found that Takao Ozawa was not White, despite his very light skin color, because he was not a Caucasian, found that Thind was not White, despite the fact that he was a Caucasian:

> What we now hold is that the words "free white persons" are words of common speech, to be interpreted in accordance with the understanding of the common man, synonymous with the word "Caucasian" only as that word is popularly understood. ... whatever may be the speculations of the ethnologist, [Caucasian] does not include the body of people to whom the appellee belongs. It is a matter of familiar observation and knowledge that *the physical group characteristics* of the Hindus render them readily distinguishable from the various groups of persons in this country commonly recognized as white.

That is, White people knew who White people were, and neither Japanese nor South Asians were White people.[78]

For Bhagat Singh Thind, the consequences were not harsh. He continued to live in the United States as a resident non-citizen. He earned a PhD, wrote several books and many pamphlets, lectured across the country on metaphysics blending Sikh beliefs with Emerson and Thoreau, lived in Hollywood, and was guru to members of the emerging movie industry.[79] But not everyone had it so good. The federal government hunted out Asian Indians and denaturalized at least sixty-five of those who had been awarded citizenship. Vaisho Das Bagai was so disheartened that he left a note that read in part: "But now they come to me and say, I am no longer an American citizen. ... What have I made of myself and my children? We cannot exercise our rights, we cannot leave this country. Humility and insults, who are responsible for all of this? I do not choose to live a life of an interned person. ... Is life worth living in a gilded cage? Obstacles this way, blockades that way, and the bridges burnt behind." Then he killed himself.[80]

Racial and gender hierarchies reinforced one another. For most of California's history it was illegal for Whites and Asians to marry. So when Gladys Emery, daughter of the Archdeacon of Grace Cathedral, wanted to marry Gunjiro Aoki, son of the head of the Japanese Episcopal mission in San Francisco, in 1909, they had to run away to the Northwest to do so. They were physically beaten and run out of Gladys's home town of Corte Madera, California. Chased by mobs and reporters up the coast, they were run out of Portland, too. Finally they found a minister in Seattle who would marry them. But on marrying an "alien ineligible to citizenship," Gladys Emery Aoki lost her own U.S. citizenship and became just such an alien herself. The couple had five children and the marriage lasted more than two decades until Gunjiro's death. In 1933, at the age of forty-five, the widow Aoki applied to be reinstated as a U.S. citizen. A federal judge agreed to do so, but she had to change her name to Oakie to complete the re-investiture into the White race.[81]

The placement of Mexican Americans with regard to Whiteness has always been a more complicated calculus. As we saw in Chapter 4, the Treaty of Guadalupe Hidalgo granted U.S. citizenship status like that of native Whites to former Mexican citizens following the U.S.-Mexican War. But that legal status was always limited by the practical, social relegation of Mexican Americans to a subordinate racial standing (and in fact, many former Mexican citizens did not ever receive the formal American citizenship they were promised by that treaty). By the end of the nineteenth century, Mexican Americans clearly were not White in the American racial system. Yet a legal decision by a West Texas federal court in 1897 did recognize them as just a bit different from other non-White peoples. *In re Rodriquez* declared that Mexican citizens, though not exactly White, could still be naturalized, because of the treaty.[82]

Racialist Pseudoscience and Its Offspring

As such distinctions evolved, they came increasingly to depend on a development within the scientific community that began in the Enlightenment in Europe and expanded with the European push for colonies around the world in the nineteenth century: pseudoscientific racial thinking.[83] That is, people styling themselves as scientists made what they presented as racial distinctions and created hierarchies of those racial groups using supposedly scientific methods, categories, and ideas. (It should be remembered that the scientific class did not enjoy in those days quite the high regard for intellectual dispassion and investigatory care that they were granted in later decades, and in any case, that there is not a great deal of similarity between the methods of scientists in those days and these.)

The founding father of this movement was Karl Linne, a Swedish botanist and path-breaking scientist who took for himself the grander name Carolus Linnaeus, perhaps with the thought that he ought to have a name that sounded like a philosopher's. In the 1750s Linnaeus did future generations the estimable service of creating a system for classifying all living things into a nested hierarchy of categories. Every organism belonged to one of two kingdoms, plant or animal. Then, proceeding downward through a multiplying hierarchy, organisms were divided into various phyla, the phyla into classes, the classes into orders, and thence to families, genera, and species. Supposedly, the species were fully distinct one from another. It was all very tidy, and it was quite an efficient device for organizing information about a multitude of organisms. For generations, neither working scientists nor the thinking public had reason to question Linnaeus's system. True, species were not quite as sealed off from one another as the system represented them to be, and true, there were a lot of organisms like bacteria that were neither plant nor animal, but still the system had a kind of elemental beauty to it. It was not exactly a tested scientific theory so much as it was abstract philosophizing based on a lot of data about the structures of north European plants and much less about other organisms. Yet it was useful for organizing a lot of information, and people thought of it as scientific.[84]

Subsequent generations of European scientists elaborated Linnaeus's system in several ways. On one hand, working biologists examined innumerable species, delimited them with care, discovered new ones, explored the relationships among them, and so on—all against the intellectual backdrop of Linnaeus's categories. That is, they developed the science of biology and what they called natural history. Taking off in another direction, philosophical people with the inclination to think about human beings worked Linnaeus's idea of species one step further, down to asserting that there were several distinct races of humankind, each with a separate physiognomy, intellect, and moral character. These were the pseudoscientific racialist speculators. Georges-Louis Leclerc, comte de Buffon, a French aristocrat and amateur naturalist, published his *Histoire Naturelle, Generale et Particuliere* in forty-four volumes between 1748 and 1804. He argued that all humans were one species, but that they were divided into several races, each with its own location on the planet, its own physical type, character, and intellectual propensities. The sources of the physical, intellectual, and moral differences, thought Buffon, came mainly from climate.[85]

Johann Friedrich Blumenbach, working in the 1770s, decided that there were precisely five races—European, Mongolian, Ethiopian, American, and Malay—into which all human beings could be divided. He decided further that Europeans had been the original race, and that the others had diverged and degenerated from European stock. Finally, he divided each race up into what he called "nations": what people much later would come to call "ethnic groups."[86] Next up was Georges Léopold Cuvier, who decided that the Europeans, who by now were being called "Caucasians," were the most beautiful of the races. They were called Caucasians, partly because some thought those mountains their point of origin, but mainly because the people from those mountains were the most beautiful White people in Cuvier's eyes: "Various nations in the vicinity of Caucasus, the Georgians and Circassians, are … the handsomest on earth." Cuvier was a scientist and chancellor of the University of Paris, but this racial speculating sounds as if Cuvier had left science behind somewhere and wandered into poetry.[87]

The villain of the piece, if there be one, was another French aristocrat, Joseph Arthur, comte de Gobineau. In a massively influential treatise, *The Inequality of Human Races* (1853 to 1855), Gobineau arranged the races in a strict hierarchy of intellect, ability, and morality: Whites, Asians, Indians of the Americas, Malays, and Africans. Race, he said, explained everything in human affairs and human history. Some of his chapter titles give the flavor of his ideas: "Degeneration: The Mixture of Racial Elements," "Racial Inequality is Not the Result of Institutions," "Some Anthropologists Regard Man as Having a Multiple Origin," "Racial Differences are Permanent," "The Human Races are Intellectually Unequal," "The Different Languages are Unequal, and Correspond Perfectly in Relative Merit to the Races that Use Them." And again, when he spoke of race and beauty: "Those who are most akin to us come nearest to beauty; such are the degenerate Aryan stocks of India and Persia, and the Semitic people who are least infected by contact with the black race. As these races recede from the white type, their features and limbs become incorrect in form; they acquire defects of proportion which, in the races that are completely foreign to us, end by producing an extreme ugliness." Richard Wagner welcomed Gobineau into his Bayreuth circle when he wore out his welcome in France, and Adolf Hitler admired his writing in a later generation.[88]

By the time these ideas reached Gobineau, what had hitherto been science—speculative science, to be sure, but arguably science nonetheless—was shading over into something quite different: popular intellectual underpinnings for a racialized public policy. Perhaps in part because of such public popularity, the racialist ideas of Blumenbach, Gobineau, and the others continued to shape scientific orthodoxy, especially among avatars of the growing discipline of physical anthropology. So one saw books like *The Races of Europe* (1899), by William Ripley, a professor of sociology at MIT and of anthropology at Columbia. Ripley's book had a lot of pictures of "racial types"—not just five big races, but subsidiary ethnic groups, and maps that showed the distribution of people according to their cephalic indexes. The cephalic index was an attempt to make racial and ethnic distinctions look more like science by quantifying them. One selected a "typical" member of an ethnic group, measured the breadth and length of that person's head, and calculated the relationship of those two numbers as a percent. Each head shape was supposed to have its own characteristic temperament and intellectual capability.[89]

A. H. Keane, in a 1901 book, *Ethnology*, which became the standard textbook on its subject for generations, presented the family tree of humankind (which he called "hominidae," perhaps because that sounded more scientific than "humankind"). He presented Anglo-Saxons as the central branch of the human species, with Anglo-Americans and other worldwide colonizers as their fullest expression. Slavs branched off earlier and were further removed from the Anglo-Saxon core group; Southern Europeans, Semites, and Ainu before that; Polynesians before that; Asians before that; and Africans (with subgroups including Australian aborigines and Melanesians) having diverged so long ago as to be almost a separate species. He presented, of course, no data except skin color and prejudice on which to base his schema or the historical relationships he supposed to have existed between peoples (Figure 6.14).[90]

Vice-president of the British Anthropological Institute and a professor of Hindustani at University College, London, Keane laid out his ideas about the current state of the races in a table I have reproduced as Table 6.4.

Keane laid religion and temperament alongside eye shape, nose shape, and skin color, as if they were all genetically determined. He used big words that sounded scientific (brachycephalous, orthognathus, mesodont, and so on). But he revealed his underlying social agenda—to excuse slavery and colonial domination of Whites over darker peoples—in the final row: temperament. Dividing a welter of peoples into four ideal physical types, and masking his enterprise in a cloud of pseudoscientific jargon, he expected his reader to follow him as he leapt to conclude that each type had a characteristic temperament that explained its social position. Hence, African-descended people were "Sensuous, indolent, improvident; fitful, passionate, and cruel … easy acceptance of the yoke of slavery; science and art undeveloped." Europeans, by contrast, were "Active, enterprising, imaginative," and either "serious, steadfast, solid and stolid" or "fiery, impulsive, fickle"—but in either case good at science and the arts. Africans were biologically destined to be slaves, said Keane and other pseudoscientists. Europeans were biologically destined to be scientists and poets. If it were in their genes, the implication was, it was no one's fault. This passed for science in turn-of-the-century America and Britain.

Pseudoscience Becomes Popular Knowledge

As such ideas became accepted scientific orthodoxy, they became unquestioned popular orthodoxy. Consider the map shown in Figure 6.15, which appeared in the

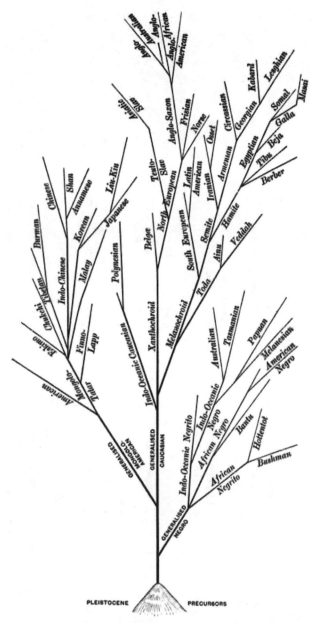

FAMILY TREE OF THE HOMINIDÆ.

Figure 6.14 Family tree of humankind.

1904 *Annual Report* of the U.S. Commissioner-General of Immigration. Its "grand division of race" presents the peoples who came to the United States as "Slavic," "Teutonic," "Iberic," "Keltic," "Mongolic," and "Hebrew," as if each of these "racial" distinctions had some scientific meaning. Similarly, one of the forty-one volumes of the 1910–1911 report of the Dillingham Commission, a comprehensive report on

Table 6.4 Racial Types in Pseudoscience

	Ideal Negro Type	Ideal Mongol Type	Ideal American Type	Ideal Caucasic Type
Hair	a. Short, jet black, frizzly, flat in transverse section, little or no beard; b. Reddish brown, woolly	Coarse, black, lustreless, lank, round in transverse section, beardless, but moustache common	Very long, coarse, black, lank, nearly round in section; beardless	a. Long, wavy, soft, flaxen; b. Long, straight, wiry, black; both oval in section; both full bearded
Color	a. Blackish; b. Yellowish brown	Yellowish	Coppery, yellowish	a. Florid; b. Pale
Skull	a. Dolichocephalous: 72 b. Brachycephalous: 83	Brachycephalous: 84	Mesaticephalous: 79	a. Dolichocephalous: 74 b. Brachycephalous: 83
Jaws	Prognathous: 60	Mesognathous: 68	Mesognathous: 72	Orthognathous: 76
Cheek bone	Small, moderately retreating	Prominent laterally	Moderately prominent	Small; unmarked
Nose	Very broad, flat, platyrrhine: 56	Very small, mesorrhine: 52	Large, bridged or aquiline, mesorrhine: 50	Large, straight or arched, leptorrhine: 46
Eyes	Large, round, prominent, black; yellowish cornea	Small, black, oblique, outerangle slightly elevated, vertical field of skin over inner canthus	Small, round, straight, sunken, black	a. Blue; b. Black: both moderately large and always straight
Teeth	Large (marcodont)	Medium (mesodont)	Medium (mesodont)	Small (microdont)
Stature	a. Above average: 5 ft. 10 in. b. Dwarfish: 4 ft.	Below the average: 5 ft. 4 in.	Above the average: 5 ft. 8 in.	a. Above average: 5 ft. 8 in. b. Average: 5 ft. 5 or 6 in.
Speech	Agglutinating of various prefix and postfix types	Agglutinating chiefly with post fixes; isolating with tones	Polysynthetic mainly	Chiefly inflecting; some agglutinating
Religion	Non-theistic; nature and ancestry worship; fetishism and witchcraft prevalent	Polytheistic; shamanism; Buddhism; Transmigration	Polytheistic; animism; nature worship	Monotheism: Judaism; Christianity; Mohammedanism
Temperament	Sensuous, indolent, improvident; fitful, passionate, and cruel, though often affectionate and faithful; little self-respect, hence easy acceptance of the yoke of slavery; science and art undeveloped	Sluggish, somewhat sullen, with little initiative but great endurance; generally frugal, thrifty and industrious, but moral standard low; science slightly, art and letters moderately developed	Moody, taciturn, wary; deep feelings masked by an impassive exterior; indifference to physical pain; science slightly, art moderately, letters scarcely at all developed	Active, enterprising, imaginative; a. serious, steadfast, solid and stolid; b. fiery, impulsive, fickle; science, art and letters highly developed in both.
	a = Negro; b = Negrito.			a = Xanthochroi; b = Melanochroi.

Source: A. H. Keane, *Ethnology* (Cambridge, U.K.: Cambridge University Press, 1901), 228.

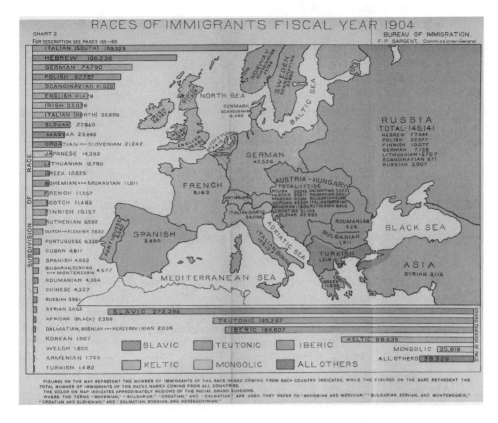

Figure 6.15 U.S. Government's map of immigrant origins.

U.S. immigration, was a *Dictionary of Races or Peoples* that purported to lay out a definitive list of races and ethnic groups, their locations in the world, their characters, physiognomies, and other material.[91]

It was a short step from pseudoscientific ideas that had made their way into public life to using those ideas to advocate particular public policies. In fact, there were published in the first decades of the twentieth century a slew of racist screeds against immigrants in general, Southern and Eastern European immigrants especially, and Asian immigrants most especially. Social and marital mixing among divergent ethnicities was a topic of particular scorn. None of the attacks was more pointed than Alfred Schultz's diatribe against race mixing and immigration, which he called "racial suicide." The book's full title tells its story: *Race or Mongrel? A brief history of the rise and fall of the ancient races of earth; a theory that the fall of nations is due to intermarriage with alien stocks; a demonstration that a nation's strength is due to racial purity; a prophecy that America will sink to early decay unless immigration is rigorously restricted.*[92]

One of the classic texts was Madison Grant's *The Passing of the Great Race.* Published first in 1916 and then in several later editions, *Passing* had an enormous influence on American public opinion, medical practice, and public policy. Grant argued that Europeans—and particularly a subset of them that he called at various stages Aryans, Nordics, and Teutons—were the central figures in all that was good, true, and beautiful in human history. He followed racial scientists in assigning scientific-sounding names to peoples—Dolicho-lepto, Lappanoid, and so on—and in assorting all European peoples into three groups: Nordics (Homo sapiens europeau), Alpines (Homo sapiens alpinus), and Mediterraneans (Homo sapiens mediterraneus). He arranged them according to what he believed to be their ancient linguistic roots, as well as their typical physical stature; eye, hair, and skin color; nose and face shape; and cephalic index. He claimed that each group, in addition to possessing a distinctive physical type, also possessed a particular temperament and set of intellectual capabilities. Teutons, for instance, were a branch of the Nordic race of Europeans. They were tall of frame and had long heads and high, narrow faces. Their hair ran from flaxen to chestnut but never to black, their eyes from blue to grey to green. They were gifted in intellectual and artistic pursuits. The common feature of all Nordics was that their languages descended from ancient Aryan roots. This set them apart from other European races in his schema.

One can catch the flavor of Grant's polemic in this excerpt, in which he dismisses the notion that non-Nordic immigrants could assimilate and become good Americans:

> With a pathetic and fatuous belief in the efficacy of American institutions and environment to reverse or obliterate immemorial hereditary tendencies, these newcomers were welcomed and given a share in our land and prosperity. The American taxed himself to sanitate and educate these poor helots, and as soon as they could speak English, encouraged them to enter into the political life, first of municipalities, and then of the nation.
>
> The result is showing plainly in the rapid decline of the birth rate of native Americans because the poorer classes of Colonial stock, where they still exist, will not bring children into the world to compete in the labor market with the Slovak, the Italian, the Syrian, and the Jew. The native American is too proud to mix socially with them, and is gradually withdrawing from the scene, abandoning to these aliens the land which he conquered and developed. The man of the old stock is being crowded out of many country districts by these foreigners, just as he is to-day being literally driven off the streets of New York City by the swarms of Polish Jews. These immigrants adopt the language of the native American; they wear his clothes; they steal his name; and they are beginning to take his women, but they seldom adopt his religion or understand his ideals, and while he is being elbowed out of his own home the American looks calmly abroad and urges on others the suicidal ethics which are exterminating his own race.

There was a German edition, and it has been said that *The Passing of the Great Race* was Adolf Hitler's favorite book and one of the works that inspired Nazi racial policies in Germany.[93]

Race or Mongrel? and *The Passing of the Great Race* were but early examplars in a very long line of popular polemics against non-Nordic immigration, based on spurious recourse to so-called science, stretching from that day to this. Lothrop Stoddard published an equally influential polemic, *The Rising Tide of Color against White World Supremacy*, in 1920. Section and chapter titles reveal the theme and tone: "The Rising Tide of Color," "The Ebbing Tide of White," "The Shattering of White Solidarity," "The Deluge on the Dikes," "The Crisis of the Ages." The book is resplendent with brightly colored maps showing racial distributions and nearly hysterical prose warning of fecund Asian and African hordes bent on taking over the world that hitherto had rightly been owned by White people.[94] Other books in this stream bore titles like *The Conflict of Colour, The Revolt Against Civilization: The Menace of the Under Man, The Mongol in Our Midst, Racial Realities in Europe, The Twilight of the White Races, The Racial Elements in World History, The Alien in Our Midst, Clashing Tides of Colour, Apes Men and Morons*, and *Twilight of Man*.[95]

Perfecting Humans

Not all pseudoscientific racism was directed toward blocking further immigration to the United States. Some of these ideas were used on unfortunate members of subordinate races and classes already here, in the form of a new pseudoscience: eugenics.[96] Eugenics grew to become a dominant influence from the 1920s through the 1950s in several scholarly circles: biology, anthropology, sociology, law, and social work. The idea was that science could gauge the heredity of individuals, use that knowledge to judge their mental abilities and their degree of physical perfection, and then use *that* knowledge to perfect the human race by weeding out the unfit and selecting the fittest for special benefits, including increased access to procreation. Originally the brainchild of Francis Galton, a British aristocrat and adventurer who mapped parts of Africa and studied how weather worked, the idea of perfecting the race by selective breeding took hold in the United States, Britain, and Germany more than in other countries. Eugenicists purported to bring together all the sciences in order to direct human evolution (Figure 6.16).

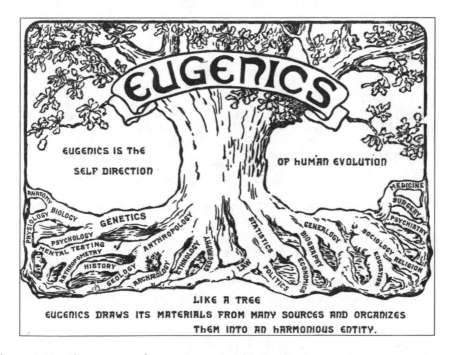

Figure 6.16 The science of eugenics, according to the Race Betterment Foundation, 1921.

Figure 6.17   The "Minnesota Baby" won the competition at the First National Conference on Race Betterment in 1914.

Some White Americans competed in the 1910s and 1920s, as Germans did in the 1930s and 1940s, to have babies who would be judged the finest physical and mental representatives of their race (Figure 6.17).

There was never a national, government-sponsored program in the United States, as there was in Germany, to breed Aryan super-babies. But there were attempts to prevent breeding by people whom eugenicists deemed to be inferior. The anti-immigrant campaign of the 1910s and 1920s was argued partly in eugenic terms. Eugenicists imposed a medical model of defective genetics on homosexuals. And, beginning in 1907, 30 states passed laws that empowered governments to force sterilization on women who were deemed to be "degenerates," "feeble-minded," "morally delinquent," or otherwise unfit. From Massachusetts to Hawai'i, girls and women were incarcerated; labeled "incorrigible" or "feeble-minded" because they appeared to enjoy sex or had borne babies out of wedlock; and sterilized—64,000 in all, most of them poor, and many of them women of color. American eugenicist Henry Laughlin helped take the show on the road, as one of the authors of the Nazi regime's "race hygiene" law; 2 million Germans were sterilized as a result.

Eugenics was the force behind the vogue of intelligence testing that swept the nation in the wake of World War I and has been with us ever since.[97] The first intelligence test was created in France by two Galton devotees, Alfred Binet and Theodore Simon. Charged by the French government in 1904 to devise a method by which to detect "mentally deficient" children, Simon and Binet devised a standardized series of questions and problems that, they said, could determine the "mental age" of a particular child. The goal was then to devise particular curricula to fit the educational needs of children of different mental ages. Binet perceived there to be a great deal of variability in mental age within any social group (and indeed within a given person over time), but those distinctions were lost as his test was brought to America in 1908 by H. H. Goddard, a former schoolteacher and University of Southern California (U.S.C.) football coach who was doing research at the Training School for Feeble-minded Girls and Boys in Vineland, New Jersey.

Goddard distributed thousands of English-language copies of the test across the country and began a lifelong campaign to bring it into every arena of American life. He and other advocates convinced the U.S. Army to use a similar test in the assignment of soldiers during World War I. As Lewis Terman, another devotee of intelligence testing, put it, "If the Army machine is to work smoothly and efficiently, it is as important to fit the job to the man as to fit the ammunition to the gun."[98] In 1912, Goddard convinced the authorities at Ellis Island to let him test immigrants, using two assistants. One assistant would scan the room for people who, to his eyes, looked stupid. They were pulled out of line and tested by the second assistant. If the test found them to be, in Goddard's terminology, an "idiot," an "imbecile," or a "moron," they were denied entry to the country. Goddard claimed that 40 percent of steerage passengers were "feeble-minded." As a result, the numbers of would-be entrants who were sent back skyrocketed.[99] Carl Brigham, one of the Army testers, contended that the tests indicated an ethnic difference in intelligence. Echoing the categories of Madison Grant, he concluded that the Alpine and Mediterranean "races"—that is, people of central and southern European origin—were "intellectually inferior to members of the Nordic race."[100]

New versions of the Binet-Simon test, including the famous Stanford-Binet test devised by Terman, made their way into business hiring practices and classrooms across the country. Goddard, Terman, Brigham, and others not only convinced the American public that intelligence was a measurable quantity. Without much scientific evidence, they also persuaded people that intelligence was an inherited, not an acquired trait, and that different groups of people—including races—tended to have different amounts of intelligence per capita. These ideas—founded in racial prejudice and nourished by dubious science—have not died. Goddard's and Terman's tests are the direct ancestors of today's SAT and GRE examinations.

Even scholars who held benign attitudes toward immigrants and peoples of color found their ideas all wrapped up with pseudoscientific racialist thinking. Caroline Bond Day, a Radcliffe-educated instructor at all-Black Atlanta University, was a protégé of the anthropometrist Earnest Hooton. Hooton described Day as "an approximate mulatto, having about half Negro and half White blood." The fractions seemed important to both Day and her mentor. Hooton sponsored the publication of Day's *Study of Some Negro-White Families in the United States* by Harvard's Peabody Museum. It is an inexpressably detailed accounting of the body parts of several hundred people whom Day interviewed, measured, and photographed, all of whom she marked as having some racial mixture. She displayed hundreds of pictures of racially mixed people, tying them together in family trees and listing them by racial fractions ("Jewett Washington, 7/16 N 9/16 W"), across scores of quarto pages. The book offered nearly a hundred tables recording detailed measurements of body parts for various categories of people. There were four tables on lips alone ("Lips, Integumental Thickness," "Lips, Membranous Thickness," "Lips, Eversion," "Lip Seam"), eleven on noses, and of course, cephalic indexes. Day's work is a monument to misbegotten precision and the piling up of data without thinking about what it is for.[101] Julie Kelley made a similar study of "Eyefold Inheritance in Inter-Racial Marriages" among Asians in Hawai'i, with similar photographs, measurements, and tables. Sidney Gulick, one of the great defenders of Asian immigrants against their critics, nonetheless felt compelled to preface his book on race in Hawai'i with thirty-two race-fractionated photographs, and to include sections on such issues as "Psycho-Physical Race Differences," "Psychological Race-Differences," "Intelligence Tests on Race-Mixtures," and "Comparative Racial Intelligence (IQ)."[102]

Beginning in the 1920s, mainstream social science struck back, with a systematic refutation of pseudobiological ideas about race. Frank Hankins made a head-on assault in 1926 with *The Racial Basis of Civilization: A Critique of the Nordic Doctrine*. He inveighed against "Aryanism ... Gobinism ... Teutonism ... Celticism ... Gallicism ... Anglo-Saxonism and Nordicism" on philosophical, scientific, and pragmatic grounds. Legendary anthropologist Franz Boas and a generation of disciples made their careers (and the discipline of cultural anthropology) out of confronting and gradually undercutting racialist pseudoscience and substituting cultural analysis. In mainstream academic circles, pseudoscientific racialist ideas had been fairly conclusively refuted by the 1940s, although it took another two decades for the public to begin to catch on.[103]

Even so, throwbacks to pseudoscientific racism continued to pop up now and then. For more than four decades beginning in the late 1930s, Harvard anthropologist Carleton Coon wrote a series of big books to an ever-shrinking audience, in which he pushed a pseudoscientific racial angle of analysis. The books lacked the vitriol and obvious policy agenda of Grant and Stoddard, but Coon's analysis was not much different than theirs. Despite his pretense to objectivity, Coon did have a barely hidden policy agenda. In 1959 he joined a number of colleagues in forming the International Society for the Advancement of Ethnology and Eugenics, with the expressed purpose of linking race and intelligence in order to win a reversal of the *Brown v. Board of Education* ruling that aimed to end school segregation.[104] Sociobiology in the 1980s and its stepchild of the 1990s, evolutionary psychology, expanded upon several of the tracks laid down by Keane, Grant, Stoddard, and Galton. But in scholarly circles, these have remained minority opinions.[105]

If the number of purportedly scientific treatments based on racialist pseudoscientific ideas has declined, policy advocacy based partly on racialist pseudoscience is still quite common. Stretching from Richard Herrnstein and Charles Murray's 1994 screed against affirmative action, *The Bell Curve*, through Peter Brimelow's *Alien Nation* (1995), Samuel Huntington's *The Clash of Civilizations* (1996), and Jon Entine's *Taboo: Why Black Athletes Dominate Sports and Why We're Afraid to Talk About It* (2000), to Patrick Buchanan's *The Death of the West: How Dying Populations and Immigrant Invasions Imperil Our Country and Civilization* (2002), popular racism based partly on long-discredited pseudoscience has been a regular feature on best-seller lists. The ilk of Madison Grant and Lothrop Stoddard have not disappeared.[106]

Anti-Immigrant Movements

A series of anti-immigrant movements swept across the United States from the 1900s through the 1920s. Drawing from the deep well of American nativism, the anti-Chinese movement of the 1870s and 1880s came back to life in the new century as the anti-Japanese movement. Anti-immigrant sentiment broadened, as the open-hearted impulses of the settlement house movement to teach immigrants life skills gave way to an increasingly militant Americanization movement during World War I. After the war, the anti-immigrant tide swelled, resulting in a drastic curtailment of further immigration from several parts of the world.

The Anti-Japanese Movement

First came the anti-Japanese movement. Japanese immigrants were few in number, but they became the object of a lot of immigration policy. Initially greeted by West Coast racist Whites as a welcome improvement over Chinese laborers, the Japanese who came between the 1890s and the 1910s soon found they had inherited the entire anti-Chinese program.[107] They were criticized as unassimilable, unclean, immoral drivers-down of White people's wages. All this came as a shock to the Japanese government, which had carefully nurtured a positive international image in the hope of avoiding the quasicolonial fate that had befallen China. The Japanese authorities had been extremely careful to allow only educated, solvent migrants to go abroad, and had used consular staff to monitor them carefully. Nonetheless, the post-1900 drive to renew the Chinese exclusion act spilled over into more generalized protests against, and calls for the expulsion of, all Asian immigrants. The Asiatic Exclusion League lumped Japanese and Chinese together on a racial basis as a threat to the welfare of White American workers:

> The conditions of life are, in the last analysis, determined by the conditions of labor. ... The Caucasian and the Asiatic races are unassimilable. Contact between these races must result, under the conditions of industrial life obtaining in North America, in injury to the former. ... The preservation of the Caucasian race upon American soil, and particularly upon the West shore thereof, necessitates the adoption of all possible measures to prevent or minimize the immigration of Asiatics to America.[108]

The *San Francisco Chronicle* whipped up its readers with lurid headlines:

"Japanese a Menace to American Women"
"The Yellow Peril—How Japanese Crowd out the White Race"
"Brown Men an Evil in the Public Schools"
"Brown Artisans Steal Brains of Whites"
"Crime and Poverty Go Hand in Hand with Asiatic Labor"[109]

Gangs of White thugs beat Japanese immigrants and tourists on the streets of San Francisco and other Western cities. They broke windows and looted stores. Progressive politician Grover Johnson added a sexual dimension to the race-baiting. Some Japanese youths were trying to learn English. Since few adult classes were available, teenagers were sometimes placed in elementary schools with native children who had similar English skills. Johnson complained: "I am responsible to the mothers and fathers of Sacramento County who have their little daughters sitting side by side in the school rooms with matured Japs, with their base minds, their lascivious thoughts, multiplied by their race and strengthened by their mode of life. ... I have seen Japanese twenty-five years old sitting in the seats next to the pure maids of California. ... I shudder to think of such a condition."[110] Johnson and the Asiatic Exclusion League pressed Congress to exclude all Asians.

Under mounting public pressure, the San Francisco school board acted in 1906 to segregate Japanese and Korean children by requiring them to attend the school the city had already established for Chinese and Black children. The Japanese government lodged a furious protest with President Theodore Roosevelt. Roosevelt shared the exclusionists' belief in Anglo-Saxon racial superiority, but as one who spoke loudly and carried a very small stick, he was loath to offend the leaders of Asia's new military powerhouse, which had just thumped a European power in the Russo-Japanese war. He sent a cabinet member to San Francisco to investigate and persuaded the San Francisco school board to reverse their segregation order for Japanese students. In return, Roosevelt persuaded the Japanese government to sign the Gentlemen's Agreement, as it was called, in which Japan promised to tighten up its emigration policy, halting the migration abroad of working men.

The anti-Japanese forces were temporarily mollified. The Gentlemen's Agreement did not, however, ban wives and children from joining their family members in the United States. In the ensuing decade and a half, thousands of Japanese women and children did just that. This seemed like betrayal to the anti-Japanese forces. In 1913 they prevailed upon the California legislature to pass the Alien Land Law. The law, quickly copied by Washington and several other states, forbade "aliens ineligible to citizenship"—that is, Asians—to buy real estate or lease it for more than three years. U. S. Webb, California's attorney general and a co-author of the law, made clear its intent: "to limit their [Japanese immigrants'] presence by curtailing their privileges which they may enjoy here; for they will not come in large numbers and long abide with us, if they may not acquire land."[111]

Many Issei became discouraged by all this abuse and started planning their return to Japan. Others, however, saw the holes in the law and set about circumventing it. The Issei were ineligible for citizenship, but their children, the Nisei, were American citizens by birth. It was an easy matter to buy land in the name of minor children and appoint oneself as trustee. Others made arrangements with citizen neighbors or set up dummy corporations with Nisei paper leaders but with

Issei in fact in control. The White population tried to tighten the land law via a 1920 initiative, but that proved equally unenforceable. The Japanese stayed in West Coast agriculture, but they came increasingly under pressure as the century progressed. There followed an ever-escalating national debate about whether or not Japanese and other Asians ever could become members of American society. That culminated in 1924, in a national decision that they could not.[112]

The Americanization Campaign

One of the usual processes through which any immigrant went was the gradual putting off of the ways of her or his old country and taking on the language, clothing, posture, habits, and ideals of the new. In this sense, Americanization was an unavoidable and perhaps unproblematic part of the migration experience. Even if one did not intend to stay, one inevitably changed during one's sojourn in the United States. Yet Americanization did not everywhere and for everyone mean the same thing. In the lands that were seized from Mexico, Americanization during the 1850s to 1870s meant not individual change for the immigrants, but massive change for society: the wholesale replacement of local language, customs, laws, and institutions with American imports as the United States ingested its colonial domain.

Beginning in eastern cities and spreading throughout the country in the 1900s, 1910s, and 1920s, White reformers conducted a campaign to Americanize immigrant peoples.[113] It began with a spirit of benevolent condescension and ended in a spirit of attack and condemnation. The roots of the Americanization campaign can be found in certain strains of reform dating from the Second Great Awakening—the desire to uplift the toiling masses and make them good citizens with middle-class White values.[114] Those missionary-minded reformers who went south after the Civil War to establish schools for newly freed slaves were operating in the same spirit as were teachers at Indian boarding schools and turn-of-the-century settlement house workers. Home missionaries working out of inner-city churches, along with settlement house workers, ran night schools to teach the English language, American history and geography, and everyday cultural skills to immigrants.

This was all done in the name of helping people who were new to the country find their way in America. But there was also an element of social control. The idea underlying the Americanization movement was to remake immigrants and racially subject peoples into persons capable of functioning smoothly in America culturally, so that they would form a dependable servant class who could communicate with their social betters. This was especially true as the Americanization idea moved into the workplace. The Ford Motor Company ran an Americanization program through its Ford Sociological Department that was designed, in historian Stephen Meyer's words, "for the resolution of a key industrial problem—the problem of work-discipline and of the adjustment of new workers to the factory environment. ... when the programs emanated from within factory gates, they had their darker side. The issue was not simply different national or ethnic cultures, but also pre-industrial and industrial cultures." Americanization meant getting immigrant workers to accept the time clock and assembly line discipline (Figure 6.18).[115]

Scholars conspired in the Americanization movement. The emerging discipline of sociology went to work after World War I at the behest of the Carnegie Foundation and produced a series of studies designed to measure and promote the

Figure 6.18 An Americanization class at the Holcomb Steel Company.

Americanization of immigrant peoples in the areas of schooling, community formation, culture, agriculture, health, household maintenance, the press, citizenship, the legal system, and industrial relationships.[116] These studies, though often sympathetic to immigrants, nonetheless treated them as an undifferentiated mass. Who particular immigrants were and how they lived their lives—these were not issues. The issue was how to turn immigrants into Americans, by systematically analyzing every arena of social life and then making plans to transform it into undifferentiated Americanness. Many other scholarly studies, notoriously those undertaken by members of the University of Chicago department of sociology and their academic offspring at Stanford, U.S.C., the University of Washington, and the University of Hawai'i, were all part of a related attempt to study immigrants in order to understand them—less for the purpose of empowering them than in order to control them.[117]

The ugly side of the Americanization movement became especially evident after World War I's anti-German hysteria and the 1919 Red Scare brought a hard edge of anti-immigrant feeling into public discourse. Gradually, in the late 1910s and 1920s, the Americanization movement was transformed from immigrant advocacy into part of the longstanding anti-immigrant movement. According to Robert MacNeil and William Cran, in the "Good English Makes Good Americans" campaign, "Children earned points for snitching to teacher on language errors of their classmates." The Chicago Woman's Club American Speech Committee introduced the following loyalty oath for schoolchildren:

I love the United States of America. I love my country's flag. I love my country's language. I promise:

1. That I will not dishonor my country's speech by leaving off the last syllables of words.
2. That I will say a good American "yes" and "no" in place of an Indian grunt "um-hum" and "nup-um" or a foreign "ya," or "yeh" and "nope."
3. That I will do my best to improve American speech by avoiding loud, rough tones, by enunciating distinctly, and by speaking pleasantly, clearly, and sincerely.
4. That I will learn to articulate correctly as many words as possible during the year.[118]

The mood of the Americanization movement had shifted decisively, from helping immigrants function in the U.S. context to making darn sure they conformed to American ways.

The Campaign for Immigration Restriction

The anti-Japanese movement and the Americanization campaign were two major threads in a broad movement that led ultimately to immigration restriction. Opposition to immigrant peoples has been a major theme in American history. We have witnessed earlier episodes, such as Benjamin Franklin's railing against Germans and the anti-Catholic movement of the 1850s and after. Often, the immigrant-bashing sentiment was overwhelmed by the we-are-a-nation-of-immigrants rhapsody sung by George Washington, Hector St. John de Crèvecoeur, Emma Lazarus, and countless others. But, then, if the immigrants in question were not White, the tune changed. From the anti-Chinese movement to the Alien Land Laws and beyond, dark-skinned immigrants were not welcomed in the United States.

The First World War temporarily interrupted the flow of migrants from Europe. The American public emerged from the war exhilarated, with an exalted idea of American prowess on the international stage, but uninterested in the world at large. The Red Scare of 1919 was couched largely in terms of the menace of a foreign ideology—Bolshevism—that some saw as a threat to American institutions and ideals. Anti-immigration writers railed against what they regarded as a horde of unassimilable foreigners, whipping out the arguments of Grant, Stoddard, and the rest.[119]

The Dillingham Commission Report set the wheels in motion for restricting immigration.[120] Congress had commissioned the report in 1907 to investigate and make recommendations for immigration policy reform. Headed by U.S. Senator William P. Dillingham and including two other senators, three Congress members, and three others appointed by the president, the U.S. Immigration Commission and its staff returned a forty-two volume report in 1911. They had taken testimony from hundreds of expert witnesses—sociologists, economists, business leaders, diplomats, and policy people, but not many immigrants. They surveyed economic conditions that led to migration out of Europe, the status of children, steerage conditions, and state and federal laws regarding immigration. The largest portion of the study (eighteen volumes) examined the impact of immigrants on numerous U.S. industries, from iron and steel to meatpacking to glove manufacturing. There was a special volume on Japanese immigrants, and two devoted to the theories of scientific racism.

The commission's recommendations became the basis of wholesale changes in immigration policy. The summary recommendation read in part: "While the American people, as in the past, welcome the oppressed of other lands, care should be taken that immigration be such both in quality and quantity as not to make too difficult the process of assimilation. ... [L]egislation concerning the admission of aliens should be based primarily upon economic or business considerations."[121] Following specific Dillingham Commission recommendations, in 1917 Congress required (over President Wilson's veto) that any would-be immigrant must be literate in some language in order to enter. It created an Asiatic Barred Zone—everything except the Philippines and Japan, which the United States was still handling gingerly—from which no immigrants at all would be allowed. Four years later, Congress passed an Emergency Quota Act to cut the immigration flow. It provided "That the number of aliens of any nationality who may be admitted ... in any fiscal year shall be limited to 3 percentum of the number of foreign-born persons of such nationality resident in the United States as determined by the United Census of 1910." It set a total cap of 350,000 per year, down more than two-thirds from prewar levels; 55 percent were to come from Northwest Europe, 45 percent from the rest of the world (mainly Southern and Eastern Europe).[122]

That set the stage for a culture-shattering debate over race, alleged cultural proclivities, and who was fit to be an American. The South Carolina Grand Dragon of the Ku Klux Klan, then a powerful and respected force in American public life, set the terms of the anti-immigrant debate on racial and what he believed to be cultural grounds. Some people, he argued, could not ever become real Americans and must be kept out:

In my opinion a law should be enacted restricting immigration to the United States for a period of at least ten years. ... The immigrants who come to this country form communities by themselves and congregate in the great cities. Paupers, diseased and criminals predominate among those who land upon American soil. They have a very low standard of morals, they are unable to speak our language and a great majority of them are unable to read and write their own language. ...

There are more than 14,000,000 foreign born in the United States. ... How do we expect to naturalize and make good citizens of those 14,000,000 foreigners who are already in this country unless we require them to speak our language and print their newspaper and magazines in English? We can never have a homogeneous population unless we require every man, woman and child in America to speak the English language. And it will be a most powerful means to stopping the spread of unsound doctrines, the spread of anarchy and Bolshevism. ...

Of the 805,000 admitted to the United States in 1921 more than half, 432,000, were Jews, Italians, Armenians, Greeks, Japanese, Chinese, and Finns, races which generation after generation maintain their own churches, customs, languages, schools, and social affiliations. ... [L]ast year 53,254 Hebrew aliens came to the United States. ... The Japanese question is another great menace. ...

The present 3 percent admission law on the basis of the 1910 census is the first attempt of Congress to restrict immigration. It was passed just at the time when a flood of destitute, restless wanderers and adventurers had an eye on the United States. This law substantially checked the alien flood, but it has not given the relief needed.[123]

Senator Ellison DuRant Smith made the case for a new law, the Johnson–Reed Act, shortly before it was passed in 1924:

[T]he time has arrived when we should shut the door. ... Americanize what we have, and save the resources of America for the natural increase of our population. ... [O]ur particular ideas, social, moral, religious, and political, have demonstrated ... that we have the highest ideals of any member of the human family or any nation. ... [We are] the descendants of those who cleared the forests, conquered the savage, stood at arms and won their liberty from their mother country, England. I think we now have sufficient population in our country for us to shut the door and to breed up a pure, unadulterated American citizenship. ... . It is the breed of the dog in which I am interested. I would like for the Members of the Senate to read the book just recently published by Madison Grant, *The Passing of the Great Race*. Thank God we have in America perhaps the largest percentage of any country in the world of the pure, unadulterated Anglo-Saxon stock. ... It is for the preservation of that splendid stock that has characterized us that I would make this not an asylum for the oppressed of all countries.[124]

A few old Progressives and new liberals argued against it, but the Johnson–Reed Act passed easily, and the United States launched on a new future—White and Northwest European on purpose. The act reduced the proportion of the population allowed in from each nationality to 2 percent—not of the 1910 census, but of the 1890 census, before South and East Europeans had begun to appear in large numbers. Furthermore, it lowered the total ceiling to 165,000 people. And it banned Asians entirely (except Filipinos, who were still residents of an American colony and so came outside the quotas). The impact of the Johnson–Reed Act's initial quotas is apparent in Table 6.5.

The lines were clear and they were racial: Northwest Europeans were welcome in as large numbers as cared to come (indeed, the German and British quotas were never filled); Southern and Eastern Europeans were not welcome and would only be tolerated in very small numbers; and Asians were banned entirely.

The argument of the day was that the United States was being inundated by a tidal wave of barely assimilable foreigners. The tide must be stopped, reversed if possible. Was that conviction in fact accurate? It seems that the supporters of immigration restriction were playing fast and loose with the facts. Were immigrants a larger percentage of the American people in the early decades of the twentieth century than they had been in previous eras? Not by much. Table 6.6 gives the number of immigrants who entered the United States each decade, along with the number of immigrants who came in that decade per 100 U.S. residents at the start of the decade.

In two decades (the 1880s and the 1900s), immigration numbers bumped high enough that slightly more than 10 immigrants entered the country per 100 U.S.

Table 6.5 Initial Immigration Quotas in the Johnson–Reed Act (Total: 164,667)

Northwest Europe and Scandinavia		Eastern and Southern Europe		Other Countries	
Country	Quota	Country	Quota	Country	Quota
Germany	51,227	Poland	5,982	Africa (not Egypt)	1,100
Britain	34,007	Italy	3,845		
Ireland	28,567	Czechoslovakia	3,073	Armenia	124
Sweden	9,561	Russia	2,248	Australia	121
Norway	6,453	Yugoslavia	671	Palestine	100
France	3,954	Romania	603	Syria	100
Denmark	2,789	Portugal	503	Turkey	100
Switzerland	2,081	Hungary	473	Egypt	100
The Netherlands	1,648	Lithuania	344	New Zealand and Pacific	100
Austria	785	Latvia	142		
Belgium	512	Spain	131	All others	1,900
Finland	471	Estonia	124		
Danzig (free city)	228	Albania	100		
		Bulgaria	100		
Iceland	100	Greece	100		
Luxembourg	100				
Total Number	142,483	**Total Number**	18,439	**Total Number**	3,745
Total Percentage	86.5%	**Total Percentage**	11.2%	**Total Percentage**	2.3%

Source: Statistical Abstract of the United States (Washington, DC: Government Printing Office, 1929), 100.

residents already here. The numbers for those decades were about the same size as the comparable numbers for the period 1840 to 1860. For other parts of the period under discussion in this chapter, the percentages of immigrants added to the U.S. population were actually *below* the averages for the entire nineteenth century.

If newcoming immigrants were not so many in number, what about the cumulative effect of all the immigrants who had come in previous decades? Table 6.7 gives the percentages of foreign-born people who lived in the United States during each census year, compared to the total U.S. population that year.

The percentage of foreign-born people in the U.S. population in the first few decades of the twentieth century—the era of the drive to restrict immigration—hovered around 14 percent, not much more than at any time in the second half of the nineteenth century. There was an immigrant tide, but it was hardly a tsunami.

One cannot escape the conclusion that the Immigration Act of 1924 was based more on fears generated by racialist pseudoscience than by the actual scale or sources of immigration. President Harry Truman looked back on this event with disdain a generation later:

Table 6.6 Immigrants Compared to U.S. Residents, 1820–2000

Decade	Number of Immigrant Arrivals	Immigrants per 100 U.S. Residents
1820–1830	151,824	1.6
1831–1840	12,866,020	4.7
1841–1850	1,713,251	10.0
1851–1860	2,598,214	11.2
1861–1870	2,314,824	7.1
1871–1880	2,812,191	7.3
1881–1890	5,246,613	10.5
1891–1900	3,687,564	5.9
1901–1910	8,795,386	11.6
1911–1920	5,735,811	6.2
1921–1930	4,107,209	3.9
1931–1940	528,431	0.4
1941–1950	1,035,039	0.8
1951–1960	2,515,479	1.7
1961–1970	3,321,677	1.9
1971–1980	4,493,314	2.2
1981–1990	7,338,062	3.2
1991–2000	9,095,417	3.7

Source: Appendix B, Table 2.

The idea behind this discriminatory policy was, to put it baldly, that Americans with English or Irish names were better people and better citizens than Americans with Italian or Greek or Polish names. It was thought that people of West European origin made better citizens than Rumanians or Yugoslavs or Hungarians or Balts or Austrians. Such a concept is utterly unworthy of our traditions and our ideals. It violates the great political doctrine of the Declaration of Independence that "all men are created equal." It denies the humanitarian creed inscribed beneath the Statue of Liberty proclaiming to all nations, "Give me your tired, your poor, your huddled masses yearning to breathe free."[125]

The anti-immigrant movement that culminated in the 1920s remade the U.S. population for the first time along racial lines. The numbers of immigrants entering the United States from all sources dropped drastically: from 587,150 total per year in the years 1921 to 1924, to 293,768 per year in the last six years of the decade, and then down to 52,843 in the depression decade of the 1930s. They did not begin to creep up again until the 1950s (Appendix B, Table 2). The sources changed in accordance with the principles of the Johnson–Reed Act. Whereas the top sending countries between 1890 and 1920 had been Italy, Russia, and Austria-Hungary, between 1930 and 1960 they were Germany and Canada (Appendix B, Table 6). The biggest numerical losers were Southern and Eastern Europe: immigration from Italy declined 97 percent, from more than 2 million in the 1900s to barely 57,000 in the 1940s; and from Austria-Hungary it declined 99 percent, from more than 2 million

Table 6.7 Foreign-Born as Percentage
of the U.S. Population, 1850–2000

Year	Foreign-Born as Percentage of Total U.S. Population
1850	9.7
1860	12.7
1870	14.4
1880	13.3
1890	14.7
1900	13.6
1910	14.7
1920	13.2
1930	8.4
1940	8.8
1950	6.9
1960	5.4
1970	4.7
1980	6.2
1990	8.0
2000	11.1

Source: Appendix B, Table 3.

to 28,000 (Appendix B, Tables 12 and 13). The percentage of foreign-born people in the U.S. population declined steadily until the 1970s. It has still not rebounded to what were consistent percentages throughout American history (early twenty-first century anti-immigrant hysteria to the contrary).[126]

Interpretive Issues

During the period 1870 to 1930, then, hierarchy that drew its source from pseudo-scientific racism was cemented in American society: hierarchy by some types of Whites such as English-descended Americans over Irish, Italians, Jews, and others; and hierarchy of Whites in general over peoples of color. These hierarchies took many forms, including Jim Crow segregation of Black and White in the South, as well as sometimes less formal segregation of Black, White, Red, Yellow, and Brown in the West. The hierarchy was legislated at the national level by the Immigration Act of 1924, but it was also reflected in myriad local episodes and movements. A few issues that came to prominence in this period remain to be explored.

Orientalism

First is Orientalism.[127] This has been a persistent theme in Western culture, and it had much to do with the way that Japanese, Chinese, and other Asian-descended peoples were treated in the United States. More enduring than the imagery that has been laid on other immigrant groups, the idea of the Oriental has continued to affect Asian-descended Americans to this day. The idea that there is a fundamental divide between East and West is a very old one in Mediterranean culture. It goes back at least to Herodotus's account of the war between Greece and Persia in the fifth century BCE. Herodotus portrayed Greeks as individuals: people with names and identities, members of city-states, possessors of personalities, whether brave or craven. The Persians, in Herodotus's account, were a faceless horde swarming over the landscape, devoid of individual identities, feelings, or human impulses.

Edward Said described the degree to which the idea of the Orient was an unexamined assumption in European culture: "'Oriental' was canonical; it had been employed by Chaucer and Mandeville, by Shakespeare, Dryden, Pope, and Byron. It designated Asia or the East, geographically, morally, culturally. One could speak in Europe of an Oriental personality, an Oriental atmosphere, an Oriental tale, Oriental despotism, or an Oriental mode of production, and be understood." Durkheim and Marx believed in it, as did Disraeli and Teddy Roosevelt. In the idea of the Orient, everything from the Bosporus to Honolulu and from Tokyo to the Nile became one undifferentiated place. People as utterly unlike one another as Egyptians, Koreans, Bengalis, and Vietnamese somehow were melded together into a single, faceless mass in the White imagination. It perhaps need not be noted that Vietnamese, Koreans, Bengalis, and Egyptians did not see one another as part of the same group at all.

In the nineteenth century Europeans of various sorts, including European Americans, encountered a multitude of different peoples in Asia on various colonial trajectories. They reinvigorated Orientalism as one particular kind of racist justification for imperial conquest and exploitation—the British in India, the French and Dutch in Southeast Asia, and everyone in China. One heard that "Life is cheap in the Orient." One learned of "Oriental coolies" as a distinctive type of labor—cheap, exploitable, faceless, disposable, and without human individuality or will. In the eyes of Western traders, according to Stuart Miller, Orientals were "ridiculously clad, superstitious ridden, dishonest, crafty, cruel, and marginal members of the human race who lacked the courage, intelligence, skill, and will to do anything about the oppressive despotism under which they lived or the stagnating social conditions that surrounded them." Missionaries wanted to save Orientals from their natural state: "lechery, dishonesty, xenophobia, cruelty, despotism, filth, and intellectual inferiority."

Such ideas endure. They have framed the experiences of Asians in the United States from the 1850s to the 2000s. White people cannot tell Asian Americans apart; Asian Americans can tell White people apart. More than any other people except Arab Americans, Asian Americans have been regarded as eternal foreigners in the United States. The anti-Japanese movement made much of the alleged unassimilability of Asians into American culture and values. To this day, hardly an Asian American lives who has not heard, and more than a few times, some version of the following questions: "Where are you from?" If the answer is "Chicago," inevitably a follow-up is asked: "No, where are you really from?" by which the White questioner means, "What foreign country is your real home?"

Orientalism came to contain a positively articulated vector that is no less pernicious. Sometimes it is the myth of the model minority, the super-achieving Asian American—pity the poor Chinese American kid who is not good at math. Sometimes it is White fascination with things Oriental. Asians are supposed to be more spiritual than other people. So not only Bhagat Singh Thind could make a good living for five decades as guru to the stars (and the Dalai Lama has a large, hip following today). The cover of a recent catalogue hawking hyper-pricey paintings shown at a Boston gallery is dominated by a picture of a man of indeterminate heritage—Afghan? Pakistani? he could be Jewish—dressed all in black, his face illuminated from above, eyes closed, with dark hair flowing down over his shoulders, his hands raised in gentle blessing. Faux Chinese calligraphy swirls around him in the air. Breathless copy tells us that Oprah Winfrey, Elton John, Kelsey Grammar, Emeril Legasse, and Tiger Woods all own the work of Jamali. The catalogue explains:

> Jamali was raised in the foothills of the Himalayas near the Khyber Pass. ... [H]e went to live in primitive conditions in the desert. For five years, Jamali lived among the Sufi, a people devoted to worship through dance. The Sufi's belief in a life of inner calm and reflection was to have great influence on the young Jamali and his future art. ... By 1976, Jamali recognized his calling, and he devoted himself to a life of painting, discipline, and meditation. ... Reminiscent of the Sufi, "Whirling Dervishes," Jamali dances over the surface of his paintings in a meditative state.[128]

Here, commercialized Orientalism lays over each other several stereotyped ideas from Hinduism, Islam, Buddhism, and the New Age. It's a great shtick. Like Bhagat Singh Thind, Jamali seems to have made Orientalism work for him. The novels of James Michener (*Tales of the South Pacific*, *Sayonara*) and Arthur Golden's *Memoirs of a Geisha* are equally Orientalist fantasies.[129]

Such Orientalist ideas, whether silly and benign in cases like Jamali's, or more often, harshly punitive as in the anti-Chinese and anti-Japanese movements, have limited non-Asian Americans' ability to see Asian (and for that matter, Arab) Americans clearly. They are old ideas, but they have not gone away.

Ethnicity on Display:
Ethnic Festivals, World's Fairs, and Human Zoos

The first decades of the twentieth century brought forth a great flowering of ethnic festivals.[130] For some groups and at some times, ethnic festivals provided a means to glue the community together in nostalgic remembrance of the old country. For others, it was a means to claim a place for themselves in the American cultural pantheon by having an ethnic festival of one's own.[131] On some occasions, by contrast, festivals that had minority ethnic content were celebrated by White Americans as means to mask White hegemony.

Many immigrant communities cemented their group cohesion by staging parades and fiestas. For Filipinos, it was Rizal Day, named after revolutionary martyr José Rizal. Rizal Day began in the Philippines as a way to show American-revolution-style patriotism in an attempt to convince the United States to award Philippine independence. Filipino students brought the festival to the United States in the 1910s and 1920s. They celebrated it with parties and speeches, with Filipino food and displays of the flag of the Philippines. It was a way of maintaining expatriate Filipino solidarity across class lines. Later, in the 1930s and after, as many Filipinos turned toward staying in the United States, the celebrations lost their flavor of old country politics and became more a domestic American ethnic festival, an expression of belonging in America by virtue of being an ethnic community. Much the same was true of Norway Days and other Norwegian American ethnic celebrations that flourished in the 1920s. Especially as the second and third generations came to be tied only loosely to the Norwegian community, Norse leaders sponsored community celebrations to keep up interest even as it waned.

Cinco de Mayo, a minor holiday in Mexico, became the Mexican American national celebration, a time for parades, dances, speeches, music, singing, and food, and for Mexicans in any given American town to come together. It seems to have begun in the 1860s or 1870s, not long after a small Mexican army defeated a much larger French army at the Battle of Puebla. By the early decades of the twentieth century Cinco de Mayo was celebrated in Mexican American communities across the Southwest. It did not become the Mexican American national holiday until the 1970s, when community leaders were looking for an ethnic festival to symbolize their community.

On the other hand, sometimes festivals were presented as performances of minority ethnicity when in fact they more accurately expressed White hegemony. Honolulu civic leaders began to sponsor the Mid-Pacific Carnival in 1904, and it grew throughout the first half of the century. A weeklong series of parades and fairs, it purported to celebrate the history of Hawai'i and also to present in patriotic display the formation and growth of the American nation. Each of the islands' ethnic groups was encouraged to have concurrent celebrations of its own, and Whites freely dressed up in the other people's ethnic costumes. In the analysis of historian Lori Pierce:

> The muddle of ethnic images reinforced the ideal of American national life as the blending and melting of distinct ethnic groups. So a Euro-American dressed as a geisha or a Native American provided the opportunity for Americans to assert the literal melting pot, blending and mixing internal ethnic consciousness with external ethnic symbols. Ethnicity was represented by a free-floating set of signifiers not permanently attached to anything or anyone. …
>
> The erasure of the Hawaiian nation, legally and symbolically, was a necessary step in the creation of an American pattern of ethnicity and racial formation in Hawai'i. All non-Whites, but especially Hawaiians, were transformed from immigrants and natives into ethnic Americans. No longer loyal to their former homelands, they were being tutored in the knowledge of democratic institutions that would ultimately transform them into Americans.
>
> The discourse of aloha asserted the equality of ethnic groups through assimilation. Every group in Hawai'i was equally welcome and had an equal claim on the right to be in Hawai'i. Hawaiians themselves were incorporated into this system of ethnic equality in order to undermine their prior claim to the right to control the political and social destiny of Hawai'i.

California's Ramona pageants and Old Spanish Days in Santa Barbara are similar examples of ethnic festivals as masks over conflicted racial histories. The Ramona pageant, which has been performed annually since 1923 in the little desert town of Hemet, retells the story of Helen Hunt Jackson's sentimental 1884 novel. Ramona, a half-Indian, half-White woman, falls in love with Alessandro. Her adopted family opposes the match because he is a full Indian. They elope, suffer a series of outrages at the hands of Whites who are invading the territory in the 1840s, Alessandro is murdered, and Ramona is rescued by her half-brother Felipe. The Ramona pageant celebrates Indians—but hardly anyone in Hemet was an Indian any more when the festival began. The pageant is a nostalgic appropriation of Indian history by White civic boosters. At the same time, many local Mexican Americans took part in the pageant, and so it served as a kind of glue for the Mexican community.

Santa Barbara's Old Spanish Days, also called Fiesta, are a fictional celebration of a mythical Castillian past. Begun in 1924, just a year after the first Ramona pageant, the festival has expanded from a parade to a weeklong celebration of "our city's heritage from Spanish founders." At the dawn of the twenty-first century, 40 percent of Santa Barbara's residents are Latinos, but Fiesta is not a celebration of their past. In fact, they are left out of the festival, except as menial laborers. Santa Barbara has a rich history beginning with the Chumash Indians, and continuing through the Spanish, Mexican, and American periods with succeeding waves of immigrants, racial strife, and domination. None of that actual history is told in Old Spanish Days. Fiesta claims Spanishness, erases Mexicans, and refigures them as docile Indians, safely dead for a century and a half. From the beginning, Fiesta was the brainchild of White boosters who wanted to celebrate the myths of heroes like Zorro, a Spanish nobleman, and use them to bring tourists to Santa Barbara. It might have been a Ramona pageant, a tulip festival, or Norway Days. It had pretensions to ethnic content, but it did not have the ethnic history of any of the people in town.

So ethnic festivals, which became popular across America in the first quarter of the twentieth century, sometimes acted as means by which immigrants commemorated their heritage and glued their ethnic groups more tightly together. Sometimes those groups used them to claim places for themselves in what was often called the American melting pot. And sometimes, such festivals were concocted wholesale by White people as means to enhance commerce.

Tourist dollars were the targets of two other venues of ethnic display that proliferated in the last quarter of the nineteenth century and the first quarter of the twentieth century: world's fairs and expositions and human zoos.[132] As the United States became a power in the world and took on imperial ambitions, Americans became fascinated by the variety of peoples out there in the world. From the Philadelphia Centennial Exhibition in 1876, through the 1893 Chicago Columbian Exposition and the 1904 St. Louis World's Fair, to Seattle's Alaska-Yukon-Pacific Exposition in 1909, international expositions brought many peoples to the United States and put them on exhibit. "Ethnological" displays of human beings, mounted by promoters but bearing the imprimatur of anthropologists, taught fascinated Americans that the peoples of Africa, Asia, the Middle East, and the Pacific were primitive barbarians, and so endorsed racial segregation at home and imperial war abroad. Brochures for the St. Louis fair's Philippine exhibit promised "47 Acres. 1200 Natives. 40 Different Tribes. 6 Philippine Villages. … Better than a trip through the Philippine Islands (Figure 6.19)."

It was a short step from such mass voyeurism to museum displays of living human beings. Ota Benga was a Pygmy, brought from his home in the Congo forest by an American missionary, Samuel Phillips Verner. Later exhibited in the monkey house at the Bronx Zoo, Ota Benga ultimately committed suicide when he came to understand that he would never be allowed to return to Africa. Ishi, a Yahi Indian, was found in the wilds of Northern California in 1911 and spent the rest of his days

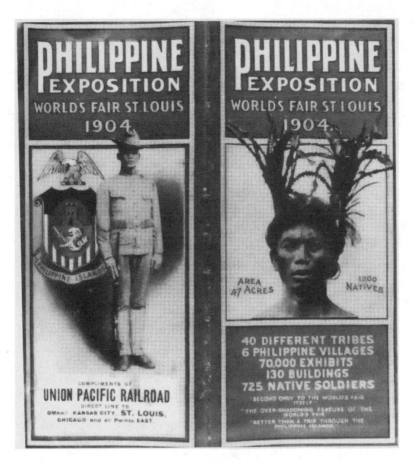

Figure 6.19 Brochure for the Philippine exhibit at the St. Louis World's Fair.

as the museum guest and study object of the anthropologist Alfred Kroeber. In 1897, explorer Robert Peary brought six Greenland Inuit back to New York from his Arctic expedition. They were exhibited in a ship in the harbor and then at the American Museum of Natural History. People poked and prodded them, felt their clothes, watched them eat, listened to them speak among themselves, and marveled at their strangeness. Four of the six died in captivity and their bones were put on display. Human zoo exhibits appeared in Berlin, Paris, Tokyo, New York—in the great cities of every imperial power. They were a vivid expression of the objectification of human beings that was so essential to make racial domination work at home and imperialism work abroad.

Racializing Religion: Jews as White and Not

Finally, it is worth taking a moment to consider the racial position of Jews in American society. I do not mean the racial position of Jews in Europe, the Middle East, Central Asia, or some other place. I believe that a persuasive case can be made that Jews constituted something like a different racial group in those places throughout most of their history there.[133] Rather, I am concerned here to explore briefly the racial position of Jews in the United States, especially as it revealed itself in these crucial decades for the making of hierarchy in American society. This is a critical issue with regard to their access to membership in American civic culture. Were American Jews White people, or were they something else? I have been at pains in earlier parts of this book to point out that Irish and Italians were always White people in the United States, contrary to some of the more extreme formulations of some recent scholars. They were discriminated against, surely, but never was their eligibility for membership in American society questioned. What about Jews?

Some writers have contended that Jewish Americans have been racialized as something other than White in U.S. history.[134] They note that the United States has always defined itself as a more-or-less Christian nation. A steady drumbeat of anti-Semitism has waxed and waned but never quite died away, from the founding generation down to the early twenty-first century. Early in the nineteenth century, three states put some limits on Jewish voting. In the era of Jim Crow, Jews were secondary targets, after Blacks, of organizations like the Ku Klux Klan. Conspiratorially minded American Gentiles, from the Populist era to our own, have inveighed against a conspiracy of Jewish bankers (allied sometimes with Jewish Communists) against White Protestant working people. Some of the motivation for the episodic attacks on the movie industry and the press by right-wing Christians can fairly be attributed to the perception that Jews have been especially prominent in Hollywood and in New York writing circles. Quotas on Jews in Ivy League student bodies and university faculties, a glass ceiling for Jews in some Gentile-run corporations, rules barring Jews from membership in some elite clubs—all these are evidence that Jews were not quite the same as other Whites in America. If Jews were White people, then they lived at the nether edge of Whiteness.[135]

On the other hand, Jews were prominent members of the inner circle of American revolutionaries and leaders of the new republic. During the antebellum period, Jews served in several state legislatures and in both houses of Congress. They were advisors to governors and presidents. In the era of industrial capitalism, they built large corporations and sat on the boards of others. In the twentieth century, they were judges and cabinet members—all fairly unproblematically and all long before any people of color. Despite some limitations, they mixed socially with the White Gentile elite. Perhaps most pointedly, no one ever questioned whether or not Jews were White for the purpose of naturalization. White people brought court cases that challenged the right of Japanese and South Asian immigrants to receive citizenship through naturalization. The courts decided they were not White. White people brought court cases that challenged the right of Arab and Armenian immigrants to receive citizenship through naturalization. The courts declared that they were White. No one ever brought a court case to challenge the right of Jews to naturalization. Jews were White.

When considering the racial position of Jewish Americans, some writers have made much of the case of Leo Frank.[136] Frank was a Cornell graduate and a member of Atlanta's highly assimilated Jewish upper crust. He was manager and part-owner of a pencil factory where, in April 1913, the body of a fourteen-year-old Gentile White girl, Mary Phagan, was found in the basement. Initial suspicions pointed elsewhere, but in the end Frank was tried and convicted of the crime. When, two years later, the governor commuted Frank's sentence, a mob including many prominent Gentile Whites seized the prisoner and lynched him. There is no question that both the

Successful despite [handwritten marginalia]

trial and the lynching were motivated by vicious anti-Semitism. That is what Frank's attorneys argued in the trial, albeit without success. But when Jim Conley, a Black janitor, took the stand and said, "Mr. Frank, you are a white man and you done it," he spoke the perception of Black Southerners on the racial position of Jews, if not on the guilt or innocence of Leo Frank. Frank was convicted of a crime he likely did not commit, largely because he was a Jew, and he was lynched for the same reason. But still, in the racial regime of the South at the time, he was unquestionably a White man.

The Frank case points, not to Jews being non-White, but toward another issue: the racialization of religion.[137] At various times in U.S. history, a group that is set off from other Americans primarily on the basis of religious difference has experienced that difference being reified further. The religious identity of Jews is written more indelibly on their character than is the religious identity of Presbyterians or Catholics. Those others are seen as more or less voluntary denominational choices among a variety of more or less equally American alternatives. But being Jewish carries a deeper stain. Even if one converts to Christianity, a Jew is somehow still a Jew.

Certain religions in America have been racialized at various times in our history. Judaism has often been one, although it has very recently begun to be domesticated as part of a "Judeo-Christian heritage" formulation that seeks to sound liberal and inclusive, while its real purpose is to keep Muslims, Buddhists, Hindus, and others barred from full membership in American society. These latter religions have been racialized consistently. We will return to the dramatic and tragic racialization of Islam in Chapter 9.

Jewish and Arab Americans throughout U.S. history have not experienced anything like the disabilities suffered by people of color: African, Asian, Mexican, or Native Americans. But they have—Jews episodically from the beginning and Arabs pretty consistently in the last third of a century—experienced the racialization of their perceived religious identity to the point that some other Americans have placed them outside the community of full Americans.

Chapter 7

White People's America, 1924-1965

The decades after the enactment of the Johnson–Reed Act were the time when the racial and ethnic hierarchies that had been generated in earlier eras took their firmest hold on the body civic. Over the course of two generations, the immigrant stream was vastly reduced, and took on precisely the shape that the framers of the Johnson–Reed Act had hoped for: almost all White people, and those mainly Northwest Europeans and Canadians. Life inside the United States for peoples of color was not pleasant, as segregation ruled the lives of most African Americans, attacks were mounted on Indian tribes' right to exist, Mexican Americans' freedom to stay in the United States was circumscribed, and Japanese Americans suffered mass imprisonment on account of their race. But cracks gradually appeared in White hegemony in the two decades following the Second World War, until finally the racist system of immigration limitation was overturned in 1965.

Recruiting Citizens

The Johnson–Reed Act had its intended effect. The idea behind the immigration quota system was not just to keep down the numbers of immigrants, but to reshape the American population racially and ethnically. The plan was to continue to encourage Northwest European immigrants, whom the framers of the act believed to be fit candidates for U.S. citizenship, and to forbid or strictly limit the numbers of other groups, whom they regarded as unfit. Table 7.1 shows the result.

Overall immigration declined 94 percent from its high of nearly 9 million in the first decade of the century. But immigration from countries whose populations were mainly White and Protestant declined far less. German immigration declined less than three-fourths despite the difficulty people had affording travel during the Depression, from a high of 412,202 in the 1920s to 114,058 in the 1930s, and it rebounded quickly after that. Canadian immigration never again reached its 1920s height, but still totaled 108,527 in the Depression decade and was back to 377,952 by

Table 7.1 Immigration by Selected Countries and Regions, 1921–1960

Decades	Germany	Canada	Britain	Italy	Mexico	All Europe	All Asia	Total
1901–1910	341,498	179,226	525,950	2,045,877	49,642	8,056,040	323,543	8,795,386
1911–1920	143,945	742,185	341,408	1,109,524	219,004	4,321,887	247,236	5,735,811
1921–1930	412,202	924,515	339,570	455,315	459,287	2,463,194	112,059	4,107,209
1931–1940	114,058	108,527	31,572	68,028	22,319	347,566	16,595	528,431
1941–1950	226,578	171,718	139,306	57,661	60,589	621,146	37,028	1,035,039
1951–1960	477,765	377,952	202,824	185,491	299,811	1,325,727	153,249	2,515,479

Source: Appendix, Tables 2, 7, 8, 9, 10, 12, 22, 23.

the 1950s. By comparison, Italian immigration dropped far more drastically—from more than 2 million in 1901 to 1910 to less than 60,000 in the 1940s (a decrease of more than 97 percent). Asian immigration, never very large in number but always figuring large in political rhetoric, dropped 95 percent, from 323,543 in the first decade of the century to 16,595 in the 1930s.

The drop in the number of foreign-born people in the U.S. population followed behind: from a high of 14.7 percent in 1910, the foreign-born population declined to 8.4 percent in 1930, 6.9 percent in 1950, and 4.7 percent in 1970.[1] The Johnson–Reed Act's exclusions and quotas did what they were supposed to do. For a substantial window of time—the entire rest of the twentieth century—the United States had fewer foreign-born people than ever before in its history. Moreover, the racially inflected government policy succeeded in making those newcomers who did manage to enter Whiter, more Protestant, and more North European of origin than they had been before 1924.

Second Generations and Third

With immigration from places other than Northwest Europe banned or severely restricted, the question of assimilating the American born became the dominant issue in most immigrant communities. Some of the groups that were most sharply cut off, such as Italians, East European Jews, Poles, and Japanese, formed discrete generations: an immigrant generation born mainly before about 1900; a second generation born in the United States mainly in the 1910s, 1920s, and 1930s; and a third generation born mainly after World War II. Japanese Americans even developed a taxonomy for their generations: Issei for the immigrant generation, Nisei for the second, and Sansei for the third.

It was widely recognized, inside and outside these communities, that each of the generations was developing its distinctive patterns in language, education, occupations, sex roles, and identity choices. What was frequently called "the problem of the second generation"—the identity issues of immigrants' children—became one of the great themes of American literature.[2] Every ethnic group (and indeed every person) experienced life in the second generation somewhat differently, yet certain themes abide. Classic second-generation issues revolve around how individuals negotiated the transition from the homes of their parents, shaped by old-country patterns, to the world of American schools and streets.

Members of the second generation (and of what would in the 1990s come to be called the 1.5 generation—people born in the old country, brought as children to the United States and reared here) typically went to American public schools. Most often, school was the first place they heard English regularly and learned to speak it. Albert Elias remembered his childhood in Los Angeles' Chávez Ravine:

> In church they spoke Spanish. In the store, Spanish. At the cleaners, all Spanish. When I went to school, I had to learn English. We didn't speak English at home, everybody was Mexican. We went barefooted to kindergarten, and all we did was paint and play games. They were trying to teach us the ABCs and the numbers and I couldn't understand the teacher. But in the first grade, I started right away. When you are a kid, you learn fast. By the second grade I was already bilingual, reading and writing. And the teachers, Miss Bodine, Miss Tucker, Miss Lummis, none of them spoke Spanish. My parents were

proud. They were trying to learn from us. I taught my mom and dad to speak English. They could defend themselves after they learned.[3]

An immigrant family was likely to have several children. Typically, the older children would be fairly fluent in their parents' language and also in English. Later children in the family commonly could understand their parents' tongue but were less likely to speak it fluently, hearing in Yiddish or Italian or Chinese and responding in English. This frequently made for a communication gap between younger siblings and their parents, whose grasp of English was seldom complete. Among themselves, members of the second generation spoke mainly English.

Creole cultures grew up in immigrant communities in the 1920s to 1940s, with people speaking mixtures of the old and new languages. The grammar base was mainly English, but it sometimes included constructions that were inflected by the immigrant tongue. Yiddish is the classic example, and a vehicle through which a large number of words and constructions entered American English. Standard American English now includes such Yiddish or Yiddish-type words as *kibitz*, *bagel*, *mish-mash*, *schmaltz*, *schlemiel*, *chutzpah*, and *beatnik*. American English expressions that bear the marks of Yiddish construction include: "Get lost." "You should live so long." "I need it like a hole in the head." "My son, the doctor." "Al*right* already." "OK by me." "Excuse the expression." "On him it looks good." "Wear it in good health."[4]

For almost every immigrant group, members of the second generation went to school longer than had their parents. This was as true for those groups who came with a lot of education, such as Jews, Japanese, and British, as it was for those who came with little, such as Poles and Italians. The American public education system was then one of the top two or three in the world in the sense that it delivered high-quality education to a large majority of children (despite sharp inequities between regions, between social classes, and between urban and rural areas). The world of school was a magical place for many immigrant children. In school they learned how to be Americans, how to speak American, how to dress and walk like an American. Immigrant children in public schools in New York, Chicago, Atlanta, Miami, Houston, Denver, Minneapolis, San Francisco, and Honolulu saluted the flag, pledged allegiance, learned to read, write, and play baseball, and listened to teachers who had been indoctrinated by the Americanization movement.

Second-generation members of some immigrant groups—stereotypically Asian Americans and Jews but others as well—embraced the opportunity school offered. They had high attendance rates, they graduated, and a significant minority went on to college at the public universities that grew throughout the century. For other groups, the commitment to school was more tenuous. Richard Alba explains that the attitudes toward school of parents who hailed from southern Italy carried over to American cities:

> From the perspective of the [Italian] family, the school appeared to pose a threat because of its potential to inject new values into a traditional society, disrupting the accepted hierarchy of authority within the family and interfering with the transmission of its values and mores from one generation to the next. The ultimate danger was of fission within the basic social atom, if the younger generation became alienated from its elders. … The emphasis on knowledge that was practical (and hence preparation for an adult trade) as well as moral (compatible with the strict family ethos) did not disappear in America. For

this reason, the use that Italian families made of American schools was very different from that made by Jews. ... [E]astern European Jews swarmed to take advantage of every educational opportunity, flooding libraries and night schools, and it was not long before they were knocking on the doors of the most prestigious colleges and universities. The contrast with Italians could not be greater. Italian children had high rates of truancy and frequently left school as early as the law allowed, with the obvious consequences that their ultimate education attainment was quite low. Even as late as 1930, only 11 percent of Italian Americans who entered New York City high schools graduated from them, at a time when over 40 percent of all the city's high school students stayed through to receive their diplomas.[5]

By contrast, Jewish and Asian kids flocked to public libraries after school, like Danny Saunders and Reuven Malter in Chaim Potok's *The Chosen* reading theology and psychology and debating ideas, or Jade Snow Wong in *Fifth Chinese Daughter* reading voraciously to prepare herself for college at Mills.[6] The public library was free, it was a place to be in the company of other members of the second generation and hang out, and it was a place to which their parents could not object. It was also a place of ideas, of exploring, and of learning how to be an American. And, like the public school, it led to other opportunities, whether those were office jobs or admission to City College or UCLA.

American education meant the opportunity for social mobility. The second generation of every American immigrant group moved up in occupational status. Second-generation members of those groups, like Jews and Japanese, who started their lives in America with substantial social capital in the form of education, moved further than those like Poles and Italians who began with less social capital. But in all groups at least some people began to move out of body work and into the ranks of the lower middle class. Sometimes this meant the creation of a middle class that served the ethnic community—shopkeepers, restaurateurs, lawyers, dentists and others who served a clientele made up mainly of other members of the ethnic group. This was not necessarily an easy transition, for the immigrants had built an ethnic enclave economy and were loath to share control of it with the next generation. In most immigrant communities, there was a struggle for control when the second generation came of age. In every group, young members of the second generation also tended to mistake their parents' accented English, cultural conservatism, and naiveté about American youth culture for lack of competence. Immigrants were tough, hardworking people who had traveled thousands of miles and wrested a living for themselves and their families from a sometimes hostile American environment, yet their children seldom appreciated those facts fully. Such misplaced second-generation contempt for their elders tended to exacerbate intergenerational struggles over economic succession.[7]

In agricultural areas, only a minority of American-born children remained on the farm; more moved to town and either worked for wages or started small businesses. In urban areas, for many immigrants, education (and especially higher education, which became available to many after World War II) meant entry into the general U.S. economy. Often, members of the second generation entered civil service occupations, as teachers, public servants, police, and fire fighters. They worked for public utilities and as social workers. The public sector was generally more open to immigrants' children than was private business before the 1970s.

As the second generation came of age, they moved out from immigrant neighborhoods and into more mixed neighborhoods. The children of Italian immigrants left their family homes in Boston's North End and moved out to working-class suburbs like Malden, Chelsea, and Revere. Second-generation Seattle Chinese and Japanese Americans moved northeast from Chinatown and Yesler Way, onto Capitol Hill, and south to Beacon Hill and Rainier Valley. Second-generation Jews who had grown up in New York's Lower East Side moved uptown in Manhattan and across the river to Brooklyn. The ethnic neighborhoods persisted as the homes of older people and as commercial centers, where one could eat in ethnic restaurants, buy groceries, and hear the old tongue on the streets. But many in the younger generations moved on as they became more prosperous and more integrated into the larger economy.

Family shape began to change. Members of the second generation had fewer children on the average than did their parents, and they approached the native White American nuclear family norm. Most immigrant households had articulated a multigenerational ideal: for immigrants who came from agricultural backgrounds in Eastern and Southern Europe or in Asia, the ideal was to have grandparents, parents, and children all living under one roof. Few immigrant households, in fact, held to that pattern, for the grandparents were most often back in the old country, but the immigrants nonetheless communicated that ideal to their children. The result was that members of the second generation were more likely than other, nonimmigrant Americans, to form multigenerational households when they came of age. Yet over time the multigenerational ideal faded and each immigrant group in its distinctive way began to more nearly approximate native American nuclear family patterns.

Sex roles also began to change. Every immigrant people was characterized by a significant degree of patriarchy, although Northern Europeans perhaps less than the others. In the United States, the feminist movement of the first decades of the century led to a degree of female emancipation. The longing of many a second-generation woman for more autonomy and a greater public role can be felt in the words of Sara Smolinsky in Anzia Yezierska's novel, *Bread Givers*. Sara takes a job and a room on her own in the city, explaining to the reader: "This door was life. It was air. The bottom starting point of becoming a person. I simply must have this room with the shut door." She speaks of "my burning ambition to rise in the world!" Her mother comes to visit and the two women have this exchange:

"Only come to see me soon."

"I'd do anything for you. I'd give you away my life. But I can't take time to go 'way out to Elizabeth. Every little minute must go to my studies."

"I tore myself away from all my work to come to see you."

"But you're not studying for college."

"Is college more important than to see your old mother?"

"I could see you later. But I can't go to college later. Think only of the years I wasted in the shop instead of school, and I must catch up all that lost time."

"You're young yet. You have plenty of time."

"It's because I'm young that my minutes are like diamonds to me. I have so much to learn before I can enter college. But won't you be proud of me when I work myself up for a school teacher, in America?"

"I'd be happier to see you get married. What's a school teacher? Old maids—all of them. It's good enough for *Goyim*, but not for you."

"Don't worry, I'll even get married some day. But to marry myself to a man that's a person, I must first make myself for a person."[8]

All these changes—language, education, social class, residence, family patterns, gender roles—made for a certain element of identity change, although that new identity was not always fully validated by other Americans who continued to see the second generation as immigrants. The members of the second generation of various immigrant groups were, in the middle decades of the twentieth century, in George Sánchez's words, "becoming Mexican American" and, in John Bukowczyk's, changing their identity "from Polish to Polish-American." The classic second-generation tale is one of yearning to be accepted as an American. John Okada, in the 1957 novel *No-No Boy*, put the issue succinctly in the words of his protagonist Ichiro. As a child in the bosom of his family, Ichiro felt only his Japanese identity. But as he grew up, "There came a time when I was only half Japanese because one is not born in America and raised in America and one does not speak and swear and drink and smoke and play and fight and see and hear in America among Americans in American streets and houses without becoming American and loving it. But I did not love it enough, for ... I was still half Japanese. ... I wish with all my heart ... that I were American."[9]

If second-generation children of immigrants from many groups had several issues in common, the same could not be said so easily of their children, members of the third generation. For many immigrant groups, particularly the South and East Europeans and Asians whose entry was cut off after 1924, the third generation was born in the 1940s and 1950s and came of age in the 1960s. Marcus Lee Hansen famously described "The Problem of the Third Generation Immigrant":

The sons and the daughters of the immigrants were really in a most uncomfortable position. They were subjected to the criticism and taunts of the native Americans and to the criticism and taunts of their elders as well. ... Whereas in the schoolroom they were too foreign, at home they were too American. ... The problem was solved by escape. As soon as he was free economically, ... the son struck out for himself. He wanted to forget everything: the foreign language that left an unmistakable trace in his English speech, the religion that continually recalled childhood struggles, the family customs. ... [They] wanted to lose as many of the evidences of foreign origin as they could. ... The leaders among the natives proclaimed loudly: It is wonderful how these young people catch the spirit of American institutions. The leaders among the foreign-born sighed and said to themselves: This apostasy means nothing good. ...

After the second generation comes the third and with the third appears a new force and a new opportunity. ... [It is an] almost universal phenomenon that what the son wishes to forget the grandson wishes to remember. ... [With the third generation comes a] resurgence of national spirit. ... Whenever an immigrant group reaches the third generation stage in its development a spontaneous and almost irresistible impulse arises which forces the thoughts of many people of different professions, different positions in life and different points of view to interest themselves in that one factor which they have in common: heritage—the heritage of blood.

This is a very tidy theory, and some have used it to explain the resurgence of ethnic identity among third-generation Japanese Americans, Jews, Poles, and others in the 1960s and 1970s. As we shall see in Chapter 9, the story of the third generation is not that simple.[10]

Recruiting Guest Workers

The immigration laws were designed to favor the entry of White people from Northwest Europe and Canada whom the majority of White Americans regarded as fit candidates for U.S. citizenship. But still labor was needed, especially in the fields and growing cities of the West. To fill that need, business leaders mounted efforts from time to time to recruit guest workers from places like the Philippines and Mexico. The idea was that they would come and work and then go home. White leaders assumed that such people were not the stuff of which Americans were made, and in time they would go back where they came from. If they did not go back when they were supposed to, then they would have to be forcibly sent back.

Mexicans

Mexican Americans possessed a strange in-between racial status, formally entitled to certain of the privileges of White people but not to complete membership in American society.[11] Many could trace ancestors back to before the time when the Southwest became part of the United States; others had come much more recently, since the era of the Mexican Revolution. By and large, Mexicans were not viewed by other Americans as worthy of inclusion in American society. But they did present a ready supply of workers, and so episodically throughout the twentieth century they were encouraged to come to the United States to work—but not to stay.

For most of American history, people moved freely back and forth across the southern and northern borders without incurring the attention of government authorities. The United States did not keep much in the way of records along either border until after 1908. In the following decades, both Mexican and Canadian migration into the United States grew substantially, although the Canadian numbers were about twice as high as those from Mexico. Recorded Mexican entries grew from less than 50,000 in the period 1901 to 1910 to nearly 460,000 in 1921 to 1930; Canadian entries rose from about 180,000 in 1901 to 1910 to more than 920,000 in 1921 to 1930 (Table 7.1). No one kept track of how many people left the United States for Canada or Mexico.

There were a couple of key differences between the Mexican and Canadian population movements. The Canadians migrated mainly into New England and the Middle West. Although some of them formed distinct ethnic communities such as St. Paul's Little Canada, and although French Canadians did encounter some discrimination in New England, for the most part Canadians, whether Anglophone or Francophone, blended quickly into the native White population and most became U.S. citizens. Mexicans, by contrast, came mainly to the Southwest and were viewed by Anglos as irredeemably foreign. Mexicans came across the border to fill jobs in a growing western economy that had previously been filled by Asian immigrants (and to a lesser extent by Southern and Eastern Europeans), and that might still have been filled by them if immigration from those countries had not been cut off. Western agriculture was becoming increasingly intertwined with the structures of corporate capitalism. Agribusiness leaders sought a foreign work force that they could intimidate into docility, and Mexican immigrants filled that bill.[12] If there was a substantial Canadian immigrant presence in the West, it has eluded historians' notice.

Customary thinking about immigration has drawn a formal line between Mexicans and Mexican Americans, and in fact that line had both legal and social meaning. Mexican Americans, legally speaking, were those who had been born in the United States, plus those who had immigrated and then become naturalized citizens. Mexicans were migrants: some permanent, some seasonal, some daily commuters back and forth across the border in places like El Paso-Ciudad Juárez. They were still citizens of Mexico, perhaps with an ambition to become American citizens one day and perhaps not. People inside Mexican American communities distinguished between these populations, as do many historians. But as David Gutiérrez points out, the relationships between people of Mexican descent who had lived long in the United States and those who had recently crossed the border were complex, and there was always a lot of fellow feeling between them. In any case, most White Americans lumped them together. Economic, residential, and social segregation drew a racial, not a citizenship line.[13] Carey McWilliams did not distinguish between the two populations, and he described the roots of the racial line between Mexican and White as economic:

> The basic factor retarding the assimilation of the Mexican immigrant, at all levels, has been the pattern of his employment. ... [O]nly a *particular class* of employers has employed Mexican labor in the Southwest: large-scale industrial enterprises; railroads; smelters; copper mines; sugar-beet refineries; farm-factories; large fruit and vegetable exchanges. These concerns have employed *many* Mexicans, in gangs, crews, and by families. ... [T]he jobs for which Mexicans were employed en masse had certain basic characteristics: they were undesirable by location (as section-hands on the desert sections of the rail lines or unskilled labor in desert mines and cement plants); they were often dead-end types of employment; and the employment was often seasonal or casual. ... In effect, Mexicans [in the California citrus industry] work, not for individual citrus growers, but for the California Fruit Growers Exchange. The exchange bears about the same relationship to "farming" that the typical industrial plant in which Mexicans are employed bears to "business": it is highly organized; it represents an enormous capital investment; and it is an enterprise which provides no ladder of advancement for field and packing-house employees.

McWilliams called such agricultural enterprises "factories in the field."[14]

Both Mexican citizens and Mexican Americans were recruited for such work. In order to maintain control over this racialized underclass, whether on factory farms, in mines, on railroads, or in processing and manufacturing plants, the Anglo population cooperated in segregating Mexican Americans. As McWilliams described it:

> To keep Mexicans earmarked for exclusive employment in a few large-scale industries in the lowest brackets of employment, their employers have set them apart from other employees in separate camps, in company towns, and in segregated *colonias*. Traditionally, Mexicans have been paid less than

Anglo-Americans for the same jobs. ... [E]mployers have limited the immigrants' chance for the type of acculturation that comes from association with other workers on the job. ... Segregated residential areas have resulted in segregated schools.[15]

Every town with a substantial Mexican-derived population had a *colonia* or *barrio*, a densely populated slum with ramshackle housing, few sewers or paved streets, desperate crowding, and substandard schools (Figure 7.1). Perhaps a third of the population of such places were immigrants; the majority were American-born. Oxnard, California, and many other towns have such *colonias* to this day. Schools were not segregated just because neighborhoods were segregated. Many towns and cities across the Southwest, from Houston to Los Angeles, had established separate, subpar schools for Mexican American children, even where, as in California, racial segregation was specifically barred by law.[16]

Mexican Americans did body labor under worse conditions and for lower pay and benefits than Anglo workers. At the depths of the Depression, many were forced off the land and into cities in search of employment. They were shunned by the American Federation of Labor (ALU); only the Industrial Workers of the World (IWW) and the Congress of Industrial Organizations (CIO) would take them on. Mexican American workers organized separate unions, often affiliated with the CIO, throughout the 1930s and 1940s. White southern politicians made sure that the most important New Deal worker protections did not apply to Blacks and Mexicans, by exempting agricultural and domestic work from the National Labor Relations Act and the Society Security Act. The 1930s saw a sharp decline in the numbers

Figure 7.1 House and yard of a Mexican family in San Antonio, Texas, 1939.

of Mexican immigrants. From a high of 459,287 in the 1920s, the migrant number dropped 95 percent to just 22,319 in the following decade. There were no jobs.

Repatriation

It was not just that a whole lot fewer people were coming into the United States from Mexico. Various agencies and levels of the American government began forcing Mexicans, both U.S. citizens and noncitizens, to leave.[17] As the Depression deepened in 1930, President Herbert Hoover began a "repatriation" program to rid the country of indigent foreign nationals. Three years later President Franklin Roosevelt stopped federal support for the program, but it continued under state and local auspices. The motive was to cut the numbers of people on the public dole. In 1931 Los Angeles County estimated that 60,000 people were on public assistance; 6,000 of them were foreign citizens, and most of those were Mexicans. In fact, the government did not distinguish between Mexican citizens and U.S. citizens of Mexican ancestry. Carey McWilliams reported that "over thirty-five thousand from Los Angeles County" were deported to Mexico. "The repatriation program is regarded locally as a piece of consummate statecraft. The average per family cost … is $71.14, including food and transportation. It cost Los Angeles County $77,249.29 to repatriate one shipment of 6024. It would have cost $424.933.70 to provide this number with such charitable assistance as they would have been entitled to had they remained—a saving of $347,684.41."[18]

Buses and trains took them to the Mexican border and dumped them. Gregg Jones wrote about the expatriation of Emilia Castaneda, a U.S. citizen who lived in Los Angeles (Figure 7.2):

> The campaign against foreign labor put her father out of work. By the time her mother died of tuberculosis in May 1935, the family didn't have money to buy flowers for the grave. Shortly afterward, her father informed Emilia and her older brother that "he had to return to Mexico," she said. "They were forcing us to return."
>
> She remembers going in the darkness to the train station with a trunk packed with their belongings. "We cried and cried," she said. "I had never been to Mexico. We were leaving everything behind." They were packed into a train that rumbled across the deserts of Arizona and New Mexico for what seemed to her like an eternity before being ushered across the border into Mexico.
>
> They returned to her father's home state of Durango. She was shocked by the poverty and primitive conditions as they moved from one relative to another, living in rooms with dirt floors, without plumbing or running water. She had to drop out of school to help provide for the family—cooking and washing clothes for her father and brother and working as a domestic.

Castaneda had to learn Spanish from scratch, for she and other American children of Mexican ancestry at her California elementary school had been forbidden to speak it. Castaneda was one of the few expatriate children who returned to the United States; she came as a war worker in 1944 at age seventeen.[19]

Altogether, as many as half a million people were expelled from states all across the Southwest. No one knows what part of that number were American

Figure 7.2 Mexican American families await expatriation in the Los Angeles train station, 1932.

citizens—One-quarter? One-third? More? Nor does anyone know how many of them succeeded in making their way back to the United States in subsequent years.

The Bracero Program

Expulsion turned to recruitment again when the economy boomed during World War II.[20] Wartime brought a labor shortage, as men went off to fight at the same time industrial and agricultural production was expanding. Tens and then hundreds of thousands of Whites and Blacks moved out of the South, into industrial and farm jobs in the North and West. Agencies of government took it upon themselves to support the war effort by ensuring a supply of workers in crucial industries. In the West, the biggest unmet needs were for temporary workers to plant and harvest crops and to build and maintain railroad lines. On August 4, 1942, the governments of Mexico and the United States signed an agreement by which Mexican guest workers would come to fill slots in these American industries. Thus began the Bracero Program. "Bracero" derives from "brazo," the Spanish word for arm. Literally it meant "arm-man," and more conventionally was translated as "farmhand." Braceros, in the eyes of employers and policy makers, were literally arms for temporary hire, not human beings to whom American society owed anything. They would come when called, work, and then go away.

The Bracero Program was not in fact a single government program, but rather a series of initiatives by the Immigration and Naturalization Service (INS) and the

Departments of State, Labor, and Agriculture. In theory, employers sent representatives south of the border to work with Mexican officials in recruiting braceros. In fact, it was much more common for workers to come north illegally on their own and then to be legalized on the spot—the term used was "paroled"—once they had found work in the United States. This maneuver was supported by the INS, and saved employers millions of dollars in recruitment costs.

Working conditions for braceros were bad—worse, even, than for other farm workers. They lived in tents or board shacks without running water, heat, or electricity. They had no medical care. They worked ten-hour days with minimal breaks. Government officials were supposed to inspect farms and rail sites in order to guarantee that workers were housed well and paid prevailing wages; they did not. One former bracero later recalled that "I saw one [government official] come by the farm in the twenty months I worked for that particular rancher. He never said a word to any of us; he just talked to the farmer, stared at us and laughed. We could only smile; none of us had any idea what they could be saying or thinking. I only know that our conditions did not change from the time we first arrived to the time we left."[21] Braceros were typically paid wages one-quarter to one-half below those of native farm workers, food allowances were illegally deducted from their wages, and sometimes the wages were not paid at all. American citizen farm workers—those of Mexican descent as well as others—tended to resent braceros, for they felt that Mexican farm workers made it harder for resident workers to organize and demand decent wages and living conditions. The AFL-CIO attempted to prevent the Bracero Program, and later tried unsuccessfully to end it.

Only 4000 Bracero recruits came to the United States that first year, but the program jumped to more than 50,000 in 1943 (Figure 7.3), and ultimately reached a height of more than 400,000 each year in the late 1950s. Over the entire period of the Bracero Program, 1942 to 1964, a total of 5,207,753 people signed bracero contracts and came to the United States as guest workers. That was 89 percent of the population of Mexican migrants who entered the United States during those years.[22]

The braceros were supposed to go back to Mexico when their contracts expired. Toward that end, the U.S. government withheld 10 percent of their wages and sent that money to the Mexican government, which was supposed to pay it to the workers on their return to their homeland. In fact, many of the workers never received these payments; at least $6 million received by the Mexican government went unaccounted for. Far more money that was owed to braceros simply disappeared into farmers' pockets amid faulty bookkeeping or malfeasance. Some former braceros were still trying to get the payments a half-century later.[23]

The Border

The United States has always had porous borders. The land borders of the lower forty-eight states, after all, total 5525 miles. It would be impossible to patrol or fence it all, and few people have ever wanted to do that. One can walk across the U.S.–Canadian border with impunity almost anywhere in the Okanogan country in eastern Washington or the vast stretches of high plains in eastern Montana and North Dakota. In many places one can drive unhindered from one country to the other. People herd cattle back and forth across that border daily, as they have for generations. There are modest checkpoints on some of the roads, but most of the land is simply open. The coastal zones are scarcely more secure. It is no great feat to pilot

Figure 7.3 The Farm Security Administration brought these Mexican workers north to harvest and process sugar beets in 1943.

a small boat across Passamaquoddy Bay from St. George, New Brunswick, to Eastport, Maine; from Thetis Island, British Columbia, to Friday Harbor, Washington; or for that matter, from Cuba to Miami if the weather is good—and it is unlikely anyone will even notice you, much less stop you.

The anti-immigrant movement of the 1920s created some demand for border control. Mae Ngai argues that "immigration restriction, particularly national-origin and numerical quotas, remapped the nation ... by emphasizing as never before the nation's contiguous land borders and their patrol." What had been a wide zone of interaction and movement gradually came to be seen as a sharp line of division. But the main impetus behind the creation of the U.S. Border Patrol was Prohibition, not immigration.[24] For twenty years the U.S. Customs Service had maintained a small force of about 75 "line riders." They were authorized to apprehend unauthorized Chinese immigrants, but their main task was keeping out illegal cattle (the United States placed a high tariff on imported cattle to prop up the American beef industry). Prohibition between 1919 and 1933 brought rampant bootlegging, most especially across the border from Canada, and so Congress created the Border Patrol in 1924 as an arm of the INS and expanded the number of patrollers to 450. The force increased only very gradually from that year until 1940, when the INS was transferred from the Labor Department to the Justice Department and the Border Patrol ranks were raised to 1500 officers.[25] Even with this expanded force, the Border Patrol always limited its activities to selected spots and selected targets. It was much more interested in interdicting bootleggers and other smugglers than it was in keeping Mexicans or Canadians from coming across to work.

Until the 1950s the Bracero Program was an emergency wartime measure to increase worker numbers in agribusiness and on Southwest railroads. Most people expected the program to end when the wartime labor shortage ended, but farm, railroad, and factory owners got used to having thousands of exploitable laborers who could be used to undercut the wages of Mexican Americans and other U.S. citizens who worked in those same industries. Agribusiness leaders prevailed upon the Truman and Eisenhower administrations to continue the program long after the wartime justification had receded. Labor leaders and assimilationist, middle-class Mexican American organizations like the League of United Latin American Citizens (LULAC) opposed extension of the Bracero Program. With that extension came also an expansion of the unauthorized immigration that had accompanied the Bracero Program from the beginning, as wives and children joined the men who had gone to work in the United States. In an era marked by Cold War xenophobia and a casual approach to constitutional niceties, a public call came for barring "wetbacks"—so-called because they were presumed to have swum the Rio Grande—from the country. In a publicity play by the INS for more funding and manpower, the Border Patrol commenced Operation Wetback in 1954. Officers swept into Mexican American neighborhoods, conducted warrantless searches, and hauled off tens of thousands of people who could not produce papers. Families were broken up, communities terrorized. In the end, the Border Patrol bragged that they had apprehended 1.1 million unauthorized Mexican immigrants and deposited them deep in Mexico's interior. The INS secured its increased funding.[26]

Operation Wetback highlighted the fact that there were elements of both tension and solidarity between Mexican Americans and new Mexican immigrants, legal or unauthorized. Perhaps the border did not become a sharply defined line even after 1924, but the act of crossing into the United States and leaving Mexico behind has long been an issue in the back of many Mexican American minds. Nearly all Mexican Americans have been conscious of a family history of crossing, made all the more poignant by Anglos' racial rejection of their right to full membership in American society. Yet they have not been without negative feelings of their own toward new immigrants. Something of the sense of ambivalence—of fellow-feeling mixed with disdain—felt by some Mexican Americans toward those who came across the border after them comes through in Albert Elias's telling of his family history:

In 1911 when my mom was about ten, her dad came to El Paso as a wetback. He had no work and no money, so he tried the border. He never returned. They don't know if he got killed or he remarried or what. He left three kids with my grandmother, and no money. That is when she sold my mother to a rich family in El Paso. That's how they got some money to survive. My grandmother sold my mom when she was twelve because they weren't making it. "I'll give you my daughter for some money and she will work for you" is how it went. She was there until she was nineteen or twenty years old. She did everything: take care of the kids, wash, iron, clean house. That is where she learned how to cook. My mom was a good cook. With the money she was making, she brought her sister and brother out of Mexico to El Paso. She really wasn't a slave. It was like a contract.

My mom would tell me the story about when she was a little girl and her dad left to find work. He was saying good-bye to the family, good-bye to everybody. They lived in a little poor ranch house by a hill. He walked away. He didn't have a horse. He went for the border walking, and turned around and waved at her. My mom loved her dad so much that she used to get little rocks and put them around the footprints of her dad where he left them. Every day, she would follow them out and place little rocks. My mom used to cry when she would tell that story. Then cattle, rain, people trampling over it, and finally my mom went out there one day, and she couldn't find the footprints anymore. He never came back. The guy disappeared. And it happens right now. All these wetbacks that come here, I would say that half of them don't go back. They start making money here, they see all these women. Why go back to that misery over there. I would say half and half, they don't go back. So how do you figure that.[27]

This ambivalence is somewhat similar to the mixed feelings that late-nineteenth-century German Jews felt toward East European Jews: a feeling of brother- and sisterhood, tempered by some resentment.

The mixture of peoples and cultural styles in the border region gave rise to distinctive border cultures in several parts of the Southwest.[28] In south Texas and northern Mexico that hybrid went by the names Norteño, Conjunto, and Tejano. From the middle decades of the nineteenth century, thousands of German, Czech, and Polish immigrants migrated into the region. They brought, among other things, engineering skills, beer, accordions, harmonicas, and brass bands playing polkas. The 1930s saw the rise of Conjunto, an accordion-driven polka music that wedded oompah bands to Mexican string ensembles. Their music, rich in folk themes, became, in the words of musicologist Manuel Peña, "a powerful symbol among the Texas-Mexican working class." The 1930s saw the first flowering of this music, which morphed several times and came again in new power in the 1990s as it burst the bounds of its region and became a national fad under the name Tejano.

Filipinos and Puerto Ricans

Another zone of mixing was California. In that region, almost anywhere there were Mexicans there also were Filipinos. Historian Rudy Guevarra speaks eloquently of "burritos and bagoong"—mixed Mexican-Filipino neighborhoods and families. In the barrios of San Diego, East Los Angeles, Porterville, Stockton, Salinas, and dozens of other locations, Filipinos and Mexicans worked and lived side by side. They inhabited a similar class and racial position. Filipino immigrant men married Mexican women, immigrant and native, and they formed a mixed community. Intermarriages continued for generations, mixing families and cultures from the 1930s through the end of the twentieth century. Some identified more as Mexicans, some as Filipinos, but they all knew they were mixed. Guevarra recalled a cousin's birthday party:

My family and friends were gathered around in the backyard when the Mexican trio showed up to play at my aunt's house in Barrio Logan. Ice-cold bottles of Corona and Pacifico were passed around while the musicians played. Some of us began dancing to the old Mexican corridos and rancheros, while others whistled and cheered us with gritos. The evening was progressing well when I noticed an odd expression on the faces of the musicians. They exchanged surprised looks when they saw the food being served to the guests. It was not the typical Mexican cuisine of carne asada, beans, salsa, and tortillas, but steamed rice, lumpia, pansit, and pan de sal. Nevertheless, they continued playing while we ate Filipino food and danced to the Mexican music. ... We had it all, rice and beans, tacos and lumpia, soy sauce and salsa.

Few people outside such mixed communities realize that the United Farm Workers (UFW) began with a merger of Filipino and Mexican unions, or that the union began with a Mexican American president and two vice presidents, one Filipino and one Mexican. The UFW is part of the complex history of the Mexican American labor struggle, and it is also part of the complicated history of the Filipino American labor struggle.[29]

Like Mexicans, Filipinos who came to work endured extraordinary hardships. Carlos Bulosan told of his life as a laborer in California at a time when White Americans wanted Filipinos to leave the country:

It was now the year of the great hatred: the lives of Filipinos were cheaper than those of dogs. They were forcibly shoved off the streets when they showed resistance. The sentiment against them was accelerated by the marriage of a Filipino and a girl of the Caucasian race. ... the state legislature [passed] a law forbidding marriage between members of the Malayan and Caucasian races. This action was followed by neighboring states, until ... New Mexico was the nearest place to the Pacific Coast where Filipino[s] could marry Caucasian women.

This was the condition in California when José and I arrived in San Diego. I was still unaware of the vast social implications of the discrimination against Filipinos. ... In San Diego, where I tried to get a job, I was beaten upon several occasions by restaurant and hotel proprietors. ...

From San Diego, José and I traveled by freight train to the south. We were told, when we reached the little desert town of Calipatria, that local whites were hunting Filipinos at night with shotguns. A countryman offered to take us in his loading truck to Brawley, but we decided it was too dangerous. We walked to Holtville where we found a Japanese farmer who hired us to pick winter peas.

It was cold at night and when morning came the fog was so thick it was tangible. But it was a safe place and it was far from the surveillance of vigilantes. Then from nearby El Centro, the center of Filipino population in the Imperial Valley, news came that a Filipino labor organizer had been found dead in a ditch.

I wanted to leave Holtville, but José insisted that we work through the season. I worked but made myself inconspicuous. At night I slept with a long knife under my pillow. ...

One day a Filipino came to Holtville with his American wife and their child. It was blazing noon and the child was hungry. The strangers went to a little restaurant and sat down at a table. When they were refused service, they stayed on, hoping for some consideration. But it was no use. Bewildered, they walked outside; suddenly the child began to cry with hunger. The Filipino went back to the restaurant and asked if he could buy a bottle of milk for his child.

"It is only for my baby," he said humbly.

The proprietor came out from behind the counter. "For *your* baby!" he shouted.

"Yes, sir," said the Filipino.

The proprietor pushed him violently outside. "If you say *that* again in my place, I'll bash in your head!" he shouted aloud so that he would attract attention. "You goddamn brown monkeys have your nerve, marrying our women. Now get out of this town!"

"I love my wife and my child," said the Filipino desperately.

"*Goddamn* you!" The white man struck the Filipino viciously between the eyes with his fist.

Years of degradation came into the Filipino's face. All the fears of his life were here—in the white hands against his face. Was there no place where he could escape? Crouching like a leopard, he hurled his whole weight upon the white man, knocking him down instantly. He seized a stone the size of his fist and began smashing it into the man's face. Then the white men in the restaurant seized the small Filipino, beating him unconscious with pieces of wood and with their fists.

He lay inert on the road. When two deputy sheriffs came to take him away, he looked tearfully back at his wife and child.

I was about to go to bed when I heard unfamiliar noises outside. Quickly I reached for José's hand and whispered to him to dress. José followed me through the back door and down a narrow irrigation ditch. We crept on our bellies until we reached a wide field of tall peas, then we began running away from the town. We had not gone far when we saw our bunkhouse burning.

We walked all the cold, dark night toward Calexico.[30]

Ever since the United States seized the Philippines in 1898, Filipino patriots had been agitating for independence. The United States contended that Filipinos were not prepared for self-government and insisted on a period of "tutelage," in which the colonizers remade as much of Filipino society as possible. They spread the English language throughout the islands. They introduced an American-style education system and government apparatus. Finally, in 1934, the United States acceded to the Filipino demand for independence, which would be granted ten years later (in fact, it took until 1946 because the Japanese seized the islands during World War II). The 1934 Tydings-McDuffie Act gave the promise of independence after a decade, and it also immediately changed the status of Filipinos in the United States. Up to that point they had been U.S. nationals: they were not citizens with the right to vote, but they could come and go between the United States and the Philippines at a time when other migrants from Asia were banned. The Tydings-McDuffie Act changed their status to aliens ineligible to citizenship, the same as other Asians. They were not completely barred from the country initially; they would be granted a token annual quota of fifty until independence; thereafter Filipinos were to be barred from the United States like other Asians. The following year Congress attempted to repatriate Filipino workers as they had Mexicans, but only 2200 agreed to go.[31]

Puerto Ricans were guest workers too.[32] The United States acquired Puerto Rico as spoils of the Spanish American War, along with Guam and the Philippines. Each of these new dominions traced its own path thenceforward, but Puerto Ricans, like Filipinos and Guamanians, held a status somewhere between enjoying the full benefits of U.S. citizenship and having the independent status of foreign nationals. Like Filipinos and residents of Guam, Puerto Ricans could come and go freely between their homeland and the United States. This did not begin to happen in large numbers until the 1920s. In 1920, there were roughly 12,000 Puerto Ricans residing in the continental United States; ten years later it was 53,000; by 1944, the number topped 90,000, and it continued to expand rapidly in the postwar years.[33]

The forces driving the Puerto Rican migration resembled those described in Lucie Cheng and Edna Bonacich's model described in Chapter 1; it was akin to the processes that brought U.S. dominance to the Philippines and Hawai'i, and Filipinos and Hawaiians to the continental United States. An infusion of American capital into Puerto Rico, mainly taking the form of large sugar plantations, disrupted what had formerly been a subsistence economy. Peasants became factory-farm workers or were cast off the land. They made their way along the channels of empire to the United States. They worked under contract in agriculture as far west as Arizona and Hawai'i, but their main involvements were as seasonal migrants in farm work in the East and Midwest. Some began to work in factories, and dense *colonias* grew up near their places of employment, in locations such as Manhattan's Lower East Side and near the Brooklyn Navy Yard. Others entered service industries in hotels and restaurants. World War II brought a burst of movement as thousands of migrants came to work in unskilled positions in war industries. Puerto Rican migration to the continent continued to expand after the war with cheap air travel. New *colonias* were built, as East Harlem became Spanish Harlem and the South Bronx became home to tens of thousands of Puerto Ricans. The same was true for depressed pockets of northern New Jersey, Chicago, Los Angeles, Miami, Philadelphia, and other urban centers.

Puerto Ricans were always a racially mixed people: Spanish, Indian, and African of origin. Under the Spanish, that meant a certain element of hierarchy based on class reinforced by skin color. But under the Americans, binary racial distinctions—White over everybody else—became the order of the day. That carried over into the United States, where Puerto Ricans were treated simply as people of color: not as dark and therefore not as disprivileged as Blacks, but nonetheless plenty dark and the objects of discrimination and disdain from Whites. The color and language of Puerto Ricans made White America reluctant to grant Puerto Ricans either independence or full citizenship.

At various times there has been a vocal Puerto Rican independence movement, and there has frequently been an equally fervent move by island business leaders to become the fifty-first state of the union. Both have foundered, not only on the conflict between these impulses, but also on U.S. unwillingness to change a relationship that is advantageous to continental Americans, as well as the conviction of many Whites that Puerto Ricans were fit neither for full U.S. citizenship nor for independence. Because they possessed a limited version of U.S. citizenship after 1917, and because of the ease of travel between the United States and Puerto Rico, Puerto Rican Americans remained tied with unusual tightness to their ancestral homeland. Not infrequently, Puerto Ricans who lived and worked much of their lives in New York or Chicago retired to the island from which they or their parents came.

Indians or Citizens?

Citizenship was also at issue for Native peoples in the middle decades of the twentieth century.[34] Indians, like members of other racial and ethnic minorities, served in the United States armed forces in World War I. It was a point of particular pride for Blacks and Indians to don uniforms and fight for their country, even though their country did not show much sign of wanting them. When the war ended in 1919, Carlos Montezuma, a Yavapai Indian, wrote to his fellow Native American soldiers:

> Brave warriors, you left your humble homes ... to fight for the principles that throbbed in your hearts, namely, freedom, equality, democracy, humanity, and justice. ... You have demonstrated to the world by taking up arms for your country and standing shoulder to shoulder with your pale face comrades that the Indian race is not helpless and incompetent for freedom and citizenship. ...
>
> Now, what is your duty? Carry on the fight—not as you experienced in the front, but for the freedom and citizenship of your race. What did you fight for? Freedom. ... Your sacrifice for your country would be a mockery were you to stop this side of freedom of your people. They have not equal rights, they have not democracy, they have not humanity and they have not justice. ... You have been loyal to your country. Your country is indebted to you. ... Your mission, at this hour, is to preach the gospel of truth that your race is ready for freedom and citizenship. ...You should proclaim this truth everywhere and let it be heard in the hall of Congress. You have fought a good fight for your country, now it is your turn to ask the country to give you what you have helped to win for your race. ... [S]tand before the world and ask the people of the United States to let your people go free from under the bondage of the Indian Bureau, so that they may enjoy the rights and privileges of citizenship.[35]

Not all Indians—in fact, probably not a majority—looked upon the acquisition of individual U.S. citizenship with the sanguinity of Carlos Montezuma. But some White politicians picked up the theme. In 1924 the U.S. Congress passed the Indian Citizenship Act, by which all Indians who had not already taken allotments under the Dawes Act and so become U.S. citizens, nor had won citizenship by virtue of military service, were deemed to be American citizens henceforth. At a stroke, Indians became U.S. citizens, but the meaning of that change took some time to establish. It is unquestionable that they were not accorded the full rights of White citizens, especially in those places that had a lot of Indians. Arizona, New Mexico, and Utah denied the vote to Indian citizens for two more decades, with the approval of the federal courts. And many tribes remained intact despite substantial progress in pursuing allotment; continued tribal membership cast doubt on the fullness of U.S. citizenship for Native peoples.

Doubts were sharpened when, in 1928, the Meriam Report showed widespread Indian poverty and distress, and put the lie to the promise of allotment that Indians would become self-supporting, productive American citizens.[36] Awash in criticism from several sides, the federal government had asked Lewis Meriam and a team of investigators to study the situation of Native peoples and make recommendations. Meriam's report is a pungent blend of condemnation of the allotment policy and condescending stereotypy toward Indians. It judges reservation culture harshly, but lays the ultimate blame on government incompetence and White cupidity. The report's summary read in part:

> An overwhelming majority of the Indians are poor, even extremely poor, and they are not adjusted to the economic and social system of the dominant white civilization. ...

Health. The health of the Indians as compared with that of the general population is bad. ... both the general death rate and the infant mortality rate are high. Tuberculosis is extremely prevalent. Trachoma. ...

Living Conditions. The prevailing living conditions among the great majority of the Indians are conducive to the development and spread of disease. ... the diet of the Indians is bad. ... The use of milk is rare, and it is generally not available even for infants. ... a diet consisting mainly of meats and starches. ... there is great overcrowding. ... Sanitary facilities are generally lacking. ...

Economic Conditions. The income of the typical Indian family is low and the earned income is extremely low. ... He generally ekes out an existence through unearned income from leases of his land, the sale of land, per capital payments from tribal funds, or in exceptional cases through rations given him by the government. ... a little agriculture, a little fishing, hunting, trapping, wood cutting, or gathering of native products, occasional labor and hauling, and a great deal of just idling. ... In justice to the Indians it should be said that many of them are living on lands from which a trained and experienced white man could scarcely wrest a reasonable living. ... Frequently the better sections of the land originally set apart for the Indians have fallen into the hands of the whites, and the Indians have retreated to the poorer lands remote from markets. ... [Most Indians use] primitive systems of irrigation. ... If the modern irrigation enterprise has been successful from an economic standpoint, the tendency has been for whites to gain possession of the land. ... The remoteness of their homes often prevents them from easily securing opportunities for wage earning. ... Even the boys and girls graduating from government schools have comparatively little vocational guidance or aid in finding profitable employment. When all these factors are taken into consideration it is not surprising to find low incomes, low standards of living and poor health.

After surveying the problems Indians suffered, Meriam and his colleagues evaluated the causes:

Suffering and Discontent. Some people assert that the Indians prefer to live as they do; that they are happier in their idleness and irresponsibility. The question may be raised whether these persons do not mistake for happiness and content an almost oriental fatalism and resignation. The survey staff found altogether too much evidence of real suffering and discontent to subscribe to the belief that the Indians are reasonably satisfied with their condition. ...

The Causes of Poverty. The economic basis of the primitive culture of the Indians has been largely destroyed by the encroachment of white civilization. The Indians can no longer make a living as they did in the past by hunting, fishing, gathering wild products, and the extremely limited practice of primitive agriculture. The social system that evolved from their past economic life is ill suited to the conditions that now confront them. ... Several past policies adopted by the government in dealing with the Indians have been of a type which, if long continued, would tend to pauperize any race. Most notable was the practice of issuing rations to able-bodied Indians. Having moved the Indians from their ancestral lands to restricted reservations as a war measure, the government undertook to feed them. ... The Indians at the outset had to accept this aid as a matter of necessity, but promptly they came to regard it as a matter of right. ... They felt, and many of them still feel, that the government owes them a living, having taken their lands from them, and that they are under no obligation to support themselves. ... When the government adopted the policy of individual ownership of the land on the reservations, the expectation was that the Indians would become farmers. ... It almost seems as if the government assumed that some magic in individual ownership of property would in itself prove an educational civilizing factor. ... Many Indians were not ready to make effective use of their individual allotments. Some of the allotments were of such a character that they could not be effectively used by anyone. ... The solution was to permit the Indians through the government to lease their lands to whites. In some instances government officers encouraged leasing, as the whites were anxious for the use of the land. ... Surplus land remaining after allotments were made was often sold and the proceeds placed in a tribal fund. Natural resources, such as timber and oil, were sold. ... the government ... often took the easiest course of managing all the Indians' property for them. The government kept the Indians' money for them at the agency. When the Indians wanted something they would go to the government agent, as a child would go to his parents, and ask for it. The government agent would make all the decisions.[37]

Initially, the administration of Republican President Herbert Hoover took some ineffective half steps. A more adequate response had to wait for the election of Franklin Roosevelt. In 1933, the federal government, led by Interior Secretary Harold Ickes and Commissioner of Indian Affairs John Collier, proposed what they called the Indian New Deal. The following year it came into effect through the Indian Reorganization Act. The act set up mechanisms for electing tribal governments on an American small-town model that served with less federal oversight than had previous reservation administrations. It introduced agricultural loans and other economic development programs, as well as vocational training. And it brought the allotment system to a halt.

Indian responses were mixed. Some, like South Dakota Sioux attorney Ramon Roubideaux, disliked the Indian Reorganization Act:

As far as the Indian Reorganization Act is concerned, I think this is possibly one of the best intentioned but unfortunate happenings that could have possibly taken place as far as the Indian people are concerned. Although it did stop the sale of Indian lands and did stop the allotment system, it created a socialistic society and set the Indian people apart from the mainstream of American life and made them a problem. It has substituted in place of the governing system that the Indians had prior to the Indian Reorganization Act a white man's idea of how they should live. ... [The Indian] was somehow made to feel that he was inferior, that he wasn't able to compete. So that the whole system emphasized the activities of the Indians as a whole for the benefit of the whole, rather than the individual private enterprise system of our American system. He wasn't taught to be a capitalist, which he must be taught in order for him to survive in this country. ... Everything they've done has been under the wing of the Government. ... Everything is planned for him, he never develops this mind of his.

Winnebago leader Alfred DuBray had a more positive evaluation of the Indian New Deal:

> Many were against, and many were for it. … it was very difficult because it was such a radical change from their way of life. Really, their customs and practices up to that point—most of all their governing procedures in the tribe—were handled through tribal leaders, designated by the chiefs, the leaders from one generation to another. They looked to the tribal chiefs … to guide them in their procedures. They had no formal government of any kind. … [The Indian New Deal] had a lot of advantages, in that many of the people would have loan funds available—huge amounts. Farm programs were developed through this; cattle-ranging programs were initiated. Education loans were beginning to be made available for the Indian youngsters who had never had any opportunity before to attend higher institutions. There was a new feeling there in education. And, of course, mainly the tribal governing body got busy there and established the governing body, voted on their representatives and their council meetings.

Despite the mixed response, and despite clear shortcomings to reorganization—such as the fact that traditional leaders were often bypassed and tribal decisions had to be ratified by the Bureau of Indian Affairs (BIA)—it is undeniably true that the Indian New Deal brought a larger measure of self-determination to Native peoples and halted the centuries-long decline in tribal autonomy.[38]

There were many Whites who thought all this a very bad idea. They were eager for what they called "the Indian problem" to go away. The tribes were the problem. Both policy makers and the White public, enraptured with the idea of individualistic capitalist culture and busy fighting the Cold War, insisted that Indians should be forced to leave the land and become anonymous individual citizens, detached from any ancestral identity or group affiliation. This sentiment resulted in the Indian New Deal being abruptly reversed in 1954.[39] There was always a constituency in Congress—indeed, there is still—for ending any special treatment for Indian tribes, including the right to own and govern tribal lands. Some of this has been principled after a fashion; the advocates reasoned that Indians were individual citizens and should be treated as such. The only check on those who would obliterate the tribes has been the existence of treaties signed between the United States and sovereign Indian nations that required that Indian tribes be recognized—a check whose effectiveness waxed and waned with White public opinion.

Some scholars have given much of the credit for the termination policy to BIA Commissioner Dillon Myer. Myer had served during World War II as head of the War Relocation Authority, jailer-in-chief for incarcerated Japanese Americans (see below). Historian Brian Dippie wrote that "Myer … was convinced that the reservations were concentration camps because he administered them, as he had the Japanese internment centers, as though they were. Thus the Indians had to be 'freed' from the prisons Myer erected around them in his mind."[40] Others credited Utah Senator Arthur Watkins, handmaiden to western business interests, or Myer's successor at the BIA, Glenn Emmons. Whoever deserves the blame, in 1953 Congress passed and a year later the BIA put into effect a termination policy. The members of each Indian tribe in turn would be notified that the tribe's independent existence was about to end. Members would be encouraged to vote on plans for distributing tribal land and resources. In a matter of a few months or years, the tribes would cease to exist.

The advocates of termination thought it a bold and exciting plan. It proved a recipe for disaster. Under termination, the Menominee tribe became simply Menominee County, Wisconsin. The state's political leaders pushed termination in order to free up reservation land for White ownership and to add that land to the state's tax rolls. The government put termination to a vote among tribe members, and those who voted were unanimous in their opposition to the move. Nonetheless, the government went ahead and terminated the tribe. The Menominee lost treaty rights that had been theirs for a century. Their once-prosperous timber business languished. And theirs became the poorest county in Wisconsin. Between 1954 and 1962, Congress terminated the federal trust relationship to sixty-one tribes and bands. In the 1970s, the government admitted it had made a mistake and reversed termination for the Menominee and several other large tribes.[41]

The necessary accompaniment to termination was relocating Indians into cities, since most of them were being thrown off tribal lands. A federal program in 1952 sought to encourage Indians to go to cities like Chicago, Seattle, Minneapolis, and Los Angeles and to help them make the transition with counseling and job referrals. Some Indians made a successful transition to work in offices and factories and became more-or-less undifferentiated dwellers of cities and suburbs: White people with some Indian ancestry, if you will. Others, however, were less successful, and ended up as a new phenomenon—the urban Indian—poor, rootless, jobless, and perhaps homeless.

World War II

The Second World War brought a mixed experience for immigrants and people of color: increased economic opportunity for some, intensified racial abuse for many. On one hand, the war meant jobs for a lot of African and Mexican Americans who had previously languished in marginal agricultural labor. A massive move by White and Black laborers out of the rural South that had begun during the Depression and Dust Bowl years exploded during the war.[42] Workers left the farms and went to southern cities such as Houston and Birmingham. They moved on, many along channels grooved by earlier migrations, north to Chicago, New York, and Pittsburgh. Some blazed new trails west to Seattle, San Francisco, and Los Angeles, where shipbuilding, steel, and aircraft manufacturing were making sleepy port towns into booming cities. Many thousands of Whites left farms in the Midwest and ended up working in cities, too. Whites got most of the best-paying factory jobs, but there was plenty of work left over for Blacks, as well as for the growing number of Mexicans who left farms and railroads and moved to cities during the war. Altogether, it was the greatest countryside-to-city migration in U.S. history. The Fair Employment Practices Commission never quite lived up to its New Deal promise to end racial discrimination in the workplace, but it did hold down White employers' attempts to activate a color line in hiring and wages.

Rooting out the Zoot

Nonetheless, discrimination and abuse continued. Blacks and Mexicans were far more likely to be working as janitors, as domestics, or in small businesses, at lower wages, and without union protections, than were White workers. A spate of riots against people of color marred the war period. The most spectacular of these were the Los Angeles Zoot Suit Riots.[43] Zoot suits were extreme clothing worn in the late 1930s and early 1940s by young minority-group men: Blacks, Asians, and pre-eminently Mexican Americans. Styled after jazz musicians, they included wide-brimmed felt hats, double-breasted jackets with huge padded shoulders tapering to narrow waists, pants that flared wide at the hips and tapered tight at the ankles, and accessories such as long metal chains dangling nearly to the ground. Robin Kelley reflected on the oppositional mentality that lay beneath the suit of the zoot:

> The zoot suiters and hipsters who sought alternatives to wage work and found pleasure in the new music, clothes, and dance styles of the period were "race rebels" of sorts, challenging middle-class ethics and expectations, carving out a distinct generational and ethnic identity, and refusing to be good proletarians. ... The combination of his suit and body language encoded a culture that celebrated a specific racial, class, spatial, gender, and generational identity. ... zoot suiters during the war were primarily young black and Latino working-class males whose living spaces and social world were confined to ... ghettos, and the suit reflected a struggle to negotiate these multiple identities in opposition to the dominant culture. ... While the suit itself was not meant as a direct political statement, the social context in which it was created and worn rendered it so. The language and culture of zoot suiters represented a subversive refusal to be subservient. ... [I]t had become an explicitly un-American style. By March 1942, because fabric rationing regulations instituted by the War Productions Board forbade the sale and manufacturing of zoot suits, wearing the suit ... was seen by white servicemen as a pernicious act of anti-Americanism.[44]

The zoot suit was an emblem of minority youth rebellion, one much resented by Whites.

One night in August 1942 (the same month the Bracero Program was inaugurated), Los Angeles police found the dying body of José Díaz at the Sleepy Lagoon, an abandoned gravel pit on the Los Angeles River where Mexicans went to swim because they were barred from the city's public pools. Díaz had either fallen on the rocks or been beaten to death. Police quickly arrested and charged twenty-four Mexican American youths with murder. They beat at least two of them severely. They alleged that Díaz had been a gang member, that his death was a gang killing, and that these youths were members of a rival gang that perpetrated the deed. In January, after a trial attended by celebrities and trumpeted in newspapers coast to coast, twelve of the twenty-four Mexican American defendants were convicted.

That June, Navy men on shore leave ran amok through Mexican neighborhoods, beating up anyone they saw who was wearing a zoot suit or otherwise could be identified as part of the counterculture of minority youth. Carey McWilliams described the first night:

> [A]bout two hundred sailors decided to take the law into their own hands. ... Coming down into the center of Los Angeles from the Naval Armory in Chavez Ravine ... they hired a fleet of twenty taxicabs. Once assembled, the "task force" proceeded to cruise straight through the center of town en route

to the east side of Los Angeles where the bulk of the Mexicans reside. Soon the sailors in the lead-car sighted a Mexican boy in a zoot-suit walking along the street. The "task force" immediately stopped and, in a few moments, the boy was lying on the pavement, badly beaten and bleeding. The sailors then piled back into the cabs and the caravan resumed its way until the next zoot-suiter was sighted, whereupon the same procedure was repeated. In these attacks, of course, the odds were pretty uneven: two hundred sailors to one Mexican boy. Four times this same treatment was meted out and four "gangsters,"—two seventeen-year-old youngsters, one nineteen, and one twenty-three,—were left lying on the pavements for the ambulances to pick up.[45]

The rioting continued night after night for ten days, egged on by the *Los Angeles Times* and protected by police. Soldiers and White civilians joined the rioters, and some Mexican Americans fought back. Hundreds were injured and hundreds arrested—Mexican American assault victims, not the rioters. In the fullness of time, the Sleepy Lagoon convictions were overturned, but no one was held responsible for the Zoot Suit Riots.[46]

There were many such attacks on people of color during World War II. A massive race riot in Detroit during the hot summer of 1943 involved tens of thousands of White and Black people and injured scores. Despite such racial hostility at home, Black, Mexican, Asian, and Native American soldiers served with distinction in the war. When Jose Lopez killed more than 100 German soldiers at the Battle of the Bulge and earned the Congressional Medal of Honor, presumably none of his comrades cared that he was an illegal immigrant from Mexico. Yet, on his return to civilian life, Lopez, like other soldiers of color, faced discrimination at many turns.[47] During World War II a Black U.S. Army Air Force unit was stationed near Salina, Kansas. Lloyd Brown and some other Black airmen went into town to a lunch counter on Santa Fe Street:

> As we entered, the counterman hurried to the rear to get the owner, who hurried out front to tell us with urgent politeness: "You boys know we don't serve colored here."
>
> Of course we knew it. They didn't serve "colored" anywhere in town when our all-black outfit first came to Salina in the fall of 1942 to open up the Smoky Hill Army Air Field just out of town. The best movie house did not admit Negroes and the other one admitted them only to the balcony. There was no room at the inn for any black visitor, and there was no place in town where he could get a cup of coffee.
>
> "You know we don't serve colored here," the man repeated. He was still very polite, but he sounded aggrieved that we had not been polite enough to leave.
>
> We ignored him, and just stood there inside the door, staring at what we had come to see—the German prisoners of war who were having lunch at the counter. There were about ten of them. They were dressed in fatigues and wore the distinctive high-peaked caps of Rommel's Afrika Korps. No guard was with them. ...
>
> We continued to stare. This was really happening. It was no jive talk. It was the Gospel truth. The people of Salina would serve these enemy soldiers and turn away black American GI's. ...
>
> If we were *untermenschen* in the Nazi Germany, they would break our bones. As "colored" men in Salina, they only break our hearts.[48]

Neither an Accident, Nor a Mistake

The most egregious attack on people of color during the war—indeed, the most shameful attack on any immigrant people in U.S. history—was the incarceration of the entire West Coast Japanese American population during World War II.[49] Legal scholar Eugene V. Rostow later called it "our greatest wartime mistake."[50] It was not a mistake, nor was it an accident. It was simply one part of the long history of anti-Asian injustice and violence perpetrated by White Americans. That history began with the attacks on Chinese immigrant workers in San Francisco and Los Angeles, in the goldfields, and in Rock Springs, Wyoming. It continued through the anti-miscegenation laws, the anti-Japanese movement, the San Francisco schools crisis, the alien land laws, the banning of all Asian immigration, and attacks on Filipino workers. These anti-Asian movements continued after World War II and into the twenty-first century (see Chapter 9).

Immediately after the bombs stopped falling on Pearl Harbor, the FBI entered Japanese neighborhoods on the West Coast and in Hawai'i and began hauling off people they called "dangerous aliens"—consular officials, leaders of community organizations, Buddhist priests, business owners, Japanese language school teachers, even tea ceremony instructors. Japanese communities were left leaderless and terrified. A Nisei college student reported:

> The strain and tension on the men in the community was terrific. Most of them had a little parcel of food, night shirt, etc., ready in case they were next on the list. It was pathetic to see their faces. It was as if they were awaiting an execution. …
>
> Now came rumors that the FBI would ransack houses. Everyone became frantic. I think every family must have gone through their homes in search of incriminating articles. Of course most were harmless, yet the FBI agents had a funny way of interpreting innocent articles. We must have burned 50 or 75 books, merely because they were written in Japanese. I spied mother with tears burning pictures of her relatives back in Japan, looking at them one by one for the last time and burning them.[51]

The FBI bagged 1500 people on December 7 and 8, and a total of more than 5000 by the end of the winter (Figure 7.4). They hauled these people off without hearings or charges being filed and confined them in camps run by the INS in places like Bismarck, North Dakota, and Missoula, Montana. The FBI and Naval Intelligence had been scouting Japanese neighborhoods for more than a year, talking with people, reading Japanese newspapers, and compiling lists of individuals who would be arrested if war came. They enlisted the cooperation of a politically conservative, hyper-patriotic group of young Nisei, the Japanese American Citizens League, who aspired to take over community leadership from their parents' generation. When war came, they arrested those people, and that was the end of government interest in Japanese Americans, for a time.

After the immediate uproar over Pearl Harbor died down, other Americans went about mobilizing for war and could not be bothered with Japanese Americans. But as the winter wore on and the Allies lost battle after battle in the Pacific, some began to fear the United States would lose the war—or worse, be invaded. Navy Secretary Frank Knox made a quick trip to Hawai'i and reported that "treachery"

Figure 7.4 "FBI Takes Father Away," watercolor by Gene Sogioka.

by Japanese in the islands, "the most effective fifth column work that's come out of this war," was responsible for the Pearl Harbor disaster. He knew it was a lie—that the defeat was the result of incompetence and lack of preparedness in the American command, as well as daring creativity on the part of Japanese strategists, but he said it anyway, and he was believed.[52] Soon West Coast newspapers began trumpeting fantasy headlines (these appeared in the *Los Angeles Times* that winter):

JAP BOAT FLASHES MESSAGE ASHORE

TWO JAPS WITH MAPS AND ALIEN LITERATURE SEIZED

CAPS ON JAPANESE TOMATO PLANTS POINT TO AIR BASE[53]

Demagogues found sinister intent in the location of many Japanese American homes near shipyards, factories, railroad tracks, and airports—conveniently forgetting that those were the slums to which they had been segregated. California Attorney General Earl Warren (later the governor and still later Chief Justice of the U.S. Supreme Court) reasoned that the complete lack of spying by Japanese Americans was proof positive that they were all involved in a carefully timed plot to destroy U.S. defenses by massive and simultaneous acts of sabotage.

Hysteria was fed by greed. Japanese Americans owned farms and businesses that some of their neighbors coveted. Austin Anson of the Grower-Shipper Association of Salinas, California, said while lobbying for the mass incarceration of Japanese Americans: "We're charged with wanting to get rid of the Japs for selfish reasons. We might as well be honest. We do. It's a question of whether the white man lives on the Pacific Coast or the brown men. They came into this valley to work, and they stayed to take over."[54]

Through the winter of 1942, a demand grew to oust Japanese Americans from the Pacific Coast. Its main perpetrators were the Chamber of Commerce, anti-immigrant organizations, the American Legion, White farmers' groups, and the Native Sons of the Golden West. They were abetted by newspaper people like Henry McLemore of the *San Francisco Examiner*: "I am for immediate removal of every Japanese on the West Coast to a point deep in the interior. I don't mean a nice part of the interior either. Herd 'em up, pack 'em off and give 'em the inside room in the badlands. Let 'em be pinched, hurt, hungry and dead up against it. ... Let us have no patience with the enemy or with anyone whose veins carry his blood. ... Personally, I hate the Japanese, and that goes for all of them."[55]

A decision was reached in Washington to imprison the entire Japanese American people. It was President Franklin Roosevelt's decision, and he had the help of his military advisors, including West Coast military defense commander Lt. Gen. John L. DeWitt. DeWitt claimed "military necessity" although he never demonstrated there was such a necessity. Instead, he offered the justification that "A Jap's a Jap. They are a dangerous element, whether loyal or not. There is no way of determining their loyalty. ... It makes no difference whether he is an American; theoretically he is still a Japanese, and you can't change him."[56]

On February 19, 1942, Roosevelt issued Executive Order 9066, which authorized DeWitt to exclude anyone he liked from the West Coast. On March 2, DeWitt designated California, the western third of Washington and Oregon, and the southern third of Arizona as territory that people of Japanese ancestry must leave. For a couple of weeks some Japanese Americans packed up and headed east, but they found they had nowhere to go. Idaho Governor Chase Clark said, "The Japs live like rats, breed like rats and act like rats. We don't want them buying or leasing land or becoming permanently located in our state."[57]

DeWitt ordered a curfew for Japanese Americans and announced that the Army would remove them. That spring, 112,000 Japanese Americans—two-thirds of them American-born U.S. citizens—were herded into concentration camps (Figure 7.5). Signs went up in their neighborhoods and they learned they had two days to two weeks before they had to leave. They were forced to sell their homes and belongings, give them to friends, or abandon them. They were allowed to take only what they could carry. Most of them lost everything.

They were tagged (each family lost its name and got a number in its place), taken by bus, train, or car caravan under armed guard to assembly centers—converted fairgrounds and racetracks, where they lived under the stands or in livestock stalls behind newly erected fences. Miné Okubo and her brother arrived at Tanforan Racetrack south of San Francisco. They were stripped, searched for weapons, given a medical exam, and led away to their new home.

The ground was wet from the downpour of the day before. Those who had come on that day were drenched and their baggage was soaked. ...

The guide left us at the door of Stall 50. We walked in and dropped our things inside the entrance. The place was in semidarkness; light barely came through the dirty window on either side of the entrance. A swinging half-door divided the 20 by 9 ft. stall into two rooms. The roof sloped down from a height of twelve feet in the rear room to seven feet in the front room; below the rafters an open space extended the full length of the stable. The rear room had housed the horse and the front room the fodder. Both rooms showed signs of a hurried

Figure 7.5 A child on the day of her imprisonment.

whitewashing. Spider webs, horse hair, and hay had been whitewashed with the walls. Huge spikes and nails stuck out all over the walls. A two-inch layer of dust covered the floor, but on removing it we discovered that linoleum the color redwood had been placed over the rough manure-covered boards.

We opened the folded spring cots lying on the floor of the rear room and sat on them in the semidarkness. We heard someone crying in the next stall.[58]

Meanwhile, the War Relocation Authority (WRA), a government agency created specially for this purpose, built ten more permanent camps for the Japanese American inmates in desolate locations in the mountains, swamps, and deserts of the West (Figure 7.6). Over the summer of 1942 the Army transferred its prisoners to the WRA. In those camps they waited out the war behind barbed wire. Gradually the White hysteria subsided as America's war fortunes turned, and the WRA became embarrassed to be holding tens of thousands of U.S. citizens and law-abiding residents in makeshift jails without any of them having been charged, much less convicted, of any crime. They administered a loyalty oath and let some of the American-born Nisei out of the camps on furlough, to work or go to school in the Midwest and East. Finally, as the war was winding down, they closed the camps and shoved the remaining inmates back into the arms of the American public who had so recently imprisoned them on account of their race.

All the while the lives and constitutional rights of Japanese Americans were being trashed, almost all other Americans remained silent. The American Civil Liberties Union took a pass. Legendary liberal Supreme Court Justice William O. Douglas looked the other way. Only a few brave individuals like attorney Wayne Collins

Figure 7.6   The Manzanar concentration camp.

spoke out (Collins led unsuccessful legal challenges to the internment). One who did speak was Supreme Court Justice Frank Murphy, who wrote in dissent: "This exclusion of 'all persons of Japanese ancestry, both alien and non-alien,' from the Pacific Coast area on a plea of military necessity in the absence of martial law ought not to be approved. Such exclusion goes over 'the very brink of constitutional power' and falls into the ugly abyss of racism."[59] Another was Black conservative gadfly George Schuyler, who wrote in his *Pittsburgh Courier* column:

> All minority groups in the United States ought to be deeply concerned over the drive being conducted by viciously reactionary elements to take away the citizenship of native-born citizens of Japanese ancestry. …
>
> These Japanese-American citizens are NOT in concentration because of the commission of any crime against the state. The contention that 70,000 citizens among the millions of whites on the Pacific Coast constituted a danger is a fantastic falsehood. These people are the most industrious, thrifty, and best behaved citizens in this country. … They had farms, businesses, and service jobs and professions. They sent their children to school and college and did all possible to measure up to American standards. They were put in concentration camps SOLELY because of "race," and the principle behind their jailing is exactly the same as that behind the jailing, torture and murder of the Jews under Hitler's jurisdiction.[60]

Schuyler and Murphy were joined by a few church people and some left-wing labor leaders, but few others, and their opposition was fruitless.

Some have wondered why Japanese Americans put up little resistance to their incarceration. Gordon Hirabayashi, Minoru Yasui, and Fred Korematsu were three individuals who did, in fact, challenge their imprisonment in court. All three got as far as the U.S. Supreme Court, and all three found the court amenable to ignoring the Constitution in their cases.[61] More widespread resistance to the initial incarceration was impossible to mount in the first months of the war, given the hysterical American public, the overwhelming might of the United States compared to the tiny Japanese American population, the fact that the Issei community leaders had all been taken away in the war's first days, and the collaboration of key Nisei leaders in the Japanese American Citizens League (JACL).[62]

Once the Japanese American population was massed inside the concentration camps, some people did resist. There were strikes and riots in some of the camps, and government troops came in, shot into crowds, and incarcerated protestors. Frank Emi, Mits Koshiyama, Yosh Kuromiya, and other outspoken Nisei refused to be drafted into the U.S. Army so long as their families were in prison camps, and they did time in federal penitentiaries because of their refusal.[63] Far more Nisei thought that the thing to do was to accept their situation and try to redeem the Japanese American image by fighting in the war. The 442nd Regimental Combat Team, an all-Nisei unit, fought in Europe, sustained more than 100 percent casualties, and earned more battlefield decorations than any unit in U.S. Army history. Other Nisei served in the Pacific, using their language skills to work behind enemy lines and to interrogate prisoners.[64]

Was the internment justified? Not for a minute. It was not a matter of security. No one brought an actual charge of espionage or sabotage against any Japanese American during the war, although some individuals surely must have had pro-Japanese sentiments. All the people arrested as Japanese agents were White. If the same ancestry standard had been applied to people whose families had come from Italy and Germany, America's other enemies in the war, then Dwight Eisenhower, Joe DiMaggio, New York City Mayor Fiorello LaGuardia, and millions of others would have been jailed. Instead, only a couple of thousand Italian and German foreign nationals were arrested. The difference was race. It is worth noting that in Hawai'i, where Japanese-descended people made up 36 percent of the population—the one place where they could have done some real damage—only a few Issei were interned. The Hawai'i Japanese were just too vital to the local economy.

What was the cost of this sordid episode? Precise numbers are, or course, not to be had, but very rough guesses are available. The American war effort lost the services of roughly 75,000 adults for an average of three years—225,000 person-years. A government commission estimated direct Japanese American property losses at between $1 and $3 billion in 1983; that did not include lost income or opportunities, just property that was stolen, destroyed, confiscated, or sold under duress at less than fair value. The loss of American constitutional liberties was enormous. For forty years, law students learned that the Japanese American concentration camp cases demonstrated that, in wartime, the guarantees of due process in the Constitution amounted only to paper promises. Two of the cases—*Korematsu* and *Hirabayashi*—were overturned in the 1980s, but events of the new century suggest that the Bill of Rights is once again disposable. Japanese American families and communities took a particularly hard hit. Most families did not recover economically for two decades, and psychological scars lasted far longer. West Coast Japanese communities never recovered their prewar population, nor their economic and cultural vitality.

In time, the public image of Japanese Americans more than recovered (see Chapter 8). But even Nisei war service did not convince most White Americans at first. In 1945 Dan Inouye was headed home after the war and tried to get a haircut.

> I went into a barbershop in one of the towns ringing San Francisco—and got as far as the door.
>
> "Are you Chinese?" the man said to me.
>
> I looked past him at the three empty chairs, the other two barbers watching us closely. "I'm an American," I said.
>
> "Are you Chinese?"
>
> "I think what you want to know is where my father was born. My father was born in Japan. I'm an American." Deep in my gut I knew what was coming.
>
> "Don't give me that American stuff," he said swiftly. "You're a Jap and we don't cut Jap hair."
>
> I wanted to hit him. I could see myself—it was as though I were standing in front of a mirror. There I stood, in full uniform, the new captain's bars bright on my shoulders, four rows of ribbons on my chest, the combat infantry badge, the distinguished unit citations—and a hook where my hand was supposed to be. And he didn't cut Jap hair. To think that I had gone through a war to save his skin—and he didn't cut Jap hair.
>
> I said, "I'm sorry. I'm sorry for you and the likes of you." And I went back to my ship.[65]

European Refugees and Displaced Persons

Several hundred thousand Europeans left their homelands as refugees in the 1930s and 1940s.[66] Some made it to America before the war broke out; others came after, fleeing the war's devastation. The rise of Fascism in Italy, Nazism in Germany, and their relatives in nearby lands drove several hundred thousand people out of their home countries. Some went elsewhere within Europe—France or Switzerland or England. Some came to the United States. Many who made this move were wealthy people for whom leaving did not mean starting their lives over from scratch, just moving their bank accounts and places of residence. Some were prominent intellectuals who could readily find jobs in North America. Even a very partial list of such people reads like a Who's Who of mid-century American intellectual and cultural life:

Theodore Adorno. German social scientist and philosopher. Expelled by the Nazis 1934. To America 1938. Returned to Germany 1952.

Hannah Arendt. German political scientist. To U.S. 1941.

Béla Bartók. Hungarian composer and pianist. To U.S. 1940.

Bruno Bettleheim. Austrian psychoanalyst. To U.S. 1939.

Ernst Bloch. German philosopher. Left Germany 1933. Lived in Czechoslovakia, France, U.S. Returned to Germany 1949.

Bertolt Brecht. German writer. To Denmark 1933. To Hollywood 1941. Returned to Germany 1947.

Marc Chagall. Russian émigré painter. Lived in Paris from 1922. To U.S. 1941. Returned to France 1948.

Salvador Dali. Spanish painter. Lived in U.S. during World War II.

Peter F. Drucker. German management consultant, author, and social critic. To U.S. 1937.
Albert Einsten. German physicist. To U.S. 1933.
Erik Erikson. German psychoanalyst. To U.S. 1933.
Enrico Fermi. Italian nuclear physicist. To U.S. 1939.
Erich Fromm. German psychoanalyst. To U.S. 1934.
Kurt Gödel. Austrian mathematician. To U.S. 1940.
Karen Horney. German psychoanalyst. To U.S. 1932.
Kurt Lewin. German psychologist. To U.S. 1932.
Thomas Mann. German writer. To U.S. 1939. To Switzerland 1952.
Herbert Marcuse. German philosopher. To U.S. 1934.
Ludwig Mies van der Rohe. German architect. To U.S. 1938.
Karl Polanyi. Austrian social scientist. To U.S. 1940. Later to Canada.
Fritz Redl. Austrian psychoanalyst. To U.S. 1936.
Theodore Schocken. German publisher. To U.S. 1938.
Igor Stravinsky. Russian composer. To U.S. 1939.
Leo Szilard. Hungarian nuclear physicist, biologist. To U.S. 1937.
Edward Teller. Hungarian nuclear physicist. To U.S. 1935.
Paul Tillich. German theologian. To U.S. 1933.
Arturo Toscanini. Italian conductor. To U.S. 1937.[67]

The United States did not always lay out a welcome for every individual, but the United States did benefit from grabbing what historian Benjamin Zulueta calls "brains at a bargain."[68] American science, engineering, music, painting, psychology, and weapons research could not have blossomed as they did in the middle decades of the twentieth century were it not for the contributions of refugee intellectuals. Name a big prize—Nobel, Pulitzer, Field Medal—and many if not most of the American winners in those years were refugee intellectuals. Many of them were Jews fleeing the oncoming Holocaust. Between 1933 and 1938, more than 102,000 German Jews moved abruptly to the United States. Several thousand more went to Britain, Canada, and Latin America.

Not all Jews were as lucky as these. Repeatedly after the rise of Hitler in 1933, American Jewish leaders and international observers warned that Jews in Germany and surrounding countries were being attacked and their lives were in jeopardy. The U.S. President and State Department, in the words of Vice President Walter Mondale a generation later, "failed the test of civilization."[69] Except for a few highly visible and highly valuable people like those listed above, the United States did everything it could to keep refugees out. In 1939, American nativists in Congress even beat back a modest proposal to take in ten thousand Jewish children. That same year, 930 Jewish passengers on the liner *St. Louis* shipped out of Germany looking for a country that would take them. They tried Cuba and the United States and were denied permission to land. In despair they went back to Germany to await the Holocaust, where 6 million Jews died, including many from the *St. Louis*.

One of the few who made it out was Carl Cohen, a mathematician, Judaic scholar, and member of the underground resistance to Hitler's regime. He was arrested fifteen times and spent months in jail. Friends forged visas to a Latin American country and got him exit documents from Germany in 1939. He went first to Holland, then England. There he taught math and Hebrew in the underground economy (he had no work permit) and saved until he could bring his wife out of Germany. His parents died in a concentration camp before he could get them out. A distant cousin got papers for Cohen and his wife to leave England and come to the United States. But when they got off the boat in Boston, U.S. authorities would not let his wife enter because she was in a wheelchair. She had a physical defect that offended the eugenic sensibilities of immigration officials. It took five weeks of anxious pleading to convince them to relent. Cohen ended up a Harvard math instructor.[70]

After the war, the refugee trickle turned to a flood. More than 20 million people in Europe were homeless and stateless at the war's end. Many were malnourished or ill. Many could not return to the places they had lived before the war. This was especially true for concentration camp survivors—for instance, nearly 1000 Jews who tried to return to Poland were killed by their neighbors between the end of the war and spring 1947. Borders were moving and people had lost their homes. Millions of ethnic Germans were expelled from Central and Eastern Europe. A couple of thousand Italians became refugees when their part of northeast Italy was given to Yugoslavia after the war. Many displaced persons ended up in what were called DP camps; such camps did not go out of business until 1957. A directive by President Harry Truman, followed by a series of successive Displaced Persons Acts, beginning in 1948, opened the way for more than half-million people to come to the United States outside the Johnson–Reed Act's quota system (200,000 more went to Canada). They went through more than two dozen steps in screening and preparation before arriving in the United States.

Truman spoke for the better impulses of the American people when he announced the 1945 directive:

> The war has brought in its wake an appalling dislocation of populations in Europe. … Every effort is being made to return the displaced persons and refugees in the various countries of Europe to their former homes. The great difficulty is that so many of these persons have no homes to which they may return. … The United States shares the responsibility [with a number of countries of Europe] to relieve the suffering. To the extent that our present immigration laws permit, everything possible should be done at once to facilitate the entrance of some of these displaced persons and refugees into the United States. In this way we may do something to relieve human misery. … I consider that common decency and fundamental comradeship of all human beings require us to do what lies within our power. … This period of unspeakable human distress is not the time for us to close or to narrow our gates. I wish to emphasize, however, that any effort to bring relief to these displaced persons and refugees must and will be strictly within the limits of the present quotas.[71]

That is, Truman wanted Americans to take in refugees, but mainly refugees who fit within the racially inflected guidelines of the 1924 law. There was no talk at all about taking in large numbers of people from China and Japan, for example, where the devastation was every bit as great as it was in Central Europe, any more than a later generation would talk about taking in significant numbers of refugees fleeing genocide in Rwanda or the Sudan.

The Displaced Persons Act of 1948 established two principles that would guide U.S. immigration laws ever after: preference for persons who had occupational skills the U.S. economy needed, and preference for relatives of people who were already U.S. citizens or residents. In 1948, the first preference among these refugees who came outside the quota system went to "Eligible displaced persons who have been previously engaged in agricultural pursuits and who will be employed in the United States in agricultural pursuits." Second preference went to "Eligible displaced persons who are household, construction, clothing, and garment workers, and other workers needed in the locality in the United States in which such persons propose to reside, or eligible displaced persons possessing special educational, scientific, technological or professional qualifications." Third preference outside the quota system went to "Eligible displaced persons who are the blood relatives of citizens or lawfully admitted alien residents of the United States."[72]

On the one hand, the Displaced Persons Acts brought tens of thousands of Holocaust survivors like Elie Wiesel to the United States. Wiesel was a young boy in Romania when the war started. In 1944 the Nazis came, arrested his family, and took them in a cattle car to Auschwitz. Wiesel's father, mother, and a sister died in the camps. He lived for some years in a French orphanage before he was reunited with his two remaining sisters. He attended the Sorbonne and began a career in Paris as a journalist. In 1955 an Israeli paper sent him to New York as its American correspondent. He stayed on in America and became the most renowned American voice for peace in the last third of the twentieth century. The author of more than thirty books, he lectured kings and presidents and was awarded the Nobel Peace Prize.[73]

On the other hand, some postwar European émigrés received plusher treatment. Werner von Braun was one of the pioneers of German rocketry who helped design and build the V-2 rocket that terrorized England in the latter stages of the war. When the war ended, U.S. officials spirited von Braun and 116 other Nazi scientists to the United States, where they became key figures in developing American rocketry, including the Redstone, Jupiter, and Saturn rockets that launched U.S. astronauts into space. The U.S. government seems to have worked closely with former Nazi officials after the war. The U.S. recruited former Nazis, some of them war criminals according to reports on government documents, to work for the FBI, Central Intelligence Agency, and other intelligence agencies, first in Europe, and then in the United States. The FBI and CIA arranged for many of them to move to the United States over the protests of the Immigration and Naturalization Service. In the postwar anti-Communist climate, the CIA, and especially FBI director J. Edgar Hoover, overruled the INS. He wanted "to keep these people in the country so they could report on any Communist trends inside their own community," according to historian Norman Goda.[74]

Von Braun became an American hero, but some of the little guys did pay for their sins in the end. One of the most notorious of the Nazi-connected postwar entrants was John Demjanjuk. A Ukrainian who apparently worked in a Nazi prison camp and may have been one of the sadistic guards in the notorious Treblinka death camp, Demjanjuk entered the United States in the late 1940s and lied about his Nazi past. Nazi hunters unmasked him in the 1970s, whereupon he fought a twenty-five-year holding action until he lost his U.S. citizenship in 2002 and was ordered deported in 2005.

The case of Josias Kumpf was a troubling one. When confronted forty years after he became an American citizen, Kumpf admitted he had been a member of the SS and a guard at the Trawniki camp, where hundreds of Jews were forced to strip naked, dig mass graves, and lie down in them; then they were machine-gunned and covered with several feet of earth. But Kumpf said he had been conscripted on pain of death into the Nazi war machine. He said he had only guarded people at Trawniki, never taken part in the murders. After the war, when U.S. immigration officials asked him if he had served in the German army, he said yes, he had. They never asked him if he had been in the SS or if he had been a concentration camp guard, and he had not volunteered the information.

In May 2005, a U.S. federal judge revoked Kumpf's American citizenship, on the ground he had lied on his immigration application, and started proceedings toward deporting him. Vivian Chakin was one Jew who survived Trawniki, but she lost her parents and her brother in the death camps. Her opinion was that, whether Kumpf had killed people or not, whether he was compelled or not, "He had a good life. He had a family. That's what all my people never had. That's what my brother never had. So why not let him feel a little bit of the suffering? Shouldn't he be punished at last?"[75]

Cracks in White Hegemony

Cracks began to appear in White native hegemony. Without the quota system being overturned, some of the groups that had been racially excluded quietly received small quotas and the right to naturalize. This was first a matter of wartime politics. At a time when the United States was fighting a war against Japan in the name of democracy, it was unseemly that the nation barred Chinese, citizens of the major U.S. ally in Asia, from entry into the country and from naturalization. So in December 1943 Congress repealed Chinese exclusion. Two months later the Roosevelt administration set a token quota of 105 annual entrants from the world's largest country—Chinese were no longer completely banned, but almost none of them would be allowed to come even so. In 1946, Congress applied a similar formula to South Asians, who were subjects of the British crown and whose country had hosted a major staging area for the war. They did the same for Filipinos, who had fought valiantly and suffered terribly in the war. In both cases, token numbers would be allowed to enter, and those here could now apply for naturalization. All other Asians—Koreans, Japanese, Southeast and Southwest Asians—remained barred.

Another crack opened with the passage of the first of several War Brides Acts in 1945. U.S. soldiers and sailors went abroad during the war and remained in Europe and Asia after the war had ended. There they did all the things that soldiers and sailors do, including meeting, dating, and mating local women. Thousands of GI children were born in Italy, Germany, France, and England, thousands more in Japan, where the occupation went on into the 1950s. Some Americans abroad sought to marry their girlfriends and bring them home to the United States. The War Brides Acts were intended to facilitate this. They provided that, "Regardless of section 9 of the Immigration Act of 1924, any alien admitted under section 1 of this Act shall be deemed to be a non-quota immigrant." These laws were aimed mainly at helping GIs who married women in Europe. The U.S. military worked hard to prevent servicemen in Asia from marrying their girlfriends, and threw up barriers to bringing them or their children back with them when their tour of duty was over. One unintended consequence of the War Brides Act was the reuniting of thousands of Chinese families. Exclusion had kept Chinese American citizen men whose wives and children were in China from bringing their families to the United States, in some cases for decades. The War Brides Acts meant that these men, most of whom served in the European theater, could send to China for their families and bring them over outside the tiny Chinese quota.[76]

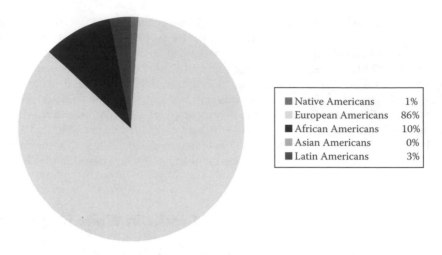

■ Native Americans	1%
▨ European Americans	86%
■ African Americans	10%
▨ Asian Americans	0%
■ Latin Americans	3%

Figure 7.7 Population by race in 1950, 153.2 million.

Figure 7.7 gives the racial makeup of the United States in 1950, during the early years of the Cold War and at the height of the impact of the Johnson–Reed Act.

The Cold War: Competing for the World's Peoples

During the Cold War, the United States competed for the loyalties, and increasingly for the company, of the world's peoples, as it opened America's doors selectively to certain classes of immigrants—primarily people with skills the American economy needed and people whom Americans defined as refugees from Communism.[77] From the latter 1940s through the 1980s, U.S. foreign policy and a considerable measure of domestic policy—including immigration and naturalization policy—were dictated by the titanic showdown between the United States and the Soviet Union.

Beginnings of Immigration Reform

So far as immigration is concerned, the 1952 McCarran-Walter Act was the centerpiece of that showdown.[78] Pat McCarran, a U.S. Senator from Nevada, was a crazed anti-Communist and an architect of the Cold War. He led the Congress in pursuit of a new immigration law that would solidify the racial hierarchies of the 1924 Johnson–Reed Act, yet remove the language of Nordic superiority that law had expressed, for Hitler's defeat had made such sentiments disreputable around the world. Congressmember Walter Judd, a Minnesota Republican and former missionary in China, seized the moment to try to end the exclusion of Asians. The result was a law that kept the quota system very much intact, but introduced the idea of an Asia-Pacific Triangle, extending from Japan to Indonesia and west to Afghanistan. Each country within that triangle would receive a quota, but only a tiny one of 100 people. McCarran and other reformers did not want to appear to be discriminating, but they did not want a lot of Asians coming into the country, either. Moreover, these quotas were racialized. Someone of European ancestry was accounted to the quota of his or her country of residence, not birth or ancestry. By contrast, someone of

Chinese ancestry who had been born and lived in Brazil was charged against the Chinese quota, not the Brazilian. Still, for the first time, at least every nation did receive a quota, even if 85 percent of the slots were reserved for Northwest Europeans. And the category "aliens ineligible to citizenship" was erased; all peoples would be allowed to naturalize.

McCarran and his supporters wanted an immigration policy that would give the United States an advantage in the Cold War. As Judd put it, they were trying to "influence greatly the battle for men's minds and hearts that is going on between the two philosophies of life and government that are locked in mortal struggle in our world." Part of that struggle was to drain the brains of many of the world's countries and bring their skills to the United States, rather than having them remain in their countries of origin or be plucked by the Soviets. Accordingly, the act established a preference system within the national/racial quota system. First preference went to people with scientific or professional skills that the United States needed. After that, the act established a preference for reuniting the families of American citizens and resident foreigners, and the closest of family members (spouses and minor children) did not count against the quotas at all. The latter provisions meant that the numbers of Asians began to creep up faster than Congress intended, as Asian immigrants, including those long residents of the United States, applied for naturalization and then sent for their families.

The act also had a sharply anti-Communist, antisubversive aspect. It provided for the expulsion and deportation of:

Aliens who are, or at any time have been, members of any of the following classes:

(A) Aliens who are anarchists;
(B) Aliens who advocate or teach, or who are members of or affiliated with any organization that advocates or teaches, opposition to all organized government;
(C) Aliens who are members or affiliated with (i) the Communist Party of the United States, (ii) any other totalitarian party of the United States, (iii) the Communist Political Association, (iv) the Communist or any other totalitarian party of any State of the United States, of any foreign state, or of any political or geographical subdivision of any foreign state. ...
(D) Aliens ... who advocate the economic, international, and governmental doctrines of world communism or the establishment in the United States of a totalitarian dictatorship, or who are members of or affiliated with any organization that advocates the economic, or international, and governmental doctrines of world communism. ...
(E) Aliens who write or publish, or cause to be written or published, or who knowingly circulate, distribute, print, or display ... any written or printed matter, advocating or teaching opposition to all organized government, or advocating or teaching ... the overthrow by force, violence, or other unconstitutional means of the Government of the United States or of all forms of law.[79]

President Harry Truman opposed the McCarran-Walter Act on the grounds that it enshrined racial discrimination, it was not much of an improvement over the

Johnson–Reed Act, and it included tools for harassing people with unpopular political views. Truman vetoed the measure, saying:

> I want our residents of Japanese ancestry, and all our friends throughout the Far East, to understand this point clearly. I cannot take the step I would like to take, and strike down the bars that prejudice has erected against them, without, at the same time, establishing new discriminations against the peoples of Asia and approving harsh and repressive measures directed at all who seek a new life within our boundaries. ... The only consequential change in the 1924 quota system which the bill would make is to extend a small quota to each of the countries of Asia. But most of the beneficial effects of this gesture are offset by other provisions in the bill. The countries of Asia are told in one breath that they shall have quotas for their nationals, and in the next, that the nationals of the other countries, if their ancestry is as much as 50 percent Asian, shall be charged to these quotas. It is only with respect to persons of oriental ancestry that this invidious discrimination applies. ... Admission to our citizenship would be made more difficult; expulsion from our citizenship would be made easier. Certain rights of native born ... Americans would be limited. All our citizens returning from abroad would be subject to serious risks of unreasonable invasions of privacy. ... Such powers are inconsistent with our democratic ideals.[80]

The law also effectively banned entry by gays and lesbians, although Truman did not protest that feature. The McCarran-Walter Act became law by a Congressional override of the President's veto. Meanwhile, Truman set a commission to work on the immigration system, in pursuit of his own vision. Just before he left office in 1953, the commission returned a report, *Whom Shall We Welcome*, that proposed ending the national origins quota system entirely and substituting an overall cap. Its summary recommendations read in part:

1. The national origins quota system should be abolished.
2. There should be a unified quota system, which would allocate visas without regard to national origin, race, creed, or color. ...
5. The maximum annual quota of visas [251,162 under this proposal, as opposed to 154,657 under the 1924 act] should be distributed ... on the basis of the following five categories:

> The Right of Asylum; Reunion of families; Needs in the United States; Special Needs in the Free World; General Immigration.

The commission also advocated trying to regularize and humanize the deportation procedures. At the time, all these recommendations went nowhere, for Dwight Eisenhower was soon President and Congress was still in Republican hands. More than a decade later, however, the recommendations in that report set the initial terms for a much more liberal policy (see below).[81]

The debate over the McCarran-Walter Act was waged in the same terms as the 1924 Immigration Act. Neither those who wanted to keep immigrants out nor those who had more liberal inclinations envisioned the numbers of immigrants rising as rapidly as they in fact did. McCarran-Walter envisioned a bit over 2 million immigrants over the period 1952 to 1965; the commission called for about 3.25 million in that time. As it happened, 3.5 million migrants came legally in that period, two-thirds of them outside the quota system—either as people with skills, close family members, or refugees.

Draining Asian Brains

Part of the Cold War thrust, following the Chinese Communist Revolution of 1949, was an effort to save Chinese people with special skills by bringing them to the United States.[82] An advocacy group calling itself Aid Refugee Chinese Intellectuals was organized in 1952 by Walter Judd and others with a missionary-inspired burden for China, with the goal to bring Chinese men and women of science and letters out of China and Hong Kong and to settle them in Taiwan and the United States. Bringing in such people and their skills amounted to, in historian Benjamin Zulueta's phrase, acquiring "brains at a bargain."[83] But encouraging Chinese to immigrate ran counter to a hundred years of agitation for racial exclusion.

These two conflicting impulses were wrapped up in the dealings of the U.S. government with one of world's premier rocket scientists, H. S. Tsien. In 1935, Tsien came to the United States on a scholarship—one of thousands of such Chinese overseas students in that era. He studied at MIT and Cal Tech. He held a top-level security clearance working on government projects during and after World War II, and he was one of the U.S. scientists chosen to debrief German scientists at the end of the war. He helped found the Jet Propulsion Laboratory (JPL) in Pasadena, where he made revolutionary advances in rocketry, engineering cybernetics, fluid dynamics, and other fields.

In 1949, Tsien became a U.S. citizen and head of the JPL. Then, at the height of the Cold War, his career came crashing down. The government revoked his security clearance, on the ground that he had known students who were Communists during his undergraduate years, and probably on the ground that he was Chinese of origin. He lived under virtual house arrest from 1950 to 1955—his phone tapped, his mail opened, his family followed. A tug of war took place between immigration officials, who wanted to deport him, and defense officials, who did not want his knowledge to fall into Communist Chinese hands. In 1955 the INS and anti-Chinese suspicion won. There was no evidence that Tsien was anything but a loyal American, but they deported him anyway. Sent back to a very different China than the one he had left two decades earlier, he found work doing the only thing he knew: making rockets. Tsien designed and supervised the construction of China's Silkworm missile (which later was sold to various other countries, including Iran) and its first satellite system, which tracked and controlled China's fleet of Intercontinental Ballistic Missibles (ICBMs). For all that Americans desired to save Asians from Communism during the Cold War years, in this case they failed spectacularly, to the everlasting detriment of U.S. strategic interests.[84]

Saving Cubans from Communism

After Castro's revolution in 1959, a lot of Americans wanted to save Cubans from Communism, too.[85] More than 200,000 people did leave Cuba for the United States during the 1960s, and "flee" was the word most often used to describe their departure.

María Cristina García interviewed several members of that first flow of Cubans. A fifty-five-year-old grandmother told of her exit experience:

> At the airport, the *milicianos* [the state police] made us disrobe and they checked all our personal belongings. Everybody … even babies in diapers … even old people. They were so arrogant, those *milicianos*. But we didn't say anything because if we did, they wouldn't let us leave. On the plane everybody was quiet. … We were all heartbroken. Many people were crying; others just sat there staring off into space. We were leaving our country for who knows how long. We were leaving everything behind. Halfway into the flight the pilot announced that we were in U.S. territory … that we were now free … and then everybody started clapping and cheering. Some men started cursing Fidel Castro … and his mother.

Deborah Carrera recalled: "When we got to Miami, the first thing [the immigration authorities] did was interview me. I declared myself to be against Fidel. That sealed my fate forever. I could never return because if I did I would be sent to prison." Most were allowed to take only a little money and a suitcase out of the country. One remembered: "We stayed in a fleabag hotel in Miami Beach. … It cost us about $5 a night. It was the only place we could afford. I would sit there every day and just look at the ocean. All I did was cry. The only thing that kept me going were the children. They depended on me. The hotel eventually threw us out because the neighbors complained that the baby cried too much. Everywhere we looked, the signs said 'No children.'"[86]

Most Cubans regarded themselves not as immigrants but as exiles at first. Hundreds if not thousands of Cuban exiles were implicated in the attempt to invade Cuba and overthrow Castro at the Bay of Pigs in April 1961. The invasion attempt failed miserably, with mismanagement on all sides. One hundred twenty would-be invaders died and another 1125 were taken prisoner. Soon they were sentenced to thirty years in prison each. Mounting a public relations campaign inside the United States, Cuban community leaders raised $53 million with which to ransom the captives; the last soldiers were repatriated to the United States just before Christmas 1962. From that time to this, many have remained Cubans in the United States rather than Cuban Americans—exiles dedicated to the overthrow of the Castro government and to one day returning home. As we shall see in Chapter 8, each year that exile quality dimmed. A new Cuban American generation arose that took on greater involvement in American life.

U.S. authorities tried at first to spread Cuban refugees out over the country, but quickly they clustered in South Florida. The climate there was like home, they were close to Cuba, and they could stand poised to go back. Very quickly, a small but significant pre-1959 Cuban community in Miami grew into an ethnic submetropolis—the second-largest concentration of Cubans after Havana. Cuban stores and restaurants, smells and sounds of Cuba came to dominate several Miami neighborhoods.

Their status as refugees from Communism helped Cubans to have success in the United States. It is true that those Cubans who came in the 1960s were among the best-educated and most upper-class groups in U.S. immigration history. Those people who had prospered under the Batista regime had the most to lose when the Communists took power, and they were the most likely to leave. Lawyers, doctors, bankers, politicians, business leaders, and their families made up the largest portion of the first wave of Cuban migrants. Since they brought with them substantial social capital, one would expect them to prosper in the United States. But their success here went beyond that advantage. The U.S. government defined Cubans as political migrants fleeing Communism. This they saw as a virtue and they contrasted Cubans to people like Mexicans and Haitians, whom they regarded as economic migrants merely seeking a better standard of living. Cold War imperatives dictated that the United States should favor the political migrants over the economic migrants. Florida was a poor state and had a dismal social service system, but the federal government rapidly changed that for Cuban migrants.

Silvia Pedraza-Bailey compared the economic and social fortunes of Mexican and Cuban migrants in painstaking detail and with mathematical precision. She found out that, even when she controlled for premigration education and economic status, Cubans had greater success in the United States than did Mexicans. The difference, she learned, was the carefully targeted network of support systems that the U.S. government set up to help Cubans adjust: a resettlement program, housing assistance, bilingual education, retraining to help doctors and other professionals earn American credentials, college tuition loans, and a fast track to citizenship. Such support systems were available to Cubans because they were defined by the government as refugees fleeing Communism; Mexicans did not have such things because they were defined as economic migrants and there was no political capital to be had from supporting them.[87]

The Civil Rights Movement

The African American civil rights movement is one of the most important features of United States social and political history. Indeed, it is a feature of world history, for it influenced independence movements and minority rights struggles all over the globe. Its origins can be traced, perhaps, to the founding of the National Association for the Advancement of Colored People (NAACP) in 1909, although one could pick any date between 1863 and 1954 as a starting point. It continued as a movement by African American leaders and an increasing number of everyday Black citizens through the 1930s and 1940s. Then in the 1950s the civil rights movement burst into flower and took over the center of the American social and political agenda. The broad outlines of that movement are well known, but their relation to still broader notions of inclusion and exclusion in American society should be explored here. I will note a number of milestones of the Civil Rights Movement that set the stage for a very large change in U.S. immigration policy in 1965.[88]

African Americans set about organizing to dismantle the powerful, all-encompassing system of racial oppression that Whites had erected after Reconstruction. Most White Southerners seemed more or less immune to appeals to conscience or assertions of Black people's rights as citizens. Because Whites controlled Southern politics utterly, Blacks could not achieve their rights by addressing either state governments or the federal legislature. They most often turned to the courts, which were no more liberal but which had fewer people they had to convince in any particular instance.

Gunnar Myrdal described a perceptual disjunction near the center of the quest for Black freedom. White priorities in maintaining dominance arranged themselves according to near-unanimous agreement on what Myrdal called the "Rank Order of Discriminations":

Rank 1. Highest in this order stands the bar against intermarriage and sexual intercourse involving white women.

Rank 2. Next come the several etiquettes and discriminations, which specifically concern behavior in personal relations. (These are the barriers against dancing, bathing, eating, drinking together, and social intercourse generally; peculiar rules as to handshaking, hat lifting, use of titles, house entrance to be used, social forms when meeting on streets and in work, and so forth. These patterns are sometimes referred to as the denial of "social equality" in the narrow meaning of the term.)

Rank 3. Thereafter follow the segregations and discriminations in use of public facilities such as schools, churches and means of conveyance.

Rank 4. Next comes political disfranchisement.

Rank 5. Thereafter come discriminations in law courts, by the police, and by other public servants.

Rank 6. Finally come the discriminations in securing land, credit, jobs, or other means of earning a living, and discriminations in public relief and other social welfare activities.

… [T]he closer the association of a type of interracial behavior is to sexual and social intercourse on an equalitarian basis, the higher it ranks among the forbidden things. Next in importance to the fact of the white man's rank order of discriminations is the fact that *the Negro's own rank order is just about parallel, but inverse, to that of the white man.* … Negroes are in desperate need of jobs and bread, even more so than of justice in the courts, and of the vote. These latter needs are, in their turn, more urgent even than better schools and playgrounds, or, rather, they are primary means of reaching equality in the use of community facilities. Such facilities are, in turn, more important than civil courtesies. The marriage matter, finally, is of rather distant and doubtful interest.

There is a certain condescension toward Blacks and accommodation to White racial-sexual fears in Myrdal's formulation. But it was not far off the mark enunciated in the same year by a dozen Black writers in *What the Negro Wants*: the four freedoms (of speech, of worship, from want, from fear), power over their own lives economically, full citizenship, political equality.[89] Whites' calculation that intimate interpersonal threat was the main issue may help explain the inhuman ferocity with which they defended their domination of African Americans. Black people's goals in the civil rights struggle centered on items that were more mundane: jobs, the right to vote, access to good education and health care, the opportunity to build businesses and join unions. Matters of etiquette and social intimacy were much further down their list.

Hardly a reader with any knowledge of U.S. history will be unfamiliar with milestones of the Civil Rights Movement such as these:

- May 17, 1954. *Brown v. Board of Education*. U.S. Supreme Court ruled that segregated schools are inherently unequal.
- May 31, 1955. Brown II. Supreme Court instructed states to begin desegregating schools "with all deliberate speed," the meaning of which was interpreted variously.

- August 28, 1955. Emmett Till, a fourteen-year-old Chicagoan visiting relatives in Mississippi, spoke to a White woman in a candy store, an offense for which he was seized, tortured, killed, and dumped in a river. His killers were known (indeed, they bragged about their deed in a national magazine) but they are not punished.
- December 5, 1955–December 21, 1956. Montgomery Bus Boycott to end segregation on public transportation in that Alabama city.
- March 12, 1956. Southern Manifesto. Ninety-six Southern members of Congress called the *Brown* decision an "unwarranted exercise of power by the court, contrary to the Constitution" and vowed to preserve segregation and "the Southern way of life."
- August 29, 1957. Congress passed a weak and unenforceable Civil Rights Act, albeit the first such legislation since Reconstruction.
- September 24, 1957. President Dwight Eisenhower sent federal troops to Little Rock, Arkansas, to help ensure that Elizabeth Eckerd and eight other Black youths were able to enroll in Central High School.
- February 1, 1960. Four freshmen from North Carolina A&T—Ezell Blair, Jr., Francis McCain, Joseph McNeil, and David Richmond—sat at the Whites-only lunch counter in Woolworth's in Greensboro. They were not served. Others joined them, and after several days of protests the restaurant was integrated. The Greensboro sit-ins were followed by others in Atlanta, Nashville, and throughout the South.
- Summer 1961. Freedom Rides. Black activists integrated interstate buses in several Southern states. They were beaten by White mobs while police watched, bombed, and 300 of them were jailed.
- September 30, 1962. James Meredith entered the University of Mississippi as its first Black student. President John Kennedy sent federal troops and federalized the Mississippi National Guard to quell White rioters.
- January 1963. While being sworn in as Alabama Governor, George Wallace vowed, "Segregation now! Segregation tomorrow! Segregation forever!" During the campaign he promised to "stand in the schoolhouse door" to prevent African Americans from entering White schools.
- May 3, 1963. Birmingham Police Commissioner Eugene "Bull" Connor directed his officers to attack marching children with truncheons, dogs, and fire hoses.
- August 28, 1963. March on Washington. Martin Luther King's "I Have a Dream" speech electrified the one-quarter million in attendance and a national audience on television.
- September 15, 1963. Whites bombed the 16th Street Baptist Church in Birmingham, Alabama, killing four little girls: Addie Mae Collins, Denise McNair, Carole Robertson, and Cynthia Wesley.
- Summer 1964. Mississippi Freedom Summer. Hundreds of Southern civil rights activists and Northern sympathizers conducted voter registration drives in rural areas. On June 21, voter registration workers James Chaney, Andrew Goodman, and Michael Schwerner were abducted and killed by members of the Ku Klux Klan.
- July 2, 1964. Civil Rights Act. President Lyndon Johnson signed a meaningful law to protect people's rights against discrimination. It outlawed segregation of restaurants, schools, parks, playgrounds, libraries, or any other public

facility. It prohibited discrimination by employers or labor unions on account of race, color, religion, national origin, or sex. It had strong federal enforcement powers. It promised a beginning toward equal treatment.

- January–March 1965. Selma, Alabama. Hundreds of Black and White people marched from Selma to the state capitol in Montgomery to publicize their attempts to register Black voters. White police and mobs of citizens attacked and beat the marchers, and two were killed.
- February 21, 1965. Malcolm X was killed.
- August 6, 1965. Voting Rights Act. The President and Congress responded to the escalating violence in the South by passing a law that outlawed all racial discriminations in voter registration. U.S. Attorney General Nicholas Katzenbach immediately deployed federal registrars in several Southern counties. Between 1960 and 1971, Black voter registration rates jumped in every Southern state—in South Carolina, from 16 to 46 percent of those eligible; in Texas, from 35 to 68 percent; in Alabama, from 14 to 55 percent; in Mississippi from 5 to 59 percent. Several times in later years, racial conservatives tried to gut the Voting Rights Act, but they were turned back each time.
- August 11–16, 1965. Watts Riots. Racial unrest spread north and west. Riots in New York, New Jersey, Chicago, and Philadelphia in 1964 were followed by a nearly week-long rampage in the biggest Black neighborhood on the West Coast.

For all that hope was engendered by the organizing, marching, protesting, petitioning, filing suit, and enduring, many Blacks felt frustration over the slow pace of change, the fact that large numbers of Blacks were left out of the new social order, and the fact that violence against Blacks did not diminish—it escalated. Some called for a new strategy. Hitherto the Civil Rights Movement had concentrated on legal challenges, voter registration drives, and nonviolent resistance to segregation. By 1965, some African American leaders began calling for Black Power. Among the speakers for this movement, none was more eloquent than Stokely Carmichael:

> For too many years, black Americans marched and had their heads broken and got shot. They were saying to the country, "Look, you guys are supposed to be nice guys and we are only going to do what we are supposed to do—why do you beat us up, why don't you give us what we ask, why don't you straighten yourselves out?" After years of this, we are at almost the same point—because we demonstrated from a position of weakness. We cannot be expected any longer to march and have our heads broken in order to say to whites: come on, you're nice guys. For you are not nice guys. We have found you out.[90]

Walter Mosley described the frustration that drove the Watts riot:

> For most people the pain they experience is just inside them. I hit you in the head but that's you and me. You could leave, find another man. You could go to work and none of the other women got a big knot on their heads. But if you come from down in Watts or Fifth Ward or Harlem, every soul you come upon has been threatened and beaten and jailed. If you have kids they will be beaten. And no matter how far back you remember, there's a beatin' there waiting for you. And so when you see some young man stopped by the cops and some poor mother cryin' for his release it speaks to you. You don't know that woman, you

don't know if the man bein' arrested has done something wrong. But it doesn't matter. Because you been there before. And everybody around you has been there before. And it's hot, and you're broke, and people have been doin' this to you because of your skin for more years than your mother's mother can remember. ...

This is a tough place. ... You got working men and women all fenced in together, brooding about what they see and what they can't have. Almost every one of them works for a white man. Every child is brought up thinking that only white people make things, rule countries, have history. They all come from the South. They all come from racism so bad that they don't even know what it's like to walk around with your head held high. They get nervous when the police drive by. They get angry when their children are dragged off in chains.

Almost every black man, woman, and child you meet feels that anger. But they never let on, so [White people have] never known. This riot was sayin' it out loud for the first time. That's all. ...

If everybody in the world despises and hates you, sees your features as ugly and simian, makes jokes about your ways of talking, calls you stupid and beneath contempt; if you have no history, no heroes, and no future where a hero might lead, then you might begin to hate yourself, your face and features, your parents, and even your child. It could all happen and you would never even know it. And then one hot summer's night you just erupt and go burning and shooting and nobody seems to know why.[91]

Still, despite the hopelessness that brought rage to the streets of Watts and Newark, as well as calls for more militant Black strategies, the Civil Rights Movement did bring the beginnings of some institutional and social change in the United States. At least for a time in America, it changed social etiquette: it was now, briefly, impolite for Whites to express racist attitudes toward Blacks and other people of color. Some social changes came that seemed to matter a lot to Whites and not very much to Blacks, like the right to join social clubs and to marry across racial lines.[92] And measures like the Civil Rights Act and especially the Voting Rights Act began to wring substantive changes from the American racial system. Within a decade, the face of the South was being remade, with Blacks a factor in politics in many locations and Black faces on school boards and in formerly White college classrooms.

Racial Fairness and the Immigration Act of 1965

One of the changes that came along with all this was a radical revision in America's immigration rules in 1965.[93] Rare indeed is the act of government that can be laid at the feet of altruism. The Immigration and Nationality Act of 1965 is one. As Nathan Glazer and Roger Daniels noted, "[T]hree pieces of legislation in 1964 and 1965— the Civil Rights Act of 1964 and the Voting Rights Act and the Immigration Act of 1965—represent a kind of high-water mark in a national consensus of egalitarianism, one from which much of the country has receded in subsequent years."[94]

While still a U.S. Senator in 1958, John F. Kennedy had been the author of record on a book, *A Nation of Immigrants*, which called for reform of the racial-national quota system. It is a paean to America's history as an immigrant nation.

Table 7.2 Preference Systems in the 1952 and 1965 Immigration Acts

Immigration and Nationality Act, 1952

Guiding principles: skilled occupations and family reunification.

Exempt from preference requirements and numerical quotas: spouses and unmarried minor children of U.S. citizens.

Preferences within the quota system:

1. Highly skilled immigrants whose services are urgently needed in the U.S. and the spouses and children of such immigrants. 50%.
2. Parents of U.S. citizens over age 21 and unmarried adult children of U.S. citizens. 30%.
3. Spouses and unmarried adult children of permanent resident aliens. 20%.
4. Brothers, sisters, and married children U.S. citizens and accompanying spouses and children. 50% of numbers not used in preferences 1-3.
5. Nonpreference: applicants not entitled to any of the above. 50% of the numbers not uses in 1–3, plus any not used in 4.

Immigration Act of 1965

Guiding principles: family reunification and skilled occupations.

Exempt from preference requirements and numerical quotas: spouses, unmarried minor children, and parents of U.S. citizens.

Preferences within the quota system:

1. Unmarried adult children of U.S. citizens. 20%.
2. Spouses and unmarried adult children of permanent resident aliens. 20% (25% after 1980).
3. Members of the professions and scientists and artists of exceptional ability. 10%.
4. Married children of U.S. citizens. 10%.
5. Brothers and sisters of U.S. citizens over 21. 24%.
6. Skilled and unskilled workers in occupations for which labor is in short supply in U.S. 10%.
7. Refugees from communist or communist-dominated countries, or the Middle East. 6%.
8. Nonpreference: applicants not entitled to any of the above. Since there are more preference applicants than can be accommodated, this has not been used.

Adapted from Roger Daniels, *Coming to America*, 2nd ed. (New York: HarperCollins, 2002), 342.

It portrays immigrants, whatever their provenance, as virtuous and hardworking. It highlights the similarities between immigrants from various places rather than their differences. In July 1963, Kennedy as President asked Congress to amend the 1952 Act; his main proposal was to eliminate national quotas. Under the heading "Elimination of discrimination based on national origins" Kennedy contended:

> The use of a national origins system is without basis in either logic or reason. It neither satisfies a national need nor accomplishes an international purpose. In an age of interdependence among nations, such a system is an anachronism, for it discriminates among applicants for admission into the United States on the basis of accident of birth.

... [T]he system is heavily weighted in favor of immigration from northern Europe and severely limits immigration from southern and eastern Europe and from other parts of the world. An American citizen with a Greek father or mother must wait at least eighteen months to bring his parents here to join him. ... Meanwhile, many thousands of quota numbers are wasted because they are not wanted or needed by nationals of the countries to which they are assigned.

After John Kennedy was assassinated in November 1963, his brother Robert published a revised edition of *A Nation of Immigrants*, which the younger Kennedy introduced with these words: "Our attitude toward immigration reflects our faith in the American ideal. We have always believed it possible for men and women who start at the bottom to rise as far as their talent and energy allow. Neither race nor creed nor place of birth should affect their chances."[95]

Kennedy's successor Lyndon Johnson continued and expanded most of the martyred president's civil rights agenda, including immigration reform. The law that resulted, the Hart-Cellar Act of 1965, abolished the discriminatory national origins quotas. It ended the Asia-Pacific Triangle. It divided the globe into the Eastern Hemisphere (Europe, Africa, Asia, and Australia), which was given a total cap of 170,000 entrants, and the Western Hemisphere (North and South America), which was granted a maximum of 120,000 each year. No more than 20,000 visas could be issued to the residents of any single Eastern Hemisphere country in any year. It was equally significant that people who had close family members already in the United States, as well as people who had skills the American economy needed, would be allowed to enter outside the numerical limitations (see Table 7.2 for preferences outside the hemispheric cap system). So, for instance, in 1977, 275,531 people entered under the numerical limitation—within the prescribed number. But another 117,857 entered outside the cap as family members of people already here, or as people with skills, and 4,701 came as refugees, also outside the cap.[96]

The Immigration Act of 1965 laid the ground for a massive change in the size and shape of immigration into the United States, to which we will turn in Chapter 8.

Chapter 8

New Migrants from New Places Since 1965

The 1965 Immigration Act removed the racist shape that immigration and citizenship laws had gradually taken on over the previous century. This had a profound (and for almost all Americans unexpected) impact on American society. A great new wave of immigrants came to the United States, mainly from Latin America and from Asia. This great movement of new peoples, along with the civil rights revolution, made for the beginnings of new social relationships and a new system of ethnic hierarchy.

The shape of immigration in the period after the 1965 immigration law was startlingly different from earlier eras.[1] As a result of the 1924 Johnson–Reed Act, in the 1950s more than half of the immigrants came from Europe, and most of the rest came from Canada. By the 1970s, a new pattern had been set: nearly half from Latin America, another third from Asia, and most of the rest from Europe (although a growing number also began to come from Africa).

Meanwhile, the overall number of migrants soared, from 2.5 million in the 1950s to 9 million in the 1990s. By the end of the century, the raw numbers were even higher than they had been a century earlier, at the height of the great wave from Europe. The annual average number of immigrants for the period 1901 to 1910 was 879,539; for 1991 to 2000, it was 909,542. But the United States to which they were coming was more than three times larger: 248,709,873 people in 1990 as compared to 75,994,575 in 1900. This meant that, in the first decade of the twentieth century, 11.6 immigrants came to the country for every 100 people already here. For the last decade of the same century, the number was only 3.7 per 100. Late twentieth- and early twenty-first-century U.S. immigration, legal and illegal, was quite large in absolute numbers, but it was much, much smaller in terms of its relative impact on the existing U.S. population than had been that earlier migration—a simple statistic thoroughly ignored by those who would close the door during the restriction hysteria yet to come.[2]

Table 8.1 shows the origins of U.S. immigrants by decade from 1951 to 2000. In the 1950s, because of the racist provisions of the Johnson–Reed Act, more than half the migrant flow came from Europe, with another 40 percent coming from the

Table 8.1   Immigration by Region of Origin, 1951–2000

Decade	Europe		Asia		Americas	
1951–1960	1,325,727	52.7%	153,249	6.1%	966,944	39.6%
1961–1970	1,123,492	33.8%	427,642	12.9%	1,716,374	51.7%
1971–1980	800,368	17.8%	1,588,178	35.3%	1,982,735	44.1%
1981–1990	761,550	10.4%	2,738,157	37.3%	3,615,225	49.3%
1991–2000	1,359,737	14.9%	2,795,672	30.7%	4,486,806	49.3%

Decade	Africa	Oceania	Total	
1951–1960	14,092*	12,976*	2,515,479	100%
1961–1970	28,954*	25,122*	3,321,677	100%
1971–1980	80,779*	41,242*	4,493,314	100%
1981–1990	176,893*	45,205*	7,338,062	100%
1991–2000	354,939*	55,845*	9,095,417	100%

Source: Appendix B, Table B.4.

* Less than .1%

Americas, mainly Canada. Immigration from Asia was almost nonexistent, and immigration from Mexico was only beginning to perk up. European immigration bottomed out in the 1980s at just over 10 percent of the total, then rebounded to 15 percent a decade later. Asian migration topped out at 37 percent in the 1980s and declined to 31 percent in the 1990s. Migration from the Americas was the largest piece of the inflow: holding steady at about half of the total. Table 8.2 shows a snapshot of the countries that sent the largest numbers of immigrants to the United States in 1998.

For the 1990s, about one-third (34 percent) of the growth of U.S. population was from immigration, legal and illegal. That means, of course, that two-thirds were due to births within the United States. Of those children who were born in the United States, 78 percent were born to native-born Americans and 22 percent were born to parents who had migrated earlier.[3]

Many Americans seem to be under the misapprehension that the United States in the late twentieth and early twenty-first centuries has had a higher proportion of immigrants than other countries in the developed world. American leaders have always been fond of reminding us that we are a nation of immigrants (and so we are, as acknowledged in the title of this book). But at the same time, it is just not true that the United States in recent decades has been unique, or even outstanding, among the world's rich nations in the proportion of its population that has come from immigration. In 2000, for example, 11.1 percent of the U.S. population was foreign born, the highest percentage in the current surge, but still below the percentages of foreign-born people in the U.S. population any time between 1860 and 1920. Compare that to 10.1 percent in the Netherlands, 11.3 percent in Sweden, 18.8 percent in Canada, 23.0 percent in Australia, and 59.3 percent in Israel. We are an immigrant nation, but we are not *the* immigrant nation *par excellence*. We are a lot like other industrial nations in our percentage of foreign-born residents, and not higher than we have been at many other times in our history.[4]

Table 8.2 Major Sources of U.S. Immigrants, 1998

Source	Number
Americas	
Mexico	131,575
Jamaica, Haiti, Dominican Republic	48,982
Cuba	17,375
Colombia	11,836
Canada	10,190
Peru	10,154
Asia	
China	42,159
India	36,482
Philippines	34,466
Vietnam	17,689
South Korea	14,268
Pakistan	13,094
Europe	
Russia	11,529
United Kingdom	9,018
Poland	8,469
Ukraine	7,448
Africa	
Nigeria	7,746

Source: "New Americans: Their Origins and Destinations," *National Geographic* (September 2001), 52–53.

What is really different about the United States is the source of its immigrants. In the United States in 2000, 54 percent of the foreign-born people came from the Americas (mainly south of the Rio Grande), 26 percent from Asia, and just 16 percent from Europe. In Australia, the foreign-born residents in 2001 were 51 percent from Europe, 29 percent from Asia, 11 percent from Oceania, and 4 percent came from the Americas. For Canada in 2001, 41 percent of the foreign-born residents had come from Europe, 37 percent from Asia, and 16 percent from the Americas. America's immigrants in the late twentieth century and early twenty-first century came predominantly from places where people wore brown or yellow skin; both Canada and Australia were new homes to many Asians—proportionately more than the United States—but they had few Latin Americans and a whole lot of Europeans.[5]

The conclusion is inescapable. If many Americans in those years had a problem about immigration, their problem was not so much about the number of immigrants—which was not in fact so large compared to either American history or the experiences of other nations—but about the races of those immigrants.

Some Migrants We Know

The stories of four people who were active in American public life in the 1990s and 2000s give a sense of a certain range of immigrant experiences in the era after the 1960s. All are still alive at this writing. The first two are men of money: Rupert Murdoch and George Soros. Murdoch is a migrant entrepreneur, who turned a family fortune gained in the Australia newspaper business into a multibillion dollar media empire on three continents.[6] He is in some people's eyes the embodiment of all that is best about the United States: wealth, enterprise, success, and engagement in public life. In the words of one admirer, John Lanchester: "Rupert Murdoch is not so much a man, or a cultural force, as a portrait of the modern world. He is the way we live now; he is the media magnate we deserve."

Murdoch began life in Melbourne, the son of Sir Keith Murdoch, Australia's most influential media mogul, who owned the Melbourne *Herald* and *Weekly Times* as well as other papers. Rupert Murdoch was schooled at English academies and Oxford, and returned home on his father's death in 1952 to take over the family news business. For the next twenty years and more, Murdoch bought one Australian newspaper after another, then television stations, and founded a national newspaper, *The Australian*, until he controlled 70 percent of the Australian news market.

In the 1960s, Murdoch began to venture into the British press. He acquired *News of the World*; the tabloid *The Sun*; *The Times*; and *The Sunday Times*. Starting in the United States in 1973, he acquired the *San Antonio News*, then the *New York Post*, and later *TV Guide*. He founded the weekly tabloid *National Star* and later the conservative political magazine, *The Weekly Standard*. In the 1990s, he ventured into broadcasting in the United States, founding the Fox TV Network, buying the Fox film studio (and later the Los Angeles Dodgers baseball team), and starting Fox Sports television and the right-wing cable talk show outlet, Fox News Channel. As the new century dawned, Murdoch sold off the Dodgers, but he also founded or acquired Britain's multichannel BSkyB network, the Star satellite network in Asia, and U.S. publisher HarperCollins.

No one is more powerful in shaping public opinion in the United States and in the world than Rupert Murdoch. Although Murdoch took out U.S. citizenship in the 1970s (the law required him to be a U.S. citizen in order to buy some American media outlets), he seems very much a citizen of several nations. He owns the largest single share of the news media in Australia, Britain, and the United States, and has significant holdings in other nations as well. As Lanchester put it, "he is in a sense not located anywhere." He uses words like "we" and "our country" freely in the United States, the U.K., and Australia and travels constantly around the globe. His outlets push hard for conservative political agendas in all three of the countries whose media markets he dominates.

Like Murdoch, George Soros is a billionaire.[7] And like Murdoch, Soros has long been involved in politics in several countries, although Soros seems personally committed to the United States rather than to Murdoch-style transnational citizenship. He was born in Budapest in 1930 as György Schwartz, although the family changed their name in 1936, to lessen their visibility as Jews as Nazi influence spread to Hungary. The family spoke Esperanto, and sought to help build an open, tolerant, international world. They survived World War II, and then young George went to England to get out from under the Soviet occupation of his homeland and to seek his future. In 1956 he moved on to the United States. He pursued a business career, and ultimately became one of America's richest people by speculating in financial markets. Soros founded Soros Fund Management, which creates and renews his extraordinary wealth.

Always both philosophically and politically inclined, Soros formed the Open Society Institute to further his capitalistic and democratic aims. He wrote several books, among them *Opening the Soviet System* (1990), *Underwriting Democracy: Encouraging Free Enterprise and Democratic Reform Among the Soviets and in Eastern Europe* (1991), *The Crisis of Capitalism: Open Society Endangered* (1998), *Open Society: Reforming Global Capitalism* (2000), and *The Bubble of American Supremacy: Correcting the Misuse of American Power* (2004). He gave more than $5 billion to promote democracy in Eastern Europe and the former Soviet Union, and was a prime supporter for the Solidarity movement in Poland, the Czech human rights group Charter 77, and the Rose Revolution in Georgia. Turning to his adopted homeland, he campaigned for more openness and equity in the American economy and politics. In 2003–2004, he contributed more than $20 million to groups that were attempting to defeat the election of U.S. President George W. Bush.

The other pair of immigrants in this sketch are people of politics: Arnold Schwarzenegger and Gary Locke. Schwarzenegger is the poster boy for the overlapping of politics and celebrity that occurred in the last decades of the twentieth century.[8] He was a celebrity first. Born in Thal, Austria, a small town near Graz, he became a bodybuilder and, in 1967 at age twenty, winner of the Mr. Universe pageant. He moved to Los Angeles in 1968 and trained further, winning Mr. Universe three more times and Mr. Olympia seven times. He also began working in movies and was the subject of the documentary *Pumping Iron* (1977). He played Hercules, then gathered small roles as hit men and mobsters before breaking through as a muscular action hero in dozens of movies, from *Conan the Barbarian* (1982) and *The Terminator* (1984) to *Predator* (1987) and *Kindergarten Cop* (1990).

Schwarzenegger became involved in politics in the 1990s as Chairman of President George H. W. Bush's Council on Physical Fitness and Sports, and in a similar job under California Governor Pete Wilson. His first run for office was in 2003, when he was elected largely on name recognition from a large field of would-be successors to recalled Governor Gray Davis. He made much of his immigrant beginnings in the campaign, although his chief opponent, Cruz Bustamante, was the child of Mexican immigrant field workers and had grown up under circumstances far more like those of most immigrants than had Schwarzenegger.[9] The new governor and his Kennedy-family wife, TV newsperson Maria Shriver, brought glamour to Sacramento, and the promise to clean up politics. In his first three years in office, Schwarzenegger was unable to achieve any of his major goals, and his political career remained pegged to the vicissitudes of celebrity and the ebb and flow of the California economy.

Like Schwarzenegger, Gary Locke was governor of a western state.[10] Locke is not an immigrant himself, but like Schwarzenegger's erstwhile rival Cruz Bustamante, Locke is an immigrant son. His grandfather migrated to Washington from Toisan, a rural district near Hong Kong; his mother came a generation later from Hong Kong. He grew up in a central Seattle housing project and then a lower-middle-class neighborhood. While his father ran a tiny grocery store, his mother tended five children. Public schools led to a scholarship to Yale and then a law degree. He was first an assistant county prosecutor in Seattle, then a six-term state legislator, then

King County Executive. At each stop Locke was highly regarded for nonideological mastery of the details of making government work. His politics were not far from Schwarzenegger's: liberal on social issues, conservative on fiscal responsibility. Where they differed was in Locke's command of the details of governing, his ability to build working coalitions, and his devotion to public education. And where Schwarzenegger turned celebrity into a brief political career, Locke was a career politician.

In giving the Democratic Party's response to President George W. Bush's State of the Union message in 2003, Locke emphasized his immigrant roots and told a tale of striving and uplift: "My grandfather came to this country from China nearly a century ago and worked as a servant. Now I serve as governor just one mile from where my grandfather worked. It took our family 100 years to travel that mile. It was a voyage we could only make in America. The values that sustained us—education, hard work, responsibility and family—guide me every day." Then he went on to criticize the Bush administration's record on terrorism, the war in Iraq, what he called "upside down economics," and, above all, education.[11] In 2003, while widely regarded as a politician with a national future, Locke stepped away from the political arena in order to spend time with his wife and three small children.

These four members of the immigrant stream are known to most publicly literate Americans. Most, however, do not think of Soros or Murdoch as an immigrant, and they might not think that about Schwarzenegger if he had not made an issue of it in his campaign. Locke, on the other hand, was widely noted to be the child of immigrants and as the nation's first Chinese American governor.

From Asia

The Locke family was part of the earlier wave of Asian migration to the United States—immigrants before the Johnson–Reed Act, paper sons and daughters thereafter, and some families reunified after World War II. Following the removal of racial restrictions on immigration in 1965, the number of migrants coming from several Asian countries exploded (Table 8.3).[12]

Filipinos were the largest in number, with 1.5 million people coming to the United States between 1961 and 2000. Chinese (from the People's Republic, Hong Kong, and Taiwan combined) were next, at 1.3 million, followed by Asian Indians

Table 8.3 Asian Immigration by Major Countries, 1961–2000

Country	1961–1970	1971–1980	1981–1990	1991–2000
China	109,771	237,793	444,942	528,893
India	27,189	164,134	250,786	363,060
Japan	39,988	49,775	47,085	67,942
Korea	34,526	267,638	333,746	164,166
Philippines	98,376	354,987	548,764	503,945
Vietnam	4,340	172,820	280,782	286,145
All Asia*	427,642	1,588,178	2,738,157	2,795,672

Source: Appendix B, Tables 8, 16, 17, 18, 19, 20, 21.

* Includes other countries besides those listed individually above.

and Koreans (about 800,000 each), and Vietnamese (700,000). Of the major Asian American groups, only Japanese came in very small numbers in this period; that may be due to the robustness of the Japanese economy and a falling birthrate, both of which made it feasible for people to seek their fortune at home. The numbers for all these groups (and for several Asian nationalities with smaller numbers, such as Thais, Cambodians, and Indonesians) climbed, decade by decade—except for Filipinos and Koreans, who peaked in the 1980s and declined thereafter as their home economies perked up and, in the case of Filipinos, as opportunities began to open in other parts of the world.

Fleeing War in Vietnam and Southeast Asia

Only very tiny numbers of people migrated to the United States from any of the countries of Southeast Asia before the 1970s. Thailand, Indonesia, Vietnam, Burma, Laos, Cambodia, Malaysia—there was a great deal of movement back and forth among these places (and also southern China and the Philippines) throughout modern history. Every nation in mainland Southeast Asia had a substantial Chinese minority, who often played a middleman role as small shopkeepers. In some places, the Chinese blended into the local society, intermarried, and became more or less indistinguishable from other local citizens. But in more places ethnic Chinese people continued to stand separate from the rest of the local populace. Even after many generations in Burma or Thailand, for instance, they often maintained economic and kinship ties back to China. Other groups besides the Chinese lived long outside their places of origin: Vietnamese in Cambodia and Laos, Cambodians in Laos and Vietnam, Laotians in both those other places, Indians in Malaysia and Indonesia. In addition, ethnic minorities without homelands of their own—like Hmong, Miao, and Karen—lived in several countries where they were dominated by other ethnic groups.[13]

All this moving around within Southeast Asia, however, was not a prelude to migration across the Pacific to the United States. That development required the additional spur of a colonial war gone bad. The U.S. war in Vietnam, which stretched from the mid-1950s to the fall of Saigon in 1975, is yet one more example of the nexus between racism, colonialism, and migration that we have seen in earlier chapters. In short order, between 1975 and 2000, hard on the heels of a racially inflected colonial war, nearly three-quarters of a million people left their homes in Vietnam and came to the United States. Several tens of thousands of people from Cambodia, Laos, and Thailand joined them.[14]

The U.S. war in Vietnam was misbegotten from the start.[15] When the Japanese army surrendered at the end of World War II, many Vietnamese, like other formerly colonized peoples, hoped and expected to win national independence. The United States was the leader of the victors, and the late U.S. President, Franklin Roosevelt, had promised as much. France had different ideas, and instead reimposed its prewar colonial regime. Thus began a war between the French and a group of guerrillas calling themselves the Viet Minh who had just fought the Japanese. It ended in total French defeat in 1954. The United States brokered a peace agreement in Geneva and took over much of the French role (including a defeat of its own twenty-one years later). Initially Vietnam was partitioned, with most of the partisans who had fought the Japanese and French going to the North and a pro-U.S. proxy government installed in the South. In 1956, the United States cancelled the southern portion of the nationwide elections that had been agreed upon at Geneva, because their candidate for national leadership, South Vietnamese President Ngo Dinh Diem, a former functionary of the French colonial government, seemed certain to lose.

War then began on a small scale and escalated very slowly. On one side stood a cadre of guerrilla fighters, former Viet Minh, who went back to their southern homes, where they kept their weapons and fought on under the name National Liberation Front (NLF); the United States and its allies called them Viet Cong. The NLF acquired the support of the Democratic Republic of Vietnam (the North), which was led by a charismatic former guerrilla fighter who took the name Ho Chi Minh. In time they added the backing of the Soviet Union, and most members of the NLF and North Vietnamese government eventually converted to Marxist ideology. On the other side, in the South, stood the Republic of Vietnam, led by Ngo Dinh Diem and backed by the United States. The United States began to send military advisors to train South Vietnamese troops in 1961, under President John Kennedy. Diem was assassinated with U.S. approval, and a series of saviors of their nation were installed, one after another, as President of the Republic of Vietnam. The fighting increased, and so did American troop commitments. The 1964 U.S. presidential election was partly a referendum on the war, with Republican Barry Goldwater advocating massive nuclear attacks against North Vietnam (and losing the election) and Kennedy's successor, Lyndon Johnson, taking a softer line (and winning).

Nevertheless, by 1965 the United States had more than half a million troops in Vietnam, and still the war got bigger and bigger, with no end in sight. Throughout, the United States insisted on understanding Vietnam as a Cold War issue, with the forces of international communism on one side and those of international capitalism on the other. Most Vietnamese saw it as a war of national liberation from colonialism, although some were pleased to embrace the American anticommunist rhetoric. From 1965 on, an antiwar movement grew within the United States; meanwhile, the NLF and their northern allies grew stronger in the field. In 1968, a winter NLF offensive took several provincial capitals and, briefly, the U.S. Embassy in Saigon. That spring saw massive demonstrations by U.S. college students and other Americans against the war. These led to President Johnson dropping out of the race for re-election. The assassination of the Democratic front-runner, Robert Kennedy, led to the election of Republican Richard Nixon, who promised but did not have a secret plan to end the war. The demonstrations grew larger and louder, until in 1970 Nixon instituted a draft lottery. The lottery made it certain that particular young men would be drafted, but it released others from that jeopardy. The antiwar movement fizzled, a few remnants turned nihilistic and violent, and the United States was still losing the war. In search of an exit strategy, Nixon's generals turned the fighting over to the South Vietnamese army, which was quickly overwhelmed. In April of 1975, as the final U.S. withdrawal was underway (Figure 8.1), this sign appeared on a wall in Berkeley: "Will the last Marine leaving Vietnam please turn out the light at the end of the tunnel?"

The U.S. war in Vietnam generated a mighty flood of refugees. Many of the first wave were people who had collaborated with the American regime in the South: members of the government, people who worked for the American forces, businesspeople who made money off the booming war economy, women and men who had personal friendships (even family relationships) with Americans, and so on. The United States had postponed making evacuation plans for fear of engendering

Figure 8.1   Helicopter leaves the U.S. Embassy in Saigon, April 1975.

public panic. No one in the American command expected the South Vietnamese army to melt away as quickly as it did. By April 1975, it was clear that South Vietnam was going to fall. The current president, Nguyen Van Thieu, resigned and fled to England, and many other high-ranking officials made preparations to leave. U.S. helicopters evacuated American citizens and their dependents, along with selected Vietnamese people. Many high officials of the South Vietnamese government and army made it out with the retreating American troops. But many more were left behind, like the man being pushed from the helicopter by a U.S. embassy officer in Figure 8.1.

In that first wave some 125,000 Vietnamese refugees, plus 5,000 people from neighboring Cambodia, were taken to a U.S. military base on Guam. Most of those people were soon flown on to the United States. After processing at military bases scattered around the United States, those with substantial amounts of money were free to enter the country as immigrants. Those without cash had to find sponsors; churches and individuals stepped up. As a matter of policy and to minimize ethnic visibility and possible backlash, the government tried to spread the refugees across the entire country, to every state, city, and rural district. Lang Ngan recalled her experiences:

On April 25th, near the end of the war, my supervisor called me in, and told me that by six o'clock that evening, we had to meet, to get to the airport by nine the next morning. I had worked for the U.S. Embassy in Saigon for seven years. If we had stayed, we would have been persecuted by the new government. There was no time to talk to friends or relatives because the evacuation was supposed to be secret, and we were not allowed to tell our relatives. We couldn't even take our money out of the bank. ... I was allowed to take my family, because I was single. My father, my mother, myself and six brothers and sisters. ... We were transported by military cargo plane. At the time, the evacuation was so sudden the U.S. government didn't have a chance to prepare for our arrival. So we were taken to a military camp in the Philippines. ... [and then on] to Wake Island, and screened for admittance. ...

We arrived at the camp in Arkansas on May fourth [eight days after leaving Vietnam]. ... Because I could speak English, I started helping many of those who couldn't, translating for them. I met the representative from the International Rescue Committee, and started to work as a volunteer for IRC. I ended up in New York because the IRC offered me a job. ... [We found] an apartment in Flushing, Queens. ... a family of nine [in] one bedroom... [O]ur parents ... had a lot of difficulty adjusting. They felt isolated, because there were no Cantonese-speaking people in the building, and in the daytime, when all the children were in school there was nothing for them to do. ... As for my siblings, they knew that if I couldn't support them I would give them away. ... They felt lucky. So they worked hard. ... We wore whatever people gave us. ... The children studied very hard to catch up in school. ... We had no furniture—just a few chairs and a used sofa that the supervisor gave us, and broken TV. And the rest were mattresses. ... All my younger sisters and brothers have done very well in school. ... My sister got a full scholarship to MIT from Bell Labs. I have one brother who got an electrical engineering degree from Columbia, and the other finished at City College. One other brother is going to medical school at New York Med. ... [I married and we] now own a two family house. My husband and I live in one side, my parents in the other.[16]

It was hard, but things seem to have worked out for Lang and many others who left Vietnam in that first wave.

Over the first few years of residence in the United States, Vietnamese people undercut the government scattering policy and gradually clustered in a few cities. Washington, D.C., and its suburbs were an early point of concentration, as quite a number of that first wave of refugees had ties to U.S. government people. Other places with large Asian populations soon began to nurture Vietnamese communities: Seattle, Boston, Los Angeles, the San Francisco Bay Area, New York (anywhere they could speak Vietnamese and get Asian groceries). In time, every major U.S. city had a Vietnamese colony, although none was so prominent a part of the local landscape as Little Saigon in Orange County, near Los Angeles. By the end of the century, Vietnamese names were appearing in state politics in Texas and California, in the graduation rolls of elite universities, in the middle echelons of businesses, and on the roster of at least one NFL team. Given that American Vietnamese communities were started mainly by members of this first refugee wave, it is perhaps not surprising that Vietnamese Americans are alone with Cuban Americans as just about the only immigrant groups that have consistently supported conservative causes and the Republican Party.

The second wave of refugees consisted mainly of ethnic Chinese who were purged from Vietnam, ostensibly because as businesspeople they constituted a capitalist influence in the newly socialist country. In fact, their forced emigration was based as much on ethnicity as it was on class. More than one-quarter of a million ethnic Chinese refugees were taken in by the People's Republic of China. Tens of thousands more fled in boats—the first so-called "boat people"—across the South China Sea to Hong Kong, Thailand, Malaysia, Singapore, Indonesia, and the Philippines. A third wave—boat people again, and also people who fled overland through Cambodia to Thailand—began to come in the early 1980s. Many of these were people who were not faring well under the new Vietnamese government. Some were family members of people who had been sent to re-education camps. Others had their property seized or had other grievances against the government. The trip was never an easy one. Le Tan Si recalled:

> Around 9:00 pm on June 4, 1979, our boat departed in good weather with fifty-eight people on board. ... [On the second day] the overworked engine broke down. Our boat drifted downwind, and so did my life. During this period, I left my life to chance. ... It was raining and the wind was blowing and, because our boat's engine was broken, the boat bobbed up and down with the waves. ... I wondered if my death was near. Our supply of food and water was gradually decreasing as our boat drifted on the sea, so we starved. ... . Thai fishermen tried to help us repair our engine, but they were not able to; however, they took our engine apart. Then they gave us lunch and some cans of water, and they told us that they would help us. ... . [They] towed our boat. ... into Thailand's territorial waters. Ten minutes later, the Thai "fishermen" displayed guns, knives, and hooks. ... They quickly took our valuables, such as rings, earrings, chains, watches, and bracelets. ... The pirates raped the Vietnamese girls and women on our boat, and killed the people who struggled with them.

Another boat of Thai fishermen who encountered Le's boat did try to help them by repairing their engine and giving them some food and water. Le's party made it to a Malaysian island, where they were able to trade gasoline for some food, cigarettes, and water. After they had spent a night on the beach, a Malaysian patrol boat came and towed them away toward a refugee camp. But then "the patrol boat's captain refused to guide our boat to their refugee camp, because their government had stopped accepting refugees. There were about thirty thousand Vietnamese refugees in the refugee camp, so the camp was full." The patrol boat promised to tow them to Singapore, but after thirty hours at sea it cast them adrift. "We again resigned ourselves to our fate. I thought about death. ... Finally, our boat came to unknown islands, about 9:00 P.M. on June 14. I saw that there were many Vietnamese people on those islands, and then I learned that I had arrived in Indonesia. I really had survived, because I was a legal refugee in the Indonesian refugee camp."[17]

The U.S. government belatedly (and only partially) recognized that American soldiers and civilians had fathered tens of thousands of children in Vietnam and other Asian countries during the war, and that the United States bore some responsibility for such people.[18] Life was often hard indeed for young Vietnamese people whose features bore paternal traces of the recent enemy. Many found themselves shut out of even basic education and jobs, as well as discriminated against socially. They were beaten and abused, ridiculed and spat upon in the street, and shunned by neighbors and family members.

In 1982, the U.S. Congress passed the Amerasian Act, which was intended to allow entry to the United States by anyone of part-American parentage who could prove paternity. But many records in Vietnam had been lost in the war or destroyed immediately afterward, some by mothers trying to hide their children's paternity and so ward off persecution. It also forced the young Amerasians to leave Vietnam alone, leaving their family behind. And it classified them as immigrants, not refugees, so it made it impossible for them to get the resettlement help that other Vietnamese were receiving. Altogether, the Amerasian Act assuaged some American guilt but did little actually to help Amerasians in Vietnam, and very few were able to come to the United States under its provisions. Some Amerasians did manage to come as refugees in the 1980s under the Orderly Departure Program, along with non-Amerasian Vietnamese.

Half a dozen years later, Congress tried again, with the Amerasian Homecoming Act, which classified Amerasians as both refugees and immigrants, let them bring family members, and relaxed the proof of paternity requirement in cases where people's features bore signs of either White or Black parentage. Once the U.S. government took responsibility for them, more than 100,000 people entered the United States from various parts of Asia—mainly from Vietnam, but also from every other Asian country where U.S. troops were stationed except Japan. About one third of them were Amerasians and the others were their mothers or siblings.

The U.S. stationed troops in several East and Southeast Asian countries at various times from the 1940s into the twenty-first century. In all of them, Amerasian children appeared. But the 1982 Amerasian Act applied only to Vietnam, and the 1988 Homecoming Act left out Japan, because the U.S. government did not want to insult America's close Asian ally by implying what was obvious to all who knew the situation: that there was terrible racial prejudice in Japan against racially mixed people. Despite these efforts on the part of the U.S. government and a guilt-ridden populace, almost certainly more Amerasians stayed on in Vietnam than made it to the United States. Most Amerasians never heard about the U.S. programs, for word did not spread outside a few large cities. Others who might have left were unable to or uninterested in leaving.

Not just Vietnamese people came to the United States as refugees on account of the U.S.-Vietnam War. Between 1975 and 1982, more than half a million people fled Cambodia and Laos overland for camps in Thailand.[19] The politics and human misery behind those great movements of people are complex and harrowing. In Cambodia, the United States helped overthrow the elected government of Prince Norodom Sihanouk and installed a friendly military dictatorship, which fell in turn to the Khmer Rouge, a communist guerrilla army. When the Khmer Rouge took over in 1975, they promptly emptied the capital city, Phnom Penh, and turned its urban population out into the countryside for supervised labor and "re-education." Any connection with the Americans or the former French colonial regime, any sign of education or international knowledge, was reason for punishment, re-education, or death. More than 1 million Cambodians were executed, starved, or died at hard labor in what came to be called "the killing fields." In 1977, war broke out with neighboring Vietnam, and in 1979 the Vietnamese took over the country and installed a puppet government. The Khmer Rouge took to the countryside and continued to fight.

The politics were different in Laos, but the result was similar: government in upheaval after the U.S.-Vietnam War, lives in chaos, and people on the move. Amidst all the suffering and warfare, hundreds of thousands of Cambodians, lowland Lao, and minority mountain peoples poured across the border into Thailand. Many more perished in the mountains and jungles, trying to get out. One Lao described the border crossing:

> When I escaped, I encountered many problems because Laos and Thailand are separated by the Mekong River. I had to use a wooden log to swim across the river at night. I had to swim as quietly as possible. I was very afraid that I would get caught by the Communists while trying to get across the river. All I could bring along with me was 600 Baht [Thai money, which was equal to $30 at that time]. What I left behind in Laos were a wooden house, household supplies, and other belongings, which were confiscated by the Communists.[20]

Another Lao spoke of life in a Thai refugee camp with his wife and three children:

> We had a small room. We got food from the United Nations. The food wasn't good but was enough for us to survive. ... My job was cutting wood. Sometimes the Thai bosses cheated the Laotian workers. They didn't want to pay us. If they paid, they paid a very low salary because we were Laotian refugees. My three children went to school in the camp offered by the United Nations. They studied English. ... The situation in the camp was very bad. There was a lot of robbery, even killings. A lot of Lao Hmong were killed in camp because the Lao Hmong had silver that they used for making jewelry. There wasn't enough food. My wife stayed home and took care of the children. We waited for our parents to escape for about two years, but they didn't. Then we decided to register to go to another country. My friends told us not to stay in Thailand. We applied to go to France, Argentina, and the United States.[21]

Only a minority managed to be accepted for resettlement in the United States.

The Hmong constituted a special case among such refugees.[22] They were a minority people who came late to Southeast Asia and lived in the mountains in Laos and Vietnam. Most had very little education if any. Hmong men were recruited by the CIA to fight against the NLF and North Vietnamese, then abandoned by the United States despite promises to the contrary. Exposed to the wrath of new communist regimes in Laos and Vietnam, many fled. I remember speaking with a Hmong mother in the nursery of a St. Paul church in the spring of 1984. We spoke about our children. She told me my little son was pretty and asked me if I had other children. I said yes, I had a daughter who was just as pretty. When I complimented her on her baby daughter and asked her if she had other children, she grew quiet. Yes, she said. She had seven children once. But one was killed in the fighting. One died in the jungle, and one wasted away in the refugee camp. Just four made it to America. This new baby brought the family back up to five (Figure 8.2).

Those Hmong who came to the United States as refugees attracted considerable interest from scholars and social workers. They clustered in just a few places—urban Minnesota and certain rural districts in California were prominent among them. Xang Mao Xiong complained to his daughter, Maijue Xiong, about life in America:

> A problem that we Hmong parents face today in America is disciplining our children. It is so difficult! Not only are our children not listening to us, but we parents can be thrown in jail for trying to teach them what is right. In Laos,

Figure 8.2 This Hmong story cloth tells of people leaving their village fleeing soldiers, and hiding in the jungle where they lived in lean-to shelters. Then they left the jungle, swam the Mekong River, and lived in a refugee camp in Thailand. After applying for resettlement, they board buses that will take them to a plane bound for America.

we disciplined our children by a good beating. If a child fights with other children or with his parents, or steals, then he or she receives a beating. After a few such beatings, children learn their lesson and become better persons. But today, here in America, if we hit our children, if they are smart they will tell their teacher or call the police. ...

Another major problem I have experienced since arriving in the United States is speaking and understanding English. I did not even know the difference between "yes" and "no" when I first came, yet I was required to find a job to support my family. I did not have the least idea where to start looking. ... Luckily, there were two Hmong ... who worked in Isla Vista for a social service agency called Indochina. This agency helped find employment for the new arrivals—for Cambodians, Vietnamese, lowland Lao, and Hmong.

My very first job in America, at which I am still employed, had very, very low pay. I started at $3.15 an hour. Though the pay was low, I was tired of being on welfare. I was tired of filling out forms and making monthly reports, tired of having to get papers signed for not working. If I did not fill out those papers and get them signed each month, my family and I would be removed from the welfare rolls. I decided, therefore, to take the job. No more papers! I could buy what I wanted without having to report to the welfare department. I was not used to depending on the government for financial support. In Laos, we had grown our own crops and earned our living by the sweat of our brow.[23]

In the United States, the stories of the various Southeast Asian migrant peoples bear certain similarities. Most came here because they suffered dislocation as a result of the U.S. war in Vietnam. Most had a harrowing time getting out of their country of origin. Those who came as refugees benefited from some initial government help, and sometimes the help of sponsors who helped them adjust to life in America. Almost all made as quick a transition as they could to supporting themselves, often at low-skill, low-pay jobs. Unlike in Southeast Asia, here most women got jobs outside the home; sometimes they were able to earn as good a living as were the men. Many refugees lived in public housing. Almost all the children went to public school. Gradually, most Southeast Asian refugee families made the move from poverty to lower-middle-class status. It was easy for none of them.

U.S. Census figures for 2000 list 1,122,528 ethnic Vietnamese as living in the United States, 171,937 Cambodians, 168,707 Lao, and 169,428 Hmong. Yet many Southeast Asian Americans do not have such simple, clear mono-ethnicities as such figures imply. Consider the family of a friend of mine. My friend is in her twenties, born in Australia. Her parents moved to the United States when she was small and took U.S. citizenship. They had lived previously in Laos and in a Thai refugee camp; she has brothers born in both those places. The family name sounds Thai, but in fact they made that up at some point in their travels. My friend's parents were born of mixed ethnic Vietnamese and Chinese stock and lived their early lives in Vietnam. Australia was their first stop out of the refugee camp. Later they were able to move to the United States, landing finally in California. Currently, some of the family's relatives live in various places in Southeast Asia, some in Australia, some in Europe, and some in the United States. My friend, when she came of age, had the choice to claim Thai, Australian, or U.S. citizenship. Had she pushed the matter, she probably could have been awarded Vietnamese or Chinese citizenship instead (or in addition). When a family reunion was held in Paris, there was no single language that all the family could use to communicate; every conversation needed a translator.[24]

Draining Brains from the Philippines

More than twice as many Filipinos as Vietnamese came to the United States during the last third of the twentieth century, although not under such dramatic conditions. Their migration was driven by rather a different set of neocolonial links.[25] The Philippines had long enjoyed—or suffered, depending on one's perspective—a colonial relationship with the United States, one that did not disappear with the end of a formal political connection in 1946. For example, when dictator Ferdinand Marcos was overthrown by the People Power revolt in 1986, it was the U.S. ambassador who delivered the news and arranged for Marcos's safe conduct out of the country—to the United States, where he lived in honored exile until his death. The Philippines had an American-style government and an American-style educational system, with textbooks that glorified the United States. It had American chain stores long before they became worldwide phenomena. Jessica Hagedorn and other fictionists and political observers have written caustically about the Filipino worship of things American. Philippines citizens have a long and unique history of special service in the U.S. Navy.

The Philippines played a subsidiary role in the U.S. war on Vietnam, as a staging area for U.S. troops and ships, as host for military men and women on R&R, and as the place where many American war wounded were sent for treatment. This meant, among other things, that the Philippines overbuilt its capacity to train nurses during the war (most of the doctors came from the United States, but most of the nurses were trained locally). When the war was over, that capacity remained, and so thousands of Filipino nurses went elsewhere looking for work. The destination of choice, given the colonial history, was the United States. At the time, the United States was experiencing a shortage of qualified nurses; it got so bad, in fact, that in 1989, Congress passed the Immigration Nursing Relief Act to try to recruit foreign nurses to come to the United States (much as two decades earlier, Germany had recruited Korean nurses and engineers to fill postwar shortages in that country).

Maribel Carcellar described her conflicted feelings as she left home, family, and country after nursing school to seek her fortune in the United States:

> I am a nurse. I come from Barrio Concepcion. ... My townfolks are farmers. ... I want to serve my people. ... But what is in store for me here? What will assure me that I will not be abandoned? Will I be able to help an aging mother? How about my brothers and sisters? ... Will I be able to live as decently as my profession demands? This is half the trouble. Am I accepted in society as other professionals are? ...
>
> My wants and needs are human. I want to be socially secure. I must live a life worthy of my profession. Will my salary allow this? I do not exchange service for money. But to keep body and soul fit to further the kingdom of God on this earth, I must be secure. That is why I take the first opportunity to go abroad. ...
>
> Have I forgotten the ideal of nursing? ... Have I turned my back on trembling hands stretched out for help? Have I given [up] hope that my country could prosper with my help? No. But to improve our nation, we must first discipline and improve ourselves. I leave to broaden my outlook, aid my family financially, advance in my nursing experience and come back to the obscure

toil and grind of a nurse, earning one-fourth of what I luxuriously enjoyed but for a brief moment.[26]

Some fairly prominent brains were drained. Perhaps the most famous Filipino health professional was not a nurse but a doctor, Josefina Magno. She received medical training in the Philippines and came to the United States in 1969 in her forties, to do advanced study in oncology. She stayed on in the United States and designed the first American hospice programs, in Arlington, Virginia, and later in Detroit. She founded the International Hospice Institute and was first director of the National Hospice Organization.[27]

By the latter 1980s, well over 25,000 Filipino nurses had come to the United States, and three-quarters of the foreign-trained nurses in the United States came from the Philippines. Scarcely a hospital in any major American city was without a corps of Filipino nurses. Thus, the post-1965 Filipino immigration boom was distinctive from its 1930s predecessor in two ways: it was largely middle-class, and it was led by females. Some brought their families; some came alone. Some of the latter made families here. The entire process was one piece of the colonial relationship between the two countries: educated and highly skilled professionals who might have been of use to their home country were trained for jobs that the United States needed filled, and then siphoned off by U.S. immigration policy and neocolonial connections into the U.S. labor pool. The reward for the individuals was a middle-class life in the United States. The cost to the Philippines was the loss of their talents.

The massive movement of Filipino women (often followed by their families) to the United States in the last quarter of the twentieth century was just one part of a growing Filipina worldwide diaspora. Tens of thousands of others went out to work, primarily as domestic servants, but many as entertainers or in other fields, in Hong Kong, Japan, the Arabian Peninsula, and to a lesser extent in Europe. Rhacel Parreñas writes that "Filipino women are the quintessential service workers of globalization." Nigel Harris says, "Filipinas are everywhere, a genuine labor force—maids gossiping and smoking on their day off in downtown Hong Kong or Singapore, working Japanese farms, running the duty-free shops of Bahrain, cleaning most of the world's cities from London to São Paolo." The work is hard. Ana Vengco described her daily tasks:

> I do cleaning, and this is from morning until early evening. Every day is the same. It is physically exhausting. Especially when I am mopping, my back aches and I get calluses on my hands. After ironing, you are just exhausted, and then you do something strenuous again like washing piles of dishes. Sometimes you feel numb all over from your hands to your feet. You are standing the whole day. We also do lifting like heavy chairs, mattresses, rugs. You have to roll those rugs and take [them] outside to the balcony and bang on [them].

Women abroad earn money they can send back to their families in the Philippines, but the personal costs are high. Rosemarie Samaniego spoke of her desire to see her children:

> When the girl that I take care of calls her mother "Mama," my heart jumps all the time because my children also call me "Mama." I feel the gap caused by

our physical separation especially in the morning, when I pack [her] lunch, because that's what I used to do for my children. … I begin thinking that at this hour I should be taking care of my very own children and not someone else's, someone who is not related to me in any way. … [W]e—the Filipino women over here—feel that all the time. The work that I do here is done for my family, but the problem is they are not close to me but are far away in the Philippines. Sometimes, you feel the separation and you start to cry. Some days, I just start crying while I am sweeping the floor because I am thinking about my children in the Philippines. Sometimes, when I receive a letter from my children telling me that they are sick, I look up out the window and ask the Lord to look after them and make sure they get better even without me around to care after them. [Starts crying.] If I had wings, I would fly home to my children. Just for a moment, to see my children and take care of their needs, help them, then fly back over here to continue my work.[28]

A large slice of the Filipinos who came to the United States after 1965 came as domestics or other body laborers, but there was an even more substantial portion who were middle class on arrival. For the former, it took a generation or more to move into middle class positions. The migrants were numerous enough that they supported concentrations in places like Daly City, a San Francisco suburb, and National City near San Diego. By the 1990s, Union City, California, and half a dozen other places with large numbers of Filipinos even had Jollibee, a Manila-based fast-food chain restaurant. The Filipina population also participated in an increasing number of intermarriages, mainly with White men. Filipino community organizations such as Seattle's Filipino Youth Activities Drill Team and San Jose Polynesian dance contests integrated the children of both old-time Filipinos and the post-1965 new wave.

One issue that animated community politics consistently in the 1990s and 2000s was the matter of securing medical and pension benefits to aging Filipino veterans who had fought in World War II at the side of Americans. Some 5000 Filipino veterans (4000 of them living in the Philippines) did receive such benefits because they were wounded in battle or were members of a particular unit, the Old Philippine Scouts. But some 42,000 others, those few who survived into the twenty-first century among the 250,000 Filipino soldiers who once fought with the Americans, who endured the Bataan Death March with the Americans, and who fought on throughout the war in guerrilla resistance against the Japanese, did not. U.S. President Franklin Roosevelt promised these benefits early in the war, but Congress reneged in 1946. Faustino "Peping" Baclig, a seventy-nine-year-old survivor of Bataan, complained in 2001: "We were fighting, eating and dying together with the Americans. Why are we not recognized? Is it because we are Filipino? Because of our color?" Two years later, President George W. Bush signed a bill granting partial benefits to a small number from among those who were still alive.[29]

From Korea

Like the Filipinos who migrated to the United States in the last third of the twentieth century (or the Jews who came a century earlier), most Korean immigrants were people of some education who came with moderate social capital.[30] This was one of the effects of the 1965 Immigration Act, which emphasized importing people with skills, as well as reunifying families. South Korea emerged only slowly from the devastating civil war (attended by great powers on both sides) of the years 1950 to 1953. Hundreds of thousands of refugees tried to make new lives out of the war's rubble. Since 1 million fled to the south from the north, and hundreds of thousands more returned from Manchuria and Japan where they had lived overseas for decades, South Korea by 1960 was one of the most densely populated nations on earth. In the 1960s, the South Korean government adopted an economic development policy that promoted emigration to relieve overpopulation and encouraged remittances from overseas workers to enhance the national balance sheet. At the same time they fostered foreign investment in Korean industry, and the United States was a big source of such investment.

Despite South Koreans having one of the highest educational levels in Asia, wages were low and working conditions were poor as the country tried to build an industrial base. As late as the 1970s there was no minimum wage (workers in South Korea earned about one-tenth of what they did in the United States); the standard work week was forty-eight hours; minors worked as young as age thirteen; there were no pensions or health benefits; and working conditions were often dirty and dangerous. Meanwhile, the South Korean government suppressed dissent in the name of anticommunism. The government kept the price of rice low so that people had something to eat, but this meant that farmers had a hard time making it and many left the land, flooding Seoul and other cities.

Meanwhile, opportunities opened elsewhere. Germany called several tens of thousands of highly skilled Koreans, particularly engineers, to work on five-year visas. Others went to Latin America. After 1965, the U.S. racial bar on Asians dropped. During the 1970s, 267,638 Koreans migrated to the United States in search of better pay and better ways to use their skills; in the following decade the number climbed to 333,746 (Table 8.3). Initially, more than one-third of those who came were allowed into the United States because the law gave preference to professionals and skilled workers. By the 1980s, that flow was joined by an increasing number of family members who came under the part of the preference system that encouraged reunification of families.

Although many Korean immigrants came with college degrees, many did not find work in the areas of their skills. Others preferred to be their own bosses. A striking number of Korean migrants ended up in a few small business niches: as greengrocers, owners of mom-and-pop liquor stores, in wig manufacturing, nail salons, and so on. In cities like New York and Los Angeles, immigrants brought savings with them from Korea, worked at menial jobs in the United States and saved their earnings, pooled their savings with family members, and bought small shops. There they toiled long hours. A typical liquor store would be open seven days a week, at least from seven a.m. to midnight. The owner would be in the store all that time—waiting on customers, stocking shelves, cleaning up, and doing the books. A family member or two would be there much of the time, helping out. Children would go to public school and come home to the store to do their homework and work the counter. Many such stores were located in poor inner-city neighborhoods where the Koreans stood out racially from their Black or Latino clientele. Since their profit margins were small and prices were higher than the chain stores that refused to locate in the inner city, Korean grocers became the object of animosity from some customers. Throughout the 1980s and 1990s, incidents of conflict between Korean small businesspeople and, especially, Black Americans proliferated.

Perhaps half the Koreans who came to America in these decades were Christians before they left home.[31] Most of those were Protestants—Presbyterians and Methodists, mainly. Protestant churches became the centers of Korean American communities across the United States. Churches and pastors proliferated. Even Buddhists, Confucianists, shamanists, and people of no particular religious conviction went to church, because that is where the Korean community was to be found. There, people spoke in Korean and told news of home. There, the smells and sounds of food and family were to be had. Protestant pastors became the most influential leaders of Korean American communities. Some of them enunciated a particularly nationalistic version of Protestant Christianity, linking Korean identity to godliness. By the 1990s, Korean Americans were top leaders in the U.S. Presbyterian hierarchy, and on many college campuses Protestant organizations like Young Life and Campus Crusade for Christ had been all but taken over by Korean American students.

The numbers of new Korean immigrants dropped by more than half in the 1990s, perhaps less because of changing conditions in Korea (although the economy there had also grown) than because Koreans sensed less welcome in the United States than they had previously imagined. This was the direct result of a riot that took place in Los Angeles in 1992.[32] Southern California is home to the largest concentration of Korean Americans, not only in the bustling midtown business district called Koreatown, but also in suburbs throughout the region. On March 3, 1991, several squads of Los Angeles police converged on a car driven by a twenty-five-year-old Black man, Rodney King. He had been speeding. They hauled King from his car, shot him with a stun gun, and kicked and clubbed him for many minutes. This kind of incident was not unusual in Los Angeles or any other major American city. What was unusual this time was that the beating was caught on videotape by an amateur photographer from a nearby apartment. The tape aired on television news across the country and shocked many Americans. In time, four police officers were charged with brutality.

When the judge granted a change of venue from central Los Angeles to Simi Valley, a White flight suburb at the extreme north end of Los Angeles County, friends of the African American community collectively groaned, for they knew that the chance of the officers being convicted had dropped from near certain to near zero. And so it came to pass. On April 29, 1992, the jury of ten Whites, one Latino, and one Asian American allowed itself to be convinced that the police had not attacked King: the victim himself had been in control of the murderous beating they heaped on him. The officers went free. In anger and despair, tens of thousands of Black Angelenos took to the streets of South Central. They were joined by large numbers of Latinos and some Whites. Some called the event a riot, others called it an uprising. Sympathetic demonstrations rocked cities across the country. In Los Angeles, three days of violence left 58 people dead, more than 2000 injured, nearly 12,000 people arrested, and nearly $1 billion in property damage.

All manner of businesses were looted and torched: clothing stores, supermarkets, fast-food restaurants, and electronics outlets. Yet the national news media focused on a particular racial confrontation, not between Black and White but between African Americans and Korean Americans. Koreatown was not far from South Central, and Korean families also owned many small grocery and liquor stores within the Black ghetto. Hundreds of Korean businesses were put to the torch, as were thousands of others. TV news played endless pictures of Korean business-people on rooftops guarding their property with rifles, keeping darker rioters at bay. Richard Rhee, owner of a market on the corner of Fifth and Western, defended his property. "Burn this down after thirty-three years? They don't know how hard I've worked. This is my market and I'm going to protect it." The *Los Angeles Times* reported, "From the rooftop of [Rhee's] supermarket, a group of Koreans armed with shotguns and automatic weapons peered onto the smoky streets. Scores of others, carrying steel pipes, pistols and automatic rifles, paced through the darkened parking lot in anticipation of an assault by looters" like the ones that had taken several nearby businesses.[33]

Korean Americans were not, in fact, the main target of the rioters. Only one Korean American was killed and forty-six injured, although Korean businesses did sustain more than 40 percent of the property damage. These were tragedies, to be sure, but not the central story of the riots they were made out to be. Still, the violence capped a long period—not only in Los Angeles but in New York and other cities where Koreans owned small businesses in poor Black neighborhoods—of intercommunal animosity. Korean and Black leaders moved quickly to demonstrate solidarity and establish dialogue, but for many years afterward Black-Korean animosity and fear continued to fester.

One issue that animated some Korean Americans in the 1990s and early 2000s was the possibility of re-establishing contact with family members in the North. When the war ended in 1953, millions of people were displaced and countless families were lost to each other for two generations. In the 1990s, relations between the North and the South began to thaw just a bit. A few people made visits back and forth. And some neutral parties arranged for a few overseas Koreans to visit their long-lost relatives.[34]

Korean Americans coined a new phrase in the lore of American immigration: "the 1.5 generation." Generation has long been one of the themes by which observers and ethnic group members alike have described life for immigrant families and communities. A considerable portion of Chapter 7 of this book, in fact, is devoted to just that kind of analysis. The migrant group constitutes the first generation, who come to America with the main life task of finding a way to build a life in the new and strange place. They find a way to earn a living, learn at least the fundaments of the English language and American behavioral expectations, and try to ward off the lack of acceptance that comes from some natives and subdue their own longing for home. Their children, the second generation, often see themselves more as part of the new place than of their parents' homeland. For them, the main life task is how to become (and be accepted as) full members of American society.

Yet in every immigrant group there has been also a third group: people who were born in the old country, but who were brought to the United States as young children. Such people are not exactly members of either the first generation or the second, although they have some qualities of each. It was Korean Americans in the 1990s who gave that in-between set of people a name: *ilchom ose*, the 1.5 generation.[35] One popular stereotype of 1.5 generation members was that they were marginal people, at home neither in Korea, nor among non-Korean Americans, nor really even among Korean Americans of the immigrant generation. More often, 1.5-generation people saw themselves as intercultural bridges. They were likely to speak Korean better and they were more likely to understand and affirm the nuances of Korean culture than were children born here. They were more likely to feel comfortable working in Korean-owned businesses and participating in Koreatown affairs. One 1.5-generation Korean told an interviewer: "We as 1.5s can understand the needs of the Korean American community, but at the same time understand how to deal with the American culture. Our method of communicating with non-Koreans is more likely to bridge the relationship with the [Korean] community and the others [non-Korean Americans]. But the first generation still will not let go of the control and still treat us like children."[36]

From South Asia

To an even greater extent than Filipinos or Koreans, the million or so South Asians who came to the United States after 1965 constituted a middle-class migration.[37] "South Asians" refers collectively to people who trace their ancestry to various parts of the Indian subcontinent and its environs, including India, Pakistan, Bangladesh, Sri Lanka, Nepal, Bhutan, Nepal, and Sikkim. The most numerous of these by far were Indians—although that designation included an array of religious, ethnic, or caste groups, notably Sikhs, who are quite distinctive from all the others. Indian immigration between 1970 and the end of the century totaled more than three-quarters of a million people.

The South Asian migration to the United States was but one part of a large and long-standing movement of South Asian peoples to and from many points of the globe. Table 8.4 gives the populations of Indian origin who lived in ten countries late in the twentieth century.

Throughout the nineteenth and twentieth centuries, Indians moved along the corridors of the British Empire and later the Commonwealth—to harvest sugar in Fiji and rubber in Malaysia, to build railroads in East Africa and roads in South Africa. They stayed on in all those places and many more. Many of them became educated and members of the local petty middle class, although like the Chinese in Southeast Asia they often remained a people apart, with ties back to India and also to other points in the Indian diaspora.

Table 8.4 The Indian Diaspora

Fiji	345,000
Guyana	389,000
Burma	415,000
Trinidad	453,000
Mauritius	664,500
United States	815,000
Great Britain	850,000
South Africa	1,033,000
Malaysia	1,462,300

Populations are from censuses taken between 1980 and 1994 at the various locations.

Source: Padma Rangaswamy, *Namasté America: Indian Immigrants in an American Metropolis* (University Park: Pennsylvania State University Press, 2000), 20.

As India's economy grew in the 1970s and 1980s, it produced a growing number of graduates from universities and technical schools, more than could be employed domestically. People looked abroad for opportunities. Many thousands went to the United Kingdom. By the 1990s, more than 30,000 each year were coming to the United States. Some came for more education, and South Asian graduate students became commonplace at American universities. Many stayed on to work, for their professional skills fit them for the 1965 law's preference system. Other Indians, usually those who lacked the educational credentials and upper-class background of the professional-class migrants, occupied economic niches such as motel operators throughout the South and East, convenience store managers across the country, and cab drivers in New York City. Others became businesspeople. Indian doctors, engineers, scientists, and academics were to be found all over the country. But Indians also clustered in big cities that had diversified economies.

New York was paramount among these, with nearly 200,000 Indian residents in 1990. Johanna Lessinger described their occupations:

> Industries ... hire Indian engineers, while computer firms want Indian software designers. Scientific employers claim that young Indian scientists are often brighter, better-prepared and more hardworking than their American counterparts. (The young Indian employees are sometimes bitter to find they have been offered lower salaries than American coworkers; employers often assume immigrants will accept any job offered them.)
>
> New York's numerous hotels and motels offer Indians both jobs and chances to invest. The city's banking, insurance and finance industry hires Indians; its enormous public health system needs Indian doctors, nurses, pharmacists, anesthesiologists and accountants. The city and state bureaucracies hire Indians as clerks, managers and administrators. Indians are found on the faculties of the city's universities and medical schools. New York, with its large garment and jewelry sectors, makes room for Indian importer/manufacturers of textiles, clothing, leather garments and gemstones. ...
>
> Indians ... use family labor to operate Hallmark card shops, newsstands and candy stores, grocery stores and delicatessens, clothing boutiques, health food shops, gas stations and muffler repair shops, restaurants and coffee shops. ... [O]ther people are obliged to work for ... very low wages. ... Indian immigrants, including college graduates, work as waiters, deli countermen, shop clerks, newsstand employees, security guards or taxi drivers. ... hotel night clerks, shop assistants or domestic servants.[38]

There were other centers of Indian American population as well: Los Angeles had 60,000; the San Francisco Bay Area, 50,000; Washington, D.C., 34,000; Houston, 25,000; Philadelphia, 20,000. By 1990, Indians in metro Chicago numbered 56,462. They made up about one-sixth of the Asian American population of the city itself—and nearly one-third of the Asian population in the suburbs. Padma Rangaswamy described the transformation of one part of North Chicago:

> I was strolling along Devon Avenue one summer day in 1990, marveling at the sights and sounds and smells of India. For a few moments, I forgot that I was in Chicago. The sight of richly embroidered saris in the windows, the sound of Hindi film music blaring from the video shops, and the smell of spices frying

in ghee in the restaurants magically transported me back home; I felt I was in one of New Delhi's busiest bazaars in Karol Bagh or Connaught Place. I recalled that I had visited a lone Indian shop on this very street, twenty years ago, eagerly seeking out an Indian face in the crowd. Now it was the white face that had become a rarity.[39]

It is important to note that the neighborhood she described was not mainly an Indian residential area, but rather a commercial district where Indian and Pakistani Americans came to shop, eat, and visit with friends. And others came there as well: Gandhi Electronics advertised its sales staff's ability to speak Polish. Still, in those twenty years, Indians and other South Asians were transformed from a tiny minority and occasional cultural curiosity to an unremarkable part of the fabric of American society.

Indian American computer scientists and entrepreneurs were among the most prominent figures in the U.S. technology boom of the 1990s. With no particular apology to Emma Lazarus, but surely with gratitude for her memorable poem, let me offer this amended version to characterize one facet of South Asian immigration to the United States since the 1970s:

> Give me your energetic, your entrepreneurial,
> Your huddled capitalists yearning to make money,
> The very brightest from your teeming universities,
> Send these to me,
> I lift my halogen lamp beside the Silicon Valley.

Many Indian migrants came from backgrounds of at least modest privilege in India, and many achieved upper-middle-class status in the United States. For such people, traveling back and forth to India or other points in the diaspora, maintaining ties to extended family and home, was economically easier than for most immigrants who came from other locations such as China or Central America. Padma Rangaswamy, for instance, spent most of the 1970s in Chicago but some of that time in India; most of the 1980s in India but some in Chicago. By the 1990s she was back in Chicago most of the time—but not all the time.

From China

China is not one place but many, and it is home to many different peoples.[40] Before the 1965 Immigration Act, the vast bulk of the Chinese American population traced its origins to Guangdong Province and a few small districts around the Pearl River delta, Hong Kong, and Canton. That did not change immediately with the new law, for the People's Republic was just then embarking on a decade of internal chaos called the Great Proletarian Cultural Revolution. Domestic politics in China twisted and whirled. Tens of millions of young people were sent down from cities into the countryside, political struggle ran wild, as Mao Zedong battled to maintain a climate of permanent revolution. Meanwhile, the United States was fighting a war in Vietnam it chose to blame in part on the Chinese. Relations between the two countries were deeply hostile, and almost no one was allowed to travel from one to the other until well into the 1980s.

So those Chinese who came to the United States in the 1960s—109,771 of them—did not come from mainland China. Most came from Hong Kong or Taiwan, where the governments were friendly to the United States. Other ethnic Chinese came from Singapore and other parts of Southeast Asia. The numbers grew with each decade: 237,793 in the 1970s; 444,942 in the 1980s; and 528,893 in the 1990s (Table 8.3). And they began to come from the Chinese mainland as well—at first just a trickle and then in the 1990s a growing stream.

Chinese Americans had long been segregated in central-city ghettos that were glorified only slightly by being called Chinatowns. On one hand, most non-Chinese Americans saw these as glitzy-shabby showplaces of exotic culture and foreign intrigue. On the more prosaic level of the people who lived packed into these densest of urban neighborhoods, they were simply monoethnic slums, albeit filled with familiar sounds and smells. School boards in Seattle and San Francisco did their best to provide quality education at Bailey Gatzert and Commodore Stockton, the Chinatown schools, but they suffered all the deprivations of aging inner-city slum schools, plus the added challenge of instructing many students who first learned English when they began to attend. Chinese from earlier migrations were limited mainly to working-class occupations, although a small second generation was beginning to go to college in the 1960s and make its way out of Chinatown's confines.

When new migrants came from China, the first place they congregated was near Chinatown. Often they could not speak Cantonese, but at least the written language, some food, and people's appearance seemed familiar. Victor and Brett Nee interviewed residents of San Francisco's Chinatown in the 1970s and wrote about "Why Chinese Restaurants Are Cheaper." One recent immigrant described his vocation:

> I am looking forward to my future, although I am now a dishwasher. This is not really what I want to do, but my family needs my support. I remember I first applied for a job as an X-ray technician in Mary Help hospital. ... four months after I got to this country. ... I asked my friend to go with me because I wanted him to be my translator. The manager of the X-ray department asked me some questions about X-ray knowledge because he wanted to see how much I had known. All the questions which he asked, I answered, they were about ninety percent correct. But the manager didn't accept me to work in the hospital because I couldn't answer them in English. The manager said, "I believe your X-ray knowledge is good enough to work as an X-ray technician, but you can't speak English well. I suggest you go to school, when your English gets better, you may apply again." The problem for me ... is that I have to support my family. Because of my family I have to work hard every day. I don't have enough time to study and when I am studying I have too many worries about my family.

At the time, Mary Help had a largely Chinese-speaking clientele, with whom, presumably, an English-only technician would have as much difficulty communicating as this man's manager did with him.[41]

Like this man, other non-English-speaking ghetto residents had few options in the American economy. They were forced to accept wages in Chinese restaurants, garment factories, and produce markets that fell far below state standards, with no health care, retirement, or other benefits. In 1980, a man's shirt sold at Macy's for about twenty-eight dollars. Macy's bought it wholesale for twelve dollars. The distributor paid six dollars to the sweatshop owner, who in turn paid sixty cents for the materials and fifty cents to the woman who sewed the shirt. Sweatshop operators—often wealthy Chinese Americans—rationalized the exploitation by saying they were providing jobs to women who could not get other employment, and offering flexibility so they could tend their children at the same time. The Nees talked with Jennie Lew, one such seamstress:

> She began working in the garment factories … when Donna [her oldest daughter, now twenty] got old enough to keep an eye on the younger ones. Of course, she worked off and on, she says. She'd stop for four or five months whenever a new child was born. … She followed pretty much the same schedule every day while she was working. She'd get up at seven and make breakfast for her husband and the kids. She'd walk the older ones to school, go to the factory at nine, and work for two hours until eleven. At eleven, she'd pick the kids up from school, make lunch for them at home, walk them back to school, and be at work again at one. At five, she would take another hour off to cook supper for everybody. At six or six-thirty she'd go back to work again, sew until ten, then come home to bed. On Saturday she would put in about five hours, and take home something to sew on Sunday. She was paid by piece-rate, not by the hour, earning between $4.50 to $8 per dozen depending on the complexity of the pattern.[42]

Jennie Lew and her family were lucky. They lived in Ping Yuen, a housing project that had bigger and better-maintained apartments than most Chinatown residences. They had four small rooms. Mr. Lew slept in one, Jennie and the three youngest children in another, with the three older children occupying a single room behind the living room. Jennie's daughter Donna was junior mama from age five, in charge of her younger siblings while mom and dad were at work, and in the Nees's eyes, already worn out and nervous by age twenty. In working-class immigrant families—Chinese, Mexicans, Dominicans, and many others—such a role for the oldest daughter was commonplace. The stress this responsibility placed on such girls, having not only to take care of their siblings from a very young age, but often to act as translators for their parents, even as decision makers regarding the family future, was life-stunting.[43]

In the 1990s, a complex illegal web formed that brought tens of thousands of people out of the People's Republic of China, parked them in cargo containers and the holds of rusty freighters, and moved them across the globe—to Europe, to Latin America, to Southeast Asia, and also to the United States.[44] Families in China pooled all their life savings to hire a "snakehead," or smuggling kingpin, to take one young relative to the United States. In the 1980s, the going price was $18,000; by 2005 it had reached $70,000. The family paid half the fee up front and the rest was due when the migrant arrived safely in America. Thousands did, usually after traveling several weeks at sea. If they could not pay the other half (and very few could) they became the property of the smuggling ring's American side. They would be hired out to Chinese restaurants, garment factories, and other employers—off the books, paid far below the minimum wage. Most worked multiple jobs and about eighty hours a week, and they remained in bondage for several years.

Peter Kwong told of Zheng, a schoolteacher who left his wife and daughter in Fujian and arrived in the United States in 1993. Four years later Zhen was working ten hours a day, seven days a week, as a dishwasher in a Manhattan restaurant. Then he did a six-hour shift as a night watchman. He lived in a one-room, windowless apartment with nineteen other single men in triple-decker bunks. He ate only ten cents' worth of bread a day. If people like Zheng were lucky, they might over several years pay off the indenture and then begin saving to bring over another family member. People like Zheng comprised a cheap, movable, disposable workforce. They were docile and guaranteed not to complain, because they were scared their snakeheads or employers would beat them, turn them over to immigration authorities, or worse, kill their relatives in China. This was not just an individual or family tragedy, nor was it a first step on an inexorable upward path to middle-class status—that is self-comforting American mythology. People like Zheng and Jenny Lew were the reason why Chinese restaurants offered sumptuous food at bargain prices, and why American-made T-shirts did not cost $50 apiece.

Heading toward the other end of the class spectrum were a totally different set of Chinese people who came on visas as university students. This began with Taiwanese and Hong Kong students in the 1960s and 1970s, but in the 1990s they were joined by a steady flow of graduate students from the Chinese mainland. In the 1980s and 1990s, every major American university came to have a colony of overseas Chinese students, young men and women, unlike mainly male migration of a century before. Many of them studied science and engineering, so when their education was finished they were able to win work visas that ended in permanent residency and, for many, American citizenship. Many such former students, now middle-class, began to move into the suburbs in the 1970s—across San Francisco Bay to Milpitas and down to Silicon Valley; across Lake Washington from Seattle to Bellevue and Renton; and out of Los Angeles to Monterey Park, America's first suburban Chinatown. In the 1970s, Monterey Park was an all-White bedroom community. By the end of the 1980s, it had a majority-Asian citizenry, as did nearby San Gabriel. These towns and others in the San Gabriel Valley were quickly dotted with signs (including street signs) in Chinese, Korean, Vietnamese, and other Asian languages. A person could live for years in Monterey Park and speak no more than a few words of English. Asian Americans became council members and mayors. These were middle-class places, but they were nearly as ethnically homogeneous as working-class Chinatown had been.[45]

A Model Minority?

One of the burdens that is laid on Asian American immigrants is the myth of the model minority.[46] In a famous 1966 *New York Times Magazine* article, sociologist William Petersen trumpeted the Japanese American "success story." Japanese Americans, observed Petersen, had the highest educational achievement level of any American racial group, higher family income than anyone except Whites, and the lowest levels of criminality and juvenile delinquency. All this success was due, suggested Petersen, to the superiority of Japanese American culture. In a similar vein, George DeVos and William Caudill asserted that, "Because of the compatibility between Japanese and American middle-class cultures, individual Nisei probably have a better chance of succeeding than individuals from other ethnic groups where the underlying cultural patterns are less in harmony with those of the American middle class." Petersen concluded, "By any criterion of good citizenship that we choose, the Japanese-Americans are better than any group in our society, including native-born whites." From that time forward, the popular press regularly echoed that kind of sentiment and extended it to Chinese, Koreans, and other Asian Americans.[47]

There are, of course, ways in which such a characterization has some measure of accuracy. Throughout the second half of the twentieth century, the average educational level achieved by most Asian American groups—whether measured by years of schooling completed or grade point average—was indeed higher than the average for Whites, Blacks, or Latinos. There was a notable concentration of Asian Americans in scientific and technical fields. In 2006, after many years of gradually approaching parity, Asian Americans passed Whites and became the most numerous racial group among students admitted to the elite University of California system (the percentages were—Asians 36.0, Whites 35.6, Latinos 17.6, Blacks 3.4, Native Americans 0.6).[48] At century's end, although Asian American income was not as high as White American income on a per capita basis, family income was indeed a bit higher, because in a typical Asian American family more people worked, and Asian American children often lived together with their parents into their working years. One reason that many observers gave for this measure of material success was Confucian culture, which stressed family solidarity, commitment to education, and hard work—the sorts of virtues about which Gary Locke spoke early in this chapter.

In 1992, however, the U.S. Commission on Civil Rights pointed to several problems with the model minority image.[49] In the first place, a lot of people used the Asian model minority idea simply as a club with which to beat up on other racial minorities. William Petersen's immediate objective in 1966 was to discredit the African American civil rights movement one year after the Watts riots. Thomas Sowell and other writers suggested that the problem with Blacks and Native peoples in terms of achieving material success in America was that they lacked the proper cultural orientation, the family commitment, the competitive drive. Dispossession, genocide, slavery, segregation, and continuing discrimination were not the problem. What African and Native Americans really needed was to become more like Chinese or Jewish Americans.[50]

Second, the image of Asian Americans as uniformly successful left out a lot of people, and it mistook some of the roots of what success has existed. It ignored the fact, for example, that a lot of South Asians and Koreans came to the United States with a lot of education and some money saved, or that post-1965 Filipinos were mainly an educated group. By contrast, some groups like the Hmong came with nothing on either account, and their struggle tended to go unnoticed.

Third, emphasis on the model minority myth has diverted attention from the very real, ongoing discrimination that many Asian Americans continue to face. The widespread idea that Asian Americans are excellent at technical tasks but have limited creative or leadership capacities made for a glass ceiling in business, entertainment, and other fields. Asians could be great cinematographers like Dong Kingman, but they could not be the movie star unless they played harmless, semi-buffoon roles like Jackie Chan or stereotypical Kung Fu fighters like Jet Li.[51] Asian American TV journalists could hold a microphone under an umbrella at the site of a breaking story, but the men, at least, could not be the main studio anchors. Asian American businessmen could head up the technical divisions of major corporations, but they could not be CEOs. Such patterns persist.

Fourth, as Timothy Fong wrote, "the model minority stereotype places undue pressure and anguish on young Asian Americans who think they have to achieve in school. This has been linked with mental health issues for teenagers and even suicides."[52] A corollary is that the model minority image tended to limit young Asian Americans to certain kinds of endeavors—such as math, science, business, and engineering—where Asians are supposed to be naturally gifted. Pity the poor Asian kid who is not good at math. The model minority fixation left little room either in Asian American communities or in the wider society for Asian American athletes, artists, or grunge rock stars (although we began to see some prominent Asian American athletes as the century drew to a close, such as Olympic champion speed skater Apolo Anton Ohno, golfer Tiger Woods, NFL linebacker Dat Nguyen, NBA center Yao Ming, and pro hockey star Paul Kariya).

The cost of the model minority image—whether the pressures came from American society at large or from within Asian American families and communities—was sometimes tragically intense. A 2003 movie, *Better Luck Tomorrow*, told a story fresh from the headlines. Half a dozen potentially Ivy-League-bound Asian American high school seniors, out of boredom with the emptiness of their lives as suburban overachievers, got involved in a web of deception and crime that ended in a senseless death. In 2006, a Korean immigrant set afire the family SUV with the immigrant, his eleven-year-old daughter, and ten-year-old son inside. "He said life was too much to handle," said Jasmine Jung, operator of a café near the man's business. This man had started a successful business making T-shirts. He had bought a Mercedes and a house in pricey Hancock Park. His children attended expensive private schools. He was a success. But the business went bankrupt, he lost the house, his wife filed for divorce, and he apparently sought a desperate way out. Sociologist Edward Chang commented, "Korean immigrants live under tremendous pressure to earn a living and to educate their young." Another Koreatown small businessman, Lee Han Ok, noted that "In Korea, coming to America means being successful and making a lot of money. But when you get here, you understand that it's not easy." Other Americans, of course faced equally intense pressures, and most people—Asian Americans and non-Asians—did not have such extreme reactions. But the added pressure of the model minority image must be at least partly to blame for tragedies such as these.[53]

From the Americas

Perhaps a Model Minority: Migrants from Mexico

Migrants from Mexico were more numerous in the final third of the twentieth century than those from any other single source.[54] From 450,000 in the 1960s, their number swelled to 2.2 million in the 1990s (Table 8.5). The Mexican American resident population grew accordingly, from 4.5 million in 1970 to 25.3 million at the end of the century. By far the majority of Mexican Americans—74 percent in 1990, 60-plus percent a decade later—were American-born native citizens, contrary to the assumption of many non-Mexican Americans that they were almost all foreigners. And, contrary to the farmworker stereotype, nine out of ten lived in cities. Yet, although most were U.S. natives, the numbers of migrants were also large. For some observers, Mexican migrants were simply a new set of huddled masses, yearning to breathe free and work hard to make lives in America. Their children represented America's future. For some others, the surge across the southwest border amounted

Table 8.5 Immigration from the Americas, 1961–2000

Origin	1961–1970	1971–1980	1981–1990	1991–2000
Mexico	453,937	640,294	1,655,843	2,249,421
Cuba	208,536	264,863	144,578	169,322
Other Caribbean	261,677	476,263	727,473	809,465
Central America	101,330	134,680	468,088	526,915
South America	257,940	295,741	461,847	539,656
Canada	413,310	169,939	156,938	191,987

Sources: Appendix B, Table 22, 23, 24, 25, 26, 27.

to an invasion, even "reverse manifest destiny"—Mexicans threatening to seize back the lands that Americans had taken away in 1848.[55]

The main force driving migration was a low standard of living in Mexico and other neighboring countries to the south, in contrast to the lush wealth that seemed available in the United States. The Mexican economic and political systems veered between chaos and modest, uneven prosperity repeatedly over the last third of the twentieth century. Mexico City grew into one of the world's great centers of international commerce. The continuing development of global capitalism within Mexico, especially after the implementation of the North American Free Trade Agreement (NAFTA) in 1994, brought U.S. investment into the border region of northern Mexico, destabilized the economies of other regions, and drew many thousands of people northward in search of work. To take one example, Ciudad Juárez, across the Rio Grande from El Paso, was a town of 250,000 in 1960; its population exploded to 1.2 million by the end of the century. The effects on other regions and sectors of the Mexican economy were devastating. After NAFTA, Mexico saw the value of its exports skyrocket—from a trade deficit to the United States of $1.7 billion in 1993 to a surplus of $49.6 billion in 2005. Meanwhile, Mexico lost 2.8 million farm jobs, compared to a gain of only 700,000 jobs in export manufacturing. Mexican and American capitalists were thriving, but Mexican farmers were losing out to U.S. agriculture. These economic forces, the direct results of international trade policy, pushed Mexicans out of agriculture and northward in search of jobs. Add to this the abuse that many Mexican peasants, particularly Indians, faced at the hands of police, prosecutors, and soldiers, and Mexico had a recipe for exodus.[56]

As it had been since it was invented in the mid-nineteenth century, the U.S.-Mexico border was not a line between separate countries, but a shared zone of movement and interaction by people and goods.[57] People from border communities on the Mexican side moved north to work in American homes, factories, and fields—leaving friends, homes, and family on the southern side. Some migrants returned home again and again; many never intended their move north to be a permanent one. Some people from deep in the heart of Mexico joined them in the trek northward.

Many are the stories of the crossing. Martín was a teenager in San Luis Potosí when his father told him in 1980:

"I have a friend who told me that it was easy to sneak across the border. Since you're the oldest, it's your responsibility to accompany me." ... My mother's face was covered in tears as she stood before us. ... I had to drop out of school when there was no more money to buy books. I started to go look for work with my father. Jobs were scarce and poorly paid, but we managed to put aside a little money to travel north. ... I got even more excited when my father told me that we would be going to Los Angeles. I knew that Hollywood was in Los Angeles, and I thought that I might be able to meet some of the stars.

When the time to leave had come, the family gathered.

At that moment, I felt a sharp pain between my ribs. Everyone in my family was crying except for me. Suddenly, a kind of sadness that I had never felt before came over me. I might never see my brothers and sisters, my mother, my friends, or even the city that I grew up in ever again. ... It was difficult for me to breathe. We left just before dawn. My mother made every effort to appear calm. She handed us a big bundle filled with bologna sandwiches, and she filled up a bottle with water for us to drink on the road. I wanted to hug her and keep holding onto her like I did when I was a boy. But those days were gone. ... I asked my mother for her blessing, and I kissed her hand as I left. I never looked back.

A bus to Mexicali took two days and most of their money. Two strangers, filthy men from Mexico City and Michoacan, approached them at the train station and told them they could help them get across. The strangers took the father and son to a coal car and showed them where they could ride under the car. The men took up positions in four corners of the undercarriage.

It was an acute angle of iron, a tiny draft sill that we could barely squeeze into. We were in a kind of squatting, ducking position. It was the only place where the inspectors on this and the other side of the border could not see us. ... [W]e saw an enormous wheel in front of us. ... [After three hours squatting in darkness] suddenly, a thunderous noise jarred us. ... other railcars being attached to the car that we were in. ... There were eight thunderclaps, eight colossal collisions, eight times that we thought we were going to be shot out from our sills and end up under the giant wheel.

They held on for many hours, fighting off fatigue. Had they relaxed their muscles even a fraction, they would have been killed. When the train was in motion, Martín and his father shouted encouragement to each other, told stories of home, recounted movies they had seen and meals the family had enjoyed together. When the train stopped and the inspectors banged on the sides of their hiding places, they hung on tight and tried not to make a sound. After nearly two days clinging to the bottom of the train, they reached San Bernardino, California. Then they walked, more than fifty miles to El Monte. They begged for two dollars to take the bus into central Los Angeles. There they knew the name of a woman who ran a hotel. She gave them a place to stay. In a few months they were doing day labor. Looking back, Martín summed up his experience crossing over:

I didn't cry when I first left home; the idea of going to the United States was so attractive to me. I didn't cry when I said goodbye to my mother either. But I'm crying now. The tears are flowing, and there's no way to stop them. I don't want to stop them. It's as if by telling my story, I've been made to live it all over again. I cry out of sadness for all those who now cross the border in a thousand different ways, but I also cry for joy because I made it alive. I married a girl from Jalisco. I have three beautiful children. A good job. I'm going to become a citizen very soon. I tell you all of this so that those who are already here in the United States do not mislead those who are still in Mexico. The road is hard, very hard. God bears witness to how hard it truly is.[58]

Others came by many routes, most of them dangerous. Some commuted daily, walking through the Rio Grande shallows from Ciudad Juárez to El Paso each morning to work in kitchens and homes, then back each evening by the same route. Hundreds at a time ran through gates operated by the Border Patrol near San Diego, secure in the hope that a few would be caught and most would get through. Others scaled the walls that U.S. authorities erected near population centers. One I know came, at age three, curled up inside the spare tire of a Chevy truck. Some crawled miles through sewer pipes haunted by swarms of rats.

American political leaders cried out against Mexican immigrants, as we shall learn in Chapter 9. The government response was a futile attempt to keep out Mexicans called Operation Gatekeeper. Beginning in 1994, the Clinton administration's Immigration and Naturalization Service (INS) built a high steel wall topped by barbed wire across the entire San Diego-Tijuana border area. It constructed similar walls near El Paso-Ciudad Juárez and Brownsville-Matamoros. Between 1994 and 2005, the U.S. government tripled the number of agents in the Border Patrol as well as their funding. It concentrated those people and resources around these urban crossings. Those who wanted to come and work were pushed out into the deserts of eastern California, Arizona, and New Mexico where the danger of the crossing increased. More and more they were forced to rely on smugglers called *coyotes*, who were often unscrupulous. In the desert heat and mountain terrain their death rate was multiplied more than five times, to more than five hundred deaths in 2004.

Forty-five-year-old Miguel F. Rivera Zurita was one. He left his mother in Santa Maria Asuncion, a village in Oaxaca, on February 21, 2004, and began the return to Portland, Oregon, where his wife and six children awaited him. The family had come to Portland in the late 1980s. They had no papers and no prospect of getting any, since they arrived after a 1986 amnesty for illegal immigrants. Miguel worked as a mechanic and he picked strawberries. When he learned his mother was dying of cancer, he flew to Mexico to see her one last time, then began the 2500-mile return trip. He went with a smuggler and seventeen others by bus to Sonora, then began walking northward, carrying water and extra clothing for the cold desert nights. He could not keep up with the younger men and soon fell behind. Another crosser found his decomposed body on April 8, two weeks after his mother had died.[59]

So those Americans already residing north of the border got to fan our fears about Mexicans and feel as if we were doing something to keep out a menace. We spent a ton of money. And all we really did was kill a lot of Mexicans. The migrant flow continued, because the economic and social forces that drove it did not abate.[60]

Like other prosperous Western countries in the 1990s and 2000s, the United States was adopting a lifeboat mentality.[61] We were attempting to beat back what some of us saw as hordes of foreign people whom we feared would overrun our country. Most Americans gave little thought either to what were the consequences for those people we beat back or whether or not such people actually constituted a threat. Mexicans were just one group among many foreign migrants, but it was on them that most of the animus fell. It is ironic, tragic—or perhaps just hypocritical—that the prosperity and comfort of Americans relied heavily on the labor of those same migrants.

Despite late-century attempts to turn them back, Mexican migrants came in steadily increasing numbers throughout the period under consideration in this chapter. Once they had made their way here, their major needs were jobs and places to live. Most Mexican migrants found body work in the cities and suburbs and on the farms of the Southwest. They did construction work and picked crops. They cooked, waited on tables, and washed dishes in restaurants. They were janitors and hotel maids. They ran steam presses and sewing machines. They worked the counter at K-Mart and McDonald's. They joined the U.S. military and died in America's wars—many in a desperate bid to earn citizenship—in numbers far outstripping their proportion of the population. They worked in mines, chemical plants, and chicken processing factories. They cut lawns and cleaned homes. In 1970, 14 percent of Orange County domestics were Latinas; by 2000, that number had skyrocketed to 86 percent. There was always lots of work—indeed, the American economy depended on Mexican migrant labor—although the work they found was seldom clean, it often was not safe, and it seldom paid well. Comedian Sandra Tsing Loh has a telling joke about the working lives of Mexican and other Central American migrants: "Hillary Clinton said it takes a village to raise a child. But in the case of Los Angeles, it's a Guatemalan village."[62]

Immigrant neighborhoods were not always safe, either. Many migrants were packed into substandard housing in decaying neighborhoods. Employers frequently abused their workers and police were as likely to knock down a door as to knock on it. Mexican migrants' diet was poorer than other Americans' and so was their overall health. Migrant children were less likely to be born in hospitals, less likely to receive vaccinations, and more likely to suffer poisoning from lead paint or DDT. HIV rates were higher than for either Whites or American-born Mexicans. Factory jobs, such as those at the Union Carbide mill in King City, California, paid better than most Mexican migrants could achieve elsewhere, but even those came with risks: in the King City case, asbestos poisoning. Migrant neighborhoods received a smaller share of city services such as sewer construction and road repair, than did middle-class, Anglo neighborhoods. And police often felt free to visit violence on Mexicans that they would not have visited on Whites.[63]

In many Mexican immigrant districts, gangs flourished among young men and boys. Far too frequently, journalists and politicians have resorted to the stereotype of the immigrant gangster. This distorted image was applied once upon a time to Irish and Jewish immigrants, and it is still applied today to Italians to some extent (hence, *The Sopranos*). This stereotypical fixation was applied to greater and lesser degrees to Vietnamese, Russian, and Mexican Americans in the last third of the twentieth century and the first years of the twenty-first. It is true that there were Mexican gangs and there was a Russian mob, just as it is true that the Sons of Liberty, the Ku Klux Klan, and the Enron gang were made up predominantly of English immigrants and their descendants. For all the ethnically charged hand-wringing, there is no particular connection between immigration and crime.[64]

By the 1990s, Mexican Americans, many of them migrants, were spreading across the country. There had long been Mexican American colonies in places like Detroit, Chicago, Milwaukee, and St. Paul. From the 1910s, Mexican migrants had gone where there were jobs, and industrial jobs in steel, autos, and grains were among the best to be had. But until late in the century the bulk of the permanently resident Mexican American population lived in a swath across the Southwest from Texas to California. That began to change in the 1990s, as new immigrants found work in the South, Midwest, and Northeast in ever-increasing numbers. Mexican migrants found work at the Tyson's chicken processing plant in Springdale, Arkansas, alongside Lao and Marshall Islanders. They did day labor on Long Island and every sort of urban job in New York City and Chicago. They slaughtered hogs and packed bacon in Denison, Iowa, and Tar Heel, North Carolina. They worked construction on the Gulf Coast. Mexican migrants made up 41 percent of the population of Dodge City, Kansas, in 2000; 16 percent of Grand Island, Nebraska; and 19 percent of Worthington, Minnesota.

The migrants who came to work in these places were mainly male, overwhelmingly young, and often uneducated. They did the most unpleasant, backbreaking, and dangerous work. Often, as in the Tyson chicken plants, the filthiest and most monotonous jobs were reserved for Mexican and Asian women. In most places outside urban centers, migrants and Anglos lived segregated lives and had little to do with each other. Sometimes the local White population had fears and misconceptions about Mexicans. Sometimes, the migrants suffered violence at their hands. On July 5, 2003, a group of White teenagers set the house of a Mexican family on fire in Farmingville, Long Island, one of several anti-immigrant incidents in the area. On September 30, 2005, two Georgia men beat five Mexican farmworkers to death and injured six others in midnight raids on trailer parks. Despite such incidents and the hard, dangerous nature of the work, Mexican migrants continued to flood into rural districts across the country. That was where the jobs were.[65]

The post-1965 Mexican migrants went through many of the same processes of cultural adjustment and economic advance as their Asian contemporaries and other previous immigrant groups. They married or sent for family members, had children who grew up in the United States. One friend of mine was smuggled into the country very young and spent most of her first decade in the United States living with her family under a bridge. They worked in the fields and she went to public school. By the time she reached her late twenties she had earned a college degree and was managing a small business. It is true that Mexican Americans were harder hit by economic recessions than were Whites and they took longer to recover lost jobs and earnings. It is also true that Mexican American high school students had a 40 percent dropout rate at the turn of the century, compared to 22 percent for Whites, 16 percent for Asians, and 43 percent for Blacks. Yet taking a long view, a RAND Corporation study found that Mexican Americans achieved the same kind of intergenerational economic mobility in the second half of the twentieth century as had European immigrants several decades earlier.[66]

The very large numbers of Mexican Americans and their increasing integration into society had an effect on American cultural and political life. Many Mexicans and other Latinos were noncitizens and so political participation was slow in coming, but they were a cultural and economic force nonetheless. By the 1990s, Cinco de

Mayo was celebrated in every major American city, and even rural Whites knew the difference between tacos and burritos. Spanish-language cable television networks like Telemundo and Univision drew in millions of viewers daily—not just Latinos, but also Anglos who understood enough Spanish to consume their products. The largest Spanish-language newspaper, *La Opiñion* in Southern California, reached 100,000 in daily circulation and spurred major chains like Gannett and Knight-Ridder to launch competing Spanish-language papers. Marketing to Latinos became a major push in mainstream advertising. Magazines such as *Latina*, *Tu Ciudad*, and *Hispanic Trends* catered to young, hip Latinos in business and the arts. Much of the marketing was framed in terms of a Latino panethnicity (see Chapter 9), but the main population force behind the move was Mexican American.[67]

Mexican Americans affected many aspects of American life. They became a large enough part of higher education to support a network of Latino fraternities and sororities, as well as college magazines directed at Latino students. A Mexican American entrepreneur, Arte Morcno, bought the Los Angeles Angels baseball team. Soccer actually became a popular spectator sport, thanks in large part to the Mexican American fans who turned out to support the Los Angeles Galaxy, Chivas U.S.A, and Real Salt Lake. The Nielsen company was forced by public demand to include Univision shows in its TV rating system. Latino rappers and rock bands played to packed houses with racially mixed audiences. By early in the new century, a Mexican American actress like Eva Longoria could become a mainstream American heartthrob while maintaining an outspoken commitment to Mexican American identity politics, where a generation earlier Raquel Welch had been forced to hide her ancestry. UPN shot soap operas in Spanish and many mainstream film companies made bilingual movies.[68]

Perhaps nowhere was the trend more apparent than in politics. Mexican American political participation was long more potential than actual; many people were not citizens, and many citizens either did not register or did not vote. Only one major city, San Antonio, elected a Mexican American mayor, Henry Cisneros, in 1981. But as the century turned, Mexican Americans and other Latinos began to flex some muscle. Both political parties sought Mexican American votes, but Democrats had more success. Longtime activists like Los Angeles County Supervisor Gloria Molina and California Lieutenant Governor Cruz Bustamante were joined in the 1990s and after by a host of new faces. The most conspicuously successful early in the new century was Antonio Villaraigosa, a bright, articulate, and telegenic former legislator who became Mayor of Los Angeles in 2005. Villaraigosa took pains to run as a candidate of all the peoples of Los Angeles, not just Mexicans, and indeed one found Villaraigosa-for-Mayor signs in shop windows in Koreatown and Little Persia. But the political arrival of Mexican Americans was palpable. Villaraigosa was not the only Mexican face in Los Angeles politics. The city council president and four other council members, the president of the school board, the chair of the county board of supervisors, sheriff, and transit board chair all were Mexican Americans.[69]

Mexican Americans constituted a growing voting bloc that both parties coveted after the turn of the century. Bill Richardson, governor of New Mexico, emphasized the Mexican side of his ancestry and prepared to run for President. President George W. Bush tried to pry loose Mexican American voters by emphasizing his ability to speak some Spanish, supporting Christian values in the public sphere, and appointing Mexican Americans to high posts such as U.S. Attorney General. The fate of Mexican Americans in U.S. politics and their dominant party affiliation are anybody's guess. What is not uncertain is that they will be a crucial political force for decades to come.[70]

For all that other Americans may not have seen them that way, one must observe that Mexican Americans had many of the qualifications that one might associate with a Model Minority: strong family values, embrace of hard work, Christian commitment, a bootstrap mentality, significant elements of success in American economic and public life. This is not to recommend recycling the Model Minority tag; Asian Americans have been misunderstood partly because of that label. Rather, it is to suggest that Mexican Americans over the last several decades of the twentieth century and into the twenty-first century contributed enormously to American life and achieved a substantial measure of success despite manifest discrimination and growing opposition from other Americans.

Migrants or Exiles? From Cuba

Mexican migrants have not been welcome in recent decades despite their persistent presence and manifest contributions. From 1960 on, however, other Americans were far more eager to embrace another group of migrants from Latin America: Cubans.[71] The Cuban migration was much smaller: fewer than 800,000 Cubans came between 1961 and 2000, compared to 5 million Mexicans (see Table 8.5). However, Cubans were viewed from the outset not as a threat or a social burden but as an opportunity for America to demonstrate its virtues, so other Americans went to extraordinary lengths to make Cubans welcome. Their motive was the Cold War.

As we saw in Chapter 7, Fidel Castro's 1959 Marxist revolution led many middle- and upper-class Cubans to flee to the United States. Here, thanks to more than $1 billion in ethnically targeted federal aid over the next two decades, they made a swift transition to American life. They gained credentials, jobs, homes, businesses, and places of achievement in American politics. Still, many Cubans regarded themselves as exiles, clinging to a hope of returning home once Castro had died or his regime had been toppled. María Cristina García described the scene in Miami in 1991:

> Talk of returning was all over the exile community. A popular political button selling in Little Havana showed Castro toppled by a series of dominoes, with the slogan "¡El próximo!" (The next one). One of the most widely read books in Miami was comedian Guillermo Alvarez Guedes's *El día que cayó Fidel Castro* (The day Fidel Castro was overthrown), and two of the most popular plays on Miami's *vodevil* circuit were *A Cuba me voy hoy mismo ... que se acabó el comunismo* (I'm leaving for Cuba this very minute ... communism is finished) and *En los 90 Fidel revienta* (In the 1990s Fidel expires). CANF, Alpha 66, the Junta Patriótica Cubana, the Cuban Municipalities in Exile, and other exile organizations began drafting versions of Cuba's new constitution and transitional government.[72]

Theirs was destined to be a long wait.

The exodus of large numbers of Cubans after Castro came to power in 1959 was followed by a steady trickle of migrants in the ensuing decades. Because of American opposition to Castro's government, U.S. law regarded any and all Cubans who floated to America on homemade rafts or came in small boats as by definition refugees fleeing communism. As such, if they succeeded in placing their feet on U.S. soil they could not be deported, unlike migrants from almost any other part of the world. In 1980, Castro, in a bid to get the United States to lift its embargo on trade with Cuba, announced that anyone who wanted to leave the island was free to do so and designated the port of Mariel as the embarkation point. Cubans in Florida brought cabin cruisers, sailboats, fishing boats, even freighters across the ninety miles to Mariel and brought out 1,700 boatloads of migrants—124,776 people in all. The Carter administration was unprepared for all this. It did not award this set of migrants the full refugee status that had been accorded to previous Cuban migrants, so they did not receive full resettlement benefits. The Marielitos were housed in camps and prisons until they could be processed and released into American society. It appears that between 1 and 2 percent may have had criminal pasts in Cuba, and the American people were less willing to step up to sponsor these migrants than they had been for earlier refugees, either from Cuba or those from Southeast Asia. It is not clear whether the fact that about 30 percent of the Marielitos were Black (as compared to 3 percent of the Cubans who came in the 1960s) discouraged other Americans from supporting their incorporation into the United States. Whatever the case, the very small number of Mariel migrants who were found to have criminal pasts were detained indefinitely, some to the end of the century. Although that number was small, the criminal image stuck to all the Marielitos in the minds of many non-Cuban Americans.[73]

The political nature of Cuban migration, and the continuing political exploitation of Cuban American loyalties in U.S. Cold War domestic politics, meant that Cubans maintained a dual identity longer than was common for immigrant groups. They were both Cuban exiles and Cuban Americans. Nonetheless, in time the intense identification with Cuba, and the rabid opposition to Castro, began to fade. For a time in the 1990s, some Cuban Americans were allowed to visit their relatives in Cuba, but then the second President Bush cut off travel and trade again. By the end of the century, enough migrants had continued to come, and continued to concentrate in South Florida, that two generations with distinct agendas had emerged in that region. The old guard, those who had come in the 1960s and 1970s, still remained implacably opposed to Castro. Anticommunism and longing for home were the grounds of their identity and the glue that held together their community. But the younger generation, made up of both the old guard's children and new post-1980 migrants, took a softer line. They focused less on Cuban politics and more on making lives in the United States.[74]

Meanwhile, Cuban Americans were making ever-deeper inroads into American politics and culture. Cuban émigrés had taken out American citizenship, were running for office, and held many key posts in South Florida government. They constituted a critical bloc of dependable votes for the Republican Party in what was otherwise a swing state in national elections, and they may be credited with putting George W. Bush over the top in the 2000 presidential election. Cuban musicians like the Buena Vista Social Club and Cuban Americans like the Miami Sound Machine and Gloria Estefan topped the jazz and pop charts. Cuba's most popular export may have been baseball players, including members of a dozen major league teams at any given time.[75]

There remained, however, periodic political outbursts, such as the furor over Elián Gonzalez. In November 1999, six-year-old Elián accompanied his mother and several others as they attempted to reach the United States by small boat. The boat capsized near Florida and most of the passengers, including Elián's mother, drowned. After a brief hospital stay, Elián was released into the care of his great-uncle Lazaro Gonzalez in Miami. When the boy's father, Juan Miguel Gonzalez, learned of his son's situation, he demanded that Elián be returned to his care in Cuba. There followed six months of pushing and pulling between the U.S. and Cuban governments and various forces on the American political scene. Anti-Castro activists and right-wing speakers denounced any attempt to return Elián to Cuba as a betrayal of his mother's bold attempt at freedom. American immigration and child custody laws, however, were clear: the father had custody. When the great-uncle and his supporters in the Cuban exile community refused to give the boy up, federal agents stormed his house, took Elián by force, and returned him to his father who was then staying outside Washington, DC. Father and son returned to Cuba in June 2004.[76]

The Elián Gonzalez controversy demonstrated the continued saliency of anti-Castro feeling among many Cuban Americans. Yet, despite the hopes of many in the Cuban American community, Castro held on—nearly forty years at this writing, with few signs of diminished capacity despite having reached his eightieth year. And many Cuban Americans were turning to the task of integrating themselves into American society as permanent citizens.

From Other Parts of Latin America and the Caribbean

These were unprecedented times for immigration from other parts of the Western Hemisphere, too. In the period 1961 to 2000, 1.2 million people migrated from Central America, 1.6 million from South America, and 2.3 million from the Caribbean outside Cuba. Numbers from individual countries waxed and waned with local politics and economics, but the number of migrants from each of those regions increased steadily, decade by decade. Only the numbers coming in from Canada dropped in this period (see Table 8.5).

Tens of thousands poured out of Nicaragua into Costa Rica, and out of Guatemala into Mexico. In the 1970s and 1980s, Central American peasants fled the countryside as armies contested for control of several countries. In Honduras, El Salvador, and Guatemala, right-wing dictatorships backed by the U.S. government sent death squads into Indian villages, killing many and driving out thousands of people who fled northward. These migrants were refugees, every bit as much as were the Cubans who floated to Miami. But political commitments to support their national governments made it impossible for the United States to acknowledge that they were in fact political or ethnic refugees fleeing for their lives. In the Nicaraguan case the emigrants were searching for a way to make a living, as the Nicaraguan economy could not support that country's population in the 1990s. By 2005 there were 400,000 desperately poor Nicaraguans living in La Carpio and other Costa Rican slums; they made up 10 percent of Costa Rica's total population. Others moved northward toward Mexico and the United States, joining a stream of other Central Americans and Mexicans.

In the 1990s and 2000s, hundreds of thousands of Central Americans, many of them women with small children, sought jobs in Mexico and the United States. Their men gone already, they left their children behind with relatives with the hope to go north, find jobs, send money back to support them, and perhaps one day send for the children to join them in the north. After years of waiting, many such children could wait no longer for their parents to send for them, so they set out on their own. Sonia Nazario, a journalist who traveled north with some such children and wrote their story, estimated that perhaps 48,000 unaccompanied minors entered the United States illegally each year from Mexico and Central America around the turn of the century. She told the story of Enrique, a Honduran boy whose mother went to work in the United States, never to return. His was a life of loneliness and longing, of dysfunction and drugs until, at age seventeen, he set out to go to America and find her. He was one of the older ones attempting the trip—others Nazario interviewed were as young as four. Enrique hitched rides on freight cars, begged and stole to eat, forded rivers even though he could not swim, endured beatings, robbery, and fear. Some he encountered died or were left along the way. Enrique was also blessed by the generosity of poor strangers who had little to give but who shared what they had nonetheless. He floated across the Rio Grande in an inner tube and made his way eventually to North Carolina, where his mother worked.[77]

Migrants came from the Caribbean, too, in unprecedented numbers. Puerto Ricans had been making homes in New York and other eastern cities for a couple of generations before the 1965 immigration act. Thereafter, the going and coming from San Juan to New York expanded numerically and geographically. In time there were Puerto Rican populations in every major American city. The same was true for Dominicans, Jamaicans, and other Caribbean peoples. They made up separate communities in many cities of the East, South, and Midwest—often taken for Black by other Americans because of their phenotype, but possessing a separate identity and a Caribbean culture that set them apart from Southern-derived African Americans.[78]

Differential treatment, based partly on race and partly on ideology, can be seen in the operation of U.S. refugee policies toward Cubans and Haitians.[79] Throughout the Reagan, Clinton, and two Bush presidencies, Haiti was in crisis. For much of that time, it was not only the poorest country in the Western Hemisphere but also a very dangerous place in which to live. Persecution of people who opposed the Haitian government was commonplace. As in Cuba, many Haitians longed to migrate to the United States, and some took to the waves in desperation. But where the United States granted refugee status to any Cuban who made it to American soil, it refused to do the same for Haitians. Because the United States had friendly relations with the Haitian government, the United States only fitfully was willing to recognize that many of the Haitians who fled their country were in fact legitimate political refugees. Instead, almost all of them were interdicted by the Coast Guard and taken back to Haiti against their will. Part of this differential treatment was spurred by ideological differences with Cuba's government, but critics charged that part of the difference in policy was due to the fact that Cubans were mainly White and Haitians were Black. The policy continued into the new century. In April 2006, U.S. immigration officials caught forty-six unauthorized migrants on a South Florida beach: one Cuban, one Jamaican, and forty-four Haitians. One of the refugees, Donald Joseph, said "I'd rather spend fifty years in prison than be sent back to Haiti." Nonetheless, the Haitians and the Jamaican were slated to be sent back. The lone Cuban could remain, because the Cuban Adjustment Act provided that any Cuban illegal immigrant who managed to set foot on U.S. soil would, simply because he or she was Cuban, be allowed to stay and qualify for permanent U.S. residency.[80]

Another feature of Caribbean migration was the long-term maintenance of networks connecting the islands and towns from which people came and the lives they made in the United States. Nina Glick Schiller and Georges Eugene Fouron refer to this as "transborder citizenry" pursued in a context of "long-distance nationalism," and the extended family relationships on which they are built as "transnational kinship." By this they mean to highlight the ongoing webs of connectedness between the places from which people came—in this case, in Haiti—and their other homes in the United States. People moved back and forth, they sent money home, they intervened in homeland politics, at the same time they built new lives and connections for themselves in the United States. Peggy Levitt calls the participants in such networks "transnational villagers." She details the ways that residents of Miraflores, a village on the south coast of the Dominican Republic, benefited from their connections to hundreds of former residents and their families in the Jamaica Plain, a neighborhood in Boston. They owned TVs and VCRs. They had better phone service and schools than residents of Santo Domingo, the national capital. They had intimate knowledge of the landscape and weekly business of a place that was nearly two thousand miles away. Carol Williams refers to the financial connection as "the new foreign aid." Williams tells the story of Dieuseul Lundi, who, "since he left for the U.S. 33 years ago … has pumped tens of thousands of dollars back onto Haiti through an extended family of at least three dozen people. On trips home, he resembles a one-man foreign aid program." In fact, Williams estimates: "Handouts from 1.5 million Haitian émigrés in the U.S., half of them in Florida, are estimated at $1 billion a year—five times more than all foreign aid to Haiti. … These payments amount to 2½ times the national budget and at least 20% of Haiti's gross domestic product."[81]

That kind of connectedness between the land of origin and the United States also characterized many other kinds of migrants in this period. Mexicans, Micronesians, South Asians, Taiwanese, and others kept up ties to home, sent money back, hosted relatives who came to join them in the United States, visited home regularly, communicated via phone and internet, and remained involved in the lives of the places from which they had come. To take just one example, early in the new century a youth football game took place in a Micronesian community in Southern California. Throughout the game, one of the spectators could be heard describing the action into a cell phone. The call, it turned out, was being made to a radio station in the Marshall Islands, where it was broadcast live throughout the island chain as play-by-play reporting.[82]

From Europe

European immigration declined steadily after the 1965 immigration act until it ticked up again in the 1990s. It dropped from 1.3 million in the 1950s to 761,550 in the 1980s, then rebounded to 1.3 million again the following decade. Among the major traditional European sending countries, migration from Great Britain, Germany, Ireland, Italy, and Scandinavia all declined fairly steadily (Table 8.6).[83]

The only major European country that saw a surge in migration to the United States after 1965 was Russia (before 1989 the Soviet Union). Emigration to the United States totaled 671 people in the 1950s, 2,465 in the 1960s, 38,961 in the 1970s, and 57,677 in the 1980s. It skyrocketed to 462,874 in the 1990s—more than one-third of the total for all of Europe.[84]

The key was the fall of communism in 1989. People in countries like Russia, the Ukraine, and members of the former eastern bloc suddenly had permission to cross

Table 8.6 Immigration from Europe and Africa, 1961–2000

Decade	Europe	Africa
1961–1970	1,123,492	28,954
1971–1980	800,368	80,779
1980–1990	761,550	176,893
1991–2000	1,359,737	354,939
Total 1961–2000	4,045,147	641,565

Source: Appendix B, Table B.4.

borders if they wished. The political chaos and economic upheaval that followed the collapse of communism in Russia and other nations of Eastern Europe—and that continued in the Russian case well into the twenty-first century—set hundreds of thousands of people on their way to new homes. Many ethnic Jews from Russia and other states of the former Soviet Union moved to Israel, but far more came to the United States. The majority of Russian migrants to the United States in this period, however, were not Jews. They were simply people who migrated for economic reasons to a place where they saw better opportunities.[85]

This is not to say that there were no immigrants from other parts of Europe, just that Russians came to constitute the largest single chunk. Several thousand Poles fled Poland during the 1980s and came to the United States. Many of them were supporters of Solidarity, the workers' democratic movement that eventually toppled the Polish communist government. Thousands more came as refugees or, more often, as illegal immigrants from the countries of the former Yugoslavia. Natasha Radojcic left just as Yugoslavia was breaking into civil war in 1989, at twenty-two years old, with $1000 in her sock. She lived on a rented mattress in Queens for $50 a week and worked a series of jobs—babysitter, receptionist, and sex-toy shop cashier—until she hit upon the lucrative and not-very-demanding career of personal trainer. That left her time to practice her English, go to college, and eventually write a novel. English people also continued to come, and as before they enjoyed the privileges of native White status immediately upon arrival.[86]

One group of Russian, Ukrainian, and other East European migrants who caught the attention of news reporters and human rights activists were women in sex work. Sex for hire is a consistent feature of human history, and it is legal in many parts of the globe, although most people acknowledge it is an industry ripe for the abuse, especially, of young women with few resources. In the aftermath of the breakup of the Soviet Union and the eastern bloc, the economic distance between rich and poor in those countries exploded, at the same time that emigration controls were removed. Women from poor families, or people wanting to get out of the country and experience the world, went looking for jobs abroad. Unscrupulous recruiters, often on the Internet, offered jobs in Britain as nannies or entrance into American universities. Women responded to the ads, and before long they found themselves standing in the snow out behind the Hamburg train station or working in brothels in Madrid or Kuala Lumpur or Houston. Similar poverty, at the same time as increased geographical mobility, in places like Thailand, the Philippines, even Korea, and several countries in South America and Africa had a similar result: thousands of women going abroad to live in virtual slavery and perform sex for a fee.[87]

The Irish have long had a special place in the story of American immigration, but that place began to change in the last years of the twentieth century. Ireland had a poor economy—one of the poorest in Europe—and was still exporting people as late as the 1980s. One of those was Jim Sheridan, an aspiring filmmaker who crept across the border from Canada illegally in the early 1980s with his wife and two small daughters. They lived in poverty in New York City among immigrants from all over the world. In the fullness of time, Sheridan did in fact become a famous director, with commercial and artistic triumphs such as *My Left Foot*. Later he and his family made a much-lauded film, *In America*, about their struggles as illegal immigrants. Tens of thousands of other Irish immigrants came without papers in the 1970s and 1980s. They came on tourist visas and simply stayed on, secure in the knowledge that, even if the U.S. government went looking for illegal immigrants, they were unlikely to care about such people if they came from Europe. Then in the years after the turn of the century, two things happened: the U.S. government got a bit more serious about tracking and putting limits even on European migrants who lacked papers (things like denying people driver's licenses) and the Irish economy boomed. Irish migrants began to flow back whence they came: 26,000 more Irish people migrated into Ireland than out in 2002. It was an astonishing turnabout after 150 years of out-migration. As Catroina Condon, a corporate receptionist before returning to County Westmeath, said, in America "It's longer hours, less money, and a lot of the time you see people working for their wage just to pay their rent, to pay their health insurance." Said Anne Cullen, an Irish New Yorker for seven years, "Everybody's leaving and nobody's coming over anymore." Almost her entire extended family had reversed course and gone back to the Old Sod.[88]

From Africa

In Chapter 2, Table 2.4 reports an estimate that about 315,000 Africans came to British North America as slaves between 1620 and 1780.[89] Even the highest estimates for African slaves who migrated into the territory that became the United States during the entire slave era are less than half a million. Immigration and Naturalization Service figures from the last four decades of the twentieth century record 641,565 African migrants to the United States—more willing immigrants in recent decades than unwilling migrants during the entire slave epoch. This does not mean, of course, that recent African migration is as significant a part of U.S. immigration history as the slave migration of centuries ago. Given the huge natural increase in the African American population that has occurred over the past two centuries, the recent African migration constitutes only a small fraction—about 7 percent—of the total Black population in the United States.[90]

The current African migration began in the 1970s, when students from several African countries began coming in large numbers to American universities. Some of them stayed on in the United States with the new skills they had acquired; others returned to their countries of origin, where they often took leadership positions in business, government, and religious institutions and encouraged others to follow their path. In that and the following decades they were joined by an increasing number of refugees. Ethiopians fled the Marxist dictatorship that seized power and terrorized much of the citizenry beginning in the 1970s. In 1983, 90 percent of the African refugees were from Ethiopia; altogether, nearly 40,000 Ethiopians fled to the

United States by the end of the century. But other countries contributed refugees as well. Nigeria fought a bloody civil war against its Igbo minority. Igbo and other Nigerians went into exile in other African countries, Europe, and the United States. A civil war and U.S. intervention in Somalia in 1991 led to thousands of Somalis leaving that country; several thousand of them ended up in the United States (others went to Sweden, Finland, and elsewhere in Europe). When Liberia descended into civil war in the 1990s, thousands left that country, as well.

A particularly poignant story was that of the so-called Lost Boys of Sudan. As this is written, a conflict between the Sudanese government and its proxy militias, on the one hand, and the residents of Darfur in the country's western deserts has raged for many months and killed scores, perhaps hundreds of thousands. That is only the latest war in Sudan. Throughout most of the 1980s and 1990s, the government waged a relentless attack on the southern region of the country. Hundreds of thousands of people were killed and rendered homeless, their villages torched and crops destroyed. One six-year-old boy, Acik Ateng Nai, lost his parents in a raid in 1997. According to his biographer:

> He hid for days in a swamp, then joined the other fleeing children. Nai and his friends never saw their families again. They didn't stop walking for nearly two months. As they slowly made their way across the harsh terrain to safety in Ethiopia, the scorching sand blistered Nai's bare feet. Older boys tried to help by tying pieces of goat skin under his toes. The boys ate whatever roots and plants they could find along the way, but Nai says the unforgiving thirst was worse than the hunger. They found brief refuge in Ethiopia, but were driven out when troops attacked their camp, forcing them to flee on foot back toward Sudan. Chased by soldiers, the boys ran to the banks of the Gilo River. "We didn't want to enter, but there was shooting and people were pushing us," recalls Nai. Many drowned before reaching the other side. Crocodiles ate dozens of others.

Of the 20,000 boys who began the journey, only 12,000 reached the safety of a refugee camp in Kenya about a year later.

> They arrived rail-thin and knobby-kneed, their legs and feet ravaged by infected sores. For the next ten years, the sprawling mud-hut settlement of 70,000 refugees from Rwanda, Ethiopia, Somalia and Sudan became the boys' home. Each day was a struggle. Malaria regularly swept through the camp. Refugees were stung repeatedly by scorpions and camel spiders, which came out by the hundreds at night. The boys had to guard their bimonthly UN rations, barely enough for one meal a day.

After ten years in the camp, Nai was one of the 4000 lucky ones who was selected for entry into the United States. He was sent to Grand Rapids, Michigan, where he got his first shoes in a decade, his first jacket ever. Supported by food stamps and a Catholic charity, Nai studied for a GED and learned about telephones and refrigerators. He got a job working for a big-box retailer and got off food stamps. He looked forward to qualifying for a green card and eventual U.S. citizenship.[91]

Some of the refugees came on tourist visas and then claimed asylum once they were inside the United States. This was the most common method used by women

Table 8.7 Leading Sending Countries of African Immigrants, 1996

Nigeria	10,221
Guinea	6,606
Equatorial Guinea	6,186
Ethiopia	6,086
South Africa	2,966
Liberia	2,206
Sudan	2,172
Somalia	2,170
Sierra Leone	1,918
Morocco	1,783
Kenya	1,666
Algeria	1,059
Central African Republic	1,012
All Africa	52,889

Source: U.S. Office of Immigration Statistics, *Statistical Yearbook: 2001* (Washington, DC: Government Printing Office, 2001).

from several parts of Africa whose asylum claims were based on the fact that they would have suffered female genital mutilation had they remained. Such mutilation was a common practice among several peoples of East and West Africa, to limit women's sexual experience and to mark their dependence on men. In 1996, Fauziya Kasinga fled Togo and ended up in a U.S. jail, where she claimed asylum on the grounds she was fleeing genital mutilation and an arranged marriage to a man who already had wives and was generations older than she. The Board of Immigration Appeals granted her petition, and gradually fear of female genital mutilation came to be considered a legitimate basis of an asylum claim. Other women claimed spousal abuse as the basis of their asylum claims, but their petitions were less frequently successful.[92]

Table 8.7 shows the leading countries in terms of migrants sent to the United States in a fairly typical year.

Thus African immigrants came in by many means. Some were students who found jobs and stayed on. Some overstayed visitor's visas and remained without documents. Some of those received documents as part of the general amnesty of 1986. Beginning in that year, the Immigration and Naturalization Service granted several thousand immigrant visas in a so-called "diversity lottery" among applicants from places with small numbers of immigrants. Increasingly in the 1990s, people who had come and achieved permanent residency or citizenship were sending back to Africa for family members under the family reunification policy.

The largest concentrations of Africans were in a few large cities such as New York, Chicago, Washington, San Francisco, and Los Angeles. Those who came as refugees were purposely spread out across the country by the INS. Those who were members of the educated elite often found professional work, but others drove taxis, opened restaurants and small shops, worked for Wal-Mart, and hawked food and household goods on city streets.

Most African immigrants, like most of those who came from the Caribbean, had to address a major identity issue: whether or not to identify with American Blacks. When Agba Mangalabou arrived from his native Togo via a stop in Europe in 2002, he complained that he was being misidentified: "In Germany, everyone knew I was African. Here, nobody knows if I'm African or American."[93] Some elite African migrants bristled at being identified with African Americans who had descended from slaves, for they believed themselves superior to such people. But in time, especially as a second generation began to grow up in the United States and experience the American racial system as their primary social matrix, most Africans took on at least some elements of solidarity with African Americans.

One of the things that Africans often experienced in common with American-derived Blacks was racist abuse. Such treatment sewed the seeds of a potential identify shift for African migrants and their children. In September 1996 a twenty-year-old young man left Guinea for the United States. Amadou Diallo came from a middle-class family. He had been educated in good schools and had traveled as far as Thailand. Though a certain measure of success likely awaited him if he stayed home, Diallo told his uncle, "I think I can do more good for the family in America than I can here," and so he went. Like Jim Sheridan, he was an immigrant without papers. His goal was to earn enough money to go to school, learn to be a computer technician, get a job, and then send for his mother and other relatives. He earned a living selling bootlegged videos on 14th Street in Manhattan. In a bit more than two years' time Diallo had saved $3000 by living as cheaply as he could in a tiny studio apartment he shared with a roommate. Then on February 4, 1999, he was confronted in the vestibule of his apartment building in the Bronx by four police officers, who were not in uniform and apparently did not identify themselves. They said later that Diallo pulled a gun, though none was found at the scene. He died in a hail of bullets (forty-one were shot; nineteen hit their mark). The officers went free.

African American leaders from Harry Belafonte to Jesse Jackson protested, to no avail. African immigrant leaders were considerably more muted in their criticism. One African immigrant scholar, Violet Showers Johnson, asked in frustration, "[H]ow capable are African immigrants in understanding and embracing the collective Black traumatized past[?]... [T]he majority of African immigrants are unable to examine the Diallo incident within the larger context of race and racism." Another, an NYU professor named Manthia Diawara, remarked that:

Amadou Diallo's death left a sour taste in my mouth. Just as my success story in America could have been his, the tragedy that had befallen him could have been mine, as a black man in America—albeit an African. Little do the Amadou Diallos of the world know that the black man in America bears the curse of Cain, and that in America they, too, are considered black men, not Fulanis, Mandingos, or Wolofs. They cut Amadou Diallo down like a black American, even though he belonged to the Fulani tribe in his native Guinea. There is a lesson here for all of us to learn.

The relationship of African immigrants and African Americans was a complex one, highlighted but not resolved in the wake of the Diallo killing.[94]

Continuing Involvements Abroad

Like Dominicans and Micronesians going back and forth, sending money home, and receiving news from abroad, migrants from many parts of the world remained involved in the affairs from the places from which they had come. Migrants and their American-born children visited back home ever more frequently, in an era of comparatively low-cost jet travel and as their economic fortunes in the United States allowed. Since U.S. immigration policy favored middle-class migrants over body workers, more and more had the ability to make such trips. The public schools in Ventura, California, got used to sending Mexican American children home with large homework packets in mid-December, for they knew that some families would be taking the children back home for an extended holiday.[95] Some countries that had ties to U.S. populations—Taiwan, Korea, and Israel were prominent examples— sponsored low-cost "heritage tours" for teenagers and young adults. These trips gave youths an opportunity to visit an overseas place either from which their parents had come or with which their religious culture was associated, to do some cultural learning, to interact with others from their ethnic group, and quite often to receive an element of political indoctrination.

Immigrant peoples in the United States often remained connected to old country politics. The involvement of American Jews with the state of Israel—visiting, sending money, being active in American politics on Israel's behalf, even fighting in Israel's army—has been the major political activity among American Jewry since the late 1940s. Few Americans questioned the appropriateness of such activity, except in a very few cases when someone was alleged to be spying on behalf of the Israeli government. In similar fashion, thousands of Irish Americans remained interested in Irish politics and many sent money to the Irish Republican Army or its political wing, Sinn Fein. Not only Jews but Palestinians and other Arab Americans have informed themselves daily about Middle East politics and tried to influence U.S. policy makers. Former Muslims who had converted to Christianity formed a satellite radio network to beam religious conversion and pro-American messages into Iran and other Muslim countries. An Afghan-born State Department and Pentagon official, Zalmay Khalilzad, was sent back home as U.S. ambassador to Afghanistan to help create the post-U.S.-invasion government of Hamid Karzai; later he became U.S. ambassador to Iraq. In the 1990s, some U.S. citizens went back to the lands of their birth as the former Soviet Bloc disintegrated, in order to stand for election in Russia, Georgia, Poland, and other countries.[96]

A substantial number of Americans who had come from other places voted in old-country elections. For some, that meant voting by absentee ballots, as U.S. citizens do while abroad. But some countries with special ties to U.S. populations managed to create polling places within the United States. It was celebrated widely when Iraqi Americans voted in Iraq's first post-invasion elections in January 2005. There was not much comment when Armenian Americans voted in presidential elections in Armenia from California polling stations.[97] U.S. public opinion was more divided over the legitimacy of Mexican Americans voting in Mexican elections. Some anti-Mexican activists used the idea that Mexican Americans who were not yet U.S. citizens might vote in their home elections as evidence that Mexicans were inappropriate immigrants and alleged that their loyalties lay elsewhere. But most observers more or less agreed with University of California San Diego scholar Wayne Cornelius:

Who cares where they vote? The near-unanimous vote last week by the Mexican Congress to allow immigrants in the United States to vote in presidential elections is a major step toward consolidating Mexico's democracy—and Americans should celebrate it. Through the power of absentee ballots, Mexicans who live here may be able to change the policies that drove many of them to seek work in the U.S., and that would have long-term consequences for migrant flows.

In the end, the Mexican government forbade candidates to campaign in the United States, although their U.S. supporters did hold a few events without the candidates present, and Mexican American voter turnout in the 2006 Mexican presidential election was low.[98]

Many immigrants tried to affect the political fortunes of their home countries more informally. Chinese immigrants, some of them veterans of the 1989 Tiananmen Massacre, tried to influence homeland politics and force a turn toward democracy, but they met dwindling support among Chinese Americans by the end of the century. Similarly, some Taiwanese Americans made loud objections to U.S. visits by Taiwanese politicians whose policies they opposed, but few listened. Some Chinese Americans did go back to China to try to influence policies there or to spread Christianity, and they were sometimes jailed for their activities. Homeland politics consumed Orange County's Little Saigon and the Long Beach Cambodian community from time to time. U.S. Filipinos were active for and against dictator Ferdinand Marcos, for two decades. Later they mourned the passing of Cardinal Jaime Sin, the man who did more than anyone else to push Marcos from power and restore Philippine democracy. Utah's Sudanese marched on the state capital to demand the U.S. government call for an investigation into the mysterious death of Sudan's vice president.[99]

Where Americans had the most impact on their ancestral countries was not politics but economics. Some of this was at the level of high finance and major corporate initiatives. Ihsan Khan, a cab driver in Washington, D.C., came to the United States in 1977 penniless and returned decades later as one of Pakistan's wealthiest citizens, thanks to having won the Lotto in 2001. He used much of the money to help rebuild his village of Batagram after a devastating earthquake in 2005 and he became its mayor. Former Fullerton, California, Mayor Julie Sa, the daughter of Chinese American immigrants, was a top candidate to head up a special economic zone in North Korea. In 2003, Russian-born U.S. citizen Simon Kukes took over as head of the Russian oil giant Yukos.[100]

Far more money and personal involvement went into sending money back home to help out families and communities from which people came. Table 8.8 shows the money sent home by emigrants abroad to twenty-three Latin American nations in 2004.

According to the Inter-American Development Bank, in 2004 about $45 billion in remittances came into Latin American countries. Most of that money was sent home by migrants living and working in the United States. The total was larger than all foreign investment and foreign aid combined. In 2005, San Francisco-based Bank of America eliminated all transfer fees to Mexico for its customers and made it possible to transfer money to a Mexican account through any B of A bank machine. This made it easy for Mexicans working in the United States to send money home. Jose Antonio and Olga Lidia Mendoza were sending money home to Jose Antonio's

Table 8.8 Remittances to Latin America by
Overseas Migrants, 2004 (millions of dollars)

Mexico	16,613
Brazil	5,624
Colombia	3,857
Guatemala	2,681
El Salvador	2,548
Dominican Republic	2,438
Ecuador	1,740
Jamaica	1,497
Peru	1,360
Honduras	1,134
Haiti	1,026
Nicaragua	810
Paraguay	506
Bolivia	422
Costa Rica	306
Argentina	270
Venezuela	259
Panama	231
Guyana	143
Uruguay	105
Trinidad and Tobago	93
Belize	77
Surinam	51

Source: "When Cash Crosses Over," editorial,
Los Angeles Times (May 21, 2005).

parents, so that they could build a house in the village that would accommodate the extended family. A news report from Pachuca said:

Jose Antonio and Olga Lidia Mendoza have never set foot on the arid hillside lot they own here along Ejido Street near the corner of Agrarian Reform. They have never taken in the spectacular view of Pachuca's old mining center in the valley below. The Mexican couple live in Los Angeles County and have not been home in years. Having managed a risky border crossing with two young children and no documents, they prefer to stay put for now, clinging to his $225-a-week job as a chef at a Japanese restaurant in Diamond Bar. What they do know precisely, though, is the computerized blueprint of their future home, which is rising from the tiny lot here by an innovative form of remote control: With help from an engineer at no extra cost, Mexicans and Mexican Americans in California can design homes or businesses for construction in Mexico and order the building materials for next-day delivery to relatives who oversee the projects.

Parents and siblings planned to move into the house when it was finished, and save space for Jose Antonio and Olga Lidia to join them when they retired.[101]

Village clubs in the United States sent money to Mexico to build farm cooperatives and provide hurricane relief. The money may not have quite made up for the people who were missing from their homes for years and decades, but with one in five Mexican families receiving at least some contributions from relatives abroad, it seemed a permanent feature of the landscape. The flow of remittances was not limited to Mexico or to Latin America. Individuals and district associations sent money back to China to build schools and hospitals. More than one in ten Filipinos lived abroad, and they sent back more than $10 billion a year.[102]

Partly, this was the fruit of the capitalist globalization that accelerated during the last third of the twentieth century. Check the tag on your shirt collar: your clothes were likely made, or the fabric woven, or the pieces assembled, in Malaysia or Sri Lanka or the Dominican Republic. If not, the seamstress may have been an immigrant who worked in a sweatshop in Chinatown or New Jersey. U.S. textile firms were among the first to go global, beginning in the 1970s and accelerating ever since. In the new century, even highly skilled jobs such as copy editing were being outsourced to India. It was not just Nike factories being opened in Southeast Asia. Non-U.S. companies increasingly came into the United States as well: Honda and Toyota opened plants in the 1980s. Rupert Murdoch's News Corp. bought American media outlets. Jollie-B came from the Philippines in the 1990s. The North American Free Trade Agreement (NAFTA) and the growing Latino market brought Grupo Gigante, a supermarket chain, and Grupo FAMSA, an electronics and furniture retailer, to Southern California. Grupo Sanborns bought CompUSA and Cemex bought U.S. cement companies. And individual Americans went abroad in search of work and lifestyles. Jewish American Joshua Bornstein outsourced himself to India to work for a computer firm, one of more than 10,000 expatriates working in Bangalore. Thousands of Americans bought homes on the coast of Mexico and as far away as the Dodecanese Islands where they retired at a fraction of the cost of an American retirement.[103]

These transborder citizens and many others gave the lie to the hoary American myth of one-way migration. Some migrants, to be sure, were uprooted and never returned. They put the past behind them and strove single-mindedly to become undifferentiated Americans. But by far the majority maintained substantial elements of connectedness between their homes in the United States and the places they also regarded as homes in other countries. They communicated with relatives there (and elsewhere in the diaspora), shared the fruits of their economic progress, even got involved in ancestral-country politics. As we have seen throughout this book, this is not new in American immigration history. It has been thus since the generations of William Penn and George Washington. What has changed in the last several decades has been not the fact of transnational connecting, of coming and going, of Over There being connected with Over Here. What has changed is the velocity and torque with which these patterns have operated in our era of cheap global transportation and instant communication—the speed and frequency of visits, emails, and phone calls, the strength of impact a person might have on two or more places at nearly the same time. Thus, in the late twentieth and early twenty-first centuries, it was unremarkable that a transnational citizen like Simon Kukes or Rupert Murdoch should rise to prominence simultaneously on both sides of an immense ocean.

Chapter 9

Redefining Membership Amid Multiplicity Since 1965

In the decades after the 1965 Immigration Act and the civil rights movement, Americans found that melting pot ideology could no longer adequately address the diverse populations that had come to make up the United States. True to the assimilationist vision, some bars between racial and ethnic groups did begin to fall. But the fortunes of African Americans remained in decline, and new, panethnic groups such as Asian Americans and Latinos began to form. Meanwhile, some White people began to speak out against the multiracial reality of modern America. Anti-immigrant sentiment, always present, once again gained supporters and took on a racist tone. At the same time, the racial rules began to morph: even as the last of five broad panethnicities were coalescing, multicultural and multiracial movements seemed to blur some racial distinctions.

Immigration Reform, Again and Again

After the 1965 Immigration Act's effects became clear—a significant increase in the number of migrants and, in the eyes of some, an even more significant shift in the sources and races of the bulk of those immigrants—U.S. public policy discussions included repeated attempts to reduce what some regarded as runaway immigration. The notion that immigration was out of control was a feature of some people's thinking and argument throughout the last third of the twentieth century and into the twenty-first century. Oftentimes it was cast in terms of there being too many immigrants. But just beneath the surface—and often not hidden at all—was an opinion on the part of some Americans that these were the wrong kinds of immigrants, coming from the wrong places, bearing the wrong racial marks.

This opinion was one of the forces that gave rise to a series of adjustments to the country's immigration laws after 1965.[1] The fundamental principles enunciated in the 1965 law did not change—the law did not renew its embrace of the formal racist principles of the 1924 law—but the details did undergo a series of modifications. Also included were a few laws to accommodate special circumstances, such as refugees.

First, the refugee acts. Immediately after World War II, refugee acts were directed to allow displaced Europeans to enter the United States. After 1959, Congress added Cubans fleeing that country's new communist government. In 1966, the administration of Lyndon Johnson sponsored legislation to allow Cuban refugees to have permanent resident status and smooth the path to U.S. citizenship for those Cubans who wanted it. In 1975, mindful that the unsuccessful U.S. war in Southeast Asia had created many other people whose lives and livelihoods would be in jeopardy under new regimes, Congress passed the Indochinese Migration and Refugee Assistance Act, which created a program for resettling refugees from Vietnam, Cambodia, and Laos. In 1980, the Refugee Act began to make a more permanent provision for the consequences of the mass refugee movements that had taken place in the 1960s and 1970s, and would also occur in the 1980s and 1990s. Previously, the refugee laws had been based on the idea of individuals fleeing persecution by hostile governments. Their numbers were assumed to be small, and they had previously been counted against the 20,000-person ceilings allowed in from single countries, except when large inflows were specifically exempted by an act of Congress. Yet the new refugee flows were much larger: 400,000 from Cuba, 340,000 from Vietnam, 110,000 from Laos, 70,000 each from Cambodia and the Soviet Union, 30,000 from Yugoslavia, and so on. The 1980 act allowed for a more flexible total cap of 50,000 refugees from wherever they might come in the world to be counted separately, outside the national quotas. It also adopted the United Nations' definition of a refugee as a person who had a "well-founded fear of persecution" on account of race, religion, nationality, or membership in a social movement or political group. So, theoretically at least, one did not need to be fleeing communism, just fleeing persecution, although it did not often work out that way in practice.[2]

The first significant amendment to the 1965 Immigration Act came in 1976, when Congress decided to get a little more control over who was coming from within the Western Hemisphere. It kept the same overall hemispheric caps: 170,000 total from the Eastern Hemisphere and 120,000 from the Western Hemisphere. But now it chose to apply the 20,000 per-country limit and the seven-point family and job skills preference system to Western Hemisphere migrants as well as those from the East. This set migrants from all countries on more or less the same footing.

Beginning with the presidency of Ronald Reagan, a national discussion developed in which some people asserted there were too many people coming into the United States, that immigration was getting out of control. President Reagan said on July 30, 1981, months after taking office: "Our nation is a nation of immigrants. More than any other country, our strength comes from our own immigrant heritage and our capacity to welcome those from other lands. No free and prosperous nation can by itself accommodate all those who seek a better life or flee persecution. We must share this responsibility with other countries."

Reagan set up a task force to study immigration policy and make recommendations. He continued:

— We shall continue America's tradition as a land that welcomes peoples from other countries. We shall also, with other countries, continue to share in the responsibility of welcoming and resettling those who flee oppression.

— At the same time, we must ensure adequate legal authority to establish control over immigration: to enable us, when sudden influxes of foreigners occur, to decide to whom we grant the status of refugee or asylee; to improve our border control; to expedite (*consistent with fair procedures and our Constitution*) return of those coming here illegally; to strengthen enforcement of our fair labor standards and laws; and to penalize those who would knowingly encourage violation of our laws. The steps we take to further these objectives, however, *must be consistent with our values of individual privacy and freedom.*

— We have a special relationship with our closest neighbors, Canada and Mexico. Our immigration policy should reflect this relationship.

— We must also recognize that both the United States and Mexico have historically benefited from Mexicans obtaining employment in the United States. A number of our States have special labor needs, and we should take these into account.

— *Illegal immigrants in considerable numbers have become productive members of our work force.* Those who have established equities in the United States should be recognized and accorded legal status. At the same time, in doing so, we must not encourage illegal immigration.[3]

Reagan's statement did not reflect hostility to immigrants. It eloquently affirmed the primacy of constitutional protections for due process and individual rights. It spoke specifically to friendship and cooperation with Mexico and Canada. And it specified approvingly the contributions of Mexicans and of unauthorized migrants to American society. It was, in many ways, a continuing of the doctrines of welcome, fairness, and nondiscrimination that had been embodied in the 1965 act. Yet, as in so many of Reagan's early initiatives in various areas including taxes, social services, and international affairs, this did represent the beginnings of what would become a dramatic policy change from previous ways of conceiving of these issues. It set a path toward ever-increasing restrictions on immigration, especially immigration from Mexico, that would mount and mount over the next quarter century. In the end, there would be an assault on immigrants in general and Mexicans in particular. Many of those constitutional protections, much of the respect for individual rights, and the special friendly relationship with Mexico would be obliterated.

The fruit of Reagan's initiative was the 1986 Immigration Reform and Control Act (which came to be called IRCA). True to Reagan's promise, it tried to stop employers, except employers of seasonal agricultural laborers, from hiring immigrants who lacked papers. And it provided punishments for those nonagricultural employers who hired any further unauthorized migrants in the future. At the same time, IRCA provided amnesty for 3 million current undocumented migrants and set them on a path to citizenship, with temporary resident status to be followed by the possibility of permanent residency.

IRCA temporarily mollified those people who wanted to choke off immigration further, but before long they were calling for more. Over the decade and more following Reagan's speech, xenophobes mounted an insistent mobilization campaign against immigrants who lacked documents, and against Mexican immigrants in particular. The first fruit of that campaign was the 1994 passage of California's Proposition 187, what some advocates called the "Save Our State" initiative. Its preamble read in part: "The People of California find and declare ... : That they have suffered and are suffering economic hardship by the presence of illegal aliens in the state. That they have suffered and are suffering personal injury and damage by the criminal conduct of illegal aliens in the state." The proposition promised "to prevent illegal aliens in the United States from receiving benefits or public services in the State of California."

The language of immigration reform had taken quite a turn in the decade or so since Ronald Reagan offered a much friendlier vision. Reagan had spoken of America as an immigrant nation and praised the essential contributions made by immigrants who did not have papers, especially Mexicans. Now the voters of California—mainly Whites, but some Blacks and American-born Latinos, too—blamed "illegal aliens" (mainly Mexicans) for unspecified and terrible crimes against the rest of the body civic, and proposed, if not to banish them from the republic, at least to make sure that they did not receive any government benefits such as enrollment in schools, food stamps, and access to state-supported medical care. The proposition was approved by 59 percent of the electorate, cementing California's reputation as a national trendsetter and also as a place where no extremism was too outrageous to find its adherents. Governor Pete Wilson rode to re-election by a wide margin on the strength of his strong support of Proposition 187. Yet, in fairly short order, the League of United Latin American Citizens sued Wilson, and most of Proposition 187 was found to be unconstitutional on two grounds: it violated the federal government's prerogative to be in charge of immigration policy, and it violated the Fourteenth Amendment, which guaranteed equal protection of the law to all persons, not just citizens.[4]

The U.S. Constitution was in fact on the side of the defenders of immigrants. Nonetheless, a chill set in over the migrant population of California. For a time, immigrant children were afraid to go to school and there were many reports of discrimination against Latino customers and job candidates, citizen and noncitizen. As soon as Proposition 187 was struck down, some politicians went to work to try to resurrect its most punitive provisions at the national level. The results came in 1996 with the immigration provisions of the Personal Responsibility and Work Opportunity Act and the Illegal Immigration Reform and Immigrant Responsibility Act. The Personal Responsibility and Work Opportunity Act focused on benefits. It said, among other things, that illegal immigrants could not apply for or receive federally sponsored loans, contracts, business licenses, retirement, welfare, health, disability, food assistance, or unemployment benefits. Exceptions were provided for emergency medical care, disaster relief, and a few other items. The law further required the states to deny such benefits on the same basis as the federal government unless those states passed specific subsequent laws to enable undocumented immigrants to receive such payments. The law went further and denied some benefits even to legal immigrants (except for refugees, people who had been working in the United States for more than ten years, and veterans). It said they could not be eligible for Supplemental Security Income and food stamps until they became citizens.

The Illegal Immigration Reform and Immigrant Responsibility Act focused on enforcement. It increased the number of Border Patrol agents by 1000 a year for the following 5 years, which would double the number of agents, and provided for a new corps of agents to investigate and prosecute immigrant smugglers. It authorized construction of a $12 million fence in three tiers (the first tier was already in place) along fourteen miles of the U.S.-Mexico border near San Diego and exempted that fence from endangered species and environmental protection laws. It provided for a national immigrant identification card with a fingerprint on it. It allowed the Immigration and Naturalization Service (INS) to "enter into agreements with state and local governments for help in investigating, arresting, detaining and transporting illegal immigrants"—in effect, trying to make the local police an arm of *la migra*. It made it a felony carrying hard jail time to smuggle illegal immigrants into the United States, granted broad authority for the INS to do undercover investigations, and hired federal lawyers to prosecute the offenders. It attempted to strengthen the sanctions on employers of immigrants without documents. It denied legal status to anyone who was in the United States without papers and barred people who had been deported from re-entering for up to ten years. And it streamlined procedures by which people could be deported, including denying people the right to a hearing or access to the court system, and limited judicial review of administrative deportation orders. It even set up a pilot program for using closed military bases as INS detention camps.[5]

These laws—in particular the Personal Responsibility and Work Opportunity Act—seemed to be in violation of the Fourteenth Amendment, as was Proposition 187. The detention and deportation features of the Illegal Immigration Reform and Immigrant Responsibility Act seemed clear violations of the due process clause of the Fifth Amendment. But these laws did express a clearly developing opinion among some segments of the American electorate that, Constitution or no, immigrants without papers must be kept out of the country, and that those who were already here must be punished, together with anyone who helped them.

The Clinton administration tried in its last years in office to dial back from this extreme phase of immigrant bashing. According to a *New York Times* summary:

> Reflecting the shift away from the anti-immigrant sentiments of the early 1990s and responding to intense criticisms that budget reforms in 1996 had been made at the expense of immigrants, Congress and the president modified some of the drastic welfare cuts enacted in 1996, which had been targeted at the foreign born. The Balanced Budget Act of 1997 restarted the Supplemental Security Income for the disabled as well as Medicaid benefits for 420,000 legal immigrants who were present in the country on August 22, 1996. The Agricultural Research Act of 1998 once again provided food stamps for 225,000 legal immigrant children, senior citizens, and persons with disabilities.[6]

Some of the cuts were later restored by Congress or the President, although never to the levels at which they had existed prior to the anti-immigrant 1990s. The 1965 national consensus in favor of immigrants had turned decisively against them, and seemed destined not to turn back. Several of these issues would rear their heads again in the new century.

Panethnic Power

In the early chapters of this book we traced the formation of two panethnic groups or races over the first couple of centuries of American history. In the crucible of slavery, Mandingo and Wolof and Bambara and Fon became Africans and then Negroes.

They were, in part, forced together and treated as if they were one undifferentiated Black mass by Whites, and they also developed a common interest to treat each other as comrades and even kin in order to survive their enslavement. Language, culture, religion, tribe, and social class all tended to merge in slavery.[7]

Reflexively, European-derived Americans banded together, too. English and Scots, Irish and Germans, and a dozen other peoples became, in America, simply White people. The dimensions and place of the White race in the United States were clear, at the very latest, by the time that Congress in 1790 limited naturalization to "free, white persons"—a standard from which it did not budge for many decades, and which then included all the peoples we today think of as White Americans.[8] Native Americans, by contrast, did not fully form a single panethnic group in those centuries, for all that Whites racialized them together and killed them interchangeably. Well into the twentieth century, Native peoples continued to hold to tribal identities, even as they also knew that they were treated by outsiders as if they were one.

All this began to change after the middle of the twentieth century. In Chapter 7 we saw the rise of the Civil Rights and Black Power movements in the 1950s to 1970s, expressing racial pride and solidarity and trying to improve the lot of African Americans and bring them the full rights of American citizenship. Those movements were echoed in the 1970s and after by several other movements of racial and ethnic mobilization. Among them were the Chicano movement, the Asian American movement, the Native American movement, and the White pride movement.

The Chicano Movement[9]

In March 1968, 10,000 students walked out of their classrooms in East Los Angeles. They stayed out for a week, protesting crumbling buildings, inadequate labs and textbooks, irrelevant curriculum, indifferent teachers, a 50 percent dropout rate, and a central district administration that seemed to take no interest in improving their situation. They proclaimed "Chicano Power" and demanded "Education for All."

This was a new step for Americans of Mexican descent. Since the 1930s, middle-class reformers had led the community and pursued a self-help strategy of asserting that Mexican Americans were White people and on that basis were entitled to full undifferentiated status as citizens. Now, these working-class youngsters were saying they were Brown, proud of it, and united in their determination to overturn the racial system that plagued them. And they were using a new word, "Chicano," to mark their identity.

The inspiration for their activism, says Ian Haney López, was "the civil rights movement's indirect influence on racial common sense. Since the mid-1950s, the spectacle of black protesters encountering violent repression had transfixed the nation. This imagery linking together protest, legal violence, and race became embedded in common sense."[10] Together with the antiwar movement of the Vietnam era, the Civil Rights and Black Power movements energized young Mexican Americans. The antiwar connection was crucial. As Lea Ybarra and Nina Genera wrote in 1972:

> We know something about what the war cost us—55,000 American dead, over 300,000 wounded—many of them disabled for life. And the war cost us two hundred billion dollars. Nixon will spend seven billion dollars more on this war

this year alone. That is money we needed here, for new schools and hospitals, better medical aid for our people, better education for our children. ... While our bombers tear apart Vietnam, this war also tears apart our own nation. ... It has meant, up to the present, death for more than 11,000 Chicanos. In other words, Chicanos have accounted for more than 20% or this country's casualties while they make up only 10% of the country's population.

In fact, at that time the Mexican American percentage of the population was considerably smaller than 10 percent, but the point is well taken that Mexican Americans were drafted at a higher rate, assigned to combat duty more often, and suffered substantially higher casualty rates than other Americans.[11]

In the last years of the 1960s, groups of young Mexican Americans who were angry about the abuse that their people had received in the United States for a century and a quarter formed activist groups in every urban *barrio* and farm town across the Southwest. They heard about each other and took encouragement from each other's example and ideas, but they had little formal connection with one another. Their sense of themselves as community leaders was different from their parents' and grandparents' generations. They were not the League of United Latin American Citizens, which had blandly stressed anonymity and citizenship, framed in the English language. Rather, they took names that spoke of Brown nationalism, the Spanish language, and Indian and working-class origins: the Brown Berets, the Young Lords, the Movimiento Estudiantil Chicano de Aztlán (MECHA), the Alianza de los Pueblos, and La Raza Unida.

Each had a specific location and constituency—poor Mexican Americans in a particular part of California, Colorado, Texas, Arizona, or New Mexico—and a specific program for changing conditions for the betterment of poor Brown people in their locale. They spoke of uniting the people of Aztlán, a legendary homeland of the Mexican people that some said lay in what had become the American Southwest.[12] Many of the groups' ideas were radical and utopian. White people found all this unnerving, for they feared that the radicalism meant violence would be directed against them (as if violence against Mexicans had not been the order of the day for more than a century).

These activists from poor Mexican American towns and *barrios* were joining a movement that had been building in the fields of California, in the mines of Arizona, and elsewhere across the Southwest since the 1950s. Working-class Mexican Americans had been organizing in unions to press for better wages, sanitary conditions, housing, regulated hours, and safety conditions—all the things that other workers had won since the New Deal but that had been denied to workers in industries dominated by Mexicans and Blacks.[13] The archetype of Mexican American union activity was the United Farm Workers. Cesar Chavez, Dolores Huerta, and other Mexican American farm workers formed the National Farm Workers Association in California's San Joaquin Valley in 1962. Four years later they merged with a Filipino union, the Agricultural Workers Organizing Committee, led by Philip Vera Cruz, to form the United Farm Workers Organizing Committee, which in turn became the United Farm Workers of America (UFW) in 1973. The UFW led organizing drives in California fields throughout the 1960s and 1970s. The most famous nationally was their strike against grape growers, which began in 1965 and escalated into a national boycott of table grapes. In 1970 the UFW achieved recognition and negotiated a contract that concluded the strike, with substantially better pay and working conditions for field workers. Later the UFW organized strikes and boycotts in the lettuce industry and other crops. Chavez and the UFW adhered to a strict ethic of nonviolence, and by the latter stages of his life in the 1980s, Chavez had come to be seen as a saintly figure by millions of Americans, with streets and schools named after him.[14]

This was all very political, but everyday Mexican Americans began to think of themselves differently, too. Carol Jacquez knew she was not White as she grew up in Chávez Ravine, a Chicano barrio near central Los Angeles, in the 1940s. But she knew she was not exactly Mexican either. When young activists began to articulate a new identity, she took to it, although not with the sort of political interpretation they may have envisioned.

> My dad … remembered going to the movies when Thursday night was Mexican night and that was the only time they could go. This was in the 1930s near Downey, here in California. … When we Latinos were categorized as "white" by the federal government, it became a problem. Because that threw us in with the big population that does relatively well. So to differentiate ourselves we became *Chicanos*. Mexicans in Mexico feel that they have the true culture. They call us transplants and *Pochos*. The *gringos* viewed us not really as equals. And we really didn't want to call ourselves "white." To call ourselves Mexicans wasn't right either. So we became Chicanos, and created this mythical land of Aztlán."[15]

Latino Panethnicity[16]

One result of the Chicano movement was a vast increase in the participation of Mexican Americans in politics, beginning on a small scale in the 1970s and then taking off in the 1980s and 1990s. Members of the American-born generations ran for city council and sheriff, for state legislatures in places like California and Texas, and a few ran for Congress. They became political strategists and campaign workers, usually in the Democratic Party. Meanwhile, other groups who hailed from other parts of Latin America also were entering the political scene. In South Florida they were mainly Cubans, they were mainly Republicans, and they developed tremendous political influence there. In New York, New Jersey, and Chicago they were more likely to be Puerto Rican or Dominican, and they had less opportunity to dominate local politics. In the 1970s there were some quite radical Puerto Rican nationalist organizations, although they never made as powerful an impact on the political scene as did Chicano activists in the West. In the western states quite a number of people came into the United States from other parts of Central America as well, but they tended not to become so involved in the American political scene as were Mexicans, Puerto Ricans, or Cubans.

These peoples were all different from one another, they formed utterly distinct communities, they had very different histories, immigration patterns, class structures, relationships to the Catholic Church, they even spoke different versions of Spanish, yet non-Latinos tended to lump them together. The census called them all "Hispanics," although that is not a label that most of them accepted for themselves. "Latinos" was a more widely accepted term, although it was "Latins" in South Florida. Increasingly, especially after the 1990s, Latinos in Congress and other parts of public life began to work together, or at least to talk with one another. One could see the bare beginnings of a new panethnic identity forming. It was premature to talk about a "Latino community," for there was no single community yet. But the outlines of common identity were beginning to take shape. College boys began to join pan-Latino fraternities. Commentators—including Mexican, Cuban, and Puerto Rican American commentators—began to speak and write about Latinos, if not as a single entity, than as a bunch of groups who had a lot of issues and interests in common.

The Asian American Panethnic Movement

"How many Asian Americans were there in 1950?" goes an old joke. The answer: "Zero. The idea hadn't been invented yet."[17] In 1950 there were several groups of people who would later come to be regarded, and most of whom would come to think of themselves, as Asian Americans. There were several hundred thousand Chinese Americans, Japanese Americans, and Filipino Americans, and smaller numbers of other peoples such as Indians and Koreans whose ancestry led back to Asian countries. But they were not anything like a single social group. During World War II, most Filipino and Chinese Americans very much disliked Japanese Americans for reasons having to do with the actions of their ancestral homelands' governments and armies during that war. When Japanese Americans were hauled off to prison camps, Chinese shopkeepers put signs in their windows saying "We Are Chinese American." It is true that White people saw Chinese, Japanese, and Filipinos all as "Orientals" and tended to treat them as an undifferentiated mass, but that was a failure of White people's perception, not evidence of a meaningful social grouping as understood from the side of Chinese, Filipinos, or Japanese.

In the two decades that followed the war, however, those three peoples did in fact begin to have common experiences that led them to form another panethnicity: Asian Americans. In the 1950s and 1960s, a generation grew up in American streets and schools, and they were very often the same streets and schools.[18] In Seattle, it was the Central Area, from Chinatown to Rainier Valley to Beacon Hill, where working-class Filipino, Chinese, and Japanese American families lived nearby one another. In San Francisco, it was Chinatown, Russian Hill, and the Western Addition. In Los Angeles it was the span from Chinatown through Little Tokyo and on to Boyle Heights. In Honolulu the district ran from Makiki to Kalihi. Youth of the American-born generation went to school together, played ball together, ran the streets together, and were treated by their teachers and other Whites as if they were all one set of people. The other racial group with whom they interacted in those same schools and neighborhoods were African Americans; although there were friendships between Blacks and Asians, they remained distinct peoples.

It was in the 1960s that Asian Americans first went to college in large numbers. There—at UCLA, Berkeley, San Francisco State, the University of Washington, and other urban, public West Coast colleges—in the second half of the 1960s, they became politicized by the Civil Rights movement and the Vietnam War. They saw that the Civil Rights and Black Power movements had resulted in some of the problems of Black communities beginning to be addressed. And the student activists who were forming Black student unions and agitating for Black studies courses were very often people they had known in high school. It was a short step for those Asians from witnessing such activism on the part of Black friends to becoming activists themselves.

As with Chicanos, the Vietnam War was crucial. Asians were not overrepresented among those drafted and killed, as was the case for Blacks and Chicanos. But the rhetoric of the war was racialized, and the racism was directed against Asians. Americans heard endlessly of "gooks" and "slopes" (derogatory terms for Asians), and that "life is cheap in the Orient." Asian GIs came home to tell of being the targets of suspicion and racist slurs from their comrades in arms. A sheltered Chinese American girl of nineteen joined an antiwar group in 1970 and passed out leaflets in a West Coast suburb. She was told repeatedly by White people she encountered, "But how can you be against the war? We're doing this for *you people*." Until that moment, she had never thought of herself as being part of the same people as the Vietnamese. Her antiwar work was political work, not ethnic work. But this experience made her rethink her identity. She remained Chinese in her own mind, but she began to see herself as Asian American, too.

A Third World Student Strike at San Francisco State in 1968 and 1969, demanding specific programs of study oriented to Blacks, Asians, American Indians, and Chicanos, was quickly copied by students at Berkeley, the University of Washington, and other schools. Out of that flurry of organizing came ethnic studies programs and the first concerted attempt by the academy to address the experiences of people of color in the United States. Those programs gave theoretical coherence and institutional support to the Asian American panethnicity that had been emerging. At the same time, young Asians began to turn their attention back to the communities from which they had come. Some of that attention was directed along ethnic-specific lines, as when Chinese Americans went into Oakland's Chinatown to run youth athletic programs and medical clinics for the elderly. But some crossed ethnic lines, as when Chinese, Japanese, and Filipinos demonstrated together throughout the 1970s and even fought against police to keep developers from razing the International Hotel, a residence for old, poor, single Filipino men in San Francisco. Increasingly, social service and political efforts took on a pan-Asian caste: the Asian American Mental Health Training Center, the Asian American Law Caucus, and the Asian American Political Alliance. Partly it was a matter of numbers: perhaps Filipinos alone could not garner much attention, but Asians *together* had about three times as many constituents. Increasingly it became a matter of a self-consciously chosen additional identity as Asian Americans. Other, less overtly political entities began to make the change: the National Asian American Telecommunications Association, the Asian American Women's Business Roundtable, the Westminster Asian American Church, and so on.

Sometimes common racialized experiences led Asian Americans to react together as one. A marker for Asian American panethnic community formation was the murder of Vincent Chin. On the night of June 19, 1982, Chin met some friends in a Detroit bar to celebrate his upcoming wedding. The American car industry was then in desperate straits; Americans were buying Japanese cars on the grounds that they were cheaper and better made than the American variety. Thousands were out of work, and they blamed the Japanese—not the Japanese government or the Japanese auto industry, but anyone they saw as a Japanese person. Chin was a Chinese American. Two White autoworkers, Ronald Ebens and Michael Nitz, accosted Chin and called him a "Jap." They chased him out of the bar, caught him, and beat him to death with a baseball bat. None of the facts are in dispute, and Ebens and Nitz were convicted of relatively minor offenses, yet neither of them served time in jail. The murder of Vincent Chin galvanized Asian Americans across the country. It became clear to them that they were at risk as Asians in American society. The fact that Chin was Chinese, not Japanese, did not keep him from being killed. The fact that he was a native-born American, not a foreigner, did not keep him from being killed. And the thought that a judge found it understandable, perhaps even reasonable, that Nitz and Ebens would kill him, cast a chill through the hearts of Asian Americans everywhere.

By the 1980s, the idea that Asian Americans were a single panethnic group that had a lot in common across lines of ancestral ethnic nationality had become a fairly unremarkable feature of life, not only on the West Coast but in communities all across the nation.

Righting Old Wrongs: The Fruits of Panethnicity

One of the things that Asian Americans did as they came together into a panethnic group was to try to right some wrongs that had plagued the various Asian American peoples. Perhaps Chinese exclusion, the Rock Springs massacre, and the Alien Land Law were too far in the past to be addressed at this late date. But some grievances from recent generations were certainly available for redress. The most obvious target—the most egregious abuse—was the World War II imprisonment of substantially all the continental Japanese American population. Advocates—many of them Japanese Americans but other Asians and some sympathetic Whites as well—took two tacks: judicial and legislative.

The judicial approach was initiated by a law professor who found some documents that suggested government lawyers had lied to the courts and suppressed evidence that would have kept Gordon Hirabayashi, Minoru Yasui, and Fred Korematsu—three Nisei who protested their incarceration—out of jail in the 1940s. A group of Asian American lawyers reopened the cases and won reversals in two of the three (Yasui died while his was still in process). Korematsu said to the court: "Your Honor, I still remember forty years ago when I was handcuffed and arrested as a criminal here in San Francisco. ... As long as my record stands in federal court, any American citizen can be held in prison or concentration camps without a trial or a hearing. ... I would like to see the government admit that they were wrong and do something about it so this will never happen again to any American citizen of any race, creed or color." Seattle Judge Donald Voorhees, in ruling for Hirabayashi, wrote: "It is now conceded by almost everyone that the internment of Japanese Americans during World War II was simply a tragic mistake for which American society as a whole must accept responsibility. If, in the future, this country should find itself in a comparable national emergency, the sacrifices made by Gordon Hirabayashi, Fred Korematsu, and Minoru Yasui may, it is hoped, stay the hand of a government again tempted to imprison a defenseless minority without trial and for no offense."[19]

The other prong of the attack was to try to get the government, through Congress and the president, to apologize and make some form of restitution. In 1976, President Gerald Ford made the apology: "An honest reckoning ... must include a recognition of our national mistakes as well as our national achievements. ... We now know what we should have known then—not only was the evacuation wrong, but Japanese Americans were and are loyal Americans." Five years later Japanese and other Asian American community leaders convinced Congress to appoint a commission to study the internment. More than 750 people testified at those hearings, including government officials, scholars, and most importantly, former inmates.

In the end, the commission recommended several steps, including a payment of $20,000 to each surviving former internee. Skillful pressure by a number of community organizations and Democratic politicians finally convinced Congress, and in 1988 President Ronald Reagan signed the redress legislation, including the $20,000 token payment.[20] The money wasn't the issue—it represented only a tiny fraction of actual Japanese American financial losses. For most Japanese Americans and for many other Asians, the issues were remembrance and accountability. Poet Nikki Nojima Louis wrote:

Breaking the Silence
honored by our ancestors
is a lamentation;
not of battles lost or won,
but a remembrance of the lives of those
    who have passed before us. ...
Breaking the silence
is also a tribute to their perseverance. ...
We do this, not to rake up old coals,
but to see with new eyes:
the past
can no more be denied.[21]

Symbolic though the payments were, carefully limited though they were to those prison camp survivors who were still alive when the redress law passed, this small measure of blame-taking on the part of the U.S. government raised the fear in some quarters that the government would soon be called on to pay reparations for African American slavery and Native American genocide. Among African Americans, some people who had been calling for slavery reparations began to gain some traction. In an April 2000 episode of *The West Wing*, Jeff Breckinridge (played by Carl Lumbly) was being interviewed for a Justice Department job. He had written a jacket blurb for a book that advocated slavery reparations. He said in his defense: "My father's fathers were kidnapped outside a village called Wimbabwa, brought to Guinea, sold to a slave trader from Boston, and bought by a plantation owner in Wadsworth, South Carolina, where they worked for no wages." After calculating the number of slaves held times the number of hours worked and the market value of manual labor, he figured, "Someone owes me and my friends 1.7 trillion dollars." Slavery reparations did not, however, actually hit the political stage in a serious way. Like Chinese exclusion, it lay too far in the past, and perhaps like the slaughter and dispossession of American Indians, the price of redress for so vast a wrong was higher than America could imagine paying. The modest reparations paid to Japanese Americans did not set a precedent.[22]

Native American Political and Cultural Resurgence

Just as the Mexican American population was inspired to create a more activist Chicano identity and Asian Americans were inspired to a panethnic movement of their own—so, too, Native Americans experienced a resurgence that derived in part from the example of the civil rights movement.[23] In each decade after the 1960s, the number of people who called themselves Indians on the U.S. census went up: from 523,591 in 1960; to 792,730 in 1970; 1,364,033 in 1980; 1,878,285 in 1990; and 2,447,989 in 2000.[24] Not only was there a resurgence in the number of Native Americans, but these decades also saw an increase in the strength of Indian identity and in people's involvement with their tribes and with new pan-Indian communities.

The 1960s and 1970s saw a sharp rise and a new aggressiveness take hold of Native American political activism. Some of the action was on behalf of specific tribes, but much of it was the work of coalitions of people from several tribes, and many of the activists were urban dwellers. One example was the occupation of Alcatraz, a decommissioned federal penitentiary on a rock in San Francisco Bay. According to the 1868 Fort Laramie Treaty between the United States and the Sioux, any abandoned federal facility was supposed to revert to Indian ownership. With that broken promise in mind, on the morning of November 20, 1969, Adam Fortunate Eagle, Richard Oakes, and seventy-six other Indians landed on Alcatraz and proclaimed it Indian land. Recalling the price that the Dutch had paid for Manhattan, they had in hand a "Proclamation from the Indians of All Tribes" that said they would pay "twenty four dollars in glass beads and red cloth" for the island. The proclamation pointed out that Alcatraz resembled most reservations—it was barren, waterless, and without health care facilities or schools. "Further, it would be fitting and symbolic that ships from all over the world, entering the Golden Gate, would first see Indian land, and thus be reminded of the true history of this nation. This tiny island would be a symbol of the great lands once ruled by free and noble Indians."[25] For the next year and a half, Alcatraz indeed became a symbol of Indian activism and a gathering place where both urban and reservation Indians came to dance, teach Native ways to their children, and exchange ideas about culture and politics. Their numbers dwindled as the novelty wore off and dissension mounted among the occupiers of this cold, joyless, waterless rock. On June 11, 1971, twenty federal marshals stormed the island and forcibly removed the last fifteen holdouts.

A second case of Native American activism was the standoff between members of the American Indian Movement (AIM) and the FBI on the Pine Ridge Sioux Reservation in South Dakota. AIM was founded in Minneapolis in 1968 by a group of urban Indians from several tribal backgrounds, including Dennis Banks, Clyde Bellecourt, Eddie Benton-Banai, and George Mitchell. Bellecourt's brother Vernon remembered:

> [I]n Minneapolis, in the Indian ghetto community [e]verything was deteriorating rather than getting better. There were police harassment and brutality. ...
>
> I watched what [AIM was] doing, and I could see the pride in these young men and women. Then I looked at myself, I was making money and living in White suburbia. ... So I went up to Minnesota. ... I got so involved I started letting my hair grow long, and I stopped wearing a tie and started to sort of deprogram myself, to become just a simple person. ... more humble.
>
> When AIM was forming, one of the first things they zeroed in on was police-community relations. Young men and women in the community formed the AIM patrol. ... They would listen to the police calls, and when they heard there was going to be an arrest ... they'd show up with cameras and take pictures of the police using more than normal restraint on the people. They got evidence of beatings and of ripping people around with handcuffs too tight, ripping their wrists. It was very vicious. This sometimes becomes a way of life for the police.

They just fall into it. They think that's the way Indians have to be treated. So AIM would show up and have attorneys ready. ... They would have a bondsman there, and they'd start filing law suits against the police department.[26]

AIM was involved with the Alcatraz takeover; a 1972 march on Washington to protest broken treaties that ended in AIM members occupying Bureau of Indian Affairs (BIA) headquarters; the "Longest Walk" in 1978 from San Francisco to Washington to raise national awareness of Native people's problems; and late-century attempts to get sports teams to stop using Indian mascots and names. But the most famous moment in AIM history was the fight with the FBI at Pine Ridge. On February 27, 1973, 250 Indians led by AIM occupied the reservation town of Wounded Knee, near the site where U.S. troops massacred three hundred Lakota (i.e., Sioux) men, women, and children in 1890. There was a long history of violence against Lakota people in the area by police and surrounding Whites. For example, in January that year, Wesley Bad Heart Bull was fatally stabbed in nearby Buffalo Gap and a White man arrested, but the police refused to take testimony from an Indian who had witnessed the crime, and they charged the White man only with second-degree manslaughter. When AIM members and other Indians protested, a fight broke out and forty Indians were charged with rioting—including Bad Heart Bull's mother. She faced forty years in prison, while the man accused of killing her son was only looking at ten.

Meanwhile, back on the reservation, tribal chairman Richard Wilson was charged with corruption by a faction characterizing themselves as traditionalists. When the traditionalists asked AIM to come into the reservation, Wilson turned to the federal government to oust them. The FBI, U.S. Marshals, and BIA dispatched 200 officers, whose armaments included machine guns, helicopters, and armored personnel carriers. They surrounded the insurgents, and finally removed them after a series of gun battles that left two Indians dead and a standoff that had lasted two and a half months. Conflict continued at Pine Ridge between AIM and some tribal members on one side and Wilson's administration and the FBI on the other. Several dozen local Indians died by violence and hundreds were beaten. Two AIM leaders, Dennis Banks and Russell Means, were arrested on dubious charges that were promptly dismissed. Two years later, in June 1975, two FBI agents drove into an AIM encampment, guns blazed, and the agents and one Indian were dead. AIM leader Leonard Peltier was ultimately incarcerated for the officers' deaths. Although evidence was spotty and probably fabricated, and few observers thought he had actually caused the deaths, Peltier was still in jail thirty years later. International human rights organizations listed him as a political prisoner.[27]

Along with the political activity came cultural renewal. City Indians went back to reservations, learned some of the old ways, and began to rebuild pride in their Indianness. One Indian told Robert White:

There was a time when I just didn't want to be an Indian. ... The forces out there were much greater than I; the movies portraying us as savages. When you are laughed at you become inferior. But ... in the summer of 1965, Cozy revived some tribal habits that hadn't been practiced for thirty-five years. He was inspired by a tribal elder named Mary Moore, who had been taught the old dances by her grandmother. ... We got her to teach us some dances. ... Our kids didn't want to do them because as soon as they got into their costumes, the neighbors would come by going, "woo-woo-woo" at them. We've held Indian ceremonial days here every August since, and you don't hear any "woo-wooing" now. We are contributors. We have something to be proud of. People come from all over the place to see us, and they applaud.[28]

Leonard Peltier spoke of the importance of culture: "With me spiritualism was always there, but with everyone it was underground. But I still went to ceremonies, we would hold them at night with guards. My grandmother was a strong traditionalist. But then, spiritualism exploded and became much more popular in the 1960s. It was always there to some extent. What we learned was that for our whole Indian movement, survival was to have a spiritual movement." One Indian returned to the reservation after living in the Bay Area:

> I became a Sun Dancer, a museum curator. My boys are Sun Dancers. One is a keeper of our sacred tribal pipe. ... I brought them back to live on the reservation so they will know racism, pain, the hardcore stuff of life around here. ... A real Indian lives in an Indian environment, learns spiritual ways, is discriminated against because of his looks, is shaped when he's young to be quiet because of racism. We pay a penalty. There's a positive aspect—the spiritual side. ... That's what I came back for.

Frances Wise linked cultural revival with the Red power movement: "They killed a lot of the traditional Indian ways here in Oklahoma. When I was growing up, there was the Native American Church, but it was so interlaced with Christianity. I wanted to connect with Indian spiritual ways. That's what Alcatraz, Native American Rights Movement, and AIM led us to—a spiritual renewal. The renewal of Indian spirituality is the legacy of that time." Tribes taught both children and adults old dances, chants, stories, medical practices, tribal histories, and the languages that had been suppressed. They reclaimed the bones of their ancestors from anthropological museums. Twenty-first century Chumash built canoes on old models and paddled among the Channel Islands to places where their ancestors once lived. Makahs taught boys to be men by hunting one whale a year off Cape Flattery, in defiance of circling boats full of White environmentalists.[29]

In addition to cultural revivals on many reservations, powwows proliferated into a regular circuit of events near cities from Boston to Honolulu. These were intertribal affairs, performed by and for local urban Indians, but also with non-Indians in attendance. At such events, practitioners of traditional tribal music, costumes, and dances exchanged skills and designs, so that considerable intertribal culture began to develop.

The Native American renewal movement also brought changes in the material circumstances of some tribes.[30] Whereas political activism and cultural renewal occurred both within specific tribal populations and on a pan-Indian basis, economic development was mainly a tribal affair. Some of the economic change surrounded reassertion of old rights that had been granted Indian tribes in the nineteenth century. For instance, in 1854 and 1855, the U.S. government induced the Puyallup, Nisqually, and other Northwest Indians to accept reservations, in return for which they were to receive perpetual rights to fish in their "usual and accustomed places." Two decades later the salmon canning industry became mechanized, and both commercial practice and state laws encouraged commercial and sport fishery on the ocean at the expense of Indian fishing on rivers. As more salmon were caught before they reached rivers on their way to spawn, Indians caught fewer and fewer, and they were punished by state game officials when they did. This went on for nearly a century. Finally, in 1974, after two decades of court battles and a decade of "fish-ins," federal courts determined that the treaties must be obeyed, and that commercial and sport fishers must be limited so that 50 percent of the designated total annual catch could get through to Indian fishers upstream.[31]

In similar proceedings throughout the 1970s especially, Native groups reasserted rights to land, water, timber, grazing rights, hunting rights, and minerals under the earth. Thirty-four so-called "energy tribes" lived on reservations where one could find 50 percent of the potential uranium reserves, 30 percent of the coal west of the Mississippi, and 20 percent of the natural gas and oil. Coal, gas, and oil were exploited by outside companies throughout most of the twentieth century, and uranium from the dawn of the atomic age. For most of that time, the tribes in question received far less than market value for the minerals that were stripped from their lands, and they were left with scarred, radioactive, and polluted landscapes. Beginning in the 1970s, by a combination of tribal activism and the conscientious efforts of some officials of the federal government, some of the inequities in mining contracts began to be renegotiated. The Environmental Protection Agency (EPA) and tribes working together began, very belatedly, to address environmental destruction. Some tribes made the painful decision to halt or curb mineral development in the interest of preserving the land and the health of the people. Others went on in the boom-and-bust cycles of energy minerals.[32]

Meanwhile, activists like Blackfoot Elouise Cobell agitated to get the U.S. government to live up to its trust responsibilities. The BIA had for more than a hundred years taken Indian lands and leased them to Whites. The payments were supposed to be made at market value, and they were supposed to go to Native tribes and individuals. In fact, the government failed to collect the payments, failed to collect them at the proper rates, failed to keep records, and failed to make the payments to the Indian owners. Finally, at the dawn of the twenty-first century, a class action lawsuit brought by Cobell and others drew federal attention. Judges chastised the Department of Interior and BIA, and the Indians seemed likely to receive several billion dollars in back payments one day, although the government resisted its responsibilities to the last.[33]

Perhaps the most lucrative engine of tribal economic development proved to be gambling. Outlawed in most parts of most states, gambling was nonetheless an attractive pastime for millions of Americans. Many Indian tribes had long sold gasoline and cigarettes on their reservations to passing motorists at below the prices charged in most states, because they were not required to collect state taxes on such sales. In the 1990s, many tribes seized on their right as quasisovereign entities to build casinos as tourist destinations. The politics of each tribe and casino differed, but in the end Indian gambling became a multibillion dollar industry with outposts all over the country.[34]

Tribal economic development projects—whether they were paid for by gambling revenues, mining contracts, grazing and timber leases, or government support—brought a host of tribal benefits: museums, schools, irrigation, public health projects, medical clinics, college scholarships, and many others. In 2003 the 157-member Santa Ynez Band of Chumash used revenues from its Santa Barbara wine country casino to hire a linguist to teach children the Chumash language that had all but died out.[35] Despite all the change and renewal, problems remained for Native

Americans. Among the five major American racial groups, Native people suffered the highest rate of infant mortality, alcoholism, and illiteracy. Despite all the progress and a growing number of rich Indians with political influence, Indians as a whole were still last in average income, education, and life expectancy.

For some, tribal membership had become more appealing, because some tribes now had resources that they had long lacked. For others, it was a sense of political engagement or spiritual renewal. So culture, politics, and economics all drew people back to Indianness in the last third of the twentieth century, some to the reservation and others to urban, pantribal assertions of identity. This raised the question of "Who is an Indian?" and that sometimes resulted in controversy. The most prominent feature of late twentieth-century Indian identity change was the formation of a lasting Indian panethnicity, with pantribal institutions—AIM is one example, but others proliferated, including Native American or American Indian studies programs at many universities, the National Indian Education Association, the Native American Rights Fund, the American Indian Science and Engineering Society, the Association of American Indian Physicians, and many others. Native peoples in these decades achieved a degree of connectedness and common identity that was not possible when Tecumseh tried to unite Indians against European Americans early in the nineteenth century. They were even able to mount a campaign for, and then to build the National Museum of the American Indian, which opened on the Mall in Washington, D.C., in 2004 and was a monument to pan-Indian cooperation and mutual identity support.

At the same time a lot of people came to see themselves as part of an Indian panethnicity, most also maintained one (or sometimes more) tribal affiliations, so like most Asian Americans they had two levels of ethnic identity. Their tribal affiliation might or might not include formal enrollment. Each tribe had its own rules for who could be an enrolled member, based more or less on degree of tribal ancestry. But old documentation was sometimes sketchy, and practically speaking, one's social membership was based more on kinship than on blood quantum. A man might not be entitled to tribal benefits, but if he lived with his grandmother on the reservation, he had a place of belonging there. Similarly, a woman might be nearly full-blood by ancestry, but if her people had been off the reservation for two or three generations, her authenticity was in question.

It was pretty easy to spot and deal with White tribal wannabes, New Age religionists, and other bogus pretenders. But what about Seth Prince, whose grandfather left Choctaw country in eastern Oklahoma in the 1940s, whose grandfather and father both married White women, who grew up in a White suburb, attended college, and worked as a journalist on the West Coast? He was pretty thoroughly deracinated, yet he could write, "I was born an Indian, and I will die one. But in between, I need to figure out what that means to me." By his own testimony, Indianness amounted to family stories, some memories of relatives, and photographs, but not to any personal knowledge of Indian people, places, or ways. His cousin Elizabeth Prince was even more articulate on this issue: "From the earliest moments of my single digit years there were certain things I knew. I knew my name. I knew who my parents were. I knew I was a girl. I knew I was an Indian. If someone had asked me to define 'Indian,' I most likely would have said, 'I am an Indian. My father is an Indian.' Indian was just one of the things I knew that I was. To me, it was a good thing to be."[36]

Sometimes identity for mixed people was more fraught still. A controversy roiled through the 1990s and 2000s over the place of the so-called "Cherokee

Freedmen." When the Cherokee were banished on the Trail of Tears, they were a racially mixed multitude (see Chapter 4). Many of the walkers were African-descended slaves. But many of the free Cherokees were partly African descended, too, and the mixing continued, to the point where by the twentieth century almost all Cherokees living in Oklahoma probably had quite a bit of Indian ancestry and some African too. Late in the twentieth century, some Cherokees who regarded themselves as racially pure or mixed only with White tried to deny tribal membership to other Cherokees whom they regarded as partly Black, in a fairly blatant adoption of White racial prejudices against African Americans. The fight by Cherokees whose features spoke of Africa to regain recognition from their tribe carried into the new century.[37]

Another fight for recognition was waged by Indians whose tribes had fallen out of bureaucratic history. Many tribes lost federal and state recognition, either because they never signed treaties or because eugenics-inspired administrators tried to erase their identities in the first half of the twentieth century. Some, like the Lumbee in North Carolina, did manage to gain federal recognition after long legal battles. Others, like the Juaneño in California, the Duwamish, Snohomish, and Chinook around Puget Sound, and the Chickahominy and Rappahannock in Virginia, still seek tribal status.[38]

African Americans after Civil Rights

Beginning in the 1970s, the impulse toward equality that had been intellectual, spiritual, moral, and political during the Civil Rights Movement became glorylessly bureaucratic. The age of organizing and boycotts and marches—of civil rights as movement and public persuasion—was largely over. In its place, there grew a host of humdrum social and political structures, which operated in a national political climate that turned ever more conservative and uninterested in racial equity. But that did not mean that the substance of the leveling impulse was entirely lost. Some might even say the opposite was true. The gains made by African Americans in the period 1950 to 1975, important as they were, were in some ways symbolic. African Americans desegregated a host of institutions, from schools to sports leagues, and so they gained access to the company and attention of White people in ways they had not known previously. They gained the legal right to vote and, increasingly, the ability to challenge discrimination in court. But they did not cure Black poverty, the income gap, abuse from police and the prison system, or most of the other substantial disabilities they faced. Between 1975 and the end of the century, although much of the public clamor had died down, African Americans continued to make some substantial gains.

To be sure, some elements of symbolism remained (and symbols are not insignificant). The 1980s were marked by the regular appearance of Black (and Asian and Latino) models in mainstream newspaper and magazine ads for the first time. Bill Cosby became a national middle-class father figure by virtue of a television show not very different from the very White 1950s series *Father Knows Best*. In the 1990s Michael Jordan emerged as the global face of American identity—more an icon of Americanness than Mickey Mantle or Frank Sinatra had been two generations earlier. When Bill Clinton took office, America for the first time had a President who did not look visibly uncomfortable in close proximity to Black people. In 1998, Franklin

Raines became the first Black CEO of a Fortune 500 company when he took the helm at Fannie Mae.[39] Oprah Winfrey became America's big sister and one of the world's richest women. In the new century, at long last, plans were laid for a National Museum of African American History and Culture, a symbol on the Mall of African Americans' place in the republic.

Some African American gains in this period were very solid. The long-term fruit of the Voting Rights Act was to put African Americans in sheriff's offices and city councils across the country. African Americans became regular players in the political system. By the end of the period, there were many more Black Congress members, and for a time even a Republican. There were Black cabinet members with considerable prominence and influence. And when the Voting Rights Act came up for renewal in 2006, Republicans did their very best to kill it.[40]

African Americans' income went up steadily over these decades, but they did not make much progress against the Whites' head start. In 1959, Black household income averaged 52 percent of White household income; in 1970 the figure was 64 percent; in 1982, 55 percent; in 1992, 58 percent; in 2004, 62 percent.[41]

Likewise, the educational achievement of African American students, as well as access to higher education, improved markedly over this period, although they still did not reach anything like parity with Whites. Table 9.1 shows the percentages of White, Black, and Latino Americans who earned bachelor's degrees or higher from 1980 to 2004. Over that period, Whites rose from 25.0 percent to 32.2 percent; Blacks from 11.5 percent to 18.1 percent; and Latinos from 7.7 percent to 12.3 percent. For Latinos and Blacks, that was an increase of nearly 60 percent over their 1980 figures. But at the end of the period they still lagged far behind Whites. Blacks graduated from college at only a bit more than half the rate for Whites, and Latinos barely more than one-third the rate for Whites. These figures do not include the fact that Black males took part in higher education at a dramatically lower rate than Black females. For Black men, the figures were even more dismal. This is not a simple half-empty/half-full story. African Americans and Latinos were making educational gains, but they were still very far behind Whites and Asians. So it went in other areas like housing and health care: Blacks made some progress in the last quarter of the twentieth century, but still they lagged far behind Whites by any measure of social well-being.[42]

The growth in higher education made for a larger African American middle class than had previously existed. And it was a different kind of middle class. As late

Table 9.1 Percentage Earning Bachelor's Degree or Higher, by Race, 1980–2004

Race	1980	1990	Percent Increase 1980–1990	2000	Percent Increase 1980–2000	2004	Percent Increase 1980–2004
White	25.0	26.4	5.6	34.0	36.0	32.2	28.8
Black	11.5	13.4	16.5	17.8	54.8	18.1	57.4
Latin Americans	7.7	8.2	6.5	9.7	26.0	12.3	59.7

Source: "America's Children: Key National Indicators of Well-Being, 2005: Higher Education," US Department of Education, National Center for Education Statistics, 2005.

as the 1950s, the small Black middle class was made up primarily of professionals—doctors, teachers, undertakers, pastors, and others—who lived in Black communities, served their neighbors, and constituted a leadership cohort for those communities. Integration in higher education, beginning in the 1960s, meant that people who in an earlier generation might have received their training at Howard or Fisk now were going to Northwestern, Clemson, or the University of Michigan. Members of the new, more numerous Black middle class were more likely to work as engineers at Boeing or underwriters at Prudential than they were to be dentists in Black ghettoes. And they were increasingly likely to live in mostly White suburbs. This meant that their life experiences nearly replicated those of members of the White middle class, and indeed they interacted fairly freely with such people. It also meant that the older Black communities were left without much of the leadership group that they had known in previous generations. Thus a gap opened up between an increasingly impoverished and unserved Black working class, concentrated in the lowest-paying sectors of the economy, and a Black middle class that was integrating itself into the wider society with some success.[43]

There were many areas where the promise of the civil rights movement went unfulfilled. From the 1980s on, segregation, which had been in decline, increased for the Black working class. So did the levels of crime and violence in neighborhoods where working-class African Americans had to live. As high as one in four young Black men was "in the system"—either under investigation, being tried for a crime, in jail, or on probation or parole. White people's centuries-long fears of Black men were carefully nurtured, as when the presidential campaign of George Bush the elder in 1988 ran notorious ads featuring sinister pictures of recidivist Willie Horton to scare White voters and discredit his opponent Michael Dukakis. Working-class Black people were incarcerated at stunningly high rates, as other Americans eagerly built ever more prisons, without regard to effectiveness, fairness, or expense. As if living in poverty and crime-ridden neighborhoods were not difficult enough for Black working families, they also continued to suffer violence at the hands of many city police departments. There were regular incidents like the 1992 beating of Rodney King in every part of the country. Racial profiling—singling out Blacks and Latinos for traffic stops, searches, and harassment—were standard police procedure almost everywhere. The life experiences of working-class and middle-class Blacks diverged sharply in these decades, although they did share the common experience of being harassed by the police for driving while Black.

The level of social acceptance into mainstream American society that came to middle-class African Americans after the civil rights decades made for a broadening of the range of opinion with Black America. Previously, Black conservatives were exceedingly rare. But in the 1980s and 1990s, when hard-right conservatism dominated the political scene, a new crop of Black conservatives like Ward Connerly, Clarence Thomas, Thomas Sowell, John McWhorter, and Shelby Steele found there was a very comfortable—even honored—living to be made telling White people, in essence, "It's not your fault. Black people need to clean up their own act. You have no responsibility for their situation."[44] In those decades the White majority, still dominant, turned decisively away from the leveling agenda of the Civil Rights era. White conservatives from Newt Gingrich to David Horowitz appropriated the memory of Martin Luther King Jr. and used his words, in ways he surely would have hated, to justify ignoring the manifest racial inequities that persisted. Horowitz's words were typical: "Martin Luther King, in my view, was a conservative, because

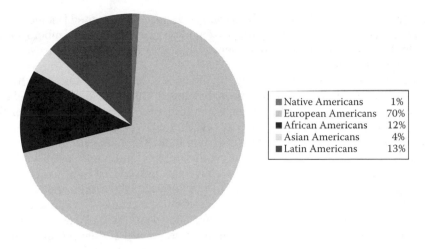

■ Native Americans	1%
■ European Americans	70%
■ African Americans	12%
■ Asian Americans	4%
■ Latin Americans	13%

Figure 9.1 Population by race in 2000, 281.6 million.

he stood for … belief in the content of your character—the value that conservatives defend today."[45]

Figure 9.1 gives the racial composition of the U.S. population in the 2000 census, after three-plus decades of a less racially restricted immigration policy and some elements of domestic racial reform.

Disgruntled White People

David Horowitz's comments above reflected the fact that, alongside all the racial egalitarianism and panethnicity building, some White Americans were becoming ever more disgruntled. First, there were the White ethnic movements as counterpoints to race-making by peoples of color, then there was immigrant bashing and a fight against affirmative action.

Not the KKK: White Ethnic Movements

White Americans did not fail to notice the labors of Black racial activists in the 1960s (they were less aware of the work of Asian, Latino, or Native American racial activists). Some noted the gains made by assertive Blacks with approbation, some with alarm. In the 1970s, a particular subset of White people came to the political fore in response to racial activism by peoples of color.[46] They were sometimes called "White ethnics," by which was meant people who were White but who, because of their class and ethnic origins, did not enjoy the same social standing as Anglo-Americans. They were Poles and Slovaks and Italians and other peoples whose ancestors came from Eastern and Southern Europe. Most of them were by that time members of the third generation. Many of them lived in the industrial cities of the East and Midwest. Most either were working class themselves or had grown up in working-class households, gotten some education, and made places for themselves in the lower middle class. They grew up in union households and their parents had voted Democratic. In the Nixon years they were turning to the Republican Party in huge numbers; others would in the 1980s be called "Reagan Democrats," and almost all of them eventually made the party switch.

Part of their turn was driven by a politics of resentment. Many felt that the needs of Black working people had been addressed—perhaps had been overcompensated for. No one seemed to know that there were also a lot of hardworking White people in America who did not have very much. When was *their* turn going to come? Michael Novak proclaimed their arrival in a 1971 manifesto, *The Rise of the Unmeltable Ethnics*: "Long ignored by the ethnic superculture, millions of white ethnics—Poles, Italians, Greeks, and Slavs—have now proved that they are a dynamic force in American politics and culture. In the 1960s ... the blacks and the young had their day. The seventies will be the 'decade of the ethnics.'"[47] The unmeltable ethnics, however, were not the Ku Klux Klan. They were not racial terrorists. They were not against Blacks so much as for their own people. If they resented anyone most, it was surely the Anglo-American business elite who controlled American culture and the economy, and who ignored them as if they did not exist. They nursed class resentments at not being completely included in the dominant White group. They had ethnic status resentments: why did Spiro Agnostopolous have to change his name to Spiro Agnew in order to be a fit candidate for political office?

The national symbol of the White ethnic movement was Archie Bunker, hero of America's most popular TV show, *All in the Family*. Bunker was crude but intelligent, loudmouthed but warmhearted, bigoted but not mean. He celebrated the virtues of White, working-class culture and manhood. *All in the Family* was just one of many expressions of the White ethnic movement in popular culture in the seventies. The *Godfather* movies, Irving Howe's *World of Our Fathers*, and other books and movies attracted vast audiences because they celebrated White ethnic subcultures and purported to take the reader or viewer inside those exotic worlds.

The White ethnic movement was closely related to an intellectual and political movement that came to be called neoconservatism. Novak was one of its avatars, as were other former Cold War liberals like Nathan Glazer and Irving Kristol.[48] The 1990s saw the rise of another intellectual offshoot of the White ethnic movement: the Whiteness studies movement. This was a more left-leaning movement, at least in its origins. Whiteness studies scholars noted that a lot of attention had been paid over the previous few decades to the histories, cultures, and social situations of African Americans and other peoples of color, but that no one seemed to be looking at the nature of White people's privilege or the way that they maintained racial dominance. The second half of that decade and first years of the new century saw an explosion of literary, scholarly, and hortatory works devoted to examining the workings of White racial privilege.[49]

Immigrant Bashing

Some political analysts would like to imagine that anti-immigrant hysteria is a new thing in the twenty-first century.[50] Some would suggest it is a reasonable response to what they believe to be a great surge in immigration. We should be cautious about such an assumption. Quite consistently in the years since World War II—even before the 1965 immigration law, at a time when the U.S. foreign-born population hovered around a record low 6 percent—xenophobes on the right have railed about a nation awash in foreigners who were destroying the very nature of the American republic. For instance, shortly after mid-century, Mary Barclay Erb wrote a book titled, *While America Sleeps ... Foundations Crumble*, which made this argument:

> The period between 1929, when the national origins quota system provision of the 1924-enacted law became effective, and 1945, when it was virtually cancelled out in a splurge of refugee admissions,—even now continuing from Cuba—constitutes the only era during which this Nation has taken forceful action to keep America American.
>
> Today [before the impact of the 1965 law was felt] the racial fabric of the population of the United States is being mongrelized to an extent which, inevitably and at a rapid rate, is substantially altering the ethnic character and makeup of our society. We are fast moving away from our historic pattern of Northern and Northwestern Europe's Anglo-Saxon dominance in the blood of our people. Increasingly, there is being added to the racial mix of Americans historically disproportionate strains of Southern and Eastern Europe, the Orient and Africa.[51]

After 1965, as we have learned, the numbers of immigrants did go up, but it was not such an enormous surge as some have imagined. The big change after 1965 was not in the numbers but in the origins and races of the new immigrants. Many were brown and yellow; fewer were White. Consider then these words from the pen of Peter Brimelow:

> [C]urrent immigration policy is Adolf Hitler's posthumous revenge on America. ... Today [since the 1965 immigration act] U.S. government policy is literally dissolving the people. ...
>
> The mass immigration so thoughtlessly triggered in 1965 risks making America an *alien nation*—not merely in the sense that the numbers of aliens in the nation are rising to levels last seen in the nineteenth century; not merely in the sense that America will become a freak among the world's nations because of the unprecedented demographic mutation it is inflicting on itself ... but, ultimately, in the sense that Americans will no longer share in common [culture, language, and ancestry]. ...
>
> Race is destiny in American politics. Its importance has only been intensified by the supposedly color-blind civil rights legislation of the 1960s. ... any change in the racial balance must obviously be fraught with consequences for the survival and success of the American nation. It is simply common sense that Americans have a legitimate interest in their country's racial balance. It is common sense that they have a right to insist that their government stop shifting it [in favor of dark-skinned people]. Indeed, it seems to me that they have a right to insist that it be shifted back.[52]

Brimelow was himself an immigrant from England. He was not arguing against immigrants. He just thought that all immigrants to this country—indeed, all Americans—ought to be White, and of British descent if possible. Otherwise the nation was doomed, he thought, to cultural fratricide, political dismemberment, and economic impoverishment. Yet Brimelow was not some far-out crank. He was a smart, successful journalist who wrote for *Fortune* and *The National Review*. His book *Alien Nation*, from which the quotes are taken, attracted a top New York publishing house and sold more than 60,000 copies. In addition to its openly racist agenda, it was studded with factual mistakes, gross exaggerations, logical non sequiturs, and downright fabrications. And it was believed by many Americans.

Patrick Buchanan was at various times a presidential speechwriter, pundit, Republican candidate for president, and distinguished party elder. He also wrote of "the death of the West," which he saw coming because

> immigrant invasions imperil our country and civilization. ... Uncontrolled immigration threatens to deconstruct the nation we grew up in and convert America into a conglomeration of peoples with almost nothing in common— not history, heroes, language, culture, faith, or ancestors. Balkanization beckons. ... A sense that America, too, is pulling apart along the seams of ethnicity and race is spreading. ... Not only ethnically and racially, but culturally and morally, we are no longer one people or "one nation under God." ... In half a lifetime, many Americans have seen their God dethroned, their heroes defiled, their culture polluted, their values assaulted, their country invaded, and themselves demonized as extremists and bigots.[53]

Buchanan singled out Mexican migrants as the heart of the problem:

> Mexicans not only come from another culture, but millions are of another race. History and experience teach us that different races are more difficult to assimilate. ... Unlike the immigrants of old, who bade farewell forever to their native lands when they boarded the ship, for Mexicans, the mother country is right next door. Millions have no desire to learn English or to become citizens. America is not their home; Mexico is; and they wish to remain proud Mexicans. They have come here to work. Rather than assimilate, they create Little Tijuanas in U.S. cities. ... Uncle Sam is taking a hellish risk in importing a huge diaspora of tens of millions from a nation [Mexico] vastly different from our own. ... Our children will live with the consequences, balkanization, the end of America as we know her.[54]

To be fair, Buchanan saw lots else wrong with America besides its changing racial makeup, and he directed his pen against all that he didn't like, but he explicitly linked what he saw as the moral decimation of the republic to a large in-flow of what he regarded as racially inappropriate immigrants. Their presence in America was what was bringing down the house of virtue and turning the United States into a mongrel nation.

Samuel Huntington extended Brimelow and Buchanan's line of argument, and gave it an intellectual veneer, in an influential 2004 *Foreign Policy* article, promptly followed by a best-selling book, *Who Are We?* Huntington's concern was mainly with the survival of what he saw as America's founding values, which he identified with British political tradition and Protestant culture.

> America was created by 17th- and 18th-century settlers who were overwhelmingly white, British, and Protestant. Their values, institutions, and culture provided the foundation for and shaped the development of the United States

in the following centuries. They initially defined America in terms of race, ethnicity, culture, and religion. Then, in the 18th century, they also had to define America ideologically to justify independence from their home country, which was also white, British, and Protestant. Thomas Jefferson set forth this "creed" ... in the Declaration of Independence. ...

By the latter years of the 19th century ... the ethnic component had been broadened to include Germans, Irish, and Scandinavians, and the United States' religious identity was being redefined more broadly from Protestant to Christian. ...

Most Americans see the creed as the crucial element of their national identity. The creed, however, was the product of the distinct Anglo Protestant culture of the founding settlers. Key elements of that culture include the English language; Christianity; religious commitment; English concepts of the rule of law ... ; and dissenting Protestant values of individualism, the work ethic, and the belief that humans have the ability and the duty to try to create a heaven on earth.

Mexican immigrants, in Huntington's view, were different from all previous waves of immigrants, in that they did not subscribe to this creed. Indeed, they were not capable—culturally, perhaps racially, he is not clear as to the reason—of entering into American society on these terms. Huntington's arguments against Mexicans (and Buchanan's and Brimelow's) were not very different from Madison Grant's and Lothrop Stoddard's in the 1910s against Italians and Jews. They were not very different from Benjamin Franklin's argument against Germans in the 1750s, or from Samuel F. B. Morse's against people with names like Buchanan in the 1830s.[55]

Historian Otis Graham explicitly linked the anti-immigrant views of the 1990s and 2000s with those earlier anti-immigrant sentiments. He believed that the Johnson–Reed Act of 1924 was the best response to inappropriate (that is, South and East European) immigration run amok a century ago. He characterized even that immigration wave as "mostly positive" by comparison with recent years, but saw late twentieth-century Latino and Asian immigration as "mostly negative" for reasons cultural and racial. He longed for a return to racial bars and national quotas based on race. He even went the other critics one better by blaming the September 11, 2001, attacks on the World Trade Center and Pentagon on the 1965 Immigration Act and our too-open border with Mexico: "The costs of America's porous borders were stunningly piled even higher on the morning of September 11, 2001. While Mexican President Fox traveled northward to Washington on his mission to open America's southern border to his surplus population, Islamic terrorists commandeered jetliners and struck the World Trade Center in New York and the Pentagon, killing nearly three thousand persons."[56]

It was the same story, told over and over again—whether by Morse or Grant or Erb or Huntington—with the same tone of urgency amid assertions that America was under an unprecedented threat from alien hordes streaming across our borders. It was sometimes written with polish, but at heart it was crude, racist fear-mongering. Yet none of these writers wanted to own up to the racism that lay at the heart of their arguments.[57]

White Americans have always been more comfortable with and welcoming of some kinds of immigrants than others. I spent a fair amount of time around the U.S. embassy in Beijing and the State Department's office in Hong Kong in the years

1987 to 1989, and I also had dealings with the embassy in Copenhagen in 2000. Formally, the bureaucratic situations faced by would-be immigrants were the same in all three locations. They had to have their papers in order, wait in line, fill out forms, be interviewed, endure background checks, have people vouch for them, and wait months for clearance to come to the United States. But there was a huge difference in the reception the different candidates received. In both Chinese locations, although many of the U.S. officials were good souls, they were under instructions to be suspicious and to do their very best to discourage any Chinese who wanted to come to the United States. By contrast, in Copenhagen, the Americans fairly fell over themselves trying to make Danish candidates welcome. It may be that Bill Clinton's State Department had a more welcoming attitude toward immigrants in general than did Ronald Reagan's or the elder George Bush's. But I am fairly certain that not far beneath the surface lurked a bedrock White American conviction that Northwest Europeans made more appropriate immigrants than did Chinese.

Many Americans' preference for White immigrants is related to a deep-seated longing for a White republic, which in turn is linked to the idea of the nation-state. According to that line of thinking, a country must be made up of a single ethnic people, and linguistic and racial boundaries are necessarily coterminous with national political boundaries. This powerful fiction has guided national self-representation in Europe since the eighteenth century and in much of the world since the twentieth century. Thus France presents itself as uniformly Gallic and Germany as Teutonic, although both national fictions mask complex ethnic mosaics that came together within single states. Once the states had come together politically, they imposed national homogeneity and refused to recognize variety. So it was also with Turkey and China—diverse peoples were brought forcibly under one national government, which solidified its right to rule by imposing a national language and identity on its various peoples and refusing to recognize their diversity or to tolerate expressions of difference. This assumption, that racial and cultural homogeneity are necessary to a successful country, is almost never questioned. It helps to explain the emotional preference many Americans have for White immigrants over those whose skin is darker.[58]

Fighting Affirmative Action

One of the complaints that all these White writers had was about affirmative action for racial minorities. As with most issues considered in this chapter, there is a huge literature on the history, conduct, possibilities, and performance of affirmative action ideas and programs, written mainly by committed advocates or relentless opponents.[59] It is not my intention to review and evaluate the history and merits of affirmative action as social policy. Let me instead make just a few observations.

"Affirmative action" was a term coined by President Lyndon Johnson in 1965 to describe efforts he asked the government to make to begin to redress the centuries of disabilities that Black Americans had suffered. In a commencement address at Howard University, he celebrated the passage of the Civil Rights and Voting Rights Acts, and then went on:

> But this victory—as Winston Churchill said of another triumph for freedom—"is not the end. It is not even the beginning of the end. But it is, perhaps, the end of the beginning."

That beginning is freedom; and the barriers to that freedom are tumbling down. Freedom is the right to share, share fully and equally, in American society—to vote, to hold a job, to enter a public place, to go to school. It is the right to be treated in every part of our national life as a person equal in dignity and promise to all others.

But freedom is not enough. You do not wipe away the scars of centuries by saying: Now you are free to go where you want, and do as you desire, and choose the leaders you please.

You do not take a person who, for years, has been hobbled by chains and liberate him, bring him up to the starting line of a race and then say, "you are free to compete with all the others," and still justly believe that you have been completely fair.

Thus it is not enough just to open the gates of opportunity. All our citizens must have the ability to walk through those gates.

This is the next and the more profound stage of the battle for civil rights. We seek not just freedom but opportunity. We seek not just legal equity but human ability, not just equality as a right and a theory but equality as a fact and equality as a result.[60]

Most of the actual implementation of affirmative action policies in the federal government was done under conservative President Richard Nixon, in particular through the office of Undersecretary of Labor Arthur Fletcher. States and localities also built affirmative action plans of their own, as did many thousands of businesses across the nation. Initially they were directed primarily at giving African Americans entrée to jobs, education, contracts, and the like. But before long there were affirmative action programs for White women, Latinos, Native Americans, and other groups. Sometimes they were crude tools—quotas and designated set-asides. More often, they simply injected an element of special consideration into a selection system. On balance, affirmative action seems to have resulted in some modest gains for Blacks and other peoples of color (although not for Asians, who were seldom included). Affirmative action programs may be credited with helping solidify the growth of the new Black middle class. The most substantial gains from affirmative action, according to several studies, were made by middle-class White women.

It is important to remember that, though the term "affirmative action" was invented in the 1960s, the fact of affirmative action was not new in American society then. What was new was the beneficiaries. Jack Ohma, cartoonist for the Portland *Oregonian*, marked the issue neatly in six panels: "(1) He didn't do that well in high school. (2) He was a 'C' student. (3) He got into a big school under a preferential system. (4) He then performed fairly well academically. (5) Ultimately, quotas worked for him. He is now a productive citizen." The last panel is a picture of President George W. Bush saying "Is this a great country, or what?" One need look no further than the White House to be reminded that this country has always had affirmative action for the sons of wealthy White families.[61]

During the Depression, affirmative action was extended to White working people. As Ira Katznelson and Mary Poole showed definitively, all the New Deal and Fair Deal programs of the 1930s and 1940s were highly discriminatory in favor of Whites and against Blacks and Latinos. For instance, the Social Security Act raised the status of unemployment insurance and social security, differentiated them from welfare, and aimed them specifically at those sectors of the economy where Whites worked. Not only those programs but laws about minimum wages and rights to unionize did not apply in the areas, such as field labor and domestic service, where most Blacks and Mexicans worked. Work rules and veterans' benefits were slanted in favor of White workers. Katznelson wrote of the GI Bill:

> It is indisputable that the GI Bill offered eligible African Americans more benefits and more opportunities than they possibly could have imagined in the early 1940s. Yet the way in which the law and its programs were organized and administered, and its ready accommodation to the larger discriminatory context within which it was embedded, produced practices that were more racially distinct and arguably more cruel than any other New Deal-era program. The performance of the GI Bill mocked the promise of fair treatment. The differential treatment meted out to African Americans sharply curtailed the statute's powerful egalitarian promise and significantly widened the country's large racial gap.[62]

That is, White soldiers got far more benefit from the GI Bill than did Black soldiers because of the discriminatory structure of American higher education at the time. That, in Katznelson's view, was affirmative action for White people.

Despite this long history of government and private business giving favor to Whites, a lot of White people still regard affirmative action as an affront and an injustice directed against White people. Patrick Buchanan had quite a different take on the provenance of affirmative action than do most historians.

> In the 1950s, [what] African Americans. ... wanted, demanded, was to be full and equal members of our national family, to which they and their people had contributed all their lives. America said yes. Black and white together, America went out and buried Jim Crow. ... But when the valid grievances had been redressed and the legitimate demands for equal rights under law had been met, America's attention moved elsewhere. Civil rights became yesterday's story. To recapture the nation's attention, new demands had to be invented, and when they were met, still newer demands. Desegregation was now no longer enough. Affirmative action, quotas, set-asides, equality of result in jobs, pay and income.[63]

Buchanan professed not to like revisionist history, but he certainly practiced it fluently. At the very least, he had a more optimistic view than did Lyndon Johnson of the life chances that faced African Americans in 1965. Peter Brimelow was more blunt. He defined affirmative action as "government-mandated discrimination against white Americans." White people, in his estimation, were the victims who needed to be protected against discrimination.[64]

Sentiments like these led to an anti-affirmative action movement that waxed and waned from the 1970s through the 2000s. A series of legal challenges resulted in rules carefully circumscribing the scope allowed to affirmative action efforts, at the same time they upheld the constitutionality of the general principle of taking positive action to redress past injustices. An attempt by White Republicans to amend the U.S. Constitution to outlaw affirmative action failed in the early 1980s, but several states passed laws or constitutional amendments in the 1990s that forbade those state governments to practice racial affirmative action. At the same time, most large private corporations continued to practice some carefully limited aspects of affirmative action, particularly those directed to enhance gender, rather than racial, equity.

Affirmative action may be good social policy or it may be bad social policy. It may have good effects or ill. It may be fair or not fair. It may be a reasonable approach to address enduring racial discrimination, or it may be meanness directed against suffering White people. But affirmative action is not new, nor has it historically been aimed primarily to benefit people of color. The movement against affirmative action did not come on the scene until people of color began to share in the benefits of affirmative action that had traditionally gone to White people.[65] Anti-affirmative action became an emblem of the disgruntlement that many White people felt at all the racial changes they perceived to be taking place around them in the last quarter of the twentieth century.

New Issues in a New Era

Changes in Racial Etiquette

Something about American racial etiquette changed dramatically over the second half of the twentieth century. For the first time, it became impolite to express racial, religious, or gender bigotry openly. It was one of the fruits of the civil rights era. It was not a complete transformation. Homophobic feeling and utterance were still alive and well in the twenty-first century, and race- and gender-related feelings of resentment and domination often lingered not all that far below the surface. But overt expressions of racism were now seen as impolite. Nice people just didn't express racist feelings or act on them overtly any more, even if they felt them privately. This new racial etiquette led to innumerable statements by public servants and private citizens that began with the preamble, "I'm not a racist, but ..."—which would of course be followed by an expression of what would appear to any neutral observer to be a racist sentiment. No one living in these times could be unaware of such expressions, but most of us were too polite to talk about it. In fact, it came increasingly to be seen as impolite if one spoke up about racism at all.

Thus an initiative sponsored by the arch-conservative American Civil Rights Institute in 2003 tried to get California to stop talking about race. Proponents of Proposition 54, the so-called "Racial Privacy Initiative," proclaimed that "Americans are tired of talking about race." The law, had it passed, would have provided that "The state shall not classify any individual by race, ethnicity, color or national origin in the operation of public education, public contracting or public employment." The idea, its authors contended, was that racism would go away if people just stopped talking about it. Opponents claimed the initiative would just make it impossible for educators, public health officials, economists, sociologists, or political leaders to collect data that would help them ascertain how various segments of the population were faring. California's voters defeated Prop 54 by a margin of 64 to 36 percent. They seem to have recognized that there was some utility to keeping racial statistics despite Prop 54's attempt to change the subject.[66]

Multiculturalism

In the last third of the twentieth century, multiculturalism became a national civic commitment.[67] Whereas the United States had always in fact been a congeries of

419

many peoples, for much of their history, Americans maintained a rhetorical posture of normative Whiteness. Thus it was possible for Americans to speak of theirs as a "White Republic" (see Chapter 3), even though it contained a lot of non-White people. Multiculturalism, one aspect of the changing racial etiquette that followed the civil rights movement, embraced the idea that America was made up of a lot of different kinds of people and that there was nothing wrong with that—indeed, that there was something good and strong about embracing the multicultural fact of America's existence.

Multiculturalism began in the 1980s as an effort to present the narrative of American self-understanding on a basis that included as many different kinds of people as possible and that did not give privilege to one group over the others. Thus, U.S. history textbooks, for example, began to include the insights of a generation of scholars who had studied not just government immigration policies but the lives of immigrants; not just Civil War politics but the lives of slaves and ex-slaves, and also of soldiers, Yankee and Confederate; not just Progressive-era legislation but the lives of middle-class White women; and so on and on. It was a move away from an elite narrative to one that included ordinary people, and more kinds of people, in the American story. Similarly, multiculturalism meant that, in addition to studying a canon of great literary figures (almost all of whom were White and male) that ran from Chaucer through Shakespeare to Twain and Hemingway, literature scholars and teachers found virtue and insight, beauty and relevance in poetry by White women and by people of color. Rick Simonson and Scott Walker wrote in favor of "multicultural literacy." Proponents of older views of history and culture, they wrote:

> seem to think that most of what constitutes contemporary American and world culture was immaculately conceived by a few men in Greece, around 900 BC, came to its full expression in Europe a few centuries later, and began to decline around the middle of the nineteenth century. ... Most Americans are now aware of the contributions of repressed cultures, more alert to how history has been rewritten and molded to the vision of the majority population, and accustomed to the notion that culture, like language, changes, and that we ought to be sensitive to those changes.[68]

Lawrence Levine wrote of the changes that had taken place in university education as a result of the multicultural movement:

> The United States has always been a multicultural, multiethnic, multiracial society, but in our own time these truths—and their implications for higher education—have become increasingly difficult to ignore. As the university becomes more open to and representative of the diverse peoples, experiences, traditions, and cultures that compose America, its impulse to find explanations for those parts of our history and our culture we have ignored grows proportionately. It has to enable its students to comprehend the nature of the society they're part of, the history of groups and traditions they will interact with, the meaning of ideas and experiences they will inevitably encounter.[69]

Multiculturalism quickly came under attack from the intellectual and political right.[70] They argued that multiculturalism was "dumbing down" the curriculum by including inferior writings from non-White-male writers, and perhaps in so doing leaving out some of the writers that conservatives cherished most. Columnist Charles Krauthammer called it a "new tribalism" that threatened to balkanize national culture. Richard Bernstein complained about what he saw as a "dictatorship of virtue"—a perhaps well-meaning attempt to be inclusive that resulted in a tyranny of political correctness run amok. Alvin Schmidt's analysis was blunt, and summarized the conservatives' objections:

> Multiculturalism is a leftist political ideology that sees all cultures, their mores and institutions, as essentially equal. No culture is considered superior or inferior to any other; it is merely different. ... Multiculturalism encourages immigrants and other minorities to retain their foreign cultures by not assimilating to the Euro-American culture. ... Americans need to know that multiculturalism is attacking and even eradicating the foundation of their nation's morality, laws, and ethics, for the multiculturalists have an intense hatred of anything that reflects biblical values. ... If multiculturalism continues to infiltrate America's basic institutions with its potentially divisive ideology, neo-pagan principles, and multi-morality, [America] will surely lose its soul.[71]

Multiculturalism came under criticism from the left, too. James Kyung-Jin Lee, for example, argued that a general embrace of diversity by American society had not done much to ameliorate the difficult social situations faced by people of color. By the beginning of the twenty-first century, even the very White Republican Party had come to embrace pigmented people in prominent places: Secretaries of State Colin Powell and Condoleeza Rice, Attorney General Alberto Gonzalez, Supreme Court Justice Clarence Thomas, Justice Department ideologue John Yoo, and many others. The fact that people such as they held prominent positions, Lee argued, gave racial cover to government policies that were profoundly hurtful to Blacks, Latinos, and other peoples of color. As Viet Thanh Nguyen wrote, "Even as Americans became more and more sensitized to the difference and diversity of the nation, and even as multicultural literature flourished, the plight of the poor and of many populations of color worsened." Racial etiquette had changed, but there was a real question whether racial change had taken place. Über-White TV character Ally McBeal could, in the 1990s, kiss a boyfriend whose Blackness was carefully not marked, and that was racial progress of a sort over the days when such a relationship would not have appeared on television. President George W. Bush could appoint three people of color to his cabinet. Yet, at the same time, an ever-higher percentage of Blacks, Indians, and Latinos lived in poverty.[72]

From whatever angle the criticism came, the fact was that America had become a multicultural place, and Americans knew it. It was not a White republic, and it could not pretend to be one any longer. The change was real, and it spread across the country and the culture, despite attempts to hold back the tide of history. A Macy's ad, chosen at random, included pictures of five models: blond, Black, Asian, Latina, and multiracial. The *Chicago Tribune* revealed that, in addition to the phone company's regular yellow-page business directory, there were versions directed to Polish, Romanian, Serbian, Korean, Pakistani, Asian American, and Spanish language customers. When California ran a gubernatorial free-for-all in 2003, the top half-dozen candidates included two immigrants with thick accents (Arianna Huffington and eventual winner Arnold Schwarzenegger) and son of immigrant Mexican laborers

(Cruz Bustamante) whose first language growing up in the fields had been Spanish. When two professional soccer teams met in Los Angeles, the match was preceded by a mass where the star attraction was a Mexican religious relic, La Virgen de Zapopan, imported specially for the occasion.[73]

On Martin Luther King Way in Seattle's Rainier Valley, Viet-Wah Superfoods exemplified the new America that had come to be since 1965. Out front in 2003 was a sign proclaiming "Grocery" in two-foot-high letters, in English, Vietnamese, Chinese, Thai, Lao, Khmer, Hmong, and Spanish. Inside the shelves were stocked with every variety of Asian vegetables, roots, spices, and canned goods, with origins stretching from Hokkaido to the Bosporus, plus Fruit Loops, Cheetos, Coke, and Wonder Bread. The workers were mainly Southeast Asians, the cashiers were all Black. In the same strip mall were a hair-braiding salon and an African American beauty products store; a bakery with signs in English and two Southeast Asian languages; a Korean nail salon; two Vietnamese restaurants; a laundromat; a Cambodian-run donut shop; and a branch of the Philippine National Bank. The clientele in all those places was racially mixed. That was the multicultural nation that America in fact had become. As Nguyen wrote, "We've moved far enough in the past few decades that multiculturalism is no longer the cry of the barbarians, but the most contemporary version of realism, describing our society in all of its diversity and tragedy."[74]

The Multiracial Movement

One concomitant of multiculturalism was an increasing flexibility about racial definitions. Beginning in the 1980s and increasing apace in the 1990s and the new century, a multiracial movement brought changes in Americans' thinking about racial identities.[75] American racial thinking had been prisoner to the one-drop rule for more than a century. Both racial slavery and racial segregation had depended on each person being marked as a member of a single racial group. Government-imposed blood quantum rules for Indian tribes had been based on the same idea: either one was an Indian or one was not. The lines were supposed to be clear.

Of course, there had always been a lot of racial mixing that went on underneath the radar of the one-drop rule. Even so prominent a White supremacist as U.S. Senator Strom Thurmond, the world learned in 2003, had maintained a probably coercive sexual relationship with a Black servant woman beginning in 1924, and the couple had a daughter, Essie Mae Washington-Williams, whom Thurmond acknowledged after a fashion. But Thurmond, Washington-Williams, and their relatives felt constrained to keep the relationship secret until after the old segregationist's death at age 100.[76] The civil rights movement began to change Americans' ideas about the importance of maintaining racial separation in personal relationships. The 1967 U.S. Supreme Court decision invalidating antimiscegenation laws, *Loving v. Virginia*, both confirmed that American attitudes had begun to change, and it also spurred further change. There followed what Maria Root called a "multiracial baby boom"—ever-increasing numbers of interracial couples dating and marrying; ever-larger numbers of multiracial children being born; a steadily more common decision on the part of such people to embrace multiple racial identities; and an increasing willingness of society at large to recognize their choice.

The Gallup Poll found that disapproval of interracial marriage dropped from 72 percent in 1968 to 42 percent in 1991. The percentage who approved such marriages, according to the Roper Poll, had soared to 83 percent by 2003. A survey in 1999 and 2000 found that more than half of Americans over the age of eighteen had dated someone of another race, although the racial isolation of Whites in this regard was substantially greater than the isolation of any other racial group.[77] The number of people who identified themselves as multiracial on the U.S. Census exploded from half a million in 1970 to 6.8 million in 2000.[78] Surely, all this reflected a dramatic increase in the numbers of interracial couples and of children born to such couples. But it just as surely also reflected a much greater readiness on the part of individuals to claim attachment to more than one racial identity.

This was the product of a movement begun in the 1980s by interracially married couples, mainly Black and White. They formed support groups with names like I-Pride, the Biracial Family Network, and Multiracial Americans of Southern California, to keep each other company as they coped with maintaining interracial marriages and raising multiracial children. In time, the multiracial people formed organizations of their own, such as Hapa Issues Forum (adopting a Hawaiian word that signified multiraciality) and the Association of Multi-Ethnic Americans. Some became active in politics, lobbying for a "multiracial" box on census and school forms. They had some success, and in 1997 the U.S. Office of Management and Budget decided that, beginning with the 2000 census, individuals would no longer be required to choose a single racial box; they would be allowed to check all that applied.

They were groping toward what multiracial scholar-activist Reg Daniel called "the new multiracial identity ... beyond black and white ... beyond the one-drop rule ... [that promises to] help create a more egalitarian racial order in the United States." The idea was that, by embracing their multiraciality, people of mixed ancestry could begin to dismantle the received categories of racial hierarchy that had imprisoned intergroup relationships in America for 300 years.[79] Perhaps that was an advocate's utopian dream, but surely there were a lot of people by the end of the twentieth century, from very different and complex racial backgrounds, who were identifying themselves as multiracial—as connected to two or more of the racial groups that had been built in America. The one-drop rule seemed to be losing some of its power.

Forever Foreigners: Asians and Arabs

During the second half of the twentieth century, many Asian Americans entered the middle class. Some were new immigrants, but others were American-born citizens up to the third and fourth generation. Nonetheless, Asian Americans remained eternal foreigners in the eyes of many non-Asian Americans.[80] In Chapter 1, I described U.S. Senator Alphonse D'Amato's apparent assumption that he was an American but that Judge Lance Ito, like D'Amato the grandson of immigrants, was a foreigner because he was an Asian American. Earlier in this chapter, we saw how Vincent Chin died, in part because two White Americans assumed he was a foreigner because he was an Asian American.

In 1996, some White politicians mounted a campaign against Asian American participation in politics. A Senate committee sought to prove that Chinese Americans who worked for the Democratic Party were agents of the government of the People's Republic of China, funneling illegal foreign campaign contributions into Bill Clinton's re-election campaign. It turned out their allegations were groundless; they were based, not on any evidence, but simply on the assumption that anyone whose ancestors came from China must be somehow Chinese, not American. In the same election season, Vice-President Al Gore was excoriated for holding a fundraising dinner in the rented hall of an Asian American Buddhist temple. Never mind that other fundraisers were held in White Lutheran or Black Baptist churches. Never mind that all the contributors were American citizens. The fact that it was an Asian American religious institution, and that some of the contributors were not only Asian-descended but also Buddhists, made their participation foreign and illegitimate in the eyes of the public and the press.

U.S. Air Force Captain Ted Lieu recounted this experience in 1999:

"Are you in the Chinese Air Force?" the elegantly dressed lady sitting next to me asked. For a moment I was left speechless. We were at an awards dinner, and I was wearing my blue U.S. Air Force uniform, complete with captain's bars, military insignia and medals. Her question jarred me and made me realize that even Air Force blue was not enough to reverse her initial presumption that people with yellow skin and Asian features are somehow not American.

Unfortunately, this was not just an isolated incident. ... I have had strangers come up to me and attempt to mimic the Chinese language in a derogatory manner. I have been told countless times that I speak "good" English. ... On any given day, if I walk around with a camera, I will be mistaken for a tourist from Asia.

Most of the discrimination I have encountered centered on the view that I am not a part of this great nation, even though I grew up in Ohio, graduated from law school in Washington, DC, and received my commission in the U.S. Air Force in 1991. ...

America is a nation founded by immigrants and built on the ideal that anyone can be an American if he or she believes in the principles and values of the Constitution. Indeed, the Vietnamese American immigrant who does not yet speak "good" English but is starting a small business and believes in freedom and democracy is much more American than a fifth-generation white separatist who blew up a federal building because he had a problem with federalism.[81]

The most egregious case of abuse of an Asian American because he was assumed to be a foreigner was the matter of Wen Ho Lee, racial prisoner.[82] Lee was a scientist who came to the United States in the 1960s from his native Taiwan to get a PhD at Texas A&M. He became a U.S. citizen and took a job at Los Alamos National Laboratory, where he worked on problems in fluid dynamics. Over the next three decades he did the work of a scientist, including traveling to conferences where physicists of many nations gathered to exchange their findings. Among the scientists he met were a few from Taiwan, some from China, and quite a number from various European and Latin American countries.

In the 1990s, Los Alamos Labs came under criticism for lax security. Some critics complained that other countries—China among them—were making weapons advances that they could only have made if they had stolen secrets from Los Alamos. In 1996 the FBI began an investigation; Wen Ho Lee was soon their chief suspect, perhaps because he had met some Chinese scientists, perhaps because he was ethnically Chinese. In March 1999 the *New York Times* broke a story that, although it did not name Lee, indicated he was probably a spy, and Los Alamos fired him. In November of that year, the Justice Department brought a fifty-nine count indictment against Lee "for copying bomb secrets with intent to injure the United States and to aid a foreign country." He was called the most damaging spy since the Rosenbergs gave nuclear secrets to Russia in the early years of the Cold War. That December Lee was locked up in solitary confinement, where he remained for 278 days, denied bail, often in shackles, under 24-hour watch. He could not scratch or go to the bathroom without being observed. He faced the possibility of spending the rest of his life in prison.

Asian Americans and scientists across the country rose in criticism of the government's mishandling of Lee's case. A crackerjack defense team dismantled the government's case against their client. In the end, it turned out that what Wen Ho Lee had done was to take his work home with him. He had put it onto his home computer, something that most of his colleagues (and indeed, as FBI Director Louis Freeh) also did. The materials he downloaded to his home computer were not classified when he downloaded them, although the government classified them later as part of his prosecution. The nuclear secrets that they said he had given to the Chinese were, it turned out, all available in published articles and reports. His FBI interrogators had lied, both to Lee during questioning, and to the courts and the press about what Lee said and did. After nearly nine months of this fiasco, the government agreed to dismiss all but one count of mishandling classified information. Lee agreed to give the government a fig leaf by pleading guilty to that one count, in return for a sentence of time already served. Judge James A. Parker set Lee free and chastised the government for its misconduct:

> What was the government's motive in insisting on your being jailed pretrial under extraordinarily onerous conditions of confinement until today, when the Executive Branch agrees that you may be set free essentially unrestricted? ... I believe you were terribly wronged. ... I am truly sorry that I was led by our Executive Branch of government to order your detention last December. ... it becomes clear that the Executive Branch now concedes, or should concede, that it was not necessary to confine you last December or at any time before your trial. ... the top decision makers in the Executive Branch ... have caused embarrassment by the way this case began and was handled. ... They have embarrassed our entire nation and each of us who is a citizen of it. ... I sincerely apologize to you, Dr. Lee, for the unfair manner you were held in custody.[83]

Asians were not the only Americans who were treated as perpetual foreigners. Mexican Americans of whatever generation were subjected to the assumption that they were recent immigrants, and probably illegal ones at that, as we shall see in the Epilogue. Arab Americans and other people who "looked Middle Eastern" shared the dubious distinction of being seen by other Americans as eternally foreign.[84] Once upon a time, Arab Americans were reckoned to be White people. In 1915 a federal court decided that George Dow was White and entitled to U.S. citizenship, in the same era when other courts were deciding that Japanese and South Asians were not White. Through the 1950s and 1960s, the census listed people of Middle Eastern origin as White, and popular figures like TV comedian Danny Thomas passed unproblematically as White people.

Beginning in the 1970s, Arab Americans and other people of Middle Eastern or North African or West Asian origins found themselves increasingly racialized as nonnative, threatening, non-White people. The lines between such peoples were never quite clear in Americans' minds. Most simply lumped them all together. Most did not know that Iranians were not Arabs but Persians. Most did not know that a majority of Arab Americans were Christians, not Muslims. Most did not know that the largest number of American Muslims were South Asian in origin, not Arab, and that a quarter of American Muslims were African Americans descended from slavery. Most did not know that the most populous Muslim country in the world was not one of the Arab nations but Indonesia. Most did not know that China had as many Muslims as Iran, Iraq, Saudi Arabia, and Afghanistan combined. Arabs, Muslims, and other Middle Eastern and North African peoples all ran together in a blur in the minds of most Americans.

They began to appear foreign and threatening when Organization of the Petroleum Exporting Countries (OPEC) began raising the price of oil in 1974. Much as the killers of Vincent Chin saw his Asian ancestry and blamed him for the wrong that they imagined Japan was doing to them, so Americans in the 1970s saw Arab and other Middle Eastern Americans and blamed them for long lines and rising gas prices. Arab and other Middle Eastern Americans became darker and darker in the American imagination, and more and more foreign, year by year, through the 1980s and 1990s.

On February 15, 1986, FBI Special Agent Frank Knight hid in an engineering booth with a view of the stage of the Glendale Civic Auditorium and watched a fundraiser put on by local Arab Americans. Twelve hundred people—families with children—came together that night to sing, dance, eat ethnic food, listen to speeches about the needs of Palestinian refugees in the West Bank and Gaza, and contribute to relief organizations. Some of the participants had a political agenda. Khader Musa Hamide said, "We wanted to influence the U.S. We wanted to be like the Jews of the United States. ... To work from within the system. ... We engaged every group that was willing to listen to us, whether it was on campuses, churches, community groups and political people. Anybody who was willing to listen to us, we went to them, with literature, with dialogue, with whatever it took. Books, you name it—with dance, with food, with anything we could. We wanted to bring out the truth." Knight did not speak Arabic and could not understand what was being said at the meeting, but he decided that these people were terrorists. The following January he arranged for eight of the participants, including Hamide, to be arrested, charged with a crime for distributing copies of a magazine that was readily available in the public library and on college campuses, and turned over to immigration authorities for deportation. Over the next twenty years their cases made their way up and down the American court system. The activities in which they engaged were all legal free speech. Nonetheless, the U.S. government was still seeking to deport them nearly two decades later. The tribulations of the LA Eight foreshadowed the treatment that would be inflicted on Arab and other Middle Eastern immigrants in the anti-terrorism hysteria of the new century.[85]

During the first Iraq war, Americans did not differentiate between friendly Arabs like Kuwaitis and Saudis, oppositional Arabs like Iraqis and Syrians, and hostile non-Arabs like Iranians and Afghans. Nor did they distinguish between the governments of such countries and American citizens and permanent residents whose ancestors came from those countries. Arab and other Middle Eastern Americans were well on their way to being White people no longer. Louise Cainkar interviewed Arab Americans in Chicago between 2002 and 2004 about their racial identities. Among their responses were:

I am resentful that I have to put down white. I don't look white. I am not treated as white.

We have always been told we should be classified as other, then white. But if I go to Mississippi with my brother named Ahmed, there is no way he'd be treated as white.

Arabs are definitely not white. That categorization comes from the treatment of a community by the institutions of American society. Arabs in the schools face the same institutional racism as other students of color.

Arabs are not white. ... I don't get treated as white, so I am not white.

We are definitely not white. But the whole idea of color makes no sense to me. My neighbor is black according to census forms but she is lighter than I am. There are Arabs that are lighter than white people. ... I would consider myself brown. I would not consider myself white. My youngest and oldest child would be white and my middle child brown.[86]

In 1995, when someone blew up the Murrah Federal Building in Oklahoma City, many Americans assumed it was the work of sinister Muslim terrorists. Calls went out in Congress and the press to put Arab and Muslim Americans in concentration camps. In the next few days, 222 hate crimes were reported to have been committed against Muslims nationwide. When the perpetrator turned out to be pink-cheeked Timothy McVeigh, a Christian ex-soldier, that first racist response directed against Arab and Middle Eastern Americans was conveniently forgotten. A Chicago mother recalled:

During the Oklahoma City bombing, my son was in his world history class, I think. Two or three of the kids knew that my son was an Arab and a Muslim, and they started making smart comments about "send all those black Arabs back where they came from." ... What happened here was that the teacher was sitting back enjoying the verbal attack on my son, and saying nothing to [stop] it. Then, the next day, when it was discovered that the bomber was not an Arab or a Muslim but an American, and my son got up and tried to give back what he got the day before, the teacher was reprimanding him. ... [My sons] were born here, they were raised here, they contribute to this society. *We* contribute to this society.[87]

But they were not seen, by these White students or this White teacher, as Americans, nor as White people. The making over of Arab and Muslim Americans in the minds of other Americans, into dark-skinned, threatening, perpetual foreigners, began long before the attacks of September 11, 2001.

Publishers came out in the first years of the new century with a spate of novels and personal accounts, written by Iranian, Afghani, and other Middle Eastern exiles. Each purported to take Americans into the heart of a hostile country and acquaint them with an exotic landscape, accompanied by an immigrant from that foreign place. Books like *The Kite Runner, Standing Alone in Mecca*, and *Lipstick Jihad* all were skillfully written and immensely popular.[88] They satisfied Americans' wish to know about places and peoples we knew we had neglected (to our peril), at the same time they reassured us that those places and peoples were fundamentally messed up. In *The War at Home*, Masuda Sultan told her story of coming to the United States with her family fleeing war-torn Afghanistan at age five; being raised in Brooklyn and Queens; forced into an arranged marriage at seventeen; divorced and a college student at twenty; back in Afghanistan to meet relatives and learn her roots; and subsequent activities documenting abuses of Afghani women. It is a moving personal story, but also one that comforts the reader with the notion that America is a much better place for women than Afghanistan.[89] Such books did introduce non-Arab, non-Middle Eastern Americans to people who had walked among them, people whom they had neither noticed nor understood heretofore. But they also reinforced notions of Muslims and Middle Eastern-derived peoples as exotic, strange, unreasonable, perhaps perverse, and unalterably foreign.

Chapter 10

Epilogue

Future Uncertain
Race, Ethnicity, and Immigration at the Dawn of the Twenty-First Century

People in California talk about the "illegals," But there was always an illegality to immigration. It was a rude act, the leaving of home. ... Immigrants must always be illegal. Immigrants are always criminals. They trespass borders and horrify their grandmothers. But they are also our civilization's prophets. They, long before the rest of us ... they saw the hemisphere whole.

Richard Rodriguez[1]

"Carlos, why are you fucking with my people?"
"Because, Ahmed, it's your turn."

Carlos Mencia[2]

Projecting the Future

Historians are, I believe, righteously reluctant to make predictions about the future. We are far more reluctant than, say, economists or evangelists, who make their living on such predictions (and seldom have to bear responsibility for having been wrong). About the only thing I can be sure of about the future is that it will be different than I or anyone else can currently imagine, and in ways that will surprise us. Accordingly, in this section I will have only a very few things to say about what demographers project for the future of U.S. immigration. Any such projection depends either on conditions remaining much as they are (which surely they will not do) or on them changing in a predictable and measurable way (which is only marginally more likely). Projections far into the future are helpful for framing possibilities, but they cannot be relied on for any degree of accuracy. With those caveats in mind, let us consider what may be in our immigration future.[3]

Estimates of the number of immigrants who will come to the United States in future decades vary enormously—mainly, it seems, depending on the point that the estimator wants to make. If the soothsayer doesn't like immigrants and wants to reduce their number, then the prediction is likely to be very large, say 1.5 million people a year and an eventual foreign-born population totaling half or more of the U.S. total. Some people with a more sanguine view of immigrants estimate much smaller numbers—perhaps 400,000 to 500,000 per year, and a foreign-born population never reaching more than 15 percent of the U.S. total.[4]

It seems likely that for the foreseeable future the United States will be receiving large numbers of migrants from Mexico, Central America, and the Caribbean, and from China, the Philippines, and South Asia, as we have in the past decades. But how long those trends will continue is anybody's guess.[5] Maybe the current economic forces pushing those migrants will continue. Maybe the United States will have a depression, induced by overspending on wars and occupations abroad, tax cuts, and a calamitous terrorist attack or natural disaster. Maybe Al Gore is right about global warming, and Miami and Los Angeles will be under water. In those cases, the United States may become less attractive to immigrants than it has been lately. Perhaps the Chinese economy will heat up so hot that people who might have emigrated will decide to stay home, and people from other countries will flock there (indeed, they have already begun to do so). Perhaps new crises in some other part of the globe (Nepal? Argentina? Nigeria?) will impel new groups of people to seek refuge in the United States. No one can say for sure. Reports from Europe, Africa, and Southeast Asia suggest that a new global web of migration and asylum seeking has been building for about two decades, and it is possible that the United States may become part of that web to an extent with which it is not yet familiar.

As it happens, the U.S. Census Bureau has made projections for the racial makeup of the U.S. population in 2000, 2010, 2020, and 2050 (Table 10.1). Note that, for these projections, they have assigned each person only one racial identity, despite the increasing recognition of multiple identities, and that they have presented Latinos as a separate racial category (contrary to their usual practice). Over the four decades projected, Indians about hold steady in percentage terms, Blacks' percentage increases slightly, Whites decline steadily, and Asians and Latinos nearly double their percentage in the population by 2050.

Perhaps it will turn out that way. Figure 10.1 shows the 2050 projection graphically, so that the reader may compare it to the race distribution pie charts in earlier chapters. One thing that has been a matter of great concern to some Whites has been the thought that the United States might become a "majority minority" society. By this they mean that the percentage of Whites in the population might dip below 50 percent. As Figure 10.1 shows, even the projections for 2050 do not suggest any such eventuality. Though the census bureau predicts European Americans will number just over half of the population by 2050, their 53 percent is more than twice as large as the next-largest racial group.

Table 10.1 Projected Population by Race, 2000–2050

Group	2000		2010	
White	196,670,000	71.4%	201,956,000	67.6%
Black	33,490,000	12.2%	36,483,000	12.2%
American Indian	2,048,000	0.7%	2,300,000	0.8%
Asian and Pacific Islander	10,620,000	3.9%	14,346,000	4.8%
Latino	32,479,000	11.8%	43,688,000	14.6%
Total	275,307,000	100%	298,773,000	100%
Group	2020		2050	
White	207,145,000	63.8%	212,991,000	52.8%
Black	41,549,000	12.8%	53,466,000	13.2%
American Indian	2,550,000	0.8%	3,241,000	0.8%
Asian and Pacific Islander	18,527,000	5.6%	35,760,000	8.9%
Latino	55,156,000	17.0%	98,229,000	24.3%
Total	324,927,000	100%	403,687,000	100%

Source: Population Projections Program, U.S. Census Bureau, "Projections of the Total Resident Population by 5-Year Age Groups, Race, and Hispanic Origin with Special Age Categories" (Washington, DC: U.S. Bureau of the Census, 2000).

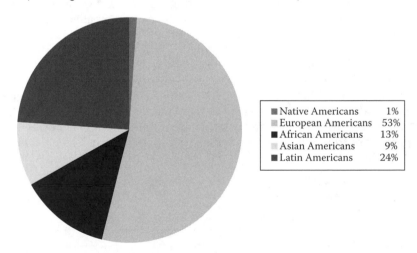

■ Native Americans	1%
▧ European Americans	53%
■ African Americans	13%
▨ Asian Americans	9%
■ Latin Americans	24%

Figure 10.1 Projected population by race in 2050, 403.7 million.

Immigration Issues

Is the United States the Immigrant Nation?

One of the most persistent features of the American self-image is that we are a nation of immigrants. As President Ronald Reagan said in 1981, "Our nation is a nation of immigrants. More than any other country, our strength comes from our own immigrant heritage and our capacity to welcome those from other lands."[6] Reagan was right in a sense. As I have contended throughout this book, immigration is one of the defining features of American history and identity. In fact, almost all Americans are immigrants or at least partially the descendants of immigrants—we are, metaphorically, almost all aliens. And as Chapter 8 described, there are a lot of immigrants in the United States now. Nonetheless, it would be a mistake to think that there are proportionately more immigrants in the United States at the dawn of the twenty-first century than there have been in earlier periods in U.S. history. In the censuses from 1860 to 1920, the foreign-born element in the U.S. population averaged nearly 14 percent. In the 2000 census, it was 11 percent. The figure was lower in the intervening years because of the racially inspired quota system. But today's numbers are still quite a bit lower than the American norm in the nineteenth century.[7]

Likewise, it would be a mistake to think that the United States is the immigrant nation *par excellence*. In fact, several nations around the globe have greater percentages of foreign-born people in their populations. To take just a few examples: El Salvador's foreign-born figure was above 10 percent in 2005; Sweden's was 11.3 percent in 2000; Canada's was 18.8; Australia's was 23.0.[8] Each of those countries began talking about immigration policy after the turn of the century, but in none of them was there the virulent anti-immigrant campaign that took shape in the United States in the 1990s.[9] What might account for the difference? One possibility is that Americans are just nastier than Canadians or Australians. More likely, it is that a much larger percentage of the American immigrants are Brown in a country that sees itself as primarily White. Table 10.2 shows the comparative percentages of migrants to Australia, Canada, and the United States by their regions of birth.

Half of Australia's foreign-born population is from Europe; for Canada, it is 41 percent; for the United States, just 16 percent. Both Canada and Australia have higher percentages of Asian immigrants, and Australia has a very large number of Pacific Islanders. Where the United States stands out is in the percentage of its immigrants who come from elsewhere in the Americas—some from Canada, certainly, but mainly from Mexico and points south. Fifty-four percent of U.S. foreign-born people are from the Americas, versus only 16 percent in Canada and a bare

Table 10.2 United States, Canadian, and Australian Foreign Born by Region of Birth, 2000–2001

Region	United States	Canada	Australia
Europe	16	41	51
Asia	26	37	29
Americas	54	16	4
Africa	3	5	4
Oceania	1	1	11

Numbers are percentages. Canada and Australia figures are from 2001; U.S. figures are from 2000.

Source: www.migrationinformation.org/globaldata/ (Web site of the Migration Policy Institute, a nonpartisan information-gathering service), March 8, 2006.

4 percent in Australia. At least some part of the animus of White Americans against immigrants documented in Chapter 9 must be on account of the origins, and perhaps the race, of those immigrants. There are other reasons as well.

Unauthorized Immigrants

No issue generated more passion in American politics in 2006 than illegal immigration.[10] The raw number of immigrants who are in the United States without papers currently is at an all-time high point. According to the Pew Hispanic Center, a foundation-funded, nonpartisan research agency, perhaps as many as 11.5 million unauthorized migrants lived in the United States as of March 2006. That was more than three times as many illegal immigrants as lived in the United States twenty-five years earlier, and nearly double the figure for 1997. Fifty-six percent of those people came from Mexico, 22 percent from other parts of Latin America, 13 percent from Asia, and 6 percent from Europe and Canada. Forty percent of the total had arrived in the United States since 2000; others had been in residence here longer, some since the 1980s or even earlier. Sixty-five percent of the people without papers held jobs, which meant that they made up 5 percent of the work force. Undocumented immigrants made up one-quarter of all farm workers; one-sixth of domestics; one-third of construction workers; and more than one-quarter of the people who worked in food processing and preparation.[11]

So as many as eleven or perhaps even 12 million unauthorized immigrants live in the United States. Do they constitute a problem for America? Possibly, but just what sort of problem depends a great deal on one's perspective. There are a lot of illegal immigrants, but not as many in proportional terms as there were a century ago. Is Diarmuid O'Scannlain a problem? His father fought with the Irish Republican Army in the Irish Revolution, then fled Northern Ireland to Canada when those provinces stayed in British hands. He crossed illegally into New York and raised a family, including his son Diarmuid. The son grew up to be a lawyer and judge, and is now the most conservative voice on the Ninth U.S. Circuit Court of Appeals.

Is Gabriel Martínez a problem? He described the circumstances of his coming to the United States:

> I was born in Jalisco, Guadalajara, Mexico, and came to the United States in 1972 as a seven-year-old immigrant with my brother as my only companion. My father had died and my mother could not raise seven children on her own, thus all of her children were sent off to be raised by various relatives in Mexico and the United States. My brother and I were sent to Southern California to live with our maternal grandmother. All this was not my choice. I had no desire to come to the United States. ...
>
> Due to my lack of English, I started kindergarten at the age of seven. At the age of eight, I was sent to work with my uncle in his flower fields. On the weekends I sold bunches of flowers on street corners to earn money and I have been working ever since. My grandmother insisted I attend private Catholic schools and I graduated from high school, but with no ambition other than to continue to work.

When he was interviewed in 2005, Martínez had married and was raising six children. He had only begun in his thirties to have an inkling that he might be capable

Figure 10.2   Gonsalo Lopez retrieves his basketball.

of doing something other than body labor. He had earned an associate's degree at a Texas community college and a B.A. from the University of Texas, and he was about to enroll in a master's program.

Is Gonsalo Lopez a problem? He is ten years old and lives in the muddy San Luis Rey River bottom near Oceanside, California. He lives with his family in a tent made out of plastic tarp with a mud floor and plays basketball on a homemade basket (Figure 10.2). His mother and sister work in the tomato fields nearby.

Are Kaprr and Titia a problem? They are a married couple, the parents of four children, three of whom were born in the United States. Kaprr and Titia came to the United States from Sierra Leone in 1991, overstayed their tourist visas, and settled down. Titia applied for asylum because of civil war back home, but was denied. They got jobs. In time they bought a house. Then, in 1997, the couple and other Sierra Leoneans were given temporary protected status: asylum for the foreseeable future, at least until the unrest at home might abate. In 2004, the Department of Homeland Security decided to begin cleaning up such people and sending them back where they came from. They let Titia and Kaprr know that they, along with other Sierra Leoneans, would have eight months to settle their affairs and return home. Then Kaprr got a permanent work visa, so he and the three younger children could stay. But Titia, her ailing mother, and the eldest daughter, a seventeen-year-old high school cheerleader, would have to go. If they remained, it would be as illegal immigrants and they would be subject to summary deportation.[12]

As for Kaprr and Titia, so for many immigrants who lack legal documents: life in America is difficult, and sometimes it is also dangerous. In the 1990s and especially after the turn of the century, as the United States fortified the border and it became harder and much more dangerous to cross, men who had come to the United States only temporarily to make some money faced a quandary: should they go back to Mexico or Central America, or should they send for their wives and children so that they could live together in the United States? The U.S. policy makers who erected the barriers clearly hoped they would go back, but higher wages, better schooling, and other attractions of life in the United States induced many to choose to reunite their families on this side of the border. In a 2005 Pew Hispanic Center survey, more than half of the illegal immigrant population were living with their families here, and fully 30 percent of the total had children who were U.S. citizens.[13]

Even immigrants with substantial roots in the United States lived a precarious existence. Anna Gorman described the plight of Paola Ordaz and her children:

> Paola Ordaz is feeling lost in America. Her husband, Alfredo Garcia, was arrested Wednesday with 28 co-workers during a raid at a Riverside-area factory run by IFCO Systems North America, where he made wooden pallets.
>
> He and his brother, Alejandro Garcia, both illegal immigrants, were immediately deported to Mexico as a result of a federal investigation into IFCO's hiring. They were among 1,187 workers taken into custody this week in a nationwide crackdown on the Dutch-based company, the largest manufacturer of wooden pallets in the United States. His wife said he's now in Tijuana and has called her twice but is afraid to cross the border illegally again for fear of landing in prison.
>
> Ordaz, 29, is left to care for three U.S.-born children under age 6, with no job, no money—not even enough for bus fare to rejoin her husband in Tijuana.[14]

Angie was a 2006 graduate of a high school in Illinois. She was class valedictorian, with a 4.7 grade point average. But she had no chance of going to college, because she was an illegal immigrant and did not have a social security number, so she could not get financial aid. Another woman worked hard at her inner-city high school, stayed away from drugs and gangs, graduated first in her class, and won a private scholarship to an Ivy League college. She was admitted to a top law school, but had to watch as others began their classes, because she, too, lacked papers and so could not get a loan to help with tuition. In 2001, California passed a law that allowed California residents from taxpaying families to pay in-state tuition and to qualify for state loans, whether or not they had immigration papers. Four years later, some out-of-state students who were U.S. citizens challenged this law in court (the outcome of the case is not yet clear). In 2002, four Arizona honor students went on a school field trip to a science fair in Buffalo, New York. In Arizona, no one questioned their status, but in Buffalo, four Mexican Americans stood out, and local officials asked to see their papers. They faced an immigration judge and the possibility of deportation. The point of all this is unclear. In the case of the four Arizona students, the United States loses out on their talents; it is a disaster for the students, as they are deported to a country they have never known; and the whole operation seems to be driven by little more than spite.[15]

Rhetorical Attacks

Some people in the United States just want unauthorized immigrants to go away—no matter when or how they came to the United States, no matter how much they have paid in taxes over the years, no matter how deeply entwined their lives are with American society, no matter whether their children are U.S. citizens, no matter how much they have to contribute here.

CNN's Lou Dobbs does a daily imitation of Fox News, railing against immigrants. In an essay for the *Arizona Republic* he wrote: "In the United States, an obscene alliance of corporate supremacists, desperate labor unions, certain ethnocentric Latino activist organizations and a majority of our elected officials in Washington works diligently to keep our borders open, wages suppressed and the American people all but helpless to resist the crushing financial and economic burden created by the millions of illegal aliens who crash our borders each year."[16]

Joining Dobbs's angry, apocalyptic vision is U.S. Rep. Tom Tancredo of Colorado. Tancredo's website rails against "the falsehood of birthright citizenship," with no sense of irony, despite his own family history. He declares that today's immigrants do not possess the same virtues that his own Italian immigrant grandparents had. He regards them as "criminals" and decries any path to citizenship as "amnesty." When the *Denver Post* ran an article about an honor student who came from a family without papers, Tancredo tried to have the family deported. He said that a reasonable response to a terrorist use of a nuclear weapon would be to bomb Mecca. He vowed to fight immigration and what he called the "cult of multiculturalism":

> I have always wanted to advance the agenda of limited government and enhanced individual freedom. ... I want our borders to be secure and those who have violated them to be deprived of the benefits lawful citizens enjoy, lest the concept of citizenship be rendered meaningless. I want immigrants seeking that citizenship to assimilate and sever their ties to their countries of origin. ... I want to do what I can to defend the West in the clash of civilizations that threatens humanity with a return to the Dark Ages.[17]

Dobbs, Tancredo, and others who don't like immigrants stress that immigrants without papers are breaking the law. Well, that's true. What they are doing is a violation. The question remains, what sort of lawbreaking is this? Is it equivalent to murder or arson? Or is it more like driving 62 in a 55 zone? No serious observer suggests that people who come to America without documents in search of jobs and a way to build their lives and feed their families are lawbreakers in the murder-and-arson sense. I don't know any certain way of judging the motivations behind immigrant-bashers' shrill screams about lawbreaking, but it is not hard to imagine that some of them, sometime in their lives, might have overstayed an expired parking meter, and perhaps even cheated on an expense account. Certainly, many of these same people thought Enron's Kenneth Lay was a business genius who committed minor but excusable indiscretions, and two decades earlier some of the same people hailed Oliver North as a "great American hero" for having lied to Congress about a matter of national security. It is hard to take seriously the lawbreaker charge against unauthorized immigrants. These people just don't like immigrants, especially Mexican immigrants. For them to call immigrants criminals is simply to inflame the policy discussion and obscure the real issues.[18]

Fortifying the Border

The usual solution that such people propose is to fortify the U.S. border with Mexico.[19] In 2005, the U.S. House of Representatives passed a bill that would erect a double fence along 700 miles of the U.S.-Mexico border; make being in the United States without papers a felony; make it a felony to help anyone without papers enter the country; establish mandatory sentences for immigration smugglers and for anyone who returned to the country without papers after having once been deported; fine employers up to $40,000 per violation for hiring undocumented workers; and impose a prison sentence of up to thirty years for any employer who is a repeat offender. Congressmember Tancredo would have gone further. His proposals included endorsing vigilante border patrols, deploying troops along the length of the border, denying all federal funds to any state that allowed in-state tuition for unauthorized immigrants, ending the family reunification feature of immigration visas, and changing the fundamental law of birthright citizenship.[20]

One of the fruits of the House bill was a move by the Bush administration to mollify their right flank by sending several thousand National Guard troops to do support work for the Border Patrol in the Southwest. Meanwhile, the Senate approved funding for 1000 more Border Patrol agents, raids were staged on workplaces across the country, and customs officers left their usual duty to hunt for illegal immigrants. Some politicians and private citizens proposed removing troops from the occupation of Iraq and redeploying them on the U.S.–Mexico border, apparently on the theory that they had had practice in the desert already.[21] Some U.S. citizens began taking the matter into their own hands. A group calling themselves the Minutemen began to take direct action against immigrants coming across the Mexican border without documents. In the spring and summer of 2005, a few hundred anti-immigrant activists brought guns, binoculars, cell phones, sunscreen, lawn chairs, and beer coolers to border areas, first in Arizona and then in California. President Bush called them "vigilantes" but they called themselves "American heroes." They promised not to shoot migrants, but only to call the Border Patrol when they spotted them. The group's founder, Jim Gilchrist, then became something of a wild card in California politics by running for the state senate from Orange County.[22]

The worst of the demagoguery is the claim that the U.S. border with Mexico needs to be militarized in order to prevent terrorism. Tom Tancredo's website proclaims, "A group of al Qaeda terrorists is attempting to infiltrate the United States from Mexico to conduct attacks in the country." The Minutemen's Gilchrist said that a border without a wall "is an invitation to terrorists who would bring us harm. It's a matter of losing security and losing the rule of law as a governing mechanism. We are literally being invaded and colonized." For all the bashing of Mexican immigrants in racist terms, no one dared assert that there are Mexican terrorists attacking Americans. In fact, on only two occasions have people accused of terrorism been arrested coming across the border—and in both instances it was the Canadian border. Yet we were doing almost nothing to increase security there; the northern border remains wide open except for a few checkpoints. All the 9/11 terrorists flew in on jumbo jets with tourist visas. Whatever sort of security problem unauthorized immigrants may present, is that problem soluble by fortifying the U.S. border with Mexico? Absolutely not. That persistent proposal—one that far predates the national security crisis that emerged after September 11, 2001—is little more than a racist dodge, an occasion for demagogues to engage in fear-mongering.[23]

The Minutemen were not the only private citizens who took it upon themselves to patrol the Mexican border. Hundreds of other would-be Texas Rangers entered the fray. In March 2003 Casey Nethercott and a group calling themselves Ranch Rescue caught two Salvadoran migrants, Edwin Alfredo Mancia Gonzales and Fatima del Socorro Leiva Medina, near the border in southern Arizona. They imprisoned the couple and, authorities charged, pistol-whipped Gonzales. The migrants later sued the Ranch Rescue vigilantes, with the support of the Southern Poverty Law Center. Nethercott ended up in prison for five years on a weapons violation, and in the civil suit a court awarded his seventy-acre ranch to Gonzales and Medina.[24]

The truth about the border is that it will always be, as it has always been, a zone of movement back and forth, not a line of separation. Carlos Gonzalez is a veteran Border Patrol officer on the Rio Grande. He has chased down and taken into custody thousands of paperless border crossers. His life is dedicated to the effort, but he knows it is in vain. He says: "We're never going to stop them, never. This was happening before I was born, and it will be happening long after I am gone. There is no way to shut the river down." The same is true for the rest of the border. The rhetoric about fortifying the border may help the careers of some American politicians, and it may feel satisfying to White racists who want to vent without having to own their racism, but it will not stop migration from our southern neighbors. It may kill some border crossers, but it will not solve any problem.[25]

Searching out the Undocumented

The border fortification effort got all the big press, but anti-immigrant activists at various levels have been taking a lot of other steps to harass undocumented migrants. In June 2004, U.S. Customs and Border Patrol officers made sweeps of immigrant neighborhoods across Southern California, many of them quite far from the border and inhabited mainly by American citizens of Mexican descent. They checked people for papers and hustled those they suspected of being unauthorized immigrants off to detention and possible deportation. Such suspicions, of course, were based on people's perceived nationality (that is, their race), so it was Mexican Americans who were targeted, whether or not they were in fact immigrants. Jim Mangia, director of St. John's Well Child and Family Center in Los Angeles, said: "There is no question that the raids spread fear and panic throughout the community. People were afraid to go to work, send their children to school and even visit the doctor. … Patients are afraid to leave their homes to pick up their diabetes medication. Parents are afraid to bring their children (many of whom are American citizens) into the clinic for immunizations." Esperanza H., a garment worker, said:

All of the garment workers were taken, regardless of their medical condition. Some were cancer patients and some of the women were pregnant. ... I felt afraid, frustrated and angry because I realized that I could have been one of the workers that were taken. ... I was too afraid to leave my house. I thought that no place was safe for the immigrant community, because they know exactly where to find us. They know where we live and work, the schools our children attend, the stores where we buy our food and the clinics where we get medical assistance. ... I am bothered that most of the detainees are Latino workers of low income, who may not know that they have rights.[26]

Federal officials stepped up deportation procedures, and thereby removed from the country many people who had been taxpaying, law-abiding residents for decades. They sharpened their targeting of employers who might hire people without papers. In 2006, they increased the penalties for people who made and sold fake ID cards (no doubt causing panic among underage college drinkers across the nation).[27]

Lawmakers and jurists cracked down on people without papers. In July 2006, Aurora Gonzalez asked Los Angeles Superior Court Judge Bruce Fink for a restraining order against her estranged husband, who was threatening to turn her over to immigration authorities if she did not come back to him. Fink ordered her out of his courtroom and said if she did not go he would have her deported himself. The U.S. government began to deport migrants, not just back to the border as previously, but to fly them deep into the interior so as to make their return more difficult. They began deporting longtime American residents, sick people, lone children. As Jennifer Chacon, a U.C. Davis law professor, said: "This concerns the people we should be the least concerned about. They are stable people with jobs: grandparents, parents, husbands. These people are not security threats."[28]

States and localities began harassing unauthorized immigrants. The poster city for this movement was Hazleton, Pennsylvania. Hazleton had been a town in decline after the closing of nearby coal mines. The population had dropped from 38,000 to 23,000 before Latinos and other immigrants began to move in from New York and New Jersey at the turn of the century and brought the number back up to 31,000. Latinos built more than fifty new businesses downtown and the population surge more than doubled the value of Hazleton homes. Yet these were brown people, and Hazleton had previously been all White—mainly Irish and Italian immigrants and their descendants. Mayor Louis Barletta began to rail against what he called an illegal immigrant crime wave (although crime had in fact gone down since the boom in Latino population) and took to wearing a bulletproof vest around town. In July 2006, Hazleton's city council passed the Illegal Immigration Relief Act, which declared that English would be the city's official language, that anyone applying to rent a dwelling would have to submit to a check of their citizenship status, that landlords who rented to illegal immigrants would be fined $1,000 a day, and that businesses who hired, rented to, or provided goods or services to illegal immigrants would lose their licenses. Said Daniel Jorge, a Dominican immigrant and realtor, "I'm sad. I loved it here. I never in my wildest dreams thought I would see this here in this city." Kim Resovsky said she and all the other White residents of Hazleton supported the new law. "The only ones who are against it are the Hispanics, and that's because it's against them."[29]

Anti-immigrant measures were passed by other states and localities. Protests against Mexicans standing on street corners selling their labor in Austin, Texas, and Orange, Redondo Beach, and Laguna Beach, California, led to laws banning day labor that were quickly overturned as unconstitutional. Police in Jaffrey, New Hampshire, took to arresting people they believed to be illegal immigrants on the charge of criminal trespassing, though a judge quickly put a stop to the practice. The Arizona electorate passed Proposition 200, which required proof of citizenship and photo ID for voting. Its aim was ostensibly to keep illegal immigrants from voting, but its main effect was to prevent thousands of U.S. citizens from exercising the franchise because they followed earlier practice and did not bring ID to the polling booth. The Arizona legislature passed bills prohibiting illegal immigrants from attending adult education classes, paying in-state tuition, or receiving child-care assistance; they barred local governments from spending funds on day labor centers that help immigrants find work; and they set up plans to build a private prison in Mexico to house illegal immigrants who were convicted of crimes. Governor Janet Napolitano vetoed the child-care and prison bills, but let the others stand.[30]

In San Bernardino, California, a petition drive tried to force a city council vote banning day labor centers, prohibiting renting to immigrants without papers, fining landlords who did, and declaring English the city language. The states of Colorado and Georgia passed laws banning non-emergency state services to anyone who could not prove he or she was a citizen. Avon Park, Florida, copied Hazleton's anti-immigrant ordinance. John Trumbo, the Sheriff of Umatilla County, Oregon, got creative: he sent a bill for $318,843 to Mexican President Vicente Fox, ostensibly to pay for the incarceration of illegal immigrants in his jurisdiction. Not to be outdone, the commissioners of Canyon County, Idaho, filed suit under racketeering laws against four companies that they said hired undocumented migrant workers. One California group that tried to mimic the Minutemen's publicity success called itself Save Our State. The brainchild of right-wing White power activist Joseph Turner, Save Our State went around Southern California lending rhetorical firepower to the border watchers, stirring up trouble in mainly Latino Baldwin Park, and helping organize the San Bernardino petition drive. Turner charged that people who objected to his tactics were "socialists" and that "They want to kick white people out of our country."[31]

A few localities extended themselves a bit toward immigrants who lacked documents. Utah and Tennessee approved laws that took away undocumented immigrants' driver's licenses, which could be used as valid identification, but they substituted driver's certificates, which could not be used as identification but would qualify holders for car insurance. Illinois and Wisconsin allowed immigrants who lacked documents to be included in state-supported housing loan programs. And the town of Maywood, California, offered itself as a sanctuary city for the undocumented. But, with the exception of Maywood's welcome, such efforts were backhanded at best, and they all paled in comparison to the anti-immigrant trend.[32]

It was reported in 2001 that, in the previous two years, Orange County, California, police departments had detained more than 4000 people whom they suspected of being unauthorized immigrants and turned them over to the Border Patrol for deportation. Some were arrested for soliciting day labor jobs, others for selling flowers on roadsides. Marcella Duque was stopped for having expired tags on her car; she and her fifteen-month-old daughter faced deportation to Colombia. Latino leaders called it racial profiling. Roberto Martinez of the American Friends Service Committee said: "It's racist; you can't call it anything else. They're not stopping white people and asking them for their papers."[33] This action by Orange County departments seems to have been self-generated, but soon the federal government got into the act, trying to recruit local law enforcement to help scour the country for immigrants without papers.

At first, outside of immigrant-bashing havens like Orange County, most police and sheriff's departments were reluctant to get into the business of checking the immigration status of people whom they apprehended. They reasoned that to become, in effect, an arm of immigration enforcement would make their jobs more difficult in immigrant communities. Yet a campaign of lobbying and financial pressure from the Department of Homeland Security gradually wore down their resistance, and several cash-strapped departments in localities with lots of immigrants finally buckled, took the money, and began screening the people they arrested for their immigration status. Los Angeles County Sheriff Lee Baca supported using local officers to enforce federal laws, saying, "How can we expect people to respect the law when we can't enforce our immigration laws?" He also pointed out that, in an era of repeated budget cuts, his department frankly needed the money. Former Los Angeles police commissioner Silvia Saucedo countered: "Once the police use immigration status only, what happens to due process, probable cause? ... We're stretched so thin, it's impossible to have the Los Angeles Police Department (LAPD) trained in federal procedures. It's not the business of the department." John Hensley, police chief of Costa Mesa, California, estimated that to use his department to enforce federal immigration laws would require him to add 30 to 40 officers to his force of 160 and cost the city millions of dollars per year. "I'm not sure how it is making Costa Mesa safer," he said.[34]

Here is how this move by the Department of Homeland Security fit into the larger picture of budgets and government spending. The federal government spent billions more than it had on fighting a war in Iraq and on Congress members' pet projects. At the same time, it drastically cut taxes on the very wealthiest Americans. Meanwhile, it cut federal allocations for roads, medical care, social welfare, and education, and pushed the responsibility for funding those items, even at reduced levels, onto states and municipalities. The states went through the same pattern (in California, for example, this meant taking some local tax proceeds away from counties and keeping them for the state). This left counties and cities across the country with ever more responsibilities and ever less money to meet them. They cut outlays for police, jails, and nearly everything else. Then Homeland Security offered money to local police and sheriff's departments if they would take on the task of looking for unauthorized immigrants. In time, a lot of departments took the money.[35]

All the anti-immigrant measures I have described above were taken with far greater vigor against Latinos generally, and Mexicans specifically, than against any other immigrant peoples. Those doing the targeting seldom distinguished between legal migrants and those without papers, between American-born citizens and immigrants. They simply targeted Mexicans, and Mexican Americans reacted with fear, depression, and anger.

In addition, the relentless bashing of Mexican immigrants and fortifying the border ran the risk of turning what had for generations been a calm relationship between friendly neighbors into a hostile encounter. The Mexican government has long acquiesced to U.S. wishes in almost everything, but there have been some signs in recent years of their patience wearing thin over the abuse of their citizens in the United States. For example, when two people died and twenty were injured at the end of a California Highway Patrol (CHP) chase of suspected undocumented immigrants in 2003, Mexican Consul General Rodulfo Figueroa accused the CHP of "gross negligence" for using spike strips in this and other pursuits that reached over 100 miles per hour. "You don't have to be a rocket scientist to know what the consequences are going to be, even if they don't hit the spikes." Even Vicente Fox, a staunch friend of the American president, nonetheless expressed outrage when, in another incident, Border Patrol officers shot across the border and killed a fleeing immigrant with bullets in the back. In those cases, the CHP and Border Patrol blamed the would-be migrants. Fox also called the House of Representatives' 2005 border fortification bill "shameful. ... To us, what has been decided in the United States Congress is a terrible sign that does not speak well of a country that calls itself democratic, and does not speak well for a country that calls itself a country of migrants."[36]

All these anti-immigrant measures may be comforting to some Americans. They may serve the political ambitions of demagogues. But the cost to the migrants is unacceptable in a civilized society. In 2005, several hundred people lost their lives trying to cross the U.S.–Mexico border, mainly because fences and Border Patrol officers drove them further and further into the desert. Thousands more were killed as they made their way across Mexico from their Central American homes. The tragedy of the entire situation is highlighted by the fact that it is utterly unnecessary. Most Americans thought that the Berlin Wall was a bad thing, because it kept people from moving to a place where they could live what they hoped would be freer, happier, and more prosperous lives. We celebrated when the wall came down and encouraged them to flood across the border. Yet many of us now want to build another wall to keep people away from what they hope will be freer, happier, more prosperous lives. There is a stunning hypocrisy at work here.[37]

The New Bracero Program

Another force in American politics has been taking a very different tack. For some years, American business leaders have been trying to get the U.S. government to create a new version of the Bracero Program. Their goal was to guarantee a dependable supply of workers in agriculture, food processing, and other low-wage, low-skill fields. Doing so, some hoped, would reduce the flow of undocumented workers by reducing the market for their labor. At the same time, bringing people in with documents that specified a fixed term would, they hoped, guarantee that one day those workers would go back where they came from.[38]

When George W. Bush assumed the presidency, creating a guest worker program in partnership with Mexican President Vicente Fox was the first item on his international affairs agenda. They were talking it up in the summer of 2001, when suddenly the September 11 attacks derailed national political discussions. In the wake of that disaster, Americans were fearful of foreigners and not in the mood to consider a program that might bring several hundred thousand more foreigners into the country each year. Presidents Bush and Fox attempted to bring the issue up again in 2004 but met a less than enthusiastic response. Then in 2005 Congress kick-started a new discussion of immigration policy by passing the build-a-fence-and-hunt-them-down plan described above.

President Bush and leaders of both parties in the Senate countered with a new version of the guest worker program that Bush and Fox had proposed five years earlier. This time, to mollify the anti-immigration people, they added stiff penalties for people without papers and their employers, as well as a 370-mile border fence. But the main features of the bill looked a lot like Bush and Fox's original proposals (and a bit like the Bracero Program of 1942 to 1964):

- a guest worker program for 1.5 million farmworkers, who would come for fixed terms but be eligible to earn legal permanent residency over time;
- 200,000 new temporary visas each year for low-skilled workers who would be required to go home at the end of their term;
- a long and difficult path to legal residency for those people who earlier had come without papers and who had been here at least five years;
- a provision that unauthorized migrants who had been here between two and five years could go back home and then reapply for legal entrance under one of these programs; and
- a requirement that anyone without papers who had been here less than two years simply had to leave.[39]

Predictably, the Senate and President's plan won support of the business and Latino communities. As Molly Ivins observed, the "Bush plan mainly aids business," because it would facilitate a regular supply of low-wage workers, primarily to agriculture but also to food processing, hotels and restaurants, and other employers. Typically, these are hard, dirty, low-paying jobs that in fact cannot find enough workers who are U.S. citizens (the 2006 harvests in Florida and California lay unpicked in the fields for want of sufficient workers, on account of the crackdown on undocumented migrants). The Chamber of Commerce supported the guest worker proposal. Surprisingly, labor leaders also supported elements of the new Bracero Program. The AFL-CIO weighed in on the positive side, apparently because they had discovered in the last decade that they could have success organizing hotel workers and others with large numbers of undocumented people among them. Generally speaking, labor and Latino leaders were more interested in the amnesty provisions, while businesspeople focused primarily on the guest worker program.[40]

Just as predictably, opposition came mainly from racial nativists. None was more clear on the subject than Pat Buchanan: "America is becoming Mexamerica. ... The immigration tsunami will make whites a minority in the U.S. ... Terrorists are among us as undocumented immigrants. ... Treat illegal immigration as an invasion and repel it. ... Stop the invasion from the south; limit immigration. ... Make English our official language. ... Use troops on borders to limit immigration. ... We're gonna lose our country." But less crude people adopted the same view. They may, like Buchanan, have had a racial agenda, but they usually framed their opposition to the Senate and the President's proposal as opposition to amnesty. Said Jim Oberweis, a cultural conservative and unsuccessful Republican Senate candidate: "The president's plan is just plain wrong. I want to be the voice for Illinois voters to tell the president we think illegal immigrants cannot be rewarded with amnesty."[41]

The American public at large did not have such strong feelings against amnesty for those undocumented people who had been living and working in the United States for a period of years. Several polls taken in 2006—by Gallup, Manhattan Institute/National Immigration Forum, *Los Angeles Times*/Bloomberg, *Time*, *Washington Post*/ABC News, CNN, NBC News/*Wall Street Journal*, and the Republican National Committee—all came to the same conclusion. Between two-thirds and three-quarters of the American public took the pragmatic position that it is a good idea to bring the stable, contributing, undocumented population onto the right side of the law through some kind of path to legal residency, with about one-quarter opposed.[42]

Steve Greenberg, cartoonist for the *Ventura County Star*, neatly summed the debate by characterizing what each party to the immigration debate is saying, alongside what they really mean:

> Republicans: It's about securing our borders from terrorists.
> (It's about securing our borders from too many Mexicans.)
> Democrats: It's about honoring our rich legacy of immigrants.
> (It's about honoring our rich windfall of Latino votes.)
> Business: It's important that we have workers for jobs Americans don't want.
> (It's important that we have workers at low wages to hold down costs.)
> Bush: Above all, we need to keep this debate civilized.
> (We need to keep this debate from converting Latinos into Democrats.)[43]

Such cynicism may be warranted. But consider the possibility that President Bush—on other issues an unbending hawk with a hard-right-wing agenda—may be acting on conscience here, as he did in vetoing federal funds for stem-cell research despite his being a minority position. In advocating a path to citizenship, he said that he wanted to show "the compassionate heart of the American people" to those who came to work; that "family values do not stop at the Rio Grande river"; and that "immigrants make us more, not less, American." Surely, his steady support of big business was part of his motivation, but there may have been a moral commitment at work here as well.[44]

Some Signs of Human Decency

Despite the fervor of the immigrant-bashers, Bush's possibly humanitarian concern is among the signs that suggest a more rational and humane approach may develop. In the winter of 2006, Los Angeles Cardinal Roger Mahony was one the first major public figures to speak back against the anti-immigrant mob. Noting that the U.S. bishops conference had supported a guest-worker program, legalizing the status of unauthorized immigrants, and increasing the number of visas for the families of current migrants, Mahony denounced the anti-immigrant movement as "hysterical." The cardinal said he would instruct his priests to refuse to ask immigrants to produce documents before serving them, as pending Congressional legislation seemed likely to require, even if it meant violating the law and going to jail. Mahony said:

> The war on terror isn't going to be won through immigration restrictions. ... The whole concept of punishing people who serve immigrants is un-American. If you take this to its logical, ludicrous extreme, every single person who comes up to receive Holy Communion, you have to ask them to show papers. It becomes absurd and the church is not about to get into that. The church is here to serve people. ... We're not about to become immigration agents. ... The church has always been in the forefront of welcoming waves of immigrants. This has been a constant theme of the church since the 1700s.

The cardinal reminded his flock that the Israelites were aliens in Egypt, and that both Old and New Testaments insist that believers have special care for strangers and aliens. "This is part of our heritage of God's care and concern for all peoples. At no point … is God asking us to build walls on borders."[45]

Not just religious leaders but some ordinary citizens began to stand up against those who would make hate a national policy. When immigration agents raided the Petit Jean Poultry plant in Arkadelphia, Arkansas, put plastic handcuffs on more than a hundred Mexican workers, and hauled them off for deportation, local citizens got angry at their government for abusing their friends and neighbors. They were a conservative, Bible-belt lot, but the meanness did not make sense to them. Said Sheriff Troy Tucker, "We take them into our public schools. We accept them into our churches. They play on our football, soccer teams. And then one day Immigration comes in and sweeps them all away." Krystle Williams helped a deported worker return to town and restart her life. She said of the immigration agents: "I think they were wrong. They should have just let them be." Arkadelphians helped their neighbors fight deportation, drove them to court, wrote pleas to political leaders, donated money, food and clothing, and took care of children while their parents were incarcerated. In time, about 60 percent of the town's Mexican residents returned. Arkadelphia was not Hazleton.[46]

Few Americans who are not themselves unauthorized immigrants know the situation of such people as well as Sonia Nazario, Pulitzer Prize-winning reporter for the *Los Angeles Times*. She rode on the tops of boxcars the length of Mexico and interviewed scores of migrants, former migrants, and would-be migrants throughout Mexico and Central America. Her analysis:

> Clearly, illegal immigration is out of control. … An estimated 850,000 people enter the U.S. illegally each year—more than double the number in the 1980s and early 1990s. … Certainly there are undeniable benefits to all this. Most people agree that U.S.-born workers won't do at least some of the backbreaking jobs that illegal immigrants take, especially for rock-bottom wages. … Immigrants' low wages keep some businesses from closing or going abroad in order to compete. … immigrant labor also lowers the cost of food and clothing for all of us, and it puts such things as child-care services within the reach of far more Americans than before. Immigrants bring new blood, ideas and ways of looking at things that drive creativity and spur advances. … And yet the downside is real too. Because they have lower incomes, immigrants and their U.S.-born children qualify and use more government services—including welfare [and public schools]—than the native-born. … pay one-third less taxes. … immigrant pay scales have lowered wages for the … neediest among the native-born.

Some of these contentions are hotly debated by other knowledgeable observers, but few would argue she is wholly off base. Nazario does stand out from the others, however, in her intimate contact with the lives and aspirations of actual unauthorized migrants. She offers this characterization of the present debate: "'Get tough' sums up one side in the debate, but it's a policy that has had little success to date. Starting in 1993, the number of agents patrolling the border and the amount of money spent on enforcement tripled. … Yet the number of illegal immigrants in the U.S. only grew more quickly. Why? More immigrants came and more stayed for good, knowing that entry and reentry would be more difficult and costly in the future." The earlier Bracero Program and previous amnesties did nothing to halt, and may have encouraged, subsequent unauthorized immigration, according to Nazario (again, there are differences of opinion among experts). Her solution is to address the underlying problem:

> [T]here is only one way to stem illegal immigration—at its source, in Mexico, Guatemala, Honduras, and wherever people are desperately poor. ... Time and again, I met migrants willing to endure months of danger and misery to reach the U.S. As long as they had any hope of success, they refused to go home. Instead of arguing about green card rules and wall heights, the U.S. should be formulating a new foreign policy. It should be aiming resources and diplomacy at improving conditions in Mexico and the few Central American countries whose migrants make up more than two-thirds of those in the U.S. illegally. Trade policies could give preference to goods from immigrant-sending countries to spur job growth. More aid could be invested there. ... [M]ost immigrants would rather stay in their home countries with their extended families, with everything they know, than take the enormous risks required to cross the border and to make a new life here. ... [I]t wouldn't take radical changes in their countries to keep them at home.[47]

Nazario is probably right, but such political changes will be hard to accomplish.

In March and April 2006, while the House and Senate were politicking, massive demonstrations erupted.[48] First, seemingly out of nowhere, between 500,000 and 1.3 million people (depending on who was estimating crowd size) took to the streets of Los Angeles on March 25. High school students and men in business suits, young mothers pushing strollers, Korean War veterans and grandmothers. Many were Mexican and Central American immigrants, documented and undocumented. Others were American-born Latinos. Many others were White or Asian or Black or Indian—college students, office workers, pastors, union members, and soccer moms. The atmosphere was familial and festive, not confrontational or hostile, although some Anglo pundits professed to feel threatened by Mexican flags amid the stars and stripes, and perhaps by Mexican music.[49] Other groups kept marching in Los Angeles and across California for several days thereafter.

Within two weeks, the demonstrations had spread across the country and become part of a national campaign for immigrants' rights. On April 10, more than 1 million people organized by churches, immigrants' rights groups, and labor organizations took to the streets in more than 100 cities on both coasts and all across the nation's heartland. Police estimated 180,000 marched in Washington, D.C.; 100,000 in New York and a similar number in Phoenix; 50,000 each in Houston and Atlanta—and 4,000 in Lincoln, Nebraska; hundreds in Tyler, Texas, Garden City, Kansas, Jonesborough, Tennessee, and Pensacola, Florida.[50]

On May 1, more than 1 million Americans turned out across the nation in support of immigrants' rights, a guest worker program, and a clear path to citizenship, and in opposition to the restrictions passed by the House.[51] Police estimated the numbers at 300,000 in Los Angeles, 400,000 in Chicago, 75,000 in Denver, 30,000 in Houston, 50,000 in the San Francisco Bay Area—and 2,000 in Las Vegas, 8,000 in Salem, Oregon, 1,000 in Detroit, and 20,000 in Orlando. The goal was to demonstrate how essential immigrants are to American economic life by skipping work on that day and marching instead. Tens of thousands of employers closed down or reduced the scope of their operations so that workers could march. Mike Lee closed his garment factory in Los Angeles Koreatown because most of his employees were Latino immigrants. And then he joined them in the march, saying, "I am also an immigrant."[52]

Many of the marchers were Latinos. "I want to come out of the shadows," said Josefina Cordoba. Jose Abrego asked, "If we didn't come, who will build the houses? We're not flowers. We're not asking to be treated delicately. We just want respect." Simon Vega left school in Lake Station, Indiana, to attend a rally in Chicago. He said: "I came here for solidarity, and everybody's an immigrant. It started at Ellis Island in New York. We want our opinions to be out there as well. Even though I'm not an immigrant, I want to help out the people."[53]

Many were not Latinos. Jose Delgado, a Chicago construction worker, said: "This is not just about Mexicans. It doesn't matter what color your skin is or what language you speak. It's about all immigrants. My struggle, and my family's struggle, is the same as what the Irish felt, what the Poles felt, what the Chinese felt. Now, we're all in the same boat." The Chicago rallies were attended by hundreds of Koreans and Chinese, and also a rowdy contingent calling themselves the Chicago Celts for Immigration Reform. Senator Barack Obama said: "To those who think we can simply close off the borders and deport, let me say this: There is no reason to fear people who have come here for the same reason as generations of Americans. They want a better future for their children." Dov Charney, president of American Apparel, the largest garment factory in the United States, and an American of European descent, gave his 3300 workers the day off with pay so they could attend the march, saying: "This is part of human history. Immigrants are Americans—that's the point. They are future Americans. We need to embrace immigrants and say, 'Hey, this is what makes LA so exciting'" (Figure 10.3). Stockbroker Dave Standifer marched in Denver. He said, "Anyone who wants to come in and work who is not considered a threat should be allowed a green card."[54]

The marchers were bolder people than any non-English immigrants America had seen in a while. Ruben Arita, a construction worker and unauthorized immigrant who joined the Washington, D.C., demonstration April 10, said: "We want to be legal. We want to live without hiding, without fear. We have to speak so that our voices are listened to and taken into account." Jaime Contreras, a former illegal immigrant from El Salvador who had achieved citizenship, said: "We're sending a strong message that we are people of dignity. All that we want is to have a shot at the American dream." Some demonstrators went so far as to lay claim to the legacy of the African American civil rights movement. Fabrian Rodriguez, an April 10 marcher and undocumented migrant from Mexico, said: "We are in the situation that Rosa Parks was in several years ago. Enough is enough." On May 1, Candido Henriquez carried a sign that said: "We are not criminals. Why do they treat us like animals? We are workers and we deserve respect." Los Angeles Mayor Antonio Villaraigosa said on May 1: "I'm mayor of all the people. But without question, I'm also someone who is a proud American, [and] also proud of where my family came from. I've never been shy about the fact that these people out here want to be part of the American dream. I support them." Marchers chanted: "Hoy marchamos, mañana votamos" (Today we march, tomorrow we vote) and "Aqui estamos y no nos vamos" (We're here and we're not leaving).

The movement harnessed the talents of thousands of activists. One prominent leader was Jesse Diaz, Jr., a fourth-generation Mexican American, one of seven children who grew up in a Seventh-Day Adventist family in Chino, California. After a troubled youth he got on an upward track in his twenties. He attended community

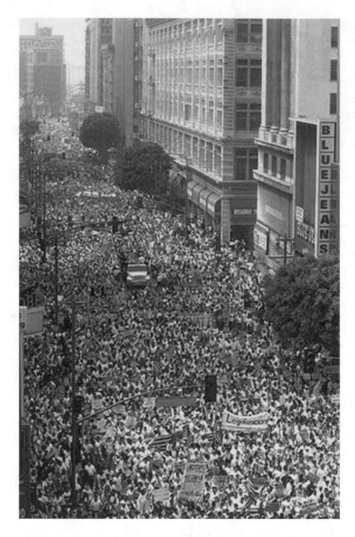

Figure 10.3   The May 1 March in Los Angeles.

college east of Los Angeles in the late 1990s and then Pitzer College on a scholarship, and ultimately found his way into a doctoral program in sociology at UC Riverside. Along the way he supported himself, his wife, and four children with day labor as a gardener. He was one of the organizers of the March 25 and April 10 marches, and a driving force behind the May 1 boycott.[55]

The demonstrators were not defying the law or other Americans. They were calling on America to be its better self. They were saying, as their blue banners proclaimed, "No Human Is Illegal" and "We Are America." They were claiming a place in American society, asking for the right to participate fully in the life of the country where they lived, where their children were born and were citizens, and where their toil contributed mightily to the lifeblood of the economy. The *New York Times* opined, "[T]hese crowds clearly had internalized at least one pillar of the American way: that peaceful dissent can spur a government to action."

The huge demonstrations caught everyone (even the organizers) by surprise. People who were supposed to be timid had stepped out of the shadows and politely claimed a place in American society. Some right-wing voices—Lou Dobbs on CNN, all the people at Fox—professed to be disgusted. Fox News anchor Brit Hume called the demonstrations "a repellant spectacle." But others, even among the most conservative leaders, recognized that something had changed in American politics, something that perhaps had been changing unacknowledged for quite some time. South Carolina Republican Senator Lindsey Graham suggested that politicians who adopted Hume's or Tancredo's posture were likely to lose out over the long run: "I understand clearly that the demographic changes are real in America and how we handle this issue in terms of fairness will be very important for the future of both parties. Those who believe that they have no political vulnerability for the moment *don't understand the future*" (italics added).

What Do Immigrants Cost?

One of the recurring points of contention with regard to immigrants—both those with documents and those without—is whether they are a net boon to or a net drag on the economic fortunes of other Americans.[56] There are some who insist that the economic impact of immigrants is mostly negative, and that this is especially the case for unauthorized immigrants. Some, like Roy Beck and Otis Graham, are frankly racist and hysterical. The sentiment of such people seems to be either that Mexicans, Latinos, and Asians are inappropriate racially and culturally to be Americans (this is not an economic argument, but somehow it leaks into their economic analysis) or that, in the words of Haydee Pavia, "We don't want them mooching off our tax dollars" (which is, more or less, an economic argument).[57] Others, however, like George Borjas, are careful economists who count up the benefits of immigrants to the economy as a whole, and then subtract several areas of cost—education and health care being the two largest. Of special concern to Borjas is the impact of immigrants on the economic fortunes of other low-skill, low-income economic groups, particularly the Black working class. Concludes Borjas:

> The economic impact of immigration is essentially a distributional one. Immigration shifts wealth away from those who compete with the skills and abilities that immigrants bring into the country, and toward those who employ or use those immigrant resources. As with many redistribution schemes, the people who lose from immigration tend to be quite diffused—there are many of them, they are dispersed geographically, and they are not well organized. In contrast, the winners are much more concentrated and better organized—many immigrants tend to be employed in a few industries, and employers in those industries probably gain substantially.

That is, big business reaps most of the gains from immigration, by being able to hire workers at substandard wages. There is merit to Borjas's argument.[58]

On the other side stand a number of economists who think that immigrants—including (and perhaps even especially) undocumented ones—are a boon to the U.S. economy. The most prominent of these was the late Julian Simon, but there are many others. Simon was probably the most careful economist to work in this area, and was an extreme conservative in all economic matters, yet he concluded after exhaustive study that immigrants were a substantial net benefit to the U.S. economy, even to working-class African Americans.[59]

Drawing on all the studies, of what can we be reasonably certain with regard to the economic consequences of immigration in contemporary America?

The immigrants of recent decades had a bimodal distribution as to education: some, like Filipinos, Koreans, and South Asians, had higher education levels than the national average; others, mainly unauthorized migrants from Mexico and Central America, had substantially lower education levels. Immigrants in general had somewhat lower incomes than did other Americans, but the gap was much larger for the undocumented than for those who came with visas. Immigrants' incomes came closer to those of other Americans as they spent more years in the United States.

Immigrants—including undocumented immigrants—paid as large or larger percentages of their income to the government in taxes than did native-born Americans, if one controls for income level. That is, rich immigrants tended to pay as much or more in taxes as did rich natives, and poor immigrants tended to pay as much or more in taxes as did poor natives. Of course, a higher percentage of immigrants than natives were poor, so that pushed the tax disparity between immigrant and native back to about even.

Contrary to the assumptions of many Americans, immigrants—including undocumented immigrants—actually used emergency rooms and prisons *less* frequently than did the native born, and so they were less of a burden on taxpayers in those areas. Immigrants' children did not cost more to educate than did the children of native-born Americans.[60]

Nelson Lim's study of the employment patterns of African Americans and immigrants found that, because they were not working in direct competition so much as in parallel sectors of the economy, immigrants did not in fact increase the unemployment level or depress the wages of working-class African Americans. Other studies, however, suggested that unauthorized immigrants might have depressed working-class Black incomes by as much as 5 percent. The range of estimates by careful economists was between "little effect" and "only a small adverse effect" on the wages of native-born Americans.[61]

Studies were unanimous in their conclusion that immigrants, including those without documents, were a boon to the health of the overall economy. California, which had the largest percentage of recent immigrants and of the undocumented, should have felt the negative impact of immigrants, if there was one, more than other states. Yet California's economy grew faster than the national average over the period 1990 to 2005. Job growth was greater. Average wages rose faster. The poverty rate declined more rapidly. Unemployment declined more rapidly than the national average. All those immigrants, and all the undocumented—a higher percentage in California than anywhere else—seem not to have had the negative effects that some predicted.[62]

There is a glitch in this generally positive picture of the economic impact of immigrants. That is, while "The majority of tax revenues paid by immigrants go to the federal government, ... the largest share of public service costs related to immigration are at the state and local level. The fiscal balance [is] positive at the federal level, but negative at the state and local government levels." Surely, this is the sort of issue that ought to be addressed.[63]

Those economists who find immigration to have negative economic consequences tend to leave out the long-term costs and contributions over the lives of the immigrants and their children. Those who consider both short- and long-term consequences inevitably see immigration in a more positive light. Wrote Simon: "The costs of schooling are somewhat higher for immigrants after the first few years in the U.S., because their families are younger than native families, on average. But when we include public retirement programs—Social Security, Medicare, and the like—immigrant families on average are seen to receive much less total welfare payments and public services than do average native families." Students of the California economy wrote: "In 20 years, today's immigrants will be more experienced and most will still be in the workforce. Their children will be out of school and in the workforce. ... The total fiscal impact of today's immigrants and their children includes current fiscal effects and future fiscal effects." Peter Francese wrote in the *Wall Street Journal*:

> Paying for the income security and medical needs of the elderly while at the same time improving the educational opportunities and well-being of children will squeeze future U.S. workers in the grip of higher federal payroll taxes, state taxes and local property taxes. ... We cannot wait 20 years to see what will happen when the baby boomers retire and ask what happened to their Social Security trust fund. The U.S. needs to admit more immigrants now to get us out of the demographic bind.[64]

There is another fiscal issue that the economists do not address, but that has begun to concern students of the law. They point out that it may hurt the U.S. economy more to spend a lot of money trying to stop migrants from entering than we can possibly afford. Charles Lindner, past president of the Los Angeles Criminal Bar Association, writes:

> What happens after an immigrant is arrested? U.S. District Judge Robert C. Brack puts it another way: "You can add Border Patrol agents, but if you do, you'd better think [downstream]. You'd better think marshals; you'd better think prosecutors, probation officers and pretrial services officers, defense lawyers, judges and clerk's staff—all of those things." ... If just 1% of the estimated 11 million illegal immigrants were arrested and convicted under the proposed [House] law, the Bureau of Prisons would be overwhelmed. In the last three years, it added more than 11,000 inmate beds. Imprisoning the new felons would require 110,000 more beds. New prisons would cost billions of dollars. ... Tough talk on immigration is cheap.[65]

On balance, it seems reasonable to conclude that immigrants amount to a very large net benefit to the United States economy as a whole. In those states and localities with very large numbers of very recent, working-class immigrants, there may be some higher costs for medical care and educating immigrants' young children over the short term. But over the lives of those immigrants and their children, the taxes they pay and the other economic contributions they make will vastly outweigh any initial costs.

Homeland Insecurity[66]

We live in an era of homeland insecurity. I mean that in two senses. First, many of the steps taken by our government since the disasters of 9/11 have stemmed from our feelings of insecurity. Second, those same steps have also created insecurity, both for the country as a whole and for the people they have targeted. The homeland security efforts of the U.S. government and the fears of the American people have fallen especially hard on immigrants, and most especially hard on those from the Middle East.[67]

In the weeks after 9/11, Arab Americans, Americans who were adherents of Islam, and people who just "looked Middle Eastern" came in for many of the same kinds of treatment that Japanese Americans suffered in 1941 and 1942, to wit:

- An elderly woman in the Los Angeles area was hauled out of her car and beaten so badly she ended up hospitalized. Her offense? Wearing the hijab.
- A Sikh American was hunted down and murdered in his gas station in Mesa, Arizona.
- An American Christian who fled his native Egypt two decades earlier partly because of religious persecution was slaughtered in his San Gabriel, California, grocery store.
- More than 1200 people of Middle Eastern origin were arrested, some on charges that were extremely specific and that might have led to convictions for terrorist involvement had they been proved true, others on the vaguest sorts of guilt-by-association thinking. None led to convictions.
- Across the country, gangs of non-Middle-Eastern-descended Americans attacked people they called "rag-heads" and "sand niggers" verbally and physically.
- A light-skinned African-American woman was accosted with her baby in a Ventura, California, supermarket and asked by her White fellow citizen, "How does it feel to have everyone hate *your kind*?"
- On a Pennsylvania highway a Sikh man was shot by another motorist.
- In Seattle a mosque was torched and worshippers were shot at.
- Throughout the land, Muslim women and men (and Sikhs and others) changed the way they dressed or stayed home, not traveling for fear of being assaulted or killed.
- In Dallas, a Pakistani grocer was shot dead.
- In Salt Lake City, a curry restaurant was fire-bombed.
- In suburban Los Angeles, two White men followed a Chicano home, chased him into his house, and beat him because they thought he "looked Arab."
- In Minneapolis, passengers on an airliner refused to take off until an Afghani refugee family was removed from the plane.
- Outside San Diego, a Sikh woman stopped at a traffic light was assaulted by two knife-wielding men who shouted, "This is what you get for what you've done to us!" and "I'm going to slash your throat," which one of them then did. She barely survived.

That was just in the few weeks following 9/11. It did not end there. More than a year later, on February 22, 2003, a gang of twenty men shouting "White power!"

attacked an eighteen-year-old Arab American boy, Rashid Alam, on a street in subur-ban Yorba Linda, California. Armed with golf clubs and baseball bats, they stomped him, jumped on his head with both feet, leaving him with a fractured jaw and mul-tiple facial bones broken.[68]

A lot of the harassment was not physical but rhetorical, yet it terrorized its victims. San Francisco schoolchildren were mocked by their classmates and even by their teachers because they were Muslims. Rev. Jerry Vines, a former president of the Southern Baptist Convention, told his fellow Baptists: "Islam is not just as good as Christianity. … Islam was founded by Muhammad, a demon-possessed pedo-phile. … Allah is not Jehovah either. Jehovah's not going to turn you into a terrorist." Right-wing cupcake Ann Coulter wrote that "We should invade their countries, kill their leaders, and convert them to Christianity" and "Deport one million Muslims." Anti-Muslim journalist Daniel Pipes said of Muslims, including American Muslims, that "Many of them are peaceable in appearance, but they all must be considered potential killers." Patrick Buchanan used 9/11 as an occasion for gratuitous immi-grant-bashing: "Our enemy, we are told, is Osama bin Laden. But though he may be the instigator and financier of terror, the war crimes of Tuesday last were carried out by men who live among us. The enemy is already inside the gates. How many oth-ers among our 11 million 'undocumented' immigrants are ready to carry out truck bombings, assassinations, sabotage, skyjackings?" Arab and Muslim American students at the University of Colorado found graffiti spray-painted on the library's columns: "Arabs Go Home," "Nuke Sandniggers," and "Blow Up Afghanistan." Four Muslim students at Orange Coast College in California, when they objected to their instructor characterizing Muslims as "terrorists," "murderers," and "Nazis," found themselves surrounded by sixty classmates, some of whom shouted, "Go back to where you came from."[69]

Muslim scholars—and scholars thought to be Muslims—came in for special abuse. The Department of Homeland Security prevented Swiss scholar Tariq Rama-dan from taking up the post he was offered at Notre Dame. Right-wing bloggers like Daniel Pipes and Campus Watch threatened Yvonne Haddad, a distinguished Arab American sociologist, a Christian, because she wrote several books about Muslims in the West. Several university professors, not all of them Arab or Muslim Ameri-cans, reported being disciplined by their departments and forbidden to speak about the Middle East and because they did not always support Israel.[70]

It was not just private citizens and institutions who were harassing Arab and Muslim Americans. Government authorities and businesses engaged in frank racial profiling. The Census Bureau gave the Department of Homeland Security special reports on the locations of Arab Americans, tabulated by the countries of their ori-gin or ancestry. The FBI spied on a prominent Palestinian American English profes-sor, Edward Said. On Christmas Day 2001, Walied Shater, a Secret Service agent of Arab American descent, was removed from an American Airlines flight on his way from Baltimore to Dallas where he was to protect President Bush. He was carrying his badge, and he had filed all the proper paperwork for the gun he carried, but he was an Arab and carried a book on Arab history, so he was detained. Virginia police demanded that college student Faiza Mohammed remove her head scarf and searched her car without a warrant. Louisiana Congressmember John Cooksey said that any airline passenger wearing "a diaper on his head" should be "pulled over" for questioning, and that "We know the faces of terrorists and where they're from. Terrorist profiling is essential for our nation's security."[71]

It is important to remember that there are ways in which the abuse of Arab and Muslim Americans in the 2000s is not like the abuse heaped on Japanese Americans in the 1940s. No one is talking about concentration camps for all Arab and Muslim Americans, partly because the Japanese American precedent is on a lot of people's minds (although the idea did cross many policy makers' minds right after the Oklahoma City bombing). In a cabinet meeting shortly after September 11, President Bush is reported to have looked at Transportation Secretary Norm Mineta, who as a boy was a prisoner in a World War II concentration camp, and reminded his colleagues that they must not do to Arab and Muslim Americans what had been done to Mineta and his family.[72]

Yet there is prejudice aplenty in our time. Crime novelist Andrew Klavan went further than most Americans would, but his sentiments underlay a lot of peoples' feelings about the racial-cultural evil of Muslims and the dispensability of civil rights in their case:

> Draft Hollywood. The nation needs more gung-ho, patriotic war movies that celebrate our fight against Islamo-fascists. ... We need some films celebrating the war against Islamo-fascism in Afghanistan and Iraq—and in Iran as well, if and when that becomes necessary. We need films like those made during World War II. ... Today we face an enemy in the grip of a belief system just as evil, just as destructive in its intent, as the system we fought back then. ... When war comes, as it always will, and when it is justified, as it is now, some nuances and shades of gray have to be set aside.[73]

Surely, that is the way many Americans see the matter.

We have seen over these years an unusual phenomenon: the racialization of a religious identity. We saw this once before in Chapter 6, in the ways that Jews were treated by non-Jewish Americans a century ago. I described in Chapter 9 how Arab Americans have long been viewed, along with Asians, as fundamentally foreign to the United States. No matter how long they have been here, they are not Americans; they are identified in the minds of other Americans with the places from which their ancestors came, to a degree that does not happen to Irish or French or British Americans. Part of the source of the difference has been the image that Arab Americans are not Christians. Never mind that more than half of Arab Americans *are* Christians; they are seen as non-Christians, and that attribution of a foreign religious identity adds to their racial foreignness.

We can see this at work in the stories of a British national and two native-born Americans: Cat Stevens, James Yee, and Brandon Mayfield. Cat Stevens is British, but was in and out of the United States freely in the 1970s, when he was one of the most popular rock musicians in the English-speaking world. Then in 1977 he converted to Islam, and two years later he took the name Yusuf Islam. He went on to start a school in Britain and become an international speaker on behalf of a peaceful branch of Islam. In 2004, Homeland Security officials detected his name on a passenger manifest and diverted his Washington-bound plane to Bangor, Maine. Here was a White guy who, because he had become a Muslim, became *persona non grata* in the United States, even though he denounced terrorism and every form of extremism.[74]

James Yee got into even more trouble. Yee was a third-generation Chinese American from the New Jersey suburbs, a former Boy Scout, a West Point graduate from a military family who served in Germany and Saudi Arabia. After he converted to Islam he became one of the U.S. Army's first Muslim chaplains and was assigned to minister to inmates at Guantanamo Bay. While there he witnessed what he regarded as abusive treatment of Muslim prisoners and spoke up on behalf of his flock to the Army brass (an act that was part of his duty as chaplain). They promptly accused him of "espionage, mutiny, aiding the enemy," and other charges and they held him in solitary confinement for two and a half months. They alleged he was part of a spy ring and that he had stolen military secrets. Eventually, they court-martialed him on assorted other trumped-up charges, which they dropped quietly six months later without comment. Yee's battalion commander said the chaplain was accused "because of his race and faith."[75]

Brandon Mayfield is a pink-cheeked young Portland lawyer. A convert to Islam, his fingerprints were in the FBI data bank because the state of Oregon licensed him to practice law. When Spanish police found a fingerprint on a bag of bomb-making materials in the aftermath of the terrorist bombings that occurred in Madrid in 2004, they sent pictures of the print to law enforcement agencies around the world. The FBI quickly decided that the fingerprint was Brandon Mayfield's. They told the Spanish police they had their man and sent a picture of Mayfield's fingerprint over the wire to Spain. The Spanish said no, the fingerprints were nothing close to a match. The FBI persisted, picked up Mayfield, and held him for two weeks before they let him go. The FBI inspector general investigated and reported that the FBI fingerprint examiners "were improperly influenced by knowledge of Mayfield's religion when they made the identification. ... One of the examiners candidly admitted that if the person identified had been someone without these characteristics, like the 'Maytag repairman,' the laboratory might have revisited the identification with more skepticism and caught the error." The FBI apologized, and Mayfield was left, like Yee, to pick up the pieces of his life.[76]

Muslims and other non-Judeo-Christian religious leaders and institutions have been finding themselves pushed out of public life, even in liberal, tolerant parts of the country. In 2004, organizers of the annual Washington County Mayors' Prayer Breakfast decided to bar Shariar Ahmed, president of Bilal Mosque in suburban Beaverton, Oregon, from offering a prayer. Later that year, Muslims across the country lowered the profile and quieted the fundraising for their annual Ramadan celebrations. Meanwhile, Muslims met more and more opposition to plans for building new mosques. The opposition spread to Hindu and Buddhist temples as well. Opponents of a suburban Los Angeles Hindu temple complained that the building "would turn Chino Hills into a 'Third World city' and a haven for terrorists."[77]

Some may object that this is religious, not racial targeting and discrimination. But there is leakage between the two categories. Anti-Muslim activists attack Yvonne Haddad because they assume she is a Muslim, although she is a Christian; they do so because she is an Arab American and because she speaks up for Muslims. Yusuf Islam, James Yee, and Brandon Mayfield are not Arabs, but they are treated as Arabs because they are Muslims. In our time, Muslim identity has been racialized by its opponents, even more viciously than Jewish identity was racialized a century ago.

How is all this affecting Arab and Muslim Americans, and others who are mistaken for being Arab and Muslim? Everyone to whom I have spoken is scared, although they are doing their best to cope with an insecure situation. Rosina Hassoun wrote in the wake of revelations of the abuse of Muslim inmates in Abu Ghraib prison: "The ability to dehumanize in this way is incomprehensible. A simple apology for crimes against humanity would not be acceptable if these prisoners had been American or white. ... Arabs have been characterized as barbarians in contrast to civilized Westerners." She confessed to be affected by "feelings of extreme alienation and isolation of Arab and Muslim Americans at this time, coupled with feelings of shame (because America is still, after all, our country too)."[78]

Jaideep Singh is a Sikh American whose ancestors came from the Punjab—that is, he is neither Arab nor Muslim. Yet he frequently is attacked verbally and sometimes physically for his turban and beard. He reveals his emotions as he tells the stories of five Men of Profile, as he calls them. Two were Sikh men, U.S. citizens, who were pulled off an airplane and detained by police, together with an Egyptian and a Latino, because the four were swarthy and had used the same restroom during a flight (the plane had only two restrooms). The other three were Muslim American medical students. A White woman said she heard them talking suspiciously in a coffee shop. She reported this to the Florida highway patrol, who mounted a manhunt, closed down an interstate highway, and arrested the three men. The subsequent investigation proved the men were just medical students and had no link to terrorism. They received no apology, but the White woman who turned them in got a commendation from Florida Governor Jeb Bush. Singh wrote:

> What were the true crimes of these five Men of Profile? Essentially, making white people uncomfortable with their mere presence—a presence defined in many white minds by their racialized identities. ... MOP do not have the same rights as other Americans. Their civil liberties, indeed the very freedom of these MOP, can be suspended, revoked, or circumscribed on the whim of virtually any white person. They can be fired from their jobs, thrown in jail without their families being told where they are being held, or even the charges against them. ... They can also be deported through a secret hearing. ... A crack has appeared in the nation's collective moral opposition to continuing use of race as a law enforcement tool, to suppress people of color and sustain white supremacy.[79]

Rosina Hassoun is more hopeful: "At the same time, it must be remembered that there are truly wonderful and culturally sensitive Americans who are as deeply disturbed at all of this as are Arab and Muslim Americans. The true test of whether the United States is an open, humane, and pluralistic democracy will be determined by the degree that the voices of decency prevail."

Patriot Games

After the tragedies on September 11, the Bush administration acted quickly to remake the law of the land. Their primary instrument was the USA PATRIOT Act.[80] It was passed by Congress without full hearings or even a complete reading, and signed by the president six weeks after September 11. The law bore the unwieldy title Uniting and Strengthening America by Providing Appropriate Tools Required to Intercept and Obstruct Terrorism Act, apparently with the aim that it would be known by its acronym, hence anyone who opposed it would be thought unpatriotic (a clever branding strategy indeed). As a *Chicago Tribune* cartoon put it: "In our polling nearly 60% of the public supports the Patriot Act. It drops around 35% when we tell them what it actually does."

The act gave U.S. Attorney General John Ashcroft, his successor Alberto Gonzales, and the newly created Department of Homeland Security virtually unlimited authority to investigate, detain, and deport whomever they liked. The act contained some sensible updates of law enforcement powers, such as broadening wiretap rules to allow for cell phones, removing barriers to communication between intelligence gatherers and law enforcement, and expanding powers to track down money laundering. But it also allowed the Justice Department to trample on the constitutional rights of U.S. citizens and, especially, of immigrants. It defined terrorism much more broadly for noncitizens than for citizens. It attempted to deny people who were not U.S. citizens the rights to free speech, political association, due process, and privacy to which they were entitled under the Constitution. As David Cole wrote, it "facilitates preventive law enforcement, but by the same token it also facilitates the punishment of innocents and the repression of political dissent." It meant that the government was free to detain or deport summarily anyone who was a member of Al Qaeda. But it also empowered them to do the same to anyone who was a member of or spoke in favor of any organization that had ever used violence. Such organizations included the African National Congress, the Irish Republican Army, the Northern Alliance in Afghanistan, the Contras in Nicaragua, and so on and on. It also empowered the government to spy with almost no limits on both citizens and noncitizens.

In 2003, the Bush administration tried to expand the Patriot Act's powers even further, but they were beaten back. In time, several of the more extreme provisions were ruled unconstitutional, but the Bush people asserted they would ignore the courts and do as they pleased anyway. In 2006, after considerable national debate, the act was renewed in all its major provisions by the Republican Congress. Under the Patriot Act and other measures taken by the government after 9/11, it became much harder for almost anyone to pass all the bureaucratic hurdles placed in front of would-be immigrants. The process of acquiring a visa or permanent residency became much slower and more capricious.

Special targets were people of Middle Eastern origin, academics, writers, students, and religious leaders. Sometimes, such people were denied entry without explanation. Other times they were summarily deported, not because they had committed a crime, but for minor visa infractions. For example, the Justice Department went into a classroom at the University of California, Irvine, hauled out two young Iranian undergraduates, and deported them. The government people said they had violated visa procedures. It turned out their crime had consisted of failing to fill in the line on their visa renewal application where they were supposed to list a street address. They had done that because they did not have a street address—they lived in a dormitory. The Attorneys General used the Patriot Act to spy on, incarcerate, and deport not just people they thought might be terrorists or know something about terrorists or agree with people the government called terrorists, but sometimes other people whom they suspected of totally unrelated violations. As Attorney General Ashcroft said, the Patriot Act was a tool they used because they had it, even though it was designed to catch terrorists and not for those other violations.

In recent years there has been considerable controversy over the treatment of the people whom the government detained.[81] The news media have covered extensively the atrocities allegedly committed by U.S. troops in Afghanistan and Iraq, in particular at Abu Ghraib prison. More to the point, for the purpose of this book on immigration, has been the undocumented abuse of Middle Eastern immigrants and others at the Guantanamo Bay prison complex and elsewhere in the immigration detention system. The government has never given a full accounting of whom it was holding at Guantanamo, what they were being held for, under what conditions they were being incarcerated, whether or with what they might be charged, or when or how they might be released. Guesses as to the total number of detainees ran upwards from 1200. It was known that the U.S. government was holding hundreds of people who were swept up in the wars in Afghanistan and Iraq, some of them probably combatants and others just unlucky people caught in the crossfire. It was suspected that some were civilians, immigrants from the Middle East, arrested while living in the United States and never charged with a crime, held in limbo indefinitely.

On June 11, 2006, newspapers across the country reported that three Guantanamo inmates had hanged themselves in their cells. They were among several hundred people whom the U.S. government had held, in violation of international law and the U.S. Constitution, for as much as four years. The victims had been subjected to force-feedings, beatings, and other varieties of what can only described as torture. They had been held without charge; without access to redress; without protection of U.S. law or the Geneva Conventions; without any idea if, when, or under what circumstances they might be released. These are the kinds of human rights violations that once moved Americans to outrage against Russian and South African jailers. Speakers for the Pentagon characterized these three suicides, as well as unsuccessful suicide attempts (forty-one in the first five months of 2006 alone), as hunger strikes, and other acts of resistance and despair, as "warfare" waged by the inmates. Orwell lives.[82]

The charge by some critics that the second Bush administration was attempting to establish a police state are surely excessive. Nonetheless, the assault on the civil liberties of both citizens and noncitizens is unprecedented in American history. President Bush or high members of his administration—Attorney General Alberto Gonzalez, Defense Secretary Donald Rumsfeld, and Vice President Dick Cheney— seem to have directed government employees to violate at least the First, Fourth, Sixth, Seventh, and Eighth Amendments to the Constitution, and they seem proud to have done so, as if they have done some great thing for the people of America and the world.[83]

In addition, the Bush administration asserts that they have a right—indeed a duty—to violate the Geneva Conventions with impunity, as well as the U.S. Uniform Code of Military Justice. Article 3 is in all four of the Geneva Conventions, and applies to all soldiers or civilians detained in wartime—including the people at Guantanamo they insisted on calling "enemy combatants" but not "prisoners of war" or "civilians." Article 3 says in part that any person detained in war "shall in all circumstances be treated humanely, without any adverse distinction bounded on race, colour, religion or faith, sex, birth or wealth. ... [T]he following acts are and shall remain prohibited at any time and in any place ... : violence to life and person, in particular ... cruel treatment and torture. ... outrages upon personal dignity, in particular, humiliating and degrading treatment."[84]

Bush's people said the Geneva Conventions were "quaint" and asserted that the president had the right, indeed the obligation, to ignore them in wartime—which, in this president's eyes, was a permanent feature of his tenure in office. The U.S. Supreme Court, made up mainly of justices appointed by George W. Bush, his father George H. W. Bush, and his mentor Ronald Reagan—said no twice, and insisted that the Guantanamo prisoners and others held by the United States in the so-called war on terror be treated according to the Geneva Conventions and the U.S. Constitution.[85]

What did the United States get for all the violations of people's rights under the Constitution and under international law? Not much. David Cole neatly summarized the so-called war on terror's effectiveness within the United States: "Of the 80,000 Arabs and Muslim foreign nationals who were required to register after September 11, the 8,000 called in for FBI interviews, and more than 5,000 locked up in preventive detention, not one stands convicted of a terrorist crime today. In what has surely been the most aggressive national campaign of ethnic profiling since World War II, the government's record is 0 for 93,000." Subsequent to Cole's writing, Zacarias Moussaoui was convicted of hoping to commit 9/11-style terrorism and Hamid Hayat, a Pakistani American born in California, was convicted of attending a terrorist training camp. So the actual record after four and a half years was better: 2 for 93,000. Not the kind of conviction rate that gets prosecutors re-elected.[86]

It is not clear how all of this will play out. Perhaps some of the other incarcerated people will turn out to be guilty of crimes, perhaps not. What is clear is that, in the new century, the U.S. government played fast and loose with the Constitution in an attempt to increase presidential power under the cover story of national security; that this has had a negative effect on the liberties of all Americans; and that its impact on Arab and other Middle Eastern Americans has been devastating indeed.

English Only?[87]

Tim runs the barber shop in a small central California town. Round-faced and pink-cheeked, he likes to talk politics. His politics are xenophobic. "You know what's wrong with America?" he declares. "We don't have one language. We need to all speak English if we want to be one country." When Tim bought the shop a few years ago from a colleague who retired, he instituted wholesale changes. Out went all the old barbers, either retired or fired. Most were past retirement age anyway and had just stayed on because they liked the place and the previous owner. Tim fired the one barber who had a couple of working decades still ahead of him, in part because Tim thought the man was gay.

Now a new squad of mostly young and docile barbers works in their places. All of them are Mexican. Tim takes a bigger cut out of their earnings than he did from the White barbers who preceded them—he even gets a share of their tips. One is a very recent immigrant, a middle-aged woman who speaks very little English. As Tim declaims on the evils of Mexican immigration, she is cutting hair only about four feet away, nearly within arm's reach. Two younger Mexican American barbers, barely out of their teens, speak English as well or better than Tim, though he does not know that. They are also in the room and they pretend not to notice. A customer asks Tim whether he has learned to speak Spanish, since he has an all-Mexican work force and lots of Mexican customers. Tim snorts, "No way. It's their job to learn English, not my job to learn Spanish."

The debate over English as the U.S. national language is not a new one. It harks back to Benjamin Franklin's railing against German immigrants and the German language in the years before the American Revolution (see Chapter 2). Ma Ferguson was a two-time Texas governor in the 1920s and 1930s. She once famously declared that "If the King's English was good enough for Jesus Christ, it's good enough for the children of Texas."[88]

The modern debate began in the 1970s. With the dawning of the multicultural ideal, schools that had a lot of immigrant children began to teach some classes in the children's native tongue. Typically, these were not for beginning kindergarteners, but for children who entered in the middle grades with some schooling behind them in Mexico, Taiwan, or wherever they came from. The children would take special classes in English and some content courses like math in the language they spoke more fluently, then gradually make a transition to all mainstream classes. Bilingual education on that model was most common. It was quite different from a tiny number of bilingual-on-purpose and foreign-language-immersion schools, like the French academy in a Midwestern city or Hawaiian language immersion programs. About the same time, voters who could speak a little English but not read it well petitioned for bilingual ballots. Some courts began to hire interpreters to work with people who came before the court but did not have fluent English skills. In places with large numbers of speakers of particular foreign languages, businesses commonly began to hire people who had some dual language skills. Hospitals, banks, fast food restaurants, and other businesses began to have on hand people who could speak Spanish in many parts of the country, Chinese in San Francisco, Polish in Chicago, and so forth.

Almost immediately, and with especial vehemence after the 1990s, some Americans made known their growing resentment against all this. They contended that America will become fragmented if we do not all speak a common language. They asserted that immigrants are not learning English. They attacked bilingual education as a dodge that holds children back, not so much educationally, but from full commitment to American society. Some began to take punitive actions. Arizona passed a law forbidding state workers to speak any language except English on the job. This included social workers and public health nurses—imagine how that hampered their attempts to serve their clients and patients. Some monolingual English-speaking shopkeepers demanded that customers speak only English on their premises. In 2005, a judge in Lebanon, Tennessee, terminated the parental rights of an immigrant mother because she did not learn English fast enough. The next year, a Senate bill declared English the official language of the United States.[89]

Let's review the evidence on language learning and retention. Recent migrants—Vietnamese and Chinese, Salvadoran and Mexican and all the others— have very uneven levels of functional English, but almost all of them are learning as much and as fast as they can. Some are having lots of success, and some are functioning no better than I have in any of the languages I have tried to learn, but they all are trying, because they recognize that English is the dominant language in the United States. Their children and grandchildren are learning English (and losing their ancestral tongues) at pretty much the same rate as did East and South European migrants a century ago, and perhaps faster than German migrants a century and a half before that. In 2000, 18 percent of the American people, and nearly 80 percent of Latinos, spoke a language other than English at home. But almost all of those people spoke some English, and more than half were fully bilingual. All the evidence indicates that bilingualism increases mental flexibility and achievement in youngsters, especially if it is bilingualism that begins very early. And several studies show that most people are English-dominant by the third generation. Given such evidence, it seems that the English-only movement is much ado about not very much.

I don't know what a good social policy is with regard to language in the United States. But I do know this social fact: at this moment, with very high numbers of people coming into the United States from Latin America and elsewhere, we are in fact a bilingual nation almost everywhere, and in some places multilingual. Just as we were in 1750. Whether it is a good idea or a bad idea, it is the fact of our demography. Witness the TV ratings from a random week in the spring of 2006. Out of the top ten most-watched shows in the Los Angeles metropolitan area, three were on English-language networks: two episodes of "American Idol" and one of "Grey's Anatomy." The other seven were all on Spanish-language KMEX. As Senator Graham might say, that is America's future. It is a bilingual future, with lots of people comfortable in English, lots in Spanish, lots in both, and some in other tongues. It's time we got used to that kind of multiplicity.[90]

If before long we will be—and it is almost certain that we will—in a situation where perhaps 20 percent of our people speak Spanish better than they speak English despite their attempts to add the latter to their skills, then we are in fact a bilingual country, as surely as is Canada or Switzerland. In this situation, it seems to me it is incumbent on every immigrant to learn as much English as he or she can. And it is incumbent on every native-born American to learn Spanish. McDonald's, ABC Television, *Cosmopolitan* magazine, and Bank of America habla español. Capitalism has spoken: they know they need to be able to communicate with their customers and their workforce. The Chicago Fire professional soccer team broadcasts its games in English, Spanish, and *Polish*. The Transportation Security Administration puts bilingual, English-and-Spanish notices in your suitcase if they open it for inspection. They know who their customers are, and they know that air safety is too important to compromise over cosmetic language status issues. The rest of us need to join them. To attempt to turn back the tide on the bilingual fact of American life is silly.

The interlocking aspect of these issues was highlighted by the March 28, 2006, issue of the *Los Angeles Times*. The first section reported on a dispute in the village of Dillingham, Alaska, over the installation of eighty surveillance cameras (one for every thirty residents) at the expense of the Department of Homeland Security. Next to that ran a banner headline followed by several pages of analysis on a bipartisan U.S. Senate bill that would create a comprehensive immigration policy—in the face of a House bill that would have made illegal immigration a felony, doubled the size of the Border Patrol, and built a 700-mile fence between the U.S. and Mexico. The Senate bill included stepped-up border enforcement (but no fence), a guest worker program, and citizenship for some immigrants who were already here without papers.

Beneath that—but still above the fold—were a picture and article describing the 40,000 students who had walked out of LA-area high schools the day before, clogging arterials and freeways in the fourth consecutive day of massive, pro-immigrant street demonstrations. The first section also included accounts of the penalty phase of the trial of convicted terror plotter Zacarias Moussaoui, Supreme Court review of the case of one Guantanamo detainee, and the potential Republican loss of Latino votes on account of the House bill. In the second section, there appeared an editorial discussing the merits of the death penalty for Moussaoui, an op-ed piece by California Governor Arnold Schwarzenegger calling for a comprehensive immigration plan that would balance border control with a guest worker program, plus a cartoon and two other opinion essays supporting immigrants and the pro-immigration demonstrators.[91] All the immigration issues I have outlined in this section were running into and across one another in the first decade of the twenty-first century.

Reprise

An image and slogan made their way onto posters and T-shirts after September 11, 2001. The image was of Goyathlay (Geronimo) and three other Chiricahua Apaches standing in the desert, holding rifles. The slogan that appeared below the picture:

HOMELAND SECURITY
Fighting Terrorism Since 1492[92]

It was a provocation, to be sure, but it signaled a link between twenty-first century politics and the politics of immigration stretching back four centuries. It reminded the viewer that the removal and annihilation of Native peoples constituted the first facts of U.S. immigration history. Immigration in the twenty-first century has consequences, and we take those consequences into account when we debate immigration policies. Immigration had consequences in the past, too, and those consequences are part of immigration's history. They are not a different part of American history. They are part of the same history.

There are several consistent themes in U.S. immigration history. Throughout American history, people have come here from a wide variety of places. There have been patterns to their coming, with lots of British and other Northwest European peoples coming in the early centuries. In the latter decades of the nineteenth century and into the twentieth century, they were joined by large numbers of migrants from certain countries in Southern and Eastern Europe. But contrary to one of the hoary myths of the American imagination, British and German migrants continued to come in large numbers throughout the latter period as well.

Migration was seldom just a one-way process. There was almost always a back-and-forth aspect to migration patterns, with people maintaining connections in their country of origin, often for a few generations, even as they were moving deeper into American society. Some never intended to stay. Others gave up and went back entirely. This was true for almost all groups, including British immigrants from the very first generations; East European Jews were an exception. There were also connections between migrants who came to the United States and those who went to other parts of the globe—Chinese who went to Hawai'i, the western United States, and Cuba, for example, or Italians who went to the United States and to Argentina.

That transnational dimension is one of the ways that the patterns of various non-White migrant peoples resemble those of White migrants. But the situations of peoples of color also were distinctly different at every point in U.S. history, and not just in the specifics of their histories as individual peoples within the American mosaic. Contrary to the mythology of the Ellis Island model, the differences for Mexicans, Asians, and others were not just that they were more recent immigrants than English, Italians, or Poles; in fact, they were not. Rather, the processes that they went through were distinctly different, and the difference was race. Every immigrant group went through a degree of acculturation and upward mobility over three or four generations—Alba and Nee are right about that. But acculturation for White groups was accompanied by lessening opposition from, and ultimately by incorporation into, the dominant Anglo-White group. That was not the case for Japanese Americans during World War II, nor for Mexican Americans in the late twentieth century and early twenty-first century, nor for Middle Eastern Americans in that same period, nor for African Americans at any time in U.S. history. White Americans didn't want them and treated them badly, not because they had failed to Americanize, but because they were not White.

Furthermore, acculturation and identity change over generations did not move immigrants from their foreign category into a single, homogeneous American identity. Rather, migrants acculturated to and changed their identities into a series of races that formed over the course of American history. The first to form was the Black race. African Americans (though not identified by that term) had become a clearly understood and meaningful social grouping by the middle of the eighteenth century. The process of making the White race was well along by 1700, and complete by the dawn of the nineteenth century. Contrary to the imaginings of some scholars, people like Irish and Italian migrants were never not-White in America, although their membership as White people became more active and perhaps more conclusive as time went on. Clearly, some groups like Jews (and Armenians in California) occupied less secure, less privileged places within the White race. For Arab and Middle Eastern Americans, their tentative place within the White race was actually revoked in the last quarter of the twentieth century.

By contrast, other groups such as Asian, Latin, and African Americans were always decidedly outside the White race. American Indians were seen as a single people far sooner in White people's imaginations than in Indians' own perceptions. European Americans treated them as an undifferentiated group almost from the beginning. But Indians saw themselves as members of competing tribes with different histories, different lineages, different languages, customs, and identities. In the early 1800s Tecumseh tried to form a pan-Indian alliance that would be powerful enough to force out the European invaders, but there was not substantial blending of Indians into a single identity until after the Civil War. The racial formation of Indians into a single group is still not complete, at least when compared to the blending that has occurred for Whites or Blacks.

The Asian American race is an idea that was invented in the 1960s out of propinquity and the common experience of orientalization, for purposes of building a political coalition to empower communities. The blending in this case is still not complete, as lots more Asian immigrants keep coming and many individuals maintain two levels of identity—say, Korean and Asian American. Likewise, the various peoples who hold Latin American ancestry are far from forming a single racial group in the United States, although some articulation of Latino commonality has begun to take place. When immigrants have come to this country, they have acculturated and changed their identities, not into a single, undifferentiated American culture and identity, but into one or another of these racial identities and cultures.

Throughout eighteenth and nineteenth centuries, the U.S. government, its institutional predecessors, and White people generally pursued a conscious policy of racial replacement. They moved out Indians and Mexicans and replaced them with Europeans and White Americans.

The central issue explored in this book is the relationship between immigration, race, and colonialism. It is one of the major issues of U.S. history. It is formative of American identity. Immigration can only be understood in light of race and colonialism. Insofar as this book may have some modest policy implications, it is that these issues must be taken into account when forming policy, and that much of the cant that passes for truth about immigration in America's past and present must be discarded. But this is emphatically a book about immigration history, not policy, about the past that was, not the future that may yet be.

The cover of this book shows a sign by a freeway near Oceanside, forty miles or so north of the California-Mexico border. Here, the Border Patrol sets up checkpoints to look for cars carrying unauthorized immigrants north toward Los Angeles. Some human smugglers drop their passengers a few hundred yards south of the checkpoint, then wait for them further north while the migrants walk overland. Some of the migrants, apparently, have run across the highway in the past, and some may have been hit by cars or nearly so. Hence the signs.

When I was growing up in the Pacific Northwest, and later living in the East and Midwest, I was familiar with highway signs very much like this one, warning motorists to watch out for deer and cattle. When I moved to California a decade ago, it was a shock to see people regarded in the same way that I was accustomed to thinking about animals of the field and forest. But that is the way that American society has come to view certain sorts of immigrants. It is not a new phenomenon: White Americans have always regarded peoples of color—African-descended people, Indians, Asians, Latin Americans—as less than fully human. They have unselfconsciously treated people of color with less respect than White people, whether those people were citizens or not. It may shock us to be reminded that this is still the case, but it confirms that race, now as ever, is the central issue in U.S. immigration history. We may regard that fact as a crime and a tragedy, but it should not be a surprise.

Perhaps this sign may remind us that we are almost all aliens. That is, almost every American can trace her or his ancestry to people who came to the United States from some other place. One of the things we have most in common is that we all came here from some other place. That makes us all guests in this land. Perhaps it will also help us see each other as something like family, for we are all in this together.

Appendices

Appendix A

Chronology of Immigration and Naturalization Laws and Decisions

Appendix B: Tables

Appendix A

Chronology of Immigration and Naturalization Laws and Decisions

1616	Virginia headright system encourages importing slaves, servants, other immigrants.
1731	Massachusetts allows citizenship after one year of residence for "all Protestants of foreign nations."
1740	British Parliament passes Plantation Act to regularize naturalization and citizenship and encourage immigration to American colonies.
1787	Constitution enshrines slavery and counts each slave as three-fifths of a person for apportionment.
1790	Naturalization Act restricts citizenship to "free white persons" who reside in the United States for five years and renounce their allegiance to their former country.
1798	Alien and Sedition Acts permit the president to deport any foreigner deemed to be dangerous.
	Revised Naturalization Act imposes a 14-year residency requirement for prospective citizens.
1802	Congress reduces the residency requirement for citizenship to five years.
1803	Louisiana Purchase.
1808	Congress outlaws bringing slaves into United States.
1819	U.S. government begins to count immigrants as they arrive.
1823	U.S. government creates Office of Indian Affairs within War Department.

1830   Congress passes Indian Removal Act.

1831–1832   Supreme Court recognizes Indian tribes as "domestic dependent nations" with retained sovereignty.

1831–1843   Removal of the Five Civilized Tribes from the Southeast to Indian Territory.

1835–1836   Americans in Texas make war and seize Texas.

1846–1848   United States fights war of aggression against Mexico.

1848   Treaty of Guadalupe Hidalgo extends U.S. citizenship to perhaps as many as 80,000 Mexican citizens of conquered territory.

1849   U.S. Supreme Court in *Passenger Cases* outlaws state taxes on immigrants, saying the right to regulate immigration is reserved to the Congress.

1850s   Know-Nothing Party fails to raise naturalization restrictions.

1854   In *People v. Hall* California Supreme Court prohibits Chinese immigrants from testifying in California courts against White people.

            In Gadsden Purchase, United States acquires southern parts of New Mexico, Arizona, and California.

1855   Castle Garden immigration station opens in New York.

1862   Homestead Act grants up to 160 acres of free land to settlers who build on the land they claim and live there for five years. This attracts immigrants. Limited to U.S. citizens and people who are eligible for naturalization and declare their intention to be naturalized — i.e., Whites.

1864   Congress legalizes importing contract laborers.

1865   Thirteenth Amendment outlaws slavery.

1868   Fourteenth Amendment ensures citizenship rights for former slaves, effectively amending "free white persons" clause.

1870   Fifteenth Amendment makes it unconstitutional to deny someone the right to vote on account of race.

            Naturalization Act limits citizenship to "white persons and persons of African descent."

            Congress prohibits army officers from holding post of Indian agent. President Grant gives control of Indian agencies to Christian missionary denominations.

1871   Congress declares that no further Indian treaties will be concluded.

1875   Page Law bars some Asian women, sets up the arguments for Chinese exclusion, and bars prostitutes and convicts.

            Court decision affirms Congressional supremacy over states in supervising immigration.

1878   In *In re Ah Yup*, federal district court in California rules Chinese are not White and therefore not entitled to naturalization.

1882   Chinese Exclusion Act bars admission of Chinese laborers (allowing entry by merchants, students, tourists) for ten years and declares

Chinese immigrants ineligible to U.S. naturalization. Passes over presidential veto.

Immigration Act places 50-cent tax on each immigrant entry and makes several categories of people ineligible to enter: "lunatics," people likely to become public charges, convicts. Authorizes Treasury Department to contract with states to process immigrants.

1885   Alien Contract Labor Law prohibits any company or individual from bringing foreigners into the United States under contract to perform labor. Exceptions: domestic servants; skilled workers who are needed to help establish a new trade or industry.

1886   In *Yick Wo v. Hopkins*, U.S. Supreme Court invalidates a San Francisco law that discriminates against Chinese laundry workers, saying it is illegal under the Fourteenth Amendment for state or local governments to deprive any person of life, liberty, or property without due process — makes no distinction between noncitizens and citizens.

Statue of Liberty dedicated.

1887   Dawes or General Allotment Act provides for breakup of Native American tribes and lands, with allotments to individuals, who are then eligible to become U.S. citizens after a twenty-five-year trust period.

1888   Scott Act expands the Chinese Exclusion Act by rescinding re-entry permits for Chinese laborers and prohibits their return. Supreme Court affirms it in 1889.

1890   Last Pennsylvania German-language public school closes.

Castle Garden Immigration Station closes.

1891   Congress establishes comprehensive federal control over immigration, including Bureau of Immigration under Treasury Department to administer immigration laws. Bars "persons suffering from a loathsome or a dangerous contagious disease," felons, polygamists, and persons guilty of "moral turpitude." Empowers BI to deport persons unlawfully entering.

1892   Chinese Exclusion Act renewed for another ten years.

Ellis Island Immigration Station opens.

1893   Americans in Hawai'i overthrow the government, imprison the Queen, and proclaim a republic.

1894   Congress establishes Bureau of Immigration within Treasury Department.

1896   U.S. Supreme Court decides in *Plessy v. Ferguson* that racial segregation is lawful.

1897   A West Texas federal court decides in *In re Rodriguez* that the Treaty of Guadalupe Hidalgo did grant U.S. citizenship rights to Mexican Americans and naturalization rights to Mexican immigrants, even though they might not be considered "White."

President Cleveland vetoes literacy test for immigration.

1898   *United States v. Wong Kim Ark.* U.S. Supreme Court finds that children of Chinese immigrants are U.S. citizens on basis of being born in the United States, despite their parents being aliens ineligible to citizenship.

United States seizes the Philippines, Guam, Puerto Rico, and Hawai'i.

1900   Organic Act extends U.S. law, including bars on Chinese immigration and on contract labor, to Hawai'i.

1901   President William McKinley is assassinated by a Polish anarchist. Congress passes the Anarchist Exclusion Act, which allows immigrants to be excluded based on their political opinions.

1902   Chinese Exclusion Act renewed for another ten years.

1903   Bureau of Immigration is placed under Department of Commerce and Labor. Congress recodifies existing immigration laws, toughens deportation powers, and bars anarchists, subversives, polygamists, and epileptics.

1904   Chinese Exclusion Act made permanent.

1906   Naturalization Act systematizes application for naturalized citizenship and makes speaking knowledge of English a requirement.

1907   Expatriation Act means that an American woman who marries a foreign national loses her U.S. citizenship. An American woman who marries an Asian citizen becomes an "alien ineligible to citizenship."

Added to the excluded list: children unaccompanied by their parents, tuberculosis patients, people with mental or physical defect likely to affect their ability to earn a living.

Congress appoints Dillingham Immigration Commission.

1907–1908   Gentlemen's Agreement. Japan agrees to stop letting laborers emigrate to United States.

1909   *In re Halladjian* court concludes that Armenians are White.

1910   White Slave Traffic Act forbids importation of women for "immoral purposes."

Angel Island Immigration Station opens in San Francisco Bay.

1911   U.S. Immigration (Dillingham) Commission publishes 42-volume report saying immigration is damaging the nation and calling for restriction of immigration from Southern and Eastern Europe.

1913   California passes Alien Land Law prohibiting "aliens ineligible to citizenship" from owning land. Other states follow: Arizona in 1917, Louisiana and Washington in 1921, New Mexico in 1922, Idaho, Montana, and Oregon in 1923, Kansas in 1925, and Arkansas, Utah, and Wyoming during World War II.

1915   Americanization/100 Percentism campaign begins under joint government-business sponsorship. Its perceived failure contributes to anti-immigrant moves of 1920s.

In *Dow v. United States*, South Carolina federal district court decides that Syrians, hence most Arabs, are White people, and therefore entitled to naturalization.

1917   Immigration Act requires literacy test (in some language) for admission — over President Wilson's veto. Creates Asiatic Barred Zone (everything except Philippines and Japan) from which immigration is barred.

State and Labor Departments issue order that requires passports of all noncitizens who seek to enter the United States and visas issued by State Department officials abroad rather than by immigration officials at port of entry.

Puerto Ricans are granted U.S. citizenship.

1918   Congress gives President broad authority to forbid entry or departure of noncitizens during wartime. Similar powers are asserted in subsequent wars.

1919   Congress grants citizenship to World War I Native American veterans.

In Red Scare, some radical noncitizens are deported.

1920   California strengthens provisions of Alien Land Law, barring aliens ineligible to citizenship (i.e., Asians) from leasing land or purchasing it in the names of minor, U.S. citizen children.

1921   Quota Act limits annual immigration to three percent of foreign born of each nationality in the United States in 1910. Imposes annual ceiling of 350,000 quota admissions: 55 percent from Northern and Western Europe, 45 percent from other countries (nearly all Southern and Eastern European). New selective measures to allow nonquota or unlimited admissions of immediate relatives of U.S. citizens and immigrants from Western Hemisphere.

1922   *Takao Ozawa v. United States*. U.S. Supreme Court rules that Ozawa is not entitled to U.S. citizenship because he was born in Japan, despite being raised in United States and in every way a model candidate.

Cable Act partially repeals Expatriation Act: for most women, their citizenship was now independent of their husbands and they could regain U.S. citizenship by naturalization, but for American women who married Asian men, the law specified that their citizenship would still follow their husbands and they could not be naturalized.

1923   *United States v. Bhaghat Singh Thind*. U.S. Supreme Court rules that Asian Indians are not eligible for naturalization on racial basis despite pseudoscientific racial placement as Aryans.

1924   Johnson–Reed Act (Second Quota Act) limits immigration further, to 2 percent of the number of each nationality group who lived in the United States in 1890. It lowers the total annual ceiling of quota immigrants to 165,000, increases the share of Northern and Western European potential immigrants to 86 percent (142,000), and decreases the share from Southern and Eastern Europe to 11 percent (18,000). It bars Asian immigration entirely (effective for Japanese and for foreign-born wives and children of U.S. citizens of Chinese ancestry). Filipinos may still come outside the quota system because they are American "nationals" — from a U.S. colony, no longer citizens of a foreign country. To take effect in 1927.

Congress grants citizenship to those Native Americans who had not already received it. Indians are able to vote in federal elections for the first time, though not in all state elections.

1925	Border Patrol is established.
1927	Johnson–Reed Act postponed to 1929.
1929	National Origins Quota system goes into full effect, recomputing quotas to fit the composition of the U.S. population in 1920; 83 percent (127,000) went to the Northern and Western European quota and 15 percent (23,000) to the Southern and Eastern European quota, with 2 percent (4,000) to other areas. Annual ceiling: 154,000.
1930	Senate investigating committee finds systematic kidnapping of Navajo children, who are placed in boarding schools.
1934	Tydings-McDuffie Act (Philippines Independence Act) provided for independence for the Philippines on July 4, 1946. Meanwhile, Filipinos lost their status as U.S. nationals and were restricted to a token quota of 50 per year.
	Mexican and Filipino forced repatriation.
	Indian Reorganization Act ends allotment, creates tribal governments and court systems.
1939	Congress defeats refugee bill to accept 20,000 children from Nazi Germany, on grounds it would exceed German quota.
1940	Smith Act (Alien Registration Act) requires all noncitizens over age 14 to be fingerprinted and broadens the grounds for deportation.
	Angel Island Immigration Station burns to the ground. It is used to house prisoners of war.
1942	President Franklin Roosevelt issues Executive Order 9066 authorizing the U.S. Army to imprison 112,000 Japanese Americans, two-thirds of them U.S. citizens and the rest ineligible to citizenship on racial grounds.
	Filipinos are reclassified so they can register for the military. Thousands sign up.
	Beginning of Bracero Program for Mexican laborers outside usual immigration controls. Also with Barbados, Jamaica, and British Honduras.
	U.S. government takes 900,000 acres of Indian lands for army facilities, gunnery ranges, nuclear testing, and Japanese American concentration camps.
	All Native, Asian, and African American men are required to register for the draft, though many cannot vote.
1943	Congress repeals Chinese exclusion and Chinese become eligible for naturalization. In 1944 a quota is set at 105 entries per year, not by

people coming from China (as with other countries) but by ethnic Chinese coming from anywhere.

In *Hirabayashi v. United States*, U.S. Supreme Court rules that curfews and detentions for Japanese Americans were constitutional on the ground of "military necessity."

1944   *United States v. Korematsu* upholds right of U.S. government to intern Japanese Americans.

Ex Parte Mitsuye Endo, Supreme Court rules that internment program was an unconstitutional violation of the habeas corpus rights of U.S. citizens of Japanese ancestry.

1945   President Truman issues executive order permitting entry of 40,000 refugees and displaced persons.

War Brides Act allows U.S. citizens who served in armed forces to bring home foreign-born wives. Aimed to facilitate marriages between U.S. soldiers and European women, it also allows Chinese American soldiers to reunite their trans-Pacific families in the United States.

1946   Luce-Cellar Act allows Asian Indians and Filipinos to become naturalized and grants quota of 100 to each country.

1948   Displaced Persons Act allows 202,000 refugees uprooted in wartime Europe to come in the next two years. Their numbers are counted against that year's and future years' quotas — effectively "quota mortgaging."

1949   Hoover Commission recommends termination of Indian tribes and integration of Native Americans as individual citizens.

1950   Internal Security Act passed over President Truman's veto. It bars admission (and provides grounds for deportation) of any foreign national who is a member of the Communist party or who might engage in activities "which would be prejudicial to the public interest, or would endanger the welfare or safety of the United States." Noncitizens must report their address annually.

Congress amends Displaced Persons Act to raise total number of visas to 341,000.

1952   McCarran-Walter Act passes over President Truman's veto, reaffirming the national-origins quota system and setting the total annual immigration limit to one-sixth of one percent of the population of the continental United States in 1920. Exempts spouses and children of U.S. citizens and people born in the Western Hemisphere from quotas, and creates system of preferences within quotas for persons with needed occupations. Ends racial limits to immigration and naturalization, giving Japan a token quota of 100.

1953   Refugee Relief Act provides 205,000 nonquota visas, ends quota mortgaging, and extends refugee status to non-Europeans.

President's Commission on Immigration and Naturalization report *Whom Shall We Welcome?* calls for an end to the quota system.

Termination becomes official U.S. Indian policy.

1954	Operation Wetback removes one million Mexican immigrants from the Southwest amid numerous civil rights violations.
	United States begins to admit Hungarian refugees.
	Ellis Island Immigration Station closes.
1959	United States begins to admit Cuban refugees.
1962	Kennedy administration ends Indian termination policy.
1964	Ends first Bracero Program.
1965	Hart-Cellar Act abolishes national origins quota system. Creates an Eastern Hemisphere system of equal visa limits per country of 20,000 annually. Places first limits on Western Hemisphere immigration. Holds total limited admissions to 290,000 per year: 170,000 from Eastern Hemisphere and 120,000 from Western Hemisphere. Establishes admissions class not subject to limitation. Revises occupation-first, family-reunion-second preference system to put family reunion first and occupations second.
1967	*Afroyim v. Rusk.* Supreme Court holds that a person with dual citizenship does not lose his or her U.S. citizenship by voting in a foreign election (in Israel in this case).
1975	Indochinese Migration and Refugee Assistance Act creates program for resettling refugees from Vietnam and Cambodia.
1976	Congress passes a law to include Laotians in Indochinese program.
	Congress passes a law to apply Eastern Hemisphere 20,000 per country limit and extend the family preference system to Western Hemisphere.
1978	Congress passes law to exclude and deport Nazi war criminals.
	Congress merges Eastern and Western Hemispheres into 290,000 worldwide total.
1980	Refugee Act places refugees outside quota system by removing "refugee" as a preference category (and so reduces the annual ceiling to 270,000 quota immigrants). Allows for 50,000 refugees per year — persons who have a "well-founded fear of persecution" on account of race, religion, nationality, or membership in a social or political movement — plus 5,000 asylum seekers.
1982	Amerasian Act recognizes the potential American citizenship of children born to Vietnamese and other Southeast Asian women who had relations with U.S. military men. The act does not make sufficient provision to bring them to the United States.
1984	Federal court overturns World War II conviction of Fred Korematsu, *ending justification for Japanese American internment.*
1986	Immigration Reform and Control Act provides amnesty for 3 million undocumented immigrants, allowing them to legalize their status, and provides punishments for employers who hire illegal immigrants.
	Federal court overturns World War II conviction of Japanese American Gordon Hirabayashi for refusing internment.

1988   Redress Act authorizes $20,000 per person token compensation for surviving Japanese Americans who were interned in World War II. Not immediately funded, but ultimately paid.

     Amerasian Homecoming Act provides for children of U.S. servicemen and their families to enter the United States from every country where U.S. troops were stationed except Japan. Nearly 100,000 enter over next three years.

1990   Immigration Act revises admissions system, creating an overall flexible cap of 700,000 persons starting in 1992, to drop to 675,000 in 1995.

1994   California voters pass Proposition 187, which prohibits providing public education, welfare, and health services to undocumented immigrants. It is later declared unconstitutional.

1996   Personal Responsibility and Work Opportunity Act embodies parts of California's Proposition 187, denies all but emergency services to unauthorized immigrants, and makes citizenship a condition of eligibility for public benefits for most authorized immigrants.

     Illegal Immigration Reform and Immigrant Responsibility Act strengthens border enforcement, makes it more difficult to gain asylum, establishes income requirements for sponsors of legal immigrants, streamlines deportation procedures, removes procedural legal protections from migrants who lack documents, and raises penalties for people who aid or employ people who lack documents.

1997   Congress restores benefits to some elderly and poor immigrants who had previously received them.

1998   Congress restores further benefits to some immigrants and allows an increased number of skilled foreign workers to enter the United States temporarily to work in industries where their skills are scarce.

2001   USA PATRIOT Act (Uniting and Strengthening America by Providing Appropriate Tools Required to Intercept and Obstruct Terrorism Act) gives Attorney General broad powers to wiretap and harass citizens, detain noncitizens (and even citizens) without charge or recourse to attorneys or courts.

2004   Homeland Security Department begins photographing and fingerprinting international visitors, including tourists, at airports, seaports, and selected border crossings.

Principal sources: Michael LeMay and Elliott Robert Barkan, eds., *U.S. Immigration and Naturalization Laws and Issues: A Documentary History* (Westport, CT: Greenwood, 1999); Reed Ueda, *Postwar Immigrant America* (Boston: Bedford, 1994): 169–172; "Landmarks in Immigration History," *Gilder Lehrman History Online*, www.gliah.uh.edu/historyonline/immigration_chron.cfm (May 15, 2002); Michael C. LeMay, *From Open Door to Dutch Door: An Analysis of US Immigration Policy Since 1820* (Westport, CT: Praeger, 1987), 17–18; *Ancestors in the Americas* website: www.cetel.org/docs.html, visited April 5, 2004 (research by UC Berkeley Asian American Studies 121).

Appendix B

Table B.1   Population by Race, Territory That Would Become
United States 1600–2000, in thousands

Year	Native	White	Black	Asian	Latino	Total
1600	2,4241[1] 100.0%					2,424
1650	2,228[2] 97.6%	53[3] 2.3%	2[4] 0.1%			2,283
1700	2,031[5] 88.4%	234 10.2%	31 1.4%			2,296
1750	1,873[6] 60.8%	964 31.3%	242 7.9%			3,079
1800	1,316[7] 19.7%	4,349[8] 65.2%	1,002 15.0%			6,667
1850	736[9] 3.1%	19,553 81.7%	3,639 15.2%			23,928
1900	657[10] 0.9%	66,809 87.4%	8,834 11.6%	114 0.1%		76,414
1950[11]	995[12] 0.5%	134,942 89.5%	15,042 10.0%	321 0.2%	1,858[13] 1.2%	153,158[14]
2000[15]	2,617[16] 0.9%	211,461 75.1%	34,658 12.3%	10,642 3.8%	35,306 12.5%	281,563

Sources:

Campbell Gibson and Kay Jung, "Historical Census Statistics on Population Totals by Race, 1790 to 1990, and by Hispanic Origin, 1970 to 1990, for the United States, Regions, Divisions, and States" Population Division, Working Paper No. 56 (Washington, DC: U.S. Census Bureau, September 2002): Table 1.

Michael R. Haines and Richard H. Steckel, Eds., *A Population History of North America* (Cambridge: Cambridge University Press, 2000).

Table B.1 (continued)   Population by Race, Territory That Would Become
United States 1600–2000, in thousands

Marcus L. Hansen, "The Population of the American Outlying Regions in 1790," in American Council of Learned Societies, "Report of Committee on Linguistic and National Stocks
in the [White] Population of the United States," in *Annual Report of the American Historical
Association for the Year 1931*, vol. 1 (Washington, DC: Government Printing Office,
1932): 398–408.

Andrew W. Lind, *Hawaii's People*, 3rd ed. (Honolulu: University of Hawai'i Press, 1967):
28.

John J. McCusker and Russell R. Menard, *The Economy of British America, 1607–1789*
(Chapel Hill: University of North Carolina Press, 1985): 54.

David E. Stannard, *Before the Horror: The Population of Hawai'i on the Eve of Western
Contact* (Honolulu: Social Science Research Institute, University of Hawai'i, 1989).

Douglas H. Ubelaker, "North American Indian Population Size, A.D. 1500 to 1985,"
American Journal of Physical Anthropology, 77 (1988): 289–294.

U.S. Census Bureau, *Overview of Race and Hispanic Origin: Census 2000 Brief*,
C2KBR/01-1 (Washington, DC: U.S. Census Bureau, March 2001): Table 1.

U.S. Census Bureau, *The Native Hawaiian and Other Pacific Islander Population: 2000*
C2Kbr/01-14 (Washington, DC: U.S. Census Bureau, December 2001): Table 4.

[1] Native population in 1600 was calculated thus:

1,801,080	Ubelaker's estimate for all North America north of Mexico
−177,100	Ubelaker's estimate for Arctic and Subarctic regions
1,623,980	
+800,000	Stannard's minimum estimate for Hawai'i at European contact
2,423,980	

Some of the Arctic Native people lived within territory that is now Alaska, and some of
the people whom Ubelaker counts as Northeast, Plains, and Northwest Coast Indians
lived in territory that is now Canada. I am assuming these groups to be very roughly the
same size. Note that Ubelaker's precontact estimates are very much smaller than those
of Russell Thornton I have used elsewhere in this book.

[2] Figures for Native Americans in 1650 and 1750 were calculated as midway between
Ubekaler's estimates for centennial years. So the total of Native peoples in what is now
both the continental US and Hawai'i in 1650 was calculated thus:

1,602,912	halfway between Ubelaker's 1600 and 1700 estimates for all North America north of Mexico
−175,275	halfway between Ubelaker's 1600 and 1700 estimates for Arctic and Subarctic regions
1,427,637	
+800,000	Stannard's minimum estimate for Hawai'i at European contact
2,227,637	

[3] White figures for 1600–1750 are from McCusker and Menard. Later figures are from
Gibson and Jung and U.S. Census.

Table B.1 (continued) Population by Race, Territory That Would Become
United States 1600–2000, in thousands

[4] Black figures for 1600–1750 are from McCusker and Menard. Later figures are from
Gibson and Jung and U.S. Census.

[5] Native population in 1700 was calculated thus:

1,404,745	Ubelaker's estimate for all North America north of Mexico
–173,450	Ubelaker's estimate for Arctic and Subarctic regions
1,231,295	
+800,000	Stannard's minimum estimate for Hawai'i at European contact
2,031,295	

[6] Figure for Native peoples in 1750 was calculated thus:

1,228,216	halfway between Ubelaker's 1700 and 1800 estimates for all North America north of Mexico
–154,459	halfway between Ubelaker's 1700 and 1800 estimates for Arctic and Subarctic regions
1,073,757	
+800,000	Stannard's minimum estimate for Hawai'i at European contact
1,872,757	

[7] Native population in 1800 was calculated thus:

1,051,688	Ubelaker's estimate for all North America north of Mexico
–135,540	Ubelaker's estimate for Arctic and Subarctic regions
916,148	
+400,000	Stannard's minimum estimate for Hawai'i 25 years after European contact
1,316,148	

[8] Here I have added to the U.S. Census figure the numbers of European-descended people
(44,000) that Hansen estimated lived in areas that would later be the United States but
that were not covered in the 1790 Census: the Louisiana Purchase, Florida, and the
Spanish Southwest.

[9] Native population in 1850 was calculated thus:

770,981	Ubelaker's estimate for all North America north of Mexico
–105,865	Ubelaker's estimate for Arctic and Subarctic regions
665,116	
+71,019	Lind's figure for Native Hawaiians in 1853
736,135	

[10] Native population in 1900 was calculated thus:

536,562	Ubelaker's estimate for all North America north of Mexico
–80,529	Ubelaker's estimate for Arctic and Subarctic regions
617,091	
+39,656	Lind's figure for Native Hawaiians in 1900
656,747	

[11] Figures for 1950 omit 49 thousand who marked "other race."

[12] Native population in 1950 was calculated thus:

799,959	Ubelaker's estimate for all North America north of Mexico
−109,214	Ubelaker's estimate for Arctic and Subarctic regions
909,173	
+86,090	Lind's figure for Native Hawaiians in 1950
995,263	

[13] Latino figure for 1950 is taken from Gibson and Jung figure for 1940 (they have no figure for 1950 or 1960).

[14] Totals for 1950 and 2000 are less than sums of categories, because a quirk of the Census Bureau's practice separated race from Hispanic origin into two different questions; some persons checked both White and Hispanic, some both Black and Hispanic, etc.

[15] Figures for 2000 omit 15,359 thousand who marked "some other race" and 6,826 who marked two or more races.

[16] Native population in 2000 was calculated thus:

2,475,956	Census figure for Native Americans
+140,652	Census figure Native Hawaiians
2,616,608	

Table B.2 Immigration by Decade or Period, 1820–2001

Decade or Other Period[1]	Number of Immigrant Arrivals	Yearly Average	Total Population at Start of Decade	Increase to Next Census	Immigrants as Percentage of Increase	Immigrants per 100 US Residents
1820–1830	151,824	13,802	9,638,453	3,227,567	4.7%	1.6
1831–1840	599,125	59,913	12,866,020	4,203,433	14.3%	4.7
1841–1850	1,713,251	171,325	17,069,453	6,122,423	28.0%	10.0
1851–1860	2,598,214	259,821	23,191,876	9,453,617	27.5%	11.2
1861–1870	2,314,824	231,482	32,645,493	5,912,878	39.1%	7.1
1871–1880	2,812,191	281,219	38,558,371	11,597,412	24.2%	7.3
1881–1890	5,246,613	524,661	50,155,783	12,791,931	41.0%	10.5
1891–1900	3,687,564	368,756	62,947,714	13,046,861	28.3%	5.9
1901–1910	8,795,386	879,539	75,994,575	15,977,691	55.0%	11.6
1903–14	*11,791,856*	*982,655*				
1911–1920	5,735,811	573,581	91,972,266	13,738,354	41.8%	6.2
1915–20	*1,602,680*	*267,113*				
1921–1930	4,107,209	410,721	105,710,620	17,064,426	24.1%	3.9
1921–24	*2,344,599*	*586,150*				
1925–30	*1,762,610*	*293,768*				
1931–1940	528,431	52,843	122,775,046	8,894,229	5.9%	0.4
1941–1950	1,035,039	103,504	131,669,275	19,028,092	5.4%	0.8
1941–45	*170,952*	*34,190*				
1946–50	*864,087*	*172,817*				
1951–1960	2,515,479	251,248	150,697,361	28,625,814	8.8%	1.7
1961–1970	3,321,677	332,168	179,323,175	23,888,751	13.9%	1.9
1971–1980	4,493,314	449,331	203,211,926	23,333,879	19.3%	2.2
1981–1990	7,338,062	733,806	226,545,805	22,164,068	33.1%	3.2
1981–88	*4,710,655*	*588,832*				
1989–90	*2,627,407*	*1,313,704*				
1991–2000	9,095,417	909,542	248,709,873	32,712,033	27.8%	3.7
2001	1,064,318		281,421,906			

Sources: 2001 Statistical Yearbook of the Immigration and Naturalization Service, M-367 (Washington, DC: GPO, 2003), 16; US Bureau of the Census, Historical Statistics of the United States, Colonial Times to 1970, Part 1 (Washington, DC: GPO, 1975), 14; US Bureau of the Census, Demographic Trends in the 20th Century, CENSR–4 (Washington, DC: GPO, 2002), A-1.

[1] The first year for which statistics are available is 1820. It is included here with the decade 1821–1830.

Table B.3 Immigrants Excluded from the United States by Cause, 1892–1954

Period	Total Excluded	Subversive or Anarchistic	Criminals	Immoral Classes	Mental or Physical Defectives	Likely to Become Public Charges	Stowaways	Attempted Entry without Inspection or without Proper Documents	Contract Laborers	Unable to Read (over age 16)	Other
1892–1900	22,515	—	65	89	1,309	15,070	—	—	5,792	—	190
1901–1910	108,211	10	1,681	1,277	24,425	63,311	—	—	12,991	—	4,516
1911–1920	178,109	27	4,353	4,824	42,129	90,045	1,904	—	15,417	5,083	14,327
1921–1930	189,307	9	2,082	1,281	11,044	37,175	8,447	94,084	6,274	8,202	20,709
1931–1940	68,217	5	1,261	253	1,530	12,519	2,126	47,858	1,235	258	1,172
1941–1950	30,263	60	1,134	80	1,021	1,072	3,182	22,441	219	108	946
1951–1954	13,678	197	1,184	117	661	120	244	10,530	9	9	607
Total	610,000	408	11,760	7,921	82,119	219,319	15,903	174,913	41,937	13,660	41,467

Source: Peter Morton Coan, *Ellis Island Interviews* (New York: Facts On File, 1997), 417.

Table B.4 Immigration by Region of Last Residence, 1820–2000

Decade	Europe	Eur %	Asia	As %	Americas	Ams %	Africa	Oceania	Total
1820–1830	106,487	70.1	36	—	11,951	7.9	17	3	151,824
1831–1840	495,681	82.7	55	—	33,424	5.6	54	9	599,125
1841–1850	1,597,442	93.2	141	—	62,469	3.6	55	29	1,713,251
1851–1860	2,452,577	94.5	41,538	1.6	74,720	2.9	210	158	2,598,214
1861–1870	2,065,141	89.2	64,759	2.8	166,6C7	7.2	312	214	2,314,824
1871–1880	2,271,925	80.7	124,160	4.4	404,044	14.4	358	10,914	2,812,191
1881–1890	4,735,484	90.3	69,942	1.3	426,967	8.1	857	12,574	5,246,613
1891–1900	3,555,352	96.4	74,862	2.0	38,972	1.0	350	3,965	3,687,564
1901–1910	8,056,040	91.6	323,543	3.7	361,888	4.1	7,368	13,024	8,795,386
1911–1920	4,321,887	75.3	247,236	4.3	1,143,671	19.9	8,443	13,427	5,735,811
1921–1930	2,463,194	60.0	112,059	2.7	1,516,716	36.9	6,286	8726	4,107,209
1931–1940	347,566	65.9	16,595	3.1	160,037	30.3	1,750	2,483	528,431
1941–1950	621,147	60.0	37,028	3.6	354,804	34.3	7,367	14,551	1,035,039
1951–1960	1,325,727	52.7	153,249	6.1	996,944	39.6	14,092	12,976	2,515,479
1961–1970	1,123,492	33.8	427,642	12.9	1,716,374	51.7	28,954	25,122	3,321,677
1971–1980	800,368	17.8	1,588,178	35.3	1,982,735	44.1	80,779	41,242	4,493,314
1981–1990	761,550	10.4	2,738,157	37.3	3,615,225	49.3	176,893	45,205	7,338,062
1991–2000	1,359,737	14.9	2,795,672	30.7	4,486,806	49.3	354,939	55,845	9,095,417
All Years	38,460,797	58.2	8,814,852	13.3	17,554,354	26.6	689,084	260,467	66,089,431

Source: 2001 Statistical Yearbook of the Immigration and Naturalization Service, M-367 (Washington, DC: Government Printing Office, 2003), 17–20. Percentages do not add up to 100 because (a) Africa and Oceania percentages were not calculated and (b) for several decades substantial numbers did not specify origin.

Table B.5   Leading Sending Regions, 1820–2000

Decade	Leading Regions and Percents		
1820–1830	Europe 70.1	Americas 7.9	
1831–1840	Europe 82.7	Americas 5.6	
1841–1850	Europe 93.2	Americas 3.6	
1851–1860	Europe 94.5	Americas 2.9	Asia 1.6
1861–1870	Europe 89.2	Americas 7.2	Asia 2.8
1871–1880	Europe 80.7	Americas 14.4	Asia 4.4
1881–1890	Europe 90.3	Americas 8.1	Asia 1.3
1891–1900	Europe 96.3	Asia 2.0	Americas 1.0
1901–1910	Europe 91.6	Americas 4.1	Asia 3.7
1911–1920	Europe 75.3	Americas 19.9	Asia 4.3
1921–1930	Europe 60.0	Americas 36.9	Asia 2.7
1931–1940	Europe 65.9	Americas 30.3	Asia 3.1
1941–1950	Europe 60.0	Americas 34.3	Asia 3.6
1951–1960	Europe 52.7	Americas 39.6	Asia 6.1
1961–1970	Americas 51.7	Europe 33.8	Asia 12.9
1971–1980	Americas 44.1	Asia 35.3	Europe 17.8
1981–1990	Americas 49.3	Asia 37.3	Europe 10.4
1991–2000	Americas 49.3	Asia 30.7	Europe 14.9
All Years	Europe 58.2	Americas 26.6	Asia 13.3

Source: 2001 Statistical Yearbook of the Immigration and Naturalization Service, M-367 (Washington, DC: Government Printing Office, 2003), 17–20.

Table B.6 Leading Sending Countries (and Subregions), 1820–2000

Decade or Period	Leading Countries (and Subregions), and Percents			
1820–1830	Ireland 35.8	Britain 18.1		
1831–1840	Ireland 34.6	Germany 25.5	Britain 12.7	
1841–1850	Ireland 45.6	Germany 25.4	Britain 15.6	
1851–1860	Germany 36.6	Ireland 35.2	Britain 16.3	
1861–1870	Germany 34.0	Britain 26.2	Ireland 18.8	
1871–1880	Germany 25.5	Britain 19.5	Ireland 15.5	Canada 13.6
1881–1890	Germany 27.7	Britain 13.3	Scandinavia 12.5	Ireland 12.5
1891–1900	Italy 17.8	Aus-Hun 16.1	Russia 13.7	Germany 13.7[1]
1901–1910	Aus-Hun 24.4	Italy 23.3	Russia 18.2	
1911–1920	Italy 19.3	Russia 16.1	Aus-Hun 15.6	Canada 12.9
1921–1930	Canada 22.5	Mexico 11.2	Italy 11.1	Germany 10.0
1931–1940	Germany 21.9	Canada 20.5	Italy 12.9	
1941–1950	Germany 21.9	Canada 16.6	Britain 13.5	
1951–1960	Germany 19.0	Canada 15.0	Mexico 11.9	
1961–1970	Caribbean 14.2	Mexico 13.7	Canada 12.4	
1971–1980	Caribbean 16.5	Mexico 14.2		
1981–1990	Mexico 22.6	Caribbean 11.9		
1991–2000	Mexico 24.7	Caribbean 10.8		
All Years	Germany 10.9	Mexico 9.3	Italy 8.2	Britain 8.0[2]

Source: 2001 Statistical Yearbook of the Immigration and Naturalization Service, M-367 (Washington, DC: Government Printing Office, 2003): 17–20.

[1] Followed by Ireland 10.5, Scandinavia 10.5.

[2] Followed by Ireland 7.2, Canada 6.8, Austria-Hungary 6.6, Russia 5.9, Caribbean 5.6, Scandinavia 3.8, South America 2.7, China 2.6.

Table B.7   European Immigration, 1820–2000

Decade	European Immigration	Percent of Total Immigration
1820–1830	106,487	70.1
1831–1840	495,681	82.7
1841–1850	1,597,442	93.2
1851–1860	2,452,577	94.5
1861–1870	2,065,141	89.2
1871–1880	2,271,925	80.7
1881–1890	4,735,484	90.3
1891–1900	3,555,352	96.7
1901–1910	8,056,040	91.6
1911–1920	4,321,887	75.3
1921–1930	2,463,194	60.0
1931–1940	347,566	65.9
1941–1950	621,147	60.0
1951–1960	1,325,727	52.7
1961–1970	1,123,492	33.8
1971–1980	800,368	17.8
1981–1990	761,550	10.4
1991–2000	1,359,737	14.9
All Years	38,460,797	58.2

Source: 2001 Statistical Yearbook of the Immigration and Naturalization Service, M-367
(Washington, DC: Government Printing Office, 2003), 17–20.

Table B.8 Asian Immigration, 1820–2000

Decade	Asian Immigration	Percent of Total Immigration
1820–1830	36	—
1831–1840	55	—
1841–1850	141	—
1851–1860	41,538	1.6
1861–1870	64,759	2.8
1871–1880	124,160	4.4
1881–1890	69,942	1.3
1891–1900	74,862	2.0
1901–1910	323,543	3.7
1911–1920	247,236	4.3
1921–1930	112,059	2.7
1931–1940	16,595	3.1
1941–1950	37,028	3.6
1951–1960	153,249	6.1
1961–1970	427,642	12.9
1971–1980	1,588,178	35.3
1981–1990	2,738,157	37.3
1991–2000	2,795,672	30.7
All years	8,814,852	13.3

Source: 2001 Statistical Yearbook of the Immigration and Naturalization Service, M-367 (Washington, DC: Government Printing Office, 2003), 17–20.

Table B.9 British Immigration, 1820–2000

Decade	British[1] Immigration	Percent of Total Immigration
1820–1830	27,489	18.1
1831–1840	75,810	12.7
1841–1850	267,044	15.6
1851–1860	423,974	16.3
1861–1870	606,896	26.2
1871–1880	548,043	19.5
1881–1890	807,357	15.3
1891–1900	271,538	7.4
1901–1910	525,950	6.0
1911–1920	341,408	6.0
1921–1930	339,570	9.7
1931–1940	31,572	6.0
1941–1950	139,306	13.5
1951–1960	202,824	8.1
1961–1970	213,822	6.4
1971–1980	137,374	3.1
1981–1990	159,173	2.2
1991–2000	151,866	1.7
All Years	5,271,016	8.0

Source: 2001 Statistical Yearbook of the Immigration and Naturalization Service, M-367 (Washington, DC: Government Printing Office, 2003), 17–20.

[1] Includes England, Wales, and Scotland; after 1925 includes Northern Ireland.

Table B.10 German Immigration, 1820–2000

Decade	German Immigration	Percent of Total Immigration
1820–1830	7,729	5.1
1831–1840	152,454	25.5
1841–1850	434,626	25.4
1851–1860	951,667	36.6
1861–1870	787,468	34.0
1871–1880	718,182	25.5
1881–1890	1,452,970	27.7
1891–1900	505,152	13.7
1901–1910	341,498	3.9
1911–1920	143,945	2.5
1921–1930	412,202	10.0
1931–1940	114,058	21.6
1941–1950	226,578	21.9
1951–1960	477,765	19.0
1961–1970	190,796	5.7
1971–1980	74,414	1.7
1981–1990	91,961	1.3
1991–2000	92,606	1.0
All Years	7,176,971	10.9

Source: 2001 Statistical Yearbook of the Immigration and Naturalization Service, M-367 (Washington, DC: Government Printing Office, 2003), 17–20.

Table B.11 Irish Immigration, 1820–2000

Decade	Irish[1] Immigration	Percent of Total Immigration
1820–1830	54,338	35.8
1831–1840	207,381	34.6
1841–1850	780,719	45.6
1851–1860	914,119	35.2
1861–1870	435,778	18.8
1871–1880	436,871	15.5
1881–1890	655,482	12.5
1891–1900	388,416	10.5
1901–1910	339,065	3.9
1911–1920	146,181	2.5
1921–1930	211,234	5.1
1931–1940	10,973	2.1
1941–1950	19,789	1.9
1951–1960	48,362	1.9
1961–1970	32,966	1.0
1971–1980	11,490	0.2
1981–1990	31,969	0.4
1991–2000	56,950	0.6
All Years	4,782,083	7.2

Source: 2001 Statistical Yearbook of the Immigration and Naturalization Service, M-367 (Washington, DC: Government Printing Office, 2003), 17–20.

[1] Includes Northern Ireland through 1925.

Table B.12 Italian Immigration, 1820–2000

Decade	Italian Immigration	Percent of Total Immigration
1820–1830	439	0.3
1831–1840	2,253	0.4
1841–1850	1,870	0.1
1851–1860	9,231	0.4
1861–1870	11,725	0.5
1871–1880	55,759	2.0
1881–1890	307,309	5.9
1891–1900	651,893	17.8
1901–1910	2,045,877	23.3
1911–1920	1,109,524	19.3
1921–1930	455,315	11.1
1931–1940	68,028	12.9
1941–1950	57,661	5.6
1951–1960	185,491	7.4
1961–1970	214,111	6.4
1971–1980	129,368	2.3
1981–1990	67,254	0.9
1991–2000	62,722	0.7
All Years	5,435,830	8.2

Source: 2001 Statistical Yearbook of the Immigration and Naturalization Service, M-367 (Washington, DC: Government Printing Office, 2003), 17–20.

Table B.13 Austria-Hungarian Immigration, 1861–2000[1]

Decade	Austria-Hungarian Immigration	Percent of Total Immigration
1820–1830		
1831–1840		
1841–1850		
1851–1860		
1861–1870	7,800	0.3
1871–1880	72,969	2.6
1881–1890	353,719	6.7
1891–1900	592,707	16.1
1901–1910	2,145,266	24.4
1911–1920	896,342	15.6
1921–1930	63,548	1.5
1931–1940	11,424	2.2
1941–1950	28,329	2.7
1951–1960	103,743	4.1
1961–1970	26,022	0.8
1971–1980	16,028	0.4
1981–1990	24,885	0.3
1991–2000	24,882	0.3
All Years	4,367,664	6.6

Source: 2001 Statistical Yearbook of the Immigration and Naturalization Service, M-367 (Washington, DC: Government Printing Office, 2003), 17–20.

[1] Migrants from Austria and Hungary were not reported until 1861, were reported together until World War I. Includes some Polish numbers, 1899–1919.

Table B.14 Scandinavian Immigration, 1820–2000

Decade	Scandinavian[1] Immigration	Percent of Total Immigration
1820–1830	283	0.2
1831–1840	2,264	0.4
1841–1850	14,442	0.8
1851–1860	24,680	0.9
1861–1870	126,392	5.5
1871–1880	243,016	8.6
1881–1890	656,494	12.5
1891–1900	371,512	10.1
1901–1910	505,324	5.7
1911–1920	203,452	3.5
1921–1930	198,210	4.8
1931–1940	11,259	2.1
1941–1950	26,158	2.5
1951–1960	55,616	2.2
1961–1970	41,801	1.3
1971–1980	14,911	0.3
1981–1990	20,552	0.3
1991–2000	23,972	0.3
All Years	2,540,338	3.8

Source: 2001 Statistical Yearbook of the Immigration and Naturalization Service, M-367 (Washington, DC: Government Printing Office, 2003), 17–20.

[1] Norway, Sweden, and Denmark.

Table B.15 Russian/Soviet Union Immigration, 1820–2000[1]

Decade	Russian / Soviet Union Immigration	Percent of Total Immigration
1820–1830	89	—
1831–1840	277	—
1841–1850	551	—
1851–1860	457	—
1861–1870	2,512	0.1
1871–1880	39,284	1.4
1881–1890	213,282	4.1
1891–1900	505,290	13.7
1901–1910	1,597,306	18.2
1911–1920	921,201	16.1
1921–1930	61,742	1.5
1931–1940	1,370	0.3
1941–1950	571	—
1951–1960	671	—
1961–1970	2,465	0.1
1971–1980	38,961	0.9
1981–1990	57,677	0.8
1991–2000	462,874	5.1
All Years	3,906,580	5.9

Source: 2001 Statistical Yearbook of the Immigration and Naturalization Service, M-367 (Washington, DC: Government Printing Office, 2003), 17–20.

[1] Includes some Polish numbers, 1899–1919, as Poland was split between Austria-Hungary, Germany, and Russia.

Table B.16 Chinese Immigration, 1820–2000

Decade	Chinese Immigration	Percent of Total Immigration
1820–1830	3	—
1831–1840	8	—
1841–1850	35	—
1851–1860	41,397	1.6
1861–1870	64,759	2.8
1871–1880	124,160	4.4
1881–1890	69,942	1.3
1891–1900	14,799	0.4
1901–1910	20,605	0.2
1911–1920	21,278	0.4
1921–1930	29,907	0.7
1931–1940	4,928	0.9
1941–1950	16,709	1.6
1951–1960	25,198	1.0
1961–1970	109,771	3.3
1971–1980	237,793	5.3
1981–1990	444,942	6.1
1991–2000	528,893	5.8
All Years	1,745,499	2.6

Source: 2001 Statistical Yearbook of the Immigration and Naturalization Service, M-367
(Washington, DC: Government Printing Office, 2003), 17–20.

Table B.17 Japanese Immigration, 1861–2000[1]

Decade	Japanese Immigration	Percent of Total Immigration
1820–1830		
1831–1840		
1841–1850		
1851–1860		
1861–1870	186	—
1871–1880	149	—
1881–1890	2,270	—
1891–1900	25,942	0.7
1901–1910	129,797	1.5
1911–1920	83,837	1.5
1921–1930	33,462	0.8
1931–1940	1,948	0.4
1941–1950	1,555	0.2
1951–1960	46,250	1.8
1961–1970	39,988	1.2
1971–1980	49,775	1.1
1981–1990	47,085	0.6
1991–2000	67,942	0.7
All Years	530,186	0.8

Source: 2001 Statistical Yearbook of the Immigration and Naturalization Service, M-367 (Washington, DC: Government Printing Office, 2003), 17–20.

[1] Data for Japan not reported until 1861.

Table B.18 Korean Immigration, 1941–2000[1]

Decade	Korean Immigration	Percent of Total Immigration
1820–1830		
1831–1840		
1841–1850		
1851–1860		
1861–1870		
1871–1880		
1881–1890		
1891–1900		
1901–1910		
1911–1920		
1921–1930		
1931–1940		
1941–1950	107	—
1951–1960	6,231	0.2
1961–1970	34,526	1.0
1971–1980	267,638	6.0
1981–1990	333,746	4.5
1991–2000	164,166	1.8
All Years	806,414	1.2

Source: 2001 Statistical Yearbook of the Immigration and Naturalization Service, M-367 (Washington, DC: Government Printing Office, 2003): 17–20.

[1] Koreans were included in Japanese numbers until 1948.

Table B.19 Asian Indian Immigration, 1820–2000

Decade	Asian Indian Immigration	Percent of Total Immigration
1820–1830	9	—
1831–1840	39	—
1841–1850	36	—
1851–1860	43	—
1861–1870	69	—
1871–1880	163	—
1881–1890	269	—
1891–1900	68	—
1901–1910	4,713	—
1911–1920	2,082	—
1921–1930	1,886	—
1931–1940	496	0.3
1941–1950	1,761	0.2
1951–1960	1,973	0.1
1961–1970	27,189	0.8
1971–1980	164,134	3.7
1981–1990	250,786	3.4
1991–2000	363,060	4.0
All Years	818,776	1.2

Source: 2001 Statistical Yearbook of the Immigration and Naturalization Service, M-367 (Washington, DC: Government Printing Office, 2003), 17–20.

Table B.20 Filipino Immigration, 1934–2000[1]

Decade	Filipino Immigration	Percent of Total Immigration
1820–1830		
1831–1840		
1841–1850		
1851–1860		
1861–1870		
1871–1880		
1881–1890		
1891–1900		
1901–1910		
1911–1920		
1921–1930		
1931–1940	528	0.1
1941–1950	4,691	0.5
1951–1960	19,307	0.8
1961–1970	98,376	3.0
1971–1980	354,987	7.9
1981–1990	548,764	7.5
1991–2000	503,945	5.5
All Years	1,530,598	2.3

Source: 2001 Statistical Yearbook of the Immigration and Naturalization Service, M-367 (Washington, DC: Government Printing Office, 2003), 17–20.

[1] Filipino migrants were not reported until 1934.

Table B.21 Vietnamese Immigration, 1952–2000[1]

Decade	Vietnamese Immigration	Percent of Total Immigration
1820–1830		
1831–1840		
1841–1850		
1851–1860		
1861–1870		
1871–1880		
1881–1890		
1891–1900		
1901–1910		
1911–1920		
1921–1930		
1931–1940		
1941–1950		
1951–1960	335	—
1961–1970	4,340	0.1
1971–1980	172,820	3.8
1981–1990	280,782	3.8
1991–2000	286,145	3.1
All Years	744,422	1.1

Source: 2001 Statistical Yearbook of the Immigration and Naturalization Service, M-367 (Washington, DC: Government Printing Office, 2003), 17–20.

[1] Filipino migrants were not reported until 1934.

Table B.22 Mexican Immigration, 1820–2000[1]

Decade	Mexican Immigration	Percent of Total Immigration
1820–1830	4,818	3.2
1831–1840	6,599	1.1
1841–1850	3,271	0.2
1851–1860	3,078	0.1
1861–1870	2,191	0.1
1871–1880	5,162	0.2
1881–1890	1,913	—
1891–1900	971	—
1901–1910	49,642	0.6
1911–1920	219,004	3.8
1921–1930	459,287	11.2
1931–1940	22,319	4.2
1941–1950	60,589	5.9
1951–1960	299,811	11.9
1961–1970	453,937	13.7
1971–1980	640,294	14.2
1981–1990	1,655,843	22.6
1991–2000	2,249,421	24.7
All Years	6,138,150	9.3

Source: *2001 Statistical Yearbook of the Immigration and Naturalization Service, M-367* (Washington, DC: Government Printing Office, 2003), 17–20.

[1] Land arrivals not completely enumerated until 1908. No Mexico data at all for 1886–1894.

Table B.23 Canadian Immigration, 1820–2000[1]

Decade	Canadian Immigration	Percent of Total Immigration
1820–1830	2,486	1.6
1831–1840	13,624	2.3
1841–1850	41,723	2.4
1851–1860	59,309	2.3
1861–1870	153,878	6.6
1871–1880	383,640	13.6
1881–1890	393,304	7.5
1891–1900	3,311	0.1
1901–1910	179,226	2.0
1911–1920	742,185	12.9
1921–1930	924,515	22.5
1931–1940	108,527	20.5
1941–1950	171,718	16.6
1951–1960	377,952	15.0
1961–1970	413,310	12.4
1971–1980	169,939	3.8
1981–1990	156,938	2.1
1991–2000	191,987	2.1
All Years	4,487,572	6.8

Source: 2001 Statistical Yearbook of the Immigration and Naturalization Service, M-367 (Washington, DC: Government Printing Office, 2003), 17–20.

[1] Land arrivals not completely enumerated until 1908.

Table B.24 Caribbean Immigration, 1820–2000[1]

Decade	Caribbean Immigration	Percent of Total Immigration
1820–1830	3,998	2.6
1831–1840	12,301	2.1
1841–1850	13,528	0.8
1851–1860	10,660	0.4
1861–1870	9,046	0.4
1871–1880	13,957	0.5
1881–1890	29,042	0.6
1891–1900	33,066	0.9
1901–1910	107,548	1.2
1911–1920	123,424	2.2
1921–1930	74,899	1.8
1931–1940	15,502	2.9
1941–1950	49,725	4.8
1951–1960	123,091	4.9
1961–1970	470,213	14.2
1971–1980	741,126	16.5
1981–1990	872,051	11.9
1991–2000	978,787	10.8
All Years	3,681,964	5.6

Source: 2001 Statistical Yearbook of the Immigration and Naturalization Service, M-367 (Washington, DC: Government Printing Office, 2003), 17–20.

[1] Does not include Puerto Rico after 1898.

Table B.25 Cuban Immigration, 1925–2000[1]

Decade	Cuban Immigration	Percent of Total Immigration
1820–1830		
1831–1840		
1841–1850		
1851–1860		
1861–1870		
1871–1880		
1881–1890		
1891–1900		
1901–1910		
1911–1920		
1921–1930	15,901	0.4
1931–1940	9,571	1.8
1941–1950	26,313	2.5
1951–1960	78,948	3.1
1961–1970	208,536	6.3
1971–1980	264,863	5.9
1981–1990	144,578	2.0
1991–2000	169,322	1.9
All Years	918,032	1.4

Source: 2001 Statistical Yearbook of the Immigration and Naturalization Service, M-367 (Washington, DC: Government Printing Office, 2003), 17–20.

[1] Not reported separately until 1925.

Table B.26 Central American Immigration, 1820–2000

Decade	Central American Immigration	Percent of Total Immigration
1820–1830	107	—
1831–1840	44	—
1841–1850	368	—
1851–1860	449	—
1861–1870	95	—
1871–1880	157	—
1881–1890	404	—
1891–1900	549	—
1901–1910	8,192	0.1
1911–1920	17,159	0.3
1921–1930	15,769	0.4
1931–1940	5,861	1.1
1941–1950	21,665	2.1
1951–1960	44,751	1.8
1961–1970	101,330	3.1
1971–1980	134,680	3.0
1981–1990	468,088	6.4
1991–2000	526,915	5.6
All Years	1,346,543	2.0

Source: 2001 Statistical Yearbook of the Immigration and Naturalization Service, M-367 (Washington, DC: Government Printing Office, 2003), 17–20.

Table B.27   South American Immigration, 1820–2000

Decade	South American Immigration	Percent of Total Immigration
1820–1830	542	0.4
1831–1840	856	0.1
1841–1850	3,579	0.2
1851–1860	1,224	—
1861–1870	1,397	—
1871–1880	1,128	—
1881–1890	2,304	—
1891–1900	1,075	—
1901–1910	17,280	0.2
1911–1920	41,899	0.7
1921–1930	42,215	1.0
1931–1940	7,803	1.5
1941–1950	21,831	2.1
1951–1960	91,628	3.6
1961–1970	257,940	7.8
1971–1980	295,741	6.6
1981–1990	461,847	6.3
1991–2000	539,656	5.9
All Years	1,789,945	2.7

Source: 2001 Statistical Yearbook of the Immigration and Naturalization Service, M-367 (Washington, DC: Government Printing Office, 2003), 17–20.

Table B.28 African Immigration, 1820–2000

Decade	African Immigration	Percent of Total Immigration
1820–1830	107	—
1831–1840	55	—
1841–1850	368	—
1851–1860	449	—
1861–1870	95	—
1871–1880	157	—
1881–1890	404	—
1891–1900	350	—
1901–1910	7,368	0.1
1911–1920	8,443	0.1
1921–1930	6,286	0.2
1931–1940	1,750	0.3
1941–1950	7,367	0.7
1951–1960	14,092	0.6
1961–1970	28,954	0.9
1971–1980	80,779	1.8
1981–1990	176,893	2.4
1991–2000	354,939	3.9
All Years	689,084	1.0

Source: 2001 Statistical Yearbook of the Immigration and Naturalization Service, M-367 (Washington, DC: Government Printing Office, 2003), 17–20.

Table B.29 Immigration and Return Migration for Various Nationalities, 1908–1924 (in thousands)

Group	Immigrants	Emigrants	Percent Emigrants
Jews	1,009	52	5.2
Irish	475	48	10.1
Scotch	362	40	11.1
Germans	765	121	15.9
Ruthenians	174	29	16.7
French	353	64	18.1
English	801	153	19.1
Scandinavians	490	101	20.5
Lithuanians	140	35	25.0
Poles	808	321	39.7
Greeks	372	176	47.4
Croats and Slovenes	230	115	50.1
Russians	220	111	50.5
Italians	2,085	1,140	54.7
Slovaks	231	128	55.5
Magyars	234	150	64.0
Rumanians	97	64	65.9
Other peoples	1,811	727	40.1
Total	10,657	3,575	33.5

Source: Liebmann Hersch, "International Migration of the Jews," in *International Migrations*, Vol. II, Walter F. Willcox, Ed. (New York: Gordon and Breach, 1969), 477.

Table B.30 Native Children of Foreign-Born Parents by Region of Parents' Birth, 1900–1970[1]

Year	Northwest Europe[2]	Eastern Europe[3]	Southern Europe[4]	Other Europe	Asia	Americas	Other	Total
1900	12,460,465	1,088,395	254,550	—	—	1,389,470	453,137	15,646,017
1910	13,574,282	2,546,232	856,178	—	—	1,843,949	74,196	18,897,204
1920	13,621,092	4,802,507	1,940,458	—	—	2,146,040	176,407	22,686,204
1930	13,588,950	6,209,008	3,035,900	101,652	—	2,717,565	96,960	25,902,383
1940	10,636,100	6,049,720	3,310,380	75,660	—	2,657,240	245,220	23,157,580
1950	10,233,700	6,324,085	3,525,805	128,030	—	2,981,040	157,300	23,589,485
1960	9,397,632	6,459,174	3,736,121	121,984	121,984	3,636,913	317,919	24,312,263
1970	7,996,826	5,939,186	3,736,742	168,082	168,082	4,281,014	913,605	23,955,930

Source: US Bureau of the Census, *Historical Statistics of the United States: Colonial Times to 1970*, Part 1 (Washington, DC: Government Printing Office, 1975), 116.

[1] Native born of foreign or mixed parentage. Whites only before 1960.
[2] United Kingdom, Ireland, Norway, Sweden, Denmark, Netherlands, Belgium, Switzerland, France, Germany.
[3] Poland, Czechoslovakia, Austria, Hungary, Yugoslavia (from 1990 its successor republics), Russia/USSR, Lithuania, Finland, Romania.
[4] Greece, Italy, Spain, Portugal.

Table B.31 Size and Percentage of Foreign-Born Population, 1850–2000

Year	Size of Foreign-Born Population	Total Population	Foreign-Born as Percentage of Total Population
1850	2,244,602	23,191,876	9.7
1860	4,138,697	32,645,493	12.7
1870	5,567,229	38,558,371	14.4
1880	6,679,943	50,155,783	13.3
1890	9,249,547	62,947,714	14.7
1900	10,341,276	75,994,575	13.6
1910	13,515,886	91,972,266	14.7
1920	13,920,692	105,710,620	13.2
1930	10,347,395	122,775,046	8.4
1940	11,594,896	131,669,275	8.8
1950	10,347,395	150,697,361	6.9
1960	9,738,155	179,323,175	5.4
1970	9,619,302	203,211,926	4.7
1980	14,079,905	226,545,805	6.2
1990	19,767,316	248,709,873	8.0
2000	31,107,889	281,421,906	11.1

Sources: Nolan Malone, Kaari F. Baluja, Joseph M. Costanzo, and Cynthia J. Davis, *The Foreign-Born Population: 2000*; Census 2000 Brief C2KBR-34 (Washington, DC: US Census Bureau, 2003), 3; *2001 Statistical Yearbook of the Immigration and Naturalization Service* (Washington, DC: Government Printing Office, 2003), 16; US Bureau of the Census, *Historical Statistics of the United States, Colonial Times to 1970*, Part I (Washington, DC: Government Printing Office, 1975), 8.

Table B.32 Foreign Born Population by Region of Birth, 1850–2000

Year	Northwest Europe[1]	Eastern Europe[2]	Southern Europe[3]	Other Europe	Asia	Canada	Latin America/ Caribbean	Other/Not Reported	Total
1850	2,021,249	2,360	8,258		1,135	147,711	20,773	43,116	2,244,602
1860	3,748,286	35,519	20,493	1,403	36,796	249,970	38,315	7,915	4,138,697
1870	4,815,171	93,664	26,155	1,678	64,565	493,464	57,871	14,711	5,567,229
1880	5,461,226	219,829	59,470	3,786	107,630	717,157	90,073	20,772	6,679,943
1890	7,165,646	633,896	208,487	12,579	113,396	980,938	107,307	27,311	9,249,560
1900	6,866,101	1,471,389	540,110	2,251	120,248	1,179,922	137,458	31,868	10,341,276
1910	6,550,304	3,670,561	1,558,105	12,871	191,484	1,209,717	279,514	43,330	13,515,886
1920	5,516,202	4,443,453	1,916,497	5,901	237,950	1,138,174	588,843	73,672	13,920,692
1930	5,336,864	4,286,728	2,108,552	16,255	275,665	1,310,369	791,840	77,876	14,204,149
1940[4]									
1950	3,261,131	3,186,177	1,653,878	185,685	275,990	1,003,038	652,286	202,723	10,420,908
1960	2,962,840	2,728,092	1,528,473	14,320	499,312	952,500	908,309	144,245	9,738,091
1970	2,369,687	1,973,129	1,343,510	20,700	824,887	812,421	1,803,970	465,998	9,619,302
1980	13,163,391	1,440,914	1,336,805	26,950	2,539,777	853,427	4,372,487	1,164,643	14,079,906
1990	18,936,845	1,253,685	1,054,141	15,351	4,979,037	753,917	8,407,837	1,276,122	19,767,316
2000	4,915,557[5]				8,226,254	829,442	16,086,346	1,049,346	31,107,573

Sources: US Bureau of the Census, *Historical Statistics of the United States: Colonial Times to 1970*, Part 1 (Washington, DC: Government Printing Office, 1975), 117–118; Campbell J. Gibson and Emily Lennon, "Historical Census Statistics on the Foreign-born Population of the United States: 1850–1990," US Bureau of the Census Population Division Working Paper No. 29 (February 1999), www.census.gov/population/www/documentation/twps0029/twps0029.html (December 17, 2003).

[1] Belgium, Denmark, France, Germany, Iceland, Ireland, Luxembourg, Netherlands, Norway, Sweden, Switzerland, United Kingdom.
[2] Albania, Austria, Bulgaria, Czechoslovakia, Estonia, Finland, Hungary, Latvia, Lithuania, Poland, Romania, Russia/USSR (from 1990 its successor republics), Yugoslavia (from 1990 its successor republics).
[3] Greece, Italy, Spain, Portugal.
[4] There are no data for this subject in the 1940 census.
[5] Regions within Europe are not differentiated in the 2000 census.

Table B.33 Jewish Population, 1654–2000

Year	Estimated Jewish Population
1654	25
1700	200–300
1776	1,000–2,500
1790	1,243–3,000
1800	2,000–2,500
1820	2,650–5,000
1826	6,000
1830	4,000–6,000
1840	15,000
1848	50,000
1850	50,000–100,000
1860	150,000–200,000
1870	200,000
1880	230,000–280,000
1890	400,000–475,000
1900	937,800–1,058,135
1910	1,508,000–2,349,754
1920	3,300,000–3,604,580
1927	4,228,029
1937	4,641,000–4,831,180
1940	4,770,000–4,975,000
1950	4,500,000–5,000,000
1960	5,367,000–5,531,500
1970	5,370,000–6,000,000
1980	5,500,000–5,920,890
1992	5,828,000
2000	6,136,000

Sources: "Jewish Population of the United States (1654–2001," *Jewish Virtual Library*, American-Israeli Cooperative Enterprise <http://www.us-israel.org/jsource/US-Israel/usjewpop1.html> (April 30, 2004); American Jewish Historical Society, *American Jewish Desk Reference* (New York: AJHS, 1999): 35; *American Jewish Year Book 2000* (New York: American Jewish Committee, 2000).

Table B.34 Jewish Immigration, 1881–1923

Year	Jewish Immigration	Year	Jewish Immigration
1881	8,193	1903	76,203
1882	31,807	1904	106,236
1883	6,907	1905	129,910
1884	15,122	1906	153,748
1885	36,214	1907	149,182
1886	46,967	1908	103,387
1887	56,412	1909	57,551
1888	62,619	1910	84,260
1889	55,851	1911	91,223
1890	67,450	1912	80,595
1891	111,284	1913	101,330
1892	136,782	1914	138,051
1893	68,569	1915	26,497
1894	58,833	1916	15,108
1895	65,309	1917	17,342
1896	73,255	1918	3,672
1897	43,434	1919	3,055
1898	54,630	1920	14,292
1899	37,415	1921	119,036
1900	60,764	1922	53,524
1901	58,098	1923	49,989
1902	57,688		

Source: Mark Wischnitzer, *To Dwell in Safety: The Story of Jewish Migration since 1800* (Philadelphia: Jewish Publication Society of America, 1948), 289.

Table B.35 Country of Birth for Foreign-Born Northeast Europeans, 1850–1990[1]

Census Year	Sweden	Norway	Denmark	Finland	Total[2]
1850	3,559	12,678	1,838	—[3]	18,075
1860	18,625	43,995	9,962	—	72,582
1870	97,332	114,246	30,107	—	241,685
1880	194,337	181,729	64,196	—	440,262
1890	478,041	322,665	132,543	—	933,249
1900	582,014	336,388	153,690	62,641	1,134,733
1910	665,207	403,877	181,649	129,680	1,380,413
1920	625,585	363,863	189,154	149,824	1,328,426
1930	595,250	347,852	179,474	142,478	1,267,818
1940					
1950					
1960	214,491	152,698	85,060	67,624	522,653
1970	127,070	97,243	61,410	45,499	216,533
1980	77,157	63,316	42,732	29,172	216,533
1990	53,676	42,240	34,999	22,313	158,299
2000					

Source: Campbell J. Gibson and Emily Lennon, "Historical Census Statistics on the Foreign-Born Population of the United States: 1850–1990," US Bureau of the Census Population Division Working Paper No. 29 (February 1999), www.census.gov/population/www/documentation/twps0029/tab04.html (December 17, 2003).

[1] Numbers are not available for 1940 and 1950.
[2] Includes Iceland.
[3] Census reports do not state where Finns were placed in immigration numbers before 1900. I presume they are in the Russian total, as Russia controlled Finland until 1917.

Table B.36 Mexicans Admitted under Bracero Program and on Permanent Visas, 1942–1964

Year	Permanent Visas	Bracero Program	Total	Bracero Percentage
1942	2,182	4,203	6,385	66.7
1943	3,985	52,098	56,083	92.9
1944	6,399	62,170	68,569	90.7
1945	6,455	49,454	55,909	88.5
1946	6,805	32,043	38,848	82.5
1947	7,775	19,632	27,407	71.6
1948	8,730	35,345	44,075	80.2
1949	7,977	107,000	114,977	93.1
1950	6,841	67,500	74,341	90.8
1951	6,372	192,000	198,372	96.8
1952	9,600	197,100	207,700	94.9
1953	18,454	201,380	219,834	91.6
1954	37,456	309,033	346,489	89.2
1955	50,722	398,650	449,372	88.7
1956	65,047	445,197	510,244	87.3
1957	49,154	436,049	485,203	89.9
1958	26,712	432,857	459,569	94.2
1959	23,061	437,643	460,704	95.0
1960	32,684	315,846	348,530	90.6
1961	41,632	291,420	333,052	87.5
1962	55,291	194,978	250,269	77.9
1963	55,253	186,865	242,118	77.2
1964	32,967	177,736	210,703	84.4
Total 1942–1964	561,554	4,646,199	5,207,753	89.2

Source: Kitty Calavita, *Inside the State: The Bracero Program, Immigration, and the INS* (New York: Routledge, 1992), 218. Note that the 1947–1950 Bracero figures are low by about 50,000 each year; they do not include illegal Mexican farm workers who worked in the United States under Bracero contracts in those years.

Table B.37 Noncitizen Spouses and Minor Children Admitted or Status Adjusted under the War Brides Acts, 1945–1950, by Regions and Select Countries

Origins	Number Admitted	Husbands	Wives	Children
Europe	87,624	234	84,517	2,873
France	8,744	23	8,581	140
Germany	14,931	6	14,175	750
Great Britain	35,469	53	34,944	472
Italy	9,728	21	9,046	661
Asia	10,202	17	9,264	921
China	5,726	5	5,132	589
Japan	467	4	458	5
Philippines	2,485	1	2,215	269
Americas	12,718	60	11,499	619
Canada	7,541	44	7,254	243
Mexico	2,300	6	2,080	214
Other regions	12,174	23	11,626	525
Australia	6,853	7	6,671	175
Total	119,963	333	114,691	4,669

Source: Xiaojian Zhao, *Remaking Chinese America: Immigration, Family, and Community, 1940–1965* (New Brunswick, NJ: Rutgers University Press, 2002), 79, from US Immigration and Naturalization Service Annual Report, 1950.

Table B.38 Southeast Asian Refugees Admitted, 1975–1992

Year	Highland Laotian[1]	Lowland Laotian[2]	Cambodian	Vietnamese	Amerasian[3]
1975	300	500	4,600	125,000	0
1976	3,000	7,100	1,100	3,200	0
1977	1,700	400	300	1,900	0
1978	3,900	4,100	1,300	11,100	0
1979	11,300	18,900	6,000	44,500	0
1980	27,200	28,300	16,000	95,200	0
1981	3,700	15,600	27,100	86,100	0
1982	2,600	6,800	20,100	42,600	0
1983	700	2,100	13,200	23,000	0
1984	2,800	4,500	19,900	24,900	0
1985	1,900	3,500	19,200	25,400	0
1986	3,700	9,200	9,800	22,800	0
1987	8,300	7,300	1,500	23,000	0
1988	10,400	4,200	2,800	17,300	400
1989	8,500	4,000	1,900	22,600	8,700
1990	5,200	3,600	2,200	27,300	13,400
1991	6,400	2,900	50	27,700	16,500
1992	6,800	500	100	27,200	17,100

Source: Jeremy Hein, *From Vietnam, Laos, and Cambodia: A Refugee Experience in the United States* (New York: Twayne, 1995), 47.

[1] Mainly Hmong, but also Mien, Tai Dam, and Lao-theung.
[2] Ethnic Lao.
[3] American-Vietnamese children born in Vietnam and accompanying relatives.

Notes

Preface

1. Thomas S. Kuhn, *The Copernican Revolution: Planetary Astronomy in the Development of Western Thought* (Cambridge, MA: Harvard University Press, 1957); Kuhn, *The Structure of Scientific Revolutions* (Chicago: University of Chicago Press, 1962).
2. Frederick Jackson Turner, *The Frontier in American History* (New York: Holt, 1920); Ray Allen Billington, *The Far Western Frontier, 1830–1860* (New York: Harper, 1956); Walter Prescott Webb, *The Great Frontier* (Boston: Houghton Mifflin, 1952). See also Richard Slotkin, *Gunfighter Nation: The Myth of the Frontier in Twentieth-Century America* (New York: Atheneum, 1992).
3. Patricia Nelson Limerick, *Legacy of Conquest: The Unbroken Past of the American West* (New York: Norton, 1987); Patricia Nelson Limerick, Clyde Milner II, and Charles Rankin, *Trails: Toward a New Western History* (Lawrence: University Press of Kansas, 1991); Richard White, *The Middle Ground: Indians, Empires, and Republics in the Great Lakes Region, 1680–1815* (Cambridge: Cambridge University Press, 1991); White, *"It's Your Misfortune and None of My Own": A New History of the American West* (Norman: University of Oklahoma Press, 1993).
4. Roger Daniels, *The Politics of Prejudice: The Anti-Japanese Movement in California and the Struggle for Japanese Exclusion* (Berkeley: University of California Press, 1962); Roger Daniels, *Not Like Us: Immigrants and Minorities in America*, 1890–1924 (New York: Ivan Dee, 1998); Roger Daniels, *Coming to America: A History of Immigration and Ethnicity in American Life*, 2nd ed. (New York: Harper Perennial, 2002); Roger Daniels, *Guarding the Golden Door: American Immigration Policy and Immigrants Since 1882* (New York: Hill and Wang, 2003); Donna R. Gabaccia, *From Sicily to Elizabeth Street: Housing and Social Change Among Italian Immigrants, 1880–1930* (Albany: SUNY Press, 1984);

Donna R. Gabaccia, Ed., *Seeking Common Ground: Multidisciplinary Studies of Immigrant Women in the United States* (Westport, CT: Praeger, 1992); Donna R. Gabaccia, *From the Other Side: Women, Gender and Immigrant Life in the United States, 1820–1990* (Bloomington: Indiana University Press, 1994); Donna R. Gabaccia, *We Are What We Eat: Ethnic Food and the Making of Americans* (Cambridge, MA: Harvard University Press, 2000); Donna R. Gabaccia, *Italy's Many Diasporas* (Seattle: University of Washington Press, 2000); Donna R. Gabaccia, *Immigration and American Diversity: A Social and Cultural History* (Oxford: Blackwell, 2002); Elliott R. Barkan, *Asian and Pacific Islander Migration to the United States: A Model of New Global Patterns* (Westport, CT: Greenwood, 1992); Elliott R. Barkan, *And Still They Come: Immigrants and American Society, 1920 to the 1990s* (Arlington Heights, IL: Harlan Davidson, 1996); Elliott R. Barkan, Ed., *A Nation of Peoples: A Sourcebook on America's Multicultural Heritage* (Westport, CT: Greenwood, 1999); Elliott R. Barkan, *From All Points, Due West: Immigration to the American West in the Twentieth Century* (Bloomington: Indiana University Press, 2007).

5. Ethnic studies scholars whose work is fundamental to the paradigm shift are legion. Among the most influential are Ronald T. Takaki, *Iron Cages: Race and Culture in Nineteenth-Century America* (New York: Knopf, 1979); Takaki, *A Different Mirror: A History of Multicultural America* (Boston: Back Bay Books, 1994); Vicki L. Ruiz, *Cannery Women, Cannery Lives: Mexican Women, Unionization, and the California Food Processing Industry, 1930–1950* (Albuquerque: University of New Mexico Press, 1987); Vicki L. Ruiz, *From Out of the Shadows: Mexican American Women in Twentieth-Century America* (New York: Oxford, 1999); Gary Y. Okihiro, *Cane Fires: The Anti-Japanese Movement in Hawaii, 1865–1945* (Philadelphia: Temple University Press, 1992); Gary Y. Okihiro, *Margins and Mainstreams: Asians in American History and Culture* (Seattle: University of Washington Press, 1994); Gary Y. Okihiro, *Common Ground: Reimagining American History* (Princeton, NJ: Princeton University Press, 2001); George Sánchez, *Becoming Mexican American: Ethnicity, Culture, and Identity in Chicano Los Angeles, 1900–1945* (New York: Oxford, 1993); Yen le Espiritu, *Asian American Panethnicity* (Philadelphia: Temple University Press, 1992); Michael Omi and Howard Winant, *Racial Formation in the United States*, rev. ed. (New York: Routledge, 1994); David G. Gutiérrez, *Wall and Mirrors: Mexican Americans, Mexican Immigrants, and the Politics of Ethnicity* (Berkeley: University of California Press, 1995); Martha Menchaca, *Recovering History, Constructing Race: The Indian, Black, and White Roots of Mexican Americans* (Austin: University of Texas Press, 2001); George Lipsitz, *The Possessive Investment in Whiteness* (Philadelphia: Temple University Press, 1998).

6. Jon Gjerde, *From Peasants to Farmers: The Migration from Balestrand, Norway, to the Upper Middle West* (Cambridge: Cambridge University Press, 1985), xiii; Dag Blanck and Philip J. Anderson, *Swedish-American Life in Chicago: Cultural and Urban Aspects of an Immigrant People, 1850–1930* (Urbana: University of Illinois Press, 1992); Richard White, *Remembering Ahanagran* (New York: Hill and Wang, 1999); Ronald T. Takaki, *Strangers from a Different Shore: A History of Asian Americans*, rev. ed. (Boston: Back Bay Books, 1998). I confess to an element of own-life-searching in my first book, *Mixed Blood: Intermarriage and Ethnic Identity in Twentieth-Century America* (Madison: University of Wisconsin Press, 1989). But subsequently I have ranged quite widely from things about which I know personally.

7. The conference was titled "Transcending Borders: Migration, Ethnicity, and Incorporation in an Age of Globalism" and it took place October 31–November 2, 2003. It was hosted by New York University and was sponsored by the Immigration and Ethnic History Society, with support from the Center for Migration Studies, American University, and other agencies.

8. For example, Nancy Foner, in a keynote address, spoke of "New York, America's classic immigrant city," and in other phrases such as "in New York, to say nothing of the United States as a whole" signaled that she was writing the New York immigration story onto the whole nation. Nancy Foner, "Then *and* Now or Then *to* Now: Migration to New York in Contemporary and Historical Perspective," paper presented to the conference, "Transcending Borders," New York, October 31, 2003.

Chapter 1

1. "Muslims Protest Border Check," "U.S. Border Fingerprint Data Faulted," and Johanna Neuman, "Canadian Cattle Cleared to Cross U.S. Border Again," all in *Los Angeles Times* (December 30, 2004).

2. Peter Kwong, *Forbidden Workers: Illegal Chinese Immigrants and American Labor* (New York: New Press, 1997), 1–10; Nancy Foner, *From Ellis Island to JFK: New York's Two Great Waves of Immigration* (New Haven, CT: Yale University Press, 2000), 17–18, 32–35; Patricia R. Pessar, *A Visa for a Dream: Dominicans in the United States* (Boston: Allyn and Bacon, 1995); Nina Bernstein, "Greener Pastures (on the Emerald Isle)" *New York Times* (November 10, 2004); Ellen Barry, "Survivors of a Sordid Venture Seek a Place," *Los Angeles Times* (April 27, 2006).

3. Nancy Abelmann and John Lie, *Blue Dreams: Korean Americans and the Los Angeles Riots* (Cambridge, MA: Harvard University Press, 1995); Edward T. Chang and Russell C. Leong, Eds., *Los Angeles—Struggles Toward Multiethnic Community: Asian American, African American, and Latino Perspectives* (Seattle: University of Washington Press, 1994); Robert Gooding-Williams, Ed., *Reading Rodney King/Reading Urban Uprising* (New York: Routledge, 1993).

4. Benjamin Z. Zulueta, "'Brains at a Bargain': Refugee Chinese Intellectuals, American Science, and the 'Cold War of the Classrooms'" (Ph.D. dissertation, University of California, Santa Barbara, 2003): 63–67; Iris Chang, *Thread of the Silkworm* (New York: Basic Books, 1995); William L. Ryan and Sam Summerlin, *The China Cloud: America's Tragic Blunder and China's Rise to Nuclear Power* (Boston: Little, Brown, 1968).

5. Francisco E. Balderrama and Raymond Rodríguez, *Decade of Betrayal: Mexican Repatriation in the 1930s* (Albuquerque: University of New Mexico Press, 1995); R. Reynolds McKay, "Texas Mexican Repatriation During the Great Depression," (Ph.D. dissertation, University of Oklahoma, 1982); Rodolfo Acuña, *Occupied America: A History of Chicanos*, 3rd ed. (New York: Harper and Row, 1988), 200–206; Barbara M. Posadas, *The Filipino Americans* (Westport, CT: Greenwood, 1999), 23–24.

6. Roger Daniels, *Guarding the Golden Door: American Immigration Policy and Immigrants Since 1882* (New York: Hill and Wang, 2004), 27–58; Roger Daniels, *Coming to America: A History of Immigration and Ethnicity in American Life*, 2nd ed. (New York: HarperCollins, 2002), 282–284.

7. Francis Paul Prucha, *The Great Father: The United States Government and the American Indians*, abr. ed. (Lincoln: University of Nebraska Press, 1986), 221; H. Henrietta Stockel, *Survival of the Spirit: Chiricahua Apaches in Captivity* (Reno: University of Nevada Press, 1993); Edward H. Spicer, *Cycles of Conquest: The Impact of Spain, Mexico, and the United States on the Indians of the Southwest, 1533–1960* (Tucson: University of Arizona Press, 1962), 229–261; Keith A. Murray, *The Modocs and Their War* (Norman: University of Oklahoma Press, 1959); Kinglsey M. Bray, "Crazy Horse and the End of the Great Sioux War," *Nebraska History*, 79 (1998), 96–115; Peter Nabokov, Ed., *Native American Testimony*, rev. ed. (New York: Penguin, 1999), 178–181.

8. Moses Rischin, *The Promised City: New York's Jews* (Cambridge, MA: Harvard University Press, 1962); Irving Howe, *World of Our Fathers: The Journey of the East European Jews to America and the Life They Found and Made* (New York: Harcourt, Brace, Jovanovich, 1976).

9. David E. Miller, Ed., *The Golden Spike* (Salt Lake City: University of Utah Press, 1973); David Howard Bain, *Empire Express: Building the First Transcontinental Railroad* (New York: Viking, 1999); Stephen E. Ambrose, *Nothing Like It in the World: The Men Who Built the Transcontinental Railroad, 1863–1869* (New York: Simon and Schuster, 2000).

10. Richard Griswold del Castillo, *The Treaty of Guadalupe Hidalgo: A Legacy of Conflict* (Norman: University of Oklahoma Press, 1990); Martha Menchaca, *Recovering History, Constructing Race: The Indian, Black, and White Roots of Mexican Americans* (Austin: University of Texas Press, 2001), 215–276; Leonard Pitt, *The Decline of the Californios: A Social History of the Spanish-speaking Californians, 1846–1890* (Berkeley: University of California Press, 1962); Albert Camarillo, *Chicanos in a Changing Society: From Mexican Pueblos to American Barrios in Santa Barbara and Southern California, 1848–1930* (Cambridge, MA: Harvard University Press, 1979).

11. Kerby A. Miller, *Emigrants and Exiles: Ireland and the Irish Exodus to North America* (New York: Oxford, 1985), 3, 281–344, 569; U.S. Census Bureau, "Irish-American Heritage Month (March) and St. Patrick's Day (March 17)" (http://www.census.gov/Press-Release/www/archives/facts_for_features/001687.html, November 11, 2004).

12. Theda Perdue and Michael D. Green, Eds., *The Cherokee Removal* (Boston: Bedford Books, 1995); Grant Foreman, *Indian Removal: The Emigration of the Five Civilized Tribes of Indians* (Norman: University of Oklahoma Press, 1953); William L. Anderson, Ed., *Cherokee Removal: Before and After* (Athens: University of Georgia Press, 1991).

13. Bernard Bailyn, *Voyagers to the West: A Passage in the Peopling of America on the Eve of the Revolution* (New York: Knopf, 1986).

14. Daniel J. Weber, *What Caused the Pueblo Revolt of 1680?* (Boston: Bedford/St. Martin's, 1999); Andrew L. Knaut, *The Pueblo Revolt of 1680: Conquest and Resistance in Seventeenth-Century New Mexico* (Norman: University of Oklahoma Press, 1995).

15. Winthrop D. Jordan, *The White Man's Burden: Historical Origins of Racism in the United States* (New York: Oxford, 1974), 26–54; Edmund S. Morgan, *American Slavery, American Freedom* (New York: Norton, 1975); Alden T. Vaughan, "The Origins Debate: Slavery and Racism in Seventeenth-Century Virginia," *Virginia Magazine of History and Biography*, 97.3 (1989), 311ff; Darlene Clark Hine, William C. Hine, and Stanley Harrold, *The African-American Odyssey*, 2nd ed. (Upper Saddle River, NJ: Prentice Hall, 2003), 51–54.

16. William Bradford, *Of Plymouth Plantation* (New York: Knopf, 1952); Francis J. Bremer, *The Puritan Experiment* (New York: St. Martin's, 1976); Alden T. Vaughan, *New England Frontier: Puritans and Indians, 1620–1675*, rev. ed. (New York: Norton, 1979).

17. An outline of this argument will appear in "Asian Americans, Religion, and Race," in *Borders, Boundaries, and Bonds: America and Its Immigrants in Eras of Globalization*, Elliott Barkan, Hasia Diner, and Alan Kraut, Eds. (New York: NYU Press, 2007).

18. J. Hector St. John de Crèvecoeur, *Letters from an American Farmer* (London, 1782), reproduced in Moses Rischin, Ed., *Immigration and the American Tradition* (Indianapolis: Bobbs-Merrill, 1976), 25–26. The power of such self-congratulatory rhetoric persists over the centuries. Whitewater prosecutor and Clinton tormentor Ken Starr wrote in his 2002 Christmas letter to family and friends: "Proudly, this nation, hewn from the vast frontier by those great generations who went before us, stands strong. ... the land of the free and home of the brave. ... We shall prevail. With apologies to no one, we already are prevailing. ... Americans come from sturdy stock. We gave the world a new birth in freedom, whereas those our forebears left behind in Europe gave us Nazism, Fascism and Communism. (Take note, England is a brave and bold exception to this hothouse of political pathologies.)" "Sincerely, Ken Starr," *Newsweek* (February 10, 2003).

19. Carl Wittke, *We Who Built America: The Saga of the Immigrant* (New York: Prentice-Hall, 1940). Louis Adamic projected a similarly celebratory attitude toward immigrants—all of them European and none of them English—in *A Nation of Nations* (New York: Harper, 1945).

20. Milton M. Gordon, *Assimilation in American Life* (New York: Oxford, 1964).

21. Peter Brimelow, *Alien Nation: Common Sense About America's Immigration Disaster* (New York: Random House, 1995), xvii, xxi, 18–19.

22. I wish no disrespect of either the late Professor Handlin or Professor Bodnar. I am very much aware of each man's contribution, and I am personally grateful to Professor Handlin for giving me my first research grant while I was still an undergraduate. But there is a blindness in their approaches. *The Uprooted*, 2nd ed. (Boston: Little, Brown, 1973), 3; Oscar Handlin, Ed., *Immigration as a Factor in American History* (Englewood Cliffs, NJ: Prentice-Hall, 1959); John Bodnar, *The Transplanted: A History of Immigrants in Urban America* (Bloomington: Indiana University Press, 1985). An otherwise outstanding recent collection of documents by eminent historian Jon Gjerde continues the erasure of the immigrant quality of Anglo-Americans; *Major Problems in American Immigration and Ethnic History* (Boston: Houghton Mifflin, 1998).

23. Emma Lazarus, "The New Colossus," quoted in Alan M. Kraut, *The Huddled Masses: The Immigrant in American Society, 1880–1921*, 2nd ed. (Wheeling, IL: Harlan Davidson, 2001), 2. For a trenchant critique of this paradigm, see Kevin R. Johnson, *The "Huddled Masses" Myth: US Immigration Law and Civil Rights* (Philadelphia: Temple University Press, 2004).

24. I am grateful to Patrick B. Miller for this phrase.

25. John Quincy Adams, to Baron Morris von Furstenwäther, June 4, 1819, reproduced in Rischin, *Immigration and the American Tradition*, 44–49.

26. Wittke, *We Who Built America*.

27. The same pattern is followed by Maldwyn Allen Jones, *American Immigration* (Chicago: University of Chicago Press, 1960); Thomas J. Archdeacon, *Becoming Americans: An Ethnic History* (New York: Free Press, 1983); Reed Ueda,

Postwar Immigrant America: A Social History (Boston: Bedford Books, 1994); Leonard Dinnerstein and David M. Reimers, *Ethnic Americans: A History of Immigration*, 4th ed. (New York: Columbia University Press, 1999). Roger Daniels begins to make a conceptual shift in *Coming to America*.

28. Thomas Muller and Thomas J. Espenshade, *The Fourth Wave: California's Newest Immigrants* (Washington, DC: Urban Institute Press, 1985).

29. Richard Alba and Victor Nee, *Remaking the American Mainstream: Assimilation and Contemporary Immigration* (Cambridge, MA: Harvard University Press, 2003), ix. See also Alba and Nee, "Rethinking Assimilation Theory for a New Era of Immigration," *International Migration Review*, 31.4 (1997), 826–74; Richard D. Alba, *Italian Americans: Into the Twilight of Ethnicity* (Englewood Cliffs, NJ: Prentice-Hall, 1985); R. Stephen Warner and Judith G. Wittner, Eds., *Gatherings in Diaspora: Religious Communities and the New Immigration* (Philadelphia: Temple University Press, 1998), 14–15 and *passim*; Russell A. Kazal, "Revisiting Assimilation: The Rise, Fall, and Reappraisal of a Concept in American Ethnic History," *American Historical Review* (April 1995), 437–471.

30. Lori Pierce refers to this as "The Eck Effect: The Racial Conundrum of Religious Diversity" in a paper given at Lake Forest College to the Second Annual Parliament of the World's Sacred Traditions (Lake Forest, IL, September 21, 2003). Cf. Diana L. Eck, *A New Religious America: How a "Christian Country" Has Now Become the World's Most Religiously Diverse Nation* (New York: HarperCollins, 2001).

31. That is explicitly the contention of Alba and Nee, *Remaking the American Mainstream*.

32. Paul Spickard, "It's the World's History: Decolonizing Historiography and the History of Christianity," *Fides et Historia*, 32.2 (summer/fall 2000), 13–29.

33. Diane Johnson, "False Promises," *New York Review of Books* (December 4, 2003), 4.

34. See Chapter 2, Table 2.1, and Appendix B, Table 9.

35. Gary B. Nash, *Red, White, and Black: The Peoples of Early America* (Englewood Cliff, NJ: Prentice-Hall, 1974); Michael A. Gomez, *Exchanging Our Country Marks: The Transformation of African Identities in the Colonial and Antebellum South* (Chapel Hill: University of North Carolina Press, 1998); Theda Perdue, *"Mixed-Blood" Indians: Racial Construction in the Early South* (Athens: University of Georgia Press, 2003); Tomás Almaguer, *Racial Fault Lines: The Historical Origins of White Supremacy in California* (Berkeley: University of California Press, 1994); Albert Camarillo, *Chicanos in a Changing Society* (Cambridge, MA: Harvard University Press, 1979); Neil Foley, *The White Scourge: Mexicans, Blacks, and Poor Whites in Texas Cotton Culture* (Berkeley: University of California Press, 1997); Menchaca, *Recovering History, Constructing Race*; David Torres-Rouff, "Making Los Angeles: Race, Place, and Municipal Power, 1822–1890" (Ph.D. dissertation, University of California, Santa Barbara, 2006); H. Craig Miner and William E. Unrau, *The End of Indian Kansas: A Study of Cultural Revolution, 1854–1871* (Laurence, KS: Regents Press, 1978); Murray R. Wickett, *Contested Territory: Whites, Native Americans, and African Americans in Oklahoma, 1865–1907* (Baton Rouge: Louisiana State University Press, 2000); William Loren Katz, *Black Indians* (New York: Atheneum, 1986); Jack D. Forbes, *Africans and Native Americans: The Language of Race and the Evolution of Red-Black Peoples*, 2nd ed. (Urbana: University of Illinois Press, 1993); James F. Brooks, Ed., *Confounding the Color Line: The Indian-Black Experience*

in North America (Lincoln: University of Nebraska Press, 2002); Arnoldo DeLeon, *Racial Frontiers: Africans, Chinese, and Mexicans in Western America, 1848–1890* (Albuquerque: University of New Mexico Press, 2002); Quintard Taylor, *The Forging of a Black Community: Seattle's Central District, from 1870 through the Civil Rights Era* (Seattle: University of Washington Press, 1994); Jacalyn D. Harden, *Double Cross: Japanese Americans in Black and White Chicago* (Minneapolis: University of Minnesota Press, 2003).

36. Will Herberg, *Protestant, Catholic, Jew*, rev. ed. (Garden City, NY: Doubleday, 1960), 42.

37. Richard D. Alba and Albert Raboteau, Eds., *Religion, Immigration, and Civic Life in Historical Comparative Perspective* (New York: Social Science Research Council and Russell Sage Foundation, 2007); I am a contributor to this volume and appreciate the editors' scholarship and friendship, even as I disagree thoroughly with the way they frame this issue. Michael Barone makes a similar interpretive move to Alba and Raboteau's, for reasons that strike me as less innocent, in *The New Americans: How the Melting Pot Can Work Again* (Washington, DC: Regnery, 2001).

38. Gomez, *Exchanging Our Country Marks*.

39. Ellis Island Immigration Museum exhibit, "The Peopling of America," October 28, 2003. The figures were compiled by Russell Menard and Henry A. Gemery. See Chapter 2, Table 2.1.

40. For related issues, see Philip J. Deloria, *Playing Indian* (New Haven, CT: Yale University Press, 1998).

41. Vine Deloria, Jr., *Custer Died for Your Sins* (New York: Avon, 1969).

42. Deloria, *Playing Indian*, 5, 7.

43. David Montejano, *Anglos and Mexicans in the Making of Texas, 1836–1986* (Austin: University of Texas Press, 1987); Almaguer, *Racial Fault Lines*; Foley, *The White Scourge*; Menchaca, *Recovering History, Constructing Race*; David J. Weber, Ed., *Foreigners in their Native Land: Historical Roots of the Mexican Americans* (Albuquerque: University of New Mexico Press, 1973).

44. Roger Rouse, "Mexican Migration and the Social Space of Postmodernism," *Diaspora*, 1.1 (1991).

45. Appendix B, Table 16; Roger Daniels, *Coming to America*, 184.

46. Lisa Lowe, *Immigrant Acts: On Asian American Cultural Politics* (Durham, NC: Duke University Press, 1996), 6; Mia Tuan, *Forever Foreigners or Honorary Whites? The Asian Ethnic Experience Today* (New Brunswick, NJ: Rutgers University Press, 1998); David J. Weber, *Foreigners in Their Native Land: Historical Roots of the Mexican Americans* (Albuquerque: University of New Mexico Press, 1973).

47. I worked in Locke's campaign.

48. Paul Spickard and W. Jeffrey Burroughs, Eds., *We Are a People: Narrative and Multiplicity in Constructing Ethnic Identity* (Philadelphia: Temple University Press, 2000); Paul Spickard and G. Reginald Daniel, Eds., *Racial Thinking in the United States: Uncompleted Independence* (Notre Dame, IN: University of Notre Dame Press, 2004); Michael Omi and Howard Winant, *Racial Formation in the United States: From the 1960s to the 1990s* (New York: Routledge, 1994); Yen Le Espiritu, *Asian American Panethnicity* (Philadelphia: Temple University Press, 1992); G. Reginald Daniel, *More Than Black? Multiracial Identity and the New Racial Order* (Philadelphia: Temple University Press, 2002); David Roediger, *The Wages of Whiteness: Race and the Making of the American Working Class* (London: Verso, 1991).

49. Ralph Waldo Emerson, *Journal*, quoted in Milton M. Gordon, *Assimilation in American Life* (New York: Oxford, 1964), 117.

50. Israel Zangwill, *The Melting Pot* (New York: Macmillan, 1909), 37, quoted in Gordon, *Assimilation in American Life*, 120.

51. *The New Face of America: How Immigrants Are Shaping the World's First Multicultural Society*, a special issue of *Time*, 142.21 (Fall 1993).

52. Gordon, *Assimilation in American Life*, 84–114.

53. Herberg, *Protestant, Catholic, Jew*, 33–34. The term "transmuting pot" belongs to George R. Stewart, *American Ways of Life* (New York: Doubleday, 1954), 23.

54. I understand this to be Michael Barone's intent expressed in the subtitle of *The New Americans: How the Melting Pot Can Work Again*.

55. Gordon, *Assimilation in American Life*, 76 and *passim*.

56. Eileen Tamura, *Americanization, Acculturation, and Ethnic Identity: The Nisei Generation in Hawai'i* (Urbana: University of Illinois Press, 1994).

57. Richard Alba, *Italian Americans: Into the Twilight of Ethnicity* (Englewood Cliffs, NJ: Prentice-Hall, 1984); David A. Hollinger, *Postethnic America: Beyond Multiculturalism* (New York: HarperCollins, 1995). Several scholars in recent years have modified the crude assimilation model, putting forth the idea of "segmented assimilation"—not becoming undifferentiated Americans, but adjusting by adopting the mores of one of a variety of immigrant enclaves. See three books by Alejandro Portes and Rubén Rumbaut: *Immigrant America*, 2nd ed. (Berkeley: University of California Press, 1996); *Legacies: The Story of the Immigrant Second Generation* (Berkeley: University of California Press, 2001); and as editors, *Ethnicities: Children of Immigrants in America* (Berkeley: University of California Press, 2001).

58. George Yancey makes that explicit claim in *Who is White? Latinos, Asians, and the New Black/Nonblack Divide* (Boulder, CO: Lynne Rienner, 2003), 9–10: "Latino and Asian Americans are beginning to approach racial issues from a majority group perspective. ... they are on their way to becoming 'white'." Richard Alba and Victor Nee, recognizing that Chinese people are not likely to become quite White, but insisting nonetheless that they will have the same status as Whites, make a more muted claim: "[A]ssimilation is not likely to require that non-Europeans come to view themselves as 'whites'. ... multiculturalism may already be preparing the way for a redefinition of the nature of the American social majority, one that accepts a majority that is racially diverse." *Remaking the American Mainstream*, 288–289.

59. Matthew Frye Jacobson, *Whiteness of a Different Color: European Immigrants and the Alchemy of Race* (Cambridge, MA: Harvard University Press, 1998).

60. Paul Spickard, "Who Is an American? Teaching about Racial and Ethnic Hierarchy," *Immigration and Ethnic History Newsletter*, 31.1 (May 1999).

61. Some of the material in this section derives from my introduction to *Pacific Diaspora: Island Peoples in the United States and Across the Pacific*, which I edited with Joanne L. Rondilla and Debbie Hippolite Wright (Honolulu: University of Hawai'i Press, 2003), 1–27.

62. James Clifford, "Diasporas," *Cultural Anthropology*, 9.3 (1994); Roger Rouse, "Mexican Migration and the Social Space of Postmodernism," *Diaspora*, 1.1 (1991); Robin Cohen, *Global Diasporas* (Seattle: University of Washington Press, 1997). On the Italian, British, and Greek diasporas, see, for example: Gloria La Cava, *Italians in Brazil* (New York: Peter Lang, 1999); Arnd Schneider, *Futures Lost: Nostalgia and Identity among Italians in Argentina* (New

York: Peter Lang, 2000); Samuel L. Baily, *Immigrants in the Lands of Promise: Italians in Buenos Aires and New York City, 1870–1914* (Ithaca, NY: Cornell University Press, 2003); Carl Bridge and Kent Federowich, Eds., *The British World: Diaspora, Culture, and Identity* (London: Frank Cass, 2003); Tony Simpson, *The Immigrants: The Great Migration from Britain to New Zealand, 1830–1880* (Auckland: Godwit, 1997); Lawrence James, *Raj: The Making and Unmaking of British India* (New York: St. Martin's Griffin, 2000); C. J. Hawes, *Poor Relations: The Making of a Eurasian Community in British India, 1773–1833* (New York: Curzon, 1996); Theodore Saloutos, *They Remember America: The Story of the Repatriated Greek-Americans* (Berkeley: University of California Press, 1956).

63. Rouse, "Mexican Migration," 13.

64. Xiaojian Zhao, *Remaking Chinese America: Immigration, Family, and Community, 1940–1965* (New Brunswick, NJ: Rutgers University Press, 2002); Adam McKeown, "Conceptualizing Chinese Diasporas," *Journal of Asian Studies*, 58 (1999), 306–337; Adam McKeown, *Chinese Migrant Networks and Cultural Change* (Chicago: University of Chicago Press, 2001). The literature on diasporas is growing rapidly. See, for example, Vijay Mishra, "The Diasporic Imaginary: Theorizing the Indian Diaspora," *Textual Practice*, 10.3 (1996), 421–447; Cohen, *Global Diasporas*; Gerard Chaliand et al., *The Penguin Atlas of Diasporas* (New York: Penguin, 1997); Nicholas Van Hear, *New Diasporas: The Mass Exodus, Dispersal, and Regrouping of Migrant Communities* (Seattle: University of Washington Press, 1998); Darshan Singh Tatla, *The Sikh Diaspora* (Seattle: University of Washington Press, 1999).

65. I recognize that some would draw distinctions between these terms, and even between "diaspora" and "diasporic," but I will treat them as roughly synonymous.

66. Sau-ling C. Wong, "Denationalization Reconsidered: Asian American Cultural Criticism at a Theoretical Crossroads," *Amerasia Journal* 21.1 and 21.2 (1995), 14–15. Elliott Barkan makes the gentler criticism that the nation-state was not the focus of most immigrants' identities. He calls them "trans*local*" rather than "trans*national*" in "America in the Hand, Homeland in the Heart: Transnational and Translocal Experiences in the American West," *Western Historical Quarterly*, 35.3.

67. Paul Mecheril and Thomas Teo, *Andere Deutsche* (Berlin: Dietz Verlag, 1994); Craig S. Smith, "French-Born Arabs Perpetually Foreign, Grow Bitter," *New York Times* (December 26, 2003); Elisabeth Schäfer-Wünsche, "On Becoming German: Politics of Membership in Germany," in *Race and Nation: Ethnic Systems in the Modern World*, Ed. Paul Spickard (New York: Routledge, 2005), 195–211; David Horrocks and Eva Kolinsky, Eds., *Turkish Culture in Germany Today* (Providence, RI: Berghahn, 1996).

68. Roger Daniels uses this mode of analysis in *Coming to America*, as does Sucheng Chan in *Asian Americans: An Interpretive History* (Boston: Twayne, 1991).

69. Edna Bonacich and Lucie Cheng, "A Theoretical Orientation to International Labor Migration," in *Labor Immigration Under Capitalism: Asian Workers in the United States before World War II*, Lucie Cheng and Edna Bonacich, Eds. (Berkeley: University of California Press, 1984), 1–56. See also L. S. Stavrianos, *Global Rift: The Third World Comes of Age* (New York: Morrow, 1981); Walter Rodney, *How Europe Underdeveloped Africa*, rev. ed. (Washington, DC: Howard University Press, 1981).

70. Alba and Nee, *Remaking the American Mainstream*, ix.

71. Yen Le Espiritu, *Asian American Panethnicity* (Philadelphia: Temple University Press, 1992). For a theoretical view of this and related processes, see Paul Spickard and W. Jeffrey Burroughs, "We Are a People," in *We Are a People: Narrative and Multiplicity in Constructing Ethnic Identity*, Paul Spickard and W. Jeffrey Burroughs, Eds. (Philadelphia: Temple University Press, 2000), 1–19. On White racial formation, see Jacobson, *Whiteness of a Different Color*; Paul Spickard, "What's Critical About White Studies?" in *Racial Thinking in the United States*, Spickard and Daniel, Eds., 248–274; Charles H. Anderson, *White Protestant Americans* (Englewood Cliffs, NJ: Prentice-Hall, 1970).

72. I have laid out my thinking on race and ethnicity more fully in *Race and Nation*. This section is drawn from that source. The reader will benefit from two works by Stephen Cornell and Douglas Hartmann: *Ethnicity and Race: Making Identities in a Changing World* (Thousand Oaks, CA: Pine Forge Press, 1998) and "Conceptual Confusions and Divides: Race, Ethnicity, and the Study of Immigration," in *Not Just Black and White: Historical and Contemporary Perspectives on Immigration, Race, and Ethnicity in the United States*, George Fredrickson and Nancy Foner, Eds., (New York: Russell Sage, 2004), 23–41.

73. Johann Friedrich Blumenbach, *The Anthropological Treatises of Johann Friedrich Blumenbach* (Boston: Milford House, 1973; orig. 1865); Joseph Arthur, comte de Gobineau, *The Inequality of Races* (New York: H. Fertig, 1915; orig. 1856); J. Philippe Rushton, *Race, Evolution, and Behavior*, 3rd ed. (Port Huron, MI: Charles Darwin Research Institute, 2000); Richard J. Herrnstein and Charles Murray, *The Bell Curve: Intelligence and Class Structure in American Life* (New York: Free Press, 1994); John Entine, *Taboo: Why Black Athletes Dominate Sports and Why We're Afraid to Talk About It* (New York: Public Affairs, 2000); Emmanuel Chukwudi Eze, Ed., *Race and the Enlightenment* (Oxford: Blackwell, 1997). Scholars such as Dinesh D'Souza and Thomas Sowell essentialize "culture" and use it to the same ends as the pseudoscientists use "race"; see D'Souza, *The End of Racism: Principles for a Multiracial Society* (New York: Free Press, 1995); Sowell, *Ethnic America* (New York: Basic Books, 1981).

For correctives, see Jonathan Marks, *Human Biodiversity: Genes, Race, and History* (New York: Aldine de Gruyter, 1995); Marks, *What It Means to be 98% Chimpanzee: Apes, People, and Their Genes* (Berkeley: University of California Press, 2002); William H. Tucker, *The Science and Politics of Racial Research* (Urbana: University of Illinois Press, 1994); Steven Fraser, Ed., *The Bell Curve Wars: Race, Intelligence, and the Future of America* (New York: Basic Books, 1995); Stephen Jay Gould, *The Mismeasure of Man*, rev. ed. (New York: Norton, 1996); Patrick B. Miller, "The Anatomy of Scientific Racism: Racialist Responses to Black Athletic Achievement," in *We Are a People*, Spickard and Burroughs, Eds., 124–141; Joseph L. Graves, Jr., *The Emperor's New Clothes: Biological Theories of Race at the Millennium* (New Brunswick, NJ: Rutgers University Press, 2001); Matt Ridley, *Nature via Nurture: Genes, Experience, and What Makes Us Human* (New York: HarperCollins, 2003).

74. See, for example, the correctives noted in the previous footnote, as well as Paul Spickard, "The Illogic of American Racial Categories," in *Racially Mixed People in America*, Maria P. P. Root, Ed. (Newbury Park, CA: Sage, 1992), 12–23; Spickard and Burroughs, "We Are a People"; Miri Song, *Choosing Ethnic Identity* (Cambridge: Polity Press, 2003); Michael Omi and Howard Winant, *Racial Formation in the United States*, rev. ed. (New York: Routledge, 1994); Stephen Cornell and Douglas Hartmann, *Ethnicity and Race* (Thousand Oaks, CA: Pine Forge Press, 1998).

75. Reginald Horsman, *Race and Manifest Destiny: The Origins of American Racial Anglo-Saxonism* (Cambridge, MA: Harvard University Press, 1981); Matthew Frye Jacobson, *Special Sorrows: The Diasporic Imaginations of Irish, Polish, and Jewish Immigrants in the United States*, rev. ed. (Berkeley: University of California Press, 2002), 177–216; Catherine Hall, Ed., *Cultures of Empire: Colonizers in Britain and the Empire in the Nineteenth and Twentieth Centuries* (New York: Routledge, 2000); see also Robert J. C. Young, *Colonial Desire: Hybridity in Theory, Culture and Race* (London: Routledge, 1995).

76. Spickard and Burroughs, "We Are a People," 2–7.

77. Of course there are meaningful differences between peoples within each of the U.S. races, as well. Korean Americans and Vietnamese Americans are quite different from one another—much more so than are, say, Irish Americans and Italian Americans. For a critique of the intellectual and political movement that would elevate differences among White people of different ethnic derivations to something like the level of racial differences, see Spickard, "What's Critical About White Studies."

78. Small, *Racialised Barriers*; Anthias and Yuval-Davis, *Racialized Boundaries*; Paul Spickard, "Mapping Race: Multiracial People and Racial Category Construction in the United States and Britain," *Immigrants and Minorities*, 15 (July 1996), 107–119.

79. Taoufik Djebali, "Ethnicity and Power in North Africa (Tunisia, Algeria, and Morocco)" in *Race and Nation*, Spickard, Ed., Rowena Fong and Paul Spickard, "Ethnic Relations in the People's Republic of China," *Journal of Northeast Asian Studies* (Fall 1994).

80. Virginia Tilley, "*Mestizaje* and the 'Ethnicization' of Race in Latin America," in *Race and Nation*, Spickard, Ed., 53–68.

81. F. James Davis, *Who Is Black? One Nation's Definition* (University Park: Pennsylvania State University Press, 1991); G. Reginald Daniel, "Passers and Pluralists: Subverting the Racial Divide," in *Racially Mixed People in America*, Root, Ed., 91–107.

82. Circe Sturm, *Blood Politics: Race, Culture, and Identity in the Cherokee Nation of Oklahoma* (Berkeley: University of California Press, 2002); James F. Brooks, Ed., *Confounding the Color Line: The Indian-Black Experience in North America* (Lincoln: University of Nebraska Press, 2002); Teresa Williams-León and Cynthia Nakashima, Eds., *The Sum of Our Parts: Mixed Heritage Asian Americans* (Philadelphia: Temple University Press, 2001); Paul Spickard, "What Must I Be? Asian Americans and the Question of Multiethnic Identity," *Amerasia Journal*, 23.1 (Spring 1997), 43–60.

83. I have drawn much of the section that follows from "We Are a People," which I wrote with W. Jeffrey Burroughs.

84. I owe this conceptual division of ethnicity into essentially three different kinds of processes with three different kinds of ethnic glue to Stephen Cornell. See his article, "The Variable Ties That Bind: Content and Circumstance in Ethnic Processes," *Ethnic and Racial Studies* (1996); also Cornell and Hartmann, *Ethnicity and Race*.

85. Abner Cohen, "The Lesson of Ethnicity," in Cohen, Ed., *Urban Ethnicity* (London: Tavistock, 1974), ix–xxiv; June Teufel Dreyer, *China's Forty Millions: Minority Nationalities and National Integration* (Cambridge, MA: Harvard University Press, 1976); Guibernau and Rex, *Ethnicity Reader*; Nathan Glazer and Daniel P. Moynihan, *Beyond the Melting Pot* (Cambridge, MA: MIT Press, 1963); William Kornblum, *Blue Collar Community* (Chicago: University of Chicago Press,

1974); Joseph Rothschild, *Ethnopolitics* (New York: Columbia University Press, 1981); William Julius Wilson, *The Declining Significance of Race*, 2nd ed. (Chicago: University of Chicago Press, 1980).

86. Alejandro Portes, "'Hispanic' Proves to Be a False Term," *Chicago Tribune* (November 2, 1989).

87. Alba, *Italian Americans*; Gordon, *Assimilation*; William Yancey et al., "Emergent Ethnicity," *American Sociological Review*, 41 (1976), 391–403.

88. Park, *Race and Culture*; E. Franklin Frazier, *Race and Culture Contacts in the Modern World* (New York: Knopf, 1957); Stephen Steinberg, *The Ethnic Myth* (Boston: Beacon Press, 1981).

89. A. L. Epstein, *Ethos and Identity* (London: Tavistock, 1978).

90. This is a refinement of the two-category analytical schema of Stephen Cornell in "Variable Ties That Bind." This analysis is carried through the history of one ethnic group in Paul R. Spickard, *Japanese Americans: The Formation and Transformations of an Ethnic Group* (New York: Twayne, 1996).

91. Rudyard Kipling, "The White Man's Burden," *McClure's Magazine* (February 1899). Kipling wrote on the occasion of United States annexation of the Philippines.

92. Schäfer-Wünsche, "On Becoming German"; Djebali, "Ethnicity and Power in North Africa"; Richard S. Fogarty, "Between Subjects and Citizens: North Africans, Islam, and French National Identity during the Great War"; and Miyuki Yonezawa, "Memories of Japanese Identity and Racial Hierarchy," all in *Race and Nation*. Fong and Spickard, "Ethnic Relations in the People's Republic of China," *Journal of Northeastern Asian Studies*.

93. Horsman, *Race and Manifest Destiny*; Matthew Frye Jacobson, *Barbarian Virtues: The United States Encounters Foreign Peoples at Home and Abroad, 1876–1917* (New York: Hill and Wang, 2000); Thomas F. Gossett, *Race: The History of an Idea in America* (Dallas: Southern Methodist University Press, 1963).

94. Antonio Gramsci, *Selections from the Prison Notebooks of Antonio Gramsci* (New York: International Publishers, 1971); Robert Blauner, *Racial Oppression in America* (New York: Harper and Row, 1972).

95. Albert Memmi, *The Colonizer and the Colonized* (Boston: Beacon, 1965); see also Nadine Gordimer, "In the Penal Colonies: What Albert Memmi Saw and Did Not See," *Times Literary Supplement* (September 12, 2003), 13–14.

96. Barone, *New Americans*; Noel Ignatiev, *How the Irish Became White* (New York: Routledge, 1995); Karen Brodkin, *How Jews Became White Folks and What That Says about Race in America* (New Brunswick, NJ: Rutgers University Press, 1998). For a corrective, see Spickard, "What's Critical About White Studies."

97. Perry Miller, *Errand into the Wilderness* (Cambridge, MA: Harvard University Press, 1956); Alden T. Vaughan, *New England Frontier: Puritans and Indians, 1620–1675*, rev. ed. (New York: Norton, 1979); Richard Drinnon, *Facing West: The Metaphysics of Indian-Hating and Empire-Building* (Norman: University of Oklahoma Press, 1997; orig. 1980), 1–61.

98. Robert Fisk, "Telling It Like It Isn't," *Los Angeles Times* (December 27, 2005).

99. For example, Cheryl Shanks, *Immigration and the Politics of American Sovereignty, 1890–1990* (Ann Arbor: University of Michigan Press, 2001); Roger Daniels and Otis L. Graham, *Debating American Immigration, 1882–Present* (Lanham, MD: Rowman and Littlefield, 2001); Juan F. Perea, *Immigrants Out! The New Nativism and the Anti-Immigrant Impulse in the United States* (New York: NYU Press, 1997).

100. The *Los Angeles Times* is a prominent exception.
101. Tuan, *Forever Foreigners or Honorary Whites?*, 1–3; "Senator D'Amato Apologizes for Faking Japanese Accent," *San Francisco Chronicle* (April 6, 1995); Melinda Henneberger, "D'Amato Gives a New Apology on Ito Remarks," *New York Times* (April 8, 1995).

Chapter 2

1. Walter Hölbling, "Thanksgiving," a poem circulated to friends, November 2003. Used with permission of the poet.
2. Lyle Campbell, *American Indian Languages* (New York: Oxford, 1997); Lyle Campbell and Marianne Mithun, Eds., *The Languages of Native America: Historical and Comparative Assessment* (Austin: University of Texas Press, 1979); Marianne Mithun, *The Languages of Native North America* (New York: Cambridge University Press, 1999). Here and elsewhere in this book, I have also used the expert essays in Frederick E. Hoxie, Ed., *Encyclopedia of North American Indians* (Boston: Houghton Mifflin, 1996), and Carl Waldman, *Atlas of the North American Indian*, rev. ed. (New York: Checkmark, 2000).
3. All three photographs come from Azusa Publishing, Inc. Kicks Iron was photographed by F. B. Fiske in about 1905. The photo of Tswawadi was taken by Charles H. Carpenter in 1904, and comes from the collection of the Field Museum of Natural History in Chicago (Neg. #13583). Mishongnovi was photographed by A. C. Vroman in 1901 and comes to us courtesy of the Seaver Center, Los Angeles County Museum of Natural History. All are used by permission of Azusa Publishing.
4. London's population ranged from 40,000 to 50,000 between 1300 and 1500, Rome's from 20,000 to 40,000. Tertius Chandler and Gerald Fox, *3000 Years of Urban History* (New York: Academic Press, 1974) 14–15, 34–35.
5. Neal Salisbury, "The Indians' Old World: Native Americans and the Coming of Europeans," *William and Mary Quarterly*, 3d ser. 53 (1996), 435–58; Lynda Norene Shaffer, *Native Americans Before 1492: The Moundbuilding Centers of the Eastern Woodlands* (Armonk, NY: M.E. Sharp, 1992); Alice Beck Kehoe, *America Before the European Invasion* (London: Longman, 2002), 163–191; Peter Nabokov with Dean Snow, "Farmers of the Woodlands," in Alvin M. Josephy, Jr., Ed., *America in 1492* (New York: Vintage, 1993), 118–145; Thomas E. Emerson, *Cahokia and the Archaeology of Power* (Tuscaloosa: University of Alabama Press, 1997); Colin G. Calloway, *One Vast Winter Count: The Native American West Before Lewis and Clark* (Lincoln: University of Nebraska Press, 2003).
6. The Hohokam in southern Arizona and the Anasazi in the Four Corners region were large, complex, agriculture-based societies like the Mississippians. They lasted several centuries but declined before the coming of the Europeans. Bruce G. Trigger and William R. Swagerty, "Entertaining Strangers: North America in the Sixteenth Century," in *The Cambridge History of the Native Peoples of the Americas. Volume I: North America. Part 1*, Bruce G. Trigger and Wilcomb E. Washburn, Eds., (Cambridge: Cambridge University Press, 1996), 325–398; Kehoe, *America Before the European Invasions*, 89–96, 138–162; Richard D. Daugherty, "People of the Salmon," in Josephy, *America in 1492*, 48–83.

7. Robert Berkhofer, Jr., *The White Man's Indian: Images of the Indian from Columbus to the Present* (New York: Knopf, 1978), 4.

8. Russell Thornton makes the following population estimates for various parts of the world about 1500 in *American Indian Holocaust and Survival: A Population History Since 1492* (Norman: University of Oklahoma Press, 1987), 37.

The Americas	75 million
China	100–150 million
Indian subcontinent	75–150 million
Southwest Asia	20–30 million
Japan	15–20 million
Rest of Asia except USSR	15–30 million
Europe except USSR	60–70 million
USSR	100–18 million
North Africa	6–12 million
Rest of Africa	30–60 million
Oceania	1–2 million
Total	407–617 million

9. These are conservative figures. Other estimates for America north of Mexico range as high as ten million. William M. Denevan, *The Native Population of the Americas in 1492*, 2nd ed. (Madison: University of Wisconsin Press, 1992), xxviii; Thornton, *American Indian Holocaust and Survival*; Russell Thornton, "North American Indians and the Demography of Contact," in *Race, Discourse, and the Origin of the Americas*, Vera Lawrence Hyatt and Rex Nettleford, Eds. (Washington, DC: Smithsonian Institution, 1995), 213–230; Thornton, "The Demography of Colonialism and 'Old' and 'New' Native Americans," in *Studying Native America*, Thornton, Ed. (Madison: University of Wisconsin Press, 1998), 17–39; David E. Stannard, *Before the Horror: The Population of Hawai'i on the Eve of Western Contact* (Honolulu: Social Science Research Institute, University of Hawai'i, 1989); Campbell Gibson and Kay Jung, "Historical Census Statistics on Population totals by Race, 1790 to 1990, and by Hispanic Origin, 1970 to 1990, for the United States, Regions, Divisions, and States," Population Division, Working Paper No. 56 (Washington, DC: U.S. Census Bureau, 2002), Table 1.

10. Kehoe, *America Before the European Invasions*, 8–21; Dean R. Snow, "The First Americans and the Differentiation of Hunter-Gatherer Cultures," in *Cambridge History of the Native Peoples of the Americas, Volume I, Part 1*, Trigger and Washburn, Ed., 61–124; E. James Dixon, *Quest for the Origins of the First Americans* (Albuquerque: University of New Mexico Press, 1993); Tom D. Dillehay, *The Settlement of the Americas: A New Prehistory* (New York: Basic Books, 2000); David E. Stannard, *American Holocaust: The Conquest of the New World* (New York: Oxford, 1992), 261–268.

11. Joel W. Martin, *The Land Looks After Us: A History of Native American Religion* (New York: Oxford, 2001); Albert Yava, Eds., *Big Falling Snow: A Tewa-Hopi Indian's Life and Times and the History and Traditions of His People*, Harold

Courlander, Ed. (New York: Crown, 1978); Paul Spickard, James V. Spickard, and Kevin M. Cragg, *World History by the World's Historians* (New York: McGraw-Hill, 1998), 6–15.

12. Ivan Van Sertima, *They Came Before Columbus: The African Presence in Ancient America* (New York: Random House, 1976); David H. Kelley, "An Essay on Pre-Columbian Contacts Between the Americas and Other Areas, with Special Reference to the Work of Ivan Van Sertima," in *Race, Discourse, and the Origin of the Americas*, Hyatt and Nettleford, Eds., 103–122; Ben R. Finney, *Sailing in the Wake of the Ancestors: Reviving Polynesian Voyaging* (Honolulu: Bishop Museum Press, 2003); David Lewis, *We, the Navigators: The Ancient Art of Landfinding in the Pacific*, 2nd ed. (Honolulu: University of Hawai'i Press, 1994); Louise Levathes, *When China Ruled the Seas: The Treasure Fleet of the Dragon Throne, 1405–1433* (New York: Oxford, 1996); Gavin Menzies, *1421: The Year China Discovered America* (New York: Morrow, 2003); Rafique Ali Jairazbhoy, *Ancient Egyptians and Chinese in America* (Totowa, NJ: Rowman and Littlefield, 1974); C. G. Leland, *Fusang: The Discovery of America by Chinese Buddhist Priests in the Fifth Century* (New York: Barnes and Noble, 1973; orig. 1875); Helge M. Ingstad, *Westward to Vinland* (New York: St. Martin's, 1969).

13. In like manner, Hawaiians will be treated as the original inhabitants of what is now the fiftieth state. Although their ancestors came to the islands in remembered time, they came several centuries before European and Asian incursions.

14. Waldman, *Atlas of the North American Indian*, 190.

15. Sherburne F. Cook and Woodrow Borah, "The Aboriginal Population of Hispaniola," in Cook and Borah, *Essays in Population History. Volume 1. Mexico and the Caribbean, 1600–1860* (Berkeley: University of California Press, 1973), 376–410; Stannard, *American Holocaust*, 58–146; Ida Altman, Sarah Cline, and Juan Javier Pescador, *The Early History of Greater Mexico* (Upper Saddle River, NJ: Prentice Hall, 2003), 53–113.

16. Altman, Cline, and Pescador, *Early History of Greater Mexico*, 185–201; David J. Weber, *The Spanish Frontier in North America* (New Haven, CT: Yale University Press, 1992), 60–91; Weber, Ed., *What Caused the Pueblo Revolt of 1680?* (Boston: Bedford/St. Martin's, 1999); Weber, Ed., *New Spain's Far Northern Frontier* (Albuquerque: University of New Mexico Press, 1979).

17. W. J. Eccles, *The French in North America, 1500–1783*, rev. ed. (East Lansing: Michigan State University Press, 1998); Eccles, *France in America* (New York: Harper and Row, 1972); Russell Shorto, *Island at the Center of the World: The Epic Story of Dutch Manhattan, the Forgotten Colony that Shaped America* (New York: Doubleday, 2004). Here and elsewhere in this chapter I have had occasion to rely also on Gary B. Nash, *Red, White, and Black: The Peoples of Early America* (Englewood Cliffs, NJ: Prentice-Hall, 1974).

18. Chrestien LeClerq, *New Relation of Gaspesia, with the Customs and Religion of the Gaspesian Indians*, trans. William F. Ganong, Ed. (Toronto: Champlain Society, 1910), 104–106, quoted in Colin G. Galloway, Ed., *The World Turned Upside Down: Indian Voices from Early America* (Boston: Bedford/St. Martin's, 1994), 50–52.

19. Berkhofer, *White Man's Indian*, 28.

20. Stannard, *American Holocaust*, 247; see also Francis Jennings, *The Invasion of America: Indians, Colonialism, and the Cant of Conquest* (New York: Norton, 1976).

21. Nash, *Red, White, and Black*, 34–43.
22. Cornelius J. Jaenen, "Amerindian Views of French Culture in the Seventeenth Century," *Canadian Historical Review*, 55 (1974), 261–291.
23. Nancy Shoemaker, *A Strange Likeness: Becoming Red and White in Eighteenth-Century North America* (New York: Oxford, 2004).
24. Charlotte J. Erickson, "English," in *Harvard Encyclopedia of American Ethnic Groups* (Cambridge: Harvard University Press, 1980), 319–336. I have used various of the essays in this encyclopedia in this chapter and throughout the book. For population figures for the entire incipient United States, see Appendix B, Table 1.
25. David Beers Quinn, *Set Fair for Roanoke: Voyages and Colonies, 1584–1606* (Chapel Hill: University of North Carolina Press, 1985).
26. David Beers Quinn, *Set Fair for Roanoke*.
27. Except where otherwise noted, information on the Jamestown encounter with Powhatan's people is taken from Edmund S. Morgan, *American Slavery, American Freedom: The Ordeal of Colonial Virginia* (New York: Norton, 1975), 44–91; David Price, *Love and Hate in Jamestown: John Smith, Pocahontas, and the Heart of a New Nation* (New York: Knopf, 2003); Helen C. Rountree, Ed., *Powhatan Foreign Relations* (Charlottesville: University Press of Virginia, 1993); Frederic W. Gleach, *Powhatan's World and Colonial Virginia* (Lincoln: University of Nebraska Press, 1997); Wesley Frank Craven, *White, Red, and Black: The Seventeenth-Century Virginian* (Charlottesville: University Press of Virginia, 1971), 39–71; Philip L. Barbour, *Pocahontas and Her World* (Boston: Houghton Mifflin, 1970); Frances Mossiker, *Pocahontas: The Life and the Legend* (New York: Knopf, 1976); Helen C. Rountree, "Pocahontas: The Hostage Who Became Famous," in *Sifters: Native American Women's Lives*, Theda Perdue, Ed. (New York: Oxford, 2001), 14–28.
28. Philip L. Barbour, Ed., *The Complete Works of Captain John Smith* (Chapel Hill: University of North Carolina Press, 1986), 1:247.
29. Vaughan, *Puritan Frontier*, 64–92; Nash, *Red, White, and Black*, 76–80; Francis J. Bremer, *The Puritan Experiment: New England Society from Bradford to Edwards* (New York: St. Martin's, 1976), 42–56.
30. Vaughan, *Puritan Frontier*, 64–92; Neal Salisbury, *Manitou and Providence: Indians and Europeans in the Making of New England, 1500–1643* (New York: Oxford, 1982); Salisbury, "Squanto: Last of the Patuxets," in *Struggle and Survival in Colonial America*, David G. Sweet and Gary B. Nash, Eds. (Berkeley: University of California Press, 1981), 228–246.
31. Thornton, *American Indian Holocaust and Survival*, 60–90; David E. Stannard, *Before the Horror: The Population of Hawai'i on the Eve of Western Contact* (Honolulu: Social Science Research Institute, University of Hawai'i, 1989); Stannard, *American Holocaust*, 95.
32. John Winthrop, "Generall Considerations for the Plantation in New England …" (1629), in *Winthrop Papers*, 5 vols., Allyn B. Forbes, Ed. (Boston: Massachusetts Historical Society, 1929–1947), 2:118; quoted in Nash, *Red, White, and Black*, 80.
33. Gleach, *Powhatan's World*.
34. Vaughan, *New England Frontier*, 123–154; Richard Drinnon, *Facing West: The Metaphysics of Indian-Hating and Empire-Building* (Norman: University of Oklahoma Press, 1997), 35–61.

35. Russell Bourne, *The Red King's Rebellion: Racial Politics in New England, 1675–1678* (New York: Atheneum, 1990); Jill Lepore, *The Name of War: King Philip's War and the Origins of American Identity* (New York: Knopf, 1998).

36. Francis Jennings, *The Invasion of America: Indians, Colonialism, and the Cant of Conquest* (Chapel Hill: University of North Carolina Press, 1975), 146–170; Stannard, *American Holocaust*, 118–119. Among the many analyses of Serbian genocide in Bosnia is *Genocide in Bosnia: The Policy of Ethnic Cleansing*, by Norman Cigar and Stjepan G. Mestrovic (College Station: Texas A & M Press, 1995).

37. Ramón Gutierrez, *When Jesus Came, the Corn Mothers Went Away: Marriage, Sexuality, and Power in New Mexico, 1500–1846* (Stanford, CA: Stanford University Press, 1991), 130–140; Jack D. Forbes, *Apache, Navaho, and Spaniard* (Norman: University of Oklahoma Press, 1994; orig. 1960), 200–249; David J. Weber, Ed., *What Caused the Pueblo Revolt of 1680?* (Boston: Bedford/St. Martin's, 1999); Weber, *The Spanish Frontier in North America* (New Haven, CT: Yale University Press, 1992), 133–145; Pekka Hämäläinen, "The Rise and Fall of Plains Indian Horse Cultures," *Journal of American History* (December 2003), 833–862.

38. Matthew Dennis, *Cultivating a Landscape of Peace: Iroquois-European Encounters in Seventeenth-Century America* (Ithaca, NY: Cornell University Press, 1993); Nash, *Red, White, and Black*, 17–25, 239–275; Theda Perdue, *"Mixed Blood" Indians: Racial Construction in the Early South* (Athens: University of Georgia Press, 2003); Amy Turner Bushnell, "Ruling 'The Republic of Indians' in Seventeenth-Century Florida," in *Powhatan's Mantle: Indians in the Colonial Southeast*, Peter H. Wood, Gregory A. Waselkov, and M. Thomas Hatley, Eds. (Lincoln: University of Nebraska Press, 1989), 134–150.

39. James Axtell, "The White Indians of Colonial America," *William and Mary Quarterly*, 3rd series, 32 (1975), 55–88.

40. Perdue, *"Mixed Blood" Indians*; Robbie Ethridge, *Creek Country: The Creek Indians and Their World* (Chapel Hill: University of North Carolina Press, 2003).

41. That is, if one does not regard Africans as a single group. See the next section, "Out of Africa," for that issue.

42. David Hackett Fischer, *Albion's Seed: Four British Folkways in America* (New York: Oxford, 1989).

43. Bernard Bailyn, *The Peopling of British North America* (New York: Knopf, 1986), 25, 40; Carl Bridenbaugh, *Vexed and Troubled Englishmen, 1590–1642* (New York: Oxford, 1968), 203–208. *Contra* Bailyn, it is worth remembering that North America was already peopled before the first British migrant left shore.

44. Walter Woodward, "Jamestown Estates," *William and Mary Quarterly*, 3rd ser., 47 (1991), 116–117.

45. Sources on the Puritans include Francis Bremer, *The Puritan Experiment: New England Society from Bradford to Edwards* (New York: St. Martin's, 1976); Alan Simpson, *Puritanism in Old and New England* (Chicago: University of Chicago Press, 1955); Edmund S. Morgan, *The Puritan Dilemma: The Story of John Winthrop* (Boston: Little, Brown, 1958); Fischer, *Albion's Seed*: 13–205; John Demos, *A Little Commonwealth: Family Life in Plymouth Colony* (New York: Oxford, 1970); William Bradford, *Of Plymouth Plantation* (New York: Knopf, 1952); Edmund S. Morgan, *Visible Saints: The History of a Puritan Idea* (New

York: New York University Press, 1963); Carol F. Karlsen, *The Devil in the Shape of a Woman: Witchcraft in Colonial New England* (New York: Norton, 1987); John Demos, *Entertaining Satan: Witchcraft and the Culture of Early New England* (New York: Oxford, 1982).

46. On the Halfway Covenant, see Edmund S. Morgan, *Visible Saints: The History of a Puritan Idea* (New York: New York University Press, 1963), 113–138.

47. Fischer, *Albion's Seed*: 207. The material for this section is taken from Morgan, *American Slavery, American Freedom*, and Fischer, *Albion's Seed*, 207–418.

48. On indentured servitude, see Abbot Emerson Smith, *Colonists in Bondage: White Servitude and Convict Labor in America, 1607–1776* (Chapel Hill: University of North Carolina Press, 1947); P. C. Emmer, Ed., *Colonialism and Migration: Indentured Labour Before and After Slavery* (Dordrecht: Martinus Nijhoff, 1986); David W. Galenson, *White Servitude in Colonial America* (Cambridge: Cambridge University Press, 1981).

49. On Bacon's Rebellion, see varying interpretations in Wilcomb E. Washburn, *The Governor and the Rebel: A History of Bacon's Rebellion in Virginia* (Chapel Hill: University of North Carolina Press, 1957); Thomas J. Wertenbaker, *Bacon's Rebellion, 1676* (Charlottesville: University Press of Virginia, 1957); Nash, *Red, White, and Black*, 127–134; Ronald Takaki, *A Different Mirror: A History of Multicultural America* (Boston: Little, Brown, 1993), 60–68; Morgan, *American Slavery, American Freedom*, 215–270; Theodore W. Allen, *The Invention of the White Race: The Origin of Racial Oppression in Anglo-America* (London: Verso, 1997).

50. Fischer, *Albion's Seed*, 419–603; Joseph E. Illick, *Colonial Pennsylvania* (New York: Scribner's, 1976); Sally Schwartz, *"A Mixed Multitude": The Struggle for Toleration in Colonial Pennsylvania* (New York: New York University Press, 1988).

51. It also encouraged migration by Africans, but as slaves rather than servants or free laborers; see below.

52. Morgan, *American Slavery, American Freedom*, 94, 171–173, 405–406.

53. Michael LeMay and Elliott Robert Barkan, Eds., *U.S. Immigration and Naturalization Laws and Issues: A Documentary History* (Westport, CT: Greenwood, 1999), 6–9.

54. Jacob Van Hinte, *Netherlanders in America*, Ed. Robert P. Swierenga, trans. Adriaan de Wit (Grand Rapids, MI: Baker Book House, 1985), 3–51; Shorto, *Island at the Center of the World*.

55. A. G. Roeber, " 'The Origin of Whatever Is Not English among Us': The Dutch-speaking and the German-speaking Peoples of Colonial British America," in *Strangers within the Realm: Cultural Margins of the First British Empire*, Bernard Bailyn and Philip D. Morgan, Eds. (Chapel Hill: University of North Carolina Press, 1991), 220–283; Don Heinrich Tolzmann, *The German-American Experience* (Amherst, NY: Prometheus, 2000), 21–94.

56. Sources on German immigration in this period include Steven M. Nolt, *Foreigners in Their Own Land: Pennsylvania Germans in the Early Republic* (University Park: Pennsylvania State University Press, 2002); A. G. Roeber, *Palatines, Liberty, and Property: German Lutherans in Colonial British America*, rev. ed. (Baltimore: Johns Hopkins University Press, 1998); Aaron Spencer Fogleman, *Hopeful Journeys: German Immigration, Settlement, and Political Culture in Colonial America, 1717–1775* (University Park: Pennsylvania State University Press, 1996); Sally Schwartz, *"A Mixed Multitude": The Struggle for Toleration in Colonial Pennsylvania* (New York: New York University Press, 1987), 81–119;

Joseph E. Illick, *Colonial Pennsylvania* (New York: Scribner's 1976), 113–136; Philip Otterness, *Becoming German: The 1709 Palatine Migration to New York* (Ithaca, NY: Cornell University Press, 2004).

57. Fogleman, *Hopeful Journeys*, esp. 80–86, 131–135, 149–153.

58. Maldwyn Jones, "Scotch-Irish," in *Harvard Encyclopedia of American Ethnic Groups*, 895–908. Other sources for this section include Fischer, *Albion's Seed*, 605–782; James G. Leyburn, *The Scotch-Irish* (Chapel Hill: University of North Carolina Press, 1963); Carl Bridenbaugh, *Myths and Realities: Societies of the Colonial South* (Baton Rouge: Louisiana State University Press, 1952), 119–196; Patrick Griffin, *The People with No Name: Ireland's Ulster Scots, America's Scots Irish, and the Creation of a British Atlantic World, 1689–1764* (Princeton, NJ: Princeton University Press, 2001); Maldwyn A. Jones, "The Scotch-Irish in British America," in *Strangers within the Realm*, 284–313; J. P. MacLean, *An Historical Account of the Settlements of Scotch Highlanders in America Prior to the Peace of 1783* (Cleveland, 1900); David Dobson, *The Scottish Emigration to Colonial America, 1607–1785* (Athens: University of Georgia Press, 1994); Tyler Blethen and Curtis W. Wood, *Ulster and North America: Transatlantic Perspectives on the Scotch-Irish* (Tuscaloosa: University of Alabama Press, 1997).

59. Samuel Johnson, *A Journey to the Western Isles of Scotland*, Ed. Mary Lascelles (New Haven, CT : Yale University Press, 1971; orig. 1775), 95.

60. James Boswell, *Journal of a Tour to the Hebrides*, Ed. Frederick A. Pottle and Charles H. Bennett (New York: McGraw-Hill, 1936; orig. 1773), 242–243; italics added.

61. Gottlieb Mittelberger, *Journey to Pennsylvania*, Ed. and trans. Oscar Handlin and John Clive (Cambridge, MA: Harvard University Press, 1960), 12–13.

62. Gottlieb Mittelberger, *Journey to Pennsylvania*, 17–19.

63. Richard Hofstadter, *America at 1750: A Social Portrait* (New York: Knopf, 1971), 22–65.

64. Mittelberger, *Journey to Pennsylvania*, 21.

65. Benjamin Franklin, *The Autobiography of Benjamin Franklin*, Ed. Louis P. Masur (Boston: Bedford/St. Martin's, 1993); Walter Isaacson, *Benjamin Franklin* (New York: Simon and Schuster, 2003); Max Weber, *The Protestant Ethic and the Spirit of Capitalism*, trans. Talcott Parsons (New York: Scribner, 1958), 79–92; Richard L. Bushman, *From Puritan to Yankee: Character and the Social Order in Connecticut, 1690–1765* (Cambridge, MA: Harvard University Press, 1967), ix; Philip J. Greven, Jr., *Four Generations: Population, Land, and Family in Colonial Andover, Massachusetts* (Ithaca, NY: Cornell University Press, 1970).

66. David Brion Davis, *In the Image of God: Religion, Moral Values, and Our Heritage of Slavery* (New Haven, CT: Yale University Press, 2001), quoted in William H. McNeill, "The Big R," *New York Review of Books* (May 23, 2002), 58.

67. I use the term "Negro" here advisedly, for it was the common term that both non-African-descended people and African-descended people used in the period under examination.

68. Venture Smith, *A Narrative of the Life and Adventures of Venture, A Native of Africa* ... (New London, CT, 1798), quoted in Thomas R. Frazier, Ed., *Afro-American History: Primary Sources*, 2nd ed. (Chicago: Dorsey, 1988), 8–9

69. Olaudah Equiano, *The Interesting Narrative of the Life of Olaudah Equiano*, Ed. Robert J. Allison (Boston: Bedford/St. Martin's, 1995; orig. 1789), 52–54.

70. Olaudah Equiano, *The Interesting Narrative of the Life of Olaudah Equiano*, 57–58.
71. Olaudah Equiano, *The Interesting Narrative of the Life of Olaudah Equiano*, 59.
72. A good place to start on the other vast slave movement out of Africa is Ronald Segal, *Islam's Black Slaves: The Other Black Diaspora* (New York: Hill and Wang, 2001).
73. Northrup, *Atlantic Slave Trade*, 133; Walter Rodney, *How Europe Underdeveloped Africa* (Washington, DC: Howard University Press, 1974), 95–118; Walter Rodney, *A History of the Upper Guinea Coast, 1545–1800* (Oxford: Oxford University Press, 1970). For contrasting views, see Patrick Manning, "Contours of Slavery and Social Change in Africa," *American Historical Review*, 88.4 (1983), 836–857; David Eltis, "Precolonial Western Africa and the Atlantic Economy," in *Slavery and the Rise of the Atlantic System*, Barbara Solow, Ed. (Cambridge: Cambridge University Press, 1991), 97–119; Henry A. Gemery and Jan S. Hogendorn, Eds., *The Uncommon Market: Essays in the Economic History of the Atlantic Slave Trade* (New York: Academic Press, 1979).
74. L. S. Stavrianos, *Global Rift: The Third World Comes of Age* (New York: Morrow), 99–121, 196–204.
75. This interpretation comes from several sources: Winthrop D. Jordan, *The White Man's Burden: Historical Origins of Racism in the United States* (New York: Oxford, 1974), 3–54; Jordan, *White Over Black: American Attitudes Toward the Negro, 1550–1812* (Chapel Hill: University of North Carolina Press, 1968), 3–98; David Brion Davis, *Slavery and Human Progress* (New York: Oxford, 1984); Betty Wood, *The Origins of American Slavery* (New York: Hill and Wang, 1997); Alden T. Vaughan, "The Origins Debate: Slavery and Racism in Seventeenth-Century Virginia," *Virginia Magazine of History and Biography*, 97.3 (1989), 311–354.
76. Allan Gallay, *The Indian Slave Trade* (New Haven, CT: Yale University Press, 2002).
77. Kenneth Morgan, *Slavery and Servitude in Colonial North America* (New York: New York University Press, 2001); Ira Berlin, *Many Thousands Gone: The First Two Centuries of Slavery in North America* (Cambridge, MA: Harvard University Press, 1998); Winthrop D. Jordan, "American Chiaroscuro: The Status and Definition of Mulattoes in the British Colonies," *William and Mary Quarterly*, 3rd ser., 19 (1962), 183–200.
78. Robert Beverley, *The History and Present State of Virginia*, Ed. Louis B. Wright (Chapel Hill: University of North Carolina Press, 1947; orig. 1705), 235–236.
79. These numbers come from a variety of sources. See those listed under Table 2.5, as well as Berlin, *Many Thousands Gone*: appendices.
80. Sources for the variety of slave patterns in the southern colonies include Berlin, *Many Thousands Gone*; Nash, *Red, White, and Black*; Morgan, *American Slavery, American Freedom*; Philip D. Morgan, *Slave Counterpoint: Black Culture in the Eighteenth-Century Chesapeake and Lowcountry* (Chapel Hill: University of North Carolina Press, 1998); Peter H. Wood, *Black Majority: Negroes in Colonial South Carolina from 1670 Through the Stono Rebellion* (New York: Knopf, 1974); Daniel C. Littlefield, *Rice and Slaves: Ethnicity and the Slave Trade in Colonial South Carolina* (Baton Rouge: Louisiana State University Press, 1981); Betty Wood, *Slavery in Colonial Georgia, 1730–1775* (Athens: University of Georgia Press, 1984).

81. Sources for this section include Gomez, *Exchanging Our Country Marks*; Douglas B. Chambers, " 'My Own Nation': Igbo Exiles in the Diaspora," in *Routes to Slavery: Direction, Ethnicity and Mortality in the Transatlantic Slave Trade*, David Eltis and David Richardson, Eds. (London: Frank Cass, 1997), 72–97; Peter Caron, " 'Of a Nation Which Others Do Not Understand': Bambara Slaves and African Ethnicity in Colonial Louisiana, 1718–1760," in *Routes to Slavery*, 98–121; "The Cultural Implications of the Atlantic Slave Trade: African Regional Origins, American Destinations and New World Developments," in *Routes to Slavery*, 122–145; Ira Berlin, "From Creole to African: Atlantic Creoles and the Origins of African-American Society in Mainland North America," *William and Mary Quarterly*, 3rd ser., 53.2 (1996); David Northrup, "Igbo Myth and Myth Igbo: Culture and Ethnicity in the Atlantic World, 1600–1850," *Slavery and Abolition*, 21.3 (December 2000); Allan Kulikoff, "The Origins of Afro-American Society in Tidewater Maryland and Virginia, 1700–1790," *William and Mary Quarterly*, 3rd series, 35 (1978), 226–259; Gwendolyn Midlo Hall, *Slavery and African Ethnicities in the Americas* (Chapel Hill: University of North Carolina Press, 2006).

82. Gomez, *Exchanging Our Country Marks*, 165.

83. Gomez, *Exchanging Our Country Marks*, 170–180.

84. Albert J. Raboteau, *Slave Religion* (New York: Oxford, 1978).

85. Tanner, *Settling of North America*, 51.

86. Ira Berlin, "Time, Space, and the Evolution of Afro-American Society on British Mainland North America," *American Historical Review*, 85.1 (1980).

87. We have more detailed knowledge of these migrants than of any others in early America, save the Puritans, thanks to the work of Bernard Bailyn and Barbara DeWolfe. See Bailyn, *Voyagers to the West: A Passage in the Peopling of America on the Eve of the Revolution* (New York: Knopf, 1986); DeWolfe, *Discoveries of America: Personal Accounts of British Emigrants to North America During the Revolutionary Era* (Cambridge: Cambridge University Press, 1997). DeWolfe collaborated on *Voyagers to the West*.

88. Richard White, *The Middle Ground: Indians, Empires, and Republics in the Great Lakes Region, 1650–1815* (Cambridge: Cambridge University Press, 1991), 223–314; Nash, *Red, White, and Black*, 239–319.

89. This was in contrast to Amherst's gentle treatment of French captives. Col. Henry Bouquet to General Amherst, July 13, 1763; Amherst to Bouquet, July 16, 1763; quoted in Francis Parkman, *The Conspiracy of Pontiac*, vol. 2 (Boston: Little, Brown, 1870), 39–40.

90. Curtin, *Atlantic Slave Trade*, 140, 234; see also Table 2.4.

91. Jordan, *White Over Black*, esp. "Unthinking Decision"; Theodore W. Allen, *The Invention of the White Race: Racial Oppression and Social Control* (London: Verso, 1994). Allen writes specifically about the early construction of the White race. Jordan concentrates on the White formation of Blackness and assigning of Blacks to slavery, but he also attends to Whiteness and the assigning of Whites to freedom. For a reflection on these authors and other students of Whiteness, see Paul Spickard, "What's Critical About White Studies," in *Racial Thinking in the United States*, Spickard and G. Reginald Daniel, Eds. (Notre Dame, IN: University of Notre Dame Press, 2004), 248–274.

92. Jon Butler, *Becoming America: The Revolution Before 1776* (Cambridge, MA: Harvard University Press, 2000), 1–49.

93. David R. Roediger, *The Wages of Whiteness: Race and the Making of the American Working Class* (London: Verso, 1991); Noel Ignatiev, *How the Irish Became White* (New York: Routledge, 1995).

Chapter 3

1. *The Lincoln-Douglas Debates of 1858*, Ed., Robert W. Johannsen (New York: Oxford, 1965), 33, 128.

2. This section is based on my unpublished study, "Black Freedom in Revolutionary America: A Legal Study," a comprehensive analysis of laws and court cases in Massachusetts, New York, Virginia, and South Carolina from the beginnings of slavery through the 1830s. See also Ira Berlin, *Many Thousands Gone: The First Two Centuries of Slavery in North America* (Cambridge, MA: Harvard University Press, 1998), 217–357; Ira Berlin, *Slaves Without Masters: The Free Negro in the Antebellum South* (New York: Pantheon, 1974), 15–107; Roger Bruns, Ed., *Am I Not a Man and a Brother: The Antislavery Crusade of Revolutionary America, 1688–1788* (New York: Chelsea House, 1977); David Brion Davis, *The Problem of Slavery in the Age of Revolution, 1770–1823* (Ithaca, NY: Cornell University Press, 1975); George M. Fredrickson, *White Supremacy: A Comparative Study in American and South African History* (New York: Oxford, 1981), 140–150; Winthrop D. Jordan, *The White Man's Burden: Historical Origins of Racism in the United States* (New York: Oxford, 1974), 134–226; Jordan, *White Over Black: American Attitudes Toward the Negro, 1550–1812* (Chapel Hill: University of North Carolina Press, 1968), 342–582; Duncan J. Macleod, *Slavery, Race and the American Revolution* (Cambridge: Cambridge University Press, 1974); William H. Pease and Jane H. Pease, Eds., *The Antislavery Argument* (Indianapolis: Bobbs-Merrill, 1965), 1–17; Henry Wiencek, *An Imperfect God: George Washington, His Slaves, and the Creation of America* (New York: Farrar, Straus and Giroux, 2003); Arthur Zilversmit, *The First Emancipation: The Abolition of Slavery in the North* (Chicago: University of Chicago Press, 1967).

3. George F. Willison, *Patrick Henry and His World* (Garden City, NY: Doubleday, 1969), 9, 264–268, 485–486; italics added.

4. U.S. Bureau of the Census, *Negro Population, 1790–1915* (Washington, DC: Government Printing Office, 1918), 45.

5. Gordon S. Wood, "Never Forget: They Kept Lots of Slaves," *New York Times* (December 14, 2003); Benjamin Quarles, *The Negro in the American Revolution* (Chapel Hill: University of North Carolina Press, 1961). Wood and Henry Wiencek suggest that it may have been George Washington's experience with African American soldiers that led him to provide for the emancipation and education of his own slaves after his death; Wiencek, *An Imperfect God*, 353.

6. Willie Lee Rose, Ed., *A Documentary History of Slavery in North America* (New York: Oxford, 1976), 61–62.

7. Carl Becker, *The Declaration of Independence* (New York: Harcourt, Brace, 1922), 212–213.

8. By the Sixteenth Amendment, the Constitution provided in 1913 for a tax on the incomes of individuals and businesses, but not a per capita tax. In the late twentieth century and the twenty-first century, flat-tax advocates reappeared in the Republican Party, a bit like flat Earth advocates.

9. Number 54, *The Federalist Papers*, by Alexander Hamilton, James Madison, and John Jay (New York: Penguin, 1961; orig. 1788), 336–337.

10. Kenneth M. Clark, "James Madison and Slavery," web site of James Madison Museum, Orange, Virginia (2000); http://www.jamesmadisonmus.org/text-pages/clark.htm (March 13, 2004); Matthew T. Mellon, *Early American Views on Slavery* (New York: Bergman, 1969).

11. Leon F. Litwack, *North of Slavery: The Negro in the Free States, 1790–1860* (Chicago: University of Chicago Press, 1961). This analysis leaves aside the question of those Whites—those who did not make property, age, gender, or literacy requirements—who were also disfranchised. Those are vital issues, but they are outside the scope of the present study.

12. Stephen A. Small, "Mustefinos Are White by Law: Whites and People of Mixed Racial Origins in Historical and Comparative Perspective," in *Racial Thinking in the United States: Uncompleted Independence*, Paul Spickard and G. Reginald Daniel, Eds. (Notre Dame, IN: University of Notre Dame Press, 2004), 76.

13. Berlin, *Slaves Without Masters*; *Revised Code of the Laws of Virginia*, 3 vols. (Richmond: Ritchie, 1819), 1.111.

14. Litwack, *North of Slavery*; Leonard Curry, *The Free Black in Urban America, 1800–1850* (Chicago: University of Chicago Press, 1981); James Oliver Horton, *Free People of Color* (Washington, DC: Smithsonian Institution Press, 1993); Gary B. Nash, *Forging Freedom: The Formation of Philadelphia's Black Community, 1720–1840* (Cambridge, MA: Harvard University Press, 1988); Eugene H. Berwanger, *The Frontier Against Slavery: Western Anti-Negro Prejudice and the Slavery Expansion Controversy* (Urbana: University of Illinois Press, 1967); Carol Wilson, *Freedom at Risk: The Kidnapping of Free Blacks in America, 1780–1865* (Lexington: University Press of Kentucky, 1994).

15. Carol V. R. George, *Segregated Sabbaths: Richard Allen and the Emergence of Independent Black Churches, 1760–1840* (New York: Oxford, 1973); W. Jeffrey Bolster, *Black Jacks: African American Seamen in the Age of Sail* (Cambridge, MA: Harvard University Press, 1997); Harry Reed, *Platforms for Change: The Foundations of the Northern Free Black Community, 1776–1865* (East Lansing: Michigan State University Press, 1994); Benjamin Quarles, *Black Abolitionists* (New York: Oxford, 1969).

16. Berlin, *Many Thousands Gone*, 44–45, 123–125.

17. Joel Williamson, *New People: Miscegenation and Mulattoes in the United States* (New York: Free Press, 1980), 5–60; Paul Spickard, *Mixed Blood: Intermarriage and Ethnic Identity in Twentieth-Century America* (Madison: University of Wisconsin Press, 1989), 235–252; U.S. Census, *Negro Population*, 220; Berlin, *Slaves Without Masters*, 46, 178. For the small minority of interracial couples who followed another pattern, see Martha Hodes, *White Women, Black Men: Illicit Sex in the Nineteenth-Century South* (New Haven, CT: Yale University Press, 1997).

18. G. Reginald Daniel, "Either Black or White: Race, Modernity, and the Law of the Excluded Middle," in *Racial Thinking in the United States*, Spickard and Daniel, Eds., 21–59; Daniel, "Multiracial Identity Brazil and the United States," in *We Are a People: Narrative and Multiplicity in Constructing Ethnic Identity*, Paul Spickard and W. Jeffrey Burroughs, Eds. (Philadelphia: Temple University Press, 2000), 153–178; Daniel, "White Into Black: Race and National Identity in Contemporary Brazil," in *Race and Nation: Ethnic Systems in the Modern World*, Paul Spickard, Ed. (New York: Routledge, 2005); Carl N. Degler, *Neither*

Black Nor White: Slavery and Race Relations in Brazil and the United States (New York: Macmillan, 1971); George M. Fredrickson, *White Supremacy: A Comparative Study in American and South African History* (New York: Oxford, 1981); Thomas E. Skidmore, *Black into White: Race and Nationality in Brazilian Thought* (New York: Oxford, 1974); Charles V. Hamilton, et al., Eds., *Beyond Racism: Race and Inequality in Brazil, South Africa, and the United States* (Boulder, CO: Lynne Rienner, 2001).

19. Theda Perdue, *"Mixed Blood" Indians: Racial Construction in the Early South* (Athens: University of Georgia Press, 2003), 31, 112, and *passim*; William Hartley and Ellen Hartley, *Osceola, the Unconquered Indian* (New York: Hawthorn, 1973).

20. Perdue, *"Mixed Blood" Indians*, 4–5; Jack D. Forbes, *Africans and Native Americans: The Language of Race and the Evolution of Red-Black Peoples* (Urbana: University of Illinois Press, 1993); Daniel F. Littlefield, Jr., *Africans and Seminoles* (Westport, CT: Greenwood, 1977); Katja May, *African Americans and Native Americans in the Cherokee and Creek Nations, 1830s to 1920s* (New York: Garland, 1996); William Loren Katz, *Black Indians* (New York: Simon and Schuster, 1996); James F. Brooks, Ed., *Confounding the Color Line: The Indian-Black Experience in North America* (Lincoln: University of Nebraska Press, 2002); Kevin Mulroy, *Freedom on the Border: The Seminole Maroons in Florida, the Indian Territory, Coahuila, and Texas* (Lubbock: Texas Tech University Press, 1993); Kenneth Wiggins Porter, *The Negro on the American Frontier* (New York: Arno, 1971). There were also many groups of "tri-racial isolates" scattered up and down the eastern seaboard from Florida to New England—small, remote groups who frequently called themselves "Indians" but whose ancestry surely included Africans and Europeans as well—such as the Lumbee, Melungeons, Brass Ankles, and many more; G. Reginald Daniel, "Passers and Pluralists: Subverting the Racial Divide," in *Racially Mixed People in America*, Maria P. P. Root, Ed. (Newbury Park, CA: Sage, 1992), 91–107.

21. *The Writings of George Washington*, Ed. John C. Fitzpatrick (Washington, DC: Government Printing Office, 1938), 27.253–54; quoted in *Immigration and the American Tradition*, Moses Rischin, Ed. (Indianapolis: Bobbs-Merrill, 1976), 43.

22. 1 Stat. 103, quoted in *U.S. Immigration and Naturalization Laws and Issues*, Michael LeMay and Elliott Robert Barkan, Eds. (Westport, CT: Greenwood, 1999), 11. Emphasis added.

23. The debate in Congress ranged over many issues and opinions, but no one seems to have questioned limiting U.S. citizenship to White people. See *Annals of Congress*, 1st Congress, 2nd Session, 1789–1790, 1109–1118; a portion of that debate is reproduced in William C. Fischer, David A. Gerber, Jorge M. Guitart, and Maxine S. Seller, Eds., *Identity, Community, and Pluralism in American Life* (New York: Oxford, 1997), 206–211.

24. James H. Kettner, *The Development of American Citizenship, 1608–1870* (Chapel Hill: University of North Carolina Press, 1978), 287–333 (quotes are on 294 and 295); Rogers M. Smith, *Civic Ideals: Conflicting Visions of Citizenship in US History* (New Haven, CT: Yale University Press, 1997).

25. Ibid.

26. Ibid., 102–3, 233–46; Alan Cowell, "Britain's First Citizenship Ceremony," *New York Times* (February 26, 2004). Emphasis added.

27. My argument in this section stands on a number of shoulders: Philip J. Deloria, *Playing Indian* (New Haven, CT: Yale University Press, 1998); Brian W. Dippie, *The Vanishing American: White Attitudes and U.S. Indian Policy* (Middletown, CT: Wesleyan University Press, 1982); Robert F. Berkhofer, Jr., *The White Man's Indian* (New York: Knopf, 1978); Eva Marie Garroutte, *Real Indians: Identity and the Survival of Native America* (Berkeley: University of California Press, 2003); S. Elizabeth Bird, Ed., *Dressing in Feathers: The Construction of the Indian in American Popular Culture* (Boulder, CO: Westview, 1996); James A. Clifton, Ed., *The Invented Indian: Cultural Fictions and Government Policies* (New Brunswick, NJ: Transaction, 1990); Shari M. Huhndorf, *Going Native: Indians in the American Cultural Imagination* (Ithaca, NY: Cornell University Press, 2001); Raymond William Stedman, *Shadows of the Indian: Stereotypes in American Culture* (Norman: University of Oklahoma Press, 1982); Ward Churchill, *Indians Are Us? Culture and Genocide in Native North America* (Monroe, ME: Common Courage Press, 1994); Alan Trachtenberg, *Shades of Hiawatha: Staging Indians, Making Americans, 1880–1930* (New York: Hill and Wang, 2004); Paige Rabmon, *Authentic Indians: Episodes of Encounter from the Late-Nineteenth-Century Northwest Coast* (Durham, NC: Duke University Press, 2005).
28. Berkhofer, *White Man's Indian*, 30; D. H. Lawrence, *Studies in Classic American Literature* (New York: Viking, 1961; orig. 1923), 38.
29. Donna Barbie, "Sacajawea: The Making of a Myth," in *Sifters: Native American Women's Lives*, Theda Perdue, Ed. (New York: Oxford, 2001), 60–76. See the Natural American Spirit website at www.nascigs.com (I visited it on February 4, 2004). The Santa Fe Tobacco Company, owned by RJ Reynolds Tobacco Holdings, freely uses Native American symbols. There is no indication anywhere in the website that anyone involved might actually be an Indian.
30. Albert L. Hurtado and Peter Iverson, Eds., *Major Problems in American Indian History*, 2nd ed. (Boston: Houghton Mifflin, 2001), 200–201; P. L. Ford, Ed., *The Writings of Thomas Jefferson* (New York, 1892–1899), 3.214, quoted in Edward H. Spicer, *A Short History of the Indians of the United States* (New York: Van Nostrand, 1969), 227.
31. Anthony F. C. Wallace, *The Death and Rebirth of the Seneca* (New York: Knopf, 1969); John Walton Caughey, *McGillivray of the Creeks* (Norman: University of Oklahoma Press, 1938).
32. Hurtado and Iverson, *Major Problems in American Indian History*, 202–203.
33. R. David Edmunds, *The Shawnee Prophet* (Lincoln: University of Nebraska Press, 1983); Edmunds, *Tecumseh and the Quest for Indian Leadership* (Boston: Little, Brown, 1984); Gregory Dowd, *A Spirited Resistance: The North American Indians' Struggle for Unity, 1745–1815* (Baltimore: Johns Hopkins University Press, 1992); Anthony F. C. Wallace, *The Long, Bitter Trail: Andrew Jackson and the Indians* (New York: Hill and Wang, 1993); Robert V. Remini, *Andrew Jackson and His Indian Wars* (New York: Viking, 2001); Sean Michael O'Brien, *In Bitterness and in Tears: Andrew Jackson's Destruction of the Creeks and Seminoles* (Westport, CT: Praeger, 2003).
34. Alexander Saxton, *The Rise and Fall of the White Republic: Class Politics and Mass Culture in Nineteenth-Century America* (London: Verso, 1990); Jacobson, *Whiteness of a Different Color*, 15–90; Dana D. Nelson, *National Manhood: Capitalist Citizenship and the Imagined Fraternity of White Men* (Durham, NC: Duke University Press, 1998).

35. Survivalist Miles Stair's opinion is typical: "Perhaps we are not a 'country' at all now, as by definition a 'country' must define its borders"; "End Times Report" (June 6, 2004) (www.endtimesreport.com, Nov. 17, 2004). Even California Governor Arnold Schwarzenegger, generally a friend of immigrants and an immigrant himself, wrote, "The first order of business for the federal government is to secure our borders"; "Next Step for Immigration," *Los Angeles Times* (March 28, 2006). At the dawn of the twenty-first century, we see a pernicious conflation of immigrants and terrorists in many minds; see U.S. Department of Homeland Security, "Undersecretary [Asa] Hutchinson Testifies Before Senate Judiciary Subcommittee on Immigration, February 12, 2004" (http://www.dhs.gov/dhspublic/display?theme=45&content=3160&print=true, November 17, 2004); Phyllis Schlafly, "Security Starts at Our Borders," The Phyllis Schlafly Report, 35.4 (Nov. 2001).

36. In parts of Texas, the border itself came and went, as the Rio Grande frequently jumped its banks until it was encased in concrete in 1968. Even today, there are huge stretches of the U.S. border with Canada where an individual can wander back and forth across the line with impunity.

37. See Appendix A. LeMay and Barkan, *US Immigration and Naturalization Laws and Issues*, 12–25; Marion T. Bennett, *American Immigration Policies* (Washington, DC: Public Affairs Press, 1963), 7–14; Michael C. LeMay, *From Open Door to Dutch Door: An Analysis of US Immigration Policy Since 1820* (New York: Praeger, 1987), 20–37; E. P. Hutchinson, *Legislative History of American Immigration Policy, 1798–1965* (Philadelphia: University of Pennsylvania Press, 1981), 11–46.

38. See Appendix B, Tables 2–6.

39. Carl Wittke, *We Who Built America* (New York: Prentice-Hall, 1940), 101.

40. Carl Wittke, *We Who Built America*, 405.

41. Carl Wittke, *We Who Built America*, 406–407.

42. These textbooks told pretty much the same old story about immigration: Jeanne Boydston, Nick Culather, Jan Lewis, Michael McGerr, and James Oakes, *Making a Nation: The United States and Its People* (Upper Saddle River, NJ: Prentice Hall, 2003); Alan Brinkley, *American History*, 10th ed. (New York: McGraw-Hill, 1999); Mark C. Carnes and John A. Garraty, *The American Nation*, 11th ed. (Glenview, IL: Longman, 2003); James West Davidson and Mark H. Lytle, *The United States: A History of the Republic*, 5th ed. (Upper Saddle River, NJ: Prentice-Hall, 1991); Robert A. Divine, T. H. Breen, George M. Fredrickson, R. Hal Williams, Ariela J. Gross, and H. W. Brands, *America: Past and Present*, 7th ed. (Glenview, IL: Longman, 2004); John M. Faragher, Susan H. Armitage, Mari Jo Buhle, and Daniel Czitrom, *Out of Many*, 4th ed. (Upper Saddle River, NJ: Prentice Hall, 2004); David Goldfield, Virginia DeJohn Anderson, Jo Ann Argersinger, Peter H. Argersinger, William L. Barney, Robert M. Weir, Carl Abbott, *The American Journey*, 3rd ed. (Upper Saddle River, NJ: Prentice Hall, 2005); James Kirby Martin, Randy Roberts, Steven Mintz, Linda O. McMurry, and James H. Jones, *America and Its Peoples: A Nation in the Making*, 5th ed. (Glenview, IL: Longman, 2003); John M. Murrin, Paul E. Johnson, James M. McPherson, Gary Gerstle, Emily S. Rosenberg, and Norman L. Rosenberg, *Liberty, Equality, Power: A History of the American People*, 4th ed. (Stamford, CT: Thomson/Wadsworth, 2005); Mary Beth North, David M. Katzman, David W. Blight, Howard P. Chudakoff, Frederik Logevall, Beth Bailey, Thomas G. Patterson, William M. Tuttle, Jr., *A People and a Nation*, 7th ed. (Boston: Houghton

Mifflin); James L. Roark, Michael P. Johnson, Patricia Cline Cohen, Sarah Stage, Alan Lawson, and Susan M. Hartmann, *The American Promise: A History of the United States*, 2nd ed. (Bedford/St. Martin's, 2002). These textbooks told rather a different story, more in line with the argument of *Almost All Aliens*: Paul S. Boyer and Madison Clifford E. Clark, Jr., *The Enduring Vision*, 5th ed. (Boston: Houghton Mifflin); James A. Henretta, David Brody, and Lynn Dumenil, *America's History*, 5th ed. (New York: Bedford/St. Martin's, 2004); Jacqueline Tyler Jones, Peter H. Wood, Elaine Tyler May, Thomas Borstelmann, and Vicki L. Ruiz, *Created Equal* (Glenview, IL: Longman, 2003).

43. Jon Gjerde, Ed., *Major Problems in American Immigration and Ethnic History* (Boston: Houghton Mifflin, 1998); Alan M. Kraut, *The Huddled Masses: The Immigrant in American Society, 1880–1921*, 2nd ed. (Wheeling, IL: Harlan Davidson, 2001); Leonard Dinnerstein, Roger L. Nichols, and David M. Reimers, *Natives and Strangers: A Multicultural History of Americans*, 4th ed. (New York: Oxford, 2003); Leonard Dinnerstein and David M. Reimers, *Ethnic Americans*, 4th ed. (New York: Columbia University Press, 1999); Frederick M. Binder and David M. Reimers, *All the Nations Under Heaven* (New York: Columbia University Press, 1995). This is true to a lesser extent even of the most revisionist of the general treatments, Roger Daniels's *Coming to America*, 2nd ed. (New York: HarperCollins, 2002). Although Daniels explicitly criticizes the Old vs. New Immigration hypothesis, he lumps Scandinavians in with Irish and Germans as "pioneers of immigration" though they mainly came later, and he does not treat British immigrants at all after the colonial period. Even George Pozzetta's masterwork, a twenty-volume compilation of essays by dozens of distinguished immigration scholars that cuts the territory up several different ways, contains not a hint of racial analysis; *American Immigration and Ethnicity*, 20 vols. (New York: Garland, 1991).

44. Katharine W. Jones examines the implications of giving privilege to English immigrants as if they were natural Americans in *Accent on Privilege: English Identities and Anglophilia in the U.S.* (Philadelphia: Temple University Press, 2001). She examines late twentieth-century English immigrants.

45. See Appendix B, Tables 14 and 16. Chinese again constituted a significant part of the immigrant stream after 1965.

46. Sources on nineteenth-century Chinese immigrants include Gunther Barth, *Bitter Strength: A History of the Chinese in the United States, 1850–1870* (Cambridge, MA: Harvard University Press, 1964); Sucheng Chan, *This Bittersweet Soil: The Chinese in California Agriculture, 1860–1910* (Berkeley: University of California Press, 1986); Ping Chiu, *Chinese Labor in Nineteenth-Century California* (Madison: State Historical Society of Wisconsin, 1963); Mary Roberts Coolidge, *Chinese Immigration* (New York: Holt, 1909); Charles McClain, Ed., *Chinese Immigrants and American Law* (New York: Garland, 1994); Charles McClain, *In Search of Equality: The Chinese Struggle Against Discrimination in Nineteenth-Century America* (Berkeley: University of California Press, 1994); Stuart C. Miller, *The Unwelcome Immigrant: The American Image of the Chinese, 1785–1882* (Berkeley: University of California Press, 1969); George Anthony Peffer, *If They Don't Bring Their Women Here: Chinese Female Immigration before Exclusion* (Urbana: University of Illinois Press, 1999); Elmer Clarence Sandmeyer, *The Anti-Chinese Movement in California* (Urbana: University of Illinois Press, 1973; orig. 1939); Alexander Saxton, *The Indispensable Enemy: Labor and the Anti-Chinese Movement in California* (Berkeley: University of

California Press, 1971); John Kuo Wei Tchen, *New York before Chinatown* (Baltimore: Johns Hopkins University Press, 1999); Benson Tong, *Unsubmissive Women: Chinese Prostitutes in Nineteenth-Century San Francisco* (Norman: University of Oklahoma Press, 1994).

47. Sources on Scandinavian immigration include Arlow W. Anderson, *The Norwegian-Americans* (Boston: Twayne, 1975); Philip J. Anderson and Dag Blanck, Eds., *Swedish-American Life in Chicago: Cultural and Urban Aspects of an Immigrant People, 1850–1930* (Urbana: University of Illinois Press, 1992); H. Arnold Barton, *A People Divided: Homeland Swedes and Swedish Americans, 1840–1940* (Carbondale: Southern Illinois University Press, 1994); Adolph B. Benson, *Americans from Sweden* (Philadelphia: Lippincott, 1950); Martin Dribe, *Leaving Home in a Peasant Society* (Södertälje, Sweden: Almqvist & Wiksell, 2000); Frederick Hale, Ed., *Danes in North America* (Seattle: University of Washington Press, 1984); Florence Edith Janson, *The Background of Swedish Immigration, 1840–1930* (New York: Arno, 1970; orig. 1931); John S. Lindberg, *The Background of Swedish Emigration to the United States* (Minneapolis: University of Minnesota Press, 1930); George R. Nielsen, *Danes in America* (Boston: Twayne, 1981); Harold Runblom and Hans Norman, Eds., *From Sweden to America* (Minneapolis: University of Minnesota Press, 1976); Ingrid Semmingsen, *Norway to America*, trans. Einar Haugen (Minneapolis: University of Minnesota Press, 1978).

48. There are only three modern monographs on the subject: Rowland Tappan Berthoff, *British Immigrants in Industrial America, 1790–1950* (Cambridge, MA: Harvard University Press, 1953); William E. Van Vugt, *Britain to America: Mid-Nineteenth-Century Immigrants to the United States* (Urbana: University of Illinois Press, 1999); Van Vugt, *British Buckeyes: The English, Scots, and Welsh in Ohio, 1700–1900* (Kent, Ohio: Kent State University, 2006). There are three edited collections of letters: Charlotte Erickson, *Invisible Immigrants: The Adaptation of English and Scottish Immigrants in 19th Century America* (Coral Gables, FL: University of Miami Press, 1972); Alan Conway, Ed., *The Welsh in America: Letters from the Immigrants* (Minneapolis: University of Minnesota Press, 1961); David A. Gerber, Ed., *Authors of Their Lives: The Personal Correspondence of British Immigrants to North America in the Nineteenth Century* (New York: NYU Press, 2006). Among the articles used to prepare this section are Maldwyn A. Jones, "The Background to Emigration from Great Britain in the Nineteenth Century," *Perspectives in American History*, 7 (1973), 3–92; Malcolm Gray, "Scottish Emigration: The Social Impact of Agrarian Change in the Rural Lowlands, 1775–1875," *Perspectives in American History*, 7 (1973), 95–174; Alan Conway, "Welsh Emigration to the United States," *Perspectives in American History*, 7 (1973), 177–271.

49. Appendix B, Table 9; Van Vugt, *Britain to America*, 8, 17.

50. Van Vugt, *Britain to America*, 3.

51. "The Emigrant's Farewell," (1839) quoted in Van Vugt, *Britain to America*, 6. There were many songs so named, with different tunes and contents.

52. Van Vugt, *Britain to America*, 2–3.

53. Mary Wrightson Adkins was my grandmother. Genealogical data from 1880 British manuscript census and these websites: www.katarre.com; www.mcguire-spickard.com/genealogy.

54. Charles H. Anderson, *White Protestant Americans* (Englewood Cliffs, NJ: Prentice-Hall, 1970), 16–18; Paul Spickard, *Japanese Americans* (New York: Twayne, 1996), 20–63.

55. See Appendix B, Tables 6 and 10. Sources for the following section include Don Heinrich Tolzmann, *The German-American Experience* (Amherst, NY: Humanity Books, 2000), 124–208; John A. Hawgood, *The Tragedy of German-America* (New York: Dutton, 1940); James M. Bergquist, "German Communities in American Cities: An Interpretation of the Nineteenth-Century Experience," *Journal of American Ethnic History*, 4.1 (1984), 9–30; Walter D. Kamphöfner, "At the Crossroads of Economic Development: Background Factors Affecting Emigration from Nineteenth-Century Germany," in *Migration Across Time and Nations*, Ira Z. Glazier and Luigi De Rosa, Ed. (New York: Holmes and Meier, 1986), 174–201; Wolfgang Köllmann and Peter Marschalck, "German Emigration to the United States," *Perspectives in American History*, 7 (1973), 497–554; Anderson, *White Protestant Americans*, 79–93; Steven M. Nolt, *Foreigners in Their Own Land: Pennsylvania Germans in the Early Republic* (University Park: Pennsylvania State University Press, 2002); Stanley Nadel, *Little Germany: Ethnicity, Religion, and Class in New York City, 1845–80* (Urbana: University of Illinois Press, 1990); Walter D. Kamphoefner, Wolfgang Helbich, and Ulrike Sommer, Eds., *News from the Land of Freedom: German Immigrants Write Home*, trans. Susan Carter Vogel (Ithaca, NY: Cornell University Press, 1991); Frederick M. Binder and David M. Reimers, *All the Nations Under Heaven: An Ethnic and Racial History of New York City* (New York: Columbia University Press, 1995), 74–92. See also Frederick C. Luebke, *Germans in the New World* (Urbana: University of Illinois Press, 1990).
56. Bruce Levine, *The Spirit of 1848: German Immigrants, Labor Conflict, and the Coming of the Civil War* (Urbana: University of Illinois Press, 1992). 15–50.
57. Kathleen Neils Conzen, *Immigrant Milwaukee, 1836–1860* (Cambridge, MA: Harvard University Press, 1976).
58. The University of Cincinnati Archives, German-Americana Collection, contains forty-three volumes of the histories of German breweries in the United States.
59. Bergquist, "German Communities in American Cities," 9.
60. Jay P. Dolan, *The Immigrant Church: New York's Irish and German Catholics, 1815–1865* (Baltimore: Johns Hopkins University Press, 1975). The ins and outs of Lutheran and pietist theological divisions and institutional struggles are desperately complex. One can get an introduction to the issues in the relevant chapters of Sydney E. Ahlstrom, *A Religious History of the American People* (New Haven: Yale University Press, 1972). See also David A. Gustafson, *Lutherans in Crisis: The Question of Identity in the American Republic* (Minneapolis: Fortress, 1993); Alan Graebner, *Uncertain Saints: The Laity in the Lutheran Church, Missouri Synod, 1900–1970* (Westport, CT: Greenwood, 1975); E. Clifford Nelson and Eugene L. Fevold, *The Lutheran Church Among Norwegian Americans* (Minneapolis: Augsburg, 1960); Todd W. Nichol, Ed., *Crossings: Norwegian-American Lutheran as a Transatlantic Religion* (Northfield, MN: Norwegian American Historical Society, 2003); Charles P. Lutz, Ed., *Church Roots: Stories of Nine Immigrant Groups that Became the American Lutheran Church* (Minneapolis: Augsburg, 1985).
61. Terry G. Jordan, *German Seed in Texas Soil* (Austin: University of Texas Press, 1966). The process continued through the end of the century. Mountain Lake, Minnesota, was founded by a group of Volga German Mennonites in 1873, as was Gackle, North Dakota, in 1904. See town websites.

62. It has been alleged that the German-language version of the Declaration of Independence was the first one publicly printed. Clyde S. Stine, "The Pennsylvania Germans and the School," in *The Pennsylvania Germans*, Ralph Wood, Ed. (Princeton, NJ: Princeton University Press, 1942), 103–127.

63. Stine, *The Pennsylvania Germans*, 105.

64. Stine, *The Pennsylvania Germans*, 120–121; Nolt, *Foreigners in Their Own Land*, 43–45.

65. Bergquist, "German Communities in American Cities," 17; Anderson, *White Protestant Americans*, 79–93; Herbert Gans, "Symbolic Ethnicity," *Ethnic and Racial Studies*, 2 (1979), 1–20.

66. Giovanni Costigan, *A History of Modern Ireland* (Indianapolis: Bobbs-Merrill, 1969).

67. Sources for this section include Timothy J. Meagher, *Inventing Irish America: Generation, Class, and Ethnic Identity in a New England City, 1880–1928* (Notre Dame, IN: Notre Dame University Press, 2001); Kerby A. Miller, *Emigrants and Exiles: Ireland and the Irish Exodus to North America* (New York: Oxford, 1985); Lawrence J. McCaffrey, *The Irish Diaspora in America* (Bloomington: Indiana University Press, 1976); Oliver MacDonagh, "The Irish Famine Emigration to the United States," *Perspectives in American History*, 10 (1976), 355–446; William V. Shannon, *The American Irish* (New York: Macmillan, 1966); Donald B. Cole, *Immigrant City: Lawrence, Massachusetts, 1845–1921* (Chapel Hill: University of North Carolina Press, 1963); Conzen, *Immigrant Milwaukee*; Oscar Handlin, *Boston's Immigrants*, rev. ed. (Cambridge, MA: Harvard University Press, 1959); Mary C. Kelly, *The Shamrock and the Lily: The New York Irish and the Creation of a Transatlantic Identity, 1845–1925* (New York: Peter Lang, 2005); J. J. Lee and Marion R. Casey, Eds., *Making the Irish American* (New York: NYU Press, 2006); Brian Christopher Mitchell, *The Paddy Camps: The Irish of Lowell, 1821–61* (Urbana: University of Illinois Press, 1988).

68. Miller, *Emigrants and Exiles*, 285.

69. Miller, *Emigrants and Exiles,* 3–4. Miller implies the song of the exile is unique to them, an essential part of Irish culture, but he has little of the crucial comparative evidence he would need to support his contention. He does not demonstrate that Irish emigrants to other places like Australia and Canada had the same melancholy resentment of exile, nor that other immigrants to the United States—say, Chinese or Koreans—did not have a similar lament.

70. Elizabeth Gurley Flynn, *Rebel Girl*, quoted in Matthew Frye Jacobson, *Special Sorrows: The Diasporic Imagination of Irish, Polish, and Jewish Immigrants in the United States*, rev. ed. (Berkeley: University of California Press, 2002), 54.

71. Donald B. Cole, *Immigrant City: Lawrence, Massachusetts, 1845–1921* (Chapel Hill: University of North Carolina Press, 1963), 27–28; Anthony F. C. Wallace, *Rockdale: The Growth of an American Village in the Early Industrial Revolution* (New York: Norton, 1978).

72. Alan Dawley, *Class and Community: The Industrial Revolution in Lynn* (Cambridge, MA: Harvard University Press, 1976).

73. Roger Daniels does this in *Coming to America*, 2nd ed. (New York: HarperCollins, 2002), 144–164.

74. The reader can explore this period in Jewish American history in many sources, among them, Jacob Rader Marcus, *The American Jew: 1585–1990* (Brooklyn: Carlson, 1995), 45–158; Abraham J. Karp, *The Jewish Experience in America*, vol. 2, *In the Early Republic* (New York: Ktav, 1969); Rudolf Glanz, *Studies in*

Judaica Americana (New York: Ktav, 1970); Stanley Feldstein, *The Land That I Show You: Three Centuries of Jewish Life in America* (Garden City, NY: Doubleday, 1979), 41–117. An important source for quantitative estimates is Avraham Barkai, "German-Jewish Migration in the Nineteenth Century," in *Migration Across Time and Nations*, Glazier and De Rosa, Eds., 202–219.

75. Jacob Rader Marcus, *The Colonial American Jew* (Detroit: Wayne State University Press, 1970); Marcus, *Early American Jewry*, 2 vols. (Philadelphia: Jewish Publication Society, 1951–1953); Hyman B. Grinstein, *The Rise of the Jewish Community of New York, 1654–1860* (Philadelphia: Jewish Publication Society, 1957); Karp, *Jewish Experience*, vol 1, *The Colonial Period*; Feldstein, *Land That I Show You*, 1–40; Marcus, *American Jew*, 1–40.

76. See Appendix B, Table 33.

77. Feldstein, *Land That I Show You*, 41–42.

78. Barkai, "German-Jewish Migration," 211.

79. I. Harold Sharfman, *Jews on the Frontier* (Chicago: Regnery, 1977).

80. The taking on of the forms and styles of congregational Protestantism was a common way for non-Christian religions to adapt to American social life. For a similar development in the twentieth century among Buddhists, see Lori Pierce, "Devoted to the Teachings of the Buddha: Buddhist Modernism in English Language Buddhist Periodicals," to be published in a volume on American Buddhism edited by Duncan Williams (advance copy courtesy of the author).

81. Joseph L. Blau, *Modern Varieties of Judaism* (New York: Columbia University Press, 1966), 60–88; Michael A. Meyer, *Response to Modernity: A History of the Reform Movement in Judaism* (New York: Oxford, 1988).

82. Eugene B. Borowitz, *Reform Judaism Today*. Volume 3. *How We Live* (New York: Behrman House, 1978), quote is from 190–191; W. Gunther Plaut, *The Growth of Reform Judaism: American and European Sources Until 1948* (New York: World Union for Progressive Judaism, 1965), 3–74.

83. Daniels, *Coming to America*, 17–18. Sucheng Chan pursues this mode of interpretation in *Asian Americans: An Interpretive History* (Boston: Twayne, 1991).

84. Dirk Hörder, "Mass Migration," in *The Settling of North America*, Helen Hornbeck Tanner, Ed. (New York: Macmillan, 1995), 102–135; Dirk Hörder, *Cultures in Contact: World Migrations in the Second Millennium* (Durham, NC: Duke University Press, 2002); Dirk Hörder, "From Immigration to Migration Systems: New Concepts in Migration History," *OAH Magazine of History*, 14.1 (Fall 1999), 5–11. Of course, the webs were more complex than this, connecting peoples outside and across this three-part division. To take just one example, Fijians, I-Kiribati, and other Pacific Islanders were taken in these same years to work under slave-like conditions in places like Australia and Chile. Paul Spickard, "Pacific Diaspora?" in Paul Spickard, Ed., *Pacific Diaspora: Island Peoples in the United States and Across the Pacific* (Honolulu: University of Hawai'i Press, 2002), 1–27.

85. John Bodnar, *The Transplanted: A History of Immigrants in Urban America* (Bloomington: Indiana University Press, 1985), 54–55.

86. *Wiley & Putnam's Emigrant's Guide* (London: Wiley & Putnam, 1845; repr. Ft. Washington, PA: Eastern National, 2001), viii.

87. Kamphoefner, Helbich, and Sommer, *News from the Land of Freedom*; reprinted in Jon Gjerde, Ed., *Major Problems in American Immigration and Ethnic History* (Boston: Houghton Mifflin, 1998), 109.

88. Walter D. Kamphöfner, *The Westfalians: From Germany to Missouri* (Princeton, NJ: Princeton University Press, 1987); Jon Gjerde, "Chain Migrations from the West Coast of Norway," in *A Century of European Migrations, 1830–1930*, Rudolph J. Vecoli and Suzanne M. Sinke, Eds. (Urbana: University of Illinois Press, 1991), 158–81; Odd S. Lovoll, "A Pioneer Chicago Colony from Voss, Norway: Its Impact on Overseas Migration, 1836–60," in *Century of European Migrations*, Vecoli and Sinke, Eds., 182–199; June Granatir Alexander, "Staying Together: Chain Migration and Patterns of Slovak Settlement in Pittsburgh Prior to World War I," *Journal of American Ethnic History*, 1 (Fall 1981), 56–83.

89. Günter Moltmann, "American German Return Migration in the Nineteenth and Early Twentieth Centuries," *Central European History*, 13.4 (1980), 378–392; Wilbur S. Shepperson, "British Backtrailers: Working-Class Immigrants Return," in *In the Trek of the Immigrants*, O. Fritiof Ander, Ed. (Rock Island, IL: Augustana College Library, 1964), 179–196; Theodore Saloutos, "Exodus U.S.A." in *Trek of the Immigrants*, Ander, Ed., 197–215; Ewa Morawska, "Return Migrations," in *Century of European Migrations*, Vecoli and Sinke, Eds., 277–292; Walter D. Kamphoefner, "The Volume and Composition of German-American Return Migration," in *Century of European Migrations*, Vecoli and Sinke, Eds., 293–311.

90. Van Vugt, *Britain to America*: 155; Charles Dickens, *American Notes and Pictures from Italy* (London: Macmillan, 1893), 223–224.

91. Philip Taylor, *The Distant Magnet: European Emigration to the U.S.A.* (New York: Harper, 1971), 131–144; Edwin C. Guillet, *The Great Migration: The Atlantic Crossing by Sailing-Ship, 1770–1860*, 2nd ed. (University of Toronto Press, 1963), 67–68.

92. Guillet, *Great Migration*, 68, 81.

93. Taylor, *Distant Magnet*, 145–166.

94. The sources on Nativism are rich and include Ray Allen Billington, *The Protestant Crusade, 1800–1860: A Study of the Origins of American Nativism* (New York: Rinehart, 1952; orig. 1938); Billington, *The Origins of Nativism in the United States, 1800–1844* (PhD dissertation, Harvard University, 1933; repr. New York: Arno, 1974); Ira M. Leonard and Ronald D. Parmet, *American Nativism, 1830–1860* (Huntington, NY: Krieger, 1971); Thomas J. Curran, *Xenophobia and Immigration, 1820–1930* (Boston: Twayne, 1975); Dale T. Knobel, *"America for the Americans": The Nativist Movement in the United States* (New York: Twayne, 1996).

95. John Higham, *Strangers in the Land: Patterns of American Nativism, 1860–1925*, 2nd ed. (New York: Atheneum, 1975), 4.

96. Thomas R. Whitney, *A Defence of the American Policy* (1856), quoted in Jon Gjerde, *Major Problems in American Immigration History* (Boston: Houghton Mifflin, 1998), 145; Samuel F. B. Morse, *Imminent Dangers to the Free Institutions of the United States Through Foreign Immigration* (New York: Clayton, 1835; repr. 1969).

97. Maria Monk, *Awful Disclosures of the Hotel Dieu Nunnery of Montreal* (Hamden, CT: Archon, 1962; orig. 1836).

98. Eric Foner, *Free Soil, Free Labor, Free Men: The Ideology of the Republican Party before the Civil War* (New York: Oxford, 1971).

99. Leonard Dinnerstein, *Antisemitism in America* (New York: Oxford, 1994), 13–34; Frederic Cople Jaher, *A Scapegoat in the New Wilderness: The Origins and Rise of Anti-Semitism in America* (Cambridge, MA: Harvard University Press, 1994).

100. Najia Aarim-Heriot, *Chinese Immigrants, African Americans, and Racial Anxiety in the United States, 1848–1882* (Urbana: University of Illinois Press, 2003), 15–29.

101. Thomas Bailey Aldrich, *The Works of Thomas Bailey Aldrich*, vol. 1 (New York: AMS Press, 1970; orig. 1907), 71–72.

102. For a summary and analysis of this intellectual movement see Paul Spickard, "What's Critical About White Studies," in *Racial Thinking in the United States*, Spickard and G. Reginald Daniel, Eds. (Notre Dame, IN: University of Notre Dame Press, 2004), 248–274. See also Theodore W. Allen, *The Invention of the White Race*, 2 vols. (London: Verso, 1994, 1997); Eric Arnesen, "Whiteness and Historians' Imagination," *International Labor and Working Class History*, 60 (2001), 3–32; Karen Brodkin, *How Jews Became White Folks and What That Says about Race in America* (New Brunswick, NJ: Rutgers University Press, 1999); Steve Garner, *Racism in the Irish Experience* (London: Pluto Press, 2004); Jennifer Guglielmo and Salvatore Salerno, Eds., *Are Italians White?* (New York: Routledge, 2003); Thomas A. Guglielmo, *White on Arrival: Italians, Race, Color, and Power in Chicago, 1890–1945* (New York: Oxford, 2003); Ira Haney Lopez, *White by Law: The Legal Construction of Race* (New York: NYU Press, 1996); Noel Ignatiev, *How the Irish Became White* (New York: Routledge, 1995); Matthew Frye Jacobson, *Whiteness of a Different Color: European Immigrants and the Alchemy of Race* (Cambridge, MA: Harvard University Press, 1998); Peter Kolchin, "Whiteness Studies: The New History of Race in America," *Journal of American History*, 89 (2002): 154–173; George Lipsitz, *The Possessive Investment in Whiteness* (Philadelphia: Temple University Press, 1998); David R. Roediger, *The Wages of Whiteness: Race and the Making of the American Working Class* (London: Verso, 1991); Alexander Saxton, *The Rise and Fall of the White Republic* (London: Verso, 1990).

103. *Oxford English Dictionary*, 2nd ed. (Oxford: Oxford University Press, 1989), 262, 264; Winthrop D. Jordan, *The White Man's Burden: Historical Origins of Racism in the United States* (New York: Oxford, 1974), 52.

104. Thomas Nast, "The Ignorant Vote: Honors Are Easy," *Harper's Weekly*, December 9, 1876), reproduced in L. Perry Curtis, Jr., *Apes and Angels: The Irishman in Victorian Culture* (Washington, DC: Smithsonian Institution, 1971), 60; Albert Bigelow Paine, *Thomas Nast: His Period and His Pictures* (New York: Harper, 1904).

105. Curtis, *Apes and Angels*.

106. Jon Gjerde, *The Minds of the West: Ethnocultural Evolution in the Rural Middle West, 1830–1917* (Chapel Hill: University of North Carolina Press, 1997), xi.

107. Milton M. Gordon, *Assimilation in American Life* (New York: Oxford, 1964), 88.

Chapter 4

1. Quoted by Richard Griswold del Castillo, *The Treaty of Guadelupe Hidalgo: A Legacy of Conflict* (Norman: University of Oklahoma Press, 1990), 108. The chapter title is taken from a sentiment widely expressed among California Chicanos. Its exact origin is obscure. Maria Herrera-Sobek recounts Chicanos

marching against California's anti-immigrant Proposition 187 chanting the slogan in 1994. Rodolfo Acuña uses the phrase in *Anything But Mexican: Chicanos in Contemporary Los Angeles* (London: Verso, 1997), 109.

2. Some Americans of more recent vintage have tried to pretend that this impulse for empire never characterized the American people. Thus, in a 2004 essay banging on George W. Bush's Iraq misadventure, Arthur M. Schlesinger, Jr., wrote: "But Americans, unlike the Romans, the British, and the French, are not colonizers of remote and exotic places. We peopled North America's vacant spaces. … But Americans, as James Bryce wrote in 1888, 'have none of the earth-hunger which burns in the great nations of Europe.' … The Americans wanted to control their own westward drive but, unlike the British and the French, could not have cared less about empire." Poppycock! The westward drive was empire, and Euro-Americans at the time called it that. Arthur M. Schlesinger, Jr., "The Making of a Mess," *New York Review of Books* (September 23, 2004), 41.

3. Quoted by Richard White, *"It's Your Misfortune and None of My Own": A History of the American West* (Norman: University of Oklahoma Press, 1991), 73.

4. Albert K. Weinberg, *Manifest Destiny: A Study of Nationalist Expansionism in American History* (Baltimore: Johns Hopkins Press, 1935), 1–2. See also Frederick Merk, *Manifest Destiny and Mission in American History* (New York: Knopf, 1963); David S. Heidler and Jeanne T. Heidler, *Manifest Destiny* (Westport, CT: Greenwood, 2003).

5. Quoted in Henry Nash Smith, *Virgin Land: The American West as Symbol and Myth* (Cambridge, MA: Harvard University Press, 1950), 44–48.

6. William Gilpin, *Mission of the North American People, Geographical, Social, and Political* (Philadelphia: Lippincott, 1873), 130 (quoting a letter of 1846), quoted in Smith, *Virgin Land*, 37. Richard Slotkin follows the career of these ideas in American popular culture in two extraordinary books: *Regeneration Through Violence: The Mythology of the American Frontier, 1600–1860* (Middletown, CT: Wesleyan University Press, 1973) and *Gunfighter Nation: The Myth of the Frontier in Twentieth-Century America* (New York: Atheneum, 1992).

7. George F. Will, "No Flinching from the Facts," *Washington Post*, May 11, 2004; Gordon W. Allport, *The Nature of Prejudice* (Garden City, NY: Doubleday, 1958); Albert Memmi, *The Colonizer and the Colonized* (Boston: Beacon, 1965). Will adds that the imperial gaze is necessarily pornographic, as were the photos of Iraqi prisoners that shook the G. W. Bush administration at its foundations. Think of pre-1970s photos in *National Geographic* or the softcore porn of Waikiki hula shows. See also Robert Young, *Colonial Desire* (New York: Routledge, 1995).

8. Gavan Daws, *Shoal of Time: A History of the Hawaiian Islands* (New York: Macmillan, 1968), 213. It is remarkable that this Christian gentleman blindly appropriated for the White race God's charge to Adam on behalf of all humankind.

9. Reginald Horsman, *Race and Manifest Destiny: The Origins of American Racial Anglo-Saxonism* (Cambridge, MA: Harvard University Press, 1981), 1–2.

10. That is not the way the Native peoples in question understood their origins. For Native understandings, see, for example, Paul Zolbrod, trans., *Dine Bahane: The Navajo Creation Story* (Albuquerque: University of New Mexico Press, 1988); Trudy Griffin-Pierce, *Earth Is My Mother, Sky Is My Father: Space, Time, and Astronomy in Navajo Sandpainting* (Albuquerque: University of New Mexico Press, 1992); Ronald Goodman, *Lakota Star Knowledge* (Rosebud, SD: Sinte Gleska University, 1992); Marsha C. Bol, *Stars Above, Earth Below: American*

Indians and Nature (Niwot, CO: Carnegie Museum of Natural History, 1998); Harold Courlander, *The Fourth World of the Hopis* (Albuquerque: University of New Mexico Press, 1971).

11. Sources for this section include: William L. Anderson, Ed., *Cherokee Removal* (Athens: University of Georgia Press, 1991); Stuart Banner, *How the Indians Lost Their Land* (Cambridge, MA: Harvard University Press, 2005); Louis Filler and Allen Guttmann, Eds., *The Removal of the Cherokee Nation: Manifest Destiny or National Dishonor?* (Huntington, NY: Krieger, 1977); Linda S. Parker, *Native American Estate* (Honolulu: University of Hawai'i Press, 1989); Theda Perdue and Michael D. Green, Eds., *The Cherokee Removal* (Boston: Bedford/ St. Martin's, 1995); Anthony F. C. Wallace, *The Long, Bitter Trail: Andrew Jackson and the Indians* (New York: Hill and Wang, 1993). Places to begin on U.S. Indian policy are: Francis Paul Prucha, *The Great Father: The United States Government and the American Indians*, abridged ed. (Lincoln: University of Nebraska Press, 1986); Wilcomb E. Washburn, Ed., *History of Indian-White Relations*, Volume 4 of *Handbook of North American Indians* (Washington, DC: Smithsonian, 1988); Brian W. Dippie, *The Vanishing American: White Attitudes and US Indian Policy* (Middletown, CT: Wesleyan University Press, 1982).

12. United States Congress, *Indian Removal Act* (May 28, 1830), Section 3, reproduced in Perdue and Green, *Cherokee Removal*, 116–117; italics added.

13. Perdue and Green, *Cherokee Removal*, 165.

14. James F. Brooks, Ed., *Confounding the Color Line: The Indian-Black Experience in North America* (Lincoln: University of Nebraska Press, 2002); Daniel F. Littlefield, Jr., *Africans and Seminoles: From Removal to Emancipation* (Westport, CT: Greenwood, 1977); Tiya Miles, *Ties That Bind: The Story of an Afro-Cherokee Family in Slavery and Freedom* (Berkeley: University of California Press, 2005); Theda Perdue, *Slavery and the Evolution of Cherokee Society, 1540–1866* (Knoxville: University of Tennessee Press, 1979); Circe Sturm, *Blood Politics: Race, Culture, and Identity in the Cherokee Nation of Oklahoma* (Berkeley: University of California Press, 2002).

15. See, for example, Ralph K. Andrist, *The Long Death: The Last Days of the Plains Indians* (New York: Collier, 1969); Merrill D. Beal, *I Will Fight No More Forever: Chief Joseph and the Nez Perce* (Seattle: University of Washington Press, 1963); Dee Brown, *Bury My Heart at Wounded Knee: An Indian History of the American West* (New York: Holt, Rinehart, and Winston, 1971); Alvin M. Josephy, Jr., *The Patriot Chiefs* (New York: Viking, 1961); Peter Matthiessen, *In the Spirit of Crazy Horse* (New York: Viking, 1983); Mari Sandoz, *Crazy Horse: The Strange Man of the Oglalas* (Lincoln: University of Nebraska Press, 1961; orig. 1942).

16. Mari Sandoz, *Cheyenne Autumn* (New York: McGraw-Hill, 1953); *Little Big Man*, directed by Arthur Penn, starring Dustin Hoffman (Paramount Pictures, 1970); Richard White, "The Winning of the West: The Expansion of the Western Sioux in the Eighteenth and Nineteenth Centuries," *Journal of American History*, 65.2 (1978), 319–343.

17. Keith A. Murray, *The Modocs and Their War* (Norman: University of Oklahoma Press, 1959); Jeff C. Riddle, *The Indian History of the Modoc War* (San Jose: Urion Press, 1998; orig. 1914); Murray L. Wax and Robert W. Buchanan, Eds., *Solving "The Indian Problem": The White Man's Burdensome Business* (New York: New Viewpoints, 1975), 6–35.

18. "Chief Joseph Speaks: Selected Statements and Speeches by the Nez Perce Chief," www.pbs.org/weta/thewest/resources/archives/six/jospeak.htm. 5/29/04.

19. Merrill D. Beal, *I Will Fight No More Forever: Chief Joseph and the Nez Perce War* (Seattle: University of Washington Press, 1966); Alvin M. Josephy, Jr., *The Nez Perce Indians and the Opening of the Northwest* (New Haven, CT: Yale University Press, 1965).

20. Russell Thornton, *American Indian Holocaust and Survival* (Norman: University of Oklahoma Press, 1987), 133.

21. Frederick E. Hoxie, *Parading Through History: The Making of the Crow Nation in America, 1805–1935* (Cambridge: Cambridge University Press, 1995), 9, 12, 14.

22. Katherine M. B. Osburn, "The Navajo at Bosque Redondo: Cooperation, Resistance, and Initiative, 1864–1868," *New Mexico Historical Review*, 60.4 (1985), 399–413.

23. *Waheenee: An Indian Girl's Story Told by Herself to Gilbert L. Wilson, North Dakota History: Journal of the Northern Plains*, 38:1–2 (1971), quoted in Peter Nabokov, *Native American Testimony*, rev. ed. (New York: Penguin, 1999), 182–183.

24. Dippie, *Vanishing American*, 12–44, 197–269 (Sprague quote, page 15); Stephen Dow Beckham, *Requiem for a People: The Rogue Indians and the Frontiersmen*, rev. ed. (Corvallis: Oregon State University Press, 1996; orig. 1971); Theodora Kroeber, *Ishi in Two Worlds: A Biography of the Last Wild Indian in North America* (Berkeley: University of California Press, 1961); Robert F. Heizer and Theodora Kroeber, Eds., *Ishi the Last Yahi* (Berkeley: University of California Press, 1979); Orin Starn, *Ishi's Brain: In Search of America's Last "Wild" Indian* (New York: Norton, 2004); Karl Kroeber and Clifton Kroeber, *Ishi in Three Centuries* (Lincoln: University of Nebraska Press, 2003); Philip J. Deloria, *Playing Indian* (New Haven: Yale University Press, 1998); Julie Schimmel, "Inventing the Indian," in *The West as America: Reinterpreting Images of the Frontier, 1820–1920*, William H. Treuttner, Ed. (Washington, DC: Smithsonian, 1991), 149–189.

25. Prucha, *Great Father*, 224–241; Emily Greenwald, *Refiguring the Reservation: The Nez Perces, Jicarilla Apaches, and the Dawes Act* (Albuquerque: University of New Mexico Press, 2002). Curtis was later Herbert Hoover's Vice President.

26. David Wallace Adams, *Education for Extinction: American Indians and the Boarding School Experience, 1875–1928* (Lawrence: University Press of Kansas, 1995); Brenda J. Child, *Boarding School Seasons: American Indian Families, 1900–1940* (Lincoln: University of Nebraska Press, 1998); Carol Devens, " 'If We Get the Girls, We Get the Race': Missionary Education of Native American Girls," *Journal of World History*, 3.2 (1992): 219–237; Clyde Ellis, *To Change Them Forever: Indian Education at the Rainy Mountain Boarding School, 1893–1920* (Norman: University of Oklahoma Press, 1996); K. Tsianina Lomawaima, *They Called It Prairie Light: The Story of the Chilocco Indian School* (Lincoln: University of Nebraska Press, 1994); Robert A. Trennert, Jr., *The Phoenix Indian School: Forced Assimilation in Arizona, 1891–1935* (Norman: University of Oklahoma Press, 1988). For a parallel attempt by Euro-Australians to erase the identities of Australian Aborigines, see Doris Pilkington/Nugi Garimara, *Rabbit-Proof Fence* (New York: Hyperion, 2002), and also the 2002 Miramax movie by the same name.

27. Edwin R. Embree, *Indians of the Americas* (New York: Houghton Mifflin, 1939), quoted in Nabokov, *Native American Testimony*, 221–224.

28. Sources for this section include: Stephen Cornell, *The Return of the Native: American Indian Political Resurgence* (New York: Oxford, 1988), 7, 62–67, and *passim*; Richard White, *The Middle Ground: Indians, Empires, and Republics in the Great Lakes Region, 1650–1815* (New York: Cambridge University Press, 1991); Robert H. Ruby and John A. Brown, *Dreamer-Prophets of the Columbia Plateau* (Norman: University of Oklahoma Press, 1989); James Mooney, *The Ghost-Dance Religion and the Sioux Outbreak of 1890*, Fourteenth Annual Report of the Bureau of Ethnology, 1892–93, Part 2 (Washington, DC: Government Printing Office, 1896); Alexander Lesser, *The Pawnee Ghost Dance Hand Game: Ghost Dance Revival and Ethnic Identity* (Madison: University of Wisconsin Press, 1978; orig. 1933); Gregory E. Smoak, *Ghost Dances and Identity* (Berkeley: University of California Press, 2006).

29. David J. Weber says that "Blacks were imported as slaves or servants, and it appears that more Blacks than Spaniards entered Mexico during the colonial period. They did not remain a distinctive minority, however, for they blended with Indian and Spanish stocks, and their descendants lost their racial identity." Gonzalo Aguirre Beltrán wrote that "black and white together never represented more than one to two percent of the total population of the country"; *La población negra de Mexico, 1519–1810* (Mexico, 1946), 200, quoted in Weber, *Foreigners in Their Native Land: Historical Roots of the Mexican Americans* (Albuquerque: University of New Mexico Press, 1973), 17, 267.

30. Sources for this section include: Teresa Palomo Acosta and Ruthe Winegarten, *Las Tejanas* (Austin: University of Texas Press, 2003); Armando C. Alonzo, *Tejano Legacy: Rancheros and Settlers in South Texas, 1734–1900* (Albuquerque: University of New Mexico Press, 1998); Arnaldo De León, *The Tejano Community* (Albuquerque: University of New Mexico Press, 1982); Martha Menchaca, *Recovering History, Constructing Race: The Indian, Black, and White Roots of Mexican Americans* (Austin: University of Texas Press, 2001); Gerald E. Poyo and Gilberto M. Hinojosa, Eds., *Tejano Origins in Eighteenth-Century San Antonio* (San Antonio: University of Texas Institute of Texan Cultures, 1991); Andrés Reséndez, *Changing National Identities at the Frontier: Texas and New Mexico, 1800–1850* (Cambridge: Cambridge University Press, 2005); James Diego Vigil, *From Indians to Chicanos* (Prospect Heights, IL: Waveland Press, 1984); Weber, *Foreigners in Their Native Land*: 1–50; David J. Weber, *The Mexican Frontier, 1821–1846: The American Southwest Under Mexico* (Albuquerque: University of New Mexico Press, 1982); Weber, Ed., *New Spain's Far Northern Frontier* (Albuquerque: University of New Mexico Press, 1979); Weber, *The Spanish Frontier in North America* (New Haven, CT: Yale University Press, 1992).

31. In speaking of the Southwest in the nineteenth century and the encounter between Mexicans and European-descended Americans, I will use the terms "Anglo-Americans" and "White Americans" interchangeably. In an earlier chapter I used "Anglo-Americans" to refer to U.S. citizens of English descent, but in the context of the U.S. encounter with Mexicans and Mexican-descended people, the White Americans in question were often of some other descent than English. The difference should be clear from context.

32. Sources for this section include Terry G. Jordan, *German Seed in Texas Soil: Immigrant Farmers in Nineteenth-Century Texas* (Austin: University of Texas Press, 1966); Michael A. Morrison, *Slavery and the American West: The Eclipse of Manifest Destiny and the Coming of the Civil War* (Chapel Hill:

University of North Carolina Press, 1997); Kevin Mulroy, *Freedom on the Border: The Seminole Maroons in Florida, the Indian Territory, Coahuila, and Texas* (Lubbock: Texas Tech University Press, 1993); Andrés Tijerina, *Tejanos and Texas under the Mexican Flag, 1821–1836* (College Station: Texas A&M University Press, 1994); Weber, *Foreigners in Their Native Land*, 51–137.

33. John Long, "The Americanization of Texas," in *The Settling of North America*, Helen Hornbeck Tanner, Ed. (New York: Macmillan, 1995), 96.

34. On that opposition, see, for example, The Legion of Liberty, *Remonstrance of Some Free Men, States, and Presses, to the Texas Rebellion, Against the Laws of Nature and of Nations* (Albany, NY: sold at the Patriot Office, 1843).

35. Richard Flores, *Remembering the Alamo* (Austin: University of Texas Press, 2002); David J. Weber, "Refighting the Alamo: Mythmaking and the Texas Revolution," in Weber, *Myth and the History of the Hispanic Southwest* (Albuquerque: University of New Mexico Press, 1988), 133–150.

36. Weber, *Foreigners in Their Native Land*, 59–60.

37. Juan N. Seguín, *A Revolution Remembered: The Memoirs and Selected Correspondence of Juan N. Seguín*, Ed. Jesús F. de la Teja (Austin: State House, 1991).

38. Weber, *Foreigners in Their Native Land*, 95–96.

39. The storied, sordid history of the Texas Rangers has been told many times. The best place to start is Julian Samora, Joe Bernal, and Albert Peña, *Gunpowder Justice* (Notre Dame, IN: University of Notre Dame Press, 1979).

40. William Starr Meyers, Ed., *The Mexican War Diary of General B. Clellan* (Princeton, NJ: Princeton University Press, 1917), 1: 102, 161–162; quoted in Rodolfo Acuña, *Occupied America: A History of Chicanos*, 3rd ed. (New York: Harper and Row, 1988), 16–17.

41. Samuel E. Chamberlain, *My Confessions* (New York: Harper and Row, 1956), 75; quoted in Acuña, *Occupied America*, 17.

42. Sources for this section include: Seymour V. Connor and Odie B. Faulk, *North America Divided: The Mexican War, 1846–1848* (New York: Oxford, 1971); Ramón Eduardo Ruiz, Ed., *The Mexican War: Was It Manifest Destiny?* (New York: Holt, Rinehart and Winston, 1963); Robert W. Johannsen, *To the Halls of the Montezumas: The Mexican War in the American Imagination* (New York: Oxford, 1985); Carol and Thomas Christensen, *The U.S.-Mexican War* (San Francisco: Bay Books, 1998); John Edward Weems, *To Conquer a Peace: The War Between the United States and Mexico* (Garden City, NY: Doubleday, 1974); Gene M. Brack, *Mexico Views Manifest Destiny, 1821–1846: An Essay on the Origins of the Mexican War* (Albuquerque: University of New Mexico press, 1975); William G. Robbins, *Colony and Empire: The Capitalist Transformation of the American West* (Lawrence: University Press of Kansas, 1994), 22–39.

43. Amelia W. Williams and Eugene C. Barker, Eds., *The Writings of Sam Houston, 1813–1863* (Austin: 1938–1941), 5: 33–34; quoted in Weber, *Foreigners in Their Native Land*, 100.

44. U.S. Congress, Senate, *The Congressional Globe*, 30th Cong., 1st sess. (1848) 98–99.

45. Sources for this section include: Griswold del Castillo, *Treaty of Guadalupe Hidalgo*; Martha Menchaca, *Recovering History, Constructing Race: The Indian, Black, and White Roots of Mexican Americans* (Austin: University of Texas Press, 2001).

46. Weber, *Foreigners in Their Native Land*, 162–168.

47. This anomaly was extended in the second half of the twentieth century to confuse the racial status of Latinos generally.

48. Clara E. Rodriguez, *Changing Race: Latinos, the Census, and the History of Ethnicity in the United States* (New York: NYU Press, 2000).

49. Neil Foley, *The White Scourge: Mexicans, Blacks, and Poor Whites in Texas Cotton Culture* (Berkeley: University of California Press, 1997); Foley, "Partly Colored or Other White: Mexican Americans and Their Problem with the Color Line," in *Beyond Black and White: Race, Ethnicity, and Gender in the US South and Southwest*, Laura F. Edwards et al. Eds. (College Station: Texas A&M University Press, 2004), 123–144. See also David Montejano, *Anglos and Mexicans in the Making of Texas, 1836–1896* (Austin: University of Texas Press, 1987); Arnoldo de León, *Racial Frontiers: Africans, Chinese, and Mexicans in Western America, 1848–1890* (Albuquerque: University of New Mexico Press, 2002).

50. Sources for this section include: Leonard Pitt, *The Decline of the Californios: A Social History of the Spanish-Speaking Californians, 1846–1890* (Berkeley: University of California Press, 1966); Albert L. Hurtado, *Indian Survival on the California Frontier* (New Haven, CT: Yale University Press, 1988); Douglas Monroy, *Thrown Among Strangers: The Making of Mexican Culture in Frontier California* (Berkeley: University of California Press, 1990); Lisbeth Haas, *Conquests and Historical Identities in California, 1769–1936* (Berkeley: University of California Press, 1995); Ramón A. Gutiérrez and Richard J. Orsi, Eds., *Contested Eden: California Before the Gold Rush* (Berkeley: University of California Press, 1998); Robert F. Heizer and Alan J. Almquist, *The Other Californians: Prejudice and Discrimination under Spain, Mexico, and the United States to 1920* (Berkeley: University of California Press, 1971); W. W. Robinson, *Land in California* (Berkeley: University of California Press, 1948); John Walton Caughey, *The Indians of Southern California in 1852* (San Marino, CA: Huntington Library, 1952); Clifford E. Trafzer and Joel R. Hyer, Eds., *"Exterminate Them": Written Accounts of the Murder, Rape, and Slavery of Native Americans During the California Gold Rush, 1848–1868* (East Lansing: Michigan State University Press, 1999); Sherburne F. Cook, *The Conflict between the California Indian and White Civilization* (Berkeley: University of California Press, 1976).

51. Albert Camarillo, *Chicanos in a Changing Society: From Mexican Pueblos to American Barrios in Santa Barbara and Southern California, 1848–1930* (Cambridge, MA: Harvard University Press, 1979); Tomás Almaguer, *Racial Fault Lines: The Historical Origins of White Supremacy in California* (Berkeley: University of California Press, 1994); David Torres-Rouff, "Making Los Angeles: Race, Space, and Municipal Power, 1822–1890" (PhD dissertation, University of California, Santa Barbara, August 2006). For broader racial processes, see James Diego Vigil, *From Indians to Chicanos: The Dynamics of Mexican American Culture*, 2nd ed. (Prospect Heights, IL: Waveland Press, 1998).

52. Weber, *Foreigners in Their Native Land*, 151–152.

53. Yellow Bird (John Rollin Ridge), *The Life and Adventures of Joaquín Murieta* (Norman: University of Oklahoma Press, 1955; orig. 1854); Susan Lee Johnson, *Roaring Camp: The Social World of the California Gold Rush* (New York: Norton, 2000), 25–53; Walter Noble Burns, *The Robin Hood of El Dorado: The Saga of Joaquin Murrieta, Famous Outlaw of California's Age of Gold* (Albuquerque: University of New Mexico Press, 1999; orig. 1932); Remi Nadeau, *The*

Real Joaquin Murieta: Robin Hood Hero or Gold Rush Gangster? (Corona del Mar, CA: Trans-Anglo Books, 1974); Frank F. Latta, *Joaquín Murrieta and His Horse Gangs* (Santa Cruz, CA: Bear State Books, 1980); Bruce Thornton, *Searching for Joaquín: Myth, Murieta and History in California* (San Francisco: Encounter Books, 2003). See also, on Gregorio Cortez, Elfego Baca, Tiburcio Vásquez, Juan Cortina, and others: Américo Paredes, *"With His Pistol in His Hand": A Border Ballad and Its Hero* (Austin: University of Texas Press, 1958); Pedro Castillo and Albert Camarillo, Eds., *Furia y muerta: Los bandidos Chicanos* (Los Angeles: Aztlán, 1973); Larry D. Ball, *Elfego Baca in Life and Legend* (El Paso: Texas Western Press, 1992); George A. Beers, *Vasquez, or The Hunted Bandits of the San Joaquin* (New York: De Witt, 1875); Eugene T. Sawyer, *The Life and Career of Tiburcio Vasquez, the California Stage Robber* (Oakland, CA: Biobooks, 1944); Jerry D. Thompson, Ed., *Juan Cortina and the Texas-Mexico Frontier, 1859–1877* (El Paso: Texas Western Press, 1994); Shelley Streeby, *American Sensations: Class, Empire, and the Production of Popular Culture* (Berkeley: University of California Press, 2002), 251–290.

54. On the recruiting of European immigrants, see Lars Ljungmark, *For Sale— Minnesota: Organized Promotion of Scandinavian Immigration, 1866–1873* (Göteborg: Läromedelsförl, 1971). Robert Bartlett points to very near parallels in the process by which West Europeans colonized outlying territories in Central Europe in the twelfth and thirteenth centuries in *The Making of Europe: Conquest, Colonization, and Cultural Change, 950–1350* (Princeton, NJ: Princeton University Press, 1993).

55. Frederick B. Goddard, *Where to Emigrate and Why* (New York: Goddard, 1869), 12. See also Patricia Hills, "Picturing Progress in the Era of Westward Expansion," in *The West as America: Reinterpreting Images of the Frontier, 1820–1920*, Ed. William H. Truettner (Washington, DC: Smithsonian, 1991), 97–148.

56. Goddard, *Where to Emigrate and Why*, quoted in Hills, "Picturing Progress," 145.

57. Frederick Hoxie, email to the author, April 12, 2004. Benjamin Horace Hibbard's magisterial *A History of the Public Land Policies* (Madison: University of Wisconsin Press, 1965; orig. 1924), has 591 pages on the organization and dispersal of U.S. public lands, but not one page on the taking of those lands from Native peoples, nor on the effect of that seizure on the former occupants. It's not part of the story.

58. A rich sampling can be had in *Ethnicity on the Great Plains*, Frederick C. Luebke, Ed. (Lincoln: University of Nebraska Press, 1980) and *European Immigrants in the American West*, Frederick C. Luebke, Ed. (Albuquerque: University of New Mexico Press, 1998). See also Frederick C. Luebke, *Immigrants and Politics: The Germans of Nebraska, 1880–1900* (Lincoln: University of Nebraska Press, 1969); Dino Cinel, *From Italy to San Francisco* (Stanford, CA: Stanford University Press, 1982); David M. Emmons, *The Butte Irish* (Urbana: University of Illinois Press, 1989); Jordan, *German Seed in Texas Soil*; Timothy J. Kloberdanz, *The Volga Germans in Old Russia and in Western North America* (Lincoln, NE: American Historical Society of Germans from Russia, 1979); Royden K. Loewen, *Family, Church, and Market: A Mennonite Community in the Old and the New Worlds, 1850–1930* (Toronto: University of Toronto Press, 1993); Robert C. Ostergren, *A Community Transplanted: The Trans-Atlantic Experience of a Swedish Immigrant Settlement in the Upper*

Middle West, 1835–1915 (Madison: University of Wisconsin Press, 1998); Dean L. May, *Three Frontiers: Family, Land, and Society in the American West, 1850–1900* (Cambridge: Cambridge University Press, 1997); O. E. Röl-vaag, *Giants in the Earth* (New York: Burt, 1929); William Toll, *The Making of an Ethnic Middle Class: Portland Jewry over Four Generations* (Albany: SUNY Press, 1982).

59. Jon Gjerde, *The Minds of the West: Ethnocultural Evolution in the Rural Middle West, 1830–1917* (Chapel Hill: University of North Carolina Press, 1997), 171.

60. Mari Sandoz, *Cheyenne Autumn* (New York: McGraw-Hill, 1953), v–vi; see also Sandoz, *Old Jules* (New York: Blue Ribbon Books, 1935). Anthony F. C. Wallace makes the connection explicit regarding the removal of southeastern Indians during an earlier period in "The Hunger for Indian Land in Andrew Jackson's America," the introduction to *The Long, Bitter Trail: Andrew Jackson and the Indians* (New York: Hill and Wang, 1993), 3–13. Jackson himself as a young lawyer moved into the town of Nashville in the Cumberland Valley in 1788, only three years after the government had forced the Cherokee to sell that valley. Two vivid memoirs by children of homesteaders make the attempt to connect with Native American experiences, although neither succeeds in getting outside its author's White perspective: Bette Lynch Husted, *Above the Clearwater: Living on Stolen Land* (Corvallis: Oregon State University Press, 2004); Jarold Ramsey, *New Era: Reflections on the Human and Natural History of Central Oregon* (Corvallis: Oregon State University Press, 2003).

61. Washington Irving, *A Tour of the Prairies* (Norman: University of Oklahoma Press, 1956; orig. 1835); Hamlin Garland, *A Son of the Middle Border* (New York: Grosset and Dunlap, 1917); Garrison Keillor, *Lake Wobegon Days* (New York: Viking, 1985).

62. It is amazing that the same White American folk wisdom that embraced the taking of land from U.S. Indians and giving it to Euro-Americans found it abhorrent when, in 1954, the democratically elected government of Guatemala proposed to take unused land from U.S. corporations like United Fruit (later United Brands, marketers of Chiquita Bananas) and give it back to the Indian peasants from whom it had been seized a generation earlier. It was sufficiently abhorrent that the American people supported a CIA-organized coup in Guatemala. See Richard H. Immerman, *The CIA in Guatemala* (Austin: University of Texas Press, 1982).

63. *Congressional Globe*, Appendix (32nd Congress, 1st Session) April 6, 1852, 410, and April 20, 1852, 438; quoted in Lawrence Bacon Lee, *Kansas and the Homestead Act, 1862–1905* (New York: Arno, 1979; orig. 1957), 23–24.

64. White, *It's Your Misfortune*, 143–145.

65. Murray R. Wickett, *Contested Territory: Whites, Native Americans, and African Americans in Oklahoma, 1865–1907* (Baton Rouge: Louisiana State University Press, 2000); William T. Hagan, *Taking Indian Lands* (Norman: University of Oklahoma Press, 2003); Banner, *How the Indians Lost Their Lands*.

66. H. Craig Miner and William E. Unrau, *The End of Indian Kansas: A Study of Cultural Revolution, 1854–1871* (Lawrence, KS: Regents Press, 1978), 133.

67. Frederick E. Hoxie, *A Final Promise: The Campaign to Assimilate the Indians, 1880–1920* (Lincoln: University of Nebraska Press, 1984); David Rich Lewis, *Neither Wolf nor Dog: American Indians, Environment, and Agrarian Change* (New York: Oxford University Press, 1994); Peter Iverson, *When*

Indians Became Cowboys: Native Peoples and Cattle Ranching in the American West (Norman: University of Oklahoma Press, 1994); Joy S. Kasson, *Buffalo Bill's Wild West* (New York: Hill and Wang, 2000).

68. Appendix B, Table 16.

69. Sources for this section include Mary Roberts Coolidge, *Chinese Immigration* (New York: Henry Holt, 1909), still the best book on the subject; Gunther Barth, *Bitter Strength: A History of the Chinese in the United States, 1850–1870* (Cambridge, MA: Harvard University Press, 1964); Sucheng Chan, *This Bittersweet Soil: The Chinese in California Agriculture, 1860–1910* (Berkeley: University of California Press, 1986); Yong Chen, *Chinese San Francisco* (Stanford, CA: Stanford University Press, 2000; de León, *Racial Frontiers*; Madeline Y. Hsu, *Dreaming of Gold, Dreaming of Home: Transnationalism and Migration Between the United States and South China, 1882–1943* (Stanford, CA: Stanford University Press, 2000); Josephine Lee, Imogene L. Lim, and Yuko Matsukawa, Eds., *Re-Collecting Early Asian America* (Philadelphia: Temple University Press, 2002); Lynn Pan, *Sons of the Yellow Emperor: A History of the Chinese Diaspora* (New York: Kodansha, 1994); Nayan Shah, *Contagious Divides: Epidemics and Race in San Francisco's Chinatown* (Berkeley: University of California Press, 2001); John Kuo Wei Tchen, *New York Before Chinatown: Orientalism and the Shaping of American Culture, 1776–1882* (Baltimore: Johns Hopkins University Press, 1999); Shih-shan Henry Tsai, *The Chinese Experience in America* (Bloomington: Indiana University Press, 1986).

70. Lee Chew, "The Biography of a Chinaman," *Independent*, 55 (February 19, 1903), 417–423; reprinted in *Plain Folk*, David M. Katzman and William M. Tuttle, Jr., Eds. (Urbana: University of Illinois Press, 1982), 164–175. Note that Mott Street was not a city, but rather a street in New York's Chinatown.

71. Karen J. Leong, " 'A Distant and Antagonistic Race': Constructions of Chinese Manhood in the Exclusion Debates, 1869–1878," in *Across the Great Divide: Cultures of Manhood in the American West*, Laura McCall, Matthew Basso, and Dee Garceau, Eds. (New York: Routledge, 2000): 131–148; Johnson, *Roaring Camp*, 35; Ronald Takaki, *Iron Cages: Race and Culture in Nineteenth-Century America* (New York: Knopf, 1979), 215–249; Jachinson W. Chan, *Chinese American Masculinities: From Fu Manchu to Bruce Lee* (New York: Routledge, 2001).

72. For a similar figure among Italian, Greek, and Mexican immigrants to the American West, see Gunther Peck, *Reinventing Free Labor: Padrones and Immigrant Workers in the North American West, 1880–1930* (Cambridge: Cambridge University Press, 2000).

73. Note that, from 1870 on, it was illegal for Chinese to marry Whites in California. In Hawai'i, Chinese immigrant men intermarried freely with the local population, formed families, and stayed on.

74. Sources for this section include Najia Aarim-Heriot, *Chinese Immigrants, African Americans, and Racial Anxiety in the United States, 1848–82* (Urbana: University of Illinois Press, 2003); Coolidge, *Chinese Immigration*; Roger Daniels, *Guarding the Golden Door: American Immigration Policy and Immigrants Since 1882* (New York: Hill and Wang, 2003); Andrew Gyory, *Race, Politics, and the Chinese Exclusion Act* (Chapel Hill: University of North Carolina Press, 1998); E. P. Hutchinson, *Legislative History of American Immigration Policy, 1798–1965* (Philadelphia: University of Pennsylvania Press, 1981); Victor Jew, "'Chinese Demons': The Violent Articulation of Chinese Otherness and Inter-

racial Sexuality in the U.S. Midwest, 1885–1889," *Journal of Social History* (2003), 389–410; Erika Lee, *At America's Gates: Chinese Immigration During the Exclusion Era, 1882–1943* (Chapel Hill: University of North Carolina Press, 2003); Robert G. Lee, *Orientals: Asian Americans in Popular Culture* (Philadelphia: Temple University Press, 1999); Michael LeMay and Elliott Robert Barkan, Eds., *US Immigration and Naturalization Laws and Issues* (Westport, CT: Greenwood, 1999); Charles McClain, Ed., *Chinese Immigrants and American Law* (New York: Garland, 1994); McClain, *In Search of Equality: The Chinese Struggle Against Discrimination in Nineteenth-Century America* (Berkeley: University of California Press, 1994); Stuart Creighton Miller, *The Unwelcome Immigrant: The American Image of the Chinese, 1785–1882* (Berkeley: University of California Press, 1969); George Anthony Peffer, *If They Don't Bring Their Women Here: Chinese Female Immigration Before Exclusion* (Urbana: University of Illinois Press, 1999); Lucy E. Salyer, *Laws Harsh as Tigers: Chinese Immigrants and the Shaping of Modern Immigration Law* (Chapel Hill: University of North Carolina Press, 1995); Elmer Clarence Sandmeyer, *The Anti-Chinese Movement in California* (Urbana: University of Illinois Press, 1939); Alexander Saxton, *The Indispensable Enemy: Labor and the Anti-Chinese Movement in California* (Berkeley: University of California Press, 1971).

75. McClain, *In Search of Equality*, 20–22.

76. Charles I. Bevans, Ed., *Treaties and Other International Agreements of the United States of America, 1776–1949* (Washington, DC: U.S. Government Printing Office, 1971), 6:682. See also Shih-shan H. Tsai, *China and the Overseas Chinese in the United States, 1868–1911* (Fayetteville: University of Arkansas Press, 1983).

77. *Daily Alta California*, May 27, 1873.

78. LeMay and Barkan, *US Immigration and Naturalization Laws*, 35; Gary Y. Okihiro, *Margins and Mainstreams: Asians in American History and Culture* (Seattle: University of Washington Press, 1994), 4–5.

79. Coolidge, *Chinese Immigration*, 265–267.

80. Megumi Dick Osumi, "Asians and California's Anti-Miscegenation Laws," in Nobuya Tsuchida, Ed., *Asian and Pacific American Experiences: Women's Perspectives* (Minneapolis: Asian/Pacific American Learning Resource Center, University of Minnesota, 1982).

81. LeMay and Barkan, *US Immigration and Naturalization Laws*, 33–34.

82. *San Francisco Chronicle* (February 25, 1878), quoted in Leong, "Distinct and Antagonistic Race," 133.

83. LeMay and Barkan, *US Immigration and Naturalization Laws*, 48–54.

84. Appendix B, Table 16; Lee, *At America's Gates*, 30–46.

85. Lee, *At America's Gates*; Madeline Y. Hsu, *Dreaming of Gold, Dreaming of Home: Transnationalism and Migration Between the United States and South China, 1882–1943* (Stanford, CA: Stanford University Press, 2000). For insight into Chinatown life, see the stories of Sui Sin Far (Edith Maude Eaton), in *Mrs. Spring Fragrance and Other Writings* (Urbana: University of Illinois Press, 1995). For later anti-Asian movements, see Roger Daniels, *The Politics of Prejudice: The Anti-Japanese Movement in California and the Struggle for Japanese Exclusion* (Berkeley: University of California Press, 1962); Gary Y. Okihiro, *Cane Fires: The Anti-Japanese Movement in Hawai'i, 1865–1945* (Philadelphia: Temple University Press, 1991); Daniels, *Prisoners Without Trial: Japanese Americans in World War II*, rev. ed. (New York: Hill and Wang, 2004).

86. See, for example, Peter Kolchin, *American Slavery* (New York: Hill and Wang, 1993); Eugene Genovese, *Roll, Jordan, Roll: The World the Slaves Made* (New York: Pantheon, 1974); Herbert Gutman, *The Black Family in Slavery and Freedom* (New York: Random House, 1976); Leslie Howard Owens, *This Species of Property* (New York: Oxford, 1976); John Blassingame, *The Slave Community*, rev. ed. (New York: Oxford, 1979); Lawrence W. Levine, *Black Culture and Black Consciousness: Afro-American Folk Thought from Slavery to Freedom* (New York: Oxford, 1977); Merton J. Dillon, *Slavery Attacked: Southern Slaves and Their Allies, 1619–1865* (Baton Rouge: Louisiana State University Press, 1990); Sterling Stuckey, *Slave Culture* (New York: Oxford, 1987); Douglas R. Egerton, *Gabriel's Rebellion: The Virginia Slave Conspiracies of 1800 and 1802* (Chapel Hill: University of North Carolina Press, 1993); Albert J. Raboteau, *Slave Religion* (New York: Oxford, 1978); Walter Johnson, *Soul by Soul: Life Inside the Antebellum Slave Market* (Cambridge, MA: Harvard University Press, 1999); Benjamin Quarles, *Black Abolitionists* (New York: Oxford, 1969); James Brewer Stewart, *Holy Warriors: The Abolitionists and American Slavery*, 2nd ed. (New York: Hill and Wang, 1997); Vincent Harding, *There Is a River: The Black Struggle for Freedom in America* (New York: Harcourt Brace Jovanovich, 1981).

87. Avalon Project, "The Fugitive Slave Act 1850" (http://www.yale.edu/lawweb/Avalon/fugitive.htm, November 25, 2004).

88. Paul Finkelman, *Dred Scott v. Sandford* (Boston: Bedford/St. Martin's, 1997); Don E. Fehrenbacher, *The Dred Scott Case* (New York: Oxford, 1978); Fehrenbacher, *Slavery, Law, and Politics: The Dred Scott Case in Historical Perspective* (New York: Oxford, 1981).

89. Leon F. Litwack, *Been in the Storm So Long: The Aftermath of Slavery* (New York: Knopf, 1979); Roger L. Ransom and Richard Sutch, *One Kind of Freedom: The Economic Consequences of Emancipation* (Cambridge: Cambridge University Press, 1977); W.E.B. Du Bois, *Black Reconstruction in America* (New York: Russell and Russell, 1966; orig. 1935); Tera W. Hunter, *To 'Joy My Freedom: Southern Black Women's Lives and Labors after the Civil War* (Cambridge, MA: Harvard University Press, 1997); Eric Foner, *Reconstruction: America's Unfinished Revolution, 1863–1877* (New York: Harper and Row, 1988); Claude F. Oubre, *Forty Acres and a Mule: The Freedmen's Bureau and Black Landownership* (Baton Rouge: Louisiana State University Press, 1978); Michael L. Perman, *Emancipation and Reconstruction, 1862–1879* (Arlington Heights, IL: Harlan Davidson, 1987).

90. Sources for this section include M. L. Marks, *Jews Among the Indians* (Chicago: Benison Books, 1992); I. Harold Sharfman, *Jews on the Frontier* (Chicago, 1977); American Jewish Historical Society, "Solomon Bibo" (Jewish Virtual Library) http://www.jewishvirtuallibrary.org/jsource/biography/Bibo.html, 10/22/04.

Chapter 5

1. Yuji Ichioka, *The Issei: The World of the First Generation Japanese Immigrants, 1885–1924* (New York: Free Press, 1988), 219.

2. *Takao Ozawa v. United States, 260 US 178* (1922); Ian F. Haney López, *White By Law: The Legal Construction of Race* (New York: NYU Press, 1996), 79–86.

3. United States Bureau of the Census, *Historical Statistics of the United States: Colonial Times to 1970* (Washington, DC: Government Printing Office, 1975), 163, 224, 230–231, 457, 589–590, 666, 693; Douglass C. North, *Growth and Welfare in the American Past*, 2nd ed. (Englewood Cliffs, NJ: Prentice-Hall, 1974), 27, 40; Mary Beth North, et al., *A People and a Nation* (Boston: Houghton Mifflin, 1982), 468.

4. Leonard Dinnerstein, Roger L. Nichols, and David M. Reimers, *Natives and Strangers: Ethnic Groups and the Building of America* (New York: Oxford, 1979), 130–131.

5. Theodore Saloutos, "Exodus U.S.A.," in *In the Trek of the Immigrants*, O. Gritiof Ander, Ed. (Rock Island, IL: Augustana College Library, 1964), 197–215. See also Theodore Saloutos, *They Remember America: The Story of the Repatriated Greek-Americans* (Berkeley: University of California Press, 1956); Hans Storhaug, "Return Migration: Numbers, Reasons and Consequences," *AEMI Journal* (2003), 1–8.

6. Mark Wyman, *Round-Trip to America: The Immigrants Return to Europe, 1880–1930* (Ithaca, NY: Cornell University Press, 1994), 17; Appendix B, Table 14.

7. Nancy L. Gree, Laura Levine Frader, and Pierre Milza, "Paris: City of Light and Shadow," in *Distant Magnets: Expectations and Realities in the Immigrant Experience, 1840–1930*, Dirk Hoerder and Horst Rössler, Eds. (New York: Holms and Meier, 1993), 34–51; Henri Bunle, "Migratory Movements Between France and Foreign Lands," in *International Migrations*, vol. 2 Walter F. Willcox, Ed. (New York: Gordon and Breach, 1969), 201–236; Michael John and Albert Lichtblau, "Vienna around 1900: Images, Expectations, and Experience of Labor Migrants," in *Distant Magnets*, Hoerder and Rössler, Eds., 52–81; Anna Reczynska, "America and the Ruhr Basin in the Expectations of Polish Peasant Migrants," in *Distant Magnets*, Hoerder and Rössler, Eds., 84–104; Franco Ramella, "Across the Ocean or over the Border: Expectations and Experiences of Italians from Piedmont in New Jersey and Southern France," in *Distant Magnets*, Hoerder and Rössler, Eds., 105–125; Donna R. Gabaccia, *Italy's Many Diasporas* (Seattle: University of Washington Press, 2000).

8. If, for example, one compares the numbers in Table 5.2 with the summary numbers in the sources from which Table 5.2 is constructed, one sees this:

	Census Summary with Germany in Eastern Europe		My Revision with Germany in Northwest Europe	
	Northwest Europe	Eastern Europe	Northwest Europe	Eastern Europe
1900	4,202,683	4,136,646	6,866,101	1,471,389
1910	4,239,067	6,014,028	6,550,304	3,670,561
1920	3,830,094	6,134,845	5,516,202	4,443,453

Scholars and policy makers have usually relied on numbers for the foreign born presented as the census makers chose to summarize them. Thus, it can hardly be a surprise that they reached the erroneous conclusion that the country was being inundated by a horde of Eastern Europeans. It was not an accurate impression. One might even say it had been prejudiced by the census makers. A detailed quantitative study of the 1920 census material on foreign-born Americans and their children is Niles Carpenter, *Immigrants and Their Children,* U.S. Bureau of the Census Monograph No. VII (Washington, DC: Government Printing Office, 1927). Analyzed critically, Carpenter's work supports the interpretation I make here, although it has always been used to support the other interpretation.

9. The degree of this misperception is evident in the selection of people June Namias included in a fine set of oral histories: *First Generation: In the Words of Twentieth-Century American Immigrants,* rev. ed. (Urbana: University of Illinois Press, 1992). Among the ethnic groups included are Armenians, Chinese, Cubans, Filipinos, Greeks, Hungarians, Indians, Italians, Japanese, Jews, Koreans, Poles, Portuguese, Russians, Spaniards, Vietnamese, and West Indians. The only Northwest Europeans are an Irish woman and a French woman. The many other immigrants from that part of the world are ignored. Joan Morrison and Charlotte Fox Zabusky show the same blindness in an equally evocative set of oral histories, *American Mosaic: The Immigrant Experience in the Words of Those Who Lived It* (Pittsburgh: University of Pittsburgh Press, 1993; orig. 1980). This is by no means a complaint about the inclusion of so many others in either volume—that is an admirable array. But the absence of Northwest Europeans distorts the representation of the actual shape of twentieth-century U.S. immigration.

10. The youngest Wrightson daughter, Mary Ellen, was my grandmother. Information on their household comes from the 1881 English manuscript census and her stories. The physical description of the landscape comes from my 1997 visit to Middlestone and the Leasingthorne Colliery. For the story of an English immigrant who remained professionally in the working class, see Samuel Gompers, *Seventy Years of Life and Labor,* abridged ed., Ed. Nick Salvatore (Ithaca, NY: ILR Press, 1985; orig. ed. 1925).

11. Stanley C. Johnson, *A History of Emigration From the United Kingdom to North America, 1763–1912* (London: Frank Cass, 1966; orig. 1913), 344–345; Charlotte J. Erickson, "English," in *Harvard Encyclopedia of American Ethnic Groups,* Stephan Thernstrom, Ed. (Cambridge, MA: Harvard University Press, 1980), 336; C. E. Snow, "Emigration from Great Britain," in *International Migrations,* Willcox, Ed., 2:239–282; E. T. McPhee, "Australia—Its Immigrant Population," in *International Migrations,* Willcox, Ed., 2:169–178; D. J. Cruickshank, "New Zealand—External Migration," in *International Migrations,* Willcox, Ed., 2:179–200.

12. Rowland Tappan Berthoff, *British Immigrants in Industrial America, 1790–1950* (Cambridge, MA: Harvard University Press, 1953), 157. Berthoff's is the only book on British immigration to the United States that takes the story past the middle of the nineteenth century.

13. Berthoff, *British Immigrants,* 10, 80–84.

14. Wilbur Shepperson, *Emigration and Disenchantment* (Norman: University of Oklahoma Press, 1965), 7.

15. Johnson, *Emigration from the United Kingdom,* 346–347.

16. For one particularly interesting group of British migrants, see P. A. M. Taylor, *Expectations Westward: The Mormons and the Emigration of their British Converts in the Nineteenth Century* (Edinburgh: Oliver and Boyd, 1965).

17. See also Appendix B, Table 10.

18. Sources for this section include Don Heinrich Tolzmann, *The German-American Experience* (Amherst, NY: Humanity Books, 2000); La Vern J. Rippley, *The German-Americans* (Lanham, MD: University Press of America, 1984; orig. 1976); Frederick C. Luebke, *Germans in the New World: Essays in the History of Immigration* (Urbana: University of Illinois Press, 1990); Walter D. Kamphoefner, Wolfgang Helbich, and Ulrike Sommer, Eds., *News from the Land of Freedom: German Immigrants Write Home* (Ithaca, NY: Cornell University Press, 1992); G. A. Dobbert, "German-Americans Between New and Old Fatherland, 1870–1914," *American Quarterly*, 19.4 (1967), 663–680; Karen Schniedewind, "Migrants Returning to Bremen: Social Structure and Motivations, 1850 to 1914," *Journal of American Ethnic History*, 12.2 (Winter 1993), 35–55; Michael Ermarth, "Hyphenation and Hyper-Americanization: Germans of the Wilhelmine Reich Veiw German-Americans, 1890–1914," *Journal of American Ethnic History*, 21.2 (Winter 2002), 33–58; F. Burgdörfer, "Migration Across the Frontiers of Germany," in *International Migrations*, Willcox, Ed., 2:313–389; Russall A. Kazal, *Becoming Old Stock: The Paradox of German-American Identity* (Princeton, NJ: Princeton University Press, 2004).

19. Charles Thomas Johnson, *Culture at Twilight: The National German-American Alliance, 1901–1918* (New York: Peter Lang, 1999).

20. Tolzmann, *German-American Experience*, 288; Frederick C. Luebke, *Bonds of Loyalty: German-Americans and World War I* (DeKalb: Northern Illinois University Press, 1974); Franziska Ott, "The Anti-German Hysteria: The Case of Robert Paul Prager," in *German Americans in the World Wars*, Don Heinrich Tolzmann, Ed. (Munich: K. G. Saur, 1995), vol. 1, 237–365; Clemens Work, *Darker Before Dawn: Sedition and Free Speech in the American West* (Albuquerque: University of New Mexico Press, 2005).

21. Tolzmann, *German-American Experience*, 268–295; Kamphoefner, Helbich, and Sommer, *News from the Land of Freedom*, 23–26. See also Phyllis Keller, *States of Belonging: German-American Intellectuals and the First World War* (Cambridge, MA: Harvard University Press, 1979). The migration to the United States in this period of the Dutch replicated in miniature the shape and issues of German migration (save the World War I situation), and came to assume local importance in some Midwestern states like Michigan, Wisconsin, and Iowa. See Robert P. Swierenga, Ed., *The Dutch in America: Immigration, Settlement, and Cultural Change* (New Brunswick, NJ: Rutgers University Press, 1985); Suzanne M. Sinke, *Dutch Immigrant Women in the United States, 1880–1920* (Urbana: University of Illinois Press, 2000).

22. Sources for this section include Donald B. Cole, *Immigrant City: Lawrence, Massachusetts, 1845–1921* (Chapel Hill: University of North Carolina Press, 1963); D. A. E. Harkness, "Irish Emigration," in *International Migrations*, Willcox, Ed., 2:261–282; Matthew Frye Jacobson, *Special Sorrows: The Diasporic Imagination of Irish, Polish, and Jewish Immigrants in the United States* (Berkeley: University of California Press, 2002); Lawrence J. McCaffrey, *The Irish Diaspora in America* (Bloomington: Indiana University Press, 1976); Timothy J. Meagher, *Inventing Irish America* (Notre Dame, IN: University of Notre Dame Press, 2001); Kerby A. Miller, *Emigrants and Exiles: Ireland and the Irish Exodus to North America* (New York: Oxford, 1988); David Roediger and James Barrett, "Making New Immigrants 'Inbetween': Irish Hosts and White Panethnicity, 1890 to 1930," in *Not Just black and White:*

Historical and Contemporary Perspectives on Immigration, Race, and Ethnicity in the United States, Nancy Foner and George M. Fredrickson, Eds. (New York: Russell Sage, 2004), 167–196; Arnold Schrier, *Ireland and the American Emigration, 1850–1900* (Minneapolis: University of Minnesota Press, 1958); William V. Shannon, *The American Irish* (New York: Macmillan, 1966); Barbara Miller Solomon, *Ancestors and Immigrants: A Changing New England Tradition* (Cambridge, MA: Harvard University Press, 1956); Stephan Thernstrom, *The Other Bostonians: Poverty and Progress in the American Metropolis, 1880–1970* (Cambridge, MA: Harvard University Press, 1973); Richard White, *Remembering Ahanagran: A History of Stories* (Seattle: University of Washington Press, 2004; orig. 1998).

23. Kerby A. Miller, "Paddy's Paradox: Emigration to America in Irish Imagination and Rhetoric," in *Distant Magnets*, Hoerder and Rössler, Eds., 264–293.

24. Miller, "Paddy's Paradox," 265. The reference is to David N. Doyle, *Irish Americans, Native Rights, and National Empires: The Structure, Divisions and Attitudes of the Catholic Minority in the Decade of Expansion, 1890–1901* (New York: Anno Press, 1976).

25. Cole, *Immigrant City*, 51–53.

26. William L. Riordian, *Plunkitt of Tammany Hall* (New York: Dutton, 1963), xx, 3, 36, 37.

27. On ethnic political machines, see, for example, Blaine A. Brownell, *Bosses and Reformers: Urban Politics in America, 1880–1920* (Boston: Houghton Mifflin, 1973); Fletcher Dobyns, *The Underworld of American Politics* (New York: Dobyns, 1932); Alex Gottfried, *Boss Cermak of Chicago* (Seattle: University of Washington Press, 1962); Paul M. Green and Melvin G. Holli, Eds., *The Mayors: The Chicago Political Tradition* (Carbondale: Southern Illinois University Press, 1995).

28. The play on words mocks the ancient creed: "One, Holy, Catholic, and Apostolic." Jay P. Dolan, *The American Catholic Experience* (Garden City, NY: Doubleday, 1985), 143, 180, 302–303.

29. Miller, "Paddy's Paradox," 265–266.

30. Jacobson, *Special Sorrows*, 25.

31. Irish World (Jan. 29, 1898), 1, and (March 12, 1898), 4, both quoted in Jacobson, *Special Sorrows*, 32.

32. Sources for this section include Richard D. Alba, *Italian Americans* (Englewood Cliffs, NJ: Prentice-Hall, 1985); Josef J. Barton, *Peasants and Strangers: Italians, Rumanians, and Slovaks in an American City, 1890–1950* (Cambridge, MA: Harvard University Press, 1975); John W. Briggs, *An Italian Passage: Immigrants to Three American Cities, 1890–1930* (New Haven, CT: Yale University Press, 1978); Dino Cinel, *From Italy to San Francisco* (Stanford, CA: Stanford University Press, 1982); Francesco Cordasco and Eugene Bucchioni, Eds., *The Italians: Social Backgrounds of an American Group* (Clifton, NJ: Augustus M. Kelley, 1974); Alexander DeConde, *Half Bitter, Half Sweet: An Excursion into Italian-American History* (New York: Scribner's, 1971); Donna Gabaccia, *From Sicily to Elizabeth Street: Housing and Social Change Among Italian Immigrants, 1880–1930* (Albany: SUNY Press, 1984); Richard Gambino, *Blood of My Blood: The Dilemma of the Italian-Americans* (Garden City, NY: Doubleday, 1974); Thomas A. Guglielmo, *White on Arrival: Italians, Race, Color, and Power in Chicago, 1890–1945* (New York: Oxford, 2003); Thomas Kessner, *The Golden Door: Italian and Jewish Immigrant Mobility in*

New York City, 1880–1915 (New York: Oxford University Press, 1977); Salvatore J. LaGumina, *The Immigrants Speak: Italian Americans Tell Their Story* (New York: Center for Migration Studies, 1979); Gary Mormino, *Immigrants on the Hill: Italian Americans in St. Louis, 1882–1982* (Urbana: University of Illinois Press, 1986); Humbert S. Nelli, *From Immigrants to Ethnics: The Italian Americans* (New York: Oxford University Press, 1983); Nelli, *Italians in Chicago, 1880–1930* (New York: Oxford, 1970); Gunther Peck, *Reinventing Free Labor: Padrones and Immigrant Workers in the North American West, 1880–1930* (Cambridge: Cambridge University Press, 2000); Andrew F. Rolle, *The Italian Americans* (Belmont, CA: Wadsworth, 1972); S. M. Tomasi, *Perspectives in Italian Immigration and Ethnicity* (New York: Center for Migration Studies, 1977); Virginia Yans-McLaughlin, *Family and Community: Italian Immigrants in Buffalo, 1880–1920* (Ithaca, NY: Cornell University Press, 1978).

33. Donna R. Gabaccia, *Italy's Many Diasporas* (Seattle: University of Washington Press, 2000); Dino Cinel, "The Seasonal Emigrations of Italians in the Nineteenth Century: From Internal to International Destinations," *Journal of Ethnic Studies*, 10.1 (1982), 43–67; J. S. McDonald, "Italy's Rural Social Structure and Emigration," *Occidente*, 12.5 (1956), 437–456; Grazia Dore, "Some Social and Historical Aspects of Italian Emigration to America," *Journal of Social History* (1968), 95–122. On late-twentieth-century Italian regionalism, see Ann Cornelisen, *Strangers and Pilgrims: The Last Italian Migration* (New York: McGraw-Hill, 1980); Alessandro Portelli, "The Problem of the Color-Blind: Notes on the Discourse of Race in Italy," in *Race and Nation: Ethnic Systems in the Modern World*, Paul Spickard, Ed. (New York: Routledge, 2005), 355–363.

34. Gabaccia, *Italy's Many Diasporas*, 60–70; Anna Maria Ratti, "Italian Migration Movements, 1876 to 1926," in *International Migrations*, Willcox, Ed., 440–470.

35. Cinel, *From Italy to San Francisco*, 196–227; Paola Sesia, "White Ethnicity in America: The Italian Experience," in *Berkeley History Review*, 2 (1982), 18–32; Mormino, *Immigrants on the Hill*, 28–55.

36. Micaela di Leonardo, *The Varieties of Ethnic Experience: Kinship, Class, and Gender Among California Italian-Americans* (Ithaca, NY: Cornell University Press, 1984), 58.

37. Rudolph J. Vecoli, "Italian American Workers, 1880–1920: Padrone Slaves or Primitive Rebels?" in *Perspectives in Italian Immigration and Ethnicity*, Tomasi, Ed., 25–49; Gunther Peck, *Reinventing Free Labor: Padrones and Immigrant Workers in the North American West, 1880–1930* (Cambridge: Cambridge University Press, 2000); Gabaccia, *Italy's Many Diasporas*, 58–80.

38. LaGumina, *Immigrants Speak*, 5–11.

39. Betty Boyd Caroli, *Italian Repatriation from the United States, 1900–1914* (New York: Center for Migration Studies, 1973); Dino Cinel, *The National Integration of Italian Return Migration, 1870–1929* (Cambridge: Cambridge University Press, 1991); Victor Von Borosini, "Home-Going Italians," in *The Italians*, Cordasco and Bucchioni, Eds., 113–119.

40. Morrison and Zabusky, *American Mosaic*, 65–67.

41. Yans-McLaughlin, *Family and Community*, 18. Yans-McLaughlin is arguing specifically against Oscar Handlin's tale of peasant migrant dislocation and social dysfunction when thrown into urban, industrial America, which he presented in *The Uprooted*, 2nd ed. (Boston: Little, Brown, 1973). Handlin's inter-

pretation followed two generations of sociologists, led by University of Chicago scholars such as William I. Thomas, who wrote with Florian Znaniecki, *The Polish Peasant in Europe and America*, abr. ed. (Urbana: University of Illinois Press, 1984; orig. 5 vols., 1918–1920). For a first take on a post-disorganization analysis, see Rudolph Vecoli, "Contadini in Chicago: A Critique of The Uprooted," *Journal of American History*, 51 (1964), 404–417. Gabaccia, *From Sicily to Elizabeth Street*, xv–xvi; Nelli, *From Immigrants to Ethnics*, 131.

42. Gabaccia, *From Sicily to Elizabeth Street*, xv.

43. Kessner, *The Golden Door*, 155; Humbert S. Nelli, "Italians," in *Harvard Encyclopedia of American Ethnic Groups*, Thernstrom, Ed., 548–549. On community building, see Dominic Candeloro, *Chicago's Italians* (Charleston: Arcadia, 2003); Cinel, *From Italy to San Francisco*; Cordasco and Bucchioni, *The Italians*, 121–279; Gabaccia, *From Sicily to Elizabeth Street*; Guglielmo, *White on Arrival*; Mormino, *Immigrants on the Hill*; Nelli, *Italians in Chicago*; Christopher M. Sterba, " 'More Than Ever, We Feel Proud to Be Italians': World War I and the New Haven Colonia, 1917–1918," *Journal of American Ethnic History*, 20.2 (Winter 2001), 70–106; Rudolph J. Vecoli, "The Formation of Chicago's 'Little Italies'," *Journal of American Ethnic History*, 2.2 (Spring 1983), 5–20; Yans-McLaughlin, *Family and Community*.

44. Yans-McLaughlin, *Family and Community*, 261–262.

45. Sources for this section include Henry Pratt Fairchild, *Greek Immigration to the United States* (New Haven, CT: Yale University Press, 1911); Ionna Laliotou, *Transatlantic Subjects: Acts of Migration and Cultures of Transnationalism Between Greece and America* (Chicago: University of Chicago Press, 2004); Charles C. Moskos, *Greek Americans: Struggle and Success* (Englewood Cliffs, NJ: Prentice-Hall, 1980); Peck, *Reinventing Free Labor*; Theodore Saloutos, "Causes and Patterns of Greek Emigration to the United States," *Perspectives in American History*, 7 (1973), 379–437; Saloutos, *The Greeks in the United States* (Cambridge, MA: Harvard University Press, 1964); Saloutos, *They Remember America*; Alice Scourby, *The Greek Americans* (Boston: Twayne, 1984).

46. The Turkish genocide carried out against Armenians is one of the harrowing tales of modern history. For Armenian immigration, see Michael J. Arlen, *Passage to Ararat* (New York: Ballantine, 1975); Arra S. Avakian, *The Armenians in America* (Minneapolis: Lerner, 1977); Donal E. Miller and Lorna Touryan, *Survivors: An Oral History of the Armenian Genocide* (Berkeley: University of California Press, 1993). For Assyrians, see Mary C. Sengstock, *Chaldean-Americans: Changing Concepts of Ethnic Identity* (New York: Center for Migration Studies, 1982).

47. Saloutos, "Greek Emigration," 544.

48. Saloutos, *They Remember America*, 90–93. For other Balkan immigrant groups, see: June Granatir Alexander, "Staying Together: Chain Migration and Patterns of Slovak Settlement in Pittsburgh Prior to World War I," *Journal of American Ethnic History*, 1 (fall 1981), 56–83; Emily Greene Balch, *Our Slavic Fellow Citizens* (New York: Charities Publication Committee, 1910); Barton, *Peasants and Strangers*; Branko Mita Colakovic, *Yugoslav Migrations to America* (San Francisco: R and E Research Associates, 1973); Gerald Gilbert Govorchin, *Americans from Yugoslavia* (Gainesville: University of Florida Press, 1961); Victor R. Greene, *The Slavic Community on Strike: Immigrant Labor in Pennsylvania Anthracite* (Notre Dame, IN: University of Notre Dame Press, 1968); Marie Prisland, *From Slovenia—to America* (Chicago: Slovenian

Women's Union of America, 1968); George J. Prpic, *The Croation Immigrants in America* (New York: Philosophical Library, 1971); Prpic, *South Slavic Immigration in America* (Boston: Twayne, 1978). For a very different set of migrant experiences, by people from the opposite end of southern Europe, see Marilyn Halter, *Between Race and Ethnicity: Cape Verdean American Immigrants, 1860–1965* (Urbana: University of Illinois Press, 1993); Jerry R. Williams, *And Yet They Come: Portuguese Immigration from the Azores to the United States* (New York: Center for Migration Studies, 1982).

49. For Eastern European groups not treated in detail here, see Balch, *Our Slavic Fellow Citizens*; Barton, *Peasants and Strangers*; Julianna Puskás, "Hungarian Images of America: The Sirens' Song of Tinkling Dollars," in *Distant Magnets*, Hoerder and Rössler, Eds., 180–198; Puskás, *Ties That Bind, Ties That Divide: 100 Years of Hungarian Experience in the United States*, trans. Zora Ludwig (New York: Holmes and Meier, 2000).

50. Sources for this section include Balch, *Our Slavic Fellow Citizens*; John J. Bukowczyk, *And My Children Did Not Know Me: A History of the Polish-Americans* (Bloomington: Indiana University Press, 1987); Bukowczyk, Ed., *Polish Americans and Their History* (Pittsburgh: University of Pittsburgh Press, 1996); Bukowczyk, *The Poles in America*, special issue of *Journal of American Ethnic History*, 16.1 (Fall 1996); Caroline Golab, *Immigrant Destinations* (Philadelphia: Temple University Press, 1977); Victor Greene, *For God and Country: The Rise of Polish and Lithuanian Ethnic Consciousness in America, 1860–1910* (Madison: State Historical Society of Wisconsin, 1975); Jacobson, *Special Sorrows*; Helena Znaniecki Lopata, *Polish Americans* (Englewood Cliffs, NJ: Prentice-Hall, 1976); Karen Majewski, *Traitors and True Poles: Narrating a Polish-American Identity, 1880–1939* (Athens: Ohio University Press, 2003); Dominic A. Pacyga, *Polish Immigrants and Industrial Chicago: Workers on the South Side, 1880–1922* (Chicago: University of Chicago Press, 2003); Thomas and Znaniecki, *Polish Peasants in Europe and America*.

51. Felix Klezl, "Austria," in *International Migrations*, 390–410.

52. Balch, *Our Slavic Fellow Citizens*, 133; Pacyga, *Polish Immigrants and Industrial Chicago*, 17; Bukowczyk, *And My Children Did Not Know Me*, 15.

53. Balch, *Our Slavic Fellow Citizens*, 263, 461. A question nags: Why is it that more Polish Americans lived in New York than in Chicago, and more lived in Pennsylvania than in Illinois, yet almost all the writing about Polish Americans is about Chicago? See, for example, Bukowczyk, *And My Children Did Not Know Me*; Greene, *For God and Country*; Lopata, *Polish Americans*; Pacyga, *Polish Immigrants and Industrial Chicago*; Thomas and Znaniecki, *Polish Peasant*. What is it about Polish life in Chicago that generates such focused interest? Because I don't have the ghost of an answer to this question, I will leave it in a footnote, but someone surely ought to figure this out.

54. Pacyga, *Polish Immigrants and Industrial Chicago*, 15–42.

55. Victor Greene, "Poles," in *Harvard Encyclopedia of American Ethnic Groups*, Thernstrom, Ed., 787–803.

56. Kraków Diocese Archives, cited in Wyman, *Round-Trip to America*, 17–18.

57. Anna Reczynska, "America and the Ruhr Basin in the Expectations of Polish Migrants," in *Distant Magnets*, Hoerder and Rössler, Eds., 84–104. See also Ewa Morawska, "From Myth to Reality: America in the Eyes of East European Peasant Migrant Laborers," in *Distant Magnets*, Hoerder and Rössler, Eds., 241–263; Jacobson, *Special Sorrows*.

58. Reczynska, "Expectations of Polish Migrants."

59. Something of history can be read in place names. A tour of the map of southern Minnesota and northern Wisconsin recalls yesteryear's boosterism (Excelsior, Welcome), patriotism (Adams, Monroe, Monticello), religious commitment (St. Peter, East Bethel), ersatz Indianness (Minnetonka, Winnebago), and the landscape and fauna (Little Falls, Coon Rapids). But it also includes rural communities that speak of specific immigrant roots: New Prague, Heidelberg, Kilkenny, Hamburg, New Ulm, Poland, Little Canada, Caledonia, Scandia, Pilsen, Lindstrom, Pulaski. Many Midwestern states boast a similar array.

60. Bukowczyk, *And My Children Did Not Know Me*, 20.

61. Polish workers seem not to have depended on labor contractors so much as did Italians, Greeks, Chinese, Japanese, and others; Bukowczyk, *And My Children Did Not Know Me*, 20–23.

62. Pacyga, *Polish Immigrants and Industrial Chicago*, 111–57. On community and institutional life, see also Lopata, *Polish Americans*, 33–67; Thomas and Znaniecki, *Polish Peasant*, 239–255.

63. William J. Galush, "Polish Americans and Religion," in *Polish Americans and Their History*, Bukowczyk, Ed., 80–92; Greene, *For God and Country*; Dolan, *American Catholic Experience*, 183–814; Pacyga, *Polish Immigrants and Industrial Chicago*, 127–143.

64. Sources for this section include Lucy S. Dawidowicz, Ed., *The Golden Tradition: Jewish Life and Thought in Eastern Europe* (Boston: Beacon, 1967); Milton Doroshkin, *Yiddish in America: Social and Cultural Foundations* (Rutherford, NJ: Fairleigh Dickinson University Press, 1969); Stanley Feldstein, *The Land That I Show You: Three Centuries of Jewish Life in America* (Garden City, NY: Doubleday, 1978); Nathan Glazer, *American Judaism*, 2nd ed. (Chicago: University of Chicago Press, 1972); Louis Greenberg, *The Jews in Russia* (New York: Schocken, 1976; orig. 1944, 1956); Liebmann Hersch, "International Migration of the Jews," in *International Migrations*, Willcox, Ed., 471–520; Irving Howe, *World of Our Fathers* (New York: Harcourt, Brace, Jovanovich, 1976); Jacobson, *Special Sorrows*; Ava F. Kahn, Ed., *Jewish Life in the American West* (Seattle: University of Washington Press, 2002); Kessner, *The Golden Door*; Jacob Rader Marcus, Ed., *The Jew in the American World* (Detroit: Wayne State University Press, 1996); Simon Kuznets, "Immigration of Russian Jews to the United States," *Perspectives in American History*, 9 (1975), 33–124; Isaac Metzker, Ed., *A Bintel Brief* (New York: Ballantine, 1971); Moses Rischin, Ed., *Grandma Never Lived in America: The New Journalism of Abraham Cahan* (Bloomington: Indiana University Press, 1985); Rischin, *The Promised City: New York's Jews*, 1870–1914 (Cambridge, MA: Harvard University Press, 1962); Jonathan D. Sarna, Ed., *The American Jewish Experience* (New York: Holmes and Meier, 1986); Chaim L. Waxman, *America's Jews in Transition* (Philadelphia: Temple University Press, 1983); Michael R. Weisser, *A Brotherhood of Memory: Jewish Landsmanshaftn in the New World* (New York: Basic, 1985). Vivid personal accounts can be found in fiction, autobiography, and film, including Mary Antin, *From Plotzk to Boston* (Boston: Clarke, 1899); Antin, *The Promised Land* (Boston: Houghton Mifflin, 1912); Abraham Cahan, *The Rise of David Levinsky* (New York: Harper and Row, 1960; orig. 1917); Cahan, *Yekl and The Imported Bridegroom* (New York: Dover, 1970; orig. 1896, 1898); M. E. Ravage, *An American in the Making: The*

Life Story of an Immigrant (New York: Dover, 1971; orig. 1917); Joan Micklin Silver, dir., *Hester Street* (New York: First Run Features, 1974); Anzia Yezierska, *Bread Givers* (New York: Persea, 1975; orig. 1925). Some sentences are modified from my book *Mixed Blood: Intermarriage and Ethnic Identity in Twentieth-Century America* (Madison: University of Wisconsin Press, 1989), 172–173.

65. Leonard Dinnerstein and Richard Reimers, *Ethnic Americans*, 2nd ed. (New York: Columbia University Press, 1982), 163–165.

66. Hersch, "International Migration of the Jews," 479; see also Kuznets, "Immigration of Russian Jews," 39.

67. Waxman, *American Jews in Transition*, 33.

68. Howe, *World of Our Fathers*, 11. East European Judaism's God was a bit more transcendent than Howe is comfortable describing. There was a mystical side, too, that came out particularly in Hasidism. See Dawidowicz, *Golden Tradition*, 93–110; Jerome R. Mintz, *Legends of the Hasidim* (Chicago: University of Chicago Press, 1968).

69. Mark Zborowski and Elizabeth Herzog, *Life Is with People: The Culture of the Shtetl* (New York: Schocken, 1952); Davidowicz, *Golden Tradition*, 5–90. The stories of Sholem Aleichem tell of shtetl life: *Tevye's Daughters* (New York: Crown, 1949). For a somewhat broader view of East European Jewish life in this period, see Isaac Bashevis Singer, *Crown of Feathers* (New York: Farrar, Straus and Giroux, 1973); Singer, *Gimpel the Fool* (New York: Noonday, 1957); Singer, *The Magician of Lublin* (London: Secker and Warburg, 1961); Singer, *The Slave* (New York: Farrar, Straus and Giroux, 1962).

70. Antin, *Promised Land*, 8.

71. Arthur A. Goren, "Jews," in *Harvard Encyclopedia of American Ethnic Groups*, Thernstrom, Ed., 571–598.

72. Quoted in Howe, *World of Our Fathers*, 27.

73. Kuznets, "Immigration of Russian Jews," 113.

74. Kuznets, "Immigration of Russian Jews," 95.

75. Howe, *World of Our Fathers*, 87.

76. Jewish immigrant women, by contrast, had a lower literacy rate (66 percent) than did Gentile immigrant women (74 percent); Kuznets, "Immigration of Russian Jews," 115.

77. Howe, *World of Our Fathers*, 148–168.

78. Howe, *World of Our Fathers*, 305.

79. Howe, *World of Our Fathers*, 305–306.

80. Lucy S. Dawidowicz, "The Jewishness of the Jewish Labor Movement in the United States," in *American Jewish Experience*, Sarna, Ed., *American Jewish Experience*, 158–166; Howe, *World of Our Fathers*, 287–359.

81. Michael R. Weisser, *A Brotherhood of Memory: Jewish Landsmanshaftn in the New World* (New York: Basic, 1985); Doroshkin, *Yiddish in America*, 136–169; Marcus, *Jew in the American World*, 340–380.

82. Howe, *World of Our Fathers*, 417–551; Doroshkin, *Yiddish in America*, 82–135; Marcus, *Jew in the American World*, 381–392.

83. Moses Rischin, "Germans versus Russians," in Sarna, *American Jewish Experience*, 120–132; Rischin, *Promised City*, 95–111; Avraham Barkai, "German-Jewish Migration in the Nineteenth Century, 1830–1910," in *Migration Across Time and Nations*, Ira Z. Glazier and Luigi De Rosa, Eds., (New York: Holmes and Meier, 1986), 202–219.

84. I will have little to say about Danes, Finns, and Icelanders here. On Danish immigrants, see Thomas Peter Christensen, *A History of the Danes in Iowa* (New York: Arno, 1979; orig. 1952); Kristian Hvidt, *Flight to America: The Social Background of 300,000 Danish Emigrants* (New York: Academic, 1975); Kristian Hivdt, *Danes Go West: A Book about the Emigration to America* (Skorping: Rebuild National Park Society, 1976); George R. Nielsen, *The Danish Americans* (Boston: Twayne, 1981). On Finns, see A. William Hoglund, *Finnish Immigrants in America*, 1880–1920 (Madison: University of Wisconsin Press, 1960); Ralph J. Jalkanen, Ed., *The Finns in North America* (Hancock, MI: Michigan State University Press, 1969); Michael G. Karni and Doublas J. Ollila, Eds., *For the Common Good: Finnish Immigrants and the Radical Response to Industrial America* (Superior, WI: Tyomies Society, 1977); Reino Kero, *Migration from Finland to North America in the Years Between the United States Civil War and the First World War* (Turku, Finland: Turun Yliopisto, 1974); Carl Ross, *The Finn Factor in American Labor, Culture, and Society* (New York Mills, MI: Parta, 1977). On Icelanders, see Thorstina Jackson Walters, *Modern Sagas: The Story of the Icelanders in North America* (Fargo, ND: North Dakota Institute for Regional Studies, 1953).

85. Sources for this section include H. Arnold Barton, *A Folk Divided: Homeland Swedes and Swedish Americans*, 1840–1940 (Carbondale: Southern Illinois University Press, 1994); John S. Lindbert, *The Background of Swedish Emigration to the United States* (Minneapolis: University of Minnesota Press, 1930); Robert C. Ostergren, *A Community Transplanted: The Trans-Atlantic Experience of a Swedish Immigrant Settlement in the Upper Middle West, 1835–1915* (Madison: University of Wisconsin Press, 1988); Harald Runblom and Hans Norman, Eds., *From Sweden to America* (Minneapolis: University of Minnesota Press, 1976).

86. Peg Meier, Ed., *Bring Warm Clothes: Letters and Photos from Minnesota's Past* (Minneapolis: Minneapolis Tribune, 1981), 194; italics added.

87. Morrison and Zabusky, *American Mosaic*, 3–8.

88. G. William Carlson, private communication with the author, 1982. Needless to say, this mix of progressive politics, unionism, and evangelical faith was lost somewhere in the last third of the twentieth century. For the longstanding bond of progressivism and evangelicalism, now abandoned, see Timothy L. Smith, *Evangelism and Social Reform: American Protestantism on the Eve of the Civil War* (Baltimore: Johns Hopkins University Press, 1980); Ernest R. Sandeen, Ed., *The Bible and Social Reform* (Chico, CA: Scholars, 1982).

89. Sources for this section include Jon Gjerde, *From Peasants to Farmers: The Migration from Balestrand, Norway, to the Upper Middle West* (Cambridge: Cambridge University Press, 1985); L. DeAne Lagerquist, *In America the Men Milk the Cows: Factors of Gender, Ethnicity, and Religion in the Americanization of Norwegian-American Women* (New York: Carlson, 1991); Odd S. Lovoll, *The Promise of America: A History of the Norwegian-American People*, rev. ed. (Minneapolis: University of Minnesota Press, 1999); Ingrid Semmingsen, *Norway to America*, trans. Einar Haugen (Minneapolis: University of Minnesota Press, 1978).

90. Ole Beim was my great-grandfather. This account is taken from his letters and from family stories.

91. Tomás Almaguer, *Racial Fault Lines: The Historical Origins of White Supremacy in California* (Berkeley: University of California Press, 1994); Gordon Morris Bakken and Brenda Farringson, Eds., *Racial Encounters in*

the *Multi-Cultural West* (New York: Garland, 2000); Arnoldo De León, *Racial Frontiers: Africans, Chinese, and Mexicans in Western America, 1848–1890* (Albuquerque: University of New Mexico Press, 2002); Neil Foley, *The White Scourge: Mexicans, Blacks, and Poor Whites in Texas Cotton Culture* (Berkeley: University of California Press, 1997); Robert F. Heizer and Alan J. Almquist, *The Other Californians: Prejudice and Discrimination under Spain, Mexico, and the United States to 1920* (Berkeley: University of California Press, 1971); Carey McWilliams, *Factories in the Fields* (Santa Barbara: Peregrinc Smith, 1971; orig. 1935); Ronald Takaki, *Pau Hana: Plantation Life and Labor in Hawaii* (Honolulu: University of Hawai'i Press, 1983).

92. Sources for this section include Susie Lan Cassel, Ed., *The Chinese in America* (Walnut Creek, CA: AltaMira, 2002); Sucheng Chan, Ed., *Entry Denied: Exclusion and the Chinese Community in America, 1882–1943* (Philadelphia: Temple University Press, 1991); Yong Chen, *Chinese San Francisco, 1850–1943* (Stanford, CA: Stanford University Press, 2000); Lucy M. Cohen, *Chinese in the Post-Civil War South* (Baton Rouge, LA: LSU Press, 1984); Clarence E. Glick, *Sojourners and Settlers: Chinese Migrants in Hawaii* (Honolulu: University Press of Hawaii, 1980); Sarah M. Griffith, "Border Crossings: Race, Class, and Smuggling in Pacific Coast Chinese Immigrant Society," *Western Historical Quarterly*, 35 (2004), 473–492; Marlon K. Hom, *Songs of Gold Mountain: Cantonese Rhymes from San Francisco Chinatown* (Berkeley: University of California Press, 1987); Madeline Y. Hsu, *Dreaming of Gold, Dreaming of Home: Transnationalism and Migration Between the United States and South China, 1882–1943* (Stanford, CA: Stanford University Press, 2000); S. W. Kung, *Chinese in American Life* (Seattle: University of Washington Press, 1962); Him Mark Lai, *Becoming Chinese American: A History of Communities and Institutions* (2004); Erika Lee, *At America's Gates: Chinese Immigration During the Exclusion Era, 1882–1943* (Chapel Hill: University of North Carolina Press, 2005); Rose Hum Lee, *The Chinese in the United States of America* (Hong Kong: Hong Kong University Press, 1960); Huping Ling, *Chinese St. Louis* (Philadelphia: Temple University Press, 2004); Ling, *Surviving on the Gold Mountain: A History of Chinese American Women and their Lives* (Albany: SUNY Press, 1998); James W. Loewen, *The Mississippi Chinese* (Cambridge, MA: Harvard University Press, 1971); Stanford M. Lyman, *Chinese Americans* (New York: Random House, 1974); Mildred Crowl Martin, *Chinatown's Angry Angel: The Story of Donaldina Cameron* (Palo Alto, CA: Pacific Books, 1977); Charles J. McClain, *In Search of Equality: The Chinese Struggle Against Discrimination in Nineteenth-Century America* (Berkeley: University of California Press); Ruthanne Lum McCunn, *Chinese American Portraits: Personal Histories, 1828–1988* (Seattle: University of Washington Press, 1988); McCunn, *Thousand Pieces of Gold* (San Francisco: Design Enterprises, 1981); Adam McKeown, *Chinese Migrant Networks and Cultural Change: Peru, Chicago, Hawaii, 1900–1936* (Chicago: University of Chicago Press, 2001); Victor G. Nee and Brett DeBary Nee, *Longtime Californ': A Documentary Study of an American Chinatown* (New York: Pantheon, 1973); Lucy E. Salyer, *Laws Harsh as Tigers: Chinese Immigrants and the Shaping of Modern Immigration Law* (Chapel Hill: University of North Carolina Press, 1995); Nayan Shah, *Contagious Divides: Epidemics and Race in San Francisco's Chinatown* (Berkeley: University of California Press, 2001); Paul C. P. Siu, *The Chinese Laundryman* (New York: NYU Press, 1987; orig. 1953); Betty Lee

Sung, *Mountain of Gold* (New York: Macmillan, 1967); Shih-shan Henry Tsai, *The Chinese Experience in America* (Bloomington: Indiana University Press, 1986); K. Scott Wong and Sucheng Chan, Eds., *Claiming America: Constructing Chinese American Identities During the Exclusion Era* (Philadelphia: Temple University Press, 1998); Judy Yung, *Unbound Feet: A Social History of Chinese Women in San Francisco* (Berkeley: California, 1995).

93. Richard Dillon's *The Hatchet Men* (New York: Coward McCann, 1962) is one example of Chinatown exoticist fantasy. The back cover read: "Chinatown, 1880, a world as vanished as Pompeii—where the hair is worn in a queue to the waist, where the full sleeve of a silken kimono hides a razor-sharp weapon. It was a world of 20 men for every woman, where tranquility was sought in the opium pipe and dish. It was a world controlled by the famed and feared tongs, whose dynasty of mayhem, assassination, extortion, gambling, prostitution and vendetta flourished just south of the Golden Gate—a hell so flagrant that nothing short of an earthquake could quell it." A far more accurate picture of Chinatown life can be found in the stories of Edith Maude Eaton, a Chinese-White woman who wrote under the pen name Sui Sin Far; see *Mrs. Spring Fragrance and Other Writings* (Urbana: University of Illinois Press, 1995; orig.1912).

94. Hsu, *Dreaming of Gold, Dreaming of Home.*

95. Sterling Seagrave, *The Soong Dynasty* (New York: Harper and Row, 1985).

96. On paper children and the trans-Pacific Chinese family, see Tung Pok Chin and Winifred C. Chin, *Paper Son* (Philadelphia: Temple University Press, 2000); Xiaojian Zhao, *Remaking Chinese America: Immigration, Family, and Community* (New Brunswick, NJ: Rutgers University Press, 2002).

97. This section is drawn from the first four chapters of my book *Japanese Americans* (New York: Twayne, 1996), which includes a comprehensive bibliography on Japanese American history. Other sources consulted include Eichiro Azuma, *Between Two Empires: Race, History, and Transnationalism in Japanese America* (New York: Oxford, 2005); Ted W. Cox, *The Toledo Incident of 1925* (Corvallis, OR: Old World Publications, 2005); Roger Daniels, *The Politics of Prejudice: The Anti-Japanese Movement in California and the Struggle for Japanese Exclusion* (New York: Atheneum, 1968; orig. 1962); Masayo Umezawa Duus, *The Japanese Conspiracy: The Oahu Sugar Strike of 1920* (Berkeley: University of California Press, 1999); Louis Fiset and Gail M. Nomura, Eds., *Nikkei in the Pacific Northwest* (Seattle: University of Washington Press, 2005); Yuji Ichioka, *The Issei: The World of the First Generation Japanese Immigrants, 1885–1924* (New York: Free Press, 1988); Kazuo Ito, *Issei: A History of Japanese Immigrants in North America* (Seattle: Japanese Community Service, 1973); Tooru J. Kanazawa, *Sushi and Sourdough* (Seattle: University of Washington Press, 1989); Akemi Kikumura, *Through Harsh Winters: The Life of a Japanese Immigrant Woman* (Novato, CA: Chandler and Sharp, 1981); Yukiko Kimura, *Issei: Japanese Immigrants in Hawai'i* (Honolulu: University of Hawai'i Press, 1988); Harry H. L. Kitano, *Japanese Americans*, 2nd ed. (Englewood Cliffs, NJ: Prentice-Hall, 1976); Henry Kiyama, *The Four Immigrants Manga* (Berkeley, CA: Stone Bridge Press, 1999); Daniel M. Masterson and Sayaka Funada-Classen, *The Japanese in Latin America* (Urbana: University of Illinois Press, 2004); Charles McClain, Ed., *Japanese Immigrants and American Law* (New York: Garland, 1994); Alan Takeo Moriyama, *Imingaisha: Japanese Emigration Companies and Hawaii* (Honolulu: University of Hawai'i Press, 1985); William Petersen, *Japanese Americans*

(New York: Random House, 1971); Frederick Samuels, *The Japanese and the Haoles of Honolulu (New Haven, CT: College and University Press, 1970); Mitziko Sawada, Tokyo Life, New York Dreams: Urban Japanese Visions of America, 1890–1924* (Berkeley: University of California Press, 1996); Linda Tamura, *The Hood River Issei* (Urbana: University of Illinois Press, 1993); Robert A. Wilson and Bill Hosokawa, *East to America: A History of the Japanese in the United States* (New York: Morrow, 1980).

98. Quoted in Chizuko Lampman, *The East*, vol. 2, no. 4 (1966), 71–75; Cited in Kitano, *Japanese Americans*, 13.

99. Quoted in Ito, *Issei*, 32.

100. It is the subject of a novel by revered Japanese American writer Yoshiko Uchida, *Picture Bride* (New York: Simon and Schuster, 1987) and a movie.

101. Sources for this section include Rodolfo Acuña, *Occupied America: A History of Chicanos*, 3rd ed. (New York: Harper and Row, 1988), 141–197; Albert Camarillo, *Chicanos in a Changing Society* (Cambridge, MA: Harvard University Press, 1979); Lawrence A. Cardoso, *Mexican Emigration to the United States, 1897–1931* (Tucson: University of Arizona Press, 1980); Sarah Deutsch, *No Separate Refuge: Culture, Class, and Gender on an Anglo-Hispanic Frontier in the American Southwest, 1880–1940* (New York: Oxford, 1987); William Deverell, *Whitewashed Adobe: The Rise of Los Angeles and the Remaking of its Mexican Past* (Berkeley: University of California Press, 2004); Foley, *White Scourge*; Manuel Gamio, *The Life Story of the Mexican Immigrant* (New York: Dover, 1971; orig. 1931); Gamio, *Mexican Immigration to the United States* (Chicago: University of Chicago Press, 1930); Juan R. García, *Mexicans in the Midwest, 1900–1932* (Tucson: University of Arizona Press, 1996); Gilbert G. González, *Culture of Empire: American Writers, Mexico, and Mexican Immigrants, 1880–1930* (Austin: University of Texas Press, 2004); Juan Gonzalez, *Harvest of Empire: A History of Latinos in America* (New York: Penguin, 2000); David G. Gutiérrez, *Walls and Mirrors: Mexican Americans, Mexican Immigrants, and the Politics of Ethnicity* (Berkeley: University of California Press, 1995); Benjamin Heber Johnson, *Revolution in Texas: How a Forgotten Rebellion and Its Bloody Suppression Turned Mexicans into Americans* (New Haven, CT: Yale University Press, 2003); John Martinez, *Mexican Emigration to the U.S., 1910–1930* (San Francisco: R and E Research Associates, 1971); Carey McWilliams, *North From Mexico* (Philadelphia: Lippincott, 1949); Natalia Molina, *Fit to Be Citizens? Public Health and Race in Los Angeles, 1879–1939* (Berkeley: University of California Press, 2006); Douglas Monroy, *Rebirth: Mexican Los Angeles from the Great Migration to the Great Depression* (Berkeley: University of California Press, 1999); David Montejano, *Anglos and Mexicans in the Making of Texas, 1836–1986* (Austin: University of Texas Press, 1987); Peck, *Reinventing Free Labor*; George J. Sánchez, *Becoming Mexican American: Ethnicity, Culture and Identity in Chicano Los Angeles, 1900–1945* (New York: Oxford, 1993); Paul S. Taylor, "Critique of the Official Statistics of Mexican Migration To and From the United States," in *International Migrations*, Willcox, Ed., 581–590; David Torres-Rouff, "Making Los Angeles: Race, Space, and Municipal Power, 1822–1890," (PhD dissertation, University of California, Santa Barbara, 2006); Zaragosa Vargas, Ed., *Major Problems in Mexican American History* (Boston: Houghton Mifflin, 1999), 176–271; Vargas, *Proletarians of the North: A History of Mexican Industrial Workers in Detroit and the Midwest, 1917–1933* (Berkeley: University of California Press, 1993).

102. The Zorro story is the story of popular bandit Joaquin Murieta (see Chapter 4) overlaid by the Californio myth of Castillian origins. On the legend of Zorro, see Isabel Allende, *Zorro* (New York: HarperCollins, 2005); Sandra Curtis, *Zorro Unmasked* (New York: Hyperion, 1998); Johnston McCulley, *The Mark of Zorro* (New York: Forge Books, 1998; orig. 1952); Alex Toth, *Zorro* (Berkeley, CA: Image Comics, 2001); John Whitman, *The Mask of Zorro* (San Francisco: Chronicle Books, 1998); William Yenne, *The Legend of Zorro* (Lincoln: University of Nebraska Press, 1991). On the changes in racial status over the course of the nineteenth century and into the twentieth century, see Torres-Rouff, "Making Los Angeles"; Almaguer, *Racial Fault Lines*; Camarillo, *Chicanos in a Changing Society*; Deverell, *Whitewashed Adobe*; Martha Menchaca, *Recovering History, Constructing Race: The Indian, Black, and White Roots of Mexican Americans* (Austin: University of Texas Press, 2001).

103. Acuña, *Occupied America*, 141. Hawai'i did not achieve a White plurality—and statehood—for another half century.

104. Gutiérrez, *Walls and Mirrors*, 40; Cardoso, *Mexican Emigration*, 38.

105. Gamio, *Life Story*, 45–47.

106. Gamio, *Life Story*, 55–57.

107. Sources for this section include Almaguer, *Racial Fault Lines*; Richard A. Buitron, Jr., *The Quest for Tejano Identity in San Antonio, Texas, 1913–2000* (New York: Routledge, 2004); Neil Foley, "Straddling the Color Line: The Legal Construction of Hispanic Identity in Texas," in *Not Just Black and White: Historical and Contemporary Perspectives on Immigration, Race, and Ethnicity in the United States*, Ed. Nancy Foner and George M. Fredrickson (New York: Russell Sage, 2004), 341–357; Foley, *White Scourge*; Ariel J. Gross, "Texas Mexicans and the Politics of Whiteness," *Law and History Review*, 21.1 (2003); Rudy Guevarra, "Burritos and Bagoong: Mexipinos and Multiethnic Identity in San Diego, California," in *Crossing Lines: Race and Mixed Race Across the Geohistorical Divide*, Marc Coronado, Rudy Guevarra, Jeffrey Moniz, and Laura Szanto, Eds. (Santa Barbara: UC Santa Barbara Multiethnic Student Outreach, 2003), 73–96; Ira F. Haney López, "Hernandez v. Brown," *New York Times* (May 22, 2004); Haney López, *White by Law: The Legal Construction of Race* (New York: NYU Press, 1996); Martha Menchaca, "Chicano Indianism: A Historical Account of Racial Repression in the United States," *American Ethnologist*, 20.3 (1993), 583–603; Menchaca, *Recovering History, Constructing Race*; Gail Pollard-Terry, "Documenting Mexico's Strong African Legacy," *Los Angeles Times* (February 21, 2005); Montejano, *Anglos and Mexicans*; Charles Montgomery, "Becoming 'Spanish-American': Race and Rhetoric in New Mexico Politics, 1880–1928," *Journal of American Ethnic History,* 20.4 (Summer 2001), 59–84; George Sánchez, *Becoming Mexican American*; Monica Sánchez, "Are Mexican Americans Whites?" (student paper, UC Santa Barbara, June 2005); Clare Sheridan, " 'Another White Race': Mexican Americans and Whiteness in Jury Selection," *Law and History Review*, 21.1 (2003); Sheridan "Contested Citizenship: National Identity and the Mexican Immigration Debates of the 1920s," *Journal of American Ethnic History*, 21.3 (Spring 2002), 3–35; Steven H. Wilson, "Brown over Other White: Mexican Americans' Legal Arguments and Litigation Strategy in School Desegregation Lawsuits," *Law and History Review*, 21.1 (2003).

108. Deutsch, *No Separate Refuge*, 5.

109. José Vasconcellos, *The Cosmic Race* (Baltimore: Johns Hopkins University Press, 1997); Virginia Q. Tilley, "Mestizaje and the 'Ethnicization' of Race in Latin America," in *Race and Nation*, Paul Spickard, Ed. (New York: Routledge, 2005), 53–66. G. Reginald Daniel reminds us that all human populations are mixed in *More Than Black? Multiracial Identity and the New Racial Order* (Philadelphia: Temple University Press, 2002).

110. Montgomery, "Becoming 'Spanish-American,'" 63. One can discern a similar racial move by already resident Mexican Americans against more recent immigrants in the support by elements of Chicano communities for California's Proposition 187 in the 1990s or calls for border controls in the 2000s.

111. *Lone Star*, John Sayles, director (Castle Rock Entertainment, 1996).

112. Foley, "Straddling the Color Line," 341.

113. Linda Gordon, *The Great Arizona Orphan Abduction* (Cambridge, MA: Harvard University Press, 1999).

114. Sources for this section include Teodoro A. Agoncillo, *History of the Filipino People*, 8th ed. (Quezon City: Garotech, 1990); Ruben Alcantara, *Sakada: Filipino Adaptation in Hawaii* (Washington, DC: University Press of America, 1981); Manuel Buaken, *I Have Lived With the American People* (Caldwell, ID: Caxton, 1948); Carlos Bulosan, *America Is In the Heart* (Seattle: University of Washington Press, 1973; orig. 1946); California Department of Industrial Relations, *Facts About Filipino Immigration Into California* (San Francisco: R and E Research Associates, 1972; orig. 1930); Sharon Delmendo, *The Star-Entangled Banner: One Hundred Years of America in the Philippines* (New Brunswick, NJ: Rutgers University Press, 2004); Virgilio Menor Felipe, *Hawai'i: A Filipino Dream* (Honolulu: Mutual Publishing, 2002); Dorothy B. Fujita-Rony, *American Workers, Colonial Power: Philippine Seattle and the Transpacific West, 1919–1941* (Berkeley: University of California Press, 2003); Stanley Karnow, *In Our Image: America's Empire in the Philippines* (New York: Ballantine, 1989); Bruno Lasker, *Filipino Immigration* (Chicago: University of Chicago Press, 1931); Charles McClain, Ed., *Asian Indians, Filipinos, Other Asian Communities and the Law* (New York: Garland, 1994); Barbara M. Posadas, *The Filipino Americans* (Westport, CT: Greenwood, 1999); Miriam Sharma, "Labor Migration and Class Formation Among the Filipinos in Hawaii, 1906–1946," in *Labor Immigration Under Capitalism*, Lucie Cheng and Edna Bonacich, Ed. (Berkeley: University of California Press, 1984), 579–611; Sharma, "The Philippines: A Case of Migration to Hawaii, 1906 to 1946," in *Labor Immigration Under Capitalism*, Ed. Cheng and Bonacich, 337–358; Angel Velasco Shaw and Luis H. Francia, Eds., *Vestiges of War: The Philippine-American War and the Aftermath of an Imperial Dream, 1899–1999* (New York: NYU Press, 2002).

115. Myrna Oliver, "Julio 'Jay' Ereneta, 103; One of the State's Last World War I Veterans," *Los Angeles Times* (April 29, 2005).

116. Lasker, *Filipino Immigration*, 5–6.

117. Scholars have focused either on the Mexican American community or on the Filipino American community and failed to see the ways they interlocked. This history is just being written for the first time by Rudy Guevarra, "Mexipino: A History of Multiethnic Identity and the Formation of the Mexican and Filipino Communities of San Diego, 1900–1965," PhD dissertation, in progress, University of California, Santa Barbara; see also Guevarra, "Burritos and Bagoong." There were also Indipino communities in the Pacific Northwest.

118. Lasker, *Filipino Immigration*, 15; Fujita-Rony, *American Workers, Colonial Power*, 1–3; Nellie Foster, "Legal Status of Filipino Intermarriages in California," in Charles McClain, Ed., *Asian Indians, Filipinos, Other Asian Communities and the Law*, 5–18.

119. Guevarra, "Mexipino: A History of Multiethnic Identity and the Formation of the Mexican and Filipino Communities of San Diego, 1900–1965," PhD diss. in progress, University of California, Santa Barbara; Paul Spickard, *Mixed Blood: Intermarriage and Ethnic Identity in Twentieth-Century America* (Madison: University of Wisconsin Press, 1989), 6, 107, 345, 351, 374–375.

120. Mary Paik Lee, *Quiet Odyssey: A Pioneer Korean Woman in America* (Seattle: University of Washington press, 1990); Wayne Patterson, *The Ilse: First-Generation Korean Immigrants in Hawai'i, 1903–1973* (Honolulu: University of Hawai'i Press, 2000).

121. Joan M. Jensen, *Passage from India: Asian Indian Immigrants in North America* (New Haven, CT: Yale University Press, 1988); Karen Isaksen Leonard, *Making Ethnic Choices: California's Punjabi Mexican Americans* (Philadelphia: Temple University Press, 1992).

122. Sources for this section include Colin G. Calloway, *First Peoples* (Boston: Bedford/St. Martin's 1999); Stephen Cornell, *The Return of the Native: American Indian Political Resurgence* (New York: Oxford, 1988); Brian W. Dippie, *The Vanishing American: White Attitudes and U.S. Indian Policy* (Middletown, CT: Wesleyan University Press, 1982); Alexandra Harmon, *Indians in the Making: Ethnic Relations and Indian Identities Around Puget Sound* (Berkeley: University of California Press, 1998); Frederick E. Hoxie, *A Final Promise: The Campaign to Assimilate the Indians, 1880–1920* (Lincoln: University of Nebraska Press, 1984); Hoxie, *Parading Through History: The Making of the Crow Nation, 1805–1935* (Cambridge: Cambridge University Press, 1995); Hoxie, Peter C. Mancall, and Hames H. Merrell, Eds., *American Nations: Encounters in Indian Country, 1850 to the Present* (New York: Routledge, 2001); Albert L. Hurtado and Peter Iverson, Eds., *Major Problems in American Indian History*, 2nd ed. (Boston: Houghton Mifflin, 2001); Francis Paul Prucha, *The Great Father: The United States Government and the American Indians*, abr. ed. (Lincoln: University of Nebraska Press, 1986); S. Lyman Tyler, *A History of Indian Policy* (Washington, DC: Bureau of Indian Affairs, 1973).

123. The Bureau of Indian Affairs was created in 1824 by Secretary of War John C. Calhoun. At various times it has also been called the Indian Bureau, the Indian Office, the Indian Service, the Board of Indian Commissioners; the Indian Desk, and the Office of Indian Affairs. Sharon O'Brien, "Bureau of Indian Affairs," in *Encyclopedia of North American Indians*, Frederick E. Hoxie, Ed. (Boston: Houghton Mifflin, 1996), 87.

124. Thomas Biolsi, "The Birth of the Reservation: Making the Modern Individual Among the Lakota," *American Ethnologist*, 22.1 (1995), 28–53; Hoxie, *Final Promise*, 185; Melissa L. Meyer, "Signatures and Thumbprints: Ethnicity Among the White Earth Anishinaabeg, 1889–1920," *Social Science History*, 14.3 (1990), 305–345; David Rich Lewis, "Reservation Leadership and the Progressive-Traditional Dichotomy: William Wash and the Northern Utes, 1865–1928," *Ethnohistory*, 38.2 (1991), 124–140.

125. Theodore Roosevelt, *The Winning of the West*, 6 vols. (New York: Putnam's, 1920; orig. 1910), Volume 1, Appendix A to Chapter 4; italics added.

126. David Wallace Adams, *Education for Extinction: American Indians and the Boarding School Experience, 1875–1928* (Lawrence: University Press of Kansas, 1995); Margaret L. Archuleta, Brenda J. Child, and K. Tsianina, Eds., *Away from Home: American Indian Boarding School Experiences, 1879–2000* (Phoenix: Heard Museum, 2000); Brenda Child, *Boarding School Seasons: American Indian Families, 1900–1940* (Lincoln: University of Nebraska Press, 1998); Sherman Coolidge, "The Function of the Society of American Indians," quoted in Calloway, *First Peoples*, 370–371; Carol Devens, "'If We Get the Girls, We Get the Race': Missionary Education of Native American Girls," *Journal of World History*, 3.2 (1992), 219–237; Lisa E. Emmerich, "'Right in the Midst of My own People': Native American Women and the Field Matron Program," *American Indian Quarterly*, 15 (1991), 201–216; Frederick E. Hoxie, "Exploring a Cultural Borderland: Native American Journeys of Discovery in the Early Twentieth Century," *Journal of American History*, 79 (1992), 969–995. It is worth noting that many of the leaders of African independence movements—people like Kenneth Kaunda of Zambia, Julius Nyerere of Tanzania, Kwame Nkrumah of Ghana, and Jomo Kenyatta of Kenya—were educated in missionary schools.

127. Harold E. Driver, "On the Population Nadir of Indians in the United States," *Current Anthropology* 9.4 (1968), 330; Russell Thornton and Joan Marsh-Thornton, "Estimating Prehistoric American Indian Population Size for United States Area: Implications of the Nineteenth Century Population Decline and Nadir," *American Journal of Physical Anthropology*, 55 (1981), 48.

128. And some were recorded as White. Anthropologist Max Stanton tells of three brothers in Dulac, Louisiana. All were Houma Indians, had a French last name, and shared the same father and mother. All received their racial designations at the hands of the medical people who assisted at their births. The oldest brother, born before 1950 at home with the aid of a midwife, was classified as a Negro, because the state of Louisiana did not recognize the Houma as Indians before 1950. The second brother, born in a local hospital after 1950, was assigned to the Indian category. The third brother, born eight miles away in a New Orleans hospital, was designated White on the basis of the French family name. See Paul Spickard, "The Illogic of American Racial Categories," in *Racially Mixed People in America*, Maria P. P. Root, Ed. (Newbury Park, CA: Sage, 1992), 12–23; Max Stanton, "A Remnant Indian Community: The Houma of Southern Louisiana," in *The Not So Solid South: Anthropological Studies in a Regional Subculture*, J. K. Moorland, Ed. (Athens: University of Georgia Press, 1971), 82–92.

129. Biolsi, "Birth of the Reservation"; James F. Brooks, Ed., *Confounding the Color Line: The Indian-Black Experience in North America* (Lincoln: University of Nebraska Press, 2002; Circe Sturm, *Blood Politics: Race, Culture, and Identity in the Cherokee Nation of Oklahoma* (Berkeley: University of California Press, 2002); Pauline Strong and Barrik Van Winkle, "'Indian Blood': Reflections on the Reckoning and Refiguring of Native North American identity," *Cultural Anthropology*, 11.4 (1996), 547–576; Terry P. Wilson, "Blood Quantum: Native American Mixed Bloods, " in *Racially Mixed People in America*, Maria P. P. Root, Ed. (Newbury Park, Calif.: Sage, 1992), 108–125. The U.S. government made the same move in Hawai'i, but there restricted membership in the Hawaiian people to only those who could demonstrate 50 percent Hawaiian ancestry. In time, many Native American tribes adopted the blood quantum idea as their own.

130. Dippie, *Vanishing American*.
131. Sources for this section include S. Elizabeth Bird, Ed., *Dressing in Feathers: The Construction of the Indian in American Popular Culture* (Boulder, CO: Westview, 1996); Ward Churchill, *Acts of Rebellion* (New York: Routledge, 2003); Philip J. Deloria, *Playing Indian* (New Haven, CT: Yale University Press, 1998); Deloria, *Indians in Unexpected Places* (Lawrence: University Press of Kansas, 2004); Dippie, *Vanishing American*; Eva Marie Garroutte, *Real Indians: Identity and the Survival of Native America* (Berkeley: University of California Press, 2003); Shari M. Huhndorf, *Going Native: Indians in the American Cultural Imagination* (Ithaca, NY: Cornell University Press, 2001); Bonita Lawrence, *"Real" Indians and Others: Mixed-Blood Urban Native Peoples and Indigenous Nationhood* (Lincoln: University of Nebraska press, 2004); Paige Sylvia Raibmon, *Authentic Indians: Episodes of Encounter from the Late-Nineteenth-Century Northwest* (Durham, NC: Duke University Press, 2005).
132. Patrick B. Miller, *The Playing Fields of American Culture* (New York: Oxford, forthcoming; advance copy courtesy of the author). See also Carol Spindel, *Dancing at Halftime: Sports and the Controversy over American Indian Mascots* (New York: NYU Press, 2000); C. Richard King and Charles Fruehling Springwood, *Team Spirits: The Native American Mascots Controversy* (Lincoln: University of Nebraska Press, 2001; Jason Edward Black, "The Mascotting of Native America: Construction, Commodity, and Assimilation," *American Indian Quarterly*, 26.4 (2002), 605–622.
133. Simon Pokagon, *The Red Man's Greeting* (Hartford, MI: E. H. Engle, 1893), quoted in *Talking Back to Civilization: Indian Voices from the Progressive Era*, Frederick E. Hoxie, Ed. (Boston: Bedford/St. Martin's, 2001), 31. See also Joy S. Kasson, Buffalo Bill's Wild West (New York: Hill and Wang, 2000), 161–219. On the Columbian Exposition, see Stanley Appelbaum, *The Chicago World's Fair of 1893: A Photographic Record* (New York: Dover, 1980); Reid Badger, *The Great American Fair: The World's Columbian Exposition and American Culture* (Chicago: Nelson Hall, 1979); Norm Bolotin, *The World's Columbian Exposition: The Chicago World's Fair of 1893* (Washington, DC: Preservation Press, 1992); Neil Harris, et al., *Grand Illusions: Chicago's World's Fair of 1893* (Chicago: Chicago Historical Society, 1993); Christopher Robert Reed, *"All the World is Here!": The Black Presence at White City* (Bloomington: Indiana University Press, 2000).
134. Carlos Montezuma, "The Duty of Every Indian Soldier Who Entered the War," Wassaja (February 1919), quoted in *Major Problems in American Indian History*, Hurtado and Iverson, Eds., 359–360.
135. Sources for this section include Carey McWilliams, *Factories in the Field: The Story of Migratory Farm Labor in California* (Santa Barbara: Peregrine Smith, 1971; orig. 1935); Martha Menchaca, *The Mexican Outsiders* (Austin: University of Texas Press, 1995), 59–77; David Torres-Rouff, "Race in the Making of Los Angeles" (PhD dissertation, UC Santa Barbara, 2006); and the sources listed under the immediate previous sections.
136. Ronald Takaki, *Pau Hana: Plantation Life and Labor in Hawaii* (Honolulu: University of Hawai'i Press, 1983.); Masayo Umezawa Duus, *The Japanese Conspiracy: The Oahu Sugar Strike of 1920* (Berkeley: University of California Press, 1999).

Chapter 6

1. That is the tendency in works such as: Nelson Lichtenstein, Susan Strasser, and Roy Rosenzweig, *Who Built America? Working People and the Nation's Economy, Politics, Culture, and Society* (New York: Worth, 2000); James Barrett, *Work and Community in the Jungle: Chicago's Packinghouse Workers, 1894–1922* (Urbana: University of Illinois Press, 1987); Anthony Bimba, *The Molly Maguires* (New York: International, 1932); James R. Green, *The World of the Worker: Labor in Twentieth-Century America* (New York: Hill and Wang, 1980); David Brody, *Workers in Industrial America* (New York: Oxford, 1980); Melvyn Dubofsky, *Industrialism and the American Worker, 1865–1920* (Arlington Heights, IL: AHM, 1975); Herbert G. Gutman, *Work, Culture and Society in Industrializing America* (New York: Random House, 1976); Victor R. Greene, *The Slavic Community on Strike: Immigrant Labor in Pennsylvania Anthracite* (Notre Dame, IN: University of Notre Dame Press, 1968). Not all labor historians make this mistake; see, for example, Zaragosa Vargas, *Labor Rights Are Civil Rights: Mexican American Workers in Twentieth-Century America* (Princeton, NJ: Princeton University Press, 2005); Cole, *Immigrant City*.

2. Ewa Morawska, "From Myth to Reality: America in the Eyes of East European Peasant Migrant Laborers," in *Distant Magnets: Expectations and Realities in the Immigration Experience, 1830–1940,* Ed., Dirk Hoerder and Horst Rössler (New York: Holmes and Meier, 1993), 241–263.

3. John DeWitt Warner, "The 'Sweating System' in New York City," *Harper's Weekly* (February 9, 1895), 135–136. For a latter-twentieth-century sweatshop tour, see Victor G. Nee and Brett DeBary Nee, *Longtime Californ': A Documentary History of San Francisco's Chinatown* (New York: Pantheon, 1973), 289–319.

4. Sources for this section include Roland Tappan Berthoff, *British Immigrants in Industrial America* (Cambridge, MA: Harvard University Press, 1953); Edna Bonacich and John Modell, *The Economic Basis of Ethnic Solidarity: Small Business in the Japanese American Community* (Berkeley: University of California Press, 1980); E. P. Hutchinson, *Immigrants and Their Children, 1850–1950* (New York: Wiley, 1956); Thomas Kessner, *The Golden Door: Italian and Jewish Immigrant Mobility in New York City, 1880–1915* (New York: Oxford, 1977); John Modell, *The Economics and Politics of Racial Accommodation: The Japanese of Los Angeles, 1900–1942* (Urbana: University of Illinois Press, 1977).

5. Far too much has been made of one particular occupational avenue to upward mobility: organized crime. Some have seen this as a sort of immigrant entrepreneurship off the back of the truck, a way to take that first step on the ladder of social mobility. On the over-identification of Italians and crime via the Mafia myth, see Richard Gambino, *Blood of My Blood: The Dilemma of the Italian-Americans* (Garden City, NY: Doubleday, 1974), 274–312; Francis A. J. Ianni, "The Mafia and the Web of Kinship," *Public Interest* (Winter 1971), 78–100.

6. Liebmann Hersch, "International Migration of the Jews," in *International Migrations* vol. 2, Walter F. Willcox, Ed. (New York: Gordon and Breach, 1969), 493.

7. These were all the socially significant ethnic groups. Warner et al., found that the town had eighty African Americans and no Indians or Asians. On Canadian immigration, see Jacques Ducharme, *The Shadows of the Trees: The Story of French-Canadians in New England* (New York: Harper, 1943); Nora Faires, "Poor Women, Proximate Border: Migrants from Ontario to Detroit in the Late Nineteenth Century," *Journal of American Ethnic History*, 20.3 (Spring 2001), 88–109; Sheila McManus, "Mapping the Alberta-Montana Borderlands: Race, Ethnicity and Gender in the Late Nineteenth Century," *Journal of American Ethnic History*, 20.3 (Spring 2001), 71–87; Bruno Ramirez, "Canada in the United States: Perspectives on Migration and Continental History," *Journal of American Ethnic History*, 20.3 (Spring 2001), 50–70; Ramirez, *Crossing the 49th Parallel: Migration from Canada to the United States, 1900–1930* (Ithaca, NY: Cornell University Press, 2001). On Azoreans and Cape Verdeans, two formally Portuguese groups that came mainly to New England in this period, see Marilyn Halter, *Between Race and Ethnicity: Cape Verdean American Immigrants, 1860–1965* (Urbana: University of Illinois Press, 1993); Jerry R. Williams, *And Yet They Come: Portuguese Immigration from the Azores to the United States* (New York: Center for Migration Studies, 1982).

8. W. Lloyd Warner, J. O. Low, Paul S. Lunt, and Leo Srole, *Yankee City*, abr. ed. (New Haven, CT: Yale University Press, 1963; orig ed. 5 vols., 1941–1959), 394–400.

9. Sources for this section include Sydney E. Ahlstrom, *A Religious History of the American People* (Garden City, NY: Doubleday, 1975), 208–223; Alfred Bloom, "Shin Buddhism in America," in *The Faces of Buddhism in America*, Charles S. Prebish and Kenneth K. Tanaka, Eds. (Berkeley: University of California Press, 1998), 31–47; Rudiger v. Busto, "DisOrienting Subjects: Reclaiming Pacific Islander/Asian American Religions," in *Revealing the Sacred in Asian and Pacific America*, Jane Naomi Iwamura and Paul Spickard, Eds. (New York: Routledge, 2003), 9–28; Donald B. Cole, *Immigrant City: Lawrence, Massachusetts, 1845–1921* (Chapel Hill: University of North Carolina Press, 1963); Jay P. Dolan, *The American Catholic Experience* (Garden City, NY: Doubleday, 1985), 127–320; Brian Masaru Hayashi, *'For the Sake of Our Japanese Brethren': Assimilation, Nationalism, and Protestantism among the Japanese of Los Angeles, 1895–1942* (Stanford, CA: Stanford University Press, 1995); Howe, *World of Our Fathers*; Tetsuden Kashima, *Buddhism in America* (Westport, CT: Greenwood, 1977); Gary Laderman and Luis León, Eds., *Religions and American Cultures*, vol. 1, 27–204; Leo Trepp, *A History of the Jewish Experience*. rev. ed. (New York: Behrman House, 1973), 387–414; Wyman, *Round-Trip to America*. See also Paul Spickard, "Asian Americans, Religion, and Race," in *Borders, Boundaries, and Bonds*, Elliott R. Barkan, Hasia Diner, and Alan Kraut, Eds. (New York: NYU Press, 2007).

10. Louise H. Hunter, *Buddhism in Hawai'i* (Honolulu: University of Hawai'i Press, 1971); Ronald Takaki, *Paul Hana: Plantation Life and Labor in Hawai'i* (Honolulu: University of Hawai'i Press, 1983); Edward D. Beechert, *Working in Hawai'i* (Honolulu: University of Hawai'i Press, 1985).

11. Masayo Umezawa Duus, *The Japanese Conspiracy: The Oahu Sugar Strike of 1920* (Berkeley: University of California Press, 1999); Samuel Gompers, *Seventy Years of Life and Labor* (New York: Dutton, 1925); Victor R. Greene, *The Slavic Community on Strike: Immigrant Labor in Pennsylvania Anthracite*

(Notre Dame, IN: University of Notre Dame Press, 1968); Peck, *Reinventing Free Labor*; Zaragosa Vargas, *Labor Rights Are Civil Rights: Mexican American Workers in Twentieth Century America* (Princeton, NJ: Princeton University Press, 2005).

12. The progressive-era reformers were indefatigable writers. See, for example, Jane Addams, *Twenty Years at Hull-House* (New York: Macmillan, 1910); Arthur C. Holden, *The Settlement House: A Vision of Social Justice* (New York: Macmillan, 1922); Jacob A. Riis, *How the Other Half Lives* (New York: Hill and Wang, 1957); Upton Sinclair, *The Jungle* (Boston: Bedford/St. Martin's, 2005; orig. 1906); Lillian D. Wald, *The House on Henry Street* (New York: Holt, 1915); Robert A. Woods, Ed., *Americans in Process: A Settlement Study* (Boston: Houghton Mifflin, 1903); Woods, *The Neighborhood in Nation-Building: The Running Comment of Thirty Years at the South End House* (Boston: Houghton Mifflin, 1923). For analyses, see Robert H. Bremner, *From the Depths: The Discovery of Poverty in the United States* (New York: NYU Press, 1956); Rivka Shpak Lissak, *Pluralism and Progressives: Hull House and the New Immigrants, 1890–1919* (Chicago: University of Chicago Press, 1989).

13. Marie Hall Ets, *Rosa: The Life of an Italian Immigrant*, quoted in Lichtenstein et al., *Who Built America?*, 2.213.

14. Sources for this section (not for this stereotype) include Hasia Diner, *Erin's Daughters in America* (Baltimore: John's Hopkins University Press, 1983); Yen Le Espiritu, *Asian American Women and Men* (Thousand Oaks, CA: Sage, 1997); Nancy Foner, *In a New Land: A Comparative View of Immigration* (New York: NYU Press, 2005), 89–105, 156–179; Kathie Friedman-Kasaba, *Memories of Migration: Gender, Ethnicity, and Work in the Lives of Jewish and Italian Women in New York, 1870–1924* (Albany: SUNY Press, 1996); Donna Gabaccia, *From the Other Side: Women, Gender, and Immigrant Life in the US, 1820–1990* (Bloomington: Indiana University Press, 1994); Gabaccia, Ed., *Seeking Common Ground: Multidisciplinary Studies of Immigrant Women in the United States* (Westport, CT: Greenwood, 1992); Martha Gardner, *The Qualities of a Citizen: Women, Immigration, and Citizenship, 1870–1965* (Princeton, NJ: Princeton University Press, 2005); Sheba Mariam George, *When Women Came First: Gender and Class in Transnational Migration* (Berkeley: University of California Press, 2005); Evelyn Nakano Glenn, *Issei, Nisei, War Bride: Three Generations of Japanese American Women in Domestic Work* (Philadelphia: Temple University Press, 1996); Susan Glenn, *Daughters of the Shtetl: Life and Labor in the Immigrant Generation* (Ithaca, NY: Cornell University Press, 1990); Linda Gordon, *The Great Arizona Orphan Abduction* (Cambridge, MA: Harvard University Press, 1999); Thomas Kessner and Betty Boyd Caroli, "New Immigrant Women at Work: Italians and Jews in New York City, 1880–1905," *Journal of Ethnic Studies*, 5.4 (1978); Huping Ling, *Surviving on the Gold Mountain* (Albany: SUNY Press, 1998); Mirjana Morokvasic, "Women in Migration: Beyond the Reductionist Outlook," in *One Way Ticket: Migration and Female Labour*, Annie Phizacklea, Ed. (London: Routledge and Kegan Paul, 1983), 13–31; Thaddeus C. Radzilowski, "Family, Women, and Gender: The Polish Experience," in *Polish Americans and Their History*, John J. Bukowczyk, Ed. (Pittsburgh: University of Pittsburgh Press, 1996), 58–79; Vicki L. Ruiz, and Ellen Carol DuBois, *Unequal Sisters: A Multicultural Reader in US Women's History*, 3rd ed. (New York: Routledge, 2000);

Barbara A. Schreier, *Becoming American Women: Clothing and the Jewish Immigrant Experience, 1880–1920* (Chicago: Chicago Historical Society, 1995); Pamela Sharpe, Ed., *Women, Gender and Labour Migration* (London: Routledge, 2001); Suzanne Sinke, "Migration for Labor, Migration for Love: Marriage and Family Formation across Borders," *OAH Magazine of History* (Fall 1999), 17–21; Sinke with Stephen Gross, "The International Marriage Market and the Sphere of Social Reproduction," in *Seeking Common Ground*, Gabaccia, Ed., 67–87; Sydney Stahl Weinberg, "The Treatment of Women in Immigration History: A Call for Change," in *Seeking Common Ground*, Gabaccia, Ed., 3–22; Judy Yung, *Unbound Feet: A Social History of Chinese Women in San Francisco* (Berkeley: University of California Press, 1995).

15. Dorothy B. Fujita-Rony, *American Workers, Colonial Power: Philippine Seattle and the Transpacific West, 1919–1941* (Berkeley: University of California Press, 2003), 1–3.

16. Gabaccia, *From the Other Side*, 11.

17. Friedman-Kasaba, *Memories of Migration*, 7; Gabaccia, *From the Other Side*, 59.

18. John J. Bukowczyk, *And My Children Did Not Know Me: A History of the Polish-Americans* (Bloomington: Indiana University Press, 1987), 24–25.

19. Sources on the picture bride phenomenon include Alice Yun Chai, "Picture Brides: Feminist Analysis of Life Histories of Hawai'i's Early Immigrant Women from Japan, Okinawa, and Korea," in *Seeking Common Ground*, Gabaccia, Ed., 123–138; Isabel Kaprielian-Churchill, "Armenian Refugee Women: The Picture Brides, 1920–1930," *Journal of American Ethnic History*, 12.3 (Spring 1993), 3–29; Laurie M. Mengel, "Issei Women and Divorce in Hawai'i, 1885–1908," *Social Process in Hawai'i*, 38 (1997), 17–39; Suzanne Sinke, "Migration for Labor, Migration for Love: Marriage and Family Formation Across Borders," *OAH Magazine of History*, 14.1 (Fall 1999), 17–21; Sinke with Stephen Gross, "The International Marriage Market and the Sphere of Social Reproduction," in *Seeking Common Ground*, Gabaccia, Ed., 67–87; Paul Spickard, *Japanese Americans* (New York: Twayne, 1996), 32–37; Yoshiko Uchida, *Picture Bride* (New York: Simon and Schuster, 1987). In fact, mail-order brides were a feature of the White native population as it spread across the North American continent as well. Famous in Seattle's history are the eleven women that Asa Mercer brought west from New York to become brides of some of that city's first citizens. See Murray Morgan, *Skid Road* (New York: Viking: 1951); William C. Speidel, *Sons of the Profits* (Seattle: Nettle Creek Publishing, 1967), 107–108.

20. Mengel, "Issei Women and Divorce."

21. Gordon, *Great Arizona Orphan Abduction*.

22. George Anthony Peffer, *If They Don't Bring Their Women Here: Chinese Female Migration Before Exclusion* (Urbana: University of Illinois Press, 1999); Karen J. Leong, "'A Distinct and Antagonistic Race': Construction of Chinese Manhood in the Exclusionist Debates, 1869–1878," in *Across the Great Divide: Cultures of Manhood in the American West*, Matthew Basso, Laura McCall, and Dee Garceau, Eds. (New York: Routledge, 2001), 131–148.

One hears echoes of the gendered quality of the anti-Chinese movement in the anti-Arab movement of the twenty-first century. Like the anti-Asianists of the nineteenth century, modern-day anti-Arabists do not even recognize their prejudice. Where once the cry of ostensibly concerned citizens was that "Chinese women are all prostitutes," now one hears from well-meaning people that "Arab women are all brutally oppressed." Most Arab American women would beg to differ, but their voices go largely unheard. See Nada Elia, "The 'White' Sheep of the Family: But *Bleaching* Is Like Starvation," in *This Bridge We Call Home*, Gloria E. Anzaldúa and Analouise Keating, Eds. (New York: Routledge, 2002), 223–231; Jennifer Kawaja, director *Under One Sky: Arab Women in North America Talk About the Hijab* (Montreal: National Film Board of Canada, 2000); Kathleen Moore, "The *Hijab* and Religious Liberty: Anti-Discrimination Law and Muslim Women in the United States," in *Muslims on the Americanization Path?*, Yvonne Yazbeck Haddad and John L. Esposito, Eds. (Atlanta: Scholars Press, 1998), 129–158.

23. David M. Brownstone, Irene M. Franck, Douglass L. Brownstone, *Island of Hope, Island of Tears* (New York: Penguin, 1986); Peter Morton Coan, *Ellis Island Interviews* (New York: Facts On File, 1997); *Island of Hope—Island of Tears* (Washington, DC: Guggenheim Productions, n.d.).

24. *Island of Hope—Island of Tears*.

25. *Carved in Silence* (San Francisco: Felicia Lowe Productions, 1996); Roger Daniels, "No Lamps Were Lit for Them: Angel Island and the Historiography of Asian American Immigration," *Journal of American Ethnic History*, 17.1 (Fall 1997), 3–18; Him Mark Lai, Genny Lim, and Judy Yung, *Island: Poetry and History of Chinese Immigrants on Angel Island, 1910–1940* (San Francisco: Chinese Culture Foundation, 1980); Lee, *At America's Gates*.

26. *Carved in Silence*; Chinese examination stations at Malone, N.Y., and Richford, Vt., *Annual Report of the Commissioner-General of Immigration* (Washington, DC: Government Printing Office, 1904), loose picture.

27. Lai, et al., *Island* 56, 100, 126.

28. Mark Stolarik, Ed., *Forgotten Doors: The Other Ports of Entry to the United States* (Philadelphia: Balch Institute Press, 1988); Ramirez, *Crossing the 49th Parallel*; Sui Sin Far (Edith Maude Eaton), *Mrs. Spring Fragrance and Other Writings* (Urbana: University of Illinois Press, 1995; orig. 1912); Bernard Marinbach, *Galveston: Ellis Island of the West* (Albany: SUNY Press, 1983).

29. "Early History of the Border Patrol" (U.S. Immigration and Naturalization Service Fact Sheet, May 1999); "US Border Patrol History" (U.S. Customs and Border Protection, July 15, 2003) www.customs.gov/xp/cgov/border_security/border_patrol/history.xml, September 25, 2005.

30. Brook Thomas, *Plessy v. Ferguson* (Boston: Bedford/St. Martins, 1997), 41–60.

31. Sources for this section include Pete Daniel, *The Shadow of Slavery: Peonage in the South, 1901–1969* (Urbana: University of Illinois Press, 1972); Allison Davis, Burleigh B. Gardner, and Mary R. Gardner, *Deep South*, abr. ed. (Chicago: University of Chicago Press, 1965; orig. 1941); Donald P. DeNevi and Doris A. Holmes, Eds., *Racism at the Turn of the Century* (San Rafael, CA: Leswing, 1973); John Dollard, *Caste and Class in a Southern Town*, 3rd ed. (Garden City, NY: Doubleday, 1957; orig. 1937); W.E.B. DuBois, *Black Reconstruction in America* (New York: Russell and Russell, 1966); John Hope Franklin, *Reconstruction After the Civil War* (Chicago: University of Chicago Press, 1961); Thomas R. Frazier, Ed., *Afro-American History*, 2nd ed. (Chicago: Dorsey, 1988); Glenda Elizabeth Gilmore, *Gender and Jim Crow* (Chapel Hill: University of North Carolina Press, 1996); Herbert G. Gutman, *The Black Family in Slavery and Freedom, 1750–1925* (New York: Pantheon, 1976);

Grace Elizabeth Hale, *Making Whiteness: The Culture of Segregation in the South, 1890–1940* (New York: Random House, 1998); Darlene Clark Hine, William C. Hine, and Stanley Harrold, *The African-American Odyssey*, 2nd ed. (Upper Saddle River, NJ: Prentice Hall, 2003); Leon F. Litwack, *Been in the Storm So Long: The Aftermath of Slavery* (New York: Knopf, 1979); Litwack, *Trouble in Mind: Black Southerners in the Age of Jim Crow* (New York: Knopf, 1998); Neil R. McMillen, *Dark Journey: Black Mississippians in the Age of Jim Crow* (Urbana: University of Illinois Press, 1989); Donald G. Nieman, Ed., *African Americans and the Emergence of Segregation, 1865–1900* (New York: Garland, 1994); Hortense Powdermaker, *After Freedom: A Cultural Study in the Deep South* (Madison: University of Wisconsin Press, 1993; orig. 1939); Roger Ransom and Richard Sutch, *One Kind of Freedom: The Economic Consequences of Emancipation* (Cambridge: Cambridge University Press, 1977); Joel Williamson, *A Rage for Order: Black-White Relations in the American South since Emancipation* (New York: Oxford, 1986); C. Vann Woodward, *The Strange Career of Jim Crow*, 3rd ed. (New York: Oxford, 1974).

32. It is important to note that all the features of southern post-Civil War segregation were used against Blacks in northern cities during the slavery era, and most of the features of segregation were also retained and often expanded in the Northeast, Midwest, and West after the Civil War. See James Oliver Horton and Lois E. Horton, *In Hope of Liberty: Culture, Community, and Protest Among Northern Free Blacks, 1700–1860* (New York: Oxford, 1997); Leon G. Litwack, *North of Slavery: The Negro in the Free States, 1790–1860* (Chicago: University of Chicago Press, 1961).

33. Joel Williamson, *New People: Miscegenation and Mulattoes in the United States* (Baton Rouge: Louisiana State University Press, 1995; orig. 1980).

34. Sources on lynching include W. Fitzhugh Brundage, Ed., *Under Sentence of Death: Lynching in the South* (Chapel Hill: University of North Carolina Press, 1997); William D. Carrigan, *The Making of a Lynching Culture: Violence and Vigilantism in Central Texas, 1836–1916* (Urbana: University of Illinois Press, 2004); William D. Carrigan and Clive Webb, "*Muerto por Unos Desconocidos* (Killed by Persons Unknown): Mob Violence against Blacks and Mexicans," in *Race, Ethnicity, and Gender in the US South and Southwest,* Laura F. Edwards, William D. Carrigan, Clive Webb, Stephanie Cole, Sarah Deutsch, and Neil Foley (College Station: Texas A&M University Press, 2004), 35–74; Monica Davey, "Minnesota Memorial Stirs Racial Tensions," *Oregonian* (December 7, 2003); Philip Dray, *At the Hands of Persons Unknown: The Lynching of Black America* (New York: Random House, 2002); Hale, *Making Whiteness*, 199–239; James H. Madison, *A Lynching in the Heartland* (New York: Palgrave/St. Martin's, 2001); Jonathan Markovitz, *Legacies of Lynching: Racial Violence and Memory* (Minneapolis: University of Minnesota Press, 2004); Michael J. Pfeifer, *Rough Justice: Lynching and American Society, 1874–1947* (Urbana: University of Illinois Press, 2004), 155–183; Stewart E. Tolnay and E. M. Beck, *A Festival of Violence: An Analysis of Southern Lynchings, 1882–1930* (Urbana: University of Illinois Press, 1995), 273; Walter White, *Rope and Faggot: The Biography of Judge Lynch* (Notre Dame, IN: University of Notre Dame Press, 2001; orig. 1929).

35. W. J. Cash, *The Mind of the South* (New York: Knopf, 1941), 188–119.

36. Matthew Frye Jacobson, *Whiteness of a Different Color: European Immigrants and the Alchemy of Race* (Cambridge, MA: Harvard University Press, 1998); David Roediger, *The Wages of Whiteness: Race and the Making of the American Working Class*, rev. ed. (London: Verso, 1991); James R. Barrett and David Roediger, "Inbetween Peoples: Race, Nationality and the 'New Immigrant' Working Class," *Journal of American Ethnic History*, 16.3 (Spring 1997), 3–44.

37. This exercise is reported more fully in Paul Spickard, "Who Is an American? Teaching about Racial and Ethnic Hierarchy," *Immigration and Ethnic History Newsletter*, 31.1 (May 1999).

38. Jacobson, *Whiteness of a Different Color*, 140; italics added.

39. David A. J. Richards, *Italian Americans: The Racializing of an Ethnic Identity* (New York: NYU Press, 1999); Noel Ignatiev, *How the Irish Became White* (New York: Routledge, 1995); Karen Brodkin, *How Jews Became White Folks and What That Says About Race in America* (New Brunswick, NJ: Rutgers University Press, 1998); see also David R. Roediger, *Working Toward Whiteness: How America's Immigrants Became White* (New York: Basic Books, 2005). For a corrective, see Paul Spickard, "What's Critical about White Studies," in *Racial Thinking in the United States*, Spickard and G. Reginald Daniel, Ed. (Notre Dame, IN: University of Notre Dame Press, 2004), 248–274.

40. See, for example, Madison Grant, *The Passing of the Great Race, or The Racial Basis of European History* (New York: Scribner's, 1918), 148–166; Alfred P. Schultz, *Race or Mongrel* (Boston: Page, 1908), 109–123; Peter Roberts, *Immigrant Races in North America* (New York: Association Press, 1912); Lothrop Stoddard, *Racial Realities in Europe* (New York: Scribners, 1924), 94–122.

41. Thomas A. Guglielmo, *White on Arrival: Italians, Race, Color, and Power in Chicago, 1890–1945* (New York: Oxford, 2003), 27ff.

42. J. Alexander Karlin, "The Italo-American Incident of 1891 and the Road to Reunion," *Journal of Southern History*, 8 (1942), 242–246; Dray, *At the Hands of Persons Unknown*, 130–132, 207–214.

43. These numbers are Dray's. An earlier accounting by Walter White, in the first and perhaps overall the best lynching study, suggested an even larger percentage of Whites among those lynched. White recorded 4951 lynchings between 1882 and 1927: 3513 Black (71 percent) and 1438 White (29 percent). See White, *Rope and Faggot*, 267; Pfeifer, *Rough Justice*, 155–183.

44. Other sources on lynching are found in note 37. Carrigan and Webb, "*Muerto por Unos Desconocidos*," estimate a "lynching rate" for Mexican Americans of 27.4, versus an African American rate of 37.1, for the period 1880–1930.

45. Jennifer Guglielmo and Salvatore Salerno, *Are Italians White? How Race Is Made in America* (New York: Routledge, 2003).

46. Vincenza Scarpaci, "Walking the Color Line: Italian Immigrants in Rural Louisiana, 1880–1910," in Guglielmo and Salerno, Eds., *Are Italians White?* 60–76; Thomas A. Guglielmo, "No Color Barrier: Italians, Race, and Power in the United States," in Guglielmo and Salerno, Eds., *Are Italians White?* 29–43.

A book on Japanese Americans in Chicago, taken together with a comment on that book by another scholar, brings up an issue that has some relevance here. Jacalyn Harden, an African American anthropologist, spoke of Japanese Americans' "vexed position as sometimes 'colored,' sometimes white (for example, the Japanese American soldier who was instructed to use the white washrooms at boot camp in Alabama during World War II, while thousands were being relocated to internment camps)." To which an African American historian responded: "Well, racialization is unevenly deployed, isn't it? What's the Jim Crow etiquette in a situation like that? Offend the White pissers by making them expose themselves to a Chinaman? Or offend the Chinaman who is clearly not friend, but not necessarily foe, by making him piss with Blacks? Individual cases mean very little, of course. If they put up a sign on the Negro restroom that said 'Niggers and Japs'—now that would mean something. But no, I don't think getting to pee with White men makes you White, any more than getting lynched like a Black man makes you Black." The first quote is from Jacalyn D. Harden, *Double Cross: Japanese Americans in Black and White Chicago* (Minneapolis: University of Minnesota Press, 2003): dust cover. The second person asked to remain anonymous; the analysis came in a private communication with the author, February 27, 2004.

47. Bukowczyk, *And My Children Did Not Know Me*, iv.
48. Among the studies of Black migration in this period are Eric Arnesen, *Black Protest and the Great Migration* (Boston: Bedford/St. Martin's, 2003); John Bodnar, Roger Simon, and Michael P. Weber, *Lives of Their Own: Blacks, Italians, and Poles in Pittsburgh, 1900–1960* (Urbana: University of Illinois Press, 1982); James Borchert, *Alley Life in Washington: Family, Community, Religion, and Folklife in the City, 1850–1970* (Urbana: University of Illinois Press, 1980); Albert S. Broussard, *Black San Francisco* (Lawrence: University Press of Kansas, 1993); Douglas Henry Daniels, *Pioneer Urbanites: A Social and Cultural History of Black San Francisco* (Philadelphia: Temple University Press, 1980); Neil Fligstein, *Going North: Migration of Blacks and Whites from the South, 1900–1950* (New York: Academic Press, 1981); Peter Gottlieb, *Making Their Own Way: Southern Blacks' Migration to Pittsburgh, 1916–1930* (Urbana: University of Illinois Press,1987); James R. Grossman, *Land of Hope: Chicago, Black Southerners, and the Great Migration* (Chicago: University of Chicago Press, 1989); Florette Henri, *Black Migration: Movement North, 1900–1920* (Garden City, NY: Doubleday, 1975); Daniel M. Johnson and Rex R. Campbell, *Black Migration in America* (Durham, NC: Duke University Press, 1981); Kenneth L. Kusmer, *A Ghetto Takes Shape: Black Cleveland, 1870–1930* (Urbana: University of Illinois Press, 1978); Carole Marks, *Farewell—We're Good and Gone: The Great Black Migration* (Bloomington: Indiana University Press, 1989); Gilbert Osofsky, *Harlem: The Making of a Ghetto, Negro New York, 1890–1930*, 2nd ed. (New York: Harper and Row, 1971); Nell Irvin Painter, *Exodusters: Black Migration to Kansas After Reconstruction* (Lawrence: University Press of Kansas, 1976); Allan H. Spear, *Black Chicago: The Making of a Ghetto, 1890–1920* (Chicago: University of Chicago Press, 1967); Quintard Taylor, *The Forging of a Black Community: Seattle's Central District from 1870 through the Civil Rights Era* (Seattle: University of Washington Press, 1994); Taylor, *In Search of the Racial Frontier: African Americans in the American West, 1528–1990* (New York: Norton, 1998); Joe William Trotter, Jr., *Black Milwaukee: The Making of an Industrial Proletariat, 1915–45* (Urbana: University of Illinois Press, 1985); Trotter, Ed., *The Great Migration in Historical Perspective* (Bloomington: Indiana University Press, 1991).
49. Marks, *Farewell—We're Good and Gone*, 122. The numbers continued to climb, as Black migration out of the South continued. There was another large expansion of the flow during World War II, and this time there was a significant flow to cities in the West as well. The migration did not begin to recede until the 1960s or later.

50. Bodnar, Simon, and Weber, *Lives of Their Own*, 69; Paul Spickard, *Japanese Americans* (New York: Twayne, 1996), 65–68; George Sánchez is currently working on a book on Boyle Heights.

51. Sarah Deutsch, *No Separate Refuge: Culture, Class, and Gender on an Anglo-Hispanic Frontier in the American Southwest, 1880–1940* (New York: Oxford, 1987), 4; Arthur Schlesinger, Jr., "The American Empire? Not So Fast," *World Policy Journal*, 22.1 (April 2005), electronic version. The fantasy of American exceptionalism is apparent in the pronouncements of President George W. Bush in November 2005. Wire services reported: "President Bush vigorously defended U.S. interrogation practices in the war on terror Monday and lobbied against a congressional drive to outlaw torture. … 'Any activity we conduct is within the law.'" That is, because they were Americans, what they were doing was not torture. "Bush Defends Detainee Policy," CNN.com (November 7, 2005). The ultimate absurdity in the dream of American exemption from the ways of human history is on view in Francis Fukuyama's wildly successful 1992 book, *The End of History and the Last Man* (New York: Free Press).

52. Stephen Kinzer, *Overthrow: America's Century of Regime Change from Hawaii to Iraq* (New York: Times Books, 2006). The debate can be traced in J. Rogers Hollingsworth, Ed., *American Expansion in the Late Nineteenth Century: Colonialist or Anticolonialist?* (New York: Holt, Rinehart and Winston, 1968); Thomas G. Paterson, *American Imperialism and Anti-Imperialism* (New York: Crowell, 1974); E. Berkeley Tompkins, *Anti-Imperialism in the United States: The Great Debate, 1890–1920* (Philadelphia: University of Pennsylvania Press, 1970).

53. Frederick Jackson Turner, *The Frontier in American History* (New York: Henry Holt, 1958; orig. 1920), quoted in James Chace, "Tomorrow the World," *New York Review of Books* (November 21, 2002), 33.

54. Rudyard Kipling, "The White Man's Burden," *McClure's Magazine*, 12 (February 1899), 290–291.

55. Quoted in Samuel Flagg Bemis, *A Diplomatic History of the United States* (New York: Henry Holt, 1936), 472. Not that Germany was not a rival in Southeast Asia at that time, and that the Philippines had the highest percentage of believing Christians of any nation outside Europe and the Americas. Not all White Americans bought this self-excusing nonsense. It is perhaps not surprising that Mark Twain waxed biting and satirical in this poetic reaction to the U.S. war on the Philippines, written about 1900. It is to be sung to the tune of "The Battle Hymn of the Republic":

> Mine eyes have seen the orgy of the launching of the Sword;
> He is searching out the hoardings where the stranger's wealth is stored;
> He hath loosed his fateful lightnings, and with woe and death has scored;
> His lust is marching on.
> I have seen him in the watch-fires of a hundred circling camps.
> They have builded him an altar in the Eastern dews and damps;
> I have read his doomful mission by the dim and flaring lamps;
> His night is marching on.
> I have read his bandit gospel writ in burnished rows of steel;
> "As ye deal with my pretensions, so with you my wrath shall deal";
> Let the faithless son of Freedom crush the patriot with his heel;
> Lo, Greed is marching on!

> We have legalized the strumpet and are guarding her retreat;
> Greed is seeking out commercial souls before his judgment seat;
> O, be swift, ye clods, to answer him! be jubilant my feet!
> Our god is marching on!
> In a sordid slime harmonious, Greed was born in yonder ditch,
> With a longing in his bosom—and for others' goods an itch—
> As Christ died to make men holy, let men die to make us rich—
> Our god is marching on.

Mark Twain, *A Pen Warmed-Up in Hell: Mark Twain in Protest*, Ed. F. Anderson (New York: Harper and Row, 1972), 4.

56. Sources for this section include Teodoro A. Agoncillo, *A History of the Filipino People*, 8th ed. (Quezon City: Garotech, 1990), 129–383; Dorothy B. Fujita-Rony, *American Workers, Colonial Power: Philippine Seattle and the Transpacific West, 1919–1941* (Berkeley: University of California Press, 2003); Willard B. Gatewood, Jr., "Black Americans and the Quest for Empire, 1898–1903," *Journal of Southern History*, 38 (1972), 545–566; Julian Go and Anne L. Foster, Eds., *The American Colonial State in the Philippines* (Durham, NC: Duke University Press, 2003); Frank H. Golay, Ed., *The United States and the Philippines* (Englewood Cliffs, NJ: Prentice-Hall, 1966); Thomas F. Gossett, *Race: The History of an Idea in America* (New York: Schocken, 1965), 210–338; Louis R. Harlan, "Booker T. Washington and the White Man's Burden," *American Historical Review*, 71 (1966, 441–467; Matthew Frye Jacobson, *Barbarian Virtues: The United States Encounters Foreign Peoples at Home and Abroad, 1876–1917* (New York: Hill and Wang, 2000); Stanley Karnow, *In Our Image: America's Empire in the Philippines* (New York: 1989); Philip W. Kennedy, "Race and American Expansion in Cuba and Puerto Rico, 1895–1905," *Journal of Black Studies*, 1 (1971), 306–316; Philip W. Kennedy, "The Racial Overtones of Imperialism as a Campaign Issue, 1900," *Mid-America*, 48 (1966), 196–205; Paul A. Kramer, *The Blood of Government: Race, Empire, the United States, and the Philippines* (Chapel Hill: University of North Carolina Press, 2006); Christopher Lasch, "The Anti-Imperialists, the Philippines, and the Inequality of Man," *Journal of Southern History*, 24 (1958), 319–331; Eric T. L. Love, *Race over Empire: Racism and US Imperialism, 1865–1900* (Chapel Hill: University of North Carolina Press, 2004); George P. Marks, "Opposition of Negro Newspapers to American Philippine Policy, 1899–1900," *Midwest Journal*, 4 (1951–52), 1–25; Michael C. Robinson and Frank N. Schubert, "David Fagen: An Afro-American Rebel in the Philippines, 1899–1901," *Pacific Historical Review*, 44 (1975), 68–83; Thomas Schoonover, *Uncle Sam's War of 1898 and the Origins of Globalization* (Lexington: University Press of Kentucky, 2003); Angel Velasco Shaw and Luis H. Francia, Eds., *Vestiges of War: The Philippine-American War and the Aftermath of an Imperial Dream, 1899–1999* (New York: NYU Press, 2002); Peter W. Stanley, *A Nation in the Making: The Philippines and the United States, 1899–1921* (Cambridge, MA: Harvard University Press, 1974); James C. Thomson, Jr., Peter W. Stanley, and John Curtis Perry, *Sentimental Imperialists: The American Experience in East Asia* (New York: Harper and Row, 1981), 106–120; Richard E. Welch, Jr., *Response to Imperialism: The United States and the Philippine-American War, 1899–1902* (Chapel Hill: University of North Carolina Press, 1979); Rubin Francis Weston, *Racism in U.S. Imperialism* (Columbia: University of South Carolina Press, 1972).

57. I owe this argument to Matt Jacobson; see *Barbarian Virtues*, 175–177 and *passim*.

58. *Congressional Record*, Senate, January 9, 1900, 704–711; reprinted in *Major Problems in Asian American History*, Lon Kurashige and Alice Yang Murray, Eds. (Boston: Houghton Mifflin, 2003), 139–142. At the close of the Spanish-American War, the U.S. also acquired Guam and Puerto Rico; see Laura Briggs, *Reproducing Empire: Race, Sex, Science, and US Imperialism in Puerto Rico* (Berkeley: University of California Press, 2002); Ronald Fernandez, *The Disenchanted Island: Puerto Rico and the United States in the Twentieth Century* (New York: Praeger, 1993); Robert F. Rogers, *Destiny's Landfall: A History of Guam* (Honolulu: University of Hawai'i Press, 1995), 108–126.

59. Edmund Wilson was writing during the war on Vietnam about American pretensions in mainland Southeast Asia, but he might easily have been writing about the Philippines at the end of the nineteenth century or Iraq at the dawn of the twenty-first century when he wrote: "Our talk about bringing to backward peoples the processes of democratic government and of defending the 'free world' is as much an exploit of Anglo-Saxon hypocrisy as anything ever perpetrated by the English"; "Preface" to *Europe Without Baedeker* (New York: Farrar, Straus and Giroux, 1966).

60. Sources on U.S. colonialism in Hawai'i include Helena G. Allen, *The Betrayal of Lili'uokalani, Last Queen of Hawai'i* (Honolulu: Mutual, 1982); Michael Dougherty, *To Steal a Kingdom: Probing Hawaiian History* (Waimanalo, HI: Island Style Press, 1992); Michael Kioni Dudley and Keoni Kealoha Agard, *A Call for Hawaiian Sovereignty* (Honolulu: Na Kane O Ka Malo Press, 1993); Rona Tamiko Halualani, *In the Name of Hawaiians: Native Identities and Cultural Politics* (Minneapolis: University of Minnesota Press, 2002); Lilikala Kame'eleihiwa, *Native Land and Foreign Desires* (Honolulu: Bishop Museum Press, 1992); Lili'uokalani, *Hawai'i's Story by Hawai'i's Queen* (Rutland, VT: Tuttle, 1964); Jon Kamakawiwo'ole Osorio, *Dismembering Lahui: A History of the Hawaiian Nation to 1887* (Honolulu: University of Hawai'i Press, 2002); Noenoe K. Silva, *Aloha Betrayed: Native Hawaiian Resistance to American Colonialism* (Durham, NC: Duke University Press, 2004); Haunani Kay Trask, *From a Native Daughter: Colonialism and Sovereignty in Hawai'i* (Monroe, ME: Common Courage Press, 1993).

61. Lori Pierce, "Creating a Racial Paradise: Citizenship and Sociology in Hawai'i," in *Race and Nation: Ethnic Systems in the Modern World*, Paul Spickard, Ed. (New York: Routledge, 2005), 69–86.

62. The connection is the same as that frequently noted by North and West African-derived, European-born citizens. It was enunciated by North African-descended French citizens with especial clarity in the wake of the Paris riots of fall 2005: "We are here because you were there"; see Gregory Rodriguez, "We're Here Because You Were There," *Los Angeles Times* (November 20, 2005). The riots were the result of European-descended Europeans making a racial distinction between themselves and the descendants of North African immigrants, and discriminating against those North African-descended citizens on that basis.

63. For similar development of racial systems in the process of empire making at various other points around the globe, see Spickard, *Race and Nation*, especially 14–16, 135–211.

64. *Omaha Progress* (October 3, 1899), quoted in Rene G. Ontal, "Fagen and Other Ghosts: African-Americans and the Philippine-American War," in *Vestiges of War*, Shaw and Francia, Eds., 118–133; Robinson and Schubert, "David Fagen"; Marks, "Opposition of Negro Newspapers"; Paul A. Kramer, "Empires, Exceptions, and Anglo-Saxons: Race and Rule between the British and United States Empires, 1880–1910," *Journal of American History* (March 2002), 1315–1353. For similar dynamics in Australia in the same years, see Gregory D. B. Smithers, "'A Bloody Useless Blackfella': Race and Miscegenation in the United States and Australia, 1890s–1930s" (paper presented to the American Historical Association/Pacific Coast Branch, Corvallis, Oregon, July 2005).

65. Some important legal milestones, such as *Plessy v. Ferguson* (1896) were treated in earlier sections; others, such as the Gentlemen's Agreement (1907–08) and the Alien Land Law (1913), will appear later in this chapter. Sources for this section include Kate Holladay Claghorn, *The Immigrant's Day in Court* (New York: Harper, 1923); Ian F. Haney López, *White by Law: The Legal Construction of Race* (New York: NYU Press, 1996); Bill Ong Hing, *Defining America Through Immigration Policy* (Philadelphia: Temple University Press, 2004); Bill Ong Hing, *Making and Remaking Asian American Through Immigration Policy, 1850–1990* (Stanford, CA: Stanford University Press, 1993); Kevin R. Johnson, *The "Huddled Masses" Myth: Immigration and Civil Rights* (Philadelphia: Temple University Press, 2004); Erika Lee, "American Gatekeeping: Race and Immigration Law in the Twentieth Century," *Not Just Black and White: Historical and Contemporary Perspectives on Immigration, Race, and Ethnicity in the United States*, Nancy Foner and George M. Fredrickson, Ed. (New York: Russell Sage, 2004), 119–144; Erika Lee, "Immigrants and Immigration Law: A State of the Field Assessment," *Journal of American Ethnic History*, 18.9 (1999), 85–114; Eithne Luibhéid, *Entry Denied: Controlling Sexuality at the Border* (Minneapolis: University of Minnesota Press, 2002); John S. W. Park, *Elusive Citizenship: Immigration, Asian Americans, and the Paradox of Civil Rights* (New York: NYU Press, 2004); Lucy E. Salyer, *Laws Harsh as Tigers: Chinese Immigrants and the Shaping of Modern Immigration Law* (Chapel Hill: University of North Carolina Press, 1995); Cheryl Shanks, *Immigration and the Politics of American Sovereignty* (Ann Arbor: University of Michigan Press, 2001).

66. Hing, *Making and Remaking Asian America*, 203.

67. "Cornelius Cole," *San Francisco Chronicle* (October 23, 1870), quoted in Peffer, *If They Don't Bring Their Women*, 75.

68. *Transactions of the American Medical Association*, 27 (1876), 106–107, quoted in Stuart Creighton Miller, *The Unwelcome Immigrant: The American Image of the Chinese, 1785–1882* (Berkeley: University of California Press, 1969), 163.

69. Peffer, *If They Don't Bring Their Women*, back cover; Mildred Crowl Martin, *Chinatown's Angry Angel: The Story of Donaldina Cameron* (Palo Alto, CA: Pacific Books, 1977). See also Leong, "Distinct and Antagonistic Race"; Nayan Shah, *Contagious Divides: Epidemics and Race in San Francisco's Chinatown* (Berkeley: University of California Press, 2001).

70. Michael LeMay and Elliott Robert Barkan, Eds., *US Immigration and Naturalization Laws and Issues* (Westport, CT: Greenwood, 1999), 99–100, 135–136.

71. *In re Ah Yup*, 1 F. Cas. 223 (C. C. D. Cal. 1878); Park, *Elusive Citizenship*, 59ff; Haney López, *White by Law*, 5–6, 209–212. See also *In re Hong Yen Chang*, 84 Cal. 163, 24 Pac. 156 (1890); *In re Gee Hop*, 71 F. 274 (N. D. Cal. 1895); *In re Fisher*, 21 F. 2d 1007 (N. D. Cal. 1927).

72. *Wong Kim Ark v. United States*, 169 U.S. 649 (March 28, 1898).

73. *In re Halladjian*, 174 F. 735 (C. C. D. Mass. 1909); *United States v. Cartozian*, 6 F. 3d 919 (D. Or. 1925). Alex Fabros is writing a PhD dissertation at the University of California, Santa Barbara, on race and ethnic succession in Fresno. For a rich evocation of Armenian American culture in this period, see William Saroyan, *My Name Is Aram* (New York: Harcourt, 1937). See also Michael J. Arlen, *Passage to Ararat* (New York: Random House, 1975); Peter Balakian, *Black Dog of Fate: An American Son Discovers His Armenian Past* (New York: Basic, 1997); Berge Bulbulian, *The Fresno Armenians* (Fresno: California State University, 2000); Charles Mahakian, *History of the Armenians in California* (San Francisco: R and E Research Associates, 1974); Robert Mirak, "On New Soil: The Armenian Orthodox and Armenian Protestant Churches in the New World to 1915," in *Immigrants and Religion in Urban America*, Randall Miller and Thomas Marzik, Eds. (Philadelphia: Temple University Press, 1977).

74. *Ex parte Dow*, 211 F. 486 (E. D. S. C. 1914); *In re Dow*, 213 F. 355 (E. D. S. C. 1914); *Dow v. United States*, 226 F. 145 (4th Cir. 1915). See also *In re Najour*, 174 F. 735 (N. D. Ga. 1909); *In re Mudarri*, 176 F. 465 (C. C. D. Mass. 1910); *In re Ellis*, 1797 F. 1002 (D. Or. 1910); *Ex parte Shahid*, 205 F. 812 (E. D. S. C. 1913); Sarah Gualtieri, "Becoming 'White': Race, Religion and the Foundations of Syrian/Lebanese Ethnicity in the United States," *Journal of American Ethnic History*, 20.4 (2001), 29–52; Haney López, *White By Law*, 72–77; Gregory Orfalea, *Before the Flames: A Quest for the History of Arab Americans* (Austin: University of Texas Press, 1988); Therese Saliba, "Resisting Invisibility: Arab Americans in Academia and Activism," in *Arabs in America*, Michael W. Suleiman, Ed. (Philadelphia: Temple University Press, 1999), 304–319; Helen Hatab Samhan, "Not Quite White: Race Classification and the Arab-American Experience," in Suleiman, *Arabs in America*, 209–226; Michael W. Suleiman, "Early Arab-Americans: The Search for Identity," in *Crossing the Waters: Arabic-Speaking Immigrants to the United States* (Washington, DC: Smithsonian Institution, 1987).

75. *In re Ahmed Hassan*, 48 F. Supp. 843 (E. D. Mich. 1942); *Ex parte Mohriez*, 54 F. Supp 941 (D. Mass. 1944).

76. Yuji Ichioka, *The Issei: The World of the First Generation Japanese Immigrants, 1885–1924* (New York: Free Press, 1988), 1–2; Haney López, *White By Law*, 79–86; Park, *Elusive Citizenship*, 121–124. See also *In re Saito*, 62 F. 126 (C. C. D. Mass. 1894); *In re Yamashita*, 30 Wash. 234, 70 Pac. 482 (1902); *In re Buntaro Kumagai*, 163 F. 922 (W. D. Wash. 1908); *In re Knight*, 171 F. 299 (E. D. N. Y. 1909); *Bessho v. United States*, 178 F. 245 (4th Cir. 1910); *In re Young*, 195 F. 645 (W. D. Wash. 1912); *In re Young*, 198 F. 715 (W. D. Wash. 1912); *Sato v. Hall*, 191 Cal. 510, 217 Pac. 520 (1923).

77. *In re Alverto*, 198 F. 688 (E. D. Pa. 1912); *In re Lampitoe*, 232 F. 382 (S. D. N. Y. 1916); *In re Mallari*, 239 F. 416 (D. Mass. 1916); *In re Rallos*, 241 F. 686 (E. D. N. Y. 1917); *United States v. Javier*, 22 F. 2d 879 (D. C. Cir. 1927); *De La Ysla v. United States*, 77 F. 2d 988 (9th Cir. 1935); *De Cano v. State*, 110 P. 2d 627 (Wash. 1941).

78. Emphasis added. Thind, by the way, was not a Hindu but a Sikh. *United States v. Thind*, 261 U.X. 204 (1923); Haney López, *White By Law*, 86–94; Park, *Elusive Citizenship*, 124–27; Joan M. Jensen, *Passage from India: Asian Indian Immigrants in North America* (New Haven, CT: Yale University Press, 1988), 246–269; Jennifer Snow, "The Civilization of White Men: The Race of the Hindu in *United States v. Bhagat Singh Thind*, in *Race, Nation, and Religion in the Americas*, Henry Goldschmidt and Elizabeth McAlister, Eds. (New York: Oxford, 2004), 259–280. See also *In re Balsara*, 171 F. 294 (C. C. S. D. N. Y. 1909); *United States v. Dolla*, 177 F. 101 (5th Cir. 1910); *United States v. Balsara*, 180 F. 694 (2nd Cir. 1910); *In re Akhay Kumar Mozumdar*, 207 F. 115 (E. D. Wash. 1913); *In re Sadar Bhagwab Singh*, 246 F. 496 (E. D. Pa. 1917); *In re Mohan Singh*, 257 F. 209 (S. D. Cal. 1919); *In re Thind*, 268 F. 683 (D. Or. 1920); *United States v. Akhay Kumar Mozumdar*, 296 F. 173 (S. D. Cal. 1923); *United States v. Ali*, 7 F. 2d 728 (E. D. Mich. 1925); *United States v. Gokhale*, 26 F. 2d 360 (2nd Cir. 1928); *Wadia v. United States*, 101 F. 2d 7 (2nd Cir. 1939); *Kharaiti Ram Samras v. United States*, 125 F. 879 (9th Cir. 1942).

79. Bhagat Singh Thind died in 1967. His books and pamphlets were mainly self-published, and many are still available from a website operated by his son David Bhagat Thind. The books include: *Divine Wisdom*, 3 vols. (2nd ed. 1929; orig. 1925); *The Enlightened Life* (2004); *House of Happiness* (2nd ed. 2003; orig. 1931); *Jesus the Christ in the Light of Spiritual Science*, 3 vols. (3rd ed. 2003); *The Pearl of Greatest Price* (2nd ed. 2003; orig. 1958); *Radiant Road to Reality*, (4th ed. 2003; orig. 1939); *Science of Union with God* (2nd ed. 2003; orig. 1953); *Tested Universal Science of Individual Meditation in Sikh Religion* (2005); *Troubled Mind in a Troubling World and Their Conquest* (2004); and *Winners and Whiners in This Whirling World* (2005).

80. Ronald Takaki, *Strangers from a Different Shore: A History of Asian Americans*, rev. ed. (Boston: Little, Brown, 1998), 300.

81. Brenda Wong Aoki, "Uncle Gunjiro's Girlfriend," *Nikkei Heritage* (National Japanese American Historical Society), 10.4 (Fall 1998), 8–9; "Miss Emery, Her Mother And Her Japanese Fiancee," *Seattle Post-Intelligencer* (March 27, 1909); "How American Women and Japanese Husbands Live in Lake Washington Colony," *Seattle Sunday Times* (June 20, 1909), Magazine, p. 3; "US Judge Restores Citizenship to Wife in East-West Marriage," *San Francisco Chronicle* (November 11, 1933), quoted in Aoki, "Uncle Gunjiro's Girlfriend."

82. *In re Rodriguez*, District Court, W. D. Texas (May 33, 1897); Neil Foley, *The White Scourge: Mexicans, Blacks, and Poor Whites in Texas Cotton Culture* (Berkeley: University of California Press, 1997); Thomas A. Guglielmo, "Fighting for Caucasian Rights: Mexicans, Mexican Americans, and the Transnational Struggle for Civil Rights in World War II Texas," *Journal of American History*, 92.4 (2006), 1212–1237; Benjamin Heber Johnson, *Revolution in Texas: How a Forgotten Rebellion and Its Bloody Suppression Turned Mexicans into Americans* (New Haven: Yale University Press, 2003); Martha Menchaca, *Recovering History, Constructing Race: The Indian, Black, and White Roots of Mexican Americans* (Austin: University of Texas Press, 2001); Charles Montgomery, "The Trap of Race and Memory: The Language of Spanish Civility on the Upper Rio Grande," *American Quarterly*, 52.3 (2000), 478–513; John M. Nieto-Phillips, *The Language of Blood: The Making of Spanish-American Identity in New Mexico, 1880s–1930s* (Albuquerque: University of New Mexico Press,

2004); Clara E. Rodríguez, *Changing Race: Latinos, the Census, and the History of Ethnicity in the United States* (New York: NYU Press, 2000); George J. Sánchez, *Becoming Mexican American* (New York: Oxford, 1993).

83. Useful sources on the history of racial theory and pseudoscientific racialism include Bruce Baum, *The Rise and Fall of the Caucasian Race* (New York: NYU Press, 2006); Emmanuel Chukwudi Eze, Ed., *Race and the Enlightenment* (Oxford: Blackwell, 1997); Thomas F. Gossett, *Race: The History of an Idea in America* (New York: Schocken, 1965); Stephen Jay Gould, *The Mismeasure of Man*, rev. ed. (New York: Norton, 1996); Joseph L. Graves, Jr., *The Emperor's New Clothes: Biological Theories of Race at the Millennium* (New Brunswick, NJ: Rutgers University Press, 2001); John P. Jackson Jr., Ed. *Science, Race, and Ethnicity* (Chicago: University of Chicago Press, 2002); James C. King, *The Biology of Race* (Berkeley: University of California Press, 1981); Jonathan Marks, *Human Biodiversity: Genes, Race, and History* (New York: Aldine de Gruyter, 1995); Ashley Montagu, *Man's Most Dangerous Myth: The Fallacy of Race* (New York: World, 1964); Marion O'Callaghan, Ed., *Sociological Theories: Race and Colonialism* (Paris: Unesco, 1980); Audrey Smedley, *Race in North America*, 2nd ed. (Boulder, CO: Westview, 1999); William H. Tucker, *The Science and Politics of Racial Research* (Urbana: University of Illinois Press, 1994).

84. Linneaus's masterwork is *Systema Naturae* (1758), translated as *The System of Nature* (London: Lackington, Allen, 1806).

85. Georges-Louis Leclerc, comte de Buffon, *A Natural History, General and Particular*, 2nd ed. (London: Strahan and Cadell, 1785).

86. Johann Friedrich Blumenbach, *On the Natural Varieties of Mankind* (New York: Bergman, 1969; orig. English 1865; orig. German 1775); Blumenbach, *The Anthropological Treatises of Johann Friedrich Blumenbach* (Boston: Milford House, 1973, orig. 1865).

87. Georges Léopold Cuvier, *Le Règne Animal* (1817), translated into English as *Animal Kingdom* (London: W. S. Orr, 1840). Quotation is taken from Eze, *Race and the Enlightenment*, 105.

88. Arthur de Gobineau, *The Inequality of Human Races* (New York: Fertig, 1999; English orig. 1915; French orig. 1853–55), v–vl, 151; Michael D. Biddiss, *Father of Racist Ideology: The Social and Political Thought of Count Gobineau* (New York: Weybright and Talley, 1970); Biddiss, Ed., *Gobineau: Selected Political Writings* (New York: Harper and Row, 1970).

89. William Z. Ripley, *The Races of Europe* (New York: Appleton, 1899).

90. A. H. Keane, *Ethnology* (Cambridge: Cambridge University Press, 1901), 224.

91. United States Commissioner-General of Immigration, *Annual Report, 1904* (Washington, 1904), endpaper; United States Congress, *Reports of the Immigration Commission* (61st Congress, 3rd Session), Volume 5: *Dictionary of Races or Peoples* (Washington, 1910–11).

92. Alfred P. Schultz, *Race or Mongrel?* (Boston: Page, 1908).

93. Madison Grant, *The Passing of the Great Race, or The Racial Basis of European History* (New York: Scribner's, 1916); quote is from 80–81. The German edition is *Der Untergang der grossen Rasse: Die Rassen als Grundlage der Geschichte Europas* (München: J. F. Lehmanns Verlag, 1925).

94. Lothrop Stoddard, *The Rising Tide of Color Against White World Supremacy* (New York: Scribner's, 1920).

95. B. L. Putnam Weale, *The Conflict of Colour* (New York: Macmillan, 1910); Lothrop Stoddard, *The Revolt Against Civilization: The Menace of the Under Man* (New York: Scribner's, 1923); F. G. Crookshank, *The Mongol in Our Midst* (New York: Dutton, 1924); Lothrop Stoddard, *Racial Realities in Europe* (New York: Scribner's, 1924); Maurice Muret, *The Twilight of the White Races* (New York: Scribner's, 1926); Hans F. K. Günther, *The Racial Elements in World History* (London: Methuen, 1927); Madison Grant and Charles Stewart Davison, Eds., *The Alien in Our Midst, or "Selling our Birthright for a Mess of Pottage"* (New York: Galton, 1930); Lothrop Stoddard, *Clashing Tides of Colour* (New York: Scribner's, 1935); Earnest Albert Hooton, *Apes, Men and Morons* (New York: Putnam's, 1937); Hooton, *Twilight of Man* (New York: Putnam's, 1939).

96. Sources on eugenics include Edwin Black, *War Against the Weak: Eugenics and America's Campaign to Create a Master Race* (New York: Four Walls Eight Windows, 2003); Laura Briggs, *Reproducing Empire: Race, Sex, Science, and U.S. Imperialism in Puerto Rico* (Berkeley: University of California, 2002); Susan Currell and Christina Cogdell, Eds., *Popular Eugenics* (Columbus: Ohio State University Press, 2006); Amy L. Fairchild, *Science at the Borders: Immigrant Medical Inspection and the Shaping of the Modern Industrial Labor Force* (Baltimore: Johns Hopkins University Press, 2003); Mark H. Haller, *Eugenics* (New Brunswick, NJ: Rutgers University Press, 1963); Daniel J. Kevles, *In the Name of Eugenics* (Cambridge, MA: Harvard University Press, 1986); Nancy Ordover, *American Eugenics: Race, Queer Anatomy, and the Science of Nationalism* (Minneapolis: University of Minnesota Press, 2003); Alexandra Minna Stern, *Eugenic Nation: Faults and Frontiers of Better Breeding in Modern America* (Berkeley: University of California Press, 2005); Tukufi Zuberi, *Thicker Than Blood: How Racial Statistics Lie* (Minneapolis: University of Minnesota Press, 2001), esp. Chapters 3–5.

97. Sources on intelligence testing include Alfred Binet, *The Development of Intelligence in Children*, trans. Elizabeth S. Kite (Baltimore: Williams and Wilkins, 1916); N. J. Block and Gerald Dworkin, Eds., *The IQ Controversy* (New York: Pantheon, 1976); Jeffrey M. Blum, *Pseudoscience and Mental Ability* (New York: Monthly Review, 1978); Paul L. Boynton, *Intelligence: Its Manifestations and Measurement* (New York: Appleton, 1933); Hans J. Eysenck, *Intelligence* (New Brunswick, NJ: Transaction, 1998); Jefferson M. Fish, Ed., *Race and Intelligence* (Mahwah, NJ: Lawrence Erlbaum, 2002); Henry H. Goddard, *The Criminal Imbecile* (New York: Macmillan, 1915); Goddard, *Feeble-mindedness: Its Causes and Consequences* (New York: Macmillan, 1914); Goddard, *The Kallikak Family: A Study in Heredity of Feeble-Mindedness* (New York: Macmillan, 1912); Goddard, *School Training of Defective Children* (Yonkers-on-Hudson, NY: World Book, 1914); Stephen Jay Gould, *The Mismeasure of Man*, rev. ed. (New York: Norton, 1996); Seymour W. Itzkoff, *The Decline of Intelligence in America* (Westport, CT: Praeger, 1994); Nicholas Lemann, *The Big Test: The Secret History of the American Meritocracy* (New York: Farrar, Straus and Giroux, 2000); Henry L. Minton, *Lewis M. Terman: Pioneer in Psychological Testing* (New York: NYU Press, 1988); Ashley Montagu, Ed., *Race and IQ* (New York: Oxford, 1999); J. David Smith, *Minds Made Feeble: The Myth and Legacy of the Kallikaks* (Rockville, MD: Aspen Systems, 1985); Theta H. Wolf, *Alfred Binet* (Chicago: University of Chicago Press, 1973); Leila Zenderland, *Measuring Minds: Henry Herbert Goddard and the Origins of American Intelligence Testing* (Cambridge: Cambridge University Press, 1998).

98. Quoted in Kevles, *In the Name of Eugenics*, 81.

99. Henry H. Goddard, "Mental Tests and the Immigrant," *Journal of Delinquency*, 2 (1917), 243–277; Gould, *Mismeasure*, 165. Historian Patrick Miller writes, "Goddard claimed that he could spot a moron amidst the mass of immigrants coming through Ellis Island—not just with the test but by eye—which may give new meaning to the word 'moron.'" Private communication with the author, April 14, 2004.

100. Carl Campbell Brigham, *A Study of American Intelligence* (Princeton, NJ: Princeton University Press, 1923), 197, quoted in Kevles, *In the Name of Eugenics*, 82–83. African Americans also were supposedly inferior to Whites. But differential access to education played a part. Midwestern Blacks scored higher on Brigham's measures of intelligence than did Southern Whites.

101. Caroline Bond Day, *A Study of Some Negro-White Families in the United States* (Cambridge, MA: Peabody Museum, 1932).

102. Julie P. Kelley, "A Study of Eyefold Inheritance in Inter-Racial Marriages" (MS thesis, University of Hawai'i, 1960); Sidney L Gulick, *Mixing the Races in Hawaii* (Honolulu: Hawaiian Board, 1937). See also Louis Wirth's chapter on "The Jewish Type" in *The Ghetto* (Chicago: University of Chicago Press, 1926).

103. Frank H. Hankins, *The Racial Basis of Civilization: A Critique of the Nordic Doctrine* (New York: Knopf, 1926); Franz Boas, *Race, Language, and Culture* (New York: Free Press, 1940); Edward H. Beardsley, "The American Scientist as Social Activist: Franz Boas, Burt G. Wilder, and the Cause of Racial Justice," *Isis*, 64 (1973), 50–66; Elazar Barkan, *The Retreat of Scientific Racism* (Cambridge: Cambridge University Press, 1992).

104. Carleton Stevens Coon, *The Races of Europe* (New York: Macmillan, 1939); Coon, *The Story of Man* (New York: Knopf, 1954); Coon, *The Origin of Races* (New York: Knopf, 1962); Coon, *The Living Races of Man* (New York: Knopf, 1965); Coon, *Racial Adaptations* (Chicago: Nelson-Hall, 1982); Wesley Critz George, *The Biology of the Race Problem* (Richmond, VA: Patrick Henry Press, 1962); John P. Jackson, Jr., *Science for Segregation: Race, Law, and the Case Against Brown v. Board of Education* (New York: NYU Press, 2005); Carleton Putnam, *Race and Reason* (Washington, DC: Public Affairs, 1961); Putnam, *Race and Reality* (Washington, DC: Public Affairs, 1967).

105. Pierre L. van den Berghe, *The Ethnic Phenomenon* (New York: Elsevier, 1981); J. Barkow, Leda Cosmides, and John Tooby, *The Adapted Mind: Evolutionary Psychology and the Generation of Culture* (New York: Oxford, 1992).

106. Richard J. Herrnstein and Charles Murray, *The Bell Curve: Intelligence and Class Structure in American Life* (New York: Free Press, 1994); Peter Brimelow, *Alien Nation: Common Sense about America's Immigration Disaster* (New York: Random House, 1995); Samuel P. Huntington, *The Clash of Civilizations* (New York: Simon and Schuster, 1996); Jon Entine, *Taboo: Why Black Athletes Dominate Sports and Why We're Afraid to Talk About It* (New York: Public Affairs, 2000); Patrick J. Buchanan, *The Death of the West: How Dying Populations and Immigrant Invasions Imperil Our County and Civilization* (New York: St. Martin's, 2002). Cultural historian Patrick Miller refers to these books as "airplane reading for bigots" (private communication with the author, 2006).

107. Sources on the anti-Japanese movement include Roger Daniels, *The Politics of Prejudice: The Anti-Japanese Movement in California and the Struggle for Japanese Exclusion* (Berkeley: University of California Press, 1962);

Montaville Flowers, *The Japanese Conquest of American Opinion* (New York: Doran, 1917); Bill Ong Hing, *Making and Remaking Asian America Through Immigration Policy, 1850–1990* (Stanford, CA: Stanford University Press, 1993); Yamato Ichihashi, *Japanese in the United States* (Stanford, CA: Stanford University Press, 1932); Ichioka, *Issei*; Charles McClain, Ed., *Japanese Immigrants and American Law* (New York: Garland, 1994); Jesse F. Steiner, *The Japanese Invasion* (Chicago: McClurg, 1917). Some of the language in this section is taken from Paul Spickard, *Japanese Americans* (New York: Twayne, 1996), 27–30, 57–63.

108. Asiatic Exclusion League of North America, *Preamble and Constitution, 1905*, quoted in Eliot G. Mears, *Resident Orientals of the American Pacific Coast* (Chicago: University of Chicago Press, 1928), 435. It should be noted that, while much of the driving force behind the anti-Asian movements came from labor organizations and anti-Japanese sentiment came articulated in the language of twin defenses of American working people and the White race, one large labor organization—the Industrial Workers of the World—adamantly opposed race discrimination.

109. *San Francisco Chronicle*, February 13–March 13, 1095, passim, quoted in Roger Daniels, *Asian America* (Seattle: University of Washington Press, 1988), 116.

110. Quoted in Daniels, *Politics of Prejudice*, 47.

111. Quoted in Robert Higgs, "Landless by Law: Japanese Immigrants in California Agriculture to 1941," *Journal of American Economic History*, 38 (1978), 215. See also Charles McClain, Ed., *Japanese Immigrants and American Law: The Alien land Laws and Other issues* (New York: Garland, 1994).

112. Japanese were not the only Asians who came under attack in the first decades of the twentieth century. Throughout the 1920s and into the 1930s, Filipinos were subject to repeated assaults and harassment by angry Whites. See Bruno Lasker, *Filipino Immigration* (Chicago: University of Chicago Press, 1931), esp. 13–20.

113. Sources for this section include James R. Barrett, "Americanization from the Bottom Up: Immigration and the Remaking of the Working Class in the United States, 1880–1930," *Journal of American History* (1992), 996–1020; Clifford S. Griffin, "Religious Benevolence as Social Control," *Mississippi Valley Historical Review*, 44 (1957), 423–444; John Higham, *Strangers in the Land: Patterns of American Nativism, 1860–1925* (New Brunswick, NJ: Rutgers University Press, 1998; orig. 1955), 234–263; Stephen Meyer, "Efforts at Americanization in the Industrial Workplace, 1914–1921," *Journal of Social History*, 14.1 (1980); Anne-Elizabeth Murdy, *Teach the Nation: Pedagogies of Racial Uplift in US Women's Writing in the 1890s* (New York: Routledge, 2002); Eileen H. Tamura, *Americanization, Acculturation, and Ethnic Identity: The Nisei Generation in Hawai'i* (Honolulu: University of Hawai'i Press, 1994); Frank Van Nuys, *Americanizing the West: Race, Immigrants, and Citizenship, 1890–1930* (Lawrence: University Press of Kansas, 2002). See also note 12.

114. David Brion Davis, Ed., *Ante-Bellum Reform* (New York: Harper and Row, 1967); Paul E. Johnson, *A Shopkeeper's Millennium: Society and Revivals in Rochester, New York, 1815–1837* (New York: Hill and Wang, 1978); Henry F. May, *Protestant Churches and Industrial America* (New York: Harper, 1967); Timothy L. Smith, *Revivalism and Social Reform* (Baltimore: Johns Hopkins University Press, 1980); Ronald G. Walters, *American Reformers* (New York: Hill and Wang, 1978).

115. Meyer, "Efforts at Americanization."

116. Published by Harper and Brothers between 1920 and 1924, the volumes were Frank V. Thompson, *Schooling of the Immigrant*; John Daniels, *America via the Neighborhood*; William I. Thomas, *Old World Traits Transplanted*; Peter A. Speek, *A Stake in the Land*; Michael M. Davis, Jr., *Immigrant Health and the Community*; Sophonsba B. Breckinridge, *New Homes for Old*; Robert E. Park, *The Immigrant Press and Its Control*; John Palmer Gavit, *Americans by Choice*; Kate Holladay Claghorn, *The Immigrant's Day in Court*; and William M. Leiserson, *Adjusting Immigrant and Industry*.

117. Examples of these studies, many of them quite distinguished, include: Romanzo C. Adams, *Interracial Marriage in Hawai'i* (New York: Macmillan, 1937); Adams, *The Peoples of Hawai'i* (Honolulu: Institute for Pacific Relations, 1933); Emory S. Bogardus, *Essentials of Americanization* (Los Angeles: University of Southern California Press, 1919); St. Clair Drake and Horace R. Cayton, *Black Metropolis: A Study of Negro Life in a Northern City* (New York: Harcourt, Brace, 1945); Clarence E. Glick, *Sojourners and Settlers: Chinese Migrants in Hawai'i* (Honolulu: University Press of Hawai'i, 1980); Rose Hum Lee, *The Chinese in the United States of America* (Hong Kong: Hong Kong University Press, 1960); Andrew W. Lind, *Hawai'i's Japanese* (Princeton, NJ: Princeton University Press, 1946); Lind, *Hawai'i's People* (Honolulu: University of Hawai'i Press, 1955); Jitsuichi Masaoka and Preston Valien, Eds., *Race Relations* (Chapel Hill: University of North Carolina Press, 1961); Mears, *Resident Orientals*; S. Frank Miyamoto, *Social Solidarity among the Japanese in Seattle* (Seattle: University of Washington Press, 1984; orig. 1939); Robert Ezra Park, *Race and Culture* (New York: Free Press, 1964); Park and Herbert Miller, *Old World Traits Transplanted* (New York: Harper, 1921); Edward B. Reuter, *Race Mixture* (New York: McGraw-Hill, 1931); Paul C. P. Siu, *The Chinese Laundryman* (New York: NYU Press, 1987; orig. 1953); William Carlson Smith, "Changing Personality Traits of Second Generational Orientals in America," *American Journal of Sociology*, 33 (1928); Steiner, *Japanese Invasion*; William I. Thomas and Florian Znaniecki, *The Polish Peasant in Europe and America*, 4 vols. (Chicago: University of Chicago press, 1918–1920). Each of these scholars nurtured dozens of students in similar tasks; some, such as Bogardus and Lind, built student factories that put out dozens of studies. For analysis, see Lori Pierce, "Creating a Racial Paradise: Citizenship and Sociology in Hawai'i," in *Race and Nation: Ethnic Systems in the Modern World*, Paul Spickard, Ed. (New York: Routledge, 2005), 69–86; Henry Yu, *Thinking Orientals: Migration, Contact, and Exoticism in Modern America* (New York: Oxford, 2001).

118. Robert MacNeil and William Cran, *Do You Speak American?* (New York: Harcourt, 2005), 95–96.

119. Sources on the anti-immigration movement include pre-eminently, Roger Daniels, *Guarding the Golden Door: American Immigration Policy and Immigrants Since 1882* (New York: Hill and Wang, 2004); also Otis L. Graham, *Unguarded Gates: A History of America's Immigration Crisis* (Lanham, MD: Rowman and Littlefield, 2004); John Higham, *Strangers in the Land: Patterns of American Nativism, 1860–1925* (New Brunswick, NJ: Rutgers University Press, 1992; orig. 1955); Kevin R. Johnson, *The "Huddled Masses" Myth: Immigration and Civil Rights* (Philadelphia: Temple University Press, 2004); Desmond King, *Making Americans: Immigration, Race, and the Origins of the Diverse Democracy* (Cambridge, MA: Harvard University Press, 2000); Dale

T. Knobel, *America for the Americans: The Nativist Movement in the United States* (New York: Twayne, 1996); Eithne Luihéid, *Entry Denied: Controlling Sexuality at the Border* (Minneapolis: University of Minnesota Press, 2002); Mae M. Ngai, *Impossible Subjects: Illegal Aliens and the Making of Modern America* (Princeton, NJ: Princeton University Press, 2004).

120. *Reports of the Immigration Commission*, 42 vols. (Washington, DC: Government Printing Office, 1911); Robert F. Zeidel, *Immigrants, Progressives, and Exclusion Politics: The Dillingham Commission, 1900–1927* (DeKalb: Northern Illinois University Press, 2004).

121. *Reports of the Immigration Commission*, vol. 1, pp. 45–48.

122. Michael LeMay and Elliott Robert Barkan, Eds., *US Immigration and Naturalization Laws and Issues* (Westport, CT: Greenwood, 1999), 133–135.

123. LeMay and Barkan, *US Immigration and Naturalization Laws and Issues*, 141–144.

124. Speech by Ellison DuRant Smith, April 9, 1924, *Congressional Record*, 68th Congress, 1st Session, vol. 65 (Washington, DC: Government Printing Office, 1924), 5961–5962.

125. Quoted in Hing, *Defining America Through Immigration Policy*, 3.

126. See Appendix B, Tables 2, 6, 12, 13, 31.

127. Sources on Orientalism include Herodotus, *The Persian Wars*, trans. Aubrey de Selincourt (Baltimore: Penguin, 1954); Christina Klein, *Cold War Orientalism: Asia in the Middlebrow Imagination, 1945–1961* (Berkeley: University of California Press, 2003; Robert G. Lee, *Orientals: Asian Americans in Popular Culture* (Philadelphia: Temple University Press, 1999); Karen J. Leong, *The China Mystique: Pearl S. Buck, Anna May Wong, Mayling Soong, and the Transformation of American Orientalism* (Berkeley: University of California Press, 2005); Douglas Little, *American Orientalism: The United States and the Middle East Since 1945* (Chapel Hill: University of North Carolina Press, 2002); Sheng-Mei Ma, *The Deathly Embrace: Orientalism and Asian American Identity* (Minneapolis: University of Minnesota Press, 2000); A. L. Macfie, *Orientalism* (London: Longman, 2002); A. L. Macfie, Ed., *Orientalism: A Reader* (New York: NYU Press, 2000); Stuart Creighton Miller, *The Unwelcome Immigrant: The American Image of the Chinese, 1785–1882* (Berkeley: University of California Press, 1969); *Orientalism and the Legacy of Edward Said*, special issue of *Amerasia Journal*, 31.1 (2005); Edward Said, *Orientalism* (New York: Pantheon, 1978); Mia Tuan, *Forever Foreigners or Honorary Whites? The Asian Ethnic Experience Today* (New Brunswick, NJ: Rutgers University Press, 1998); Mari Yoshihara, *Embracing the East: White Women and American Orientalism* (New York: Oxford University Press, 2002).

128. *Jamali: Mystical Expressionism* (Boston: Rizolli International Publications, 1997). Needless to say, this characterization of Sufis is wildly off the mark.

129. James A. Michener, *Hawaii* (New York: Random House, 1959); *Sayonara* (New York: Random House, 1954); *Tales of the South Pacific* (New York: Macmillan, 1946); Arthur Golden, *Memoirs of a Geisha* (New York: Knopf, 1997).

130. Sources on ethnic festivals include Olivia Cadaval, *Creating a Latino Identity in the Nation's Capital: The Latino Festival* (New York: Garland, 1998); Pamela R. Frese, Ed., *Celebrations of Identity: Multiple Voices in American Ritual Performance* (Westport, CT: Bergin and Garvey, 1993); David Glassbert, *American Historical Pageantry: The Uses of Tradition in the Early*

Twentieth Century (Chapel Hill: University of North Carolina Press, 1990); Rosemary Gong, *Good Luck Life: The Essential Guide to Chinese American Celebrations and Culture* (New York: HarperCollins, 2005); Ramón Gutiérrez and Geneviève Fabre, Eds., *Feasts and Celebrations in North American Ethnic Communities* (Albuquerque: University of New Mexico Press, 1995); Lon Kurashige, *Japanese American Celebration and Conflict: A History of Ethnic Identity and Festival in Los Angeles, 1934–1990* (Berkeley: University of California Press, 2002); Shelley Sang-Hee Lee, "Cosmopolitan Identities: Japanese Americans in Seattle and the Pacific Rim, 1900–1924," (PhD dissertation, Stanford University, 2005); Kenneth H. Marcus, "Ethnic Identity on Stage: The Art of the Mexican Players and the Ramona Pageant," paper presented to the Pacific Coast Branch-American Historical Association, Corvallis, OR (August 6, 2005); Valerie Menard, *The Latino Holiday Book* (New York: Marlowe, 2000); Lori Pierce, "'The Whites Have Created Modern Honolulu': Ethnicity, Racial Stratification, and the Discourse of Aloha," in *Racial Thinking in the United States*, Paul Spickard and G. Reginald Daniel, Eds. (Notre Dame, IN: University of Notre Dame Press, 2004), 124–154; April R. Schultz, *Ethnicity on Parade: Inventing the Norwegian American through Celebration* (Amherst: University of Massachusetts Press, 1995); Dorothy Gladys Spicer, *Folk Festivals and the Foreign Community* (New York: The Womans Press, 1923).

131. Kwanzaa is one of these, created in 1966 as a pan-African American alternative to Christmas and Hanukah. Elizabeth Pleck, "Kwanzaa: The Making of a Black Nationalist Tradition, 1966–1990," *Journal of American History*, 20.4 (2001), 3–28.

132. Sources for this section include Rosemarie K. Bank, "Representing History: Performing the Columbian Exposition," *Theatre Journal*, 54 (2002), 589–606; Phillips Verner Bradford and Harvey Blume, *Ota Benga: The Pygmy in the Zoo* (New York: Dell, 1992); Janet M. Davis, *The Circus Age: Culture and Society Under the American Big Top* (Chapel Hill: University of North Carolina Press, 2002); Joy S. Kasson, *Buffalo Bill's Wild West* (New York: Hill and Wang, 2000); Theodora Kroeber, *Ishi in Two Worlds: A Biography of the Last Wild Indian in North America* (Berkeley: University of California Press, 1961); Robert W. Rydell, *All the World's a Fair: Visions of Empire at American International Expositions, 1876–1916* (Chicago: University of Chicago Press, 1984); *The Secret Museum of Mankind* (Salt Lake City: Gibbs Smith, 1999; orig. 1941?); Carol Spindel, *Dancing at Halftime: Sports and the Controversy over American Indian Mascots* (New York: NYU Press, 2000); Judith Snodgrass, *Presenting Japanese Buddhism to the West: Orientalism, Occidentalism and the Columbian Exposition* (Chapel Hill: University of North Carolina Press, 2003); Louis S. Warren, *Buffalo Bill's America: William Cody and the Wild West Show* (New York: Knopf, 2005); Orin Starn, *Ishi's Brain: In Search of America's Last "Wild" Indian* (New York: Norton, 2005).

133. On North Africa, see Taoufik Djebali, "Ethnicity and Power in North Africa: Tunisia, Algeria, and Morocco," in *Race and Nation: Ethnic Systems in the Modern World*, Paul Spickard, Ed. (New York: Routledge, 2005), 135–154.

134. Matthew Frye Jacobson, *Whiteness of a Different Color: European Immigrants and the Alchemy of Race* (Cambridge, MA: Harvard University Press, 1998); Karen Brodkin, *How Jews Became White Folks and What That Says About Race in America* (New Brunswick, NJ: Rutgers University Press, 1998).

135. David Gerber, *Anti-Semitism in America* (Urbana: University of Illinois Press, 1986); Leonard Dinnerstein, *Uneasy at Home* (New York: Columbia University Press, 1987); Richard Hofstadter, *The Age of Reform* (New York: Knopf, 1955), 70–81.

136. Jacobson, *Whiteness of a Different Color*, 63–68; Jeffrey Melnick, *Black-Jewish Relations on Trial: Leo Frank and Jim Conley in the New South* (Jackson: University Press of Mississippi, 2000); Steve Oney, *And the Dead Shall Rise: The Murder of Mary Phagan and the Lynching of Leo Frank* (New York: Pantheon, 2003).

137. On the racialization of religion, see Henry Goldschmidt and Elizabeth McAlister, Eds., *Race, Nation, and Religion in the Americas* (New York: Oxford, 2004).

Chapter 7

1. Appendix B, Table 31.
2. For literary treatments, see Julia Alvarez, *How the García Girls Lost Their Accents* (New York: Workman, 1991); Sandra Cisneros, *Caramelo* (New York: Knopf, 2002); Cisneros, *The House on Mango Street* (New York: Vintage, 1989); Cisneros, *Woman Hollering Creek and Other Stories* (New York: Vintage, 1991); Alfred Kazin, *A Walker in the City* (New York: Harcourt, Brace, 1951); Maxine Hong Kingston, *The Woman Warrior* (New York: Knopf, 1976); C. Y. Lee, *The Flower Drum Song* (New York: Farrar, Straus and Cudahy, 1957); Gus Lee, *China Boy* (New York: Dutton, 1991); Pardee Lowe, *Father and Glorious Descendant* (Boston: Little, Brown, 1943); Lin Yutang, *Chinatown Family* (New York: John Day, 1948); Bernard Malamud, *The Assistant* (New York: Farrar, Straus and Giroux, 1957); Toshio Mori, *Yokohama, California* (Seattle: University of Washington Press, 1985; orig. 1949); John Okada, *No-No Boy* (Rutland, VT: Tuttle, 1957); Chaim Potok, *The Chosen* (New York: Simon and Schuster, 1967); Richard Rodriguez, *Days of Obligation: An Argument with My Mexican Father* (New York: Viking, 1992); Rodriguez, *Hunger of Memory* (New York: Godine, 1982); Henry Roth, *Call It Sleep* (New York: Cooper Square, 1934); Ramon Eduardo Ruiz, *Memories of a Hyphenated Man* (Tucson: University of Arizona Press, 2005); Monica Sone, *Nisei Daughter* (Boston: Little, Brown, 1953); Amy Tan, *The Joy Luck Club* (New York: Putnam's, 1989); Yoshiko Uchida, *A Jar of Dreams* (New York: Macmillan, 1981); Uchida, *The Best Bad Thing* (New York: Macmillan, 1983); Jade Snow Wong, *Fifth Chinese Daughter* (Seattle: University of Washington Press, 1989; orig. 1945); Anzia Yezierska, *Bread Givers* (New York: Doubleday, 1925).

   Analytical treatments include Richard D. Alba, *Italian Americans* (Englewood Cliffs, NJ: Prentice-Hall, 1985); John J. Bukowczyk, *And My Children Did Not Know Me* (Bloomington: Indiana University Press, 1987); Niles Carpenter, *Immigrants and Their Children, 1920* (Washington, DC: Government Printing Office, 1917); Mary Yu Danico, *The 1.5 Generation: Becoming Korean American in Hawai'i* (Honolulu: University of Hawai'i Press, 2004); Mario T. García, *Mexican Americans: Leadership, Ideology and Identity, 1930–1960* (New Haven, CT : Yale University Press, 1989); Bill Hosokawa, *Nisei: The Quiet Americans* (New York: Morrow, 1969); Harry H. L. Kitano, *Japanese Americans*, 2nd ed. (Englewood Cliffs, NJ: Prentice-Hall, 1976); Karen Isaaksen Leonard, *Making Ethnic Choices: California's Punjabi Mexican Americans*

(Philadelphia: Temple University Press, 1992); Daisuke Kitagawa, *Issei and Nisei* (New York: Seabury, 1967); Lon Kurashige, *Japanese American Celebration and Conflict* (Berkeley: University of California Press, 2002); Timothy J. Meagher, *Inventing Irish America: Generation, Class, and Ethnic Identity in a New England City, 1880–1928* (Notre Dame, IN: University of Notre Dame Press, 2001); Deborah Dash Moore, *At Home in America: Second Generation New York Jews* (New York: Columbia University Press, 1981); Alejandro Portes and Rubén G. Rumbaut, *Legacies: The Story of the Immigrant Second Generation* (Berkeley: University of California Press, 2001); George J. Sánchez, *Becoming Mexican American* (New York: Oxford, 1993); Miri Song, *Helping Out: Children's Labor in Ethnic Businesses* (Philadelphia: Temple University Press, 1999); Paul Spickard, "The Nisei Assume Power: The Japanese American Citizens League, 1941–1942," *Pacific Historical Review*, 52 (1983), 147–174; Everett V. Stonequist, *The Marginal Man: A Study in Personality and Culture Conflict* (New York: Scribner's, 1937), 96–106; Edward K. Strong, *The Second-Generation Japanese Problem* (Stanford, CA: Stanford University Press, 1934); W. Lloyd Warner, J. O. Low, Paul S. Lunt, and Leo Srole, *Yankee City*, abr. ed. (New Haven: Yale University Press, 1963), 425; Judy Yung, *Unbound Feet: A Social History of Chinese Women in San Francisco* (Berkeley: University of California Press, 1995).

3. Don Normark, *Chávez Ravine, 1949* (San Francisco: Chronicle Books, 1999), 76.

4. Leo Rosten, *The Joys of Yiddish* (New York: Pocket Books, 1968), ix–xiv and *passim*; Robert MacNeil and William Cran, *Do You Speak American?* (New York: Harcourt, 2005).

5. Alba, *Italian Americans*, 59–60.

6. Potok, *The Chosen*; Wong, *Fifth Chinese Daughter*.

7. Spickard, "Nisei Assume Power."

8. Yezierska, *Bread Givers*, 171–172.

9. Okada, *No-No Boy*, 34–35; Sánchez, *Becoming Mexican American*; Bukowczyk, *And My Children Did Not Know Me*, 65. They were not, in my estimate moving "into the twilight of ethnicity"; cf. Alba, *Italian Americans: Into the Twilight of Ethnicity.*

10. Marcus Lee Hansen, "The Problem of the Third Generation Immigrant," *Augustana Historical Society Publications* (Rock Island, IL: Augustana Historical Society, 1938), 5–20; Michael Novak, *The Rise of the Unmeltable Ethnics* (New York: Macmillan, 1973).

11. Sources for Mexican migrants in this period include Rodolfo E. Acuña, *A Community Under Siege: A Chronicle of Chicanos East of the Los Angeles River, 1945–1975* (Los Angeles: UCLA Chicano Studies Center, 1984); John H. Burma, Ed., *Mexican-Americans in the United States* (Cambridge, MA: Schenkman, 1970); Edward J. Escobar, *Race, Police, and the Making of a Political Identity: Mexican Americans and the Los Angeles Police Department, 1900–1945* (Berkeley: University of California Press, 1999); Neil Foley, *The White Scourge: Mexicans, Blacks, and Poor Whites in Texas Cotton Culture* (Berkeley: University of California Press, 1997); Ernesto Galarza, *Barrio Boy* (Notre Dame, IN: University of Notre Dame Press, 1971); García, *Mexican Americans*; Richard Griswold del Castillo, *La Familia: Chicano Families in the Urban Southwest 1848 to the Present* (Notre Dame, IN: University of Notre Dame Press, 1984); David G. Gutiérrez, *Walls and Mirrors: Mexican*

Americans, Mexican Immigrants, and the Politics of Ethnicity (Berkeley: University of California Press, 1995); Carey McWilliams, *North from Mexico* (Philadelphia: Lippincott, 1948); David Montejano, *Anglos and Mexicans in the Making of Texas, 1836–1986* (Austin: University of Texas Press, 1987); Vicki L. Ruiz, *From Out Of The Shadows: Mexican Women in Twentieth-Century America* (New York: Oxford, 1998); *Salt of the Earth*, dir. Herbert Biberman (Oak Forest, IL: MPI Home Video, 1987; orig. 1953); Sánchez, *Becoming Mexican American*; Zaragosa Vargas, *Labor Rights Are Civil Rights: Mexican American Workers in Twentieth-Century America* (Princeton, NJ: Princeton University Press, 2005); Zaragosa Vargas, Ed., *Major Problems in Mexican American History* (Boston: Houghton Mifflin, 1999).

12. Grant McConnell, *The Decline of Agrarian Democracy* (Berkeley: University of California Press, 1953).

13. Gutiérrez, *Walls and Mirrors*.

14. McWilliams, *North from Mexico*, 215; McWilliams, *Factories in the Field: The Story of Migratory Farm Labor in California* (Santa Barbara: Peregrine Smith, 1971; orig. 1935).

15. McWilliams, *North from Mexico*, 215–216.

16. David Torres-Rouff, "Making Los Angeles: Race, Space, and Municipal Power, 1822–1890" (PhD dissertation, University of California, Santa Barbara, 2006); Alicia Rivera, "The *Lemon Grove* Case and School Segregation in the Southwest," *Journal of Latino-Latin American Studies*, 1.3 (2004), 105–118.

17. Sources for the repatriation interlude include Francisco E. Balderrama and Raymond Rodríguez, *Decade of Betrayal: Mexican Repatriation in the 1930s* (Albuquerque: University of New Mexico Press, 1995); Camille Guerin-Gonzales, *Mexican Workers and the American Dream: Immigration, Repatriation, and California Farm Labor, 1900–1939* (New Brunswick, NJ: Rutgers University Press, 1994); Abraham Hoffman, *Unwanted Mexican Americans in the Great Depression: Repatriation Pressures, 1929–1939* (Tucson: University of Arizona Press, 1974).

18. Carey McWilliams, "Getting Rid of the Mexicans," *American Mercury*, 28 (March 1933).

19. Gregg Jones, "Apology Sought for Latino 'Repatriation' Drive in '30s," *Los Angeles Times* (July 15, 2003).

20. Sources on the Bracero program include Henry P. Anderson, *The Bracero Program in California* (Berkeley: School of Public Health, University of California, 1961); Kitty Calavita, *Inside the State: The Bracero Program, Immigration, and the INS* (New York: Routledge, 1992); Deborah Cohen, "Caught in the Middle: The Mexican State's Relationship with the United States and Its Own Citizen-Workers, 1942–1954," *Journal of American Ethnic History*, 20.3 (Spring 2001), 110–132; Richard B. Craig, *The Bracero Program: Interest Groups and Foreign Policy* (Austin: University of Texas Press, 1971); Barbara A. Driscoll, *The Tracks North: The Railroad Bracero Movement of World War II* (Austin: CMAS Books, 1999); Ernesto Galarza, *Strangers in Our Fields*, 2nd ed. (Washington, DC: Joint United States-Mexico Trade Union Committee, 1956); Erasmo Gamboa, *Mexican Labor and World War II: Braceros in the Pacific Northwest, 1942–1947* (Austin: University of Texas Press, 1990); Richard H. Hancock, *The Role of the Bracero in the Economic and Cultural Dynamics of Mexico* (Stanford, CA: Hispanic American Society, 1959).

21. Edward Lara, "The Bracero Program" (student paper, UC Santa Barbara, 2001).
22. Appendix B, Table 36.
23. Gariot Louima, "Bracero Protest 'Caravan' Comes to LA," *Los Angeles Times* (April 11, 2002); "Mexican Migrants Who Worked in US Push for Old Savings," *New York Times* (February 15, 2004); James F. Smith, "Ex-Migrants Sought for Class-Action," *Los Angeles Times* (March 15, 2001); Laura Wides, "Braceros Rally for Drive to Recover Millions in Missing Wages," *Los Angeles Times* (February 5, 2001); "Braceros Will Get $3,500," *Los Angeles Times* (October 28, 2005).
24. Mae Ngai, *Impossible Subjects: Illegal Aliens and the Making of Modern America* (Princeton, NJ: Princeton University Press, 2004). Kelly Lytle Hernandez is writing a history of the Border Patrol. While we wait for her book, we will have to make do with such as these: Clifford Alan Perkins, *Border Patrol: With the US Immigration Service On the Mexican Boundary 1910–54* (El Paso: Texas Western Press, 1978); Mary Kidder Rak, *Border Patrol* (Boston: Houghton Mifflin, 1938); Rak, *They Guard the Gates* (Evanston, IL: Row, Peterson, 1941). See also Joseph Nevins, *Operation Gatekeeper: The Rise of the "Illegal Alien" and the Making of the US-Mexico Boundary* (New York: Routledge, 2002).
25. The numbers of Border Patrol agents did not jump dramatically again until the 1990s; they went from 3,651 in 1991 to 9,212 in 2000 and 11,200 in 2005; Nevins, *Operation Gatekeeper*, 197; www.cbp.gov (January 10, 2006). Sui Sin Far wrote a vivid account of smuggling Chinese workers across the Canadian border into upstate New York in "The Smuggling of Tie Co," a 1912 story that was reprinted in *Mrs. Spring Fragrance and Other Writings* (Urbana: University of Illinois Press, 1995), 104–109.
26. Juan Ramon García, *Operation Wetback: The Mass Deportation of Mexican Undocumented Workers in 1954* (Westport, CT: Greenwood, 1980); Gutiérrez, *Walls and Mirrors*.
27. Normark, *Chávez Ravine*, 54.
28. Sources on the borderlands and border culture include Ramiro Burr, *Tejano and Regional Mexican Music* (New York: Billboard Books, 1999); Rosa Linda Fregoso, *MeXican Encounters: The Making of Social Identities on the Borderlands* (Berkeley: University of California Press, 2003); Jefferson Morgenthaler, *The River Has Never Divided Us* (Austin: University of Texas Press, 2004); Manuel Peña, *Música Tejana* (College Station: Texas A&M University Press, 1999); Manuel Peña, *The Texas-Mexican Conjunto: History of a Working-Class Music* (Austin: University of Texas Press, 1985); Dorothy Lee Pope, *Rainbow Era on the Rio Grande* (Brownsville, TX: Springman-King, 1971), 89–128; Guadalupe San Miguel, Jr., *Tejano Proud: Tex-Mex Music in the Twentieth Century* (College Station: Texas A&M University Press, 2002); Andrew Grant Wood, Ed., *On the Border: Society and Culture Between the United States and Mexico* (Lanham, MD: SR Books, 2004).
29. Rudy P. Guevarra, Jr., "Burritos and Bagoong: Mexipinos and Multiethnic Identity in San Diego, California," in *Crossing Lines: Race and Mixed Race Across the Geohistorical Divide*, Marc Coronado, Rudy P. Guevarra, Jr., Jeffrey Moniz, and Laura Furlan Szanto, Eds. (Santa Barbara: University of California Santa Barbara Multiethnic Student Outreach, 2003), 73–96; Craig Scharlin and Lilia V. Villanueva, *Philip Vera Cruz* (Los Angeles: UCLA Labor Center, 1994).

30. Carlos Bulosan, *America Is in the Heart* (Seattle: University of Washington Press, 1973; orig. 1946), 143–145.

31. Linda España-Maram, *Creating Masculinity in Los Angeles's Little Manila: Working-Class Filipinos and Popular Culture, 1920s–1950s* (New York: Columbia University Press, 2006); Barbara M. Posadas, *The Filipino Americans* (Westport, CT: Greenwood, 1999); James C. Thomson, Peter W. Stanley, and John Curtis Perry, *Sentimental Imperialists: The American Experience in East Asia* (New York: Harper and Row, 1981).

32. So were workers from Barbados, Jamaica, and British Honduras—all of these countries sent workers to the United States under the Bracero Program. Sources on Puerto Rican immigration include Joseph P. Fitzpatrick, *Puerto Rican Americans* (Englewood Cliffs, NJ: Prentice-Hall, 1987); History Task Force, Centro de Estudios Puertorrriqueños, *Labor Migration Under Capitalism: The Puerto Rican Experience* (New York: Monthly Review Press, 1979); Joan Moore and Harry Pachon, *Hispanics in the United States* (Englewood Cliffs, NJ: Prentice-Hall, 1985); Clara E. Rodríguez, *Puerto Ricans: Born in the USA* (Boulder, CO: Westview, 1991); Edward Rivera, *Family Installments* (New York: Morrow, 1982); Virginia E. Sánchez Korol, *From Colonia to Community: The History of Puerto Ricans in New York City*, rev. ed. (Berkeley: University of California Press, 1994); Stan Steiner, *The Islands: The Worlds of the Puerto Ricans* (New York: Harper and Row, 1974).

33. Census figures for Puerto Rican Americans were:

1930	52,774
1940	69,967
1950	301,375
1960	887,661
1970	1,391,463
1980	2,013,945
1990	2,651,815

Sánchez Korol, *From Colonia to Community,* 213, 216.

34. Sources on American Indians in this period include Vine Deloria, Jr., and Clifford Lytle, *The Nations Within: The Past and Future of American Indian Sovereignty* (New York: Pantheon, 1984); Brian W. Dippie, *The Vanishing American: White Attitudes and US Indian Policy* (Middletown, CT: Wesleyan University Press, 1982); Frederick E. Hoxie, Peter C. Mancall, and James H. Merrell, Eds., *American Nations: Encounters in Indian Country, 1850 to the Present* (New York: Routledge, 2001); Albert L. Hurtado and Peter Iverson, Eds., *Major Problems in American Indian History*, 2nd ed. (Boston: Houghton Mifflin, 2001); Mark Edwin Miller, *Forgotten Tribes: Unrecognized Indians and the Federal Acknowledgment Process* (Lincoln: University of Nebraska Press, 2004); Peter Nabokov, *Native American Testimony*, rev. ed. (New York: Penguin Putnam, 1999); James S. Olson and Raymond Wilson, *Native Americans in the Twentieth Century* (Urbana: University of Illinois Press, 1984); Donald L Parman, *Indians and the American West in the Twentieth Century* (Bloomington:

Indiana University Press, 1994); Francis Paul Prucha, *The Great Father: The United States Government and the American Indians*, abridged ed. (Lincoln: University of Nebraska Press, 1986).

35. Carlos Montezuma, "The Duty of Every Indian Soldier Who Entered the War," *Wassaja* (February 1919), quoted in Hurtado and Iverson, *Major Problems in American Indian History*, 359–360. See also Michael T. Smith, "The History of Indian Citizenship," *Great Plains Journal*, 10 (Fall 1970), 25–35.

36. Additional sources on the Indian New Deal include Thomas Biolsi, *Organizing the Lakota: The Political Economy of the New Deal on the Pine Ridge and Rosebud Reservations* (Tucson: University of Arizona Press, 1992); John Collier, *From Every Zenith: A Memoir and Some Essays on Life and Thought* (Denver: Sage, 1963); Randolph C. Downes, "A Crusade for Indian Reform, 1922–1934," *Mississippi Valley Historical Review*, 32 (1945), 331–354; Laurence M. Hauptman, *The Iroquois and the New Deal* (Syracuse, NY: Syracuse University Press, 1981); Lawrence C. Kelly, *The Assault on Assimilation: John Collier and the Origins of Indian Policy Reform* (Albuquerque: University of New Mexico Press, 1983); Donald L. Parman, *The Navajos and the New Deal* (New Haven, CT: Yale University Press, 1976); Kenneth Philp, Ed., *Indian Self Rule* (Salt Lake City: Howe Brothers, 1986); John C. Savagian, "The Tribal Reorganization of the Stockbridge-Munsee: Essential Conditions in the Re-Creation of a Native American Community, 1930–1942," *Wisconsin Magazine of History* (August 1993), 39–62; Graham D. Taylor, *The New Deal and American Indian Tribalism: The Administration of the Indian Reorganization Act, 1934–1945* (Lincoln: University of Nebraska Press, 1980).

37. Lewis Meriam, *The Problem of Indian Administration* (Baltimore: Johns Hopkins University Press, 1928), 3–8.

38. Nabokov, *Native American Testimony*, 327–329.

39. Additional sources on the termination campaign include Richard Drinnon, *Keeper of Concentration Camps: Dillon S. Myer and American Racism* (Berkeley: University of California Press, 1987); Peter Iverson, "Building Toward Self-Determination in the 1940s and 1950s," *Western Historical Quarterly*, 16.2 (1985), 163–173; Harry A. Kersey, Jr., *An Assumption of Sovereignty: Social and Political Transformation Among the Florida Seminoles, 1953–1979* (Lincoln: University of Nebraska Press, 1996); League of Women Voters, "The Menominee: A Case Against Termination," *The National Voter*, 22.5 (Jan.–Feb. 1973), 17–20; John Wooden Legs, "Back on the War Ponies," *Indian Affairs* (1960), 3–4.

40. Dippie, *Vanishing American*, 337.

41. Nabokov, *Native American Testimony*, 344–347.

42. Sources on Black and White migration during these years include Keith E. Collins, *Black Los Angeles: The Maturing of the Ghetto, 1940–1950* (Saratoga, CA: Century Twenty One Publishing, 1980); Sherna Berger Gluck, *Rosie the Riveter Revisited: Women, the War and Social Change* (New York: Twayne, 1987); James N. Gregory, *American Exodus: The Dust Bowl Migration and Okie Culture in California* (New York: Oxford, 1989); Arnold R. Hirsch, *Making the Second Ghetto: Race and Housing in Chicago, 1940–1960* (Cambridge: Cambridge University Press, 1983); Amy Kesselman, *Fleeting Opportunities: Women Shipyard Workers in Portland and Vancouver During World War II and Reconversion* (Albany: SUNY Press, 1990); Gretchen Lemke-Santangelo,

Abiding Courage: African American Migrant Women and the East Bay Community (Chapel Hill: University of North Carolina Press, 1996); Shirley Ann Wilson Moore, *To Place Our Deeds: The African American Community in Richmond, California, 1910–1963* (Berkeley: University of California Press, 2000); Gerald D. Nash, *The American West Transformed: The Impact of the Second World War* (Bloomington: Indiana University Press, 1986), 37–55, 88–107; Josh Sides, *LA City Limits: African American Los Angeles from the Great Depression to the Present* (Berkeley: University of California Press, 2003); Quintard Taylor, *In Search of the Racial Frontier: African Americans in the American West* (New York: Norton, 1998), 251–277.

43. Sources on the Zoot Suit Riots include Patricia Rae Adler, "The 1943 Zoot-Suit Riots: Brief Episode in a Long Conflict," in *An Awakened Minority: Mexican-Americans,* 2nd ed., Mauel P. Servín, Ed. (Beverly Hills, CA: Glencoe, 1974), 142–158; Stuart Cosgrove, "An Interpretation of the Causes of the Zoot Suit Wars," *History Workshop Journal,* no. 18 (Autumn 1984), 77–91; Edward J. Escobar, *Race, Police, and the Making of a Political Identity: Mexican Americans and the Los Angeles Police Department, 1900–1945* (Berkeley: University of California Press, 1999), 155–290; Mauricio Mazón, *The Zoot-Suit Riots: The Psychology of Symbolic Annihilation* (Austin: University of Texas Press, 1984); McWilliams, *North From Mexico,* 227–258; Eduardo Obregón Pagán, *Murder at the Sleepy Lagoon: Zoot Suits, Race, and Riot in Wartime LA* (Chapel Hill: University of North Carolina Press, 2003); Vargas, *Labor Rights Are Civil Rights,* 203–251; Daniel Yi, "Zoot Suits Dress Up His Memories of Wartime," *Los Angeles Times* (June 2, 2003).

44. Robin D. G. Kelley, *Race Rebels: Culture, Politics, and the Black Working Class* (New York: Free Press, 1996), 163–166; for corrections to some of Kelley's more extreme flights of fancy, see Paul Spickard, "Not Just the Quiet People: The Nisei Underclass," *Pacific Historical Review,* 68.1 (1999), 78–94.

45. McWilliams, *North From Mexico,* 245.

46. David Stannard describes an eerily similar 1931 precursor to the Sleepy Lagoon murder and the Zoot Suit Riots in *Honor Killing: How the Infamous "Massie Affair" Transformed Hawai'i* (New York: Viking, 2005).

47. Harvard Sitkoff, "The Detroit Race Riot of 1943," *Michigan History,* 53 (1969), 183–206; John Morton Blum, *V Was for Victory: Politics and Culture During World War II* (New York: Harcourt Brace Jovanovich, 1976), 199–207; Robert L. Allen, *The Port Chicago Mutiny* (New York: Amistad, 1993); Raúl Morín, *Among the Valiant: Mexican Americans in World War II and Korea* (Los Angeles: Borden, 1963); Myrna Oliver, "Jose M. Lopez, 94; Battle of the Bulge Hero Killed 100 German Soldiers," *Los Angeles Times* (May 18, 2005).

48. Lloyd L. Brown, "Brown v. Salina, Kansas," *New York Times* (February 26, 1973), 31.

49. The literature on the Japanese American concentration camp episode is voluminous. Concise summaries are found in Paul Spickard, *Japanese Americans* (New York: Twayne, 1996), 93–132, 178–181; and Alice Yang Murray, *What Did the Internment of Japanese Americans Mean?* (Boston: Bedford/St. Martin's, 2000), 1–26. The best single introduction to the subject is Roger Daniels, *Prisoners Without Trial: Japanese Americans in World War II* (New York: Hill and Wang, 1993). Other essential treatments include Drinnon, *Keeper of Concentration Camps*; Louis Fiset, *Imprisoned Apart: The World War II Correspondence*

of an Issei Couple (Seattle: University of Washington Press, 1997); Jeanne Wakatsuki Houston and James D. Houston, *Farewell to Manzanar* (Boston: Houghton Mifflin, 1973); Peter Irons, *Justice at War: The Story of the Japanese American Internment Cases* (New York: Oxford, 1983); Daisuke Kitagawa, *Issei and Nisei: The Internment Years* (New York: Seabury, 1967); Alexander H. Leighton, *The Governing of Men* (Princeton, NJ: Princeton University Press, 1945); Richard S. Nishimoto, *Inside an American Concentration Camp: Japanese American Resistance at Poston, Arizona*, Lane Ryo Hirabayashi, Ed. (Tucson: University of Arizona Press, 1995); Greg Robinson, *By Order of the President: FDR and the Internment of Japanese Americans* (Cambridge, MA: Harvard University Press, 2001); Dorothy S. Thomas and Richard Nishimoto, *The Spoilage: Japanese-American Evacuation and Resettlement During World War II* (Berkeley: University of California Press, 1946); U.S. Commission on Wartime Relocation and Internment of Civilians, *Personal Justice Denied* (Washington, DC: Government Printing Office, 1982); Yoshiko Uchida, *Desert Exile: The Uprooting of a Japanese-American Family* (Seattle: University of Washington Press, 1982); Michi Weglyn, *Years of Infamy: The Untold Story of America's Concentration Camps* (New York: Morrow, 1976). The best film treatment is *Rabbit in the Moon*, dir. Emiko Omori (POV/National Asian American Telecommunications Association, 1999).

50. Eugene V. Rostow, "The Japanese American Cases—A Disaster," Yale Law Journal, 54 (1995), 489–533.

51. Quoted in Leighton, *Governing of Men*, 19.

52. Daniels, *Prisoners Without Trial*, 28.

53. Quoted in Roger Daniels, *Concentration Camps USA: Japanese Americans and World War II* (New York: Holt, Rinehart and Winston, 1971), 33–34.

54. Quoted in Morton Grodzins, *Americans Betrayed: Politics and the Japanese Evacuation* (Chicago: University of Chicago Press, 1949), 27.

55. Quoted in Jacobus tenBroek, Edward N. Barnhart, and Floyd W. Matson, *Prejudice, War and the Constitution* (Berkeley: University of California Press, 1954), 75.

56. Quoted in Allan R. Bosworth, *America's Concentration Camps* (New York: Norton, 1967), 171.

57. Quoted in Audrie Girdner and Anne Loftis, *The Great Betrayal* (New York: Macmillan, 1969), 115.

58. Miné Okubo, *Citizen 13660* (New York: Columbia University Press, 1946), 33–36.

59. *Korematsu v. United States*, 323 US 233, quoted in *Major Problems in Asian American History*, Lon Kurashige and Alice Yang Murray, Eds. (Boston: Houghton Mifflin, 2003), 299. Murphy pointed to what James Michener much later called "a hideous circumlocution" in the exclusion order—"aliens or non-aliens." Michener continued: "What in the hell is a nonalien? What could he possibly be but a citizen? I had read this pompous phrase years ago without catching its irony" (in forward to *American in Disguise*, by Daniel I. Okimoto, New York: Weatherhill, 1971), ix. Historian Benjamin Zulueta responded: "Why [don't we] catch it until decades later? The only people who really catch the irony are the ones who get caught in it, and for them calling it an irony borders on the insulting" (personal communication with the author, September 4, 2003).

60. George S. Schuyler, "Views and Reviews" *Pittsburgh Courier* (May 29, 1943). Schuyler cited Congressmember John Rankin of Mississippi and Senator Tom Stewart of Tennessee as two who had introduced bills to take away the Nisei's citizenship and expatriate them to Japan. He likened them to "Nazis" and warned that they might support the efforts of Mississippi Senator Theodore Bilbo to take away Black citizenship as well.

61. On these cases and their ultimate reversal decades later because of misconduct on the part of government prosecutors, see Peter Irons, *Justice at War: The Story of the Japanese American Internment Cases* (New York: Oxford, 1983); Irons, Ed., *Justice Delayed: The Record of the Japanese American Internment Cases* (Middletown, CT: Wesleyan University Press, 1989). On the wider issue of resistance, see Spickard, "The Nisei Assume Power."

62. The role of the JACL in collaborating with the WRA is documented in Spickard, "Nisei Assume Power."

63. They did not object to military service, and some of them served with honor in the Korean War and during the 1950s, but they did refuse to join the Army while their families were in jail without charge. William Minoru Hohri, *Resistance: Challenging America's Wartime Internment of Japanese-Americans* (Lomita, CA: Epistolarian, 2001).

64. Masayo Umezawa Duus, *Unlikely Liberators: The Men of the 100th and 442nd* (Honolulu: University of Hawai'i Press, 1987); Franklin Odo, *No Sword to Bury: Japanese Americans in Hawai'i during World War II* (Philadelphia: Temple University Press, 2004).

65. Daniel K. Inouye, *Journey to Washington* (Englewood Cliffs, NJ: Prentice-Hall, 1968), 207–208.

66. Sources on 1940s-era European refugees include Joseph Berger, *Displaced Persons: Growing Up American After the Holocaust* (New York: Scribner, 2001); Haim Genizi, *America's Fair Share: The Admission and Resettlement of Displaced Persons, 1945–1952* (Detroit: Wayne State University Press, 1993); Ella E. Schneider Hilton, *Displaced Person: A Girl's Life in Russia, Germany, and America* (Baton Rouge: Louisiana State University Press, 2004); Anna D. Jaroszynska-Kirchmann, "Displaced Persons, Émigrés, Refugees, and Other Polish Immigrants," in *Polish Americans and Their History*, John J. Bukowczyk, Ed. (Pittsburgh: University of Pittsburgh Press, 1996), 152–179; Tony Kushner and Katharine Knox, *Refugees in an Age of Genocide* (London: Frank Cass, 1999); Michael R. Marrus, *The Unwanted: European Refugees in the Twentieth Century* (New York: Oxford, 1985); Sarah A. Ogilvie and Scott Miller, *Refuge Denied: The St. Louis Passengers and the Holocaust* (Madison: University of Wisconsin Press, 2006); Mark Wyman, *DP: Europe's Displaced Persons, 1945–1951* (Ithaca, NY: Cornell University Press, 1998).

67. Donald Fleming and Bernard Bailyn, Eds., *The Intellectual Migration: Europe and America, 1930–1960* (Cambridge, MA: Harvard University Press, 1969), 675–720.

68. Benjamin C. Zulueta, *Forging the Model Minority: Chinese Immigrants, American Science, and the Cold War* (unpublished manuscript, courtesy of the author, 2006).

69. Roger Daniels, *Coming to America*, 2nd ed. (New York: HarperCollins, 2002), 296.

70. June Namias, *First Generation*, rev. ed. (Urbana: University of Illinois Press, 1992), 109–119.

71. Michael LeMay and Elliott Robert Barkan, Eds., *US Immigration and Natu-ralization Laws and Issues* (Westport, CT: Greenwood, 1999), 204–205.

72. LeMay and Barkan, *Immigration and Naturalization Laws*, 211–213.

73. Elie Wiesel, *All Rivers Run to the Sea: Memoirs* (New York: Schocken, 1996).

74. Elizabeth Olson, "Documents Show US Relationship With Nazis During Cold War," *New York Times* (May 14, 2004); Robert Breitman, Norman Goda, Timothy Naftali, and Robert Wolfe, *US Intelligence and the Nazis* (Washington, DC: National Archives Trust Fund for the Nazi War Crimes and Japanese Imperial Government Records Agency, 2004).

75. "US Asks for Deportation of Demjanjuk," *New York Times* (December 18, 2004); "Suspected Nazi Guard to Be Deported," *Los Angeles Times* (December 29, 2005); Richard B. Schmitt, "Nazi Concentration Camp Guard Arrested in Michigan." *Los Angeles Times* (July 3, 2003); Richard A. Serrano, "A Nazi's Day of Judgment," *Los Angeles Times* (July 12, 2005). For a moving account of the emotional weight carried by many German postwar migrants, see Ursula Hegi, *Tearing the Silence: On Being German in America* (New York: Touchstone, 1998).

76. Paul R. Spickard, *Mixed Blood: Intermarriage and Ethnic Identity in Twenti-eth-Century America* (Madison: University of Wisconsin Press, 1989), 123–158; Evelyn Nakano Glenn, *Issei, Nisei, War Bride: Three Generations of Japanese American Women in Domestic Service* (Philadelphia: Temple University Press, 1986); Elfrieda Berthiaume Shukert and Barbara Smith Scibetta, *War Brides of World War II* (New York: Penguin, 1989); Xiaojian Zhao, *Remaking Chinese America: Immigration, Family, and Community, 1940–1965* (New Brunswick, NJ: Rutgers University Press, 2002), 78–123. See Appendix B, Table 37.

77. Sources on immigration policy and race during the Cold War include Daniels, *Guarding the Golden Door*, 81–128; Mary L. Dudziak, *Cold War Civil Rights: Race and the Image of American Democracy* (Princeton, NJ: Princeton University Press, 2000); Michael Gill Davis, "The Cold War, Refugees, and US Immigration Policy, 1952–1965" (PhD dissertation, Vanderbilt University 1996); Graham, *Unguarded Gates*; Hing, *Defining America Through Immigration Policy*, 73–92; Michael L. Krenn, Ed., *Race and US Foreign Policy During the Cold War* (New York: Garland, 1998); Ngai, *Impossible Subjects*; Brenda Gayle Plummer, *Rising Wind: Black Americans and US Foreign Affairs, 1935–1960* (Chapel Hill: University of North Carolina Press, 1996); Plummer, Ed., *Window on Freedom: Race, Civil Rights, and Foreign Affairs* (Chapel Hill: University of North Carolina Press, 2003); Mayme Sevander with Laurie Hertzel, *They Took My Father: Finnish Americans in Stalin's Russia* (Minneapolis: University of Minnesota Press, 2004; orig. 1992); Reed Ueda, *Postwar Immigrant America* (Boston: Bedford/St. Martin's, 1994); U.S. Senate Judiciary Committee, *US Immigration Law and Policy: 1952–1986* (Washington, DC: Government Printing Office, 1988).

78. Michael J. Ybarra, *Washington Gone Crazy: Senator Pat McCarran and the Great American Communist Hunt* (Hanover, NH: Steerforth, 2004).

79. Quoted in Hing, *Defining America Through Immigration Policy*, 74.

80. Harry S. Truman, "Veto of McCarran-Walter Act" (June 25, 1952), *Public Papers of the Presidents* (June 25, 1952), 441–447; reprinted in Michael LeMay and Elliott Robert Barkan, Eds., *US Immigration and Naturalization Laws and Issues* (Westport, CT: Greenwood, 1999), 228–231.

81. U.S.. Presidential Commission on Immigration and Naturalization, *Whom Shall We Welcome* (Washington, DC: Government Printing Office, 1953). The commission reflected some of the views of the Progressive Party, which carried on New Deal ideals into the first years of the Cold War. A 1948 party statement said in part:

> —The Progressive Party advocates the right of the foreign born to obtain citizenship without discrimination.
>
> —The Progressive Party advocates the repeal of discriminatory immigration laws based upon race, national origin, religion, or political belief.
>
> —The Progressive Party recognizes the just claims of Japanese Americans for indemnity for the losses suffered during their wartime internment, which was an outrageous violation of fundamental concepts of justice.
>
> —The Progressive Party supports legislation facilitating naturalization of Filipinos, Koreans, Japanese, Chinese, and other national groups now discriminated against by law.

Campaign Handbook of the Progressive Party (New York: Progressive Party National Headquarters, 1948), reprinted in *US Immigration and Naturalization Laws and Issues*, LeMay and Barkan, Eds., 216.

82. Benjamin C. Zulueta, *Forging the Model Minority: Chinese Immigrants, American Science, and the Cold War* (Honolulu: University of Hawai'i Press, forthcoming; advance copy of manuscript courtesy of the author); Iris Chang, *Thread of the Silkworm* (New York: Basic Books, 1995); William L. Ryan and Sam Summerlin, *The China Cloud: America's Tragic Blunder and China's Rise to Nuclear Power* (Boston: Little, Brown, 1968).

83. Geraldine Fitch, "Brains at a Bargain," *Rotarian*, 89 (December 1956), 17–19.

84. Another episode in Cold War interventionism is the rise in those years of an international adoption industry. This effort was frequently characterized by its advocates as an attempt to save Asian or East European babies from Communism, sometimes to bring children from backward places the benefits of superior, White American civilization. The historical study of adoption is just beginning to blossom; see E. Wayne Carp, *Family Matters: Secrecy and Disclosure in the History of Adoption* (Cambridge, MA: Harvard University Press, 2000); Carp, Ed., *Adoption in America: Historical Perspectives* (Ann Arbor: University of Michigan Press, 2004); Barbara Melosh, *Strangers and Kin: The American Way of Adoption* (Cambridge, MA: Harvard University Press, 2002). Sociological analyses include Joyce Ladner, *Mixed Families: Adopting Across Racial Boundaries* (Garden City, NY: Doubleday, 1978); Adam Pertman, *Adoption Nation: How the Adoption Revolution is Transforming America* (New York: Basic Books, 2000); Rita J. Simon and Rhonda M. Roorda, *In Their Own Voices: Transracial Adoptees Tell Their Stories* (New York: Columbia University Press, 2000). On Korean international adoptions in this period, moving personal expressions can be found in Tanya Bishoff and Jo Rankin, Eds., *Seeds from a Silent Tree: An Anthology by Korean Adoptees* (Glendale, CA: Pandal Press, 1997); Thomas Park Clement, *The Unforgotten War* (published by the author, 1998); Susan Soon-Keum Cox, *Voices from Another Place* (St. Paul: Yeong and Yeong, 1999); Sara Dorow, Ed., *I Wish for You a Beautiful Life: Letters from the Korean Birth Mothers of Ae Ran Won to Their Children* (St. Paul: Yeong and Yeong, 1999); Heinz Insu Fenkl, *Memories of My Ghost Brother*

(New York: Dutton, 1996); Elizabeth Kim, *Ten Thousand Sorrows* (New York: Doubleday, 2000); Jane Jeont Trenka, *The Language of Blood* (St. Paul, MN: Borealis Books, 2003).

85. Sources on Cuban migration include Cheris T. Brewer, "'Castro's Loss Is Our Gain': Accepting, Assisting, and Resettling Cuban Refugees, 1959–1978," (MA thesis, Washington State University, 2005); María Cristina García, *Havana USA: Cuban Exiles and Cuban Americans in South Florida, 1959–1994* (Berkeley: University of California Press, 1994); Alejandro Portes And Robert L. Bach, *Latin Journey: Cuban and Mexican Immigrants in the United States* (Berkeley: University of California Press, 1985).

86. García, *Havana USA*, 17–19.

87. Silvia Pedraza-Bailey, *Political and Economic Migrants in America: Cubans and Mexicans* (Austin: University of Texas Press, 1985).

88. Places to begin on the civil rights movement include Daisy Bates, *The Long Shadow of Little Rock* (New York: David McKay, 1962); Taylor Branch, *Parting the Waters: America in the King Years: 1954–63* (New York: Simon and Schuster, 1988); *Brown v. Board of Education, Fifty Years After*, special issue of *Journal of American History*, 91.1 (June 2004); Clayborne Carson, *In Struggle: SNCC and the Black Awakening of the 1960s* (Cambridge, MA: Harvard University Press, 1981); William H. Chafe, *Civilities and Civil Rights: Greensboro, North Carolina, and the Black Struggle for Freedom* (New York: Oxford, 1981); Dudziak, *Cold War Civil Rights*; Glenn Feldman, Ed., *Before Brown: Civil Rights and White Backlash in the Modern South* (Tuscaloosa: University of Alabama Press, 2004); David J. Garrow, *Bearing the Cross: Martin Luther King, Jr., and the Southern Christian Leadership Conference* (New York: Morrow, 1986); Richard Kluger, *Simple Justice: The History of "Brown v. Board of Education" and Black America's Struggle for Equality* (New York: Knopf, 1976); Chana Kai Lee, *For Freedom's Sake: The Life of Fannie Lou Hamer* (Urbana: University of Illinois Press, 1999); Patrick B. Miller, Elisabeth Schäfer-Wünsche, and Therese Frey Steffen, Eds., *The Civil Rights Movement Revisited* (Münster, Germany: Lit Verlag, 2001); Anne Moody, *Coming of Age in Mississippi* (New York: Dial, 1968); James T. Patterson, *Brown v. Board of Education: A Civil Rights Milestone and its Troubled Legacy* (New York: Oxford, 2000); Charles M. Payne, *I've Got the Light of Freedom: The Organizing Tradition and the Mississippi Freedom Struggle* (Berkeley: University of California Press, 1995); Howell Raines, *My Soul Is Rested: Movement Days in the Deep South Remembered* (New York: Putnam, 1977); *Reporting Civil Rights: American Journalism, 1941–1973*, 2 vols. (New York: Library of America, 2003); Jo Ann Gibson Robinson, *The Montgomery Bus Boycott and the Women Who Started It* (Knoxville: University of Tennessee Press, 1987); Harvard Sitkoff, *The Struggle for Black Equality, 1954–1992*, rev. ed. (New York: Hill and Wang, 1993); Juan Williams, *Eyes on the Prize: America's Civil Rights Years, 1954–1965* (New York: Viking, 1987); Williams, *Thurgood Marshall* (New York: Times, 1998).

89. Gunnar Myrdal, *An American Dilemma: The Negro Problem and Modern Democracy* (New York: Harper and Row, 1962; orig. 1944), 60–61 (italics in original); Rayford W. Logan, Ed., *What the Negro Wants* (Notre Dame, IN: University of Notre Dame Press, 2001; orig. 1944).

90. Stokely Carmichael, "Power and Racism," *New York Review of Books* (September 22, 1966); see also Floyd B. Barbour, Ed., *The Black Power Revolt* (Boston: Extending Horizons Books, 1968); Stokely Carmichael and Charles V. Hamilton, *Black Power* (New York: Knopf, 1967).

91. Walter Mosley, *Little Scarlet* (Boston: Little, Brown, 2004), 50–51, 82–83, 271.

92. On *Perez v. Sharp*, *Loving v. Virginia*, and the other cases where couples succeeded in overturning the states' anti-miscegenation laws, see: Kevin R. Johnson, Ed., *Mixed Race America and the Law* (New York: NYU Press, 2003); Randall Kennedy, *Interracial Intimacy: Sex, Marriage, Identity, and Adoption* (New York: Pantheon, 2003); Rachel F. Moran, *Interracial Intimacy: The Regulation of Race and Romance* (Chicago: University of Chicago Press, 2001); Dana Orenstein, "Void for Vagueness: Mexicans and the Collapse of Miscegenation Law in California," *Pacific Historical Review*, 74.3 (2005), 367–407; Charles F. Robinson II, *Dangerous Liaisons: Sex and Love in the Segregated South* (Fayetteville: University of Arkansas Press, 2003); Renee C. Romano, *Race Mixing: Black-White Marriage in Postwar America* (Cambridge, MA: Harvard University Press, 2003); Spickard, *Mixed Blood*; Peter Wallenstein, *Tell the Court I Love My Wife: Race, Marriage, and the Law—An American History* (New York: Palgrave Macmillan, 2002).

93. Sources on the 1965 act include Daniels, *Guarding the Golden Door*; Graham, *Unguarded Gates*; Hing, *Defining America Through Immigration Policy*; Shanks, *Immigration and the Politics of American Sovereignty*; U.S. Senate, *US Immigration Law and Policy*.

94. Roger Daniels, *Coming to America*, 2nd ed. (New York: HarperCollins, 2002), 338.

95. John F. Kennedy, *A Nation of Immigrants*, rev. ed. (New York: Harper and Row, 1964), x, 102–103.

96. Daniels, *Coming to America*, 344.

Chapter 8

1. Sources for this section include Nancy Foner, *From Ellis Island to JFK: New York's Two Great Waves of Immigration* (New Haven, CT : Yale University Press, 2000); Nathan Glazer, Ed., *Clamor at the Gates: The New American Immigration* (San Francisco: ICS Press, 1985); Darrell Y. Hamamoto and Rodolfo D. Torres, Eds., *New American Destinies: Contemporary Asian and Latino Immigration* (New York: Routledge, 1997); Guillermina Jasso and Mark R. Rosenzweig, *The New Chosen People: Immigrants in the United States* (New York: Russell Sage, 1990); Alejandro Portes and Rubén G. Rumbaut, *Immigrant America*, 2nd ed. (Berkeley: University of California Press, 1996); Alejandro Portes and Rubén G. Rumbaut, *Legacies: The Story of the Immigrant Second Generation* (Berkeley: University of California Press, 2001); David M. Reimers, *Other Immigrants: The Global Origins of the American People* (New York: NYU Press, 2005); David M. Reimers, *Still the Golden Door: The Third World Comes to America* (New York: Columbia University Press, 1985); Rubén G. Rumbaut and Alejandro Portes, Eds., *Ethnicities: Children of Immigrants in America* (Berkeley: University of California Press, 2001). Sources of numbers include Jeffrey S. Passel and Roberto Suro, "Rise, Peak, and Decline: Trends in US Immigration 1992–2004" (report by Pew Hispanic Research Center,

Washington, DC, 2005); Population Projections Program, U.S. Census Bureau, "Projections of the Total Resident Population by 5-Year Age Groups, Race, and Hispanic Origin with Special Age Categories" (Washington, DC: US Bureau of the Census, 2000).

2. See Appendix B, Table 2.

3. Steven A. Camarota, "Immigrants in the United States—2000," on Web site of the Center for Immigration Studies, a nonpartisan information-gathering service (www.cis.org/articles/2001/back101.html, June 27, 2002). See also Jeffrey S. Passel and Roberto Suro, "Rise, Peak, and Decline: Trends in US Immigration, 1992–2004," (report by Pew Hispanic Center, Washington, DC, September 27, 2005).

4. Website of the Migration Policy Institute, www.migrationinformation.org/globaldata/ (March 8, 2006); Appendix B, Table 31; https://www.cia.gov/cia/publications/factbook/index.html (November 23, 2006).

5. www.migrationinformation.org/globaldata/.

6. Sources on Murdoch include Neil Chenoweth, *Rupert Murdoch: The Untold Story of the World's Greatest Media Wizard* (New York: Crown, 2002); Thomas Kiernan, *Citizen Murdoch* (New York: Dodd, Mead, 1986); John Lanchester, "Bravo l'artiste," *London Review of Books* (February 5, 2004), 3–7; *Outfoxed: Rupert Murdoch's War on Journalism*, dir. Robert Greenwald (Cinema Libre Studio, 2004); Bruce Page, *The Murdoch Archipelago* (New York: Simon and Schuster, 2003); William Shawcross, *Murdoch: The Making of a Media Empire*, rev. ed. (New York: Simon and Schuster, 1997); Jerome Tuccille, *Rupert Murdoch* (New York: Fine, 1989); Michael Wolff, *Autumn of the Moguls: My Misadventures with the Titans, Poseurs and Money Guys who Mastered and Messed up Big Media* (New York: Harper, 2003).

7. Sources on Soros include: Eric Alterman, "Target: George Soros," *The Nation* (December 29, 2003), 10; Michael T. Kaufman, *Soros: The Life and Times of a Messianic Billionaire* (New York: Knopf, 2002); Richard Rainey, "Financing His Own Anti-Bush Campaign," *Los Angeles Times* (September 29, 2004); Robert Slater, *Soros: The Unauthorized Biography* (New York: McGraw-Hill, 1997); George Soros, *The Bubble of American Supremacy: Correcting the Misuse of American Power* (New York: Public Affairs, 2003); Soros, *The Crisis of Global Capitalism* (New York: Public Affairs, 1998); Soros, *On Globalization* (New York: Public Affairs, 2002); Soros, *Open Society: Reforming Global Capitalism* (New York: Public Affairs, 2000); Soros, *Opening the Soviet System* (London: Weidenfeld and Nicholson, 1990); Soros, *Underwriting Democracy: Encouraging Free Enterprise and Democratic Reform Among the Soviets and in Eastern Europe* (New York: Free Press, 2004).

8. Sources on Schwarzenegger include Laurence Learner, *Fantastic: The Life of Arnold Schwarzenegger* (New York: St. Martin's, 2005); and the daily *Los Angeles Times* throughout the first six years of the twenty-first century.

9. Alan Zarembo, "Slow but Steady Approach Has Served Bustamante Well," *Los Angeles Times* (August 30, 2003).

10. As yet there has been no biography of Gary Locke. Helen Zia has considerable material on Locke in *Asian American Dreams: The Emergence of an American People* (New York: Farrar, Straus and Giroux, 2000), 280–300. I have known Locke and his family since 1963 and worked in his gubernatorial campaigns. I also use materials here from many issues of the *Seattle Times*. See especially the first section of the July 23, 2003, issue.

11. "Democrats Respond to Bush's State of the Union," *Washington Post* (January 28, 2003).

12. Sources on Asian immigration include Karin Aguilar-San Juan, Ed., *The State of Asian America* (Boston: South End Press, 1994); Angelo N. Ancheta, *Race, Rights, and the Asian American Experience* (New Brunswick, NJ: Rutgers University Press, 1998); Tony Carnes and Fenggang Yang, Eds., *Asian American Religions* (New York: NYU Press, 2004); Jane Naomi Iwamura and Paul Spickard, Eds., *Revealing the Sacred in Asian and Pacific America* (New York: Routledge, 2003); Lisa Lowe, *Immigrant Acts: On Asian American Cultural Politics* (Durham, NC: Duke University Press, 1996); Pyong Gap Min and Jung Ha Kim, Eds., *Religions in Asian America* (Walnut Creek, CA: AltaMira Press, 2001); Paul Ong, Edna Bonacich, and Lucie Cheng, Eds., *The New Asian Immigration in Los Angeles and Global Restructuring* (Philadelphia: Temple University Press, 1994); Edward J. W. Park and John S, W. Park, *Probationary Americans: Contemporary Immigration Policies and the Shaping of Asian American Communities* (New York: Routledge, 2005); Lisa Sun-Hee Park, *Consuming Citizenship: Children of Asian Immigrant Entrepreneurs* (Stanford, CA: Stanford University Press, 2005); Joanne L. Rondilla and Paul Spickard, *Is Lighter Better: Skin-Tone Discrimination among Asian Americans* (Lanham, MD: Rowman and Littlefield, 2007); Linda Trinh Vo and Rick Bonus, Eds., *Contemporary Asian American Communities* (Philadelphia: Temple University Press, 2002); Jean Wu and Min Song, Eds., *Asian American Studies* (New Brunswick, NJ: Rutgers University Press, 2000); David K. Yoo, Ed., *New Spiritual Homes: Religion and Asian Americans* (Honolulu: University of Hawai'i Press, 1999); Min Zhou and James V. Gatewood, Eds., *Contemporary Asian America* (New York: NYU Press, 2000); Helen Zia, *Asian American Dreams* (New York: Farrar, Straus and Giroux, 2000); and the full runs of *Amerasia Journal* and the *Journal of Asian American Studies*.

13. Sources on ethnic minorities in mainland Southeast Asia include Paul J. Bold, *China and Southeast Asia's Ethnic Chinese* (Westport, CT: Praeger, 2000); David Brown, *The State and Ethnic Politics in Southeast Asia* (New York: Routledge, 1994); Cam Truong, *The Thai in the Northwestern Region of Vietnam* (Hanoi: Social Science Publishing House, 1978); *Ethnic Minorities in Vietnam* (Hanoi: Culture Publishing House, 1959); Clifford Geertz, *The Religion of Java* (Gelncoe, IL: Free Press, 1960); Institute of Ethnology, *Handbook on Ethnic Groups in Vietnam* (Hanoi: Social Science Publishing House, 1983); Institute of Ethnology, *Ethnic Minorities in Vietnam (Northern Provinces)* (Hanoi: Social Science Publishing House, 1978); Institute of Ethnology, *Ethnic Minorities in Vietnam (Southern Provinces)* (Hanoi: Social Science Publishing House, 1984); Joel S. Kahn, Ed., *Southeast Asian Identities* (New York: St. Martin's, 1998); Khong Dien, *Population and Ethno-Demography in Vietnam* (Chiang Mai, Thailand: Silkworm Books, 2002); Meng Tarr Chou, "The Vietnamese Minority in Cambodia," *Race and Class*, 34 (1992), 33–48; Sherri Prasso, *Violence, Ethnicity, and Ethnic Cleansing: Cambodia and the Khmer Rouge* (Cambridge: Cambridge University, 1995); Christine Su, "Becoming Cambodian: Ethnicity and the Vietnamese in Kampuchea," in *Race and Nation: Ethnic Systems in the Modern World*, Paul Spickard, Ed. (New York: Routledge, 2005), 273–296; Leo Suryadinata, Ed., *Ethnic Chinese as Southeast Asians* (New York: St. Martin's, 1997); W. E. Wilmott, *The Chinese in Cambodia* (Vancouver: University of British Columbia Publications Center, 1968.

14. See Appendix B, Table 21. Books on Southeast Asian immigrants often embody examination and comparison of Vietnamese, Cambodian, and Laotian American experiences. Those used here include Nathan Caplan, John K. Whitemore, and Marcella H. Choy, *The Boat People and Achievement in America: A Study of Family Life, Hard Work, and Cultural Values* (Ann Arbor: University of Michigan Press, 1989); Daniel F. Detzner, *Elder Voices: Southeast Asian Families in the United States* (Walnut Creek, CA: AltaMira, 2004); David W. Haines, Ed., *Refugees as Immigrants: Cambodians, Laotians, and Vietnamese* (Totowa, NJ: Rowman and Littlefield, 1989); Jeremy Hein, *From Vietnam, Laos, and Cambodia: A Refugee Experience in the United States* (New York: Twayne, 1995).

Sources on Vietnamese immigrants include Duong Van Mai Elliott, *The Sacred Willow: Four Generations in the Life of a Vietnamese Family* (New York: Oxford, 1999); James M. Freeman, *Changing Identities: Vietnamese Americans, 1975–1995* (Boston: Allyn and Bacon, 1995); Freeman, *Hearts of Sorrow: Vietnamese-American Lives* (Stanford, CA: Stanford University Press, 1989); Freeman and Nguyen Dinh Huu, *Voices from the Camps: Vietnamese Children Seeking Asylum* (Seattle: University of Washington Press, 2003); Bruce Grant, *The Boat People* (New York: Penguin, 1979); Le Ly Hayslip, *When Heaven and Earth Changed Places* (New York: Doubleday, 1989); Nazli Kibria, *Family Tightrope: The Changing Lives of Vietnamese Americans* (Princeton, NJ: Princeton University Press, 1993); Patrick Du Phuoc Long and Laura Ricard, *The Dream Shattered: Vietnamese Gangs in America* (Boston: Northeastern University Press, 1996); Robert S. McKelvey, *A Gift of Barbed Wire: America's Allies Abandoned in South Vietnam* (Seattle: University of Washington Press, 2002); Paul James Rutledge, *The Vietnamese Experience in America* (Bloomington: Indiana University Press, 1992); Nguyen Van Vu and Bob Pittman, *At Home in America* (Nashville: Broadman, 1979); Min Zhou and Carl L. Bankston III, *Growing Up American: How Vietnamese Children Adapt to Life in the United States* (New York: Russell Sage, 1998).

15. Sources on U.S.-Vietnam relations and the Vietnam War are many. Among those used here are Mark Philip Bradley, *Imagining Vietnam and America: The Making of Postcolonial Vietnam, 1919–1950* (Chapel Hill: University of North Carolina Press, 2000); Frances Fitzgerald, *Fire in the Lake: The Vietnamese and the Americans in Vietnam* (Boston: Little, Brown, 2002; orig. 1973); George C. Herring, *America's Longest War: United States and Vietnam, 1950–1975*, 2nd ed. (New York: McGraw-Hill, 1985); Hugh Higgins, *Vietnam*, 2nd ed. (London: Heinemann, 1982); Frederik Logevall, *Choosing War: The Lost Chance for Peace and the Escalation of War in Vietnam* (Berkeley: University of California Press, 1999); Frederik Logevall, *The Origins of the Vietnam War* (New York: Longman, 2001); Robert J. McMahon, Ed., *Major Problems in the History of the Vietnam War* (Lexington, MA: Heath, 1990); Charles E. Neu, *America's Lost War: Vietnam, 1945–1975* (Arlington Heights, IL: Harlan Davidson, 2005); James S. Olson and Randy Roberts, *Where the Dominos Fell: America and Vietnam, 1945–1990* (New York: St. Martin's, 1991); Gareth Porter, Ed., *Vietnam: A History in Documents* (New York: New American Library, 1981); Harrison E. Salisbury, Ed., *Vietnam Reconsidered* (New York: Harper and Row, 1984); Marilyn B. Young, *Vietnam Wars, 1945–1990* (New York: Harper, 1991); Marilyn B. Young, John J. Fitzgerald, and A. Tom Grunfeld, Eds., *The Vietnam War: A History in Documents* (New York: Oxford, 2003).

The parallels between the American misadventure in Vietnam and the disaster in Iraq a generation later are so many and so obvious that they would appear crudely comical, were their consequences not so tragic.

16. Lang Ngan, "The Success Story," in *Asian American Experiences in the United States*, Ed. Joann Faung Jean Lee (Jefferson, NC: McFarland, 1991), quoted in *Major Problems in Asian American History*, Lon Kurashige and Alice Yang Murray, Eds., (Boston: Houghton Mifflin, 2003), 390–392.

17. Le Tan Si, "A Terrifying Escape," in *The Far East Comes Near*, Lucy Nguyen Hong-Nhiem and Joel Martin Halpern, Eds. (Amherst: University of Massachusetts Press, 1989), quoted in *Major Problems*, Kurashige and Yang Murray, Eds., 294–297.

18. Sources on Amerasians in Vietnam and the United States include Thomas A. Bass, *Vietnamerica: The War Comes Home* (New York: Soho, 1996); Robert S. McKelvey, *The Dust of Life: America's Children Abandoned in Vietnam* (Seattle: University of Washington Press, 1999); Kien Nguyen, *The Unwanted: A Memoir* (Boston: Little, Brown, 2001); Kieu-Linh Caroline Valverde, "Doing the Mixed-Race Dance: Negotiating Social Spaces Within the Multiracial Vietnamese American Class Typology," in *The Sum of Our Parts: Mixed Heritage Asian Americans*, Teresa Williams-León and Cynthia L. Nakashima, Eds., (Philadelphia: Temple University Press, 2001), 131–44; Valverde, "From Dust to Gold: The Vietnamese Amerasian Experience," in *Racially Mixed People in America*, Maria P. P. Root, Ed. (Newbury Park, CA: Sage, 1992), 144–161. For a haunting evocation of these people's experience, see *The Beautiful Country*, dir. Hans Peter Moland (Sony Pictures Classics, 2004).

19. Sources on Cambodian Americans and other Southeast Asian peoples in the U.S. and elsewhere include Sucheng Chan, *Survivors: Cambodian Refugees in the United States* (Urbana: University of Illinois Press, 2004); Sucheng Chan and Audrey U. Kim, Eds., *Not Just Victims: Conversations with Cambodian Community Leaders in the United States* (Urbana: University of Illinois Press, 2003); Chanrithy Him, *When Broken Glass Floats: Growing Up Under the Khmer Rouge* (New York: Norton, 2000); *The Killing Fields*, dir. Roland Joffé (Warner Home Video, 1984); Aihwa Ong, *Buddha Is Hiding: Refugees, Citizenship, the New America* (Berkeley: University of California Press 2003); Robert Proudfoot, *Even the Birds Don't Sound the Same Here: The Laotian Refugees Search for Heart in American Culture* (New York: Peter Lang, 1990); Nancy J. Smith-Hefner, *Khmer American* (Berkeley: University of California Press, 1999); Pascal Khoo Thwe, *From the Land of Green Ghosts* (London: HarperCollins, 2003); Usha Welaratna, *Beyond the Killing Fields* (Stanford, CA: Stanford University Press, 1993).

20. Caplan, *Boat People and Achievement*, 7–8.

21. Caplan, *Boat People and Achievement*, 13–14.

22. The literature on Hmong in Laos, Vietnam, and the United States grows—some might say all out of proportion to the size of the Hmong population. But the Hmong are a remarkable people, and this literature includes some of the best writing on any Southeast Asian people in the United States, including Sucheng Chan, et al., *Hmong Means Free: Life in Laos and America* (Philadelphia: Temple University Press, 1994); Nancy D. Donnelly, *Changing Lives of Refugee Hmong Women* (Seattle: University of Washington Press, 1994); Lillian Faderman and Ghia Xiong, *I Begin My Life All Over: The Hmong and the American Immigrant Experience* (Boston: Beacon Press, 1998); Anne Fadiman, *The*

Spirit Catches You and You Fall Down: A Hmong Child, Her American Doctors, and the Collision of Two Cultures (New York: Farrar, Straus and Giroux, 1997); Jo Ann Koltyk, *New Pioneers in the Heartland: Hmong Life in Wisconsin* (Boston: Allyn and Bacon, 1998); Tim Pfaff, *Hmong in America: Journey from a Secret War* (Eau Claire, WI: Chippewa Valley Museum Press, 1995); Keith Quincy, *Harvesting Pa Chay's Wheat: The Hmong and America's Secret War in Laos* (Spokane, WA: Eastern Washington University Press, 2000); Quincy, *Hmong: History of a People* (Spokane, WA: Eastern Washington University Press, 1995); William A. Smalley, Chia Koua Vang, and Gnia Yee Yang, *Mother of Writing: The Origin and Development of a Hmong Messianic Script* (Chicago: University of Chicago Press, 1990).

23. Xang Mao Xiong and Maijue Xiong, "The Xiong Family of Lompoc," in Chan, *Hmong Means Free*, 101–102.

24. T. C. Huo tells the story of a boy who was a member of just such a multinational refugee family in his powerful novel, *Land of Smiles* (New York: Penguin, 2000).

25. Sources on Filipino immigrants include Peter Bacho, *Dark Blue Suit and Other Stories* (Seattle: University of Washington Press, 1997); Benjamin V. Cariño, "The Philippines and Southeast Asia: Historical Roots and Contemporary Linkages," in *Pacific Bridges: The New Immigration from Asia and the Pacific Islands*, James T. Fawcett and Benjamin V. Cariño, Eds. (Staten Island, NY: Center for Migration Studies, 1987), 305–325; Catherine Ceniza Choy, *Empire of Care: Nursing and Migration in Filipino American History* (Durham, NC: Duke University Press, 2003); Yen Le Espiritu, *Filipino American Lives* (Philadelphia: Temple University Press, 1995); Espiritu, *Home Bound: Filipino American Lives Across Cultures, Communities, and Countries* (Berkeley: University of California Press, 2003); Stephen Griffiths, *Emigrants, Entrepreneurs, and Evil Spirits* (Honolulu: University of Hawai'i Press, 1988); Jessica Hagedorn, *Dogeaters* (New York: Pantheon, 1990); Hagedorn, *The Gangster of Love* (Boston: Houghton Mifflin, 1996); Melinda L. de Jesús, Ed., *Pinay Power* (New York: Routledge, 2005); Paul Ong and Tania Azores, "The Migration and Incorporation of Filipino Nurses," in *The New Asian Immigration in Los Angeles and Global Restructuring*, Ong, Edna Bonacich, and Lucie Cheng, Eds. (Philadelphia: Temple University Press, 1994), 164–195; Ong, Lucie Chang, and Leslie Evans, "Migration of Highly Educated Asians and Global Dynamics," *Asian and Pacific Migration Journal*, 1 (1992); Richard C. Paddock, "The Overseas Class—The New Foreign Aid: Philippines," *Los Angeles Times* (April 20, 2006) ; Barbara M. Posadas, *The Filipino Americans* (Westport, CT: Greenwood, 1999); James A. Tyner, "The Global Context of Gendered Labor Migration from the Philippines to the United States," *American Behavioral Scientist*, 42.4 (1999).

26. Choy, *Empire of Care*, 89–90.

27. Elaine Woo, "Dr. Josefina B. Magno, 83; Pioneer of Hospice Care for Dying Patients in the US," *Los Angeles Times* (August 3, 2003).

28. Rhacel Salazar Parreñas, *Servants of Globalization: Women, Migration, and Domestic Work* (Stanford, CA: Stanford University Press, 2001), 1, 119, 155; Nigel Harris, *The New Untouchables: Immigration and the New World Worker* (New York: Penguin, 1995), 15.

29. David Pierson, "Filipino Vets Battle for Benefits," *Los Angeles Times* (May 28, 2001); Richard Simon, "Filipino Veterans of WWII Win a Battle in Struggle for Benefits," *Los Angeles Times* (December 17, 2003).

30. Sources on Korean immigrants include Mary Yu Danico, *The 1.5 Generation: Becoming Korean American in Hawai'i* (Honolulu: University of Hawai'i Press, 2004); Won Moo Hurh and Kwang Chung Kim, *Korean Immigrants in America* (Rutherford, NJ: Fairleigh Dickinson University Press, 1984); Elaine H. Kim and Eui-Young Yu, *East to America: Korean American Life Stories* (New York: New Press, 1996); Ilsoo Kim, *New Urban Immigrants: The Korean Community in New York* (Princeton, NJ: Princeton University Press, 1981); Ho-Youn Kwon, Kwang Chung Kim, and R. Stephen Warner, Eds., *Korean Americans and Their Religion* (University Park: Pennsylvania State University Press, 2001); Pyong Gap Min, *Caught in the Middle: Korean Merchants in America's Multiethnic Cities* (Berkeley: University of California Press); Min, *Changes and Conflicts: Korean Immigrant Families in New York* (Boston: Allyn and Bacon, 1998); Sharon A. Suh, *Being Buddhist in a Christian World: Gender and Community in a Korean American Temple* (Seattle: University of Washington Press, 2004).

31. The reasons for Korea having the highest percentage of Christians of any Asian nation except the Philippines have to do with the fact that colonialism in Korea came not at the hands of the West, but from Japan. On Korean American Christianity, see Karen J. Chai, "Competing for the Second Generation: English-Language Ministry at a Korean Protestant Church," in *Gatherings in Diaspora: Religions, Communities and the New Immigration*, R. Stephen Warner and Judith G. Wittner, Eds. (Philadelphia: Temple University Press, 1998), 295–332; Won Moo Hurh and Kwang Chung Kim, "Religions Participation of Korean Immigrants in the United States," *Journal for the Scientific Study of Religion*, 29 (1990), 19–34; Ai Ra Kim, *Women Struggling for a New Life: The Role of Religion in the Cultural Passage from Korea to America* (Albany, NY: SUNY Press, 1996); Grace Ji-Sun Kim, *The Grace of Sophia: A Korean North American Woman's Christology* (Cleveland: Pilgrim Press, 2002); Illsoo Kim, *New Urban Immigrants*, 187–207; Jung Ha Kim, *Bridge-Makers and Cross-Bearers: Korean-American Women and the Church* (Atlanta: Scholars Press, 1997); Ho-Youn Kwon, Kwang Chung Kim, and R. Stephen Warner, Eds., *Korean Americans and Their Religions* (University Park: Pennsylvania State University Press, 2001); Pyong Gap Min, "A Comparison of Korean Immigrant Protestant, Catholic, and Buddhist Congregations in New York," in *Religion and Incorporation of Immigration of Immigrants*, Jose Casanova and Aristide Zolberg, Eds. (New York: NYU Press, forthcoming; advance copy courtesy of the author); Min, "Immigrants' Religion and Ethnicity: A Comparison of Korean Christian and Indian Hindu Immigrants," in *Revealing the Sacred in Asian and Pacific America*, Jane Naomi Iwamura and Paul Spickard, Eds. (New York: Routledge, 2003), 125–141; Min, "The Structure and Social Functions of Korean Immigrant Churches in the United States," *International Migration Review*, 26 (1992), 1370–1394; Pyong Gap Min and Jung Ha Kim, Eds., *Religions in Asian America* (Walnut Creek, CA: AltaMira Press, 2001); Andrew Sung Park, *Racial Conflict and Healing: An Asian-American Theological Perspective* (Maryknoll, NY: Orbis, 1996); Soyoung Park, "'Korean American Evangelical': A Resolution of Sociological Ambivalence Among Korean American College Students," in *Asian American Religions*, Tony Carnes and Fenggang Yang, Eds. (New York: NYU Press, 2004) 182–203; Eui-Hang Shin and Hyung Park, "An Analysis of Causes of Schisms in Ethnic Churches: The Case of Korean-American Churches," *Sociological Analysis*, 49 (1988), 234–248;

Sharon A. Suh, *Being Buddhist in a Christian World: Gender and Community in a Korean American Temple* (Seattle: University of Washington Press, 2004). In addition, David Yoo and Ruth Chung have edited a collection of articles on Korean American religion that will soon be published by the University of Illinois Press.

32. On Black-Korean tensions and the Los Angeles riots, see Nancy Abelmann and John Lie, *Blue Dreams: Korean Americans and the Los Angeles Riots* (Cambridge, MA: Harvard University Press, 1995); Edward T. Chang and Jeannette Diaz-Veizades, *Ethnic Peace in the American City* (New York: NYU Press, 1999); Moon H. Jo, "Korean Merchants in the Black Community: Prejudice Among the Victims of Prejudice," *Ethnic and Racial Studies*, 15 (1992), 395–410; Heon Cheol Lee, "Black-Korean Conflict in New York City" (PhD dissertation, Columbia University, 1993); Kyeyoung Park, "Use and Abuse of Race and Culture: Black-Korean Tension in America," *American Anthropologist*, 98 (1996), 492–499; In-Jin Yoon, *On My Own: Korean Businesses and Race Relations in America* (Chicago: University of Chicago Press, 1997).

33. Ashley Dunn, "Looters, Merchants Put Koreatown Under the Gun," *Los Angeles Times* (May 2, 1992).

34. Helie Lee, *Still Life With Rice* (New York: Simon and Schuster, 1996); Gordon Y. K. Pang, "Group Hopes to Reunite Families," *Honolulu Advertiser* (March 21, 2006).

35. The term seems to have been invented in the 1970s (accounts conflict), but it became widely used only later.

36. Danico, *1.5 Generation*, 179.

37. Sources on South Asian immigrants include Margaret Abraham, *Speaking the Unspeakable: Marital Violence Among South Asian Immigrants in the United States* (New Brunswick, NJ: Rutgers University Press, 2000); Shamita Das Dasgupta, Ed., *A Patchwork Shawl: Chronicles of South Asian Women in America* (New Brunswick, NJ: Rutgers University Press, 1988); Chitra Banerjee Divakaruni, *Arranged Marriage* (New York: Doubleday, 1995); Margaret A. Gibson, *Accommodation Without Assimilation: Sikh Immigrants in an American High School* (Ithaca, NY: Cornell University Press, 1988); S. Mitra Kalita, *Suburban Sahibs: Three Immigrant Families and Their Passage from India to America* (New Brunswick, NJ: Rutgers University Press, 2003); Madhulika S. Khandelwal, *Becoming American, Being Indian: An Immigrant Community in New York City* (Ithaca, NY: Cornell University Press, 2002); Prema A. Kurien, *Kaleidoscopic Ethnicity: International Migration and the Reconstruction of Community Identities in India* (New Brunswick: Rutgers University Press, 2002); Jhumpa Lahiri, *Interpreter of Maladies* (Boston: Houghton Mifflin, 1999); Johanna Lessinger, *From the Ganges to the Hudson* (Boston: Allyn and Bacon, 1995); *Mississippi Masala*, dir. Mira Nair (Columbia TriStar Home Video, 1991); Aminah Mohammad-Arif, *Salaam America: South Asian Muslims in New York* (London: Anthem, 2002); Bharati Mukherjee, *Jasmine* (New York: Ballantine, 1989); Vijay Prashad, *The Kharma of Brown Folk* (Minneapolis: University of Minnesota Press, 2000); Bandana Purkayastha, *Negotiating Ethnicity: Second-Generation South Asian Americans Traverse a Transnational World* (New Brunswick, NJ: Rutgers University Press, 2005); Padma Rangaswamy, *Namasté America: Indian Immigrants in an American Metropolis* (University Park: Pennsylvania State University Press, 2000); Sharmila Rudrappa, *Ethnic Routes to Becoming American: Indian Immigrants and the*

Cultures of Citizenship (New Brunswick, NJ: Rutgers University Press, 2004); Lavina Dhingra Shankar and Rajini Srikanth, Eds., *A Part, Yet Apart: South Asians in Asian America* (Philadelphia: Temple University Press, 1998); Gurinder Singh Mann, Paul David Numrich, and Raymond B. Williams, *Buddhists, Hindus, and Sikhs in America* (New York: Oxford, 2002).

38. Lessinger, *From the Ganges to the Hudson*, 17–18.

39. Rangaswamy, *Namasté America*, xiii; 55, 81.

40. Sources on Chinese immigrants include Iris Chang, *The Chinese in America* (New York: Viking, 2003); Shenglin Chang, *The Global Silicon Valley Home: Lives and Landscapes Within Taiwanese American Culture* (Stanford, CA: Stanford University Press, 2006); Ko-Lin Chin, *Smuggled Chinese: Clandestine Immigration to the United States* (Philadelphia: Temple University Press, 1999); Timothy P. Fong, *The First Suburban Chinatown* (Philadelphia: Temple University Press, 1994); Kenneth J. Guest, *God in Chinatown* (New York: NYU Press, 2003); Peter Kwong, *Forbidden Workers: Illegal Chinese Immigrants and American Labor* (New York: New Press, 1997); Kwong, *The New Chinatown* (New York: Noonday, 1987); Jan Lin, *Reconstructing Chinatown* (Minneapolis: University of Minnesota Press, 1998); Chalsa M. Loo, *Chinese America: Mental Health and Quality of Life in the Inner City* (Thousand Oaks, CA: Sage, 1998); Victor G. and Brett DeBary Nee, *Longtime Californ'* (New York: Pantheon, 1973); Wanning Sun, *Leaving China: Media, Migration, and Transnational Imagination* (Lanham, MD: Rowman and Littlefield, 2002).

41. Nee and Nee, *Longtime Californ'*, 279–280.

42. Nee and Nee, *Longtime Californ'*, 290–295.

43. Miri Song begins to explore the junior mama phenomenon in *Helping Out: Children's Labor in Ethnic Businesses* (Philadelphia: Temple University Press, 1999), but the main focus of her analysis is elsewhere. This important subject awaits examination.

44. Sources on illegal Chinese migrants include Chin, *Smuggled Chinese*; Kwong, *Forbidden Workers*; Sam Howe Verhovek, "22 Chinese Stowaways found at Cargo Facility in Seattle," *Los Angeles Times* (April 6, 2006); Xiao-huang Yin, "The Invisible Illegal Immigrants," *Los Angeles Times* (April 2, 2006).

45. Fong, *First Suburban Chinatown*; Chang, *Global Silicon Valley Home*; David Pierson, "Dragon Roars in San Gabriel," *Los Angeles Times* (March 31, 2006).

46. On the model minority myth, its provenance and consequences, see Rudy V. Busto, "The Gospel According to the Model Minority? Hazarding an Interpretation of Asian American Evangelical College Students," *New Spiritual Homes*, David Yoo, Ed. (Honolulu: University of Hawai'i Press, 1999); Caplan, Whitmore, and Choy, *Boat People and Achievement*; Lucie Cheng and Philip Q. Yang, "The 'Model Minority' Deconstructed," in *Ethnic Los Angeles*, Roger Waldinger and Mehdi Bozorgmehr, Eds. (New York: Russell Sage, 1996), 305–344; Timothy P. Fong, *The Contemporary Asian American Experience: Beyond the Model Minority* (Upper Saddle River, NJ: Prentice Hall, 1998); Charles Hirschman and Morrison G. Wong, "The Extraordinary Educational Attainment of Asian Americans," *Social Forces*, 65 (1986), 1–27; Jayjia Hsia and Samuel S. Peng, "Academic Achievement and Performance," in *Handbook of Asian American Psychology*, Lee C. Lee and Nolan W. S. Zane, Eds. (Thousand Oaks, CA: Sage, 1998), 325–358; Won Moo Hurh and Kwang Chung Kim, "The Success Image of Asian Americans," *Racial and Ethnic Studies*, 12 (1984), 512–538; Stacey J. Lee, *Unraveling the "Model Minority" Stereotype: Listening*

to Asian American Youth (New York: Teachers College, Columbia University, 1996); Vivian S. Louie, *Compelled to Excel: Immigration, Education, and Opportunity Among Chinese Americans* (Stanford, CA: Stanford University Press, 2004); Keith Osajima, "Asian Americans as the Model Minority: An Analysis of the Popular Press Image in the 1960s and 1980s," in *Reflections on Shattered Windows: Promises and Prospects for Asian American Studies*, Gary Y. Okihiro, Ed. (Pullman: Washington State University Press, 1988), 165–174; Lisa Sun-Hee Park, *Consuming Citizenship: Children of Asian Immigrant Entrepreneurs* (Stanford, CA: Stanford University Press, 2005); William Petersen, *Japanese Americans: Oppression and Success* (New York: Random House, 1971); Mia Tuan, *Forever Foreigner or Honorary White? The Asian Ethnic Experience Today* (New Brunswick, NJ: Rutgers University Press, 1999); Wendy Walker-Moffat, *The Other Side of the Asian American Success Story* (San Francisco: Jossey-Bass, 1995); Deborah Woo, *Glass Ceilings and Asian Americans* (Walnut Creek, CA: AltaMira Press, 2000); David K. Yoo, "Testing Assumptions: IQ, Japanese Americans, and the Model Minority Myth in the 1920s and 1930s," in *Remapping Asian American History*, Sucheng Chan, Ed. (Walnut Creek, CA: AltaMira, 2003), 69–86; Benjamin Zulueta, *Forging the Model Minority: Chinese Immigrants, American Science, and the Cold War* (to be published by the University of Hawai'i Press, advance copy courtesy of the author).

47. Petersen, "Success Story, Japanese-American Style," *New York Times Magazine* (January 9, 1966); William Caudill and George DeVos, "Achievement, Culture, and Personality: The Case of the Japanese Americans," *American Anthropologist*, 58 (1956), 1102–1126. Hard on the heels of Petersen's paean to Japanese American wonderfulness, another writer lauded similar virtues in Chinese Americans: "Success Story of One Minority in the US," *US News and World Report* (December 26, 1966), 73–78. The theme continued: "Asian-Americans: A Model Minority," *Newsweek* (December 6, 1982), 39–51; D. A. Bell, "The Triumph of Asian-Americans," *New Republic*, 22(July 15, 1985), 24–31; Robert B. Oxnam, "Why Asians Succeed Here, *New York Times Magazine* (November 30, 1986); D. Divorky, "The Model Minority Goes to School, *Phi Delta Kappan*, 70 (1988), 219–222; Stephen G. Graubard, "Why Do Asian Pupils Win Those Prizes," *New York Times* (January 29, 1988).

48. Rebecca Trounson, "UC System Accepts Record 55,242 Calif. Applicants for Fall Term," *Los Angeles Times* (April 20, 2006). Asians had outnumbered all other groups for several years at the top two campuses in the system, Berkeley and UCLA, as well as at UC Irvine. Asians also amounted to more than one-quarter of Harvard's entering class.

49. U.S. Commission on Civil Rights, *Civil Rights Issues Facing Asian Americans in the 1990s* (Washington, DC: Government Printing Office, 1992).

50. Thomas Sowell, *Ethnic America* (New York: Basic Books, 1981). See also Nathan Glazer and Daniel Patrick Moynihan, *Beyond the Melting Pot* (Cambridge, MA: MIT Press, 1975).

51. Jachinson Chan, *Chinese American Masculinities* (New York: Routledge, 2001).

52. Fong, *Contemporary Asian American Experience*, 57.

53. *Better Luck Tomorrow*, dir. Justin Lin (Paramount Home Entertainment, 2003); Hemmy So, "Koreans Stunned by Tragedy," *Los Angeles Times* (April 8, 2006).

54. Sources on Mexican migration include Rodolfo F. Acuña, *Anything But Mexican: Chicanos in Contemporary Los Angeles* (London: Verso, 1996); Alejandro Portes and Robert L. Bach, *Latin Journey, Cuban and Mexican Immigrants in the United States* (Berkeley: University of California Press, 1985); David E. Hayes-Bautista, *La Nueva California: Latinos in the Golden State* (Berkeley: University of California Press, 2004); Silvia Pedraza-Bailey, *Political and Economic Migrants in America: Cubans and Mexicans* (Austin: University of Texas Press, 1985); David M. Reimers, *Other Immigrants: The Global Origins of the American People* (New York: NYU Press, 2005), 101–124; Roberto Suro, *Strangers Among Us: Latino Lives in a Changing America* (New York: Knopf, 1999); Zaragosa Vargas, *Major Problems in Mexican American History* (Boston: Houghton Mifflin, 1999).

55. U.S. Census Bureau press release (April 20, 2005); U.S. Census Bureau, *We The People: Hispanics in the United States*, CENSR-18 (Washington, DC: U.S. Department of Commerce, 2004); Nicole Gaouette, "Latinos Boost US Population," *Los Angeles Times* (May 10, 2006); Richard Montoya, Ric Salinas, and Herbert Sigüenza, *Culture Clash's Zorro in Hell* (Berkeley Repertory Theatre, 2006); David Kelly, "Vision That Inspires Some and Scares Others: Aztlan," *Los Angeles Times* (July 7, 2006).

56. Sources on the economics, politics, and consequences of NAFTA include David Bacon, *The Children of NAFTA: Labor Wars on the US/Mexico Border* (Berkeley: University of California Press, 2004); Celia W. Dugger, "Report Finds Few Benefits for Mexico in NAFTA," *New York Times* (November 19, 2003); William Greider, *The Case Against Free Trade: GATT, NAFTA, and the Globalization of Corporate Power* (Berkeley, CA: North Atlantic Books, 1993); Marla Dickerson, "Placing Blame for Mexico's Ills: The Economic Policies of the US," *Los Angeles Times* (July 1, 2006); Peter Hakim and Robert Elitan, Eds., *The Future of North American Integration: Beyond NAFTA* (Washington, DC: Brookings, 2002); Rachel Kamel and Anya Hoffman, Eds., *The Maquiladora Reader: Cross-Border Organizing Since NAFTA* (Philadelphia: American Friends Service Committee, 1999); Frederick W. Mager, *Interpreting NAFTA* (New York: Columbia University Press, 1998); "Mexico Adrift," (editorial) *New York Times* (December 28, 2003); William A. Orme, *Understanding NAFTA* (Austin: University of Texas Press, 1996); "Rural Mexico: Indigenous Peasants Abused, Amnesty Says," *Seattle Times* (June 26, 2004); Sidney Weintraub, *NAFTA's Impact on North America: The First Decade* (Washington, DC: Center for Strategic and International Studies, 2001).

57. Sources on the U.S.-Mexican border include Alicia Alarcón, *The Border Patrol Ate My Dust*, trans. Ethriam Cash Brammer de Gonzales (Houston: Arte Público Press, 2004); J. P. Bone, *Illegals* (Berkeley: Mindfield, 1996); Ken Ellingwood, *Hard Line: Life and Death on the US-Mexico Border* (New York: Pantheon, 2004); Luis D. D. León, *La Llorona's Children: Religion, Life, and Death in the US-Mexican Borderlands* (Berkeley: University of California Press, 2004); David E. Lorey, *The US-Mexican Border in the Twentieth Century* (Wilmington, DE: Scholarly Resources, 1999); Ruben Martinez, *Crossing Over: A Mexican Family on the Migrant Trail* (New York: Henry Holt, 2001); Joseph Nevins, *Operation Gatekeeper: The Rise of the "Illegal Alien" and the Making of the US-Mexico Boundary* (New York: Routledge, 2002); *El Norte*, dir. Gregory Nava (Cinecom International Films, 1983); Victor M. Ortiz-González, *El Paso: Local Frontiers at a Global Crossroads* (Minneapolis: University of

Minnesota Press, 2004); Pablo Vila, Ed., *Ethnography at the Border* (Minne-apolis: University of Minnesota Press, 2003). I am also grateful to students who have written papers and told me stories about their own experiences crossing over.

58. Alarcón, *Border Patrol Ate My Dust*, 1–15.

59. Alex Pulaski, "Borders and Legalities Multiply Oregon Family's Grief," *Oregonian* (April 24, 2004).

60. Joseph Nevins, *Operation Gatekeeper: The Rise of the "Illegal Alien" and the Making of the US-Mexico Boundary* (New York: Routledge, 2002); Ken Elling-wood, *Hard Line: Life and Death on the US-Mexico Border* (New York: Pan-theon, 2004); Claudia Smith, "Operation Gatekeeper's Darker Side," *San Diego Union-Tribune* (October 16, 1997); Claudia Smith, "Is America Losing Its Soul in Its Attempt to Control the Border?" *San Diego Union-Tribune* (September 10, 1998); Erin Texeira, "The Hidden Toll," *Los Angeles Times* (November 2, 2000); Scott Gold and Ken Ellingwood, "Trapped in Trailer, 18 Migrants Die," *Los Angeles Times* (May 15, 2003); Patrick O'Driscoll and Haya El Nasser, "Summer Can Be Lethal for Illegals," *USA Today* (May 19, 2003); Richard Boudreaux, "Deadly Journey of Hope," *Los Angeles Times* (October 13, 2004); "Crosses on the Border," editorial, *New York Times* (June 1, 2004); Richard Marosi, "Border Crossing Deaths Set a 12-Month Record," *Los Angeles Times* (October 1, 2005); Nick Madigan, "Early Heat Wave Kills 12 Illegal Immigrants in the Arizona Desert," *New York Times* (May 26, 2005); CBS News, "Dying To Get In," *60 Minutes* (December 8, 2005); Nicholas Riccardi, "Migrants Survive Arizona Desert," *Los Angeles Times* (July 20, 2006).

61. Britain, France, Germany, Spain, Austria, Sweden, Ireland, Denmark, and Italy are among the European nations that had repeated, escalating political and humanitarian crises over immigration and membership through the 1990s and 2000s. See, for example, Alessandro Portelli, "The Problem of the Color-Blind," in *Race and Nation: Ethnic Systems in the Modern World*, Paul Spickard, Ed. (New York: Routledge, 2005), 355–363; Charles A. Kupchan, "Europe Turns Back the Clock," *Los Angeles Times* (May 30, 2006); Judy Dempsey, "Racial Attack on Politician Angers Germans," *International Herald Tribune* (May 22, 2006); A. Eatwell, "Ministers Rush Through Urgent Plan as Migrants Sail 1,200 Kilometers to Spain," *El Pais* (May 16, 2006); Renwick McLean, "A Surge of Migrants Hits Canary Islands," *International Herald Tribune* (May 16, 2006); Miguel Gonzalez, "Military Embarks on Migrant Early Warning Patrols," *El Pais* (May 18, 2006); Meg Clothier, "Racism in Russia is Out of Control," *Reuters* (May 4, 2006); Jeffrey Fleishman, "Cultural, Religious Dis-cord Shades European Need for Immigrants," *Los Angeles Times* (April 28, 2006); Tracy Wilkinson, "A Sister's Sacrifice," *Los Angeles Times* (April 22, 2006); Jeffrey Fleishman, "In Germany, Citizenship Tests Stir Up Muslims, and Cultural Debate," *Los Angeles Times* (April 9, 2006); Jeffrey Fleishman, Ralph Frammolino, and Sebastian Rotella, "Outraged Europeans Take Dimmer View of Diversity," *Los Angeles Times* (September 5, 2005); Graham Bowley, "Euro-pean Commission Seeks Faster Repatriation of Some Migrants," *International Herald Tribune* (September 2, 2005); Katrin Bennhold, "French Police Evict 40 Africans," *International Herald Tribune* (September 3, 2005); Ranwick, "Five Killed in Mass Attempt to Cross From Morocco to Spanish Enclave," *New York Times* (September 30, 2005); Craig S. Smith, "Morocco Again Expels Africans Trying Risky Path to Europe," *New York Times* (October 17, 2005); Michael

Kamber and Marc Lacey, "For Mali Villagers, France Is a Workplace and Life-line," *New York Times* (September 11, 2005); Tracy Wilkinson, "Muslims' Slice of Italy's Life," *Los Angeles Times* (October 28, 2005); "French Riots Rage for Ninth Night," *Los Angeles Times* (November 5, 2005); Richard Bernstein, "Officials Cautious on Violence in Germany and Belgium," *New York Times* (November 7, 2005); Craig S. Smith, "Spain's African Enclaves Are Migrants' Portals to Europe," *New York Times* (November 5, 2005); Jeffrey Fleishman, "A Mutual Suspicion Grows in Denmark," *Los Angeles Times* (November 12, 2005); Olivier Roy, "Get French or Die Trying," *New York Times* (November 9, 2005); Craig S. Smith, "What Makes Someone French?" *New York Times* (November 11, 2005); Jeffrey Fleishman, "In Berlin, a Cultural Wall Sets Turks Apart," *Los Angeles Times* (December 22, 2005); Elisabeth Rosenthal, "A Poor Fit for an Immigrant: After 20 Years of Hard Work in Italy, Still Not Italian," *New York Times* (January 1, 2006); Ian Fisher, "Flow of Muslim Immigrants Strains the Reputation for Tolerance of a Small Italian Town," *New York Times* (August 27, 2005); John Daniszewski, "Britain Issues Criteria for Deportation," *Los Angeles Times* (August 25, 2005).

62. Esmeralda Bermudez, "Blanca Aguilar: Child Labor Crusade Springs from Fields," *Oregonian* (May 10, 2004); Frank Cancian, *Orange County House-cleaners* (Albuquerque: University of New Mexico Press, 2006); Lisa Girion, "Once Surrounded by Asbestos, Now Surrounded by Their Fears," *Los Angeles Times* (September 25, 2004); Daniel Hernandez, "For Some, Avalon Is Alca-traz," *Los Angeles Times* (February 24, 2005); Jerry Hirsch, "Farm Labor Con-tractor, Union in Pact," *Los Angeles Times* (April 12, 2006); James C. McKinley, Jr., "Mexican Pride and Death in US Service," *New York Times* (March 22, 2005); Zeke Minaya, "Marine Corps Pfc. Fernando Hannon, Wildomar; Killed in Explosion," *Los Angeles Times* (August 22, 2004); Julian E. Barnes, "Newest US Citizens Take Oath in Iraq," *Los Angeles Times* (July 5, 2006); Sam Qui-nones, "Drifting In on Katrina's Wind, Laborers Alter the Streetscape," *Los Angeles Times* (May 1, 2006); *Real Women Have Curves*, dir. Patricia Cardoso (HBO Films, 2003); Rone Tempest, "Saddened Town Adds Name to Monument Honoring War Dead," *Los Angeles Times* (November 12, 2003); Kevin Thomas, "The Political Is Personal in 'Bread and Roses,'" *Los Angeles Times* (May 11, 2001); Catherine Trevison, "From Wanting Out to Getting Out," *Oregonian* (November 17, 2003); Paula L. Woods, "Seen but Not Seen," *Los Angeles Times* (June 11, 2006); Sandra Tsing Loh quote is from Héctor Tobar, *Translation Nation* (New York: Riverhead, 2005), 343.

63. Sharon Bernstein, "HIV on the Rise Among Migrants," *Los Angeles Times* (November 2, 2004); Marla Cone, "DDT Study Finds New Hazard," *Los Ange-les Times* (July 5, 2006); Girion, "Once Surrounded by Asbestos"; Kathleen Hennessey, "Barriers to Latino Home Buying," *Los Angeles Times* (Septem-ber 15, 2004); Claire Hoffman, "Grape Grower Agrees to Settle EEOC Sexual Harassment Case," *Los Angeles Times* (June 16, 2005); Lee Romney, "Poor Neighborhoods Left Behind," *Los Angeles Times* (September 18, 2005); "No Indictment in Death of Immigrant," *Los Angeles Times* (May 3, 2002).

64. On the press's and the politicians' fascination with Mexican American gangs, see Nick Anderson, "Ad Brings Stereotype Charge," *Los Angeles Times* (Octo-ber 9, 2004); Arian Campo-Flores, "Gangland's New Face," *Newsweek* (Decem-ber 8, 2003); Chris Kraul, Robert J. Lopez, and Rich Connell, "LA Violence Crosses the Line," *Los Angeles Times* (May 15, 2005); Claudia Kolker, "Danc-

ing for Pay, Dying by the Hand of a Demon," *Los Angeles Times* (July 31, 1999); Charlie LeDurr, "100 Members of Immigrant Gang Are Held," *New York Times* (March 15, 2005); Anne-Marie O'Connor, "Past Haunts Immigrant Who Says He Cut Gang Ties," *Los Angeles Times* (April 21, 2000); Tony Perry, "Mexican Mafia Charges Filed," *Los Angeles Times* (June 17, 2006); Dan Weikel, "INS Frees Man After Nine Months," *Los Angeles Times* (May 24, 2000).

65. Genaro C. Armas, "Hispanic Population Still Burgeoning," *Oregonian* (October 8, 2003); Esmeralda Bermudez, "Five Men Arrested in Housing Scam," *Oregonian* (March 15, 2004); Esmeralda Bermudez, "Hillsboro Survey Finds Gripes on Gain in Latino Population," *Oregonian* (November 18, 2003); Steven Bodzin, "Latino Immigrants Filling Southern Niches, Study Finds," *Los Angeles Times* (July 27, 2005); "A Chance to Reach Out," *New York Times* (April 24, 2005); Mike Davis, "Magical Urbanism: Latinos Reinvent the US Big City," *National Labor Review*, no. 234 (March April 1999), 3–43; Lawrence Downes, "The 185 Tequilas of Alida Yougez," *New York Times* (January 8, 2006); Leon Fink, *The Maya of Morgantown: Work and Community in the Nuevo New South* (Chapel Hill: University of North Carolina Press, 2003); Stephen Franklin, "'Jobs that Americans Won't Do' Filled by Desperate Migrants," *Chicago Tribune* (January 17, 2005); Jeffrey Gettleman, "Obscure Law Used to Jail Day Laborers in Georgia," *Los Angeles Times* (August 21, 2001); William Grimes, "In This Small Town in Iowa the Future Speaks Spanish," *New York Times* (September 14, 2005); "A High Death Rate for Hispanic Pedestrians in the South," *New York Times* (December 4, 2005); Peter Y. Hong, "Latinos Finding New Home in Suburbs, Study Shows," *Los Angeles Times* (July 31, 2002); "Hope and Ashes in Farmingville," *New York Times* (June 27, 2004); "In Georgia, Immigrant Recalls Night of Death and Violence," *New York Times* (October 2, 2005); John McCormick and John Keilman, "Latinos Drive Growth," *Chicago Tribune* (August 11, 2005); Robin Pogrebin, "Lured by the Work, but Struggling to Be Paid," *New York Times* (October 17, 2005); Grogory Rodriguez, "*La Nueva* New Orleans," *Los Angeles Times* (September 25, 2005); Ann M. Simmons, "Latinos in New Orleans, Suburb Feel Slighted," *Los Angeles Times* (September 20, 2005); Stephanie Simon, "Latinos Take Root in Midwest," *Los Angeles Times* (October 24, 2002); Stephen Striffler, "We're All Mexicans Here: Poultry Processing, Latino Migration, and the Transformation of Class in the South," paper presented to anthropology department, University of California, Santa Barbara (February 5, 2004); Zaragosa Vargas, *Proletarians of the North: A History of Mexican Industrial Workers in Detroit and the Midwest, 1917–1933* (Berkeley: University of California Press, 1993); Víctor Zúñiga and Rubén Hernández-León, Eds., *New Destinations: Mexican Immigration in the United States* (New York: Russell Sage, 2005).

66. Duke Helfand, "Nearly Half of Blacks, Latinos Drop Out, School Study Shows," *Los Angeles Times* (March 24, 2005); Ruben Navarette, "Latino Immigrants Have Done Just Fine in Pursuing Dreams," *Los Angeles Times* (May 27, 2003); Rand Corporation, "Rand Study Shows Hispanic Immigrants Move Up Economic, Educational Ladder As Quickly As Other Immigrant Groups" press release (May 22, 2003); Dianne Solis, "Latinos Lag Whites in Job Growth Recovery," *Oregonian* (October 8, 2003).

67. Arlene Dávila, *Latinos Inc.: The Marketing and Making of a People* (Berkeley: University of California Press, 2001); "Latin USA: How Young Hispanics Are Changing America," Brook Larmer, "Latino America," John Leland and

Veronica Chambers, "Generation Ñ," "Critical Más," Christy Haubegger, "The Legacy of Generation Ñ," *Newsweek* (July 12, 1999); Aliert Brown-Gort, "As American as Cinco de Mayo," *Chicago Tribune* (May 4, 2005); Jennifer Delson, "Parade Caps Celebration of Mexican Culture," *Los Angeles Times* (September 26, 2005).

68. Stuart Silverstein, "Chancellor Tackles Image Problems," *Los Angeles Times* (May 27, 2003); "A New Campus 'Vida,'" *Newsweek* (September 13, 2004); Lisa Helm, "Greeks Go Latin—Or Vice Versa," *Newsweek* (November 1, 2004); "Academe's Hispanic Future," *Chronicle of Higher Education*, 50.14 (November 28, 2003); Kimi Yoshino, "Love of the Game Brings Angels' Buyer to Baseball," *Los Angeles Times* (May 15, 2003); Bill Plashke, "Touched by Moreno," *Los Angeles Times* (May 23, 2003); "This Is *American* Soccer?" *Los Angeles Times* (March 13, 2005); Paul Gutierrez, "Bachelors of Starts," *Los Angeles Times* (May 28, 2005); Lauren Gustus, "Trying to Make a Connection: Real Salt Lake's Relationship with Utah's Latinos," *Salt Lake Tribune* (August 3, 2005); Meg James, "Nielsen Bows to Latino Viewers," *Los Angeles Times* (December 20, 2005); Meg James, "Networks Have an Ear for Spanish," *Los Angeles Times* (September 11, 2005); Reed Johnson, "A Post-NAFTA Star," *Los Angeles Times* (May 28, 2006).

69. Noam N. Levey, "Q & A: Supervisor Gloria Molina," *Los Angeles Times* (April 14, 2006); Jenifer Warren and Dan Morain, "His Is a Tale of Timing and Gradual Change," *Los Angeles Times* (September 7, 2003); Steve Lopez, "Shedding Some Light on Bustamante's Dark Activist Past," *Los Angeles Times* (September 3, 2003); Patrick McGreevy, "Latinos, Flexing Political Muscle, Come of Age in LA," *Los Angeles Times* (June 27, 2005); Nicolle Gaouette, "Latino Clout at Polls Lagging, Study Says," *Los Angeles Times* (June 28, 2005); Steve Hymon, "Sons Live Out a Dream," *Los Angeles Times* (May 7, 2006); Jim Newton, "Speaker Villaraigosa Enters Race for Mayor," *Los Angeles Times* (October 17, 1999); several articles on Villaraigosa victory, *Los Angeles Times* (May 19, 2005); "Latino Power: LA's New Mayor—and How Hispanics Will Change American Politics," cover story, *Newsweek* (May 30, 2005); John M. Broder, "New Mayor Talks His Way Across Los Angeles's Divides," *New York Times* (May 30, 2005); Patrick McGreevy, "Villaraigosa Wins Over Crowds in Nation's Capital," *Los Angeles Times* (June 2, 2005); Jessica Garrison and Daniel Hernandez, "World Press Fits Villaraigosa Into the Big Picture," *Los Angeles Times* (June 30, 2005); several articles on Villaraigosa taking office, *Los Angeles Times* (July 2, 2005); Daniel Hernandez, "Villaraigosa Aims to Make Most of 'Latino Mayor' Role," *Los Angeles Times* (October 12, 2005).

70. David Kelly, "He's the Non-Candidate on Everyone's Radar," *Los Angeles Times* (September 4, 2003); Jennifer Senior, "The Life of the Party?" *New York Times* (May 9, 2004); Mark Z. Barabak, "A New New Democrat Looks West and Forward," *Los Angeles Times* (August 14, 2005); Ronald Brownstein, "Latino Clout, Improved Economy Soften GOP Stance on Immigration," *Los Angeles Times* (July 19, 1999); Rubén Martínez, "The Ties That Bind Latinos," *Los Angeles Times* (August 5, 2001); Sarah Kershaw, "A Vital Bloc, Realizing Its Power, Measures Its Suitors," *New York Times* (February 2, 2004); James Rainey, "'Hope Is On the Way,' Edwards Assures Latinos in Los Angeles," *Los Angeles Times* (July 17, 2004); Ronald Brownstein and Kathleen Hennessey, "Latino Vote Still Lags Its Potential," *Los Angeles Times* (September 25, 2004); Ricardo Alonso-Zaldivar, "Bush Snags Much More of the Latino Vote, Exit Polls Show,"

Los Angeles Times (November 4, 2004); "Hispanic Voters Think Again," *Los Angeles Times* (November 11, 2004); David Stout, "Senate Rift Deep in Debate Over Attorney General Nominee," *New York Times* (February 1, 2005); Richard B. Schmitt, "Ethnic Roots to Show at Hearings," *Los Angeles Times* January 6, 2005); Fernando J. Guerra, "The 'Browning' of US Politics," *Los Angeles Times* (May 3, 2005).

71. Sources on Cuban immigration include Cheris T. Brewer, "'Castro's Loss Is Our Gain': Accepting, Assisting, and Resettling Cuban Refugees, 1959–1978" (MA thesis, Washington State University, 2005); María Cristina García, *Havana USA: Cuban Exiles and Cuban Americans in South Florida, 1959–1994* (Berkeley: University of California Press, 1996); José Llanes, *Cuban Americans* (Cambridge, MA: Abt, 1982); James S. Olson and Judith E. Olson, *Cuban Americans* (New York: Twayne, 1995); Pedraza-Bailey, *Political and Economic Migrants*; Portes and Bach, *Latin Journey*; Alex Stepick, Guillermo Grenier, Max Castro, and Marvin Dunn, *This Land Is Our Land: Immigrants and Power in Miami* (Berkeley: University of California Press, 2003); María de los Angeles Torres, *The Lost Apple: Operation Pedro Pan, Cuban Children in the US, and the Promise of a Better Future* (Boston: Beacon, 2004).

72. García, *Havana USA*, 163.

73. John-Thor Dahlburg, "Cuban Americans Applaud Ruling by High Court," *Los Angeles Times* (January 15, 2005); Linda Greenhouse, "Supreme Court Rejects Mariel Cubans' Detention," *New York Times* (January 13, 2005); Alex Larzelere, *The 1980 Cuban Boatlift* (Washington, DC: National Defense University Press, 1988).

74. Arian Campo-Flores, "Dance of the Cubans," *Newsweek* (March 10, 2003); John-Thor Dahlburg, "Plea for Unity Among Cuban Exiles," *Los Angeles Times* (January 14, 2003); John Pain, "Cuban Americans Try to Beat Trip Limits," *Oregonian* (June 30, 2004); John M. Glionna, "Bush's Cuban American Support May Be Slipping," *Los Angeles Times* (September 21, 2004); Miguel Bustillo, "Some Cuban Exiles Give Up the Wait," *Los Angeles Times* (August 2, 2006); Carol J. Williams, "Change in Cuba Policy Floated," *Los Angeles Times* (August 10, 2006); Carol J. Williams, "In Miami, Graying Anti-Castro Movement Is Losing Steam," *Los Angeles Times* (August 11, 2006).

75. Yes, it is true that a young Fidel Castro possessed a good enough curve ball that he was drafted and offered a bonus by the New York Giants. He chose instead to go to law school and pursue a career in revolution.

76. The Elian Gonzalez controversy was a daily news feature for several months. See, for example,, Joseph Contreras and Russell Watson, "A Little Boy in the Middle," *Newsweek* (December 20, 1999); "Miami Kin File Petition to Fight Boy's Return to Cuba," *Los Angeles Times* (January 8, 2000); John J. Goldman, "Elian's Grandmothers Fly to NY, Ask for His Release," *Los Angeles Times* (January 22, 2000); Jack Kelley, "Quest for Freedom Knows No Bounds," *USA Today* (March 10, 2000); Hector Tobar and Mike Clary, "Many Latinos Resent Exiles' Clout, Favor Elian's Return," *Los Angeles Times* (April 15, 2000); Richard Serrano and Mike Clary, "Stalemate Over Fate of Elian Continues," *Los Angeles Times* (April 15, 2000); Esther Schrader, "'Cult of Elian' Devotees Hold Out Hope for a Miracle," *Los Angeles Times* (April 16, 2000); "Elián's Ordeal," cover story, *Newsweek* (April 17, 2000); Mike Downey, "With Friends Like These, Little Elian Needs No Enemies," *Los Angeles Times* (April 19, 2000); Richard Serrano and Eric Lichtblau, "Elian's Father Asks Public to Urge

Reunion," *Los Angeles Times* (April 21, 2000); Richard A. Serrano, "Elian, Dad Reunited After Raid," *Los Angeles Times* (April 23, 2000); Anna Quindlen, "The Sins of the Fathers," *Newsweeek* (April 24, 2000); Robert Scheer, "Everyone Is Using the Little Boy," *Los Angeles Times* (April 25, 2000); "Seizing Elian," cover story, *Newsweek* (May 1, 2000); Evan Thomas, "Cashing In on Little Elián," *Newsweek* (May 8, 2000); Mike Clary, "Cuban Americans United in Frustration," *Los Angeles Times* (May 23, 2000); Esther Schrader, "Elian Returns to Cuba After Appeal Rejected," *Los Angeles Times* (June 29, 2000); John-Thor Dahlberg, "Little Havana Hasn't Forgiven or Forgotten the Seizure of Elian," *Los Angeles Times* (February 1, 2005).

77. Bone, *Illegals*; María Cristina García, *Seeking Refuge: Central American Migration to Mexico, the United States, and Canada* (Berkeley: University of California Press, 2006); Sonia Nazario, *Enrique's Journey* (New York: Random House, 2006); Sonia Nazario, "Enrique's Journey," series, *Los Angeles Times* (September 29–October 7, 2002); *El Norte*; Stephen Kinzer, "The Trouble with Costa Rica," *New York Review of Books* (June 8, 2006).

78. Sources on Puerto Rican migrants include María Teresa Babín and Stan Steiner, Eds., *Borinquen: An Anthology of Puerto Rican Literature* (New York: Knopf, 1974); Arlene Dávila, *Barrio Dreams: Puerto Ricans, Latinos, and the Neoliberal City* (Berkeley: University of California Press, 2004); Edward Rivera, *Family Installments: Memories of Growing Up Hispanic* (New York: Morrow, 1982); Clara E. Rodríguez, *Puerto Ricans: Born in the USA* (Boulder, CO: Westview, 1991); Virginia E. Sánchez Korrol, *From Colonia to Community: The History of Puerto Ricans in New York City*, rev. ed. (Berkeley: University of California Press, 1994); Aurora Levins Morales, *Remedios: Stories of Earth and Iron from the History of Puertorriqueñas* (Cambridge, MA: South End Press, 2001); Stan Steiner, *The Islands: The Worlds of the Puerto Ricans* (New York: Harper, 1974); Carmen Teresa Whalen and Víctor Vázquez-Hernández, Eds., *The Puerto Rican Diaspora* (Philadelphia: Temple University Press, 2005).

Sources on Dominicans, Jamaicans, and other West Indians include Julia Alvarez, *How the García Girls Lost Their Accents* (New York: Workman, 1991); Holger Henke, *The West Indian Americans* (Westport, CT: Greenwood, 2001); Philip Kasinitz, *Caribbean New York: Black Immigrants and the Politics of Race* (Ithaca, NY: Cornell University Press, 1992); Petty Levitt, *The Transnational Villagers* (Berkeley: University of California Press, 2001); Silvio Torres-Saillant and Ramona Hernández, *The Dominican Americans* (Westport, CT: Greenwood, 1998); Milton Vickerman, *Crosscurrents: West Indian Immigrants and Race* (New York: Oxford, 1999); Mary C. Waters, *Black Identities: West Indian Immigrant Dreams and American Realities* (New York: Russell Sage, 1999).

79. Sources on Haitians include Karen McCarthy Brown, *Mama Lola: A Vodou Priestess in Brooklyn* (Berkeley: University of California Press, 1991); Michel S. Laguerre, *American Odyssey: Haitians in New York City* (Ithaca, NY: Cornell University Press, 1984); Nina Glick Schiller and Georges Eugene Fouron, *Georges Woke Up Laughing: Long-Distance Nationalism and the Search for Home* (Durham, NC: Duke University Press, 2001); Tekle Mariam Woldemikael, *Becoming Black American: Haitians and American Institutions in Evanston, Illinois* (New York: AMS, 1989); Flore Zéphir, *The Haitian Americans* (Westport, CT: Greenwood, 2004).

80. Brian Haas, Macollvie Jean François, and Tal Abbady, "46 Immigrants Caught in Upscale Florida Town," *Los Angeles Times* (April 18, 2006); Ruth Ellen Wasem, "US Immigration Policy on Haitian Migrants," Congressional Research Service Report for Congress (January 21, 2005); David G. Savage, "Haitian Intercept Policy Backed by High Court Immigration," *Los Angeles Times* (June 22, 1993); Mark Dow, "Occupying and Obscuring Haiti," *New Politics*, 5.2 (1995); Sarah Bermeo, "Clinton and Coercive Diplomacy: A Study of Haiti," Woodrow Wilson School of Public and International Affairs, Princeton University (April 24, 2001); Carolle Charles, "Political Refugees or Economic Immigrants? A New 'Old Debate' Within the Haitian Immigrant Communities *but* with Contestations and Division," *Journal of American Ethnic History*, 25.2–3 (2006), 190–208.

On the racial dimension of the differential treatment accorded Haitians, see Stepick et al., *This Land Is Our Land*, 102–104. The U.S. Supreme Court ruled in 1985, in the case *Jean et al. v. Nelson*, that the INS was indeed violating the equal protection clause of the Fifth Amendment, in that the court judged the reason INS was treating Haitians differently with regard to parole from detention was made on the basis of race and national origin; LeMay and Barkan, *US Immigration and Naturalization Laws and Issues*, 280–281.

81. Schiller and Fouron, *Georges Woke Up Laughing*; Levitt, *Transnational Villagers*; Carol J. Williams, "The Benefactor," *Los Angeles Times* (April 18, 2006).

82. Matt Kester, personal communication. For theoretical insights into this phenomenon, see James Clifford, "Diasporas," *Cultural Anthropology*, 9.3 (1994), 302–338; Roger Rouse, "Mexican Migration and the Social Space of Postmodernism," *Diaspora*, 1.1 (1991); Vijay Mishra, "The Diasporic Imaginary: Theorizing the Indian Diaspora," *Textual Practice*, 10.3 (1996), 421–447; Robin Cohen, *Global Diasporas: An Introduction* (Seattle: University of Washington Press, 1997); Nicholas Van Hear, *New Diasporas: The Mass Exodus, Dispersal, and Regrouping of Migrant Communities* (Seattle: University of Washington Press, 1998); Darshan Singh Tatla, *The Sikh Diaspora* (Seattle: University of Washington Press, 1999); Paul Spickard, "Pacific Diaspora?" in *Pacific Diaspora: Island Peoples in the United States and Across the Pacific*, Spickard, Ed. (Honolulu: University of Hawai'i Press, 1–27); Shengling Chang, *The Global Silicon Valley Home: Lives and Landscapes Within Taiwanese American Trans-Pacific Culture* (Stanford, CA: Stanford University Press, 2006).

83. Appendix B, Tables 9–14.

84. Appendix B, Table 15.

85. Russian Americans and people from other Eastern European countries inherited some of the gangster stereotype from Italian Americans. It was as little warranted in their case as it had been for Italians, but that did not stop TV shows like *Law and Order* from portraying countless menacing Ukrainian and Russian criminal masterminds. The 2003 remake of *The Italian Job* (dir. F. Gary Gray, Paramount Pictures), included a sinister Ukrainian crime figure, of which a huge Samoan named Skinny Pete says fearfully, "If there's one thing I know, it's never to mess with mother nature, mother-in-laws, or mother-freaking Ukrainians." The Ukrainian in question proceeds to eliminate multiple characters in grisly ways. On the reputed Albanian mob in New York, see Kareem Fahim, "Beating Them at Their Own Game," *New York Times* (January 3, 2006).

86. On recent Polish migration, see Mary Patrice Erdmans, *Opposite Poles: Immigrants and Ethnics in Polish Chicago, 1976–1990* (University Park: Pennsylvania State University Press, 1998). On Balkan migrants, see T. Christian Miller, "Kosovo Families Adjusting to Life in the Valley," *Los Angeles Times* (May 30, 1999); T. Christian Miller and Ann M. Simmons, "Relief Camps for Africans, Kosovars Worlds Apart," *Los Angeles Times* (May 21, 1999); Natasha Radojcic, "The Many Faces of New York: Rented Mattress in an Adopted City," *International Herald Tribune* (November 24, 2004). For a penetrating look at how recent immigrants from Britain use their Englishness strategically to their advantage—to be even Whiter and hence more privileged than other White Americans—see Katharine W. Jones, *Accent on Privilege: English Identities and Anglophilia in the US* (Philadelphia: Temple University Press, 2001).

87. Sources on sex work and migration include Ruben Abati, *Trapped: A Compendium of Issues on Illegal Migration and Human Trafficking* (Lagos, Nigeria: Society for Enlightenment of Youths on Dangers Abroad); Laura Agustín, "The Plight of Migrant Women: They Speak, but Who's Listening?" in *Women@ Internet: Creating New Cultures in Cyberspace*, W. Harcourt, Ed. (London: Zed, 1999); Laura Agustín, "Working in the European Sex Industry: Migrant Possibilities," *OFRIM/Suplementos* (June 2000); Anti-Slavery International, *The Migration-Trafficking Nexus* (London: Anti-Slavery International, 2003); Muhadjir Darwin, Anna Marie Wattie, Susi Eja Yuarsi, *Cross-Border Mobility and Sexual Exploitation in the Greater Southeast Asia Sub-Region* (Yogyakarta, Indonesia: Center for Population and Policy Studies, Garjah Mada University, 2003); Melissa Hope Ditmore, *Encyclopedia of Prostitution and Sex Work* (Westport, CT : Greenwood, 2006); Kristina Kangaspunta, *Trafficking in Persons: Global Patterns* (United Nations Office on Drugs and Crime, April 2006); Kamala Kempadoo, Jyoti Sanghera, Bandana Pattanaik, Eds., *Trafficking and Prostitution Reconsidered: New Perspectives on Migration, Sex Work and Human Rights* (Boulder, CO: Paradigm Publishers, 2005); Gilbert King, *Woman, Child for Sale: The New Slave Trade in the 21st Century* (New York: Chamberlain, 2004); David Kyle and Rey Koslowski, Eds., *Global Human Smuggling* (Baltimore: Johns Hopkins University Press, 2001); Barbara Limanowska, *Trafficking in Human Beings in South Eastern Europe* (Sarajevo, Bosnia and Herzegovina: Unicef, 2003); Vincenzo Musacchio, "Migration, Prostitution and Trafficking in Women," *German Law Journal*, 5.9 (2004), 1015–1030; Organización Internacional par las Migraciones, *Migración, Prostitución y Trata de Mujeres Dominicanas en la Argentina* (Buenos Aires: OIM, 2003); Leah Platt, "Regulating the Global Brothel," *American Prospect* (Summer 2001); Birgit Sauer, "Trafficking in Women and Prostitution," project of the Institute for Human Sciences, Vienna; Penelope Saunders, "Migration, Sex Work and Trafficking in Persons," www.walnet.org/csis/papers/saunders-migration.html (July 10, 2006); Siriporn Skrobanek, Nataya Boonpakdee, Chutima Jantateero, *The Traffic in Women: Human Realities of the International Sex Trade* (London: Zed, 1997); Craig S. Smith, "Turkey's Growing Sex Trade Snares Many Slavic Women," *New York Times* (June 26, 2005); Dag Stenvoll, project leader, "Prostitution, Gender and Migration: Russian Women Selling Sex in Norway," policy research working group (Bergen: Rokkansenteret, 2006); Sally Stoecker and Louise Shelley, *Human Traffic and Transnational Crime: Eurasian and American Perspectives* (Lanham, MD: Rowman and Littlefield, 2005); United Nations International Office for Migration, *Migrant Trafficking and Human*

Smuggling in Europe (UNIOM, 2000); Washington State Task Force Against Trafficking in Persons, *Human Trafficking: Present Day Slavery* (Olympia, WA: Office of Crime Victims Advocacy, 2004).

Some would argue that the more than 350 Internet companies, such as the Svetlana Agency, that were offering international dating and pen pal services were promoting a softer-core version of sex for hire, women advertising themselves overseas in the hope of attracting husbands who would bring them to America. See Nicole Constable, *Romance on a Global Stage: Pen Pals, Virtual Ethnography, and "Mail Order" Marriages* (Berkeley: University of California Press, 2003).

88. *In America*, dir. Jim Sheridan (Fox Searchlight Pictures, 2002); Stephanie Merritt, "In the Pain of the Father," *The Observer* (October 12, 2003); Nina Bernstein, "An Irish Face on the Cause of Citizenship," *New York Times* (March 16, 2006); Nina Bernstein, "Greener Pastures (on the Emerald Isle): As American Dream Fades, More Irish Immigrants Are Going Home," *New York Times* (November 10, 2004).

89. Sources on recent African migration include Rogaia Mustafa Abusharaf, *Wanderings: Sudanese Migrants and Exiles in North America* (Ithaca, NY: Cornell University Press, 2002); John A. Arthur, *Invisible Sojourners: African Immigrant Diaspora in the United States* (Westport, CT: Praeger, 2000); Nate Carlisle, "Utah's Sudanese Urge Probe of Death," *Salt Lake Tribune* (August 3, 2005); Helene Elliott, "Marathoner Is Nothing if Not Enduring," *Los Angeles Times* (June 24, 2005); April Gordon, "The New Diaspora—African Immigration to the United States," *Journal of Third World Studies*, 15 (1998), 79–103; Jon D. Holtzman, *Nuer Journeys, Nuer Lives: Sudanese Refugees in Minnesota* (Boston: Allyn and Bacon, 2000); Violet Showers Johnson, "What, Then, Is the African American? Immigration and the Transformation of Black America," Joseph R. Gladden Jr. Public Lecture, Agnes Scott College, Decatur, Georgia (April 4, 2006); Chidinma Offoh-Robert, "African/Nigerian Immigrant Students in Higher Education," (PhD dissertation, University of California, Santa Barbara, 2004); Ann M. Simmons, "African Immigrants Upset at Service Center Closure," *Los Angeles Times* (September 3, 2005); Tibbert L. Speer, "A Cracked Door: US Policy Welcomes Only Africa's Brightest and Richest," *Emerge*, 6 (August 31, 1995), 36; Paul Stoller, *Money Has No Smell: The Africanization of New York City* (Chicago: University of Chicago Press, 2002).

90. Sam Roberts, "More Africans Enter US Than in Days of Slavery," *New York Times* (February 21, 2005).

91. Donatella Lorch, "Out of Africa," *Newsweek* (March 19, 2001); Reimers, *Other Immigrants*, 232–260; Ann M. Simmons, "Sudanese Refugees Reunite to Plan Future," *Los Angeles Times* (May 31, 2005); Simmons, "Years Later, 'Lost Boy' Finds Kin, but What About His Mom?" *Los Angeles Times* (June 11, 2005).

92. Sources on female genital mutilation and its involvement in migration and asylum claims include Amnesty International, "Female Genital Mutilation—A Human Rights Information Pack," www.amnesty.org/ailib/intcam/femgen/fgm1.htm (July 10, 2006); Efua Dorkenoo, *Cutting the Rose: Female Genital Mutilation: The Practice and Its Prevention* (London: Minority Rights Group, 1994); feminist.com, "Spotlight on Female Genital Mutilation," www.feminist.com/violence/spot/fgm.html (July 10, 2006); Fran P. Hosken, *Stop Female Genital Mutilation: Women Speak* (Lexincton, MA: Women's International News, 1995); Religious Tolerance.org, *Debates about FGM*, www.

religioustolerance.org/fem_cirm.htm (July 10, 2006); Nahid Toubia and Susan Izett, *Female Genital Mutilation: An Overview* (Geneva: World Health Organization, 1998); Alice Walker and Pratibha Parmar, *Warrior Marks: Female Genital Mutilation and the Sexual Blinding of Women* (San Diego: Harcourt Brace, 1996).

93. Roberts, "More Africans Enter." Note that the difference was both that the American did not see his Africanness and that his African identity was more obvious in Europe because there were very few local Blacks.

94. Violet Showers Johnson, "Forty-One Shots Through the American Dream: Black Immigrants' Narratives about the Diallo Killing," paper presented to the Society for Multi-Ethnic Studies: Europe and the Americas (Pamplona, Spain, May 20, 2006); Kadiatou Diallo, *My Heart Will Cross This Ocean: My Story, My Son, Amadou* (New York: Ballantine, 2004); Sidney L. Harring, "The Diallo Incident: Another 'Tragic Accident' in New York's War on Street Crime?" *Social Justice*, 21.1 (2000).

95. Sandra Murillo, "No Holiday From Homework," *Los Angeles Times* (December 23, 2002).

96. Jeffrey Blankfort, "The Influence of Israel and Its American Lobby over US Middle East Policy," paper presented to Islamic Human Rights Commission Conference, London School of Oriental and African Studies (July 2, 2006); Stephen Schwartz, *Is It Good for the Jews? The Crisis of America's Israel Lobby* (Garden City, NY: Doubleday, 2006); Louis Sahagun, Kelly Niknejad, and David Streitfeld, "Former Muslims Reach Out," *Los Angeles Times* (March 27, 2006); Halima Kazem, "US Ambassador, 'Viceroy of Afghanistan,' Turns to Iraq," *Los Angeles Times* (June 21, 2005); Michael Massing, "The Storm Over the Israel Lobby," *New York Review of Books* (June 8, 2006); Stephen Braun and Laura King, "Soldier Was Determined to Fight for Israel," *Los Angeles Times* (August 12, 2006); Edmund Sanders, "US Outsider Surprises Congo," *Los Angeles Times* (August 1, 2006).

97. P.J. Huffstutter, "Expatriates Eager to Rock the Iraqi Vote," *Los Angeles Times* (January 10, 2005); Steven R. Weisman, "Many Iraqis to Cast votes in US," *New York Times* (January 13, 2005); Maria L. La Ganga, "They Drove 22 Hours for a Defining Moment," *Los Angeles Times* (January 30, 2005); Michael Krikorian, "Local Armenians Flock to Polls for Presidential Runoff," *Los Angeles Times* (March 6, 2003).

98. The U.S. Supreme Court was explicit in a 1967 case, *Afroyim v. Rusk*, that American citizens were allowed to vote in elections in other countries where they held dual citizenship; Michael LeMay and Elliott Robert Barkan, Eds., *US Immigration and Naturalization Laws and Issues* (Westport, CT: Greenwood, 1999), 264–266; Wayne A. Cornelius, "Who Cares Where They Vote?" *Los Angeles Times* (July 3, 2005); Ken Ellingwood, "Getting Out the Cross-Border Vote," *Los Angeles Times* (June 28, 2000); Jennifer Mena, "Mexico's 2006 Race Comes to Santa Ana," *Los Angeles Times* (July 5, 2002); "North-of-the-Border Voting," editorial, *Los Angeles Times* (March 18, 2005); Sam Quinones, "Mexican Emigres Cheer, Shrug at New Voting Right," *Los Angeles Times* (July 2, 2005); Sam Enriquez, "US Is Off-Limits for Candidates in Mexico Elections," *Los Angeles Times* (September 22, 2005); Sam Enriquez and Sam Quinones, "Mexico's Absentee Voter Drive Slow in US," *Los Angeles Times* (November 26, 2005); "Mexico's Absentee Total Low," *Los Angeles Times* (February 17, 2006).

99. David Pierson, "Change in China, Change in LA," *Los Angeles Times* (June 4, 2005); David Pierson, "Lee Visit Stirs Up Taiwan Debate," *Los Angeles Times* (October 22, 2005); Mai Tran, "Emigres Oppose Visit by Leader of Vietnam," *Los Angeles Times* (June 8, 2005); Mai Tran, "Vietnamese Activist's Release is Sought," *Los Angeles Times* (July 13, 2006); Jia-Rui Chong and David Pierson, "Activist is Indicted in Coup Plot," *Los Angeles Times* (June 2, 2005); David Pierson, "Man Indicted in Phnom Penh Attacks Active in GOP Causes," *Los Angeles Times* (June 3, 2005); Jia-rui Chong and David Pierson, "Fraud Alleged in Rebel Funding," *Los Angeles Times* (June 9, 2005); Wendy Lee, "Southland Filipinos Mourn Influential Cardinal," *Los Angeles Times* (June 22, 2005); Nate Carlisle, "Utah's Sudanese Urge Probe of Death," *Salt Lake Tribune* (August 3, 2005).

100. Barbara Demick, "Californian May Oversee North Korea Economic Zone," *Los Angeles Times* (September 8, 2004); John M. Glionna, "Where to for Lotto Winner? Back Home to Help His Town," *Los Angeles Times* (November 30, 2005); James Cox and Bill Nichols, "US Citizen Heads Russian Oil Titan," *USA Today* (November 5, 2003); Evelyn Iritani, "Expatriates Play Key Role in India's Economic Rise," *Los Angeles Times* (August 12, 2006).

101. "When Cash Crosses Over," editorial, *Los Angeles Times* (May 21, 2005); "Banks Without Borders," editorial, *Los Angeles Times* (January 31, 2005); Richard Boudreaux, "Migrants' Dollars Cross Border, Brick by Brick," *Los Angeles Times* (June 1, 2003); Chris Kraul, "Tapping Generosity of Emigrants," *Los Angeles Times* (June 8, 2000); Ginger Thompson, "A Surge in Money Sent Home by Mexicans," *New York Times* (October 28, 2003); Ginger Thompson, "Mexico's Migrants Profit From Dollars Sent Home," *New York Times* (February 23, 2005); Lisa Richardson, "Yucatan Emigres Seek to Aid Wilma's Victims," *Los Angeles Times* (October 27, 2005); Reed Johnson, "A Parade of Human Loss," *Los Angeles Times* (April 7, 2006).

102. Richard C. Paddock, "The Overseas Class," *Los Angeles Times* (April 20, 2006); Paddock, "For Filipinos, Thoughts of a Paycheck Outweigh the Dangers," *Los Angeles Times* (July 15, 2004).

103. Leslie Earnest, "Made in LA, for Now," *Los Angeles Times* (January 16, 2005); David Streitfeld, "Office of Tomorrow Has an Indian Address," *Los Angeles Times* (August 29, 2004); Amy Waldman, "A Young American Outsources Himself to India," *New York Times* (July 17, 2004); Michael F. Corbett, *The Outsourcing Revolution* (Chicago: Dearborn, 2004); Ron French, *Driven Abroad: The Outsourcing of America* (Berkeley: RDR Books, 2006); Steven Hill, "The American Dream … in Mexico," *Los Angeles Times* (May 20, 2005); Evelyn Iritani, "Hot Housing Market Crosses the Border," *Los Angeles Times* (October 10, 2005); Evelyn Iritani, "They're Building in Baja," *Los Angeles Times* (February 21, 2006).

Chapter 9

1. Sources on immigration law changes in this period include Roy Beck, *The Case Against Immigration* (New York: Norton, 1996); Roger Daniels, *Coming to America*, 2nd ed. (New York: HarperCollins, 2002); Roger Daniels, *Guarding the Golden Door: American Immigration Policy and Immigrants since 1882* (New York: Hill and Wang, 2004); Otis L. Graham, Jr., *Unguarded Gates: A*

History of America's Immigration Crisis (Lanham, MD: Rowman and Littlefield, 2004); Bill Ong Hing, *Defining America Through Immigration Policy* (Philadelphia: Temple University Press, 2004); Charles Hirschman, Philip Kasinitz, and Josh DeWind, Eds., *The Handbook of International Immigration: The American Experience* (New York: Russell Sage, 1999); Kevin R. Johnson, *The "Huddled Masses" Myth: Immigration and Civil Rights* (Philadelphia: Temple University Press, 2004); Susanne Jonas and Suzie Dod Thomas, Eds., *Immigration: A Civil Rights Issue for the Americas* (Wilmington, DE: Scholarly Resources, 1999); Erika Lee, "American Gatekeeping: Race and Immigration Law in the Twentieth Century," in *Not Just Black and White*, Nancy Foner and George M. Fredrickson, Eds. (New York: Russell Sage Foundation, 2004), 119–144; Michael LeMay and Elliott Robert Barkan, Eds., *US Immigration and Naturalization Laws and Issues* (Westport, CT : Greenwood, 1999); John S. W. Park, *Elusive Citizenship: Immigration, Asian Americans, and the Paradox of Civil Rights* (New York: NYU Press, 2004); Cheryl Shanks, *Immigration and the Politics of American Sovereignty, 1890–1990* (Ann Arbor: University of Michigan Press, 2001); Reed Ueda, *Postwar Immigrant America* (Boston: Bedford/St. Martin's, 1994).

2. LeMay and Barkan, *US Immigration and Naturalization Laws and Issues*, 210–213, 245–249, 263–264, 267–269, 271–275, 280–281.

3. LeMay and Barkan, *US Immigration and Naturalization Laws and Issues*, 276–277, italics added.

4. LeMay and Barkan, *US Immigration and Naturalization Laws and Issues*, 296–301; Philip Martin, "Proposition 187 in California," *International Migration Review*, 29.1 (1995), reprinted in *New American Destinies*, Darrell Y. Hamamoto and Rodolfo D. Torres, Eds. (New York: Routledge, 1997), 325–332; Kent A. Ono and John M. Sloop, *Shifting Borders: Rhetoric, Immigration, and California's Proposition 187* (Philadelphia: Temple University Press, 2002).

5. LeMay and Barkan, *US Immigration and Naturalization Laws and Issues*, 301–310.

6. Michael Janofsky, "Legal Immigrants Would Regain Aid in Clinton Plan," *New York Times* (January 25, 1999); Jonathan Peterson, "White House to Try to Restore Food Aid to Legal Immigrants," *Los Angeles Times* (January 11, 2002).

7. Michael Gomez, *Exchanging Our Country Marks* (Chapel Hill: University of North Carolina Press, 1998); Gwendolyn Midlo Hall, *Slavery and African Ethnicity in the Americas* (Chapel Hill: University of North Carolina Press, 2005).

8. Theodore W. Allen, *The Invention of the White Race*, 2 vols. (London: Verso, 1994, 1997); Thomas A. Guglielmo, *White on Arrival* (New York: Oxford, 2003); Noel Ignatiev, *How the Irish Became White* (New York: Routledge, 1995); Ian F. Haney López, *White by Law* (New York: NYU Press, 1996); Matthew Frye Jacobson, *Whiteness of a Different Color* (Cambridge, MA: Harvard University Press, 1998); Winthrop D. Jordan, *White Over Black* (Chapel Hill: University of North Carolina Press, 1968); David R. Roediger, *The Wages of Whiteness* (London: Verso, 1991).

9. Sources on the Chicano movement include Oscar Zeta Acosta, *Revolt of the Cockroach People* (New York: Vintage, 1989; orig. 1973); Rodolfo Acuña, *Anything but Mexican* (London: Verso, 1996); Acuña, *A Community Under Siege: A Chronicle of Chicanos East of the Los Angeles River, 1945–1975* (Los

Angeles: UCLA Chicano Studies Research Center, 1984); Rudy V. Busto, *King Tiger: The Religious Vision of Reies López Tijerina* (Albuquerque: University of New Mexico Press, 2005); Ian F. Haney López, *Racism on Trial: The Chicano Fight for Justice* (Cambridge, MA: Harvard University Press, 2003); Susan E. Keefe and Amado M. Padilla, *Chicano Ethnicity* (Albuquerque: University of New Mexico Press, 1987); Laura Pulido, *Black, Brown, Yellow, and Left: Racial Activism in Los Angeles* (Berkeley: University of California Press, 2006); Arnulfo D. Trejo, Ed., *The Chicanos: As We See Ourselves* (Tucson: University of Arizona Press, 1979); Zaragosa Vargas, *Major Problems in Mexican American History* (Boston: Houghton Mifflin, 1999).

10. Haney López, *Racism on Trial*, 10–11.

11. Lea Ybarra and Nina Genera, "La batalla esta aqui: Chicanos and the War," in Vargas, *Major Problems in Mexican American History*, 389–390.

12. Guillermo Lux and Maurilio E. Vigil, "Return to Aztlán: The Chicano Rediscovers His Indian Past," in *Chicanos*, Trejo, Ed., 1–17; David Kelly, "Vision That Inspires Some and Scares Others: Aztlan," *Los Angeles Times* (July 7, 2006).

13. Ira Katznelson, *When Affirmative Action Was White* (New York: Norton, 2005).

14. Jacques E. Levy, *Cesar Chavez: Autobiography of La Causa* (New York: Norton, 1975); Craig Scharlin and Lilia V. Villanueva, *Philip Vera Cruz* (Los Angeles: UCLA Labor Center, 1992); Miriam Pawel, "UFW: A Broken Contract," *Los Angeles Times* (January 8–11, 2006).

15. Don Normark, *Chávez Ravine, 1949* (San Francisco: Chronicle Books, 1999), 50.

16. Sources on Latino panethnicity include William V. Flores and Rina Benmayor, Eds., *Latino Cultural Citizenship* (Boston: Beacon, 1997); Juan Gonzalez, *Harvest of Empire: A History of Latinos in America* (New York: Penguin, 2000); David E. Hayes-Bautista, *La Nueva California: Latinos in the Golden State* (Berkeley: University of California Press, 2004); Roberto Suro, *Strangers Among Us: Latino Lives in a Changing America* (New York: Knopf, 1998); Héctor Tobar, *Translation Nation: Defining a New American Identity in the Spanish-Speaking United States* (New York: Riverhead, 2005); Ken Ellingwood, "Throughout the Country, Latinos See Their Clout Build in Political Arena," *Los Angeles Times* (November 17, 2002); Alan Feuer, "Little but Language in Common," *New York Times* (September 6, 2003); Ian Haney López, "The Birth of a 'Latino Race'," *Los Angeles Times* (December 29, 2004); Lisa Helem, "Greeks To Latin—Or Vice Versa," *Newsweek* (November 1, 2004); Mireya Navarro, "Census Reflects Hispanic Identity That Is Hardly Black and White," *New York Times* (November 9, 2003); Eric Pape, "So Far From God, So Close: Mexican Immigrants Are Transforming New York City's Latino Presence," *Los Angeles Times Magazine* (August 3, 2003); Richard Rodriguez, *Brown: The Last Discovery of America* (New York: Viking, 2002); Rachel L. Swarms, "Hispanics Are Perplexed by Census Racial Categories," *Los Angeles Times* (October 24, 2004); Luis R. Torres, "One Crime, a Million 'Hispanic' Suspects," *Los Angeles Times* (August 26, 2003).

17. Sources on Asian American panethnicity and the Asian American movement include Karin Aguilar-San Juan, Ed., *The State of Asian America: Activism and Resistance in the 1990s* (Boston: South End Press, 1994); Edwin G. Burrows, *Chinese and Japanese in Hawaii during the Sino-Japanese Conflict* (Honolulu: Institute of Pacific Relations, 1939); Doug Chin, *Seattle's International*

District: The Making of a Pan-Asian American Community (Seattle: International Examiner Press, 2001); Yen Le Espiritu, *Asian American Panethnicity* (Philadelphia: Temple University Press, 1992); *The Fall of the I-Hotel*, dir. Curtis Choy (National Asian American Telecommunications Association, 1993); Emma Gee, Ed., *Counterpoint: Perspectives in Asian American* (Los Angeles: UCLA Asian American Studies Center, 1976); Philip Kan Gotanda, *Yankee Dawg You Die* (New York: Dramatists Play Service, 1991); Russell Jeung, *Faithful Generations: Race and New Asian American Churches* (New Brunswick, NJ: Rutgers University Press, 2005); Edward J. W. Park and John S. W. Park, *Probationary Americans: Contemporary Immigration Policies and the Shaping of Asian American Communities* (New York: Routledge, 2005); Lavina Dhingra Shankar and Rajini Srikanth, *A Part, Yet Apart* (Philadelphia: Temple University Press, 1998); Amy Tachiki et al., Eds., *Roots: An Asian American Reader* (Los Angeles, UCLA Asian American Studies Center, 1971); Linda Trinh Vo, *Mobilizing Asian American Community* (Philadelphia: Temple University Press, 2004); Karen Umemoto, "'On Strike!' San Francisco State College Strike, 1968–1969: The Role of Asian American Students," *Amerasia Journal*, 15.1 (1989), 3–41; U.S. Commission on Civil Rights, *Civil Rights Issues Facing Asian Americans in the 1990s* (Washington, DC: Government Printing Office, 1992); Linda Trinh Vo, *Mobilizing an Asian American Community* (Philadelphia: Temple University Press, 2004); William Wei, *The Asian American Movement* (Philadelphia: Temple University Press, 1992); Helen Zia, *Asian American Dreams* (New York: Farrar, Straus and Giroux, 2000).

18. This is described in detail in Paul Spickard, *Japanese Americans* (New York: Twayne, 1996), 65–68, 135–138. See also Quintard Taylor, *The Forging of a Black Community* (Seattle: University of Washington Press, 1994).

19. Peter Irons, *Justice at War: The Story of the Japanese American Internment Cases* (New York: Oxford University Press, 1983); Peter Irons, Ed., *Justice Delayed: The Record of the Japanese American Internment Cases* (Middletown, CT: Wesleyan University Press, 1989); Eric Yamamoto, Margaret Chon, Carol L. Izumi, Jerry Kang, Frank H. Wu, *Race, Rights and Reparation: Law and the Japanese American Internment* (New York: Aspen, 2001). Quotes are from *Justice Delayed*, 25–26, 46.

20. Roger Daniels, Sandra C. Taylor, and Harry H. L. Kitano, Eds., *Japanese Americans: From Relocation to Redress*, rev ed. (Seattle: University of Washington Press, 1991); Leslie T. Hatamiya, *Righting a Wrong: Japanese Americans and the Passage of the Civil Liberties Act of 1988* (Stanford, CA: Stanford University Press, 1993); William Minoru Hohri, *Repairing America: An Account of the Movement for Japanese-American Redress* (Pullman: Washington State University Press, 1988); Mitchell T. Maki, Harry H. L. Kitano, and S. Megan Berthold, *Achieving the Impossible Dream: How Japanese Americans Obtained Redress* (Urbana: University of Illinois Press, 1999); Roy Miki, *Redress: Inside the Japanese Canadian Call for Justice* (Vancouver: Raincoast Books, 2005); Robert Sadamu Shimabukuro, *Born in Seattle: The Campaign for Japanese American Redress* (Seattle: University of Washington Press, 2001); Yasuko I. Takezawa, *Breaking the Silence: Redress and Japanese American Ethnicity* (Ithaca, NY: Cornell University Press, 1995).

21. Nikki Nojima Louis, "Breaking the Silence," in Takezawa, *Breaking the Silence*, vii.

22. Boris J. Bittker, *The Case for Black Reparations* (Boston: Beacon, 2003); Roy L. Brooks, *Atonement and Forgiveness: A New Model for Black Reparations* (Berkeley: University of California Press, 2004); Randall Robinson, *The Debt: What America Owes to Blacks* (New York: Dutton, 2000); Ronald P. Salzberger and Mary C. Turck, Eds., *Reparations for Slavery* (Lanham, MD: Rowman and Littlefield, 2004); John Torpey, Ed., *Politics and the Past: On Repairing Historical Injustices* (Lanham, MD: Rowman and Littlefield, 2003).

23. Sources on Native American activism and panethnic resurgence include Fergus M. Bordewich, *Killing the White Man's Indian: Reinventing Native Americans at the End of the Twentieth Century* (New York: Anchor, 1996); Colin G. Calloway, *First Peoples* (Boston: Bedford/St. Martin's, 1999); Ward Churchill, *Acts of Rebellion* (New York: Routledge, 2003); Stephen Cornell, *The Return of the Native: American Indian Political Resurgence* (New York: Oxford, 1988); Vine Deloria, *Behind the Trail of Broken Treaties: An Indian Declaration of Independence* (New York: Delacorte, 1974); Hazel Hertzberg, *The Search for an American Indian Identity: Modern Pan-Indian Movements* (Syracuse, NY: Syracuse University Press, 1971); Patricia Penn Hilden, *From a Red Zone* (Trenton, NJ: Red Sea Press, 2006); Frederick E. Hoxie, Ed., *Encyclopedia of North American Indians* (Boston: Houghton Mifflin, 1996); Frederick E. Hoxie, Peter C. Mancall, and James H. Merrell, Eds., *American Nations* (New York: Routledge, 2001); Albert L. Hurtado and Peter Iverson, Eds., *Major Problems in American Indian History* (Boston: Houghton Mifflin, 2001); Bruce Johansen and Roberto Maestas, *Wasi'chu: The Continuing Indian Wars* (New York: Monthly Review, 1979); Troy R. Johnson, *The Occupation of Alcatraz Island: Indian Self-Determination and the Rise of Indian Activism* (Urbana: University of Illinois Press, 1996); Troy R. Johnson, "The Roots of Contemporary Native American Activism," *American Indian Culture and Research Journal*, 20.2 (1996), 127–154; Troy R. Johnson, Joane Nagel, and Duane Champagne, Eds., *American Indian Activism* (Urbana: University of Illinois Press, 1997); Alvin M. Josephy, Joane Nagel, and Troy R. Johnson, Eds., *Red Power: The American Indians' Fight for Freedom*, 2nd ed. (Lincoln: University of Nebraska Press, 1999); MariJo Moore, Ed., *Genocide of the Mind: New Native American Writing* (New York: Nation Books, 2003); Peter Nabokov, *Native American Testimony*, rev. ed. (New York: Penguin, 1999); Joane Nagel, *American Indian Ethnic Renewal: Red Power and the Resurgence of Identity and Culture* (New York: Oxford, 1997); Paul Chaat Smith and Robert Allen Warrior, *Like a Hurricane: The Indian Movement from Alcatraz to Wounded Knee* (New York: New Press, 1996); Stan Steiner, *The New Indians* (New York: Dell, 1968); Carl Waldman, *Atlas of the North American Indian*, rev. ed. (New York: Checkmark, 2000).

24. These are the numbers who told the census they were Indians and did not acknowledge another identity. When the option of claiming more than one identity became available in 2000, 1,867,876 people claimed Native identity in combination with another racial identity, for a total of 4,315,865. Russell Thornton, *American Indian Holocaust and Survival* (Norman: University of Oklahoma Press, 1987), 160; U.S. Bureau of the Census, "Census Bureau Releases 1990 Census Counts on Specific Racial Groups," CB91–125 (Washington, DC: Government Printing Office, June 12, 1991), Table 1; Stella U. Ogunwole, U.S. Bureau of the Census, *We the People: American Indians and Alaska Natives in the United States*, CENSR-28 (Washington, DC: Government Printing Office, February 2006), Table 1.

25. "A Proclamation from the Indians of All Tribes, Alcatraz Island, 1969," in *Major Problems in American Indian History*, Hurtado and Iverson, Eds., 455–456.

26. Nabokov, *Native American Testimony*, 375–376.

27. *Voices from Wounded Knee, 1973* (Rooseveltown, NY: Akwesasne Notes, 1974); Mario Gonzalez and Elizabeth Cook-Lynn, *The Politics of Hallowed Ground: Wounded Knee and the Struggle for Indian Sovereignty* (Urbana: University of Illinois Press, 1998). On the denouement, see *Incident at Oglala: The Leonard Peltier Story*, dir. Michael Apted (Live/Artisan Studio, 1992); John William Sayer, *Ghost Dancing the Law: The Wounded Knee Trials* (Cambridge, MA: Harvard University Press, 1997).

28. Robert White, *Tribal Assets: The Rebirth of Native America* (New York: Holt, 1990), 136–137.

29. Quotes are from Nagel, *American Indian Ethnic Renewal*, 187–212; see also Steven Chawkins, "Paddlers Cross Channel in Their Ancestor's Wake," *Los Angeles Times* (September 12, 2004); Clyde Ellis, "'We Don't Want Your Rations, We Want This Dance': The Changing Use of Song and Dance on the Southern Plains," *Western Historical Quarterly*, 30 (1999), 133–154; Sonia Krishnan, "Pillars of Indian Culture Honored," *Seattle Times* (May 8, 2005); Edgar Sandoval, "Some Latinos Seek Their Pre-European Past," *Los Angeles Times* (June 19, 2000).

30. Sources on tribal economic development include Stephen Cornell and Joseph P. Kalt, Eds., *What Can Tribes Do? Strategies and Institutions in American Indian Economic Development* (Los Angeles: UCLA American Indian Study Center, 1992); Cornell and Kalt, *Reloading the Dice: Improving the Chances for Economic Development on American Indian Reservations* (Cambridge, MA: Harvard Project on American Indian Economic Development, 2003); Cornell and Kalt, *Sovereignty and Nation-Building: The Development Challenge in Indian Country Today* (Cambridge, MA: Harvard Project on American Indian Economic Development, 2003); Cornell and Kalt, *Two Approaches to Economic Development on American Indian Reservations: One Works, the Other Doesn't* (Tucson: Native Nations Institute, 2006); White, *Tribal Assets*.

31. Fay G. Cohen, *Treaties on Trial: The Continuing Controversy Over Northwest Fishing Rights* (Seattle: University of Washington Press, 1986).

32. Marjane Ambler, *Breaking the Iron Bonds: Indian Control of Energy Minerals* (Lawrence: University Press of Kansas, 1990); Ward Churchill and Winona LaDuke, "Native North America: The Political Economy of Radioactive Colonialism," in *The State of Native North America* (Boston: South End Press, 1992); Peter H. Eichstaedt, *If You Poison Us: Uranium and Native Americans* (Santa Fe: Red Crane Books, 1994); Donald A. Grinde and Bruce E. Johansen, *Ecocide of Native America: Environmental Destruction of Indian Lands and Peoples* (Santa Fe: Clear Light, 1995); John K. Wiley, "Mining's Dark Legacy for Tribe," *Oregonian* (December 2, 2003).

33. Robert Gehrke, "Judge Holds Norton in Contempt," *Seattle Post-Intelligencer* (September 18, 2002); Tom Gorman, "Land Battle Splits Shoshone Nation," *Los Angeles Times* (July 22, 2002); J. Michael Kennedy, "Return of the Warrior," *Los Angeles Times* (July 7, 2002); Henry Weinstein, "Appeals Court Removes Judge from Indian Trust Fund Case," *Los Angeles Times* (July 12, 2006); Henry Weinstein, "Judge Orders Indian Trust Fund Action," *Los Angeles Times* (February 24, 2005).

34. William R. Eadington, Ed., *Indian Gaming and the Law* (Reno: Institute for the Study of Gambling and Gaming, 1990); Joseph G. Jorgenson, "Gaming and Recent American Indian Development," *American Indian Culture and Research Journal*, 22.3 (1998), 157–172; Steven Andrew Light, *Indian Gaming and Tribal Sovereignty* (Lawrence: University Press of Kansas, 2005); W. Dale Mason, *Indian Gaming: Tribal Sovereignty and American Politics* (Norman: University of Oklahoma Press, 2000); Tony Perry, "$2-Million Donation Fits Tribe's Bold Profile," *Los Angeles Times* (September 3, 2003); Sam Howe Verhovek, "Plan for Off-Reservation Casino Causes Stir in Oregon," *Los Angeles Times* (May 30, 2005).

35. William Overend, "Casino Money Is Fueling Chumash's Interest in Past," *Los Angeles Times* (June 16, 2003).

36. Seth Prince, "American Native," *Oregonian* (February 1, 2004); see also Patricia Penn Hilden, *When Nickels Were Indians: An Urban, Mixed-Blood Story* (Washington, DC: Smithsonian, 1995); Eva Marie Garroutte, *Real Indians: Identity and the Survival of Native America* (Berkeley: University of California Press, 2003).

37. "Blood Feud," *Wired* (September 2005); Karen Kaplan, "Ancestry in a Drop of Blood," *Los Angeles Times* (August 30, 2005); Brent Staples, "When Racial Discrimination Is Not Just Black and White," *New York Times* (September 12, 2003); Circe Sturm, *Blood Politics: Race, Culture, and Identity in the Cherokee Nation of Oklahoma* (Berkeley: University of California Press, 2002).

38. Karen L. Blu, *The Lumbee Problem: The Making of an American Indian People* (Cambridge: Cambridge University Press, 1980); Alexandra Harmon, *Indians in the Making: Ethnic Relations and Indian Identities around Puget Sound* (Berkeley: University of California Press, 1998); Laurence M. Hauptman and Jack Campisi, "There Are No Indians East of the Mississippi," in Hauptman, *Tribes and Tribulations* (Albuquerque: University of New Mexico Press, 1995), 94–108; David McKibben, "For Juaneño Indians, Unity Proves Elusive," *Los Angeles Times* (October 10, 2005); Bobbi Nodell, "Duwamish Take to Canoes in Celebration of Their Past," *Seattle Times* (September 1, 2002); Emma Schwartz, "Virginia Tribes Fight for Sovereignty," *Los Angeles Times* (October 12, 2004); Paul Shukovsky, "McDermott Bill Would Recognize Duwamish," *Seattle Post-Intelligencer* (September 20, 2002); Tomas Alex Tizon, "A Rift Among History's Voiceless," *Los Angeles Times* (April 11, 2005).

It is worth noting that many of the issues and trends described in this section for continental Native peoples had parallels in the same period for Native Hawaiians. See Peggy Myo-Young Choy, Candace Fujikane, Momiala Kanahele, and Jonathan Okamura, Eds., *Whose Vision? Asian Settler Colonialism in Hawai'i*. Special issue of *Amerasia Journal, 26.2* (2000); Michael Kioni Dudley and Keoni Kealoha Agard, *A Call for Hawaiian Sovereignty* (Honolulu: Na Kane O Ka Malu Press, 1993); George H. S. Kanahele, *Ku Kanaka: Stand Tall: A Search for Hawaiian Values* (Honolulu: University of Hawai'i Press, 1986); J. Kehaulani Kauanui, *Rehabilitating the Native: The Politics of Hawaiian Blood and the Question of Sovereignty* (Durham, NC: Duke University Press, in press; advance copy courtesy of the author); Poka Laenui, *Another View on Hawaiian Sovereignty and Self-Determination* (Waianae, Hawai'i: privately printed, 1994); Davianna Pomaika'i McGregor, "Recognizing Native Hawaiians: A Quest for Sovereignty," in *Pacific Diaspora*, Paul Spickard,

Joanne Rondilla, and Debbie Hippolite Wright, Eds. (Honolulu: University of Hawai'i Press, 2002), 331–354; Jonathan Kamakawiwo'ole Osorio, "'What Kine Hawaiian Are You?' A Mo'olelo about Nationhood, Race, History, and the Contemporary Sovereignty Movement in Hawai'i," *Contemporary Pacific*, 13.2 (2002), 359–379; Haunani-Kay Trask, *From a Native Daughter: Colonialism and Sovereignty in Hawai'i* (Monroe, ME: Common Courage Press, 1993); Thurston Twigg-Smith, *Hawaiian Sovereignty: Do the Facts Matter?* (Honolulu: Goodale, 1998).

39. Clifton Wharton headed TIAA-CREF from 1987 to 1993, and it had sufficient assets to be included in Fortune's list, but the magazine did not include companies not registered with the Securities and Exchange Commission at that time. Tony Chapelle, "The State of the Black CEO," *Black MBA* (2001), www.blackmbamagazine.com (July 23, 2006).

40. Melanie Eversley, "For Miss. Town, Voting Law Helped," *USA Today* (August 5, 2005); "Bad New Days for Voting Rights," *New York Times*, editorial (April 18, 2004); Peter Wallsten and Johanna Neuman, "Voting Rights Act Renewal Divides GOP," *Los Angeles Times* (July 12, 2006); Johanna Neuman, "Voting Rights Act Renewal Wins House Approval," *Los Angeles Times* (July 14, 2006).

41. Reynolds Farley, *Blacks and Whites: Narrowing the Gap?* (Cambridge, MA: Harvard University Press, 1984), 199; U.S. Census, Public Information Office, "Income Stable, Poverty Race Increases, Percentage of Americans Without Health Insurance Unchanged," press release (August 30, 2005). See also Martin Carnoy, *Faded Dreams: The Politics and Economics of Race in America* (Cambridge: Cambridge University Press, 1994); Andrew Hacker, *Two Nations: Black and White, Separate, Hostile, Unequal* (New York: Ballantine, 1995).

42. The Asian figure hovered around 50 percent. Angela Provitera McGlynn, "The Gender Gap in Higher Education: More Striking Among Blacks and Latinos," *Hispanic Outlook in Higher Education Magazine* (June 9, 2004); Manning Marable, "Blacks in Higher Education: An Endangered Species?" (July 2002) www.manningmarable.net (July 23, 2006).

43. Lawrence B. De Graaf, "African American Suburbanization in California, 1960 through 1990," in *Seeking El Dorado: African Americans in California*, Lawrence B. De Graaf, Kevin Mulroy, and Quintard Taylor, Eds. (Los Angeles: Autry Museum of Western Heritage, 2001), 405–449; E. Franklin Frazier, *Black Bourgeoisie* (New York: Free Press, 1957); Douglas G. Glasgow, *The Black Underclass* (New York: Vintage, 1981); Bill E. Lawson, Ed., *The Underclass Question* (Philadelphia: Temple University Press, 1992); Mary Pattillo-McCoy, *Black Picket Fences: Privilege and Peril Among the Black Middle Class* (Chicago: University of Chicago Press, 2000); Alphonso Pinckney, *The Myth of Black Progress* (Cambridge: Cambridge University Press, 1984); William Julius Wilson, *The Declining Significance of Race*, 2nd ed. (Chicago: University of Chicago Press, 1980); William Julius Wilson, *The Truly Disadvantaged: The Inner City, the Underclass, and Public Policy* (Chicago: University of Chicago Press, 1987).

44. Ward Connerly, *Creating Equal: My Fight Against Race Preferences* (San Francisco: Encounter Books, 2000); Thomas Sowell, *Ethnic America* (New York: Basic Books, 1981); G. Reginald Daniel and Josef Manuel Castañeda-Liles, "Race, Multiraciality, and the Neoconservative Agenda," in *Mixed Messages: Multiracial Identities in the "Color-Blind" Era*, David Brunsma, Ed. (Boulder, CO: Lynne Rienner, 2006), 125–145; Thomas Sowell, *Race and Economics* (New

York: Longman, 1975); John H. McWhorter, *Losing the Race: Self-Sabotage in Black America* (New York: Free Press, 2000); John H. McWhorter, *Winning the Race: Beyond the Crisis in Black America* (New York: Gotham, 2006); Shelby Steele, *The Content of Our Character: A New Vision of Race in America* (New York: Harper Perennial, 1991); Shelby Steele, *A Dream Deferred: The Second Betrayal of Black Freedom in America* (New York: HarperCollins, 1998); Shelby Steele, *White Guilt: How Blacks and Whites Together Destroyed the Promise of the Civil Rights Era* (New York: HarperCollins, 2006). For correctives, see Derrick Bell, *Faces at the Bottom of the Well: The Permanence of Racism* (New York: Basic Books, 1992); Stephen L. Carter, *Reflections of an Affirmative Action Baby* (New York: Basic, 1991); Cornel West, *Race Matters* (New York: Vintage, 1994).

45. Horowitz's comments came on CNN's *Crossfire* (September 5, 1994), cited in Paul Rockwell, "The Right Has a Dream: Martin Luther King as an Opponent of Affirmative Action," academic.udayton.edu/race (1995; retrieved July 24, 2006).

46. Sources on the White ethnic movement include Michael Novak, *The Rise of the Unmeltable Ethnics* (New York: Macmillan, 1971); William Kornblum, *Blue Collar Community* (Chicago: University of Chicago Press, 1974); Matthew Frye Jacobson, *Roots Too: White Ethnic Revival in Post-Civil Rights America* (Cambridge, MA: Harvard University Press, 2006); Mary C. Waters, *Ethnic Options: Choosing Identities in America* (Berkeley: University of California Press, 1990); Matt Wray and Annalee Newitz, Eds., *White Trash* (New York: Routledge, 1997).

47. Novak, *Unmeltable Ethnics*, back cover.

48. Nathan Glazer, *Affirmative Discrimination: Ethnic Inequality and Public Policy* (New York: Basic Books, 1975); Glazer, *Ethnic Dilemmas, 1964–1982* (Cambridge, MA: Harvard University Press, 1983); Glazer, *Clamor at the Gates: The New American Immigration* (San Francisco: ICS Press, 1985); Irving Kristol, *Reflections of a Neoconservative* (New York: Basic Books, 1983); Kristol, *Neoconservatism: The Autobiography of an Idea* (New York: Free Press, 1995).

49. I have analyzed the Whiteness studies movement at length in "What's Critical About White Studies," in *Racial Thinking in the United States*, Paul Spickard and G. Reginald Daniel, Ed. (Notre Dame, IN: University of Notre Dame Press, 2004), 248–274. Among the best examples of this movement are Theodore W. Allen, *The Invention of the White Race*, 2 vols. (London: Verso, 1994, 1997); Tomás Almaguer, *Racial Fault Lines: The Historical Origins of White Supremacy in California* (Berkeley: University of California Press, 1994); Karen Brodkin, *How Jews Became White folks and What That Says about Race in America* (New Brunswick, NJ: Rutgers University Press, 1998); Philip J. Deloria, *Playing Indian* (New Haven, CT: Yale University Press, 1998); Joe R. Feagin, Hernán Vera, and Pinar Batur, *White Racism*, 2nd ed. (New York: Routledge, 2001); Neil Foley, *The White Scourge: Mexicans, Blacks, and Poor Whites in Texas Cotton Culture* (Berkeley: University of California Press, 1997); Elizabeth Hale, *Making Whiteness: The Culture of Segregation in the South, 1890–1940* (New York: Vintage, 1998); Noel Ignatiev, *How the Irish Became White* (New York: Routledge, 1995); Matthew Frye Jacobson, *Whiteness of a Different Color: European Immigrants and the Alchemy of Race* (Cambridge, MA: Harvard University Press, 1998); Robert Jensen, *The Heart of Whiteness:*

Confronting Race, Racism, and White Privilege (San Francisco: City Lights, 2005); George Lipsitz, *The Possessive Investment in Whiteness: How White People Profit from Identity Politics* (Philadelphia: Temple University Press, 1998); David Roediger, *The Wages of Whiteness: Race and the Making of the American Working Class* (London: Verso, 1991); Alexander Saxton, *The Rise and Fall of the White Republic* (London: Verso, 1990); Tim Wise, *White Like Me* (New York: Soft Skull Press, 2005).

50. Sources on immigrant bashing include Nicholas Capaldi, Ed., *Immigration: Debating the Issues* (Amherst, NY: Prometheus, 1997); John Crewdson, *The Tarnished Door: The New Immigrants and the Transformation of America* (New York: Times Books, 1983); Gordon H. Hanson, *Why Does Immigration Divide America?* (Washington, DC: Institute for International Economics, 2005); John C. Harles, *Politics in the Lifeboat: Immigrants and the American Democratic Order* (Boulder, CO: Westview, 1993); David Heer, *Immigration in America's Future* (Boulder, CO: Westview, 1996); Robert S. Kahn, *Other People's Blood: US Immigration Prisons in the Reagan Decade* (Boulder, CO: Westview, 1996); Juan F. Perea, Ed., *Immigrants Out! The New Nativism and the Anti-Immigrant Impulse in the United States* (New York: NYU Press, 1997); David M. Reimers, *Unwelcome Strangers: American Identity and the Turn Against Immigration* (New York: Columbia University Press, 1998); Mary E. Williams, Ed., *Immigration: Opposing Viewpoints* (San Diego: Greenhaven, 2004).

51. Mary Barclay Erb, *While America Sleeps … Foundations Crumble* (Washington, DC: Goetz, 1966), 30. Erb also wrote *Invasion Alert* (Washington, DC: Goetz, 1965).

52. Peter Brimelow, *Alien Nation: Common Sense About America's Immigration Disaster* (New York: Harper Perennial, 1996), xvii, xxi, 264. Italics in original. See also Brimelow, "Time to Rethink Immigration?" *National Review* (June 22, 1992), 30–46.

53. Patrick J. Buchanan, *The Death of the West* (New York: St. Martin's, 2002), 3–5.

54. Buchanan, *Death of the West*, 125–127. Buchanan predicted a similar dire fate for Europe: "[A]s the millions pour into Europe from North Africa and the Middle East, they will bring their Arab and Islamic culture, traditions, loyalties, and faith, and create replicas of their homelands in the heartland of the West. Will they assimilate, or will they endure as indigestible parts of Africa and Arabia in the base camp of what was once Christendom?" (page 100).

55. Samuel P. Huntington, "The Hispanic Challenge," *Foreign Policy* (March–April 2004); Huntington, *Who Are We? The Challenges to America's National Identity* (New York: Simon and Schuster, 2004). I will quote from the article, as it has pith. For incisive analysis of Huntington's stance, see Louis Menand, "Patriot Games: The New Nativism of Samuel P. Huntington," *The New Yorker* (May 17, 2004), 92–98.

56. Otis L. Graham Jr., *Unguarded Gates: A History of America's Immigration Crisis* (Lanham, MD: Rowman and Littlefield, 2004), xii, xv, 165. Other immigrant bashers from this period included Roy Beck, *The Case Against Immigration* (New York: Norton, 1996); Richard D. Lamm and Gary Imhoff, *The Immigration Time Bomb* (New York: Dutton, 1985); Jared Taylor, Ed., *The Real American Dilemma: Race, Immigration, and the Future of America* (Oakton, VA: New Century Foundation, 1998).

57. Buchanan, *Death of the West*, 218–220. When a listener commented after Graham's plenary address to the Organization of American Historians in Washington, D.C., on April 20, 2006, to the effect that his argument was tied together by racism at its logical core, he shouted that the listener had no intellectual legitimacy because he had marked the racism. It is almost enough to make one long for the forthrightness of Bull Connor or George Wallace. Professor Graham did own up to being "mean-spirited."

58. Geoff Eley and Ronald Grigor Suny, *Becoming National* (New York: Oxford, 1996); Ernest Gellner, *Nations and Nationalism* (Ithaca, NY: Cornell University Press, 1983); E. J. Hobsbawm, *Nations and Nationalism since 1780*, 2nd ed. (Cambridge: Cambridge University Press, 1990); Anthony D. Smith, *The Ethnic Origins of Nations* (Oxford: Blackwell, 1986); Howard Eissenstadt, "Metaphors of Race and Discourse of Nation: Racial Theory and State Nationalism in the First Decades of the Turkish Republic," in *Race and Nation: Ethnic Systems in the Modern World*, Paul Spickard, Ed. (New York: Routledge, 2005), 239–256; Peter C. Perdue, *China Marches West: The Qing Conquest of Central Eurasia* (Cambridge, MA: Harvard University Press, 2005).

59. Sources on affirmative action include Terry H. Anderson, *The Pursuit of Fairness: A History of Affirmative Action* (New York: Oxford, 2004); Herman Belz, *Equality Transformed: A Quarter-Century of Affirmative Action* (New Brunswick, NJ: Transaction, 1991); William G. Bowen and Derek Bok, *The Shape of the River: Long-Term Consequences of Considering Race in College and University Admissions* (Princeton, NJ: Princeton University Press, 1998); Steven M. Cahn, Ed., *Affirmative Action and the University* (Philadelphia: Temple University Press, 1993); Carter, *Affirmative Action Baby*; Connerly, *Creating Equal*; George E. Curry, Ed., *The Affirmative Action Debate* (Reading, MA: Addison-Wesley, 1996); Terry Eastland and William J. Bennett, *Counting by Race: Equality from the Founding Fathers to Bakke and Weber* (New York: Basic, 1979); Lynne Eisaquirre, *Affirmative Action: A Reference Handbook* (Santa Barbara, CA: ABC-Clio, 1999); Richard A. Epstein, *Forbidden Grounds: The Case Against Employment Discrimination Laws* (Cambridge, MA: Harvard University Press, 1992); Kathanne W. Greene, *Affirmative Action and Principles of Justice* (New York: Greenwood, 1989); Rachel Kranz, *Affirmative Action* (New York: Facts on File, 2002); Andrew Kull, *The Color-Blind Constitution* (Cambridge, MA: Harvard University Press, 1992); Frederick R. Lynch, *Invisible Victims: White Males and the Crisis of Affirmative Action* (New York: Praeger, 1991); Paul D. Moreno, *From Direct Action to Affirmative Action: Fair Employment Law and Policy in America, 1933–1972* (Baton Rouge: Louisiana State University Press, 1997); Albert G. Mosley and Nicholas Capaldi, *Affirmative Action: Social Justice of Unfair Prejudice?* (Lanham, MD: Rowman and Littlefield, 1996); Kul B. Raj and John W. Critzer, *Affirmative Action and the University* (Lincoln: University of Nebraska Press, 2000); Barbara Reskin, *The Realities of Affirmative Action in Employment* (Washington, DC: American Sociological Association, 1998); Philip F. Rubio, *A History of Affirmative Action, 1619–2000* (Jackson: University Press of Mississippi, 2001); Girardeau Spann, *The Law of Affirmative Action* (New York: NYU Press, 2000); Richard F. Tomasson, Faye J. Crosby, and Sharon D. Herzberger, *Affirmative Action: The Pros and Cons of Policy and Practice* (Washington,

DC: American University Press, 1996); Robert J. Weiss, *We Want Jobs: A History of Affirmative Action* (New York: Garland, 1997); Tim Wise, *Affirmative: Racial Preference in Black and White* (New York: Routledge, 2005).

60. Ira Katznelson, *When Affirmative Action Was White* (New York: Norton, 2005), 174–175.

61. Jack Ohma, editorial cartoon reproduced in the *Seattle Times* (January 20, 2003). Bush had two sorts of preference going for him when he applied to Yale: his father and grandfather were influential alumni (his grandfather had just retired as U.S. Senator from Connecticut, the state where Yale is located), and he was awarded points for geographical diversity since he was from Texas. C. Wright Mills, *The Power Elite* (New York: Oxford, 1956); G. William Domhoff, *The Higher Circles: The Governing Class in America* (New York: Random House, 1970); G. William Domhoff, *The Powers That Be: Processes of Ruling-Class Domination in America* (New York: Random House, 1978); G. William Domhoff, *Who Rules America?* 5th ed. (New York: McGraw-Hill, 2005); Peter W. Cookson and Caroline Hodges Persell, *Preparing for Power: America's Elite Boarding Schools* (New York: Basic Books, 1987); Arthur Powell, *Lessons from Privilege: The American Prep School Tradition* (Cambridge, MA: Harvard University Press, 1998). I do not mean to suggest that the younger Bush has not been a fine president, only that he could not possibly have gotten to that position on his sterling qualities alone, had it not been for the extreme privilege with which he was blessed from birth.

62. Katznelson, *When Affirmative Action Was White*, 140–141; Mary Poole, *The Segregated Origins of Social Security* (Chapel Hill: University of North Carolina Press, 2006).

63. Buchanan, *Death of the West*, 218.

64. Brimelow, *Alien Nation*, 219.

65. The anti-affirmative action movement has been directed primarily against racial affirmative action. With respect to a few professions—police, fire fighters, perhaps engineers—anti-affirmative action impulses may have gender targets, but gender is not usually where the resistance has occurred.

66. Sources on Proposition 54 and the assault on racial analysis include several issues of *The Egalitarian*, the American Civil Rights Institute's newsletter; David A. Hollinger, "Race, Politics, and the Census," *Chronicle of Higher Education* (March 17, 2006); Patricia J. Williams, "Racial Privacy," *The Nation* (June 17, 2002); Gregory Rodriguez, "Prop. 54 Could Undermine Racial Gains," *Los Angeles Times* (August 31, 2003); and materials on pro- and anti-Prop 54 websites www.racialprivacy.org and www.defeat54.org (October 2003).

67. Sources on multiculturalism include Alba Amoia and Bettina L. Knapp, *Multicultural Writers Since 1945* (Westport, CT: Greenwood, 2004); Charlotte Crabtree and Gary B. Nash, *National Standards for United States History* (Los Angeles: UCLA National Center for History in the Schools, 1994); Antonia Darder and Rodolfo D. Torres, *After Race: Racism After Multiculturalism* (New York: NYU Press, 2004); Curtiss Paul DeYoung, Michael O. Emerson, George Yancey, and Karen Chai Kim, *United by Faith: The Multiracial Congregation as an Answer to the Problem of Race* (New York: Oxford, 2003); Henry Louis Gates, Jr., *Loose Canons: Notes on the Culture Wars* (New York: Oxford, 1992); Avery F. Gordon and Christopher Newfield, Eds., *Mapping Multiculturalism* (Minneapolis: University of Minnesota Press, 1996); Sneja Gunew, *Haunted Nations: The Colonial Dimensions of Multiculturalisms* (New York:

Routledge, 2004); Roger Hewitt, *White Backlash and the Politics of Multiculturalism* (Cambridge: Cambridge University Press, 2005); Mike Hill, *After Whiteness: Unmaking an American Majority* (New York: NYU Press, 2004); Gerald P. Kernerman, *Multicultural Nationalism* (Vancouver: UBC Press, 2005); James Kyung-Jin Lee, *Urban Triage: Race and the Fictions of Multiculturalism* (Minneapolis: University of Minnesota Press, 2004); Donald Macedo, *Literacies of Power* (Boulder, CO: Westview, 1994); Michael T. Maly, *Beyond Segregation: Multiracial and Multiethnic Neighborhoods in the United States* (Philadelphia: Temple University Press, 2005); Satya P. Mohanty, Linda Martin Alcoff, Michael Hames-Garcia, and Paul M. L. Moya, Eds., *Identity Politics Reconsidered* (New York: Palgrave Macmillan 2006); Gary B. Nash, Charlotte Crabtree, and Ross E. Dunn, *History on Trial: Culture Wars and the Teaching of the Past* (New York: Knopf, 1997); Ronald Takaki, *A Different Mirror: A History of Multicultural America* (Boston: Little, Brown, 1993).

68. Rick Simonson and Scott Walker, Eds., *Multicultural Literacy* (St. Paul, MN: Graywolf Press, 1998), x–xi.

69. Lawrence W. Levine, *The Opening of the American Mind: Canons, Culture, and History* (Boston: Beacon, 1996), xviii–xix.

70. Prominent opponents of multiculturalism include Richard Bernstein, *Dictatorship of Virtue: Multiculturalism and the Battle for America's Future* (New York: Knopf, 1994); Allan Bloom, *The Closing of the American Mind: How Higher Education Has Failed Democracy and Impoverished the Souls of Today's Students* (New York: Simon and Schuster, 1987); Dinesh D'Souza, *Illiberal Education: The Politics of Race and Sex on Campus* (New York: Free Press, 1991); Nathan Glazer, *We Are All Multiculturalists Now* (Cambridge, MA: Harvard University Press, 1997); E. D. Hirsch, Jr., *Cultural Literacy* (Boston: Houghton Mifflin, 1987); John J. Miller, *The Unmaking of Americans: How Multiculturalism has Undermined America's Assimilation Ethic* (New York: Free Press, 1998); Arthur Schlesinger, Jr., *The Disuniting of America* (New York: Norton, 1992).

71. Alvin J. Schmidt, *The Menace of Multiculturalism* (Westport, CT: Praeger, 1997), 4, 7.

72. James Kyung-Jin Lee, *Urban Triage: Race and the Fictions of Multiculturalism* (Minneapolis: University of Minnesota Press, 2004); Viet Thanh Nguyen, review of *Urban Triage*, *Amerasia Journal*, 32.1 (2006), 136–139; Daniel Klaidman, "Homesick for Texas," *Newsweek* (July 12, 2004), 32.

73. "Have a Great Weekend Sale," *Los Angeles Times* (March 5, 2006); Charles Leroux, "Let Your Dedos Do the Walking," *Chicago Tribune* (March 23, 2004); Matea Gold and Joe Mathews, "At Fresno Rally, Bustamante Switches Spotlight to Himself," *Los Angeles Times* (September 8, 2003); Jonathan Abrams, "La Virgen Is Queen of Court," *Los Angeles Times* (July 16, 2006); Suketu Mehta, "The Meltingest Pot," *New York Times* (October 5, 2003).

74. Nguyen, review of *Urban Triage*, 139.

75. The places to begin on the multiracial movement include G. Reginald Daniel, *More Than Black? Multiracial Identity and the New Racial Order* (Philadelphia: Temple UP, 2002); Maria P. P. Root, Ed., *Racially Mixed People in America* (Newbury Park, CA: Sage, 1992); Maria P. P. Root, Ed., *The Multiracial Experience* (Thousand Oaks, CA: Sage, 1995); Teresa Williams-León and Cynthia L. Nakashima, Eds., *The Sum of Our Parts: Mixed Heritage Asian Americans* (Philadelphia: Temple University Press, 2001); Naomi Zack,

Race and Mixed Race (Philadelphia: Temple University Press, 1993). Other prominent writings on multiracial people and the movement include Gloria Anzaldúa, *Borderlands/La Frontera: The New Mestiza* (San Francisco: Aunt Lute Press, 1987); Katya Gibel Azoulay, *Black, Jewish, and Interracial* (Durham: Duke University Press, 1997); Carol Camper, Ed., *Miscegenation Blues: Voices of Mixed Race Women* (Toronto: Sister Vision, 1994); Sui Sin Far, *Mrs. Spring Fragrance and Other Writings* (Urbana: U of Illinois Press, 1995); Jack D. Forbes, *Black Africans and Native Americans: Color, Race and Caste in the Evolution of Red-Black Peoples* (New York: Basil Blackwell, 1988); Kip Fulbeck, *Paper Bullets* (Seattle: University of Washington Press, 2001); Kip Fulbeck, *Part Asian – 100% Hapa* (San Francisco: Chronicle Books, 2006); Lise Funderburg, *Black, White, Other: Biracial Americans Talk About Race and Identity* (New York: Morrow, 1994); Patricia Penn Hilden, *When Nickels Were Indians: An Urban, Mixed-Blood Story* (Washington, DC: Smithsonian, 1995); Margaret L. Hunter, *Race, Gender, and the Politics of Skin Tone* (New York: Routledge, 2005); Jayne O. Ifekwunigwe, Ed., *'Mixed Race' Studies* (New York: Routledge, 2004); Kevin R. Johnson, *How Did You Get to be Mexican? A White/Brown Man's Search for Identity* (Philadelphia: Temple University Press, 1999); Yelena Khanga, *Soul to Soul: The Story of a Black Russian American Family, 1865–1992* (New York: Norton, 1992); Karen Isaaksen Leonard, *Making Ethnic Choices: Punjabi-Mexican Americans* (Philadelphia: Temple University Press, 1994); James McBride, *The Color of Water: A Black Man's Tribute to His White Mother* (New York: Riverhead, 1996); Robert S. McKelvey, *Dust of Life: America's Children Abandoned in Vietnam* (Seattle: University of Washington Press, 1999); Barack Obama, *Dreams from My Father: A Story of Race and Inheritance* (Tokyo: Kodansha, 1995); Nguyen, *Unwanted*; Clara E. Rodríguez, *Changing Race: Latinos, the Census, and the History of Ethnicity in the United States* (New York: NYU Press, 2000); David Parker and Miri Song, Eds., *Rethinking 'Mixed Race'* (London: Pluto Press, 2001); Maria P. P. Root and Matt Kelley, Eds., *Multiracial Child Resource Book* (Seattle: Mavin, 2003); Miri Song, *Choosing Ethnic Identity* (London: Polity, 2003); Paul Spickard, *Mixed Blood: Intermarriage and Ethnic Identity in Twentieth-Century America* (Madison: University of Wisconsin Press, 1989); Spickard and Daniel, *Racial Thinking*; Barbara Tizard and Ann Phoenix, *Black, White, or Mixed Race?* (New York: Routledge, 1993); Dorothy West, *The Wedding* (New York: Doubleday, 1995); Gregory Howard Williams, *Life on the Color Line* (New York: Penguin, 1995); Joel Williamson, *New People: Miscegenation and Mulattoes in the United States* (New York: Free Press, 1980); Loretta Winters and Herman DeBose, Eds., *New Faces in a Changing America: Multiracial Identity in the 21st Century* (Thousand Oaks, CA: Sage, 2003); Marguerite Wright, *I'm Chocolate, You're Vanilla: Raising Healthy Black and Biracial Children in a Race-Conscious World* (San Francisco: Jossey-Bass, 1998).

76. Jeremiah Marquez, "Strom Thurmond Was Her Father, Says Mixed-Race Woman," *Oregonian* (December 14, 2003); Jacob Jordan, "Thurmond Daughter Feels 'Free'," *Oregonian* (December 18, 2003); Marie Cocco, "Strom's Daughter: A Life Separate, Unequal," *Oregonian* (December 18, 2003); Charles Coulter, "Race Watch," *Kansas City Star* (December 18, 2003); Marilyn W. Thompson, "The Long Road to Truth," *Washington Post* (January 4, 2004).

77. Maria Root, "Within, Between, and Beyond Race," in *Racially Mixed People*, Root, Ed., 3–11; Charlotte Astor, "Gallup Poll: Progress in Black/White Relations, but Race is Still an Issue," *US Society and Values*, 2.3 (August 1997); Alison Stein Wellner, "US Attitudes Toward Interracial Dating Are Liberalizing," Population Reference Bureau report (June 2005); George Yancey, "Who Interracial Dates," *Journal of Comparative Family Studies*, 33.2 (2002), 177–190; Sharon M. Lee and Barry Edmonston, "New Marriages, New Families: US Racial and Hispanic Intermarriage," *Population Bulletin*, 60.2 (2005).

78. U.S. Census Bureau, *The Two or More Races Population: 2000* (Census 2000 Brief C2KBR/01-6; Washington, 2001).

79. Daniel, *More Than Black?*, 191–194.

80. Sources on Asian Americans and the eternal foreigner theme include Michael Chang, *Racial Politics in an Era of Transnational Citizenship: The 1996 "Asian Donorgate" Controversy in Perspective* (Lanham, MD: Lexington Books, 2004); Darrell Y. Hamamoto, *Monitored Peril: Asian Americans and the Politics of Representation* (Minneapolis: University of Minnesota Press, 1994); K. Connie Kang, "US Asians Seen as 'Alien,' Study Finds," *Los Angeles Times* (March 2, 2000); Mia Tuan, *Forever Foreigners or Honorary Whites? The Asian Ethnic Experience Today* (New Brunswick, NJ: Rutgers University Press, 1998).

81. Ted W. Lieu, "Are You in the Chinese Air Force?" *Washington Post* (June 19, 1999).

82. The best sources on Lee's tribulations are his autobiography, written with Helen Zia, *My Country Versus Me* (New York: Hyperion, 2001), and the *Los Angeles Times* accounts by Robert Scheer, e.g.,"What's Been Done to Lee Is Outrageous" (November 23, 1999); "Why Was Lee Indicted, and Not Deutch?" (February 8, 2000); "CIA's Deutch Heedlessly Disregarded Security" (February 29, 2000); "Case Against Lee Is Flying Out Window" (April 18, 2000); "Lee Does Penance for Justice Dept.'s Sins" (July 25, 2000); "Wong One Is on Trial in Lee Case" (August 25, 2000); "How Can Lee—How Can We—Forget What the Government Did?" (September 14, 2000); "China Spying Story: All the Excuses Fit to Print" (February 6, 2001); "The Persecution of Wen Ho Lee, Redux" (August 7, 2001); "Lee: Guilty Until Proved Innocent" (August 17, 2001).

Analytical accounts include Neil Gotanda, "Comparative Racialization: Racial Profiling and the Case of Wen Ho Lee," *UCLA Law Review*, 47 (2000), 1689–1703; Dan Stober and Ian Hoffman, *A Convenient Spy: Wen Ho Lee and the Politics of Nuclear Espionage* (New York: Simon and Schuster, 2001); Spencer K. Turnbull, "Wen Ho Lee and the Consequences of Enduring Asian American Stereotyped," in *Asian American Politics*, Don T. Nakanishi and James S. Lai, Ed. (Lanham, MD: Rowman and Littlefield, 2003), 303–316; Cheuk-Yin Wong, "The Los Alamos Incident and Its Effects on Chinese American Scientists," in *Chinese American Voices*, Judy Ung, Gordon Chang, and Him Mark Lai, Eds. (Berkeley: University of California Press, 2006), 416–422; Frank H. Wu, "Profiling Principle: The Prosecution of Wen Ho Lee and the Defense of Asian Americans," in *Asian American Politics*, Nakanishi and Lai, Ed., 297–301.

Other journalistic accounts include Angela Oh, "Spy Charges Fueled Search for Scapegoats," *Los Angeles Times* (June 21, 1999); Author?, "FBI Made Wen Ho Lee Think He Failed Polygraph," *Washington Post* (January 8, 2000); James Glanz, "Asian-American Scholars Call for Boycott of Labs," *New*

York Times (May 31, 2000); Bob Pool, "Rally Denounces Charges in Spy Case," *Los Angeles Times* (June 9, 2000); James Glanz, "Fallout in Arms Research: Amid Race Profiling Claims, Asian-Americans Avoid Labs," *New York Times* (July 16, 2000); James Sterngold, "Defense Argues Ethnicity Made Scientist a Suspect," *New York Times* (August 16, 2000); James Sterngold, "Agent Concedes Faulty Testimony in Secrets Case," *New York Times* (August 18, 2000); Bob Drogin, "Science Academies Decry Lee's Treatment," *Los Angeles Times* (September 1, 2000); Bob Drogin, "Scientist to Accept Plea Deal; Likely to Be Freed Today," *Los Angeles Times* (September 11, 2000); Bob Drogin, "How FBI's Flawed Case Against Lee Unraveled," *Los Angeles Times* (September 13, 2000); Bob Drogin, "Wen Ho Lee Freed; Judge Scolds US Over Case Tactics," *Los Angeles Times* (September 14, 2000); "A Case of Shame," editorial, *Los Angeles Times* (September 14, 2000); Robert L. Jackson, "Clinton Criticizes Justice Dept. Over Wen Ho Lee Case," *Los Angeles Times* (September 15, 2000); Gish Jen, "Wen Ho Lee, Still Not So Very Free," *New York Times* (September 15, 2000); Anthony Lewis, "It Did Happen Here," *New York Times* (September 16, 2000); James Sterngold, "Asian-Americans Demanding Bias Inquiry in Scientist's Case," *New York Times* (September 18, 2000); Michael Isikoff, "Into the Sunshine," *Newsweek* (September 25, 2000); Bob Drogin and Eric Lichtblau, "Reno, Freeh Insist Wen Ho Lee Posed 'Great Risk' to US," *Los Angeles Times* (September 27, 2000); Matthew Purdy, "The Making of a Suspect: The Case of Wen Ho Lee," *New York Times* (February 4, 2001); Matthew Purdy, with James Sterngold, "The Prosecution Unravels," *New York Times* (February 5, 2001); Michael Isikoff, "The Lee Case: A Damning Report," *Newsweek* (August 27, 2001); Adam Liptak, "Scientist, News Media Settle Suit on Privacy," *New York Times* (June 3, 2006).

83. Court transcript, quoted in Lon Kurashige and Alice Yang Murray, Eds., *Major Problems in Asian American History* (Boston: Houghton Mifflin, 2003), 440–441.

84. Sources on Arab, other Middle Eastern, and Muslim Americans include Nabeel Abraham and Andrew Shryock, Eds., *Arab Detroit* (Detroit: Wayne State University Press, 2000); André Aciman, *False Papers* (New York: Farrar, Straus and Giroux, 2000); Ibrahim Aoudé, "Arab Americans and Ethnic Studies," *Journal of Asian American Studies*, 9.2 (2006), 141–156; Michael Arlen, *Passage to Ararat* (New York: Ballantine, 1975); Peter Balakian, *Black Dog of Fate: An American Son Uncovers His Armenian Past* (New York: Broadway, 1997); *Brothers and Others*, dir. Nicolas Rossier (Arab Film Distribution, 2002); Louise Cainkar and Sunaina Maira, "Targeting Arab/Muslim/South Asian Americans: Criminalization and Cultural Citizenship," *Amerasia Journal*, 31.3 (2005), 1–27; G. Patricia de la Cruz and Angela Brittingham, *The Arab Population: 2000*, U.S. Census 2000 Brief C2KBR-23 (Washington, DC: Government Printing Office, 2003); Firoozeh Dumas, *Funny in Farsi* (New York: Random House, 2003); Yvonne Yazbeck Haddad, Ed., *The Muslims of America* (New York: Oxford, 1991); Yvonne Yazbeck Haddad and Adair T. Lummis, *Islamic Values in the United States* (New York: Oxford University Press, 1987); Elaine C. Hagopian, *Civil Rights in Peril: The Targeting of Arabs and Muslims* (Chicago: Haymarket, 2004); Ron Kelley, Ed., *Irangeles: Iranians in Los Angeles* (Berkeley: University of California Press, 1993); Hanif Kureishi, *My Son the Fanatic* (London: Faber and Faber, 1997); Sunaina Maira and Magid Shihade,

"Meeting Asian/Arab American Studies," *Journal of Asian American Studies*, 9.2 (2006), 117–141; Amir Marvasti and Karyn D. McKinney, *Middle Eastern Lives in America* (Lanham, MD: Rowman and Littlefield, 2004); C. Eric Lincoln, *The Black Muslims in America*, 3rd ed. (Trenton, NJ: Africa World Press, 1994); Kathleen M. Moore, *Al-Mughtaribun: American Law and the Transformation of Muslim Life in the United States* (Albany: SUNY Press, 1995); Vijay Prashad, "Ethnic Studies Inside Out," *Journal of Asian American Studies*, 9.2 (2006), 157–176; Jack G. Shaheen, *Arab and Muslim Stereotyping in American Popular Culture* (Washington, DC: Center for Muslim-Christian Understanding, Georgetown University, 1997); Jack Shaheen, *The TV Arab* (Bowling Green, OH: Bowling Green State University Popular Press, 1984); Jack Shaheen, *Reel Bad Arabs: How Hollywood Vilifies a People* (New York: Olive Branch Press, 2001); Evelyn Shakir, *Bint Arab: Arab and Arab American Women in the United States* (Westport, CT: Praeger, 1997); Garbi Schmidt, *Islam in Urban America* (Philadelphia: Temple University Press, 2004); Michael W. Suleiman, Ed., *Arabs in America* (Philadelphia: Temple University Press, 1999); Richard Brent Turner, *Islam in the African-American Experience* (Bloomington: Indiana University Press, 1997).

85. Peter H. King, "18 Years Waiting for a Gavel to Fall," *Los Angeles Times* (June 29, 2005); King, "Live of Worry, Sadness,' Why?'" *Los Angeles Times* (June 30, 2005).

86. Louise Cainkar, "The Social Construction of Difference and the Arab American Experience," *Journal of American Ethnic History*, 25.2–3 (2006), 243–278.

87. Schmidt, *Islam in Urban America*, 33; *A Rush to Judgment: A Special Report on Anti-Muslim Stereotyping, Harassment and Hate Crimes Following the Bombing of Oklahoma City's Murrah Federal Building, April 19, 1995* (Washington, DC: Council on American-Islamic Relations, 1995).

88. Khaled Hosseini, *The Kite Runner* (New York: Riverhead, 2003); Azadeh Moaveni, *Lipstick Jihad: A Memoir of Growing up Iranian in America and American in Iran* (New York: Public Affairs, 2005); Asra Q. Nomani, *Standing Alone in Mecca: An American Woman's Struggle for the Soul of Islam* (San Francisco: HarperCollins, 2005).

89. Masuda Sultan, *My War At Home* (New York: Washington Square Press, 2006).

Chapter 10

1. Richard Rodriguez, "Pocho Pioneer," in *The Late Great Mexican Border: Reports from a Disappearing Line*, Bobby Byrd and Susanna Mississippi Byrd, Eds. (El Paso: Cinco Puntos Press, 1996), 224; quoted in Joseph Nevins, *Operation Wetback* (New York: Routledge, 2002), 165.

2. Carlos Mencia, "It's Your Turn" (www.carlosmencia.com, July 12, 2005). Comedian Mencia explains: "America is a giant game of tag. Somebody is always It. Somebody is always on the bottom getting fucked by everybody at the top. And on September tenth of two thousand and one, that was niggers and spics on the bottom of that fucking totem pole. We were fucking *It*. And then the goddam buildings collapsed and they showed the pictures of the nineteen hijackers and that's when Carlos and Tyrone went 'Fuck you, puta! You're It. It's your turn.'"

3. Some readers may make the mistake of thinking that *Almost All Aliens* is about American immigration policy. It is not. It is about immigrants, and not in the present day. Specifically, this is a history of immigration into the United States, and of the racial and colonial dynamics that have shaped both the immigrant flow itself and how we Americans have chosen to think about immigrants and ourselves. It is not that I lack opinions about current immigration policy. No informed American can fail to have such opinions. But this book is not about them. It is an attempt to take a clear, nonideological look at immigration in America's past. If a clear understanding of the past should tend to support particular policy options in the present or future, then that is a matter for another book.

   Nonetheless, I would be failing to complete the historical task if I did not attempt to bring this history up as far as possible in time—that is, up to the middle of 2006, when this manuscript is being completed. A lot has been happening on the immigration front in the last few years. Still, for years so recent as these, we have not yet the degree of clarity that hindsight will likely bring. So I shall treat the immediate past few years as part of the extended present. In this chapter, then, I do not pretend to be setting out a history of immigrant lives and experiences in the early twenty-first century. Rather, I will make some observations and ask some questions regarding what seem to be important issues relating to immigration and race in our era, and into the future so far as we can project. I have read scores of books on immigrant experiences and immigration policies in our era, but my main sources for this chapter are the pages of the daily newspaper, as well as conversations with hundreds of immigrants, immigration officials, and other Americans. At the very end, I shall do a little summing up of the issues I have explored in the book as a whole.

4. Leon Kolankiewicz, "Immigration, Population, and the New Census Bureau Projections," Center for Immigration Studies press release (Washington, June 2000); Steven A. Camarota, "Immigration in an Aging Society," Center for Immigration Studies press release (Washington, April 2005).

5. Republican strategist Matthew Dowd, for one, thinks that a sharply declining fertility rate in Mexico heralds a decline in that country's population growth, hence in pressure for Mexicans to migrate in search of work; Matthew Dowd, "The Mexican Evolution," *New York Times* (August 1, 2005).

6. *The Papers of the Presidents, Ronald Reagan, 1981*, volume 1 (Washington, DC: Government Printing Office, 1982), 676–677, quoted in Michael LeMay and Elliott Robert Barkan, Eds., *US Immigration and Naturalization Laws and Issues* (Westport, CT: Greenwood, 1999), 276–277.

7. See Appendix B, Table 31.

8. www.migrationinformation.org/globaldata/ (website of the Migration Policy Institute, a nonpartisan information-gathering service), March 8, 2006.

9. White native Australians did mount some racially motivated riots in 2006: "Racial Unrest in Sydney," *Los Angeles Times* (December 12, 2005); "Violence Rages in Australia for 2nd Night," *Associated Press* (December 12, 2005); Eva Sallis, "Australia's Dangerous Fantasy," *New York Times* (December 17, 2005).

10. Sources on illegal immigration include Alicia Alarcón, trans. Ethriam Cash Brammer de Gonzales, *The Border Patrol Ate My Dust* (Houston: Arte Público Press, 2004); J. P. Bone, *Illegals* (Berkeley: Mindfield, 1996); Leo R. Chavez, *Shadowed Lives: Undocumented Immigrants in American Society*, 2nd ed. (n.p.: Wadsworth, 1998); Marc Cooper, "Last Exit to Tombstone," *LA Weekly* (March 31, 2005); James R. Edwards, Jr., "Two Side of the Same Coin: The Connection

Between Legal and Illegal Immigration," Center for Immigration Studies report (February 2006); Ken Ellingwood, *Hard Line: Life and Death on the US-Mexico Border* (New York: Pantheon, 2004); Helen Hayes, *US Immigration Policy and the Undocumented: Ambivalent Laws, Furtive Lives* (Westport, CT: Praeger, 2001); Christian Joppke, "How Immigration is Changing Citizenship," *Ethnic and Racial Studies*, 22.4 (1999), 629–652; David Kyle and Rey Koslowski,, Eds., *Global Human Smuggling* (Baltimore: Johns Hopkins University Press, 2001); Peter Kwong, *Forbidden Workers: Illegal Chinese Immigrants and American Labor* (New York: New Press, 1997); Rubén Martínez, *Crossing Over: A Mexican Family on the Migrant Trail* (New York: Picador, 2001); Jeffrey S. Passell, *Unauthorized Migrants: Numbers and Characteristics* (Washington, DC: Pew Hispanic Center, 2005); Luis Alberto Urrea, *Across the Wire: Life and Hard Times on the Mexican Border* (New York: Anchor, 1993); U.S. Immigration and Naturalization Service, "Illegal Alien Resident Population," (June 28, 2001); Michael Welch, *Detained: Immigration Laws and the Expanding INS Jail Complex* (Philadelphia: Temple University Press, 2003).

11. Jeffrey S. Passel, "Estimates of the Size and Characteristics of the Undocumented Population," Pew Hispanic Center report (March 21, 2005); Maura Reynolds and Nicole Gaouette, "Immigration Bill Is on Hiatus With the Senate," *Los Angeles Times* (April 8, 2006); Carlos Gutierrez-Jones and Josef Castañeda-Liles, "Basic Facts about Immigration," aad.english.ucsb.edu/basicfacts.html (May 2, 2006).

12. Ashbel S. Green, "Diarmuid O'Scannlain: Conservative Helps Balance Liberal Court," *Oregonian* (January 26, 2004); Nina Bernstein, "Most Mexican Immigrants in New Study Gave Up Jobs to Take Their Chances in US," *New York Times* (December 7, 2005); Anna Gorman and Jennifer Delson, "Policies on Illegal Immigration at Odds," *Los Angeles Times* (November 27, 2005); Douglas McGray, "Exit Date," *New York Times* (May 2, 2004).

13. Bill Ong Hing, "An Immigrant's Death Trap," *Chicago Tribune* (January 2, 2006); Nicholas Riccardi, "Why Illegal Immigrants Fear Leaving," *Los Angeles Times* (April 12, 2006); Anna Gorman, "Deportation to Nowhere," *Los Angeles Times* (November 6, 2005); Anna Gorman, "The Great Divide of Citizenship," *Los Angeles Times* (May 7, 2006); Steve Lopez, "Nuances of Immigrant Debate Lost in the Fury," *Los Angeles Times* (June 1, 2005).

14. Sam Quinones, "Deportation of Illegal Workers Leaves Families in Quandary," *Los Angeles Times* (April 22, 2006); Nicole Gaouette, "What Was Behind the Big Raid," *Los Angeles Times* (April 22, 2006).

15. Don Terry, "I'm Still Crossing the Border," *Chicago Tribune* (July 23, 2006); Steve Lopez, "Immigrant a Graduate of the US System," *Los Angeles Times* (May 11, 2005); Kate Taylor, "For These Top Students, Dreams Falter," *Oregonian* (June 8, 2004); Nicholas Riccardi, "A Test of Origins Has Left Star Students in Free-Fall," *Los Angeles Times* (July 19, 2005); Dan Frosch, "Four Arizona Students From Mexico Forestall Their Deportation," *New York Times* (July 22, 2005); Anne-Marie O'Connor, "Illegal Immigrants Enter Twilight Zone as Teenagers," *Los Angeles Times* (May 19, 2000); Jill Leovy, "Bill Seeks to Legalize Immigrant Students," *Los Angeles Times* (May 21, 2001); Jill Leovy, "Tuition Law Praised, Attacked," *Los Angeles Times* (October 31, 2001); Stuart Silverstein, "Out-of-State Students Sue Over Tuition," *Los Angeles Times* (December 15, 2005); Rachel L. Swarns, "Suit Challenges California's Tuition Rule for Illegal Immigrants," *New York Times* (December 15, 2005).

16. Tim Rutten, "Lou Dobbs: Bile Across the Border," *Los Angeles Times* (April 1, 2006).

17. Tancredo.house.gov/irc/nationalsecurity.html (August 1, 2006); Mark Z. Barabak, "GOP Lawmaker Relishes Role as a Flamethrower," *Los Angeles Times* (December 27, 2005); "Tancredo: It They Nuke Us, Bomb Mecca," foxnews.com (July 18, 2005); Tom Tancredo, *In Mortal Danger: The Battle for America's Border and Security* (Nashville: WND Books, 2006), 9.

18. Andrés Martinez, "We're Partners in This Crime," *Los Angeles Times* (May 18, 2005); Georgie Anne Geyer, "Running Out of Excuses for Illegal Entry," *Oregonian* (November 28, 2003).

19. Sources on border issues include Peter Andreas and Timothy Snyder, Eds., *The Wall Around the West: State Borders and Immigration Controls in North America and Europe* (Lanham, MD: Rowman and Littlefield, 2000); John J. Bukowczyk, Ed., *Permeable Border: The Great Lakes Basin as Transnational Region, 1650–1990* (Pittsburgh: University of Pittsburgh Press, 2005); Teresa Hayter, *Open Borders: The Case Against Immigration Controls*, 2nd ed. (London: Pluto Press, 2004); Kevin R. Johnson, "Open Borders?" *UCLA Law Review*, 50 (2003); Robert Lee Maril, *Patrolling Chaos: The US Border Patrol in Deep South Texas* (Lubbock: Texas Tech University Press, 2004); Belinda I. Reyes, Hans P. Johnson, and Richard Van Swearingen, *Holding the Line? The Effect of the Recent Border Build-Up on Unauthorized Immigration* (San Francisco: Public Policy Institute of California, 2002).

20. Teresa Watanabe and Anna Gorman, "'86 Amnesty Frames Immigration Debate," *Los Angeles Times* (June 3, 2006); Tancredo's program included **"Begin Building a Border Security Fence**: Put troops on the border. … Mandate passport usage for everyone traveling internationally. Make volunteer border patrol a sanctioned federal activity. … **Enforcing the Law Throughout the Country**: Require a federal response when local law enforcement asks to have illegal aliens arrested. Restrict federal money that goes to local governments that have illegal alien sanctuary policies. … Make DUI a deportable offense. Increase penalties for the smuggling of illegal aliens; Increase penalties for terrorists who are illegal aliens. … Make unlawful presence in the United States a felony. **Stopping Businesses from Hiring Illegals**: Make employment verification mandatory. … Increase the penalty for employers who hire illegal aliens. Make businesses that hire illegal aliens ineligible for future guest workers. **Reducing the Incentive to Come Illegally**: Disallow all federal funding for states that offer in-state tuition to illegal aliens. … eliminate Social Security totalization for illegal aliens. … **Restoring the Meaning of Citizenship**: End birthright citizenship for illegal aliens. Eliminate dual citizenship. Make English the official language. … **Reforming Legal Immigration**. Eliminate the visa lottery. Eliminate chain migration [i.e., family reunification preferences]. Eliminate H-1B visas [temporary work permits]. Eliminate unskilled worker green cards. Create a Department of Immigration"; Tancredo, *In Mortal Danger*, 187–189. So much for limited government.

21. "First Guard Members Arrive to Fortify Border," *Los Angeles Times* (June 4, 2006); Peter Nicholas, "Governor Refuses Bush Request for Border Troops," *Los Angeles Times* (June 24, 2006); Nicole Gaouette, "Senate Approves Border Security Bill," *Los Angeles Times* (July 14, 2006); Nicole Gaouette, "Nationwide Raids Intensify Focus on the Employment of Illegal Immigrants," *Los Angeles Times* (April 21, 2006); John Pomfret, "Special Agent Has Tunnel Vision," *Washington Post* (April 20, 2006).

22. Jim Gilchrist and Jerome R. Corsi, *Minutemen: The Battle to Secure America's Borders* (Los Angeles: World Ahead Publishing, 2006); Ricardo Alonso-Zaldivar, "US to Bolster Arizona Border Security," *Los Angeles Times* (March 30, 2005); Timothy Gean, "Wanted: Border Hoppers. And Some Excitement, Too," *New York Times* (April 1, 2005); David Kelly, "Citizen Border Patrols Hurry Up … and Wait," *Los Angeles Times* (April 3, 2005); David Kelly, "Border Watchers Capture Their Prey—the Media," *Los Angeles Times* (April 5, 2005); "A West Too Wild," editorial, *New York Times* (April 11, 2005); Peter Nicholas and Robert Salladay, "Gov. Praises 'Minuteman' Campaign," *Los Angeles Times* (April 29, 2005); "'Minutemen' End Unofficial Border Patrol, but Plan to Return," *New York Times* (May 1, 2005); Anna Gorman, "Volunteers to Patrol Border Near San Diego," *Los Angeles Times* (May 5, 2005); Leslie Berestein, "New Buzz in the Immigration Debate," *San Diego Union-Tribune* (May 13, 2005); Jennifer Delson and Mai Tran, "After Minuteman Melee, Protesters Have New Beef," *Los Angeles Times* (May 27, 2005); Scott Gold, "Border Watchers Gear Up for Expanded Patrol," *Los Angeles Times* (July 3, 2005); Richard Marosi, "'California Minutemen' Begin Patrol," *Los Angeles Times* (July 17, 2005); "Border Patrol Considering Use of Volunteers, Official Says," *New York Times* (July 21, 2005); "US Bars Plan to Let Civilians Patrol Borders," *New York Times* (July 22, 2005); Sarah Vowell, "Lock and Load," *New York Times* (July 23, 2005); "Marchers Protest Border Patrol Group," *New York Times* (July 24, 2005); Anna Gorman and Richard Marosi, "Minuteman-Style Border Patrol Is Over in No Time," *Los Angeles Times* (September 18, 2005); Jean O. Pasco, "Border Activist a Wild Card in OC Election," *Los Angeles Times* (October 2, 2005); Jean O. Pasco, "Minuteman a Wild Card in OC Race," *Los Angeles Times* (October 6, 2005).
23. Tancredo.house.gov/irc/nationalsecurity.html (August 1, 2006); Rich Connell and David Haldane, "Rallies Draw Dueling Protesters in Clashes Over Illegal Immigration," *Los Angeles Times* (January 8, 2006); Beth Duff-Brown and Pauline Arrillaga, "At Canadian Crossings, Scant 9/11 Upgrades," *San Francisco Chronicle* (July 4, 2005).
24. Andrew Pollack, "2 Illegal Immigrants Win Arizona Ranch in Court," *New York Times* (August 19, 2005); Beth DeFalco, "Ranch of Foe of Immigrants Given to Nemeses," *San Francisco Chronicle* (August 20, 2005).
25. Miguel Bustillo, "Agents' Chase Never Ends," *Los Angeles Times* (August 13, 2006).
26. "Immigrant Sweeps Trigger Fear and Damage Communities," *ACLU Open Forum*, 80 (August–September 2004).
27. "Despite Neighbors' Help, a Family is Deported," *Los Angeles Times* (September 2, 2004); Ann M. Simmons, "Deportation May Cut Short an Immigrant Success Story," *Los Angeles Times* (September 29, 2004); Chuck Bartels, "60 Wal-Mart Stores Raided; 300 Arrested," *Oregonian* (October 24, 2004); Jennifer Mena, "On the Run, but Not Out of Reach," *Los Angeles Times* (November 1, 2004); Nicole Gaouette, "New Federal Rules Target Hiring of Illegal Immigrants," *Los Angeles Times* (June 9, 2004); Anna Gorman, "Employers of Illegal Immigrants Face Little Risk of Penalty," *Los Angeles Times* (May 29, 2005); Eric Lipton, "New Checks Planned for Illegal Workers and Their Employers," *Los Angeles Times* (December 2, 2005); Anna Gorman, "Employers of Illegal Workers in a Catch-22," *Los Angeles Times* (March 6, 2006); Steve Lopez, "Hapless Chinese Immigrants Can't Escape the Party Line," *Los Angeles Times* (May 26, 2002); Nick Madigan, "160 Migrants Found at an Upscale Home" *New York Times*

(February 13, 2004); Solomon Moore and Hector Becerra, "House Crammed with Illegal Immigrants Raided in Watts," *Los Angeles Times* (April 22, 2004); Steve Lopez, "Shirking the Cost of Human Bondage," *Los Angeles Times* (April 23, 2004); Greg Krikorian, "Chinese Smuggled Into Port Arrested," *Los Angeles Times* (April 5, 2005); Andrew Blankstein and Anna Gorman, "70 Illegal Migrants Found in Raid," *Los Angeles Times* (March 4, 2006); Anna Gorman, "Fake ID Trade Makes a Name for Itself," *Los Angeles Times* (November 29, 2005). The crackdown on makers and users of fake identification compelled one to wonder whether this meant that the Bush twins were bound for jail.

28. Sam Quinones, "It Wasn't the Court Order She Sought," *Los Angeles Times* (July 20, 2006); Sam Quinones, "Experts Criticize Judge's Deportation Threat," *Los Angeles Times* (July 21, 2006); Sam Quinones, "Volunteer Judge Who Threatened to Deport Woman Is Dropped," *Los Angeles Times* (July 22, 2006); Mark Stevenson, "US Deportation Program Draws Anger from Mexican Government," *Oregonian* (September, 27, 2003); Chris Kraul, "Illegal Immigrants Receive a One-Way Ticket to Mexico," *Los Angeles Times* (July 13, 2004); David G. Savage, "Supreme Court Upholds Strict Deportation Law," *Los Angeles Times* (June 23, 2006); "Kids, Shackles and Shame," editorial, *Los Angeles Times* (June 26, 2003); Jennifer Mena, "Deported Man, Getting Day in Court, Asks to Continue Caring for HIV-Stricken Boy," *Los Angeles Times* (July 22, 2003); "Bring 'Papa' Back for Ill Boy," *Los Angeles Times* (July 30, 2003); Henry Weinstein, "Contesting the Bar to Asylum," *Los Angeles Times* (August 21, 2006).

29. Ellen Barry, "City Vents Anger at Illegal Immigrants," *Los Angeles Times* (July 14, 2006).

30. Steven Greenhouse, "Day Laborer Battle Runs Outside Home Depot," *New York Times* (October 10, 2005); Jennifer Delson, "Dayworker Arrests Followed Complaints, Orange Officials Say," *Los Angeles Times* (February 28, 2006); Anna Gorman, "Judge Blocks Arrests of Day Laborers," *Los Angeles Times* (May 3, 2006); Jennifer Delson, "Protest Aims at Laborer Center," *Los Angeles Times* (July 17, 2005); Pam Belluck, "Town Uses Trespass Law to Fight Illegal Immigrants," *New York Times* (July 13, 2005); Pam Belluck, "Towns Lose Tool Against Illegal Immigrants," *New York Times* (August 13, 2005); David Kelly, "Illegal Immigrant Measure Upheld," *Los Angeles Times* (December 23, 2004); Rubén Martínez, "The Kindness of Strangers," *New York Times* (December 24, 2004); Nicholas Riccardi, "Eligible to Vote in Arizona? Prove It," *Los Angeles Times* (November 5, 2005); "Arizona: Limits on Immigrants," *New York Times* (May 13, 2005); "Arizona Governor Vetoes Measures on Immigration," *New York Times* (May 22, 2005); Ellen Barry, "It's 'Get These People Out of Town,'" *Los Angeles Times* (August 16, 2006); Molly Selvin, "Suit Targets Hiring of Illegal Farmworkers," *Los Angeles Times* (August 23, 2006).

31. Ashley Powers, "Vote on Migrant Issues Is Forced," *Los Angeles Times* (May 5, 2006); Ashley Powers, "Immigrant-Rights Activist Slaps Opponent, Police Say," *Los Angeles Times* (June 24, 2006); Ashley Powers, "Law Aimed at Migrants Faces Hurdle," *Los Angeles Times* (June 27, 2006); Nicholas Riccardi, "Immigration Hard-Liners on a High," *Los Angeles Times* (September 12, 2001); David Kelly, "Illegal Immigration Fears Have Spread," *Los Angeles Times* (April 25, 2005); David Kelly, "Colorado Activists Push Immigration Initiative," *Los Angeles Times* (September 13, 2005); Nicholas Riccardi, "Court Kills Measure to Deny Immigrant Services," *Los Angeles Times* (June 13, 2006); Jenny Jarvie,

"Georgia Law Chills Its Latino Housing Market," *Los Angeles Times* (June 19, 2006); Chris Livingston, "A Florida Mayor Turns to an Immigration Curb to Fix a Fading City," *New York Times* (July 10, 2006); Tomas Alex Tizon, "Mr. Fox, Cough Up $300,000," *Los Angeles Times* (May 12, 2006); "Group Calls Metrolink Monument Anti-American, Demands Removal," *San Diego Union-Tribune* (May 14, 2005); David Pierson and Patricia Ward Biederman, "Protest Over Art Forces Police to Draw the Line," *Los Angeles Times* (May 25, 2005); David Pierson and Wendy Lee, "A Monumental War of Words," *Los Angeles Times* (June 25, 2005); Wendy Thermos, "Immigration Protest in Baldwin Park Is Peaceful," *Los Angeles Times* (June 26, 2005); Fred Alvarez, "A Street-Fighter Mentality on Illegal Immigration," *Los Angeles Times* (June 27, 2005); Rich Connell and David Haldane, "Rallies Draw Dueling Protesters in Clashes Over Illegal Immigration," *Los Angeles Times* (January 8, 2006).

32. "Utah Senate Approves Immigrant Driver's Card," *New York Times* (February 20, 2005); Shaila Dewan, "Immigrants in Tennessee Issued Certificates to Drive," *New York Times* (May 9, 2005); P. H. Huffstutter, "Putting a Roof Over Illegal Immigrants," *Los Angeles Times* (May 11, 2006); Anna Gorman, "Despite Illegal Status, Buyers Get Home Loans," *Los Angeles Times* (August 9, 2005); Hector Becerra, "Welcome to Maywood, Where Roads Open Up for Immigrants," *Los Angeles Times* (March 21, 2006); Ted Rohrlich, "Protest Targets Maywood's Stance," *Los Angeles Times* (August 27, 2006).

33. H. G. Reza, "Minor Offenders in Orange County Taken to Border Patrol; Many Are Deported," *Los Angeles Times* (February 12, 2001).

34. Randy Jurado Ertll and Marvin Andrade, "Don't Make the Police an Arm of the INS," *Los Angeles Times* (December 16, 2001); Solomon Moore, "LAPD Enlisted in Fight on Human Smuggling," *Los Angeles Times* (January 25, 2004); Robert Pear, "US Is Linking Immigrant Patients' Status to Hospital Aid," *New York Times* (August 10, 2004); Solomon Moore, "Baca's Plan to Screen Inmates OKd," *Los Angeles Times* (January 26, 2005); Charlie Le Duff, "Police Say Immigrant Policy Is Hindrance," *New York Times* (April 7, 2005); Richard Winton, "Department Clarifying Rule on Immigrants," *Los Angeles Times* (March 31, 2005); Andrew Blankstein, "Proposed LAPD Immigrant Policy Change Raises Fears," *Los Angeles Times* (April 7, 2005); Jack Leonard, "County May Resume Immigration Training for Jailers," *Los Angeles Times* (June 7, 2005); Lance Pugmire, "Immigration Check at Inland Jail is OKd," *Los Angeles Times* (September 21, 2005); David Haldane, "Immigrant Measure Spurs New Protest," *Los Angeles Times* (January 6, 2006); Richard Simon, "State Would Again Lose Funds for Jailed Illegal Immigrants," *Los Angeles Times* (February 7, 2006); Jennifer Delson, "Border Battle Is New Turf for Costa Mesa Mayor," *Los Angeles Times* (March 5, 2006); Patrick McGreevy, "Group Targets LAPD's Rule to Ignore Residency Status," *Los Angeles Times* (March 30, 2006); Jennifer Delson, "Migrant Fight Taxes OC City's Police Chief," *Los Angeles Times* (April 5, 2006); Susannah Rosenblatt, "Inmate Screening to Focus on Legal Status," *Los Angeles Times* (April 12, 2006); Jennifer Delson, "Group Disputes Costa Mesa's Stance on Immigration," *Los Angeles Times* (August 15, 2006).

35. John Decker, manuscript in progress (to be published by the University of California Press), advance copy courtesy of the author.

36. Anna Gorman, "Mexican Official Condemns Use of Spike Strips in Border Chases," *Los Angeles Times* (March 11, 2003); Ashley Powers and Seema Mehta, "Fatal Crash Ends Border Patrol Chase," *Los Angeles Times* (April 14,

2005); Richard Marosi, "Mexico Seeks Probe Into Shooting of Man at Border," *Los Angeles Times* (January 4, 2006); Ginger Thompson, "Mexico Investigates Death of Man Shot in US by Border Patrol Agent," *New York Times* (January 4, 2006); Richard Marosi, "At Border, Fatal Shot Still Rings," *Los Angeles Times* (January 9, 2006); Michard Marosi, Robert J. Lopez, and Rich Connell, "Reports Cite Incursions on US Border," *Los Angeles Times* (January 26, 2006); Ginger Thompson, "Mexican Leader Condemns US for Migrant Bill Passed by House," *New York Times* (December 20, 2005); "Cheap Border Politics," editorial, *New York Times* (December 21, 2005).

37. Wayne A. Cornelius, "An Immoral Policy on Illegal Entry," *Los Angeles Times* (June 8, 2003); Jonathan Glancey, "Walls Always Tumble Down," *Los Angeles Times* (May 26, 2006); Richard Marosi, "A Harsher Border Crossing," *Los Angeles Times* (August 20, 2006); Maura Reynolds and Richard Marosi, "Drop in Illegal Border Crossings a Sign of Success, Bush Aide Says," *Los Angeles Times* (August 24, 2006).

38. Sources for this section include several hundred articles in the *Los Angeles Times*, *New York Times*, *Oregonian*, *San Diego Union-Tribune*, and *Washington Post* over the period 2001–2006.

39. Nicole Gaouette, "Senate Passes Sweeping Bill on Immigration," *Los Angeles Times* (May 26, 2006); Teresa Watanabe and Anna Gorman, "'86 Amnesty Frames Immigration Debate," *Los Angeles Times* (June 3, 2006).

40. Molly Ivins, "Bush Plan Mainly Aids Business," *Oregonian* (January 15, 2004); Adam Geller, "Many Businesses Support Bush's Immigration Plan," *Oregonian* (January 19, 2004).

41. Pat Buchanan, quoted by "On The Issues," www.issues2000.org/Celeb/Pat_Buchanan_Immigration.htm (November 17, 2004); Richard W. Stevenson and Steven Greenhouse, "Plan for Illegal Immigrant Workers Draws Fire From Two Sides," *New York Times* (January 8, 2004); Louis Uchitelle, "Plan May Lure More to Enter US Illegally, Experts Say," *New York Times* (January 9, 2004); Rachel L. Swarns, "Outcry on Right Over Bush Plan on Immigration," *New York Times* (February 21, 2004).

42. Mark Z. Barabak, "Guest-Worker Proposal Has Wide Support," *Los Angeles Times* (April 30, 2006); Tamar Jacoby, "Amnesty Is Not a Four-Letter Word," *Los Angeles Times* (July 29, 2006).

43. Steve Greenberg, "A Shadow Debate for a Shadow Economy," *Ventura County Star*, reproduced in the *Los Angeles Times* (April 2, 2006).

44. "A Passion for Immigration Reform," *New York Times* (December 29, 2004); Paul Donnelly, "Make a Green Card the Real Payoff for Guest Workers," *Los Angeles Times* (February 12, 2001).

45. Teresa Watanabe, "Immigrants Gain the Pulpit," *Los Angeles Times* (March 1, 2006); Teresa Watanabe, "Mahony's Lenten Message Irritates Some at Service," *Los Angeles Times* (March 2, 2006); "A Cardinal Truth," editorial, *Los Angeles Times* (March 3, 2006). Mahony's support for undocumented immigrants went deeper than the 2006 debate, and it had echoes among not only other Catholic leaders but also some Protestants: Roger Mahony, "Immigrant Workers Deserve Legal Status and Respect," *Los Angeles Times* (June 8, 2000); Ricardo Alonso-Zaldivar, "US, Mexican Bishops Urge Bush to Resume Migration Negotiations," *Los Angeles Times* (January 25, 2003); Teresa Watanabe, "Catholic Leaders Hope to Sway Immigration Debate," *Los Angeles Times* (March 4, 2006); Arin Gencer and Steve Padilla, "Mass Draws on 'Justice for

Immigrants' Program," *Los Angeles Times* (April 6, 2006); Stephanie Simon, "Faith Shapes Views at a Church of Immigrants," *Los Angeles Times* (April 19, 2006).

46. Molly Hennessy-Fiske, "The Town That Didn't Look Away," *Los Angeles Times* (July 23, 2006); Hilda M. Muñoz, "Giving Shelter to the Most Vulnerable Children," *Los Angeles Times* (May 25, 2003); Eric Schlosser, "A Side Order of Human Rights," *New York Times* (April 6, 2005).

47. Sonia Nazario, "The Love Left Behind," *Los Angeles Times* (April 2, 2006). Another immigration expert who weighed in on the side of migrants was Wayne A. Cornelius, "Flailing at This Piñata: Scapegoating Mexico Is Easy, But It Doesn't Get Us Anywhere," *Los Angeles Times* (May 29, 2005).

48. This section is taken from the *Los Angeles Times* and *New York Times* reports during the period.

49. Teresa Watanabe and Hector Becerra, "500,000 Cram Streets to Protest Immigration Bills," *Los Angeles Times* (March 26, 2006); Anna Gorman, Michelle Keller, and Kelly-Anne Suarez, "Many Stories, a Single Theme," *Los Angeles Times* (March 26, 2006).

50. Sources on the April 10 demonstrations include Maura Reynolds and Faye Fiore, "Across the US: 'We Are America,'" *Los Angeles Times* (April 11, 2006); "People Power," *New York Times* (April 12, 3006). Rachel L. Swarns, "Immigrants Rally in Scores of Cities for Legal Status," *New York Times* (April 11, 2006); and a collection of photos and information at www.latimes.com (April 11, 2006).

51. These demonstrations occupied most of the front sections of the *Los Angeles Times*, *New York Times*, and *Chicago Tribune*, on May 2, from which my account is drawn.

52. Daniel Yi, "Koreatown Immigrants Blending In," *Los Angeles Times* (May 2, 2006).

53. Anna Gorman, Marjorie Miller, and Mitchell Landsberg, "Immigrants Raise Their Banners in Massive Rally," *Los Angeles Times* (May 2, 2006); "In Chicago, Many Absences at School," *New York Times* (May 2, 2006).

54. P. J. Huffstutter, "Cities' Immigrants Spoke One Language This Time," *Los Angeles Times* (May 2, 2006); Claire Hoffman, "Apparel Factory Chief Gives Day Off," *Los Angeles Times* (May 2, 2006); "In Denver, Fears of Deportation," *New York Times* (May 2, 2006).

55. Ashley Powers, "Activist's Persistence a Driving Force in Boycott," *Los Angeles Times* (May 1, 2006).

56. I am going to speak in conceptual terms in this section, rather than descend into mathematical detail, for I am analyzing the arguments of other scholars, not presenting my own. Sources on the economic impact of immigration include Gordon H. Hanson, *Why Does Immigration Divide America? Public Finance and Political Opposition to Open Borders* (Washington, DC: Institute for International Economics, 2005); David Heer, *Immigration in America's Future* (Boulder, CO: Westview, 1996); *The Impact of Immigration on the California Economy* (Palo Alto, CA: Center for the Continuing Study of the California Economy, 2005); Kevin F. McCarthy and Georges Vernez, *Immigration in a Changing Economy* (Santa Monica, CA: Rand, 1997); Passell, *Unauthorized Migrants*; Steven Shulman, Ed., *The Impact of Immigration on African Americans* (New Brunswick, NJ: Transaction, 2004); James P. Smith and Barry Edmonston, Eds., *The New Americans: Economic, Demographic, and Fiscal*

Effects of Immigration (Washington, DC: National Academy Press, 1997); *We The People: Helping Newcomers Become Californians* (Sacramento, CA: Little Hoover Commission, 2002).

57. Haydee Pavia, letter to the editor, *Los Angeles Times* (December 27, 2003).

58. George Borjas, *Heaven's Door: Immigration Policy and the American Economy* (Princeton, NJ: Princeton University Press, 1999), 212. Other writers with a negative assessment of the economic impact of immigrants include Beck, *The Case Against Immigration*; Steven A. Camarota, *Immigration from Mexico: Assessing the Impact on the United States* (Washington, DC: Center for Immigration Studies, 2001); Graham, *Unguarded Gates*; Christopher Jencks, "Who Should Get In?" *New York Review of Books* (November 29, 2001); Roger Lowenstein, "The Immigration Equation," *New York Times* (July 9, 2006); Robert J. Samuelson, "The Changing Face of Poverty," *Newsweek* (October 18, 2004); Dan Stein, "Immigration Is Fueling Poverty Rate," *Los Angeles Times* (July 6, 1999).

59. Writers with a positive assessment of the economic impact of immigrants include Vernon M. Briggs Jr. and Stephen Moore, *Still an Open Door? US Immigration Policy and the American Economy* (Washington, DC: American University Press, 1994); Tim Cavanaugh, "No Border, No Problem," *Los Angeles Times* (May 23, 2006); James Flanigan, "Immigrants Benefit US Economy Now as Ever," *Los Angeles Times* (July 4, 2005); Michael Hiltzik, "Clearing Out Bad Data on Illegal Immigrants," *Los Angeles Times* (December 22, 2003); Michael Hiltzik, "The Truth About Illegal Immigrants," *Los Angeles Times* (December 15, 2005); Tamar Jacoby, "A Law That Means Business," *Los Angeles Times* (July 12, 2005); Robert Scheer, "Surprise! Immigration Hasn't Ruined Us," *Los Angeles Times* (February 22, 2000); Julian Simon, *The Economic Consequences of Immigration*, 2nd ed. (Ann Arbor: University of Michigan Press, 1999); Kenneth Swift, "Saving Social Security? Now That's a Job for Immigrants," *Los Angeles Times* (April 23, 2006).

60. Rong-Gong Lin II, "Mexican Immigrants Not Burdening ERs, Study Says," *Los Angeles Times* (October 14, 2005); David R. Francis, "Recent Immigrants Less Likely to Go to Prison than Natives," *NBER Digest* (Cambridge, MA: National Bureau of Economic Research, 1998).

61. Nelson Lim, "On the Back of Blacks? Immigrants and the Fortunes of African Americans," in *Strangers at the Gates*, Roger Waldinger, Ed. (Berkeley: University of California Press, 2001), 186–227; Camarota, *Immigration from Mexico*, 5–6; Otis Graham's guess of 30 percent was wildly off the mark: Graham, *Guarding the Gates*, 113.

62. *Impact of Immigration*.

63. *Impact of Immigration*, 8.

64. Simon, *Economic Consequences*, 367; *Impact of Immigration*, 8; Peter Francese, quoted in Nicholas Capaldi, Ed., *Immigration: Debating the Issues* (Amherst, NY Prometheus, 1997), 171; Kenneth Swift, "Saving Social Security? Now That's a Job for Immigrants," *Los Angeles Times* (April 23, 2006). I made essentially this same argument in an op-ed piece for the *Minneapolis Star-Tribune* in 1984.

65. Charles L. Lindner, "Police the Border, Flood the Courts," *Los Angeles Times* (July 16, 2006).

66. Material for this section comes from hundreds of articles drawn from the *Los Angeles Times*, *New York Times*, and other newspapers from September 2001 to summer 2006. I will give individual citations only to major books, sources of quotations, and materials on specific, limited subtopics.

67. Tram Nguyen, *We Are All Suspects Now: Untold Stories from Immigrant Communities After 9/11* (Boston: Beacon, 2005).

68. Laurie Goodstein and Gustav Niebuhr, "Attacks and Harassment of Middle-Eastern Americans Rising," *New York Times* (September 14, 2001); Eric Slater and Rebecca Trounson, "Calm Urged as Muslims Face Threats," *Los Angeles Times* (September 14, 2001); Hector Becerra, "Arizona Sikh Man Dead in Suspected Hate Attack," *Los Angeles Times* (September 16, 2001); "Driver Slams Car Into Mosque in Ohio," *Reuters* (September 17, 2001); Joe Mozingo, "Slain Egyptian Was a Fixture in San Gabriel," *Los Angeles Times* (September 19, 2001); Mike Anton, "Collateral Damage in War on Terrorism," *Los Angeles Times* (September 22, 2001); Richard A. Serrano, "Assaults Against Muslims, Arabs Escalating," *Los Angeles Times* (September 28, 2001); Jeff Coen, "Hate-Crime Reports Reach Record Level," *Chicago Tribune* (October 9, 2001); Deborah Kong, "FBI Probes Apparent Hate Crime Deaths," *Associated Press* (October 10, 2001); Curt Anderson, "Hate Crimes Targeting Muslims, Middle Easterners Surged in 2001, FBI Says," *Associated Press* (November 25, 2002); William Lobdell and Christine Hanley, "Assault Was Hate Crime, Police Say," *Los Angeles Times* (March 4, 2003).

69. Cristi Hegranes, "Suffer the Little Muslims," *San Francisco Weekly* (August 17–23, 2005); "Church Head Won't Repudiate Comments," *New York Times* (June 12, 2002); Lynette Clemetson and Keith Naughton, "Patriotism vs. Ethnic Pride: An American Dilemma," *Newsweek* (September 24, 2001); Ann Coulter, "Detainment Isn't Enough," www2.uclick.com/client/cap/ac/ (October 5, 2001); Peggy Noonan, "Profiles Encouraged: Under the Circumstances, We Must Be Wary of Young Arab Men," *Wall Street Journal* (October 19, 2001); Patrick J. Buchanan, "US Pays the High Price of Empire," *Los Angeles Times* (September 18, 2001); "Racial Backlash Flares at Colleges," *CNN Web News* (September 21, 2001); William Lobdell, "Teacher's Terrorism Remarks Stir Academic Freedom Debate," *Los Angeles Times* (September 30, 2001); "Immigration Policy Paved Way for Sept. 11 Attack," *Lodi News-Sentinel* (October 6, 2001). Even the normally restrained President George H. W. Bush chimed in on occasion, as when he glibly referred to U.S. foreign and domestic policy as all part of the "war against Islamic fascists"; Louis Sahagun, "Muslims Upset by Bush's Remarks," *Los Angeles Times* (August 11, 2006).

70. "Banned Muslim Scholar Resigns from US Post," *Los Angeles Times* (December 15, 2004); Jonathan Dowd-Gailey, "Yvonne Haddad: America's Islam 'Sensitivity' Trainer," *FrontPage Magazine* (December 14, 2005); Brock Read, "Columbia U. Professor, Criticized for Views on Israel, Is Banned From Teacher-Training Program," *Chronicle of Higher Education* (February 22, 2005).

71. Lynette Clemetson, "Homeland Security Given Data on Arab-Americans," *New York Times* (July 30, 2004); Alexander Cockburn, "The FBI and Edward Said," *Nation* (February 2006); David Price, "How the FBI Spied on Edward Said," counterpunch.com (January 13, 2006); Sam Howe Verhovek, "Once Appalled by Race Profiling, Many find Themselves Doing It," *New York Times* (September 23, 2001); Henry Weinstein, Michael Finnegan, and Teresa Watanabe,

"Racial Profiling Gains Support as Search Tactic," *Los Angeles Times* (September 24, 2001); Sandy Banks, "En Route to a Newfound Prejudice," *Los Angeles Times* (October 7, 2001); "Congressman Cooksey Again Calls for Racial Profiling: An Ugly Appeal," *Washington Post* (October 11, 2001); Mona Charen, "Columnist Says Pull Over 'Middle Eastern-Looking' Drivers," *Washington Times* (October 18, 2001); Florangela Davila, "Bank Accused of Profiling," *Seattle Times* (January 12, 2002); Sharon Begley, "The Latest Trouble With Racial Profiling," *Newsweek* (January 14, 2002); Lori Hope, Did I Save Lives or Engage in Profiling?" *Newsweek* (April 1, 2002); Fareed Zakaria, "Freedom vs. Security: A Delicate Balance: The Case for 'Smart Profiling' as a Weapon in the War on Terror," *Newsweek* (July 8, 2002).

72. Not all Americans shared President Bush's sentiment. Congressmember Howard Coble of North Carolina remarked in a radio interview that, while he did not support imprisoning all Arab Americans, said that he thought the World War II imprisonment of Japanese Americans was entirely appropriate. Janet Hook, "Internment Remarks by Lawmaker Anger Peers," *Los Angeles Times* (February 7, 2003); Wendy Thermos, "Honda Seeks GOP Action Over Remarks on Internment," *Los Angeles Times* (February 16, 2003). It is disappointing to note that many historians did not even catch the parallel to the events of 1941 and 1942. The *Journal of American History*'s first take on September 11, *History and September 11th*, edited by Joanne Meyerowitz (Philadelphia: Temple University Press, 2003), did not even mention the Japanese American experience in World War II.

73. Andrew Klavan, "Draft Hollywood," *Los Angeles Times* (May 7, 2006).

74. Mark Hosenball and Michael Isikoff, "Homeland Security's Info: Miles from Nowhere," *Newsweek* (October 4, 2004); Leslie Miller, "The Former Cat Stevens Gets Plane Diverted," *Associated Press* (September 21, 2004).

75. Chris Plante, "US Army Muslim Chaplain Arrested," *CNN.com* (September 22, 2003); "US Drops All Charges Against Muslim Chaplain," *CNN.com* (May 6, 2004); Laura Parker, "The Ordeal of Chaplain Yee," *USA Today* (May 16, 2004); "Charges Dropped in Guantanamo Case," *Los Angeles Times* (September 17, 2004); Teresa Watanabe, "Ex-Chaplain, Once Jailed by Army, Defends His Patriotism," *Los Angeles Times* (October 23, 2005); James Yee with Aimee Molloy, *For God and Country: Faith and Patriotism Under Fire* (New York: Public Affairs Press, 2005); Joseph Lelyveld, "The Strange Case of Chaplain Yee," *New York Review of Books* (December 15, 2005).

76. Sarah Kershaw and Eric Lichtblau, "US Lawyer Is Arrested in Madrid Bombing Inquiry," *New York Times* (May 7, 2004); Kershaw and Lichtblau, "Arrest in Bombing Inquiry Was Rushed, Officials Say," *New York Times* (May 8, 2004); Kershaw and Lichtblau, "Arrest and Release in Bombing Center on Fingerprint Match," *New York Times* (May 22, 2004); Maria Newman, "Error Tied US Lawyer to Spain Blasts; Judge Voids Case," *New York Times* (May 24, 2004); Joseph Rose, "FBI Apologizes to Mayfield," *Oregonian* (May 25, 2004); Les Zaitz, "FBI Traces Fingerprint Error," *Oregonian* (May 26, 2004); Anjana Malhotra, "Material Witness Law Is Being Abused," *Oregonian* (May 27, 2004); Joseph Rose, "Residue of Arrest Clutters Mayfield's Present, Future," *Oregonian* (May 28, 2004); Les Zaitz, "FBI Case Against Oregon Lawyer Built on Blurry Fingerprint, Logic," *Oregonian* (May 30, 2004); Mark Larabee, "Portland Cases Fuel Rights Debate," *Oregonian* (May 31, 2004); Sarah Kershaw, "Spain and US at Odds on Mistaken Terror Arrest," *New York Times* (June 5,

2004); Tomas Alex Tizon, "Portland, FBI Unit to Part Ways," *Los Angeles Times* (April 28, 2005); Tomas Alex Tizon, "Report Says Mistaken Arrest Was Due to FBI's Sloppy Work," *Los Angeles Times* (January 7, 2006).

77. Richard Colby, "Prayer Organizers Disinvite Muslim; Mayor Bows Out," *Oregonian* (April 24, 2004); Jill Smith, "Events Push Mosque Leader into Spotlight," *Oregonian* (May 10, 2004); Teresa Watanabe, "US Muslims Temper Ramadan Giving With Caution," *Los Angeles Times* (November 6, 2004); Donna Leinwand, "Muslims See New Opposition to Building Mosques Since 9/11," *USA Today* (March 9, 2004); Hugo Martín, "Hindu Temple Plans Uncertain," *Los Angeles Times* (October 4, 2004).

78. Rousina Hassoun, "The Impact of Revelations of Abuse on Arab and Muslim Americans," written for *Anthropology News* and circulated among friends, May 8, 2004.

79. Jaideep Singh, "American Apartheid for the New Millennium: Men of Profile," paper presented to the Asian and Pacific Islander American Religions Research Initiative, Berkeley, August 2003.

80. Quotes on the USA PATRIOT Act are from David Cole, *Enemy Aliens: Double Standards and Constitutional Freedoms in the War on Terrorism* (New York: New Press, 2003), 57–71; the cartoon is from Tribune Media Services and was reprinted in the fall 2005 newsletter of the Southern California ACLU. Other sources for this section include Robert P. Abele, *A User's Guide to the USA PATRIOT Act and Beyond* (Lanham, MD: University Press of America, 2005); Stewart A. Baker, *Patriot Debates* (Chicago: American Bar Association, 2005); Howard Ball and Mildred Vasan, Eds., *The USA PATRIOT Act* (Santa Barbara: ABC-CLIO, 2004); Walter Brasch, *America's Unpatriot Acts: The Federal Government's Violation of Constitutional and Civil Rights* (New York: Peter Lang, 2005); Samuel Dash, *The Intruders: Unreasonable Searches and Seizures from King John to John Ashcroft* (New Brunswick, NJ: Rutgers University Press, 2004); John Yoo, *The Powers of War and Peace: The Constitution and Foreign Affairs After 9/11* (Chicago: University of Chicago Press, 2005); Jonathan Peterson, "New Immigration Initiative May Not Provide More Safety," *Los Angeles Times* (October 31, 2001); Eric Lichtblau, "Justice Officials Introduce Tighter Immigrant Policy," *Los Angeles Times* (November 1, 2001); David Jackson, "US to Crack Down on Immigration," *Dallas Morning News* (November 1, 2001); Cara Mia DeMassa, "Muslims Condemn INS Detentions, Say USA Patriot Act Went Too Far," *Los Angeles Times* (December 22, 2002); David G. Savage, "Justice Dept. May Pursue Wider Power to Arrest Terror Suspects," *Los Angeles Times* (February 8, 2003); Patrick J. McDonnell, "INS Ends Life as Separate Agency," *Los Angeles Times* (March 1, 2003); "FBI Casts Wide Net to Battle Terrorism," *Los Angeles Times* (March 16, 2003); Renee Tawa, "Pro-Constitution, anti-Patriot," *Los Angeles Times* (May 28, 2003); Roger B. Schmitt, "Stiffer Terror Laws Urged," *Los Angeles Times* (June 6, 2003); Richard B. Schmitt, "Planned Sequel to Patriot Act Losing Audience," *Los Angeles Times* (July 29, 2003); Margaret Noel, "League of Women Voters: Repeal Parts of Patriot Act," *Oregonian* (October 23, 2003); Michael Isikoff, "Patriot Act Helps the Feds in Cases with No Tie to Terror," *Newsweek* (December 1, 2003); Nina Bernstein, "Crime Database Misused for Civil Issues, Suit Says," *New York Times* (December 17, 2003); Ashbel S. Green, "Deportation Effort Jails US Citizen for Month," *Oregonian* (February 12, 2004); Bill Fletcher Jr., "Actor Finds He's Target of US Customs," *Oregonian* (February 20, 2004); Timothy

Egan, "Computer Student on Trial for Aid to Muslim Web Sites," *New York Time* (April 27, 2004); Nicholas D. Kristof, "May I See Your ID?" *New York Times* (March 17, 2004); William Greider, "Under the Banner of the 'War' on Terror," *Nation* (June 21, 2004); Janet Hook, "House GOP Leaders Kill Effort to Limit Patriot Act," *Los Angeles Times* (July 9, 2004); Richard B. Schmitt, "Provision of Patriot Act Is Ruled Unconstitutional," *Los Angeles Times* (September 30, 2004); Kevin Sack, "Chasing Terrorists or Fears?" *Los Angeles Times* (October 24, 2004); Steve Hymon, "Rights a Victim of Terror War, US Judge Says," *Los Angeles Times* (November 7, 2004); David Cole, "Uncle Sam Is Watching You," *New York Review of Books* (November 18, 2004); Rachel L. Swarns, "Program's Value in Dispute as a Tool to Fight Terrorism," *New York Times* (December 21, 2004); Eric Lipton, "Nominee Says US Agents Abused Power After 9/11," *New York Times* (February 3, 2005); Eric Lichtblau, "Justice Dept. Defends Patriot Act Before Senate Hearings," *New York Times* (April 5, 2005); "Revising the Patriot Act," editorial, *New York Times* (April 10, 2005); "Guilty Until Proven Innocent," editorial, *New York Times* (April 12, 2005); Nicole Gaouette, "Immigration Overhaul Seen as Key to Domestic Security," *Los Angeles Times* (July 14 2005); David Cole, "What Bush Wants to Hear," *New York Review of Books* (November 17, 2005); Nicole Gaouette, "Senators Oppose Extending Patriot Act," *Los Angeles Times* (November 18, 2005); Rick Schmitt and Mary Curtius, "Bush Defends Eavesdropping as Defense Against Terrorism," *Los Angeles Times* (December 18, 2005); Peter Wallsten, "GOP Ranks Breaking Over Bush's Tactics," *Los Angeles Times* (December 18, 2005); Bob Drogin, "Lawmakers Urge Review of US Spy Program," *Los Angeles Times* (December 19, 2005); Siobhan Gorman, "Legal Support for Bush's Spy Actions Is Thin, Report Says," *Los Angeles Times* (January 7, 2006); Frank Rich, "The Wiretappers That Couldn't Shoot Straight," *New York Times* (January 8, 2006); Maura Reynolds, "Gonzales Defends Spying as 'Limited and Lawful,'" *Los Angeles Times* (February 7, 2006); "Names on US Terror List Quadruple," *Los Angeles Times* (February 15, 2006); Maura Reynolds, "Renewal of Patriot Act Passes Senate," *Los Angeles Times* (March 3, 2006); Bruce Craig, "Scholars Become Targets of the Patriot Act," *American Historical Association Perspectives* (April 2006).

81. Sources on the detainees issue include Cole, *Enemy Aliens*; Mark Dow, *American Gulag: Inside US Immigration Prisons* (Berkeley: University of California Press, 2004); Michael Ignatieff, "Lesser Evils," *New York Times* (May 2, 2004); Steven H. Miles, *Oath Betrayed: Torture, Medical Complicity, and the War on Terror* (New York: Random House, 2006); and several hundred newspaper and magazine articles.

82. Julian E. Barnes and Carol J. Williams, "Guantanamo's First Suicides Pressure US," *Los Angeles Times* (June 11, 2006).

83. The pieces of the Bill of Rights that have been violated are: The First Amendment protection rights to free speech and a free press, and the right peaceably to assemble. The Fourth Amendment right to be secure in one's person, house, papers, and effects; the right to be free from unreasonable searches and seizures and from warrants issued without probable cause and particular descriptions of the place to be searched and the person or thing to be seized. The Fifth Amendment right not to be deprived of life, liberty, or property without due process of law. The Sixth Amendment rights to a speedy and public jury trial, to be informed of the nature and cause of the accusation, to be confronted with

the witnesses against one, to have the subpoena power, and to be assisted by counsel. The Seventh Amendment right to a jury trial. The Eighth Amendment prohibition against cruel and unusual punishment. It is important to note that, while the Constitution limits some rights to citizens of the United States, it does not make such a limitation on any of the rights listed here. The Fourteenth Amendment reinforces that distinction, when it declares the government shall not "deprive any *person* of life, liberty, or property, without due process of law; nor deny to any *person* within its jurisdiction the equal protection of the laws" (italics added). "Person," not "citizen." The Constitution is in shreds.

Sources on the war on the Bill of Rights include Elaine Cassel, *The War on Civil Liberties: How Bush and Ashcroft Have Dismantled the Bill of Rights* (Chicago: Lawrence Hill Books, 2004); Cole, *Enemy Aliens*; Peter H. Irons, *War Powers: How the Imperial Presidency Hijacked the Constitution* (New York: Metropolitan, 2005); Arthur M. Schlesinger Jr., *War and the American Presidency*, rev. ed. (New York: Norton, 2005); Geoffrey B. Stone, *Perilous Times: Free Speech in Wartime From the Sedition Act of 1798 to the War on Terrorism* (New York: Norton, 2004); Melvin I. Urofsky, Ed., special issue of *Journal of Supreme Court History*, 28.3 (2003).

84. United Nations High Commission for Human Rights, www.unhchr.org (August 8, 2006); Richard B. Schmitt, "Congress Faces Dilemma on Terror Trials," *Los Angeles Times* (July 2, 2006).

85. David G. Savage, "High Court Rejects Bush's Claim That He Alone Sets Detainee Rules"; Julian E. Barnes, "Military Fought to Abide by War Rules"; Carol J. Williams, "Lonely Victory of US Navy Lawyer"; "Bush vs. the Constitution"; Rosa Brooks, "The Geneva Convention 'Catch'"; Harvey Silvergate, "Court Says No to an Imperial Presidency"; all *Los Angeles Times* (June 30, 2006); Henry Weinstein, "Wiretap Project Ruled Illegal," *Los Angeles Times* (August 18, 2006).

86. David Cole, "Are We Safer?" *New York Review of Books* (March 9, 2006), 17; Rone Tampest and Eric Bailey, "Conviction for Son, Mistrial for Father in Lodi Terror Case," *Los Angeles Times* (April 26, 2006); Richard B. Schmitt, "For the Justice Department, a Welcome Conviction," *Los Angeles Times* (April 26, 2006); Richard A. Serrano, "With Judgment, Moussaoui Is Silenced at Last," *Los Angeles Times* (May 5, 2006).

87. Sources on the language debate include Richard Alba, John Logan, Amy Lutz, and Brian Stults, "Only English by the Third Generation? Loss and Preservation of the Mother Tongue Among the Grandchildren of Contemporary Immigrants," *Demography*, 39.3 (2002), 467–484; Richard Alba and Victor Nee, *Remaking the American Mainstream: Assimilation and Contemporary Immigration* (Cambridge, MA: Harvard University Press, 2003); Dennis E. Baron, *The English-Only Question: An Official Language for Americans* (New Haven, CT: Yale University Press, 1990); James Crawford, Ed., *Language Loyalties: A Source Book on the Official English Controversy* (Chicago: University of Chicago Press, 1992); Nicholas Capaldi, Ed., *Immigration: Debating the Issues* (Amherst, NY: Prometheus, 1997), 251–305; *The English Only Movement: An Agenda for Discrimination* (Washington, DC: League of United Latin American Citizens, 1989); Carmen Fought, *Chicano English in Context* (New York: Palgrave Macmillan, 2002); Richard D. Lamm and Gary Imhoff, *The Immigration Time Bomb* (New York: Dutton, 1985); Robert MacNeil and William Cran, *Do You Speak American?* (New York: Harcourt, 2005); Allan A. Metcalf,

Chicano English (Arlington, VA: Center for Applied Linguistics, 1979); Joyce Penfield and Jacob L. Ornstein-Galicia, *Chicano English* (Philadelphia: J. Benjamins, 1985); Alejandro Portes and Rubén C. Rumbaut, *Immigrant America*, 2nd ed. (Berkeley: University of California Press, 1996), 192–231; Roberto R. Ramirez, *We the People: Hispanics in the United States* (Washington, DC: U.S. Census Bureau, 2004); Ronald Schmidt, *Language Policy and Identity Politics in the United States* (Philadelphia: Temple University Press, 2000); Hyon B. Shin and Rosalind Bruno, *Language Use and English-Speaking Ability: 2000* (Washington, DC: U.S. Census Bureau, 2003); Raymond Tatalovich, "Official English as Nativist Backlash," in *Immigrants Out! The New Nativism and the Anti-Immigrant Impulse in the United States*, Juan F. Perea, Ed. (New York: NYU Press, 1997), 78–102; Tatalovich, *Nativism Reborn? The Official English Language Movement and the American States* (Lexington: University Press of Kentucky, 1995); Lucy Tse, *"Why Don't They Learn English?" Separating Fact from Fallacy in the US Language Debate* (New York: Teachers College Press, Columbia University, 2001).

88. en.wikiquote.org/wiki/wikiquote.org/wiki/Ma_Ferguson (April 8, 2006), quoting Texas Governor Ann Richards's Mount Holyoke College commencement address, May 28, 1995.

89. Ellen Barry, "Learn English, Judge Tells Moms," *Los Angeles Times* (February 15, 2005); Ellen Barry, "Judge Who Ordered English Lessons Restores Custody," *Los Angeles Times* (April 27, 2005).

90. "By the Numbers: TV Rankings," *Los Angeles Times* (March 22, 2006).

91. Tomas Alex Tizon, "80 Eyes on 2,400 People"; Nicole Gaouette and Maura Reynolds, "Immigration Fight Heats Up"; Cynthia H. Cho and Anna Gorman, "Massive Student Walkout Spreads Across Southland"; Teresa Watanabe and Hector Becerra, "How DJs Put 500,000 Marchers in Motion"; Richard A. Serrano, "Moussaoui Says He Was to Fly 5th Plane"; David G. Savage, "High Court to Review Guantanamo Case"; Janet Hook, "A Hard GOP Line Could Erode Latino Vote"; "Execute Moussaoui?" (editorial); Arnold Schwarzenegger, "Next Step for Immigration"; Jeff Danziger, "New Citizens" (cartoon); Gustavo Arellano, "The Protests of Allegiance"; Joel Stein, "500,000 People, and No One Called Me?"—all in *Los Angeles Times* (March 28, 2006).

92. Among the marketers were The Native Press (www.cafepress.com), West Wind World (www.westwindworld.com), and Coyotes Corner (www.coyotescorner.com).

Illustration Permission Acknowledgments

Every effort has been made to contact copyright holders for their permission to reprint illustrations in this book. The publishers would be grateful to hear from any copyright holder who is not acknowledged here and will undertake to rectify any errors or omissions in future editions or printings of this book.

Figure 1.1   "The new face of America" according to *Time*. Reprinted with permission of *Time*, Inc.

Figure 1.2   Bonacich and Cheng's conceptual diagram of international labor migration. Reprinted with permission of Edna Bonacich and Lucie Cheng.

Figure 2.1   Tribal groups. From *Encyclopedia of North American Indians*, ed. Frederick E. Hoxie, Copyright 1996 by Houghton Mifflin Company. Reprinted with permission of Houghton Mifflin Company. All rights reserved.

Figure 2.2   Kicks Iron. Reprinted with permission of Azusa Publishing.

Figure 2.3   Tswawadi. Reprinted with permission of Azusa Publishing.

Figure 2.4   Mishongnovi. Reprinted with permission of Azusa Publishing.

Figure 2.6   Indian trade routes. From *Encyclopedia of North American Indians*, ed. Frederick E. Hoxie, Copyright 1996 by Houghton Mifflin Company. Reprinted with permission of Houghton Mifflin Company. All rights reserved.

Figure 2.12 Slave coffle. Reprinted with permission of Culver Pictures.

Figure 2.13 Slave ship. Reprinted with permission of New York Historical Society.

Figure 2.14 U.S. imports of slaves per decade, 1620–1860. Reprinted with courtesy of Helen Hornbeck Tanner.

Figure 3.2   Natural American Spirit ad. Reprinted courtesy of Reynolds American, Inc.

Figure 3.3   Leaving Queenstown. Reprinted with courtesy of Nostalgia Press.

Figure 3.4   Irish squatters in Central Park. From the J. Clarence Davies Collection. Reprinted with courtesy of the Museum of the City of New York.

Figure 5.10 Triangle fire victims. Reprinted with courtesy of Brown Brothers.

Figure 5.11 Alamo City Employment Agency. Reprinted with courtesy of H. L. Summerville, Photography Collection, Harry Ransom Humanities Research Center, University of Texas, Austin.

Figure 5.12 Mexican and U.S. rail networks. Mexican emigration to the United States, 1897–1931, by Lawrence Cardoso, Copyright 1980 Arizona Board of Regents. Reprinted with permission of the University of Arizona Press.

Figure 5.13 Filipinos and Mexicans worked side by side in the fields. Reprinted courtesy of U.S. Department of Agriculture.

Figure 6.2 Striking Polish miners armed with sticks and rocks lost the fight to goons armed with guns, Shenandoah, Pennsylvania, 1888. Reprinted with courtesy of Brown Brothers.

Figure 6.3 "This Hungarian immigrant mother had plenty to do, caring for her children and managing her home." Reprinted courtesy of National Park Service, Sherman Collection.

Figure 6.4 An Ellis Island interrogator is flanked by an interpreter and a man aspiring to enter. Reprinted with courtesy of Brown Brothers.

Figure 6.5 Immigrants were subjected to a medical exam. Reprinted with courtesy of Brown Brothers.

Figure 6.6 Chinese boy being interrogated at Angel Island. Reprinted with courtesy of National Archives.

Figure 6.10 The lynching of Lige Daniels, August 3, 1920, Center, Texas. Reprinted with courtesy of the Pixel Press.

Figure 7.2 Mexican American families await expatriation in the Los Angeles train station, 1932. Reprinted with courtesy of Los Angeles Public Library, Security Pacific Historical Collection.

Figure 7.4 "FBI Takes Father Away," watercolor by Gene Sogioka. Reprinted with courtesy of Estate of Gene Sogioka, Cornell University Library Department of Rare Books and Manuscripts.

Figure 8.1 Helicopter leaves the U.S. Embassy in Saigon, April 1975. Reprinted with courtesy of Popperfoto and Helen Hornbeck Tanner.

Figure 8.2 Hmong story cloth. Reprinted with courtesy of Science Museum of Minnesota.

Figure 10.2 Gonsalo Lopez retrieves his basketball. Reprinted with courtesy of Don Bartlett, *Los Angeles Times Magazine*.

Figure 10.3 The May 1 March in Los Angeles. Reprinted with courtesy of the *Los Angeles Times*.

Also by Paul Spickard

Mixed Blood: Intermarriage and Ethnic Identity in Twentieth-Century America

A Global History of Christians
(with Kevin M. Cragg)

Japanese Americans: The Formation and Transformations of an Ethnic Group

World History by the World's Historians
(with James V. Spickard and Kevin M. Cragg)

Is Lighter Better? Skin-Tone Discrimination among Asian Americans
(with Joanne L. Rondilla)

As Editor

Pacific Island Peoples in Hawai'i

Pacific Islander Americans: A Bibliography
(with Debbie Hippolite Wright and others)

We Are a People: Narrative and Multiplicity in Constructing Ethnic Identity
(with W. Jeffrey Burroughs)

Pacific Diaspora: Island Peoples in the United States and across the Pacific
(with Joanne L. Rondilla and Debbie Hippolite Wright)

Revealing the Sacred in Asian and Pacific America
(with Jane Naomi Iwamura)

Racial Thinking in the United States: Uncompleted Independence
(with G. Reginald Daniel)

Race and Nation: Ethnic Systems in the Modern World

Affect and Power: Essays on Sex, Slavery, Race and Religion
(with David J. Libby and Susan Ditto)

Index

Numbers in bold are from created images; while numbers in italics are photographs.